ESSENTIALS OF TREASURY MANAGEMENT®

FOURTH EDITION *Second Printing*

Mark K. Webster, CCM, CPA, CSP, *Editor*

Association for Financial Professionals®

4520 East-West Highway, Suite 750, Bethesda, Maryland 20814, USA

TEL: +1 301.907.2862 FAX: +1 301.907.2864

www.AFPonline.org

Association for Financial Professionals®

ESSENTIALS OF TREASURY MANAGEMENT®, FOURTH EDITION

Second Printing, April 2014

All inquiries should be addressed to:

Association for Financial Professionals

4520 East-West Highway, Suite 750, Bethesda, MD 20814, USA

TEL: +1 301.907.2862 **FAX:** +1 301.907.2864 **E-MAIL:** AFP@AFPonline.org

www.AFPonline.org

ISBN 978-0-615-80037-0

Copy Editor: Angie Woodward, The Caviart Group (awoodward@thecaviartgroup.com)
Graphic Design and Layout: Rob Myers (robkmyers@hotmail.com)

AUTHOR'S ACKNOWLEDGMENTS

This is the second edition of the *Essentials of Treasury Management (ETM)* that I've had the privilege to work on. And I'll admit to having been in the business long enough to remember when the first *Essentials of Cash Management*, a much thinner book, was published. The interesting thing about working on this edition of *ETM* is that, as long as I've been in the business, I'm still learning new things. Writing this edition of the book has made me really take a look at things that I thought I knew or assumed I knew and challenge some of my basic assumptions. It's made me examine some of the facts and principles about treasury management and get back to root causes about why they were true instead of just asserting that they were true. It's also reaffirmed my joy in the work that I do. I believe that the process has been good both for me and for the content of the book that you hold in your hands.

Obviously a project like this couldn't be done without the support and funding of the Association for Financial Professionals (AFP), headed by Jim Kaitz. I also can't say enough about the time and effort put into the project by Donna Berzellini, CTP, Managing Director, Certification, and Stacy Saul, Director of Examinations. They kept me on track and managed the schedule. Donna, especially, helped make sure I questioned some of those assumptions mentioned previously as she reviewed every chapter. She also went out of her way to send me articles, clippings, and various AFP resources that were helpful in drafting this book. My thanks, also, to all of the other AFP staff members who helped in many ways with the development and production of this edition of *ETM*.

My thanks to the CTP Body of Knowledge (BOK) Committee who reviewed the work as it progressed and provided valuable insights into what needed to be in the text. My special thanks to Robert Venema, CTP, Assistant Treasurer & Executive Director, Cash Management of Kaiser Permanente, the chair of the BOK Committee. Robert reviewed every chapter and was present for almost every review meeting. Without his efforts this book would not be what it is. The other members also did yeoman's work and are listed in the front of this book. Thanks also to Fred Butterfield, CTP, Trust Company of America, who, while not on the committee, did provide thoughts and research on some of the material during the development process.

My thanks to my partners at the Treasury Alliance Group LLC (TAG) for their support in writing this edition of *ETM*. Some of the material and exhibits in the book are provided courtesy of TAG, and my partners were always available if I had an issue that I needed help with.

Finally, my thanks to my family and relatives and especially to my wife, Brenda, who has put up with me over the last year as I worked on this edition of *ETM*. Without her support, encouragement, and patience, this book would never have been written.

Mark K. Webster, CCM, CPA, CSP

ABOUT THE AUTHOR

Mark K. Webster, CCM, CPA, CSP

Mark Webster is a Partner in Treasury Alliance Group LLC, a consulting firm that specializes in payments and treasury management. He has over 35 years of experience in all areas of payments and treasury and risk management, and he has worked with domestic and international clients in a wide variety of industries, including financial services, retail, insurance, and government. The former head of the treasury management consulting practice at Coopers & Lybrand, Mark has led bank operations and payments consulting practices as a partner at both PricewaterhouseCoopers and Capco. He has significant financial services industry experience, having worked for both regional and money center banks in a variety of roles, including Chief Information Officer, Treasury Services Product Manager, and head of Payments Operations and Check Processing.

Mark is a board member and past president of NEOTMA, the Northeast Ohio Treasury Management Association, and served on the CTP Body of Knowledge Committee of the AFP. He is a past chairman of the Affiliates Council of NACHA, The Electronic Payments Organization, and was a voting member of NACHA's Rules and Operations committee for many years. He is the principal author of *Essentials of Treasury Management, 4th Edition*, and has authored articles on the payments industry, treasury management, risk management, and operational transformation for a variety of publications. He is a frequent speaker and lecturer on both a local and national level and has served on the faculty of The Payments Institute, The Institute of International Payments, the Treasury Management Series at the Haas Business School at the University of California, and The Global Treasury Forum.

Mark is a Certified Cash Manager (Permanent), a Certified Public Accountant in the state of Ohio, and a Certified Systems Professional, and was a recipient of the Elijah Watts Sells award for national excellence when he sat for the CPA exam. He received his Masters of Business Administration with honors from Cleveland State University and attended Northwestern University for his undergraduate studies.

MEMBERS OF THE 2014-2016

Certified Treasury Professional (CTP) Body of Knowledge (BOK) Committee and Associate Editors

Robert Venema, CTP
Chair, BOK Committee
Assistant Treasurer & Executive Director, Cash Management
Kaiser Permanente
Oakland, CA

Renee Adcock, CTP
Director, Corporate Treasury Solutions
PricewaterhouseCoopers
Tampa, FL

Kathe Bender, CTP
Vice President, Operational Risk Manager
TD Bank
Mt Laurel, NJ

Debra Crow, CTP
Vice President, Treasurer
Yahoo!
Sunnyvale, CA

James Gilligan, CTP
Assistant Treasurer
Kansas City Power & Light Company
Kansas City, MO

Rue Jenkins
Assistant Treasurer
Costco Wholesale Corporation
Issaquah, WA

Terri Mimms, CTP
Past Chair, BOK Committee
Chair, Certification Committee
Assistant Director of Treasury Operations
Purdue University
West Lafayette, IN

Tom Minneman, CTP
Consultant
Certes Financial Pros
Minneapolis, MN

Maureen O'Boyle, CTP
Castro, CA

Michelle Palombo, CTP, AAP
Managing Director, Electronic Banking
BNY Mellon
Pittsburgh, PA

Rick Perillo, CTP
Manager, International Treasury
Crane Co.
Stamford, CT

Hugo Rios, CTP
Banking Analyst, Treasury Division
Ontario Financing Authority
Toronto, ON
CANADA

Donald Rossi, CTP
Treasury Manager
National Geographic Society
Washington, DC

Ernest Smith, CTP
Senior Vice President, Regional Sales Manager, Treasury Management Services
BBVA Compass
Dallas, TX

Tom Wolfe, III, CTP
Senior Director, Global Treasury
Marriott Vacations Worldwide Corporation
Lakeland, FL

OTHER SUBJECT MATTER EXPERT CONTRIBUTORS

Fred Butterfield, CTP
Treasury Manager
Trust Company of America
Centennial, CO

Jim Washam, PhD, CTP
Interim Dean, College of Business
Arkansas State University
State University, AR

TABLE OF CONTENTS

PART II: THE TREASURY MANAGEMENT ENVIRONMENT

PART IV: RISK MANAGEMENT

LIST OF EXHIBITS

CHAPTER 1

CHAPTER 4

CHAPTER 5

CHAPTER 7

CHAPTER 8

CHAPTER 9

CHAPTER 10

CHAPTER 11

CHAPTER 12

CHAPTER 13

CHAPTER 14

CHAPTER 15

CHAPTER 16

CHAPTER 18

CHAPTER 19

CHAPTER 20

PART I
Introduction to Treasury Management

INTRODUCTION
Introduction to the Study of Treasury Management

CHAPTER 1
The Role of Treasury Management

INTRODUCTION
Introduction to the Study of Treasury Management

I. INTRODUCTION

II. THE EVOLVING ROLE OF THE TREASURY PROFESSIONAL

III. ORGANIZATION OF *ESSENTIALS OF TREASURY MANAGEMENT*

IV. SUMMARY

I. INTRODUCTION

Treasury management covers the various tools, techniques, and skills needed to manage an enterprise's overall financial holdings. The field, and as a result this book, covers a wide variety of topics.

The terms *treasury management* and *cash management* are often used synonymously but are actually quite different. Treasury management covers all aspects involved in managing an entity's financial assets (the treasury), while cash management is a subset of treasury management that focuses primarily on the day-to-day management of the entity's cash flow and liquidity. Cash management typically includes collections, disbursements, banking, and short-term borrowing and investment. Treasury management is the broader topic that goes beyond simple cash management to deal with longer-term borrowing and investing, capital management, and operational, financial, and reputational risk. The ultimate objective of both treasury management and cash management is to maximize the enterprise's liquidity while minimizing cost and risk within the overall framework of the firm's strategic plan.

II. THE EVOLVING ROLE OF THE TREASURY PROFESSIONAL

This book presents and discusses all of the various aspects of treasury management. It covers the generally accepted principles and practices used to manage a firm's liquidity, capital, and risk management functions. As such, it also represents the body of knowledge that needs to be mastered to earn the Certified Treasury Professional (CTP) credential. The CTP certification, which is administered by the Association for Financial Professionals (AFP), serves as a benchmark of competency in the finance profession and is recognized as the leading credential in corporate treasury worldwide.

Because the management of treasury functions takes place in a dynamic, ever-evolving environment, the related body of knowledge changes over time. The evolution of the profession is apparent not only in the rapid expansion of the day-to-day methodologies and tools treasury professionals use, but also in the types of responsibilities boards of directors and chief executive officers place on treasury professionals. This ongoing change creates a need to periodically update any book or text that discusses the profession.

The AFP facilitates an update of the CTP body of knowledge every three years based on an in-depth job analysis study conducted with a wide variety of treasury professionals and industry experts. The job analysis process provides a systematic procedure of identifying and validating the performance domains of the treasury professional and the knowledge and skills that are necessary to execute job responsibilities. The analysis includes:

- Field interviews with practitioners to create an inventory of critical responsibility and knowledge domains
- Development and execution of a comprehensive survey sent to a diverse cross-section of practitioners from various industries, geographic regions, and professional roles
- Analysis of the results

Survey respondents (nearly 1,000 for the most recent survey) validate the job tasks and responsibilities, and rank the importance of each. Treasury practitioners with experience in the various subject areas then work with the content editor, who is also a subject-matter expert, to update the actual body of knowledge.

As reflected in the title, this is the fourth edition of *Essentials of Treasury Management*. Each edition of this book is updated to reflect the changes that have occurred in the profession since the previous edition. As in previous editions, one of the goals of this book is to explain how and why particular methods and analytical tools are used, including when it is appropriate to use them and how the results should be interpreted. The objective of all business decisions should be to increase the economic value of the business, either immediately or over the long term. This goal applies no less to treasury responsibilities and decisions than it does to other areas of a firm's operations.

Economic value in the marketplace is tied directly to financial performance. Financial markets weigh a firm's performance relative to market participants' expectations for that firm. A treasury professional has to weigh considerations of cost, efficiency, risk, and expected return on investment when choosing among treasury management tools and investment and borrowing alternatives, as well as when making decisions that affect the timing of cash flows. The treasury professional must make choices with an understanding of their impact on firm value, while simultaneously ensuring an adequate level of safety represented by appropriate liquidity and risk mitigation practices.

It should also be noted that while this book focuses primarily on the typical for-profit corporation, many of the principles and practices in the treasury area also apply in the not-for-profit and government sectors. The organizational goals may be slightly different, but the concept of providing best-practice treasury operations in the most efficient manner is consistent.

III. ORGANIZATION OF *ESSENTIALS OF TREASURY MANAGEMENT*

This book is organized into five major parts. Part I, Introduction to Treasury Management, which includes this introduction, presents an overview of the role of treasury management and discusses how the treasury function fits within an entity's overall management structure.

Part II, The Treasury Management Environment, discusses the external environment in which treasury operates. This includes an overview of the legal and regulatory environment as well as a discussion of the major players and markets with which treasury has to interact.

Part III, Working Capital Management, discusses the tools and techniques used to manage an entity's short-term financial assets, including but not limited to cash and other liquid assets. As it has evolved, the treasury management profession has gone beyond traditional cash and liquidity management to broader working capital activities. This includes the various activities that correspond to what is traditionally referred to as the *cash management function* of treasury management.

Part IV, Risk Management, focuses on the various areas of risk that face treasury operations. Risk management has always been a key concern of treasury professionals, and developments over the last few years in both the financial markets and the economy have made risk management even more important than in the past. There are, in fact, risk management implications to virtually all treasury decisions. Part IV discusses traditional financial risk management, but also presents issues related to operational and enterprise risk management that are now typically part of the treasury mandate.

Finally, Part V, Financial Management, goes beyond the day-to-day operations of corporate cash management and looks at the overall issues of financial management in an organization. This material is important for two primary reasons. First, the tasks and responsibilities of treasury management have a significant impact on an entity's overall financial management, and an entity's financial management goals and objectives have a corresponding impact on the overall operations and objectives of treasury. Second, as treasury management continues to evolve, many of the tasks that historically were considered solely the purview of finance are becoming part of the treasury mandate. As such, the traditional tools of financial management have become an important part of the knowledge base of any treasury professional.

Each chapter in this book discusses a particular facet of treasury management. Each starts with a high-level overview of the material to be presented and ends with a summary of the key issues discussed. Each chapter also includes a number of questions intended to test the reader's understanding of the material presented. Diagrams and charts are included where appropriate. In addition, the book includes a glossary of key terminology used in the profession.

IV. SUMMARY

The topic of treasury management covers the various tools, techniques, and skills needed to manage an enterprise's overall financial holdings. This book presents the current body of knowledge required by an effective treasury professional in fulfilling that function, based on a survey of working treasury professionals. The body of knowledge is constantly growing and evolving as the role of treasury management grows and evolves to meet the needs of a changing business environment.

CHAPTER 1
The Role of Treasury Management

I. INTRODUCTION

treasury, n. Pronunciation: /ˈtrɛʒərɪ/

Etymology: Middle English < Old French tresorie (11th cent. in Godefroy), < Old French tresor, treasure n. (after medieval Latin *thesauria* : see thesaury n.) + *ie*, -y suffix.

1. A room or building in which precious or valuable objects are preserved, *esp.* a place or receptacle for money or valuables (now Hist.); *transf.* the funds or revenue of a state or of a public or private corporation.

2. *fig.* A repository of 'treasures'; a thesaurus; a 'treasure-house', 'storehouse'.

3. (Now with cap. initial.) The department of state which controls the collection, management, and expenditure of the public revenue; *spec.* that of the United Kingdom; also that of the United States.[1]

As the above definition implies, the term *treasury* has its roots in a room or place that was used to store money or valuables. The term *treasury management* covers the safeguarding and efficient use of financial assets for the benefit of a company and its various stakeholders. In today's world, where financial assets are typically deposited with an external agency such as a financial institution (FI), rather than being kept in an internal store room or safe, treasury management also involves dealing with banks, brokers, and other third-party financial services providers.

In the short term, treasury professionals in any organization perform critical daily liquidity management tasks that help ensure the availability of adequate cash resources needed to sustain the organization's ongoing operational activities. In the long term, treasury professionals perform critical finance functions that ensure the availability of funds and information necessary to sustain senior management's initiatives that support the organization's overall financial objectives.

This chapter discusses the basic role and objectives of treasury management, the potential structure of treasury, and the relationship between treasury management and general corporate financial management. It closes with a discussion of corporate governance and its impact on treasury.

II. THE ROLE AND ORGANIZATION OF TREASURY MANAGEMENT

A. Overall Goal and Objectives

The primary goal of treasury management is to manage the cash and related financial assets of an organization as efficiently as possible to provide the financial flexibility needed to achieve the organization's objectives in a manner consistent with the organization's overall strategic plan. No matter how wealthy or efficiently run a business or organization may be, there is a limited and fluctuating amount of cash and liquid assets available at any given time. Treasury's responsibility is to manage and use that pool of resources as efficiently and effectively as possible.

1. From *Oxford English Dictionary Online*, s.v. "treasury," accessed November 19, 2012, http://oed.com.

The major objectives of treasury management include:

- **Maintain Liquidity:**[2] Ensure the company's ability to meet current and future financial obligations in a timely and cost-effective manner.
- **Optimize Cash Resources:** Establish policies and procedures, and implement strategies that manage holdings of nonearning cash balances while providing adequate liquidity. Invest excess cash balances to generate interest income, or pay down debt to reduce interest expenses.
- **Maintain Access to Short-Term Financing:** Establish and maintain reliable access to short-term borrowing facilities at the lowest cost possible. Use short-term borrowing facilities to finance a company's working capital gap created when the operating cycle produces cash outflows that precede cash inflows.
- **Manage Investments:** Invest excess funds in a prudent manner for both short- and long-term needs. The preservation of principal is the primary objective, followed by ensuring liquidity and maximizing overall return. Investment activities should also be conducted in accordance with a board-approved investment policy.
- **Maintain Access to Medium- and Long-Term Financing:** Maintain access to medium- and long-term debt and equity financing to support planned asset expansion as well as the firm's existing asset base. Provide the financial flexibility necessary to exert strategic action when investment opportunities arise.
- **Manage Financial Risk:** Identify, measure, analyze, and mitigate or remediate a company's exposure to many types of financial risk (e.g., interest rate, foreign exchange [FX], counterparty, and operational). As discussed later in this book, this includes protecting overall financial assets from loss or theft.
- **Coordinate Financial Functions and Share Financial Information:** Collaborate with other internal divisions and departments to coordinate financial functions and share financial information. Effective communication with other divisions and functions is essential to ensure the achievement of treasury's goal to utilize cash as efficiently as possible.
- **Manage External Vendors:** Manage relationships with external vendors, including but not limited to banks and other financial institutions, to make the most effective use of financial assets while minimizing risk and expense.

Collectively, the first four objectives listed above are often referred to as *working capital management*, which is discussed in detail in Part III, Working Capital Management. Together they focus on the effective management of the cash conversion cycle (illustrated in Exhibit 1.1) and are often referred to as *treasury operations or cash management.*

2. *Liquidity* is usually defined as the ability to quickly convert an asset into cash without a significant loss of value. As a result, assets that can easily be bought or sold are referred to as *liquid assets*. By definition, cash is typically considered completely liquid.

EXHIBIT 1.1 **CASH CONVERSION CYCLE**

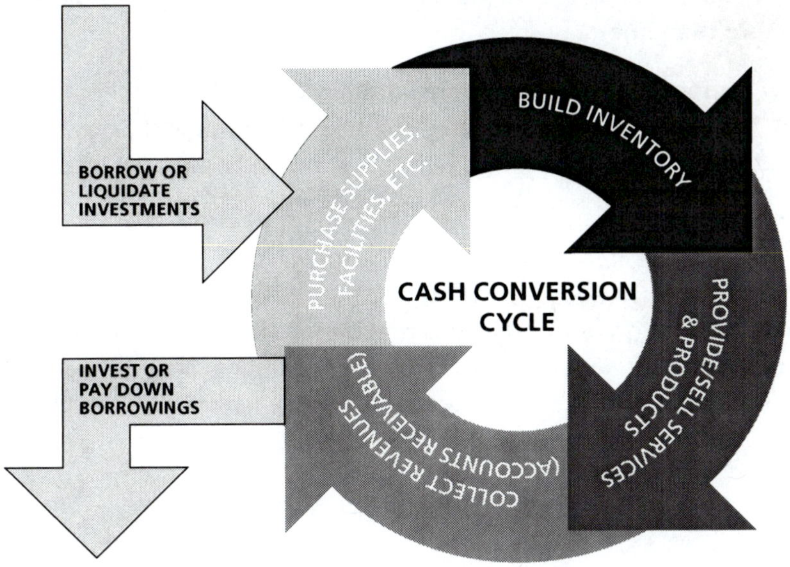

While the other objectives are very important and are also discussed in detail later in this book, working capital management is the foundation of effective treasury management. Without access to cash to pay vendors and employees, companies cannot operate. Many profitable companies have been forced to close their doors because of insufficient liquidity due to poor cash management.

B. Treasury Operations/Cash Management

Regardless of how the cash management function is organized, daily cash management typically involves the following six tasks, which are discussed in detail later in this book:

- Preparing a cash position worksheet
- Monitoring cash balances on deposit at financial institutions
- Collecting, concentrating, and disbursing cash
- Investing and borrowing funds on a short-term basis when needed
- Researching and reconciling exception items, such as unexpected charges on bank accounts, missing deposits, and uncleared checks
- Coordinating efforts with other finance areas, such as accounts receivable, accounts payable, tax, and accounting

C. Bank Relationship Management

Depending upon the specific company and its operations, treasury is often responsible for managing a number of external vendor relationships. Chief among those is bank relationship management, since all companies need at least one bank in order to operate and many have more than one.

The treasury management function is normally responsible for opening, maintaining, and closing all bank accounts for the organization within the authority that has been delegated to it by the board of directors or owners of the company, as well as managing the ongoing relationship with the various banks that house those accounts.

D. Reporting and Information Sharing

Treasury professionals need to gather information from many sources to complete their various tasks. Effective treasury management requires information sharing and cooperation with other internal departments and functions, such as purchasing, accounts receivable, accounts payable, risk management, pension management, internal audit, human resources/payroll, tax, financial planning and analysis, legal, and accounting (general ledger). Typical internal collaboration is shown in Exhibit 1.2.

EXHIBIT 1.2 **INTERNAL COLLABORATION**

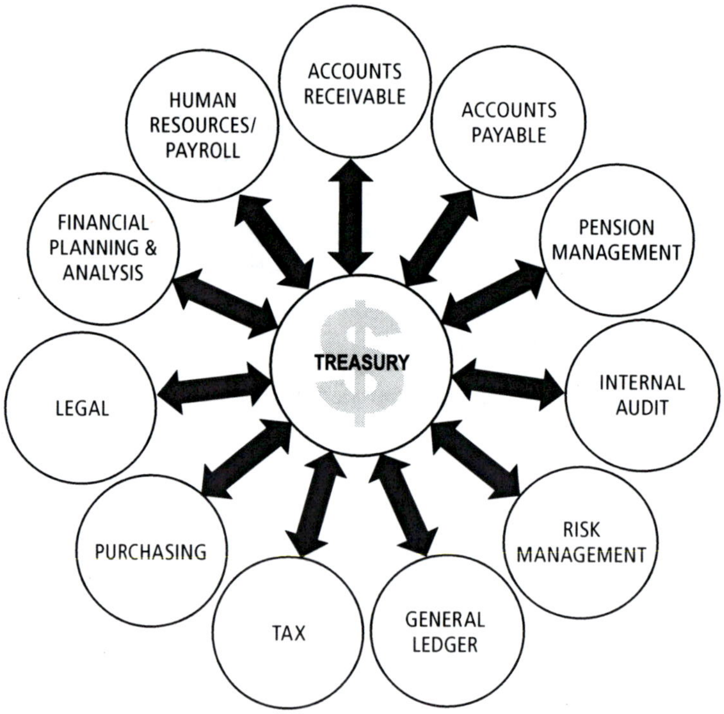

The activities of these other departments directly impact the cash management function. Most of these functions/departments typically report to managers outside the treasury area, such as the controller or chief financial officer. Therefore, individuals responsible for funds management must interact daily with these departments to ensure that overall treasury management objectives are met.

While treasury needs to collect information from many of these entities, it is equally important for treasury to share information regarding cash management and other functions with various internal stakeholders. This is often done using an organization's intranet or ERP (enterprise resource planning) systems, which are discussed in more detail in later chapters of this book.

Collaboration with a variety of external entities, such as financial institutions, financial markets, rating agencies, and third-party providers, is also critical to successful treasury management. These relationships, illustrated in Exhibit 1.3, play a key role in providing information or services that enable treasury to perform its daily functions.

EXHIBIT 1.3 **EXTERNAL COLLABORATION**

III. FINANCE AND TREASURY ORGANIZATION

The organization of the treasury and finance function varies significantly among industries and companies, but should be structured to facilitate the achievement of its overall objectives.

A. Financial Professionals in an Organization

In most large organizations, the senior finance officer is the chief financial officer (CFO). Alternatively, some firms may use the title *director of finance* or *vice president of finance.* The treasurer and the controller normally report directly to the CFO. Some companies have a flatter organizational structure where functions such as treasury, accounting, information systems, strategic planning, investor relations, and financial analysis all report directly to the CFO. Exhibit 1.4 illustrates a typical reporting structure at a large organization.

EXHIBIT 1.4 **SAMPLE FUNCTIONAL ORGANIZATION OF THE FINANCE FUNCTION**

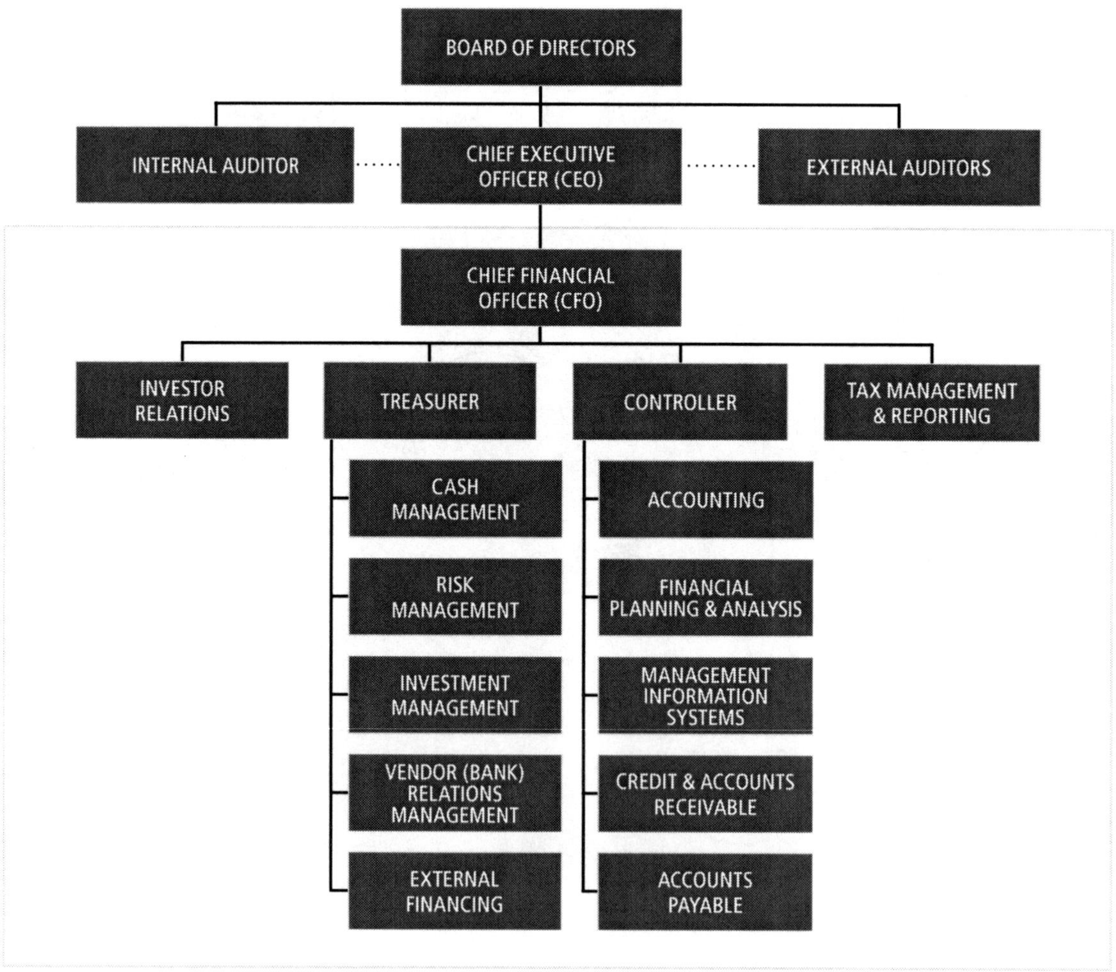

Note that this exhibit is intended to be illustrative and is not necessarily representative of any specific company. Note also that this exhibit focuses on function and not title. Titles can be confusing in that one organization may refer to its senior financial officer as the CFO while another may use *controller*, *comptroller*, or *vice president of finance*. In smaller companies, the structure may be considerably flatter, and it is not uncommon for some of these functions to be combined, with each position carrying a greater number of responsibilities. However individual companies are structured and however the actual titles may vary, most companies will have the following functions somewhere within their organization.

1. CHIEF FINANCIAL OFFICER (CFO)

The CFO is generally a member of the executive management team and reports to the chief executive officer (CEO). In a large company, the CFO usually oversees the treasury, risk, tax, investor relations, financial planning, and accounting functions.

The CFO plays an important role in strategic planning and is pivotal to the capital budgeting and financial planning process. Capital budgeting involves assessing the economic significance of proposed investments in new assets to determine whether they will increase the firm's value. This is accomplished by applying financial and statistical tools to measure the benefits and risks associated with a proposed investment.

Additionally, the CFO is responsible for accurate financial reporting. The United States (US) Sarbanes-Oxley Act of 2002 (SOX) makes the CFO of a publicly traded company listed on a US stock exchange personally responsible for the accuracy and completeness of financial statements, and for the development and implementation of adequate internal financial controls. Many other countries and exchanges have similar requirements.

2. TREASURER

The treasurer is primarily responsible for:

- Managing overall financial risk, including FX risk
- Arranging external financing, both short- and long-term
- Managing relationships with banks and other service providers
- Overseeing day-to-day liquidity and cash management
- Investing for the short and long term
- Developing and implementing treasury policies and procedures
- Managing domestic and international payments

In some companies, the treasurer may also be responsible for a variety of other functions, including management of dividend disbursements, insurance, and pension or retirement fund assets, as well as general risk management. In a large company, oversight of many of these responsibilities may be delegated to an assistant treasurer (AT) or a manager of treasury operations.

3. ASSISTANT TREASURER (AT) OR MANAGER OF TREASURY OPERATIONS

Many organizations are large enough to have a separate position designated as *AT* or *manager of treasury operations.* This position generally is responsible for the day-to-day operational aspects of the treasury department's duties described previously, thereby enabling the treasurer to focus on more strategic issues. Some organizations may have more than one AT—in some cases, one for international treasury and one for domestic treasury operations.

4. CASH MANAGER

The cash manager directs day-to-day cash management operations to include daily cash administration, management of current accounts, and in many cases bank relations. Depending upon the size of the company, the cash manager may report to the AT, or may be an AT and report directly to the treasurer.

5. CONTROLLER

The controller's primary function is financial reporting, but the function is often also responsible for accounts payable, accounting, budgeting, and coordinating with external auditors. In some companies, accounts receivable, financial planning and analysis (FP&A), and financial information systems may also report to the controller. In other companies, these functions report directly to the CFO.

6. RISK MANAGER

Overall financial risk management is treasury's responsibility, but specific risk areas, such as enterprise risk management, insurance, business continuity planning, and disaster recovery, may each be assigned to a separate risk manager. Reporting to the treasurer or CFO, the risk manager may evaluate and negotiate all insurance policies and coverage levels, as well as oversee disaster recovery and contingency planning.

7. INTERNAL AUDITOR

The internal auditor manages the internal audit function, which ensures that controls and operating procedures are established to protect the company from losses caused by inefficiency, inaccuracy, or fraud. The internal auditor typically reports directly to the board of directors to assure the auditor's independence and objectivity. In addition to an internal audit function, companies typically have audit committees of their boards that follow and monitor internal auditing functions.

8. CREDIT MANAGER

The credit manager preserves and collects accounts receivable, sets corporate credit policies, approves the extension of credit terms and exposure limits to customers, and establishes information systems to monitor accounts receivable. The credit manager typically reports to the controller, but could report to the treasurer or sales manager. One control consideration with this arrangement is that the sales manager could influence the credit manager to give a higher-than-prudent credit line to a customer in order to achieve certain sales goals. A company should have controls in place if this reporting relationship exists.

9. ACCOUNTS RECEIVABLE MANAGER

The accounts receivable manager is responsible for monitoring and collecting accounts receivable created through credit sales. This person is generally responsible for the accurate posting of all payments made on accounts and the reconcilement of the payments to the invoices. This task is sometimes referred to as the *application of payments.* The organizational placement of the accounts receivable area and the reporting lines can vary from company to company. The treasury and cash management areas must often interface with accounts receivable in order to pass along remittance data that accompanies payments received.

10. ACCOUNTS PAYABLE MANAGER

The accounts payable manager ensures that payments are made to vendors and suppliers in a manner that is consistent with the credit terms. This process involves maintaining lists of authorized vendors and suppliers, reviewing incoming invoices, matching invoices to approved purchase orders, reviewing invoices for proper approval, and scheduling payments. The accounts payable manager typically reports to the controller.

11. INVESTOR RELATIONS MANAGER/OFFICER

The investor relations manager makes sure that both stock investors and bondholders receive up-to-date information on the company, especially any reporting that is required by regulatory authorities. In addition, the investor relations manager typically provides access to annual reports, manages regular investor briefings, and answers questions that current or potential investors may have regarding the company. This position typically reports to the CFO.

B. Treasury Organizational Structure

1. PROFIT CENTER VERSUS COST CENTER

Treasury operations can be set up as a cost or profit center. A cost center is the most common approach because treasury usually is regarded as a support function to the organization and is not expected to return a profit to the company. The downside to this approach is that management may focus on the cost of treasury operations and not the value provided by the function, leading to difficulties in obtaining appropriate budget and staff.

Alternatively, treasury may be organized as a profit center for companies heavily involved in global finance, trade, or risk management, or for those companies that are financial services providers. Companies that engage in these activities have extensive dealings in money, capital, FX, interest rate, or commodities markets that require the buying/selling/holding of securities or the use of derivatives and other hedging instruments to increase earnings and/or reduce losses. The rationale for establishing treasury as a profit center is that it should generate income from either its trading operations or from hedging and/or speculative activities. The potential downside to this approach is that there may be pressure to produce significant profits from trading or investment activities at the expense of the best interests of the organization.

2. CENTRALIZED VERSUS DECENTRALIZED

A company that operates geographically dispersed sales offices with limited personnel may centralize its treasury functions at the company's headquarters, and multinational companies may centralize all treasury operations in one country. A centralized treasury offers the advantages of stronger control, economies of scale, and lower operating costs. The advantages can be even greater for multinationals as there may be significant tax advantages based on the location of treasury. However, a centralized treasury grants less autonomy to field office personnel or subsidiaries.

A company with autonomous subsidiaries and/or multiple operational entities (e.g., manufacturing, distribution, marketing, sales, and finance) may operate with a decentralized treasury structure, using guidelines and/or policies established by the company headquarters. Local subsidiary personnel can offer the advantages of possessing familiarity with local business and banking practices, as well as intimate knowledge of languages, customs, and cultures. In a decentralized structure, field personnel are responsible for some daily treasury functions, but there is typically a duplication of efforts—and resources—across units. Decentralized or foreign offices also may have a heavier burden in regards to compliance efforts, due to span-of-control issues and the increased need for coordination.

For the purpose of both information and control, local treasury operations generally submit periodic financial management reports to the home office. Typically, these reports summarize bank balances and transaction activities, as well as providing information on key treasury functions, such as cash forecasting, borrowing, investment, and FX activities. Best practice is for the home office to review local offices periodically to ensure conformance with policies, procedures, and controls. The internal audit function in large corporations generally serves this purpose.

Some large multinational corporations operate regional treasury centers that combine aspects of centralized and decentralized systems (i.e., while each region is centralized, overall treasury operations are decentralized to the regional centers). These regional centers typically provide treasury services to specific subsidiaries within a designated geographic area (e.g., North America, Europe, Asia-Pacific, Latin America, the Middle East, or Africa).

The advent of enterprise-wide accounting and information systems combined with the growth of automated treasury management systems has resulted in the introduction of hybrid centralized treasury systems with decentralized or distributed input and output. In this case, local personnel are responsible for entering local information, including payment and funds transfer requests, into a common treasury management or accounting system, while a centralized treasury staff manages and is responsible for overall treasury operations and cash management. Where needed, local equipment can be added to such an operation to allow for local printing and distribution of payments and reports.

3. SHARED SERVICES CENTERS (SSCs)

A shared services center is a department or operation within a multiunit organization tasked with supplying multiple business units and their respective divisions and departments with specialized services, such as information technology (IT), human resources (HR), or accounts payable (A/P) services. In some companies this includes day-to-day treasury operations (cash management) and other treasury functions, which may be operated as SSCs.

Shared services involve more than just centralized processing or operations. Services such as treasury, HR, or IT that are often duplicated within multiple operating units are consolidated in a shared services center, and the funding and management are shared across the enterprise. The resulting SSC becomes an internal service provider and is, in effect, another vendor or supplier to the various operating units that use its services.

Shared services centers are typically deployed for a variety of reasons:

- To reduce the costs of multiple or duplicate operations
- To standardize processes
- To increase the quality and timeliness of services
- To create a higher degree of strategic flexibility

SSC costs are typically charged back to operating units based on some form of transfer pricing, and overall service is managed based on specific service level agreements (SLAs) that specify how and when the service involved will be provided. In many cases SSCs are outsourced (i.e., operated or provided by an external third party).

IV. CORPORATE GOVERNANCE

Corporate governance refers to the principles and processes by which any organization (for-profit or not-for-profit) is governed. It provides the guidelines for managing a company so that the company can fulfill its stated goals and objectives in a manner that adds to the value of the company and is also beneficial for all stakeholders in the long term. The stakeholders in this case include all interested parties: the board of directors, management, stockholders or shareholders of for-profit companies, donors to not-for-profits, customers, employees, and even society in general. Management of the company assumes the role of trustee or fiduciary for all of the other stakeholders.

A. The Challenges of Corporate Governance

One of the key challenges in corporate governance relates to the separation of ownership and control that exists in most large companies. Stockholders own the company, but executive officers control the company's operations. Separation of ownership and control is a potential challenge in large, widely held corporations (versus small, closely held companies) because management may be able to make decisions with little or no oversight by the owners. Governance is also a challenge for not-for-profit entities. These organizations seek to serve the public good, with their boards generally serving as oversight for the public. The same kinds of conflicts that exist in the for-profit sector can exist here between the public and internal management.

It may be more appropriate to think of stockholders as investors rather than owners. This is a somewhat subtle, but important, difference. An investor orientation focuses on asset returns and the composition of investment portfolios. This orientation tends to make most investors passive shareholders, which sometimes may induce members of management to take actions that benefit themselves at shareholders' expense (e.g., managing short-term profits to maximize employee bonuses in a manner that reduces the long-term value of the organization, or ignoring a very profitable merger offer that would eliminate current management jobs). This generally is referred to as the *agency problem* between management and stockholders because the managers are legally the agents of the owners.

To protect stockholders, corporate governance procedures establish a set of checks and balances to place limits on executive prerogatives and to monitor management performance. Important components include the board of directors (especially independent directors), shareholder meetings, independent external auditors, and regulatory agencies. Most recent failures in corporate governance can be traced back to a failure on the part of one or more of these components. Therefore, an organization should have a chief audit executive accountable for internal auditing who reports directly to the board of directors' audit committee. The board should provide sufficient funding and other resources for the audit process, including periodic private sessions to discuss risks and controls with the chief auditor.

The board of directors also has the responsibility to act in the best interests of shareholders. In the United States, this is generally interpreted as maximizing shareholder wealth, or maximizing the company's stock price over the long term. In other countries, the objectives and responsibilities of the board may be more broad-based.

In many countries, the other stakeholders in the company (e.g., employees/unions, bondholders, bankers, local community, and governments) may also be considered in the company's decision process regarding such issues as salaries and benefits, capital expansion, or product offerings. In planned or socialist economies, the government may be the primary decision maker for companies in that country.

B. Role of the Board of Directors in Treasury Operations

In most large organizations, the board of directors serves as the general authority for all operations, including treasury. Ultimately, it is the board's responsibility to approve business policies, major initiatives, and contracts. In order to facilitate day-to-day operations, the board will delegate authority for specific functions to treasury, generally via a board resolution. In such a resolution, the board typically grants the treasury function the authority to:

- Open, close, and modify bank accounts
- Establish credit facilities
- Oversee investments
- Issue debt and equity securities
- Devise, implement, and execute risk management strategies

It is important to note that this delegation is typically not open ended but subject to specific limitations and regular review by the board, which should be clearly spelled out in board-approved policy statements. At the end of the day, overall responsibility and related oversight is still the responsibility of the board, but even its authority may be limited by the company's original articles of incorporation and corporate charter.

C. Role of Independent Directors

As noted above, independent directors are one of the key components of good corporate governance. In many countries, independent directors (also referred to as *external or nonexecutive directors*) are a regulatory requirement. In the United States, any company listed and traded on the New York Stock Exchange (NYSE) is required to comply with the NYSE basic standards regarding independent directors. The United Kingdom (UK) Corporate Governance Code has similar requirements for British corporations. While the specific rules and regulations regarding independent directors may vary by country and stock exchange, many global companies look to NYSE regulations for guidance if they have any thought of ever potentially trading on the NY exchange.

As part of the requirements for listing, many exchanges have established basic standards for the role of independent directors of listed companies. Financial professionals at listed companies, or those at companies considering listing on one of the exchanges, must understand these requirements and expectations. Failure to adhere to these standards could cause significant public embarrassment for the company, as well as a significant loss of investor capital. CEOs must certify to the listing exchange(s) that their companies comply with these standards.

There is a significant downside for companies that ignore these standards, but there are many benefits for companies that meet and exceed them. Compliant companies are better positioned to attract and retain shareholders because adherence to the standards lowers investors' assessment of ownership risk while improving their sense that the company will be durable.

For a director to be considered independent under the NYSE standards, the board must determine that the director has no material relationship with the listed company, either directly or as a partner, shareholder, or officer of the organization. Independent directors must meet in regular executive sessions without management present. A director cannot be considered independent unless he or she has not been an employee or an independent auditor of the company for a continuous five-year period, which is referred to as a *cooling-off period.*

For NYSE listed companies, independent directors must constitute a majority of a board. Companies must have a nominating committee and a compensation committee (or committees of the company's own determination with the same responsibilities), as well as an audit committee, each comprised solely of independent directors who possess meaningful finance and/or accounting experience.

V. SUMMARY

The primary goal of treasury management is to manage the cash and related financial assets of an organization as efficiently as possible to provide the financial flexibility needed to achieve the organization's objectives in a manner consistent with the organization's overall strategic plan. Treasury management includes cash management—the subset of treasury management that deals with day-to-day liquidity—as well as broader treasury roles, such as long-term borrowing and investment, and financial risk management.

This chapter discussed the role of treasury management within an organization. It also presented an overview of the typical roles and functions of both treasury management and finance, and reviewed the relationship between the two. The chapter closed with a discussion of corporate governance.

EXHIBIT 1.5 **RELATIONSHIP OF CASH MANAGEMENT, TREASURY MANAGEMENT, FINANCIAL MANAGEMENT, AND CORPORATE GOVERNANCE**

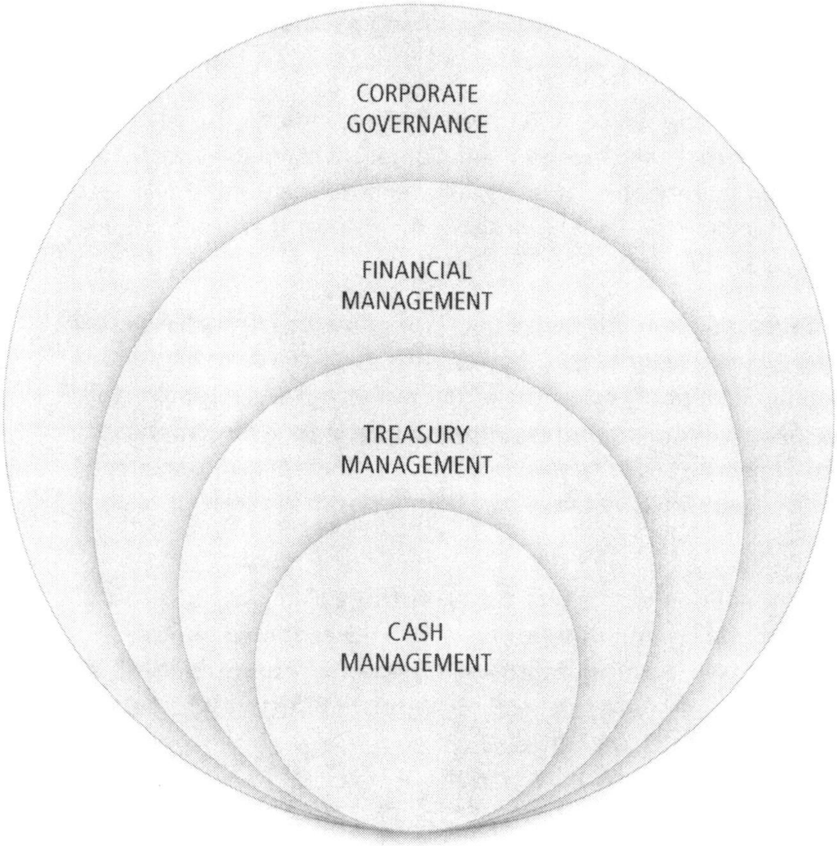

Treasury can be organized in a variety of ways, but the overall roles and functions remain the same. Exhibit 1.5 provides a visual depiction of the relationship between cash management, treasury management, financial management, and corporate governance. The board of directors, or its equivalent, has overall authority for setting the direction of a company and authorizing contractual relationships. The portion of that authority related to control of financial assets and bank accounts is typically delegated to finance and treasury within approved limits and guidelines.

TEST YOUR UNDERSTANDING: CHAPTER 1

Answers are on pages 639–641.

1. What are the major objectives of treasury management?
2. Which of these objectives make up working capital management?
3. Why is effective management of working capital critical to an organization?
4. What are the typical primary responsibilities of a treasurer?
5. What are the typical responsibilities of a credit manager?
6. What are some typical activities for which a board of directors might grant authority to individuals within treasury operations?
7. What are the six tasks involved in daily cash management?
8. What is the downside of making treasury a cost center?
9. Why are shared services centers (SSCs) typically deployed?
10. Define corporate governance.
11. What is required for a director to be considered independent under NYSE standards?
12. What are the major checks and balances that limit and monitor management performance?

PART II
The Treasury Management Environment

CHAPTER 2
Regulatory and Legal Environment

I. INTRODUCTION

II. GENERAL REGULATORY ENVIRONMENT

A. General Types of Financial Institution (FI) Regulations
B. Issues Affecting Financial Regulation

III. PRIMARY REGULATORS AND STANDARD SETTERS OF INTERNATIONAL FINANCIAL MARKETS

A. Central Banks
B. Financial Stability Board (FSB)
C. Bank for International Settlements (BIS)
D. Basel Committee on Banking Supervision (BCBS)
E. European Payments Council (EPC) and Single Euro Payments Area (SEPA)
F. European Securities and Markets Authority (ESMA)
G. International Association of Deposit Insurers (IADI)
H. International Organization of Securities Commissions (IOSCO)
I. Financial Action Task Force (FATF)
J. International Association of Insurance Supervisors (IAIS)

IV. US LEGAL AND REGULATORY ENVIRONMENT

A. Regulatory Agencies
B. US Legal Environment

I. INTRODUCTION

As discussed in Chapter 1, The Role of Treasury Management, the treasury profession requires that practitioners work with a large number of internal and external partners. This part of the book, The Treasury Management Environment, introduces some of the key external groups with which practitioners need to work and examines some of the various issues faced in managing those relationships.

The financial services industry, which is discussed in more detail in Chapter 3, Banks and Financial Institutions, is a key supplier of products and services used by treasury professionals. Historically, the financial services industry and its relationships with corporate customers have been very highly regulated. Because this regulation has a significant impact on how financial institutions (FIs) operate, it is important that treasury professionals understand the regulatory environment faced by their various financial services providers.

This chapter provides an overview of the legal and regulatory issues that impact FIs and their treasury management customers on a daily basis. It begins with an overview of financial services regulation in general, including the major issues that the various regulators supervise. The next section provides a high-level overview of the various types of regulators and discusses their impact on treasury management. Because of the global impact of the US market and the fact that US financial services regulations have often been used as models by other countries around the world, the following section examines the US financial services regulatory system as an example of the regulatory and legal structure that treasury professionals may have to deal with. The final sections of the chapter provide overviews of corporate tax considerations and insolvency/bankruptcy laws and regulations.

II. GENERAL REGULATORY ENVIRONMENT

In order to understand the financial regulatory environment better, it is important to clarify the general role that FIs serve in the economy. Their primary role is to provide a mechanism for savers of capital to transfer that capital to those who might best use it. In one instance, it may be some consumer's savings being used to help other consumers purchase a house or car. In another instance, it may be the pension savings of a worker being used to provide the equity capital for a company to expand its production facilities. Because this vital role of capital transfer is fundamental to the efficient functioning of the economy, FIs generally are regulated closely by monetary and other government authorities.

The most common type of FI is the commercial bank. In the most general case, a bank accepts deposits from both consumers and businesses, and then lends some portion of those deposits to other consumers and businesses. The acceptance of deposits and provision of loans are the primary criteria used to define a *bank*, sometimes referred to as a *depository institution*. In some cases, a bank may be limited to servicing certain sectors or customer bases, but the deposit/loan criteria are still present. For the purpose of this chapter, the term *bank* will be used to represent any FI that provides both the deposit and loan functions.

A bank makes its profit by charging a higher rate on the money it lends than it pays for the deposits it accepts. A bank obviously has some risks in this process, specifically default/credit risk (if the borrower does not repay the loan) and liquidity risk (if depositors withdraw their deposits with little notice). From a bank's point of view, these risks could result in the possible failure of the bank. From the perspective of the economy in general, the risks from bank failures include depositors losing their money and potentially a collapse of the entire banking system.

The primary job of bank regulators, therefore, is to monitor the risks (both credit and liquidity) relating to potential bank failures and to implement safeguards that can help to reduce the overall risk of systemic failure (i.e., the collapse of the entire banking system). There are several approaches regulators can take to address these risks, and most countries impose regulatory oversight of some type on the traditional banking functions. As is discussed in more detail below and in Chapter 3, Banks and Financial Institutions, this oversight results in restrictions on the banks' actions in order to manage the overall riskiness of the financial system and reduce the impact of potential bank failures.

A. General Types of Financial Institution (FI) Regulations[1]

Much of the following discussion relates primarily to the regulation of banks, which are the primary type of FIs. Other FIs will be discussed where applicable.

There are five general areas in which the regulation of FIs is usually concentrated. These are:

1. Monitoring and managing the overall safety and soundness of the banking system
2. Setting and implementing monetary policy
3. Determining guidelines for the chartering of banks and other depository FIs
4. Allocating credit toward certain sectors of the economy and protecting consumers
5. Protecting investors purchasing securities through FIs

These areas are outlined in more detail below. It is important to understand that laws and regulations relating to these areas will vary significantly from country to country. While there are ongoing efforts to coordinate the international regulatory environments, as a sovereign nation, each country has the right to enact whatever laws and/or regulations it deems necessary for the banks operating in that country. A multinational bank, therefore, may have to abide by many sets of regulations, depending on where it operates.

1. MONITORING AND MANAGING THE OVERALL SAFETY AND SOUNDNESS OF THE BANKING SYSTEM

The purpose of regulations with respect to safety and soundness is to protect both depositors and borrowers against the risk of failure by banks in the system.

One of the primary regulatory approaches is the setting of minimum capital levels required of banks operating within the country. Capital requirements determine how much capital (usually defined as equity funds) the owners of a bank must contribute to the business. This is typically in the form of a ratio of capital to at-risk assets (loans and other investments). The higher the ratio of capital to assets, the lower the risk on the part of the bank. Many regulators use the concept of tiers of capital, with common equity being the first tier (most stable) and other long-term capital (less stable sources, such as preferred stock or long-term debt) forming a second tier. This concept of tiered capital is a key component of global regulation of the banking industry.

1. This section is derived partly from: Anthony Saunders and Marcia Cornett, *Financial Institutions Management: A Risk Management Approach*, 6th ed. (New York: McGraw-Hill/Irwin, 2008).

A second regulatory approach related to the safety and soundness of the banking system is to ensure proper investment policies and diversification on the part of each bank (e.g., that the bank makes loans that are properly priced for default risk). In most countries, the regulatory authorities will monitor the quality of the loan and investment portfolios of the banks closely, and will generally place restrictions on how much can be loaned or invested in a particular company or industry sector. These are referred to as *impairment of capital rules*. The basic idea is to limit the chances that the failure of one large company, and the resulting defaults on its loans, could lead to a bank's failure.

As the result of the failure of a number of large financial institutions in the Recession of 2009, there was increased discussion on the part of regulatory authorities globally of increasing the restrictions on certain types of bank investment activities—specifically, proprietary trading (i.e., trading securities on the bank's own account), hedge funds, and private equity businesses—that were thought to have contributed to the recession. One of the earliest proponents of these types of restrictions was Paul Volcker, who served as chairman of the US central bank from 1979 to 1987. The US implementation of this restriction, called the *Volcker rule*, is discussed in the context of US banking regulations later in this chapter.

The third layer of protection with respect to safety and soundness is generally in the form of some type of deposit insurance for investors' funds held by the bank. In some countries, this deposit insurance may be called a *deposit guarantee*, but the intent is the same. The basic idea is primarily to protect the assets of smaller deposit customers (typically consumers, although corporate accounts are also typically covered up to a certain amount) who would be most harmed by a bank failure. To this end, most of these regulations do place some limit on the amount of funds that will be guaranteed. The concept of deposit insurance, however, brings along with it the concept of moral hazard. If the depositors know that their money is insured regardless of which bank they use, there is very little incentive on their part to investigate the bank's creditworthiness. From the banker's perspective, the moral hazard issue is that the bank may undertake a higher level of risk (i.e., make riskier loans or investments) knowing that if the bank fails, the government will protect depositors.

Ultimately, the key benefit of deposit insurance or a guarantee is that it increases the overall confidence in the banking system, especially on the part of smaller depositors. Depositor confidence in any bank is critical to that bank's survival. A lack of consumer confidence can lead to "a run on the bank" in which a large number of depositors demand the return of their deposits all at once. Since banks are in the business of lending deposits out to other customers, they rarely have enough currency on hand to pay off a large group of depositors at once and can be forced out of business. During the Great Depression, many banks were forced to close due to a run on the bank, rather than actual insolvency. During times of financial crisis, some regulators have increased the levels of deposit insurance in order to bolster this confidence and prevent a panicked withdrawal of funds by depositors.

Along with these protections, most regulators impose some type of monitoring and surveillance. This is usually in the form of on-site examinations, as well as requirements that the FI produce accounting statements and other operational and financial reports on a regular basis to be evaluated off-site. The degree of monitoring and regulation can vary significantly from country to country.

2. SETTING AND IMPLEMENTING MONETARY POLICY

Banks and other financial institutions play a key role in the implementation of monetary policy set by a country's central bank. Monetary policy includes the actions taken by the central bank to control the money supply and interest rates in that country. The issue that arises for the monetary authorities is that the money supply of a country is usually much greater than just the amount of currency (notes and coin) in circulation. This is a result of the ability of the commercial banking system to effectively multiply the deposits that it holds. This multiplication is done by lending deposits out to companies and individuals, who in turn redeposit those funds back into the system so that they can be lent out a second time, and so on. This multiplication of deposits basically allows banks to create money and increase the overall money supply in any given country. The more loans that financial institutions make, the larger the money supply. A certain amount of growth is critical to economic growth, but too much growth can lead to inflation and other economic problems. Determining the "proper" size of the money supply in any country is a key element of monetary policy.

In order to manage this multiplication of deposits, most central banks impose reserve restrictions on the commercial banks operating within their systems. For each unit of deposits, some percentage must be maintained as reserves (i.e., not loaned out or invested). These reserves may either be held at the commercial bank, or in many countries, at the central bank. This requirement increases the safety of the overall monetary system and allows the central bank to better control the money supply by changing the reserve requirement, either raising the percentage to contract the supply of money in circulation, or lowering it to encourage lending.

3. DETERMINING GUIDELINES FOR THE CHARTERING OF BANKS AND OTHER DEPOSITORY INSTITUTIONS

The chartering process generally refers to the establishment or opening of banks and other depository institutions (e.g., credit unions or savings banks) and the guidelines as to the types of financial services they are allowed to offer. The chartering process and the types of charters available can vary significantly from country to country. Some countries have very clear distinctions between different types of depository institutions and their services, while other countries allow single institutions to offer a broader range of services. Chartering regulations also typically specify the amount of capital needed to open a bank and may also limit the ownership of banks in a country by foreign entities.

4. ALLOCATING CREDIT TOWARD CERTAIN ECONOMIC SEGMENTS AND PROTECTING CONSUMERS

Many countries have, as part of their financial regulation, a mandate to support certain sectors of the economy, such as housing or farming. Regulations relating to allocation of credit may require that a certain percentage of loans be made to specific sectors, or there may be limits on interest rates, prices, or fees in that sector. Ultimately, these types of regulations may have significant impacts on the lending policies of banks operating within the country.

Consumer protection regulations are designed to protect consumers, who are frequently assumed to lack bargaining power and are therefore considered "vulnerable" when entering into financial transactions. In many cases, consumer protection regulations are linked to those related to credit allocation. The goal is to provide acceptable access for consumers to financial services, credit, and financial information. These regulations may also be used to prevent financial discrimination against certain sectors of the population.

5. PROTECTING INVESTORS PURCHASING SECURITIES THROUGH FINANCIAL INSTITUTIONS (FIs)

Regulations relating to investor protection are generally aimed at those FIs that provide investment banking or brokerage services. Depending on the country, banks may have restrictions on offering some of these services to depositors, and some FIs only provide investment services. (This is discussed in more detail in Chapter 3, Banks and Financial Institutions.) The investor protection regulations are designed to protect investors who purchase securities through various types of FIs. In addition to banks, the FIs in this case include investment banks, brokerages, mutual funds, or pension funds. The most common types of investor protection regulations shield investors against abuses such as insider trading, lack of disclosure, outright malfeasance, and breach of fiduciary responsibilities.[2]

B. Issues Affecting Financial Regulation

As discussed in the previous section, each country has its own set of laws and regulations relating to the chartering and operation of banks within its borders. While there is some level of international cooperation between the various regulatory authorities, there is no true central regulatory authority, which can lead to inconsistencies in various jurisdictions and duplication of regulatory efforts. Ongoing developments and crises in the global financial community have made the problem even more complex.

In the past, a large amount of global business flowed through banks or insurance companies, and there was a limited range of investment vehicles trading in regulated markets. The development of private equity funds, hedge funds, sovereign funds, and other, often unregulated, investment opportunities has produced a much greater challenge in the regulation of financial markets. In addition, instruments such as derivatives make it much easier for an FI to manage risk on a far greater scale and in more complex ways.

Some of the other features of the current global financial environment are:

- A growing dominance of a few, very large FIs that operate in more than one country
- Cross-border ownership[3] of most securities exchanges
- Technology that allows an FI to conduct business virtually anywhere in the world

Couple these changes with the integration of the global economy, and the challenges faced by regulators can easily be seen. The 2010 debt crisis in Greece, Portugal, and Spain and the resulting impact on the euro zone, and ultimately on the global economy, are prime examples of the fact that global financial money and capital markets are highly integrated.

2. In some countries, additional protection may be provided against the failure or bankruptcy of brokerages. The protection is generally limited to cash accounts and lost securities, and does not normally include protection from loss of investment security value due to market fluctuations.
3. Historically, securities exchanges existed in individual countries and were locally owned, either by investors, financial institutions, and/or regulators. The trend toward global trading has resulted in the consolidation of many of the existing exchanges across national borders, resulting in cross-border ownership. An example would be the merger of the New York Stock Exchange (NYSE) with Euronext, a group of European stock exchanges, in 2007 and its pending merger with IntercontinentalExchange, Inc.

III. PRIMARY REGULATORS AND STANDARD SETTERS OF INTERNATIONAL FINANCIAL MARKETS

While each country maintains its own regulatory structure, there are a number of organizations that work cooperatively to try to better manage FIs internationally. This section introduces some of the primary regulators, organizations, and standard-setting groups in the area of global financial markets.

A. Central Banks

A central bank (sometimes referred to as a *monetary authority*) is an entity that is responsible for implementing and managing a country's monetary policy—in other words, the country's money supply and interest rates. In many countries, the central bank is also responsible for overseeing its country's commercial banking and payment systems. Examples of central banks include the European Central Bank (ECB), the Bank of England, the Federal Reserve Bank (the Fed) in the United States, and the People's Bank of China.

Central banks typically bear responsibility for one or more of the following functions:

- **Monetary Policy:** Many central banks are responsible for implementing the country's chosen monetary policy, including controlling the size of the money supply and overall interest rates. This is typically done using tools such as managing reserve requirements, buying and selling government securities (handled in the United States by the Federal Reserve Bank's Federal Open Market Committee, or FOMC), and setting an official interest rate used for lending to financial institutions.
- **Currency Issuance:** Many central banks are responsible for issuing currency, which they "sell" to FIs and other investors in exchange for government bonds. The income derived from this activity is called *seigniorage* and is used to support the central bank or remitted to the local government.
- **Supervision and Regulation:** Some central banks, such as the Fed, are directly responsible for supervising and regulating the country's commercial banks.
- **Government Services:** Some central banks provide financial services to their own government, taking the place of commercial banks. They are in effect the government's bank. This can include providing basic deposit and safekeeping services, as well as the sale and redemption of government securities.
- **Depository Institution Services:** Some central banks provide various services to FIs. These services can include the operation of clearing and settlement systems (discussed in more detail in Chapter 4, Payment Systems), the provision of coin and currency, and the holding of reserve balances.

B. Financial Stability Board (FSB)[4]

The FSB (based in Basel, Switzerland) was established to provide international coordination of national financial authorities and international standard-setting bodies. It works to develop and promote the implementation of effective regulatory, supervisory, and other financial sector policies. The FSB has members from the financial authorities of the G20[5] nations, as well as from international organizations such as the World Bank, International Monetary Fund (IMF), the Bank for International Settlements (BIS), the Organisation for Economic Co-operation and Development (OECD), and others.

4. Information on the FSB was obtained from its website (http://www.financialstabilityboard.org, accessed October 15, 2013). Additional details on FSB members and standards can also be found at this site.
5. The Group of Twenty, or G20, is a group of finance ministers and central bank governors from 20 major global economies that have met periodically since 2008 to discuss global economic issues.

The primary goals of the FSB are to (1) maintain financial stability, (2) promote the openness and transparency of the financial sector, (3) implement international financial standards, and (4) conduct periodic peer reviews. The FSB provides an agenda for strengthening financial systems and the stability of international financial markets, but actual changes to regulations must be enacted by the relevant national financial authorities.

C. Bank for International Settlements (BIS)[6]

The Bank for International Settlements was established in 1930 to deal with international financial issues resulting from the First World War. It is the world's oldest international financial institution and remains the principal center for international central bank cooperation.

Currently, the BIS's activities focus on fostering cooperation among central banks and, increasingly, other agencies in pursuit of monetary and financial stability. Since 1930, central bank cooperation at the BIS has taken place through the regular meetings in Basel of central bank governors and experts from central banks and other agencies. In support of this cooperation, the BIS has developed its own research in financial and monetary economics and makes an important contribution to the collection, compilation, and dissemination of economic and financial statistics.

In the monetary policy field, cooperation at the BIS in the immediate aftermath of the Second World War and until the early 1970s focused on implementing and defending the Bretton Woods[7] system. In the 1970s and 1980s, the focus was on managing cross-border capital flows following the oil crises and the international debt crisis. The 1970s crises also brought the issue of regulatory supervision of internationally active banks to the fore, resulting in the 1988 Basel Capital Accord and its "Basel II" revision of 2001–06. More recently, the issue of financial stability in the wake of economic integration and globalization, as highlighted by the 1997 Asian crisis, has received a lot of attention and led to the third round of Basel Capital Accords.

Apart from fostering monetary policy cooperation, the BIS has always performed "traditional" banking functions for the central bank community (e.g., gold and foreign exchange transactions), as well as trustee and agency functions. The BIS was the agent for the European Payments Union (EPU, 1950–58), helping the European currencies restore convertibility after the Second World War. Similarly, the BIS has acted as the agent for various European exchange rate arrangements, including the European Monetary System (EMS, 1979–94), which preceded the move to a single currency. Finally, the BIS has also provided or organized emergency financing to support the international monetary system when needed.

6. Information on the BIS was obtained from its website (http://www.bis.org, accessed October 15, 2013). Additional details on BIS and its subcommittees, secretariats, and standards can also be found at this site.
7. The Bretton Woods Agreements established the rules used to govern monetary relations among the world's major financial powers following the Second World War. The International Monetary Fund (IMF) and the International Bank for Reconstruction and Development (IBRD), both now part of the World Bank, were established as part of the Bretton Woods Accords.

In addition to its operational role, the BIS sponsors several committees that support its overall mandate. Some of the principal committees are listed below.

1. GROUP OF GOVERNORS AND HEADS OF SUPERVISION (GHOS)

The Group of Governors and Heads of Supervision is the governing body of the Basel Committee, which is discussed below, and is comprised of central bank governors and (non-central bank) heads of supervision from member countries. The GHOS's secretariat is based at the Bank for International Settlements in Basel, Switzerland.

2. COMMITTEE ON THE GLOBAL FINANCIAL SYSTEM (CGFS)

The Committee on the Global Financial System is a central bank forum for the monitoring and examination of broad issues relating to financial markets and systems. It helps to elaborate appropriate policy recommendations to support the central banks in the fulfillment of their responsibilities for monetary and financial stability. In carrying out this task, the committee places particular emphasis on assisting central bank governors in recognizing, analyzing, and responding to threats to the stability of financial markets and the global financial system.

3. COMMITTEE ON PAYMENT AND SETTLEMENT SYSTEMS (CPSS)

The CPSS is a BIS-hosted standard-setting body for payment and securities settlement systems. It also serves as a forum for central banks to monitor and analyze developments in domestic payment, settlement, and clearing systems, as well as in cross-border and multicurrency settlement schemes.

D. Basel Committee on Banking Supervision (BCBS)[8]

The BCBS was originally established in 1974 in response to the liquidation of the Herstatt Bank in Cologne, Germany. The failure of the Herstatt Bank highlighted the potential systemic risk that could be caused by the failure of one large international bank between the time terms of a financial contract (such as an FX trade) were agreed and the time of actual settlement. The term *Herstatt risk* is now used to refer to foreign exchange settlement risk, especially between bank counterparties. In response to that situation, the G10[9] banded together and formed a standing committee, the BCBS, under the sponsorship of the BIS.

The BCBS operates as a standard-setting body under the BIS and provides a forum for regular cooperation on banking supervisory matters. Its objective is to reduce systemic risk, enhance the understanding of key supervisory issues, and improve the quality of banking supervision worldwide. It does so by exchanging information on national supervisory issues, approaches, and techniques, as well as developing guidelines and supervisory standards, primarily in the area of capital adequacy.

In 1988 the BCBS published an initial set of minimum capital requirements for banks. This was originally known as the *1988 Basel Capital Accord*, and eventually *Basel I*. Basel I established minimum capital ratios for large banks based upon the credit risk of the various assets of each bank. These initial capital standards were put into effect by the G10 countries in 1992.

8. Information on the BCBS was obtained from the BIS website (http://www.bis.org/bcbs/index.htm, accessed October 15, 2013).
9. The Group of Ten, or G10, is a group of nations that joined together in 1962 and agreed to make financial resources available to the IMF for borrowing to help stabilize the global economy.

In 2004, the BCBS published the second set of Basel Accords, typically referred to as *Basel II*. Basel II expanded the risk ratings implemented by Basel I and added an assessment of operational risk to the existing credit risk evaluation in establishing core capital requirements for major banks. Basel II was based upon three so-called pillars:

- Minimum capital requirements to address credit and operational risk
- Supervisory review, which provided a framework for dealing with and evaluating risk
- Market discipline, which focused on disclosure requirements regarding risk metrics and capital adequacy

The third Basel Accords (Basel III) extended Basel II to address stress testing and market liquidity risk, as well as capital adequacy. Basel III is a comprehensive set of reform measures, developed in 2011 in response to the global financial crisis of the late 2000s (referred to in this book as the *Recession of 2009*) and scheduled to be implemented through 2018, to strengthen the regulation, supervision, and risk management of the banking sector. As part of Basel III, core capital requirements were increased by approximately 2%, and minimum leverage and liquidity requirements were introduced.

Basel III's stated goals are to:

- Improve the banking sector's ability to absorb shocks arising from financial and economic stress, whatever the source
- Improve risk management and governance
- Strengthen banks' transparency and disclosures

The reforms target:

- Bank-level regulation, which will help raise the resilience of individual banking institutions to periods of stress
- System-wide risks that can build up across the banking sector, as well as the procyclical amplification of these risks over time

These two approaches to supervision are complementary, as greater resilience at the individual bank level reduces the risk of system-wide shocks.

E. European Payments Council (EPC) and Single Euro Payments Area (SEPA)[10]

The European Payments Council (EPC) is the coordination and decision-making body of the European banking industry in relation to payments. The purpose of the EPC is to support and promote the Single Euro Payments Area (SEPA). The EPC develops payment schemes and frameworks that help to realize the integrated euro payments market. In particular, the EPC defines common positions for the cooperative space of payment services.

10. Some information in this section was obtained from the EPC's website (http://www.europeanpaymentscouncil.eu, accessed October 15, 2013).

The Single Euro Payments Area (SEPA) is the name of the European Union (EU) payments integration initiative. The SEPA vision was set out by EU governments in the Lisbon agenda in March 2000, which aimed to make Europe more dynamic and competitive. The legislative framework of SEPA is contained in the European Payment Services Directive (PSD).

Following the introduction of euro notes and coins in 2002, the political drivers of the SEPA initiative—EU governments, the European Commission (EC), and the European Central Bank (ECB)—have focused on the integration of the euro payments market. Since then, the political drivers have called upon the payments industry to bolster the common currency by developing a set of harmonized payment schemes[11] and frameworks for electronic euro payments, in line with the following overall vision for SEPA:

- Integrating the multitude of existing national euro credit transfer and euro direct debit schemes into a single set of European payment schemes is a natural step toward making the euro a single and fully operational currency. The PSD currently sets February 2014 as the final date for migration of both credit transfers and direct debits to the SEPA debit and credit schemes.
- Creating a single standard for payment cards across national borders aims at ensuring a consistent customer experience when making or accepting payments with cards throughout the euro area.
- The SEPA program seeks to incentivize increased use of electronic payment instruments by standardizing practices while reducing the cost of wholesale cash distribution.

SEPA focuses on the technical, legal, and commercial barriers to paying and/or receiving euros cross-border within SEPA boundaries. SEPA establishes minimum standards and common pricing for payments processing within the EU, and consists of two primary concepts:

- Creation of standard credit and debit payment schemes (both high- and low-value)
- Creation of a common payment card framework (both debit and credit)

While SEPA only applies within the EU, any organization that does business within that area is potentially impacted. SEPA currently consists of the 28 EU member states plus nonmembers such as the Czech Republic, Denmark, Iceland, Norway, Liechtenstein, Switzerland, and Monaco. A complete listing of SEPA member states is provided in Appendix 2.1.

F. European Securities and Markets Authority (ESMA)[12]

ESMA is an independent EU authority that contributes to safeguarding the stability of the European Union's financial system by ensuring the integrity, transparency, efficiency, and orderly functioning of securities markets, as well as enhancing investor protection. In particular, ESMA fosters supervisory convergence, both amongst securities regulators and across financial sectors, by working closely with the other European supervisory authorities competent in the fields of banking (the European Banking Authority, or EBA) and insurance and occupational pensions (the European Insurance and Occupational Pensions Authority, or EIOPA).

ESMA's work on securities legislation contributes to the development of a single rule book in Europe. This serves two purposes. First, it ensures the consistent treatment of investors across the EU, enabling an adequate level of protection of investors through effective regulation and supervision. Second, it promotes equal conditions of competition for financial services providers, as well as ensuring the effectiveness and cost efficiency of supervision for supervised companies. As part of its role in standard setting and reducing the scope of regulatory arbitrage, ESMA strengthens international supervisory cooperation. Where requested in European law, ESMA undertakes the supervision of certain entities with pan-European reach.

11. A payment scheme is a method of making or receiving a payment (i.e., a payment system) and is discussed in more detail in Chapter 4, Payment Systems.
12. Information on ESMA was obtained from its website (http://www.esma.europa.eu, accessed October 15, 2013).

Finally, ESMA also contributes to the financial stability of the European Union, in the short, medium, and long term, through its contribution to the work of the European Systemic Risk Board (ESRB), which identifies potential risks to the financial system and provides advice to diminish possible threats to the financial stability of the EU. ESMA is also responsible for coordinating actions of securities supervisors or adopting emergency measures when a crisis situation arises.

ESMA is partially responsible for the implementation and administration of the European Market Infrastructure Regulation (EMIR), which was adopted by the European Parliament and Council in 2012. EMIR is intended to increase the stability of the over-the-counter (OTC) derivatives market throughout Europe, and implements reporting and clearing obligations for OTC derivatives analogous to the requirements of the Dodd-Frank Act in the United States (discussed later in this chapter).

G. International Association of Deposit Insurers (IADI)[13]

The International Association of Deposit Insurers (IADI) was formed in May 2002 to enhance the effectiveness of deposit insurance systems by promoting guidance and international cooperation. Members of IADI conduct research and produce guidance for the benefit of those jurisdictions seeking to establish or improve a deposit insurance system. Members also share their knowledge and expertise through participation in international conferences and other forums.

IADI currently represents 70 deposit insurers from 69 jurisdictions. IADI is a not-for-profit organization constituted under Swiss law and is domiciled at the Bank for International Settlements in Basel, Switzerland.

Deposit insurance is a tool implemented by many countries to protect their depositors against loss from the failure of a bank or other financial institution. The amount of protection and the specific details of what is covered vary by country. Deposit insurance is generally only provided on deposit accounts and does not typically cover mutual funds or other types of investments. The main purpose of deposit insurance, as discussed earlier in this chapter, is to increase depositor confidence and reduce the risk of a potential run on a given bank, thus helping to insure overall financial stability.

H. International Organization of Securities Commissions (IOSCO)[14]

IOSCO is recognized as the international standard setter for securities markets. Its membership regulates more than 95% of the world's securities markets, and it is the primary international cooperative forum for securities market regulatory agencies. IOSCO members are drawn from and regulate more than 100 jurisdictions. IOSCO provides comprehensive technical assistance to its members, in particular those that regulate emerging securities markets.

13. Information on IADI was obtained from its website (http://www.iadi.org, accessed October 15, 2013).
14. Information on IOSCO was obtained from its website (http://www.iosco.org/about/, accessed October 15, 2013).

Through members' efforts, IOSCO strives to establish and apply rigorous standards of regulation, effectively monitor international security transactions, and strengthen enforcement against offenses.

I. Financial Action Task Force (FATF)[15]

The FATF is an international organization composed of members from more than 30 countries. The primary purpose of this intergovernmental group is the development and promotion of policies, at both national and international levels, to combat money laundering and terrorist financing.

Since its creation, the FATF has spearheaded the effort to adopt and implement measures designed to counter the use of the financial system by criminals, primarily through anti-money laundering efforts. It monitors members' progress in implementing necessary measures, reviews money laundering and terrorist-financing techniques and countermeasures, and promotes the adoption and implementation of appropriate measures globally. In performing these activities, the FATF collaborates with other international bodies involved in combating both money laundering and the financing of terrorism.

In US regulations, money laundering is defined as "any financial transaction which generates an asset or a value as the result of an illegal act, which may involve actions such as tax evasion or false accounting."[16] In some countries (e.g., England), money laundering does not even need to involve money, but can include any economic good. Courts in several major countries have ruled that money laundering has been committed by private individuals, drug dealers, businesses, corrupt officials, members of criminal organizations (e.g., the Mafia), and even states. Essentially, any business through which money laundering could occur would come under possible regulation.

Money laundering is a diverse and complex process involving three stages:

- **Placement:** The physical deposit of cash proceeds from illegal activities into an FI
- **Layering:** A series of financial transactions designed to separate cash proceeds from their criminal or terrorist origins
- **Integration:** Creating what appears to be a legitimate explanation for the source of funds (e.g., showing that funds were donated for a charitable purpose)

For money laundering to be successful, there must not be a paper trail that connects these three stages.

As an example, an organization that has large amounts of illegal cash might employ apparently innocent individuals (often referred to as *smurfs*) to use the cash to buy chips to gamble at legal casinos. The smurfs will take the proceeds and deposit them into legitimate bank accounts and declare them as gambling winnings, often paying income tax on the money to make it appear legitimate. The resulting deposits now appear to have a legitimate source and can in turn be transferred out of the country using normal banking channels.

J. International Association of Insurance Supervisors (IAIS)[17]

The IAIS is a standard-setting group that represents insurance regulators and supervisory entities of some 190 jurisdictions in nearly 140 countries, constituting the great majority of the world's insurance premiums. Its primary objective is to encourage cooperation among the members on both the international and domestic levels. This cooperation helps to ensure the maintenance of efficient, fair, safe, and stable insurance markets, ultimately benefiting and protecting policyholders.

15. Information on FATF was obtained from its website (http://www.fatf-gafi.org, accessed October 15, 2013).
16. From "Money Laundering: A Banker's Guide to Avoiding Problems," published by the Office of the Comptroller of the Currency (OCC), December 2002 (http://www.occ.gov/topics/bank-operations/financial-crime/money-laundering/money-laundering-2002.pdf).
17. Information on the IAIS was obtained from its website (http://www.iaisweb.org/, accessed October 15, 2013).

IV. US LEGAL AND REGULATORY ENVIRONMENT

Due to its overall size and the number of international organizations that do business there, the US market has a global impact. Additionally, US financial services regulations have often been used as models by other countries around the world. While the specific details may vary, many of the principles embodied in US financial services laws and regulations are implemented elsewhere. This section of the chapter will briefly examine the US regulatory system as an example of regulatory and legal impact in the financial services industry specifically and treasury management generally.

Historically, the US Congress and federal regulatory agencies have imposed restrictions on FIs to help align and enforce the regulatory objectives presented at the beginning of this chapter. In addition to those basic objectives, financial regulations in the United States have also sought to prevent any concentration of economic and political power, as well as encourage institutional specialization. Essentially, the Congress enacts legislation and the regulatory agencies develop regulations based on that legislation. From the Glass-Steagall Act of 1933 until the Gramm-Leach-Bliley Act of 1999 (GLB), US FIs served very distinct functions. During those 66 years, the functions of commercial lending and deposit taking, securities underwriting, mortgage origination, and insurance underwriting were legally required to be carried out by separate FIs. This changed in 1999 when GLB removed the barriers among the functions of commercial banking, investment banking, and insurance, allowing FIs a broader range of products and more direct competition.

The landscape of financial regulation in the United States was impacted further by the passage of the Dodd-Frank Wall Street Reform and Consumer Protection Act of 2010 (Dodd-Frank Act). This wide-ranging legislation, passed in the wake of the Recession of 2009, affected almost all types of FIs and significantly changed the regulatory framework for financial activities in the United States.

A. Regulatory Agencies

The United States has a dual banking system. *Dual* refers to the fact that banks are either federally or state chartered. At the federal level, bank supervision is shared primarily by three agencies: the Office of the Comptroller of the Currency (OCC), the Board of Governors of the Federal Reserve System, and the Federal Deposit Insurance Corporation (FDIC). The Financial Stability Oversight Council (FSOC), which helps oversee these primary bank regulators, is a newly created agency under the Dodd-Frank Act charged with monitoring systemic risk in financial systems and making recommendations to other regulatory entities.

In addition to the primary regulators mentioned previously, there are a number of agencies and regulatory bodies that are responsible for monitoring specific depository FIs or certain financial services. These include the Consumer Financial Protection Bureau (CFPB), the Office of Foreign Assets Control (OFAC), the Financial Crimes Enforcement Network (FinCEN, the US FIU[18]), the National Credit Union Administration (NCUA), state banking boards and commissions, and the Department of Justice (DOJ).

18. An FIU, or financial intelligence unit, is a specialized government agency established in many countries to deal with the problems of money laundering and similar financial crimes.

There are a large number of other regulators focused on specific segments of the financial environment. These include such agencies/organizations as the Securities and Exchange Commission (SEC), the Commodity Futures Trading Commission (CFTC), and the Financial Industry Regulatory Authority (FINRA).

1. COMMODITY FUTURES TRADING COMMISSION (CFTC)

The CFTC was created by Congress in 1974 as an independent agency with the mandate to regulate commodity futures and options markets in the United States. As part of the Dodd-Frank Act, the CFTC is required to work with the SEC to regulate over-the-counter derivatives so that irresponsible practices and excessive risk taking can no longer escape regulatory oversight.

2. CONSUMER FINANCIAL PROTECTION BUREAU (CFPB)

The CFPB is an independent consumer protection entity within the Fed that was created in 2010 by the Dodd-Frank Act. The primary reason behind the CFPB's creation was to consolidate and strengthen consumer protection responsibilities and oversee the enforcement of federal laws intended to ensure the fair, equitable, and nondiscriminatory access to credit for individuals and communities.

To achieve this objective, the CFPB has the authority to examine and enforce regulations for banks and credit unions with assets exceeding $10 billion and all mortgage-related businesses (e.g., lenders, servicers, and mortgage brokers), payday lenders, and student lenders, as well as other nonbank financial companies that are large, such as debt collectors and consumer reporting agencies. Banks and credit unions with assets of $10 billion or less will be examined for consumer complaints by their appropriate regulator.

3. DEPARTMENT OF JUSTICE (DOJ)

The DOJ, as well as the Fed, reviews and approves proposed bank mergers and holding company acquisitions to determine their impact on competition as part of antitrust legislation. The Federal Bureau of Investigation (FBI), a bureau of the DOJ, plays a central role in investigating FI fraud and theft, as well as in enforcing key money laundering legislation.

4. FEDERAL DEPOSIT INSURANCE CORPORATION (FDIC)

The FDIC, which was established in 1933 as part of the Glass-Steagall Act, is an independent agency of the federal government whose primary role is to protect depositors from losses caused by bank insolvency. The FDIC's responsibilities include:

- Providing deposit insurance for all insured FIs
- Supervising selected depository institutions[19]
- Acting as a trustee in the event of bank failures

The FDIC administers the Deposit Insurance Fund (DIF). Insured institutions pay a premium into the fund that is based on their level of deposits and risk profile, as determined by the type and mix of assets and liabilities the institution holds. The fund is backed by the full faith and credit of the US government and covers deposits in checking and savings accounts up to a maximum of $250,000 per depositor, as of 2013.

19. The FDIC has direct supervisory authority over state-chartered banks that are not members of the Federal Reserve System, and backup authority over national and Fed member banks.

5. FINANCIAL CRIMES ENFORCEMENT NETWORK (FinCEN)

FinCEN serves as the US financial intelligence unit (FIU) and is the primary agency (operating as a bureau of the Treasury) that oversees and implements policies to prevent and detect money laundering by criminal or terrorist organizations. It does this by enforcing counter-money laundering legislation (e.g., the Bank Secrecy Act), which requires reporting large and/or suspicious monetary transfers conducted at banks. FinCEN also provides intelligence and analytical support to law enforcement agencies in the form of reports that are used to build investigations and plan new strategies that combat money laundering.

6. FINANCIAL INDUSTRY REGULATORY AUTHORITY (FINRA)[20]

FINRA is the largest independent regulator for all securities firms and registered securities representatives doing business in the United States. It was created in 2007 through the consolidation of the National Association of Securities Dealers (NASD) and the member regulation, enforcement, and arbitration functions of the New York Stock Exchange (NYSE). FINRA's mission is to provide investor protection and market integrity through effective and efficient regulation, as well as through compliance and technology-based services.

FINRA is involved in most aspects of the securities business, including:

- Registering and educating industry participants (i.e., brokers, registered investment advisors, etc.)
- Examining brokerage firms
- Writing and enforcing rules related to federal securities laws
- Informing and educating the investing public
- Providing trade reporting and other industry utilities
- Administering the primary dispute resolution forum for investors and registered firms

FINRA also performs market regulation under contract for the NASDAQ Stock Market, the NYSE MKT (formerly known as the *American Stock Exchange*), the International Securities Exchange, and the Chicago Climate Exchange.

7. FINANCIAL STABILITY OVERSIGHT COUNCIL (FSOC)

The FSOC's primary responsibility is to prevent systemic risk from threatening the financial system by identifying threats to financial stability and gaps in regulations, and facilitating coordination across federal and state agencies. It does not directly regulate institutions; instead, this is the primary role of the Fed, FDIC, OCC, and others. While the FSOC has a strong systemic oversight role, it has limited enforcement power and can only make recommendations to the primary regulators.

8. NATIONAL CREDIT UNION ADMINISTRATION (NCUA)

The NCUA is an independent federal agency that charters and supervises federal credit unions. The NCUA is backed by the full faith and credit of the US government. It also operates the National Credit Union Share Insurance Fund (NCUSIF), insuring the savings of account holders in all federal credit unions and many state-chartered credit unions.

20. Information on FINRA comes from its website (http://www.finra.org/AboutFINRA/, accessed October 15, 2013).

9. OFFICE OF FOREIGN ASSETS CONTROL (OFAC)

OFAC is an office of the Treasury Department that administers and enforces economic and trade sanctions against targeted foreign countries, terrorist-sponsoring organizations, and international narcotics traffickers. Based on US foreign policy and national security goals, OFAC can impose controls on financial transactions and freeze foreign assets under US jurisdiction. The role of OFAC was expanded under the USA PATRIOT Act, which is covered later in this chapter.

10. THE SECRET SERVICE

The Secret Service was created in 1865 to suppress counterfeit currency. Now part of the US Department of Homeland Security, its mission statement includes the charge to "safeguard the nation's financial infrastructure and payment systems to preserve the integrity of the economy." In addition to dealing with counterfeit currency, the Secret Service also deals with credit card fraud, check fraud, and identity theft.

11. SECURITIES AND EXCHANGE COMMISSION (SEC)

The SEC, which is governed by the securities laws of 1933, 1934, and 1940, is a federal agency designed to maintain a fair and orderly market for investors by regulating and supervising securities sales. The SEC's responsibilities include:

- Registering public offerings of debt or equity securities by banks, bank holding companies, and other corporations
- Setting financial disclosure standards for corporations that sell securities to the public
- Requiring companies with publicly owned securities to file quarterly and annual financial statements
- Regulating mutual funds and investment advisors
- Monitoring insider trading to enforce related regulations

While the role of most agencies that oversee the financial services industry relate to protecting depositors, the SEC focuses on protecting people who invest in stocks, bonds, and derivative instruments. In general, the SEC requires publicly traded companies to disclose all relevant financial information to investors.

B. US Legal Environment

A wide range of laws and regulations affects FIs and, as a result, their customers. Many laws date back to the 1913 Federal Reserve Act, which provided the foundation for the current banking system.

The most sweeping banking regulation, however, was the Dodd-Frank Act, which significantly changed the regulatory landscape and revamped the federal government's approach to consumer protection in the financial arena. This section provides an outline of significant US federal legislation relating to the financial services industry. The discussion is divided into seven basic areas:

1. Legislation regarding regulation and supervision of FIs and financial services
2. Legislation governing payment systems and instruments
3. Legislation relating to financial crimes, money laundering, and financial disclosure
4. Federal Reserve regulations
5. Regulations relating to investments and securities
6. The Uniform Commercial Code
7. Unclaimed property (escheatment) legislation

1. LEGISLATION REGARDING REGULATION AND SUPERVISION OF FINANCIAL INSTITUTIONS (FIs) AND FINANCIAL SERVICES

a. Federal Reserve Act (1913)

The Federal Reserve Act established the Federal Reserve System and provided the foundation for the current banking system. It requires all banks with a national charter granted by the OCC to become Reserve banks, and thus become subject to Fed regulation, supervision, and reserve requirements. The act also empowered the Federal Reserve to create a national check collection and settlement system through member banks.

b. Glass-Steagall Act (also known as the Banking Act of 1933)

The Glass-Steagall Act was passed to address major issues and problems with the financial services industry stemming from the Great Depression. As initially written, the act:

- Prohibited commercial banks from underwriting securities except for government issues
- Prohibited securities firms from engaging in bank-like activities, such as deposit gathering
- Required the Fed to establish interest rate ceilings on all types of accounts and prohibit the payment of interest on demand deposits (provisions of this act were incorporated in Federal Reserve Regulation Q, known as *Reg Q*)
- Created the FDIC to guarantee deposits up to a stipulated maximum amount in order to restore faith in the banking system after numerous Depression-era bank failures

The Gramm-Leach-Bliley Act of 1999, discussed below, repealed almost all of Glass-Steagall with the exception of deposit insurance under the FDIC.

c. Anti-tying Amendments to the Bank Holding Company Act (1970)

The term *tying* refers to the act of requiring an organization or individual to purchase a product or service in order to be allowed to obtain a second different product. Under the 1970 amendments to the Bank Holding Company Act, the federal government prohibits tying in financial services, in an effort to increase competition and remove unfair banking practices. In general, the regulations provide that a financial institution may not condition the extension of credit on the requirement that the borrower obtains other services from the FI. There are some very broad exclusions to the general rule as a result of what is called the *traditional bank product* exception. Under this exception, banks may condition the terms, including price, of an offer based on the requirement that the customer purchase or use other products from the bank, as long as all of the products are available separately to the same customer.

d. Gramm-Leach-Bliley Act (1999)

The Gramm-Leach-Bliley Act eliminates many of the provisions of the Glass-Steagall Act, especially those that created barriers among the functions of commercial banking, investment banking, and insurance. Specifically, it:

- Permits the creation of financial holding companies (FHCs) that can engage in any activity that the Fed considers financial in nature or incidental to it
- Establishes the Fed as the primary regulator of FHCs, which are subject to consolidated capital requirements at the parent company level and bank-style risk management at all levels
- Allows easier entry by foreign banks into the US financial services market
- Includes key provisions relating to consumer protection, including specific regulations regarding the protection of nonpublic personal information

e. Dodd-Frank Wall Street Reform and Consumer Protection Act (2010)

This sweeping legislation was enacted in response to concerns related to the financial services industry in the wake of the Recession of 2009. The act had a major impact on the regulation of banks and other FIs, and brought financial consumer protection under a single authority.

One of the primary objectives of the Dodd-Frank Act was to bring more transparency and accountability to the derivatives market. Specifically, with respect to derivatives, the act:

- **Closes Regulatory Gaps:** It provides the Securities and Exchange Commission (SEC) and the Commodity Futures Trading Commission (CFTC) with authority to regulate over-the-counter (OTC) derivatives, so that irresponsible practices and excessive risk taking can no longer escape regulatory oversight.
- **Requires Central Clearing and Exchange Trading:** It requires central clearing and exchange trading for derivatives that are cleared or settled through exchanges. It also provides a role for both regulators and clearinghouses to determine which contracts should be cleared.

  In recognition of the fact that many companies enter into OTC derivatives for important economic reasons, including but not limited to risk management, the act provides an exception to the central clearing requirement for some "end users." To qualify for the exception, the end user must not be a financial entity, the derivatives must be used only for hedging purposes, and the company must satisfy reporting requirements established by the CFTC.
- **Requires Market Transparency:** It requires data collection and publication through clearinghouses or swap repositories to improve market transparency, and provides regulators with important tools for monitoring and responding to risks.
- **Adds Financial Safeguards:** It increases the safety of the system by ensuring that dealers and major swap participants have adequate financial resources to meet responsibilities. The act also provides regulators with the authority to impose capital and margin requirements on swap dealers and major swap participants, but not on end users.
- **Sets Higher Standards of Conduct:** It establishes a code of conduct for all registered swap dealers and major swap participants when advising a swap entity. When acting as counterparties to a pension fund, endowment fund, or state or local government, dealers are to have a reasonable basis to believe that the fund or governmental entity has an independent representative advising it.

Specific effects of various provisions of this act are discussed throughout this book. At the time of publication, much of the enabling regulations of Dodd-Frank had yet to be enacted.

As part of the broader act, the so-called Durbin Amendment to Dodd-Frank is a provision intended to limit debit card interchange fees and increase competition in payment processing. The Durbin Amendment's limits on interchange fees are discussed in Chapter 4, Payment Systems.

Another piece of the act, known as the *Volcker rule* after the former Fed chairman who first suggested it, would limit a financial institution's ability to engage in proprietary trading for its own portfolio and to own or invest in a hedge fund or private equity fund. The final legislation eliminated the restrictions on hedge and private equity funds. There has been much discussion regarding the Volcker rule, and although draft regulations have been approved, the rule had not yet been implemented by the time of publication of this book.

2. LEGISLATION GOVERNING PAYMENT SYSTEMS AND INSTRUMENTS

a. Electronic Fund Transfer Act (EFTA) (1978)

The EFTA defines the rights and responsibilities of customers using all electronic funds transfer (EFT) services except wire transfers. Further, it limits customer liability for unauthorized banking transactions involving automated teller machines (ATMs) and point-of-sale (POS) terminals, provided the customer promptly notifies the bank or other institution that issued the card. Provisions of this act are incorporated in Federal Reserve Regulation E.

b. Depository Institution Deregulation and Monetary Control Act (DIDMCA) (1980)

The DIDMCA impacts both FIs and treasury professionals. For the financial services industry, it:

- Requires all deposit-taking institutions to maintain reserves at the Fed
- Makes Fed services such as the discount window and check clearing available to all deposit-taking institutions
- Mandates the Fed to reduce and/or price payment system float and price previously free Fed services according to the standards of a tax-paying vendor

c. Electronic Signatures in Global and National Commerce (E-Sign) Act (2000)

The purpose of the E-Sign Act is to grant digital signatures the same legal status as handwritten ink signatures. It establishes the legal certainty of electronic commerce (e-commerce) transactions and provides a measure of confidence around the enforceability of electronic transactions. Digital signatures are not facsimile signatures but electronic files used to "sign" electronic documents, and are discussed in Chapter 14, Information Technology in Treasury.

d. Check Clearing for the 21st Century Act (Check 21) (2003)

Check 21, which is discussed in Chapter 4, Payment Systems, provided the basis for electronic clearing of checks by allowing the substitution of a copy or image of a check for the original document in the clearing process. The act was intended to speed and facilitate the clearing of checks by eliminating the need to exchange physical paper, and improve the overall efficiency of the payment system.

3. LEGISLATION RELATING TO FINANCIAL CRIMES, MONEY LAUNDERING, AND FINANCIAL DISCLOSURE

a. Bank Secrecy Act (BSA) (1970) and Money Laundering Control Act (MLCA) (1986)

The purpose of the BSA and the MLCA is to control the flow of illegal money, essentially occurring when money is laundered to conceal criminal activities, usually related to drug trafficking, tax evasion, or terrorist activities. While the initial money laundering regulations were directed toward FIs, their impact has broadened over time.

The primary intent of the BSA is to deter money laundering and the use of secret foreign bank accounts. By requiring all FIs to report any suspicious financial transactions, a paper trail is created to assist in detecting and monitoring illegal activities. It is important to note that the term *FI* is very broadly defined, and as a result, the act covers many businesses not normally thought of as FIs. The act requires any trade or business organization that receives $10,000 or more in cash to file IRS Form 8300, identifying from whom that cash was received, on whose behalf the transaction was conducted, a description of the transaction, and the method of payment.

The MLCA enhanced the BSA by making it a crime to structure transactions in such a way as to avoid the reporting requirements of that act—in effect, defining money laundering and making it a federal crime. FIs are liable for substantial civil and criminal penalties if they fail to comply with the reporting provisions of anti-money laundering regulations. The MLCA also requires FIs to establish effective "know your customer" guidelines, be aware of parties to large-value funds transfers, and file currency transaction reports (CTRs) and criminal referrals. As noted below, the USA PATRIOT Act extended many of the provisions of the MLCA to nonfinancial businesses potentially handling large-value transactions, such as car, boat, plane, and jewelry dealers. Specifically, FIs and other covered organizations must monitor and report the following:

- Activity that is inconsistent with a customer's business
- Attempts by customers to avoid reporting or record-keeping requirements
- Unusual or multiple funds transfer activities
- Customers who provide insufficient or suspicious information

b. USA PATRIOT Act (2001)

In response to the September 11, 2001, attacks on the United States, Congress passed wide-ranging legislation designed to improve overall security, and granted the FBI and the DOJ increased latitude in intelligence-gathering activities. This legislation is named the *Uniting and Strengthening America by Providing Appropriate Tools Required to Intercept and Obstruct Terrorism Act (USA PATRIOT Act)*. The primary impact for FIs is the substantial number of amendments added to the provisions of existing money laundering legislation, such as the BSA. These amendments are intended to make it easier to prevent, detect, and prosecute international money laundering and the financing of terrorism.

Some provisions of the USA PATRIOT Act are that it:

- Imposes significant obligations upon nonbank FIs, including broker-dealers, credit card companies, and check-cashing services (nonbank FIs were not covered previously by BSA). It also includes nonfinancial entities potentially handling large-value transactions, such as car, boat, plane, and jewelry dealers.
- Makes all foreign banks with accounts in the United States subject to US jurisdiction, including the power to obtain records and information regarding customers.
- Prohibits US banks from maintaining, either directly or indirectly, correspondent accounts for any foreign shell banks, which are defined as foreign banks without a physical presence in any country.
- Prevents US credit card system operators from authorizing foreign banks to issue or accept US credit cards without taking steps to prevent usage by terrorists.
- Requires banks to know their customers, resulting in increased due diligence before taking on new business.

c. Sarbanes-Oxley Act (SOX) (2002)

The primary purpose of SOX is to improve disclosure and financial reporting in the wake of a series of dramatic financial scandals between the years 2000 and 2002. SOX brought about numerous changes to SEC rules and regulations and created the Public Company Accounting Oversight Board (PCAOB). Specifically, publicly traded firms must:

- Disclose in annual reports the code of ethics applicable to senior financial officers. Companies that change or waive the code must disclose the event by filing a Form 8-K with the SEC or posting a notice on the company's website.
- Disclose in annual reports whether the audit committee has a financial expert.
- Establish and maintain adequate internal controls for financial reporting.
- Require audit committees to preapprove all audit and non-audit services provided by the auditor, and be briefed by auditors on the company's accounting, including alternative approaches that might be preferable to the company's current methods.

SEC Regulation G, which implements much of SOX, requires public companies to reconcile pro forma financial information to financial statements. Companies that issue earnings releases must file them on Form 8-K. Finally, all off-balance-sheet arrangements (OBSAs) that may have a material current or future effect on the financial statements or liquidity must be included in the management's discussion and analysis (MD&A) section of the financial statements. While SOX is a US regulation, because it applies to any company traded on a US stock exchange, it has a significant international impact.

d. The Red Flags Rule[21]

The Federal Trade Commission (FTC), the federal bank regulatory agencies, and NCUA have issued regulations (the Red Flags Rule) requiring FIs and creditors to develop and implement written identity theft prevention programs, as part of the Fair and Accurate

21. Information on the Red Flags Rule was obtained from the FTC website (http://www.ftc.gov/bcp/edu/pubs/business/alerts/alt050.shtm, accessed August 20, 2013).

Credit Transactions Act of 2003 (FACT). The programs must provide for the identification of, detection of, and response to patterns, practices, or specific activities—known as *red flags*—that could indicate identity theft.

The rule applies to FIs and creditors with consumer accounts designed to permit multiple payments or transactions—or any other account for which there is a reasonably foreseeable risk of identity theft. Under the rule, an *FI* is defined as a state or national bank, a state or federal savings and loan association, a mutual savings bank, a state or federal credit union, or any other entity that holds a transaction account belonging to a consumer. Most of these institutions are regulated by the federal bank regulatory agencies and NCUA.

e. Foreign Account Tax Compliance Act (FATCA) (2010) and the Report of Foreign Bank and Financial Accounts (FBAR)

FATCA was implemented to address tax noncompliance by US taxpayers with foreign bank accounts. The act requires US taxpayers to file an annual report (IRS Form TD F 90-22.1, known as an *FBAR*) of all foreign financial accounts and offshore assets. The act also requires foreign financial institutions to report financial accounts held by US taxpayers or foreign entities that are substantially owned by US taxpayers. US persons (including businesses) must file an FBAR if the person had a financial interest in or signature authority over at least one account located outside of the United States and the aggregate value of all financial accounts exceeded $10,000 at any time during the year. There is a general exception for corporate signers who are included in a consolidated FBAR filed by their organization.

4. FEDERAL RESERVE REGULATIONS

The Fed defines and enforces several key banking regulations that impact treasury professionals. Some of the major regulations[22] include:

a. Regulation D

Regulation D implements the reserve requirement provision of the Federal Reserve Act of 1913, and imposes uniform reserve requirements on all depository institutions, with different levels of reserves for different types of deposits. The Fed uses this regulation to control the supply of money.

b. Regulation E

Regulation E implements provisions of the Electronic Fund Transfer Act of 1978, which establishes the rights, responsibilities, and liabilities of parties engaging in consumer-related EFTs, and also protects consumers using systems such as ATMs, automated clearinghouse (ACH), and credit cards. Regulation E also establishes the guidelines for the documentation of electronic transfers.

c. Regulation J

Regulation J implements the check collection and settlement provision of the Federal Reserve Act of 1913, and establishes procedures, duties, and responsibilities for check collection and settlement through the Federal Reserve System.

d. Regulation Q

Regulation Q implemented the interest-bearing account restriction of the Glass-Steagall Act of 1933 and barred the paying of interest on any corporate demand deposit accounts. Interest rate ceilings initially set by this regulation on all commercial bank deposit accounts were partially phased out in 1986 by the DIDMCA, and the final restrictions on corporate demand deposits were removed by the Dodd-Frank Act in 2010.

22. Details on all Federal Reserve regulations may be found at http://www.frbservices.org.

e. Regulation Y

Regulation Y implements various provisions of the Bank Holding Company Act of 1956, the Change in Bank Control Act of 1978, and subsequent revisions covering the acquisition of control of banks and bank holding companies. It defines and regulates the nonbanking activities in which bank holding companies and foreign banking organizations in the United States may engage, including anti-tying restrictions.

f. Regulation Z

Regulation Z applies to the Truth in Lending Act of 1968 (TILA), which is concerned with promoting informed use of credit by consumers. This regulation covers the use of all types of consumer lending, including credit cards, home mortgages, student loans, and installment loans. For treasury professionals, the primary impact of this regulation relates to credit cards offered to their customers; for educational institutions, the impact relates to the use of student loans.

Regulation Z was updated in February of 2010 in order to implement the Credit Card Accountability Responsibility and Disclosure Act of 2009 (Credit CARD Act). As a result, Regulation Z also:

- Protects consumers from unexpected increases in credit card interest rates by generally prohibiting increases in a rate during the first year after an account is opened, as well as any increases in a rate that applies to an existing credit card balance
- Prohibits creditors from issuing a credit card to a consumer who is under the age of 21 unless the consumer can make the required payments or obtains the signature of a parent or other cosigner who is able to do so
- Requires creditors to obtain a consumer's consent before charging fees for transactions that exceed the credit limit
- Limits the high fees associated with subprime credit cards
- Bans creditors from using the two-cycle billing method to impose interest charges[23]
- Prohibits creditors from allocating payments in ways that maximize interest charges

g. Regulation BB

Regulation BB implements the provisions of the Community Reinvestment Act of 1977 as revised in 1995, and requires banks to help meet the credit needs of the entire community in which they do business.

h. Regulation CC

Regulation CC implements the provisions of the Expedited Funds Availability Act of 1987, which establishes rules designed to speed the collection and return of checks, and mandates banks to return unpaid checks expeditiously. This regulation also imposes the same return procedures to payable through drafts (PTDs) that apply to checks, and establishes endorsement standards for banks and companies to follow when depositing and clearing checks.

23. Two-cycle billing, also known as *double-cycle billing*, is a process used by some creditors to calculate interest charges based on the average balance of the account over two billing periods (the current and prior period), instead of using only the current period. Two-cycle billing effectively wipes out any grace period for account balances and tends to increase the amount of interest charged on credit accounts.

5. REGULATIONS RELATING TO INVESTMENTS AND SECURITIES

a. Fair Disclosure, Regulation FD[24]

On August 15, 2000, the SEC adopted Regulation FD to address the selective disclosure of information by publicly traded companies and other issuers. Regulation FD provides that when an issuer discloses material nonpublic information to certain individuals or entities—generally, securities market professionals, such as stock analysts, or holders of the issuer's securities who may well trade on the basis of the information—the issuer must make public disclosure of that information.

b. SEC Rule 2a-7, Money Market Funds (MMFs), and Net Asset Value (NAV)

During the Recession of 2009, the Reserve Primary Fund, one of the world's largest MMFs, "broke the buck," which is a slang term meaning that the fund's NAV dropped to less than $1.00 per share. In real terms, the fund did not have sufficient cash and was unable to sell assets quickly enough to pay out all of the redemptions requested by investors. (NAV is discussed in Chapter 5, Money Markets.)

As a result of this situation, the SEC reviewed Rule 2a-7, which controlled many of the money market funds. In 2010, the SEC announced more stringent rules for 2a-7 funds, including specific liquidity requirements, tougher asset quality requirements, a shorter average time to maturity, and monthly Internet-accessible reporting of the assets held in the fund. All of these changes affected the fund but had little to no direct effect on the investor.

On June 5, 2013, the SEC voted to add additional restrictions on 2a-7 funds. (At the time of writing, other non-US securities regulators, such as the European Securities and Markets Authority [ESMA], are considering making similar changes.) The proposal contained two potential regulatory changes, either or both of which may eventually be implemented. One alternative would require funds to adopt a floating NAV, calculated daily, rather than continuing the stable NAV of $1.00 per share. This change would require investors to calculate and record gains/losses on their short-term investments just as they do with the assets in their long-term portfolio. The second alternative would require funds to establish redemption limitations that would reduce the amount of money an investor could withdraw in a single request. As an example, if the investor wanted to withdraw $10 million, the limitation would require the fund to pay out $9.5 million in its usual settlement period, and hold the remaining $500,000 for up to 30 days before paying it to the investor. (The figures used are an example only; no percentages have been set at this writing.) The second alternative also includes potential liquidity fees and redemption gates. In the event that liquid assets of a money market fund fall below 15% of its total assets, the fund would potentially have to impose a 2% fee on all redemptions and could impose a temporary suspension (or redemption gate) of no more than 30 days on all redemptions.

At the time of publication, regulatory changes are still being reviewed, and the effective date of any final changes is expected to be sometime in 2015.

6. THE UNIFORM COMMERCIAL CODE (UCC)

The UCC is a uniform set of laws governing commercial transactions in the United States. It defines the rights and duties of all parties in a commercial transaction and provides a statutory definition of commonly accepted business practices. Because of the size of the US economy, the UCC has significant impact globally, and various portions of it have been used as a model in developing global trade agreements, such as the United Nations (UN) Convention on Contracts for the International Sale of Goods and international standards regarding letters of credit.

24. Information in this section was taken from the SEC's website (http://www.sec.gov/answers/regfd.htm, last modified August 30, 2004).

Because the UCC is a generalized standard, it did not take effect until the actual laws were enacted separately in each US state, but every state in the United States has enacted some version of the UCC.

a. Article 3: Negotiable Instruments

The primary provisions of Article 3 involve negotiable instruments, accord and satisfaction, and how banks handle unauthorized signatures. Article 3 is especially relevant for companies using automated bank or third-party lockbox processors because it defines exactly what constitutes a negotiable instrument, such as a draft, check, certificate of deposit, or note.

Initially, checks were permitted to constitute payment made in full (accord and satisfaction) when a message to that effect was written on the face of the check and the check was deposited. However, this provision allowed for the possibility of inadvertent accord and satisfaction when the customer wrote "paid in full" on a check for a disputed claim, especially for checks collected through a lockbox. The revised section of Article 3 prevents inadvertent accord and satisfaction if the payee discovers the error and returns the payment to the payor within 90 days.

Article 3 also clarifies that a bank's failure to examine a forged drawer's signature is not a failure to exercise ordinary care if it does not violate the bank's procedures and if the procedures do not vary from general banking practices unreasonably. A bank can charge a customer's account only for properly payable checks. Therefore, items with unauthorized signatures do not pass this test. However, a bank customer may be held liable if it does not exercise ordinary care related to check issuance and does not notify the bank of any potential discrepancies in a timely manner.

b. Article 4: Bank Deposits and Collections

The provisions of Article 4 include the rights, responsibilities, and definitions of the parties involved in the deposit and collection process. Specifically, Article 4 addresses the relationship between a bank and its customers. Article 4 defines:

- When a bank may charge a customer's account
- The bank's liability to a customer for failing to honor a good check
- The customer's right to stop payment
- The bank's option not to pay an item more than six months old (stale-dated)
- A customer's duty to report an unauthorized signature or alteration

A bank customer has the duty to examine bank statements within a reasonable time, not to exceed 30 days after the statement is sent, and to report any unauthorized signatures or alterations. This makes it imperative that companies accurately reconcile bank accounts on a timely basis.

c. Article 4A: Funds Transfers

Article 4A provides a legal framework that outlines the risks, rights, and obligations of parties in connection with wholesale ACH credit transfers, Fedwire transfers, and transactions handled through the Clearing House Interbank Payments System (CHIPS). Two primary provisions of Article 4A are security procedures and consequential damages:

- **Security Procedures:** A bank must make such procedures available to the customer. Further, the bank and the customer must agree that the procedures are commercially reasonable for verifying payment. Some common security measures include the use of personal identification numbers (PINs), callbacks, encryption, and message authentication.
- **Consequential Damages:** Banks generally are not responsible for consequential damages, which are losses resulting from an action or error made by the bank beyond the actual loss. However, a bank incorrectly executing a payment order remains liable for interest losses or incidental expenses. (A bank is liable for consequential damages only when it agrees to assume this liability in a written agreement with the customer.)

d. Article 5: Letters of Credit (L/Cs)

Article 5 covers US commercial L/Cs requiring documentary drafts and defines an L/C, documentary draft, and documentary demand for payment. It also defines the various roles of an L/C issuer, the applicant for whom the credit is issued, the beneficiary of the credit, and the advising and confirming banks. Article 5 does not cover standby L/Cs.

e. Article 9: Secured Transactions

Article 9 covers secured transactions, which occur when a lender or creditor requires some type of security or collateral for money it lends or goods it sells. Under this article, any business that requires such a security interest must file a UCC-1 financing statement with its state's office of assessments and taxation. The UCC-1 financing statement form lists collateral specifically assigned to secure the loan. It is a legal document signed by the borrower and lender that helps determine who has a right to the assets in the event of default.

7. UNCLAIMED PROPERTY (ESCHEATMENT) LEGISLATION

In the business world, escheat statutes primarily impact banks or companies that hold unclaimed assets of customers or employees. The most general occurrence of escheat is when an entity (e.g., a bank) holds money or property (e.g., an account in that bank) and the property goes unclaimed for some specified period of time (generally referred to as a *dormant account*). In many jurisdictions, if the owner cannot be located, such property can be escheated to the government. Many states maintain websites and databases that allow individuals and companies to search for funds that have been escheated.

For nonbank organizations, escheat is the process of turning over to a state authority (in the United States) unclaimed or abandoned payroll checks, stocks and shares whose owners cannot be traced, or unclaimed/unused rebates, customer purchase deposits or down payments, and gift cards/certificates. It is important to realize that the state involved is the residence state of the customer or owner of the item being escheated, not the state of residence of the organization holding the property. Every company is required to file unclaimed property reports with each appropriate state annually and to make a good faith effort to find the owners of dormant accounts. The escheating criteria are driven by individual state regulations and, in many cases, the penalties and interest assessed by the state for failure to comply are often more than the actual amount of unclaimed property.

V. TAX CONSIDERATIONS

Multinational companies must deal with tax codes in all the countries where they have sales, employees, and/or operations. This section introduces some of the critical issues that should be considered.

A. Unitary Taxes and Foreign Tax Credits

A unitary tax is a tax on a corporation's global income. Some countries levy unitary taxes on corporations operating in their borders in order to prevent them from avoiding taxes by transferring income to another country with a low or no corporate tax. A unitary tax can, however, result in multiple taxation of the same income. To help deal with this problem, some countries with unitary taxes also provide a tax credit for local taxes paid on income earned by foreign operations.

A US company's income derived from its non-US operations typically is included in its tax return to determine the amount of US income tax due. If income from foreign sources has already been subjected to foreign income taxes, the same income is taxed twice. To relieve the effect of double taxation, US tax law grants a US company a tax credit against its total US income tax liability for foreign income taxes paid by the parent and its subsidiaries. This credit is called the *foreign tax credit*. It is allowed only for foreign income taxes that do not exceed US tax rates.

To attract multinational businesses and thereby obtain employment opportunities for their citizens, a number of countries offer tax incentives for subsidiaries that perform certain administrative and financial functions within the host country. The laws governing the taxation of nondomestic income are extremely complex. Treasury professionals are advised to consult with tax experts.

B. Capital Tax

In some foreign countries, particularly those experiencing an upsurge in economic growth, companies are assessed a capital tax on the initial capital used to establish a new venture, and on subsequent incoming capital or repatriated capital. A capital tax is used as a fiscal tool by some countries to augment tax collections. The tax can also be used by a government to slow foreign direct investment in a country.

C. Asset Tax and Turnover Tax

Despite the fact that a company may not show a profit or owe income tax on an international project, many foreign countries still impose an asset tax. Even though a company may not produce operating profits, it may still owe taxes on the value of accumulated real property or business equipment, or on the value of a financial portfolio. There also may be a turnover tax, which is essentially a sales tax on goods and services.

D. Withholding Tax

Companies may be required to pay taxes when moving funds outside a foreign country. The amount can vary from 1% to almost 35% of the repatriated flow. Some countries refer to these taxes as *lifting fees*. They are charged whenever funds are transferred from a resident (domestic) account to a nonresident (foreign) account. Depending on the company's overall foreign tax credit position, some offset may be available on the withholding tax.

E. Sales and Use Taxes

Sales taxes are charged at the point of purchase for certain goods and services, and the tax amount is typically calculated by applying a percentage rate to the taxable price of a sale. In most cases, sales taxes are collected from the buyer by the seller, who then remits the tax to the appropriate government agency/agencies. Sales taxes are commonly charged on sales of goods, but may be charged on sales of services as well.

A use tax is imposed directly on the consumer of goods that were purchased without paying sales tax (generally items purchased from a vendor in another state or over the Internet and delivered to the purchaser by mail or common carrier). Corporations operating in many locations may have to comply with sales and use tax regulations for all the locations in which they operate.

F. Other Taxes

Another tax commonly used by many countries is a value-added tax (VAT), which is a type of sales tax. A separate tax is charged at each discrete stage of production and/or distribution based on the increased value (i.e., value added) occurring at that stage. Other taxes that a company might incur include a transfer tax (in the event of the sale of a company) and perhaps, in the future, an Internet transaction tax on sales.

VI. BANKRUPTCY (INSOLVENCY) LAWS

Bankruptcy, or insolvency, affects many organizations each year.[25] A company becomes insolvent if it does not have enough assets to pay its debts or if it cannot pay its debts on their contractual due dates. The terms *bankruptcy* and *insolvency* are often used interchangeably, but in some jurisdictions, such as the United Kingdom, *bankruptcy* refers only to personal insolvency while the general term *insolvency* applies to both corporate and personal insolvency. In addition to the typical financial problems that may force a firm into bankruptcy, management teams may be able to use the bankruptcy laws to protect either the firm's stakeholders or its management.

Insolvency laws vary from country to country but generally insolvency begins when a firm has not been able to meet scheduled payments on its debt. Insolvency may also occur when a firm's projections of cash flows indicate that it will not be able to meet debt payments at some time in the near future. The management and the board of directors are the key decision makers in this process. The major creditors may be involved in the decision concerning insolvency in many cases, and the creditors will force the firm into insolvency in some cases.

Creditors are typically divided into classes based on the seniority (or priority) of their claims on the distressed company's assets. Secured creditors have a legal security interest in specific assets (i.e., specified in a mortgage or lien) and can take possession of those assets in the event of default of the debt related to those assets. Unsecured creditors do not have an interest in any specific assets, but rather a general claim on any remaining assets after the secured assets are removed. Senior debt is paid before junior debt, and subordinated debt is generally the last to get paid. A listing of the priority of claims in the event of a company's liquidation is provided later in this section.

25. Bankruptcy legislation covers organizations of all kinds, as well as individuals. For the purposes of this book, the primary focus will be on business bankruptcy. This discussion will use US bankruptcy as a model for the overall discussion. Specific issues regarding insolvency or bankruptcy should be researched in the country involved.

A. Critical Issues in a Business Bankruptcy Decision

Some of the critical issues that management, the board of directors, and creditors need to address in a bankruptcy are as follows:

- Is the firm's inability to meet scheduled debt payments a temporary cash flow problem, or is it a permanent problem caused by long-term economic and business trends?
- If the problem is temporary, a short-term restructuring arrangement may work, but the impact on the long-term value of the firm must be considered.
- The company may be worth more if liquidated; thus, selling off its pieces may maximize its value to both the bondholders and shareholders.
- Which is the proper procedure for bankruptcy filing if it is required—formal or informal (discussed in more detail in Section VI.E of this chapter)?
- Who will be in charge of the firm during the reorganization—existing management, a special bankruptcy trustee, or special restructuring management?
- What type of bankruptcy is most appropriate for the organization in question?

B. Bondholders' Rights

The bondholders' rights in bankruptcy are normally senior to those of the equity holders, especially if the bondholders have liens or mortgages on assets owned by the distressed firm. The creditors of a firm generally have the right to force a firm into bankruptcy if scheduled debt payments are not made or if the condition of the firm is such that debt payments may be in default in the near future. This is known as an *involuntary bankruptcy* and is initiated when three or more creditors of the firm petition the federal bankruptcy court to begin proceedings against the firm. This process is actually quite rare in the United States, as creditors that initiate unjustified involuntary bankruptcy proceedings may be held liable for damages to the firm. Voluntary bankruptcy, where the management of the firm petitions the courts for bankruptcy protection, is generally the norm.

C. Shareholders' Rights

Generally, shareholders have limited rights in the event of financial distress for their firm. They have the lowest-priority claim on both the earnings stream and the assets of the firm. Preferred stockholders do have a higher claim on the firm's assets in liquidation than do common shareholders. There are cases where firms under reorganization have been turned over to the creditors and all, or virtually all, of the claims of the shareholders were voided in the process.

D. Types of Bankruptcy in the United States

In the United States, there are several types of bankruptcy available for corporations, municipalities, and individuals. The following are the most common:

- **Chapter 7:** Liquidation of a firm
- **Chapter 9:** Financially distressed municipalities (city, county, and state government bankruptcies)
- **Chapter 11:** Business reorganization
- **Chapter 13:** Adjustment of debts for individuals with regular income (personal bankruptcy)
- **Chapter 15:** Establishment of bankruptcy trustees (for bankruptcies that involve companies, assets, or individuals in more than one country)

Firms filing for bankruptcy have a choice between liquidation under Chapter 7 of the US Bankruptcy Code and reorganization under Chapter 11 of the code. The firm's management makes the initial choice of which type of bankruptcy to file. The reorganization procedure in bankruptcy is designed to allow failing firms that are in temporary financial difficulty, but are worth saving, to continue operating while the claims of the creditors are settled using a collective procedure.

1. CHAPTER 11 BANKRUPTCY (REORGANIZATION)

When a firm files to reorganize under Chapter 11, the existing management typically remains in control. Creditors may petition the bankruptcy court to appoint a trustee, but they must show grounds for suspecting that management is stealing the firm's assets or making preferential transfers to favored creditors. Incompetence of the existing management in running the business is not considered a sufficient reason for appointing a trustee.

Firms that file under Chapter 11 must adopt a reorganization plan. There are two separate procedures for formulating such a plan: the unanimous consent procedure and the cram-down procedure.

a. Unanimous Consent Procedure

Under the unanimous consent procedure, all classes of creditors and equity holders must consent to the reorganization plan, with a two-thirds vote of all members in each class required for consent. The assumption under this plan is that the firm's assets will have a higher value if it reorganizes and continues operating than if it liquidates.

Management is in a strong bargaining position in the negotiations over the reorganization plan because only management can propose a plan during the first four months of the filing, and extensions of this time frame are often granted in this process. Only after all parties have voted on management's initial plan, which may take another two months, can other parties propose alternative plans.

Management can threaten to transfer the firm's bankruptcy filing from Chapter 11 to Chapter 7 if creditors do not agree to the plan. This threat is often most effective in prodding unsecured creditors to agree since they may receive little or nothing in liquidation due to their position in the liquidation hierarchy. Finally, management usually remains in control of the firm during this entire process. Secured creditors may fear that the market value of their lien assets will decline below the market value of their liabilities if the process drags on.

b. Cram-Down Procedure

The cram-down procedure is generally executed by secured creditors and comes into play when a reorganization plan fails to meet the standard for approval by all classes under the unanimous consent procedure, or when the firm is insolvent and the old equity must be eliminated. In a cram-down case, if at least one class of creditors has voted in favor of a plan, then the court may confirm the plan (or a modified version of it) as long as each dissenting class is treated fairly and equitably. The fair and equitable standard closely reflects the absolute priority rule, covered later in this chapter, in that it requires that all unsecured creditors either receive full payment on the face value of their claims or that all lower rankings receive nothing. It also requires that secured creditors retain their pre-bankruptcy liens on assets or that they receive periodic cash payments equal to the value of their claims.

Cram-down plans usually involve higher transaction costs than unanimous consent plans because the bankruptcy court is likely to require appraisals by outside experts and more court hearings before approving them.

2. CHAPTER 7 BANKRUPTCY (LIQUIDATION)

As opposed to a Chapter 11 reorganization, which strives to preserve the firm as a going entity, Chapter 7 liquidation is a total shutdown of the firm and the orderly liquidation of its assets.

Chapter 7 of the US Bankruptcy Code is designed to accomplish three objectives:

- Provide safeguards against the withdrawal of assets by the owners of the bankrupt firm.
- Provide for an equitable distribution of the assets among creditors.
- Allow insolvent debtors to discharge all of their obligations and start over unhampered by a burden of prior debt.

The distribution of assets in liquidation under Chapter 7 of the code is governed by the following priority of claims (also known as the *absolute priority rule*):

1. Secured creditors are entitled to the proceeds of the sale of specific property pledged for a lien or a mortgage. If the proceeds do not fully satisfy the secured creditors' claims, then the remaining balance of such claims is treated as a general creditor claim, under item #9 below.
2. Trustee's costs to administer and operate the bankrupt firm are reimbursed next.
3. Next are expenses incurred after an involuntary liquidation has begun but before a trustee is appointed.
4. Wages are paid to workers if earned within three months prior to the filing of the bankruptcy petition (subject to current limits).
5. Claims for unpaid contributions to employee benefit plans that should have been paid within six months prior to filing are upheld. These claims, plus wages in item #4, may not exceed current per-wage-earner limits.

6. Unsecured claims for customer deposits, not to exceed current maximum limits, are honored next.
7. Taxes due to federal, state, county, and any other government agency are paid.
8. Unfunded pension plan liabilities have a claim priority over that of the general creditors for an amount up to 30% of the book value of the common and preferred equity. Any remaining, unfunded pension claims are ranked with the general creditors.
9. Next are general, or unsecured, creditors, which include holders of trade credit, unsecured loans, the unsatisfied portion of secured loans, unfunded pension liabilities, and debenture bonds. This is the final category before equity holders. Holders of subordinated debt also fall into this category, but their claims may be junior to certain holders of senior debt.
10. Preferred stockholders can receive an amount up to the par value of the preferred stock.
11. Common stockholders receive the remaining funds, if any.

E. Formal versus Informal Bankruptcy Procedures

Bankruptcy procedures can be either formal or informal.

1. FORMAL BANKRUPTCY

In a formal bankruptcy procedure, the case is filed and taken before a bankruptcy court for adjudication. The assets are distributed in accordance with the absolute priority rule as outlined in Chapter 7 of the US Bankruptcy Code. The priorities of claims are outlined in the preceding section. There are several types of formal procedures:

- **Free Fall:** In this case, a firm goes (or is forced) into bankruptcy and has no structured plan for coming out of bankruptcy.
- **Prearranged:** In this case, management has arranged a tentative deal with some of the creditors or parties, but not with all of them. Generally, these deals are done on an informal basis and are not legally binding.
- **Prepackaged (Prepac):** In this case, management files with the SEC a formal plan that all classes of creditors have voted on and accepted. Essentially, the firm goes to court with all of the details worked out and with everyone agreeing to the plan.

2. INFORMAL BANKRUPTCY

It is possible to perform a reorganization or a liquidation informally. An informal reorganization typically involves a firm that is fundamentally sound, but is undergoing temporary financial difficulties. This is often done outside of bankruptcy in an agreed-upon write-off of some portion of the firm's debts by its creditors.

The firm's creditors work directly with management to establish a plan for returning the firm to a sound financial basis. These plans usually involve some restructuring of the firm's debt, with creditors agreeing either to reduce or reschedule debt payments in order to ensure the firm's continuing operation.

Informal liquidation or assignment is an alternative to Chapter 7 liquidation procedures. In this case, title to the distressed firm's assets is transferred to a third party (called an *assignee* or *trustee*) who liquidates the assets through a sale or public auction. The assignee/trustee then distributes the proceeds to creditors on a pro rata basis, according to the seniority of the claims. The informal liquidation is usually only appropriate for smaller firms and does not automatically result in a full and legal discharge of all the debtor's liabilities.

VII. SUMMARY

Financial services providers and the various services that they offer are highly regulated around the world, as are many of the day-to-day activities that are an integral part of treasury operations.

This chapter provided an overview of the legal and regulatory issues that impact FIs and their treasury management customers on a daily basis. This included a discussion of financial services regulators both globally and within the United States. The chapter also provided a high-level overview of some of the key US laws and regulations that impact treasury professionals. The chapter closed with an overview of corporate tax issues and a discussion of insolvency and its impact on organizations.

APPENDIX 2.1: SEPA MEMBER STATES

COUNTRY/TERRITORY	BIC[26]	IBAN	CURRENCY CODE
Åland Islands	FI	FI	EUR
Austria	AT	AT	EUR
Azores	PT	PT	EUR
Belgium	BE	BE	EUR
Bulgaria	BG	BG	BGN
Canary Islands	ES	ES	EUR
Croatia	HR	HR	HRK
Cyprus	CY	CY	EUR
Czech Republic	CZ	CZ	CZK
Denmark	DK	DK	DKK
Estonia	EE	EE	EUR
Finland	FI	FI	EUR
France	FR	FR	EUR
French Guiana	GF	FR	EUR
Germany	DE	DE	EUR
Gibraltar	GI	GI	GIP
Greece	GR	GR	EUR
Guadeloupe	GP	FR	EUR
Hungary	HU	HU	HUF
Iceland	IS	IS	ISK
Ireland	IE	IE	EUR
Italy	IT	IT	EUR
Latvia	LV	LV	LVL
Liechtenstein	LI	LI	CHF

26. The BIC and IBAN columns include the country code used in the Bank Identification Code (BIC) and International Bank Account Number (IBAN) for each country/territory. BIC and IBAN are discussed in Chapter 3, Banks and Financial Institutions. The currency code identifies the base currency of each country/territory.

COUNTRY/TERRITORY	BIC	IBAN	CURRENCY CODE
Lithuania	LT	LT	LTL
Luxembourg	LU	LU	EUR
Madeira	PT	PT	EUR
Malta	MT	MT	EUR
Martinique	MQ	FR	EUR
Mayotte	YT	FR	EUR
Monaco	MC	MC	EUR
Netherlands	NL	NL	EUR
Norway	NO	NO	NOK
Poland	PL	PL	PLN
Portugal	PT	PT	EUR
Réunion	RE	FR	EUR
Romania	RO	RO	RON
Saint Barthélemy	BL	FR	EUR
Saint Martin (French part)	MF	FR	EUR
Saint Pierre and Miquelon	PM	FR	EUR
Slovakia	SK	SK	EUR
Slovenia	SI	SI	EUR
Spain	ES	ES	EUR
Sweden	SE	SE	SEK
Switzerland	CH	CH	CHF
United Kingdom	GB	GB	GBP

TEST YOUR UNDERSTANDING: CHAPTER 2

Answers are on pages 642–647.

1. What is the primary role that financial institutions (FIs) play in the economy, and why are they regulated?
2. What is a central bank?
3. What is the Financial Stability Board?
4. What are the principal committees of the Bank for International Settlements?
5. Describe the main features of the third Basel Accords (Basel III).
6. What is SEPA?
7. What is the FATF, and what does it do?
8. Describe the three stages of money laundering.
9. What are the five general areas in which financial institution regulation is typically concentrated?
10. What are the major provisions of the Gramm-Leach-Bliley Act?
11. What is the Durbin Amendment?
12. What are the main provisions of the USA PATRIOT Act?
13. What is the Red Flags Rule?
14. Discuss the impact of Sarbanes-Oxley (SOX) legislation on publicly traded firms.
15. List and discuss the key Fed regulations that impact treasury professionals.
16. What is the Uniform Commercial Code?
17. What are escheatment statutes, and how do they impact banks and companies?
18. List the most common types of bankruptcies allowed by US federal legislation.
19. Describe the three types of formal bankruptcy.
20. What is a capital tax?

CHAPTER 3
Banks and Financial Institutions

I. INTRODUCTION

Because banking and financial services are a critical part of the treasury function, banks and other financial institutions (FIs) represent a key element of the treasury management environment.

The dictionary[1] defines *financial institution* as:

> an enterprise specializing in the handling and investment of funds (as a bank, trust company, insurance company, savings and loan association, or investment company)

Although the term *financial institution* is often used synonymously with *commercial bank*, as the definition makes clear, the term *financial institution* covers a number of different types of companies that provide a variety of services to treasury professionals. This chapter presents an overview of the various types of FIs and a brief description of the different roles they fill and the services they provide. Many of these services are explored in more detail in later chapters of this book, where coverage includes how they are actually used by treasury professionals.

In general, throughout this book, the terms *FI* and *bank* will be used interchangeably to refer to an organization that provides a range of financial services to the public. Explicit terms such as *insurance company, broker-dealer,* or *investment company* will be used when referring to a particular type of FI that provides specific services.

II. FINANCIAL INSTITUTIONS: FUNCTIONS AND SERVICES

Historically, FIs—primarily commercial banks—have dominated the marketplace for treasury-related products and services because they controlled access to the various payment and financial delivery systems around the world. As the regulatory environment discussed in the last chapter changed, the services that the various FIs were able to offer also changed, and some of the distinctions between types of FIs became less important. For example, traditionally retail financial institutions began to offer services to businesses, while commercial banks began offering investment and insurance products. This section outlines the key functions and services of the major types of FIs. It begins by presenting a broad overview of the general role of FIs in a global environment and continues on to provide an outline of FI functions, services, and organization.

A. Global Financial Institutions (FIs)

Unfortunately, there is no such thing as a truly global bank or FI. That is, there is no single institution that operates everywhere in the world. For the purpose of this book, a *global FI* is defined as one that operates in multiple countries in more than one part of the world, providing services to both domestic and multinational corporations. An FI with substantial operations outside its home country would be considered a global bank or FI according to this definition.

1. From *Merriam-Webster Unabridged Dictionary*, s.v. "financial institution," accessed March 1, 2013, http://unabridged.merriam-webster.com/unabridged/financial%20institution.

The primary services offered by global FIs are depository accounts, transaction services, lending, foreign exchange (FX), information reporting, and investment banking. Depending on the general banking structure and regulations in each country, how these services are offered may vary considerably. There may also be different types of institutions specializing in or serving different markets (i.e., large business, small business, consumer, etc.). In most cases, there is also a functional split between commercial banking (depository accounts, transactions, and lending) and investment banking (underwriting of stocks and bonds, as well as brokerage services). FX services may be provided by a separate entity or combined with the other transaction services offered through an FI.

In addition to the functions listed above, FIs may provide a wide range of other services to their business customers, depending upon the local regulatory restrictions. These could include trade services, agent and fiduciary services, risk management, and consulting. Many of these banking services are discussed in greater detail later in this chapter.

Most global FIs have similar service offerings, but there may be some differences from country to country. The primary reason for these differences is the fact that each country has its own set of regulations and guidelines for banking within that country. FIs operating within a given country are required to follow the guidelines of that country, even if they are providing services internationally and may be headquartered in a different country. Although the requirements for opening bank accounts may vary by country, the general practice is that most large FIs follow KYC (or "know your customer") guidelines based on standards established by the Financial Action Task Force (FATF), which are discussed in the previous chapter.

Most large global banks offer a wide range of services to their customers, although the specific services available can vary by country. The relationship between banks and their customers also can vary by country. In some countries (e.g., Austria, Germany, and Switzerland), banks are permitted to own a minor or even a controlling ownership position in corporations through equity investments. FIs in many countries are allowed to lend a large percentage of their capital base to a single customer (generally referred to as a *legal lending limit*). Though these guidelines vary, banks often are allowed to lend up to 25% of the bank's capital base to any one non-related company. In the United States, in contrast, the legal lending limit is 15% in most cases.

Banking systems in most countries are characterized by a few large banks that operate on a nationwide basis. In addition, FIs are generally allowed to pay interest on positive balances, and accounts often have automatic overdraft provisions for negative balances. Banks in many countries also offer foreign currency accounts, where deposit balances may be held in a currency other than that of the country of location. Many banks also offer multicurrency accounts, where a customer can maintain balances in several currencies in one account. Another type of deposit account typically offered is a nonresident account, which is one that is owned by people or institutions from outside the country in which the FI is chartered.

A company operating on a global basis will often have to manage a variety of currencies in different locations. It may be able to manage these currency needs in its home country if foreign currency accounts are offered by its banks; it may choose to maintain accounts in foreign currencies in the country of that currency; or it may use some combination of the two approaches. A multinational firm's actual banking structure (the number and location of FIs that it uses to provide operating services) will depend upon the types of collections and disbursements undertaken by the firm, the locations and currencies of the financing and investments utilized by the firm, and the legal and tax regulations of the specific countries involved.

B. Commercial Banks

In the United States, a commercial bank is an FI possessing a federal or state charter that accepts deposits and makes commercial loans. Although the rules and charters may vary, there are similar FIs in most countries. A commercial bank may also offer other services, which are outlined below. The term *commercial bank* applies to FIs ranging from small, single-site community banks with several million dollars in assets to large, multinational FIs with a global footprint and trillions in assets.

Large FIs are typically owned by bank holding companies that provide an even wider range of products and services in partnership with their nonbank subsidiaries. FIs operate in a highly regulated environment, which is covered in Chapter 2, Regulatory and Legal Environment.

1. DEPOSIT ACCOUNTS

There are two basic types of depository accounts:

- Current accounts, referred to as *checking or demand deposit accounts (DDAs)* in the United States
- Noncurrent or time deposit accounts (TDAs)

a. Current or Demand Deposit Accounts (DDAs)

A DDA, or checking account, is both a store of value (deposits) and, perhaps more importantly for treasury management purposes, a vehicle through which an account holder uses a bank to transfer funds to, and receive deposits from, a third party. The method of payment can be by cash, check, debit card, internal book transfer, or electronic transfer.

Depending upon the local regulations, DDAs may be interest-bearing or non-interest-bearing. Prior to 2010 and the passage of the Dodd-Frank Act, the US Federal Reserve prohibited the payment of interest on demand deposits held by for-profit companies in the United States, in what was known as *Reg Q*. While Reg Q has since been repealed, most US-based corporate DDAs still do not earn interest on deposited funds. In addition, most large government or not-for-profit entities do not earn interest on their deposits because they use the same types of deposit accounts that are used by large corporations. In lieu of actual interest payments, many US-based banks provide earnings credits or analysis credits, which can be used to offset charges for bank services. This practice is discussed in more detail in Chapter 7, Relationship Management and Vendor Selection.

It is also important to note that another major difference between DDAs in the United States and those in other countries is the process of handling overdrafts. An overdraft occurs when items are presented against a DDA in excess of the balance in that account. In most countries, the general practice is to incorporate both an investment rate and a credit agreement with the DDA so that any positive balances are paid interest, while negative DDA balances result in an automatic loan and are charged some rate of interest. This type of arrangement is not generally available in the United States for corporate holders of DDA accounts unless specific lending arrangements have been previously agreed upon.

b. Noncurrent or Time Deposit Accounts (TDAs)

Time deposit accounts are accounts that must be maintained at an FI for a contractually specified period of time. These accounts usually allow withdrawal only with prior notification and may charge a penalty if the withdrawal requirements are not met. A certificate of deposit (CD) is a type of TDA and is used widely by savers. It represents the bank's obligation to pay a fixed or variable interest rate over some period of time.

For CDs under $100,000, the rate is typically nonnegotiable by the depositor and is generally fixed through the tenor of the certificate. The maturity date is a specified date in the future, not a length of time. Interest rates and maturities on CDs valued at more than $100,000 are typically negotiable, and the interest rate may be fixed or variable. For larger institutional investors, fully negotiable CDs are offered generally in $1 million blocks with maturities ranging from 14 days to 5 years. Most are offered with maturities of 12 or fewer months and are traded in an active secondary market.

FIs also offer other types of TDAs, such as savings accounts and money market deposit accounts (MMDAs), primarily for their retail and small business customers.

c. Nonresident Accounts

A nonresident account, either current or noncurrent, is an account with an FI in a given country held by an entity whose legal headquarters, residence, or tax status is outside of the country where the account is held. An example of this might be a UK-based company with a nonresident account at a bank in China. Rules regarding nonresident bank accounts vary by country, currency, and purpose of the account. Accounts denominated in US dollars, euros, and British pounds are often held by nonresidents from and in various countries. Common uses for nonresident accounts include currency hedging and commercial collections and payments.

d. Account Identification

Since most financial transactions involve transferring value from one bank account to another bank account at some point in the process, it is important to be able to uniquely identify specific banks and the related accounts within those banks. This is typically done through the use of some form of bank identification code and individual account numbers within each bank. Unfortunately, there is no one international standard for bank identification codes and account number formats. They vary not only from country to country but also from bank to bank, which can at times lead to difficulties in uniquely identifying specific accounts. A number of generally accepted standards have developed in various parts of the world to help deal with this issue:

- The Bank Identification Code, or BIC, is a unique identifier that specifies precisely the financial institutions involved—in some cases down to the branch level—in a financial transaction. The most commonly used BIC is known as the *SWIFT code* because the system is administered by the Society for Worldwide Interbank Financial Telecommunication (SWIFT).

  A SWIFT code consists of eight or eleven characters, as follows:

  - First four characters—bank code (alphabetic only)
  - Next two characters—ISO 3166-1 alpha-2 country code (alphabetic only)
  - Next two characters—location code (alphanumeric)
  - Last three characters—branch code, optional ("XXX" for primary office) (alphanumeric)

  When an eight-character code is used, it refers to the primary or head office of a given bank.

- A routing transit number (RTN),[2] is a nine-digit bank code used in the United States to identify individual banks for purposes of routing check and electronic transactions to the proper financial institution. US banks will typically have both an RTN and a SWIFT BIC. Canadian banks use an eight-digit system managed by the Canadian Payments Association in a similar fashion. Refer to Exhibit 4.1 in the next chapter for further details.

- The International Bank Account Number (IBAN) is a way to identify bank accounts across national borders. It was originally adopted by the European Committee for Banking Standards (ECBS), and later adopted as an international standard by the International Organization for Standardization (ISO). As with the BIC, the current standard is managed by SWIFT. The IBAN was initially developed to simplify payments within the European Union under SEPA, which is discussed in Chapter 2, Regulatory and Legal Environment. It has since also been implemented by most European countries and many other countries, especially in the Middle East and in the Caribbean.

  The IBAN consists of up to 34 alphanumeric characters: first the two-letter ISO 3166-1 alpha-2 country code, then two check digits, and finally a country-specific Basic Bank Account Number (BBAN). The BBAN format is decided by each national banking community under the restriction that it must be of a fixed length of case-insensitive alphanumeric characters. It includes the domestic bank account number, branch identifier, and potential routing information.

2. RTNs are also often referred to as *ABA numbers* because the system was originally developed and managed by the American Bankers Association. The system is now managed by Accuity.

2. CREDIT SERVICES

Commercial banks, by definition, are broad-based lenders. They offer a wide range of business loans that vary by type of borrower, use of proceeds, and loan maturities. Banks provide medium- to long-term secured and unsecured loans to businesses for the purchase of property, plant, and equipment. The source of repayment is generally from cash flows of the company, but in some cases may be restricted to cash flows generated by the asset being financed. The loans are typically collateralized by the company's property, plant, or equipment, but again in some cases the collateral may be limited to the specific asset that is being financed (e.g., equipment loans or property loans). Leasing divisions of banks provide an alternative to medium- and long-term loans for financing capital equipment. Leasing is covered in more detail in Chapter 20, Financial Decisions and Management. FIs also provide mortgage financing[3] for commercial real estate.

In addition, banks offer short-term working capital loans to fund cash shortfalls that occur when cash outflows precede cash inflows. In seasonal businesses, an expansion of the investment in inventory and accounts receivable precedes the cash inflow that occurs when accounts receivable convert to cash. This topic is covered in more detail in Chapter 8, Introduction to Working Capital Management.

Short-term business borrowing (typically with a term of less than a year) can take several forms. For example, a business may borrow a specific amount to be repaid by a specific date (commonly referred to as a *term loan or note*). Alternatively, a business may secure a revolving line of credit (commonly referred to as a *revolver*), meaning it can borrow up to a specified amount, repay all or part of the outstanding balance, and borrow again at any time. In this case, the business typically must pay off the revolver in full by a specified date.

3. INVESTMENT BANKING SERVICES

FIs are an integral part of the investment banking process for the commercial paper (CP) and municipal securities markets. (Section C below offers more details on the investment banking process.) CP consists of unsecured, discounted, short-term promissory notes issued by companies or commercial bank holding companies, typically with maturities not exceeding 270 days. FIs typically act as agents to place CP with investors. As discussed in more detail in Chapter 11, Short-Term Investing and Borrowing, CP is rated for default risk by various credit rating agencies, and the rating has a significant effect on the interest rate.

Municipal securities (commonly called *munis*) are bonds or notes issued by city, county, or state government entities and generally have some type of income tax exemption for any interest paid on them. Municipals are also rated for default risk.

FIs also offer loan sales and private placements. Loan sales involve the structuring of lending facilities so that short-term loans can be sold to other banks and investors. Private placements are the direct sales of long-term notes to institutional investors, such as insurance companies and hedge funds.

4. TRANSACTION PROCESSING

As discussed in more detail in Chapter 4, Payment Systems, FIs typically provide transaction-processing services, such as check, card, and electronic payment processing, to their customers. In most countries, FIs control access to the various payment systems, and any payment other than a strictly cash transaction must go through an FI at some point in the process.

3. Mortgage lending differs from other property lending in that a mortgage loan is secured by a specific lien (known as a *mortgage*) on a specific piece of property.

5. TRADE SERVICES

Large FIs often provide a wide range of services to facilitate the payment and collection of trade obligations. These are more typically used for international business, but sometimes they are also used domestically. The topic of trade services and trade financing is covered in more detail in Chapter 8, Introduction to Working Capital Management.

- **Trade or commercial letters of credit (L/Cs)** are documents issued by a bank, guaranteeing the payment of a customer's draft up to a stated amount for a specified period, provided that certain conditions are met. In effect, the issuing bank is substituting its good name and credit on behalf of its customer's.
- **Standby L/Cs or guarantees** (also known as *clean L/Cs*) are performance contracts issued by banks ensuring that certain terms and conditions will be met by the bank's customer. Though these guarantees are generally used by companies involved in large capital construction projects, they are suitable any time certain contract conditions must be met and when there is no tangible collateral to seize for nonpayment or nonperformance.
- A **documentary collection** is a trade-services payment method that processes the collection of a draft[4] and accompanying shipping documents through international correspondent banks. Instructions regarding the specifics of the transaction are contained in a collection letter that accompanies the documentation. It is the responsibility of the seller (exporter) to determine the specific instructions used in the collection letter.
- A **banker's acceptance (BA)** is a negotiable, short-term instrument used primarily to finance the import of foreign goods, the export of domestic goods, or the storage of readily marketable staples. A BA is created when a bank "accepts" payment responsibility for a draft issued in connection with an L/C or documentary collection.

6. FOREIGN EXCHANGE (FX) SERVICES

Large banks, especially those with global networks, are major participants in the FX markets. They offer FX services to customers to facilitate international business and trade. These services allow companies to buy or sell internationally traded currencies for either immediate (spot market) or future (forward market) use. In addition, these banks offer risk management services, such as forward options and swap contracts, that assist international clients in hedging, or protecting, FX exposures. These services are discussed in more detail in Chapter 16, Financial Risk Management.

4. A draft is a written order or instruction drawn by a creditor (borrower) directing a debtor or lender to pay a sum of money to a third party.

7. RISK MANAGEMENT SERVICES

Fluctuations in exchange rates, interest rates, or commodities prices can impact a company's financial performance significantly. For example, currency movements against the US dollar can impact the profitability of a US company that operates in international markets. To control these risks, banks and other FIs offer a variety of products, such as forwards, futures, swaps, and options. These instruments are known as *derivatives* because their market value is derived from an underlying asset, which may be a foreign currency, commodity, or class of instruments carrying a particular interest rate. Derivatives are covered in more detail in Chapter 16, Financial Risk Management.

8. FIDUCIARY SERVICES

A fiduciary is an individual or institution to which certain property is given to hold in trust according to a trust agreement. Not all fiduciaries are FIs, but FIs often provide these services. As a fiduciary, an FI has duties and responsibilities that are legally enforceable and must be executed in a prudent and timely manner.

Fiduciary services, more commonly referred to as *trust services,* represent one of the many roles performed by FIs. Trust departments offer a wide range of services to corporate customers, including:

- Establishing and managing employee pension plans or qualified employee benefit plans
- Acting as a corporate trustee for corporate bond or preferred stock issues
- Monitoring compliance with bond indenture agreements, which are the contractual arrangements between bond issuers and bondholders
- Acting as a transfer agent by keeping records of each purchase and sale of stocks and bonds, including maintaining records of a corporation's shareholders by name, address, and number of shares
- Acting as a registrar by compiling and maintaining lists of current stockholders and bondholders for the purpose of remitting dividend and interest payments
- Acting as a paying agent, whereby an FI receives funds from an issuer of stocks or bonds to pay dividends to stockholders and to pay principal and interest to bondholders
- Offering custody services (such as providing safekeeping for securities), and buying, selling, receiving, and delivering securities based on terms outlined in a custody agreement

9. CONSULTING SERVICES

Some banks provide a range of formal consulting services for corporate customers in areas such as treasury management, FX, risk management, and corporate financial structure.

10. OTHER FINANCIAL SERVICES

Depending upon local regulations, FIs can act as brokers and dealers for various investment securities and foreign currencies, as well as providing insurance and other types of underwriting services. As discussed in Chapter 2, Regulatory and Legal Environment, the types of services that FIs can offer are often limited by law and tying restrictions.

C. Investment Banks and Brokerage Firms

Investment banks and brokerage firms provide a wide range of financial services related to the issuance and trading of securities. Generally, the investment banking functions discussed in this book are much broader than the narrow range of investment banking services that can typically be offered under the commercial bank framework. Investment banking services may also be offered through the investment banking arm of a commercial bank's holding company.

Companies in this area tend to specialize in either investment banking or securities brokerage. Investment banking is also called *corporate finance*. Some firms choose to serve either institutional or retail customers, while others are full-service firms that fulfill the needs of all customers.

1. INVESTMENT BANKS

An investment bank is a financial intermediary that performs a variety of services, such as (1) underwriting, by acting as an intermediary between an issuer of securities and the investing public; (2) facilitating mergers, acquisitions, divestitures, and other corporate reorganizations; and (3) acting as a broker/financial advisor for institutional clients. The investment banking process relating to the issuance of stocks and bonds generally has three distinct components: origination, underwriting, and distribution. These topics (which are also discussed in Chapter 6, Capital Markets) are explained below.

a. Origination

Origination involves consultation with a company raising funds about the characteristics of the issue and any underlying documents. The investment bank also monitors market conditions and advises the company about the best time to bring the issue to market in order to maximize the price per issued share and the amount of funds the firm wishes to raise.

b. Underwriting

Underwriting is the act of purchasing all or part of a block of securities issued by a company. Under a full-underwriting arrangement, the investment bank or syndicate (group) of investment banks owns the entire issue. The company has all the money it will receive and may set about the business of using the money as it intends. At that point, the investment bank (or syndicate) assumes the price and marketability risks of the issue. Price risk means it may not be possible for the investment bank to sell the entire issue of bonds or stock at the anticipated market price, which can jeopardize its profitability. Marketing risk means that it may not be possible to sell all the shares, which also places profitability at risk.

If the investment bank or syndicate is not confident it can sell the entire issue, it may try to assist the company on a best-efforts basis. In this case, the company pays a fee directly to the investment bank as compensation for advising the firm and marketing the issue. The investment bank does not underwrite the issue. Rather, it simply sells as many shares as possible through a selling group of brokerage firms up to a specified limit.

c. Distribution

Distribution is the term applied to a securities sale to investors by an investment bank or a syndicate of investment banks. When a syndicate is formed, one of the investment banks serves as the lead bank (also called the *lead underwriter*). The lead bank assumes most management functions and receives most of the fees. Once the underwriting syndicate owns the new securities, each member investment bank uses its distribution system to sell the issue.

For full-service investment banks that offer both the underwriting/distribution function (referred to as the *sell side* of the house) and the investment advisory or management function (referred to as the *buy side*), there is a potential for conflict of interest. There have been numerous instances where the sell side has influenced the recommendations made by the buy side in order to enhance a firm's profitability. As discussed in the previous chapter, this is a violation of securities regulations and ethics guidelines regarding insider trading in the United States and in many other countries.

Ideally, any research or recommendations provided by the buy side should be completely independent of any activities on the sell side of a firm. The two sides of the transaction must be separated by internal controls and procedures (sometimes referred to as a "wall") that prevent each party from acquiring material nonpublic information (MNPI) from the other side of the transaction and acting upon it. It is important to understand that merely possessing MNPI is not a crime. The crime resides in the act of using the information. An analyst or trader could receive MNPI and not act on it and not be in violation of the law.

Having MNPI but not using it sometimes occurs when a research analyst is "brought over" to work for the underwriting department in order to focus on a particular company. This is known as "bringing someone over the wall" since the individual is being moved from one side of the internal control process (the "wall") to the other. The purpose of such a transfer is to add a knowledgeable opinion to the underwriting process, thereby adding value to it. Once the underwriting process is complete, the research employee who has been "brought over the wall" is not allowed to comment on any information learned in the underwriting process until it has become public knowledge.

Another issue that can arise is insider trading, which is the illegal trading of securities based on information that has not yet been made public (i.e., MNPI). Enforcement of insider trading varies by country. For example, in the United States, the SEC monitors and disciplines those who engage in insider trading and enforces related regulations, while in the United Kingdom, enforcement is handled by the Financial Services Authority (FSA).

2. INSTITUTIONAL AND RETAIL BROKERAGE FIRMS

Brokerage firms specialize in the sale of securities. They execute the distribution, or selling, side of an investment bank's intermediation function. The distribution function applies to the initial public offering (IPO) of securities by privately owned firms becoming publicly owned companies, and to existing public companies issuing new securities and debt offerings.

Brokerage firms can be institutional or retail brokers and either discount or full-service firms. Institutional brokers are brokers whose clients are mostly large institutions, such as FIs, hedge funds, and large corporations. Typically, institutional brokers deal with large blocks of securities or transactions that may require special handling. Retail brokers typically handle smaller investment accounts and transactions for individuals, and may have offices in multiple locations, as well as research services to assist retail clients. Typically, retail commissions (as a percentage of the transaction) are relatively high compared to those charged by institutional brokers because there are more individual retail transactions to process and the average dollar size per transaction is usually smaller. The rate charged by institutional brokers may be lower, but the actual commissions received will be higher, due to the larger dollar volumes of the institutional transactions.

Discount brokerages let investors make trades at reduced prices, but provide little or no investment advice. Full-service brokerages have research analysts who are industry specialists. They provide investment advice to institutions and individual investors. As noted in the previous section on distributions, research is for sale and has some guarantee of independence; there should be no linkages between the part of the firm that offers investment advice and the part that is involved in the distribution of new securities. Some full-service brokerages also manage investment portfolios for institutions and individuals.

D. Credit Unions

Credit unions are not-for-profit financial corporations in the United States, chartered by either federal or state agencies. The National Credit Union Association (NCUA) charters and supervises federal credit unions (about 60% of the total), while the remaining 40% are chartered at the state level. Additionally, NCUA insures the deposits for all federally chartered credit unions and almost all of the state-chartered corporations through the National Credit Union Share Insurance Fund (NCUSIF).

Membership in a credit union was originally restricted to individuals with a common affiliation, such as an employer, association, community organization, or geographic location, but membership was later expanded to include businesses. Credit unions can provide financial services similar to those offered by other types of FIs and can potentially provide access to various payment networks to a company affiliated with them. Members/owners often enjoy higher savings and lower lending rates compared to banks.

E. Special-Purpose Financial Institutions

There are a variety of other FIs that focus on specific markets or populations.

1. INDUSTRIAL BANKS

An industrial bank, also known as an *industrial loan company*, is an FI with a limited scope of services. Industrial banks sell certificates that are labeled as *investment shares* and can also accept customer deposits. They then invest the proceeds in installment loans for consumers and small businesses. Industrial banks differ from commercial lenders because they accept deposits. They also differ from commercial banks because they do not offer checking accounts. Because of their limited scope of services, they do not fall under general banking regulatory authority, are locally chartered, and may be owned by nonbank holding companies.

2. CAPTIVE FINANCE COMPANIES

A captive finance company is a type of industrial bank that is a subsidiary of a large industrial corporation and that finances purchases solely of the corporation's products. These FIs typically raise funds in the CP market and lend to other companies and individuals that purchase products from the parent corporation. Having a captive finance company allows a company to extend credit to customers without putting itself directly at risk. Companies such as Ford Motor Credit, General Electric (GE) Capital, and Hyundai Motor Finance are examples of captive finance companies.

3. FACTORS

A factor is another type of nonbank financial intermediary. Factors are entities that provide short-term financing to companies by purchasing accounts receivable at a discount.

4. INSURANCE COMPANIES

Insurance companies are also considered nonbank FIs. From a corporate perspective, they are primarily long-term lenders to companies. They are significant investors in real estate, particularly commercial real estate such as shopping centers, as well as long-term bonds. Insurance companies have started to compete with banks for short- and medium-term loans. They provide mortgage funding, leasing services, guaranteed investment contracts (similar to bank CDs, generally paying interest for one to five years), and universal life insurance policies with long-term savings features.

III. SUMMARY

Financial institutions are a critical part of the treasury management environment. In addition to providing a wide variety of credit and noncredit services, they typically provide companies access to various payment systems. This chapter presented an overview of the major types of financial institutions and the services that they typically provide to treasury professionals. The discussion included a review of commercial banks, investment banks, and brokerages, as well as credit unions and special-purpose financial institutions. Historically, commercial banks have been the predominant financial institution used by treasury professionals because they provide transaction services as well as credit (lending) services, but as regulations have changed, other types of FIs have entered the treasury services arena.

TEST YOUR UNDERSTANDING: CHAPTER 3

Answers are on pages 648–651.

1. What is a global financial institution, and what are the primary services that it offers?
2. What are the two types of depository accounts?
3. What are the different types of credit services offered by commercial banks?
4. What are the typical trade services offered by large financial institutions?
5. What are the three components of the investment banking process?
6. Describe the services offered by commercial bank trust departments to their commercial customers.
7. What is a bank identification code? Describe the most commonly used bank identification code.
8. What is an IBAN?
9. What is a captive finance company?

CHAPTER 4
Payment Systems

V. LARGE-VALUE ELECTRONIC FUNDS TRANSFER (EFT)/WIRE TRANSFER SYSTEMS

A. Real-Time Gross Settlement (RTGS) Systems

B. Clearing House Interbank Payments System (CHIPS)

C. TARGET2 and the Single Euro Payments Area (SEPA)

D. Continuous Linked Settlement (CLS)

E. Society for Worldwide Interbank Financial Telecommunication (SWIFT)

VI. SMALL-VALUE TRANSFER OR AUTOMATED CLEARINGHOUSE (ACH) SYSTEMS

VII. CARD-BASED PAYMENT SYSTEMS

A. Credit Cards

B. Debit Cards/EFTPOS

C. Other Varieties of Payment Cards

D. Payment Card Industry Data Security Standard (PCI DSS)

E. Merchant Card Fees

VIII. SUMMARY

APPENDIX 4.1: CHECK RETURN REASONS

APPENDIX 4.2: FEDWIRE FORMAT EXAMPLE

APPENDIX 4.3: FEDGLOBAL ACH PAYMENTS COUNTRIES

APPENDIX 4.4: BANKING AND PAYMENT SYSTEMS INFORMATION FOR SELECTED COUNTRIES

I. INTRODUCTION

Because the movement of funds is a fundamental part of the treasury function, it is important for treasury professionals to understand how payment systems operate and how to use the mechanisms employed to manage the collection and disbursement of funds (discussed in Chapter 10, Collections, Concentration, and Disbursements).

This chapter begins by presenting an overview of how payment systems work in general. It then takes a detailed look at the more common payment systems, including checks, cards, and electronic payments, and examines the various features and functions that distinguish each one. Cash (both coin and currency)—although technically not a payment system[1]—is also discussed, because it is a major payment method and is especially critical to treasury professionals that have any involvement in retail business.

II. PAYMENT SYSTEMS OVERVIEW

A payment system is a series of processes and technologies that transfer monetary value from one party to another. Payments are typically made in exchange for the provision of goods or services, or to satisfy a legal obligation. They can be made in any number of currencies, using a variety of methods, such as cash, checks, electronic transfers, and cards. What makes a payment system a system is that it uses cash substitutes, such as checks or electronic messages, to instruct the debits and credits that transfer value from one party to another. Cash payments are not, per se, a payment system, since the value transfer happens as part of the transfer of the coin or currency, but they constitute a critical payment method nonetheless. In fact, because of the inherent value of cash and the associated need for accounting and safekeeping, most companies have implemented significant processes around the handling of cash payments.

For noncash payments, the value that is being transferred is typically stored in depository accounts at an FI. The FIs, in turn, are connected into the various types of payment systems, and process payments on behalf of their customers or depositors. As an example, most FIs are connected to a variety of electronic and paper-based messaging and payment systems, such as Fedwire, TARGET2, SWIFT, Visa, MasterCard, and many others.

A. Basic Payments

In the simplest case, payments involve four participants:

- The **payor** makes the payment and has his/her account debited for the value of the transaction.
- The **payor's financial institution** (often referred to as the *paying bank*[2]) processes the value transfer on the payor's behalf.
- The **payee or beneficiary** is the receiver of the payment whose account is credited for the value of the transaction.

1. Because the value of coin and currency is inherent in the physical cash and not some related bank account, the exchange of cash is a valid method of payment but is not a payment system because it does not require the use of any outside agency, such as a financial institution.
2. The term *bank* is used here and throughout this chapter, even though the FI involved may well be a different form of financial institution, because the term *paying bank* is the traditional term used to identify the payor's financial institution. This usage goes back to the time when checks were the primary payment system and only commercial banks could process checks. In today's world all types of financial institutions process payments and the terms *originating FI and receiving FI* are often used in place of *paying* and *receiving bank*.

- The **payee's financial institution** (often referred to as the *receiving bank* or *receiving FI*) processes the transaction on behalf of the payee and generally holds the value in an account.

This simple case is illustrated in the four-corner payment system model shown in Exhibit 4.1.

EXHIBIT 4.1 **FOUR-CORNER PAYMENT SYSTEM MODEL**

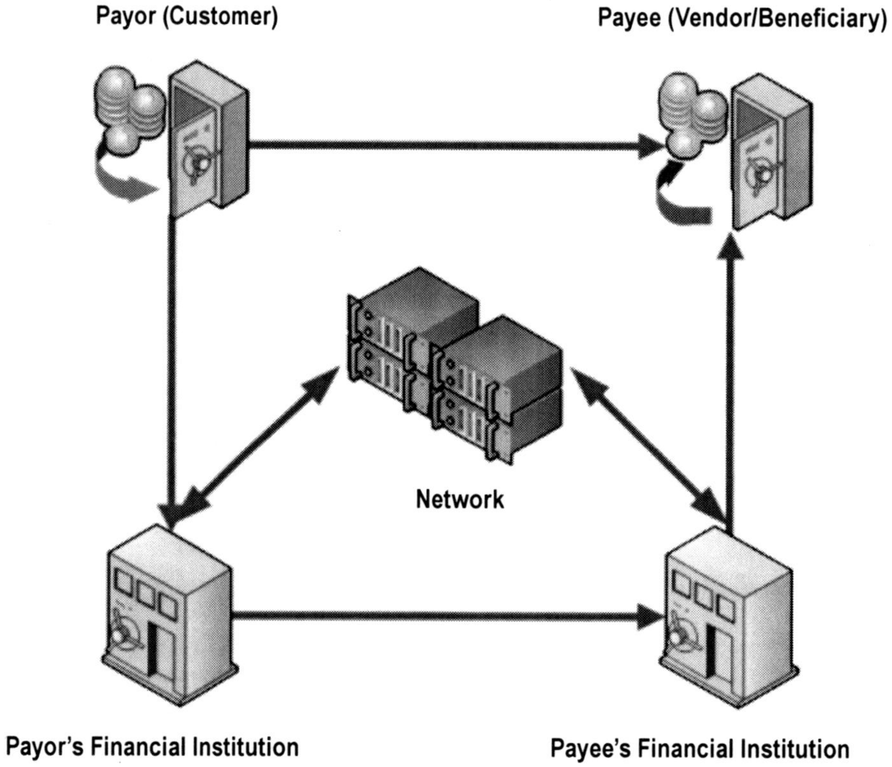

While the FIs may choose to transfer payment instructions and funds directly with each other, there can be additional parties and intermediaries in the transaction that help facilitate matters. Exhibit 4.1 refers to these intermediaries as the *network*.

In the real world the network includes central banks such as the US Federal Reserve (Fed), the European Central Bank (ECB), or the Bank of England, and commercial entities such as CHIPS (Clearing House Interbank Payments System) or Visa. There are also transaction facilitators (e.g., SWIFT), which include information transmission mechanisms, and payment systems (e.g., Fedwire in the United States and BOJ-NET in Japan), which also include information transmission capabilities. There may also be entities outside of the four-corner model that participate in the payment process, such as payroll processors, check printers, and systems providers.

B. The Payment Process

From a systems standpoint, there are four elements in the payment process:

- **Payment instructions** are the information contained in an electronic transfer (e.g., a wire or ACH [automated clearinghouse] transaction) or a check. These instructions are from the payor and tell the paying bank to transfer value to the beneficiary through the receiving bank.
- **Payment generation** is where the instructions are entered into the payment system itself.
- **Clearing** is the process where the FIs use the payment information to transfer money between themselves on behalf of the payor and the beneficiary, either directly or through some external network.
- **Settlement** is the final step in the process and occurs when the beneficiary's bank account is credited and the payor's bank account is charged.

C. Settlement versus Finality

It is important to understand the difference between settlement and finality of payment. *Settlement or availability* refers to the actual movement of funds from the payor's account to the payee's account—in other words, the time at which the payee can actually use the money involved. *Finality* refers to the point in time when the payor knows that the money involved cannot be taken back or retracted by the payor or the payor's bank. Settlement becomes final when a payment is unconditional and irrevocable.

Finality varies depending on the payment system and the parties involved in the transaction. Payment systems that offer immediate and irrevocable value are called *real-time gross settlement (RTGS) systems* and are typically wire transfer systems. Others, such as check- or card-based systems, typically provide immediate information, with value following at a later time. But the value is contingent on the payor or the payor's bank not attempting to retract the payment, a right which can exist for several months or more, depending upon the specific payment system.

The actual transfer of funds, or settlement, can be handled in several different ways. In a domestic transfer, one in which all parties are in the same country, settlement is often handled between the FIs using common accounts held at their central bank.

Alternatively, financial institutions can use depository accounts with each other, called *correspondent accounts*, to settle their customers' funds transfers. While this is more commonly used for cross-border payments involving more than one country, correspondent accounts can also be used to process domestic payments.

In a correspondent banking relationship, two banks have accounts with each other for the purpose of clearing and settlement of payment items between the banks. Generally, smaller banks with limited access to other clearing methods will maintain a correspondent relationship with a larger bank to enable more efficient clearing. In most international funds transfers, correspondent banks play a key role in the settlement process. These correspondent relationships may be reciprocal (i.e., both banks move value both ways and have accounts with each other) or one-way (i.e., a small bank may have an account with a larger bank for clearing purposes).

D. Types of Payments

There are a variety of different payment systems that can be used to make a payment, and each has different operating characteristics, risks, rules, and settlement mechanisms. In addition to cash, payments are typically grouped into one of the following four types of payment systems:

- **Checks or drafts** are payments that are initiated when one party writes a check to pay another, and they are one of the oldest forms of noncash payment systems. They are still used throughout the world and are most widely used in the United States, where they still represent the largest number of commercial or business payments.
- **RTGS (real-time gross settlement) or large-value electronic payments** are what most people mean when they refer to *wire transfers*. Wires have existed since the late 1800s with the invention of the telegraph, but did not become widely used until the early 1900s.
- **Low-value electronic payments,** often referred to as **automated clearinghouse, or ACH, payments,** were introduced in the early 1970s and were designed to replace checks with electronic payments. Unlike wires, which are processed individually and immediately (in real time), ACH payments are value-dated and processed in batches, and typically take one to two days to settle. Originally ACH payments were intended for "small" payments, such as payroll and consumer transactions. Today, many companies use ACH transactions to replace wires and other payment systems when the payment amount is known at least one day prior to the transaction date, due to the lower cost of ACH transactions.
- **Card-based payments** are payments that settle through one of the large card-processing networks such as Visa, MasterCard, China UnionPay, or American Express, or through one of the ATM (automated teller machine) or POS (point-of-sale) systems such as STAR, NYCE, or PULSE in the United States, Interac in Canada, or Telstra in Australia. Originally, card transactions were all credit card payments and were initiated through the presentment of a plastic credit card. Today, card payments come in a wide variety of alternatives, such as debit cards, prepaid cards, and payroll cards—some of which, despite the name, no longer use a physical card.

Payments are also often differentiated based upon the identities of the various parties involved in the payment transactions:

- **Business-to-business (B2B)** are payments from one business to another, typically for vendor payments. While this represents the smallest volume of payments in number, it typically represents the largest individual payments by value. Historically, B2B payments have been either by check or wire transfer, but over time, checks are being replaced by other electronic and/or card-based payments.
- **Business-to-consumer (B2C)** are payments from businesses to consumers or individuals, typically for things such as payroll.
- **Consumer-to-business (C2B)** are payments from consumers to businesses, typically for purchases and bill payments. Historically, these were largely cash and check payments in the United States, or cash and giro payments[3] in Europe. Now, small-dollar transactions at the point of sale are still often cash, but the majority of the other payments are either card payments at the point of sale or electronic through an FI for bill payments.

3. Giro (or postal giro, since many giro systems are run by the postal system within a country) is a method of transferring money by instructing a bank to directly transfer funds from one bank account to another without the use of checks. Giro payments are initiated by the payor and can be one-time payments or can be recurring standing instructions for a series of payments.

- **Consumer-to-consumer (C2C)**, or sometimes **person-to-person (P2P)**, are payments from one individual to another for individual transactions, including income payments (e.g., babysitting or lawn mowing) and various personal payments (e.g., gifts).
- **Business-to-government (B2G)** and **consumer-to-government (C2G)** are payments for such things as taxes, fines, and other government fees.
- **Government-to-business (G2B)** are usually vendor payments.
- **Government-to-consumer (G2C)** are various government-issued payments such as retirement, social security, and welfare payments.

The large majority of government payments are either electronic or card-based.

III. CASH PAYMENTS

Cash transactions involve the use of currency and coin in physical form and are primarily used by consumers for small amounts. Generally, each country has its own currency, which is used for cash transactions within that country. In some regions, a common currency may be used across a number of countries within that region (e.g., the euro within most of Europe). In some countries, the common currency in use may be that of another country, often a major trading partner (e.g., Ecuador and Panama use the US dollar as their primary currency). In most cases, cash payment systems are self-sufficient, meaning that cash is the payment instrument and that when the payor gives cash to the payee for a transaction, the physical transfer of the cash represents both the clearing network and the final settlement—no other settlement infrastructure is needed for that particular transaction.

Many types of companies (e.g., retailers, grocers, and restaurants) receive a significant portion of their payments in the form of cash. In some countries, cash payments may be the normal method of payment for many types of transactions, both business and consumer. In addition, it is still common in some countries for payrolls to be paid in cash.

The popular conception is that because cash transactions are "self-settling" (i.e., they do not require an FI or network and are final at the time of presentment), they are less expensive than other types of payments. Any retailer can explain that the opposite is true. Because cash has an intrinsic value on its own, it represents a security risk and needs to be both accounted for and safeguarded. Cash collected by a company must generally be safeguarded at the collection point until it can be transported to a bank and into the company's bank account. The cost of this process, which includes everything from locked cash drawers and dual-control procedures to specialized safes and armored cars, can actually be quite high. Additionally, FIs typically charge their corporate customers a fee to receive, count, and verify cash deposits. As a result, when all costs are considered, cash is potentially a high-cost payment system for most companies.

IV. CHECK-BASED PAYMENTS

Checks (or cheques) are the traditional method that payors, also referred to as *makers* (because they "make" the check), have used to access their accounts. While the volume of checks being written is declining over time, it is still the primary method used for B2B payments in the United States. Checks are also used in many other countries around the world, but the overall volume of checks is much lower than in the United States.

Depending upon the country, check payments are usually available to depositors in one or two days, but finality can take several weeks or longer, due to stop payment orders and overdraft returns by the paying bank. (See Appendix 4.1 for a more complete list of potential return reasons.)

EXHIBIT 4.2 **CHECK PAYMENT SYSTEM**

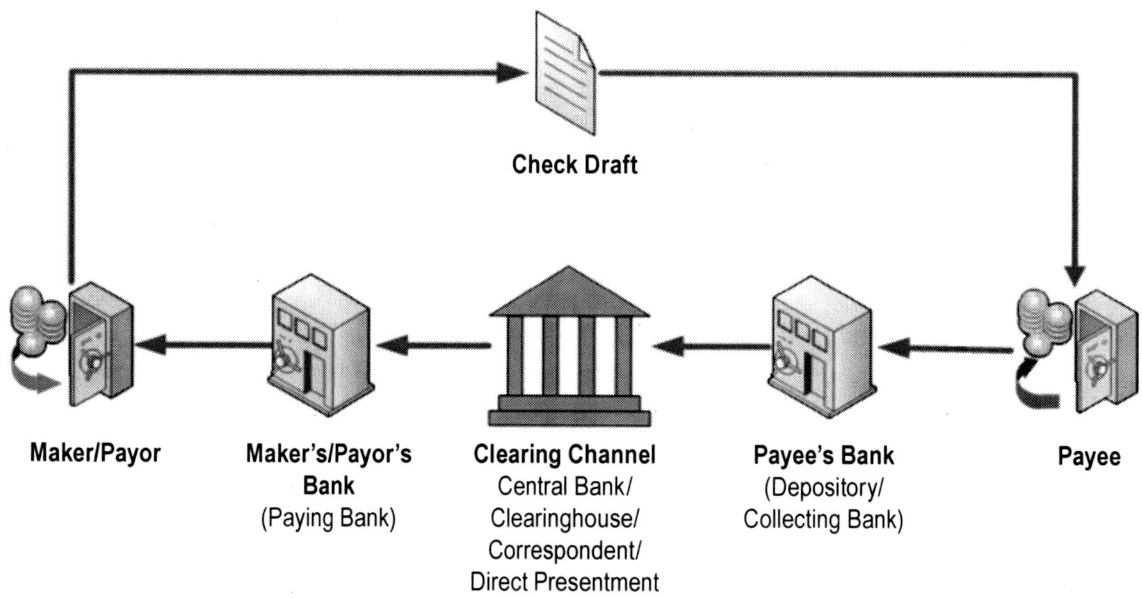

As illustrated in Exhibit 4.2, the process of clearing a payment through the check payment system begins with the deposit or "paying in" of a check—drawn on a domestic bank in local currency—into a payee's account at the payee's bank, referred to as the *bank of first deposit* (also known as the *depository or collecting bank*). The check may be deposited either as a physical check or (in the United States) potentially as a check image, using a process referred to as *remote deposit capture (RDC)*. (RDC is discussed later in this chapter.)

If the payee has not already scanned the check and deposited it as an electronic image, the check is either scanned at the teller counter, or batched and sent through a reader/sorter at the bank of first deposit, which captures the MICR line information and captures an image of the check. During this scanning process, the amount of the check is captured and added to the information contained in the MICR line on the bottom of each check.

The MICR line is a specially formatted line of machine-readable information on the bottom of a check that contains all the information necessary to process the check through the check-clearing system. It is called the *MICR line* because it is printed with a special magnetic ink used for magnetic ink character recognition, or MICR. Today, many check readers actually use optical character recognition, or OCR, to capture the information in a MICR line. Magnetic ink is still used to print the MICR line, however, because of the large number of MICR readers still in use. Check images can only be read via OCR, since the image does not contain any magnetic ink. Exhibit 4.3 illustrates a sample US business check and the elements of the MICR line.[4] Comparable MICR lines are used in other countries.

4. US consumer checks differ from business checks in that they are slightly smaller (6 inches versus 8.5 inches) and lack the initial, or auxiliary on-us, field in the MICR line.

EXHIBIT 4.3 SAMPLE US BUSINESS CHECK

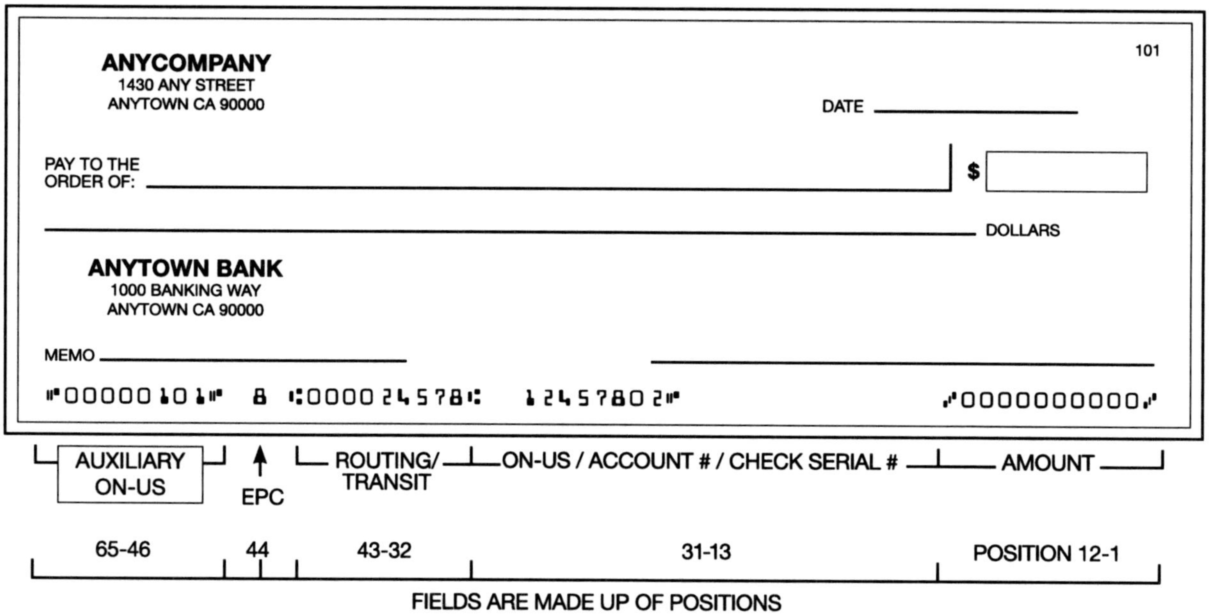

AUXILIARY ON-US FIELD

- This is an eight-digit field used on business checks.
- This number is frequently the check number.
- It assists the drawee bank in providing a variety of account reconciliation services.
- It is a key in providing stop payment and positive pay services.
- It is necessary to prevent check conversion.

EXTERNAL PROCESSING CODE (EPC)

This is a single-digit optional field for special purposes, such as image processing codes, located to the immediate left of the routing number.

ROUTING NUMBER

Also known as the *American Bankers Association (ABA) number* or *routing transit number (RTN)*, the routing number is a nine-digit code that identifies which financial institution the check is drawn upon. The format of the ABA is as follows:

The first two digits of the nine-digit ABA number must be in the ranges 00 through 12, 21 through 32, 61 through 72, or 80.

The digits are assigned as follows:

- 00 is used by the United States government.
- 01 through 12 identify the drawee bank's Federal Reserve district.
- 21 through 32 were assigned only to thrift institutions.
- 61 through 72 are used for electronic transactions.
- 80 is used for traveler's checks.

The third digit represents the particular office of a Federal Reserve Bank serving the drawee bank. The fourth digit historically referred to whether items were given immediate or deferred availability by the Fed.

The following four digits, or digits 5 through 8 of the nine-digit number, designate the specific bank location, served by the designated Federal Reserve office, to which the item must be delivered for payment. Banks can have more than one RTN if they have multiple check-processing locations.

The last digit is known as the *check digit*. This is a mathematical calculation used to verify the accuracy of the routing number.

ON-US/ACCOUNT NUMBER

This field contains the customer account number as assigned to the payor by the drawee bank.

ENCODED AMOUNT OF CHECK

This number should agree with the amount written on the check by the payor. The amount is typically encoded on the check by the depository bank and appears in the lower right-hand corner of the processed check.

After initial capture via scanning or reader/sorter, the checks and/or images are then sorted according to the rules of the country's check system and the actual clearing channel used to collect the payments (discussed in more detail later in this chapter), and are sent through the clearing channel as cash letters. A cash letter is typically a file of check images and related control information but can also be used to refer to a physical bundle of checks and related control documents. This processing is typically done at the bank of first deposit.

Historically, for settlement to occur, the original check had to be presented to, and be accepted by, the bank on which the check was drawn, referred to as the *paying bank*. Thus, the key event in the check-clearing process was presentment—the physical delivery of a check to the paying bank. This resulted in the creation of a logistical system to physically transport a large number of checks from one bank to another, every night. The term *cash letter* derives from the fact that bundles of physical checks were sent to a paying bank in exchange for "cash" or some form of bank credit.

This situation has changed in many countries with the introduction of image check processing,[5] which has largely replaced the exchange of physical checks with the exchange of check images. Another result of image check processing has been the development of ancillary services, such as remote deposit capture (RDC). In its most simple terms, RDC is a service (available primarily in the United States) that allows a payee to scan any check it receives as payment and transmit the scanned images to a bank for posting and clearing, instead of having to deposit physical checks. Originally designed for larger commercial deposits, RDC is now often available for consumer and small-business depositors as well.

Regardless of whether the check is paper or an image, value is subtracted from the paying bank's account at the time of presentment through a central bank (e.g., the Federal Reserve), a correspondent bank, or some other clearing channel. Following presentment, the paying bank posts the check to the payor's account. Most check processing is automated, and banks rely on account holders to report fraudulent checks, forged endorsements, and alterations.

The paying bank has a limited period of time to conduct a review of the paid check/image and either authorize final payment, or refuse payment and return the check to the bank of first deposit. Returned checks (referred to as *return items*) may be redeposited or charged back to the depositor's account, depending on the return reason. In the United States, banks have until midnight of the business day following the day of receipt of a check (either as an image or a physical document) to complete their review and return any checks, roughly 36 hours.[6] This compares with the United Kingdom, where the return deadline is six days from the date the check was deposited at the payee's bank. While other countries have similar rules governing check processing, there are often local variations on such issues as processing time and return requirements. As a result, it is important

5. In the United States, this change occurred in 2004 with the enactment of the Check Clearing for the 21st Century Act (referred to as *Check 21*). While Check 21 did not specifically authorize image presentment of checks, it did create a new negotiable instrument called an *image replacement document (IRD)*. An IRD is a paper reproduction of the original check that contains an image of the front and back of the original check and is the legal equivalent of the original check. As a result, US banks can legally exchange images electronically instead of shipping paper checks, and can use the images to print an IRD when or if someone in the clearing process needs a physical document.
6. The guidelines for returned check items are based on the Federal Reserve's Reg CC.

that treasury professionals know and understand the rules and regulations that apply to any checks that they may use or receive in the normal course of business. Local FIs are usually one of the best sources of this information.

A. On-Us Check Clearing

"On-us" check clearing involves a single bank and occurs when a payee deposits a check in an account at the same bank on which it is drawn. The bank simultaneously debits the payor's account and credits the payee's account. The depositor typically receives same-day or immediate availability, if funds are available, and processing fees are often lower than for other checks that require additional processing.

"On-we" check clearing is similar to on-us but involves a group of banks that use a common third-party vendor to process their checks for them. Since all of the banks' checks are processed at the same time and same place, they can be treated as if they were on-us items, typically resulting in same-day or immediate availability for the depositing company.

B. Transit Check Clearing

Deposited checks drawn on other FIs are referred to as *transit checks* and require more processing than on-us or on-we checks. As discussed above, the bank of first deposit must sort these checks into cash letters, which must then be transmitted to the paying bank either directly or via intermediary processors, such as a central bank, a clearing facility, or a correspondent bank (collectively referred to as *clearing channels*) for final settlement.

Four major clearing channels are available in the United States for processing transit checks:

- **Clearinghouse:** Clearinghouses are either formal or informal associations formed by banks in a geographic area to permit the exchange of items drawn on the member participants. Member banks make daily, or sometimes more frequent, presentments to the clearinghouse. The net value (i.e., face amount of items submitted less items received, calculated on a bank-by-bank basis) is transferred between the banks by debiting and crediting correspondent accounts or through reserve accounts that each bank maintains with the local Federal Reserve Bank.
- **Correspondent Bank:** In correspondent bank clearing, the collecting bank maintains a depository account with another bank. The collecting bank sends cash letters to the correspondent bank, which presents the items to the paying bank through a local clearinghouse or the Fed. The collecting bank's depository account at the correspondent bank is then credited with the proceeds of the checks.
- **Direct Send or Direct Exchange:** As an alternative to using the clearing channels just discussed, collecting banks may arrange to send cash letters directly to a paying bank or to a nonlocal Federal Reserve Bank. This process, also referred to as *direct presentment*, enables banks to meet various deposit deadlines and achieve faster clearing times. The collecting bank maintains a depository account with the paying bank or nonlocal Federal Reserve Bank, which is credited with the proceeds of the checks. If the cash letter arrives early enough in the day, the paying bank must settle the same day.
- **Federal Reserve System (Fed):** The Fed also acts as a check-clearing agent. Depository banks can send cash letters to the Fed, which will then clear the checks and transfer values from paying banks to depository banks.

As a result of image processing and electronic presentment of checks in the United States, many checks now clear the same day, with the remainder settling in one day. Finality, however, can still take several weeks due to returned items of various types. Similar options are typically available in most countries with the proviso that the Federal Reserve System is typically replaced by that country's central bank or some other equivalent processor.

C. Foreign Checks

Foreign checks are any checks deposited into a bank in one country that are drawn on a bank in another country. Foreign checks may also be drawn in a foreign currency (e.g., a check in British pounds deposited with a US bank for credit to a US dollar bank account). These checks are normally treated as "collection items"[7] and processed outside of the normal check-clearing systems. This typically means that the depository bank that receives the foreign check will send the item to a correspondent bank (or a foreign branch of the depository bank, if it has one) in the country in which the foreign check is payable. The correspondent bank will, in turn, process the foreign check locally and eventually remit the proceeds to the depository bank. Because these checks are subject to both foreign exchange (FX) costs and extra processing fees, the bank of first deposit typically will not credit the payee's account until it actually receives and converts the proceeds of the check to its base currency. As a result, these checks can take days or even weeks to clear and normally clear for significantly less than the face amount of the check.

One exception to this process is US dollar checks that are drawn on a Canadian bank but have a US MICR line[8] and are deposited into a US bank—these are processed through standard check-processing channels.

D. Endpoints

An endpoint is the location of the paying bank where final settlement occurs. The endpoint is determined by the routing information, such as the RTN or sort code[9] on the check.

E. Deadlines and Deposit Timing

There are two check deposit-related deadlines established by banks that determine when funds become available: the ledger cutoff time and the deposit deadline. All of the times and deadlines discussed in this section are assumed to be local times at the point of deposit and apply to deposits[10] of checks, either as images or physical documents. Each bank sets deadlines based on competitive and operational considerations. A particular banking day may start at some time other than midnight, but banking days are always reckoned as 24-hour days—never as fractional days. It is important to know when a banking day begins and ends because, for example, a deposit made to an interest-bearing account will earn interest for that day irrespective of when the deposit was made during the banking day.

7. A collection item (also called a *noncash item*) is any item presented to a bank for deposit that the bank will not provisionally credit to the depositor's account. Payment must be received from the payor's bank before the item is credited to the payee's account.
8. Several Canadian banks have requested and been assigned US RTNs.
9. A sort code is the name given by banks in the United Kingdom to the bank codes used to route money transfers and payments between banks. It is similar to an RTN in US banks. RTNs are discussed in Chapter 3, Banks and Financial Institutions.
10. The term *deposit* typically refers to deposits of checks and/or cash. Electronic payments are normally "received" rather than deposited, and while they may be subject to processing deadlines, they are not usually subject to deposit deadlines and/or availability schedules.

A bank's ledger cutoff is the time of day when a deposit must be received in order to be posted to the ledger balance of the depositor's account. This time can vary within a bank depending on where and how the items are received. Items deposited after the ledger cutoff time are considered to be received by the bank on the next banking day. For example, if a bank has a published ledger cutoff time of 3:00 p.m., then a deposit made at 2:00 p.m. Friday will be credited to the ledger balance on Friday. However, a deposit made to the same bank account on Friday at 3:30 p.m. would not be credited to the ledger balance until Monday, which is the next banking business day. Ledger balances are granted provisional credit based on the anticipated settlement and finality of the item. The deposit deadline is the time within the banking day when an item must be ready for transit at the depository bank's processing center to qualify for the availability stated in the availability schedule.

F. Availability Schedules

Availability schedules specify, for each drawee endpoint, when a bank grants available credit or collected balances for deposited items. Each bank is free to set its own availability schedule based on its own processing schedules, capabilities, and pricing decisions. In order to receive the availability stated on the schedule, the deposited item must have been received by the assigned deposit deadline. If the deposit deadline is missed, then availability is delayed. Checks are generally assigned somewhere between zero- and one-day availability for businesses, although in rare cases some items may be assigned two-day availability.

Most banks assign availability using the proof-of-deposit (POD) method. Under the POD method, availability is assigned to each check as it is processed. Availability is determined based on the time and day of deposit and the check's drawee endpoint. Some banks may negotiate special availability for selected high-volume customers.

The Fed has availability schedules for US banks, correspondent banks have availability schedules for other banks, and banks have availability schedules for customers. Many banks have multiple availability schedules depending on the customer and the volume of business. Because the availability schedule impacts float[11] balances, the schedule a bank offers to a particular customer is part of the pricing decision.

G. Balances and Float

Balance measurements and float calculations are determined by the relationship of the time that a check is deposited to the deadlines set by the depository institution (in contrast, electronic payments are typically available when posted):

- **Ledger balances** are bank balances that reflect all entries to a bank account, regardless of whether the deposited items have been collected and are available for withdrawal. Ledger balances are important for accounting purposes, but not for funds availability or bank compensation purposes. A negative ledger balance results in a ledger overdraft, for which substantial charges can be assessed.
- **Available balances** reflect the amount of funds available for withdrawal from an account, based on the bank's availability schedule and/or local regulations that require specific availability for certain funds (e.g., Reg CC in the United States; other countries typically have similar regulations).
- **Collected balances** refer to the average ledger balance minus the deposit float. Neither *collected balances* nor *deposit float* are regulatory terms. Rather, they are items used by US banks to determine earnings credits on account analysis statements (discussed in more detail in Chapter 7, Relationship Management and Vendor Selection).

11. *Float* is defined as the time interval between when a transaction is initially processed and when the value of that transaction is available for use or charged to an account.

H. Other Check-Processing Factors That Influence Availability

Several other factors may impact funds availability:

- **RDC/Image Capture:** A depositor may elect to use RDC or some other form of image capture for deposited items. Remote deposit capture typically adds the dollar amount to the MICR data captured with each check prior to deposit. Items that are preprocessed using RDC—or some other method of capturing the MICR and payment information—may receive faster availability, a later cutoff time, a later deposit deadline, and/or lower service charges because the customer is, in effect, performing a labor-intensive task for the bank.
- **Reject Items:** Checks that are rejected by a bank's automated check-processing equipment are likely to miss critical deposit deadlines, resulting in delays in availability and additional processing fees. The reason for this is that reject items must be repaired and reprocessed. Most reject items arise either because of physical defects in the MICR line or because the MICR line does not meet banking industry specifications.
- **As-Of Adjustments:** When a check takes longer to clear than the initial availability that was granted, a bank may add the additional time as part of the collected-balance calculation. This practice is referred to as making an *as-of adjustment*. If a bank originally granted one-day availability but actually cleared the check in two days, then one more day of float is added when calculating collected balances. As-of adjustments are important because they can impact the funds available for use by a depositor. As discussed in Chapter 7, Relationship Management and Vendor Selection, because as-of adjustments normally reduce available balances, they can also increase bank fees and in extreme cases even result in overdrafts.
- **Value Dating:** Value dating, which is discussed in more detail in Chapter 7, Relationship Management and Vendor Selection, is the practice of debiting or crediting a particular transaction on some date other than the processing date. For example, in Canada it is standard practice to charge a payor's account for the value of a check as of the date the check was deposited, rather than the date it was actually processed by the bank.

I. Additional Paper-Based Instruments

A number of other payment instruments have check-like attributes (e.g., a MICR line and RTN) and typically clear through the same channels as checks. These include:

- **Payable through Draft (PTD):** A PTD is a payment instrument resembling a check that is drawn against the payor rather than the bank. It is handled like a check through the clearing process, but the responsibility for paying the draft lies with the payor, referred to as the *drawee* in the case of drafts. The primary reason companies use drafts is to preserve the right to review the items prior to final payment. Insurance companies often use this type of instrument for claims reimbursement because drafts provide insurers with an opportunity to verify signatures and endorsements before honoring the items.

- **Remotely Created Check (RCC):** RCCs, also known as *pre-authorized drafts*, are a type of check used to draw or draft against a payor's account. The check is unsigned, and the payee, rather than the payor, initiates the transaction. RCCs are typically created for a one-time payment, such as a late bill payment or debt settlement. Because they do not bear a signature and can be created without the knowledge of the payor, RCCs are very vulnerable to fraud. As a result, many banks refuse to accept them for deposit. According to Reg CC (in the United States) and most clearinghouse agreements, any bank that transfers or presents a remotely created check warrants that the check is authorized by the person on whose account the check is drawn.
- **Money Order:** A money order is a prepaid instrument issued by various third parties such as banks, postal services (the postal services of both the United States and India are large issuers of money orders), or consumer outlets (e.g., convenience stores and check-cashing agencies). The purchaser is the instrument's payor, and the money order is the obligation of the issuer.
- **Traveler's Check:** Traveler's checks are prepaid instruments similar to money orders. Two signatures usually are required by the purchaser: one at issuance and one at the time the check is used to pay for goods or services. Some traveler's check issuers are moving to replace the checks with various types of stored-value cards to improve processing times and reduce fraud.
- **Sight Draft/Time Draft:** A sight draft is usually presented in combination with other documents that verify the terms of a transaction have been met. If all the documentation is in order, then the draft is payable upon presentment (i.e., at sight). A time draft is the same as a sight draft except it is not payable until a specified future date. Sight and time drafts are used primarily to support international trade, and are discussed in more detail in Chapter 10, Collections, Concentration, and Disbursements. Time drafts are used for transactions that call for delayed payment.
- **Cashier's Check/Certified Check:** A cashier's check, also known as an *official bank check*, is a check drawn on a bank's own funds. A certified check is drawn on a depositor's checking account, and funds are withdrawn from the depositor's account at the time of certification, to assure payment with a certification or guarantee by the bank. Both carry the signature of a bank officer certifying the check to be genuine and guaranteeing payment. Due to the higher processing costs of certified checks, most banks have replaced them with cashier's checks.
- **Government Warrant:** In government finance, a warrant is an order to pay that instructs a treasurer to pay the warrant holder on demand or after a maturity date. Warrants deposited in a bank are routed (based on the MICR line information) to a collecting bank that processes them as collection items. The collecting bank presents the warrants to the government entity's treasury department for payment each business day. In the United States, warrants are typically issued by state treasurers for payroll purposes, for A/P to vendors, for tax refund payments to taxpayers, and for payments to owners of unclaimed monies.

V. LARGE-VALUE ELECTRONIC FUNDS TRANSFER (EFT)/WIRE TRANSFER SYSTEMS

Processing large-value electronic funds transfers involves two key elements: clearing and settlement. Clearing is the transfer and confirmation of information between the payor's bank (sending FI) and the payee's bank (receiving FI). Settlement is the actual transfer of funds between the payor's FI and the payee's FI. Settlement discharges the obligation of the payor FI to the payee FI with respect to the payment order. Final settlement is irrevocable and unconditional. The finality of the payment is determined by the transfer system's rules and applicable law. The illustration shown in Exhibit 4.4 assumes that the funds transfer takes place within one country. In this case the transaction information and ultimate settlement is all handled through the country's central bank or equivalent. For transactions involving more than one country, referred to as *cross-border payments*, the transaction information is sent via an external system such as SWIFT or CLS (as discussed below), and settlement is handled through correspondent bank accounts.

EXHIBIT 4.4 **LARGE-VALUE FUNDS TRANSFER SYSTEM**

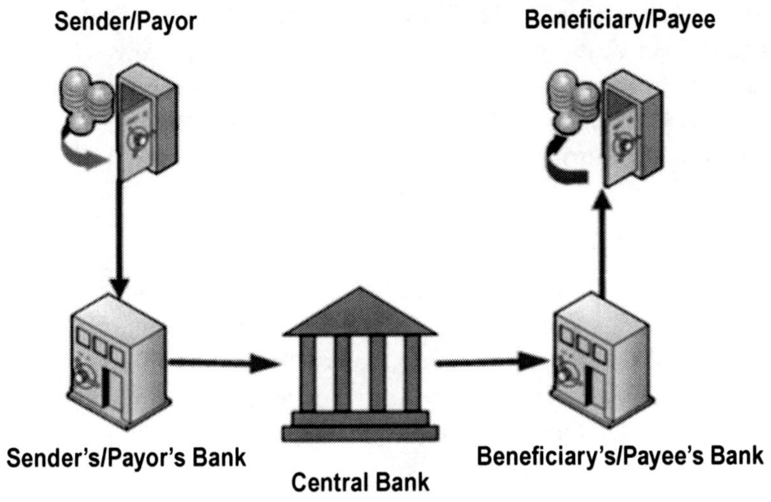

Large-value funds transfer systems can be either real-time gross settlement (RTGS) systems or net settlement systems.

Gross settlement occurs when each transaction results in a separate value transfer between the payor and payee. In most gross settlement systems, the settlement is on a real-time basis, resulting in a real-time gross settlement system. Payments in an RTGS system are considered final at the time they are processed.

Net settlement occurs when many transactions are combined and then sorted by sending and receiving banks. At the end of day (or at another agreed-upon point in time), the net amount either owed by or owed to each bank is determined and only the net amount of value is actually transferred. At this point, electronic credit transactions are considered to be final. Electronic debits may be reversible under certain, specified circumstances. All of the individual transactions are, of course, accounted for on a bookkeeping basis, with each bank making the necessary debits and credits to individual accounts.

A. Real-Time Gross Settlement (RTGS) Systems

Real-time gross settlement means that the clearing and settlement of each transaction occur continuously during the processing day. Payment to the receiving participant (payee) is final and irrevocable when the RTGS processor (central bank or equivalent) either credits the amount of the payment order to the receiving bank's account or sends notice to the receiving bank, whichever is earlier.

There are similar public and private large-value transfer systems in most countries around the world. Examples include Fedwire in the United States, CHAPS in the United Kingdom, LVTS in Canada, and CNAPS in China.[12]

Large-value RTGS payment systems are used by companies to facilitate major transactions that are time sensitive and where the irrevocable receipt of value is required. Because a payment made through these systems is final and irrevocable once made—and because the amounts can be significant—special care and diligence is required in the issuance and processing of wire transfers. An example of an RTGS payment transaction message via the US Fedwire is provided in Appendix 4.2, along with an explanation of the appropriate Fedwire format for the message.

B. Clearing House Interbank Payments System (CHIPS)

CHIPS is a US-based privately owned wire transfer system that settles its transactions through the Federal Reserve Bank. Like Fedwire, CHIPS handles both the transmission of funds transfer instruction messages among financial institutions, as well as the settlement of the payment between the institutions, and is a real-time settlement system that is final at the time of the transaction. CHIPS claims to be the main electronic funds transfer system for processing international US dollar funds transfers made among international banks in the United States. To access CHIPS, an FI must have a US presence. As of 2013, CHIPS has 46 banks, representing 19 countries, as members.

C. TARGET2 and the Single Euro Payments Area (SEPA)

TARGET2[13] is the European RTGS system and went live in November 2007. TARGET2, along with its predecessor TARGET, was developed as part of the implementation of SEPA, the Single Euro Payments Area. SEPA, an initiative of the European Union, is intended to ensure that electronic payments within the euro zone are handled in a standardized and inexpensive manner across all countries of the euro zone. In effect, cross-border payments within the SEPA boundaries are treated as if they were in-country rather than cross-border payments. TARGET2 is based on a common operating platform developed and operated by Banca d'Italia, Banque de France, and Deutsche Bundesbank on behalf of the Eurosystem.

D. Continuous Linked Settlement (CLS)

Beginning in the mid-1990s, central banks became increasingly concerned that the high level of settlement risk in existing practices, coupled with an unexpected event or failure, could trigger a serious disruption of the global FX markets and financial system liquidity. In an FX transaction, settlement risk is the risk that one party to the transaction pays out the currency it sold but does not receive the currency it bought. The exposure to a single counterparty, even if for a limited time, can be very large relative to the capital of the parties to the transaction. The solution to address this concern was the development of a risk-reducing, multicurrency FX settlement service. This solution is called *continuous linked settlement (CLS)*. CLS allows a simultaneous exchange of the payments for both sides of the underlying financial transactions (e.g., FX contracts, non-deliverable forward [NDF] contracts, and over-the-counter [OTC] derivative contracts), thereby eliminating settlement risk.

The CLS process is managed by CLS Group Holdings AG and includes the CLS Bank International (CLS Bank). It is regulated by the central banks in the countries in which it operates. The group was formed in 1997, and the system has been operating since 2002. As of 2013, CLS membership includes 64 member banks and 17 central banks.

12. *CHAPS* refers to the UK's Clearing House Automated Payment System, *LVTS* refers to Canada's Large Value Transfer System, and *CNAPS* refers to the China National Advanced Payment System.
13. TARGET2 is the second generation of the Trans-European Automated Real-time Gross settlement Express Transfer (TARGET) system.

E. Society for Worldwide Interbank Financial Telecommunication (SWIFT)

SWIFT is not, strictly speaking, a payment system. It is a communication system used by most of the banks in the world to transmit payment instructions, among other things, and is therefore often thought of, incorrectly, as an international wire transfer or funds transfer system. SWIFT is an industry-owned, cooperative, interbank telecommunication network that enables banks to send authenticated electronic messages in standard formats. The information that moves through SWIFT ultimately results in value being transferred from one party to another, generally through correspondent banks, hence the perception that it is a payment system.

SWIFT was created in Brussels in 1973, supported at that time by more than 200 large banks in 15 countries. As of 2012, SWIFT included more than 9,000 banking organizations, security institutions, and corporate customers in more than 209 countries. SWIFT communications contain payment-related information, but do not actually transfer value. Communications that are initiated and received by member banks are known as *SWIFT messages*. These messages cover a wide range of international banking services, and include balance reporting, letters of credit (L/Cs), documentary collections, and foreign exchange (FX) transactions. Through the SWIFT network, a company can request a bank to initiate a balance transfer or foreign payment.

For corporate customers, SWIFT provides a limited membership that allows a corporation to utilize SWIFT's multibank platform to exchange financial information with its banks through one standardized platform. This may allow the corporation to reduce or eliminate transaction costs while increasing the speed of payment and minimizing the necessity of maintaining multiple bank connections in order to send/receive information and initiate payments.

VI. SMALL-VALUE TRANSFER OR AUTOMATED CLEARINGHOUSE (ACH) SYSTEMS

Small-value transfer systems are electronic networks for the exchange of smaller payment instructions among FIs, typically on behalf of consumers. Many countries have small-value transfer systems—Bacs in the United Kingdom, ECG (Electronic Clearing) in Hong Kong, and ACH in the United States. Small-value transfer payments, usually referred to as *ACH payments or non-time-critical payments*, are payment instructions to either debit or credit a deposit account. They are typically batch-processed, value-dated electronic funds transfers between originating and receiving FIs. An additional feature of most ACH systems is that an ACH transaction is capable of transferring more information about a payment than can normally be transmitted via most paper-based instruments or most wire transfers.

ACH transactions can either be credits, such as payroll payments, that are originated by the account holder who is sending funds (the payor), or they can be debits, such as mortgage or loan payments, that are originated by the account holder who is receiving funds (payee). SEPA debit and credit schemes (discussed in Chapter 2, Regulatory and

Legal Environment) fall into the category of ACH transactions. All ACH systems allow for the processing of credit transactions, but not all systems allow for pre-authorized debits.

A giro payment, available in some countries, is the functional equivalent of an ACH credit. The payor, typically a consumer, authorizes his/her bank to pay the payee, typically a business, through a direct transfer. Although the original authorization from the customer may be received through either paper or electronic bill payment systems, the payment itself is electronic and is usually sent through the country's ACH system. Although the term *giro* is still widely used in many countries, separate giro-processing systems have largely been replaced by ACH systems.

Because ACH transactions can be originated as either credits or debits, the terms *payor* and *payee* are not used to identify the parties to an ACH transaction. Instead, as shown in Exhibit 4.5 below, which shows the flow of an ACH credit transaction, the terms *originator* and *receiver* are used. In a similar manner, the financial institutions involved in an ACH transaction are not referred to as the *depository and paying banks*. Rather, they are called the *originating depository financial institution (ODFI)* and the *receiving depository financial institution (RDFI)*. Unlike checks, which are always created by the payor and move money to the payee, ACH transactions can be either created by the payor to send money to the payee (called *ACH credits* or *credit mandates*), or created by the payee to take money from the payor (called *ACH debits or debit mandates*).

EXHIBIT 4.5 **CREDIT TRANSACTION IN AN ACH PAYMENT SYSTEM**

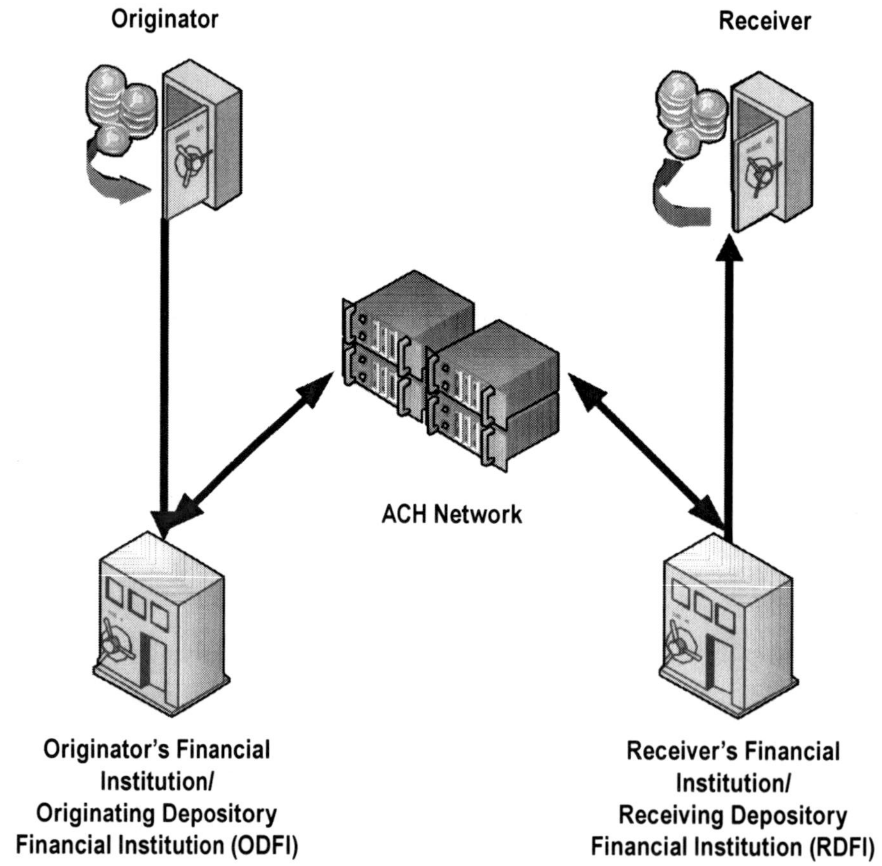

ACH transactions are typically sent in batches by FIs and third-party service providers to ACH operators for processing one or two business days before settlement dates. The ACH operators then deliver the transactions to the receiving institutions at defined times.

Companies use ACH payments for a wide range of transactions, including the issuance of payroll credits and pre-authorized debits. While the value of ACH payments is usually less than that of large-value wires, there is still a considerable range of checks and balances that apply to ACH payments. These include debit filters and blocks, which restrict the ability of somebody who knows a business's routing transit number and account number from withdrawing money from the account using an ACH transaction.

Although ACH systems typically operate within a specific country, it is possible to send ACH transactions between countries in what are referred to as *cross-border ACH transactions*. This is accomplished through the use of a "gateway" bank or service provider who will receive transactions in one country and then forward them to the ACH system of another country. The US Federal Reserve Bank provides this service, called *FedGlobal ACH Payments*, to over 35 countries as of 2013 (see Appendix 4.3 for the list of countries), and many global banks provide a similar service for their customers.

The standard option for distributing cross-border payments between deposit accounts is known as an *account-to-account transfer.* An account-to-receiver option is also offered and allows funds from accounts at a US depository financial institution to be retrieved by any receiver either at a participating bank location or at a trusted, third-party provider in certain receiving countries.

The FedGlobal service also provides a range of transaction currency options:

- **Fixed-to-Variable:** US dollars are converted to a variable amount of a destination currency based on a competitive exchange rate. Settlement is between participating US financial institutions and the Federal Reserve Banks, in US dollars.
- **Fixed-to-Fixed—US Dollar to US Dollar:** Payments are both transferred and received in US dollars. Settlement is between participating US financial institutions and the Federal Reserve Banks, in US dollars.
- **Fixed-to-Fixed—Foreign Currency to Foreign Currency:** Payments are both transferred and received in foreign currency. The FX rate and settlement are managed and processed by participating US financial institutions and the respective foreign gateway operators via their foreign correspondent banks.

As discussed, small-value or ACH systems are typically value-dated and take one or more days for transactions to settle. The growth in acceptance of Internet services and online banking has created a demand for small-value systems that settle more quickly than the traditional ACH systems. In response to this demand, many countries are looking at various options to provide some form of same-day or near real-time transaction. An example of this is the Faster Payments Service in the United Kingdom. Faster Payments is a joint development of CHAPS, the UK ACH system, and VocaLink, a large British telecom company, and uses an Internet-based system to provide immediate online payments to customers. Faster Payments was developed by British banks in response to a government demand to reduce the clearing time for ACH transactions. Other countries are looking at similar changes.

In the US ACH system there are two ACH operators: the Federal Reserve Bank processes most of the ACH transactions, while a private operator, the Electronic Payment Network (EPN), processes the remainder. NACHA, the Electronic Payments Association (formerly the National Automated Clearing House Association), is a trade organization that is responsible for managing the development, administration, and governance of the ACH system. NACHA is a membership organization of financial institutions and other stakeholders in the ACH system. In addition to administering the rules, standards, and procedures that enable the system to work on a daily basis, NACHA also is responsible for enforcing the rules and various risk management processes.

VII. CARD-BASED PAYMENT SYSTEMS

Credit and debit cards are payment cards issued to individuals and businesses for the purchase of goods, payment for services, and/or access to cash advances and withdrawals. Any vendor may issue credit or debit cards; however, bank-issued cards are the most widely used. A credit card is issued against a line of credit that the institution or merchant has extended, whereas a debit card is issued against a deposit account belonging to the cardholder. Charge cards are a special type of credit card in which the outstanding balance must be paid off each month.

A. Credit Cards

Banks and financial service companies are the primary issuers of credit cards, although some major retailers and oil and fuel service companies issue them as well. The two primary bank-issued cards used in the United States are Visa and MasterCard. The main nonbank card is American Express (Amex), which is issued primarily from Amex itself, though some of its specialty cards may be associated with bank lines of credit. All three of these cards are offered and accepted on a global basis. China UnionPay is the principal bank card agency in China and, although relatively new, has become one of the largest card issuers and processors in the world, with cards also accepted on a global basis. The Japan Credit Bureau (JCB) card is bank-issued and used in about 20 countries, including the United States. Finally, the Discover card is issued primarily by Discover Financial Services and is US-based.

In general, bank-issued cards, Amex, and Discover are known as *open-loop cards* because they are accepted anywhere the card logo is displayed. Cards issued by gas companies, department stores, and other retailers are considered *closed-loop cards*[14] if the card is accepted only by the issuing company. While several major retailers offer their own card programs, many retailers have moved to issuing private-label or co-branded cards through programs that are run by large banks. Many of the large oil companies issue their own credit cards for fuel purchases, and there are several fuel service companies that provide card services to corporate and government entities.

There are several participants in a credit card transaction. Exhibit 4.6 describes these participants and their roles in the credit process.

14. Although they are open-loop cards because they are accepted by many merchants, Amex and Discover are sometimes called *closed-loop cards* in reference to the fact that Amex and Discover are both the issuer and the processor for their cards. The now-standard definition of *closed-loop cards* refers to cards that are only accepted by the company that issued them.

EXHIBIT 4.6 **PARTICIPANTS IN A CREDIT CARD TRANSACTION**

CARDHOLDER	A CARDHOLDER RECEIVES A CARD FROM THE ISSUING BANK.
CARD ISSUER	ISSUING BANKS UNDERWRITE AND ISSUE CARDS TO INDIVIDUAL AND BUSINESS CARDHOLDERS WHO MEET CREDIT STANDARDS, OR IN THE CASE OF DEBIT CARDS, HOLD BANK ACCOUNTS WITH THAT FINANCIAL INSTITUTION. THE ISSUING BANK MAINTAINS THE INDIVIDUAL CARD ACCOUNTS, BILLS AND COLLECTS PAYMENTS FROM CARDHOLDERS, AND MONITORS THE PERFORMANCE OF CREDIT CARD RECEIVABLE PORTFOLIOS.
MERCHANT	MERCHANTS ARE BUSINESSES THAT ACCEPT CARDS AS A METHOD OF PAYMENT. MERCHANTS CAN INCLUDE "BRICK AND MORTAR" MERCHANTS (THOSE WITH A PHYSICAL STOREFRONT PRESENCE), E-COMMERCE MERCHANTS (THOSE CONDUCTING TRANSACTIONS ON THE INTERNET), OR MOTO MERCHANTS (THOSE WHO PROCESS ORDERS BY MAIL ORDER OR TELEPHONE ORDER).
MERCHANT ACQUIRER	IN ADDITION TO ISSUING CARDS, BANKS CAN ALSO ACT AS ACQUIRING BANKS FOR BUSINESSES THAT ACCEPT CREDIT CARD PAYMENTS. THE MERCHANT ACQUIRING BANK QUALIFIES BUSINESSES (REFERRED TO AS *MERCHANTS*) THAT ACCEPT CREDIT CARD PAYMENTS. THE MERCHANT ACQUIRING BANK PROVIDES MERCHANTS WITH CREDIT CARD TERMINALS, WHICH MAY BE PURCHASED OR LEASED, AND MAINTAINS DEPOSIT ACCOUNTS THROUGH WHICH THE CREDIT CARD PAYMENTS SETTLE.
ACQUIRING PROCESSOR	MANY MERCHANTS AND MERCHANT ACQUIRING BANKS USE THIRD-PARTY PROCESSORS TO MANAGE THE DAILY SETTLEMENT, AS WELL AS THE INFORMATION FLOWS, RELATED TO CREDIT CARD ACTIVITIES.
ISSUER PROCESSOR	THE ISSUER PROCESSOR PROVIDES A SYSTEM FOR CARD ISSUERS TO BOARD ACCOUNTS, PROVIDES AUTHORIZATIONS, AND OFFERS RISK MANAGEMENT TOOLS TO ISSUERS TO MANAGE THEIR CARD PORTFOLIOS EFFECTIVELY.
NETWORK OPERATOR	NETWORK OPERATORS MAINTAIN COMMUNICATION NETWORKS TO SUPPORT CARD TRANSACTION ACTIVITIES, SUCH AS AUTHORIZATION, CLEARING, AND SETTLEMENT. NETWORK OPERATORS INCLUDE VISA, MASTERCARD, DISCOVER, STAR, NYCE, PULSE, ACCEL/EXCHANGE, INTERLINK, AND OTHERS.

In addition to the clearing and settlement processes common to all payments, credit card transactions add a third major process: authorization. Credit card transaction processes are illustrated in Exhibit 4.7.

EXHIBIT 4.7 CREDIT CARD TRANSACTION PROCESS

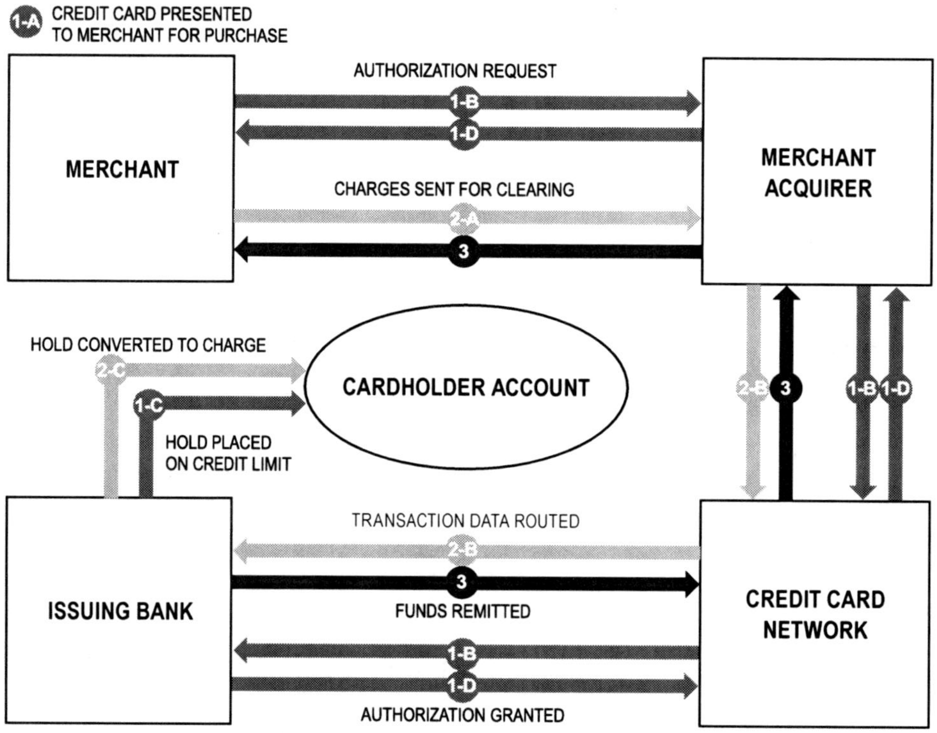

AUTHORIZATION PROCESS

STEP 1-A: CREDIT CARD PRESENTED TO MERCHANT FOR PURCHASE
STEP 1-B: AUTHORIZATION REQUEST
STEP 1-C: HOLD PLACED ON CREDIT LIMIT
STEP 1-D: AUTHORIZATION GRANTED

CLEARING PROCESS

STEP 2-A: CHARGES SENT FOR CLEARING BY MERCHANT
STEP 2-B: TRANSACTION DATA ROUTED TO ISSUING BANK
STEP 2-C: HOLD CONVERTED TO CHARGE

SETTLEMENT PROCESS

STEP 3: FUNDS REMITTED THROUGH NETWORK TO MERCHANT

AUTHORIZATION
CLEARING
SETTLEMENT

The authorization process starts when a customer pays for a purchase using a card (Step 1-A). This process is essentially the equivalent of the payment instruction and generation process outlined for payments in the earlier discussion of the payment process. The merchant submits an online authorization request for the charge amount to its merchant acquiring bank, which is also known as the *merchant acquirer* (Step 1-B). The request usually is transmitted through a POS terminal or other electronic communication system. That authorization request is routed through the appropriate card network and subsequently to the issuing bank. The issuing bank reviews the cardholder's account and approves or declines the transaction. If approved, the issuing bank places a hold on the cardholder's credit limit (Step 1-C, referred to as *open-to-buy*) for the amount of the charge. If the purchase is made with a debit card, the issuing bank places a hold on the cardholder's available funds. Then, an authorization response is routed back through the network to the merchant (Step 1-D).

The second major step in a card transaction is the clearing process—the communication of payment information through a card-processing network or channel. Card transaction data are submitted electronically by the merchant to the merchant acquirer, typically at the end of the business day (Step 2-A). The merchant acquirer then forwards the data through the network operator to the issuing bank (Step 2-B). Depending upon the type of card used, the acquirer uses one of several networks, such as Visa, MasterCard, or American Express. When the issuing bank receives the transaction data, it converts the hold on the customer's account to a charge that will appear on the cardholder's monthly billing statement (Step 2-C).

The final step in a card transaction is the settlement process, in which the funds are transferred from the issuing bank to the merchant via the merchant acquirer. The network operator establishes net positions of all settlement participants (issuers/acquirers), collects funds from the issuing bank, and makes transfers to the merchant acquirer through the ACH, Fedwire, or other similar system. Settlement usually occurs the next day, following submission of the clearing transaction to the network operator (Step 3). If the card transaction involves more than one currency (i.e., it is a cross-border transaction where a card issued in one country is used for purchases in another country), any foreign currency exchange is handled as part of the settlement process.

The merchant receives settlement either gross or net of any allocated fees. These fees, which are discussed in more detail later in this chapter, include interchange fees due to the issuing bank, any network assessment fees due to the network operator, and any transaction fees due to the merchant acquirer.

If the amount that the merchant receives is the net settlement, then the transaction value is less the fees. If the terms are gross settlement, then the merchant receives full transaction value, and a periodic invoice is received for the amount of the fees due to the respective parties.

Cardholders can dispute a charge assessed to their accounts, which may result in a charge-back to the merchant. Generally, cardholders have a window of anywhere from 60 to 120 days to dispute a transaction. A merchant has an established time period to respond to this charge-back and provide evidence to the validity of the charge, as well as have the charge re-presented by the merchant acquirer. Certain card networks permit up to two charge-back cycles. Then, the process of pre-arbitration and arbitration may occur.

B. Debit Cards/EFTPOS[15]

Debit and credit cards have similar features, but debit cards, often referred to as *EFTPOS* in many parts of the world, access funds directly from a cardholder's checking or savings deposit account. Debit cards may be signature-based and/or personal identification number (PIN)-based. Regardless of the manner of usage, the transaction still debits funds from the cardholder's checking or savings account.

- **Signature-Based:** Signature debit cards bear the logos of Visa, MasterCard, or Discover, and are processed in the same manner as credit card transactions using those network operators. The customer signs a receipt at checkout time.
- **PIN-Based:** A PIN debit transaction facilitates consumer authorization and authentication through the entry of a PIN at the POS terminal. Authorization and clearing are generally immediate and are facilitated by network operators, such as Maestro (owned by MasterCard), Interlink (owned by Visa), NYCE, STAR, and ACCEL/Exchange.

C. Other Varieties of Payment Cards

Some variants of payment cards include purchasing (or procurement) cards, smart cards, and stored-value cards, such as payroll cards, health reimbursement account cards, and gift cards. These and other cards are discussed below.[16]

- **Purchasing Cards:** Purchasing cards (also known as *procurement cards* or *p-cards*) are credit cards used by businesses for the purchase of supplies, inventory, equipment, and service contracts. Typically, p-cards are used for varying purchases, either low- or high-value, with spending limits established on an individual card basis. Purchases can be limited to approved vendors and suppliers, as determined by the merchant category code of the vendor or supplier. The principal benefit of a p-card for a company is the replacement of the traditional time-consuming, labor-intensive, paper-based requisition process. Additionally, companies may negotiate a rebate based on charge volume and average transaction size, and they may be able to effectively delay payment since purchased items will not be paid for until the end of the billing cycle. The principal benefit for an employee is that essential goods and services can be obtained quickly and conveniently without a complicated purchase order process.
- **Travel and Entertainment (T&E) Cards:** These credit cards, sometimes just called *travel cards*, are used by businesses for employee travel purposes. Travel cards may be incorporated into a company's p-card program (typically referred to as *one-card programs*), or they may be issued as a separate card. These cards work very similarly to p-cards. Card issuers may send companies a regularly scheduled data file of transactions that have been charged by employees for automatic loading, as well as send reconciliation details directly into the company's employee expense system. Rebates may also be offered in a travel card program. T&E cards, as with p-cards, often can have restrictions on use based on company policy.
- **Fleet Cards:** Fleet cards are similar to T&E cards but are designed to be used for expenditures related to trucks and cars, such as fuel and repairs, and in some cases, other driver expenses, such as food and lodging. Fleet card systems often capture added information, such as vehicle mileage and location.

15. *EFTPOS* refers to electronic funds transfer (EFT) at the point of sale (POS).
16. Several of these payment cards are also discussed in Chapter 10, Collections, Concentration, and Disbursements.

- **Ghost Cards or Virtual Cards:** These are variations on the p-card that do not involve the use of an actual card. With a ghost card system, a card number is given to a specific vendor and is then used for electronic purchasing and billing purposes.
- **Departmental (Unnamed) Cards:** This is another variation on the p-card in which each department is given its own p-card for general use by that department. The card is linked to the department rather than to an individual, and unlike most cards, there is no individual's name on the card.
- **Single-Use Cards:** Most credit card companies offer their account holders the ability to generate a single-use or disposable card number to provide additional purchasing security. These card numbers look like regular credit card numbers, including embedded expiration dates and security codes, but they will only work for a single use. Single-use cards are often used by A/P departments to pay vendors. Since the number is only good for a set amount and a set period of time, it is a mechanism for fraud control.
- **Stored-Value Cards (SVCs):** These debit cards may be offered by financial institutions, retailers, and other service providers, and they can be branded, open-loop cards (e.g., Visa or MasterCard), or private-label, closed-loop cards (e.g., Starbucks or other merchant gift cards). Generally, open-loop cards can be used almost anywhere while closed-loop cards can only be used at one selected merchant or group of merchants. Gift cards are one of the most commonly used types of stored-value card. The payroll card (or pay card), another stored-value card type, is offered as an alternative payment method to employees who do not have bank accounts and therefore cannot accept direct deposit of funds for their paychecks. The key benefits to employers of moving employees to payroll cards versus checks include reduced payroll costs and lower levels of payroll-related fraud. Another use for stored-value cards is for employee benefit programs, such as flexible spending accounts and health care expense reimbursements. Depending upon the specific card and issuer, SVCs can be either reloadable (i.e., the holder of the card can add more value) or non-reloadable (i.e., the value of the card is limited to the amount originally placed on it).
- **Chip Cards or Smart Cards:** These payment devices are typical payment cards with the addition of a computer chip with related circuitry that can be used to store information for security or transaction processing. In the early 1990s, Europay, MasterCard, and Visa agreed to develop common specifications for smart cards as either debit or credit cards. This system, called *EMV*, was initially released in 1994 and has been upgraded several times since then. With the exception of a few countries, such as the United States, EMV-compliant cards and equipment are widespread. Because not all countries or even all merchants in a country are capable of reading the chip on chip cards, these cards also typically have a magnetic stripe on them in addition to the chip. While Visa and other card issuers have indicated that they intend to start issuing chip cards in the United States, widespread acceptance of such cards is dependent upon merchant installation of equipment that will read the chips. Visa, which has been one of the strongest proponents of EMV in the United States, has announced that it will require that all processors be capable of handling EMV data as of 2015.

D. Payment Card Industry Data Security Standard (PCI DSS)

As a result of several system breaches and compromises of data in card networks, the card industry created a governing body to establish and administer a series of strict requirements for the security of card data. Merchants are required to go through an audit of their systems and applications to confirm they are compliant with the Payment Card Industry Data Security Standard (PCI DSS).

The PCI DSS is a worldwide information security standard defined by the Payment Card Industry Security Standards Council. The standard was created to help organizations that process card payments prevent payment card fraud through increased controls around the data they hold and exchange. The standard applies to all organizations that store, process, or transmit cardholder information from any card branded with the logo of one of the major card brands.

Failure to comply with standards or a breach of security can result in substantial fines and possible termination of the acceptance of payment cards.

E. Merchant Card Fees

Merchant card fees are a complex subject and are affected by a large number of variables, including such things as the type of card being accepted, the amount of the transaction, the way the card is being processed, and the merchant's contract with its bank and/or acquiring processor (sometimes referred to as a *merchant processor*).

The major components of merchant card fees are:

- Interchange fees (referred to simply as *interchange*)
- Assessments
- Processor fees or markups

Interchange typically accounts for the largest portion of overall card fees and represents a fee that is paid to the issuing bank for each transaction. These fees are established by the card brands (Visa, MasterCard, etc.) and go directly to the issuing bank to cover its costs in issuing cards and processing card transactions. Interchange fees vary depending upon the method of acquisition and card type. The lowest fees are generally set for cards that the merchant is able to swipe at the point of sale (referred to as *"card present" transactions*.) This allows for accurate transmittal of the data and reduced security concerns (i.e., the actual card is present at the time and point of the transaction, and the cardholder authorizes the transaction). Card transactions accepted over the phone or via the Internet, referred to as *"card not present" transactions* or originally *mail order or telephone order (MOTO) transactions*, may be assessed higher fees due to the increased risk (e.g., fraud and data errors) from the transaction. In determining interchange fees, *card type* refers to whether the card is a standard card versus a reward card (i.e., cards that offer rewards or points back to the user), as there are typically higher fees on reward cards than on standard (i.e., non-reward) cards, but it also includes whether the card is a debit or credit card. As discussed in Chapter 2, Regulatory and Legal Environment, recent US regulations have impacted interchange fees for debit cards, and as a result, debit card interchange fees are limited to roughly $0.24 per transaction.[17] Credit card fees are typically higher, and while there may be a fixed fee involved, interchange is usually a percentage of the card transaction itself. For example, as of 2012, the Visa interchange fee for a standard, swiped consumer credit card in the United States was 1.51% + $0.10.

17. At the time of publication, a recent US court case ruled that the current debit interchange limits were improperly set and invalid. The ruling was being appealed, and the issue will probably be in the courts for several years.

Assessment fees typically are calculated as a percentage of the amount of the transaction and are set by the network operators, such as MasterCard, Visa, STAR, or Interlink. These fees can vary based on the type of industry, the method of acceptance, and other factors. The assessment fees are intended to reimburse the network operators for their services and for brand management. Like interchange, assessments do not vary by card processor or acquirer, since they are set by the network operator.

Processor fees or markups, also referred to as *transaction fees*, are set by the individual card processor or merchant acquirer and are the fees charged to process the transaction on the merchant's behalf. These fees are usually based on the expected transaction volume of a given merchant. This is the only portion of merchant card fees that is truly negotiable. Transaction fees vary significantly from processor to processor.

Merchant fees are typically charged as either bundled pricing or "interchange-plus" pricing. In bundled fees, the merchant is charged one fee by its card processor that covers all of the cost components of the transaction. This type of fee is also referred to as the *merchant discount*, as it is typically subtracted directly from any card settlement. Obviously, merchant discount will be greater than card interchange, in some cases much greater. Smaller merchants or companies with small card volumes tend to pay higher fees. In many cases, the merchant discount is quoted as a flat percentage even though the underlying interchange can vary by transaction. As a result, bundled fees are often quoted high to cover any potential changes in interchange. In interchange-plus pricing, the merchant pays the actual amount of any interchange and assessment fees, plus a stated fee to the card processor. This fee can be either a fixed amount per transaction or a percentage of the value of the transactions.

In addition to the fees already discussed, merchants are also subject to a number of miscellaneous fees for such things as returns, charge-backs, and disputes, as well as for supplies and equipment costs for terminals and card scanners. In some cases these may be included in bundled pricing.

VIII. SUMMARY

This chapter began with a discussion of the basics of how payment systems work, including a discussion of settlement versus finality. A payment system is a series of processes that transfer monetary value from one party to another. *Settlement* is defined as the point at which funds are transferred between the two parties to a transaction and are available for use by the receiving party. This is distinctly different from finality, which is the point at which funds belong to the receiving party and cannot be recalled for such things as non-sufficient funds or fraud.

The remainder of the chapter provided an overview of cash payments as well as each of the major types of payment systems: paper-based (e.g., checks), large-value transfer systems (e.g., wire transfers), small-value transfer systems (e.g., ACH), and card-based systems. Appendix 4.4 provides an overview of the actual payment systems used in several major countries, as an example of how these systems vary. Within each payment system there are often multiple channels for processing and settling transactions, such as direct presentment versus central bank clearing for checks, or Fedwire versus CHIPS for US wire transfers. Specific issues relevant to each type of payment, including but not limited to timing, settlement, and finality, were also covered.

APPENDIX 4.1: CHECK RETURN REASONS

Not Sufficient Funds/Non-sufficient Funds (NSF): At the time the check was presented to the account holder's bank, there were not enough funds in the account to pay the check or draft. NSF checks can be redeposited unless the front of the item is stamped "Do Not Redeposit."

Uncollected Funds (UCF or UF)/Uncollected Funds Hold (UFH): Items are returned because funds in the account are not yet collected and available. UCF checks can be redeposited.

Stop Payment/Stop Pay: The person who originally wrote the check or authorized the draft has revoked his/her authorization. Stop pay checks cannot be redeposited.

Closed Account/Account Closed: The account holder's bank account that was associated with the check is closed. Closed-account items cannot be redeposited.

Unable to Locate Account/Unable to Locate (UTL): The bank cannot find any account with that account number in its records. UTL checks cannot be redeposited.

Frozen Account/Blocked Account: The account is blocked or frozen due to legal action. A bank can be required to freeze an account due to a divorce judgment, tax lien, wage garnishment, court order, or other legal reason. Checks stamped "Frozen Account" cannot be redeposited.

Stale-Dated Check/Stale Check/Expired Check: The check is past the expiration date as set by the check issuer. Some checks are valid only if cashed or deposited within 7 days, 30 days, 90 days, or 180 days. Checks with this time limit may be returned as stale-dated or expired checks, and cannot be redeposited.

Post-Dated/Post-Dated Check: The date on the check is for a future date. Future-dated checks can be returned as post-dated checks. Checks that are returned and stamped "Post-Dated" or "Post-Dated Check" can be redeposited on or after, but not before, the date of the check.

Endorsement Missing/Missing Endorsement: The depositor did not endorse the check. Checks stamped "Endorsement Missing" may be redeposited after adding an appropriate endorsement.

Endorsement Irregular/Irregular Endorsement: There is a problem with the endorsement, such as the endorsement is illegible, the signature does not match the payee name on the check, or the endorsement is not in the correct location. Checks with irregular endorsement may be redeposited after the endorsement issue has been resolved.

Signature(s) Missing: The required signature or signatures on a check are not present. Some checks can be returned for signature missing when two signatures are required to write a check on a particular account and only one signature appears on the check. A check with signature(s) missing cannot be redeposited until the proper signature or signatures are collected.

Signature(s) Irregular: A signature does not match the account holder's, or the signature appears damaged, altered, or otherwise obscured. "Signature(s) Irregular" checks cannot be redeposited. A new item must be obtained from the maker of the check.

Noncash Item/Not Cash Item (NCI): An invalid check, such as a rebate coupon, promotional check, or gift certificate, is deposited in error as a real check. NCI items cannot be redeposited.

Altered Item/Fictitious Item: The check does not match the account holder's records or the bank's records as far as the amount, date, or terms of the check, and is being returned in dispute of its validity. Any alteration can void the check at the discretion of the paying bank. A cross-out, alteration, or change should be initialed by the account holder, but does not always stop returns, especially with high-dollar items. Altered/fictitious items may not be redeposited.

Not Authorized/Unauthorized: The account holder disputed the item during the payment presentment process, or the account has a block such as "No Drafts" or "No Debits." Items returned as not authorized or unauthorized cannot be redeposited.

Refer to Maker (RTM): The account holder must contact the maker of the check to determine why the check was returned. Checks returned as "Refer to Maker" cannot be redeposited.

APPENDIX 4.2: FEDWIRE FORMAT EXAMPLE

The sample shown is a relatively simple US domestic wire going directly from one bank to another. Additional tags and data elements are available and used for more complex payments. In the event that the business function code (tag {3600}) is CTP (Customer Transfer Plus), an additional field with a tag of {8200} is used, with the ability to transmit up to 8,994 characters of formatted remittance data. For further information on the Fedwire format, refer to the latest Fedwire Funds Service Format Reference Guide from the Federal Reserve Bank, available at www.frbservices.org.

Definition of Fed Tag Values	Fed Tag[18]	Value
Transaction Dollar Amount: Total wire value with no decimal and no commas (12 positions) (Example: $250.00 = 000000025000)	**{2000}**	**000000025000**
Sending Bank's ABA Number (9 positions), and **Sending Bank's Name**	{3100}	000123790 ABC BANK
Receiving Bank's ABA Number (9 positions), and **Receiving Bank's Name**	**{3400}**	**129999999** **XYZ BANK**
Business Function Code (Transaction Type) (Example: CTR = Customer Transfer, nonbank beneficiary)	**{3600}**	**CTR**
Beneficiary Information (BNF): Beneficiary's account number at receiving bank, including: ***ID Code*** (If ID code is present, identifier is mandatory, and vice versa.) ***Identifier*** (34 characters) ***Name*** (35 characters) ***Address*** (3 lines of 35 characters each)	**{4200}**	**123456789** Company X
Reference to Beneficiary (RFB): Remittance or other reference information (up to 16 characters)	**{4320}**	ABC123456789
Originator Information (ORG): Originating customer account number from sending bank; name of originating company; and originator's address, city, state, and zip code	{5000}	12345 ABC COMPANY 123 ABC PLAZA NEW YORK NY 10258
Originator to Beneficiary Information (OBI): Additional beneficiary (remittance) information (up to 4 lines of 35 characters each)	**{6000}**	XYZ9999998

18. In the "Fed Tag" and "Value" columns, bold font indicates a mandatory field.

APPENDIX 4.3: FEDGLOBAL ACH PAYMENTS COUNTRIES

- Argentina
- Austria
- Belgium
- Brazil
- Canada
- Colombia
- Costa Rica
- Cyprus
- Czech Republic
- Denmark
- El Salvador
- Finland
- France
- Germany
- Greece
- Guatemala
- Honduras
- Ireland
- Italy
- Luxembourg
- Malta
- Mexico
- Netherlands
- Nicaragua
- Panama
- Peru
- Poland
- Portugal
- Slovakia
- Slovenia
- Spain
- Sweden
- Switzerland
- United Kingdom
- Uruguay

APPENDIX 4.4: BANKING AND PAYMENT SYSTEMS INFORMATION FOR SELECTED COUNTRIES[19]

A. China

1. BANKING

The Chinese central bank is the People's Bank of China (PBC). Bank supervision is performed by the China Banking Regulatory Commission (CBRC). China applies central bank reporting requirements. These are managed by the State Administration for Foreign Exchange (SAFE), according to the rules set out in the Regulations on Foreign Exchange System of the People's Republic of China (2008) and relevant regulations. Resident entities are permitted to hold foreign currency bank accounts domestically and outside of China, but residents must first gain approval from SAFE for foreign currency bank accounts held abroad. Nonresident entities are permitted to hold foreign currency bank accounts within China. Nonresidents can hold fully convertible renminbi (CNY) trade settlement accounts inside and outside of China but these accounts are subject to restrictions and PBC approval.

China has five major commercial banking institutions, which control over 44% of the country's banking assets. There are also 3 government-controlled policy banks, established in 1994. There are 12 joint-stock commercial banks, 83 rural commercial banks, 223 rural cooperative banks, 349 village and township banks, and 2,646 rural credit cooperatives, as well as 147 city commercial banks that specialize in retail and corporate commerce. The government indirectly controls the country's commercial banks by maintaining a majority share in each bank. There is an increasing foreign banking presence in China—77 foreign banks have established branches in China and approximately 200 have representative offices. Foreign banks, if incorporated locally, are able to offer CNY retail products to Chinese residents and are subject to national treatment.

2. PAYMENTS

China's three main interbank payment clearing systems are CNAPS-LVPS, CNAPS-BEPS[20] and the Local Clearing House system (LCHs). The RTGS-based China Domestic Foreign Currency Payment System (CDFCPS) was introduced in July 2008 for eight international currencies. In addition, a new "Super e-banking" online interbank clearing system for real-time Internet payments and account enquiries was introduced in August 2010. The system linked up the individual online payment systems of approximately 120 financial institutions during 2012.

The most important cashless payment instruments in China are debit cards among individuals, checks between local institutions, and electronic credit transfers for intercity payments. Economic expansion in China's large cities has led to a growth in the use of electronic payments, such as Internet, telephone, and mobile payments.

19. Information in this appendix was obtained from the executive summaries of the selected countries' *Cash and Treasury Management Country Reports* as provided by AFP for its members through its AFP Country Profiles (http://www.afponline.org/pub/country/profiles.html). The executive summaries used were dated (last updated) August 30, 2013, except for India, which was dated July 31, 2013.
20. HVPS (High-Value Payment System) and BEPS (Bulk Electronic Payment System) are the application systems of the China National Advanced Payment System (CNAPS).

B. India

1. BANKING

The Reserve Bank of India (RBI) is fully owned by the Indian government and is charged with maintaining monetary stability by directing lending and deposit rates. In addition, the RBI is responsible for FX management, currency issuance, and regulation of the financial system via the Board for Financial Supervision. The RBI compiles balance-of-payments data as required by the Foreign Exchange Management Act. Banks that undertake FX transactions must submit returns and supporting documents.

Residents and nonresidents may hold accounts denominated in Indian rupees (INR) or in a foreign currency both in India and abroad. However, there are a number of restrictions on the different types of accounts permitted. India's banking system is dominated by state-owned commercial and development banks, which provide the majority of financing for domestic and foreign companies. Around 40 foreign banks have established operations in India, but there are restrictions on acquisitions and the expansion of branch networks.

2. PAYMENTS

India operates an RTGS system for high-value electronic payments, as well as a number of payment systems for processing paper-based and retail electronic instruments. India is in the process of converting its check-clearing systems to image processing and expects to be complete by the end of 2013. India's vast geography requires a network of more than 10,000 access points to its various payment systems. Checks and drafts are the most commonly used instruments for commercial transactions in India, but cash is the dominant payment method for medium- and small-value transactions. In the retail sector, payment cards have increased in popularity in the last three to four years. Debit cards are the most commonly used cashless payment instrument in terms of volume, and credit transfers are the mostly widely used in terms of value.

C. Japan

1. BANKING

The Japanese central bank is the Bank of Japan (BOJ). Bank supervision is performed by the Financial Services Agency. Japan does apply some central bank reporting requirements. These are managed by the Ministry of Finance (MOF) through the BOJ, according to the rules set out in the Foreign Exchange and Foreign Trade Act, and relevant regulations.

Resident entities may hold fully convertible foreign currency bank accounts both domestically and outside Japan. Nonresident entities may hold fully convertible domestic and foreign currency bank accounts within Japan. Japan has 4 large city banks and a decreasing number of regional banks (64), which are divided into first and second tiers generally according to size and assets. There is a significant foreign banking presence in Japan—58 foreign banks have established branches in Japan.

2. PAYMENTS

Japan's four main interbank payment clearing systems are the BOJ Financial Network System (BOJ-NET), the Foreign Exchange Yen Clearing System (FXYCS), Zengin, and the BCCSs (bill and cheque clearing systems). In addition, there are seven Japanese banks that are settlement members of CLS Bank.

The most important cashless payment instruments in Japan are electronic credit transfers in terms of value and, in terms of volume, payment cards. Checks are primarily used for business-to-business transactions, while direct debits are widely used among individuals and businesses to make regular payments. Though the Japanese have been slower to adopt credit and debit cards, their usage, particularly of credit cards, is increasing rapidly. E-money is also gaining in popularity as a retail payment instrument.

D. United Kingdom (UK)

1. BANKING

The United Kingdom's central bank is the Bank of England. Prudential regulation and supervision of the banking sector is performed by the Prudential Regulation Authority (PRA), a part of the Bank of England. The United Kingdom does not impose central bank reporting requirements.

Resident entities are permitted to hold fully convertible domestic currency (pounds, or GBP) and foreign currency bank accounts within and outside the United Kingdom. Nonresident entities are permitted to hold fully convertible domestic and foreign currency bank accounts within the United Kingdom.

The United Kingdom has 154 banks (of both domestic and foreign origin) and 47 building societies. There is a significant foreign banking presence in the United Kingdom and 156 foreign banks have established branches.

2. PAYMENTS

The United Kingdom's four main payment systems are CHAPS, Bacs, the Faster Payments Service, and the Cheque and Credit Clearing Company (C&CCC) system. The most important cashless payment instruments in the United Kingdom are electronic credit transfers in terms of value and card payments in terms of volume. Checks and direct debits are also popular payment instruments in the United Kingdom. The increased use of electronic and Internet banking by consumers and businesses has led to significant growth in the use of electronic payments.

TEST YOUR UNDERSTANDING: CHAPTER 4

Answers are on pages 652–656.

1. What is a payment system?
2. Is cash a payment system? Why or why not?
3. Name the four basic participants in a payment.
4. What are the four key elements of the payment process?
5. Discuss the difference between settlement and finality.
6. List the four major categories of payments, other than cash.
7. What are on-us and on-we check clearing?
8. What are the four major clearing channels for transit checks in the United States?
9. Describe continuous linked settlement (CLS) and why it was developed.
10. What is SWIFT?
11. What are small-value transfer or ACH systems?
12. What are the three major currency options available for FedGlobal ACH payments?
13. What are the primary differences between credit, debit, and charge cards?
14. What are purchasing cards, and what are their principal benefits?
15. What is PCI DSS?
16. List the major components of merchant card fees.

CHAPTER 5
Money Markets

I. INTRODUCTION

The *money market* (or *money markets*) is defined as that part of the global financial market that deals with financial instruments that are easily converted to cash (highly liquid) and have very short maturities, typically one year or less. Money markets are used by treasury professionals to borrow or invest for periods ranging from a day to just under a year, as part of managing their organization's liquidity needs.

The term *money market securities* then refers to instruments that are traded on the various money markets, usually with a term of less than a year. These are generally debt-type securities, also known as *fixed-income securities*, as opposed to stocks or equity securities, which are traded on the capital markets (discussed in Chapter 6). Money market securities consist of negotiable certificates of deposit (CDs), banker's acceptances, government securities (e.g., US Treasury bills, also known as *T-bills*), commercial paper, municipal notes, federal funds, and repurchase agreements (repos).

There are thriving and highly developed markets in the British pound (GBP), the euro (EUR), and the US dollar (USD), and many other markets for a wide variety of short-term instruments. As a result, treasury managers have the ability to build an appropriate short-term investment strategy wherever they may operate.

This chapter provides an overview of money markets as used by treasury professionals to manage their organization's liquidity and short-term investing and financing. Managing a short-term investment portfolio is discussed in Chapter 11, Short-Term Investing and Borrowing, and the various aspects of financial risk related to these instruments are discussed in Chapter 16, Financial Risk Management.

II. GLOBAL MONEY MARKETS

This section provides a basic overview of money markets globally and includes a discussion of the various participants and a description of the major types of money market instruments.

A. Money Market Participants

Issuers of money market instruments include government entities, securities dealers, commercial banks, and other corporations (including not-for-profits) that raise funds by borrowing in the money market. These organizations also invest in this market directly through purchases of money market instruments and indirectly by investing in money market funds (MMFs).

In the money markets, investors are lenders, while issuers are borrowers. Thus, investors purchasing money market instruments are making short-term loans to issuers. In many cases, large organizations participating in the money markets are both issuers and investors, depending on their needs at a specific point in time.

A broker-dealer is an entity that trades securities for its own account or on behalf of its customers. When executing trade orders on behalf of a customer, the institution is said to be acting as a *broker*. When executing trades for its own account, the institution is said to be acting as a *dealer*. Securities bought from clients or other firms in the capacity of a dealer may be sold to clients or to other firms, acting again in the capacity of a dealer, or they may become a part of the broker-dealer's own holdings.

Broker-dealers can hold securities in their own name, in the names of their customers, or in what is termed a *street name*. In the latter case, the securities are held in the broker's name (the street name) on behalf of the broker's customer. Holding securities in street name does not affect the rights of the actual owner of the securities, but does eliminate the need to reregister or reissue securities in the name of the actual owner. This was originally done to simplify trading, as reregistration of securities could take several days in a manual environment while the securities themselves were often being traded daily. With today's electronic trading systems and the ability to change ownership names immediately, this is no longer an issue, but the practice still continues and most money market securities are held in street name. This practice also permits investors to keep their investment activities anonymous, absent any legal requirements for public disclosure.

Although many broker-dealers are independent firms solely involved in broker-dealer services, others are business units or subsidiaries of commercial banks, investment banks, or investment companies.

Broker-dealers are compensated by the fees and/or commissions they charge for their services. Broker-dealers play key roles in the money markets by placing the majority of new issues in the primary market and by providing secondary markets with the liquidity necessary for outstanding issues. Primary and secondary markets are discussed in more detail in Chapter 6, Capital Markets.

When acting as dealers, these parties also take positions in securities so they can act as the counterparty[1] in the purchase and sale of transactions. The price or yield at which the dealer will sell a security is known as the *ask price*, while the price or yield at which the dealer will purchase a security is known as the *bid price*. The difference between the two is called the *spread*, and represents the dealer's profit on a specific transaction. Dealers also enter into repurchase agreements (repos), which are money market transactions used to finance a dealer's securities inventories. Money markets and related securities fall under the jurisdiction of a variety of regulators, depending on the parties to a transaction, the securities involved, and the markets or exchanges on which the instruments are traded.

Central securities depositories (CSDs) are companies that hold securities, in either certificated or noncertificated (dematerialized) form, to enable book-entry transfer of securities. CSDs may also provide a variety of other services—such as trade matching, and clearing and settlement—to facilitate money market transactions. Examples of CSDs include the Depository Trust Company (DTC) in the United States, Euroclear in Belgium, and the Singapore Exchange (SGX) in Singapore. Nearly all short-term securities are issued in noncertificated or book-entry form.

International central securities depositories (ICSDs) are central securities depositories that settle trades in international securities as well as in domestic securities, through links to local CSDs. Clearstream, Euroclear, and SIX Securities Services (SIX SIS) are examples of ICSDs. While DTC is technically a national CSD rather than an ICSD, DTC actually holds over $2 trillion in non-US securities and in American depositary receipts from over 100 nations, due to the large number of trades that are executed in the United States.

1. A counterparty, as the name implies, is the person or entity on the other side of a financial transaction (i.e., to a buyer of securities, the counterparty is the entity selling the security).

B. Investment Risk Considerations

Most money market instruments have low default, liquidity, and price/interest rate risk, and are therefore appropriate for conservative, short-term portfolios. Such low risk levels are typically accompanied by lower returns or yields, but this is consistent with the primary need to minimize risk to principal while maintaining liquidity. An obvious exception is when investing in foreign currency money market instruments. In this case, one must also consider the risks related to foreign exchange (FX).

1. CREDIT/DEFAULT RISK

The risk that payments to investors on a security will not be made under the original terms is called *credit or default risk*. Credit risk evaluation of a security assesses the probability that the issuer might default on the obligation. Higher yields are typically associated with higher risk, as investors will require a higher return to compensate for a higher chance of loss. The greater the likelihood of default, the higher the risk premium and expected yield will be. A risk premium is the extra yield above that of a comparable risk-free security that investors require as added compensation for assuming the additional risk.

Most acceptable investment securities carry credit ratings[2] assigned by credit rating agencies, such as Moody's, Standard & Poor's (S&P), Fitch, or DBRS (formerly Dominion Bond Rating Service) (also known as *nationally recognized statistical rating organizations*, or *NRSROs*). These rating agencies, their ratings, and the factors that are used to create the ratings are discussed in more detail in Chapter 11, Short-Term Investing and Borrowing. Credit ratings are assigned to specific securities based on the issue's default risk and seniority,[3] with additional consideration given to collateral, backup lines of credit, bond insurance, or any credit enhancement provided to support the obligation. If a financial institution intermediary provides credit enhancement by issuing an instrument such as a standby letter of credit (L/C) or surety bond to guarantee the obligation of the borrower, then the obligation assumes the credit rating of the institution providing the enhancement.

Some short-term investments may be unrated, which impacts investors in several important ways. Initially, the investment must be evaluated for credit risk, which could be an involved process. Another concern is that if the security must be resold, then the new purchaser would most likely need to perform a credit risk evaluation on the security. This process could make it difficult to find a buyer—or at a minimum, delay the sale—leading to increased liquidity risk on the investment. Finally, holding unrated securities in an organization's short-term portfolio would most likely require footnotes about the securities on any audited financial statements.

2. The major exception to the use of external credit ratings on investment securities is a US Treasury security, which is generally considered free of default risk due to the size and strength of the US government. Most other sovereign issues are rated for default risk, especially for smaller countries or where the government is experiencing severe fiscal and monetary problems.
3. Seniority of debt indicates the priority of payment for that debt, especially in the event of bankruptcy. Higher-seniority debt is paid before lower-seniority debt and is thus considered to have lower default risk.

2. LIQUIDITY RISK

Liquidity risk is the risk that a security investment cannot be sold quickly without experiencing an unacceptable loss, and it can also affect the yield and pricing on a security. By definition, a *liquid security* is one that can be converted quickly and easily into cash with very little exposure to market price risk and for a small transaction cost. The primary determinants of a security's liquidity are its marketability and maturity. The existence of an active secondary market ensures that the short-term securities suitable for liquidity management purposes are readily marketable.

Most financial instruments other than MMFs have a maturity date on which the obligation they represent is redeemed. By general definition, money market securities have maturities ranging from one day to one year. Occasionally, investors employing particular strategies may hold long-term investments in a short-term portfolio. If active secondary markets do not exist, then these investments may take considerable time to liquidate and, in some cases, may have to be held until maturity. Even with active secondary markets, however, holding investments over longer periods of time increases the exposure to price/interest rate risk.

3. PRICE/INTEREST RATE RISK

Interest rate (or price) risk is the risk that arises when interest rates change for securities that are identical or nearly identical to portfolio securities. Securities with longer maturities generally are subject to greater price risk than similar securities with shorter maturities because their market values are more responsive to changes in market interest rates. Interest rate risk exists because a fixed-rate security may have to be sold prior to maturity in a market where interest rates are rising, causing a loss of principal on the sale.

Reinvestment risk is another type of price risk associated with fixed-income and money market securities. It occurs when the proceeds from an investment that has been sold, has matured, or has been redeemed prior to maturity must be reinvested after market interest rates have declined. Interest rate risk management through the use of swaps and derivatives is covered in Chapter 16, Financial Risk Management.

4. FOREIGN EXCHANGE (FX) RISK

FX risk arises when securities denominated in foreign currencies are held in an investment portfolio. FX risk is the risk of a change in the rate of exchange between the currency in which a security is denominated and the company's local currency. If the issue's currency depreciates relative to the investor's local currency, then the value of the investment declines. For example, a European investor may hold US Treasuries, which are considered free from default risk but which carry FX risk for the European investor, as the value of the investment will fluctuate based on the exchange rate between the US dollar and the euro.

This risk is present whether the investment is sold prior to maturity or is redeemed at maturity. To limit FX risk, most company investment policies permit investment in foreign securities in only two situations: (1) when the investment is issued in an economically and politically stable country, or (2) when the security is suitable as part of an overall currency hedging strategy. FX risk is discussed in greater detail in Chapter 16, Financial Risk Management.

C. Types of Money Market Instruments and Investments[4]

Exhibit 5.1 provides a comparative listing of major short-term investment alternatives for global treasury professionals. In addition to these specific short-term investments, many organizations also utilize different types of MMFs that are available globally. MMFs utilize combinations of the investments discussed below and are covered in detail later in this chapter.

4. Some information in this section is taken from: Neil Ellerbeck, "Short-Term Investment Options for Treasurers," *gtnews*, 11 March 2008, http://www.gtnews.com/.

EXHIBIT 5.1 **COMPARISON OF SHORT-TERM INVESTMENTS**

	COMMERCIAL PAPER (CP)	ASSET-BACKED COMMERCIAL PAPER (ABCP)	BANK OBLIGATIONS	GOVERNMENT PAPER (e.g., T-BILLS)	FLOATING-RATE NOTES (FRNs)	REPURCHASE AGREEMENTS (REPOS)
MATURITY	Overnight–270 days (typically <45 days)*	Overnight–270 days (typically <45 days)*	1 day–2 years	4–52 weeks	Variable	Wholly negotiable
ISSUED BY	Companies	Companies	Banks	Governments and public bodies	Companies and financial institutions	Companies and financial institutions
INTEREST RATE	Fixed	Fixed	Fixed***	Fixed	Variable, with periodic reset dates	Negotiable
INTEREST PAID	On maturity**	On maturity**	During term or on maturity**	On maturity**	During term or on maturity	On maturity**
HOW ISSUED	Discount	Discount	Interest-bearing	Discount	Interest-bearing	Specified sales and repurchase price
SECURED	No	Yes	No	No	Yes/No	Yes
ACCESS TO CAPITAL BEFORE MATURITY	Sell on secondary market	Sell on secondary market	Sell on secondary market (for negotiable certificates of deposit and BAs)	Sell on secondary market	Sell on secondary market	Negotiable
INVESTMENT RISKS****	• Credit • Price	• Credit • Liquidity • Price	• Credit • Liquidity	• Price	• Credit • Liquidity	• Credit • Liquidity

* Although not common, private-placement CP can have a term of up to 397 days.

** Interest is paid via the security being issued at a discount to face value. (Calculation of investment yield of discount securities is discussed in Chapter 11, Short-Term Investing and Borrowing.)

*** Variable rates may be available on issues with maturities of one year or more.

**** Foreign exchange risk will be an issue for any investment denominated in a currency other than the currency of the investor.

1. COMMERCIAL PAPER (CP)

Companies raise funds in the short-term money market through the issuance of CP. *Commercial paper* refers to tradable promissory notes issued by companies, as opposed to banks, and is normally an unsecured obligation or debt of the issuing company (i.e., the CP is not backed or "secured" by any collateral of the issuing company). Maturity can range from overnight to 270 days for publicly traded CP (issued in the United States under the SEC Securities Act of 1933 Section 3(a)(3)) and up to 397 days for private-placement CP (issued under Section 4(a)(2) of the same act), but most paper issued matures in less than 45 days. CP does not usually pay interest during its term. Instead, it is issued at a discounted price and the face value is paid at maturity. Therefore, the yield is a factor of the difference between the price paid and the face value over the term. Most CP is purchased for a specific maturity and is held for the full term. However, CP can be traded on the secondary market if an investor needs to access its capital value before maturity.

In terms of advantages, investment-grade CP tends to be highly liquid, and the broad range of available maturities allows investors to target the investment term very precisely. Investors can diversify risk by investing in issuers across different industries and sectors of the economy. Both Europe and the United States have highly developed CP markets, which also offer opportunities for geographic diversification.

The primary disadvantage of CP is that it is not secured against any particular asset, though it may be backstopped by some form of credit enhancement (e.g., issued with either a backup line of credit or standby letter of credit from a financial institution that will pay off the CP in the event of a default; letters of credit are discussed in more detail in Chapter 10, Collections, Concentration, and Disbursements). Therefore, most investors will want to ensure they invest in highly rated individual issues and set strict counterparty limits.

2. ASSET-BACKED COMMERCIAL PAPER (ABCP)

ABCP has most of the features of standard CP listed above, but it is secured against specific assets—usually short-term trade receivables from a single company or a range of companies. ABCP is issued through a sponsoring financial institution, referred to as a *conduit*, rather than directly by an issuing company. ABCP may be classified as either *single seller* if it is backed by assets from a single institution or *multi-seller* if it is backed by assets purchased from a number of issuers.

The primary advantage of ABCP is that it offers more security than standard CP. Investors' interests are protected by some form of asset. In addition, credit enhancement from the sponsoring bank will facilitate timely repayment at maturity. As far as disadvantages, the more complex structure of ABCP can make it harder to appraise the overall risk of the security and may require the use of third-party credit monitoring. The smaller size of the ABCP market (relative to standard CP) combined with this added complexity can also lead to increased liquidity risk for ABCP. However, investors tend to be rewarded for this extra complexity with a moderately higher rate of return than on standard CP.

3. BANK OBLIGATIONS

Banks raise funds in the money markets through time deposits, repurchase agreements (repos, covered in detail later in this chapter), and banker's acceptances (BAs). These are sometimes collectively referred to as *bank paper* or *bank obligations*. Examples of time deposits include savings accounts, certificates of deposit (CDs), and negotiable CDs. Negotiable CDs are large-value time deposits issued by banks and other financial institutions that are bought and sold on the open market. Negotiable CDs are usually traded in multiples of 100,000 or more (USD or foreign currency equivalent). While all CDs have a fixed maturity, there is an active secondary market for negotiable CDs. Nonnegotiable CDs, or retail CDs, which are issued in many different denominations to consumers and businesses, generally cannot be redeemed prior to maturity without a penalty and lack a secondary market.

Because they are deposits, investments in CDs are protected by deposit insurance (discussed in Chapter 2, Regulatory and Legal Environment), where available. Typically, however, deposit insurance limits are too low to provide significant protection against credit risk for most business investors. One solution to that issue in the United States is the Certificate of Deposit Account Registry Service (CDARS). CDARS is a private service that makes it possible to receive full FDIC insurance coverage on amounts up to $50 million by distributing the funds among CDs issued by a network of banks. The investor receives the quoted rate offered by the bank where the total deposit is made, and the service provides the investor with one periodic statement detailing the locations and amounts of the deposits.

Non-US banks and foreign branches of US banks raise funds in the global money markets through Eurodollar deposits (Eurodollars). Eurodollars are USD-denominated deposits held in financial institutions outside the United States and may be issued as negotiable Eurodollar CDs or as nonnegotiable Eurodollar time deposits, both of which are interest-bearing. Many multinational businesses invest in these foreign bank issues because they provide the ability to invest in USD-based securities that historically have had a higher rate of interest than comparable US bank securities, due to fewer regulations and a lack of US reserve requirements.

Yankee CDs are USD-denominated CDs that are sold by US branches of non-US banks. They are typically sold through the New York branches of foreign banks and carry minimum investments of $100,000. As with Eurodollar CDs, Yankees historically had a higher rate of interest than comparable US bank securities, due to regulatory differences and a lack of reserve requirements. Although that difference has largely disappeared as regulations have changed, investors may still use Yankees to provide geographic diversification in their portfolio.

A banker's acceptance (BA) arises out of commercial trade. It represents a time draft that is issued by a purchaser of goods to pay a supplier and that has been accepted by the bank on which the draft is drawn. The BA constitutes the bank's unconditional promise to pay the draft at maturity. The holder (i.e., beneficiary) of the acceptance can either wait until the maturity to receive payment in full, or sell it at discount and receive less than face value immediately. BAs are covered in more detail in Chapter 10, Collections, Concentration, and Disbursements.

4. GOVERNMENT PAPER

State and local government agencies and authorities, as well as other government entities, raise funds in the short-term money market by issuing a range of short-term paper, generally referred to as *treasury bills* or *government-issued promissory notes.*

The market for government paper in most countries tends to be liquid and highly active, with investors having the ultimate reassurance of a sovereign issuer, although sovereign risk (i.e., the risk that a government itself may default, discussed in more depth in Chapter 7, Relationship Management and Vendor Selection) is a growing issue. In most cases, short-term government paper is issued on a discount basis. A variety of maturities is generally available, depending on a government's borrowing requirements, allowing investors to match their liquidity requirements very closely. However, government issuers generally do not need to offer much relative yield to attract investors, and returns will tend to be lower than other instruments of the same maturity because of the generally low default risk.

UK gilts, US Treasuries, German bunds, Japanese government bonds (JGBs), and Brazilian government bonds are all examples of sovereign government bonds. The United States, Japan, and Europe have historically been the biggest issuers in the government bond market.[5] While US Treasury issues include T-bills, notes, and bonds, only those maturing

5. From "Everything You Need to Know About Bonds," published by PIMCO, March 2012 (http://www.pimco.com/en/education/pages/everythingyouneedtoknowaboutbonds.aspx).

within one year are classified as money market instruments. Because their liquidity and default risk are so low as to be considered near zero by the rating agencies, US Treasury securities are generally considered risk-free and serve as the benchmark against which interest rates on other debt securities are compared.

T-bills are money market instruments that are sold at a discount to their maturity value (i.e., par) and issued with original maturities of less than one year. At the time of this writing, T-bills are issued with maturities of 4, 13, 26, and 52 weeks. Newly issued Treasury offerings are sold through a multiple-price, sealed-bid auction. T-bills can be purchased on either a competitive or a noncompetitive basis. For investors submitting competitive bids, the bids are accepted starting with the highest price (i.e., lowest yield) offered, down to the lowest price necessary to sell the entire issue. Noncompetitive bids may also be submitted. In this case, the bidder is guaranteed to receive the desired amount of bills at the average price from the competitive-bid process.

Eligible banks, broker-dealers, and other private and governmental entities tender bids for specific amounts of the offered securities. Dealer bid and ask yield quotes for T-bills are published daily. An example of daily T-bill quotations that appear in the financial press is shown below:

Maturity Date	Days to Maturity	Bid Discount (Percent)	Ask Discount (Percent)	Ask Yield (Percent)
April 18	36	0.075	0.065	0.066
April 25	43	0.075	0.035	0.035
May 2	50	0.070	0.066	0.066
May 9	57	0.055	0.050	0.051

The secondary market for US Treasury securities is one of the largest in the world and has low transaction costs, which makes the bills highly marketable. They can be bought and sold in significant volumes with negligible, if any, impact on market prices and yields. Details on calculating prices, costs, and yields of T-bills and other investments are provided in Chapter 11, Short-Term Investing and Borrowing.

5. FLOATING-RATE NOTES (FRNs)

Both companies and banks issue FRNs to raise funds in the short-term market. FRNs sit at the longer end of the money market maturity spectrum, with maturities typically of one year or longer. FRNs pay a regular coupon,[6] as well as the promise of a return of their face value at maturity. The actual return, or margin, on an FRN is a combination of the coupon interest rate and the capital gain or loss that results from an FRN transaction, since FRNs are traded on the secondary market at a discount. If an FRN is trading at par (i.e., at full face value), then the return is identical to the coupon rate.

The name *floating-rate note* derives from the fact that the rate of interest resets periodically, based on a reference rate such as the London Interbank Offered Rate (LIBOR) or the Euro Interbank Offered Rate (Euribor). As a result, FRNs are sold at a quoted spread over the stated reference rate. The spread is a rate that remains constant while the reference rate can vary. FRNs can have a variety of special features, such as minimum or maximum coupon rates. Perpetual FRNs are a type of FRN that is issued with no maturity date, and investors can only recapture their capital by selling them on the secondary market.

6. A coupon payment is a regular payment of interest on the face value of the investment. Coupons are typically used in instruments with maturities of greater than one year. The name comes from the fact that historically securities were issued in paper form with coupons that represented each interest payment attached to the bond. Bondholders had to "clip" the coupon from the bond and return it to the issuer to receive the interest payment.

The variable-rate nature of FRNs makes them very appealing in an uncertain interest rate environment and when investors do not want to lock themselves into a fixed rate. FRNs tend to offer relatively attractive yields. Moreover, the regular resetting of the coupon means investors experience less capital volatility than with fixed-interest securities. The creditworthiness of FRNs is generally straightforward to ascertain because they tend to have a published credit rating. However, independent analysis is always recommended, especially when the possibility of a downgrade exists. As with CP, some FRNs are issued with credit enhancements to improve their marketability. In addition, FRNs may be secured by collateral pledged by borrowers.

Similar to fixed-rate bonds, a disadvantage of an FRN investment is that an FRN's capital value can fluctuate in the time between interest rate resets that bring the security's yield in line with the rest of the market.[7] The bid-offer spread of an FRN tends to be wider than the other instruments detailed above, and so regular trading can erode any yield advantage relatively quickly.[8] Like CDs, FRNs tend to be issued with fairly large minimum denominations. Smaller investors may be unable to achieve sufficient counterparty diversification by buying FRNs individually. In this case, it may be more appropriate to access them via an MMF.

6. REPURCHASE AGREEMENTS (REPOS)

In a typical repo, a bank or securities dealer sells government securities it owns to an investor and agrees to repurchase them at a later date and at a slightly higher price. In most cases, this type of agreement is referred to as a *repo agreement* from the perspective of the entity selling the securities and agreeing to repurchase them at a later date. From the perspective of the entity that buys the securities with a promise to sell them back at a later date, it is generally known as a *reverse repo*. Thus, the repo side of the transaction is actually a short-term borrowing arrangement while the reverse repo side is a short-term investment arrangement.

Repos usually involve the sale and repurchase of government debt (as discussed above). However, they can be based on any security with the agreement of the parties involved. Repos are classified as *overnight*, *term* (two days or longer), and *open* (no maturity date). Term repos may have any maturity agreeable to both parties, but they are rarely for periods of more than a year. An open repo has no maturity date, but rather either party can terminate the agreement on a day-by-day basis.

Because each repo is negotiated individually between two parties, there is ample opportunity to tailor a repo's maturity and interest to each party's requirements (although the rate of interest will generally be determined by market repo rates). Taking legal possession of the underlying security (usually through a broker-dealer) also gives the investor a high degree of comfort, as repos can be sold if the selling counterparty defaults on the agreement, which is referred to as *settlement risk*.[9] While repos can be set up

7. Fixed-rate bonds pay a fixed rate of interest (usually as a coupon payment) over their life. For example, a 10% bond would pay a coupon equal to 10% of its face value each year it was outstanding. Over the bond's life, only interest is paid. Then, the principal (i.e., face value) is paid at maturity.
8. *Bid-offer spread* refers to the difference in pricing for a security bought or sold through a dealer (i.e., the dealer will buy [bid] a security at one price, but sell [offer] at a higher price).
9. When the collateral is held by a broker-dealer and the funds are exchanged through that party, the arrangement is called a *tri-party repo*. This is considered to be the safest method for securing the repo.

simply with standard contracts, the investor needs to perform analysis or due diligence to determine, among other things, a fair price for, and the creditworthiness of, the exchanged security.

7. OTHER TYPES OF MONEY MARKET INVESTMENTS

There are a variety of other types of money market investments, typically using some combination of the specific instruments discussed above. These include MMFs, short-duration mutual funds, and sweep accounts.

a. Money Market Funds (MMFs)

MMFs, known as *unit trusts* in the United Kingdom and Europe, are commingled pools of money market instruments, typically held by banks or investment firms, in which fund investors have an ownership interest. Many of the investments discussed above form the basis for these types of funds. The funds may be offered in the local currency or, where allowed by local regulators, in a foreign currency.

MMFs generally have a net asset value (NAV) set at one unit of the currency of the offering, such as dollars, pounds (sterling), or euros (hence the term *unit trust*). MMFs typically strive for stability and security. As long as the NAV of a particular MMF does not fall below one unit (e.g., $1), referred to as "breaking the buck," the investor's initial investment is secure. Historically, MMFs have been secure investments, and many treasury professionals (as well as individual investors) tend to regard them as the equivalent of cash in the bank. However, as discussed in Chapter 2, Regulatory and Legal Environment, MMFs are not insured, and various regulators, such as the Securities and Exchange Commission (SEC) in the United States and the European Securities and Markets Authority (ESMA), are looking at changing the regulations regarding NAV and other MMF features. In addition, funds can differ substantially from each other in terms of risk, maturity, and return, based on the types of investments held in the fund and the financial strength of the sponsoring organization.

MMFs are typically configured to report a NAV of $1 per share. In addition, they generally may not hold securities whose maturity exceeds 397 days and must maintain a dollar-weighted average portfolio maturity of 60 days or less. A variety of funds with different yields and risk thresholds are available. In the United States, MMFs are regulated by the SEC, which under Rule 2a-7 restricts investments in MMFs by quality, maturity, and diversity. The 2010 version of this rule imposes minimum liquidity requirements, implements daily and weekly liquidity requirements, and restricts the ability of funds to purchase illiquid and lower-quality securities. Because US MMFs are so highly regulated, the total US MMF market is significantly larger than comparable markets in other parts of the world.

MMFs can provide an organization with a professionally managed, marketable securities portfolio at a low cost. MMFs charge management fees or service charges based on the investor's balance, level of activity, and services provided. For many organizations, using MMFs may be more cost-effective than managing a short-term investment portfolio (discussed in more detail in Chapter 11, Short-Term Investing and Borrowing). They are also administratively easy to use, helping to free up valuable treasury resources for other tasks.

MMFs offer daily liquidity and pay dividends (usually monthly) based on the fund's average yield for the dividend period. Because minimum investments in many MMFs tend to be substantially smaller than those required for direct investments in money market securities, organizations can tailor their short-term portfolios more easily to meet diversification and maturity requirements.

MMFs also may offer advantages over other securities when there are changing interest rate conditions. For example, when interest rates are falling, MMF managers may extend the maturities of new securities purchases in the fund's underlying portfolio (within regulatory guidelines and limits) to lock in yields. Thus, investors in the fund receive the greater return of longer-term instruments while enjoying the liquidity and stability of principal that can be associated with investments with shorter maturities. The opposite holds true in rising interest rate environments.

The economies of scale of large MMFs generally means they can obtain very competitive trading terms, helping to ensure that yield is not eroded by active management of the underlying portfolio. Moreover, most MMFs offer same-day settlement, making them just as liquid as overnight deposits, and they are credit-rated by some or all the leading rating agencies, which makes their risk profile relatively easy to appraise.

b. Short-Duration Mutual Funds

Short-duration mutual funds invest in securities with maturities that exceed the maturities of most money market instruments. In most cases, longer-maturity funds offer not only higher average returns, but also a higher risk of fluctuations in their underlying value. Unlike MMFs, these funds do not typically have a fixed unit currency value (i.e., NAV).

Quite commonly, the average maturity of securities held in a short-duration portfolio is between one and three years. These funds place the majority of their holdings in specific types of instruments, such as government issues, CDs, or CP. Some mutual fund companies offer a variety of short-duration funds based on differing average maturities or duration. They may be used by investors to implement a strategy that attempts to match investments with forecasted cash flow needs. For example, a treasury professional may place some investable cash in MMFs, other cash in a short-duration mutual fund with an average maturity of 15 months, and still other cash in a fund with an average maturity of 24 months.

c. Investment Sweep Accounts

A firm may choose to have its depository institution sweep any excess end-of-day funds into an investment account. Though sweep accounts are not actually a separate category of short-term investment, they are widely used and are diverse, offering investment in repos or other money market instruments, managed accounts, and mutual funds. Some sweeps offer tax-exempt, offshore investments.[10] Using sweep accounts generally entails minimal risk and minimal time and effort, but typically produces lower returns than active management.

10. Depending on where the sweep funds are invested and the legal agreement with the bank, these investments may or may not be covered by government deposit insurance or guarantee programs (e.g., Federal Deposit Insurance Corporation [FDIC] insurance in the United States). Treasury professionals using sweep accounts should get a clear statement from their banks as to any insurance coverage or guarantees on those accounts.

III. SHORT-TERM MONEY MARKETS IN THE UNITED STATES

The US money market is very large and efficient, with no single participant, other than the Federal Reserve System (Fed) and its monetary actions undertaken by the Federal Open Market Committee (FOMC), being big enough to impact prices. (The Fed and FOMC are discussed in Chapter 2, Regulatory and Legal Environment.) Because of its relative size and the perceived safety of US Treasury securities, the US money market is routinely accessed by treasury professionals around the world.[11]

This section of the chapter presents some issues that apply specifically to the US money market.

A. Processing and Clearing of Short-Term Investments in the United States

There are two primary entities that provide for the processing and clearing of most short-term investments in the United States. The first is the Fed's Commercial Book-Entry System (CBES) (also known as the Treasury/Reserve Automated Debt Entry System, or TRADES), which processes Treasury securities, and the second is the Depository Trust & Clearing Corporation (DTCC), the parent company of DTC (the US CSD), which processes all forms of book-entry securities.

1. COMMERCIAL BOOK-ENTRY SYSTEM (CBES)[12]

Operated by the US Treasury, CBES is a multi-tiered, automated system for purchasing, holding, and transferring marketable Treasury securities. CBES exists as a delivery system that provides for the simultaneous transfer of securities against the settlement of funds. Securities owners (or their brokers on their behalf) receive interest and redemption payments wired directly to their linked accounts.

At the top tier of CBES is the National Book-Entry System (NBES), which is operated by the Fed. For Treasury securities, the Fed operates the NBES in its capacity as the fiscal agent of the US Treasury. The Federal Reserve Banks maintain book-entry accounts for depository institutions, the US Treasury, foreign central banks, and most government-sponsored enterprises (GSEs).

At the middle tier of CBES, depository institutions hold book-entry accounts for their customers, which include brokers, dealers, institutional investors, and trusts. At the lower tier, each broker, dealer, and financial institution maintains book-entry accounts for individual customers, corporations, and other entities.

When an investor purchases securities through a broker, dealer, or financial institution, the securities are held on the book-entry system of that firm. Holding Treasury securities in this manner is known as *indirect holding* since there are one or more entities between the investor and the issuer (US Treasury). The CBES has succeeded in replacing paper securities with electronic records, eliminating the potential for theft, loss, or counterfeiting.

2. DEPOSITORY TRUST & CLEARING CORPORATION (DTCC)[13]

DTCC is an investment-industry-owned corporation that works through its subsidiaries to provide clearing, settlement, and information services for equities, corporate and municipal bonds, government and mortgage-backed securities, money market instruments, and over-the-counter derivatives. It was formed in 1999 by the combination of the Depository Trust Company (DTC) and National Securities Clearing Corporation (NSCC). DTCC is able to bring significant efficiency to the market clearing process by acting as a legal depository (i.e., holding place) for most stock and bond

11. The US Government Accounting Office (GAO) estimated that approximately 46% of all US Treasury debt was held by foreign investors as of the end of fiscal year 2011.
12. Information on CBES comes from the website for TreasuryDirect, an operation of the US Treasury Department (http://www.treasurydirect.gov/instit/auctfund/held/cbes/cbes.htm, last modified November 15, 2012).
13. Information on DTCC was obtained from its website (http://www.dtcc.com/about/business/index.php, accessed September 30, 2013).

certificates and by netting transactions among brokers, dealers, mutual funds, insurance companies, and other large institutional investors. DTCC's depository primarily provides custody and asset servicing for millions of securities issues from the United States, but it also provides servicing for some foreign items.

As an industry-owned corporation, DTCC and its subsidiaries operate on an at-cost basis, charging transaction fees for services and then returning excess revenue to its members. DTCC is owned by its member firms, including international broker-dealers, correspondent and clearing banks, mutual fund companies, and investment banks. All services provided through the clearing corporations and depository are registered with, and regulated by, the US SEC.

B. US Money Market Participants

Participants in the US money market include the same parties discussed earlier in this chapter in Section II, Global Money Markets. US issuers include the US Treasury, federal agencies and GSEs, securities dealers, commercial banks, and municipalities, as well as other corporations that raise funds by borrowing in the money market.

In addition to all of the other participants, the Fed plays a significant role in the US money market. First, the Fed is responsible for managing the initial sale and subsequent settlement of most book-entry Treasury security sales/purchases. Secondly, the Fed implements US monetary policy through the FOMC (Federal Open Market Committee). The FOMC implements its monetary policy through purchases and sales of Treasury securities in the secondary markets, often using repos, as discussed above. Finally, the Fed buys, sells, and redeems Treasury securities in its role as fiscal agent for the US Treasury. More information on the role of the Fed and the FOMC is provided in Chapter 2, Regulatory and Legal Environment.

C. US Federal Agency and Government-Sponsored Enterprise (GSE) Securities

In addition to traditional government paper, such as T-bills, the US federal government has many agencies and GSEs that issue various types of securities. Much of the federal agency and GSE debt generally carries either an explicit or an implied guarantee by the US government. Additionally, such debt instruments are created as one of two types: direct debt or asset-backed debt. Asset-backed securities require a greater degree of due diligence prior to investing and often require sophisticated analytical skills not normally associated with a typical corporate treasury function. A higher level of due diligence is required to fully investigate both the security issue and all the assets that are used as part of the collateral and/or securitization arrangements related to the asset-backed security.

The Government National Mortgage Association (GNMA, or Ginnie Mae), a wholly owned agency of the United States, provides liquidity for government-sponsored mortgage programs through its mortgage-backed securities (MBSs) plan. Individual mortgages insured or guaranteed by certain government agencies are pooled and interests in them are sold, either as MBSs or as real estate mortgage investment conduits (REMICs), supported by Ginnie Mae's guarantee. The Ginnie Mae guarantee is backed by the full faith and credit of the US government, so yields on Ginnie Mae issues are lower than those for most other MBSs.

In addition to the typical investment risks discussed in Chapter 16, Financial Risk Management, Ginnie Mae MBSs are also subject to prepayment risk and extension risk. Most MBS investment pools have an assumed rate of prepayment of the underlying mortgages built into the package. Prepayment risk arises in these types of investments because as interest rates fall, mortgage refinancings increase, resulting in a higher prepayment rate. Extension risk is the opposite problem. As interest rates rise, refinancings decrease, resulting in a lower prepayment rate and effectively extending the maturity of the investment.

Default risk is typically not a concern, due to federal government guarantees on the instrument. REMICs offer some control over these risks by allocating principal and interest payments from pools of mortgages to classes (i.e., tranches) with differing maturities and differing prepayment and interest characteristics that appeal to a variety of investment risk profiles.

The US Department of Veterans Affairs (VA) also guarantees REMICs issued through its Vendee Mortgage Trust Securitization Program. Like Ginnie Mae, the VA guarantees timely payment of principal and interest to the REMIC investor. This guarantee is backed by the full faith and credit of the federal government.

GSEs are private companies that act as financial intermediaries to provide funds for loans made in the housing, education, and agriculture sectors. GSEs do not carry the credit backing of the US government though there is a strong implication that the federal government would intervene in a crisis to help repay investors because of the importance of GSEs to public welfare.

GSE securities (i.e., bonds and sometimes equity) are issued by the Federal National Mortgage Association (FNMA, or Fannie Mae), the Federal Farm Credit Banks Funding Corporation, the Federal Home Loan Mortgage Corporation (FHLMC, or Freddie Mac), and the Federal Home Loan Banks Office of Finance to provide liquidity in support of their loan programs. At the time of this publication, GSE reform and government support of GSE securities were issues being debated at the highest levels of government. Due to price, prepayment, and extension risk, as well as the possible lack of a direct federal guarantee, a treasury professional should exercise care when investing in agency and GSE securities.

D. Municipal Notes, Variable-Rate Demand Obligations (VRDOs), and Tax-Exempt Commercial Paper (CP)

In addition to paper issued by the federal, state, and local governments, their agencies, authorities, and subdivisions raise funds in the money market through municipal notes, variable-rate demand obligations (VRDOs), and tax-exempt CP. Many municipal and not-for-profit entity issues are exempt from federal income taxes and/or state income taxes in the state of issuance, making these attractive for investors seeking tax-free income.

Maturities of three months to one year are typical for municipal notes and range up to 270 days for CP. Most of these short-term municipal issues are used by local governments to provide interim financing for general obligation bond projects (e.g., bond anticipation notes [BANs]) or short-term working capital in anticipation of future (tax) revenues (e.g., tax anticipation notes [TANs] and revenue bonds).

VRDOs are issued as long-term bonds that carry a short-term liquidity feature, or put. Generally, this put option, which is an investor's option to sell (or put) the instrument back to the issuer at par, allows for liquidation either weekly or monthly and is typically supported by a credit facility, such as a bank L/C. While interest from VRDOs is often tax-exempt, VRDOs exist as both taxable and nontaxable instruments.

Dealers provide an active secondary market for all of these short-term municipal obligations. A formula for comparing yields on taxable and tax-exempt instruments is presented in Chapter 11, Short-Term Investing and Borrowing.

IV. SUMMARY

Money markets, which represent short-term investment securities, are a key resource for treasury professionals in managing short-term liquidity and short-term borrowing and investment.

This chapter introduced the concept of global money markets by providing an overview of the participants and the various types of investments available in the global money markets. There are a variety of instruments available in the global money markets, with maturities ranging from overnight to up to two years. In addition to direct investments (e.g., commercial paper, bank and government securities, and repos), money market mutual funds and unit trusts offer treasury professionals access to a broad range of diversified securities with minimal financial restrictions.

The chapter also included a discussion of the risks of investing in money market securities. As with any investment, these securities do have some risk. However, because there is a strong secondary market for money market securities in most of the world, these investments are usually highly liquid and provide ready access to funds when needed.

The chapter concluded with a discussion of short-term money markets in the United States. Because of its relative size and the perceived safety of US Treasury securities, the US money market is routinely accessed by treasury professionals around the world.

TEST YOUR UNDERSTANDING: CHAPTER 5

Answers are on pages 657–660.

1. Who are the primary participants in the money market?
2. What is a central securities depository?
3. What are the major categories of investment risk?
4. What is a repurchase agreement (repo), and how does it work?
5. What is CP?
6. What is bank paper?
7. Describe government paper.
8. What is an FRN?
9. What is meant by the phrase "breaking the buck"?
10. Describe the Commercial Book-Entry System (CBES).

CHAPTER 6
Capital Markets

I. INTRODUCTION

II. OVERVIEW OF CAPITAL MARKETS

A. The Basics of Capital Markets
B. Key Participants in Capital Markets
C. Division of the Capital Markets
D. Securities Exchanges and Over-the-Counter (OTC) Markets

III. DEBT MARKET

A. Medium- and Long-Term Borrowing
B. Other Factors in Using Debt as a Source of Capital

IV. EQUITY (STOCK) SECURITIES

A. Common Stock
B. Preferred Stock
C. Hybrid Securities
D. Depositary Receipts (DRs)

V. SUMMARY

APPENDIX 6.1: LISTING OF THE WORLD'S TOP 10 STOCK EXCHANGES

I. INTRODUCTION

Capital markets are financial markets for the buying and selling of long-term debt (bonds) or equity-backed securities (stocks). They promote economic efficiency by channeling funds from those who do not have an immediate productive use for them to those who do. Capital markets exist in virtually all developed countries and in many developing countries, as well.[1] They are a major source of funding and investment for many types of organizations, and most countries have globalized their financial markets to attract foreign business.

Most chief financial officers and treasurers attempt to identify an appropriate mix of long-term debt and equity to finance their firms. This mix is termed a *target capital structure*. The availability and choice of debt issues has a major impact on a company's ultimate capital structure. This chapter addresses the capital markets that are used by treasury professionals to meet the capital financing needs of their firms. Issues regarding capital structure are addressed in more detail in Chapter 20, Financial Decisions and Management.

The next section of this chapter provides an overview of the operations and participants in the capital markets. The remaining sections of this chapter cover the basic characteristics of debt and equity securities (including term loans). The management and valuation of those securities is discussed in Chapter 12, Long-Term and Capital Investments.

II. OVERVIEW OF CAPITAL MARKETS

A. The Basics of Capital Markets

Financial markets are typically divided into two markets:

- **Money markets,** which include issues with maturities of one year or less (covered in Chapter 5, Money Markets)
- **Capital markets,** which include issues with maturities extending beyond one year

The capital markets, which represent a major part of the financial markets, are further subdivided into two basic segments:

- **Debt market,** which includes fixed-income capital, such as bond securities and term loans
- **Equity market,** which includes securities such as shares of common and preferred stock

Equity instruments have no fixed maturity date. However, an equity security ceases to exist when the issuing firm's life ends due to bankruptcy, merger, acquisition, or liquidation. On the other hand, capital market debt is typically sold with original maturities ranging from just over one year to as long as thirty or more years, and is issued by borrowers with various credit ratings. Longer-dated capital market instruments are usually marginally less liquid than money market instruments, due to their longer maturity.

1. Not all developing economies have capital markets. Where capital markets do not exist, banks, international financial organizations, and governmental agencies provide much of the needed development capital instead.

These markets and the exchanges upon and through which securities change hands are overseen by various regulatory bodies in the countries where they operate.

B. Key Participants in Capital Markets

The key participants in the capital markets are the issuers of the securities, the investors who buy those securities, the broker-dealers who help to make the market function, and the regulators who help to ensure a level playing field and adherence to the rules. This section provides an overview of these participants and their roles.

1. ISSUERS OF SECURITIES

The issuers of securities represent the supply side of the equation in the capital markets. The different types of issuers are outlined below. In most cases, they issue different types of securities to raise capital or funds for their organization. Issuers of debt-type securities are borrowers, while the issuers of equity-type securities are selling ownership in their enterprise. Governmental and not-for-profit (G/NFP) entities issue debt securities, while companies can issue both debt and equity securities. The purpose of this section is to introduce these market supply participants and discuss the general types of securities they issue. The characteristics and details of the securities issued by these various entities are covered in later sections of this chapter.

a. Governments (Ministries of Finance) and Central Banks: Debt Securities

Globally, governments (typically through their ministry of finance or treasury) and central banks raise funds through their respective capital markets and generally only through the debt side. Governments (sovereigns) typically issue debt of various maturities to finance fiscal deficits. In most countries, these issues are backed by the full faith and credit of the issuing government. Other governmental financing arms market similar sovereign securities for capital-raising purposes. In the United States, the Treasury Department raises funds through the sale of Treasury securities, including discounted Treasury bills (T-bills) and interest-bearing notes and bonds.

In many countries, central banks also issue their own securities to finance the acquisition of assets (particularly foreign exchange reserves). They also often conduct open market operations, which involve sales and purchases of government debt. As a result, both the government and the central bank directly influence the mix of short- and long-term securities held by the public. Some central banks issue bonds as a monetary policy instrument only, and in some countries, central banks are banned from issuing debt to finance the government.

b. Corporations: Debt and Equity Securities

Corporate entities, including commercial banks and other financial institutions, raise capital through the sale of stocks and bonds. As discussed in Chapter 5, Money Markets, corporations are major issuers of short-term debt in the commercial paper market. They are also major issuers of long-term debt in a variety of formats, but mostly in the form of five- to ten-year bond issues, although longer terms have historically been available. Term loans greater than one year are also part of this market. On the equity side, corporations are the primary issuers of both preferred and common stock, which represent ownership in those corporations. As discussed later in this chapter, these issues can take many forms, including hybrid-type securities (e.g., convertible bonds), which combine both debt and equity features into a single instrument.

c. State-Owned Enterprises: Debt Securities

A state-owned enterprise (SOE) is a company that is created by a national government in order to participate in or help support various commercial activities on the government's behalf. SOEs can be either wholly or partially owned by a government and are common in many countries around the globe. SOEs are also known as *crown corporations* (in Canada and the United Kingdom, for example) or *government-sponsored enterprises,* or *GSEs* (in the United States).

Non-asset-backed debt is issued regularly by government-sponsored agencies or entities of various types. These organizations are generally formed for a specific purpose and are often designed to support a certain economic sector (e.g., financing residential or farm mortgages, industrial development, or import/export financing). Examples include Freddie Mac and Fannie Mae[2] in the United States, Canada Post or VIA Rail Canada in Canada, or Sinosteel Corporation in China.

d. Sub-sovereign Entities: Debt Securities

Sub-sovereign entities (i.e., governmental units within a country, such as states, counties, cities, and municipal government agencies) borrow extensively in the debt markets in many countries but are not allowed in all countries. In the United States, interest paid to investors on such instruments is generally exempt from federal income taxation, which may make them more attractive to certain types of investors. Tax laws vary significantly from country to country, so investors should be sure to verify the tax implications of any securities they hold.

e. Mutual Fund Companies: Debt and Equity Securities

Mutual fund companies sell shares in many different types of money market, bond, and stock funds. Generally speaking, these types of securities do not represent a direct issuance of stocks and bonds by the mutual fund sponsor. Rather, they are shares sold by the fund, which holds aggregated securities, allowing smaller investors to diversify their investments more easily.

2. INVESTORS

The investors represent the demand side of the capital markets. They are the entities that purchase and hold the securities sold by the issuers. Investors generally are categorized as either *retail or institutional investors.*

Retail investors are typically individuals buying small amounts of stocks or bonds for their own investment portfolios. They are a large source of demand for investment vehicles and, in large measure, are relied upon by issuers as a very important source of capital. On the other hand, institutional investors come in various forms, but they can generally be described as large-scale investors (e.g., mutual fund companies, insurance companies, money managers, pension funds, corporations, and banks) that purchase large blocks of securities on behalf of others, as well as for their own portfolios.

2. *Freddie Mac* refers to the Federal Home Loan Mortgage Corporation (FHLMC), and *Fannie Mae* refers to the Federal National Mortgage Association (FNMA).

3. BROKER-DEALERS (INVESTMENT BANKING AND BROKERAGE FIRMS)[3]

Investment banking firms serve as intermediaries in most capital market transactions. They are regulated entities that distribute new issues of stocks and bonds, and maintain ongoing, secondary markets for securities. These firms fulfill several key roles:

- **Investment bankers** are professionals who are responsible for assisting issuers in the design and placement of securities issuances. This typically includes underwriting the initial offering.
- **Originators** (often referred to as *origination desks*) are a subset of trading professionals who are charged with evaluating, pricing, and managing the placement of new security issues.
- **Securities traders** maintain active, orderly, secondary markets for all equity and debt instruments.

In addition to the various individual brokerage firms, there are also syndicates (i.e., selling groups), which are groups of brokerage firms that combine their securities distribution networks in order to place new securities issues most effectively. A number of electronic trading systems, which generally run without the intervention of securities traders, have also developed in recent years.

4. REGULATORS

As discussed in Chapter 2, Regulatory and Legal Environment, the role of regulators is critical to the maintenance of fair and open markets. The regulators who watch over the capital markets are generally different from those who monitor the banking markets, and may even be different from those in the money markets, depending on the country. In most cases, the role of the capital market regulators is to provide for consistent and transparent disclosure of financial information related to the securities traded in their markets, and to ensure a fair and level playing field for all market participants.

Funds invested in capital markets are not insured by the government, and investors are expected to exercise proper due diligence in the selection of the securities they purchase.

There are some linkages between capital markets in different parts of the world, but this integration comes more from the fact that both issuers and investors operate in many different geographic markets, rather than from a true global integration of the markets themselves. While there have been some moves to try to better coordinate the world's capital markets, the reality today is that each country still regulates only those markets that operate within its own borders. The capital market regulators in key developed countries are discussed in Chapter 2, Regulatory and Legal Environment.

5. OTHER PARTICIPANTS

There are other parties involved in the securities markets that should be mentioned because of the important services they provide in the functioning and efficiency of those markets.

a. Rating Agencies

For debt securities, rating agencies play a key role in determining the credit risk, and therefore the cost/return, of those securities. Rating agencies are discussed in more detail in Chapter 11, Short-Term Investing and Borrowing.

3. Many investment banking and brokerage firms also serve as investment advisors, a totally separate function from their role as market intermediaries. Refer to Chapter 3, Banks and Financial Institutions, for more details.

b. Transaction Processors

There are also entities called *transaction processors* that are critically involved in the flow of payments from issuers to investors (e.g., payments of interest, principal, and dividends), as well as the record keeping involved in processing transactions. These trustees and agents are discussed in Chapter 3, Banks and Financial Institutions, in the section on fiduciary services.

c. Other Parties

Other parties also play a role in the efficient operation of capital markets. They can include attorneys, printing companies (e.g., for the printing of securities, official statements, or bond transcripts), proxy solicitors, and data service providers (e.g., news services or market quote services).

C. Division of the Capital Markets

Capital markets are typically distinguished by the channels and mechanisms they use to provide for the buying and selling of securities. These capital market channels are outlined below.

1. PRIMARY MARKETS

Primary markets offer newly issued debt and equity securities to investors when firms or government units sell securities to raise funds. An investment bank or a syndicate of investment banks underwrites (purchases) a securities issue and then sells shares of that issue to the investing public.

New issues represent transactions that increase the outstanding stock of a publicly traded corporation, or the indebtedness of a corporation or government entity. If new stock shares are sold by a company with shares already trading on an exchange or the over-the-counter (OTC) market, then the new shares are referred to as a *secondary or follow-on issue*. The market price of existing shares guides the price for new shares.

If a firm issues equity shares to the investing public for the first time, the issue is termed an *initial public offering (IPO)*. In this case, there is no direct market guidance as to the value of a share of stock. Instead, the firm consults with its investment bankers to select an issue price that represents the highest price per share that can be obtained while simultaneously resulting in selling all the shares in the issue. In contrast to an IPO, a seasoned offering occurs when a firm that already has outstanding stock issues new, additional equity (i.e., a secondary or follow-on issue) in the market.

When an investment bank or syndicate of investment banks underwrites a securities issue, the issuing firm receives the funds directly from the bank on the issue date and may set about using those funds for their intended purpose. The investment banks market (i.e., sell) the issue to the investing public through a network of brokerage firms, termed the *syndicate* or *selling group*. The issue is divided among the brokerage firms based on the initial syndication agreement, and the firms, in turn, allocate the securities to individual offices and their registered representatives. Both retail and institutional investors may purchase the securities.

2. SECONDARY MARKETS

After the initial offering is sold to investors, the securities can be bought and sold on the secondary market.[4] Existing debt and equity issues are traded by retail and institutional investors in secondary markets through established exchanges or through OTC markets. Since the securities are bought and sold among investors, the issuing firm neither experiences a cash flow nor a change in the number of securities outstanding.

Stock exchanges generally have a physical location and hours of business when trading can occur. Alternatively, an OTC market is an electronic information interchange, instead of a physical trading floor, that connects its trading members, and displays recent bid and ask prices for the securities it trades.

The members of OTC markets are securities firms that may choose to maintain an inventory of equity or debt securities, and stand ready to buy those same securities from investors or other dealers wishing to buy or sell them. Once a debt or equity security is issued in the primary market, any subsequent trades occur in the secondary market until the debt or security is redeemed, repurchased, called, or otherwise defeased by the firm that issued it. (Defeasance of debt is covered later in this chapter.)

3. PRIVATE MARKETS

In a private placement, or direct placement, securities are offered and sold to a limited group of investors and not offered to the general public. While the specific regulations regarding private placement vary from country to country, they generally require that private-placement securities only be sold to a limited number of high net worth investors or to *qualified institutional investors (QIIs)*, referred to in the United States as *qualified institutional buyers (QIBs)*. The investment banking firm, acting as a broker to bring the issuer and investors together, meets with prospective buyers and confirms the details of the offering. Provisions of a private issue may be tailored to meet the needs of the issuing company and the buyer(s).

Although the regulations regarding QIIs can and do vary by country, the US regulations are often used as a guideline because they tend to be among the most restrictive. According to guidelines set forth by the US Securities and Exchange Commission (SEC) in Rule 144A, a QIB is an institution that manages at least $100 million in securities, and can be a bank, thrift institution, pension fund, corporation, insurance company, investment company, or employee benefit plan, or an entity owned entirely by qualified investors. A QIB can also be a registered broker-dealer that owns and invests, on a discretionary basis, at least $10 million in the securities of issuers that are not affiliated with the broker-dealer. Private placements often require that an investor attest to its status as a QIB because such private placements may not be marketed to non-QIBs.[5]

A private issue typically will not require the preparation of a detailed prospectus and may be exempt from registration with the various local authorities, such as the SEC in the United States or the Financial Conduct Authority (FCA) in the United Kingdom, and can therefore be completed more rapidly than a public offering. Further, a private debt issue typically may have:

- Lower issuance costs (because it is usually exempt from most regulatory registration)
- Less restrictive covenants
- A more favorable purchase price for the investor (to offset the diminished liquidity of the private placement)

4. Insiders, such as company founders, owners, managers, employees, and venture capitalists, who are holding a company's stock when it goes public are typically prohibited from reselling their stock during what is referred to as a *lockup period*. The lockup is a contractual restriction that prevents insiders from selling the stock for a period usually lasting 90 to 180 days after the company goes public.
5. As of the time of this publication, recent proposals by FINRA (the Financial Industry Regulatory Authority) may expand QIB requirements and permit broker-dealers to depend upon a negative affirmation of QIB status, rather than requiring a positive confirmation for research and private placements.

D. Securities Exchanges and Over-the-Counter (OTC) Markets

Organized stock exchanges facilitate the buying and selling of equity securities. There are major securities exchanges in most developed nations. A listing of the 10 top securities exchanges in the world is provided in Appendix 6.1.

Organized exchanges function in various ways and provide four principal benefits:

- They provide a market system where the competitive forces of supply and demand determine securities prices.
- They sustain a market where frequent trading minimizes price volatility between individual trades.
- They maintain a market large enough to enable issuers to raise large amounts of capital through securities offerings.
- They furnish a regulated environment to help ensure fairness for exchange participants.

OTC markets are more decentralized than formal exchanges. They also rely upon electronic communication to conduct trading activity in an auction-style market between participating brokers and dealers. Government, municipal, and corporate debt, and some equity issuances that are not traded on exchanges, are sometimes traded in the OTC markets. Financial markets in developing countries or emerging markets are often run on an OTC basis.

III. DEBT MARKET

Organizations and governmental entities can raise debt capital in both the short-term money market and long-term capital market. In either case, debt capital typically imposes a fixed payment requirement on a company or a sovereign. For businesses, the interest portion of these payments is usually deductible as a business expense and must be paid prior to any payments to equity holders. In addition, debt holders have priority claims on a company's assets in the event of financial distress (i.e., senior debt has a higher priority than junior or subordinated debt[6]). Given the fixed nature and deductibility of debt payments, the use of debt provides financial leverage for a company. (Financial leverage and capital structure are covered in Chapter 20, Financial Decisions and Management.)

A. Medium- and Long-Term Borrowing

A wide range of sources exists for medium- and long-term borrowing. Primary sources are term loans, intermediate-term notes and bonds, and long-term bonds. It is important to understand the seniority of claims (i.e., the order in which debt will be paid in the event of liquidation) when selecting a particular form of debt. Because seniority affects the risk of a given loan (senior loans are paid before subordinated loans), it impacts the interest rate and covenants related to the debt issue. In addition, seniority is used to

6. *Subordinated debt* refers to debt that is paid after other creditors have been paid. If there are not enough resources to pay all creditors, the subordinated debt may not be paid, since the senior debt has first claim on any assets.

demarcate debt types in a bankruptcy situation when claims are made on funds that result from asset liquidation. In some cases, such as secured or collateralized debt, designated assets are used to satisfy the debt. For unsecured debt, the indenture agreement and covenants related to each debt issue generally determine the priority of claims.

1. TERM LOAN

A term loan is a loan with a fixed maturity, usually greater than one year, which can be repaid either in installments or in a single payment. In most cases, term loans are amortizing, meaning that the periodic payment represents both interest and principal so that the balance of the loan reduces over the term of the loan. Term loans are typically negotiated with a financial institution or other lender (e.g., insurance company) and are not normally bought and sold in the secondary market. Frequently, a term loan is issued for a specific financing need, such as the purchase of a new plant or new equipment, or for general expansion. Interest is paid at periodic intervals and may be fixed or variable. A term loan typically is secured by the asset being financed, and its maturity is related to the asset's useful life. Companies may prefer these loans because they are tied to the specific asset that the loan finances rather than the general assets of the company. For many organizations, leasing equipment is an alternative to term loans, especially when the equipment seller/manufacturer provides specialized leasing arrangements. It is important to note that leases do not typically constitute marketable securities and do not have an active secondary market. Thus, from the lender's perspective, they are normally illiquid.

2. MEDIUM- OR INTERMEDIATE-TERM NOTES

Companies or government entities issue medium- or intermediate-term notes with terms in the two- to ten-year range. In most cases, these notes pay interest at periodic intervals (e.g., semiannually) and are very similar to long-term bonds except for the shorter maturity. Because such securities may be traded actively or because securities dealers may stand ready to make a market in them, medium- or intermediate-term notes are deemed marketable, or liquid, securities.

3. LONG-TERM BONDS

Long-term bonds, which typically are issued for periods of 10 to 30 years,[7] represent a major source of long-term debt financing for many organizations. Unlike loans, which are negotiated with one or more specific lenders, bonds are issued like stock, and are bought and sold on the secondary market. Also unlike loans, bonds are typically not secured against any specific assets of the issuing company but are considered unsecured debt. Terms (known as *tenors*) and purposes vary widely, making it possible for an organization to issue long-term debt with characteristics and provisions that suit it best. Most long-term bonds are coupon bonds, which make regular interest payments at a fixed rate (known as the *coupon rate*) over the life of the bond. Typically, these payments are interest only and are made on a semiannual basis. The principal is repaid in full to the bondholder on the bond's maturity date.

Bonds represent a contract between the issuing entity and the bondholders. This contract is known as a *bond indenture*, which serves several purposes. It:

- Describes the bond issue
- Lists collateral (when applicable)
- Makes representations and warranties
- Specifies covenants
- States the terms by which the company will provide funds for redemption
- Sets forth the schedule of interest payment dates and amounts, the scheduled maturity date, and any early redemption or call provisions

7. In 1993 Walt Disney and Coca-Cola issued so-called century bonds with a term of 100 years. There is ongoing debate as to whether these bonds serve as debt or equity since while they are structured as debt, their long term provides an equity-like feature. A number of other entities, primarily universities, have also offered century bonds since then. Given their long term, a key question is whether the issuer will still be in existence after 100 years.

In the event of bankruptcy, bond issues have differing claim priorities depending on the seniority of the bonds and liens, or pledges, on any assets. The restrictions that are included in indentures can place limits on the use and disposition of assets, on the formulation of working capital, and on other financial policies, as well as on the ability to acquire additional financing. These restrictions can cause the security's value to fall if changing economic or competitive conditions create a risk that indenture requirements (discussed later in this chapter) may be violated.

Bonds may also be issued with a call provision that allows the issuer to call, or retire, the bonds prior to maturity. For example, callable bonds permit the issuer to retire bonds when the opportunity arises to refinance in a lower interest rate environment. Some bonds are also issued with a put provision that allows the buyer to redeem the bond prior to maturity by forcing the issuer to buy the bonds back. Both are discussed in more detail later in this chapter.

Although historically the US bond market has been the largest in the world, bonds issued in the United States now account for less than half (about 44%) of the global bond market volume. In Europe, bonds are about two-thirds of the total amount of securities outstanding in bonds and shares; in the United States, the bond market is about the same size as the stock market.[8]

The primary types of bonds are described below.

a. Mortgage Bonds

Used to finance specific assets pledged as security against the issue, mortgage bonds usually include substantial financial covenants or indenture agreements, which are discussed later in this chapter.

b. Unsecured Bonds (Debentures)

Debentures are unsecured bonds that represent general claims against the issuing organization's assets and/or cash flows, and may carry a higher interest cost (to the issuer) than secured bonds. Large, financially secure organizations issue debentures based on their reputation in the marketplace. Organizations that do not have easily securitized assets must use unsecured borrowing through the use of debentures. Debentures may be issued on a subordinated basis, indicating that the claim on assets is subordinate to designated notes payable, bank loans, or other specified debt. Unsecured bonds may include sovereign (treasury), corporate, and municipal bonds.

c. Convertible Bonds

Convertible bonds are corporate debt securities that can be converted by the holder, or sometimes the issuer, into shares of common or preferred stock at a fixed ratio of shares per bond. Convertible bonds provide the holder with a potential for capital growth. Thus, investors may accept a somewhat lower interest rate on these bonds compared to bonds that are not convertible. Convertibles are covered in Section IV of this chapter.

8. From "Types of Bonds" on the website for Investing in Bonds Europe/Association for Financial Markets in Europe (AFME) (http://www.investinginbonds.eu/Pages/LearnAboutBonds.aspx?folder_id=464, accessed February 1, 2013).

d. Sovereign Bonds

Bonds issued by a national government are referred to as *sovereign bonds* or *sovereign debt*, and are typically denominated in the currency of the issuing government. This category would include all types of government debt ranging from US government bonds to bonds issued by developing countries around the world. In addition to the traditional credit risk associated with bonds of any sort, sovereign debt also carries sovereign or political risk, and potentially foreign exchange or currency risk if issued in a currency other than the home currency of the investor. Sovereign risk is the risk that while the country may still exist at the maturity of the bond, there may be a change in monetary policy that may affect the value of the bond.

e. Sub-sovereign Bonds (Municipal Bonds)

Sub-sovereign bonds are bonds issued by any level of government below the national or central government, which includes regions, provinces, states, municipalities, etc. In the United States, these bonds are typically municipal bonds, often referred to as *munis*. Historically, the market for sub-sovereign bonds has been primarily in the United States, but the markets for these bonds is rapidly expanding around the world due to local government needs to finance day-to-day operations of public services and capital investments in roads and other infrastructure that cannot be financed by the sovereign government (due to debt ceiling limits or other restrictions).

Bonds issued by government entities are usually in the form of general obligation or revenue bonds, and may or may not be guaranteed by the national government.

- **General obligation bonds** are paid from the proceeds of general tax revenues.
- **Revenue bonds** are linked directly to, and repaid from, the revenues generated from specific public projects or services (e.g., stadiums, toll roads and bridges, or public utilities).

Sub-sovereign bonds are subject to a wide variety of national and regional provisions in their country of origin and may have tax implications. For example, most US municipal bonds are exempt from federal and, in some cases, state and local income taxes. Local regulations, especially tax considerations, should always be considered before investing in sub-sovereign debt.

f. Eurobonds

Despite their name, Eurobonds have nothing to do with the euro or the European Union.[9] A Eurobond (sometimes called an *external bond*) is an international bond that is denominated in a currency other than that of the country in which it is issued. Eurobonds are named based on their face currency (e.g., Euroyen or Eurodollar). An example of this would be a Eurodollar bond that is dominated in US dollars and issued in India by a UK-based company. In this example, the UK company could issue the bond in any country other than the United States because it is denominated in US dollars.

These bonds are typically sold simultaneously in many countries outside the country of the borrower. Eurobonds can be an effective financing tool because they give issuers the flexibility to choose the currency and country in which to offer their bond, according to the country's regulatory constraints, their own FX needs, and their preferred currency. This flexibility provides multinational organizations an ability to create "natural hedges," which are discussed in Chapter 16, Financial Risk Management.

9. At the time of publication, the European Union (EU) was discussing the possibility of issuing sovereign debt on behalf of the entire EU. Confusingly, this debt is also being referred to as *Eurobonds*.

g. Zero-Coupon Bonds

Zero-coupon bonds typically pay no periodic interest during their life. They are issued at a substantial discount below par value and pay par value at maturity. There are two advantages for the corporate issuer: (1) there is no cash outflow until maturity, and (2) the issuing company receives an annual tax deduction until maturity.[10]

The disadvantages of zero-coupon bonds are that they generally are not callable or refundable, and investors are required to pay taxes on imputed interest earnings each year, even though no actual payment is received until maturity. Thus, when held in a portfolio that is not tax-exempt, there is a negative cash flow stream (i.e., tax outflows) during the bond's life.

h. High-Yield Bonds

Also referred to as *junk bonds* or *below-investment-grade bonds* (i.e., an investment quality rating of BB+ or less from S&P, or Ba1 or less from Moody's[11]), high-yield bonds are issued by less creditworthy entities, which implies a high required yield to compensate for the additional risk. Investment-grade bonds may also become high-yield or junk bonds as a result of a ratings downgrade.

i. Other Bonds

Many other types of bonds are used for special purposes or are related to specific types of assets:

- **Income bonds** pay interest only if a company has profits, thus reducing some of the risk of issuing debt from a company's viewpoint.
- **Collateral trust bonds** are backed by securities of other companies that are owned by the firm issuing the bond.
- **Equipment trust certificates** are bonds that are secured by movable equipment (e.g., a fleet of trucks or railroad equipment). Each certificate is backed by a specific asset or group of assets (i.e., there is no blanket lien securing the issue).
- **Index bonds** have interest rates tied to an economic index and are used most often when a high level of price inflation is present or possible.
- **Economic development bonds** typically are issued by developing countries or sponsoring organizations, such as the World Bank or the International Monetary Fund (IMF), for the express purpose of fostering development of infrastructure and related projects.
- **Tax increment financing (TIF) bonds** are used primarily for local financing in which a municipality may use all or a portion of new property taxes within a designated district to assist in the project's financing.
- **Tender option bonds** (i.e., put bonds) allow the holder to redeem the bond (i.e., sell it back to the issuer) either once during its life or on specified dates. Redemption is usually at par value.

10. For US tax purposes, the Internal Revenue Service determines an estimated interest payment for each year of the zero-coupon bond. For the issuer, this results in a tax deduction; for the holder, it results in a tax liability.
11. Bond ratings are covered in detail in Chapter 11, Short-Term Investing and Borrowing.

- **Foreign bonds** are bonds sold in a particular country by a foreign borrower, but they are usually denominated in the domestic currency of the country where issued. These bonds are primarily regulated by the authorities in the country of issue.
- **Multicurrency bonds** usually are issued as (1) currency option bonds that allow investors to choose among several predetermined currencies, or (2) currency cocktail bonds that are denominated in a standard basket of several currencies (e.g., special drawing rights [SDRs][12]).

4. OTHER FORMS OF DEBT CAPITAL

Other types of debt-like instruments that can be used to raise capital are outlined below.

a. Floating- (Adjustable-) Rate Debt

Floating-rate securities (or floaters) carry interest payments that reset periodically, based on movement in a representative interest rate index, such as the London Interbank Offered Rate (LIBOR) or the US T-bill. The rate on these securities is usually stated as a spread of difference from the base index rate (e.g., LIBOR + 3%). The interest rate on floating-rate debt may be reset daily, weekly, monthly, quarterly, semiannually, or annually, typically based on the index that is used for the security.

This type of debt is attractive to an investor during periods of rising interest rates because the floating-rate debt provides a stable market value and matches current interest rates. Borrowers, on the other hand, prefer floating-rate debt because it allows them to take advantage of any drop in interest rates while matching the debt's maturity to the asset's maturity.

b. Project Financing

Project financing applies to large projects, often in the energy area (e.g., energy exploration, refineries, and utility power plants). Project financing is also used for private infrastructure (e.g., stadiums, shopping centers, toll roads, and commercial or residential developments). The typical project-financing arrangement is complex, involving several companies or sponsors forming a separate legal entity to operate the project. Lenders are paid from the project's cash flows and generally do not have recourse to the project's individual sponsors or owners.

c. Securitization

Many types of debt instruments are securitized to increase liquidity, thus lowering the cost of capital to borrowers. The primary corporate applications of securitization are accounts receivable and inventory. These are bundled together to collateralize securities, making them more liquid and attractive to investors. Securitization of debt instruments has occurred because certain financial institutions have been willing to make a market in these instruments, in particular, for commercial paper and high-yield bonds.

The resulting securities in a securitized structure are known as *asset-backed securities (ABS)*. An example of this type of security is the credit card market. A financial institution that has outstanding credit card receivables can use them as collateral for ABS that they sell to investors. The resulting cash can then be used for additional lending. This arrangement provides significant liquidity to the card issuers, which benefits both borrowers and lenders. ABS are marketed in many countries around the world, typically by financial institutions that have the ability to put together packages of debt instruments and market the resulting ABS.

12. The IMF created SDRs, an artificial currency whose asset value is based on a basket of currencies consisting of the euro, Japanese yen, British pound sterling, and US dollar.

d. Off-Balance-Sheet Financing

Off-balance-sheet financing is designed to provide financing that does not appear on the balance sheet. Examples of off-balance-sheet financing include joint ventures, research and development partnerships, sales of receivables (factoring), and operating leases (rather than purchases of capital equipment). While many companies use off-balance-sheet funding, it is often used by organizations with high current debt levels or those that have very restrictive covenants on the use of additional debt.

Operating leases are one of the most common forms of off-balance-sheet financing. In these cases, the asset itself is kept on the lessor's balance sheet, and the lessee reports only the required rental expense for use of the asset.

There are significant restrictions on the use of this type of financing as outlined in ASC Topic 840-10-15: *Leases: Scope and Scope Extensions*,[13] which requires that companies entering into certain types of leases must capitalize the leases. This means companies must restate their balance sheets to report a leased asset as a fixed asset and the present value of future lease payments as a liability, which may appear as a footnote to the financial statements. Leasing is covered in greater detail in Chapter 20, Financial Decisions and Management.

5. DEBT CONTRACT PROVISIONS

Although the use of debt instead of equity can result in a lower cost of capital for a company (this is discussed in more detail in Chapter 20, Financial Decisions and Management), it also requires the management of the organization to accept some restrictions. The only way debt holders can protect their interests effectively is to perform due diligence at the time of the initial debt contract and establish certain provisions (e.g., representations, warranties, and covenants) designed to make it difficult for the management or equity holders to engage in actions that reduce the debt's value. These provisions also give debt holders additional rights under certain deteriorating conditions (i.e., material adverse changes) or in events of default. In passing, it should be noted that this applies to all commercial debt, not just bonds.

In addition, a debt issue may have provisions for early debt retirement, principal repayment, or refinancing of the issue. The debt contract also includes a promissory note that outlines the amount of funds borrowed and the financial terms. Several examples follow.

a. Debt (Bonds and Term Loans) Indentures and Covenants

An indenture is a legal document that outlines the rights and obligations of the borrower (or bond issuer) and lender (or bondholder). It is a contract between the company and the bondholders or lenders that includes various restrictive covenants that impose constraints on the actions of the company's management. Covenants may be negative (i.e., actions the company cannot take, such as the double pledging of collateral) or affirmative (i.e., actions the company must take, such as providing regular financial statements or maintaining certain financial ratios). Covenants may also include change-of-control and most-favored-nation clauses[14] that provide the buyer/lender relief in certain circumstances.

13. *ASC* refers to the Financial Accounting Standards Board's (FASB's) Accounting Standards Codification (ASC) guidelines in the United States, and there are comparable guidelines in other countries, as discussed in Chapter 18, Financial Accounting and Reporting.
14. A most-favored-nation (MFN) covenant typically states that the bond issuer cannot offer another buyer better terms before offering those terms or better terms to the first buyer. For example, a bond or loan covenant may have an MFN clause that says that the interest rate on the existing bond or loan will be increased so that it is not less than 25 basis points lower than the interest rate on any new bonds that may be issued.

The purpose of the document is to protect lenders (and bondholders) from actions by a company's management that would heighten the risk to lenders or increase the value for equity holders or other stakeholders at the expense of the lenders. Violation of an indenture agreement is usually sufficient grounds for lenders to make the debt immediately due and payable, which may force a company into bankruptcy. And in the United States, the SEC must approve indenture agreements in public offerings and ensure that all indenture provisions are met before allowing a company to sell new securities to the general public.

Typical covenants outline:

- The assets involved
- The right of an organization to issue additional bonds
- The use of second or junior mortgages
- Sinking fund requirements[15]
- Reporting requirements
- Restrictions involving key financial ratios and liquidity
- Prepayment terms
- Restrictions on dividend policy

b. Representations and Warranties

Representations and warranties are the existing conditions at the time when the loan agreement is executed, as attested to by the borrower. Such conditions generally include:

- Affirmation of the valid, legal existence of the borrowing company
- A resolution by the borrower's board of directors authorizing the borrowing
- The authority of the corporate officers signing the documents
- The borrower's confirmation of compliance with all applicable regulations
- An indemnity protecting the lender from environmental liabilities
- Representation that the execution of the loan agreement does not violate or conflict with the charter or bylaws of the borrower, or any other loan agreements to which the borrower is a party

c. Events of Default

An event of default may occur if a borrower breaches or violates any term or condition under a debt agreement. Examples include:

- Nonpayment of interest or principal when due
- A material adverse change in the borrower's condition
- Violation of a specified covenant
- Incorrect, or misrepresentation of, representations or warranties

15. Sinking funds are arrangements for the orderly repayment of bond principal and are covered later in this chapter.

The characteristics of events of default include cure periods, remedies, and waivers of default:

- **Cure periods,** often specified in the agreement, are periods of time in which an event of default may be corrected before the lender may pursue default remedies.
- **Remedies** available to a lender normally include an acceleration of all principal and interest on the debt when a default occurs.
- **Waivers of default** may be given at the lender's discretion, typically for a fee or change in terms.

d. Material Adverse Change (MAC) Clause

A MAC clause lets a lender refuse funding or declare a borrower to be in default, even if all agreements are in full compliance, if the lender believes a material adverse change has occurred in the borrower's condition. Examples of material adverse changes that might trigger a MAC clause could include changes in laws or regulations that have a significant negative impact on the borrower or the loss of a borrower's primary customer. MAC clauses are often used as a way to renegotiate the terms of an agreement when something negative happens, rather than being used to entirely cancel the agreement.

e. Call and Put Provisions

Call provisions give the issuing entity the right to call in a bond or other issue for redemption prior to the original maturity. As compensation to investors for early redemption, a call premium is generally paid when a bond is called. The call premium usually is set on a sliding scale, with larger premiums above par required the earlier an issue is called.

The call privilege is valuable to a company because it allows redemption of a bond issue if interest rates fall or if excess cash becomes available and refinancing becomes an attractive option. As a result, bonds with call provisions typically require a higher coupon rate than noncallable bonds of similar size, duration, and quality in order to attract investors. The primary downside to the investor is that if interest rates fall and the bond is called, then the investor is forced to reinvest the call proceeds at a lower rate.

The counterpart of a call provision is a put provision that allows the holder of the debt to force the issuer to repurchase the debt at specified dates. The put provision generally provides that the debt will be redeemed at par, creating a floor price for the debt and providing greater security for the holder. Bonds with put provisions typically trade at a premium (a higher price) on the secondary market to bonds that lack such a provision.

f. Sinking Funds

The usual format for bond issues is for the borrower to pay interest only (i.e., coupon payments) for the life of the bond and then repay the principal (i.e., par or face value) at maturity. In other words, most bonds are not amortized. This means the borrower must plan to make a large lump sum payment at the issue's maturity. (This can be contrasted with term loans, which may require amortization, or repayment of principal over the life of the loan.)

Typically, sinking fund provisions in the indenture agreement require companies to call, or repurchase on the open market, a portion of the outstanding bond issue each year. In essence, this amortizes the bond's issue over its life. Other types of sinking funds require a company to make payments into a trust account, which either repurchases bonds on the open market or amasses a lump sum for retirement of the bonds at maturity.

The existence of some type of sinking fund arrangement, as specified in the bond indenture agreement, generally increases the safety of the bonds and lowers the required interest rate.

g. Refinancing

Refinancing of bonds is often done following periods of high interest rates. During high interest rate periods, many entities that must issue bonds attach call provisions that allow the bonds to be redeemed prior to maturity. When interest rates fall, companies issue new bonds at a lower interest rate and use the proceeds to retire the older, higher interest bonds. The primary purpose of these operations is to take advantage of falling interest rates and reduce a company's overall cost of debt. Loan agreements sometimes include what is known as a "make whole" provision, which requires the borrower to make an additional payment based on the net present value of the future debt payments to protect the lender's anticipated profit on the original deal.

h. Defeasance of Debt

Defeasance removes debt from an organization's balance sheet without actually retiring the debt issue. In this arrangement, the borrower places sufficient funds in escrow, usually in government securities, to pay for interest and principal on the debt issue. Because control of both the debt and escrow funds is relinquished, and payment and retirement of the debt issue is now guaranteed, this debt and the related securities can be removed from the balance sheet and do not need to be considered in relation to any restrictive covenants the organization may have regarding debt.

i. Promissory Note

The legal portion of the debt contract is typically referred to as the *promissory note*, which is an unconditional promise to pay a specified amount plus interest at a defined rate either on demand or on a certain date. A promissory note can be issued for each individual borrowing or for a total line amount against which multiple borrowings exist. A master note is a type of promissory note used to simplify the paperwork connected with loans that have multiple advanced features, such as lines of credit and revolvers.[16] A company signs one comprehensive promissory note for the total amount of the line of credit. Any loans or repayments under the note are covered by the terms of the master note.

j. Collateral

Assets used as security for the loan or bond issue are called *collateral*. They may include physical assets (e.g., plant, equipment, and inventory) or financial assets (e.g., receivables and marketable securities). The condition of the assets must be monitored, their value must be determined (usually through appraisal), and in the case of physical assets, insurance may be required.

k. Liens

In most types of secured lending, the lender has a lien or legal claim on the assets used as collateral in the event it cannot take physical possession of the assets. This may be in the form of a mortgage for larger assets or a blanket lien against inventory and receivables. If the borrower defaults on the loan or bond issue, the lender can seize the assets in lieu of repayment. To ensure these claims are valid and enforceable, the lender must generally follow a legal process

16. Revolvers, or revolving credit agreements, are covered in Chapter 11, Short-Term Investing and Borrowing.

to establish the claim by filing notice with the appropriate governmental agency. These items perfect the lien and make it enforceable in a court of law. Lenders often perform a lien search on a potential borrower to determine whether the assets being offered as collateral are pledged already to some other creditor.

B. Other Factors in Using Debt as a Source of Capital

The following section discusses various other factors that influence a company's decisions regarding debt as a source of capital.

1. CREDIT ENHANCEMENTS

A credit enhancement can be used as part of a borrowing arrangement or debt securities issue to improve the overall credit rating on the loan or issue. Through credit enhancement, the lender is provided with reassurance that the borrower will honor the obligation, through additional collateral, insurance, or a third-party guarantee. Credit enhancement reduces credit/default risk of a debt, thereby increasing the overall credit rating and lowering interest rates. While the most common forms of credit enhancement are various forms of guarantees (discussed below), the enhancement may also be in the form of a standby letter of credit or backup line of credit issued by a financial institution (typically used in commercial paper issues as discussed in Chapter 11, Short-Term Investing and Borrowing).

2. GUARANTEES

When a subsidiary of a larger company borrows funds or issues bonds, lenders may require that the parent corporation (or sister subsidiary, supplier, customer, or other entity) provide a guarantee of principal for the arrangement. (In some cases, a subsidiary may provide a guarantee for the parent.) This requirement allows lenders recourse to the parent company (or guaranteeing party) to obtain payment in the event the subsidiary is in default. There are several levels of guarantees that the parent corporation or others (i.e., the guarantee party) can make regarding the degree of protection offered to a lender:

- **Full Guarantee:** The guarantee party fully guarantees any borrowing arrangement by the subsidiary and agrees to take over the loan if the subsidiary fails to make timely payments.
- **Specific-Project Guarantee:** The guarantee party guarantees only loans relating to specific projects of the subsidiary, rather than all loans.
- **Guarantee of Payment or Collection:** The guarantee party guarantees to make payment on the loan or collect payment from the subsidiary, but only if the subsidiary formally defaults on the loan. This agreement usually requires the lender to initiate default proceedings on the subsidiary and initiate collection efforts before the parent becomes involved.
- **Comfort Letter:** A comfort letter is a letter from another party stating actions that it will or will not take on behalf of the borrower. This type of agreement is not legally enforceable.

- **Performance Guarantee:** In some cases, the lender may ask for specific performance guarantees relative to the assets being financed. Under a full guarantee, the parent fully guarantees performance by the subsidiary. Under a best-efforts guarantee, the parent agrees to use its best efforts to persuade the subsidiary to perform, but it does not guarantee subsidiary performance.
- **Personal Guarantee:** In some cases, especially for smaller, privately held companies, the lender may require a personal guarantee on the part of the owner or other principals in the business before granting a loan.

3. BOND/CREDIT RATINGS

Bond issues and other long-term debt are assigned quality ratings that reflect the default probability of the company issuing debt. Each issue is rated independently by one or more of the accredited rating agencies. There are several considerations related to ratings to think about. The first consideration is the rating criteria used by the agency. Ratings generally are based on both qualitative and quantitative factors. Given the complexity of most large companies, there is no precise mathematical formula that analysts can use to determine the rating; instead, many factors must be taken into account.

The second consideration is the importance of the ratings to both investors and the issuer's management. Many charters restrict institutional investors to buying investment-grade bonds or better, and these investors make up the bulk of the bond market. Also, an organization's bond rating is considered a direct measure of the risk of the related securities and impacts an organization's cost of capital (i.e., the rating sets the pricing—the higher the rating, the lower the cost of borrowing).

The third consideration relates to changes in ratings. Rating agencies review outstanding debt periodically and may upgrade or downgrade an issue based on changes in either an issuer or the general economic environment. Companies or government entities with downgraded ratings have a more difficult time raising additional capital in the market and have to pay a higher price for bonds issued or other debt incurred.

The topic of rating agencies and their bond and credit ratings is covered in more detail in Chapter 11, Short-Term Investing and Borrowing.

4. MATURITY MATCHING

Maturity matching involves matching the life of a debt issue to the life of any assets being financed. Generally, companies try to match maturities of debt issues and assets wherever possible to reduce a company's overall risk. The primary risk from a maturity mismatch usually results from long-term assets being funded with short-term sources. Under this scenario, the short-term debt must continually be rolled over to provide an ongoing funding source. This exposes the organization to the chance that interest rates will increase, making the cost of debt more expensive, or that the debt cannot be refinanced at all. Many companies will also follow a practice of "laddering" securities so that maturity dates of a company's debt obligations are staggered and the company is not faced with a large amount of bonds or other debt that comes due at the same time.

5. EFFECTS OF INTEREST RATE LEVELS AND FORECASTS

The general level of interest rates and economic activity impacts both the use and cost of debt for companies. Also, the forecast of future interest rates impacts both the type of capital raised by a company and the provisions that may be attached to capital issues. Organizations issuing debt must consider the issue of "flight to quality" whenever financial market conditions decline. In these times, investors move toward safe or quality investments; hence, the yield spread between high- and low-risk investments typically increases significantly. In good financial markets, the spread between high- and low-risk investments may be much smaller.[17]

6. AVAILABILITY OF COLLATERAL

Companies with large (currently unencumbered) asset bases that can be used as collateral typically borrow at lower rates than companies of the same credit quality and rating that do not have collateral. Companies with lower risk profiles have the financial strength to borrow on an unsecured basis and obtain funds at lower rates than companies and industries that are more prone to default and that therefore must resort to secured borrowing to obtain funds.

IV. EQUITY (STOCK) SECURITIES

The equity market represents the ownership of publicly owned corporations (e.g., stocks and similar securities) that are traded throughout the world, consisting of both primary and secondary markets. The market for equity securities (e.g., stocks) is truly global in nature and changes constantly as the world's exchanges continually form new alignments with each other. Many stocks are cross-listed on multiple exchanges, increasing both the availability of stock for investors and access to the markets for corporations raising funds. A large number of the equity markets have consolidated and integrated due to the formation of the European Union and market alliances.

Another trend in global equity markets is that of privatization, where government-owned assets are sold to private investors or groups. The primary rationale behind this trend is to develop capital markets, widen share ownership, raise money for the government, and change corporate governance.

A. Common Stock

Common stock represents ownership in a company. The management of a company acts as an agent for stockholders to protect their interests. Common equity usually represents a significant portion of a publicly traded company's capital base.

1. BALANCE SHEET ACCOUNTS AND DEFINITIONS

Treasury professionals must be aware of three key accounting terms relating to common stock: par value, retained earnings, and additional paid-in capital (APIC). The total amount of stockholders' equity is the sum of these accounts. It is important to realize that these accounts represent only the historical accounting value of the equity and not the current market value.

17. This movement away from riskier securities in times of economic challenge is often referred to as a *flight to quality* or a *flight to liquidity*.

The three accounting terms are defined as follows:

- **Par Value:** Par value is an arbitrary amount (usually stated in the corporate charter) that indicates the minimum amount stockholders have put up (or must put up) in the event of bankruptcy. For many publicly traded companies, this is $1 per share or $0 (no par value).
- **Retained Earnings:** This balance sheet account represents the accumulated net earnings of a corporation since its inception, less dividends paid to stockholders. This is part of the stockholders' equity and is an accounting of the money reinvested in a company in lieu of dividends paid out. It is important to understand that retained earnings are recorded as an accounting entry in the equity section of the balance sheet to reflect profits that have been invested in assets. However, they are not an available pool of funds.
- **Additional Paid-in Capital (APIC):** This account reflects the difference at the time of issue between the par value and the issuance price (less underwriting costs) of any new stock sold by a company. For example, if a company were to sell a new issue of stock with a par value of $1 and the company nets $25 per share, then a $1 per-share increase would be shown in the par value account and a $24 per-share increase would be shown in the APIC account.

In addition to the previous items, three other terms are relevant to the stockholders' equity account:

- **Book Value per Share:** This term is defined as total common stockholders' equity divided by the number of shares outstanding.
- **Market Value per Share:** This item is defined as the current price at which a share of stock is traded. Though this is not technically part of the accounting statements, it is often included in reports issued by a company and various financial reporting services.
- **Treasury Stock:** This term is defined as stock issued by a company and later reacquired. It may be held in the company's treasury indefinitely, reissued to the public, or retired. Treasury stock receives no dividends and does not carry voting power while held by the company. It is considered issued, but not outstanding; therefore, it is deducted from any capital calculations. Some jurisdictions do not permit treasury stock, and any stock reacquired by the company is considered automatically retired.

2. TYPES OF COMMON STOCK

Companies typically have only one class of common stock, but some firms issue multiple classes oriented toward the preferences of different types of investors. Classified stock is typically referred to as *Class A* or *Class B*, but these terms have no standard meaning; rather, they are specific to each company. Generally, the different classes of stock may limit voting privileges, dividends, and/or resales.

Different classes of stock may be issued to differentiate returns for various pieces (i.e., divisions) of a large, diversified company. Large, multinational corporations often issue stock in this manner to offer nondiversified investments to certain classes of stockholders.

Tracking stock is a separate stock created by a parent company to track the financial progress of a particular piece of business. Despite being part of a publicly traded entity, tracking stocks trade under unique ticker symbols. These stocks are meant to create opportunities for investors to buy into a fast-growing unit without investing in the whole company. The revenues and expenses of the segment of the company being tracked are extracted from the company's financial statements and are linked to the tracking stock for valuation purposes. However, tracking stocks do not provide stockholders with ownership in the parent company, nor do they include voting rights.

Tracking stocks are also used to create a security that mirrors some key index in the market. A popular example of this type of stock is the SPDR,[18] or Spider (SPY), which is an exchange-traded fund (ETF) that mirrors the returns of the S&P 500 index. Another example is the FXI (iShares China Large-Cap ETF), which mirrors the equity market in China (FTSE China 25).

Institutional investors (also referred to as *qualified institutional buyers* [*QIBs*] or *qualified institutional investors* [*QIIs*] and discussed earlier in this chapter) own about 70% of all common stock. Brokerage firms use different criteria for classifying institutional investors, but a typical list would include:

- Financial institutions (e.g., banks)
- Insurance companies
- Pension funds
- Registered investment companies or advisors (e.g., an individual or mutual fund with total assets of at least $100 million)

B. Preferred Stock

Preferred stock is equity, but it is different from common stock in terms of stockholder rights and its dividend payment streams. Preferred stock normally does not have voting rights. The general purpose is to raise capital through the issue of new equity while still maintaining control of a company. In terms of cash flows, it is more like debt than equity because of the fixed dividend payments. Unlike with debt, where missing interest payments can trigger loan covenants and even bankruptcy, a company does not risk bankruptcy by missing a preferred stock dividend. Another difference is that dividend payments on preferred stock do not have the tax deductibility feature that interest payments on debt do; therefore, the cost is generally much higher than that of a similar debt issue.

1. MAJOR PROVISIONS OF PREFERRED STOCK ISSUES

Preferred stockholders have priority claim on both earnings and assets before the common stockholders (but after debt holders). They are paid the specified, preferred stock dividend in full before any dividend may be paid to common stockholders. Preferred stock always has a par value. The dividend is fixed by establishing it as a percentage of the par value, and this dividend must be paid if the company has sufficient earnings to pay it. For example, if a $100 par value preferred stock certificate states that the dividend is 6% of par, then the annual dividend is fixed at $6.

Most preferred stock accumulates dividends in arrears. If a company has not paid a preferred dividend on one or more scheduled dividend payment dates, it must pay these dividends and the current dividend before it can pay any dividend to common stockholders. Many issues of preferred stock have a provision that grants voting rights and/or the right to elect a representative to the board of directors if a specified sequence of dividends is missed. The intent is to give preferred stockholders a voice in board deliberations.

18. SPDR is an acronym for *S&P's depositary receipt*.

Some preferred stock issues may be convertible into either common stock or debt under certain conditions. Either of these features offers more flexibility to the issuer of the preferred stock, as well as a unique investment opportunity to purchasers. In recent years, many new provisions have been offered to help make preferred stock more attractive to investors. These include:

- Voting rights under certain conditions
- Participation in earnings if they exceed a certain level
- Sinking funds to redeem preferred stock
- Maturity dates
- Exchange or call provisions

2. EVALUATION OF PREFERRED STOCK

From the corporate issuer's viewpoint, the main advantage of issuing preferred stock is that a company can lock in financing costs and potentially leverage the return to common stockholders due to the fixed nature of the dividends. With preferred stock, a company accomplishes this without increasing the company's default risk. Also, large portions of preferred stock issues are private issues to institutional investors. This usually means substantially lower flotation costs[19] and less stringent disclosure requirements for the issue.

From the investor's perspective, preferred stock provides a steadier and more assured income than common stock, though the pricing may be sensitive to interest rate movements, because of its similarities to debt. Also, for most US corporate holders of preferred stock, 70% of the dividend income may be excluded from federal income tax. This makes preferred stock especially attractive to institutional investors.

3. SOME PARTICULAR USES OF PREFERRED STOCK

Many companies have found the unique features of preferred stock to be an advantageous way to raise capital in certain circumstances. Financial institutions have been heavy issuers of preferred stock due to the fact that most regulatory authorities count preferred stock as regulatory capital, which is a big plus for the financial institution. In addition, most rating agencies look favorably on the use of preferred stock. Other heavy users of preferred stock financing are companies that are either young/high growth or in financial distress. In both cases, the tax advantages to debt financing are minimal to nonexistent. Thus, the cost differential between debt and preferred stock is very small. When the equity nature of preferred stock is taken into account, this form of financing can be very attractive to these users.

C. Hybrid Securities

Hybrid securities are generally created by combining the elements of two or more different types of securities into one. Typically, a hybrid will behave like a fixed-income security (bond) under certain circumstances and an equity security (stock) under other circumstances. The most common of these securities are convertibles and warrants.

1. CONVERTIBLES

Convertible securities are usually bonds or preferred stock that may be exchangeable at the holder's or issuer's option for a company's common stock under certain terms and conditions, and at a pre-stated price. The conversion does not provide any new capital for a company. Rather, it simply converts existing debt or preferred stock into common equity. The conversion ratio states the number of stock shares that one bond may be converted to if the owner chooses. The maturity value of the bond and the conversion ratio determine the issue's conversion price. For example, a $1,000 par

19. Flotation costs are those costs related to the issuance of a security by an organization. They are discussed in the section on cost of capital in Chapter 20, Financial Decisions and Management.

value bond with a conversion ratio of 20 (i.e., 20 shares of common stock per bond) implies a stock conversion price of $50 (i.e., $1,000 divided by 20 shares).

Most convertibles contain clauses that protect against dilution of value due to stock splits, stock dividends, or reduced stock prices. The typical provision states that if new common stock is sold at a price below the conversion price, then the conversion ratio must be raised (thus, the conversion price lowered) to the issue price of the new stock.

In the example above, if there was a split, then the conversion ratio has to increase to keep the value of the holdings equal. Before the split the value was $1,000. Due to the split, the conversion ratio has to be raised to 40 shares per bond so that the value remains $1,000 (the conversion price is now $25).

Convertibles are advantageous for the issuer in that they offer a firm the chance to sell debt with lower interest rates and fewer restrictive covenants in exchange for a chance for the investor to participate in potential capital gains as a company's value increases.

Convertibles also may have significant disadvantages for the issuer:

- If a company's stock price increases significantly during the convertible's life, then the company may have been better off issuing regular debt than refunding the debt with a new stock issue.
- If the convertible issue has a low coupon rate, then that rate is lost if the holders convert the bonds into stock.
- If stock prices do not rise, then a company may be locked into the debt issue, although it is typically at a lower coupon rate than regular debt.

2. WARRANTS (BONDS WITH AN EQUITY KICKER)

Warrants are company-issued options that give the warrant's owner the right to buy a stated number of shares of the company's stock at a specified price for a specified period of time. Warrants often are listed on major exchanges and trade like options.

Unlike convertibles, warrants issued with bonds represent potential additional equity capital for the issuing company. Most warrants are detachable, meaning they can be traded separately from the bond. If these warrants are exercised, then the low-coupon bond issue remains outstanding. Therefore, the warrants bring additional funds into a company while keeping debt costs low. Warrants are used extensively by small, rapidly growing companies as "sweeteners" when selling either debt or preferred stock. A bond with warrants has some characteristics of debt and equity, thus creating a hybrid security (sometimes called a *bond with an equity kicker*) that gives a company the ability to expand its mix of securities and appeal to a broader group of investors.

Warrants may dilute the value of the current stockholders' equity and the earnings per share (EPS). Some companies report a fully diluted EPS figure, which assumes that all outstanding warrants were exercised. The SEC requires that the disclosure of EPS includes:

- Information on the capital structure
- Explanation of the EPS computation
- Identification of common-stock equivalents (including convertibles, rights, and warrants)
- The number of shares converted
- Assumptions made

D. Depositary Receipts (DRs)

In order to expand the holdings of stock on a global basis, many stock exchanges offer different types of DRs. Typically equity securities, DRs are negotiable financial instruments that trade on a local exchange but actually represent stock ownership in a foreign, publicly listed company. One of the most common DRs is the American depositary receipt (ADR), which allows US investors to effectively own stocks traded on foreign exchanges. These securities are known as *global depositary receipts (GDRs)* outside the United States.

Regardless of where the original company is located, the issuing company must meet all of the requirements of the exchanges and regulatory authorities of the country where the DR is traded. It is also possible for a previously unlisted company to conduct an IPO via the DR markets, either through an exchange listing or on an OTC basis.

The DR markets offer some significant benefits, especially for issuers in countries with limited financial markets:

- They help increase global trade, including transaction volumes on both local and foreign markets.
- They offer greater exposure and the opportunity to raise capital on a global basis to companies in smaller countries.
- They help reduce market inefficiencies, especially in emerging markets, by allowing for easier global investment in those emerging markets.

V. SUMMARY

While much of the emphasis in treasury management tends to be on short-term debt and investments, capital markets are an important part of the financial infrastructure and have direct and indirect impacts on many of the decisions a treasury professional has to make.

This chapter discussed the major participants in capital markets, including issuers, who are borrowing money or selling equity; investors, who are in effect lending money or buying equity in companies; broker-dealers, who serve as middlemen in the transactions and facilitate the interaction between issuers and investors; and regulators, who set the rules and oversee the operations of the various markets.

Capital markets are typically subdivided into debt and equities. The major characteristics of each of these types of securities were also introduced. Further discussion of how to manage capital investments is provided in Chapter 12, Long-Term and Capital Investments.

APPENDIX 6.1: LISTING OF THE WORLD'S TOP 10 STOCK EXCHANGES[20]

(Ranked by Domestic Market Capitalization in 2012)

Rank	Exchange Name	Country	Domestic Market Cap (in $ Billions)
1	NYSE Euronext (US)	United States	14,086
2	NASDAQ OMX (US)	United States	4,582
3	Tokyo Stock Exchange Group	Japan	3,479
4	London Stock Exchange Group	United Kingdom	3,397
5	NYSE Euronext (Europe)	Belgium, France, The Netherlands, and Portugal	2,832
6	Hong Kong Exchanges	Hong Kong	2,832
7	Shanghai Stock Exchange	China	2,547
8	TMX Group	Canada	2,059
9	Deutsche Börse	Germany	1,486
10	Australian Securities Exchange	Australia	1,387

20. From "2012 WFE Market Highlights," published by World Federation of Exchanges, January 22, 2013 (http://www.world-exchanges.org/insight/reports/wfe-publishes-2012-global-market-highlights).

TEST YOUR UNDERSTANDING: CHAPTER 6

Answers are on pages 661–665.

1. What are the two basic segments of the capital markets?
2. Who are the key participants in the capital markets?
3. List the different issuers of securities in the capital markets.
4. What is the difference between retail and institutional investors?
5. Discuss the concept of primary markets versus secondary markets.
6. What is a QIB?
7. What are the principal benefits of organized securities exchanges?
8. What are the purposes of a bond indenture?
9. What are sovereign bonds?
10. What are Eurobonds?
11. What are floating-rate securities?
12. What are representations and warranties?
13. What is a MAC clause?
14. What is a loan guarantee?
15. Define par value, retained earnings, and additional paid-in capital.
16. What is preferred stock?
17. What are convertible securities?
18. What are depositary receipts?

CHAPTER 7

Relationship Management and Vendor Selection

I. INTRODUCTION

II. RELATIONSHIP MANAGEMENT

A. Number of Bank Relationships

B. Documentation

C. Performance Measurement and Evaluation

III. VENDOR SELECTION AND THE REQUEST FOR PROPOSAL (RFP) PROCESS

A. Getting Started

B. RFP Design

C. RFP Administration

IV. BANK COMPENSATION PRACTICES

A. Billing for Bank Services

B. Value Dating

C. Account Analysis in the US Commercial Banking System

D. Comparing and Monitoring Costs among Financial Services Providers

V. ASSESSING SERVICE PROVIDER RISK

A. Assessing Operational Risk for Service Providers

B. Assessing Financial Services Provider (FSP) Risk

C. Sovereign and Political Risk

D. Managing Confidential Information and Conflicts of Interest

E. Legal and Ethical Issues

VI. SUMMARY

APPENDIX 7.1 SAMPLE BANK SCORECARD

APPENDIX 7.2: RFP ACTIVITY INFORMATION

APPENDIX 7.3 SAMPLE UNIFORM BANK PERFORMANCE REPORT (UBPR)

I. INTRODUCTION

Treasury professionals are often responsible for dealing with a wide variety of vendors, often from around the world. Historically, commercial banks have dominated the marketplace for treasury-related products and services, including technology products such as treasury management systems. Today, however, a wide variety of nonbank financial institutions (FIs) and other vendors also provide treasury-related services. These organizations may be referred to collectively as *financial services providers (FSPs)*.

Given the importance of these vendors to treasury operations and the effort and expense involved in changing vendors, managing vendor relationships is an important part of treasury's responsibilities. And given the ever-increasing pressure to do more with less, getting the right products and services at the right price has never been more important.

This chapter starts by taking a look at managing those relationships and some of the tools that can be used to make the process more effective.

No matter how well vendors are managed, however, there will always be the need to conduct vendor selections, either to replace existing vendors or to add new vendors and capabilities. The second part of this chapter outlines a typical vendor selection process, its essential elements, and the project administration requirements. The approach contains the broad concepts suitable for bank, third-party processing, and technology selection, with some specific sections appropriate for each of these distinct segments.

The remainder of the chapter deals with the issue of bank compensation and managing FSP risk.

II. RELATIONSHIP MANAGEMENT

In most companies, treasury is the focal point for bank relationship management and for vendor management with other financial services providers, such as investment managers and custody services providers. In some organizations, an employee within treasury is assigned primary responsibility for treasury vendor management. In others, oversight of bank relationships rests directly with the treasurer. In either case, relationship management entails many responsibilities ranging from day-to-day communication regarding transaction inquiries and problem resolution to quarterly, semiannual, and/or annual performance evaluations and relationship reviews based on agreed-upon objectives.

Changing vendors, especially global financial services vendors, is a difficult and costly process. It makes sense then to devote time and effort to managing any existing vendor relations. Relationships only work well if both parties involved work at the relationship. But the cost and effort of good vendor management is typically much less than the cost and effort of changing vendors.

There are many similarities between banks and other FSPs, but bank relationships involve a number of unique considerations due to the types of documentation required, the methods of monitoring risk, and the methods of compensation, all of which are discussed later in this chapter.

For anything other than commodity products (products, such as printer paper, that do not vary from vendor to vendor), optimal vendor performance requires an in-depth knowledge on the part of the vendor (more specifically, the relationship manager) of a client's operations and needs. In addition, as previously mentioned, changing service vendors is typically a time-consuming and expensive process. Consequently, effective vendor relationships are long term. Success in every long-term relationship involves mutual accommodation. Factors that increase the mutual benefit and profitability of the relationship are:

- Open and frequent two-way communications
- Regular and timely feedback
- Documentation of expectations of both parties in agreements and legal contracts
- Fairly priced, efficient, and effective financial services/products
- Complete, candid, and timely disclosure of information by both parties

A. Number of Bank Relationships

The treasurer generally determines how many bank relationships are needed or desired for the organization's particular operation. Decision factors include the existence of multi-country operations, the costs of maintaining multiple relationships, the risk of having a "single point of failure" (concentration risk), the relative strengths and capabilities of each bank, and the organization's credit needs. Companies with a complex, over-the-counter/field bank collection and concentration system involving multiple geographies may have to deal with a large number of small FIs to obtain appropriate geographic coverage. Multinational companies may need to have multiple bank relationships to provide product and service coverage in all the countries where the company has a presence.

The types, sophistication, and geographic location of services needed by a company often dictate multiple bank relationships. Maintaining secondary bank relationships lets the treasury professional shift accounts and services if a significant problem develops with a primary provider. Allocating business to specific banks is a key part of managing the relationships. Financial services providers are fairly sophisticated in understanding what percentage of a client's business they have (often referred to as "share of wallet") and will often ask for more business if they feel they are not being given an appropriate share. It is also often worth asking specific vendors which services they would like to provide, as different vendors may be more interested in specific pieces of business.

Companies with multiple bank relationships often designate one bank as the primary, or lead, institution. While this is more common with credit relationships, some companies follow the same practice with operating services. There may be different lead institutions for credit and other services. While many companies establish multiple relationships to ensure that they have adequate credit facilities, a company's primary credit bank often serves in a lead role by selling excess credit exposure to other institutions or by acting as an agent for loan syndication.

There are internal and external costs associated with each bank relationship. These costs create the incentive for a company to optimize the number of bank relationships it maintains. In addition, banks have developed more sophisticated methods for measuring relationship profitability, resulting in lower costs for a company that obtains multiple services from one institution.

For example, the pricing of bank loans is often based on interdependent factors such as:

- Cost of funds
- Credit rating

- Total loans committed and outstanding
- Service fees
- Deposit balances maintained
- Range of other services used (e.g., foreign currency or derivatives trading)
- Loan maturity
- Revenue size and importance of the overall relationship to the lending institution
- Competition

Likewise, the pricing of depository and cash management services is based on factors such as:

- Transaction volumes
- Customization
- Exception-handling requirements
- Cost of providing the service
- Operational overhead
- Deposit balances maintained
- Value of other services used (e.g., global trade services, letters of credit, and custody services)
- Credit relationship
- Revenue size and importance of the overall relationship to the FI

B. Documentation

Among the important documents integral to an FI relationship are service agreements, account resolutions, signature cards, articles of incorporation from the customer, and contracts for depository accounts. The complexity and number of documents required typically increases as the number of countries involved increases. For example, FIs in many European countries will require a statement of beneficial interest.[1] The complexity of and the need to frequently update documentation has led to the development of eBAM (electronic bank account management), which is discussed in Chapter 14, Information Technology in Treasury.

The remainder of this section deals specifically with operational documentation needed for current accounts. The components of credit agreements are discussed in Chapter 11, Short-Term Investing and Borrowing.

1. ACCOUNT RESOLUTIONS

An account resolution, usually made at the board of directors' level, is the basic account or service authorization empowering a representative of the business to enter into

1. *Beneficial interest or ownership* refers to control over funds or accounts and is separate from signature authority or legal title. It recognizes that the entity in whose name an account is opened with a bank is not necessarily the person who ultimately controls the funds or who is ultimately entitled to the funds. Many countries require a statement of beneficial interest whenever a bank account is opened.

agreements for financial services. The resolution specifies the functions that can be performed by specific individuals or job titles, the people authorized to open and close accounts, and the entire scope and limitations of the relationship.

The account resolution may be general or specific with regard to actions that the FI may take on behalf of the company. It can be a standard form used by FIs to serve all commercial customers or it can be customized for a given company. Some companies have developed their own standard resolutions for use with all FIs, although a bank's acceptance of a company's resolution is subject to negotiation.

In an effort to simplify and reduce the documentation needed to manage an operating relationship, many banks now use a master agreement that spells out overall operating requirements and authorizes the FI to operate on behalf of the company signing the agreement. Once the master agreement is in place, additional accounts or services are covered by separate operating agreements that are addenda to the existing master agreement.

2. SIGNATURE CARDS AND SERVICE AGREEMENTS

Banks require companies to furnish signatures of authorized signers (or specimens of both facsimile and computerized signatures) for all accounts. In conjunction with any signature card, FIs typically provide a standardized set of service agreements to companies when relationships are established and accounts are opened. Service agreements are contracts—legal documents that describe the requirements and expectations of both the purchaser and provider of a specific service or services. There may be a master service agreement relating to the overall relationship and then separate service agreements for each specific service area (e.g., deposit accounts, card services, and lockboxes). These documents provide the terms and conditions of the account—many of which can be negotiated as with any other contract—as well as the responsibilities of the bank and the account holders in the maintenance of accounts. The elements of a service agreement often include:

- Compensation policies, including pricing, method of payment, payment frequency, and excess/deficit balance arrangements
- Contract length and adjustments
- Information on funds availability
- Time frames during which errors must be reported
- A bank's right of offset against accounts resulting from fees owed to it
- Liability clauses defining responsibilities for specified risks
- Other terms and conditions of the relationship

Agreement terms are amended from time to time by the bank, and notice usually is distributed with account statements and/or posted to the bank's website. Depending upon the countries in which the actual accounts are domiciled, the FI may also require incumbency certificates (documents used to confirm the identity of the signing officers of a corporation).

3. SERVICE LEVEL AGREEMENTS (SLAS)

An SLA may be a separate document or part of the service agreement. The SLA is primarily concerned with the definition of the specific services being provided and the operating metrics that can be used to measure the level of service being provided. SLAs also typically include a description of any penalties for failure to comply with the requirements of the agreement. The elements of an SLA often include:

- Operational policies and procedures (including the detailed processing requirements for each service; a list of required information and related reports; a list of individuals authorized to make changes; and a description of the issue escalation and resolution process)
- Performance standards and calculations that define agreed-upon levels of service performance and quality

4. "KNOW YOUR CUSTOMER" (KYC) AND STATEMENTS OF BENEFICIAL OWNERSHIP

Largely in response to money laundering and other related financial crimes, most countries have significantly strengthened their requirements around new bank relationships and the opening of bank accounts. These activities go under the general title of *"know your customer"* (or *KYC*) and require financial institutions to perform varying amounts of due diligence to determine the legitimacy of any new customers, as well as the identities of the individuals who have access or control over the funds in those accounts. Collectively, these due diligence efforts are usually referred to as *customer identification programs,* or *CIPs*. The nature and extent of the CIP may vary by country but will typically require a firm to provide copies of its articles of incorporation and identification of all signers on any bank accounts—through provision of copies (often certified) of driver's licenses or passports, as well as formal statements of beneficial ownership. A statement of beneficial ownership identifies the individuals that actually own or control a given bank account, which may be different from the name or names on the account.

C. Performance Measurement and Evaluation

Service quality is crucial to a company's relationship with any provider. A company must determine its performance expectations clearly with regard to quality standards. These expectations should be based on the service levels stipulated in its agreements with the vendor, as discussed above and documented in SLAs. These expectations should also have been detailed in the original request for proposal (RFP) process that was used to select the service provider.

Two of the most common types of performance measurement techniques are report cards, also referred to as *vendor scorecards*, and relationship reviews.

1. VENDOR SCORECARD

A vendor scorecard is a management tool used to measure a vendor's performance in both a qualitative and quantitative method. The primary purpose of a scorecard is to provide a quantitative measure of the service provided and the benefit received, but it also provides feedback for the service provider to better understand how the customer perceives the value/quality/cost of the service(s) provided. In addition, the scorecard provides a tool to measure the relative value of current service relationships and evaluate service providers on those issues that the organization deems to be important. Finally, the scorecard can be used in support of continuous improvement and communication between both parties, and as a way to clarify how well the service provider delivers services and deals with issues. Although treasury is typically the focal point of the scorecard process, it is important to get input and feedback from any other area of the organization that may be affected by the vendor, such as accounting, accounts payable, or accounts receivable.

A sample bank scorecard is provided in Appendix 7.1.

2. RELATIONSHIP REVIEW

A relationship review is another procedure companies use to assess service levels and provider responsiveness, both quantitatively and qualitatively. Reviews may be formal or informal. Formal reviews typically involve a quarterly, semi-annual, or annual meeting of the senior management representatives from both parties. Informal reviews typically involve weekly or monthly contacts by individuals responsible for day-to-day relationship management. Vendors also often initiate relationship reviews by preparing summaries of services, fees, error rates, and other relationship information, as well as an introduction to new products and services. Relationship reviews enable vendors and companies (clients) to discuss future strategies and needs in true two-way dialogue. The key elements of these discussions need to be the presentation of new ideas and suggestions for process improvements, as well as both the client's and vendor's plans for growth and change. These meetings are an excellent time to discuss current and planned allocation of services, as well as share of wallet.

III. VENDOR SELECTION AND THE REQUEST FOR PROPOSAL (RFP) PROCESS

Purchasing decisions can be driven by anything—drivers can range from basic work requirements (e.g., requests to open accounts for newly formed subsidiaries or the need for a new third-party custodian) to major projects (e.g., migration to a new technology platform) to even more far-reaching relationship issues (e.g., a bank's participation in the company's credit facility or the acquisition of an existing third-party vendor). Over time an ad hoc approach to vendor selection can lead to an unwieldy network of vendors, services, and technology solutions that is inefficient and costly to maintain, particularly if operations are spread across the globe.

When paired with good strategic thinking and design, the request for proposal (RFP) process is an effective tool for acquiring new products and services, including technology solutions. Well-designed RFPs help select the best products and services at fair prices and ensure long-term, mutually rewarding supplier relationships.

A. Getting Started

The discussion that follows assumes that a decision to solicit vendors has already been made and that appropriate budget and internal resources are available for the project. Once that decision has been made, the company needs to determine how it will proceed in identifying potential vendors and selecting the best alternative.

1. IS AN RFP REQUIRED?

RFPs require a lot of work by both the company and the vendors, so it can be tempting to bypass the process altogether, and frankly, RFPs may be overkill in some situations. In some cases, organizations may invite a group of providers to discuss their requirements and recommend solutions. Another approach is the request for information, or RFI, where the company provides a more formal description of its needs and asks selected vendors to provide general information as to how they could meet the company's needs. An additional option is the request for quote, or RFQ. An RFQ is used to invite suppliers into a bidding process on specific products or services. It is similar to an RFP, but it is best suited to products and services that are essentially standardized and/or commoditized, which makes each supplier's quote easily comparable to others. To increase comparability, RFQs often include the specifications of the items/services desired to ensure all the suppliers are bidding on the same item/service. The more detailed the specifications, the more accurate the quote will be and the more comparable it will be among suppliers. All of these approaches are more structured than asking a few peers at other companies what they do and going along with the majority view.

There are circumstances where any of the various approaches may be appropriate, but when selection involves a product or service that is essential to what a company does or how it does it—and especially when services rather than commodities are involved—the formal RFP process is usually worth the time and effort. (See Exhibit 7.1 for a comparison of vendor selection methods.) Many companies require a formal RFP for contracts or purchases over a certain amount. A well-designed RFP will ensure that the company has included the proper set of vendors and given them the information they require to recommend the appropriate products and services. The benefit of the RFP process goes even further by ensuring that these products and services are offered at the best price and that the relationships with all vendors are managed well.

EXHIBIT 7.1 **COMPARISON OF VENDOR SELECTION METHODS**

	Informal Review	**Request for Information (RFI)**	**Request for Quote (RFQ)**	**Request for Proposal (RFP)**
Purpose	Solicit vendors for potential solutions to existing problems	Identify vendors that are willing and able to provide products and services; typically used as a prelude to an RFP or RFQ	Solicit binding price quotes from vendors on comparable products and services	Solicit proposed solutions and proposed pricing from selected vendors
Project Type	Small	Small to large	Commodity purchases of all sizes	Large-scale purchase of products or services
Format	Informal	Structured, with information regarding problem to be addressed	Detailed product/service specifications	Detailed description of company and product/service needs
Expected Result	Suggested solutions	List of potential vendors and their qualifications	Price quote	Vendors' recommended solution(s), capabilities, and proposed pricing
Final Outcome	Change to existing services	Typically, RFP or RFQ; occasionally, contract negotiations	Purchase order	Contract negotiations and implementation

2. THE FIRST STEP

The first step in an RFP project does not involve prospective vendors. The treasury professional needs to develop and articulate a clear understanding of what is driving the decision to update/acquire new products/services or change service providers, and what the desired future state will look like. These drivers are not mutually exclusive and fall into a number of categories:

- **Strategic:**
  - o The company may need to achieve greater vendor diversity in order to reflect a broadening global footprint or reduce the potential risk of a single-vendor relationship.
  - o Acquisitions, mergers, or changes in strategic direction in one or more countries may change the scope of a company's business.
  - o Structural adjustments or realignment, such as the establishment of new holding companies in response to tax or legal initiatives, may drive the need for treasury centers and special liquidity services, such as pooling.
- **Operational:**
  - o New accounts or upgraded services at regional or local levels may be needed in order to accommodate internal process improvements or customer and vendor requirements.
  - o Administrative actions, including consolidating accounting services in a shared services center or upgrading an ERP system, may lead to process changes that justify banking platform improvements (e.g., implementing host-to-host payment processing or SWIFT connectivity).
  - o Geographic expansion of existing businesses and product lines may require banks with branch or partner networks capable of servicing more than the needs of a simple sales office.
  - o Concerns may arise regarding the level of service provided by the vendor, including such issues as frequency of errors and timeliness of reporting.
- **Treasury:**
  - o There may be a need to increase oversight and control globally in response to regulatory requirements (such as SOX or the Foreign Corrupt Practices Act [FCPA] for US companies).
  - o External pressure may demand improved liquidity management through access to internal cash and expanded bank credit facilities.
  - o The opportunity may be available to reduce the cost of treasury services by changing the mix of services purchased and leveraging the scale of the enterprise to obtain the best possible pricing.

Understanding the specific drivers and identifying key objectives allows the company to allocate the internal resources needed in the selection process, involve the necessary stakeholders, and determine the business information requirements.

The RFP process takes a significant amount of resources to do properly, and having a strong project manager to coordinate those resources is helpful. If the appropriate skill sets and resources are not available internally, there are many external consulting firms that provide excellent support in developing and administering an RFP.

3. BUSINESS REQUIREMENTS AND PROJECT PLAN

Determining a meaningful set of business requirements and a plan to meet them is essential because of the resources and time the entire RFP process can require. The business requirements function as a set of objectives, and the plan as the road map to achievement of the objectives. Clarity in both will help, as it is easy to miss deadlines or stray from the objectives. Further, when companies underestimate the amount of time required, they frustrate themselves as the process appears to drag on, and they lose credibility with vendors who are unsure of how to proceed. An external project manager or consulting firm is often helpful in addressing all of these issues.

a. Business Requirements

Business requirements spell out what the organization is trying to do (e.g., acquire a system to help manage treasury operations, find a SWIFT service bureau, or revise the global banking network). They also include the needs of the various stakeholders. In the case of a treasury management system (TMS), IT might require that the system be installed on company servers, treasury might insist that it accommodate a certain number of users globally, and legal might demand that only domestic providers be considered, for security reasons.

Business requirements are sometimes prioritized as *must have, nice to have,* and *neutral.* The requirements-gathering process provides the chance for all stakeholders to provide input—at the beginning when the project planning takes place. Requirements can change in the middle of the project, but project managers are less at the whim of stakeholders when there is a formal document in place.

The following are some representative business requirements for TMS, banking, and services RFPs:

- **TMS:**
  - o Enable visibility over the company's global cash, including daily cash position.
  - o Provide a platform for global cash forecasting.
  - o Facilitate bank account and counterparty management.
  - o Support multiple users in multiple geographies.
  - o Interface with existing systems.
  - o Operate within a software-as-a-service (SaaS) model.
- **Banking:**
  - o Provide in-country accounts with direct links to high- and low-value payment systems.
  - o Match company account needs with the bank's branch structure.
  - o Support the account structure with necessary overdraft and FX facilities.
  - o Meet specific service level and customer service requirements.
- **Third-Party Services:**
  - o Provide needed services, such as investment management and custodial services.
  - o Integrate with existing service partners.

- o Protect confidential employee data.
- o Be licensed to operate in all relevant locations.

b. Issues and Opportunities

The RFP process is typically a good opportunity to identify areas for process improvement, such as eliminating or reducing the use of paper-based products and services. More and more countries use predominantly electronic methods for both collections and payments—with notable exceptions being the United States and Canada—and the RFP is an opportunity to capitalize on this trend. It is important to highlight this within the RFP document itself (e.g., "Checks are currently used in the United Kingdom, but we intend to switch to Bacs in our future banking arrangements").

Another area to consider is leveraging existing corporate systems by centralizing payments through a global or regional hub. Host-to-host file transfer is an excellent way to take advantage of bank capabilities for straight-through processing (STP).[2]

The RFP represents an opportunity go beyond basic requirements and implement a banking structure that introduces improved treasury management techniques.

c. Project Plan Elements

The next step is to develop a project plan. Project plans identify the large and small tasks that make up the project and define completion dates, assigned resources, and task dependencies. Exhibit 7.2 provides an illustrative outline of the major steps and approximate timing for a complex global RFP. Specific projects will differ and smaller projects may require less time.

EXHIBIT 7.2 **RFP PROJECT STEPS**

Element	Time Required
Define objectives and develop project plan	1 week
Assemble project team	2 weeks
Develop business requirements	2 weeks
Obtain relevant transaction/use data	4 weeks
Develop account/systems architecture	2 weeks
Perform vendor scan	2 weeks
Create vendor long list	1 week
Determine RFP format	1 week
Develop RFP questions	1 week
Issue and administer RFP	4–6 weeks
Review and score proposals and pricing	2 weeks
Host vendor presentations	1 week
Select vendor	1 week
Implement project	3–12 months

2. *Straight-through processing* is defined as eliminating all manual intervention so that a particular process is totally electronic from beginning to end.

Keep in mind that the larger the scope of the project, the more time that will be needed to allow for the vendors to respond. Senior executives can be impatient with the process, but shortcuts are not recommended. Global RFPs require that the vendors assemble teams from several regions and business functions, and invest a considerable amount of time developing a thoughtful solution. Given that the organization is asking the vendors to design specific solutions to fit its requirements and will be working with the bank or vendor selected for many years, it is only sensible to give them the time necessary to get it right at the front end. If the organization is not able to invest the time and manage expectations for this type of timeline, then it should consider employing external resources, such as a consulting firm, or reducing the scale of the project.

d. Stakeholders

Treasury RFPs are often initiated by the corporate treasury department, and treasury often provides the project manager for the RFP. There are, however, many other stakeholders involved in a typical treasury RFP. It is important to involve all stakeholders—particularly for complex global projects—so that their expertise and buy-in can be obtained. Major stakeholders may include:

- **Business Operations:** Local or regional business managers from sales, operations, or finance who will be using the services being solicited have the first-line contact with customers and vendors. It is up to them to assist in defining the types of receivable and payable services and account locations needed. They can also provide valuable feedback on how banks and other vendors perform and are perceived in various localities around the world.
- **Tax and Legal:** Legal review of all documents and contracts is always critical. When the RFP is international and involves the movement of funds across borders and between entities, the legal and tax personnel become especially important. They will play an essential role in the initial development of the structure and should be involved in the review of bank proposals. Documentation is a mandatory part of setting up new accounts and services, and the legal department needs to participate in this process.
- **Accounting:** Bank accounts and business processes must be integrated with the company's ERP system, and all banking transactions will ultimately be reflected in the company's books, so it is important that accounting be involved with the project. Reconcilement, cash application, and payment processing are some of the key areas where bank or third-party service selection impacts accounting.
- **Systems:** IT professionals control the ERP system and govern the types of technology within the company, such as SaaS (software as a service) and client/server. They will be critical players in setting up file connectivity with the treasury's partners, such as SWIFT or host-to-host. IT is also an excellent resource in helping with an assessment of a potential vendor's systems and technology. Since IT resources can be quite scarce, it is a good idea to get them involved with the project early so they commit the necessary resources to support treasury.

- **Regulatory Compliance and Internal Audit:** The growing number and complexity of regulatory requirements, especially for multinational companies, requires input from whatever group in the firm has overall compliance responsibilities, such as for OFAC and anti-money laundering compliance requirements (discussed in more detail in Chapter 2, Regulatory and Legal Environment).
- **Supply Chain/Procurement:** This area within the organization plays a growing role in treasury projects, performing due diligence on vendor stability and negotiating contracts.

Involving the stakeholders early helps determine if the necessary resources are available within the company to handle the project internally or if outside resources in areas such as treasury, systems, legal, or tax may be required.

B. RFP Design

There are two basic elements in any RFP design: the substance of the required services and the form in which the RFP is delivered to vendors. The substance of the information required is fairly consistent among all types of RFPs, and it is important to remember that the more complete and accurate the information provided to bidders, the better the options will be for the purchaser.

1. COMPONENTS OF AN RFP

Substance of an RFP can be divided into a number of general components, such as:

- **Company Description:** This general section at the beginning of the RFP is designed to give all participants a common level of background about the company's products, services, and operating structure. Even if bidder organizations know the company well and much information can be obtained on the web, the background description is important, as the RFP will be distributed to many product areas and geographic regions within the bidder organization where the level of familiarity may not be as high. Further, it is important to ensure that each organization is working from the same information and background.
- **RFP Objectives:** The company's specific objectives need to be clearly spelled out. Examples include centralize liquidity in Europe, reduce total number of bank accounts in Asia-Pacific, manage intercompany lending, or provide netting services for a company's worldwide operations.
- **Activity Information:** This section provides vendors with the transaction information they will need to recommend a solution and provide realistic price quotes. If the company will make 10,000 EUR (euro) credits in a given month in Italy, this should be made clear. For TMS RFPs, the company should indicate the volume and types of activities, services, and modules needed, as well as the number of users. This allows the bank or TMS vendor not only to provide a good price but also to suggest the best system and connectivity model given the activity. Additional discussion of activity information specific to banking RFPs is contained in Appendix 7.2.
- **Desired Outcome:** For bank RFPs, the desired account structure should be described and diagrammed, and should be consistent with the activity information provided to the banks. For example, if a global structure for US dollar (USD) liquidity is required, the RFP should indicate the participants by region and include information on their legal statuses. TMS RFPs should provide a similar structure, including the names of the banks for which connectivity will be required.
- **Specific Questions:** Business requirements dictate whether the RFP is divided into sections based on geography (e.g., Europe, Asia-Pacific), function (e.g., technology, customer service), or both. Regardless of how the RFP is sectioned, there should be a short series of questions within each section that fulfill two objectives:

  - o To help differentiate one bidder from another. Asking if a solution will rely primarily on a bank's network of branches or the use of strategic banking partners, or asking whether the proposed solution relies on external vendor technology will help differentiate providers.
  - o To elicit a precise response from the respondent rather than a generic statement. For example, a request to provide specific information on technology initiatives relating to payment products is more useful than a general question on a bank's approach to technology. Similarly, asking if a bank can handle specific transactions such as tax payments or direct debits in a country is preferable to asking whether it has a branch or strategic partner located in that country.

- **Administrative Requirements:** The RFP should provide clear instructions on the required format and timing of the responses as well as any desired references. It should describe the expected decision-making process and selection criteria that will be employed and offer the opportunity for vendors to ask questions regarding the RFP. If technology and the scope of the RFP permit, the company should set up an e-mail address for bidder questions and share all questions—and answers—with the other vendors. It is also important to establish firm guidelines surrounding the supplementary information that can be incorporated in a response. The company wants materials relating to its particular situation and that information is not generally provided in annual reports, product brochures, or videos that the vendor may want to include. Ideally, supplemental information should be limited to no more than three to four pages of diagrams.

2. FORM OF AN RFP

Form has importance because it determines how the RFPs will be received by the vendors and how responses will be compared by the company issuing the RFP. It is relatively easy to prepare a document using a word-processing program and deliver an e-mailed or printed version to vendors. Without more detailed instructions, vendors may respond with a large, bound color proposal document, multiple copies of which are provided to the company by vendors. These can be quite beautiful to look at but extremely difficult to analyze and compare.

There are a number of options when it comes to form. For simple RFPs, a word-processing document inviting a structured response by e-mail may well make sense. As the scale and complexity of the RFP increases, the following possibilities may make more sense:

- Create the RFP as a workbook with separate spreadsheets for the instructions and various question sections. This approach can be very effective because all vendors have access to a spreadsheet program and because this format can both limit the size of the vendor's response and allow it to be easily compared with responses from other bidders. It also has the advantage of keeping most of the RFP in a single file.
- A step up in sophistication would be preparing the RFP as an Adobe Acrobat form. This provides vendors with a familiar format and an RFP document that can easily

be shared with colleagues around the world. The more recent versions of Acrobat enable RFP authors to receive a string of eXtensible markup language (XML) code as the response, to facilitate comparison of bidder submissions. A similar result can be achieved using Google Applications forms.

- At the top end, a company can host the RFP on a secure website maintained by the company or a third party. Vendors are directed to a specific URL (uniform resource locator) where the complete RFP is housed, and answer all questions relating to the RFP within forms on the site. This approach reduces the amount of paper, facilitates the ability to compare vendor responses, and is in some cases simpler for the RFP vendors themselves.

Whatever approach is taken, the design objective should be simplicity and understandability for the respondent and clear and comparable responses for subsequent analysis by the issuer, using score sheets typically created in parallel with the RFP itself.

C. RFP Administration

RFP administration is divided into six major tasks, with activity occurring at various points throughout the process:

1. Development of a vendor long list
2. Issuance of the RFP
3. Evaluation of responses and creation of a vendor short list
4. Vendor meetings and demonstrations
5. Vendor selection and contract negotiation
6. Implementation and post-project review

1. DEVELOPMENT OF A VENDOR LONG LIST

Development of a vendor long list occurs fairly early in the RFP process and is the result of what is sometimes referred to as a *market scan* of potential providers. The scan is a nonjudgmental look at the players in the market who claim to provide the type of services required by the company, such as electronic billing or payroll. This scan is then refined according to company criteria, which may exclude privately held companies or banks that do not meet certain rating requirements. The resulting list, the long list, may simply be too large for the company's requirements. The solution is to keep adding criteria—for example, existing relationship or reputation—to refine the list to a manageable level.

When the long list and the project plan are complete, it is advisable for the company to let the vendors or banks on the list know of its plans to issue an RFP. This useful courtesy will ensure that vendors have time to assemble the right team. This is particularly important in banking RFPs, as it allows the banks to plan their response and address relationship issues—such as credit availability—before the RFP is issued. Scheduling issues should be kept in mind; for example, it is never a good idea to issue a European RFP in August with a two-week response window, due to the scheduling of summer holidays.

2. ISSUANCE OF THE RFP

To this point, most of the work on the RFP has been performed within the company. This changes once the RFP has been issued to the vendors. The issuer and the vendors are now on a shared timeline with a conclusion that may have significant financial consequences at the end. Further, this can be an expensive process for participants, and vendors hope to eventually recoup their costs. Vendors may begin to probe their contacts at the issuing company to get a better sense of their competition and the company's selection criteria. They almost certainly will ask for clarification on points within the RFP.

These questions should come to the single point of contact specified by the company and be answered promptly and completely. The RFP is a tool to obtain the best goods and services, so unless the question is inappropriate, a reply is recommended. It is also recommended that all questions and answers be shared with the entire bidder pool. This ensures a level playing field for the participants and may elicit other questions that can lead to a better response.

The company should let all the participants know the rules and timeline that will be followed in the RFP process, using a high-level version of the project plan. It is also a good idea to ask all vendors for a complete list of people within their organization who need to be kept informed.

3. EVALUATION OF RESPONSES AND CREATION OF A VENDOR SHORT LIST

The purpose of the evaluation stage is to identify the vendor or vendors that best meet the needs of the RFP and will be invited in for vendor meetings and demonstrations, if necessary. All members of the project team, including operations, tax, legal, accounting, and IT, should undertake evaluation of the proposals. A best practice is to consolidate the responses into a single document or location—such as a spreadsheet, shared drive, or Sharepoint site—and then have them reviewed by the team. Prior to the review, the team should create a scoring and weighting methodology that will be used by all members of the evaluation team. Many companies actually hold formal scoring meetings in which team members have open discussions to facilitate this process.

There are four parts to a good scoring and weighting methodology:

- The areas of evaluation, such as reporting times or systems architecture
- The respondent score for that area
- The weighting of the importance of the area to the company
- Pro forma pricing review and comparison

When determining the areas of evaluation, it is a good idea to follow the basic categories of the RFP, with a few items within each area. Too many points of evaluation will lead to reviewer fatigue and too few will not provide sufficient differentiation between responses. It is also important to include an assessment of deal breakers and "must have" requirements as part of the process.

For example, branch locations may be essential to a company that has a physical presence throughout a region, but less important to a company that has centralized collections and payments through a shared services center. This brings the answers into perspective and favors the vendors that have positive answers in areas that are key decision drivers for the company, such as having a regional operations center, being part of the local clearinghouse, or offering specialized services in a region. There are no formal rules on the scale that must be used for the score and the weighting. Ranges of 1–3 or 1–5 provide for a sufficient degree of differentiation without requiring too much of reviewers. In any event, the scoring should mirror the structure of the RFP.

The scoring can be used to identify potential areas of strength or weakness that can be explored in the final meetings. If the number of vendors responding to the RFP is large, the initial scoring also can be used to select a group of finalists, often referred to as the *short list,* to make oral presentations to the entire team.

Simultaneously with the review of RFPs, references should be contacted and reviewed to ensure that any vendors selected for the short list meet the firm's expectations. This is also the appropriate time to perform any needed due diligence reviews regarding the vendor's financial capacity and stability, as well as any legal issues.

4. VENDOR MEETINGS AND DEMONSTRATIONS

A vendor presentation is normally part of the final selection process. This meeting is an excellent time to ask detailed questions and drill down into the proposal, as well as better understand how the implementation will be handled. Normally, these presentations are held at the company's headquarters, but depending on the scope of the RFP, a regional office or financial center may be appropriate.

It is very easy for meetings to stray from their purpose or run longer than expected, and this does not benefit the company or the vendors. Prior to the actual meeting, the company should distribute an agenda (and if appropriate, demonstration scripts and sample data) to all participants with clear limits on the amount of time that will be allowed. It is also a good idea to stress that the meetings are for the purposes of discussing the proposal, not to hype the vendor. Three hours is a realistic maximum, and it can be difficult to schedule more than two such meetings in a day.

Vendors should be encouraged to bring the product and the implementation specialists relevant to the proposal, and to resist the temptation to bring a large team. Linking specialists by phone can disrupt the flow of the meeting but may be the only way to bring a specialist on Africa into a meeting in San Francisco. Many companies have sophisticated videoconferencing facilities, and these can be used to very good effect.

The scoring summary prepared as part of the review process is an excellent guide for specific questions during the meetings. Simply watching how the respondent's team manages the time and addresses the questions can be quite revealing about how they would behave if awarded the business.

Immediately following the meetings, the company's evaluation team should sit down and discuss impressions and observations, and review—or adjust—the scoring, based on what was learned. Often, the team may identify additional questions for one or more of the vendors, so it may not be possible to decide on the winner within a few days. Further delays in making a decision can be caused by attempts to balance the amount of business awarded to any one respondent or by the need for executive management to review recommendations. It is important not to delay a decision without good cause, as it is both unfair to vendors and suggests a lack of clarity on the part of the company.

In many cases—and especially with selection of a TMS—it is a good idea to see a demonstration of the product or technology. This allows for scripted scenarios that are essential to evaluating a TMS and also permits daily users who may not be on the evaluation team to offer their views on the competing products and services. This stage of the process may also include site visits and other vendor meetings once the selection list has been narrowed to a reasonable number of potential vendors.

5. VENDOR SELECTION AND CONTRACT NEGOTIATION

After all of the vendor meetings and demonstrations are complete, the evaluation committee should review the updated scoring and identify the preferred vendor. Depending upon company requirements, this may require further review and ratification by senior management.

Once a vendor has been selected, the final details of any needed contracts and service requirements must be worked out with the finalist. Bear in mind that final selection is not complete until the final contracts are negotiated. As a result, many companies will not notify unsuccessful vendors of the outcome of the RFP until contracting is completed. This allows for the possibility of an alternate solution if a final agreement cannot be reached with the primary vendor. It is critical not to underestimate the time needed to complete this step. While many contracts are simple and easy to negotiate, detailed servicing agreements and software contracts can take weeks or months to finalize.

Once selection has been finalized, it is good practice and common courtesy to notify the other vendors as the company may need to consider them again sometime in the future.

6. IMPLEMENTATION AND POST-PROJECT REVIEW

The selection process is complete and the contract has been negotiated and signed, but the RFP process is not over until the implementation is complete. In terms of time and effort, implementation is often the largest part of the project. Much will depend on the type and scope of the services covered by the RFP, but implementation can often take three to four times the amount of time needed for the vendor selection portion of an RFP project, especially if the vendor involved is a new one that the company has no previous experience with. Further, depending on the type of services being acquired, significant resources from accounting, IT, or legal may be required.

Depending upon the size of the project, it may be advisable to break the implementation into sections. While there are proponents of the so-called "big bang" approach who advocate implementing everything at once, this can be problematic with a large project. Breaking implementation into pieces allows the opportunity to test new practices and procedures in one area before they are rolled out company-wide. For example, with a global banking RFP, it may be advisable to take a regional approach to implementation and solve problems that occur in one region so that they do not, or at least are less likely to, occur in others. It is important to allow sufficient time to test new processes, procedures, and especially, new software. This is a critical step that is often ignored.

It is an easy—and serious—mistake to underestimate the time and resources required for implementation. The best advice is to follow a disciplined process similar to that used for the RFP. The selected vendor is typically the best guide at this point, as the vendor will have helped other customers through similar implementations and should have well-developed project plans and resource requirements. Even with a relatively simple banking RFP, opening new accounts takes time (often months) to complete all of the needed paperwork, even though the vendor has documentation experts on its implementation team to guide the client through the process.

A best practice in any vendor selection and implementation project is to conduct a post-project review as the final step in the project. The purpose of this review is not to point fingers and cast blame, but to determine what went well and why, and what could have been done better and why. It is a learning experience for both the company and the vendor that can be used as a starting point in ongoing vendor management.

IV. BANK COMPENSATION PRACTICES

Bank compensation refers to how a bank is compensated for the total relationship, the complete "book of business" that a bank may have with a particular company. This includes credit (lending), operating services, and potentially trust and investment management services. Some banks look at compensation for each type of service separately, but the vast majority look at the profitability of the total relationship. In many cases, banks are willing to reduce the price of one product or service and use it as a loss leader with a given client in hopes of making up that loss on other more profitable business. As a result, it is important that treasury professionals look at the total cost of a relationship and manage their bank relationships accordingly. Compensation can come in the form of fees, balances, or some combination of the two. The mix can vary depending upon the desires of both the bank and the corporate customer.

A. Billing for Bank Services

All vendors are typically compensated by fees paid for services or products provided. In the case of FIs, the fees are typically netted against any actual or imputed interest earned on the accounts. Banking services are often bundled[3] and paid for with a combination of required balances in deposit accounts, augmented by value dating (discussed below). Over time, as larger banks expanded outside of their home country and began competing for services globally, many banks began to unbundle their services and charge specific fees for specific services. In an effort to help companies manage these unbundled services, TWIST[4] has been working to develop standards for electronic billing of bank services (discussed in more detail in Chapter 14, Information Technology in Treasury). Various groups, including AFP, are working to standardize international banking service descriptions and provide a standardized service code structure that can be used for billing. Designed specifically to work with the TWIST BSB format,[5] the 2011 AFP Global Service Codes™ include over 800 codes for banking services that are widely adopted across Europe, the Middle East, Africa, and the Pacific Rim.

In contrast to the corporate banking practices in most other countries—where banks charge explicit fees and pay interest on deposits—most banks in the United States provide corporations with "earnings credits" (imputed interest) that can be used to pay for services from the bank. This system developed due to the fact that, historically, US banks were legally barred from paying interest on commercial accounts by federal regulation.[6] The practice allows depositors to be compensated for the value of the balances they have at the bank, in lieu of actual interest. An example of the computation of the amount of the earnings credit is shown later in this chapter. While FIs are now able to pay actual interest on commercial accounts, there has not been a widespread demand for this feature. The option is typically available, however, and can be discussed and negotiated with a firm's bank(s).

3. Bundling of services is the practice of either charging a single fee for a group of services or charging different fees for specific services depending upon which services are used. As a result of bundling, a vendor can charge a very low price on a service that it knows is normally scrutinized and make up for it by charging a higher fee for a service that is not as likely to be examined closely.
4. The Transaction Workflow Innovation Standards Team (TWIST) is a not-for-profit industry group formed to rationalize financial industry standards by creating user-driven, nonproprietary, and internally consistent XML-based standards for the financial supply chain.
5. The TWIST BSB (bank services billing) format has been incorporated into the ISO 20022 standard discussed in more detail in Chapter 14, Information Technology in Treasury.
6. This practice was prompted by the Reg Q prohibition against paying interest on DDA accounts. This regulation was repealed in 2010, as part of the Dodd-Frank Act. At the time of this publication, there was no clear indication of the impact of the repeal on the practice of using earnings credits.

B. Value Dating

Outside the United States, banks often use value dating as compensation for services provided to customers. Under a value-dating system, a bank sets a forward value date on which the value of funds credited to an account is determined and establishes a back value date on which the value of funds debited from an account is determined. For example, when a deposit is forward valued, the date of the credit to the customer's account is later than the actual date the item is added to the customer's ledger balance at the bank. Similarly, when a withdrawal is back valued, the date of the debit to the customer's account is earlier than the actual date the item is deducted from the customer's ledger balance at the bank. This reduces available balances, which in turn reduces interest earned on the account. In effect, the bank is compensated during the value-dating period either by not having to pay interest on positive balances or by earning interest charged on negative balances. In some countries, value dating is standardized among the major clearing banks, while in other countries, it is negotiated on a customer-by-customer or item-by-item basis.

EXHIBIT 7.3 **BANK STATEMENT SHOWING VALUE DATING**

The Globe Bank
21 New Globe Walk Bankside
London SE1 9DT

Account Type: Current Account—Commercial
Account Name: ABC Ltd
Account Number: 9999888889999
Sort Code: 22-15-44
BIC: GLBKGB2XXXX

Date	Description	Paid Out	Paid In	Value Date	Account Balance
01.09.2xx1	Opening Balance				255,918.25
01.09.2xx1	Cheque	1,455.00		30.08.2xx1	254,463.25
01.09.2xx1	Cheque	2,155.00		29.08.2xx1	252,308.25
01.09.2xx1	Wire	25,000.00		01.09.2xx1	227,308.25
02.09.2xx1	Wire	35,000.00		02.09.2xx1	192,308.25
02.09.2xx1	Cheque	5,615.25		01.09.2xx1	186,693.00
02.09.2xx1	Faster Payment		500.00	02.09.2xx1	187,193.00
02.09.2xx1	Deposit		24,515.25	03.09.2xx1	211,708.25
03.09.2xx1	Cheque	1,000.00		01.09.2xx1	210,708.25
03.09.2xx1	Wire	50,000.00		03.09.2xx1	160,708.25
03.09.2xx1	Faster Payment		255.00	03.09.2xx1	160,963.25
03.09.2xx1	Deposit		55,125.00	04.09.2xx1	216,088.25
03.09.2xx1	Cheque	155.00		02.09.2xx1	215,933.25
04.09.2xx1	Wire	75,000.00		04.09.2xx1	140,933.25
04.09.2xx1	Service Charge	145.00		04.09.2xx1	140,788.25

Exhibit 7.3 provides an example of how value dating may appear on a bank statement. In this example, while the account balance shown at the end of 02.09.2xx1 (or September 2) is 211,708.25, the amount that is available for earning interest would only be 186,038.00.

This is because the deposit of 24,515.25 has a value date of September 3, and the two cheques posted after September 2 (for 1,000.00 and 155.00) were both back valued to September 2 or earlier.

While US banks do not typically value-date transactions, they achieve similar results through the use of availability of funds and as-of adjustments, which are discussed in more detail in Chapter 4, Payment Systems.

C. Account Analysis in the US Commercial Banking System

As previously noted, FIs in the United States typically provide their corporate customers with imputed interest on demand deposit account (DDA) balances. The systems that FIs use to manage the imputed credits are generically referred to as *earnings credit analysis (ECA)* systems. The rate used to calculate this imputed interest is called the *earnings credit rate (ECR)* and is typically negotiable as part of the initial vendor selection process when selecting a bank. Banks can, and often do, change ECR without any notification to their customers, resulting in unexpected fees or unused balances at the end of a billing period.

An account analysis statement is, in effect, a bank's "bill" for services rendered, but is typically referred to as an *analysis statement*. *Analysis* is the name of the process that most banks use to determine both earnings credits and charges for services rendered. An account analysis is, therefore, a record of the services provided to the customer by the bank, along with detailed information on balances and related earnings credits for those balances. This practice is typically not seen outside of the United States where invoices for services are more common. The account analysis statement typically provides the following information to a bank's commercial customers:

- Services provided
- Balances maintained
- Transaction/item volumes processed
- Charges assessed
- Earnings credit allowances

It is important to note that different FIs often use varying terminology when describing these services and/or varying definitions of identical terms. Some services and fees may be combined into a single line item or flat fee, and these combinations may vary from bank to bank. Fee structures are as varied and complex as the account analysis formats. Any fees owed after earnings credits are applied are typically debited directly from the account. In some cases, however, the bank may be willing to invoice the organization's accounts payable department for the fees. Exhibit 7.4 provides an example of an account analysis statement.

EXHIBIT 7.4 **ACCOUNT ANALYSIS STATEMENT**

ABC BANK—CORPORATE BANKING ANALYSIS

Global Manufacturing Company
1234 Main Street
Anytown, Ohio
Date: 7/1/2xx3
ECR: 1.00%

Relationship Mgr: J. Sellsalot
Company Contact: J. Cash

Days in Month: 30
Month Ending: 6/30/2xx3

BALANCE SUMMARY	
AVERAGE LEDGER BALANCE	$ 658,987.26
LESS: AVERAGE FLOAT	(55,934.89)
AVERAGE COLLECTED BALANCE	$ 603,052.37
LESS: RESERVE REQUIREMENT (10%)	(60,305.24)
AVERAGE AVAILABLE BALANCE	$ 542,747.13
LESS: BALANCE REQUIRED	(6,796,367.52)
NET AVAILABLE BALANCE	$(6,253,620.39)

EARNINGS CREDIT SUMMARY	
AVAIL. BAL. FOR EARNINGS CREDIT	$542,747.13
EARNINGS CREDIT ALLOWANCE	$ 446.09
LESS: CHARGE FOR SERVICES	(5,586.05)
NET SERVICE CREDIT	$ (5,139.96)
SERVICE CHARGE AMOUNT	$ 5,139.96

ACTIVITY	VOLUME	UNIT PRICE	FEES REQUIRED	BALANCE REQUIRED
GENERAL ACCOUNT SERVICES				
ACCOUNT MAINTENANCE FLAT FEE	4	20.00	$ 80.00	$ 97,333.43
DEPOSITORY SERVICES				
CREDITS	94	0.25	23.50	28,591.69
DEPOSITED ITEMS	1,745	0.08	139.60	169,846.83
RETURN ITEMS	15	2.00	30.00	36,500.04
DEBITS	1,598	0.10	159.80	194,423.52
STOP PAYMENTS	5	18.00	90.00	109,500.11
LOCKBOX SERVICES				
WHOLESALE LOCKBOX MAINT. FEE	3	105.00	315.00	383,250.38
ITEM PROCESSING FEE	486	0.40	194.40	236,520.23
ZBA/CONTROLLED DISBURSEMENT SERVICES				
ZBA MAINTENANCE	1	40.00	40.00	48,666.71
CONTROLLED DISBURSEMENT NOTIFICATION	1	45.00	45.00	54,750.05
FUNDS TRANSFER SERVICES				
ACH MAINTENANCE	1	55.00	55.00	66,916.73
ACH ITEMS	145	0.12	17.40	21,170.02
INCOMING WIRE TRANSFERS	24	7.00	168.00	204,400.20
OUTGOING WIRE TRANSFERS	8	12.00	96.00	116,800.11
INTERNATIONAL SERVICES				
INTERNATIONAL WIRES: OUTBOUND	26	25.00	650.00	790,834.11
INTERNATIONAL COLLECTION ITEMS	125	20.00	2,500.00	3,041,669.66
FOREIGN EXCHANGE TRANSACTIONS	87	10.00	870.00	1,058,501.04
ACCOUNT RECONCILIATION SERVICES				
RECON. MAINTENANCE—PARTIAL	1	50.00	50.00	60,833.39
CHECKS RECONCILIATION	1,247	0.05	62.35	75,859.24
TOTALS			$5,586.05	$6,796,367.52

1. ACCOUNT ANALYSIS STANDARDS

Since 1986, AFP Service Codes™ have been recognized as the standard for identifying balances and charges that appear on account analysis statements and in responding to RFPs.[7] AFP Service Codes are six-character, alphanumeric codes used by banks to provide standard, uniform references and terms for identifying, describing, and reporting bank services, as well as the associated charges. By simplifying and organizing the often varied and complex terminology used to identify bank services, the codes also help to resolve volume and pricing errors.

The Accredited Standards Committee (ASC) X12 of the American National Standards Institute (ANSI) has developed a standardized format (Account Analysis Transaction Set 822) for FIs to use when sending account analysis statements to account holders electronically. The ASC X12 822 transaction set accommodates the AFP standard account analysis format and AFP Service Codes.

It is important for organizations that receive account analysis statements to review them for accuracy in a timely manner. Commercial software packages can be used for this purpose, but many organizations accomplish the review using a database or computer spreadsheet.

2. ACCOUNT ANALYSIS TERMINOLOGY

Among the common terms used in account analysis statements are the following:

- **Average Ledger Balance:** This is the sum of the daily ending ledger balances (both positive and negative) divided by the number of days in the analysis period. Balances used in the calculation are net of any current-period adjustments.
- **Average Deposit Float:** This is the sum of the daily dollar amount of items (primarily checks) in the process of collection divided by the number of calendar or business days in the analysis period.
- **Average Collected Balance:** This is the sum of the daily ending collected balances (both positive and negative) divided by the number of days in the analysis period. In many account analysis statements, this item is calculated as the average ledger balance minus the average deposit float.
- **Reserve Requirement:** In the context of an earnings credit computation, the reserve requirement represents an FI's compensation for the level of balances it is required to maintain with the Fed.[8] Historically, reserve balances needed to satisfy an FI's reserve requirement were nonearning, hence the practice of deducting this reserve from balances that received an earnings credit. Just as FIs are now allowed to pay interest on commercial accounts, reserve banks in the United States now pay interest on reserve balances. Many banks, however, still deduct the reserve from available balances in calculating earnings credits. As with most things related to analysis statements, the amount of funds deducted for reserve requirements is usually subject to negotiation.
- **FDIC Fees:** As with the reserve requirement, FIs will sometimes charge customers so-called FDIC fees to cover the cost of federally mandated deposit insurance. While the FDIC does not object to FIs charging fees to cover such expenses, in 2012 the FDIC ordered banks to stop labeling their fees with "FDIC" and other government agency names, saying it could mislead customers into thinking those fees go directly to the government instead of to the banks themselves.
- **Service Charges:** These are the explicit fees or prices charged for services provided by an FI. Service charges are either expressed as a flat monthly fee or as a per-item or per-unit price. In the case of the latter, the unit price is multiplied by the volume to arrive at the analysis period total.

7. It should be noted that not all FIs or account analysis statements use these standards.
8. As of the date of publication, the reserve requirement was 10% of collected balances.

- **Available or Investable Balance:** The available balance, sometimes referred to as the *investable balance,* represents the balances in the customer's account that the bank was able to invest in income-producing assets during the account analysis period. Some banks calculate the investable balance as the average collected balance reduced by the reserve requirement balance. The investable balance can be a surplus or deficit.
- **Earnings Credit Allowance and the ECR:** The earnings credit allowance is the total dollar value of credit that can be used to offset the service charges incurred during the analysis period. It is calculated by multiplying the investable balance by the ECR for the period. The methods used for determining the ECR vary among FIs. A commonly used ECR is based on the 90-day T-bill rate, but banks set their ECRs based upon their own internal requirements and rates. For example, some banks reduce their ECR by the applied reserve requirement (a reserve-adjusted ECR), and calculate the earnings credit using the average collected balance instead of the investable balance.

3. ACCOUNT ANALYSIS CALCULATIONS

Integrating these definitions results in the following formula used to measure the earnings credit:[9]

$$EC = CB \times (1 - RR) \times ECR\left(\frac{D}{365}\right)$$

Where:

EC = Earnings credit

CB = Average collected balance

RR = Reserve requirement

ECR = Earnings credit rate

D = Number of days in the month (Note: Some banks use the ECR divided by 12 to determine this monthly calculation instead of using the actual number of days.)

An example of this calculation appears in Exhibit 7.5.

9. These equations are generally representative of those used for account analysis statements, though the actual calculation format may vary from bank to bank.

EXHIBIT 7.5 EARNINGS CREDIT CALCULATION

ASSUMPTIONS:

AVERAGE LEDGER BALANCE	$250,000
DEPOSIT FLOAT	$ 30,000
RESERVE REQUIREMENT	10%
EARNINGS CREDIT RATE	1%
SERVICE CHARGES FOR THE MONTH	$1,000
DAYS IN MONTH	30

AVERAGE COLLECTED BALANCE CALCULATION

AVERAGE LEDGER BALANCE	$250,000
LESS: DEPOSIT FLOAT	(30,000)
EQUALS: AVERAGE COLLECTED BALANCE	$220,000

$$\text{EARNINGS CREDIT} = \text{COLLECTED BALANCE} \times (1 - \text{RESERVE REQUIREMENT}) \times \left(\text{EARNINGS CREDIT RATE} \times \frac{\text{DAYS IN MONTH}}{365}\right)$$

$$EC = CB \times (1 - RR) \times ECR \times \left(\frac{D}{365}\right)$$

$$= \$220{,}000 \times (1 - 0.10) \times \left(0.01 \times \frac{30}{365}\right)$$

$$= \$220{,}000 \times 0.9 \times (0.01 \times 0.0822) = \$162.76$$

The $220,000 average collected balance in Exhibit 7.5 results in an earnings credit that is insufficient to cover the service provider's $1,000 charges for the month. It would be of interest to know how much the average collected balance would have to be to avoid paying fees directly (i.e., that results in an earnings credit that just equals the fees). This is determined easily by rearranging the formula to isolate the collected balances required amount. The rearranged formula is:

$$CB = \frac{SC}{ECR \times \left(\frac{D}{365}\right) \times (1 - RR)}$$

Where:

- CB = Average collected balance required to pay service charges
- SC = Monthly service charges
- ECR = Earnings credit rate
- RR = Reserve requirement
- D = Number of days in the month (Note: Some banks use the ECR divided by 12 to determine this monthly calculation instead of using the actual number of days.)

An example of this calculation is presented in Exhibit 7.6.

EXHIBIT 7.6 CALCULATION OF REQUIRED COLLECTED BALANCE

$$\text{AVERAGE COLLECTED BALANCE REQUIRED} = \frac{\text{MONTHLY SERVICE CHARGES}}{\left(\text{EARNINGS CREDIT RATE} \times \frac{\text{DAYS IN MONTH}}{365}\right) \times (1 - \text{RESERVE REQUIREMENT})}$$

$$CB = \frac{SC}{ECR \times \left(\frac{D}{365}\right) \times (1 - RR)}$$

$$= \frac{\$1,000}{\left(0.01 \times \frac{30}{365}\right) \times (1 - 0.10)} = \frac{\$1,000}{(0.01 \times 0.0822) \times 0.9}$$

$$= \frac{\$1,000}{(0.0007398)} = \$1,351,716.68$$

An average collected balance of $1,351,716.68 produces an earnings credit that offsets the $1,000 service charges. To obtain this result, the firm must increase the average collected balance by $1,131,716.68 (i.e., the $1,351,716.68 in Exhibit 7.6 minus the $220,000.00 in Exhibit 7.5). Assuming that the firm has these funds available, it must decide whether to use them to increase the average collected balance or invest them in a low-risk, short-term money market instrument. If the investment yields more than the ECR after considering any transaction costs, then the money market instrument is the better choice.

4. FEE VERSUS BALANCE COMPENSATION

Given the account analysis system and earnings credit allowance as described, there has long been a debate over whether it is better to pay for banking services with excess balances or to aggressively manage bank balances and directly invest the funds. The advantages and disadvantages of providing compensation for services using the earnings credit or direct fee payments differ depending upon whether the perspective of a company or an FI is taken.

A company may favor fee compensation when it is able to earn more interest on its investments than it can obtain in an earnings credit on collected balances. The use of fees for compensation is even more compelling when a company can use excess balances to pay down short-term debt, which typically has a significantly higher opportunity cost than the ECR. In addition, fees can be budgeted and compared with other costs, while balances are not as directly comparable.

From a company's point of view, balance compensation lets the company take advantage of excess collected balances that arise from unanticipated deposits or precautionary transaction balances. Additional reasons why a company may prefer balance compensation are:

- Some FIs price loans and other services more favorably if collected balances are maintained.
- Balance compensation is not as visible as fee expenditures for budgeting purposes, thereby "masking" or hiding the actual compensation and eliminating the need for budget dollars to cover the services.
- Earnings credits used to determine the value of collected balances to the company are not taxable, while interest earned on short-term investments or sweep accounts generally is taxable.
- ECRs may exceed available short-term investment rates.

Some of the disadvantages of balance compensation for a company include:

- ECRs are not always known until after the applicable billing period.
- Earnings in excess of analysis fees are unusable and lost to the company.
- Balances in excess of the FDIC insurance limit may be at risk of loss in the event the bank is closed.

Some FIs prefer fee compensation because deposit balances increase the liabilities on their balance sheet. This may lead to a need for additional capital to meet regulatory or other requirements. A second reason why FIs often prefer fee compensation is that fees from deposit services are viewed as a low-risk source of earnings.

The principal reason why a bank may prefer balance compensation is that deposits may be used to fund loans and investments at rates exceeding the ECR provided to an account holder.

D. Comparing and Monitoring Costs among Financial Services Providers

Companies usually compare FI service charges during their initial vendor selection process and then during periodic relationship reviews. This process is important not only to validate the reasonableness of vendor pricing over time, but also to confirm that the service provider is actually abiding by any negotiated pricing. One source for comparable bank service charge data is Phoenix-Hecht's *The Blue Book of Bank Prices. The Blue Book* is published annually and provides a comparison of various key service charges.

Developing a precise comparison of pricing, whether during the RFP and vendor selection process or during relationship reviews, can be a difficult exercise, but it can be simplified with a carefully prepared template or spreadsheet for bank fee analysis, prepared ahead of time by the treasury professional. It is often helpful to share this template with the various providers so that they understand how they are being evaluated. Banks have varying approaches to bundling products and services—the charging basis can be quite different (e.g., per-user or per-location), and terminology and descriptions for services are not standardized (e.g., *pooling, sweeping,* and *concentration* can be used interchangeably at one bank and refer to separate services and price points at another).

A well-designed comparison template also requires that prices be specified in a common currency, such as US dollars (USD) or euro (EUR). For example, a bank might suggest that since all bank services provided in Singapore are billed in Singapore dollars (SGD), these prices should also be quoted in SGD. A good counter to that request is that the primary purpose of the analysis template is comparability.

The comparison template should include comparisons for each of the primary bank charges. In general, the broad categories of bank charges are:

- Implementation
- Maintenance
- Account services
- Transaction processing
- Information delivery
- Technology

At the end of the day, the only valid method of comparing costs is to calculate the bottom-line cost of a specific set of services based on the processing volumes and balances that a company reasonably expects to have.

Adding to the difficulty of comparing and monitoring ongoing costs is the fact that while many institutions provide monthly analysis statements, others may calculate their account analysis quarterly, semiannually, or annually. If an account holder's balances fluctuate from month to month, then quarterly, semiannual, or annual analysis periods allow excess balances in one month to offset charges in other months. Consultants can help companies compare service charges from a single bank or multiple banks.

There are a number of automated tools available to help with the review and validation of bank pricing, but many companies do a very satisfactory job using spreadsheets or other more manual tools. There are also a number of third-party services that provide comparable information on bank fees that can be used to help assess the reasonableness of any fees.

V. ASSESSING SERVICE PROVIDER RISK

Service provider viability is of paramount importance because a provider failure such as an operations breakdown, information compromise, or financial failure could significantly disrupt a firm's ability to perform basic liquidity management activities and make and receive payments. Accordingly, the operating practices and creditworthiness of FIs and other companies that provide financial services must be assessed periodically.

A. Assessing Operational Risk for Service Providers

In order to monitor a service provider's operational risk, a company should request copies of the provider's SSAE 16 report (also known as an *SOC 1 Report*[10]). The Statement on Standards for Attestation Engagements (SSAE) No. 16, *Reporting on Controls at a Service Organization,* was finalized by the Auditing Standards Board of the American Institute of Certified Public Accountants (AICPA) in January 2010 and effectively replaced the previous SAS 70[11] as the authoritative guidance for reporting on service organizations.

10. An SOC 1 Report is the first of a set of Service Organization Control (SOC) Reports introduced by the AICPA. SOC 1 is designed for engagements performed under SSAE 16.
11. *SAS 70* refers to the Statement on Auditing Standards No. 70, which was the previous AICPA document that covered the review of controls and operations of third-party or external service providers.

SSAE 16 complies with the International Standard on Assurance Engagements (ISAE) No. 3402, *Assurance Reports on Controls at a Service Organization,* which was issued in December 2009 by the International Auditing and Assurance Standards Board (IAASB), part of the International Federation of Accountants (IFAC). ISAE 3402 was developed to provide an international assurance standard for allowing public accountants to issue a report for use by user organizations and their auditors (user auditors) on the controls at a service organization that are likely to be a part of the user organization's system of internal controls over financial reporting.

Service providers receive significant value from having an SSAE 16 or ISAE 3402 engagement performed and report issued. A service provider's audit report with an unqualified opinion that is issued by an independent accounting firm differentiates the service provider from its peers by demonstrating the establishment of effectively designed control objectives and activities. A service auditor's report also helps a provider build trust with its customers.

Without a current service auditor's report, a service provider may have to entertain multiple audit requests from its customers and their respective auditors. Multiple visits from user auditors can strain the organization's resources. A service auditor's report ensures that all user organizations and their auditors have access to the same information. This will satisfy the user auditor's requirements in many cases.

A customer that obtains service auditor's reports from its service providers receives valuable information regarding each provider's controls and the effectiveness of those controls. The customer receives a detailed description of the service provider's controls (in what is referred to as a *Type 1 report)* and an independent assessment of whether the controls were placed in operation, suitably designed, and operating effectively (this more detailed report is referred to as a *Type 2 report).*

The customer should provide the service auditor's report to its auditors. This will greatly assist the customer's auditors in planning the audit of the customer's financial statements. Without a service auditor's report, the customer would likely have to incur additional costs in sending its auditors to the service organization to perform additional audit procedures.

B. Assessing Financial Services Provider (FSP) Risk

Assessing the risk of FSPs is necessary because they often literally control an organization's information flows, related records, and liquid assets. The provider must have adequate backup systems and disaster recovery procedures. These procedures should be evaluated at the outset of a relationship and periodically thereafter. SLAs and contract provisions should indicate specific rights and responsibilities of the parties in the event of a service interruption. Risk management is discussed in more detail in Chapter 15, Operational and Enterprise Risk Management, but some issues relative to FSP risk are discussed here.

1. BASEL ACCORDS

As discussed in more depth in Chapter 2, Regulatory and Legal Environment, the Basel Accords are the result of a round of meetings and discussions by central bankers from around the world who originally met in Basel, Switzerland, in 1988 to talk about the need to modify capital requirements for banks, based upon perceived credit risk. These meetings and deliberations produced a set of minimal capital requirements for banks and came to be known as the *Basel Accord.* There have subsequently been two more rounds of Basel discussions, and the Basel Accords now include specific requirements around assessment of and provision for operational risk in addition to credit risk. And more discussions are planned.

2. ASSESSING FINANCIAL RISK FOR FINANCIAL INSTITUTIONS (FIs)

One of the primary publicly available tools for assessing the general financial risk of an FI in the United States is the Uniform Bank Performance Report (UBPR), published by the Federal Financial Institutions Examination Council (FFIEC). The UBPR is an analytical tool created for bank supervisory, examination, and management purposes. In a concise format, it shows the impact of management decisions and economic conditions on a bank's performance and balance sheet composition. The performance and composition data contained in the report can be used to help evaluate the adequacy of earnings, liquidity, capital, asset and liability management, and growth management. Bankers and examiners alike can use this report to further their understanding of a bank's financial condition and, through such understanding, perform their duties more effectively.[12]

By analyzing the data contained in the UBPR, the user can obtain an overall picture of the bank's financial health and discover conditions that might require further analysis and investigation. The UBPR presents three types of data for use in the financial analysis of a bank:

- Data for the specific bank
- Data for a peer group of banks similar in size and economic environment
- Percentile rankings

A thorough understanding of these data groups and their interrelationships and limitations is essential in order to use the UBPR effectively. As a general rule, any analysis should compare the bank to its peer group, consider the bank's trends over time, and recognize trends and changes in peer group averages.[13] A sample UBPR is provided in Appendix 7.3.

3. COUNTERPARTY RISK

Counterparty risk (discussed in more detail in Chapter 15, Operational and Enterprise Risk Management) is the risk to each party of a contract that the other party will not or cannot live up to its contractual obligations. This applies as much or more to contracts with FSPs, who may be acting as custodian of company funds and information, as it does to any investment decision. This is a very real risk and should be considered when evaluating a contract for services of any kind with a bank or FSP.

C. Sovereign and Political Risk

Global account management requires an understanding of sovereign and political risks. *Sovereign risk* is a broad concept that a central bank of a country could alter its monetary policy significantly or impose FX regulations that would reduce or negate the value of FX contracts or currency trades. More broadly, the concept of sovereign risk can apply to any political risk that a country will refuse to comply with an agreement to which it is a party.

Political risk is the term applied to the variety of actions that a government may take that negatively impact a company's operations and/or value. It includes the risk that a

12. From "UBPR" on FFIEC's website (http://www.ffiec.gov/UBPR.htm, last modified October 3, 2012).
13. From "A User's Guide for the Uniform Bank Performance Report," published by FFIEC, December 2008 (http://www.ffiec.gov/PDF/UBPR/UBPR_12-08.pdf).

company's operations in a foreign country may be nationalized or expropriated by the government of that country. *Nationalization* refers to a government takeover of all companies in a specific industry, often involving ore extraction, petroleum, transportation, or power generation and distribution businesses. *Expropriation* refers to a government takeover of a single company, with or without compensation. Experience suggests that when compensation is made, it is significantly less than the market value of the expropriated company. Other types of political risk include:

- **Blocked Currencies:** Profits cannot be converted from the local currency into a major trading currency.
- **Forced Reinvestment:** Funds cannot be transferred out of the country in any form, or the amount that can be transferred is limited.
- **Required Majority Ownership:** Companies must be owned by resident nationals.

Multinational companies are exposed to varying degrees of political risk depending upon attitudes and policies of the host country and the nature of the business. A company with operations in foreign countries must be knowledgeable about the laws, regulations, taxes, and customs that govern business activities, as well as the overall political and social dynamics of the countries where capital is invested.

D. Managing Confidential Information and Conflicts of Interest

Service providers often have access to confidential information about an organization's customer base. A treasurer must know if, and under what conditions, this information may be shared with affiliates of the service provider or other parties to prevent any loss of confidentiality. Some organizations document this with a nondisclosure agreement.

A conflict of interest may arise when a particular vendor serves in multiple capacities. For example, an FI with a lending relationship with a specific company also may serve as the company's bond trustee. If the borrower becomes distressed, there is a risk that the FI might protect its own interests at the expense of the bondholders and other investors. Traditionally, FIs have established a notional barrier (sometimes referred to as a "wall") against information flows between functional divisions to prevent such abuses. Employees are typically not permitted to work on both sides of the "wall," and there are internal controls about what information may be passed "over the wall."

FIs may form business alliances with vendors that have complementary areas of expertise or superior cost efficiencies. These alliances often result in the FI outsourcing services to another party or corporate entity. For example, many FIs outsource their credit card merchant processing operations to third parties. In these cases, information is shared with outside parties and disclosure to the customer is generally required.

E. Legal and Ethical Issues

In many countries, "commissions" or "fees" that would be considered bribes in the United States are ingrained deeply in the commercial culture. However, the Foreign Corrupt Practices Act (FCPA) forbids US companies from engaging in these practices. Many other countries have similar laws and regulations. US companies also must consider whether their foreign activities may come under the jurisdiction of the Office of Foreign Assets Control (OFAC). OFAC (discussed in Chapter 2, Regulatory and Legal Environment) is an office of the US Treasury Department that administers and enforces economic and trade sanctions against targeted foreign countries, terrorist-sponsoring organizations, and international narcotics traffickers, as required by legislation, foreign policy, and national security goals. OFAC has the authority to impose controls on financial transactions and freeze foreign assets under US jurisdiction.

VI. SUMMARY

This chapter provided detailed information to assist treasury professionals in conducting an RFP and vendor selection process. The RFP process is an excellent tool to assess and select financial services vendors. It requires hard work and planning and cannot be done without the help of all parts of an organization, but can produce worthwhile results. Using a formalized process helps to insure buy-in from both management and other operational units. It does take time, however, and companies need to be realistic about both commitment and expectations.

Once a financial services provider has been selected, relationship management is an important part of any treasury professional's job. Relationship management goes beyond assessing the quality of the products or services provided—it includes assessment of compensation and ongoing assessment of service provider risk. These and other key elements of relationship management were discussed in this chapter. Good relationship management takes time and effort. But given the work needed to change vendors, investing in relationship management makes a lot of sense and can provide dividends in quality of service and new ideas for customers.

APPENDIX 7.1: SAMPLE BANK SCORECARD[14]

SAMPLE BANK SCORECARD

COMPANY NAME

Bank Name: Any Bank Name

Acct Officer: Any Relationship Manager

Time Period: Any Time Period

BANKING SERVICES EVALUATION

SECTION 1	GENERAL CUSTOMER SERVICE					
	N/A	**Excellent**	**Satisfactory**	**Poor**	**Unacceptable**	**Rating**
1. Level of Competence	O Not Applicable	O Rating of 4	O Rating of 3	O Rating of 2	O Rating of 1	
2. Courteous Professional Behavior	O Not Applicable	O Rating of 4	O Rating of 3	O Rating of 2	O Rating of 1	
3. Telephone Availability	O Not Applicable	O Rating of 4	O Rating of 3	O Rating of 2	O Rating of 1	
4. Backup Coverage	O Not Applicable	O Rating of 4	O Rating of 3	O Rating of 2	O Rating of 1	
5. Response Correctness	O Not Applicable	O Rating of 4	O Rating of 3	O Rating of 2	O Rating of 1	
6. Timeliness of Response	O Not Applicable	O Rating of 4	O Rating of 3	O Rating of 2	O Rating of 1	
7. Follow Through on Commitments	O Not Applicable	O Rating of 4	O Rating of 3	O Rating of 2	O Rating of 1	
8. Overall Problem Solving	O Not Applicable	O Rating of 4	O Rating of 3	O Rating of 2	O Rating of 1	
9. Knowledge of Bank's Policies/Procedures	O Not Applicable	O Rating of 4	O Rating of 3	O Rating of 2	O Rating of 1	
10. Knowledge of Bank's Cash Mgmt Products	O Not Applicable	O Rating of 4	O Rating of 3	O Rating of 2	O Rating of 1	
Custom Field	O Not Applicable	O Rating of 4	O Rating of 3	O Rating of 2	O Rating of 1	
Custom Field	O Not Applicable	O Rating of 4	O Rating of 3	O Rating of 2	O Rating of 1	
Custom Field	O Not Applicable	O Rating of 4	O Rating of 3	O Rating of 2	O Rating of 1	
Custom Field	O Not Applicable	O Rating of 4	O Rating of 3	O Rating of 2	O Rating of 1	

Average = **Total =**

Comments: ____________________

14. The sample bank scorecard is taken from the "AFP Bank Scorecard" published in April 2009 and available through AFP's website (http://www.afponline.org/mbr/res/topics/Bank_Scorecard.html?terms=bank_scorecard).

SAMPLE BANK SCORECARD (CONTINUED)

SECTION 2	RELATIONSHIP MANAGER					
	N/A	Excellent	Satisfactory	Poor	Unacceptable	Rating
1. Knowledge of Bank's Cash Mgmt Products	O Not Applicable	O Rating of 4	O Rating of 3	O Rating of 2	O Rating of 1	
2. Ability to Match Services to our Needs	O Not Applicable	O Rating of 4	O Rating of 3	O Rating of 2	O Rating of 1	
3. Follow-up on Requests	O Not Applicable	O Rating of 4	O Rating of 3	O Rating of 2	O Rating of 1	
4. Company and Industry Knowledge	O Not Applicable	O Rating of 4	O Rating of 3	O Rating of 2	O Rating of 1	
5. Calling Frequency [Excellent = __ visits / yr]	O Not Applicable	O Rating of 4	O Rating of 3	O Rating of 2	O Rating of 1	
6. Ease of Access—General	O Not Applicable	O Rating of 4	O Rating of 3	O Rating of 2	O Rating of 1	
7. Ease of Access—Emergency	O Not Applicable	O Rating of 4	O Rating of 3	O Rating of 2	O Rating of 1	
Custom Field	O Not Applicable	O Rating of 4	O Rating of 3	O Rating of 2	O Rating of 1	
Custom Field	O Not Applicable	O Rating of 4	O Rating of 3	O Rating of 2	O Rating of 1	
Custom Field	O Not Applicable	O Rating of 4	O Rating of 3	O Rating of 2	O Rating of 1	
Custom Field	O Not Applicable	O Rating of 4	O Rating of 3	O Rating of 2	O Rating of 1	
	Average =				**Total =**	

Comments: ____

____

____

SAMPLE BANK SCORECARD (CONTINUED)

SECTION 3			TECHNICAL RELIABILITY			
	N/A	**Excellent**	**Satisfactory**	**Poor**	**Unacceptable**	**Rating**
1. Service Level Agreement (SLA) Compliance	O Not Applicable	O Rating of 4	O Rating of 3	O Rating of 2	O Rating of 1	
2. System Response Time to Inquiry	O Not Applicable	O Rating of 4	O Rating of 3	O Rating of 2	O Rating of 1	
3. Security / Ease of Application & Practical	O Not Applicable	O Rating of 4	O Rating of 3	O Rating of 2	O Rating of 1	
4. Problem Resolution	O Not Applicable	O Rating of 4	O Rating of 3	O Rating of 2	O Rating of 1	
5. Timeliness of Data Availability	O Not Applicable	O Rating of 4	O Rating of 3	O Rating of 2	O Rating of 1	
6. Communication of System Status	O Not Applicable	O Rating of 4	O Rating of 3	O Rating of 2	O Rating of 1	
7. System Outages	O Not Applicable	O Rating of 4	O Rating of 3	O Rating of 2	O Rating of 1	
Custom Field	O Not Applicable	O Rating of 4	O Rating of 3	O Rating of 2	O Rating of 1	
Custom Field	O Not Applicable	O Rating of 4	O Rating of 3	O Rating of 2	O Rating of 1	
Custom Field	O Not Applicable	O Rating of 4	O Rating of 3	O Rating of 2	O Rating of 1	
Custom Field	O Not Applicable	O Rating of 4	O Rating of 3	O Rating of 2	O Rating of 1	

Average = **Total =**

Comments: ______________________________

Direct Transmission	**N/A**	**Excellent**	**Satisfactory**	**Poor**	**Unacceptable**	**Rating**
1. FTP Access	O Not Applicable	O Rating of 4	O Rating of 3	O Rating of 2	O Rating of 1	
2. Timeliness of Transactions	O Not Applicable	O Rating of 4	O Rating of 3	O Rating of 2	O Rating of 1	
3. Security / Ease of Application & Practical	O Not Applicable	O Rating of 4	O Rating of 3	O Rating of 2	O Rating of 1	
4. Problem Resolution	O Not Applicable	O Rating of 4	O Rating of 3	O Rating of 2	O Rating of 1	
5. Overall Benefit to Customer	O Not Applicable	O Rating of 4	O Rating of 3	O Rating of 2	O Rating of 1	
Custom Field	O Not Applicable	O Rating of 4	O Rating of 3	O Rating of 2	O Rating of 1	
Custom Field	O Not Applicable	O Rating of 4	O Rating of 3	O Rating of 2	O Rating of 1	
Custom Field	O Not Applicable	O Rating of 4	O Rating of 3	O Rating of 2	O Rating of 1	
Custom Field	O Not Applicable	O Rating of 4	O Rating of 3	O Rating of 2	O Rating of 1	

Average = **Total =**

Comments: ______________________________

SECTION TOTAL **Average =** **Total =**

SAMPLE BANK SCORECARD (CONTINUED)

COMPANY NAME

Bank Name: Any Bank Name

Acct Officer: Any Relationship Manager

BANKING SERVICES EVALUATION

Time Period: Any Time Period

SCORING SUMMARY	QUALITATIVE	
	Average	**Total**
1. GENERAL CUSTOMER SERVICE	0.0	0
2. RELATIONSHIP MANAGER	0.0	0
3. TECHNICAL RELIABILITY	0.0	0
SECTION AVERAGE / TOTAL	**0.0**	**0**

SCORING SUMMARY	QUANTITATIVE	
	Average	**Total**
1. ACCOUNT ANALYSIS	0.0	0
2. BANK SAFETY AND SOUNDNESS (DR, FIN STABILITY)	0.0	0
SECTION AVERAGE / TOTAL	**0.0**	**0**

SCORING SUMMARY	PAYMENTS	
	Average	**Total**
1. DISBURSEMENT SERVICES	0.0	0
2. REMOTE DEPOSIT SERVICES	0.0	0
3. DEPOSIT SERVICES	0.0	0
SECTION AVERAGE / TOTAL	**0.0**	**0**

SAMPLE BANK SCORECARD (CONTINUED)

SCORING SUMMARY	INFORMATION REPORTING	
	Average	**Total**
1. INFORMATION REPORTING (include any type of balance reporting)	0.0	0
2. ACCOUNT RECONCILEMENT	0.0	0
3. WEB / OTHER SERVICE	0.0	0
4. POSITIVE PAY	0.0	0
SECTION AVERAGE / TOTAL	**0.0**	**0**

SCORING SUMMARY	MISCELLANEOUS	
	Average	**Total**
1. INTERNATIONAL SERVICES	0.0	0
2. INVESTMENT / BROKERAGE SERVICES	0.0	0
3. THIRD-PARTY VENDORS	0.0	0
4. CARDS COMMERCIAL	0.0	0
SECTION AVERAGE / TOTAL	**0.0**	**0**

SCORING SUMMARY	LOCKBOX	
	Average	**Total**
1. ITEM PROCESSING	0.0	0
2. INFORMATION REPORTING	0.0	0
SECTION AVERAGE / TOTAL	**0.0**	**0**

SCORING SUMMARY	TOTAL SCORES
WEIGHTED AVERAGE TOTAL	**0.0**
SECTION AVERAGE / TOTAL	**0.0**

APPENDIX 7.2: RFP ACTIVITY INFORMATION[15]

A company may be a household name in Europe and the United States, but a relative unknown in Asia-Pacific or Latin America. If prospective vendors do not realize the size and scope of the potential business, they will not devote the right resources to develop a proper response to an RFP. The RFP process addresses this in two ways: (1) through the development of business requirements—discussed in the body of Chapter 7—and (2) through the relevant transaction and use data, which demonstrate the scale and are the subject of this appendix.

Company Overview

Detailed and accurate information allows vendors to clearly assess whether they are capable of—and interested in—handling the types of transactions required. This will lead to a thorough and well-thought-out proposal that is a direct result of the RFP.

RFP activity information should develop a clear picture of the company's business footprint that may include detailed information on:

1. **Legal Entity Structure:** This portion of the activity information provides the legal names and ownership structure for the company on a global and/or regional basis, depending on the scope of the RFP. This should be outlined in a chart showing the ownership, business/product lines covered, tax/legal status (e.g., branch, subsidiary, check-the-box), functional currency, and nature of business conducted (e.g., sales, manufacturing, or distribution). Most companies have current legal entity diagrams, and treasury can add value to these by including business details on the activities performed at each entity and how the entities relate to one another—including regional financial oversight, intercompany flows, and commissionaire arrangements.
2. **Organization:** This overview shows the hierarchy of job functions, including who has responsibility for banking relationships, the management of cash at the local and regional level, and investment and borrowing decisions.
3. **Current Bank Account or Systems Architecture:** For a banking RFP, this should show all bank accounts, including the name of the bank, the branch where the account is domiciled, the currency of the account, and the average monthly cash balances. Where possible, the account hierarchies (such as zero-balancing and sweeping) should be indicated so that there is a clear picture of how the company currently manages its cash flows. For a TMS or other type of RFP, it should show the systems deployed and their interconnection.
4. **Planned Bank Account or Systems Architecture:** For a banking RFP, this can be a description or a series of diagrams of what bank structure is planned. The description should fully describe techniques that will be used, such as European pooling, local currency pooling in select countries, US dollar (USD) pooling in Asia-Pacific, entrust loan arrangements in China, cash concentration in Mexico,

15. Much of this material is provided courtesy of Treasury Alliance Group LLC and is taken from its white paper, "The Request for Proposal Process: A Treasurer's Guide," published in 2012 (http://www.treasuryalliance.com/assets/publications/cash/Treasury_Alliance_Group_RFP_Guide.pdf).

or zero balance accounts (ZBAs) in the United States. For a systems project, this should show what is desired in terms of the number of systems and how they will relate to one another.

5. **Transaction Values, Volumes, and Types:** Information provided should include the average monthly value of cash flows and the volume of transactions, along with the type of payment instruments (e.g., wire payments, ACH, and check). This information must be provided by currency (e.g., US dollars, euros, and Japanese yen), and it is advisable to list all amounts in the local currency, rather than converting them all to the company's functional currency. The required information can easily be obtained from account analyses for accounts in the United States but is more difficult to obtain for accounts in other countries. It is usually necessary to create a spreadsheet or other data request to collect the required information from international sources. This can be a somewhat frustrating exercise, and it can be tempting to rely on information from the company's ERP. Unfortunately, what is important for a treasurer may not be important to an accountant. There is really very little choice but to go through the detailed work to gather the correct information. The information should be as specific as possible. For example, it should specify whether electronic payments are local bulk payments (ACH) or cross-border transfers, delineate which transactions are intercompany or third-party, and segregate payroll volumes and amounts.

6. **Banking Services:** The services used by the business in the relevant geographies should be outlined. In addition to traditional services such as bank accounts, wire transfers, and web-based balance reporting/transaction initiation, most global companies require services such as payroll, rent guarantees, export guarantees, import letters of credit, VAT (value-added tax) reimbursements, tax payments, and specialized software. As with the transaction values and volumes, it is a good idea to structure a data request to all of the company's related operations to make sure that the inventory of services is as complete as possible. It is best to understand the full array of services needed before working with the banks.

APPENDIX 7.3: SAMPLE UNIFORM BANK PERFORMANCE REPORT (UBPR)[16]

FDIC Certificate #   FRB District/ID_RSSD   FIRST STATE BANK, THE   Summary Ratios
OCC Charter # 0   County: Summary Ratios--Page 1   2/18/2013 7:51:50 PM
Public Report

	12/31/2012			12/31/2011			12/31/2010			12/31/2009			12/31/2008		
Earnings and Profitability	BANK	PG 15	PCT	BANK	PG 15	PCT	BANK	PG 15	PCT	BANK	PG 15	PCT	BANK	PG 15	PCT
Percent of Average Assets:															
Interest Income (TE)	4.07	3.92	57	5.38	4.29	90	6.04	4.68	93	6.49	5.09	95	6.99	5.79	93
- Interest Expense	0.72	0.53	77	1.38	0.74	96	1.67	1.02	94	2.03	1.34	92	2.90	1.97	95
Net Interest Income (TE)	3.35	3.38	48	4.00	3.53	75	4.38	3.65	83	4.46	3.73	84	4.10	3.81	68
+ Noninterest Income	0.33	0.44	38	0.26	0.48	23	0.32	0.50	31	0.52	0.51	60	0.43	0.55	43
- Noninterest Expense	3.40	2.88	73	2.61	2.96	37	2.42	3.09	19	2.68	3.17	28	2.39	3.09	19
- Provision: Loan & Lease Losses	0.00	0.08	46	0.00	0.12	36	8.48	0.19	99	1.02	0.28	87	1.01	0.16	93
Pretax Operating Income (TE)	0.27	0.89	18	1.65	0.93	83	-6.20	0.86	0	1.27	0.84	67	1.13	1.11	47
+ Realized Gains/Losses Sec	0.00	0.03	71	0.00	0.02	71	0.00	0.02	75	0.00	0.02	73	0.00	0.01	75
Pretax Net Operating Income (TE)	0.27	0.94	16	1.65	0.97	82	-6.20	0.89	0	1.27	0.86	65	1.13	1.10	47
Net Operating Income	0.21	0.75	15	1.66	0.77	91	-5.01	0.72	0	0.78	0.68	51	0.71	0.89	38
Adjusted Net Operating Income	0.21	0.76	16	1.44	0.78	82	-1.72	0.73	2	0.97	0.72	59	0.57	0.89	30
Net Inc Attrib to Min Ints	0.00	0.00	99	0.00	0.00	99	0.00	0.00	99	0.00	0.00	99	N/A	0.00	N/A
Net Income Adjusted Sub S	0.21	0.63	15	1.66	0.65	97	-5.01	0.60	0	0.78	0.56	61	0.71	0.74	44
Net Income	0.21	0.75	15	1.66	0.77	91	-5.01	0.72	0	0.78	0.68	51	0.71	0.89	38
Margin Analysis:															
Avg Earning Assets to Avg Assets	93.55	91.39	61	99.57	91.34	99	94.97	91.09	78	96.21	91.82	86	96.38	93.35	83
Avg Int-Bearing Funds to Avg Assets	76.56	69.44	80	85.01	70.76	97	82.62	71.69	93	82.39	71.42	93	80.46	71.34	88
Int Inc (TE) to Avg Earn Assets	4.35	4.33	51	5.40	4.72	78	6.36	5.17	89	6.74	5.57	91	7.26	6.21	91
Int Expense to Avg Earn Assets	0.77	0.59	75	1.39	0.81	94	1.76	1.12	93	2.11	1.47	91	3.01	2.11	93
Net Int Inc-TE to Avg Earn Assets	3.58	3.73	43	4.01	3.89	57	4.61	4.03	77	4.63	4.08	78	4.25	4.09	60
Loan & Lease Analysis:															
Net Loss to Average Total LN&LS	0.00	0.15	39	0.28	0.23	71	6.78	0.35	99	1.10	0.45	81	1.56	0.28	91
Earnings Coverage of Net Losses (X)	N/A	25.90	N/A	7.54	23.57	47	0.44	14.90	11	2.70	16.28	34	1.84	24.81	20
LN&LS Allowance to LN&LS Not HFS	0.00	1.69	0	6.20	1.69	98	5.36	1.65	97	0.90	1.67	14	0.75	1.56	7
LN&LS Allowance to Net Losses (X)	N/A	21.16	N/A	19.22	16.75	72	0.77	11.87	8	0.87	11.37	13	0.48	16.47	4
LN&LS Allowance to Total LN&LS	0.00	1.68	0	6.20	1.68	98	5.36	1.64	97	0.90	1.67	14	0.75	1.56	7
Total LN&LS-90+ Days Past Due	2.34	0.21	95	0.69	0.22	83	0.32	0.18	77	3.08	0.30	96	0.49	0.27	75
-Nonaccrual	6.02	0.88	96	7.25	0.85	96	1.84	0.88	78	1.47	0.95	72	0.38	0.75	56
-Total	8.36	1.22	97	7.94	1.20	96	2.17	1.19	75	4.55	1.41	87	0.87	1.16	54
Liquidity															
Net Non Core Fund Dep New $250M	-57.52	-21.59	12	-24.57	-15.74	27	-21.08	-13.78	28	21.95	1.80	83	13.18	3.07	66
Net Loans & Leases to Assets	58.64	47.90	74	73.25	50.51	89	72.13	52.81	87	78.51	54.22	94	74.40	55.39	89
Capitalization															
Tier One Leverage Capital	10.59	11.13	51	6.64	11.35	1	4.14	11.42	0	9.35	11.73	27	9.43	12.05	26
Cash Dividends to Net Income	0.00	38.52	28	18.33	38.04	37	-3.10	39.88	2	47.20	43.12	53	26.40	56.26	29

16. The sample report is from FFIEC's website (https://cdr.ffiec.gov/public/Reports/UbprReportPrint.aspx, accessed February 18, 2013).

TEST YOUR UNDERSTANDING: CHAPTER 7

Answers are on pages 666–671.

1. What are the major factors that contribute to a successful long-term mutual relationship between companies and vendors?
2. What factors affect the pricing of bank loans?
3. What factors impact the number of bank relationships that an organization needs?
4. List some of the important documents required as part of a relationship with an FI.
5. What is an SLA?
6. What is meant by KYC?
7. What is a vendor scorecard?
8. What are the four major vendor selection methods, and what is the main purpose of each?
9. In addition to treasury, who are the major stakeholders in a treasury RFP?
10. Describe value dating.
11. What is an account analysis statement?
12. Compare and contrast average ledger balance and average collected balance.
13. Compare and contrast fee compensation and balance compensation in the United States.
14. What is political risk?
15. What is an SSAE 16 report?
16. What concerns should a treasurer have about service provider access to confidential information?

PART III
Working Capital Management

CHAPTER 8
Introduction to Working Capital Management

VI. MANAGEMENT OF CREDIT AND ACCOUNTS RECEIVABLE (A/R)

A. Relationship between Treasury and Credit Management
B. Trade Credit Policies
C. Billing and Collection Methods
D. Forms of Credit Extension
E. Cash Application
F. Considerations Pertaining to Terms of Sale
G. Financing Accounts Receivable (A/R)

VII. MANAGEMENT OF INVENTORY

A. Elements of Basic Inventory Policy
B. Inventory Financing Alternatives

VIII. MANAGEMENT OF ACCOUNTS PAYABLE (A/P)

A. Disbursement System Considerations
B. Types of A/P and Disbursement Systems

IX. MULTINATIONAL WORKING CAPITAL MANAGEMENT TOOLS

A. Multicurrency Accounts
B. Netting
C. Leading and Lagging
D. Re-invoicing
E. Internal Factoring
F. In-House Banking
G. Export Financing

X. SUMMARY

I. INTRODUCTION

Chapter 1, The Role of Treasury Management, discusses that one of the primary responsibilities of any treasury professional is to properly manage a firm's financial assets to ensure that there is sufficient liquidity to meet current and future financial obligations in a timely and cost-effective manner. This has historically been referred to as *cash management*. The broader term for this is *working capital management*.

Working capital is technically defined as current assets less current liabilities, which roughly corresponds to cash and liquid assets that can quickly be converted to cash. No matter how wealthy or efficiently run a business or organization may be, there is a limited and fluctuating amount of cash and liquid assets available at any given time. Treasury's responsibility is to manage and use that pool of resources as efficiently and effectively as possible. Understanding how a company manages that pool of cash is also helpful in cash forecasting, which is discussed in Chapter 13.

Financial managers often take a different view of current asset management than operations or sales managers. Operations managers typically prefer a large inventory of raw materials or partially finished goods to meet production quotas. Sales managers similarly favor a large inventory of finished goods to meet consumer demands and a liberal credit policy to stimulate sales. Financial managers, on the other hand, prefer to minimize inventory and accounts receivable (A/R) to minimize the cost of financing these assets. As a result, working capital management spans all areas of an organization. While treasury may lead the effort and bear the ultimate responsibility for results, effective working capital management is normally a cross-functional effort.

This chapter examines the various components that make up working capital, looks at how they interact with each other to affect the overall liquidity of a firm, and discusses various alternatives that can be used to manage them. As part of that discussion, the concept of the cash conversion cycle (CCC) is introduced, along with ways the CCC can be managed to maximize available liquidity. The chapter also covers the idea of float and discusses how it affects working capital.

II. OVERVIEW OF WORKING CAPITAL

The term *working capital* is defined as current assets less current liabilities. It is the cash and other liquid assets required by any organization to continue its operations by satisfying both upcoming operational expenses and maturing short-term debt. Working capital can be obtained (increased) by:

- Collecting cash flow from operations
- Increasing debt
- Selling assets and investments
- Selling equity

And it is used (reduced) by:

- Using cash flow in operations
- Repaying debt
- Purchasing assets and investments
- Paying dividends and buying back stock/equity

The term *current assets* generally refers to assets that are expected to be converted into cash within one year. For most organizations, the major current assets consist of accounts such as cash, marketable securities, A/R, inventory, and prepaid expenses. *Current liabilities*, in turn, generally refers to liabilities that are required to be paid for within one year. For most organizations, the primary current liabilities are accounts payable (A/P), debt maturing in less than one year, notes payable, and accrued liabilities.

A company's daily operating activities create a flow of cash through the various working capital accounts, which is called the *operating cycle* or *cash conversion cycle*, illustrated in Exhibit 8.1. For a variety of reasons discussed later in this chapter, this flow is often uneven, resulting in fluctuations in individual accounts and overall working capital. Understanding how these flows work, how the accounts interact, and how both impact working capital is critical to the job of any treasury professional. Management of these flows is critical to a company's short-term liquidity and long-term viability.

EXHIBIT 8.1 **CASH CONVERSION CYCLE**

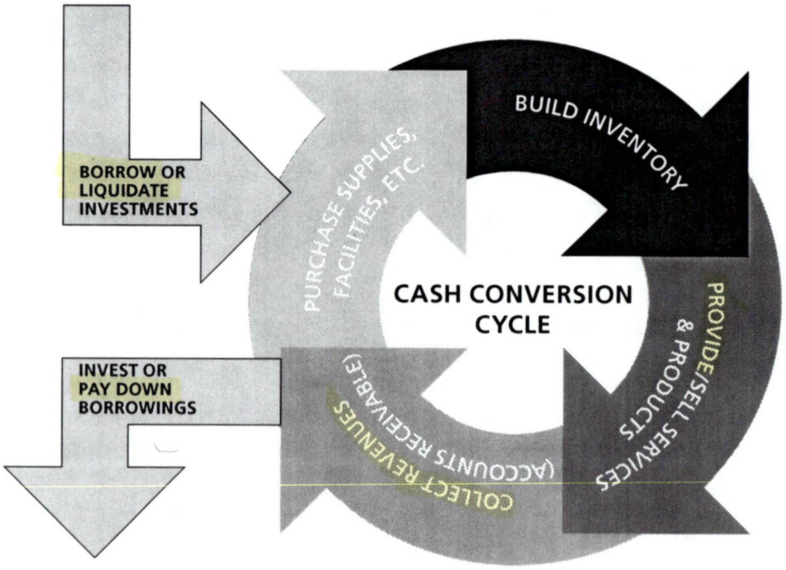

Working capital management is the management of business and financial processes aimed at maximizing or creating shareholder value by optimizing the cash locked in short-term assets and liabilities. It refers to the decisions and strategies concerning the amounts and types of investments in current assets, as well as the amounts and types of current liabilities that support the investment in current assets. It also involves the analysis of the risk/reward relationships that attach to different strategies.

Working capital strategies affect many of the financial ratios used to evaluate financial positions, particularly the current and quick ratios, which are discussed in Chapter 9, Working Capital Metrics. In addition, the risks associated with various working capital decisions may influence the company's cost of capital. A firm's credit and cash management practices may also positively or negatively impact working capital.

A high value for the current ratio (current assets divided by current liabilities) suggests a strong liquidity position. However, current assets typically have low rates of return relative to long-term or fixed assets. Current liabilities tend to carry interest rate charges that are higher than the rate of return on current assets. As a result, excessive liquidity can also cause a drag on overall financial performance. Working capital management involves balancing the need for liquidity against the lower rate of return to decide what level of liquidity is appropriate for a particular business or industry.

A. Operating Cash Flows and Timelines

There are four principal types of cash flows that treasury professionals must consider:

- **Cash outflows** include funds disbursed to employees, vendors, and suppliers; lenders; local, state, and federal tax agencies; bondholders; and shareholders. This process is typically referred to as the *purchase-to-pay timeline*. As discussed below, inventory can be a by-product of the purchase-to-pay timeline.
- **Cash inflows** include funds collected from customers, obtained from financial sources (e.g., loans or investment income), and/or received from other sources. This is typically referred to as the *order-to-cash timeline*.
- **Concentration/funding flows** involve internal transfers among operating units of a company and between a firm's various bank accounts, with the objectives of pooling funds for other purposes or funding various disbursement accounts.
- **Liquidity management flows** involve using the organization's liquidity reserves in the most effective manner. If there is a surplus of funds, treasury may either (1) invest in suitable investments, or (2) pay down existing debt. If there is a shortage of funds, then treasury may either (1) sell off investments, or (2) draw on available debt sources (e.g., credit lines or commercial paper issuance).

This chapter will focus primarily on the first two cash flows, Concentration is discussed in more detail in Chapter 10, Collections, Concentration, and Disbursements, and liquidity management is discussed in Chapter 5, Money Markets, and Chapter 11, Short-Term Investing and Borrowing.

1. PURCHASE-TO-PAY TIMELINE

For most companies, the purchase-to-pay timeline represents the time from the purchase of raw materials, retail goods, or services until payment is received and collected, as illustrated in Exhibit 8.2. Purchase-to-pay represents an outflow of cash.

EXHIBIT 8.2 PURCHASE-TO-PAY TIMELINE

Purchasing Timeline (Purchase-to-Pay)

The purchase-to-pay timeline depicted in Exhibit 8.2 is typical of many firms whether they are manufacturing a product from raw materials or purchasing retail goods for resale to consumers. In either event, the period of time between purchase and ultimate sale involves the creation of inventory, which is shown in Exhibit 8.3.

2. INVENTORY TIMELINE

EXHIBIT 8.3 INVENTORY TIMELINE

Inventory Timeline

For a manufacturing company, the process of acquiring raw materials and parts, converting them into finished goods, storing the goods as inventory, and shipping the goods when sold may be lengthy. In a retail business, the time from acquisition of retail inventory to its ultimate sale may be considerably faster. Further, for businesses that supply customers with information (e.g., from economic advice and real estate listings to an infinite variety of data), the process of filling an order may be immediate, resulting in very little actual inventory.

3. ORDER–TO-CASH TIMELINE

The order-to-cash timeline, illustrated in Exhibit 8.4, is a cash inflow and represents the final piece of the operating cycle. It includes all of the tasks involved in soliciting customers and converting inventory into sales and ultimately into cash. The actual receipt and processing of a payment (highlighted in Exhibit 8.4) is sometimes referred to as the *collection-to-cash cycle*. Management of that process is discussed in Chapter 10, Collections, Concentration, and Disbursements.

EXHIBIT 8.4 **ORDER-TO-CASH TIMELINE**

4. CASH FLOW TIMELINE

When combined, the three timelines constitute the complete cash flow timeline, illustrated in Exhibit 8.5.

EXHIBIT 8.5 **CASH FLOW TIMELINE**

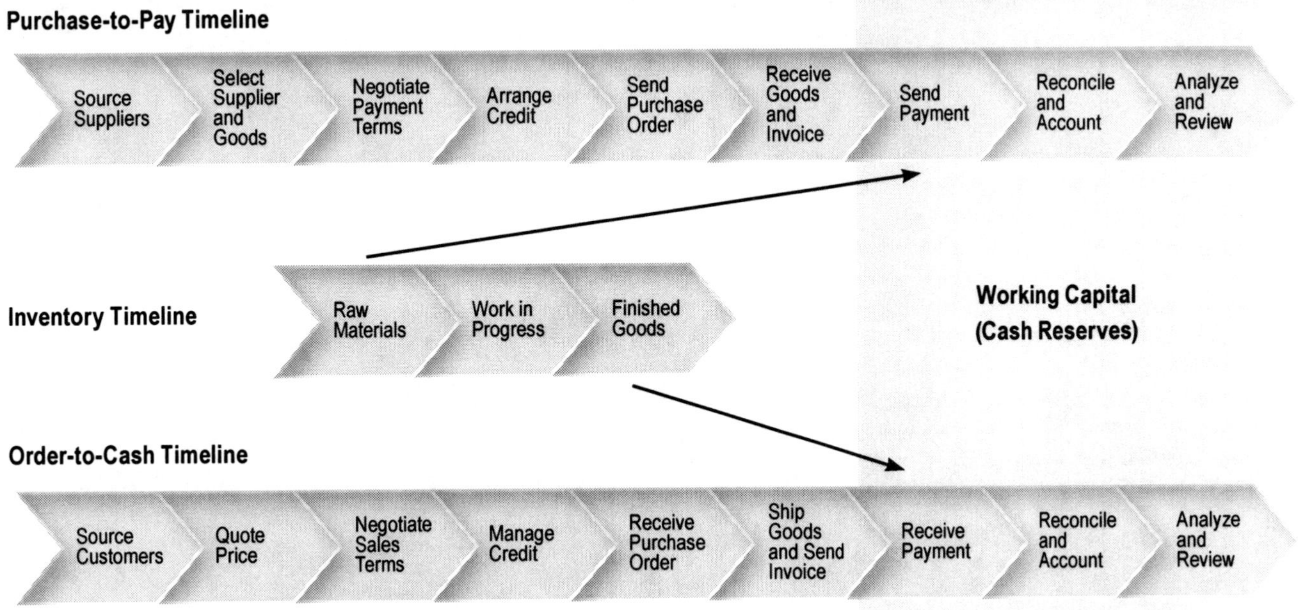

The difference between the various timelines creates working capital, which is, in effect, a reserve of cash. As discussed throughout the remainder of the chapter, treasury professionals normally do their best to optimize this cash reserve by lengthening the purchase-to-pay timeline and shortening the order-to-cash timeline.

It is important to realize, however, that purchase-to-pay and order-to-cash are opposite sides of the same coin—that is to say that one company's purchase-to-pay is another company's order-to-cash. Any actions that the first company may take to extend its purchase-to-pay timeline will automatically also extend the second company's order-to-cash timeline, and vice versa. As a result there is a constant dynamic at play as treasury professionals at different companies take actions that impact their pieces of the timeline.

B. Float

The cash flow timeline spans the interval that begins with the purchase of raw materials or parts from vendors and suppliers at the start of the operating cycle and ends when payment is received from customers at the completion of the operating cycle.

Float refers to the time interval, or delay, between the start and the completion of a specific phase or process occurring along the cash flow timeline. Float is often the result of wait time (e.g., the time lost while waiting for someone else to take action or the time needed to transmit information between two parties) and inefficiencies within a specific process, but is also often increased by the use of paper processes and delivery systems, such as the mailing of invoices to a business's customers. As the use of e-commerce and related technology has expanded, the overall level of float created by paper processes has been declining for most companies. However, float may still be created if there are delays in a certain process. For example, invoices may be sent via e-mail or another electronic format, but if the seller is slow to create those invoices and send them out, then float will occur as part of that process. Exhibit 8.6 illustrates some of the typical types of float that treasury professionals have to manage, and shows their relative length in days.

EXHIBIT 8.6 **FLOAT TIMELINE**

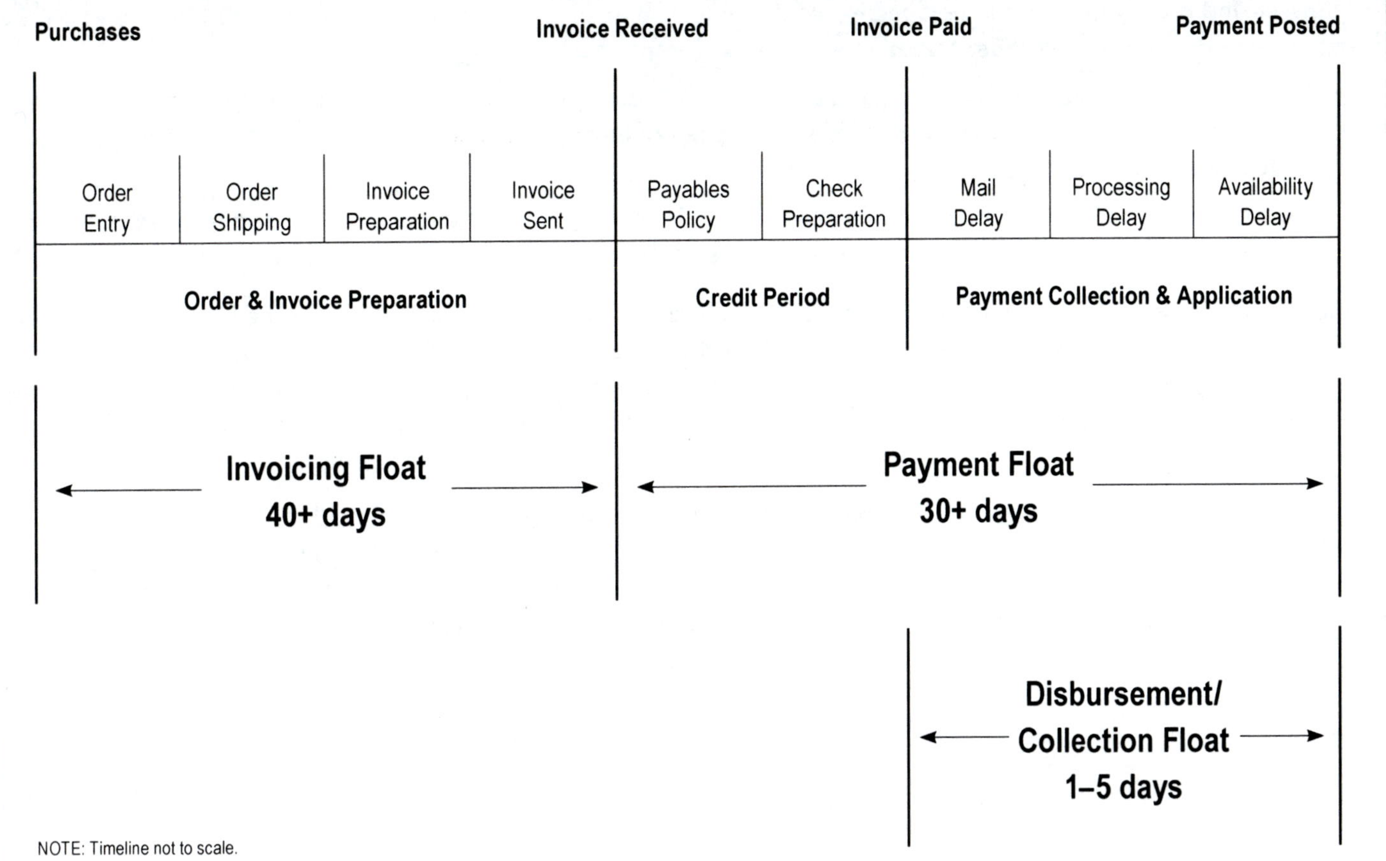

The term *float* often is used just to refer to disbursement/collection float, the period of time that occurs between the creation of a payment and the actual time when the payment is credited in good funds to the payee's account. As can be seen in Exhibit 8.6, this type of float is typically the smallest piece of float with which a treasury professional needs to be concerned.

While e-commerce has moved quickly in many countries and in many industries, some countries still rely heavily on the use of paper processes for many of their business-to-business (B2B) transactions. While it may be typical for a global organization to use electronic billing and electronic payment of invoices, the common practice in much of the world is still a mailed invoice to the buyer, with the remittance advice being mailed back to the seller. The delays inherent in this type of paper-based system result in numerous types of float that companies must manage.

1. DIFFERENT TYPES OF FLOAT

Different float terms may refer to the same or similar time intervals, but specific usage varies, depending upon whether the time period is viewed from the perspective of the seller/payee or the buyer/payor, as illustrated in Exhibit 8.7. For example, consider the term *payment float* when a check[1] is sent to pay an invoice:

- From the seller/payee's perspective, payment float (including mail, processing, and availability float) represents the delay between the time an invoice is sent to the buyer and the time the seller/payee's account is credited with available funds.
- From the buyer/payor's perspective, payment float (including mail, processing, and clearing float) represents the delay between the time an invoice is received and the time the buyer/payor's account is debited.

Collection float (for the seller/payee) represents the time interval or delay between the time the buyer/payor initiates payment and the time the seller/payee receives good funds, while disbursement float (for the buyer/payor) is the time interval or delay between the day when a payment is initiated and the day when funds are debited from the buyer/payor's account. Invoicing float represents the delay between the purchase of goods or services and the receipt of an invoice by the buyer/payor.

Information float is a separate type of float that refers to the inability to use or generate cash due to a delay in receiving related information. For example, if a customer payment has been received but not posted to accounts receivable due to lack of remittance information, the customer may not be able to make additional purchases because it may appear to have exceeded its credit limit (open-to-buy line) even though a payment has been received.

1. Checks are used in this example because check payments illustrate types of float—for example, mail and clearing (check) float—not typically seen in electronic payments.

EXHIBIT 8.7 **TWO SIDES OF FLOAT**

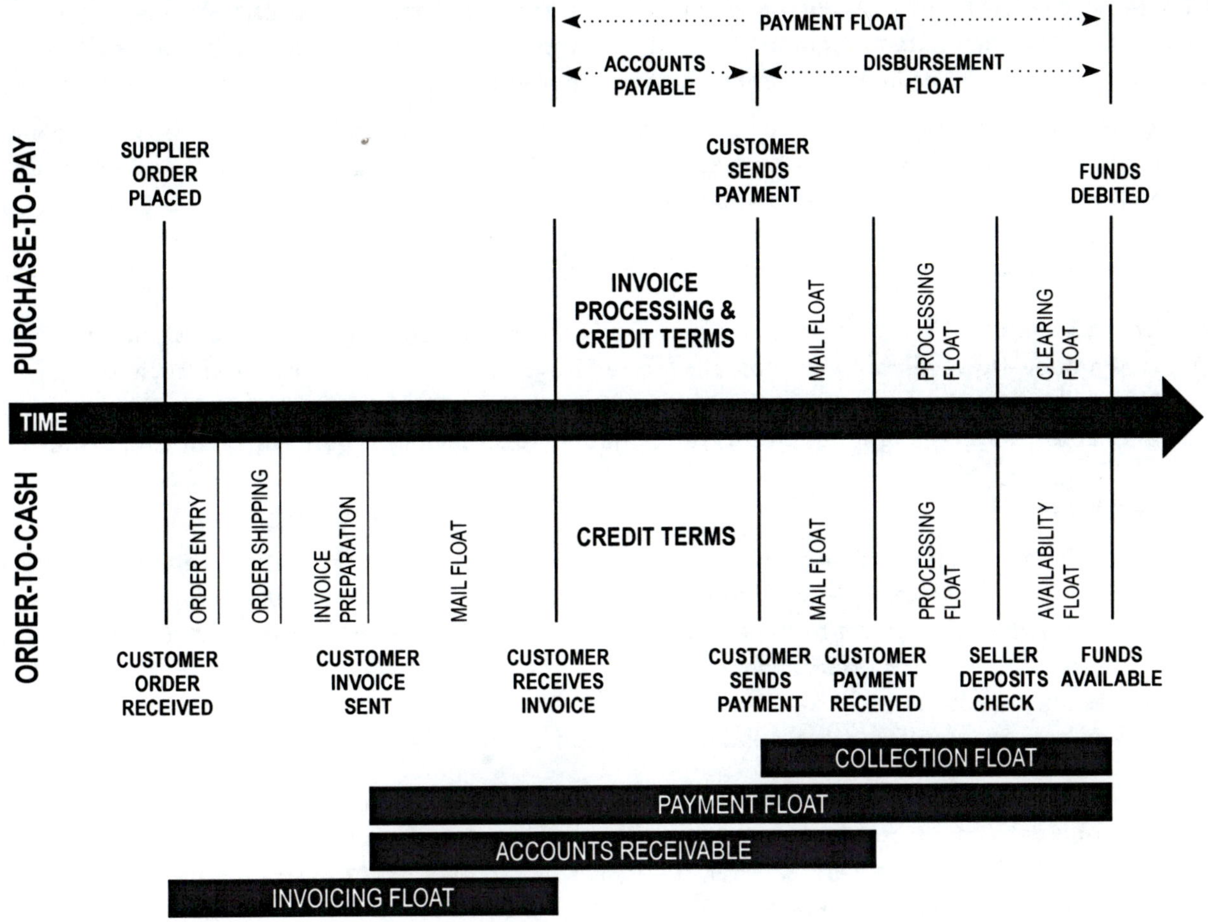

NOTE: Assumes payment by check. Timeline not to scale.

a. Collection Float

Collection float is the time interval or delay between the time the buyer/payor initiates payment and the time the seller/payee receives good funds. Collection float applies principally to paper-based payment instruments that are subject to three types of float or delays:

- **Mail Float:** The time interval or delay between the day a payment (and any related remittance information) is mailed and the day it is received by a payee or at a payee's processing site. Mail float usually ranges between as little as a day or two to many days or even weeks in the case of international payments.

- **Processing Float:** The time interval or delay between the time the payee or the payee's processing site receives the payment and the time the payment (typically a check) is deposited into the payee's account. Processing time is required to capture remittance and payor information, and to prepare the deposit. Processing float is typically one day or less, but may extend for more days if the processing system is inefficient or has any built-in processing delays, such as receiving payments at branch locations but sending them elsewhere for final processing.
- **Availability Float:** The time interval or delay between the day when a payment is deposited into a bank account and the day when the payee's account is credited with collected funds. Availability float varies but ranges from zero to two business days domestically, and even longer for international payments. As discussed in Chapter 4, Payment Systems, availability is often negotiable and is determined by the depository institution's availability schedule or the availability schedule negotiated with the institution by its customer.

The primary cost associated with collection float is opportunity cost because uncollected funds cannot be invested or used to pay down debt. However, the methods used to reduce or eliminate collection float, such as remote deposit capture (RDC) or lockbox services, should be weighed against the cost of achieving those improvements. These topics are covered in Chapter 9, Working Capital Metrics, and Chapter 10, Collections, Concentration, and Disbursements.

b. Disbursement Float

Disbursement float is the time interval or delay between the day when a payment is initiated and the day when funds are debited from the payor's account. As with collection float, disbursement float applies principally to paper-based payment instruments, which are subject to three types of delays or float: mail, processing, and clearing. Disbursement float is analogous to collection float, except that it is viewed from the payor's perspective. As illustrated in Exhibit 8.7, the mail and processing float components of disbursement float are the same as in collection float. The primary difference between collection and disbursement float is availability versus clearing float.

Clearing float is the time interval or delay between the day when a check is deposited by the payee and the day when the payor's account is debited. In most cases, the payee's account is credited with collected funds at the same time the payor's account is debited. In some cases, however, there also may be clearing float considerations related to the use of disbursements with automated clearinghouse (ACH) network credits. Some banks require that certain customers fund ACH disbursements upon initiation rather than when the actual value transfer takes place.

c. Invoicing Float

Invoicing float is the delay between the day that a customer places an order and the day that the customer actually receives an invoice for that order that can be processed for payment. The major components of invoice float are order entry and billing system delays, as well as mail float when a paper invoice is mailed to the customer. As shown in Exhibit 8.6, invoicing float is typically much larger than collection or disbursement float. The implementation of e-commerce and other technology tools, discussed in Chapter 14, Information Technology in Treasury, can significantly reduce invoicing float.

d. Payment Float

As discussed above, payment float is the period of time between the day that a bill or invoice is sent/received (depending on the perspective of the seller or buyer) and the day that payment is actually credited to the biller's bank account. By definition, payment float includes disbursement/collection float, but this is usually just a small part of the total payment float. The largest portion of payment float is typically related to the customer's payables policy and the trade (credit) terms that have been negotiated between the biller and the customer. While this delay can be the result of process inefficiencies related to receiving, verifying, and paying a specific invoice, it is more commonly caused by customers' deferring payment until a specific due date, as discussed below in the section on disbursement system considerations. Depending upon trade terms and the willingness of specific customers to delay payments, payment float can often be the largest float component in any commercial payment process. As a result, it can also provide the greatest opportunity for improvement and effective management. As with invoicing float, payment float can be significantly reduced by e-commerce, but effective management of trade terms can typically provide even greater benefit.

2. INFORMATION FLOAT

Information float is different from other types of float in that instead of referring to delays in the actual collection of funds, it refers to lack of knowledge about the funds themselves. Information float is the time between receiving good funds and the time the organization knows that it has the funds available and can actually make use of those funds. This is especially critical for global organizations due to the significant time differences they must deal with. Even when daily balance information is available from a company's global banks, it is often prior-day balances, and value may be lost by not being able to move those balances until the next business day.

For a company receiving payments on A/R, there may also be delays between the receipt of the payment and the posting of that payment to a customer's account. If the customer is close to its credit limit, this could, in turn, delay the ability of the company to sell more goods or services to that customer.

3. BENEFITS OF FLOAT REDUCTION

A company typically benefits from shortening all types of float associated with collections and lengthening all types of float associated with disbursements. However, it is important to note that suppliers have an incentive to engage in actions that minimize the company's payment float, while customers try to maximize the company's collection float. Traditionally, the rule in cash management is to collect quickly and disburse slowly, within the constraints of prudent business practices and the maintenance of good relations with trading partners and other stakeholders. Accordingly, partners along the supplier-producer-customer chain have opposing incentives. The introduction of electronic payment systems, including commercial cards, has changed this to an extent because the efficiency and benefits of the new payment methods outweigh the benefits of slower paper-based payments, resulting in quicker disbursements. This is reflected in the float-neutral calculation discussion below.

In many industries, therefore, companies are taking a win-win approach by establishing strategic partner relationships with both suppliers and customers. In these industries, the focus has shifted away from the end of the operating cycle shown in Exhibit 8.1 (sell and collect) and toward the beginning of the operating cycle (purchase and build). In other words, the focus has shifted to the areas that represent the greatest possible gains in reducing cycle time, such as just-in-time (JIT) inventory and supply chain management.[2] For those industries and companies that have realigned trading partner relationships and reengineered supply chain management, the trend is to replace checks with electronic payment methods and to replace paper invoices with electronic data interchange (EDI), thereby eliminating all paper-based float delays.

4. FOCUS OF TREASURY IN THE CASH FLOW TIMELINE

For treasury areas, however, the focus often remains on the payment portion of the cycle. Efficiencies can usually be realized in the payment process by replacing paper document flows and payments with electronic methods. In some cases, a buyer will agree to electronic payment rather than paper-based if the seller agrees to float-neutral terms, where either the timing (i.e., value date) of the payment is adjusted or a discount is offered so as to maintain whatever float the buyer was receiving with the paper payment.

Calculation Example: Float-Neutral Calculation

Assume a business transaction where the buyer can either pay by check or by electronic transfer. If the difference between the value date of the payment methods (from the buyer's perspective) is three days, then float-neutral terms would either allow the buyer to pay electronically three days later than by check or offer the buyer a discount that would make the electronic payment equivalent to the check payment. (This example assumes no difference in the cost of the payment methods to the buyer.)

If the discount approach is used, the amount of the discount will be dependent on the cost of funds (i.e., opportunity cost) for the buyer and the timing difference in days between check and electronic payments.

The general formula for determining the appropriate discount is as follows:

$$\text{Discount} = 1 - \frac{1}{1 + TD\left(\frac{r}{365}\right)}$$

Where:

TD = Total days' difference in timing between check and electronic payments

r = Opportunity cost as an annual rate

2. Supply chain management is the integration of business processes with the entire chain of channel partners, which can include suppliers, intermediaries, third-party service providers, and customers.

For this calculation, assume TD = 3 days, as suggested in the text above, and r = 12%. This results in the following discount for float-neutral terms:

$$\text{Discount} = 1 - \frac{1}{1 + 3\left(\frac{0.12}{365}\right)}$$

$$= 1 - \frac{1}{1.0009863} = 1 - 0.99901467$$

$$= 0.00098533$$

$$= 0.001 \text{ (rounded), or } 0.10\%$$

Therefore, if the buyer is allowed to take a discount of 0.10% for paying electronically, the buyer should be indifferent (at least in present value terms) between paying by check or by electronic transfer.

III. THE WORKING CAPITAL CASH CONVERSION CYCLE (CCC)

The continuous flow of cash through working capital accounts results in the CCC, which explains and calculates how much time elapses from when funds are disbursed in direct support of a revenue-generating activity until the time when funds are recovered from revenues. In this chapter, the CCC is used to show how strategies concerning inventory, receivables, and payables interact to affect the flow of cash through the company. A diagram that illustrates the relationship between the various elements of the cash conversion cycle appears in Exhibit 8.8.

EXHIBIT 8.8 **ELEMENTS OF CASH FLOW**

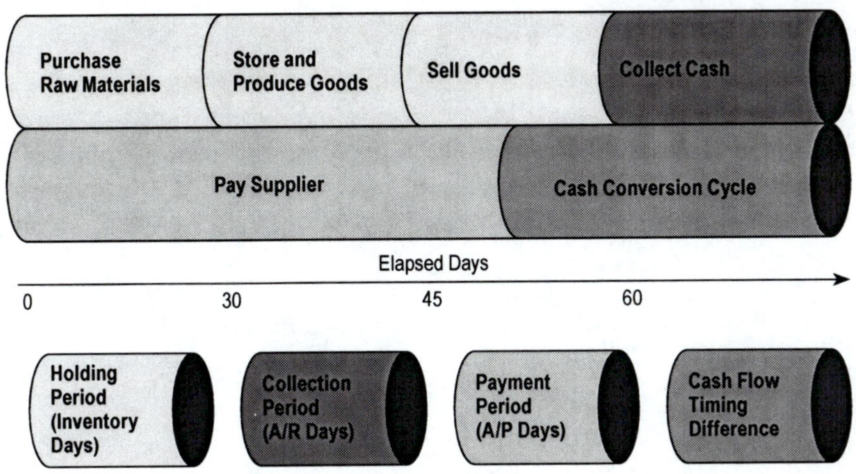

Exhibit 8.8 lays out the various elements of the cash conversion cycle in a linear fashion and shows that the cycle begins when inventory is purchased and ends when available funds are collected from A/R. If all payments were settled in cash at the time of purchase or sale, the CCC would start with the purchase of raw materials and end with the sale of finished goods. In reality, inventory is typically purchased on credit, which does not require cash, as the payment is not made until some later time through the A/P system, and sales are often on credit and not collected until some time after the actual sale is completed. As a result, while the cash conversion cycle begins with the purchase of raw materials, the CCC metric is the timing difference between the actual payment for those materials and the collection of cash from the sale of finished goods. In other words, the CCC is the period of time between disbursement for the A/P and collection of the A/R. The CCC process involves basically the same elements that were previously presented in the cash flow timeline in Exhibit 8.5, with the elements rearranged to focus on the timing differences between disbursement for product and collection for sales. This cycle should be as short as possible because the CCC influences a company's financial performance.

A. Days' Inventory (DI) or Inventory Conversion Period

For a manufacturing company, days' inventory, or the inventory conversion period (also referred to as *days' sales in inventory,* or *DSI*), is the average number of days that elapse from the purchase of raw materials until the sale of finished goods. This period of time is the sum of the average number of days that:

- Raw materials remain in inventory
- Raw materials are converted into finished goods (work-in-progress inventory)
- Finished goods remain in inventory

Any decision that affects the raw materials, work in progress, or finished goods held in inventory impacts the inventory conversion period.

For a retail business, days' inventory is the average length of time that finished goods inventory is held before sale. For a service company, the inventory conversion period is determined by the average length of time that materials are held in inventory until they are used to provide services. (In practice this may be inconsequential.) Inventory management techniques, such as just-in-time (JIT), can reduce inventory levels significantly and are covered in more detail later in this chapter.

B. Days' Receivables (DR) or Receivables Conversion Period

For manufacturing, retail, and service companies, the days' receivables, or receivables conversion period, is the average number of days required to convert a sale into a collection. Changes in A/R policies (e.g., credit standards, credit terms, or collection efforts) impact the receivables conversion period. Any changes in the competitive marketplace or general business conditions also may impact days' receivables. A related measure to days' receivables (DR) is days' sales outstanding (DSO), which measures the average amount of credit sales that are in A/R. Both DSO and DR are covered in greater detail in Chapter 9, Working Capital Metrics.

C. Days' Payables (DP) or Payables Conversion Period

For all types of companies, the days' payables, or payables conversion period, is the average number of days between the purchase/receipt of materials or supplies and issuance of payment for them.[3] Days' payables represents the actual trade credit period, which is often very different from stated trade terms. A company with trade terms of net 30 will typically have day's payables somewhat higher than 30. The ability to purchase materials on deferred payment lets the buying company delay the outflow of cash. Any strategy that delays payment lengthens the payables conversion period and shortens the CCC from the buyer's point of view. Delaying payment until near the end of the credit term or the credit discount period enables a company to:

- Use cash to reduce debt
- Invest cash on a short-term basis
- Purchase other assets

Proper payables management is important and provides an effective source of liquidity for many companies, and some companies use this form of "hidden" financing extensively. Deferring payments until the end of the established trade terms and negotiating improved trade terms are both good practices. Unilaterally paying vendors late, while a practice of some companies, is something that should be avoided if at all possible. Firms should be very cautious about stretching payables beyond agreed-upon credit terms because the act of doing so can affect vendor and supplier relationships negatively.

D. Calculating the Cash Conversion Cycle (CCC)

The formula for CCC is:

$$\text{Cash Conversion Cycle} = \text{Days' Inventory} + \text{Days' Receivables} - \text{Days' Payables}$$

CCC is the average number of days between the cash outflow for the acquisition of materials and supplies, and the cash inflow from the sale of products or services. Therefore, the cycle is a method for calculating the average length of time a company must finance a cash outflow before receiving a cash inflow. Assume the following information for a company in determining the CCC:

- Days' inventory = 45 days
- Days' receivables = 35 days
- Days' payables = 30 days

Based on these assumptions, the company's current CCC is 50 days,[4] calculated as:

$$\text{CCC} = 45 + 35 - 30 = 50 \text{ Days}$$

3. For the purposes of the CCC discussion, this text is simply looking at when payment is issued, rather than getting involved in the details of disbursement or collection float, which are discussed in more detail earlier in this chapter.
4. The example provided is typical for most retail or manufacturing companies that routinely have inventory. The calculation for service companies is identical, with the possible exception that because they do not typically carry inventory, days' inventory is 0 days. Using the original assumptions provided above for days' receivables and days' payables, the calculation becomes: CCC (for a service company) = 0 + 35 – 30 = 5 days.

Suppose the company reduces its days' inventory to 40 days by more carefully planning purchases, scheduling production runs, and managing finished goods inventories. Next, by encouraging slow-paying customers to pay within terms, the company reduces its days' receivables to 32 days. Finally, the business discovers it was taking some supplier discounts that were not to its economic advantage. It begins paying these accounts at term, which expands overall days' payables to 33 days. Through these improvements, the company reduces its CCC to 39 days, as follows:

$$\text{CCC} = 40 + 32 - 33 = 39 \text{ Days}$$

Decreased investment in inventory and A/R, and the increased process efficiency in A/P, are all sources of funds. Note that nothing about the business itself has changed. Dollar revenues, unit sales of the product or service, total purchases, and total billings remained constant. What has changed is that the company now recovers a dollar spent for materials inventory (e.g., finished goods inventory for a retail firm) in 39 rather than 50 days, which significantly reduces its investment in net working capital. Since the overall volume of business has not changed over the accounting period, total disbursements from cash balances have not changed.

Companies can also determine another measure called *cash turnover* from the CCC. The formula for cash turnover is:

$$\text{Cash Turnover} = \frac{365}{\text{Cash Conversion Cycle}}$$

In the earlier example, when the CCC was 50 days, cash turnover was 365/50, or 7.3 times per year. Reducing the CCC to 39 days increases cash turnover to 9.4 times (i.e., 365/39 = 9.4). Since total disbursements are the same, the only way cash turnover can increase is if the company is operating with a smaller amount of working capital.

Note that this example includes reducing the investment in inventory and increasing the funding provided by A/P. The net result is a reduction in current assets and in the amount of current liabilities needed to finance current assets. Increasing A/P may also help to reduce interest-bearing, short-term debt. Shortening the CCC reduced the company's investment in total assets and increased net income by lowering interest expense and inventory carrying costs.

Note also that the CCC calculation is based upon averages over a given period of time. To the extent that actual payment and receipt patterns are uneven (e.g., a company may only make disbursements once a week or at the end of a month), the CCC calculation may not match real-world numbers at a given point in time.

The CCC can be shortened by reducing the receivables and inventory conversion periods and by extending the payables conversion period. Taking these actions may improve profitability and the value of the firm. However, caution is warranted when pursuing operating policies that produce these results. The improvement in financial performance will be short-lived if some or all of the following occur:

- Lost sales due to overly strict credit and collection standards
- Production stoppages attributable to inadequate raw materials or parts inventories
- Payables stretched beyond the due date
- Foregone cost-saving trade discounts
- Higher prices assessed by vendors because individual orders are smaller or payment is slower
- Refusal to sell to customers that are good credit risks but occasionally slow in paying
- Excessive reliance on A/P in lieu of a stable base of short-term bank credit

The decision to implement policies that enhance short-term (and possibly long-term) profitability must be weighed against the considerations listed previously. If any or all of them lead to the loss of goodwill with a customer, supplier, or bank, then they are likely to be counterproductive in the long run. To avoid this consequence, treasury staff must perform a cost/benefit assessment and a qualitative analysis.

E. Evaluating the Impact of Changes to the Cash Flow Timeline

In several of the sections below, the impact of a change to the cash flow timeline is discussed. Examples of related calculations are presented in Chapter 9, Working Capital Metrics. In evaluating different cash flow alternatives, the general approach is to determine the present value of each alternative at some interest rate and choose the best alternative for the organization (i.e., the lowest present value cost or highest present value benefit). The relevant interest rate is usually referred to as the *opportunity cost* for the decision in question.

In a general financial sense, the most common opportunity cost used is the weighted average cost of capital (WACC), which is discussed in Chapter 20, Financial Decisions and Management. However, WACC may not be the proper cost to use for working capital decisions. WACC is primarily a cost of long-term capital, and for many organizations, it may be more appropriate to use some short-term measure for opportunity cost. The idea behind opportunity cost is to determine what the most attractive unused alternative is for any funds or balances that are generated as a result of the decision. Opportunity cost is discussed in more detail in Chapter 9, Working Capital Metrics.

For example, if an organization is offered different terms for paper versus electronic payments (covered earlier in this chapter), the primary consideration on the proper opportunity cost is where will the organization get the funds for paying earlier via electronic means (assuming loss of clearing float as a result of electronic payment). If the organization is generally a net borrower (on a short-term basis), then the appropriate opportunity cost would be its short-term borrowing rate (assuming it would have to borrow in order to make an earlier payment). If, on the other hand, the organization is a net investor (in the short-term), then the appropriate opportunity cost would be its short-term investment rate (assuming it would have to sell off some short-term investments to make an earlier payment).

Alternatively, some organizations may decide that using WACC for working capital decision evaluations is the best course for them. The rationale is that short-term rates may fluctuate rapidly in some economic situations, and an organization may prefer to have a rate that is more stable over time.

For the remainder of this chapter, the general term *opportunity cost* will be used to represent the cost of funds for any of the alternatives discussed. The actual opportunity cost used by an organization will vary depending on its circumstances.

IV. HOW CHANGES IN CURRENT ACCOUNTS IMPACT EXTERNAL FINANCING

Many current asset and current liability accounts vary whenever sales activity occurs. These accounts are called *spontaneous* because no specific working capital management decisions are involved in increasing these accounts. Changes in account levels occur as account activity fluctuates with a change in the level of sales activity. The magnitude of spontaneous changes significantly impacts the amount of external financing necessary for working capital.

A. Changes in Current Assets

Generally, as the volume of sales activity increases, credit sales also increase, resulting in larger dollar amounts invested in A/R. Additional sales may require increases in raw materials and parts inventories to support the production of finished goods, thereby increasing both inventory and A/P. An increase in A/R and inventory may decrease the cash account or increase short-term borrowing to support the working capital requirement. If the increased level of sales activity is permanent, then it should result in a larger investment in cash and short-term securities to provide adequate liquidity in the business to match the new sales levels. Increases in noncash current assets must be supported by reducing cash and by increasing debt and other liabilities. Conversely, a sales decrease should cause a corresponding decrease in current asset accounts, although inventory may increase in the short term while production schedules are adjusted to reflect the lower sales level.

B. Changes in Current Liabilities

A decrease in A/P results in a decrease in cash or an increase in debt to pay off the accounts, because decreases in current liabilities must be offset by decreases in an asset account or increases in other liability accounts. For example, a larger volume of sales activity typically requires a higher volume of materials purchased. If these materials are purchased on vendor credit, then the A/P account increases. Likewise, the additional labor expenses associated with increased production would increase the accrued wages account. A tax increase due to a higher level of taxable income also would increase the accrued taxes account. On the other hand, a decrease in sales activity should cause corresponding decreases in these accounts.

C. External Financing Requirements

As current asset accounts increase, the need for working capital normally increases. Further, as the company generates additional profits, the retained earnings account increases. If the need for working capital exceeds the increase in funds generated by additional profits, the difference must be financed. Therefore, the total of net increases in current asset accounts represents the total amount of financing necessary to fund working capital, assuming cash flows do not change due to fluctuations in long-term assets or liabilities.

If current assets decrease, funds have been released from investments in A/R and/or inventory, so the overall need for short-term liabilities to support current assets declines. If, however, there is a more-than-corresponding decline in non-interest-bearing current liabilities (e.g., A/P, and wages and taxes payable), then additional short- and/or long-term debt must support the current assets.

V. WORKING CAPITAL INVESTMENT AND FINANCING STRATEGIES

A treasury professional must establish a framework for assessing the risk/return trade-offs involved in working capital management. The framework must include investment and financing strategies that reflect the firm's needs and attitude toward risk taking, with consideration given to industry practices. In effect, a treasury professional makes two decisions: (1) how much working capital to have, and (2) how to finance that working capital. In practice, these decisions are made concurrently because they impact one another. The following sections address considerations surrounding how much to invest in working capital and how much working capital to finance.

A. Current Asset Investment Strategies

The extent of the company's uncertainty and risk tolerance determines its investment levels in current asset accounts. Current asset accounts tend to vary spontaneously with changes in sales, while risk is related to the stability and predictability of sales. The less stable and less predictable sales are, the higher the dollar investment in current assets must be in relation to the flow of sales. This practice helps the company ensure that its inventory can meet customers' demands in an unstable selling market.

A company must choose a current asset investment strategy that suits its business needs, risk tolerance, and management style. If the company's management is conservative, then it will select a high level of current assets to sales, which will lead to higher liquidity (i.e., safety), but lower profitability. If management prefers to take risks in the interest of generating higher profitability, then it will operate with a low current assets to sales ratio. A restrictive (or less liquid) strategy and a relaxed (or more liquid) strategy are contrasted in the following sections.

1. RESTRICTIVE CURRENT ASSET INVESTMENT STRATEGY

Under a restrictive current asset investment strategy, a company maintains low levels of current assets relative to sales. The investment in raw materials is managed as tightly as possible using JIT inventory techniques. Additionally, outstanding A/R and cash balances are kept low, reflecting a restrictive credit policy.

A restrictive current asset investment strategy may entail relatively higher risks associated with the tighter management of credit and inventory, as well as the lack of cash available for accounts payable. In particular, a restrictive credit policy may impact sales negatively. Likewise, a restrictive inventory policy may negatively impact the selection of goods available to meet consumer demands. A restrictive strategy is typically the most profitable as long as unexpected events do not drive down liquidity to the point that it causes severe problems.

2. RELAXED CURRENT ASSET INVESTMENT STRATEGY

Under a relaxed current asset investment strategy, a company maintains high levels of current assets relative to sales. Typically, these current assets consist of high levels of inventory and A/R. High levels of A/R are usually a result of a liberal credit policy, while high levels of inventory may result from concerns over replenishing raw materials or a reluctance to lose a sale due to insufficient finished goods inventory. A large investment in current assets is likely to lower investment returns, but the firm operates with less risk because of its larger liquid asset balances.

3. SELECTING A CURRENT ASSET INVESTMENT STRATEGY

Which current asset investment strategy a company selects depends upon its risk/return trade-off characteristics. The opinions of the company's creditors are important. Banks and other lenders attach importance to the firm's liquidity level because it factors into their decisions about credit extension and loan interest rates. They also consider the quality of A/R and inventories, especially when pledged as security for a loan. Many companies, especially smaller ones, are forced to pursue a restrictive strategy due to the limited availability of short-term credit or limited overall capitalization.

A company's current asset strategy may also be influenced by industry practices. In industries with high gross profit margins on sales, a liberal credit policy may offer substantial benefits, especially if the potential for additional profit greatly outweighs potential costs. This observation assumes that profits gained from additional sales exceed the costs of carrying the additional receivables and any additional bad debt costs.

B. Current Asset Financing Strategies

Decisions about how to finance permanent and fluctuating current assets define a company's working capital financing strategy. While it may seem strange to talk about "permanent" current assets, the concept is important when considering financing. For any given organization, there will be a certain minimum amount of current assets that it must have to do business. This number will vary by company and industry, but one way of identifying it is to examine the balance sheet and determine the lowest amount of current assets that a given company has had in the past several years. This base is considered *permanent current assets* and anything over that amount is considered *fluctuating current assets.* Because the company can reasonably assume that, barring major problems, the value of its current assets will not fall below the permanent base, it can consider financing current assets with longer-term debt.

The basic decision is whether to place greater reliance on short- or long-term sources of funding. Short-term debt, with an original maturity of less than one year (e.g., a line of credit), enables a firm to adjust the amount of financing to the fluctuation in current assets so it never has excess financing and never pays interest unnecessarily. On the other hand, if the company cannot obtain a multiyear revolving credit agreement (i.e., a revolver), then the line of credit must be renewed annually. Longer-term debt (e.g., an intermediate-term loan of four or five years) guarantees financing during those years. Under these conditions, however, the firm has excess financing and pays interest unnecessarily during the year if the amount of borrowing is at or approaches the estimated need when fluctuating current assets peak. In some cases, the assets themselves may be used as collateral to facilitate the process, as discussed below in the section on A/R financing.

The choice of financing depends heavily upon management's risk orientation, but it also is influenced by interest rate differentials among short-, intermediate-, or long-term debt. (This difference is referred to as the *yield curve* and is discussed in more detail in Chapter 11, Short-Term Investing and Borrowing.) A treasury professional must know whether it is less expensive to borrow from the money markets or banks continuously, or to lock in to an intermediate- or long-term rate by obtaining a term loan or accessing funds via capital markets.

Approaches to the financing decision may be classified as *maturity matching, conservative,* and *aggressive*. These policy approaches are shown in Exhibit 8.9. The top bar in the exhibit partitions current assets into permanent and fluctuating categories. The remaining bars depict the mix of short- and long-term financing associated with the three strategies. Depending on current interest rates, the forecast of future rates, and especially management's risk tolerance, any of these approaches may be appropriate at a particular time.

EXHIBIT 8.9 **ALTERNATIVE CURRENT ASSET FINANCING STRATEGIES**

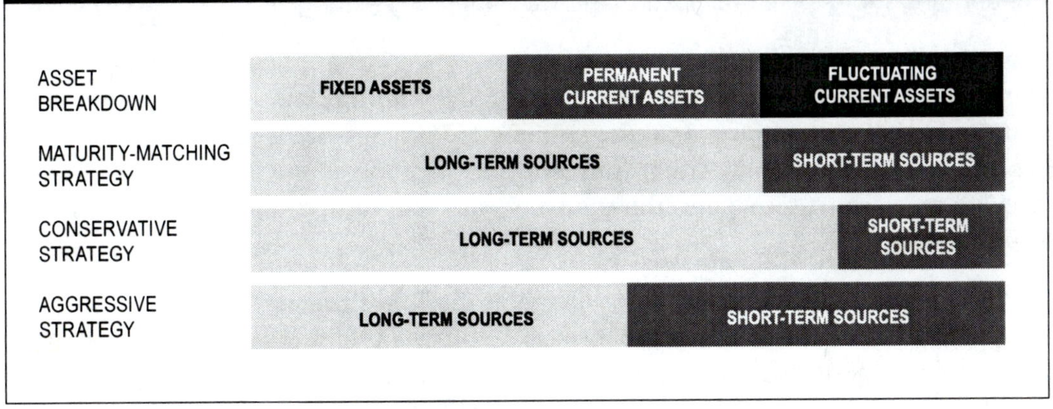

1. MATURITY-MATCHING FINANCING STRATEGY

Under a maturity-matching financing strategy, the total of permanent current assets and fixed assets are financed with long-term financing (e.g., debt and equity). Short-term financing is used to finance fluctuating current assets. This means that the amount of short-term financing at a given time mirrors the amount of fluctuating current assets at that time. This is the intention when financing with a line of credit. As fluctuating assets expand, drawing on the line increases to support that expansion. When the assets decline, funds are released and are used to pay down the line of credit.

2. CONSERVATIVE FINANCING STRATEGY

Under a conservative financing strategy, long-term financing supports fixed assets, permanent current assets, and some portion of fluctuating current assets. A company usually tries to finance the average level of fluctuating current assets with long-term sources. Short-term financing is used for the remainder of the fluctuating current assets. Since short-term financing is used for only a portion of the fluctuating current assets, this strategy generally involves the least use of short-term financing and, therefore, has higher financing costs than other approaches because long-term debt is carried when it is not needed.[5]

The relatively lower reliance on short-term financing results in a higher current ratio, but it also may result in lower profits for the company because of the higher total interest expense. It is possible, however, that interest rate risk may be mitigated if long-term debt is borrowed on a fixed-rate basis and short-term financing is acquired on a floating- or variable-rate basis.

3. AGGRESSIVE FINANCING STRATEGY

Under an aggressive financing strategy, a company finances all fixed assets with long-term debt and equity, but finances only a portion of permanent current assets with long-term

5. The higher financing costs result since there are times when the amount of funds borrowed on a long-term basis will exceed the required investment in fluctuating current assets. The excess amount will be invested in short-term investments and will most likely have a lower rate of return than the rate being paid on the long-term borrowing (assuming a normal yield curve).

financing. Short-term financing supports the remainder of the permanent current assets and all temporary current assets. This strategy utilizes more ongoing short-term financing than other financing strategies.

Short-term financing typically costs less than long-term financing because the yield curve is upward sloping most of the time. Consequently, this strategy is often the most profitable because it is the least costly. However, the greater use of short-term financing results in a lower current ratio and greater liquidity risk. The risk is associated with more volatile short-term interest rates and the need to renew credit frequently. In addition, if the lender has an annual "cleanup" period,[6] as is common with many short-term lines, the company will need to find some alternative source of financing each year to cover the cleanup.

A poor business year could eventually occur due to a recession, a change in the firm's competitive environment, or other factors. When sales slump, inventory may not be converted into cash quickly enough to avert a cash shortage. Customers that normally pay on time may pay more slowly, causing a further drain on cash. The firm may find itself stretching its A/P beyond the credit term. Profit will be down because of the sales slump and the profit-eroding influence of fixed operating expenses.

In this circumstance, the firm needs to renew its short-term financing arrangement with its bank, but now the firm may look very risky to the bank. The bank may decide it must charge the firm a higher interest rate, but its analysis may reveal that the firm cannot support a higher interest payment. If the bank finds itself in a situation where it must ration credit among its customers, the firm may end up without financing at a critical moment.

The firm invites this situation by choosing to finance itself heavily with short-term debt that must be renewed annually. However, there are variations in financing arrangements that can lessen this risk. For example, there are multiyear revolving credit agreements (usually three to five years) that let companies borrow on a short-term basis, yet classify the loan as long-term for accounting purposes. This type of borrowing arrangement does not reduce the current ratio, as does borrowing under a traditional short-term loan.

4. SUMMARY OF FINANCING STRATEGIES

A company that combines a restrictive current asset investment strategy with an aggressive financing policy may project increased profitability, but travels a risky road. Conversely, a firm that follows a relaxed current asset investment strategy combined with a conservative financing strategy may be excessively liquid, and thus be less profitable than it needs to be. Additionally, companies that have large cash balances and are excessively liquid may be perceived as takeover targets by investors who are more interested in the value of the liquid assets than the operating value of the company itself. A restrictive current asset investment strategy can be mitigated by a conservative financing strategy, and a relaxed current asset investment strategy can be somewhat offset by an aggressive financing strategy. The overall decision involves trade-offs that need to be weighed in light of management's tolerance for risk, sales stability and predictability, lender concerns, the interest rate environment, the availability of funds, supplier reliability, and other factors.

VI. MANAGEMENT OF CREDIT AND ACCOUNTS RECEIVABLE (A/R)

A/R management is linked closely to a company's credit, billing, and collection policies. Efficient A/R management requires the careful monitoring and control of accounts at both the individual and aggregate levels. A treasury professional may have responsibility for arranging the collections/bad debt function (the final stage of the A/R process), as well as have direct or indirect responsibility for financing the company's A/R.

6. Many lenders require their short-term borrowers to completely pay off or "clean up" the outstanding balance on an operating line of credit at least once a year to prove that the line is not really being used for long-term financing. Further details are discussed in Chapter 11, Short-Term Investing and Borrowing.

Trade credit is a contractual arrangement allowing a customer to take possession of a good, product, or service now and pay for it later. The company, in turn, receives a promise of future payment from the buyer, which is the basis for entering the sale as an A/R. Payment is due per the agreed-upon credit terms extended to the customer. Sales, accounting, and finance personnel are involved in credit and A/R management activities.

The primary reason for offering trade credit is to increase sales. Since most sales are made on an open account basis and many customers do not have access to other sources of financing, competition for customers usually requires that a company grant trade credit. This is especially true in industries where credit extension is the norm, such as women's clothing. Credit terms are designed to lure customers away from competitors and encourage existing customers to increase purchases. A liberal credit policy can increase sales, but it also increases account servicing costs, collection costs, and bad debt expense.

Proper management of A/R includes:

- Creating, preserving, and collecting A/R
- Maintaining up-to-date customer records
- Initiating collection procedures on past-due accounts

A. Relationship between Treasury and Credit Management

The treasury and credit management functions are separated in most companies. However, maintaining a good working relationship with departments and employees involved in credit management is important for treasury—especially because credit policies and A/R collection significantly impact the timing of cash inflows.

A company's credit manager administers policies that establish credit standards, defines the terms of trade credit extension, approves customers for credit sales, and sets individual and aggregate credit limits within policy guidelines. Since credit is used as a tool to increase sales, the credit manager usually works closely with the sales manager.

A/R is created once a sale is made and trade credit is extended. A/R management includes billing, posting remittance information, monitoring payment patterns, and collecting delinquent accounts. These duties typically fall under the responsibility of the credit manager. However, some companies outsource credit management and A/R through captive finance companies and/or factors. In either case, it is important that trade terms are negotiated and clearly established during the customer onboarding process. Failure to do so typically leads to collection problems and increased days' receivables.

The methods and tools used to monitor the overall health of A/R are covered in detail in Chapter 9, Working Capital Metrics. In addition, it is important to monitor individual accounts on a regular basis, especially with respect to possible financial distress.

B. Trade Credit Policies

To ensure consistent application and fairness, companies should maintain written credit policies and procedures that clearly define their:

- Credit standards
- Credit terms
- Discount terms
- Collection policies

1. TRADE CREDIT STANDARDS

Establishing trade credit standards is a two-stage process. First, the company must establish credit acceptance criteria that represent a maximum amount of payment risk the company is willing to assume. Second, it must decide whether to approve a credit applicant under the criteria and, if approved, set a credit limit for that applicant.

There are two key considerations when determining credit extension policies:

- If a company implements credit standards that are too strict, it may decline trade credit to customers that represent an acceptable credit risk, thereby limiting sales opportunities.
- If a company implements credit standards that are too lenient, it may grant trade credit to customers that represent an unacceptable credit risk, thereby increasing the risk of late payments and bad debt expenses.

Quantifying the costs of these risk considerations is difficult. However, credit is a sales tool and a zero default rate probably means that a company's credit terms are too strict.

a. Information Sources

A company must consider the type, quantity, and cost of information when establishing a method for analyzing credit requests. Credit information is gathered in stages from internal and external sources. At each stage, costs are weighed against expected benefits. The most important sources of internally generated credit information are a credit application (agreement) completed by the applicant and the company's own records regarding an applicant's payment history.

A company can use various external sources to help determine an applicant's creditworthiness. One primary source is an applicant's financial statements. Both audited and unaudited financial statements provide important information about corporate credit applicants because these statements and related ratios can be compared to industry averages from a variety of sources.

Trade references, or other companies from whom the applicant has purchased on credit, can provide a secondary source of information about the applicant's payment performance. Additionally, banks or other financial creditors (e.g., commercial finance or leasing companies) can provide standardized credit information about an applicant's payment history and available credit. Finally, there are various local and nationwide credit rating agencies that collect, evaluate, and report information about companies' credit histories. These credit reports include information such as payment history, financial information, maximum outstanding credit amounts, the length of time credit has been available, and any outstanding collection actions. Payment experience is provided to the rating agencies on a voluntary basis. That said, the sample used by the rating agency may be small and/or inaccurately represent the firm's overall payment history.

b. The Five Cs of Credit

Credit analysis depends upon the type of information available and the trade-offs between the costs and benefits of the analysis. The traditional factors lenders consider are known as the *five Cs of credit*, which are:

- **Character:** This is the perceived honesty or integrity of an individual applicant or a corporate applicant's officers. Character indicates an intent or willingness to pay, as evidenced by personal or corporate payment history.
- **Capacity:** Capacity represents the current and future financial resources a company or individual has available to pay obligations when they come due. This factor can be assessed using financial liquidity ratios and cash flow forecasts.
- **Capital:** Capital refers to an individual or corporate customer's short- and long-term financial resources that could be accessed if the immediate cash flow is insufficient to meet payment obligations.
- **Collateral:** This factor identifies available assets or guarantees used to secure an obligation in the event that payment terms are not met.
- **Conditions:** This factor assesses the general, existing economic environment that impacts a customer's ability to pay or the willingness of a company to grant credit.

c. Quantitative Credit Analysis

The quantitative analysis of business credit information begins with an examination of a credit applicant's financial statements, usually using ratio analysis to assess a customer's financial condition. (These ratios are discussed in more detail in Chapter 9, Working Capital Metrics, and Chapter 19, Financial Planning and Analysis.) The measures most often used include:

- Liquidity and working capital ratios (e.g., the current, quick, and cash flow to total debt ratios)
- Debt management and coverage ratios (e.g., times interest earned, long-term debt to capital, debt to total assets, and total liabilities to total assets ratios)
- Profitability measures (e.g., return on sales, return on total assets, and return on equity)

Ratios provide valuable insight when evaluated in relation to industry and country standards published by credit rating agencies and other associations. Some commercial credit analysis involves credit scoring, which is evaluated by purchasing credit reports from third-party companies or by generating credit scores based on either internal or external databases.

In the consumer sector, quantitative credit scoring models are used extensively by major issuers of retail credit, such as department stores. Credit scoring involves a four-step process:

- Differentiating standard and high-risk accounts based on the applicant's monthly income, outstanding obligations, and employment history
- Weighting the characteristics of applicants who fit into each category to establish creditworthiness

- Setting cutoff scores for clear approval or denial of credit
- Applying further analysis to applicants whose scores fall between the cutoff points

These quantitative approaches are cost-effective and aid in complying with consumer credit legislation. A formal statistical method termed *discriminant analysis* can identify factors that effectively distinguish between paying and nonpaying customers, sometimes on a region-by-region basis. Consumer credit bureaus also assess creditworthiness based on proprietary models.

In the business-to-business (B2B) world, quantitative credit scoring models[7] are becoming increasingly more common, but are still not as widespread as in the consumer sector. There are several reasons for this:

- The available databases for building commercial credit scoring models are much smaller than those used for consumer models. This makes it more difficult to develop reliable models.
- The per-transaction exposure is usually much larger in the commercial sector than in the consumer sector. While a default by one large commercial customer could have a serious impact on a small seller, this is rarely the case in the consumer sector.
- It is sometimes difficult to obtain financial information for some customers, especially for smaller, private companies.

2. CREDIT TERMS

Establishing credit terms involves designing sales contracts or agreements that clearly specify under what conditions credit terms are granted. Creating collection policies involves determining the steps involved to collect delinquent accounts or bad debts. Finally, a company must develop an information system or purchase software that monitors A/R to ensure compliance with credit terms and to detect changes in customer payment patterns at aggregate and individual customer levels.

A company also must determine the aggregate amount of credit (i.e., the credit limit) it will grant each customer. Companies usually grant a new customer credit at the lowest limit. After a period of satisfactory payment performance, credit limits increase. And companies continuously review a customer's payment history in order to adjust these limits as necessary.

a. Credit Policy Constraints

A number of factors may constrain or influence a company's credit policies. In many industries, credit terms and policies are based on industry standard practices. As a result, it is difficult for a company to vary its terms from those of its competitors. A company also must consider how offering trade credit may impact existing loan covenants. A change in A/R balances can affect working capital ratios, potentially resulting in failing to comply with covenants. There are also legal constraints that can vary significantly from country to country or even within a country.

b. Financing Implications

A company's credit terms, sales, and collection patterns determine its level of A/R. Since A/R must be financed, a company's ability to extend credit relates directly to its ability to borrow. Mismanagement of receivables can cause liquidity problems due to delayed customer payments. However, receivables also may be a source of liquidity when used as collateral for asset-based loans, when used to securitize a debt instrument, or when sold for cash to factors. Factoring is discussed in more detail later in this chapter.

7. An example of a B2B quantitative credit scoring model would be the Altman Z-Score (developed by Professor Edward Altman of New York University's Stern School of Business), which uses publicly available data to predict the probability that a publicly traded company will go bankrupt.

c. Income and Expenses Related to Granting Credit

Trade credit may increase a company's income because the extension of credit increases sales. Another potential source of income arising from credit sales is interest earned from installment payment arrangements. This interest can be a significant source of profit, especially for retail companies that provide direct financing to customers through their own private-label credit cards or installment contracts.

In addition to interest earned from credit sales, companies may assess a penalty fee for payments received after the due date. This fee is usually a percentage of the amount past due and must be stated clearly at the time of the sale and disclosed on the invoice.[8]

Further, there are costs associated with offering trade credit. On the expense side, the primary costs of A/R are carrying costs. Typically, a company determines this cost by using the marginal cost of short-term borrowing or the weighted average cost of capital (WACC). Operating and maintaining a credit department can be very expensive. Personnel costs, data and payment processing costs, and costs related to credit evaluation or obtaining credit information (if a third-party credit bureau is used) are all expenses associated with a credit department. These costs must be weighed against the cost of bad debt, which can be a significant element of A/R cost if not properly managed.

3. CUSTOMER DISCOUNTS

If a company offers discount terms, then the "cost" of discounted payments affects income. When customers take advantage of a discount, but the discount offer does not produce a general increase in sales, net revenue declines. The revenue loss may be fully or partially offset by a reduction in A/R carrying costs. Dynamic discounting takes traditional trade discounts a step further and includes the ability to vary the discount according to the date of early payment; the earlier the payment, the larger the discount. Finally, if discounts are offered, the company must determine a benchmark eligibility date. This can be the postmark date of the payment remittance or the date funds are received. Cash discounts are discussed further in Chapter 9, Working Capital Metrics.

4. PAYMENT DISCREPANCIES

In a typical B2B environment, payment discrepancies can arise from customers paying multiple invoices—each with possible adjustments—with a single payment. The costs associated with monitoring, investigating, and resolving discrepancies between invoices and customer payments can be substantial. Discrepancies must be investigated, the legitimacy of shortfalls and deductions must be ascertained, and all related bookkeeping, invoicing, and payment adjustments must be recorded. Some customers may also use these discrepancies as a reason to delay payment, thus effectively increasing their credit period.

5. MONITORING FINANCIAL DISTRESS

It is critical to monitor each credit account over time for potential financial distress. As financial distress for a particular customer increases, so does the probability of slower payments or default on the account. This monitoring should involve the tracking of

8. Interest and the interest calculation must be disclosed in the sales contract or on the invoice to allow the seller to collect interest in a court of law. Without disclosure, the seller's ability to collect is not enforceable.

payments and level of credit outstanding, as well as monitoring news and press releases issued by the customer. In many cases, the potential for financial distress may appear in the news before the customer is late on its payments.

6. COLLECTION POLICY

Costs related to delinquent account monitoring and bad debt collection impact a company's income. Though accounting conventions may vary somewhat, it is generally the case that uncollectible A/R must be charged off as bad debt. Most companies use historical collection patterns to estimate the level of losses, and create a reserve account through periodic charges to bad debt expense. The timing and volume of bad debt expense and charge-offs are important aspects of a credit policy.

The cost of collecting delinquent accounts can be significant. Companies can reduce the impact of bad debts by purchasing various types of insurance designed to cover receivables losses. Insurance premiums should be included in the cost/benefit analysis when assessing the potential profitability of credit sales.

C. Billing and Collection Methods

The major objective of a collection policy is to convert A/R into cash quickly, while minimizing collection expense and bad debt losses. The type of credit a company offers significantly impacts which collection methods it employs.

Effective A/R management includes reducing invoicing float, which is the interval between the time goods and services are sold to a customer and the time that a customer receives an invoice. The first step in collecting an account is sending accurate and timely invoices with clearly stated payment terms and remittance instructions. Delays in invoice preparation or errors on an invoice may extend the payment process by days or even weeks. This is particularly an issue with customers that use "auto-match" processes that validate invoices against purchase orders and receiving statements (referred to as *three-way match*) to authorize payment of invoices. Minor errors in an invoice can lead to lengthy delays in payment as a result. Sometimes, companies send summary statements of outstanding invoices as a reminder that payment is due. Consumer billing typically involves sending statements listing goods or services purchased during the preceding month.

Electronic bill presentment and payment (EBPP) and electronic invoice presentment and payment (EIPP) are e-commerce tools that are increasingly being used to reduce invoice and payment float and improve overall collections. These topics are discussed in more detail in Chapter 10, Collections, Concentration, and Disbursements.

When payment is not received by the due date, a company can:

- Send a duplicate invoice, or mail a form letter or a series of form letters (i.e., dunning letters)
- Call the customer or pay a personal visit
- Suspend further shipment of goods or terminate services until past-due items are paid
- Negotiate with the customer for payment of overdue amounts

A company typically employs all of these measures as it escalates its collection efforts.

Once a company has exhausted these methods, it may pursue more serious actions, such as reporting the customer's delinquent status to credit bureaus, repossessing collateral, negotiating additional corporate or personal guarantees, obtaining a lien on specific assets, initiating direct legal action, or turning delinquent accounts over to a collection agency.

D. Forms of Credit Extension

There are four basic forms of credit extension: open account or open book credit, installment credit, revolving credit, and letter of credit.

- **Open Account:** Open account, sometimes called *open book credit*, is the most common type of commercial trade credit. A seller issues an invoice as formal evidence of the obligation and records the sale as an A/R. The buyer is billed for each transaction by an invoice and/or monthly statement. Full payment of invoiced amounts is expected within the specified credit terms unless certain discounts or deductions are available to the buyer. A buyer's creditworthiness is reviewed periodically, but the buyer does not need to apply for credit each time it places an order.
- **Installment Credit:** Installment credit requires a customer to make equal periodic payments, each of which contains principal and interest components. Installment credit is used frequently for the purchase of high-value consumer durables, such as automobiles. Installment credit is liquidating, in that normal payments will eventually pay off the balance of the account over time. The seller requires the buyer to sign a contract, which specifies the credit terms of the obligation, discloses the interest rate, and lists all other costs.
- **Revolving Credit:** Under revolving credit terms, a company grants credit without requiring specific transaction approval, as long as the account remains current. An account usually is considered current if the credit outstanding is below an established credit limit and minimum payments are made on time. If the account is not paid in full by the due date, an interest charge is calculated based on the average amount outstanding over the entire period. Unlike installment credit, revolving credit is not automatically liquidating, as new purchases are added to the balance even as payments for older purchases are received and processed.
- **Letter of Credit (L/C):** The most complex form of credit extension is a commercial L/C. L/Cs are most commonly used in import/export transactions and are covered in more detail in Chapter 10, Collections, Concentration, and Disbursements.

E. Cash Application

Cash application is the process of applying a customer's payment against outstanding invoices or receivables. This process occurs via an open item or a balance-forward system.

1. OPEN ITEM SYSTEM

An open item system is most commonly used in B2B sales. Each invoice sent to a customer is recorded in the A/R file. When a payment is received, it is matched with the specific invoices being paid. Any payment discrepancies are noted (e.g., discounts, allowances, adjustments, or returns). Remittance information, which typically accompanies payments, indicates which invoices are being paid, as well as any adjustments to the payment. This application process may be manual, automated, or a combination of both. Most open accounts are cleared using the open item system.

Many companies have automated cash application programs that take the payment and remittance information and, using a series of algorithms, apply the payments by matching them to specific invoices. These algorithms also determine the priority by which invoices are credited in the event of partial payments, which can have an impact on penalties and fees for overdue accounts. A high rate of successful, automated applications greatly reduces the manual effort required to complete the cash application process.

2. BALANCE-FORWARD SYSTEM

A balance-forward system is used most often by companies selling goods and services to individual consumers. A credit limit is established for each individual. A/R outstanding balances increase as purchases are made or services are provided. Similarly, A/R balances decrease as payments are received, but payments are not matched to specific purchases. The balance-forward system is most common in revolving credit situations, such as retail credit cards.

F. Considerations Pertaining to Terms of Sale

Buyers and sellers may choose from a variety of standard sales terms that are often specified in sales agreements, invoices, and other legal or commercial documents.

1. COMMON TERMS OF SALE

The most common sales terms are:

- **Cash before Delivery (CBD):** CBD terms, sometimes referred to as *prepayment terms,* require the buyer to make full and final payment before the shipment or receipt of goods. In business-to-consumer (B2C) sales, CBD is used frequently for catalog, telephone, or Internet transactions. In B2B sales, CBD is used when the seller does not know the buyer or when the seller considers the buyer a greater credit risk than the seller is willing to accept. A variation of this is to require a substantial prepayment of the sale prior to delivery, with the balance collected at some future date. While not as risk-free as CBD, it does reduce the potential for eventual bad debt.
- **Cash on Delivery (COD):** The seller ships the goods and the buyer pays upon receipt. If the buyer refuses to pay, the goods are returned and the seller must pay the shipping and handling costs.
- **Cash Terms:** The buyer generally has 7 to 10 days to make payment. Cash terms are used frequently in the sale of perishable items or in cases where the buyer has not established a credit history with the seller.
- **Net Terms:** The seller specifies a net due date by which the buyer must pay in full. For example, terms of net 30 require the buyer to pay within 30 days from the date of invoice, date of delivery, or some other specified date.
- **Discount Terms:** In addition to specifying a net due date, the seller may offer a discount on payments made prior to that date. Terms of 2/10 net 30 mean that the total amount is due within 30 days of the invoice date, but the buyer can take a 2% discount if it pays within 10 days. For a calculation of discount terms, see Chapter 9, Working Capital Metrics.
- **Monthly Billing:** The seller issues a monthly statement covering all invoices prior to a cutoff date, typically toward the end of each month. If the seller extends proximo (or prox, meaning *in the following month*) payment terms, then the buyer must pay by a specified date during the following month. The seller may offer the buyer a discount for prompt payment. For example, if the terms are 1/10 prox 30, the buyer may take a discount of 1% if payment is made by the 10th day of the following month. However, the total due must be paid by the 30th day of the following month.

- **Draft/Bill of Lading:** Also known as a *documentary collection*, this credit term lets sellers collect payments through banking channels. Documentary collection is more common in international than domestic trade and is discussed in more detail in Chapter 10, Collections, Concentration, and Disbursements. The seller ships the goods to the buyer and sends the shipping and title documents to a bank, which transmits the documents to the buyer's bank. The buyer gains possession of the documents and thus ownership of the goods upon paying the bank or upon signing a draft agreeing to pay at a future date. Upon collection, the buyer's bank remits payment to the seller's bank. Note that a documentary collection is not guaranteed by the bank.
- **Seasonal Dating:** The seller agrees to accept payment at the end of the buyer's selling season. This lets a manufacturer provide short-term financing for a buyer's purchases and reduces the manufacturer's inventory costs. It is common in industries with distinct seasonality of sales, such as toys, greeting cards, garden supplies, sporting goods, or textbooks. Since the time between when goods are shipped to the buyer and when payment is received can be lengthy, the seller may offer a series of discounts to encourage the buyer to pay early.
- **Consignment:** Under a consignment agreement, the supplier (sometimes referred to as the *consignor*) ships goods to another party (sometimes referred to as the *consignee*) who has no obligation to pay until the goods have been sold. The supplier retains title to the goods until they are sold, at which time title is transferred to the ultimate buyer. The consignee will then deduct any commission or fees and forward the remainder to the supplier.

2. OFFERING DISCOUNTS

When offering cash discounts, the seller must evaluate the costs versus the benefits gained from receiving early payments. Standard practice involves using the gross or net method for discounted sales. Under the gross method, gross revenues are recorded on the income statement and in receivables, and discounts are recorded as an expense. In the net method, net revenues are recorded on the income statement and in receivables. Any discounts not taken are shown as income. Chapter 9, Working Capital Metrics, provides a calculation for the cost of not taking an offered discount.

G. Financing Accounts Receivable (A/R)

As previously discussed, many companies finance A/R using unsecured borrowings. If a company cannot finance A/R with unsecured borrowings, it may pledge A/R as collateral and borrow on a secured basis. Commonly referred to as *asset-based lending*, this financing method is based on the quality of the receivables. A lender evaluates the receivables to determine those acceptable as collateral for a loan, which is repaid as the company collects the receivables. A related alternative is supply chain financing, which is discussed below in inventory financing, as it applies to both inventory and A/R for specific trading partners.

Large companies—particularly those with finance subsidiaries, such as mortgage, automobile, and credit card companies—bundle and issue securities backed by receivables called *securitization*. Securitization is a financing method that frees up a company's capital and enhances its creditworthiness by using consumers' installment payments to pay off the securitized instrument's principal and interest. A variation of this practice is the actual sale of the A/R to an intermediary financial institution who packages the accounts and securitizes them.

Some companies establish a wholly owned subsidiary known as a *captive finance company* to perform credit operations and obtain A/R financing for the sale of products. Because receivables represent a significant proportion of current assets, operating a captive finance company enhances the parent's liquidity and provides access to capital at a lower cost.

Third-party financing is another option in which a company collects the information necessary to complete a credit application from a customer and forwards it to a financial institution. The financial institution decides whether to grant credit. Due to the administrative costs involved, companies using third-party financing tend to manufacture and market big-ticket items, such as production machinery. Although third-party financing frees up capital, it does mean a company relinquishes control over the credit-granting decision and foregoes direct marketing opportunities. It also means the company may have to discount the price of goods sold to compensate the third party, thus foregoing potential income.

1. CARD PAYMENTS

Card payments are fairly common in consumer or retail transactions. Increasingly, companies are accepting cards as payment for goods and services from commercial customers in a B2B environment. Typically, a company receives a payment, less the merchant discount, one to two business days following the transaction. The merchant discount is the amount a credit card company (or acquiring bank) charges a seller for the service. This amount varies depending on the method of transmission (e.g., terminal, Internet, or paper), average size of the sale, total volume, type of card used (e.g., brand type, reward, corporate, foreign, or purchasing), and business or industry type.

The advantages of accepting credit cards rather than maintaining A/R in a B2B setting are:

- The seller bears no direct costs of running a credit department.
- The seller does not have to finance A/R.
- As long as proper authorization procedures are followed, the credit card issuer absorbs bad debt losses.
- Sales typically increase by making it easier for customers to charge purchases.
- The seller is paid more quickly—typically in one to two business days following the transaction.

The disadvantages of accepting credit cards for customer financing include:

- The seller relinquishes control over the credit decision (e.g., the sale could be lost if credit is not granted).
- The seller loses promotional opportunities by not having access to a list of credit customers.
- The seller incurs discount costs and transaction fees.
- There is an expense associated with maintaining compliance with credit card data security standards.

A more detailed discussion about payment cards in general is included in Chapter 10, Collections, Concentration, and Disbursements.

2. FACTORING

Factoring involves the outright sale of receivables to a factor, a company that specializes in the financing and management of receivables. In most factoring arrangements, the buyer of the receivables has no recourse to the seller. *No recourse* or *without recourse* means that the factor must absorb the loss if a customer fails to pay. In some cases, however, the factoring arrangement stipulates that the factor has recourse, in which case the seller is liable for any bad debts the factor cannot collect. Most factoring is performed on a notification basis, meaning the seller must notify customers that the account has been sold because payment is remitted directly to the factor.

The primary benefit of factoring is that the seller can receive funds immediately upon completion of the factoring arrangement. The primary disadvantage is that the receivables will usually be sold at a significant discount. Where factoring is routinely used by a seller, the cost of this discount is usually incorporated into the sales price.

3. PRIVATE-LABEL FINANCING

In private-label financing, a third party operates the credit function in the seller's name rather than the seller administering a credit program in-house. From the customer's perspective, the credit appears to be arranged through the seller. Private-label financing lets sellers retain many of the promotional aspects of conducting credit functions while incurring none of the costs of maintaining a credit operation and/or financing A/R. However, the seller does not receive the full face value of the sale and may lose the authority to decide which customers receive credit.

VII. MANAGEMENT OF INVENTORY

The amount of inventory a company carries impacts its production and sales activities, which, for most companies, are the main source of large cash flows. The manner in which inventory is managed affects the length of the cash conversion cycle and the type of cash flow forecasting a company employs. Further, the timing and accuracy of cash flows also affect a company's liquidity needs and the maintenance thereof.

Although inventory management is generally the direct responsibility of marketing or manufacturing managers, treasury managers are responsible for obtaining inventory financing. The ability to use inventory as collateral for a loan is related directly to the type of inventory and how it is managed.

A. Elements of Basic Inventory Policy

The inventory policy of most companies includes elements such as:

1. Reasons for holding inventory
2. Types of inventory
3. Levels of inventory
4. Obsolescence and spoilage
5. Benefits and costs of inventory

1. REASONS FOR HOLDING INVENTORY

Two stages of the operating cycle of a business—the acquisition and conversion stages—involve the purchase of raw materials or finished goods, and the manufacturing and/or distribution of a final product. These stages often entail time-consuming processing steps, and the physical transport and delivery of goods. Inventories enable a company to plan these activities so they can be scheduled as efficiently as possible.

Several specific drivers affect the size of inventories maintained. One of the primary reasons for holding inventory is to provide the goods required for expected sales levels during normal operating and production cycles. Inventory may also be held as a precautionary measure, for speculative purposes, and to meet supplier requirements.

2. TYPES OF INVENTORY

Most inventories are connected with some part of the company's production process. Any item held in stock that links two or more production processes can also be thought of as inventory. The types of inventory generally are categorized as follows:

- **Raw Materials:** Raw materials inventory represents the basic input to the manufacturing process and allows arrivals to be separated from production scheduling. Partially completed components, such as subassemblies, may fall into this category instead of work in progress to give the company more flexibility in the production process.
- **Work in Progress (WIP):** WIP inventory represents items or materials that are in the process of being manufactured. This type of inventory allows different phases of the production process to be separated. The use and amount of WIP inventory are generally functions of the production process. A short, continuous process such as chemical production may have very little WIP, whereas a long batch-production process such as furniture manufacturing has a large level of WIP. WIP inventory also serves as a buffer between production stages with different processing speeds.
- **Finished Goods:** This type of inventory consists of completed items or materials available for sale, and lets a company fill orders when received rather than depend upon product completion to satisfy customer demands. Companies can manage highly variable or unpredictable demand levels more easily, which is extremely valuable in a retail environment because it allows the retailer to maintain a wide variety of goods for customers. It is important to note a significant difference in the management of finished goods inventory for generic products versus customized products. Due to limited resale value, customized product inventories must be managed much more tightly than more generic, easily sold goods.
- **Scrap or Obsolete Items:** In industries such as steel and aluminum manufacturing, scrap from production can be reused in later batches or sold to recyclers. Also, a portion of a company's inventories may become obsolete or damaged, especially in environments where there are rapid changes in existing products or introductions of new products. Obsolete or scrap inventories must be identified and dealt with independently. These inventories may be turned into cash through sales to scrap dealers or by taking tax deductions through write-offs.
- **Stores and Supplies:** Stores and supplies inventories are sometimes referred to as *indirect purchases*. These items are not used directly; rather, they support the production process. Examples include lubricating oils or maintenance materials for production machinery in a manufacturing business, or paper and other office supplies in a service business.

3. LEVELS OF INVENTORY

Since excess inventory lowers profits, prudent inventory reduction is an ongoing management objective. One of the most popular approaches is just-in-time (JIT), which attempts to minimize inventory levels by reducing the costs or uncertainties that underlie the motives for holding inventory. JIT methodology recognizes that excess inventory can be a liability rather than an asset. Therefore, JIT is not simply an inventory management system, but a production/business philosophy that treats inventory as being undesirable. Under this philosophy, excess inventory indicates poor inventory planning, poor inventory location and movement problems, inferior supplier quality, and/or unbalanced production processes.

JIT systems often are coupled with material planning systems (MPSs) that bring together long-range production planning with the current flow of materials through the production process. In today's competitive environment, a company may negotiate arrangements with suppliers to provide a continuous level of production materials on short notice, resulting in reduced carrying costs for the raw materials used to create finished goods. Some retailers link point-of-sale (POS) equipment to suppliers so that specific merchandise sales can be tracked for automated reordering. JIT and MPS methods allow for time-phased methods of planning that facilitate adjustments to changing costs.

In supplier-managed replenishment programs, the supplier maintains and tracks the inventory of materials it provides to a customer. As the inventory is used, the supplier bills the customer for the items and replenishes the supply. Title to the product is transferred at the shipping dock. The rationale for this system is that the supplier can track trends in inventory usage and manage levels of inventory more efficiently, thus reducing costs for both the supplier and the customer.

The paid-on-production process is similar to supplier-managed replenishment programs, but has some specific implications for financial managers. Paid-on-production is the process by which a payment record is created for goods and/or services based on usage rather than shipment. It is similar to consignment sales in retail, but is employed in a manufacturing environment. Title to the product is transferred during the manufacturing process rather than at the shipping dock.

The unique demands of the JIT manufacturing environment have a major impact on a company's treasury and reporting functions, especially with respect to the information system for financial management. JIT implementation often requires changes to the accounting methods used for inventory and impacts the timing of purchases. Companies using JIT purchase more frequently and buy smaller amounts, which increases the number of transactions to monitor and record. The process of evaluating the cost of inventory becomes more difficult for companies using JIT. Most companies use a rolling average of actual costs rather than traditional transaction-by-transaction cost accounting methods.

4. OBSOLESCENCE AND SPOILAGE

Any inventory policy must take into account the need to manage obsolescence and spoilage. *Obsolescence* (discussed above in types of inventory) refers to inventory that is no longer salable through normal channels because it is out of date or has been replaced with newer products. Obsolete inventory must still be tracked and eventually either written off or sold at a discount (potentially at a loss) to get it off of the books. *Spoilage* refers to inventory that is no longer salable due to damage or other defects that occur over time. Again, spoiled inventory must eventually be disposed of though write-offs or through some form of discounted sale. Spoilage is distinct from scrap, which is a normal by-product of many manufacturing processes.

5. BENEFITS AND COSTS OF INVENTORY

Inventories provide some benefits by separating elements of the purchasing, production, and shipment processes. One of the primary benefits of holding sufficient inventory is reducing stock-out costs (i.e., lost sales due to a lack of sufficient inventory). In a more positive sense, inventory (especially finished goods) may provide a competitive advantage over other companies and provide increased customer goodwill, higher sales levels, and increased profits.

There are also costs involved in maintaining varying levels of inventory. Setup or order costs are transaction costs incurred when obtaining a new batch of inventory, such as supplies for setting up a new production run. Holding costs are those related to carrying inventory, such as physical storage and handling costs, insurance, taxes, and the opportunity cost of funds invested in inventory.

Generally, the objective of inventory management is to minimize the total costs associated with the inventory while meeting a desired level of production and/or customer service. Economic order quantity (EOQ) models are typically used to calculate the optimal level of inventory, given specified ordering and holding costs. However, EOQ models can be difficult to apply because they do not account for variables such as volume discounts and blanket purchase orders that cover a schedule of deliveries.

B. Inventory Financing Alternatives

When inventory cannot be financed as part of general working capital requirements, financing alternatives may be tied directly to the amount of inventory. These financing alternatives are likely to be used by companies experiencing rapid growth, or those with seasonal operations or less financial security. The amount of credit available, as a percentage of the inventory's value, depends upon the nature of the inventory, its location, when and where transfer of title occurs, and the existence of a secondary market. Financing is usually not available for WIP inventory, but rather for raw materials and finished goods.

For many firms, A/P or trade credit granted by suppliers is typically the least expensive alternative and finances a significant portion of inventory. This spontaneous financing source increases and decreases with the level of inventory on hand. While some companies routinely delay payments to suppliers to extend the amount of financing provided, either because they cannot or chose not to pay on time, renegotiating appropriate trade terms is a much better alternative. The opportunity cost of arbitrarily delaying trade payment is the cost of lost cash discounts, lost goodwill with suppliers, and lost sales due to delayed shipments. In many cases, suppliers refuse to ship additional products unless outstanding invoices are paid promptly. Such delays often cause production delays and sales problems, which can ultimately be more expensive than alternative methods of financing.

Supply chain financing is a related form of inventory lending where a seller receives financing based upon the existence of sales contracts and purchase orders with large, financially stable, trading partners. These types of programs are typically arranged for by the buyer rather than the seller and provide lower-cost loans based upon the buyer's credit rating and financial capabilities, rather than the seller's. The seller benefits by receiving a lower interest rate, and the buyer benefits by not having to directly finance the seller and create on-balance-sheet debt.

Collateralized loans are another form of inventory financing. These loans are arranged using inventory as collateral for a loan, with the lender providing financing for some predetermined percentage of the inventory's value. The company's cash flows are viewed as the primary repayment source, and inventory is viewed as a secondary repayment source or a means of reducing the amount of loss in the event of default. A claim against the inventory is perfected in the form of a lien, which is often recorded formally with the appropriate government body. This way, the lender can act on it if the buyer defaults. Although the stated interest rate of these loans may be lower than unsecured credit, the total cost of these types of loans may be higher because of the additional expense the lender incurs in perfecting and monitoring the claim.

Inventory financing also may involve asset-based loans. Asset-based lending is based on the value of the inventory rather than the borrower's general financial strength. To enforce the claim on the inventory, the lender usually takes physical possession of it if the company defaults on the loan or files for bankruptcy. If either occurs, the lender may store the inventory at a public warehouse, which is a storage facility operated by an independent warehouse company on its own premises, or in a field warehouse rented by a company on another firm's premises. These warehouses are generally secure storage facilities where commodities, raw materials, or finished goods are held until a warehouse receipt is presented to claim them. In cases where the inventory directly supports a loan, a lender may release the materials only after the portion of the loan supported by inventory is paid.

Floor planning is a type of asset-based lending used for high-value durable goods, such as automobiles, trucks, or heavy equipment. Loans are made against each individual item, recorded by serial number, and are not fully repaid until the item is sold. Floor plan lenders typically perform periodic inventory audits.[9]

VIII. MANAGEMENT OF ACCOUNTS PAYABLE (A/P)

A/P provides a major source of short-term financing for many companies. Additionally, the treasury area generally oversees funding disbursement accounts and may manage the actual disbursement of payments.

An A/P manager's primary responsibility is to verify incoming invoices and authorize payments. Some companies call this process *vouchering*. This process generally involves the traditional three-way match, in which an invoice is matched to both an approved

9. Depending on the lender, region, or industry, there may be requirements for interim payments on the loan if the item financed is not sold within some specified period of time.

purchase order, as well as receiving and, in some cases, shipping information. This verification ensures that the items being billed to the company are authorized purchases from an approved vendor and that all items are received in satisfactory condition. The A/P function also monitors compliance with trade payment terms.

Once the approval process is complete, the invoice is vouchered for payment. In a typical B2B environment, multiple invoices are combined in a single payment. Once approved, the voucher is forwarded to the treasury manager or disbursements clerk who, in turn, generates payment.

There are two critical areas of coordination between treasury and A/P management. The first is the communication from A/P to treasury regarding the invoices vouchered for payment. The second is the communication from treasury back to A/P regarding the reconciliation of cleared items.

Companies with integrated enterprise resource planning (ERP) or accounting systems with treasury management modules often integrate these functions easily. However, many companies use either separate systems for disbursement management or treasury information software provided by banks. This software may not interface as easily with the A/P ledger. Customized interfaces or middleware (in a client-server environment) are required to facilitate the transfer of information between applications.

A company's net cost of making payments includes both opportunity costs and the administrative costs of managing A/P and disbursements processes. A description of different payment instruments and disbursement methods is included in Chapter 10, Collections, Concentration, and Disbursements.

A. Disbursement System Considerations

A disbursement system is a set of procedures that determines who may authorize payments, where and when the payments originate, how potential fraud is controlled, and how accounts are reconciled. In designing a disbursement system, an organization must keep several goals in mind:

- **Information Access:** Obtaining access to timely and accurate information regarding the status of disbursement accounts and disbursement clearings lets a company manage its cash position more effectively.
- **Fraud Prevention:** Preventing fraud means protecting company funds from unauthorized use, through written policies and internal controls, prompt bank reconciliation, and appropriate banking services (e.g., positive pay and debit blocks[10]).
- **Relationship Maintenance with Payees:** Maintaining good relationships with payees means ensuring timely payments to employees, vendors, suppliers, lenders, tax agencies, bondholders, and shareholders, as well as filing any necessary tax or other legal forms.
- **Timing of Payments:** While it is important to pay vendors in a timely fashion, it can be equally important that payments not be made before they are due. Scheduling of payments is an important function of any disbursement system. Making payments early reduces available working capital, while deferring payments increases working capital by maximizing trade credit. The use of trade credit as a source of short-term financing is discussed in Chapter 11, Short-Term Investing and Borrowing.

10. Positive pay and other fraud prevention tools are covered in more detail in Chapter 10, Collections, Concentration, and Disbursements.

B. Types of A/P and Disbursement Systems

A/P and disbursement systems may be centralized, decentralized, or a combination of both. Each system has distinct advantages and disadvantages in relation to the disbursement system goals just described.

1. CENTRALIZED A/P AND DISBURSEMENT SYSTEMS

- **Advantages:** In a centralized system, the A/P and disbursement functions are located in a single place—either at headquarters or at a centralized processing center. From this centralized location, a company receives all inbound invoices, approves them for payment, issues payments, and funds and reconciles accounts. A centralized disbursement system makes it easier to maintain control, obtain information, concentrate excess cash, provide greater access to cash position information, and improve forecasting accuracy.
- **Disadvantages:** The principal disadvantage of a centralized A/P and disbursement system is its potentially negative impact on payee relationships. Centralized systems may result in delayed payments to vendors and suppliers and/or lost discount opportunities. Technology developments and improved access to information have reduced some of these problems. There is also a need for coordination between the central A/P department and the company's field offices to resolve payment disputes.

2. DECENTRALIZED A/P AND DISBURSEMENT SYSTEMS

In a decentralized system, the A/P and disbursement functions are managed at the local or regional level. Field office managers approve invoices for payment, issue payments, and reconcile accounts. Additionally, payments are often made through a local or regional bank. Decentralized systems are often the result of mergers and acquisitions where the A/P and disbursement systems of the merging companies have not been combined.

- **Advantages:** This system gives greater autonomy to field office managers. As a result, the primary advantage is improved relationships with vendors and suppliers because items clear quickly and disputes can be resolved locally. In addition, it is easier to take advantage of discount terms that require payments to be made in a shorter time frame (typically 10 days).
- **Disadvantages:** The primary disadvantages of a decentralized system are the loss of control over information (possibly resulting in delayed payments); the lost opportunity to concentrate funds, reduce borrowing expenses, and increase investment returns; and the increased likelihood of unauthorized disbursements. Other disadvantages include the cost and complexity of redundant systems; the increased possibility of excess or idle balances at the local bank level; increased difficulty in obtaining information about a company's day-to-day cash position and cash outflows; and increased transfer, reconciliation, and administrative costs.

3. DECENTRALIZED A/P AND DISBURSEMENT SYSTEMS WITH CENTRALIZED CLEARING

The advent of enterprise-wide software packages with distributed access and data entry has created the ability for some companies to use a hybrid system in which local or regional managers oversee the A/P process and authorize payments at a local level, but the actual disbursement of payments is managed centrally and drawn on a centralized disbursement bank.

In this type of system, invoices can be received and processed locally as well as at a common A/P processing location. This ability reduces the time lag required to send locally received invoices to a central A/P site for processing or to send centrally received invoices to local managers for approval. The distributed input capability, often coupled with workflow management software, allows managers to track and approve invoices as desired and ensures that all required approvals are received before an invoice is paid.

Disbursements are made by a central A/P system, which can generate payments from a central bank account or from subsidiary accounts as necessary. Payments can be made by any payment method desired, whether electronic or paper. The addition of remote printing capabilities makes it possible to actually print checks at local offices if needed or desired. Some companies take this process a step further and outsource the actual disbursement of payments using products such as integrated payables (discussed in Chapter 10, Collections, Concentration, and Disbursements) or shared services centers (discussed in Chapter 1, The Role of Treasury Management). This approach provides increased control along with reduced excess balances, improved cash position reporting and forecasting, and increased opportunities for volume discounts on bank disbursement services.

IX. MULTINATIONAL WORKING CAPITAL MANAGEMENT TOOLS

A. Multicurrency Accounts

Multicurrency accounts, which are mentioned in Chapter 3, Banks and Financial Institutions, are a special arrangement between a bank and a company, in which the bank lets the customer receive or make payments in a range of currencies from a single account or multiple subsidiary accounts. A multicurrency agreement generally specifies four stipulations:

- The base currency in which the account is denominated
- The portfolio of currencies accepted
- The spread or margin over the spot rate to use in exchanging each currency back to the base currency
- The value date to apply to debits and credits for each transaction type and currency

These accounts simplify the management of multinational working capital by allowing a company to make and receive payments in a variety of currencies without having to worry about the foreign exchange (FX) implications of every transaction.

B. Netting

Netting is an internal company (intracompany) payables system that is designed to reduce the number of cross-border payments among company units through the elimination or consolidation of funds denominated in different currencies, thus enhancing natural hedging. Some countries impose restrictions on the use of netting systems due to their tax consequences; hence, central bank or government approval often is required. Some countries, such as China, Brazil, and India, disallow the practice altogether.

1. BILATERAL NETTING

In a bilateral netting system, purchases between two subsidiaries of the same company are netted against each other so that periodically, typically once or twice per month on preset dates, only the net difference is transferred. If the payments are in different currencies, then the total due to each subsidiary is converted to a common currency, usually that of the receiving country, to determine the net amount due.

As an example of bilateral netting, if one subsidiary of a multinational company is located in France and another is located in the United Kingdom, then payments to each other are held until one or two regularly scheduled times during the month. Prior to a settlement date, payment flows in both directions are totaled and the net amount due to one of the subsidiaries is made available with a single transfer. If there is a material FX exposure to the company after netting, then it should be hedged.

2. MULTILATERAL NETTING

A multilateral netting system is similar to a bilateral system, but it involves more than two subsidiaries. Each subsidiary informs a central treasury management center of all planned cross-border payments through an electronic system. To determine netting transactions, payments between all subsidiaries are converted into a common currency and combined into a few larger transactions. Each unit is informed of the net amount owed or due in advance of the settlement date, and the central treasury management center makes the necessary FX conversions. Multilateral netting is used primarily for intracompany transactions, but some companies' netting processes also include third-party payments and receipts. The mechanics of multilateral netting are illustrated in Exhibit 8.10.

EXHIBIT 8.10 MULTILATERAL NETTING

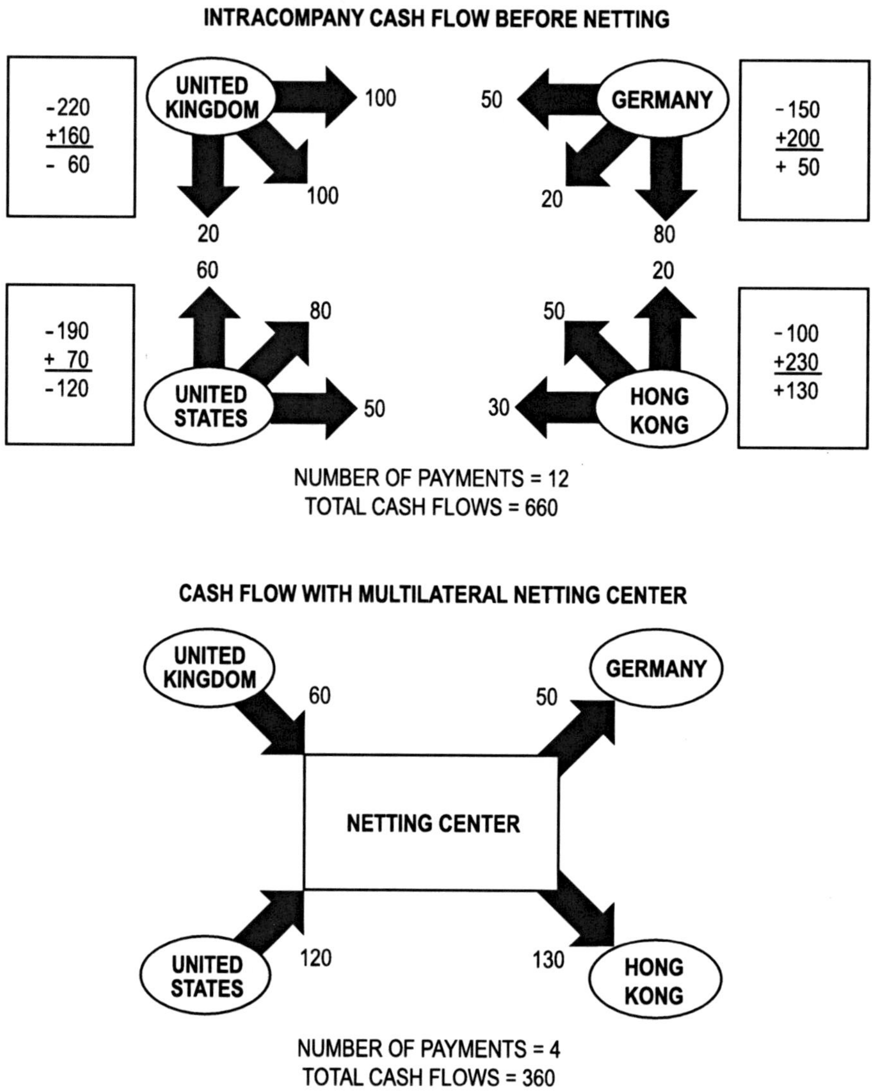

There are three principal benefits of using a netting system:

- A reduction in the number of FX transactions and cross-border wire transfers, and the resulting benefits from natural hedging
- More favorable FX rates due to the potential for larger FX trades resulting from consolidation
- Improved cash and currency exposure forecasting for both the subsidiary and the parent company as a result of the ability to preplan cross-border payments

The principal costs of netting, comprised of setup, administration, and maintenance expense, must also be taken into account.

C. Leading and Lagging

Netting systems may be used to lead and lag payments. Leading and lagging involve executing cross-border payments between subsidiaries before the scheduled payment date (leading) or after the scheduled payment date (lagging). In both leading and lagging, liquidity is shifted from one subsidiary to another. Leading is employed when a subsidiary country's currency is expected to depreciate relative to the parent company's currency. Lagging is used when a subsidiary country's currency is expected to appreciate relative to the parent company's currency. For example, if a company whose base currency is the euro has a subsidiary in Japan and expects the yen to depreciate in the near future, it will speed up (lead) payments from its Japanese subsidiary to avoid the depreciation in the yen. Likewise, if the same company expects the yen to appreciate against the euro, it may delay (lag) payments from its Japanese subsidiary to collect the benefits of the gain in the yen.

D. Re-invoicing

Re-invoicing is an intracompany method of centralizing the responsibility for monitoring and collecting international A/R to more effectively manage related FX exposures. A re-invoicing center is a company-owned subsidiary that purchases goods from an exporting subsidiary and sells the goods to an importing subsidiary. The exporting unit invoices and receives funds from the re-invoicing subsidiary in its own currency, and the importing unit is invoiced and pays funds to the re-invoicing subsidiary in its own currency. Although the title to the goods passes through the re-invoicing center, the actual goods usually are shipped directly from the exporting subsidiary to the importing subsidiary. Establishing a re-invoicing center requires local government and tax approval, and negotiations with tax authorities in all involved countries to determine how the subsidiary is taxed.

One of the primary benefits of a re-invoicing center is the centralization of FX exposures so they can be managed more effectively. The re-invoicing center also improves a company's worldwide short-term liquidity management by providing flexibility in inter-subsidiary payments. In addition, re-invoicing:

- Eases the implementation of leading and lagging arrangements

- Improves export trade financing and collections
- Reduces bank costs
- Minimizes FX risk and obtains advantaged FX rates by enabling larger trades
- Reduces payment costs

It is particularly beneficial to have the ability to set worldwide international pricing, but this practice may be regulated heavily by foreign monetary authorities. Major costs include the re-invoicing center expenses, which are incurred primarily when establishing a physical location, and administrative costs. Re-invoicing is illustrated in Exhibit 8.11.

EXHIBIT 8.11 **RE-INVOICING**

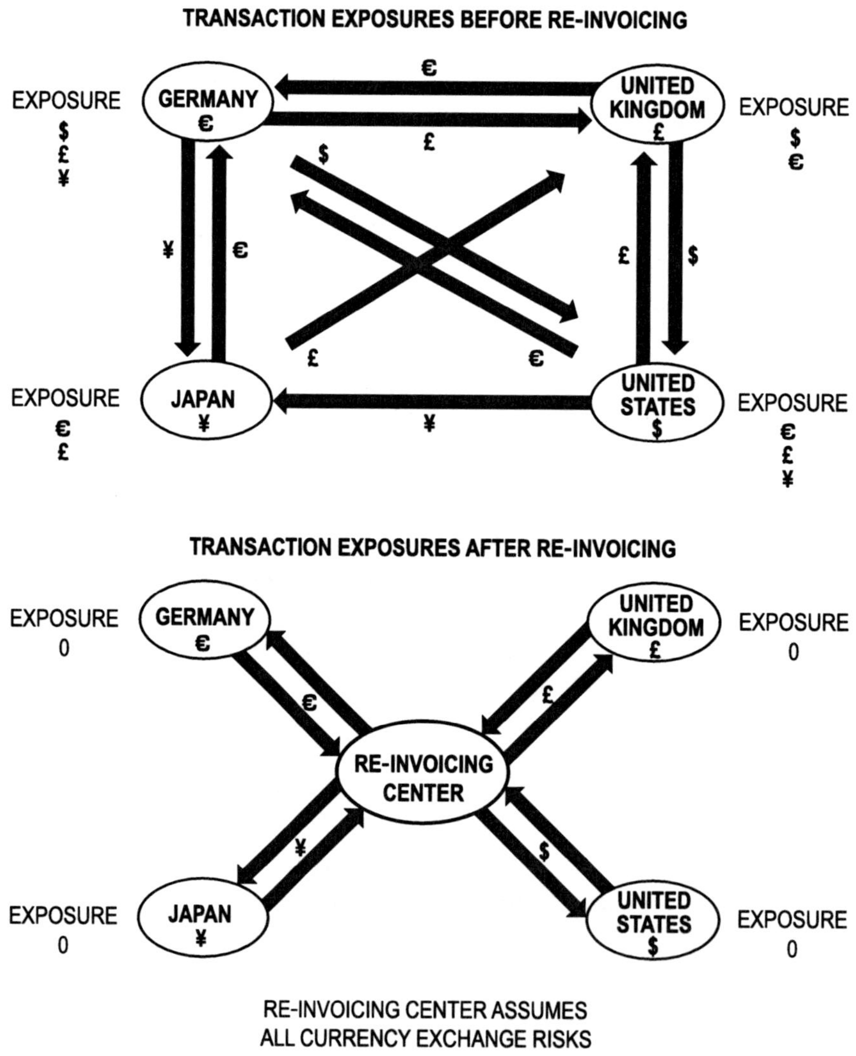

E. Internal Factoring

The concept of internal factoring is very similar to that of re-invoicing. However, rather than taking actual title to the goods, as is the case with re-invoicing, the internal factoring unit buys A/R from the exporting unit and collects funds from the importing unit. As with re-invoicing, internal factoring allows a company to:

- Implement leading and lagging arrangements
- Centralize and improve export trade financing and collections
- Minimize FX risk
- Reduce bank costs
- Reduce payment costs

Most internal factoring is done on a recourse basis, meaning that the factor can return past-due receivables and bad debts to the subsidiary for collection.

F. In-House Banking

Many large global companies have found it beneficial to establish in-house banks. In this arrangement, treasury becomes the main provider of banking services for all the company's operating entities. Because treasury manages all banking services, individual transactions of various subsidiaries can be aggregated, netted, and processed in bulk, resulting in fewer transactions and lower fees. The primary benefit is a reduction in overall banking costs. Secondary benefits include improved visibility and control over subsidiary cash assets, minimized borrowing, and an improved ability to manage internal and external FX risk. There may also be potential tax benefits to using this type of structure, as it provides for better information and tax planning related to international transactions, and some countries provide tax advantages for in-house banking facilities.

The in-house bank normally is responsible for managing international treasury management solutions, including:

- Investments/debts, especially intracompany or subsidiary-to-subsidiary loans
- Netting
- Pooling
- Re-invoicing
- FX transactions and FX risk management

The use of treasury technology, including TMS and ERP systems, to manage in-house banking operations is discussed in Chapter 14, Information Technology in Treasury.

G. Export Financing

In many countries, the government supports export activities through export loans, credit guarantees, or a combination of both.[11] The general term for entities that are established by governments to provide these services is *export credit agencies (ECAs)*.

ECAs are typically established to assist in the financing of goods and services from their country to international markets, often with a focus on smaller companies that are developing international capabilities. The basic services that the ECAs typically provide are working capital guarantees (pre-export financing), export credit insurance, and loan guarantees and direct loans (buyer financing).

The advantages of long-term export financing through an ECA include:

- The interest rate generally is fixed at a lower rate and for a longer term than would otherwise be available from commercial sources.
- Indirect government involvement can provide some protection against government appropriation or interference.

The disadvantages of long-term export financing through an ECA include:

- Additional time may be required to obtain the necessary approvals.
- The exporter may face currency exposure if the currency of the loan is different from that of the cash flow of the project being financed or the exporter's home currency.

While most ECAs are created to provide support for trade with their specific country, there are also a number of multilateral ECAs created to foster trade in multiple jurisdictions. The Multilateral Investment Guarantee Agency (MIGA), a subsidiary of the World Bank, was created to foster trade with developing countries and "South-South" trade (i.e., trade between developing countries).

X. SUMMARY

Working capital management refers to the processes and techniques needed to manage the short-term assets and liabilities of a company, literally the life blood of the company. Identifying and achieving an appropriate level of liquidity is the goal of working capital management. This involves managing the impact of changes in a variety of working capital accounts and finding the appropriate balance between excess liquidity and investment needs.

This chapter introduced the concept of the cash conversion cycle and examined how that cycle affects the operating and financing activities of a company. The concept of float was also introduced, and the various types of float were discussed. The chapter continued with a discussion of managing key working capital accounts: A/R, inventory, and A/P. The final section of the chapter discussed working capital tools that are helpful in international or cross-border trade.

11. Credit guarantees provided by export credit agencies will reimburse an exporter for sales to foreign buyers if those buyers default on payment to the exporter.

TEST YOUR UNDERSTANDING: CHAPTER 8

Answers are on pages 672–678.

1. What is meant by the term *working capital*? How can working capital be increased or decreased?
2. What is meant by the term *permanent current assets*?
3. Compare and contrast the three current asset financing strategies.
4. What are two key considerations when determining credit extension policies?
5. What are the five Cs of credit?
6. What are the four steps in the credit scoring process?
7. Compare and contrast the four basic forms of credit extension.
8. What is an open item system of cash application?
9. What are the most common terms of sale?
10. What are some of the advantages and disadvantages of accepting credit cards in a business-to-business (B2B) setting?
11. What is factoring?
12. What are the four principal types of cash flows with which treasury professionals must work?
13. What is float?
14. What is the working capital cash conversion cycle? Identify its major components.
15. What are the elements of a basic inventory policy?
16. Describe the basic types of inventory.
17. What are multicurrency accounts?
18. What are the principal benefits of using a netting system in managing multinational working capital?
19. In designing a disbursement system, what four goals must an organization keep in mind?
20. What is an export credit agency?
21. What are the benefits of establishing an in-house bank?

CHAPTER 9
Working Capital Metrics

I. INTRODUCTION

II. BASIC FINANCIAL CONCEPTS

A. Time Value of Money

B. Opportunity Cost

C. Cost of Capital

III. FUNDAMENTAL WORKING CAPITAL METRICS

A. Current Ratio

B. Quick Ratio

C. Cash Flow to Total Debt Ratio

D. Total Working Capital

IV. CALCULATION OF THE CASH CONVERSION CYCLE (CCC)

A. Days' Sales in Inventory (DSI) or Days' Inventory (DI)

B. Days' Receivables (DR)

C. Days' Payables (DP) or Days' Payable Outstanding (DPO)

D. Cash Conversion Cycle (CCC)

E. Cash Turnover

F. Days of Working Capital (DWC)

G. Cash Conversion Efficiency

V. CASH DISCOUNT CALCULATIONS

A. Costs to a Buyer of Not Taking the Cash Discount

B. Financial Impact to a Seller of Offering a Cash Discount

VI. ACCOUNTS RECEIVABLE (A/R) MONITORING AND CONTROL

A. Days' Sales Outstanding (DSO)

B. A/R Aging Schedule

C. A/R Balance Pattern

VII. COLLECTIONS AND CONCENTRATION CALCULATIONS

A. Lockbox Cost/Benefit Analysis

B. Cash Concentration Break-Even Analysis

VIII. SUMMARY

I. INTRODUCTION

This chapter discusses the basic calculations and metrics that are an essential part of working capital management and the broader topic of treasury management. Collectively, these metrics provide treasury professionals and financial analysts the tools needed to assess the effectiveness of various working capital components.

The chapter begins with some basic financial concepts, including the time value of money, which are essential to many financial analyses. The next section introduces the tools used to monitor and evaluate the various components of working capital. The remainder of the chapter presents a number of miscellaneous calculations that should be part of any treasury professional's tool kit.

II. BASIC FINANCIAL CONCEPTS

A. Time Value of Money

The time value of money is a basic financial concept that recognizes the fact that a given amount of money received today is more valuable than the same amount of money received a year from now. This is due to the fact that the money earned today can be used to earn more money, resulting in a larger amount of money in the future.

Most financial decisions involve a trade-off between present and future cash flows. For example, treasury professionals often have to decide whether to invest funds now to produce expected, future cash flows. The time value of money establishes the relationship between cash flows received at different times and allows for a valid comparison between the two. The value of a cash flow at a point in time depends upon an applicable interest rate and when the cash flow is expected to occur.

The future value (FV) of an investment made today is the expected value of that investment at a specified, future date. Calculation of FV is more complex than just multiplying the current amount times the interest rate and time period. A valid FV requires compounding based upon the assumption that any cash flows that the investment "pays" along the way will be reinvested and grow at the interest rate used for the analysis.

For example, investing $100 for two years at 10% per year yields a $10 return at the end of the first year. That $10 is added to the original amount of $100. In the second year, $110 is invested at 10% and the investment pays $11 in interest. The $11 is added to $110, which equates to an investment value of $121 at the end of year two. FV computations are based on compounding the growth of an amount invested now to see what its value will be in the future.

The formula for calculating FV is as follows:

$$FV = PV(1+i)^n$$

Where:

FV = Future value

PV = Present value or value today

i = Periodic interest rate

n = Number of periods

In the example above, the period is one year. Therefore, the FV of $100 after two years compounded at 10% per year is:

$$FV = \$100(1 + 0.10)^2 = \$100(1.21) = \$121$$

The mathematical term *$(1 + i)^n$* is called the *interest factor, compound value factor,* or *FV factor.* It has the mathematics of compounding imbedded in it and is an exponential function. The value of $100 was invested at 10% for two periods, but the ending value is not $100 + $10 + $10 = $120; rather, it is $121.

In another example, assume $2,000 is invested for three years at 6% per year. In this case, the FV factor is $(1 + 0.06)^3$ and the calculation is as follows:

$$FV = \$2,000(1 + 0.06)^3 = \$2,000(1.191) = \$2,382$$

For the next example, assume that a business expects to receive a $4,000 payment now, $5,000 at the end of one year, and $6,000 at the end of two years. It wants to determine how much the entire stream of payments will be worth at the end of the two years if invested at 8%. To determine FV, compute the value at the end of year two by recognizing that the payment now will compound at 8% for two years, the payment received after one year will compound at 8% for one year, and the payment received at the end of year two will not have any time to compound. The following calculation illustrates this example:

$$\begin{aligned} FV &= \$4,000(1 + 0.08)^2 + \$5,000(1 + 0.08)^1 + \$6,000 \\ &= \$4,000(1.1664) + \$5,000(1.08) + \$6,000 \\ &= \$4,665.60 + \$5,400.00 + \$6,000.00 = \$16,065.60 \end{aligned}$$

The inverse of FV is present value, or PV: the current value of future expected cash flows or payments. PV is used more commonly in business contexts where treasury professionals are asked to make an investment at the present time that will pay the business cash flows in the future. For example, if an individual is offered the opportunity to buy a restaurant, a chain of auto parts stores, a refinery, or any other business, then the buyer would have to estimate the net cash flows that each asset would generate in the future. Next, the buyer would relate those cash flows to the expected cost of each investment. Since (as already established above) money received tomorrow is less valuable than money received today, merely adding the future cash flows and comparing them to the current cost of the investment is inadequate. Instead, the PV of those cash flows must be calculated and added before they can be accurately compared to the cost of the investment.

FV and PV are opposite methods. FV starts in the present and moves forward in time, whereas PV starts in the future and moves back in time. This is called an *inverse or reciprocal mathematical relationship*.

FV is calculated in the equation $FV = PV(1 + i)^n$ when the PV is known. To find an unknown PV from a known FV, the PV must be isolated by first dividing both sides of the equation by the FV factor, as follows:

$$\frac{FV}{(1+i)^n} = \frac{PV(1+i)^n}{(1+i)^n}$$

Then, canceling the FV factor terms on the right-hand side of the equation yields the following:

$$PV = \frac{FV}{(1+i)^n} \text{ or } PV = FV\left[\frac{1}{(1+i)^n}\right]$$

Where:

$\frac{1}{(1+i)^n}$ is the inverse or opposite of the compound value factor $(1+i)^n$

Note that when performing PV calculations, the process of finding the present value of a future amount in the present is called *discounting*, and the interest rate used in the calculation is called the *discount rate*.

Next, returning to the cash flows used previously, below is an example of how to calculate the PV of \$2,382 to be received three years from today if the discount rate is 6%:

$$PV = \frac{FV}{(1 + i)^n} = \frac{\$2{,}382}{(1 + 0.06)^3} = \frac{\$2{,}382}{1.191} = \$2{,}000$$

A firm often must compare the economic value of cash flows from different investment alternatives occurring at various times in the future. The only way to do this with consistency is to compare their values in the present. Additional factors that need to be considered include the purchasing power of a dollar now, the costs of investment alternatives now, and how much can be raised to invest now.

PV applies, too, if one thinks of market instruments like stocks and bonds. A bond pays interest periodically and repays principal upon maturity. These payments are stretched over time, but what are they worth now? A stock may pay a stream of dividends over time and can be sold for some estimated price at some future date. Again, this is a stream of payments stretched over time, but what are these expected payments worth in the present?

The PV of a stream of payments is calculated by identifying the PVs of individual payments and adding them together to arrive at the PV for the entire series. Therefore, the PV of a series of future payments may be generalized for any number of periods as follows:

$$PV = \frac{C_1}{(1+i)^1} + \frac{C_2}{(1+i)^2} + \frac{C_3}{(1+i)^3} + \ldots + \ldots \frac{C_n}{(1+i)^n}$$

Where:

PV = Present value or value today

C_n = Cash flow C in time period n (i.e., C_3 represents the cash flow in period three)

n = Number of periods

i = Periodic interest rate (discount rate)

As an example, assume the following annual cash flows: $200 in year one, $400 in year two, and $600 in year three. If the appropriate discount rate is 12%, then the PV of the stream would be:

$$PV = \frac{\$200}{(1+0.12)^1} + \frac{\$400}{(1+0.12)^2} + \frac{\$600}{(1+0.12)^3}$$

$$= \frac{\$200}{1.12} + \frac{\$400}{1.2544} + \frac{\$600}{1.4049}$$

$$= \$178.57 + \$318.88 + \$427.08 = \$924.53$$

The sum of the cash flows is $1,200, but the sum of the cash flows discounted at 12% is $924.53. This means that if a company paid $924.53 now and received the future payments as specified in the example, it will earn a 12% rate of return on its investment. If the company required a rate of return higher than 12%, then it would not undertake the investment. Conversely, the company would fund the investment if the required rate of return was equal to or less than 12%.

B. Opportunity Cost

Opportunity cost is defined as the value of the best alternative not taken when two or more mutually exclusive alternatives are available. For example, if an investor has $100 to invest for one year and has to choose between investing in a stock that is expected to return 10% and a CD that will return 8%, the investor's opportunity cost of investing in the stock is the return that the investor would have made on the CD but did not (in other words, $8.00).

Investors in a firm's debt and equity securities expect to earn a return on their investment. How these expected rates of return are determined and how an overall rate of cost of funds is computed are discussed further in Chapter 20, Financial Decisions and Management.

Here, it is important to recognize that investors look to alternative investments in a particular risk class to discover the best rate of return available. Investors in a firm's securities have this rate available to them in the marketplace, so they lose the opportunity to invest in the available alternative when they invest in the firm's securities. The cost of the lost opportunity is an opportunity cost.

In order to continue to attract investors, a firm must provide a rate of return to them that at least equals their opportunity cost in the market.

C. Cost of Capital

Chapter 18, Financial Accounting and Reporting, introduces financial statements and points out that the liabilities and equity on one side of a firm's balance sheet are the means by which the firm's assets (the other side of the balance sheet) are financed. The sources of funding on the liabilities and equity side of the balance sheet bear a cost because investors in a firm's long-term debt and equity expect a rate of return on their investment. *Capital* is defined as the sum of the firm's long-term debt and equity.

In practice, the term *capital* describes more permanent sources of funds used by a company, such as long-term debt, preferred stock, and common equity. Common equity includes money contributed by stockholders and earnings retained in the business. The cost of capital is derived from the rates of return that investors in a firm could earn by investing in the debt and equity instruments of other companies of similar risk. The cost of capital to the firm, therefore, is based on the opportunity costs investors incur by investing in the company and is a measure of the cost a company would incur to raise funds to make investments in assets. It follows, then, that the firm must earn a rate of return at least equal to its cost of capital to justify an asset investment. This reasoning explains why the company's cost of capital is often referred to as an *opportunity cost.*

A company's overall cost of capital depends on the mix of long-term debt and equity on its balance sheet, and the costs of each. This mix is called the *capital structure* of a company. The individual cost of each capital component is determined by the perceived risks that securities market investors have about investing in the company. The primary cost associated with debt is its interest rate. The primary cost of equity is the return stockholders expect to earn on the stock they own. The cost of capital can therefore be computed as a weighted average of the effective cost of debt and the cost of equity, which is called the *weighted average cost of capital* (*WACC*). The calculation of the individual capital components and WACC is covered in Chapter 20, Financial Decisions and Management. For the purposes of the examples and calculations in this chapter, a suggested WACC, which is often used as the opportunity cost in finance calculations, will be provided.

The WACC is a very important measure. If, for example, a firm has a WACC of 10%, it means that the firm must earn a return of at least 10% on assets to satisfy investors' expectations. If the firm earns less than 10%, even if it reports accounting profits and has a positive cash flow, then investors will be disappointed and bid down the company's stock price. On the other hand, investors will be satisfied if the firm earns more than

10% on assets and may bid up the stock price. Because the ultimate goal of any for-profit organization is to create shareholder value, a treasury professional knows that the company should not invest in assets that earn less than the WACC because it will negatively impact a portion of the firm's stock value. Conversely, projects that earn more than the WACC will increase shareholder value. The WACC, then, is a fundamental performance hurdle rate assigned by investors.

To determine what the expected future cash flows from an investment are worth to the firm, the firm must first find the PV of the cash flows by discounting them at the WACC, because this is the return expectation that investors have placed on the firm. The firm's management must also be aware of the return on total assets (ROTA) relative to the WACC.[1] The only way the firm can create shareholder value is if ROTA exceeds the WACC. So, a positive rate spread between ROTA and WACC is important. The firm's senior management attempts to choose asset investments with a ROTA greater than the WACC, but the spread can also be widened by minimizing the WACC. This concept is covered in more depth in Chapter 20, Financial Decisions and Management.

III. FUNDAMENTAL WORKING CAPITAL METRICS

This section of the chapter presents a number of metrics that are used to measure and monitor working capital. In using these metrics, it is important to realize that there is no right or wrong number for a particular metric. The important issue is the direction the metric is moving over time (i.e., is it improving or getting worse). For example, if the current ratio is going down, the company is becoming less liquid, which may be a problem. It is important for management to compare metrics from period to period and understand why they are changing.

It is also important to realize that metrics vary by industry and by country. For example, days' sales outstanding (DSO) of 45 days would be very commonplace in the United States, but would be extremely good in France, where a DSO of 60+ is much more the norm. As a result, when evaluating or comparing metrics, it is important to compare metrics between comparable companies in similar geographies. Just as with credit ratings, there are a number of companies that provide comparative ratios for use in analyzing financial statements and working capital.

A. Current Ratio

The *current ratio* is defined as total current assets divided by total current liabilities. It is therefore the ratio of cash and assets expected to become cash in one year or less, to short-term liabilities that must be paid in one year or less. This ratio measures a company's ability to meet its current obligations or the degree to which current obligations are covered by current assets. The current ratio can be calculated as follows:

$$\text{Current Ratio} = \frac{\text{Total Current Assets}}{\text{Total Current Liabilities}} = \frac{\$8{,}000}{\$3{,}400} = 2.35$$

In the above example, the firm has $2.35 of cash and short-term assets for each dollar of short-term liabilities. A decline in overall economic activity or a competitive shock can slow sales. Accounts receivable and inventory would convert into cash more slowly, but the short-term liabilities must be paid on schedule. Therefore, the current ratio implies a higher level of safety when liquid assets are a greater multiple of current liabilities.

1. The ROTA calculation is discussed in Chapter 19, Financial Planning and Analysis.

B. Quick Ratio

The *quick ratio* is defined as cash plus short-term investments and accounts receivable, divided by total current liabilities. It is also known as the *acid test ratio* because it is a more stringent measure of liquidity than the current ratio. The quick ratio, which measures the degree to which a company's current liabilities are covered by its most liquid current assets (i.e., cash and assets that will convert to cash most quickly), is calculated as follows:

$$\text{Quick Ratio} = \frac{\text{Cash + Short-Term Investments + Accounts Receivable}}{\text{Total Current Liabilities}}$$

$$= \frac{\$1{,}500 + \$1{,}300 + \$1{,}700}{\$3{,}400} = 1.32$$

Inventory is not included in the numerator because it is not a financial asset like accounts receivable, as it may deteriorate or become obsolete. Unlike accounts receivable, which have an associated payment term, the receipt of cash from inventory is uncertain because sales of inventory are not known with assurance. Compared to accounts receivable, inventory is a step further away from becoming cash since, in most cases, it must convert to an account receivable and then the account receivable must convert to cash.

Prepaid expenses are assets that will not convert to cash, so they are excluded from the numerator. The firm has $1.32 of cash and very liquid assets for each dollar of short-term liabilities. Again, a higher ratio is associated with greater safety.

C. Cash Flow to Total Debt Ratio

Cash flow to total debt is defined as net income plus depreciation (and other noncash expenses, such as amortization and depletion), divided by total long- and short-term debt. Short-term debt consists of short-term notes, commercial paper, or other short-term debt obligations associated with interest. Interest and principal repayments on debt are made from the cash account. Therefore, a low ratio indicates a company's weak ability to repay debt. Studies of failed companies find that inadequate cash flow to total debt ratios are a reliable predictor of financial failure. The ratio examines the flow of cash based on the income statement to the stock of debt shown on the balance sheet. Depreciation is deducted as an expense on the income statement, but the estimate of cash flow is obtained by adding it to net income because it is not a cash outflow.

For example, in its most recent accounting cycle, a firm generated $0.184 for each dollar of interest-bearing debt, as follows:

$$\text{Cash Flow to Total Debt Ratio} = \frac{\text{Net Income + Depreciation}}{\text{Short-Term Debt + Long-Term Debt}}$$

$$= \frac{\$850 + \$200}{\$1,800 + \$3,900} = \frac{\$1,050}{\$5,700} = 0.184$$

Consider the following example. If the interest rate on the debt averages 5%, then the interest expense would be $0.05 per dollar of debt. If principal on the debt was paid off (on average) over 10 years, then the cash outflow per dollar of debt would be $0.10 per dollar of debt (the dollar of debt divided by 10 years). The sum of interest and principal per dollar of debt is therefore $0.05 + $0.10 for a total of $0.15, but the cash flow per dollar of debt is $0.184. The company can therefore service its debt, but a higher ratio would imply more safety.

D. Total Working Capital

Working capital is another measure of liquidity or safety and is defined as current assets less current liabilities. It is not a ratio—rather, it is the dollar amount by which current assets exceed current liabilities.

In the following example, if all current assets convert to cash, then the firm would have $4,600 above what is needed to pay off short-term liabilities:

$$\text{Working Capital} = \text{Current Assets} - \text{Current Liabilities}$$

$$= \$8,000 - \$3,400 = \$4,600$$

In general, firms are more liquid when they have higher working capital and related ratios (e.g., current, quick, and cash flow to total debt). It is worth noting, however, that excessively high ratios are neither necessary nor beneficial. For a manufacturing firm, current assets earn a lower rate of return than plant and equipment. Once adequate liquidity is in place, additional investment in current assets lowers the overall return on assets, which translates into a lower profit per dollar of investment.

Consider a retailing firm that purchases finished goods, marks them up, and sells them. Inventory is its most important profit-generating asset. Even so, an excessive investment in inventory creates unnecessary operating and financing costs, and lowers the overall return per dollar invested in assets.

The firm's management must assess the risk/return trade-off of liquidity versus profitability. Adequate liquidity is essential, but while increasing liquidity reduces risk, it typically also reduces profitability. The real question becomes, what is the appropriate amount of liquidity for a specific company given its current circumstances? Industry average ratios provide guidance, but desired liquidity amounts also depend upon senior management's attitude toward the liquidity-versus-profitability trade-off.

IV. CALCULATION OF THE CASH CONVERSION CYCLE (CCC)

The CCC calculates the time required to convert cash outflows (necessary to produce goods) into cash inflows (through the collection of A/R). To measure how efficiently a company uses its current assets and liabilities, add the average age of inventory (days' inventory) plus the average age of A/R (days' receivables) and subtract the average age of A/P (days' payables). The general discussion of the CCC is presented in Chapter 8, Introduction to Working Capital Management, while this chapter covers the individual component calculations. For the examples below, the financial data from the sample statements in Chapter 18, Financial Accounting and Reporting, will be used. The relevant items for these calculations are as follows (all figures are in thousands of dollars):

Annual Revenues	$15,000
Annual Cost of Goods Sold	$9,200
Cash Flow from Operations	$550
Ending Inventory	$2,600
Ending Accounts Receivable	$1,700
Ending Accounts Payable	$1,600

A. Days' Sales in Inventory (DSI) or Days' Inventory (DI)

Days' inventory (DI), also known as days' sales in inventory (DSI), is calculated as a function of the inventory value and the cost of goods sold (COGS). The inventory value used here is the ending inventory, though some forms of this ratio may use an average of the figures at the measurement period's beginning and end. The COGS, rather than sales, is used in this formula because inventory is valued on the balance sheet at its purchase or manufacturing cost rather than at its selling price.

The idea is to determine how many days it normally takes to convert available inventory into actual sales during the period (e.g., one year). Treasury professionals can find the average COGS per day by dividing the annual COGS, found on the income statement, by 365.[2] Next, this result is divided into the inventory amount on the balance sheet. Using the figures provided above, the calculation is as follows:

$$\text{Days' Inventory} = \frac{\text{Inventory}}{\text{Cost of Goods Sold}} \times 365 = \frac{\$2{,}600}{\$9{,}200} \times 365 = 103.15 \text{ Days}$$

In this case, the firm had 103.15 days of COGS in inventory.

2. Please note that this example uses annual figures for revenues and COGS. If CCC is being computed using end-of-quarter figures, then the normal convention is to use 91 days rather than 365 in all three of the CCC components. Some companies use the actual number of days for the specific quarter instead.

B. Days' Receivables (DR)

Days' receivables is calculated by determining how many days of sales reside in A/R. Accordingly, the period ending value for A/R is divided by the amount of sales (or revenues) per day. In this calculation, note that revenues are used rather than COGS because A/R is carried on the balance sheet based on the selling price. Year-end A/R is used here, but some users average the A/R balance from the most recent two balance sheets.

Days' receivables represents the number of days required to convert a sale into a cash inflow. The calculation is performed as follows:

$$\text{Days' Receivables} = \frac{\text{Accounts Receivable}}{\text{Revenues}} \times 365 = \frac{\$1{,}700}{\$15{,}000} \times 365 = 41.37 \text{ Days}$$

In this case, the firm had 41.37 days of sales in A/R.

C. Days' Payables (DP) or Days' Payable Outstanding (DPO)

Days' payables is calculated by dividing A/P by the COGS per day. The COGS denominator is used because A/P reflects the cost paid for various forms of inventory. Year-end A/P is used here, but some users average the A/P balance from the most recent two balance sheets.

The calculation is performed as follows:

$$\text{Days' Payables} = \frac{\text{Accounts Payable}}{\text{Cost of Goods Sold}} \times 365 = \frac{\$1{,}600}{\$9{,}200} \times 365 = 63.48 \text{ Days}$$

In this case, the firm had 63.48 days of COGS in A/P.

D. Cash Conversion Cycle (CCC)

The next step is to compute the CCC, or the average number of days that elapse from the time the firm pays for inputs into the production-sales cycle (parts and materials in manufacturing, or finished goods in retailing) to the time when cash is received from a sale. Using the formula presented in Chapter 8, Introduction to Working Capital Management, the CCC can be calculated as:

$$\begin{aligned}\text{Cash Conversion Cycle} &= \text{Days' Inventory} + \text{Days' Receivables} - \text{Days' Payables} \\ &= 103.15 \text{ Days} + 41.37 \text{ Days} - 63.48 \text{ Days} = 81.04 \text{ Days}\end{aligned}$$

On average during the prior year, 81.04 days elapsed from the time the company disbursed cash until it recovered cash from a sale.

E. Cash Turnover

The importance of the CCC becomes apparent when computing the *cash turnover ratio*, defined as the number of cash cycles a firm experiences in one year and calculated as follows:

$$\text{Cash Turnover} = \frac{365}{\text{Cash Conversion Cycle}} = \frac{365}{81.04} = 4.5 \text{ Times}$$

The CCC is 81.04 days. This means that from the time a dollar is spent on the inputs into the CCC, it takes 81.04 days to recover it. The dollar can be spent again once recovered, however, and this occurred 4.5 times during the last accounting period.

If the cash turnover increased to 5.5 times, then the company could spend and re-spend a dollar 5.5 times in an accounting cycle. This does not mean the volume of business has changed, but rather there has been a gain in how efficiently the company uses its investment in cash. The company still experiences the same amount of sales and spends the same amount for the inputs to production or sales. The company just uses the dollars in its cash account more intensively and operates with a smaller average cash balance.

Operationally speaking, the company would want to shorten the CCC while still operating prudently. This can be achieved by:

- Shortening days' inventory through careful purchasing and production scheduling, and through removing excess inventory of finished goods (i.e., using JIT inventory management)
- Collecting A/R faster by monitoring customer payment habits and controlling delinquencies better
- Managing A/P effectively through accepting supplier discounts only when it makes economical sense and not paying earlier than is required

F. Days of Working Capital (DWC)

Days of working capital is a measure of the number of days of sales a company has tied up in working capital and is defined as:[3]

$$\text{Days' Inventory} + \text{Days' Sales Outstanding} - \text{Days' Payables}$$

By expressing this measure in days rather than total dollars, DWC is able to be compared from company to company. Reducing DWC will free up working cash for other uses, while increasing DWC means a company will need to invest more cash in current operations.

Assuming that:

- DI = 103.15 days
- DSO = 41.37 days
- DP = 63.48 days

3. Days' sales outstanding, or DSO, is defined in Section VI.A of this chapter.

Then:

$$\text{DWC} = 103.15 + 41.37 - 63.48 = 81.04 \text{ Days}$$

Which is identical to the calculation just used to determine CCC. This is not surprising since DWC and CCC are very similar and many texts treat them as being synonymous. The major difference in the two is the use of Days' Sales Outstanding in place of Days' Receivables. For companies with little or no cash sales, the two calculations will be identical as shown in this example.

G. Cash Conversion Efficiency

Cash conversion efficiency measures how effectively a company has converted sales (or revenues) into cash. The cash flow generated by operations (i.e., operating cash flow from the statement of cash flows) is viewed as a percentage of revenue. The higher the cash conversion efficiency ratio, the greater the net cash generated per dollar of revenue. This ratio, also called the *cash profit margin*, can be calculated as follows:

$$\text{Cash Conversion Efficiency} = \frac{\text{Cash Flow from Operations}}{\text{Revenues}}$$

$$= \frac{\$550}{\$15{,}000} = 0.037\text{, or } 3.7\%$$

The calculation reveals that each dollar of cash flow resulted in $0.037 of revenue.

V. CASH DISCOUNT CALCULATIONS

A. Costs to a Buyer of Not Taking the Cash Discount

The discussion of the cash flow timeline in Chapter 8, Introduction to Working Capital Management, references cash or trade discounts. Such discounts are offered to induce payment near the beginning of the credit term. Credit terms often are expressed in the form *2/10 net 30*. This means the credit period or term is 30 days, but the buying organization may take a 2% discount if it pays the invoice within 10 days. If the buyer pays any time from day 11 through day 30, then the full invoice amount is due. This is illustrated in the calculation example below.

Calculation Example: Cost of the Cash Discount

Assume that an organization is offered the credit terms above (2/10 net 30). If the organization's opportunity cost of funds is 8% (assume this is its short-term borrowing rate), should it take the discount? Answering this question requires determining the effective cost of not taking the discount offered and paying at term instead. For example, if the invoice is $100, then the buying organization can pay within 10 days and take a 2%, or $2.00, discount. That said, the buyer's resulting invoice is $98, with an option to finance the invoice for an additional 20 days (i.e., from day 11 to day 30) at a $2.00 cost. If the buying organization chooses to pay $100 on day 30, then it has charged itself $2.00 in interest to finance the invoice for 20 days. The approximate annual cost of not taking the discount and paying at term is found as follows:

$$\text{Discount Cost} = \frac{D}{100 - D} \times \frac{365}{N - T}$$

Where:

D = Discount percentage

N = Net period

T = Discount period

Using the data in the above example, where the discount percentage is 2%, the net period is 30 days, and the discount period is 10 days, the cost of the cash discount is calculated as follows:

$$\text{Discount Cost} = \frac{2}{100 - 2} \times \frac{365}{30 - 10}$$

$$= \frac{2}{98} \times \frac{365}{20} = 0.0204 \times 18.25 = 0.3723, \text{ or } 37.23\%$$

The first term in the calculation, *D ÷ (100 – D)*, identifies the interest rate applicable to the 10-day discount period. The second term, *365 ÷ (N – T)*, annualizes the interest rate. Payment can be "postponed" by 20 days by not taking the discount, and there are 18.25 20-day periods in a year. Therefore, the interest rate applicable to the discount period is annualized by multiplying it by 18.25.

The cost of not taking the discount can be compared with the organization's 8% opportunity cost to borrow short-term funds. Since the cost to borrow is less than the cost of not taking the discount, the organization should borrow funds and take the discount.

To generalize, there are only three situations where it makes economic sense to forgo the offered discount:

- If the organization can earn a rate of return exceeding the discount rate by investing the funds in the short term instead of paying early and earning the discount.
- If the organization does not have cash available to take the discount, but has to borrow the necessary funds at an interest rate higher than the approximate cost of not taking the discount.
- If the organization has the ability to effectively change the terms by stretching out its accounts payable (A/P) terms. By paying the net amount at a later date, the paying organization is effectively reducing the implied interest rate on the transaction. However, as noted in Chapter 8, Introduction to Working Capital Management, this alternative is not one that should be exercised in the normal course of events due to the potential negative impact on vendor relations and ultimately on credit ratings.

A supplier can rather accurately estimate the firm's earning rate on short-term investments and its short-term cost of funds. Accordingly, if the supplier chooses to include a discount as a part of its credit policy, then it will construct the terms to make it economically rational for its buyer to take the discount because its intention is to induce early payment.

B. Financial Impact to a Seller of Offering a Cash Discount

Sellers offer cash discounts to induce their customers to pay before term or to be competitive. However, the seller's net benefit must also be calculated because there is a cost, in the form of lower revenue per dollar of sales, associated with offering buyers a discount for earlier payment. This is illustrated in the calculation example below.

Calculation Example: Net Benefit of Offering a Cash Discount

Assume that a seller has an opportunity cost of 8%, the average credit sale to the buyer is $100, and the credit terms are 2/10 net 30. To determine the present value (PV) of receiving the discounted payment on day 10, begin by calculating the discounted payment amount, as follows:

$$\text{Discounted Amount} = \text{Credit Sale} \times (1 - \text{Discount Amount}) = \$100 \times (1 - 0.02) = \$98.00$$

As indicated earlier in this chapter, PV can be calculated as:

$$PV = \frac{FV}{(1 + i)}$$

And the interest rate (i) for the discount period can be calculated as:

$$i = \text{Days in Discount Period} \times \frac{\text{Annual Interest}}{365}$$

$$= 10 \times \frac{8\%}{365} = 0.22\%$$

The two can be combined to calculate the PV of the discounted payment as:

$$PV_{\text{Day 10}} = \frac{\$98}{(1 + 0.22\%)} = \$97.78$$

Alternatively, the PV of receiving the full payment after 30 days is calculated as:

$$PV_{\text{Day 30}} = \frac{\$100}{(1 + 0.66\%)} = \$99.34$$

The seller can now calculate net present value (NPV) of the discount as follows:

$$NPV = PV_{Day\ 10} - PV_{Day\ 30} = \$97.78 - \$99.34 = -\$1.56$$

With these results, the seller knows its net disadvantage is $1.56 for every $100 of credit sales if the buyer takes the discount and pays by day 10 rather than waiting to pay the full amount on day 30. In other words, $1.56 is the amount of PV the seller loses if the buyer pays on the 10th day.

In this case, barring other reasons for incenting earlier payment, the seller might want to reconsider its discount terms. If the 10-day discount period and 30-day net are kept, then a discount rate of a little less than 0.5% would make the PV of payment on day 10 and day 30 about the same (i.e., consider setting the terms to 0.5/10 net 30). Following the same format as the original calculation, the PV of the discounted payment is:

$$PV_{Day\ 10} = \frac{\$99.50}{(1 + 0.22\%)} = \$99.28$$

Since the PV of the full payment on day 30 is still $99.34, the NPV of 0.5/10 net 30 is calculated as:

$$NPV = PV_{Day\ 10} - PV_{Day\ 30} = \$99.28 - \$99.34 = -\$0.06$$

VI. ACCOUNTS RECEIVABLE (A/R) MONITORING AND CONTROL

Many, but not all, companies have A/R that has to be managed. If a company has only cash or credit card sales, it may have no need for A/R. For those that do, however, monitoring and controlling a company's A/R at both an individual account and aggregate level are important to overall working capital efficiency. For example, a report of DSO identifies the overall collection rate for A/R, and an aging schedule (covered later in this chapter) helps track collection rates of individual receivables.

It is important to monitor individual accounts in order to identify:

- Errors or delays in the invoicing or payment process that are slowing collections
- Customers who may delay payment intentionally until follow-up is initiated
- A change in financial condition that may alter a customer's ability to make timely payments and require the curtailment of future credit sales

Companies also should monitor A/R on an aggregate level to identify an increase in receivables that impacts liquidity and may prompt the need for additional financing. Further, significant changes in overall A/R levels may indicate a change in the business that could affect a company's financing needs and/or cash levels. Management should analyze these changes to determine the underlying causes and take corrective actions.

Developments that may prompt significant changes in A/R include variations in sales volumes, seasonality, modifications of trade credit standards, fluctuations in economic conditions, changes in foreign currency valuations, and promotions or other sales initiatives offered by competitors. Finally, the analysis of aggregate receivables serves as the basis for forecasting the amount and timing of future cash receipts.

Another consideration for A/R management is to monitor the effectiveness of the application of payment and the overall level of write-offs or bad debt loss. The effectiveness of application of payments, discussed in Chapter 8, Introduction to Working Capital Management, can be monitored by examining the discrepancies between amounts invoiced and the actual payments applied to those invoices. While many discrepancies may be related to invoicing errors or damaged goods, accounts may be adjusted in some cases due to customers paying less than what was owed. These adjustments should be accounted for as write-offs or bad debt losses in order to properly track the overall quality of A/R. A rise in write-offs could indicate the deterioration of A/R quality.

A. Days' Sales Outstanding (DSO)

DSO, or the average collection period, is one method for measuring the quality of A/R. It is calculated by dividing outstanding A/R at the end of a period by the average daily credit sales for that period. This differs from DR, which is calculated using total sales rather than credit sales. Note that if there are no cash sales, then the two numbers are identical. DSO provides a single number that can be compared to stated credit terms, historic trends, or industry norms to indicate a company's overall collection efficiency. It may, however, be distorted by changing trends in sales volume or by strong sales seasonality.

DSO is calculated as:

$$\text{DSO} = \frac{\text{Accounts Receivable}}{\text{Daily Credit Sales for Period}}$$

Daily credit sales is typically calculated by dividing total credit sales during the period by the number of days in the period. Accounts receivable is the actual balance at the end of the period. Assuming, for example, that a company has daily credit sales of $3,444.44 and an A/R balance of $285,000, its DSO would be calculated as:

$$\text{DSO} = \frac{\$285{,}000}{\$3{,}444.44} = 82.74 \text{ Days}$$

In other words, the company takes an average of just under 83 days to convert a credit sale into cash. If the company's normal sales terms were net 90, this would be good because DSO is less than the normal sales terms. If the normal terms were net 30, this would be bad and would indicate that most of the company's credit sales were paid late. In fact, the average past due can be calculated as follows:

$$\text{Average Past Due} = \text{DSO} - \text{Average Days of Credit Terms}$$

$$= 82.74 - 30.00 = 52.74 \text{ Days}$$

B. A/R Aging Schedule

An aging schedule, which separates A/R into current and past-due receivables using set periods (typically 30-day increments), is another method for measuring A/R. Companies can analyze the aging of receivables in aggregate or on a customer-by-customer basis. An aging analysis identifies past-due accounts, which become less collectible as the age of each increases. Assuming credit terms of net 30, the aging schedule in Exhibit 9.1 reveals that 30% of the A/R is past due.

EXHIBIT 9.1 **AGING SCHEDULE**

AGE OF A/R	AMOUNT OF A/R	% OF TOTAL A/R
CURRENT	$1,750,000	70%
1–30 DAYS PAST DUE	375,000	15%
31–60 DAYS PAST DUE	250,000	10%
OVER 60 DAYS PAST DUE	125,000	5%
TOTAL	$2,500,000	100%

An aging schedule is more indicative of trends than the DSO calculation because it illustrates a pattern of distribution, rather than just providing a single number representing an average. It is possible that the DSO is consistent with credit terms extended by the firm, but a few accounts may be quite delinquent. The DSO will obscure the delinquencies, whereas the aging schedule immediately reveals them. However, an aging schedule can send the same misleading signals as DSO when sales vary significantly from month to month.

For both DSO and aging schedules, it is important to bear in mind how and when the time periods are calculated. Most companies "start the clock" at the time that they send an invoice for a particular sale. Customers, on the other hand, may start the clock on the date they receive the invoice or the actual shipment, whichever is later. Practices vary by country and industry, and it is important to understand what the common practice is before assuming that payments are late. Whatever practice is used, it is important to calculate the aging schedule based on the "past-due date" (i.e., the date on which the payment actually becomes past due), not the invoice or mail date. For example, if terms are net 30 and the company is tracking from the date of the invoice, then the payment is not past due until 30 days after the invoice date. On the 31st day after the invoice date, the payment is only 1 day past due, not 31 days past due. The latter is a fairly common mistake in creating aging reports.

C. A/R Balance Pattern

An A/R balance pattern is a forecasting tool that is used to estimate the timing of future cash flows from A/R. An A/R balance pattern specifies the percentage of credit sales during a time period (e.g., one month) that remain outstanding at the end of the current and each subsequent time period. A company's collection history determines the normal balance pattern. Management evaluates any shifts by comparing current patterns with historical norms. Companies also use balance patterns to project A/R levels, measure collection efficiency, and forecast future cash inflows. Exhibit 9.2 provides an example of an A/R balance pattern report.

EXHIBIT 9.2 **A/R BALANCE PATTERN REPORT**

INTERVAL SINCE SALE	PERCENTAGE COLLECTED
Month 0 (current month)	5%
Month 1	40%
Month 2	35%
Month 3	15%
Month 4	5%

Using the pattern in Exhibit 9.2, the following example projects there will be $50,000 of A/R outstanding (uncollected) at the end of March from January's sales:

January Sales	$250,000
January Collections (5% of Sales)	$ 12,500
February Collections (40% of Sales)	100,000
March Collections (35% of Sales)	87,500
Total Collections (80% of Sales)	$200,000
Total Outstanding Receivables from January Sales (i.e., January Sales – Total Collections)	$ 50,000

An alternative method for calculating uncollected A/R is to multiply the percentage of outstanding sales three months after the sale (100% – 80%, or 20%) by the total amount outstanding ($250,000) as follows:

$$0.20 \times \$250,000 = \$50,000$$

The previous example assumes the timely collection of all receivables. In the real world, however, a certain percentage of receivables would be past due or deemed bad debts. An A/R balance pattern may be adjusted to reflect these items.

VII. COLLECTIONS AND CONCENTRATION CALCULATIONS

There are a number of additional calculations that a treasury professional sometimes needs to use as part of managing a collection or concentration program, which are in effect tools of working capital management. Not surprisingly, these calculations all use the concept of time value of money.

A. Lockbox Cost/Benefit Analysis

The use of a lockbox system as a collection tool is discussed in Chapter 10, Collections, Concentration, and Disbursements. Assessing the suitability of using a lockbox system or network requires a cost/benefit analysis to determine whether the net benefit of reduced collection float and/or elimination of in-house processing outweighs the incremental costs of lockbox processing. The net benefit from a lockbox is the reduction in the opportunity cost of float adjusted for the difference between lockbox charges and internal processing costs. Three factors determine the opportunity cost of float:

- The dollar amount of the collected items
- The total collection time for items
- A company's current opportunity cost of funds (usually its short-term investment or borrowing rate)

Therefore, the first step in a lockbox cost/benefit analysis is to compare the differences in collection float (i.e., mail, processing, and availability float) for a company processing center versus a lockbox provider. Note, however, that in the case of a retail lockbox, float savings may not be as important as improved efficiency and lower per-item costs.

Collection float is usually measured in dollar-days and is a function of a transaction's dollar amount and the number of days of float delay. The dollar-days of float on an individual check are calculated by multiplying the dollar amount of the check by the number of days from the time the payor mails the check to the time when the payee is granted credit, or availability, of collected funds. Average daily float is calculated by dividing the sum of the dollar-days of float for all items received in a certain period by the number of days in the period. The cost of float is a product of the opportunity cost of funds and the average daily float.

An example of a lockbox cost/benefit calculation is shown in Exhibit 9.3. In the exhibit, the lockbox processor charges are the sum of a fixed cost and a variable cost based on the volume of items processed. Lockbox providers have many different methods of charging for services, but the costs can be classified as fixed or variable. Fixed monthly costs may include fees for renting the post office box, sending remittance data to the company, and providing balance reporting and account maintenance. Often, several of these costs are combined into a monthly lockbox maintenance charge. There also may be a charge for transferring funds to a concentration bank.

EXHIBIT 9.3 LOCKBOX COST/BENEFIT ANALYSIS

This exhibit shows the lockbox savings and associated costs for a company with $108,000,000 annual sales ($9,000,000 per month). Each of the items is assumed to be a batch of checks with an average check size of $9,000; the annual volume of checks is 12,000. The company's annual opportunity cost is 9%. The company's internal check-processing cost (assuming no lockbox) is $0.25 per item. The lockbox processor charges $10,000 per year plus a processing cost of $0.50 per item.

WITHOUT LOCKBOX

BATCH	DOLLAR AMOUNT	CALENDAR DAYS OF COLLECTION FLOAT WITHOUT LOCKBOX	TOTAL DOLLAR-DAYS
1	$1,500,000	x 4 =	$ 6,000,000
2	4,500,000	x 2 =	9,000,000
3	3,000,000	x 6 =	18,000,000
TOTAL DEPOSITS	$9,000,000	TOTAL FLOAT WITHOUT LOCKBOX	$33,000,000
DIVIDED BY: 30 CALENDAR DAYS =			$ 1,100,000
TIMES: OPPORTUNITY COST/INVESTMENT RATE			x 9%
EQUALS: ANNUAL COST OF FLOAT			$ 99,000

WITH LOCKBOX

BATCH	DOLLAR AMOUNT	CALENDAR DAYS OF COLLECTION FLOAT WITH LOCKBOX	TOTAL DOLLAR-DAYS
1	$1,500,000	x 3 =	$ 4,500,000
2	4,500,000	x 1 =	4,500,000
3	3,000,000	x 5 =	15,000,000
TOTAL DEPOSITS	$9,000,000	TOTAL FLOAT WITH LOCKBOX	$24,000,000
DIVIDED BY: 30 CALENDAR DAYS =			$ 800,000
TIMES: OPPORTUNITY COST/INVESTMENT RATE			x 9%
EQUALS: ANNUAL COST OF FLOAT			$ 72,000

ANNUAL COST OF FLOAT WITHOUT LOCKBOX	$ 99,000
ANNUAL COST OF FLOAT WITH LOCKBOX	(72,000)
LOCKBOX FLOAT SAVINGS	$ 27,000
FIXED LOCKBOX COST	$ (10,000)
VARIABLE LOCKBOX COST: 12,000 CHECKS x $0.50	(6,000)
ELIMINATION OF INTERNAL PROCESSING COST: 12,000 x $0.25	3,000
NET DOLLAR BENEFIT OF LOCKBOX	$ 14,000

Variable costs may include charges for deposits and per-item charges, as well as costs for services such as transmission of remittance data, photocopying, and imaging. Usually, these and other customized processing charges are calculated on a per-unit or per-occurrence basis. Some costs, such as those for deposit preparation, may be either fixed or variable depending upon the lockbox processor. Some processors use a fixed monthly fee for deposit preparation while others charge by deposit. When preparing a cost/benefit analysis, it is important to understand how the actual charges are being calculated.

Lockbox providers also differ in terms of service flexibility and quality. Only those providers meeting a customer's standard service criteria should be included in the final lockbox selection process.

A collection or lockbox study is conducted to estimate the float savings of implementing the lockbox. A collection study uses data from remittance envelopes and images of checks to obtain information, such as the location and geographic concentration of customers and the location of the customers making the largest check payments. Often, the company's existing depository institutions are asked to perform an endpoint analysis that provides information about availability on both an aggregate and item-by-item basis. Additional information necessary for the collection study includes intercity mail times and bank availability schedules.

Specialized treasury consulting companies and major cash management banks perform periodic studies to compare mail times for various combinations of cities.

Availability schedules, which can be negotiated, vary from bank to bank and must be obtained from all banks under consideration. The results of mail time studies are combined with information from availability schedules to compare providers. Banks or consulting firms use these data, in conjunction with an analysis of a company's actual remittances, to determine which cities or combinations of cities are the most effective collection sites. A computer analysis is performed to produce an optimal solution.

B. Cash Concentration Break-Even Analysis

Chapter 10, Collections, Concentration, and Disbursements, discusses that the two principal mechanisms used for concentrating or transferring cash from regional depository accounts to a central disbursement account are wire transfers and ACH debits. Both methods have advantages and disadvantages, but the principal differences are cost and speed. Wires are typically more expensive than ACH transactions, but are also typically faster.

When determining whether to use an ACH debit or a wire transfer to concentrate funds, the first step is to establish the value of funds acceleration. In this calculation, the relevant opportunity cost of funds is typically either a short-term investment rate (e.g., the US Treasury bill rate) or a short-term borrowing rate, depending upon whether the company is a net investor or net borrower. By comparing the value of accelerated funds to the incremental cost of the wire, the appropriate transfer method can be identified.

Calculation Example: Break-Even Wire Transfer Amount

Assume the following:

- The incremental cost of an ACH debit is $1.00.
- The incremental cost of a wire transfer is $10.00.
- The opportunity cost of funds is 3.5%.
- Funds are available one business day sooner with a wire transfer than with an ACH transfer.

The formula for computing the break-even wire transfer amount is as follows:

$$\text{Minimum Transfer} = \frac{\text{Wire Cost} - \text{ACH Cost}}{\text{Days Accelerated} \times \left(\dfrac{\text{Opportunity Cost}}{365\ \text{Days}}\right)}$$

$$= \frac{\$10.00 - \$1.00}{1\ \text{Day} \times \left(\dfrac{0.035}{365\ \text{Days}}\right)} = \frac{\$9.00}{1 \times 0.00009589} = \$93{,}858$$

In this example, as long as the wire transfer amount is larger than $93,858, the additional cost of the wire transfer is justified. If the amount being transferred is less than $93,858, it is more cost-effective to use an ACH transaction.

VIII. SUMMARY

This chapter presented a number of metrics or calculations that are frequently used by treasury professionals in analyzing results and making decisions. It started with a discussion of the time value of money, which represents the essential underpinnings of most financial calculations. The chapter then outlined a number of key metrics used in analyzing working capital, as well as the cash conversion cycle. The next sections examined metrics that apply to A/R, including cash discount calculations. The chapter concluded with some break-even calculations that are valuable in analyzing collection and concentration systems.

TEST YOUR UNDERSTANDING: CHAPTER 9

Answers are on pages 679–680.

1. What is meant by the term *time value of money*?
2. Explain the meaning of the term *opportunity cost*.
3. Compare and contrast the current ratio and the quick ratio.
4. How is days' receivables calculated?
5. What is the formula for the cash conversion cycle?
6. What is cash conversion efficiency?
7. What are the three situations where it makes economic sense to forego taking a cash discount?
8. Why is it important to monitor individual accounts receivable?
9. What is an A/R aging schedule?
10. When conducting a lockbox cost/benefit calculation, what are the three elements that determine the opportunity cost of float?

CHAPTER 10
Collections, Concentration, and Disbursements

I. INTRODUCTION

Chapter 4, Payment Systems, discusses the fundamentals of how payment systems work. This chapter takes a look at how those various payment systems are used to manage the day-to-day requirements of collections and disbursements. The collection of funds from customers and other sources (related to accounts receivable [A/R]) and the disbursement of funds to employees, suppliers, tax authorities, and capital markets (related to accounts payable [A/P]) are key parts of day-to-day treasury operations. Collection and disbursement products and services are also the primary types of cash management services offered by banks to their customers.

Collections and disbursements are the fundamental processes of working capital management, discussed in Chapter 8, Introduction to Working Capital Management. It is important to remember that collections and disbursements are opposite sides of the same coin. In other words, Company A's disbursements are Company B's collections. As a result, many of the same banking services and products—EFT or current (checking) accounts, for example—are important to both disbursements and collections. Concentration, or more properly, funds concentration, rounds out the suite of basic cash management services by making sure that the funds that are collected are properly situated so that they are available for disbursements—either as payments for goods and services, for investment, or for debt repayment.

This chapter starts with a discussion of general disbursement practices, which includes an overview of some of the bank products and services that are normally used by treasury professionals. It then "turns the coin over" and looks at collections and their related services. Section IV of this chapter examines concentration of funds, including the concepts of notional and physical pooling. The chapter closes with a discussion of payments fraud, which is a constant concern for all treasury professionals.

II. DISBURSEMENTS

The primary issue in disbursements is control (e.g., ensuring that disbursements are made exactly as requested by A/P, that the needed funds are available, and that payments risk/fraud is controlled). Disbursement processes include both the payment initiation and the reconciliation of the payment (e.g., verifying that the payment was processed and debited from the disbursement account accurately). Managing the information related to the disbursements and to the actual clearing and settlement of the payments is also an important part of the process.

A. Disbursement Management Products

Disbursement systems, which allow an organization to make payments, may range from a single bank account for a small business to a very complex system with multiple banks, accounts, payment methods, and financial management products for a large corporation.

1. ZERO BALANCE ACCOUNTS (ZBAs)

ZBAs are bank accounts in which the end-of-day balance is maintained at zero. Credits and debits that post to the ZBA are netted at the close of each business day. From the account holder's perspective, if there is a credit balance in the ZBA, then the ZBA will be debited and the master account will be credited. This brings the balance in the ZBA back to zero. If there is a debit balance in the ZBA, then the ZBA will be credited and the master account will be debited. Again, this end-of-day transaction returns the balance in the ZBA to zero. Funding of the ZBA is generally done automatically by the bank and typically involves only an accounting entry by the bank and the company.

ZBAs are typically disbursement accounts on which a company issues checks, initiates ACH[1] debits, or initiates wire transfers. In some cases, however, ZBAs are used for both collections and disbursements.

Multi-tiered ZBAs may be used to let companies with multiple divisions or subsidiaries initiate payments from separate accounts or segregate different types of payments, such as A/P, payroll, dividends, and taxes. A cash manager can control the balances and funding of a master account and that account's associated ZBAs as if they were all one account. This approach reduces excess balances and the need for multiple, manual transfers, while maintaining distinct information and audit trails. These specific-purpose accounts can also help protect the concentration account against fraud, through the use of debit blocks for deposit-only ZBAs or check blocks for ACH-only ZBAs. Accounts can also have debit filters to allow debits to be processed only from certain entities (e.g., only allow debits by specific tax authorities, account numbers, or company identification) or within a certain range of values.

2. POSITIVE PAY

Positive pay is a disbursement service used to combat payment (primarily check, but increasingly ACH) fraud. With this service, the company transmits a file of payment information to the disbursement bank either at or before the time of the physical distribution of checks or anticipated ACH debits. The bank matches check serial numbers and dollar amounts of checks presented for payment against the issue database and pays only those checks or ACH transactions that match all relevant criteria. Many positive pay services also offer the ability to match against the payee field (known as *payee positive pay*), as well as the serial number and the amount, in an effort to detect an altered payee. In the case of ACH positive pay, transactions are matched based on dollar amount and originator.

The standard positive pay service is typically done on a batch basis as the bank processes checks or ACH payments. A related service, known as *teller positive pay*, allows for real-time inquiry on checks by tellers at all the branches of the bank, enabling the teller to match the item to the check issue file on a real-time basis and helping to prevent the cashing of fraudulent items.

Any exceptions to the positive pay match process are conveyed to the company for its decision whether to pay or return the item. Given the limited amount of time available to return items, exceptions typically must be reviewed and "decisioned" (i.e., a determination made to pay or reject the transaction) by an established deadline that same day. Because the bank cannot process the exception items without company authorization, it is common to set up accounts with a default status of either *pay all* or *pay none*. In other words, if the company fails to notify the bank of its decision on any exception items by the deadline, the bank will either pay all of the exception items and post them to the company's account, or pay none of the exception items and return them all to the depositor. Most banks offer online access to payment transaction data and check images, to assist in this process of researching and identifying potentially fraudulent payments.

1. As discussed in Chapter 4, Payment Systems, the term *ACH transaction* is used in this text generically to include all pre-authorized, low-value debit and credit EFT transactions, including but not limited to ACH, SEPA, Bacs, ECG, and other country-specific transfer systems.

A similar service, known as *reverse positive pay*, is a process whereby the bank transmits a file of the checks presented for payment to the company on a daily or intraday basis. Within a specified time deadline, the company matches this file to a list of checks issued and notifies the bank of any items to be returned. This service, however, does not prevent fraudulent checks from being cashed at the paying bank teller line (i.e., teller positive pay) since the bank does not have access to the issue file. As with regular positive pay, when using a reverse positive pay service, the company and bank must agree on a default action if the company does not meet the required deadline—that is, should the bank pay all or pay none, bearing in mind that in the case of reverse positive pay, pay none means that all checks presented that day will be returned, not just the exception items.

It is important to note that positive pay services cannot protect against a type of fraud known as *fraudulent endorsement*. Fraudulent endorsement occurs when an authorized check is stolen or intercepted by a third party, and then that party endorses and cashes the check. So long as the check amount, the check number, and potentially the payee are not altered, this type of fraud is not usually detected by positive pay. While positive pay services do detect duplicate checks (i.e., a valid check and a forged copy), they typically cannot distinguish between the original and a copy and will pay the first check presented. Fortunately, checks returned for forged or fraudulent endorsement are not subject to the normal next-day return deadline and may be returned upon discovery of the forged endorsement, subject to any agreed-upon limits with the paying bank.

3. CONTROLLED DISBURSEMENT

Controlled disbursement is a bank service that provides same-day notification to a company of the amount of checks that will clear against its disbursement account on a given day. This product is unique to the United States and was developed due to the specific characteristics of US corporate checking accounts (i.e., the historic regulatory ban on paying interest on positive balances and the limitations on overdrawing current accounts). As discussed in Chapter 8, Introduction to Working Capital Management, the amount of time it will take a check to be presented at a company's bank for payment can vary significantly due to such issues as mail and processing float. The historic inability of US banks to pay interest on checking accounts meant that if the account was funded on the day the checks were issued, funds would lie dormant until the checks were actually presented. With controlled disbursement, the account is typically not funded each day until after the daily notification is received. The daily clearings are normally available by early or mid-morning, allowing the treasury professional to more accurately determine the organization's cash position. The disbursement bank generally receives its final cash letter of the day from the local Federal Reserve Bank early in the morning. This approach allows enough time for the payment items to be sorted and the company to be notified of its funding requirement for the account. The company must then provide adequate funds to the account to cover the value of the checks and other debits presented that day.

A company typically funds a controlled disbursement account from its concentration account, in which case an automatic, internal bank transfer is made. This is usually accomplished by setting up the controlled disbursement account(s) as ZBA(s). However, a wire transfer may be used when a company negotiates the funding of a controlled disbursement account from another bank. In some cases, funding by ACH is negotiated, but this is the exception rather than the norm. For risk control purposes, most banks require that controlled disbursement accounts be funded either from another account at the same bank or by wire transfer. When the funding account for the controlled disbursement is not at the controlled disbursement bank, a balance equivalent to an average day's clearing (or a sufficient line of credit) is often required to be maintained to reduce the bank's risk of nonpayment.

One of the principal advantages of a controlled disbursement account is that it allows a company to calculate its daily cash position early enough to take advantage of better market rates for investing or borrowing. However, there are instances where discrepancies arise between the reported disbursement clearings and the actual amount of checks presented for payment. These discrepancies typically arise from same-day presentment, over-the-counter presentment, and rejected items. Some banks carry over these adjustments until the following business day.

4. MULTIPLE-DRAWEE CHECKS

Multiple-drawee checks, also known as *payable-if-desired (PID) checks*, are checks that can be presented for payment at more than one bank. Normally, both bank names appear on the check as drawees. Uses for multiple-drawee checks include dividend checks, payroll in jurisdictions that require employees to be paid by checks that are payable locally, and payroll for employees on assignments away from the company office. Companies maintain balances and/or pay a fee at an alternate payment bank to compensate the bank for cashing multiple-drawee checks. The alternate bank requires indemnity from the paying company for any loss related to the checks, including fraud. Not all banks provide this service.

5. IMPREST ACCOUNTS

An imprest account, which is sometimes used as a petty cash account, is an account maintained at a fixed amount for a particular purpose or activity. For example, a field office may have an imprest account for local disbursements, with a balance sufficient for one or two months' expenses. Based on either an established time frame or a designated level of imprest account balances, the field office submits expenses to headquarters for approval, and headquarters replenishes the imprest account and brings it back to the fixed amount. Variations of this type of account include those used for certain types of medical claims payments, or revolving funds accounts for a company's departmental expense funds. For these revolving funds accounts, the balance in the fund is drawn down as expenses are paid over the period, and then the account is replenished to some set amount at the end of the period or when a certain balance level is hit.

B. Electronic Disbursement Products

Electronic disbursements via wire transfer and ACH are used for business-to-consumer (B2C) and business-to-business (B2B) payments, as well as for payments from governments to consumers (G2C) and businesses to governments (B2G). These forms of payments are covered in detail in Chapter 4, Payment Systems. As discussed in more detail in the section below on collections, one of the significant advantages of electronic disbursements is the ability to include remittance information with B2B payments. Additional information on some specific types of electronic disbursements is provided below.

1. DIRECT DEPOSIT (ACH) PAYMENTS

Direct deposit payments have been used widely in the United States since the early 1980s for both government and commercial payments, and are now routinely used throughout much of the world. The introduction of the SEPA credit transfer scheme in the euro zone and cross-border ACH in other countries (including the United States) has made global use of direct deposit simpler and more acceptable for many companies. Direct deposits are transfers made from a company's account to the accounts of employees, shareholders, vendors, and trading partners using ACH credit transactions. While direct deposit of payroll is the most common form of ACH payment, direct deposit can also be used for employee expense reimbursements, interest payments, tax payments, dividend distributions, and B2B transactions. Some state labor departments allow companies to mandate direct deposit of payroll. For employees without bank accounts, an alternative to direct deposit of payroll is the payroll card, discussed below.

In addition to corporate use of direct deposit, government agencies use direct deposit for benefits distributions, social security payments, and tax refunds. Two advantages of direct deposit are the low cost of the transactions and the certainty of timing.

2. TAX PAYMENTS

Many taxing authorities throughout the world allow (and in some cases, mandate) electronic payment of various types of taxes.[2] In the United States, the Electronic Federal Tax Payment System (EFTPS) is the primary method for collecting and accounting for federal taxes withheld by employers from individuals' salaries and wages, as well as corporate business, sales, and excise taxes.

Sub-sovereign or local taxing authorities are also moving toward electronic payment of taxes. In the United States, most states require companies with tax payments above certain amounts to remit them electronically. This is accomplished either by initiating an ACH credit or authorizing an ACH debit. The standard NACHA payment format for state tax payments via ACH is known as the tax payment (TXP) banking convention, yet usage and specific formats vary from state to state. Some states also accept tax payments by wire transfer. In addition, most US states now require electronic payments from employers for payroll amounts withheld, such as child support and wage garnishments.

Many banks provide specialized systems that can support and maintain multiple tax payment formats and are specifically designed to handle the timing and information requirements of tax payments.

3. WIRE TRANSFERS

As discussed in Chapter 4, Payment Systems, wire transfers (e.g., Fedwire in the United States or TARGET2 in Europe) are an important disbursement tool for companies that need to make large-value payments that are immediate and final at the time of settlement. Most banks provide a number of methods for originating wire transfers, ranging from telephone initiation to online systems (discussed in more detail in Chapter 14, Information Technology in Treasury). To meet the needs of corporate users, banks generally classify wire transfers by usage category. This classification is based on which elements of information change from wire to wire (as summarized below). Understanding the differences in the types of wires is important from a payments risk/fraud control standpoint as the level of risk varies by type of wire.

2. "Paying Taxes 2011" (a joint publication produced by the World Bank, the International Finance Corporation [IFC], and PwC) reported that 61 of 183 economies surveyed provide for electronic filing and payment of taxes, and that the number is growing steadily. The study was based on data collected as part of the *Doing Business* project by the World Bank and IFC. (From "Paying Taxes 2011," published by PwC, 2010, http://www.pwc.com/gx/en/paying-taxes/pdf/paying-taxes-2011.pdf.)

- **Repetitive Wires:** Repetitive wire transfers are used when a company makes frequent transfers to the same credit parties. In a repetitive wire, only the date and dollar amount of the wire change—all other information remains constant. The bank (or payment system, such as a treasury management system [TMS], used by the customer to originate wires) maintains a record of the debit and credit bank accounts and accepts instructions either electronically (most banks offer a web-based wire transfer system) or via telephone to initiate the transfer. A unique identifier is assigned to each instruction template that contains all of the standing information. Since only the date and the dollar amount can be changed on a repetitive wire, this type of transfer provides significant assurance that funds will not be sent to an unknown or fraudulent party.
- **Semi-Repetitive Wires:**[3] The debit and credit parties remain the same in a semi-repetitive wire transfer, but the description (e.g., a customer or an invoice number) may be changed, along with the date and the dollar amount. Semi-repetitive transfers combine the controls of repetitive transfers with the flexibility of non-repetitive transfers.
- **Non-Repetitive (Free-Form) Wires:** The debit and credit parties are different each time in a non-repetitive wire. Because all of the information is variable, this type of transfer has the highest degree of payment risk due to fraud or simple data entry errors. As a result, additional security measures are typically required to guard against both fraud and input errors. Examples of such measures are callbacks, secondary levels of approval, and segregation of duties.
- **Drawdown Wires:** A drawdown wire transfer is a request sent by a company's bank to a second bank requesting that the second bank initiate a wire transfer from either the company's account or another party's account at the second bank, sending the funds back to the first bank. The party being debited must pre-authorize the transfer; therefore, drawdown wires are most frequently used as part of a company's concentration system, since the company can authorize both sides of the transaction.
- **Standing Wires:** With a standing wire, a company establishes repetitive transfer instructions to move funds between two specified accounts automatically when previously determined criteria are met. Standing wires typically are used for concentrating funds, and the criteria could address either timing (e.g., all funds in the account at the end of the day) or a designated balance level (e.g., all funds in excess of $50,000).

C. Card Payments

As discussed in Chapter 4, Payment Systems, payment cards, both credit and debit, have become an important method of disbursing payments for consumers and for businesses. If payment cards are used in a company, it is important to have established and documented policies and procedures to provide appropriate controls. This is discussed in more detail in Chapter 17, Treasury Policies and Procedures. Some uses of cards specific to business and government payments are provided below.

1. PURCHASING CARDS

Purchasing cards (also known as *procurement cards* or *p-cards*) are credit cards used by businesses for the purchase of supplies, inventory, equipment, and service contracts. Typically, p-cards are used for varying purchases, either low- or high-value, with spending limits established on an individual card basis. Purchases can be limited to approved vendors and suppliers, as determined by the merchant category code of the vendor or supplier, and non-allowed transactions are rejected at the point of sale. The principal benefit of a p-card for a company is the replacement of the traditional time-consuming, labor-intensive, paper-based requisition process. Additionally, companies may negotiate a rebate based on charge volume and average transaction size, and they may be able to effectively delay payment since purchased items will not be paid for until the end of the billing cycle. The principal benefit for an employee is that

3. Depending upon the bank, the term *template wire* may be used to refer to either repetitive or semi-repetitive wires. This is based on the fact that a template is used to hold the fixed data for either type of wire.

essential goods and services can be obtained quickly and conveniently without a complicated purchase order process. One of the benefits of purchasing cards is the ability to eliminate the use of local petty cash funds since the cards can be used in place of most cash payments. Although p-cards are often issued to a specific individual, they typically also have the company name on the card, and purchases on the card are a liability of the company rather than the individual named on the card.

2. TRAVEL AND ENTERTAINMENT (T&E) CARDS

T&E cards (sometimes called *travel cards*) are used by businesses for employee travel purposes. Travel cards may be incorporated into a company's p-card program (typically referred to as *one-card programs*), or they may be issued as a separate card. These cards work very similarly to p-cards. Card issuers may send companies a regularly scheduled data file of transactions that have been charged by employees for automatic loading, as well as send reconciliation details directly into the company's employee expense system. Rebates may also be offered in a travel card program. T&E cards, as with p-cards, often can have restrictions on use based on company policy. Depending upon the program and the specific terms negotiated by the organization, the primary liability for T&E card purchases can be either the company or the individual cardholder. In the latter case, the company typically guarantees payment in the event that the cardholder does not make the required payments.

3. FLEET CARDS

Fleet cards are similar to T&E cards but are designed to be used for expenditures related to trucks and cars, such as fuel and repairs, and in some cases, other driver expenses, such as food and lodging. Fleet card systems typically are designed to capture added information, such as vehicle mileage and location, in addition to actual purchase information.

4. COMBINED CARDS

As the name implies, combined cards combine the features of p-cards, T&E cards, and potentially fleet cards into one card that can be issued to employees to make appropriate payments. The benefit to the employee is the convenience of only needing to carry one card. The disadvantage to the company is a potential reduction of disbursement information since multiple types of payments are being made through one channel.

5. PAYROLL CARDS AND OTHER STORED-VALUE CARDS

The payroll card (sometimes simply called a *pay card*) is a stored-value card that is offered as an alternative payment method to employees who do not have bank accounts or do not want to accept direct deposit of funds for their paychecks. The key benefits to employers of moving employees to payroll cards versus checks include reduced payroll costs and lower levels of payroll-related fraud. Other uses of stored-value cards include employee benefit programs, such as flexible spending accounts and health care expense reimbursements, on-the-spot bonus programs, and termination payments.

6. ELECTRONIC BENEFIT TRANSFER (EBT) CARDS

EBT cards are a type of stored-value card issued by government entities to disburse benefit and social support payments, such as food stamps. EBT is especially prevalent in the United States, where most state governments now use EBT systems for the disbursement of benefits under food stamp programs, but EBT is also used internationally in countries ranging in size from India and Canada to the Dominican Republic. These systems allow recipients of government transfer payments to receive benefit payments through ATMs and POS terminals.

D. Outsourced Accounts Payable (A/P) Services

Because of the complexity of many payment types and the need for extensive controls over disbursement activities, outsourcing A/P functions is quite common. Outsourcing products include freight payment services, payroll services, and integrated or comprehensive A/P.

1. FREIGHT PAYMENTS

Some banks and third parties offer a payment service called *freight payment* in which specialists pay all of a shipper's freight bills, audit bills for possible overcharges and duplicate payments, and provide reports that help a company compare costs for different routes and carriers. Manufacturers and wholesale distributors typically use this service.

2. PAYROLL SERVICES

Numerous vendors offer payroll services that handle many payroll functions, including check and direct deposit file issuance, payroll tax filing and payment, and retirement/pension account administration. Payroll services also provide employees with the required withholding forms. Many small- to medium-sized businesses outsource payroll because it is often a cost-effective and convenient service.

3. INTEGRATED OR COMPREHENSIVE ACCOUNTS PAYABLE (A/P)

An integrated or comprehensive A/P service allows a company to outsource all or part of the company's A/P and/or disbursement functions. There are two common approaches to managing an integrated or comprehensive A/P service:

- In the first approach, a company may send a data file to a financial services provider (FSP) periodically, containing a list of all payments to be made. The file contains information on when to issue a disbursement and to whom, as well as instructions on the payment method to be used (e.g., check, wire, ACH, foreign draft, or foreign currency).
- In the second approach, the FSP may maintain a database of a company's payees that includes detailed information, such as preferred payment methods, specific remittance information, and the names of receiving financial institutions. The database is updated periodically as payees are added or deleted, or as an existing payee's remittance profile changes. Under this method, when a company needs a disbursement, it sends only limited payment information to the FSP.

With either approach, the FSP issues the payments immediately or warehouses the items (i.e., holds payments until some future transaction date), according to the instructions in the data file.

4. PAYMENT FACTORIES

A payment factory is essentially a centralized A/P processing center. It is often part of a centralized treasury operation known as an in-house bank, or it may be set up as part of an organization's enterprise resource planning (ERP) system. Payment factories are often used in multinational organizations with a large number of cross-border payments. They can also be linked to multilateral netting systems or re-invoicing programs in order to reduce the number of transactions between subsidiaries of a company, as well as better control overall exposures from foreign currencies. To send payments outside the organization, a single payment file from all the operating units can be sent to a global or regional bank, which can then arrange for payments to be made in local currencies to the vendors. These topics are covered in more detail in Chapter 8, Introduction to Working Capital Management.

E. Managing Disbursement Information

Accurate and comprehensive information management is central to an effective disbursement system. Obtaining timely and accurate information about the status of disbursement accounts and disbursement clearings lets a company manage its cash position more effectively. In addition, information must be provided to the A/P function regarding the status of outstanding items.

1. BALANCE REPORTING SERVICES

Online balance or transaction reporting services, which are discussed in more detail in Chapter 14, Information Technology in Treasury, allow a bank to report transaction and balance information to corporate customers. Information is typically classified as either *same day* (i.e., transactions that have happened today; also referred to as *current day*) or *prior day* (i.e., transactions that were processed before today). By providing current information, these services not only help manage bank accounts but are an important part of fraud control as they allow treasury professionals to see transactions in real or near-real time and question suspicious or unexpected transactions.

2. INTERFACE WITH ACCOUNTS PAYABLE (A/P)

Two critical areas of interface between treasury and A/P relate to disbursements. The first is the communication from A/P regarding the invoices vouchered for payment, and the second is the communication from treasury back to A/P regarding the reconciled payments. Typically, companies with integrated ERP/accounting systems that include treasury management modules can integrate these functions. However, many companies must use either separate systems for disbursement management or bank-provided treasury information software that may not interface with the A/P ledger. In these cases, customized patches (or middleware, in a client-server environment) may be obligatory to facilitate the transfer of information between applications.

3. ACCOUNT RECONCILIATION PROGRAM (ARP)

Banks provide account reconciliation services to meet companies' information and control requirements. In a partial reconciliation program, the bank lists all items paid in numerical order by check serial number or in chronological order by date paid. For each item, the paid report generally shows the serial number (if applicable), dollar amount, and date paid. The listing is usually available as a paper report, on a CD-ROM, via a direct data transmission, or through a website.

With a full reconciliation program, a company supplies the bank with an electronic file of all payments issued, and the bank matches items paid against the file. For companies using a bank's positive pay service, this can be the same file used for that service. In addition, many banks bundle ARP services with their positive pay services since the reconciliation is effectively being done as the items are presented to the account.

Related bank services that may be used for disbursement activities include stop payments and high-order prefix sorting. A stop payment is an order given to the paying bank instructing it not to honor a specific payment that has already been issued but has not yet cleared. These orders generally are given because a check is lost or stolen, or the payor determines after the payment is issued that there is a mistake and the payment must be rescinded. Stop payments may be initiated by voice, electronically, or in writing. Written confirmation may be required by the bank for telephone instructions. Stop payments usually remain in place for only six months and must be renewed, if necessary.

A high-order prefix (divisional) sort is a service that allows a company with multiple units to use a single bank account for all of its payments and still identify individual payments by unit. Codes identifying the various units are included in the check serial number field at the beginning of the check number. The paying bank then sorts the payments by the high-order code and reports them to the company either through account reconciliation or some other reporting service. This method is used to facilitate the identification and sorting of payments by operating unit.

4. IMAGING TECHNOLOGY

As discussed above in the section on positive pay, most banks can provide images of checks that have been presented for payment to help companies in researching payments and reconciling accounts. Images of both the front and the back of a paid check are captured during the check-processing cycle. (As discussed in Chapter 4, Payment Systems, most checks in the United States are now paid based on image presentment rather than the physical check.) Paid check images (either all or selected ones) may be transmitted to a company via fax, Internet, or direct transmission. The check images may also be stored in a bank database that a company can access online for viewing or retrieving images. Imaging provides a company with faster access to disbursement check information and is particularly beneficial when used in conjunction with controlled disbursement, payable through drafts (PTDs), and/or positive pay services. Its primary use is to exchange information between the bank and customer.

III. COLLECTIONS

Organizations collect funds from a wide range of sources, and the collection system or processes employed by an organization will often depend upon the type of organization and who is making the payments. For example, B2B collection systems will look very different from collection systems that are used for consumer payments and/or retail businesses. Businesses that collect large amounts of cash and/or collect cash at a local level (e.g., fast food or retail) will require different collection processes than a large service-type business (e.g., an accounting or consulting firm). There are a number of major issues that must be addressed in any collection system:

- **Speed of Collection:** Minimizing the time it takes to collect the actual payment and have the funds available for use is a key goal for a collection system.
- **Security of the Payment:** The collection system should ensure that the payment is not diverted or stolen during the collection process. This is especially important when cash payments are involved.
- **Availability of Remittance Information:** Collecting a payment is important, but as discussed in Chapter 8, Introduction to Working Capital Management, it is equally important to know who made the payment and why, especially if the payment is for less than anticipated.
- **Cost of Collection:** Minimizing the cost of any collection system is important, but the cost must be balanced against the prior items.

A. Collecting Payments

Any organization wants to make it as easy as possible for trading partners and customers to pay it. This helps encourage prompt and timely collections. Unfortunately, it means that the organization must have the ability to receive and process as many types of payments as possible, from cash to checks to cards to EFT. As a rule, retail organizations receive most of their payments in the form of cash and cards, although some may accept checks. When the retailer has more than one location, the picture is complicated even further by the need to consolidate retail payments from the various locations into a central collection account, as discussed in the next section. Wholesale organizations tend to receive payments in the form of checks and EFT, both ACH and wire transfer; but a growing number of B2B payments are being made by procurement cards, as discussed in the disbursements section earlier in this chapter.

The situation becomes even more complex when the organization has customers and trading partners in other countries. The organization must deal with issues of foreign exchange (which are discussed in Chapter 16, Financial Risk Management), but it must also deal with the credit risk of foreign trading partners and cross-border payments, which often results in the need to deal with trade payments and letters of credit (L/Cs).

B. Domestic Collection Products[4]

Just as there are a wide variety of products that support disbursements, banks and other vendors provide a number of products to support domestic collections.

1. ARMORED CARRIERS AND VIRTUAL VAULTS

Companies with multiple retail locations use armored cars to collect deposits from their retail outlets to ensure the safety of both the collections and their staff. Because of the high cost of armored carriers, companies typically use them only for outlets with large amounts of cash receipts or where there are specific security concerns regarding the safety of employees taking deposits to local depository banks. The desire to speed up the collection cycle by having daily armored carrier pickups must be balanced against the cost of each individual pickup.

One solution to this problem that is becoming increasingly common is a product referred to as a *virtual vault*. The armored carrier, working in conjunction with the company's depository bank, provides a special safe to the retail outlet that records deposits into the safe and reports them to the armored carrier and the bank. The bank provides provisional credit at the time of the deposit into the safe, and the armored carrier picks up the contents of the safe on a reduced schedule, perhaps weekly instead of daily.

Virtual vaults also provide the ability for a bank to service retail outlets that are not near any of its branches. Working through the armored carrier, the bank can effectively accept deposits in any location that the armored carrier can service and is not limited to the geography of the bank's branches. As a result, this can also help geographically dispersed retailers handle their cash consolidation needs.

4. *Domestic collection* refers to payments received from customers and trading partners within the same country as the collecting company.

2. MERCHANT SERVICES

Merchant services is the term typically used to describe the products offered by a bank, Internet service provider, or other firm (referred to as a *merchant processor*) that processes credit and debit card transactions. While the term principally refers to the acceptance and processing of card transactions, it also often includes ancillary services such as returns and adjustments, POS terminals, supplies, and customer support.

3. REMOTE DEPOSIT CAPTURE (RDC)

RDC (discussed in Chapter 4, Payment Systems) involves using a check scanner to capture an image of check payments and then depositing them by sending the images to the company's depository bank(s). This service eliminates the need to gather the checks and take them to the bank or send them via mail or overnight delivery service. This speeds up collection time, reduces the risk that the checks will be lost or stolen in transit, and typically reduces the overall cost of check processing. As with a virtual vault, RDC allows a depository bank to service locations that are physically distant from a bank facility, alleviating the need for subsequent cash consolidation from a local field bank. In some cases, RDC scanners are being incorporated into the electronic safes used for virtual vault services, providing a consolidated service for retail organizations. The product is limited to checks denominated in US dollars.

4. CHECK CONVERSION

Check conversion involves scanning the payor's check and converting it to an ACH debit. The benefit of this is that ACH transactions are typically less expensive than check processing. Checks can be converted at the point of presentment (e.g., the retail sales counter), in the back office or deposit-processing operation, or in a lockbox operation that is receiving bill payments (see the discussion of lockbox below). Each type of conversion has a different SEC code.[5] As with RDC, check conversion is limited to checks drawn on US-domiciled accounts. Unlike RDC, which is available for both consumer and commercial checks, check conversion is limited to consumer checks under $25,000.[6]

5. MAIL PAYMENTS

Mail payments can be processed internally or outsourced to a lockbox processor as discussed in the next section. In an internal company processing center, check and payment card processing, along with deposit preparation, are performed in-house. For checks, the processing generally involves the following steps:

- Receiving and opening the mail
- Separating the payment (i.e., check) from the remittance advice, which provides information on who is paying and what they are paying
- Forwarding the remittance advice, amount, and date of payment to the A/R department
- Preparing the check for deposit (i.e., endorsement and deposit preparation), or in the case of consumer payments, preparing the check for possible conversion into an ACH debit
- Transporting the check to the organization's deposit bank, employing remote deposit capture, or converting an eligible check into an ACH debit

For payment card collections, the card information and amount must be captured and sent to the merchant processor mentioned above to start the collection process. The card transaction process itself is covered in Chapter 4, Payment Systems.

5. *SEC* is an acronym for *standard entry class*, which refers to a code that is used to distinguish different types of ACH transactions. A list of common SEC codes is provided in Appendix 10.1.
6. The technical limitation on check conversion is to checks under $25,000 that do not contain an auxiliary on-us field in the MICR line, which is basically equivalent to consumer checks, as most business checks have an auxiliary on-us field. For complete details, refer to the current NACHA operating rules and guidelines.

The primary advantage of an in-house processing center is control of the collections operation. Maintaining control may be especially important in organizations where capturing very detailed remittance information is required in order to allow A/R to apply the payments properly. The primary disadvantages are the need to provide appropriate controls (e.g., segregation of duties and security over payments), potential processing delays of internal processing, and the need to add staff to handle peak volumes of transactions.

Traditionally, in-house processing was performed either by very small companies with low volumes of check and card payments or by fairly large companies that could justify the expense of the automated equipment required to manage high volumes. The introduction of RDC and improved scanning technology, along with increased use of electronic payment and remittance transmission methods, has changed these guidelines. In today's collections environment, the choice between using an in-house processing center and a lockbox (discussed below) must be evaluated carefully to ensure the most cost-effective solution for the company.

6. LOCKBOX

A lockbox system is a collection tool in which a financial institution or third-party vendor receives payments at specified post office box (lockbox) addresses, processes the remittances, and credits the payments into a payee's account. While lockbox services are available in a number of countries, they are most widely used in the United States, due to the widespread use of paper checks.

For organizations with a large number of EFT collections, a variation of the lockbox approach, known as an *electronic lockbox*, is discussed below in the section on consolidated remittance processing.

The major advantages of a lockbox system over an internal company payment-processing center include:

- Reduced mail and processing float[7]
- Improved access to remittance information
- Reduced risk and improved security since payments are no longer received internally
- Improved control and record-keeping capabilities
- Uninterrupted service
- Scalability
- Proper segregation of duties

Lockbox procedures also establish an external audit trail for payments received and segregate check processing from other A/R functions. Generally, lockbox operators can establish business continuity plans and disaster recovery sites more readily than individual companies can, which can result in a higher level of reliability in payment processing. Finally, a lockbox is generally easier to scale up or down as business volumes change (as compared to an in-house processing center). This is especially an advantage for a seasonal business.

7. The various components of float are discussed in Chapter 8, Introduction to Working Capital Management.

Traditionally, there are three basic types of lockboxes:

- **Retail lockboxes,** which process payments that involve machine-readable remittance documents (or "coupons"), such as utility and credit card payments. These are typically consumer payments (C2B) and tend to be high-volume payments that can justify the cost of the equipment used to process and read the remittance documents.
- **Wholesale lockboxes,** which typically process B2B payments, involving a smaller number of payments, with attached remittance information that is usually not machine-readable. These tend to be large payments that can justify the cost of staff to review and extract remittance information.
- **Hybrid lockboxes,** which combine features of wholesale and retail lockboxes (e.g., smaller volumes but machine-readable remittance documents).

In addition to these three, the increased volume of electronic remittance payments has led to what is often referred to as an *electronic lockbox,* a service that combines and presents remittance information from electronic payments. While this service, which is discussed in more detail below in the section on consolidated remittance processing, is not literally a "lockbox" since there is no actual mail involved, it does have many of the reporting features traditionally associated with lockbox processing, hence the term *electronic lockbox.*

As mentioned in the previous section, the introduction of RDC and related scanning technology has led a number of companies to move away from external providers and perform their own processing in-house. While in-house processing can reduce processing and collection float, and may be less costly than a bank or third-party provider lockbox, it does not provide all of the benefits of a standard lockbox service.

7. ELECTRONIC FUNDS TRANSFER (EFT) WITH REMITTANCE INFORMATION

As previously mentioned, the availability and reliability of remittance information is a key issue in processing collections. Historically, one of the problems with EFT transactions, in both large-dollar and ACH systems, was the inability to transmit remittance information with the payment. As a result, companies received remittance information separately from the electronic payments and were forced to match and reconcile them. This is a particular problem when trading partners or customers are making partial payments or taking deductions from the face amount of an actual invoice. As a result, many of the EFT systems around the world have introduced extended remittance information capabilities largely modeled after the ISO 20022 payment standard supported by SWIFT.

8. ELECTRONIC BILL PRESENTMENT AND PAYMENT (EBPP) AND ELECTRONIC INVOICE PRESENTMENT AND PAYMENT (EIPP)

Although often thought of as disbursement products since they allow consumers or businesses to make payments electronically, EBPP and EIPP are actually a bridge between collections and disbursements that enable companies to send electronic statements and receive electronic remittances from their customers. With both products (EBPP for retail customers and EIPP for corporate customers), a company sends billing data to its customer, typically through an e-mail with a link to the company's billing portal (website). The customer can review the billing information, ask questions, and modify payment amounts as needed. Once satisfied, the customer authorizes payment electronically, typically triggering an EFT debit. EBPP and EIPP may be provided through a company's own website or a third-party vendor, often referred to as a *payment portal.* Because the collecting company, or the third-party vendor, controls both the transmission of the billing data and the subsequent collection, the remittance information is already linked to the payment, simplifying subsequent posting to A/R and reducing any exception processing.

9. CONSOLIDATED REMITTANCE PROCESSING (CRP)

Because payments come in many forms and types, organizations are often forced to deal with multiple sources of remittance information and payment data, often in widely different formats. This can result in processing delays and expensive exception item processing. One solution to this is a product often referred to as *consolidated remittance processing*. The predecessor of CRP was a service often referred to as an *electronic lockbox*. An electronic lockbox (discussed earlier in this chapter) provides a single collection point for all ACH and wire payments, and it can also process remittance advices from a variety of incoming formats into a single format for transmission to the organization's A/R department for posting and reconciliation. CRP takes this a step further by consolidating all remittance information into one stream of data in a common format. This can include not only EFT but check and card payments as well.

In some versions of CRP, the vendor (often a bank) providing the service also provides a service called *receivables matching*, in which the vendor matches a processed payment against the company's open invoices, applies the payment, and updates the A/R record.

10. IMAGING TECHNOLOGY

In addition to being used for check processing, imaging technology can also facilitate the processing of both wholesale and retail remittance information. This technology allows paper documents, such as checks and remittance advices, to be scanned, converted to digital images, and stored for subsequent distribution, handling, and processing. Having this payment information readily available is especially beneficial for organizations that must research a high volume of customer service inquiries (e.g., mortgage, insurance, and utility companies). Potential benefits of applying image technology to the remittance-processing function include:

- Reduced overall processing costs
- Increased productivity
- Improved accuracy
- Automated updating of A/R
- Improved response time to customer inquiries
- Faster resolution of lockbox discrepancies

C. Cross-Border Collections and Trade Management Products

International or cross-border payments add a significant degree of complexity to collections. In addition to all of the issues already discussed for domestic collections, cross-border collections add the risk of FX (discussed in Chapter 16, Financial Risk Management) and the risk of credit management when dealing with customers who are across a single border or on the other side of the world. As a result, in addition to all of the traditional collections products available for domestic collections, there are a number of payment mechanisms that have been developed primarily for use in international business.

The most frequently used cross-border trade payment mechanisms (i.e., open account, documentary collection, and L/C) can be explained in terms of increasing levels of protection, complexity, and cost. Open account terms are the simplest and least costly, but offer the least protection for the seller. Documentary collections are more complex and costly, but offer some protection to both parties. Finally, L/Cs, which typically include documentary collection as part of the process, are the most complex and costly vehicles for international trade, but they provide the best combined security for both parties. Exhibit 10.1 shows the hierarchy of the primary international trade payment mechanisms in terms of protection for the buyer or seller.

EXHIBIT 10.1 **HIERARCHY OF INTERNATIONAL TRADE PAYMENT METHODS**

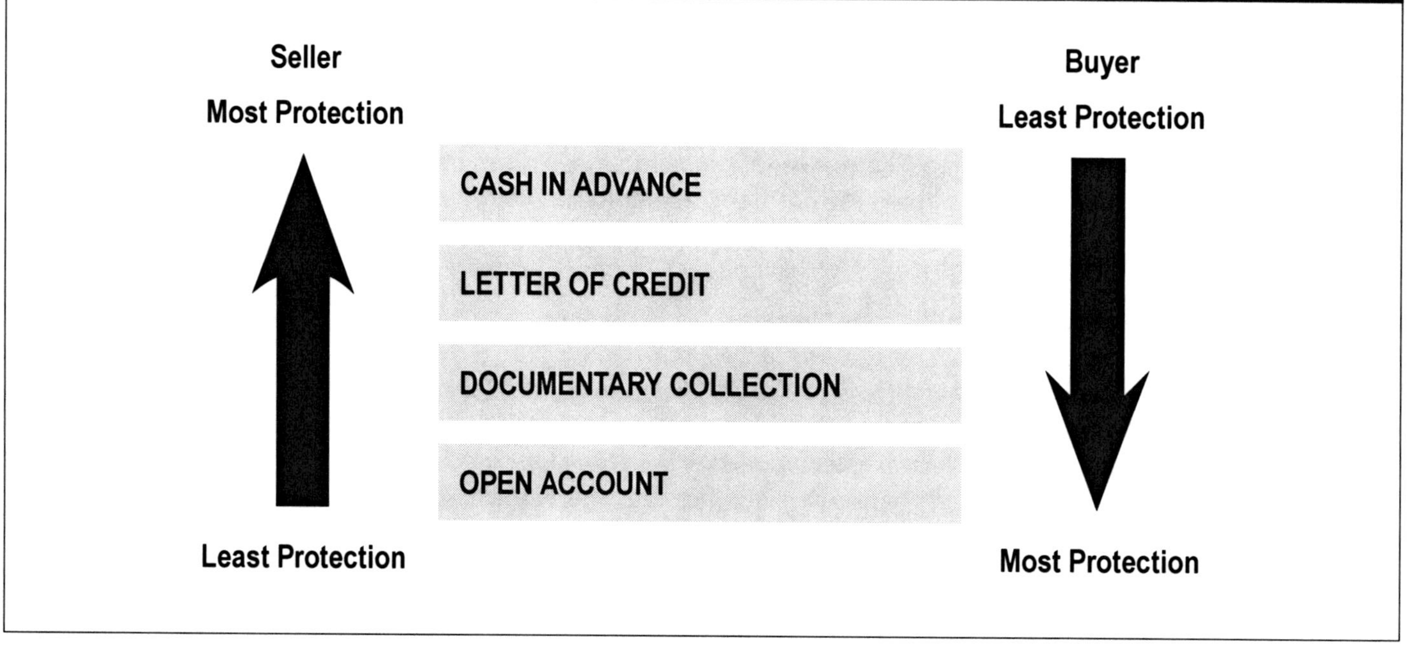

Regardless of the method of trade payment, its use must be agreed upon by the buyer and the seller. The method of payment is usually specified in the buyer's or the seller's currency, but it may be in a third currency, if acceptable to both parties.

1. OPEN ACCOUNT

As discussed in Chapter 8, Introduction to Working Capital Management, open account is the most common form of credit extension and collection. It is widely used internationally when two trading partners have an existing relationship and essentially trust each other to complete their obligations in their transactions. When there is no such relationship, especially when exporting goods to a nondomestic buyer, a seller will often require credit risk protection through either a documentary collection or an L/C.

2. DOCUMENTARY COLLECTION

Documentary collection is a trade payment mechanism that processes the collection of a draft and accompanying shipping documents through international correspondent banks. Instructions regarding the transaction specifics are contained in a collection letter that accompanies the documentation. It is the responsibility of the exporter (seller) to determine the instructions specified in the collection letter. As noted below, any discrepancies between the instructions and the actual documents presented for payment will delay and may bar any payment by the bank.

The typical information disclosed in a documentary collection letter includes:

- Name of the seller (exporter)
- Name and address of the buyer (importer)
- Information regarding the collecting bank
- Details of the documentation accompanying the collection
- Date, tenor, and value of the collection
- Details of bank and other charges to be paid by the exporter, importer, or both
- Recourse procedures in the event of nonacceptance or nonpayment
- Any nonstandard terms or conditions

Absent a formal L/C, banks that are involved in a documentary collection normally act only as collecting and paying agents and assume no direct obligation for ensuring that payment is made. Banks involved in these transactions perform different roles:

- The **remitting bank**, which is the bank of the seller/exporter, receives the collection documents from the seller. These documents are then remitted (forwarded) to the buyer's bank along with instructions for payment. The buyer's bank is referred to as the *collecting or presenting bank* in this transaction.
- The **collecting or presenting bank** (the buyer's bank, also referred to as the *issuing bank* when the transaction includes a letter of credit as discussed below) is the bank that presents the documents to the buyer. In exchange for these documents, the bank collects either cash payment in the form of a bank draft or a promise of future payment in the form of a bill of exchange.

A collection letter specifies the exact procedures to be followed before shipping documents are released to the importer (buyer). The importer usually requires physical possession of the shipping documents in order to obtain the merchandise. Documents typically are released either against payment or acceptance:

- **Documents against payment (D/P)** use a sight draft, which is a draft payable on demand, that requires the collecting bank to receive full and final payment of the amount owed prior to releasing the documents.
- **Documents against acceptance (D/A)** use a time draft, which is a draft payable on a specified future date, that must be accepted by the importer before the collecting bank may release documents. Upon maturity of the time draft, it is presented to the importer for payment.

Once full and final payment is received from the buyer (importer), the collecting bank transfers funds to the remitting bank, as instructed, for payment to the seller (exporter). Less commonly, the remitting bank advances payment to the exporter at a discount and then collects final payment on the due date. But this advance payment depends upon a preexisting credit relationship between the remitting bank and its exporter-customer.

In the event of nonpayment or nonacceptance, the exporter has the cost of remarketing the goods to another buyer or paying to have the merchandise returned. The exporter may request that the collecting bank initiate formal action against the importer for nonperformance. Exhibit 10.2 illustrates a documentary collection.

EXHIBIT 10.2 **DOCUMENTARY COLLECTION**

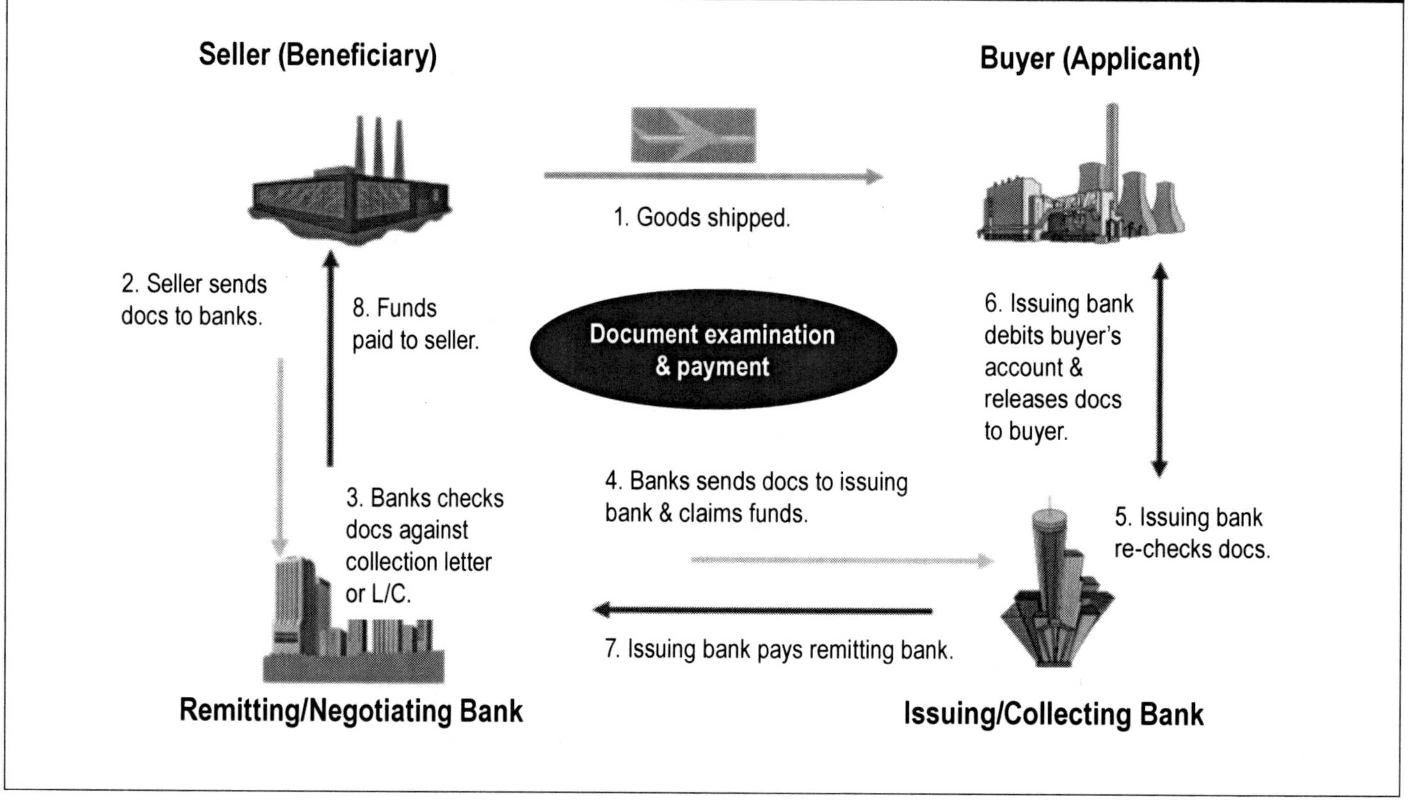

A primary difference between a documentary collection and an L/C is that the collecting bank does not guarantee payment to the seller under a documentary collection. This is one reason why documentary collections are less expensive and less complicated than L/Cs.

An issue with both documentary collections and L/Cs is discrepant documents. Whenever the documentation does not match the terms and conditions of the documentary collection or L/C, either the documentation must be updated, the agreement must be amended, or the seller must waive the discrepancy. All of these actions take time and usually involve additional costs to both parties in the transaction.

It is important to realize that with both documentary collections and L/Cs, the banks are only reviewing documents for completeness and accuracy. There is no review of the physical merchandise and no guarantee that it is not defective. As a result, buyers often include an inspection requirement as part of the terms of the collection or L/C. The collecting bank will then not process the transaction without presentation of an inspection document that indicates the goods have been inspected and meet the requirements of the collection. A current trend in the trade finance business is the ongoing consolidation and integration of logistics and trade solutions providers to allow for increased efficiency and risk reduction. These vendors provide a "one-stop shop" for customers by managing the physical movement of products as well as the information and documents needed for documentary collections and L/Cs.

3. LETTER OF CREDIT (L/C)

An L/C is a document issued by a bank, guaranteeing the payment of a customer's draft up to a stated amount for a specified period, provided certain conditions are met. The L/C substitutes a bank's credit for that of the buyer, virtually eliminating the credit risk to the seller. L/Cs are a widely used method of payment for import and export shipments and are used frequently as a financing vehicle for cross-border trade transactions.

a. Commercial Letter of Credit (L/C)

A commercial (or documentary) L/C is issued by a bank as the intended mechanism of payment in relation to a trade transaction involving the domestic or international shipment of merchandise. A commercial L/C typically requires presentment of a draft, commercial invoice, and related shipping documents; hence, it is documentary in nature. Because a bank's role in an L/C transaction is the examination of documents, not the underlying merchandise, it is the responsibility of the importer (buyer) to specify the documentation required prior to payment, which reasonably ensures the receipt of the exact merchandise ordered. Additionally, since the bank's responsibility only extends to examining and approving documents, the buyer often pays for the goods prior to receiving them.

L/Cs may be revocable or irrevocable. A revocable L/C can be canceled by the bank or the buyer at any time. This limits the credit protection available to the beneficiary of the L/C (i.e., the seller), who might ship goods only to find that the related L/C has been canceled. An irrevocable L/C can only be canceled if all parties to the transaction (i.e., the buyer, the seller, the issuing bank, and if the L/C is confirmed, the confirming bank) agree, thus providing maximum protection to the seller. Most L/Cs are irrevocable.

Banks may serve a variety of roles in L/C transactions:

- The **issuing bank** is the buyer's (importer's) bank that issues the L/C in favor of the seller (exporter).
- The **advising bank** advises the seller of an L/C in its favor.
- Other banks that may be involved in the transaction are the **negotiating bank** and the **confirming bank**.

- The advising and negotiating banks are frequently the same bank, performing dual roles. The advising/negotiating bank examines the documents presented by the beneficiary (i.e., the seller), receives payment from the issuing bank, and pays the beneficiary.
- If requested, the advising/negotiating bank may add confirmation (as the confirming bank) to an L/C. In doing so, the confirming bank commits to the seller that payment will be made if documents meet the terms and conditions of the L/C, regardless of the issuing bank's ability to pay. If an L/C is confirmed, the confirming bank will be the negotiating bank, as well.

Once documentation has been presented, the L/C may provide either immediate payment (sight draft) or deferred payment (time draft) to the seller. When the L/C requires the presentment of a sight draft, which is a draft payable on demand (or at sight), the advising/negotiating bank pays the seller immediately and is reimbursed by the issuing bank. When the L/C requires presentment of a time draft, which provides payment at a future date, the seller provides credit terms to the buyer. The seller may be able to receive payment prior to maturity by discounting (i.e., selling at a discounted value) the time draft to a local bank. At this point, the discounted L/C becomes a banker's acceptance, which is described in more detail later in this chapter. A deferred payment L/C provides presentation of one or more sight drafts at specified dates in the future and sometimes extends over several years. When medium-term financing is provided for the export of capital goods, a deferred payment L/C may be used in conjunction with a term loan agreement. Exhibit 10.3 illustrates the participants in the issuance of a typical commercial L/C. The collection/payment process is identical to that discussed above and illustrated in Exhibit 10.2.

EXHIBIT 10.3 **LETTER OF CREDIT (L/C)**

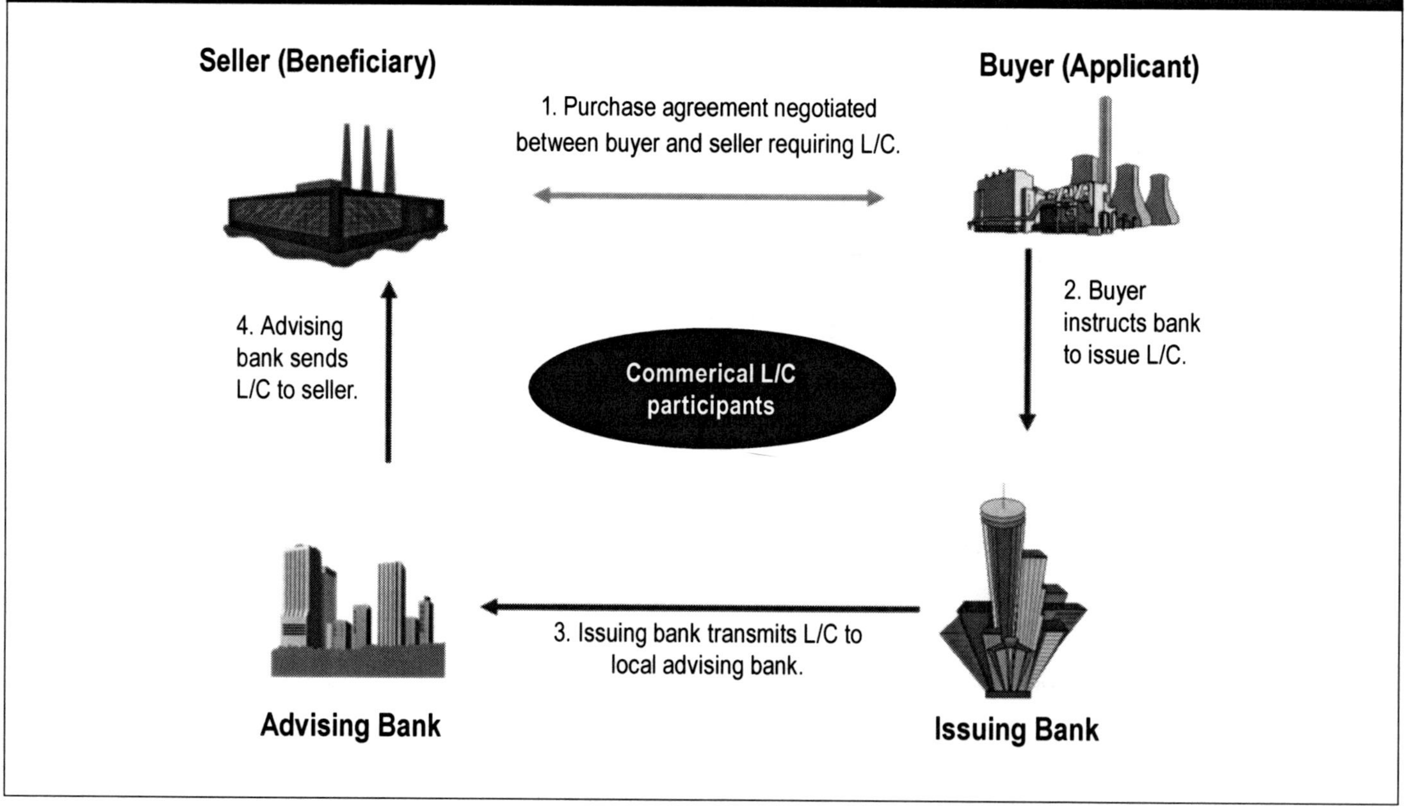

The International Chamber of Commerce (ICC) has established rules governing commercial L/Cs, known as *Uniform Customs and Practice for Documentary Credits (UCP)*. The current rules are outlined under UCP 600, and these rules affect almost every credit issued under the ICC's UCP. Most notably, UCP 600 establishes an absolute deadline of five calendar days to review documents and pay or decline a draw.

In general, standard credit language in international trade agreements should be in compliance with and refer to UCP 600 to ensure proper administration and interpretation in the event of any legal disputes.

In conjunction with UCP 600, issuers should consider the administration of standby L/Cs (see below) and ensure that they are issued under the rules of ICC's publication *International Standby Practices*: ISP98. An increasing number of banks are issuing standby L/Cs under ISP98, because the guidelines offer a number of benefits to issuers. Most importantly, the ISP98 rules are often easier and clearer to apply than the UCP rules in the context of standby L/Cs.

b. Standby Letter of Credit (L/C) or Guarantee

Standby L/Cs are variations of commercial L/Cs. While standby L/Cs can be issued by insurance companies in some countries, they are issued primarily by banks. In the United States they are referred to as *standby L/Cs* for regulatory reasons, while most of the rest of the world refers to them as *guarantees*. Once issued, a standby L/C serves as a vehicle to ensure the financial performance of a bank's customer to a third-party beneficiary. Unlike a standard L/C, which is paid upon presentment and validation of the required documents, a standby L/C or guarantee is only payable in the event that the primary entity fails to pay or perform some specified duty. A standby L/C typically requires the presentation of a sight draft and documentation that supports the beneficiary's claim of nonperformance on the part of the issuing bank's customer.

4. BANKER'S ACCEPTANCE (BA)[8]

A BA can be used to finance the import, export, or domestic shipment of goods, as well as the storage of properly titled goods. BAs are used frequently in conjunction with L/Cs requiring a time draft drawn on a bank.

A BA is created when one person signs an unconditional written order directing a bank to pay a certain sum of money on demand or at a definite time to another person, usually to finance the shipment or temporary storage of goods. The unconditional written order, also known as a *time draft*, is stamped "accepted" by the bank.

By accepting the draft, the bank agrees to pay the face value of the obligation if the buyer (the issuer and party who drew the draft) fails to make payment. Since the accepting bank assumes the risk of the buyer defaulting, it makes it easier for the buyer or seller to undertake international trade.

8. This discussion refers to standard BAs created as an acceptance of a draft and related to a trade transaction. In Canada, the term *banker's acceptance* usually refers to a short-term investment instrument issued by banks, essentially similar to a negotiable certificate of deposit in the United States.

A BA is a less expensive form of short-term financing than a loan. BAs may be held by the bank until maturity or be sold at a discount in secondary markets as short-term negotiable instruments, where the bank's credit standing is substituted for the creditworthiness of the issuer.

The cost of BA financing has two components: the discount rate (the rate earned by the investor) and the commission. Most BA financing is accomplished with eligible BAs, which have a maturity not exceeding 180 days and are sold at a nominal spread over US Treasury bills. The rates at which they trade are known as *BA rates*. Eligible underlying transactions include the import or export of goods, domestic storage transactions with the documents conveying title attached, and storage of readily marketable staples secured by warehouse receipts.

5. TRADE ACCEPTANCE

A trade acceptance is similar to a BA except it is drawn on, and accepted by, a buyer (importer). It can be used to verify a buyer's obligation to pay for purchased merchandise where the seller (exporter) is satisfied with the credit risk. Trade acceptances often are used by importers to secure financing from a bank or, similar to BAs, may even be sold to a bank or an investor at a discount prior to maturity.

6. OTHER TRADE PAYMENT METHODS

Other less frequently used cross-border trade payment mechanisms include cash in advance (cash before delivery) and consignment, as well as barter, countertrade, and trading companies:

- **Barter:** Barter involves the direct exchange of goods or services between two parties without the exchange of money. It is most frequently used when funds cannot be repatriated due to currency controls or other legal limitations. (Repatriation is discussed in Chapter 20, Financial Decisions and Management.)
- **Countertrade:** Countertrade is a method of payment used by companies that do not have access to sufficient hard currencies (i.e., internationally traded currencies) to pay for imports from other countries. For example, an exporter ships merchandise to the countertrading country. In exchange, it takes merchandise that may be sold elsewhere in the world. Pricing and foreign exchange rates are established between the trading parties. This differs from barter in that the exporter is receiving valuable goods for resale locally to recoup its costs rather than a product that it intends to keep and use for its own purposes.
- **Trading Companies:** Trading companies are used when an exporter (seller) sells products at a discount to an export trading company, which then resells the products internationally. In some cases, a global parent company will create a trading company entity that purchases products and then resells to subsidiaries of the company.

IV. CONCENTRATION OF FUNDS

The end result of collection of receipts is available funds in one or more bank accounts. To the extent that a company does all of its business with one bank in one country, those receipts can be easily combined into a pool of usable funds via ZBA or internal book transfers. Unfortunately, most companies deal with more than one bank and increasingly in more than one country. This results in pockets of money in different accounts in different banks and sometimes in different currencies. As discussed in Chapter 8, Introduction to Working Capital Management, this creates a number of problems for the treasury professional responsible for managing those funds. As a result, once an organization completes the collection of receipts, the next step is to concentrate those funds into one or more concentration accounts at the company's lead bank in preparation for future use, either for investment or disbursement. Exhibit 10.4 illustrates some of the potential transfers and accounts involved in a cash concentration system. This is a particularly complex example and includes multiple types of concentration. Most corporate systems are often much simpler.

EXHIBIT 10.4 **CASH CONCENTRATION SYSTEM**

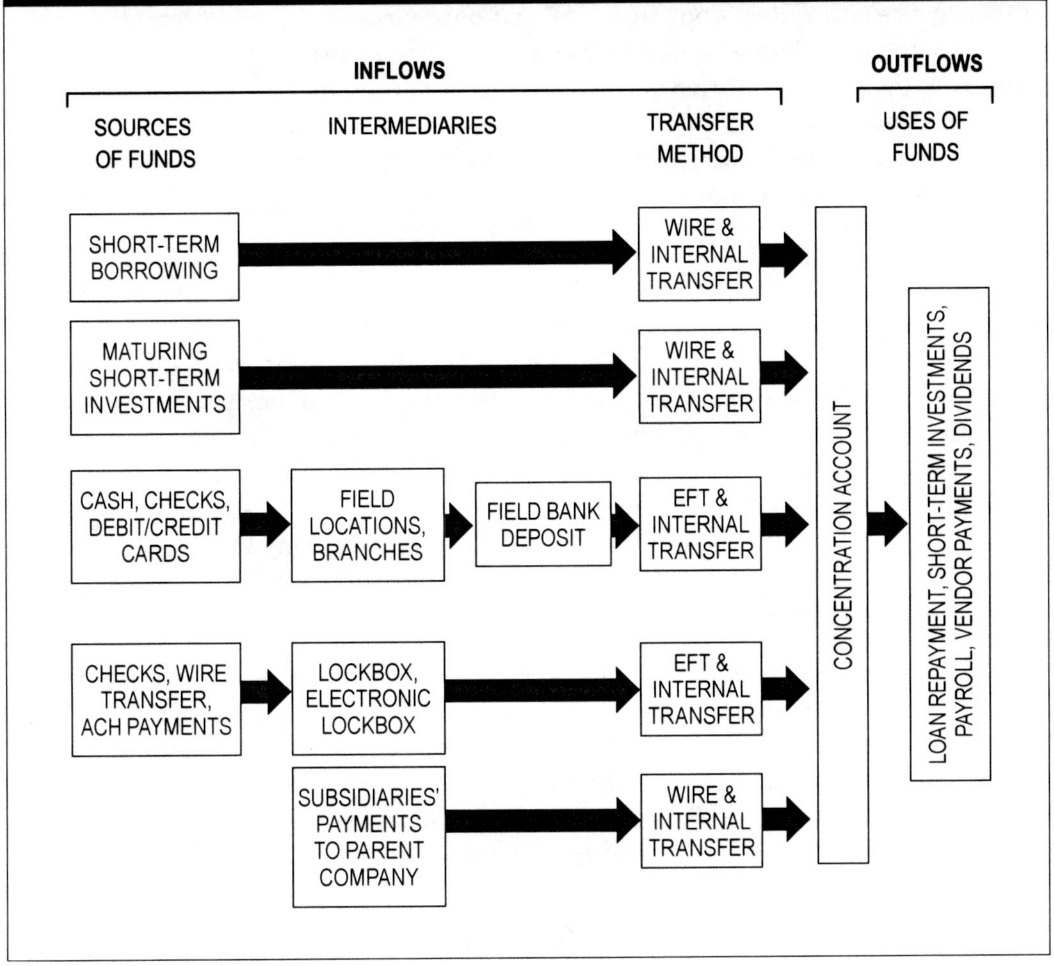

The two major objectives of a cash concentration system are to efficiently move the funds from deposit banks to the concentration bank and minimize excess bank balances. Moving all the funds into a single concentration account enables those funds to be managed more efficiently and effectively, and facilitates daily liquidity management. Concentration of funds enables a company to:

- Balance excess and deficit cash positions across multiple locations, entities, and currencies
- Invest a larger amount of funds, potentially increasing interest income
- Pay down debt faster and minimize borrowings, potentially reducing interest expense
- Take advantage of supplier and/or vendor discount terms, potentially reducing the cost of goods sold or operating expenses

A. Domestic Concentration of Funds

Domestic cash concentration systems typically transfer funds from outlying depository locations (often at different banks) to a central bank account at a company's primary bank, commonly referred to as a *concentration account*. This process is often referred to as *sweeping* (not to be confused with *sweep accounts* used in the United States for the overnight investment of surplus funds). While the need for this action is seen primarily in the United States, where companies often have to deal with a number of separate banks in dispersed geographic locations, the situation can occur in any country where an organization deals with more than one bank.

Many businesses collect receipts at field locations (over-the-counter collections) that include local offices or branches, and retail stores. Retail businesses accept cash, checks, and payment cards at the point of sale (POS). A wholesale customer or its agent may also deliver checks or cash to a vendor's office. Alternatively, a payee or a payee's agent may pick up cash or checks directly from a customer when making a delivery. Historically, these payments were all deposited into a bank located near each field location in the interest of security and convenience. These deposits were then swept into the company's main concentration account, typically through the use of wire transfers or ACH debits, as discussed below. The introduction of banking services such as RDC and virtual vaults, discussed above in the section on collection products, has simplified the process by allowing many corporations to eliminate most field bank accounts and deposit payments and funds directly into their concentration account. As a side note, it is worth mentioning that card transactions are automatically concentrated since the merchant services provider who processes card payments for the company can and typically will deposit the proceeds into a single account.

When possible, the concentration of funds is greatly simplified by using branches of the same bank in multiple locations. When a company uses multiple branches of a single bank, it can use individual accounts for each branch and link them via ZBAs (discussed above). Alternatively, the company can use a single account across all branches and use deposit reconciliation services to capture an appropriate audit trail for accounting and internal audit purposes. With deposit reconciliation services, deposit tickets carry a unique identifier for each company location, thereby enabling the bank (or the company, through its internal treasury information system) to produce location-specific deposit reports on a daily, weekly, or monthly basis for each location.

Most large retail chains transmit information on local receipts from POS terminals to headquarters. When it is not feasible to use one bank, headquarters can use this information to transmit ACH debit instructions to a concentration bank. In addition, some third-party providers specialize in gathering deposit information from field units by phone, POS terminal, or computer. After gathering the deposit data, the third party can create an ACH file that is sent directly to the concentration bank, which then processes the file through the ACH payments system. Alternatively, the deposit data can be sent to headquarters, allowing headquarters personnel to determine the transfer amounts and to prepare and transmit the ACH debit file. Some concentration banks also can receive deposit data reported by phone, e-mail, or other electronic communication directly from the field offices, and offer online access for headquarters to review deposit-reporting activity and identify non-reporting units.

A wire transfer (such as Fedwire in the United States) is an alternative to ACH when a company needs to expedite funds transfers. Wire transfers provide immediate funds and help to reduce excess balances at deposit banks. However, because wire transfers are an expensive funds transfer mechanism, they are used primarily to concentrate large dollar amounts when same-day value and finality are critical. A break-even analysis comparing both methods is provided in Chapter 9, Working Capital Metrics.

B. Global Concentration of Funds

Companies that operate in multiple countries face a much more complex situation. Liquidity management is an important treasury objective that is challenging because of the need to juggle excess and deficit cash positions across multiple entities, regulatory environments, and currencies. As a result, multinational companies generally have to use a mix of different concentration techniques depending on the banking structures and regulations in the countries in which they operate. Different types of pooling arrangements are discussed in the following section. Pooling has three basic forms: physical pooling, notional pooling, and bank overlay structure.

1. PHYSICAL POOLING

In physical pooling, funds in separate subaccounts are automatically transferred to/from a header or concentration account in order to eliminate idle cash and fund cash outflows. The participating entities are either in surplus or deficit from a transactional perspective, but the bank accounts themselves are zero balanced. Physical pooling can be used across multiple legal entities located in the same or different countries, but the funds must be in the same currency. The funds movement between the participating entities is accounted for via intercompany loans, which must be at an "arm's length" or market rate as discussed in Chapter 20, Financial Decisions and Management. This is somewhat analogous to a ZBA account structure, but differs in that there is no requirement that all the accounts belong to one entity, hence the need for intercompany loans.

2. NOTIONAL POOLING

Notional pooling achieves the same result, but it is accomplished by making balancing entries on a set of virtual accounts with no changes to the bank accounts held by company entities. The bank managing the notional pool provides an interest statement that reflects the net offset, which is similar to what would have been achieved with physical pooling. As there is no physical movement of money, intercompany loans are not required to account for the notional transactions. Banks usually require credit facilities to support any deficit balances in the pool, and notional pooling often requires extensive cross-guarantees among subsidiaries, which many companies find very difficult to implement.

Some countries, including the United States, Germany, Mexico, Japan, and Brazil, disallow notional pooling. In these cases, the physical pooling method must be used.

The chart in Exhibit 10.5 provides a high-level summary of the differences between physical and notional pooling.

EXHIBIT 10.5 **POOLING COMPARISON**

NOTIONAL POOLING		PHYSICAL POOLING
Interest is earned/paid as bank interest.	COMPENSATION	Must use "arm's length" (or market) rate, track loans, and allocate interest.
Can provide tax efficiency.	TAX	Withholding taxes can apply to intercompany loans.
Is highly complex due to involvement of banks and multiple jurisdictions.	COMPLEXITY	Greater transparency generates less regulatory concern.
Can be implemented across multiple currencies.	APPLICABILITY	Must be done on a currency-by-currency basis.
Is restricted in many countries.	AVAILABILITY	Is widely available and most common form of pooling.

3. BANK OVERLAY STRUCTURE

A bank overlay structure is an approach that combines both sweeping and pooling. It is typically used when a company's primary bank has branches in several countries, but the branches do not provide a full range of domestic banking services. A local bank is used to provide collection and disbursement transactions and accounts, and to sweep surplus funds to the primary bank. The primary bank (overlay bank) then notionally pools or physically transfers cash balances in overlay accounts, providing a multi-country solution. The exact structure of this arrangement will depend on the bank agreement and possible tax considerations. The concept is shown in Exhibit 10.6.

EXHIBIT 10.6 **BANK OVERLAY STRUCTURE**

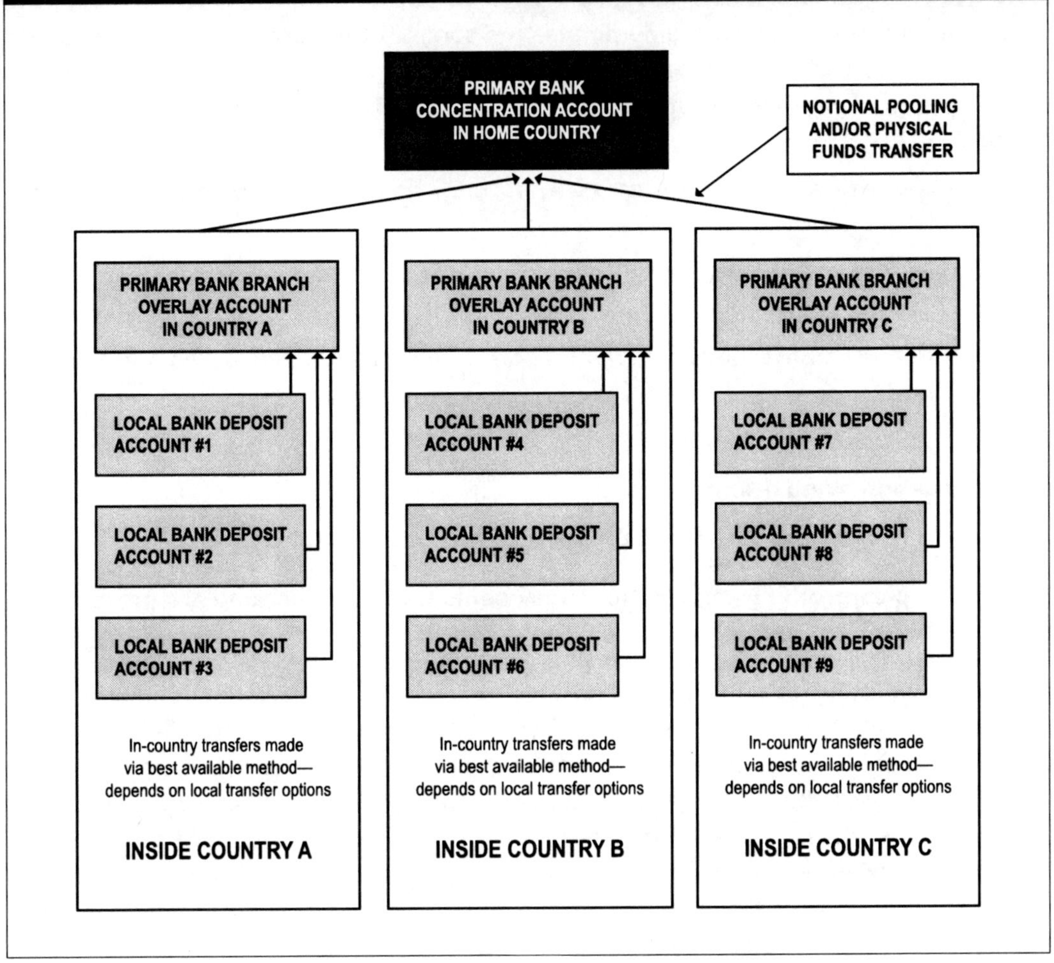

Whatever method of pooling is used in managing multinational balances, it is essential to involve tax and legal counsel in any decision making. Although the basic concepts are fairly simple, the actual execution and the related legal documentation needed can be quite complex. Even small mistakes can result in large costs in the form of unexpected fees and taxes.

V. PAYMENTS FRAUD

Payments fraud is a major concern for all organizations. The *2013 AFP Payments Fraud and Control Survey*[9] reported that the majority of all organizations in the United States (61%) were the subject of attempted or actual payments fraud, which aligns with the results of a survey by the Economist Intelligence Unit[10] that indicated that 75% of companies globally were the subject of fraud. The AFP survey also revealed that payments fraud is not limited to large companies, but is a concern for organizations of all sizes. It is very likely that this holds true throughout the world.

9. The *2013 AFP Payments Fraud and Control Survey* is available through AFP's website (http://www.afponline.orgfraud/?terms=AFP_Payments_Fraud_and_Control_Survey).
10. From the fifth Annual Global Fraud Survey, commissioned by Kroll, carried out by the Economist Intelligence Unit, and published in Kroll's "Global Fraud Report: Annual Edition 2011/12" (http://www.krolladvisory.com/media/pdfs/KRL_FraudReport2011-12_US.pdf).

The good news in the AFP survey is that the large majority of fraud attempts fail and that most of the organizations (73%) that were attacked did not lose any money. Even better news is that while some of the methods used to perpetrate payments fraud are highly sophisticated, most of them are fairly simple, and some of the best methods of detection and prevention are fairly simple and easy to use. Positive pay (preferably with payee verification), ACH filters and blocks, and daily reconciliations are among the methods most used to help detect and control payments fraud. Other best practices for fraud control include:

- Use of check stock with built-in security features, such as microprinting, holograms, and other non-photo-reproducible features
- Appropriate segregation of duties so that the person reconciling accounts is not the person who can initiate transactions from the account
- The use of dual authentication for all EFT transactions, where one person originates a transaction and a second person reviews and releases the transaction
- The reduction or elimination of non-repetitive wires
- The use of separate accounts for deposits and disbursements
- The use of a dedicated computer (i.e., not used for other purposes) for the initiation of online EFT transactions

Additional best practices designed to help control EFT and electronic payments fraud and hacking are presented in Chapter 14, Information Technology in Treasury.

A problem related to check fraud that is typically not prevented by positive pay or daily reconciliation is known as the *"holder in due course" issue*. This is a uniquely US problem that results from US law regarding negotiable instruments such as checks. The problem occurs when a third party, someone other than the payee or the depository bank, accepts or cashes a negotiable instrument (i.e., a check) that subsequently turns out to be fraudulent. As long as the third party can show that it was a "holder in due course"[11] at the time that it accepted the check, the third party may be able to collect from the maker of the check even though the actual check was fraudulent or altered. A common example of this situation is when a check-cashing store that regularly accepts and cashes payroll checks for employees of a local company accepts and cashes a forged or altered payroll check without having been given any notice or warning of any problems with the check. Positive pay will normally detect the item and allow its return, but the check-cashing store may be able to hold the company liable for the amount of the fraudulent check, assuming it is not an obvious forgery and the check casher had no reason to suspect that there was a problem with the check. While there is no sure defense against this problem, tamper-resistant check stock using non-photo-reproducible features may help reduce the problem. Another, more certain, alternative is to replace check payments with EFT or card payments.

Card payments, however, are not risk-free. Merchants that accept mail, phone, or Internet orders made with card payments may mitigate their risk of fraud by using an address verification service (AVS) that matches the address provided by the cardholder with the account billing address on record with the issuer. AVS and confirmation of the card verification value or card verification code (CVV/CVC) number printed on the reverse side of a credit card are two of the most common practices in reducing risks due to fraudulent credit card transactions.

11. The Uniform Commercial Code § 3-302 defines a *holder in due course* as "...the holder of an instrument if: (1) the instrument when issued or negotiated to the holder does not bear such apparent evidence of forgery or alteration or is not otherwise so irregular or incomplete as to call into question its authenticity; and (2) the holder took the instrument (i) for value, (ii) in good faith, (iii) without notice that the instrument is overdue or has been dishonored...and (iv) without notice that the instrument contains an unauthorized signature or has been altered...." (From "UCC § 3-302" on Cornell University Law School's website, http://www.law.cornell.edu/ucc/3/3-302, accessed September 4, 2013.)

Identity theft has become a rapidly growing source of credit card fraud loss for merchants and card issuers. Use of lost, stolen, fraudulent, or counterfeit cards and the unauthorized use of cardholders' credit card numbers constitute most credit card fraud. Businesses can reduce card losses if they take reasonable precautions in accepting and securing card payments. Specifically, a merchant should obtain authorization, an authentic signature, and an electronic imprint of the card being used. If a merchant performs any one of these actions and fraud occurs, then the card-issuing institution absorbs any losses. Card-issuing institutions reduce this risk by using complex algorithms called *neural networks*, which monitor cardholder charge patterns for unusual activity. Banks may also maintain sophisticated call center fraud units that use analysis of transaction data to detect this type of fraud as early as possible and to prevent any significant losses. Credit cards are discussed in more detail in Chapter 4, Payment Systems.

VI. SUMMARY

Disbursement and collection of receipts and related processes are an essential part of most treasury professionals' jobs. This chapter discussed some specific products that are available to assist in efficient and cost-effective disbursement and collection management. It also covered some of the payments products utilized in international trade, including L/Cs and documentary collections. Domestic sweeps and multinational pooling were introduced as methods of concentrating funds and managing cash balances across international borders. Finally, the chapter discussed some of the issues related to payments fraud and presented some best practices for avoiding related losses.

APPENDIX 10.1: US ACH STANDARD ENTRY CLASS (SEC) CODES AND PAYMENT TYPES

The US ACH system uses standard entry class (SEC) codes to distinguish between various types of transactions. Transaction formats vary by SEC code. There are standard ACH formats for C2B, B2C, and B2B payments. All ACH payment formats move funds in essentially the same manner. The most appropriate format for a particular payment is determined by the relationship between the parties, the information exchanged, and the types of ACH payment services offered by the participating banks. The major ACH formats and their related SEC codes are as follows:

- **Accounts Receivable Conversion (ARC):** To increase funds availability and reduce check handling, eligible checks received at a lockbox can be converted into electronic debits and processed as ACH debits. The company receiving the checks must notify the check writer that checks will be converted. This typically is done by including a statement to this effect on bills or invoices.
- **Back Office Conversion (BOC):** Retailers and other entities that accept checks at the point of purchase (POP) or other manned bill payment locations can convert eligible checks to ACH debits in the back office. Explanatory signage must be present at the point of presentment, and the merchant/originator must put specific verbiage on the customer receipt indicating that the check may be converted and may clear as soon as the same day.
- **Corporate Credit or Debit (CCD) or CCD Plus Addendum (CCD+):** CCD is the basic electronic payment format used for the concentration and disbursement of funds within or between companies (B2B). Only a limited amount of remittance information can be sent with the CCD format. The CCD+ is essentially a CCD with an addendum record that can hold up to 80 characters of remittance data. CCD+ is one of the formats used for the US Treasury's Vendor Express program in paying commercial suppliers to federal agencies, and for B2B payments. It is useful when only a limited amount of information must be transmitted. The CCD+ addendum record also is used to report federal and state tax payment information, in which case the addenda data conform to the tax payment (TXP) banking conventions.
- **Customer-Initiated Entry (CIE):** The CIE format is used for pre-authorized payments that are initiated by consumers using telephone bill-paying services.
- **Corporate Trade Exchange (CTX):** The CTX format is designed for B2B trade payments. It consists of a standard ACH payment transaction and a variable-length message addendum designed to convey remittance information in the Accredited Standards Committee (ASC) X12 data standard. The addendum can accommodate 9,999 records of 80 characters each. CTX is useful for payments related to multiple invoices and those with substantial invoice detail.
- **International ACH Transaction (IAT):** An IAT is an ACH debit or credit entry that is part of a payment transaction originating from, or transmitted to, an office of a financial agency located outside the territorial jurisdiction of the United States. Corporate and consumer accounts may receive IAT entries.
- **Point-of-Purchase (POP) Check Conversion:** Many retail outlets have systems that allow customers to have checks scanned, capturing the account information from the MICR line at the POP. The MICR line data are converted into an ACH debit, and the check is voided and returned to the customer, who then signs a debit authorization in the form of a register receipt.
- **Prearranged Payment and Deposit (PPD):** The PPD format is the payment application by which consumers authorize a company or a financial institution to credit or debit an account for normally recurring payments in fixed amounts. Examples of consumer PPD credits (B2C and G2C) are payroll, expense reimbursements, dividends, social security benefits, and tax refunds. Examples of consumer PPD debits (C2B) are rent and mortgage payments, subscriptions, dues and memberships, insurance premiums, installment debt payments, and utility payments.

- **Re-Presented Check Entry (RCK):** The RCK format is used to transmit ACH debit entries in place of a paper check that has been returned for insufficient or uncollected funds. The general requirements are that the item be less than $2,500 and be drawn on a consumer account. RCK originators must provide advance notice to the check writer (e.g., in a customer statement or at the point of sale) that any check returned for insufficient or uncollected funds may be collected electronically. Originators may transmit a re-presented check entry no more than twice after the first return of a paper item and no more than once after the second return of a paper item.
- **Telephone-Initiated Entry (TEL):** The TEL format is used for payments that are not pre-authorized, but are approved by consumers over the phone. TEL entries are single payments used for telephone catalog sales, ticket sales, and other one-time purchases.
- **Internet-Initiated Entry (WEB):** The WEB format is used for payments that are not pre-authorized, but are initiated by consumers using the Internet. WEB entries can be either single payments for one-time purchases or recurring payments.
- **Destroyed Check Entry (XCK):** The XCK format is used to clear and settle items that originated as checks, but the original paper item was lost or destroyed due to a catastrophic event (e.g., fire, flood, or hurricane).

TEST YOUR UNDERSTANDING: CHAPTER 10

Answers are on pages 681–687.

1. What is a ZBA?
2. What is positive pay?
3. What is controlled disbursement?
4. What are the different categories of wire transfers? Describe each.
5. What are freight payments?
6. What is a payment factory?
7. Describe the major issues that must be addressed in any collection system.
8. What is a virtual vault?
9. What is meant by the term *merchant services*?
10. What is RDC?
11. List the major steps in processing mail payments involving checks.
12. What is check conversion?
13. What are EBPP and EIPP?
14. Describe consolidated remittance processing.
15. What are the advantages of using a lockbox?
16. What information is normally included in a documentary collection letter?
17. What is a letter of credit?
18. What is the difference between a revocable and irrevocable letter of credit?
19. What is countertrade?
20. Describe the three basic forms of pooling.
21. Describe some of the best practices that can be used to control payments fraud.

CHAPTER 11
Short-Term Investing and Borrowing

I. INTRODUCTION

II. MANAGING SHORT-TERM INVESTMENTS

A. In-House versus Outsourced Management of Short-Term Investment Portfolio
B. Short-Term Investment Policies
C. Investment Strategies
D. Reporting
E. Securities Safekeeping and Custody Services
F. Investment Risk Considerations

III. PRICING AND YIELDS ON SHORT-TERM INVESTMENTS

A. Factors Influencing Investment Pricing
B. Yield Calculations for Short-Term Investments

IV. MANAGING SHORT-TERM FINANCING

A. Short-Term Funding Alternatives
B. Pricing and Costs of Principal Short-Term Financing Sources

V. DEBT FINANCING

A. Costs of Borrowing
B. Basic Components of Interest Rates
C. Base Rates
D. Short-Term versus Long-Term Borrowing
E. Loan Agreements and Covenants
F. Credit Rating Agencies (CRAs)

VI. SUMMARY

APPENDIX 11.1: LISTING OF SOME MAJOR CREDIT RATING AGENCIES

I. INTRODUCTION

As discussed in Chapter 8, Introduction to Working Capital Management, liquidity management is essential to the well-being of any firm and is a significant part of many treasury professionals' jobs. Short-term investing and borrowing is a key part of liquidity management for most firms as they will either have excess funds to invest or need to borrow to fund ongoing activities at different points in time.

As with disbursements and collections, investing and borrowing (financing) are opposite sides of the same coin. This chapter starts on the investment side with a discussion of the issues involved in managing a short-term investment portfolio. It then turns to the other side of the situation and looks at things from the issuer's or borrower's point of view, including a discussion of pricing and debt financing.

It is important to realize that many of the issues discussed in this chapter, such as debt pricing and rating agencies, also apply to longer-term investing and borrowing, which are discussed in Chapter 12, Long-Term and Capital Investments.

II. MANAGING SHORT-TERM INVESTMENTS

Chapter 5 introduced the various securities and investments that collectively are known as *money markets*, typically short-term instruments with a maturity of less than one year.[1] Short-term investments are a key part of an organization's liquidity management process. For most large organizations, this requires the management of a portfolio of various short-term investments or securities. The first step toward managing short-term investments is the development of an investment policy. Once the policy is developed, an organization may choose from two basic methods for the actual construction and ongoing management of its short-term investment portfolio: internal (in-house) or external (outsourced). As discussed below, some companies actually use a combination of the two. Each of these approaches offers varying advantages and disadvantages. The sections below describe the different methods and discuss additional steps, such as investment policies, investment reporting, and securities safekeeping.

A. In-House versus Outsourced Management of Short-Term Investment Portfolio

When using in-house management of short-term investments, an organization assumes responsibility for directly managing its own portfolio, including strategy choice, security and maturity selection, quality standards, and compliance monitoring to ensure the investment policy is followed and regulatory requirements are met. Although these decisions are guided by the organization's investment policy, the organization must be prepared to make specific decisions at all times based on current market conditions.

1. Equities, although sometimes used as a short-term investment, are typically considered long-term investments and are discussed in Chapter 12, Long-Term and Capital Investments.

1. IN-HOUSE MANAGEMENT

In-house management is generally appropriate only to the extent that the individuals charged with this responsibility have sufficient resources, training, and experience to effectively involve themselves in the relevant markets and accounting considerations or consequences for each investment choice. It can be argued, however, that hiring and managing properly trained and experienced investment professionals, along with the related administrative costs, can be expensive, especially for small companies and/or small investment portfolios. Some companies deal with this issue by investing only in money market funds (MMFs). This practice may help alleviate some of the need for market knowledge and research, but does not relieve the company of its overall responsibility to effectively manage its portfolio.

2. OUTSOURCED MANAGEMENT

The alternative to in-house management is to assign short-term investment portfolio duties to a third party, such as a money market fund manager or an outside money manager (e.g., an investment bank or registered investment advisor). While management costs or fees will be incurred, these need to be balanced against the cost needed to hire and maintain appropriate internal expertise. The use of external managers may also be dictated by the size and complexity of the organization's portfolio. External fund and money managers will typically have greater resources and experience than those usually found within an organization's treasury department. One of the most important of these resources is ready access to securities research. While in-house treasury managers can usually get access to research information from their broker-dealers, they have to know to ask for it and in some cases have to be willing to pay for it.

When making the decision to outsource short-term investment management, it is important to realize that there is a distinct difference between a broker-dealer and a registered investment advisor. As discussed in Chapter 5, Money Markets, a broker-dealer is an organization that trades securities for its own account and on behalf of its customers. A broker-dealer may provide investment recommendations to its customers, but does not have the fiduciary duty that a registered advisor does. As a result, broker-dealer recommendations are potentially going to be based upon securities that the broker-dealer has available for sale and may not address the actual wants or needs of the customer.[2]

A registered investment advisor is someone who is paid a fee to make investment recommendations for a client or group of clients. When an organization hires an investment advisor to manage its short-term portfolio, the normal practice of the industry is to have a written agreement with that advisor making the relationship between the parties clear and specifying fees, investment guidelines, and any restrictions or operating policies that the advisor must follow. Such an investment advisor has a fiduciary duty to the customer that a broker-dealer does not. It is important to note that even though the advisor has a duty to comply with the company's investment policy, the company is still responsible for monitoring the advisor's actions to ensure that compliance. A periodic review of the portfolio to verify compliance with the organization's policy is a good idea.

A potential disadvantage of outsourcing is that investment policies and guidelines must be communicated clearly to the outside manager, who must be able to make individual, tactical investment decisions within a portfolio independent of the investor client and within the policy guidelines (or exception provisions). This may become an issue when using MMFs, as the manager's investment choices may not be aligned with the client's preferences completely. Other issues can include additional reporting (especially if multiple managers are used), the compliance monitoring already noted, and general due diligence with regard to the safety and soundness of the advisor.

2. Current regulations, such as FINRA Rule 2111 in the United States, hold a broker-dealer responsible for assessing the "suitability" of a given investment before recommending it to a customer but say nothing about complying with a customer's investment policies or procedures.

3. COMBINATION OF IN-HOUSE AND OUTSOURCED MANAGEMENT

Depending upon the size of the actual investment portfolio, some companies will split the management among more than one external manager (or keep some of it in-house and outsource a portion to one or more third parties). This strategy allows an organization to compare the cost and performance of the portfolio managers over time. If one manager is significantly better or worse than the other, the company has an effective benchmark to use in renegotiating fees or reallocating the portfolio between managers. The downside of this approach is that the added cost of multiple managers may exceed the expected value of comparing the various managers. One alternative is to benchmark funds managers against industry indices, such as the Bank of America Merrill Lynch 3-Month T-Bill Index or the Barclays Capital 1–3 Year Global Treasury ex-US Capped Index, instead of each other. This approach is also helpful if the funds are allocated to various managers based on investment type, making it difficult to directly compare the managers.

B. Short-Term Investment Policies

Most organizations have some form of short-term investment policy that lays out the guidelines that treasury professionals need to follow when building and managing a short-term investment portfolio. It is also quite common to have an investment committee responsible for overseeing investment operations and management. An organization may incur substantial losses by making poor investment choices, assuming unnecessary risks, or assigning investment responsibilities to unqualified personnel. A short-term investment policy should regulate risk taking to ensure that the short-term investment portfolio is constructed and regulated in a manner that is faithful to the goals of principal preservation and liquidity maintenance. In some cases, where funds are divided among multiple managers by investment type, companies may decide to have separate policies that identify approved investments for each manager.

Formulating a short-term investment policy requires an organization to determine its tolerance for the types of risk borne, but no prudent short-term investment policy should be without the primary objective of principal preservation. Additionally, a board-approved investment policy should include the following:

- Investment objectives with respect to risk and return
- Permissible and prohibited investment vehicles or classes of investments
- Minimum and acceptable security ratings
- Maximum maturity for individual securities
- Maximum weighted average maturity or duration for the portfolio
- Maximum amounts (either by percentage, total dollar amount, or both) of the portfolio that may be invested in individual securities, companies, instrument classes, geographic areas, or industries
- Policies/guidelines for investing in foreign securities

- Specific responsibilities for implementing the policy, by organizational title
- Methods of monitoring compliance with policies, procedures, and internal controls
- Provisions for performance measurement, evaluation, and reporting
- Guidance for classification of investments in accordance with appropriate local regulatory and accounting guidance, such as the International Accounting Standards Board (IASB) guidelines globally, or the Financial Accounting Standards Board (FASB) and Governmental Accounting Standards Board (GASB) rules in the United States
- Responsibilities and reporting requirements for custodians, external investment managers, broker-dealers, and other investment counterparties
- Exception management and related approval processes

Whether a company manages its own portfolio or outsources to an investment manager, these are the key factors to include when constructing an investment policy.

As previously noted, when using an MMF instrument, it will not always be possible to align the investment policies to those of the fund completely. But given the wide variety of MMFs available, the organization should be able to find one that is fairly close in terms of investment objectives and policies. If MMFs are permitted investments, the policy should state this and clearly state the rules governing MMFs, including how the funds are to be selected, if they must be rated, and whether their composition must adhere to the overall guidelines established in the investment policy.

In addition to the basic short-term investment policy, organizations should have two other policies to round out the guidelines for the management of their short-term portfolio: a short-term investment valuation policy and a short-term investment impairment policy. While it is possible to combine these into one master policy, it often makes sense to leave them as separate policies due to their different purposes and potentially different owners (the latter two may be accounting policies rather than treasury policies).

The short-term investment valuation policy lays out the methodology that the firm will use to establish the fair market value of the various securities in its portfolio, as discussed in Chapter 17, Treasury Policies and Procedures. While this is typically easily done for the actively traded securities in the portfolio, which have publicly quoted prices and values, the methodology used may not be as clear for other securities in the portfolio that are not actively traded, (i.e., do not have a publicly quoted market price). Although these other securities may represent only a small fraction of a given portfolio, the methodology that will be used to establish their fair value should be well documented before questions are raised by auditors or other outsiders.

The impairment policy documents the actions that an organization will take when a particular investment may be impaired, as discussed below in the section on reporting. The policy should clearly define the severity and duration of an unrealized loss that will cause an impairment review, and identify the specific securities that need to be reviewed. An impairment review does not necessarily require a write-down, but leads to a quantitative analysis of the securities involved. There are always alternatives to be evaluated, and having a well-written and documented impairment policy can help avoid the unnecessary write-downs of securities that might otherwise be classified as impaired by auditors.

Additional information on investment policies and a sample short-term investment policy are provided in Chapter 17, Treasury Policies and Procedures.

C. Investment Strategies

A variety of short-term investment strategies is available to an organization, depending on its strategic objectives:

- A conservative investor may prefer a passive strategy, such as employing a buy-and-hold-to-maturity approach or investing in MMFs. As previously discussed, a company without the resources to actively manage a portfolio of short-term investments may choose to simply hold one or more MMFs.
- A more aggressive investor may prefer active portfolio management to meet specific needs or potentially earn a higher rate of return by investing in securities that might be considered too risky by other investors.
- A corporate investor that is in a high tax bracket may favor tax-based strategies in addition to those described above.

These strategies may be used individually or in combination, depending on the organization's investment needs and objectives.

1. BUY-AND-HOLD-TO-MATURITY STRATEGY

The traditional strategy for investing excess cash and preserving capital is to invest only in securities whose maturities can be expected to sufficiently fund any potential cash needs, hold those securities to maturity, and reinvest only if maturity proceeds are not needed for expenditures. This approach is referred to as a *buy-and-hold-to-maturity strategy*, or sometimes a *matching strategy*. The main advantages of this method are that funding needs are always met (as long as securities are structured or laddered properly to meet cash needs) and interim price fluctuations in the securities can largely be ignored, as the maturity will always fulfill the investment's initial return expectation. The disadvantage is that a company may carry excess liquidity and forego some potential for marginally higher yields.

When an organization matches the cash flows from maturing investments to known future expenditures, it generally allows for investing over extended periods (i.e., longer maturities), which may potentially increase yields. For this strategy to be effective, however, it requires careful forecasting of future cash flows and capital requirements. If cash is needed sooner than expected, the securities purchased to correspond with a specific cash outflow may have to be sold prematurely, perhaps at a loss. Companies that apply a matching strategy often will do so in a conservative manner, covering only a portion of the expected capital need.

2. ACTIVELY MANAGED PORTFOLIO STRATEGY

An active investment strategy (also known as a *total-return strategy*) is contrasted with the buy-and-hold strategy in that an active approach pursues enhanced returns by capturing capital gains that may arise on relatively longer-dated instruments. This strategy requires that an investor be prepared to sell holdings when their prices rise and is dependent on interest rates falling or on the relative creditworthiness of an issue improving.

One advantage to this approach is that for as long as the yield curve is sloped positively (meaning short-term rates are and remain lower than long-term rates), capital gains are possible over time. The yield curve, discussed in more detail later in this chapter, is the interest trend line that spans the full spectrum of maturities employed in the strategy. As time passes and longer-dated purchases approach maturity, their value in the secondary market increases because while their maturities are shortening, their stated interest rates remain at levels associated with longer-dated instruments. When this increase in value occurs, such securities can be sold for a premium because they now pay above the market rates for short-term investment instruments of identical maturity.[3]

The threats to cash assets from this strategy arise when time passes but prices do not rise—capital gains therefore do not materialize, and the investor's portfolio has a longer duration than intended due to the lack of capital gains. Investing in an actively managed portfolio, or using a total-return approach, is only appropriate for amounts of cash that can be seen as required no earlier than the longest-maturity security that might be purchased in such a strategy. An active short-term investment strategy requires that the in-house or outside investment manager responsible for short-term investment decisions forecast the course of interest rates over the very short term.

3. TAX-BASED STRATEGY

Depending on the investor's location and applicable tax regulations, there may be certain investments that offer tax-advantaged returns (typically in the form of returns that are exempt from income or other taxes). Where tax-advantaged investments exist, potentially higher returns may be available to certain investors. In most cases, the yield benefit of a tax-advantaged investment is related directly to an investor's marginal tax rate (see details in the yield calculation discussion in Section III.A.2 of this chapter). The use of such tax-advantaged vehicles can be employed in both passive and active strategies.

For global organizations, there may be advantages related to developing a globally based investment strategy. There are often tax advantages related to investing in one location or currency versus another, and an organization operating in many different currencies and countries must often maintain liquidity in many currencies and locations.

In India, for example, companies have the option of investing in tax-free infrastructure bonds to create a higher yield. In the United States, there are several tax-advantaged investment strategies. Besides investing in specific and federally tax-exempt municipal securities, investors may buy shares in tax-advantaged mutual funds tailored to their state of domicile. Further, for companies with a mix of income from multiple US states, portfolios of municipal securities and/or bond funds can be used to match this income mix closely, thereby minimizing overall state taxation.

Dividend capture is another tax-motivated, short-term investment strategy also available to corporations that pay taxes in the United States. A corporation may exclude from its taxable income 70–80% of the dividends received from stock owned in another corporation, as long as it owns the stock for at least 46 days of the 91-day period starting 45 days prior to the ex-dividend date.[4] Even though dividend capture requires an equity investment, the strategy is considered a short-term investment because the stock is held only long enough to capture the dividend and qualify for the dividend exclusion.

3. This would obviously not be the case if the yield curve were inverted (i.e., short-term rates above long-term rates), which has happened in the past.
4. For a 70% exclusion, the stock must be less than 20% owned by the receiving corporation. If a corporation owns more than 20% but less than 80%, then the exclusion is 80% of the dividend.

Assume, for example, that a company purchases common stock in another company after the dividend announcement, then sells it after the ex-dividend date, ensuring that at least 46 days of ownership elapses.[5] The company has then captured the dividend and will receive it on the payment date. There is little risk that the dividend will not be paid because only stock in large, reputable firms is purchased for this purpose. However, there is a risk that the stock may have to be sold at a loss, but firms using this strategy employ it frequently so that gains and losses offset one another over many transactions. The strategy should be avoided when the market is in a secular downtrend or if there is a sense that the market may be shocked by a macroeconomic or political event.

D. Reporting

Reliable investment reporting is important for all organizations to ensure that performance and risk management goals are met, as well as to satisfy external reporting requirements for public companies. An organization's investment reporting should clearly illustrate the composition of a portfolio according to maturity distribution, quality ratings, and security classes. This presentation furnishes a simplified means for assessing investment policy compliance and affords a reader a concise overview of a company's investment pool and its risk exposure.[6]

When multiple fund managers are used, the question of who is responsible for specific reporting can become an issue if it is not properly managed. Since one of the goals of the reporting is to compare the various fund managers, it is important that there be separate reporting from each manager. On the other hand, consolidated reports are needed for overall management review, including compliance review, and for external reporting for public companies. Typically each investment advisor will prepare reports for its portion of the overall portfolio. The firm's custodian, discussed in the following section, can then take the various reports and compile a consolidated version that can be used for management and external reporting.

Reporting is especially critical for companies whose stock is publicly traded, due to regulatory and exchange requirements. In periodic filings, a company must be prepared to account for investment returns as allocated to a specific reporting period.[7] For money market and other fixed-income investment portfolios, this means reporting interest income on an accrual basis rather than a cash basis. For investment vehicles that typically pay interest on dates that do not coincide with a reporting period's beginning or ending dates, interest accrual reports must be prepared by the company, and by its investment managers or brokers, that accurately show interest earned (even if unpaid) for any relevant reporting period.

5. The ex-dividend date is the date on which the stock is sold without entitlement to an upcoming dividend. Dividends are discussed in Chapter 20, Financial Decisions and Management.
6. In the United States, this reporting is covered under Accounting Standards Codification (ASC) Topic 820, which is addressed in Chapter 18, Financial Accounting and Reporting.
7. The relevant US guidelines in this area are ASC Topics 320, 820, and 825, which are covered in more detail in Chapter 18, Financial Accounting and Reporting.

An added component of investment reporting requires that any unrealized gain or loss that might be associated with investments be shown. Because market values for money market and other fixed-income instruments may fluctuate during their lives until maturity, any difference between the current market value of a holding and its adjusted cost basis must be detailed in periodic reporting. This is what is referred to as *mark-to-market accounting*, and the importance of this exercise is magnified in periods of market stress.

Under rules created by the FASB and the IASB,[8] any security holding is deemed to be impaired when its fair market value is less than its adjusted cost basis. This difference is an unrealized loss unless the security is liquidated at that current price, whereupon it becomes a realized loss. However, under certain circumstances and according to IASB and FASB requirements, unrealized losses must be reported in the same manner as realized losses (as mentioned in Chapter 18, Financial Accounting and Reporting).

If a security is deemed to be impaired (i.e., its market value is less than its adjusted cost) and this impairment is not or cannot be expected to be cured in the foreseeable future, then it must be further classified as other-than-temporary impairment (OTTI). As such, the investment's carrying value must be reduced by the amount of the unrealized loss, and this loss amount must be subtracted from net earnings.[9] As discussed above, organizations should have both valuation and impairment policies in place that spell out the actions that need to be taken to determine if specific securities are impaired and when or if a write-down is appropriate.

E. Securities Safekeeping and Custody Services

Once a security is purchased, it must be warehoused and tracked to ensure that any interest income, dividends, or other proceeds are credited properly to its owner. The common method for this is for securities to be registered in the name of an institution that holds securities on behalf of investors (sometimes referred to as the *nominee* or *street name*). In turn, these institutions are required to maintain separate books and records that evidence the specific, underlying ownership of the securities. The essential purpose of these processes is to facilitate fast and efficient transfers of securities from one broker to another.

Effective custody of securities can be accomplished by one of two basic means. The first choice is to engage a third party to provide custodial services for an investor. Here, the corporate trust department of a commercial bank serves as custodian of the securities, and collects income from the securities, redemption monies, and other cash flows associated with a particular investment on behalf of individual investor clients (including corporations). A custodian bank also serves as a conduit to the underlying investor for any notices, official information, or other actions regarding the securities it holds.

An alternative to fee-based, third-party custodians is to keep securities at the institution (usually a brokerage firm) from which they were purchased. This method affords all the same support as with a custodian bank, but such custody services are normally offered at no charge, which may be attractive to smaller organizations. This second approach is considered somewhat more risky than the first because there may be a potential for fraud, as the custodian is supposed to be the third-party control in the process.

8. The FASB rules are covered in ASC Topic 320: *Investments—Debt and Equity Securities*, and the IASB rules are covered in IAS 39: *Financial Instruments: Recognition and Measurement*.
9. For securities deemed to be temporarily impaired, this unrealized loss amount must be accounted for on the company's balance sheet rather than on its income statement.

The primary advantage of using a fee-based third party for securities custody is that reporting is consolidated and control over the investor's entire group of holdings is established. This is especially important when an organization uses multiple investment managers (as discussed in the previous section), who otherwise might execute trades through their own brokerage. Because all trades for the organization's portfolio are handled by a single custodian, it is much easier to monitor compliance with policy and operating guidelines and identify any irregularities in trading or undue concentration. Since this process requires managers (internal or external) to trade through a particular custodian rather than using their own facilities, it can be an important separation-of-duties control feature. While some organizations may be able to take advantage of complimentary custody services extended by brokerage firms to save some money, third-party custodians are often required for investors who outsource their investment management.

F. Investment Risk Considerations

As discussed in Chapter 5, Money Markets, most money market instruments have low default, liquidity, and price/interest rate risk, and are therefore appropriate for conservative, short-term portfolios. Such low risk levels are accompanied by lower returns or yields, but this is consistent with the primary need to minimize risk to principal while maintaining liquidity. An obvious exception is when investing in foreign currency money market instruments. In this case, one must also consider the risks related to foreign exchange.

The major areas of risk in short-term investments include:

- **Credit/Default Risk:** The risk that payments to investors on a security will not be made under the original terms of the security
- **Asset Liquidity Risk:** The risk that a security investment cannot be sold quickly without experiencing an unacceptable loss
- **Price/Interest Rate Risk:** The risk that arises when there are changes in interest rates for securities that are identical or nearly identical to portfolio securities
- **Foreign Exchange (FX) Risk:** The risk of a change in the rate of exchange between the currency in which a security is denominated and the company's local currency (applies to foreign currency investments only)

These risks are discussed in more detail in Chapter 5, Money Markets, and Chapter 16, Financial Risk Management.

III. PRICING AND YIELDS ON SHORT-TERM INVESTMENTS

A. Factors Influencing Investment Pricing

Yield is a measure of the return an investor derives from a financial instrument. Typically, it is stated as an annual percentage rate of return. Many factors can influence the pricing and, ultimately, the yield of an investment. These factors include default, liquidity, and price risk; the general shape of the yield curve; and the tax status of the investment. The various risk factors are discussed above, and the concept of yield curves and the impact of an investment's tax status are covered below.

1. YIELD CURVES

A yield curve is a plot of the yields to maturity on the same investment instrument or class of instruments, but with varying maturities, as of a specific date. For example, a yield curve for US Treasury instruments is a plot of yields to maturity for US Treasury bond issues with varying periods to maturity as of the close of business on a particular date. Similarly, a plot of yields to maturity for AA rated industrial bonds with various maturities is a yield curve for that class of instruments.

Refer to Exhibit 11.1. The curve in the graphs of the various yields to maturity illustrates what is called the *term structure* of interest rates. In the left panel of Exhibit 11.1, the yield to maturity on the instrument or class of instruments increases with maturity, whereas it declines with maturity in the right panel.

EXHIBIT 11.1 **YIELD CURVES**

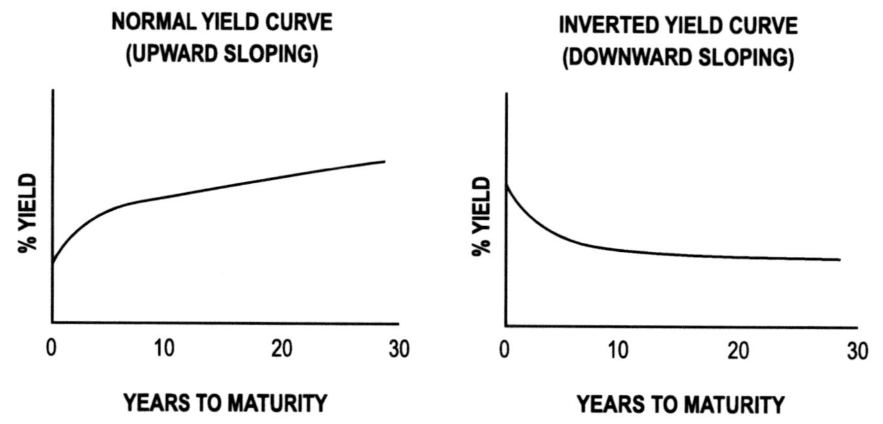

The slope, or shape, of the yield curve at any given point in time has decision implications for a treasury professional charged with executing a company's investment policy. Since short-term interest rates are more often lower than long-term rates, an upward-sloping yield curve is referred to as a *normal yield curve*. The liquidity preference theory of the term structure of interest rates holds that investors demand a yield premium in compensation for the lower liquidity that is associated with longer maturity. Thus, long-term rates are normally higher than short-term rates.

A downward-sloping yield curve is referred to as an *inverted yield curve*. In this case, investors are shifting their preferences to long-term securities (or conversely, issuers are shifting their preference to short-term borrowing). This increased demand for long-term securities causes their prices to increase and long-term yields to decline, thus pushing down the long-term end of the curve and causing an inversion. An inverted yield curve is typically a sign that the market is expecting a recession in the near future and is investing in longer-term securities to attempt to "lock in" interest rates or avoid any reduced interest rate that may occur in the short run. It is also a sign of low expectations with regards to future inflation, as expectations of high inflation would automatically increase the yields required on long-term securities (to offset the expected inflation) and create a normal, upward-sloping yield curve.

2. TAX STATUS[10]

The tax status of an investment is not related directly to liquidity, but it affects yield. Tax-exempt securities, such as US T-bills or Indian infrastructure bonds, provide a lower pretax yield than taxable securities of similar maturity and default risk, because of their tax advantage. When comparing taxable and tax-exempt instruments, the tax-exempt yield must first be converted to a taxable equivalent to allow proper comparison. The tax-exempt yield can be converted to a taxable equivalent yield as follows:

$$\text{Taxable Equivalent Yield} = \frac{\text{Tax-Exempt Yield}}{1 - \text{Marginal Tax Rate}}$$

This taxable equivalent yield can be used to compare the tax-exempt instrument with other taxable investments. For example, assume a treasury professional is choosing between a taxable security with a 4.60% yield and a tax-exempt security with a 3.20% yield of similar risk and maturity. The firm's marginal income tax rate is 35%. In this case, the tax-exempt security has a taxable equivalent yield of 4.92%, calculated as follows:

$$\text{Taxable Equivalent Yield} = \frac{0.032}{1 - 0.35} = 0.0492\text{, or } 4.92\%$$

Another approach to making this comparison is to compute the after-tax yield on the taxable security, which can then be compared directly to the tax-exempt instrument. The calculation is as follows:

$$\text{After-Tax Yield} = \text{Taxable Yield} \times (1 - \text{Investor's Marginal Tax Rate})$$

$$= 0.0460 \times (1 - 0.35) = 0.0299\text{, or } 2.99\%$$

Either method indicates that the tax-exempt security should be chosen because it has a higher taxable equivalent yield (4.92% versus 4.60%) and a higher effective after-tax yield (3.20% versus 2.99%) than the taxable security.

10. This discussion is primarily from the perspective of a US investor, to illustrate the effects of tax status, but investors outside of the United States may also have access to tax-advantaged investments, depending on local tax codes.

B. Yield Calculations for Short-Term Investments

Yield calculations for short-term investments usually are made on a simple interest basis, while yields on long-term investments are made on a compounded net present value (NPV) basis. The quoted yield for most short-term investments is a simple annual rate called a *nominal yield*, which does not reflect compounding.

Only yield calculations related to short-term investments are presented in this section. The valuation and yield calculations for long-term investments are covered in Chapter 12, Long-Term and Capital Investments.

1. YIELD CALCULATION PRINCIPLES AND EXAMPLES

The yield on any short-term investment instrument is a function of the:

- Cash flows received from the investment
- Amount paid for that investment
- Maturity or holding period

A yield is based upon how long an investor loses the use of funds (because they are committed and therefore cannot be employed in an alternative use), how much cash compensation is received for investing the funds, and over what period of time the funds were unavailable for an alternative use.

A holding period yield is the yield computed for the time a security is held. However, yields are quoted on an annualized basis, so the holding period yield is adjusted by determining how many holding periods occur in one year and using that number to annualize the yield. For example, if funds invested for one month earn a yield of 1% for the month, the annualized yield is 12% since there are 12 months in a year.

Two commonly quoted yields that are calculated using the annual yield formula are the money market yield and the bond equivalent yield. The number of days in a year is referred to as the *year basis*. Money market yield is based on a 360-day year, while bond equivalent yield is based on a 365-day year.

The use of a 360-day year has its roots in historical convention. The year was treated as consisting of 12 months, each with 30 days. Rate quotes and interest payments on money market instruments are still computed using a 360-day year. An investor's effective annual yield is computed using a 365-day year.[11]

The formulas for these basic yield calculations are:

$$\text{Holding Period Yield} = \frac{\text{Cash Received at Maturity} - \text{Amount Invested}}{\text{Amount Invested}}$$

$$\text{Annual Yield} = \text{Holding Period Yield} \times \frac{\text{Days in Year}}{\text{Days to Maturity}}$$

11. The decision to use 360 versus 365 (or in some cases 366) days in a year in various investment calculations is a standard convention based upon historical practice and not left to the discretion of the practitioner. For consistency and comparability purposes, treasury practitioners need to learn which period is appropriate for various calculations and comply with the appropriate convention.

Assume that a $100,000 T-bill currently sells for $98,800 and matures in 90 days. The holding period yield is calculated as:

$$\text{Holding Period Yield} = \frac{\$100{,}000 - \$98{,}800}{\$98{,}800} = \frac{\$1{,}200}{\$98{,}800} = 0.01215\text{, or } 1.215\%$$

A T-bill is a money market instrument, so a 360-day year basis is used to annualize the 90-day rate, as follows:

$$\text{360-Day Basis Yield} = 0.01215 \times \frac{360}{90} = 0.01215 \times 4 = 0.0486\text{, or } 4.86\%$$

To determine the yield to an investor, convert the 360-day year to a 365-day year, as follows:

$$\text{365-Day Basis Yield} = \text{360-Day Basis Yield} \times \frac{365}{360}$$

Using the data above, calculate the 365-day basis yield as follows:

$$\text{365-Day Basis Yield} = 0.0486 \times \frac{365}{360} = 0.0493\text{, or } 4.93\%$$

The higher yield on a 365-day year is logical because there are more 90-day periods in a 365-day year than there are in a 360-day year. It takes the investor a smaller proportion of the year to earn $1,200 in a 365-day year than it does in a 360-day year, so the annualized rate over a 365-day year will be higher.

Consider another example in which a newly issued $1,000,000 par (or face) value 182-day T-bill is sold for $974,216:

$$\text{Holding Period Yield} = \frac{\$1{,}000{,}000 - \$974{,}216}{\$974{,}216} = \frac{\$25{,}784}{\$974{,}216}$$

$$= 0.0265\text{, or } 2.65\%$$

$$\text{360-Day Basis Yield} = 0.0265 \times \frac{360}{182} = 0.0524\text{, or } 5.24\%$$

T-bills, commercial paper (CP), and banker's acceptances (BAs) are discounted instruments. They do not pay interest; rather, they are issued at less than par value (the discount) and pay par value at maturity. The interest earned is represented by the difference between the purchase price and the par, or maturity, value. This difference is termed the *dollar discount*. In the preceding example, the dollar discount is:

$$\begin{aligned}\text{Dollar Discount} &= \text{Par Value} - \text{Purchase Price}\\ &= \text{Cash Received at Maturity} - \text{Amount Invested}\\ &= \$1{,}000{,}000 - \$974{,}216 = \$25{,}784\end{aligned}$$

The *discount rate* is defined as the dollar discount divided by the par, or maturity, value and then annualized using a 360-day year:

$$\text{Discount Rate} = \frac{\text{Dollar Discount}}{\text{Par Value}} \times \frac{360}{\text{Days to Maturity}}$$

$$= \frac{\$25{,}784}{\$1{,}000{,}000} \times \frac{360}{182} = 0.0510, \text{ or } 5.10\%$$

The dollar discount can be related to the discount rate by rearranging the previous equation:

$$\text{Dollar Discount} = \text{Discount Rate} \times \text{Par Value} \times \frac{\text{Days to Maturity}}{360}$$

$$= 0.0510 \times \$1{,}000{,}000 \times \frac{182}{360} = \$25{,}784$$

The money market yield, based on a 360-day year, is:

$$\text{Money Market Yield} = \text{Holding Period Yield} \times \frac{360}{\text{Days to Maturity}}$$

$$= \frac{\$1{,}000{,}000 - \$974{,}216}{\$974{,}216} \times \frac{360}{182}$$

$$= 0.0265 \times 1.978 = 0.0524, \text{ or } 5.24\%$$

The bond equivalent yield, or annual yield to an investor, using a 365-day year, is:

$$\text{Bond Equivalent Yield} = \text{Holding Period Yield} \times \frac{365}{\text{Days to Maturity}}$$

$$= \frac{\$1{,}000{,}000 - \$974{,}216}{\$974{,}216} \times \frac{365}{182}$$

$$= 0.0265 \times 2.0055 = 0.0531\text{, or } 5.31\%$$

In this case, since the money market yield has been computed, the bond equivalent yield can also be calculated as:

$$\text{Bond Equivalent Yield} = \text{Money Market Yield} \times \frac{365}{360}$$

$$= 0.0524 \times \frac{365}{360} = 0.0531\text{, or } 5.31\%$$

The bond equivalent yield always will exceed the money market yield because, as noted earlier, it is computed on a 365-day year basis versus a 360-day year basis for the money market yield calculation. Furthermore, note that the money market yield always exceeds the discount rate because the holding period yield is calculated using the purchase price, which is less than par value, whereas the discount rate calculation uses par value.

2. TREASURY BILL (T-BILL) QUOTES AND YIELD CALCULATIONS

Dealers buy and sell T-bills in a secondary market and typically utilize a *bid-ask* quote framework. The *ask* quote is the discount at which the dealer will sell the T-bill, while the *bid* quote is the discount at which the dealer will purchase the same security. Both the bid and the ask quotes are based on a 360-day year basis because they are given in terms of a discount.

In addition to the bid and ask discounts, the ask yield is provided. The ask yield is the yield to an investor purchasing a T-bill at the ask discount. This yield is calculated on a 365-day year basis. Sample quotes and calculations based on a March 13 purchase date are as follows:[12]

Maturity Date	Days to Maturity	Bid Discount (Percent)	Ask Discount (Percent)	Ask Yield (Percent)
April 18	36	0.075	0.065	0.066
April 25	43	0.075	0.035	0.035
May 2	50	0.070	0.066	0.066
May 9	57	0.055	0.050	0.051

The following formulas are used to calculate the purchase price that must be paid by an investor to the dealer (or that the dealer would pay to an investor selling a T-bill):

$$\text{Discount Rate} = \frac{\text{Dollar Discount}}{\text{Par Value}} \times \frac{360}{\text{Days to Maturity}}$$

$$\text{Dollar Discount} = \text{Par Value} - \text{Purchase Price}$$

Rearranging the preceding equation to isolate the purchase price results in:

$$\text{Purchase Price} = \text{Par Value} - \text{Dollar Discount}$$

And as shown earlier in this chapter, rearranging the discount rate calculation above allows for calculation of the dollar discount using the discount rate, as follows:

$$\text{Dollar Discount} = \text{Discount Rate} \times \text{Par Value} \times \frac{\text{Days to Maturity}}{360}$$

As an example, the purchase price an investor would pay for a \$1,000,000 T-bill maturing on April 18 is based on the April 18 ask discount:

$$\text{Dollar Discount} = 0.00065 \times \$1{,}000{,}000 \times \frac{36}{360} = \$65.00$$

$$\text{Purchase Price} = \$1{,}000{,}000 - \$65.00 = \$999{,}935.00$$

12. This is the format typically used for T-bill quotations in the financial press.

If the investor sold the T-bill, then the sale price paid to the investor by the dealer would be based on the April 18 bid discount of 0.075%:

$$\text{Dollar Discount} = 0.00075 \times \$1{,}000{,}000 \times \frac{36}{360} = \$75.00$$

$$\text{Sale Price} = \$1{,}000{,}000 - \$75.00 = \$999{,}925.00$$

The ask yield, or 365-day annual yield to the investor, is determined as follows:

$$\text{Holding Period Yield} = \frac{\text{Cash Received at Maturity} - \text{Amount Invested}}{\text{Amount Invested}}$$

$$= \frac{\$1{,}000{,}000 - \$999{,}935}{\$999{,}935} = 0.00007\text{, or } 0.007\%$$

$$\text{Annual Yield} = \text{Holding Period Yield} \times \frac{365}{\text{Days to Maturity}}$$

$$= 0.00007 \times \frac{365}{36} = 0.0007\text{, or } 0.07\%$$

IV. MANAGING SHORT-TERM FINANCING

A. Short-Term Funding Alternatives

Short-term debt instruments mature within one year and are generally used by firms to finance current assets such as accounts receivable (A/R) and inventory. Any type of loan or credit arrangement can be referred to as a *credit facility.* As discussed in Chapter 8, Introduction to Working Capital Management, there are a number of alternatives to short-term debt issuance, including trade financing, internal borrowing, and the sale of receivables. These are all potential sources of liquidity funding that should be considered as part of a company's short-term funding strategy, and are summarized below.

1. TRADE CREDIT

Trade credit arises when a buyer receives goods but payment is not made to the supplier until some later date. Trade credit is the primary source of short-term financing used by many businesses. While the supplier does not advance cash to the buyer, trade credit lets a buyer use the supplier's goods or services while simultaneously using the cash it otherwise would have had to pay in advance or upon delivery. Trade credit provides a tangible economic benefit as a source of financing because the buyer may avoid liquidating investments or incurring debt over the credit period. A company buyer who pays its suppliers too quickly before the invoice's due date (assuming no discount for early payment) may be foregoing an inexpensive source of working capital. (For further detail, refer to Chapter 9, Working Capital Metrics for discussion of calculation of the value of trade discounts.)

2. INTERNAL BORROWING

Internal borrowing is often the best source of low-cost funds. Multiple units of an organization—typically separate subsidiaries of a multinational corporation that are often in different countries—may borrow and lend among themselves through an in-house bank or other internal borrowing mechanism. Termed *intracompany lending*, these arrangements are formal and typically involve promissory notes or a memorandum of understanding. They are typically priced at market rates ("arm's length" rates) to comply with tax and regulatory requirements in many jurisdictions; however, the entity as a whole retains the money.

Many laws and regulations affect domestic and cross-border intracompany lending. For example, the length of time that intracompany loans are outstanding can affect whether the repayment of principal is treated as a return of capital or a dividend for tax purposes. As discussed in Chapter 20, Financial Decisions and Management, there are also significant issues around transfer pricing (which necessitates the use of market rates) and capitalization requirements. Many jurisdictions examine these loan programs very closely, and even minor compliance problems can result in large fines. As a result, policies and documentation related to intracompany transactions should be comprehensive and designed based on advice from legal, audit, and tax professionals to avoid possible problems.

3. SELLING OF RECEIVABLES

Receivables may be sold or discounted to raise cash in two ways. First, receivables may be factored (referred to as *factoring*), which is the sale or transfer of title to A/R to a third party called a *factor*. Securitization is the second method by which receivables may be sold. Through this financing technique, a company issues debt securities backed by a pool of receivables. Receivables that are suitable for debt securitization have a predictable cash flow stream adequate to retire the issue and a historical record of low losses. More detailed information about factoring and securitization is presented in Chapter 8, Introduction to Working Capital Management.

4. COMMERCIAL BANK CREDIT

Bank credit is an important source of short-term funds for businesses. Bank borrowings are the chief source of working capital for most companies, especially middle-market and smaller companies. Larger, publicly traded organizations often find bank credit attractive because banks can customize debt structures and use information not disclosed to the public to justify underwriting the debt.

Bank loans are offered on a secured or unsecured basis. Security, provided in the form of collateral or guarantees, may be used to obtain more favorable rates by some borrowers or to make credit available to businesses that cannot access unsecured credit facilities.[13] In addition, a lender's use of private information may reduce borrowing costs.

a. Loan Syndications and Participations

For organizations requiring large credit facilities, banks may extend those facilities through loan syndications and participations.

13. Guarantees on commercial loans are covered in more detail in Chapter 6, Capital Markets.

In a loan syndication, multiple financial institutions share the funding of a single credit facility. The syndicate, or group of lenders, is led by an agent who acts as the intermediary between the company and the syndicate to negotiate credit terms and documentation, make advances and collect payments on the loan, and disseminate information. All syndicate members share common documentation, but each lender has a promissory note, making it a direct lending relationship.

In a loan participation, a financial institution purchases an interest in another lender's credit facility. The purchaser is called a *participant*, and the seller is the *lead institution*. The participant does not have a separate note and has only an indirect relationship with the borrower. A participation agreement specifies the participant's and lead institution's rights and obligations. In the case of a blind participation, the participation is not disclosed to the borrower, and the participant may not contact the borrower directly or disclose the participant's role in the credit facility.

The rationale for these arrangements is that they allow banks to offer larger loans than they could on their own (due to capital requirements) and to expand their loan portfolio beyond their usual market, creating a more diversified mix of loans. It is important for treasury professionals whose organizations have loans under syndication or participation arrangements to understand the structure of the arrangements since it will affect how they interact with the lenders.

b. Lines of Credit

i. Overview

A line of credit is an agreement in which the lender gives the borrower access to funds up to a maximum amount over a specific period of time. Lines of credit are usually revolving (see discussion below), meaning the borrower may borrow, repay, and borrow funds again up to the established limit during the commitment period. A line of credit can provide short-term financing, back up a CP program, or provide temporary liquidity.

ii. Conditions and Covenants

Requirements and conditions frequently associated with lines of credit include cleanup periods, credit sub-limits, covenants, and material adverse change (MAC) clauses. To ensure that a line is used for temporary financing, a lender may require a period of 30 to 60 consecutive days with no outstanding borrowing on the line (i.e., the cleanup period). This requirement is used mostly for middle-market and small companies to ensure that they do not use short-term financing for needs more appropriately met by long-term sources. A lender also may establish sub-limits under the line for specific uses such as letter of credit (L/C) issuance, drafts under BAs, or other purposes, which are discussed in Chapter 10, Collections, Concentration, and Disbursements. Covenants (discussed in more detail in Chapter 6, Capital Markets) used in short-term lending typically focus on maintaining certain minimum liquidity or coverage ratios, or maximum debt ratios. Finally, a MAC clause lets the lender refuse further funding or even declare the loan in default if there has been an adverse change in the borrower's credit profile.

Good internal reporting and cash forecasting are essential to ensuring a lack of unpleasant surprises in relation to ongoing compliance with loan covenants. While reporting is normally a requirement of any covenant, it is also an important management tool. It is much easier to negotiate problems with covenant violations before they actually occur than after the fact. Since covenants typically apply to an entire organization, timely and accurate reporting from any subsidiaries is an essential part of this issue.

iii. Types of Lines

Lines of credit are secured or unsecured, and uncommitted or committed. Secured lines require the borrower to pledge some form of collateral, most often current assets such as A/R and inventory. Unsecured lines do not require any collateral as part of the borrowing arrangement. The availability under some secured lines is limited by a borrowing base (sometimes referred to as *loan value*) that is negotiated as a percentage of the value of the collateral securing the line.

An uncommitted line is an agreement with a lender in which the lender offers to make funds available in the future but is not obligated to provide a specific amount. Usually, an uncommitted line is made available for a one-year period. However, funding may be refused at the lender's discretion or canceled outright, usually due to changes in the financial condition of the borrower. Hence, an uncommitted line is often called a *discretionary line of credit*. There is typically no fee for an uncommitted line unless funds are actually borrowed.

By contrast, a committed line usually involves a formal loan agreement that specifies the terms and conditions of the credit facility. It also typically requires compensation in the form of balances or fees because the lender is obligated to provide funding up to the credit limit stipulated in the agreement so long as the borrower is not in default. A commitment fee may be assessed based on the total amount or unused portion of the commitment. Typically, payment is made quarterly with varying fees, depending upon the company's creditworthiness, the stated purpose of the line, and the commitment term.

Another type of "credit" line is referred to as a *guidance line* or *operating risk exposure limit*. Guidance lines are used by banks to accommodate the credit exposure created from operating activities, such as automated clearinghouse (ACH) operations, "daylight" overdrafts,[14] returned deposits, and FX exposure. Banks initiate this type of line, rather than the customer, in order to determine the overall level of exposure the bank has relative to all of the activities (borrowing and non-borrowing) that the customer has with the bank. Often, the bank will not mention this type of line or "credit" limit unless the customer specifically asks about it. It is important, however, that treasury professionals ask about and actively manage any exposure limits to avoid potential problems with their company's ability to send wires or ACH credits from its accounts or obtain additional borrowing. This is especially true during periods of high growth or acquisitions, which may stretch or break limits that are not being managed. It is also important to note that while the guidance line is typically treated by the bank as a credit exposure that impacts overall lending to a specific customer, it does not represent any commitment on the part of the bank to lend funds to the organization in question.

iv. Compensating Balances

Compensating balances are balances maintained in the company's deposit accounts at the bank for the purpose of increasing the bank's overall revenue on the account. They generally do not earn interest or offset depository service charges. Under a compensating balance arrangement, the balance requirement can be specified as a percentage of the:

- Total line commitment
- Unused amount of the commitment
- Outstanding borrowings

14. A "daylight" overdraft occurs when a customer's available account balance becomes negative during the day, but the needed funds are deposited or become available before the end of the business day. This may happen when a bank allows a customer to initiate wires or submit ACH payment files against funds that will be deposited or become available later in the day.

If compensating balances are required by the bank, their effect is to reduce the amount of borrowed funds that are available to be used by the borrower, thereby increasing the loan's effective annual interest rate. The practice of requiring compensating balances is becoming less common over time.

v. Pricing

Pricing for a line of credit is usually negotiable. The lender may take into account various aspects of the overall lender/ borrower relationship in pricing the facility. There are three basic cost components for lines of credit:

- The all-in rate of interest
- Commitment fees, which can be on both used and unused balances
- Compensating balances

The all-in rate consists of a base rate, such as LIBOR, the US prime rate, or the Fed funds rate (all discussed later in this chapter), plus a spread that is added to, or occasionally subtracted from, the base rate. Rates on lines are normally variable and adjust immediately to changes in the base rate. While the actual rate on the loan will vary with the market, it is not unusual for a credit agreement to have a floor rate, which provides a bottom limit on how low the total interest rate can go.

The total interest paid is calculated as the all-in rate times the loan balance outstanding at any given time. Since both the rates and the loan balance can vary from day to day, daily interest will also change. Annual (or period) interest is the total of the daily interest charges during the year (or period). Total fees paid include all commitment fees, placement fees, and any issuance costs. The average usable funds of the borrowed amount is the average outstanding loan for the year less the required compensating balances. The impact of these rates and fees on loan pricing is covered later in this chapter.

c. Revolving Credit Agreements

One of the most common types of lines of credit is a revolving credit agreement, also known as a *revolver*. This is a committed line of credit (as opposed to a standby letter of credit, which is discussed in Chapter 10, Collections, Concentration, and Disbursements) established for a specified period of time, often on a multiyear basis. Revolving credits are formal, contractual commitments with loan agreements, including covenants. Usually, there is a commitment fee on the unused portion, as well as a fee for use of the borrowing facility. Though often used for short-term borrowing, the commitment term typically ranges from two to five years and may be followed by a period in which the principal is repaid systematically. If more than one year remains on a multiyear revolver, accounting guidelines typically allow balances on this agreement to be carried as a long-term liability on the borrower's balance sheet.

Revolvers contain all the characteristics of committed lines. In addition, revolvers often feature short-term, fixed-rate funding options that offer fixed-rate loans for specified periods with penalties imposed for prepayment. An example is a funding option for 90-day advances fixed at a rate equal to some preestablished spread over LIBOR. The amount of the spread varies depending on the credit risk.

5. SINGLE PAYMENT NOTES

Single payment notes usually are granted for a short period of time and specific purpose, with both the principal and interest amounts paid at maturity. Because of the limited duration and precise maturity of a single payment note, a specific cash flow event is frequently identified as the repayment source at the time the funds are advanced. Longer-term notes and term loans are covered in Chapter 6, Capital Markets.

6. REPURCHASE AGREEMENTS (REPOS)

A repo is another source of short-term funds. Securities are sold, providing the seller with cash until the securities are repurchased. Repos let companies tap into the liquidity of their investment portfolio without having to dispose of their investments in money market instruments. An equivalent transaction may be structured by using a single payment note secured by marketable securities. Repos are covered in more detail in Chapter 5, Money Markets.

7. COMMERCIAL PAPER (CP) ISSUANCE

CP as an investment is covered in Chapter 5, Money Markets. This section focuses on the use of CP as a source of short-term financing. CP is an unsecured promissory note of highly rated corporations, financial institutions, or sovereigns. While the specific characteristics of CP programs vary by country, most CP markets are modeled after the US market, which is the oldest and still the largest CP market in the world.

In the United States, there are two types of CP programs, named after the sections in the Securities Act of 1933 that provide exemptions from registration of CP with the SEC. An issuer under a 3(a)(3) program can issue CP up to 270 days in minimum amounts of $100,000. The proceeds of 3(a)(3) CP may only be used for working capital purposes. An issuer under a 4(2) program can issue CP up to 397 days in minimum amounts of $250,000. There is no restriction on how the proceeds of 4(2) CP may be used, including for construction expenditures or acquisitions. In practice, most outstanding CP has a maturity less than 30 days, but issuers continually roll over the CP into a new issue at maturity.

Characteristics of 3(a)(3) and 4(2) CP programs are outlined in Exhibit 11.2.

EXHIBIT 11.2 **CHARACTERISTICS OF 3(a)(3) AND 4(2) CP PROGRAMS**

	3(a)(3)	4(2)
Type	Public	Private Placement
Proceeds	Working Capital	No Restrictions
Maximum Maturity	270 Days	397 Days
Minimum Issuance	$100,000	$250,000
Pricing	Spread to LIBOR	Spread to LIBOR (no premium)
Investors	Accredited Investors	Institutional Investors & Qualified Institutional Buyers (QIBs)

CP programs are rated by the major credit rating agencies, which normally require each program to have a liquidity backup in the event the market would not be available to issue or reissue CP for any reason. Typical backup facilities include a revolving credit facility or a letter of credit issued by a highly rated bank. Although common, not every CP issuer has to have a backup. Some very liquid and very creditworthy organizations are able to issue CP based solely on their own resources. CP can be issued directly by corporations (i.e., sold directly to investors), but most CP is placed through dealers (selected by the issuer) who market the CP to investors for a nominal fee.

CP is sold at a discount, meaning the interest paid by the issuer on the CP is deducted from the proceeds. The discount rate on CP is always calculated on a 360-day basis. Other costs associated with a CP program include the dealer fees, backup credit facility fees, rating agency charges, and any credit enhancement costs.

Because of the effort and high fixed costs involved in establishing a CP program, CP financing is desirable only when ongoing funding needs are large. Few companies consider CP for amounts below $50 million, although individual issues under an overall program may be for smaller amounts. In addition, companies without excellent credit ratings often find commercial bank credit more attractive than CP because banks have more flexibility in structuring credit (e.g., covenants, rate adjustments, and collateral) to mitigate risk and therefore lower costs to the borrower.

8. ASSET-BASED BORROWING

Commercial finance companies and some commercial banks specialize in asset-based lending. Asset-based lines of credit in the working capital area are typically secured by A/R or inventory, and can support temporary financing needs. This topic is covered in detail in Chapter 8, Introduction to Working Capital Management.

B. Pricing and Costs of Principal Short-Term Financing Sources

A loan or other borrowing arrangement represents an investment to the counterparty (the lender or investor). Consequently, the factors that influence investment yield are the determinants of credit pricing. Pricing and fees on loans increase with default risk, price risk, liquidity, and length of maturity. A discussion of how these factors impact loan pricing (interest rates) is provided in the following section of this chapter. Factors that enter into borrowing costs yet do not impact an investor's yields include dealer and placement fees, credit enhancement, and backup credit costs.

In this section, the costs involved in two primary sources of short-term financing are covered. These sources are CP and bank lines of credit. Formulas and calculations for these sources are discussed below.

1. ANNUAL COST FOR COMMERCIAL PAPER (CP) ISSUANCE

The all-in or total costs to issue CP include the interest rate implied in the discount, a dealer fee, and a fee for credit enhancement in the form of a backup or standby L/C.

Assume that a company issues $50,000,000 of CP with a 20-day maturity at a discount of 0.396%. To calculate the annualized cost of the paper, begin by finding the amount of usable funds, which is the face amount of the CP less the discount:

$$\text{Dollar Discount} = \text{Discount Rate} \times \text{Par Value} \times \frac{\text{Days to Maturity}}{360}$$

$$= 0.00396 \times \$50{,}000{,}000 \times \frac{20}{360} = \$11{,}000.00$$

$$\text{Usable Funds} = \text{Par Value} - \text{Dollar Discount}$$

$$= \$50{,}000{,}000 - \$11{,}000 = \$49{,}989{,}000$$

Assume that the annualized dealer fee is 0.12% (12 basis points) and the cost of a backup L/C is 0.25% (25 basis points). The amount of the dealer fee and the amount of the backup L/C fee can be calculated as follows:

$$\text{Prorated Dealer Fee} = \text{Annual Fee Rate} \times \text{CP Issue Size} \times \frac{\text{Days to Maturity}}{360}$$

$$= 0.0012 \times \$50{,}000{,}000 \times \frac{20}{360} = \$3{,}333.33$$

$$\text{Prorated Backup L/C Fee} = \text{Annual L/C Rate} \times \text{CP Issue Size} \times \frac{\text{Days to Maturity}}{360}$$

$$= 0.0025 \times \$50{,}000{,}000 \times \frac{20}{360} = \$6{,}944.44$$

Based on the principle that an interest rate is how much is paid in relation to usable funds for a specified period of time, the annual interest rate on the line of credit is:

$$\text{Annual Interest Rate} = \frac{\text{Dollar Discount} + \text{Dealer Fee} + \text{Backup L/C Fee}}{\text{Usable Funds}} \times \frac{365}{\text{Days to Maturity}}$$

$$= \frac{\$11{,}000.00 + \$3{,}333.33 + \$6{,}944.44}{\$49{,}989{,}000} \times \frac{365}{20}$$

$$= 0.00042565 \times \frac{365}{20} = 0.0078\text{, or } 0.78\%$$

The annualized 0.78% rate of cost applies to the issuer. The buyer (investor) bases yield on how much is gained in relation to the amount of funds that are not usable because they are tied up in the investment. In this example, the nominal, or annual, yield to the investor (calculated on a 365-day basis) is:

$$\text{Commercial Paper Nominal Yield} = \frac{\text{Dollar Discount}}{\text{Purchase Price}} \times \frac{365}{\text{Days to Maturity}}$$

$$= \frac{\$11{,}000}{\$49{,}989{,}000} \times \frac{365}{20} = 0.0040, \text{ or } 0.40\%$$

2. ANNUAL COST FOR A LINE OF CREDIT

A line-of-credit lender will typically charge interest and a commitment fee on the line on an annual basis. While there may be other fees, as discussed below, they tend to be one-time charges rather than annual fees. Interest is charged on the used portion of the line. The commitment fee may be charged on the line or its unused portion. The overall interest rate on the line is determined by the total interest paid on the line's used portion and the amount paid for the commitment fee relative to the average used portion of the credit line over the borrowing period. In the example that follows, the commitment fee applies to the unused portion of the credit line.

Assume that a company expects to use $1,600,000 of short-term borrowings, but it wants to establish a $3,000,000 credit line to ensure adequate reserve borrowing capacity. A lender offers the company LIBOR plus a risk premium of 2.50%. It requires a commitment fee of 0.30% (30 basis points) on the unused portion of the line. LIBOR at the time of the loan is 0.70%. The rate on the used portion of the line is LIBOR plus 2.50%, or 3.20% (the all-in rate). Begin by calculating all interest and fees paid:

$$\text{Interest Paid} = \text{Average Borrowing} \times \text{All-in Rate} = \$1{,}600{,}000 \times 0.032 = \$51{,}200$$

$$\text{Fee on Unused Portion} = \text{Unused Portion} \times \text{Commitment Fee}$$

$$= \$1{,}400{,}000 \times 0.0030 = \$4{,}200$$

Next, calculate the annual interest rate as total costs relative to the amount used on the line:

$$\text{Annual Interest Rate} = \frac{\text{Interest + Fee on Unused Portion of Line}}{\text{Used Portion of Line}}$$

$$= \frac{\$51{,}200 + \$4{,}200}{\$1{,}600{,}000} = 0.0346, \text{ or } 3.46\%$$

Now, suppose that the lender is a bank that requires a 10% compensating balance—that is, the borrower must maintain a balance in its demand deposit account (DDA) or current account that is not less than 10% of the amount borrowed on the credit line. Further, assume that the company operates its DDA as a zero balance account (ZBA). Since the firm would have to hold 10% of $1,600,000, or $160,000, in its DDA, its usable funds would only be $1,440,000. The 10% compensating balance requirement means that the firm will have to borrow more than $1,600,000 on the line in order to have $1,600,000 available. The compensating balance has the following effect on the calculation of the annual interest rate:

$$\text{Annual Interest Rate} = \frac{\text{Interest + Fee on Unused Portion of Line}}{\text{Used Portion of Line} - \text{Compensating Balance}}$$

$$= \frac{\$51{,}200 + \$4{,}200}{\$1{,}600{,}000 - \$160{,}000} = 0.0385\text{, or } 3.85\%$$

The amount that must be borrowed on the line in order to have $1,600,000 available can therefore be calculated as follows:

$$\text{Available Amount} = \text{Borrowed Amount} - (\text{Compensating Balance \%} \times \text{Borrowed Amount})$$

$$= \text{Borrowed Amount} - (0.10 \times \text{Borrowed Amount})$$

$$= \text{Borrowed Amount} \times (1 - 0.10) = \text{Borrowed Amount} \times 0.90$$

Therefore:

$$\text{Borrowed Amount} = \frac{\text{Available Amount}}{0.90} = \frac{\$1{,}600{,}000}{0.90} = \$1{,}777{,}777.78$$

The larger amount borrowed increases the total interest and fees paid:

$$\text{Interest Paid} = \text{Average Borrowing} \times \text{All-In Rate}$$

$$= \$1{,}777{,}777.78 \times 0.032 = \$56{,}888.89$$

$$\text{Fee on Unused Portion} = \text{Unused Portion} \times \text{Commitment Fee}$$

$$= (\$3{,}000{,}000 - \$1{,}777{,}777.78) \times 0.0030 = \$3{,}666.67$$

Then, recalculate the annual interest rate as a total cost relative to the borrowed amount that is actually usable:

$$\text{Annual Interest Rate} = \frac{\text{Interest + Fee on Unused Portion of Line}}{\text{Used Portion of Line} - \text{Compensating Balance}}$$

$$= \frac{\$56{,}888.89 + \$3{,}666.67}{\$1{,}777{,}777.78 - (0.10 \times \$1{,}777{,}777.78)}$$

$$= \frac{\$60{,}555.56}{\$1{,}600{,}000} = 0.0378, \text{ or } 3.78\%$$

The compensating balance requirement means that a company will have to borrow more than it needs in order to have available the usable amount it needs. As a result, it will pay more in interest and fees ($60,555.56 versus $55,400.00) and it will pay a higher interest rate on the credit line (3.78% versus 3.46%).

V. Debt Financing

This section discusses the basics of debt financing and management for organizations, which is important for treasury professionals to understand due to the impact of debt usage on both the profitability and value of the organization. Most of this text will cover this topic in a general framework, with some specific information provided on issues for US-based organizations as applicable. The major differences between countries are in the interest rate measures used and some specific regulations related to the credit and debt instruments.

A. Costs of Borrowing

The primary costs of borrowing are related to the interest rate on the debt, but there are other costs that should also be considered. These include the costs of credit enhancements (e.g., guarantees or letters of credit); fees paid to credit rating agencies; legal fees; commitment and facility fees; fees paid to brokers, dealers, or investment banks for the underwriting of bond or commercial paper issues; and potentially registration and regulatory fees. On a more indirect level, any costs related to negotiating and maintaining loan covenants should also be considered. Renegotiations of covenants to cure or avoid a breach often involve significant fees. The next part of this section focuses on the determinants of the interest rate paid for a specific issue.

B. Basic Components of Interest Rates

Interest rates depend on many factors. Some of these factors come from general economic conditions, and some are dependent upon individual organization variables, such as financial position, industry, overall debt use, and environmental liabilities. To help form a basic understanding of these factors, the model below incorporates some of the most common factors into a calculation of an underlying borrowing rate on a specific issue.

For most companies, organizations, or government entities, the underlying cost of borrowing is a function of the following factors, which can be expressed as the variable r, where r is defined as:

$$r = r^*_{RF} + IP + DP + LP + MP$$

Where:

r^*_{RF} = Real risk-free rate of interest

IP = Inflation premium

DP = Default premium

LP = Liquidity premium

MP = Maturity premium

The *real risk-free rate of interest* is generally defined as the rate demanded by savers (or investors) to compensate for delaying their use of the money today, in the absence of any risk or inflation, for a one-year maturity. This base rate demanded by savers becomes the basis for the borrowing rate. Historically, this rate has generally been in the range of 1–4%, depending on general preferences for consumption today versus consumption at a later time. At the time of publication, the base rate is currently at or close to zero in most major markets due to long-term government intervention to lower rates.

The first adjustment to the real rate is for inflation, as investors want to maintain the purchasing power of the money they are investing. The combination of the real risk-free rate and a short-term rate of inflation usually matches the rate on short-term government investments (e.g., a T-Bill in the United States) for the period in question. For investments other than government securities, there is a risk of default on the part of the security issuer that must be factored into the rate of interest. As the level of default risk rises, so does the required interest rate. This is known as the *risk/return trade-off.*

While the markets for most securities of large governments (i.e., those of the G8 countries[15]) are very efficient and highly liquid, other securities are not as easily traded, resulting in higher transaction costs and, ultimately, lower liquidity. Finally, longer-term fixed instrument investments generally have more price risk (i.e., they fluctuate more in price for a given change in interest rates). As a result of this price risk, longer-term securities usually have a maturity premium in addition to the interest-rate adjustments.

15. The G8 (or Group of Eight) countries consist of Canada, France, Germany, Italy, Japan, Russia, the United Kingdom, and the United States.

As an example of these calculations, the estimated interest rates demanded by investors on various types of fixed-income investments can be determined using the information in Exhibit 11.3. Three basic types of notes or bonds will be illustrated: a US Treasury issue (i.e., a T-bill), a corporate issue, and a municipal issue, each with varying maturities. The rates displayed here are for illustration purposes only and are not necessarily representative of actual rates or spreads between different types of investments.

EXHIBIT 11.3 **RISK-FREE RATES AND PREMIUMS**

RISK-FREE RATE AND INFLATION PREMIUMS			
REAL RISK-FREE RATE	1-YEAR INFLATION	5-YEAR INFLATION	10-YEAR INFLATION
0.0%	0.5%	2.5%	4.0%

ESTIMATED DEFAULT PREMIUMS		
US TREASURIES	CORPORATE BONDS	MUNICIPAL BONDS
0.0%	2.5%	1.5%

ESTIMATED LIQUIDITY PREMIUMS		
US TREASURIES	CORPORATE BONDS	MUNICIPAL BONDS
0.0%	0.5%	1.0%

ESTIMATED MATURITY PREMIUMS		
1-YEAR ISSUE	5-YEAR ISSUE	10-YEAR ISSUE
0.0%	0.4%	0.9%

In calculating the rates for each type of investment, all of the rates in Exhibit 11.3 will be taken into account, as well as the following assumptions:

- US Treasuries are perceived to be risk-free, with no default risk.
- US Treasuries are highly liquid and thus have no liquidity risk.
- Both corporate and municipal bonds have default and liquidity risk.
- Maturity risk increases with the issue's time to maturity.

This information is combined to calculate the total cost of borrowing for each investment type, which is shown in the final column of Exhibit 11.4.

EXHIBIT 11.4 **COMPARISON OF INTEREST RATES OR YIELDS ON DIFFERENT TYPES OF INVESTMENTS**

INVESTMENT	REAL RISK-FREE RATE	INFLATION PREMIUM	DEFAULT PREMIUM	LIQUIDITY PREMIUM	MATURITY PREMIUM	COST OF BORROWING
1-YEAR TREASURY	0.0%	0.5%	0.0%	0.0%	0.0%	0.5%
5-YEAR TREASURY	0.0%	2.5%	0.0%	0.0%	0.4%	2.9%
10-YEAR TREASURY	0.0%	4.0%	0.0%	0.0%	0.9%	4.9%
1-YEAR CORPORATE	0.0%	0.5%	2.5%	0.5%	0.0%	3.5%
5-YEAR CORPORATE	0.0%	2.5%	2.5%	0.5%	0.4%	5.9%
10-YEAR CORPORATE	0.0%	4.0%	2.5%	0.5%	0.9%	7.9%
1-YEAR MUNICIPAL	0.0%	0.5%	1.5%	1.0%	0.0%	3.0%
5-YEAR MUNICIPAL	0.0%	2.5%	1.5%	1.0%	0.4%	5.4%
10-YEAR MUNICIPAL	0.0%	4.0%	1.5%	1.0%	0.9%	7.4%

The impact of the various factors on the required rates for different types of bonds can be seen in Exhibit 11.4. For example, for one-year maturity bonds, the rate for a T-bill is 0.5%, the rate for a corporate issue is 3.5%, and the rate for a municipal issue is 3.0%. The T-bill incorporates only the inflation premium as an adjustment to the real risk-free rate, while both the corporate and municipal issues reflect some amount of default risk and liquidity risk. While this chart represents rates on bonds, these rates are essentially the costs of borrowing for each different class of borrower and maturity. Whether the borrowing is in the form of a bond issue or a loan, the impact of these factors is essentially the same.

C. Base Rates

For most borrowers, the cost of funds is expressed as the sum of some base rate plus an appropriate adjustment (or spread) to account for other risks involved in the arrangement, as discussed above. The base rate will generally include the adjustments for inflation and maturity premiums, while the spread will factor in adjustments for the default and liquidity premiums. The difference between the common base rates discussed below and the T-bill rate is that the rates below are essentially interbank rates (i.e., the rate at which one bank will lend to another bank). The interbank rates will be slightly higher than the T-bill rate at any given time due to a small amount of default risk inherent in a bank-to-bank borrowing arrangement.

Economic conditions and yield curves influence the general level of interest rates and base interest rates for borrowing, such as the London Interbank Offer Rate (LIBOR) and, to a lesser extent, the Federal Reserve (Fed) funds rate or the US prime rate. The British Bankers' Association compiles LIBOR daily by averaging the interest rate quotes of at least eight banks chosen to reflect a balance by country, type of institution, reputation, and scale of marketing activity. LIBOR is quoted in numerous currencies and is released to the market in London each day.

The Fed funds rate is the interest rate US banks charge to borrow reserve balances from one another. The target rate for Fed funds is set by the Federal Open Market Committee (FOMC)[16] on a periodic basis (about eight times per year), but the actual rate charged between banks is negotiated by those banks. This is known as the *Fed funds effective rate*. The prime rate is the interest rate commercial banks charge their best corporate customers, although strong, creditworthy borrowers usually can obtain rates below prime from their financial partners. Unlike LIBOR, which fluctuates on a daily basis, the US prime rate is typically set about three percentage points above the Fed funds rate and can remain fixed for extended periods of time.

D. Short-Term versus Long-Term Borrowing

Historically, short-term interest rates are usually lower than long-term rates, so yield curves are usually normal, meaning they slope upward with maturity. This implies that there is a cost advantage to using short-term credit. When short-term rates are higher than long-term rates, the yield curve is inverted and slopes downward with maturity.

A significant responsibility for treasury professionals is to monitor interest rate cycles and the yield curve in order to make effective decisions about short- versus long-term financing. Depending on interest rate cycles and the prevailing yield curve for interest rates, a company may secure long-term, low-rate bank or institutional financing and/or obtain fixed- versus floating-rate financing. There are also several short-term financing sources (e.g., accounts payable and accruals) that have little or no interest costs.

Borrowing on a short-term basis carries two types of risks to the borrower that are avoided in longer-term borrowing:

- The first risk relates to fluctuations in market interest rates. If the company borrows on a short-term, floating-rate basis, then it will borrow at the prevailing interest rate and risk dramatic rate swings in either direction. Many companies negotiate short-term borrowing risk reduction techniques such as interest rate caps, collars, swaps, and floors to protect themselves against interest rate fluctuations. (These tools are discussed in more detail in Chapter 16, Financial Risk Management.)
- The second risk of short-term financing concerns the availability of funds. If a company relies heavily on short-term borrowing, then the short-term funds may not be available at some future point due to tightening credit standards on the part of lenders. Also, a company's credit quality may decline, thus endangering the future rollover or renewal of the credit arrangement. Some companies counter this risk by negotiating multiyear credit line commitments known as *revolving credit agreements*, which guarantee the availability of funds over a longer term.[17]

In contrast to short-term borrowing, long-term borrowing on a fixed-rate basis stabilizes interest costs, or it provides a narrow range for fluctuation in interest costs on a variable-rate, long-term loan with an interest rate collar.

16. The role of central banks such as the US Federal Reserve in setting and managing interest rates is covered in detail in Chapter 2, Regulatory and Legal Environment.
17. During the Recession of 2009, many banks rescinded these guarantees under material adverse change (MAC) clauses. As the crisis continued, banks primarily offered credit agreements of less than one year in length, as the capital requirements on these agreements were lower than those for multiyear credit agreements.

1. OPERATIONAL ADVANTAGES OF SHORT-TERM FINANCING

It is important to understand the advantages and disadvantages of short-term financing (i.e., credit facilities of less than one year) relative to long-term financing (i.e., credit facilities of at least one year). Aside from differences in cost and risk, there are operational differences in using short- versus long-term debt to finance current assets.

The primary operational advantages of short-term financing are ease of access, flexibility, and the ability to finance seasonal credit needs efficiently. For organizations borrowing funds in the United States, short-term loans are typically easier to obtain than long-term loans because the Fed does not impose reserve requirements on credit facilities of less than 365 days. This makes it easier for financial institutions to provide short-term loans with maturities of less than one year. In addition, short-term loans generally have less restrictive covenants than long-term loans because a lender's money is at risk for a shorter period of time. If funds are necessary for only a short time, then borrowing and repaying on a short-term basis lets a company maintain flexibility for future borrowing decisions. For example, to meet increased seasonal needs, a company may need financing to increase inventory and/or accounts receivable. Short-term loans are a primary tool for financing temporary, seasonal increases in current assets.

Short-term financing can also be obtained from spontaneous sources such as accounts payable and prepaid expenses, as discussed in Chapter 8, Introduction to Working Capital Management. As a company's sales grow, these sources generate funds that can offset any needed investment in current assets.

2. OPERATIONAL DISADVANTAGES OF SHORT-TERM FINANCING

An operational disadvantage of short-term financing, especially sources such as lines of credit or commercial paper, is the continuing need to renegotiate or roll over the financing. A lender may decide not to roll over the loan or renew the credit line at maturity due to changing financial variables in the company or changes in general economic conditions. In addition, lenders that provide lines of credit typically require that loans used to finance short-term working capital deficits be paid in full for a minimum period of one to three months each year (known as a *cleanup period*). Lenders do this to ensure that the firm is not using short-term debt when long-term debt may be the appropriate financing source.

Many companies find that using short-term loans to finance permanent current asset requirements is risky, as discussed in Chapter 8, Introduction to Working Capital Management. However, one approach to continued use of short-term debt that carries lower risk involves revolving loans secured by accounts receivable or inventory, referred to as *asset-based lending*. The downsides to secured borrowing are:

- The assets used as security must be monitored.
- Key ratios related to the assets must often be maintained.
- Lending is generally limited to some percentage of the asset values.

E. Loan Agreements and Covenants

Loan covenants, discussed earlier in this chapter, impose either restrictions (known as *restrictive or negative covenants*) and/or obligations (known as *affirmative or positive covenants*) on the part of an organization's management. Loan covenants generally serve as a protection for the lenders (or investors) by preventing management (acting on behalf of the equity holders) from increasing the organization's credit risk, thereby reducing the value of any existing debt securities. Because the lenders do not typically have a voice in the organization's management, they must protect themselves through covenants at the time the loan is made. For bonds, the covenants typically are determined from negotiations with the rating agency as part of the ratings process. Depending on the covenants, there may be significant restrictions on the financial decision making for an organization. These restrictions could include limits or restrictions on the:

- Ability to sell certain assets
- Right of an organization to issue additional bonds
- Use of second or junior mortgages
- Key ratios that limit flexibility in financial decision making
- Payment of dividends

It is also important to understand that the terms of the loan agreements and covenants are generally negotiable between the borrower and the lender. The advantage that the borrower has is that it usually has a better idea about the amount of the line that will be used, as well as how often it will be used. In general, if only a small portion of the credit line will be used, then it would be advantageous to agree to a higher interest rate in return for a smaller commitment fee. If, on the other hand, the borrower thinks it will be using the bulk of the line, then a lower interest rate may be negotiated in return for a higher commitment fee, assuming the commitment fee is on the unused portion of the line.

In many cases, a multiyear revolving credit agreement may be counted as long-term debt on the company's balance sheet, which can reduce the level of current liabilities, thereby improving key ratios, such as the current and quick ratios.

F. Credit Rating Agencies (CRAs)

Most publicly issued debt by corporations and municipalities is rated by one or more of the credit rating agencies.[18] These companies assign credit ratings for issuers of certain types of short- and long-term debt obligations, as well as for the debt instruments themselves. Ratings can be on either a solicited or unsolicited basis. In other words, a company that knows it is going to be issuing debt may ask one or more agencies to rate the company and may work with the agency to ensure an appropriate rating in anticipation of the future debt offering. On the other hand, some of the CRAs are beginning to rate firms based on publicly available information even when the firm has not requested a rating. This may result in a poor rating based on incomplete information. It is important to remember that a credit rating is not an investment recommendation; rather, it is an assessment of the potential for downside loss on the investment. A listing of some of the major credit rating agencies is provided in Appendix 11.1.

A rating agency will generally have access to a corporation's internal information, and the agency's analyses and subsequent rating are widely accepted by market participants and regulators. In most cases, the rating agencies have access to confidential, nonpublic information that the securities issuers provide to the agencies only for the determination of ratings. This information is not released to the general public without the issuer's permission. Financial institutions use these agency ratings when required by regulators to hold investment-grade bonds.

18. As mentioned in Chapter 5, Money Markets, in the United States CRAs are also known as *nationally recognized statistical rating organizations*, or *NRSROs*.

Part of the Dodd-Frank Wall Street Reform and Consumer Protection Act (discussed in Chapter 2, Regulatory and Legal Environment) specifically addresses the rating agencies and the potential for conflicts of interest arising because the rating agencies receive their primary revenues from the companies they rate and not the investors who use the information. The act requires the rating companies to provide greater disclosure of their rating models and methodologies, and subjects them to greater liability.

1. CLASSES OF RATINGS

- **Issuer Credit Ratings:** The rating is an opinion on the obligor's (issuer's) overall capacity to meet its financial obligations. These include counterparty, corporate credit, and sovereign credit ratings. Counterparty ratings are made on key counterparties in financial transactions, such as financial institutions and insurance companies. Corporate credit ratings are on corporate debt issuers, and sovereign ratings are on government debt issuers.
- **Issue-Specific Credit Ratings:** These ratings of specific long- and short-term securities consider the attributes of the issuer, as well as the specific terms of the issue, the quality of the collateral, and the creditworthiness of the guarantors.

2. THE RATINGS PROCESS

The ratings process includes the quantitative and qualitative analyses of the company or entity being assessed. The quantitative aspects focus mainly on financial analyses and are based on the firm's financial reports. In most cases, analysts examine the issuer's financials using proprietary models and may perform additional quantitative reviews if necessary. The qualitative side is concerned with issues not related to the financials. For a corporate issuer, this may include analyzing the quality of the management and the firm's competitiveness within its industry, as well as the expected growth of the industry and its vulnerability to business cycles, technology changes, regulatory changes, and labor relations.

For government issues (both sovereign and sub-sovereign), the typical approach is based on an analysis of the primary factors relating to government finance. These usually include the economy, overall debt levels, finances (tax revenues and expenses), financial statements, and administration/management strategies for the government entity. Other factors would include the collateral for the debt and the primary source for repayment (from general taxes or from specific revenues, such as tolls for a bridge). Each factor is evaluated individually and for its effect on the other factors in the context of the government entity's ability to repay its debt.

3. REVIEWS OF RATINGS

Ratings usually are reviewed by the rating agencies once a year based on new financial reports, new business information, or review meetings with management. These review meetings are an important part of the ongoing relationship between the organization and the rating agency. A credit watch or rating review is issued if there is a reason to believe that the review may lead to an unfavorable credit rating change.

4. CREDIT RATING SCALES

The scales used for bond credit ratings by the primary agencies recognized by the US SEC are shown in Exhibits 11.5 (long-term bonds) and 11.6 (short-term issues). Note that short-term credit uses a different system of ratings and is primarily for commercial paper, but could include debentures and other issues. The main reason for the difference in rating systems is that long-term debt has more possible options and variations that affect the ratings, and the maturity and seniority of the issue often play a major role in the ultimate ratings. Short-term issues, on the other hand, tend to be more standardized in their structure and options, so a narrow range of ratings is appropriate.

EXHIBIT 11.5 **LONG-TERM BOND CREDIT RATINGS**

Definitions	Moody's	S&P	Fitch	DBRS	JCR
Investment Grade					
Prime (Maximum Safety)	Aaa	AAA	AAA	AAA	AAA
High Grade (High Quality)	Aa1 to Aa3	AA+ to AA-	AA+ to AA-	AA	AA
Upper Medium Grade	A1 to A3	A+ to A-	A+ to A-	A	A
Lower Medium Grade	Baa1 to Baa3	BBB+ to BBB-	BBB+ to BBB-	BBB	BBB
Below or Non-Investment Grade					
Below Investment Grade	Ba1	BB+	BB+	–	–
Speculative	Ba2 to Ba3	BB to BB-	BB to BB-	BB	BB
Highly Speculative	B1 to B3	B+ to B-	B+ to B-	B	B
Substantial Risk	Caa	CCC+	CCC	CCC to C	CCC
In Poor Standing	–	CCC to CCC-	–	–	CC
Extremely Speculative	Ca	CC	CC	–	C
May Be in Default	C	C	C	–	LD
Default	–	D	DDD to D	D	D

EXHIBIT 11.6 **SHORT-TERM ISSUE CREDIT RATINGS**

Definitions	S&P	Moody's	Fitch	JCR
Investment Grade				
Highest Quality	A-1	Prime-1	F1	J-1
Good Quality	A-2	Prime-2	F2	J-2
Adequate Credit	A-3	Prime-3	F3	J-3
Speculative Grade				
Vulnerable to Changes	B-1 to B-3	NP	B	NJ
High Default Risk	C	NP	C	NJ
Under Regulatory Supervision	R	NP	RD	NJ
Default	SD or D	NP	D	NJ

VI. SUMMARY

Short-term borrowing and investing is a critical part of day-to-day liquidity management for any treasury professional. The first part of this chapter discussed the various issues related to management of short-term portfolios, including internal versus external management, investment strategies, reporting, and securities safekeeping. It also introduced some of the risks associated with managing a short-term portfolio. (These risks are covered in more depth in Chapter 15, Operational and Enterprise Risk Management, and Chapter 16, Financial Risk Management.) And it presented pricing and yield calculations and discussed yield curves and their impact on portfolio management. In the next part of the chapter, various forms of short-term borrowing were discussed, including pricing and cost calculations for typical short-term credit facilities. The final sections of the chapter covered some of the issues related to pricing of both short- and long-term borrowing, which included a discussion of credit rating agencies (or NRSROs).

APPENDIX 11.1: LISTING OF SOME MAJOR CREDIT RATING AGENCIES

- Moody's Investors Service [US]
- Standard & Poor's (S&P) [US]
- Fitch Ratings [US and UK]
- Credit Rating Information Service of India (CRISIL)
- Japan Credit Rating Agency (JCR)
- Credit Analysis & Research (CARE) [India]
- DBRS (formerly Dominion Bond Rating Service) [Canada]
- Brickwork Ratings [India]
- A.M. Best (US-based insurance companies)
- ICRA (formerly Investment Information and Credit Rating Agency of India)
- Kroll Bond Rating Agency (KBRA) [US]
- Veda (formerly Baycorp Advantage) [Australia]
- China Credit Information Service (CCIS)
- RAM Holdings (formerly Rating Agency Malaysia Berhad)
- Egan-Jones Ratings Company [US]
- The Pakistan Credit Rating Agency Limited (PACRA)

TEST YOUR UNDERSTANDING: CHAPTER 11

Answers are on pages 688–692.

1. Compare and contrast in-house and outsourced investment management.
2. What is the difference between a broker-dealer and a registered investment advisor?
3. What are the key elements in a short-term investment policy?
4. Describe the basic short-term investment strategies that are available to an organization.
5. What is a yield curve?
6. Yield on a short-term investment is a function of what three factors?
7. Name the principal types of short-term funding available to most companies.
8. What are the costs typically involved with a line of credit?
9. What are the basic components of interest rates for borrowing?
10. Compare and contrast short-term and long-term borrowing.
11. What are loan covenants?
12. What are the two major classes of credit ratings?

CHAPTER 12
Long-Term and Capital Investments

I. INTRODUCTION

Chapter 6 introduced the concept of capital markets and discussed the various types of instruments that were available for long-term investments. This chapter discusses some of the tools and techniques that are appropriate for managing long-term investments.[1]

Long-term investments are often referred to as *capital investments*. One reason for this is that they take advantage of the capital markets previously discussed. A second reason is that because these are longer-term investments, the funds involved are typically not day-to-day operating funds but longer-term (capital) assets of the company. Assets that are appropriate for long-term investment are often less liquid than those used for short-term investment and are therefore considered to be riskier since they may require that the investor have the ability to hold the asset for an indefinite period of time.

As noted at the beginning of Chapter 11, Short-Term Investing and Borrowing, many of the issues discussed in that chapter also apply to long-term investment portfolios. Differences, where appropriate, are noted as part of the discussion in this chapter.

II. MANAGING CAPITAL MARKET INVESTMENTS

A. Objectives of Capital Market Investments

When determining an organization's capital market investment objectives, it is important to remember that these goals must be expressed in terms of both risk and return, and should conform to the organization's investment policies. In addition to trying to achieve direct financial returns, organizations may have strategic reasons for specific investments (e.g., to encourage development of needed technology, support specific trading partners, or position themselves for future acquisitions or mergers). This type of strategic investing is particularly common in industries such as the high-tech and pharmaceuticals industries because of the large amount of research and development needed to develop new products.

A careful analysis of the investor's risk tolerance is a starting point for setting any of the objectives relative to investment allocations and selections. Once the tolerance for risk has been determined, the types of return required by the investor must be considered. The return objective may be stated in terms of:

- An absolute return (e.g., an annualized return of 2.5%)
- A relative return (e.g., exceeds the return on 10-year US Treasuries by 50 basis points)
- A general goal (e.g., current income, capital appreciation, capital preservation, or total return[2])

Capital preservation generally means that investors want to maintain the purchasing power of their investments while minimizing the risk of loss. While this is a suitable short-term investment management strategy, it may not always fit into the guidelines

1. Managing the financial risk in both short- and long-term portfolios is discussed in Chapter 16, Financial Risk Management.
2. When the return objective is stated in terms of a general goal, such as current income, the aim is actually to maximize that target area in order to achieve the highest possible value that is consistent with other investment requirements.

for capital investments, where the assumption is that the organization has the ability to "ride out" short-term market downturns that could be detrimental to a short-term portfolio. This assertion proves to be true, for example, when an investment portfolio consists of long-term fixed income and stock issues, which may fluctuate significantly in price over the short term but tend to produce greater income over the longer term if the investor has the ability to ride out the short-term losses to achieve the longer-term gains.

A more likely return objective for a capital investment portfolio will be some mix between current income (e.g., from annual coupon payments on bonds and dividends from stock) and capital appreciation (e.g., from a rise in the market price of securities). The investment return objective may also be impacted by the intended use for those returns. For example, if the portfolio is to be used for pension fund purposes, then the portfolio manager may want to structure the cash flows and maturities of the portfolio carefully to match the projected needs for the pension payments. As another example, if the projected use for the funds is to provide a sinking fund for repayment of a debt issue's principal, then investments would be structured specifically to meet those needs.

Exhibit 12.1 provides a list of issues that treasury professionals should consider when setting their capital market investment objectives.

EXHIBIT 12.1 **OBJECTIVES OF CAPITAL MARKET INVESTMENTS**

OBJECTIVES OF CAPITAL MARKET INVESTMENTS

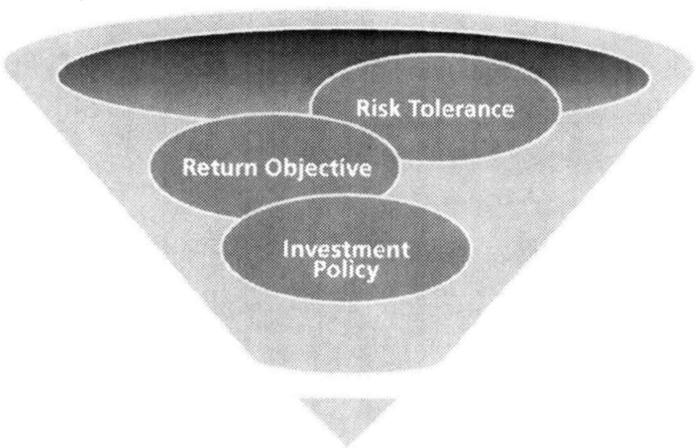

Some mix between current income and capital appreciation

ISSUES TO CONSIDER:

- Risk preferences for portfolio
- Return objectives
- Liquidity needs
- Time horizons or future needs for funds
- Tax issues
- Legal or regulatory factors (especially for pension fund investments)

As with short-term investments, organizations also need a long-term investment policy. Typically the biggest differences in the two policies will be the overall investment guidelines and the permitted investments. Some companies combine short-term and long-term policies into one policy, with separate sections for the items that vary but common requirements for such things as reporting and exception management.

B. The Asset Allocation Decision

One of the key decisions in managing a portfolio of long-term, capital market investments is that of asset allocation, or the mix between fixed-income (debt) and equity (stock) securities.[3] Although there are some variations, fixed-income securities generally tend to provide their returns in the form of income while equity investments are usually a mix of both income and capital appreciation (and potentially depreciation or loss). As a result, fixed-income securities, as the name implies, provide a relatively predictable stream of income over time.

Equities, on the other hand, have a higher potential for long-term gain, since the investor is benefiting from any increase in value of the underlying company, but equities also run the risk of a loss if the investment must be liquidated at a time when the value of the stock has declined.

The basic structure of the long-term asset allocation for any portfolio will be highly dependent on the objectives outlined for that portfolio. Generally, the longer the desired maturity of the portfolio and the greater the tolerance for risk, the higher the level of equity used in the portfolio, since equity has no maturity date and may have greater risk of short-term loss. Taxes must also be considered, especially when there are significant differences between tax rates on interest income versus capital gains.

C. Long-Term Fixed-Income (Debt) Portfolio Management

The management of a long-term fixed-income investment portfolio is also a part of some organizations' financial decision-making processes. This is especially true of entities that must manage large loss or cash reserves, such as insurance companies, financial intermediaries, or educational institutions.

Many of the policy and procedure issues related to the management of a long-term fixed-income portfolio are the same as those related to short-term investments, discussed in Chapter 11, Short-Term Investing and Borrowing. The key difference is that managing maturities and duration becomes a much bigger issue with long-term investments.

1. DURATION

Duration is one of the key measures of risk for a bond or fixed-income portfolio. It is important because it gives an estimate of the volatility of an investment, since bonds with higher durations typically have greater price volatility than bonds with lower durations (given equal credit, inflation, and reinvestment risk). Generally, the longer the duration, the more sensitive the bond or portfolio is to changes in interest rates.

3. A long-term portfolio may generate some cash due to normal operations (also referred to as *residual cash*), but cash and cash equivalents are normally considered part of short-term investment management unless and until invested in a capital asset.

Duration measures the number of years required to recover the true cost of a bond, considering the present value of all coupon and principal payments received in the future. Duration, in its simplest form, is the weighted average time to receipt of all future cash flows associated with a bond investment, including interest payments, discount accretion, premium amortization, and payment of principal. Because a bond generally pays interest periodically and may accrue additional principal if purchased at a discount to its maturity value (or depreciate if bought at a premium), it can be viewed as having an average maturity of all these cash flows that is different from its final maturity. Duration is simply the weighted average amount of time needed before all of the various cash flows from the bond pay back the initial cost of the bond.

In the simplest case, a zero-coupon bond, where all payments for the bond are made at maturity, would have a duration that was equal to the actual maturity of the bond. On the other hand, a bond that pays interest semiannually would have a much shorter duration, as part of the initial investment is returned with each interest payment. As more and more payments are received earlier in the life of the bond (through coupons or interest payments), the duration continues to shorten compared to the overall maturity of the bond.

For example, assume that an investor has purchased a three-year $10,000 bond paying a 10% annual coupon, and interest rates (for present value purposes) are currently at 5%.

The market price of the bond would be:

$$\text{Price} = \$1{,}000 / (1.05)^1 + \$1{,}000 / (1.05)^2 + \$11{,}000 / (1.05)^3$$

$$= \$952.38 + \$907.03 + \$9{,}502.21 = \$11{,}361.62$$

And its duration would be:

$$\text{Duration} = (1 \times \$952.38 / \$11{,}361.62) + (2 \times \$907.03 / \$11{,}361.62) + (3 \times 9{,}502.21 / \$11{,}361.62)$$

$$= 0.0838 + 0.1597 + 2.509 = 2.75$$

In other words, it will take 2.75 years to recover the actual cost of the bond.

As explained in Chapter 9, Working Capital Metrics, the present value (PV) of any investment is the sum total of all future financial income, each receipt discounted at a rate commensurate with the perceived risk. Chapter 9 also explains that as the receipt of a cash benefit is pushed further and further into the future, the PV of that benefit diminishes. Bonds are no exception. Therefore, the risk of recovering the full face value of the bond increases with the time to maturity. But in the interim, a percentage of the purchase price may be recovered as a function of the coupon rate of the bond. A bond with a higher coupon rate—say, 6%, or $60, per year—will return a higher percentage of the bond's current market value over a given number of years when compared to a bond of similar maturity but with a lower coupon rate—say, 3% per year. Notice that the duration on any bond that pays coupons will be less than the maturity because some amount of the payments are going to come before the maturity date.

Some of the factors that affect bond duration are:

- **Time to Maturity:** Consider two bonds, each with a cost of $1,000 and an annual yield of 5%. A bond that matures in one year would more quickly repay its true cost than a bond that matures in 10 years. As a result, the shorter-maturity bond would have a lower duration and less price risk. The longer the maturity, the higher the duration.

- **Coupon Rate:** A bond's payment is a key factor in calculating duration. If two otherwise identical bonds pay different coupon rates—say, 7% and 3%—the bond with the 7% coupon will pay back its original cost more quickly than the lower-yielding bond and will therefore have a shorter duration. All else being equal, the higher the coupon (or interest payment), the lower the duration.

The calculation of bond duration brings all these factors together in one number, providing a measurement of a bond's price sensitivity to changes in market interest rates. As a result, duration can also provide some estimate of how a bond will respond to changes in the general level of interest rates. Once a bond has been created and its interest rate (coupon rate) fixed, its value will change should it be sold in the market where yields demanded by investors have risen or fallen. When interest rates rise, the market value of existing bonds declines. This decline results in a price for lower-interest bonds that is at a discount to their final maturity value (par or 100). For an investor purchasing a discounted bond, the recaptured discount at maturity adds to the bond's total return, thus providing a return that is higher than just the stated interest rate. This outcome raises the overall yield to maturity to a level consistent with the market rate.

Conversely, when interest rates fall, existing bonds rise in market value and trade at premium prices (greater than par). When such a bond matures, an investor who bought the bond at a premium will not recover that premium amount. Thus, the return is marginally diminished to a rate below the stated interest rate but equal to the market rate.

The magnitude of these discounts and premiums for bonds can be predicted using duration. For every change in interest rates of one full percentage point (100 basis points), a bond's price will likely change at a percentage rate that is roughly equal to its duration. As an example, if interest rates rise by 100 basis points (one full percentage point), then the price of a bond with a duration of four years would fall by about 4%.

Another advantage of using duration as a risk measure for a portfolio of fixed-income securities is that it is easy to calculate the overall duration by taking a simple weighted average of the individual investments. The weights used in this calculation are the proportions of the portfolio invested in each security.

2. INTEREST RATE RISK

Duration helps treasury professionals to understand the concept of interest rate risk, or the risk from changes in market value for fixed-income investments when the general level of market rates fluctuates.

As an example, compare the price action[4] for a 1-year bond and a 10-year bond, both with the same stated interest rate (known as the *coupon rate*) of 3%. Assume that both bonds were purchased originally at par (100) for $1 million. Assume also that right after the bonds were purchased, the general rate of interest rose by 100 basis points to a new market rate of 4%.

4. The term *price action* refers to the movement of a security's price in response to various market factors.

Exhibit 12.2 demonstrates the impact on the pricing of the 1- and 10-year bonds under these circumstances. Due to its longer maturity, and therefore longer stream of coupon payments, the 10-year bond shows a much greater change in price than the 1-year bond. As discussed above, the duration measure provides a rough estimate of the impact of changes in interest rates on the price of the bond. For the 1-year bond, the duration of 0.9926 would predict a drop in the bond price of about 1% for a 1% interest rate increase, which is close to the actual percentage change. For the 10-year bond, the duration of 8.6354 indicates a much greater price drop (approximately 8.6%) for a 1% increase in interest rates—close to the 8.2% actual drop in price. Thus, higher duration equates to higher interest rate risk.

EXHIBIT 12.2 **DURATION'S IMPACT ON INTEREST RATE RISK**

Par Value	Coupon Rate	Maturity	Market Rate (Yield to Maturity)	Market Price	Gross Market Value	Change	Percentage Change	Duration
$1,000,000	3.00%	1 Year	4.00%	$99.029	$990,292.20	$(9,707.80)	-0.9708%	0.9926
$1,000,000	3.00%	10 Years	4.00%	$91.829	$918,294.79	$(81,705.21)	-8.1705%	8.6354

NOTE: Typically bonds with different maturities will not have the same coupon rate. This example uses identical rates to simplify comparability of the instruments.

3. DIVERSIFICATION

Just as with equity portfolios (discussed below and in Chapter 6, Capital Markets), diversification can help reduce the overall risk of a fixed-income portfolio. Combining a variety of investments with differing characteristics in a portfolio can significantly reduce the amount of investment risk inherent in any individual investment. The basic theory is that even if one investment loses value, others will gain value and help offset the loss.

4. FIXED-DEBT TO FLOATING-DEBT RATIO

In addition to interest rate risk, many fixed-income portfolio managers also use the ratio of fixed-rate obligations to floating-rate obligations to monitor their portfolios. This relation is usually expressed in terms of a target fixed/floating ratio. In general, the ratio of fixed-rate to floating-rate investments tends to correspond to an organization's views on long-term interest rates. A firm that thinks interest rates are going to rise is likely to have more floating-rate than fixed-rate investments in its portfolio, while a firm that expects rates to drop is more likely to invest in a higher percentage of fixed-rate obligations. In addition, companies tend to use more floating-rate debt when they have sufficient financial strength to support the additional interest rate exposure. However, the proportion of fixed- to floating-rate debt varies widely among companies, suggesting that there is as much art as science in determining the appropriate mix.

The drawback to managing a portfolio solely on the ratio of fixed-rate debt to floating-rate debt is that it only considers one operational target and fails to take into account the terms of the actual securities in the portfolio. Since bonds can vary in maturity from 1 to 30 years (or longer), the ratio of fixed-rate debt to total debt reveals very little about the debt's maturity profile and the risks associated with it. As a result, it is also important to take into account the average term to maturity of the portfolio, as well as the overall duration of the portfolio.

5. FOREIGN-CURRENCY-DENOMINATED INVESTMENTS

When foreign-currency-denominated investments are included in a portfolio, the investment manager must consider the impact of fluctuating exchange rates on the overall portfolio value. This means that in addition to default and interest rate risks, foreign exchange (FX) risk must also be considered. The use of FX derivatives for risk management is discussed in Chapter 16, Financial Risk Management.

6. USING DERIVATIVES IN A LONG-TERM FIXED-INCOME PORTFOLIO

Due to the risks associated with a long-term fixed-income portfolio, a portfolio manager will typically utilize derivative instruments to mitigate these risks. Interest rate futures, forwards, options, and swaps can be used to manage interest rate risk. Credit default swaps[5] can be used to manage credit risk, and FX futures, forwards, options, and swaps can be used to manage currency risk. Nothing comes without a cost, however. While proper use of derivatives can reduce overall risk, the cost of using them will also reduce the potential profit. The use of these instruments is discussed in more detail in Chapter 16, Financial Risk Management.

7. ASSET/LIABILITY MANAGEMENT

Whenever an investment portfolio utilizes borrowed funds as part of its overall strategy, the issue of asset/liability management arises. This is primarily an issue for banks and large financial institutions that fund their investments with either deposits or borrowed funds. In many cases, the issue is expressed in terms of a maturity mismatch; that is, the institution may be borrowing funds in the short-term markets (e.g., by using commercial paper) while using the proceeds from the financing to purchase long-term assets.

This strategy can be profitable as long as the yield curve is upward sloping (i.e., when short-term rates are lower than long-term rates), the value of the long-term assets remains stable, and short-term credit is readily available. In the Recession of 2009, however, all of these factors turned unfavorable at the same time, resulting in serious valuation and liquidity problems for many large financial institutions. In the current environment (at the time of publication), the yield curve is still fairly flat, but it is positive and short-term credit has become much more available due to government intervention.

8. SECURITIES LENDING

One technique that is available to help manage long-term assets is securities lending. Securities lending is a practice where the owner of specific securities lends them to another party. The terms of the securities lending agreement normally require the borrower to provide the lender of the securities with collateral, in the form of other securities or a letter of credit, equal to or greater in value than the securities that are being lent. The primary purpose of the loan is to allow the borrower to hedge or short-sell securities that it does not own, in anticipation of the value of the security declining. (See Chapter 16, Financial Risk Management, for a discussion of hedging and short sales.) In return, the borrower pays the lender a negotiated fee. Loaned securities are also used to cover

5. A credit default swap, or CDS, is an arrangement whereby the seller of the CDS will pay the buyer in the event of a loan default or other credit event (e.g., bankruptcy) on the part of a particular issuer. It is, in effect, a form of insurance against loss due to credit issues. A "naked" CDS is a CDS where the buyer does not actually have any investment in or exposure to the firm covered by the CDS, and is an investment vehicle rather than an insurance or hedging tool.

or eliminate "failed transactions."[6] The practice allows owners of long-term securities to earn additional income on holdings that they cannot or do not want to actually sell out of their portfolio.

D. EQUITY (STOCK) PORTFOLIO MANAGEMENT

As discussed in Chapter 11, Short-Term Investing and Borrowing, there are a variety of strategies for managing an investment portfolio. At the most general level, managing an equity portfolio usually comes down to either a passive or an active management strategy. The passive approach is basically a buy-and-hold strategy and is often related to managing the portfolio relative to an index (i.e., buy same or similar stocks to those in some well-known index, such as the Dow Jones Industrial Average or the Standard & Poor's [S&P] 500, a practice that is sometimes referred to as *index investing*). An active management strategy attempts to outperform, on a risk-adjusted basis, some benchmark portfolio, which may be an index or some other common measure.

It is beyond the scope of this book to go into the detailed discussion of managing a long-term equity portfolio. Rather, the section below discusses some of the basic concepts of equity portfolio management, as well as methods for determining the relative risk and return of equity securities, all of which should be considered in developing an overall investment strategy.

1. DEFINING AND MEASURING INVESTMENT RISK

Risk is associated with the possibility that actual results may differ from expected results and with the estimation of how large this difference may be. The risk associated with an investment in financial assets is the possibility that realized returns may differ from those expected by investors. Financial professionals use standard deviation[7] to assess the amount by which actual returns are likely to deviate from expected returns. An expected return is merely a weighted average of the returns that the market or an individual analyst thinks may occur.

Expected return and standard deviation are used to make quantitative assessments of possible investment outcomes and the degree of confidence (probabilities) that may be attached to them. Oftentimes, an investment's expected return and standard deviation are adequate for evaluating the investment merits of an asset when the asset is considered in isolation and without regard to the possibility that it is owned in combination with other assets. When an asset is owned in combination with others (called a *portfolio of assets*), a different perspective on risk is needed because the overall riskiness of a portfolio is more dependent on the covariance of the assets with each other than on the individual asset variances (or standard deviations). The covariance measures how two or more assets change relative to one another.

2. DIVERSIFICATION

One of the most common tenets of equity portfolio management is that of diversification. The basic idea is that combining stocks into a portfolio can significantly reduce the amount of investment risk. This principle is explained in more detail in the next section on the capital asset pricing model. For the purposes of the discussion on managing equity portfolios, it will be assumed that most rational investors will, if given a choice, hold a diversified portfolio of stocks. Note that while this discussion focuses on equities, a growing number of companies are including alternative investments such as real estate, commodities, and even art in their long-term investment portfolios.

6. A "failed transaction" occurs when the seller of securities is unable to deliver them on the settlement date for some reason. The seller, or its broker, can borrow the proper security to avoid the failed transaction. The borrowed securities are typically returned when the seller is able to actually deliver the originally promised securities.

7. Standard deviation is a typical statistical measure used to determine the potential variability of some variable. Technically, the standard deviation is the square root of the variance of the distribution of a particular variable. It usually is calculated from the historical (past) values of that variable and can be used to determine the future probability of some specific value for the variable in question.

3. CAPITAL ASSET PRICING MODEL (CAPM)

The CAPM describes one possible relationship between risk and the required rate of return on an asset. In the case of common stock, the CAPM is based on the concept that a sensible investor holds a diversified portfolio of stocks to mitigate risk. As more stocks are added to a portfolio, the overall riskiness and variability of the portfolio is reduced. Many studies show that company-specific return variation is almost completely eliminated in portfolios when 25 to 40 stocks in a variety of industries are owned.

The source of return variation that remains is related to fluctuations in the overall economy and stock market. The measure of this systematic risk is determined by finding the relationship between the returns on the specific stock and the stock market. The commonly used measure of the stock market for this determination is the S&P 500. Using historical data for the specific stock and the index, a regression analysis produces a statistical description of how the returns on a stock increase or decrease in response to an increase or decrease in overall stock market returns. The analysis also shows that some portion of a stock's return is related to market return in a systematic manner.

The outcome of this statistical analysis is known as the *beta* (ß) and measures how volatile a stock's return is relative to the market. The market rises and falls over time, so one may consider that the market is 100%, or one time, as volatile as itself. This means that the market, by definition, has a beta of 1.00. If a stock's return tends to rise and fall 120% as fast as the market, it would have a beta of 1.20 and be more risky than the market itself. Companies with variable earnings (e.g., technology companies or those in extractive or construction businesses) tend to have beta values greater than 1.00.

On the other hand, another company may have earnings that rise or fall only 60% as fast as the overall market, and so it will have a beta of 0.60 and be less risky than the market. Utility companies and entities that sell consumer staple goods tend to have beta values that are less than 1.00.

A company's beta will change over time if the degree of stability in its business changes. Factors that can affect a company's beta include such things as new competitors, market consolidation, getting picked up by an analyst, or being added to an index. Because beta values do change over time, a more recently computed beta is more useful than one that is a bit stale.

EXHIBIT 12.3 AVERAGE BETAS FOR SELECTED INDUSTRIES

Industry	Average Beta
Apparel	1.36
Pharmacy Services	1.17
Household Products	0.98
Power	1.35
Retail/Wholesale Food	0.68
Semiconductor	1.49
Water (Utility)	0.49

SOURCE: "Betas by Sector" as of January 2013, from NYU Stern School of Business's website (http://pages.stern.nyu.edu/~adamodar/New_Home_Page/datafile/Betas.html, accessed September 10, 2013).

Consider the examples in Exhibit 12.3. For staple goods and other products with stable usage in most economic environments, company stock beta values tend to be less than 1.00. This is because purchases of basic food and personal care products (e.g., retail/wholesale food and water industries in Exhibit 12.3) do not decrease proportionately with declines in the rate of macroeconomic growth, nor do they increase proportionately with a rise in the rate of growth. Sales and profits of department and general merchandise stores (e.g., household products industry in Exhibit 12.3) tend to mirror overall economic performance, which is reflected in an average beta of around 1.00. Purchases of industrial equipment, such as machine tools and semiconductor manufacturing equipment (e.g., semiconductor industry in Exhibit 12.3) are very sensitive to overall economic performance because revenues from sales of the end products they are used to make fluctuate with the economy. Accordingly, their profitability and stock returns are more volatile than the average for all companies, and they therefore have high beta values.

The CAPM is used to estimate the required rate of return for a diversified investor on a given company's common equity. This estimate is a function of the underlying risk-free rate of return in the economy, the risk premium the market expects above the risk-free rate, and a particular stock's beta. The relationship is linear and is expressed algebraically as:

$$r_E = r_{RF} + (r_M - r_{RF})\, ß_i$$

Where:

r_E = Required rate of return on stockholders' equity

r_{RF} = Expected rate of return on the risk-free asset (e.g., T-bill rate)

r_M = Expected rate of return on the market portfolio (e.g., S&P 500 index)

$ß_i$ = Beta value for stock i

The return on the risk-free asset typically is measured by the return on short-term government securities, such as the US T-bill. Another approach is to use a risk-free rate with a maturity that matches the asset's maturity. In this case, a long-term government security rate could be used as a risk-free rate for long-term bonds or stocks. The choice depends upon an analyst's viewpoint.

Calculation Example: Capital Asset Pricing Model (CAPM)

Suppose that the risk-free rate of return (e.g., the T-bill rate) is 2.0%, and the expected or historical rate of return on the stock market is 8.0%. Historically, Company X has had a beta of about 1.50. Given this beta, Company X's required rate of return is estimated to be:

$$r_E = r_{RF} + (r_M - r_{RF})\,\beta_i$$

$$= 0.02 + (0.08 - 0.02)(1.50)$$

$$= 0.110, \text{ or } 11.0\%$$

In the market environment represented by the risk-free rate and the expected return on the market, Company X's stock is expected to return 11.0% to satisfy investors. The required return is greater than the expected return on the market because Company X's stock is more risky than the market.

In another example, the beta of Company Y, a seller of staple food products, has averaged around 0.60 over time. Company Y's required return is therefore:

$$r_E = r_{RF} + (r_M - r_{RF})\,\beta_i$$

$$= 0.02 + (0.08 - 0.02)(0.60)$$

$$= 0.056, \text{ or } 5.6\%$$

If an investor in Company Y experienced a 5.6% return, the reward is commensurate with the systematic risk of the company. There is no basis for complaint that the return is less than the market return since the risk borne is also less than the risk represented by the market. Companies X and Y bring different levels of nondiversified, systematic risk to a portfolio. The difference in their required rates of return is based on this difference in systematic risk, as measured by their respective beta values.

The concept of CAPM is also discussed in Chapter 20, Financial Decisions and Management, to estimate the cost of equity raised for a company.

4. DETERMINING PORTFOLIO RISK AND RETURN

One of the biggest benefits of using CAPM and beta for equity portfolio management is the ability to determine a portfolio's average return and overall riskiness by simply taking the weighted average of the returns and the betas of the individual stocks.

Calculation Example: Portfolio Beta and Return

Using the two stocks from the previous example (Company X and Company Y), and assuming a two-stock portfolio consisting of 70% Company X stock and 30% Company Y stock, the calculations for the portfolio beta and expected return (expressed as a percentage return) are as follows:

$$\text{Portfolio } \beta = (\% \text{ of Co. X Stock} \times \text{Co. X } \beta) + (\% \text{ of Co. Y Stock} \times \text{Co. Y } \beta)$$

$$= (0.70 \times 1.50) + (0.30 \times 0.60) = 1.23$$

$$\text{Portfolio Return} = (\% \text{ of Co. X Stock} \times \text{Co. X Return}) + (\% \text{ of Co. Y Stock} \times \text{Co. Y Return})$$

$$= (0.70 \times 0.11) + (0.30 \times 0.056) = 0.0938, \text{ or } 9.38\%$$

It should be noted that the same portfolio return is obtained if the portfolio beta is used to calculate the required rate of return with the CAPM equation:

$$r_E = r_{RF} + (r_M - r_{RF})\,\beta_i$$

$$= 0.02 + (0.08 - 0.02)(1.23)$$

$$= 0.938, \text{ or } 9.38\%$$

III. VALUATION OF LONG-TERM SECURITIES

Publicly traded corporate securities are valued by financial markets. A security, or any economic asset, derives its value from the cash flow stream expected by investors over the asset's life and the risk associated with the possibility that the cash stream may not be realized as expected. The valuation of the anticipated cash benefit stream involves discounting the stream at the market's required rate of return, which is a function of the stream's risk. This rate of return represents an investor's opportunity cost (i.e., the rate of return that can be earned on investments of the same risk). That said, the asset's market value is the present value of the anticipated cash stream that is discounted using a rate appropriate to the stream's risk. Expressed algebraically, this idea may be represented as the summation of all the asset's cash flows over the investor's holding period, discounted at the appropriate opportunity cost. This concept can be written using the following formula:

$$PV_0 = \sum_{t=1}^{n} \frac{CF_t}{(1+k_i)^t} = \frac{CF_1}{(1+k_i)^1} + \frac{CF_2}{(1+k_i)^2} + \ldots + \frac{CF_n}{(1+k_i)^n}$$

Where:

PV_0 = Current value of the asset

CF_t = Cash flow for the asset for Periods 1 through n

k_i = Opportunity cost or required rate of return for asset type i

NOTE: In this equation, the Σ sign indicates a summation of the factor following the symbol. In this case, the variable t runs from 1 to n in the summation.

This model works for any type of asset or stream of cash flows. The investor estimates the cash flows for the asset, determines the appropriate required rate of return, and then calculates the asset's value. Asset valuation can be performed on a financial calculator or with spreadsheet software.

A. Bond or Fixed-Income Valuation

The valuation of bonds, or any other fixed-income security, is straightforward because the amount and timing of future cash flows are specified. In the case of a fixed-rate bond, the amount and timing of interest (coupon) payments and principal repayments are stated in the indenture. As noted earlier, bond interest payments usually are made semiannually. A bond's market price is the present value of the stream of interest payments plus the present value of the principal repayment, where discounting occurs at the market's required rate of return. This required rate is simply the interest rate the market is demanding over the remaining life of the bond at a particular point in time. This rate is called the *yield to maturity (YTM)*.

Putting this into a formula using the example from the section on duration earlier in this chapter, the YTM for a three-year \$10,000 bond with a 10% coupon rate selling at a market price of \$11,362 would be calculated as:

$$\$1{,}000 / (1 + \text{YTM})^1 + \$1{,}000 / (1 + \text{YTM})^2 + \$11{,}000 / (1 + \text{YTM})^3 = \$11{,}362$$

$$\text{YTM} = 0.05, \text{ or } 5\%$$

For ease of calculation, this example assumes annual payment of interest instead of the more common semiannual period. In more complicated cases, rather than trying to calculate YTM by hand, there are any number of bond calculators and computer models that will do this automatically given the input data.

If the bond has a call provision (discussed in Chapter 6, Capital Markets), then the yield to call (YTC) should also be computed. This is the yield the bond would provide if the issuer calls it prior to maturity. YTC is calculated in the same manner as the YTM discussed above but uses the call date instead of the maturity date. Since callable bonds usually are called only if interest rates have fallen, the YTC is typically lower than the YTM. One approach to analyzing callable bonds is known as *yield to worst* (*YTW*), where all the possible YTC values are computed and the assumed yield is the lowest of the potential values. This process provides a range of possible outcomes that helps the investor better understand the risk parameters of the investment.

The YTW concept can also be used with other types of bonds. In this context, YTW is the lowest possible yield that can be received on a bond without the issuer actually defaulting. This yield is calculated by making worst-case scenario assumptions on the issue by calculating the returns that would be received if all potentially negative provisions (e.g., prepayments, calls, or sinking funds) are used by the issuer.

B. Preferred Stock Valuation

Preferred stock is equity, but it has features of both debt and equity financing. Like debt, the payment stream (i.e., stream of dividends) is fixed. The annual preferred dividend is stated as a percentage of the stock's par value, but it is paid in quarterly installments to investors. Like debt, preferred stock has a claim above common stock in both going concern and liquidation situations.

Preferred stock is like equity in that bankruptcy is not a possible consequence of missing a dividend payment, the stock does not mature (except in uncommon cases), and its claim on earnings or asset liquidation values is subordinate to all debt claims. From a valuation standpoint, preferred stock is viewed as an annuity that exists into perpetuity. Its market price is found easily by capitalizing the annual interest payment at the market's required return.

Calculation Example: Preferred Stock Valuation

Assume that a $50 par value preferred stock pays a 6.6% annual dividend and that the market currently requires an 8.0% return on the stock. The preferred stock annual dividend is calculated as:

$$\text{Preferred Stock Dividend} = \text{Preferred Stock Dividend Rate} \times \text{Par Value}$$

$$= 0.066 \times \$50 = \$3.30$$

The price of the preferred stock is therefore calculated as:

$$\text{Price of Preferred Stock} = \frac{\text{Preferred Stock Annual Dividend}}{\text{Required Rate of Return}}$$

$$= \frac{\$3.30}{0.08} = \$41.25$$

Next, assume that the market's required return increased to 10.0% due to the perception of increased risk or rising inflation expectations. In this case, the market price of the stock would be recalculated as follows:

$$\text{Price of Preferred Stock} = \frac{\$3.30}{0.10} = \$33.00$$

As these calculations reveal, the market price fell when the required rate of return increased, because the only way a higher return can be achieved from a given stream of receipts is to pay less for the right to receive that stream.

C. Common Stock Valuation

Common stock valuation differs from bond and preferred stock valuation because both the timing and amount of cash flows associated with stock ownership are neither fixed nor known with certainty. A corporation's dividend policy is set by its board of directors, and the actual dividend paid may change over time. A stock investor would expect to sell the shares at some point in the future, but the selling price at that time is unknown today.

To value common stock, it is necessary to estimate the dividend stream and liquidation price, and then assign a required rate of return in order to determine the present value of the estimates. CAPM, discussed earlier in this chapter, can be used to determine the required rates of return on common equity.

In the most general case of valuing stock, the price an investor would be willing to pay is the present value of the future dividend stream[8] (i.e., the summation of all future dividends), discounted by the firm's cost of equity. This concept is shown in the following equation:

$$P_0 = \frac{D_1}{(1+k_s)^1} + \frac{D_2}{(1+k_s)^2} + \frac{D_3}{(1+k_s)^3} + \ldots + \frac{D_\infty}{(1+k_s)^\infty}$$
$$= \sum_{t=1}^{\infty} \frac{D_t}{(1+k_s)^t}$$

Where:

P_0 = Current value of the stock

D_t = Dividend for Periods 1 through ∞ (infinity)

k_s = Required rate of return for the stock

Unfortunately, this formula is difficult to solve unless some assumptions are made about the dividend stream over the life of the stock. One of the most common approaches is to assume that the dividends will grow at some constant rate in the future. If this is the case, then the dividend (D) at a time (t) in the future is simply the current dividend (D_0) multiplied by one plus the estimated growth rate (g) raised to the t power, or:

$$D_t = D_0(1 + g)^t$$

Substituting this computation into the equation from above produces the following:

$$P_0 = \sum_{t=1}^{\infty} \frac{D_0(1 + g)^t}{(1 + k_s)^t}$$

And by substituting the next expected dividend as D_1 (calculated as $D_0[1+g]$), the above equation is reduced to the following form:

$$P_0 = \frac{D_1}{(k_s - g)}$$

8. Most common stock valuation models are based upon the present value of an anticipated stream of dividends. While there are some models that value certain stocks that have no dividends, they are beyond the scope of this book.

This model works well for companies paying a steadily growing dividend, which include a significant portion of large market capitalization (large-cap) firms in the United States. To apply this calculation, an estimate is required for both the growth rate and the required rate of return for the stock. In many cases, growth can be determined from either historical growth patterns or analysts' estimates. As mentioned above, the required rate of return on the stock can be determined using CAPM.

Calculation Example: Common Stock Valuation

The calculation of a simple stock value can be determined using the following assumptions:

- Next dividend (D_0) = \$2.00
- Estimated growth rate (g) = 6%
- Return on stock (k_s) = 13%

The current value (P_0) of the common stock can therefore be calculated as:

$$P_0 = \frac{D_1}{(k_s - g)} = \frac{D_0(1 + g)}{(k_s - g)}$$

$$= \frac{\$2.00\ (1 + 0.06)}{(0.13 - 0.06)} = \frac{\$2.12}{0.07} = \$30.29$$

IV. SUMMARY

Managing long-term, or capital, investments is very different from managing a short-term investment portfolio. In managing a short-term portfolio, the primary objective is capital preservation, since the assets may need to be liquidated at any time. As a result, rate of return, while important, is a secondary concern. When managing a long-term portfolio, a greater degree of risk is acceptable in return for a higher long-term return on investment on the overall portfolio.

Therefore, while risk is still an important concern, it must be weighed against potential return for long-term investments. This chapter discussed this concept of balancing risk and return for long-term investments. It also presented an overview of how that risk/return balance impacts long-term investment objectives and described a number of tools that are available to help manage a long-term investment portfolio, including duration, beta, and CAPM—all of which help predict how the value of a particular investment may change as the overall market changes.

The chapter closed with a discussion of the valuation of a capital market asset as the present value of all of the expected cash flows received in return for the investment, including the eventual sale or redemption of the equity or security. Examples were provided of how this value is calculated for the various types of long-term securities.

TEST YOUR UNDERSTANDING: CHAPTER 12

Answers are on pages 693–696.

1. What are the typical ways of stating a return objective for a long-term portfolio?
2. What are the issues that should be considered in setting capital market investment objectives?
3. Discuss asset allocation.
4. What is duration?
5. What is the importance of the fixed-debt to floating-debt ratio?
6. Describe securities lending.
7. What is CAPM?
8. How is the value of a long-term security established?
9. How is the value of a bond established?
10. How is the value of common stock established?

CHAPTER 13
Cash Forecasting

I. INTRODUCTION

II. PURPOSE OF CASH FORECASTING

III. ISSUES AND OPPORTUNITIES IN FORECASTING

A. Simplicity
B. Collaboration and Communication
C. Duplication

IV. TYPES OF FORECASTS

A. Purpose
B. Forecasting Horizon
C. Update Frequency
D. Projected Closing Cash Position

V. THE FORECASTING PROCESS

A. Cash Flow Components
B. Degree of Certainty
C. Data Identification and Organization
D. Selection and Validation of the Forecasting Method

VI. FORECASTING METHODS

A. Short-Term Forecasting Methods

B. Medium- and Long-Term Forecasting Methods

C. Statistical Methods in Forecasting

VII. BEST PRACTICES FOR CASH FORECASTING

VIII. SUMMARY

I. INTRODUCTION

Cash forecasting assists a treasury professional in planning cash management activities, such as scheduling cash concentration transfers for field and collection accounts, funding disbursement accounts, making short-term investing and borrowing decisions, and establishing and managing target balances for purposes of bank compensation, covenant management, and regulatory requirements. Unfortunately, as important as it is, cash forecasting is still as much an art as it is a science, due to the number of assumptions that must be made and the variability in external events.

In the simplest terms, cash forecasting requires a treasury professional to take three steps:

- Estimate future cash inflows and outflows.
- Generate a pro forma cash position.
- Identify how to cover any cash deficits or use any cash surpluses. The shortfall or surplus is measured relative to the predetermined, minimum desired liquidity or target balances.

Although they have some elements in common, cash forecasts are different from the broader financial models (discussed in more detail in Chapter 19, Financial Planning and Analysis) that are often used in financial decision making. Financial models typically examine projected earnings and expenses—including earnings per share, projected taxes, and other metrics—in an effort to develop pro forma financial statements for planning purposes. Cash forecasting is more concerned with projecting actual cash flows as opposed to creating accounting statements that must comply with GAAP (Generally Accepted Accounting Principles) or IFRS (International Financial Reporting Standards) requirements.

Because they are only as accurate as the data used to create them, cash forecasts should be reviewed and updated frequently, adjusting the forecast with the most current and complete information available.

This chapter examines why forecasting is necessary and what types of forecasts are typically performed by the treasury function. The chapter continues with an overview of the forecasting process and introduces some of the principal forecasting methods. The chapter closes with a discussion of best practices in treasury forecasting.

II. PURPOSE OF CASH FORECASTING

The accurate prediction of cash inflows and outflows over time is an important part of a treasury professional's job and is essential to a variety of tasks:

- **Managing Liquidity:** Forecasting a company's net cash position at different intervals[1] to identify potential cash excesses or shortages is essential for scheduling investment decisions and anticipating borrowing requirements to meet daily obligations. It is the most important reason for cash forecasting.

1. It is important to distinguish between the interval of a forecast, which is the period covered (daily, weekly, monthly, etc.), and the frequency with which the forecast is reviewed and updated. For example, a monthly forecast may be updated weekly as new information on actual cash flows becomes available.

- **Controlling Financial Activities:** Variance analysis that compares actual cash flows with projected cash flows can help identify problems such as unanticipated inventory changes, delays in A/R collection, the mistiming of payments, and fraud or embezzlement. Early identification lets a company initiate corrective measures.
- **Meeting Strategic Objectives:** Cash flow forecasts are used to project future funding requirements and make operating decisions to support a company's strategic plan.
- **Budgeting Capital:** Forecasts of revenue, expenditures, and funding are needed to help evaluate proposed capital expenditures. This topic is discussed in more detail in Chapter 19, Financial Planning and Analysis.
- **Managing Costs:** Cash forecasts are used to help minimize excess bank balances, reduce short-term borrowing costs, and increase short-term investment income.
- **Managing Currency Exposure:** Cash flow forecasts attributable to foreign operations are used to assess the degree of foreign currency exposure and provide information for policies designed to control currency risk.
- **Complying with Regulatory Requirements:** Cash flow forecasts are frequently part of internal control procedures needed to meet various regulatory requirements, such as minimum capital requirements or requirements for imprest tax accounts. This is especially important for publicly traded companies.

III. ISSUES AND OPPORTUNITIES IN FORECASTING

A. Simplicity

The goal of a cash forecast is to create a reasonable snapshot of a company's projected cash position by currency. The key word here is *reasonable*. The necessary degree of accuracy is a function of the purpose of the forecast. A short-term forecast used to manage daily cash position has to be more precise than a long-term forecast used to determine the availability of capital for future expansion of plant or equipment. But neither of these needs to be accurate to the last decimal place. The ultimate goal is to develop a cash forecast with a degree of detail appropriate to its ultimate purpose, not a new financial statement. Spending a significant amount of time and effort trying to produce a forecast that is accurate to the decimal point when accuracy to the nearest hundred or thousand units of currency may be perfectly acceptable is not a good use of resources.

It is important to note that for companies that conduct business in more than one currency or country, forecasts need to be made by currency. Shortfalls in one currency are not automatically offset by excesses in another currency unless specific plans to do so have already been made and put into place. One of the reasons for forecasting is to manage currency exposure, and this cannot be done if everything in the forecasting model is reduced to a company's base or home currency.

B. Collaboration and Communication

Treasury is dependent upon business units to provide the information and assumptions needed to create a good forecast. Failure to know about impending payments or delays in collections can doom a forecast from the outset. This need for collaboration with other units in the company, such as A/P, A/R, tax, and financial planning and analysis (FP&A), creates a need for effective communication, clear expectations, and common terminology.

C. Duplication

Due to the many uses of a cash forecast and the similarity to financial statements, departments besides treasury (e.g., FP&A, capital budgeting, or tax departments) often develop forecasts of their own. It is important to realize that while the end purposes of the forecasts are different, the information and assumptions used are usually similar and should agree with each other. Unless the various departments that use forecasts cooperate, there is typically a duplication of effort that costs an organization in time and effort. A less obvious issue is that because the forecasts are developed by different people using different inputs and assumptions, the results are often different—sometimes significantly different. This variation in forecasts based on different assumptions can ultimately result in a lack of trust by management in any of the forecasts.

The important issue is the overall coordination of various areas in an organization that develop financial forecasts and models. It is a best practice to collaborate with other functional areas that develop forecasts to ensure access to the best available information and to help foster consistency in assumptions.

IV. TYPES OF FORECASTS

How a cash forecast is developed depends on its purpose, the forecasting horizon or time frame, and the frequency with which the forecast is updated. The type of forecast may also be affected by the company's size and industry, as well as the available forecasting tools and sources of information.

A. Purpose

Forecasts serve a variety of purposes, from making short-term investment decisions to planning long-term capital requirements and making strategic decisions about projects and long-term investments. Whatever the actual purpose, forecasts can be broken down into two major categories:

- **Predictive forecasts** attempt to predict or project what will happen in the future. They can be used to answer questions such as "How much cash will I have available to invest over the next week?" or "Will I need to borrow money against my line of credit in the next week?"
- **Analytical forecasts,** also referred to as *simulations,* are used to answer what-if questions or to predict the financial impact of a given project. They are particularly useful in strategic planning around things like capital investments or tax planning.

B. Forecasting Horizon

The time interval over which information is to be forecasted is an important consideration because a method appropriate for a short-term forecast will not be appropriate for longer-term forecasts, and vice versa. In most companies, short-term forecasting is the responsibility of treasury while longer-term forecasts are often done by FP&A or capital budgeting.

- **Short-Term Forecasting:** Short-term forecasts typically range from one to thirty days in length and predict cash receipts and disbursements, as well as the resulting balances, on a daily, weekly, or monthly basis. They aid in scheduling cash transfers, funding disbursement accounts, and making short-term investing and borrowing decisions. Short-term forecasting is also important for establishing and managing target balances for purposes of bank compensation. There is a growing trend on the part of some companies to create intraday cash forecasts in an attempt to reduce potential overdrafts and other related bank fees. This trend is supported by the availability of intraday balance reporting data from many banks (see discussion in Chapter 14, Information Technology in Treasury).
- **Medium-Term Forecasting:** Cash flow forecasts from one to twelve months in length are an integral part of cash budgeting and are considered medium-term forecasts. They project the inflows (e.g., collections from sales and other sources of funds) and outflows (e.g., expenses and other uses of funds) on a monthly basis. They are used to determine the company's need for short-term credit or the availability of funds for short-term investing. They also serve as a benchmark for performance by comparing actual cash flows to projected cash flows based on the cash budget.
- **Long-Term Forecasting:** Long-term forecasts cover any period beyond one year. They take into consideration projections of long-term sales and expenditures, as well as market factors. These forecasts are of strategic importance because they help inform decisions about which type and amount of long-term financing to obtain, and the timing of obtaining funds. Financial institutions and rating agencies also use long-term forecasts for credit analysis and evaluation purposes.

C. Update Frequency

The frequency and type of update are also important factors to consider when working with forecasts:

- **Static Forecasts:** As the name implies, a static forecast is one in which the time period of the forecast does not change but remains static even though the actual numbers or data in the forecast change over time. The period of time used in the forecast remains constant, and the forecast is updated at the end of the forecast period to show the subsequent period. A monthly (horizon) cash forecast that is done each month (frequency) is an example of a static forecast. An annual budget is another typical example of a static forecast in that the budget, which is a type of forecast, is normally always for the same 12-month period (e.g., January through December), even if the numbers are updated during the year.
- **Rolling Forecasts:** In contrast, a rolling forecast is one with a constant number of periods (weeks, months, etc.) that is updated on a regular basis and "rolls" forward. An example of a rolling forecast would be a 13-month cash forecast that is updated monthly. Assume that the initial forecast covers the 13 months from January 2xx1 through January 2xx2. Sometime during January 2xx1, the forecast will be updated and will now cover the 13 months from February 2xx1 through February 2xx2. If nothing has changed, all that happens is that January 2xx1 is dropped from the forecast and the projection for February 2xx2 is added. In reality, the forecast data for the other months in the report are typically also updated because newer information is now available.

D. Projected Closing Cash Position

A projected closing cash position statement, also known as the *daily cash forecast* or merely the *cash report,* is one particular type of cash forecast that is used by many treasury professionals. The projected closing cash position is calculated by taking the day's opening available bank balance(s), adding any expected settlements in the collection and concentration accounts (depository banks), and deducting any projected disbursement totals. Information about receipts in the process of collection, whether checks, cards, or electronic, is typically available from the prior day's balance reports. Same-day receipts, such as wire transfers and controlled disbursement totals, are typically reported on a same-day basis.

Clearings of disbursements made from accounts other than controlled disbursement accounts must be estimated. Since wire transfers are real-time transactions, notice of incoming and outgoing wires is often available through a bank reporting system or TMS. The projected closing position is used to determine whether there will be a cash surplus or a cash deficit in a particular bank account. Exhibit 13.1 is an example of a worksheet used to project the closing (or net) cash position.

EXHIBIT 13.1 **DAILY CASH FORECAST**

ACCOUNT NAME	Concentration Bank Acct	Other Accts (as needed) FL-1	FL-2	GA-1	LA-1	Total
OPENING AVAILABLE BALANCE (REPORTED BY BANK)	550,000.00	296,000.00	50,000.00	106,000.00	546,000.00	448,000.00
PLUS: CASH INFLOWS						
STORE RECEIPTS						
CREDIT CARD RECEIPTS	194,000.00	—	—	—	—	194,000.00
LOCKBOX RECEIPTS	1,375,000.00	—	—	—	—	1,375,000.00
CORPORATE RECEIPTS						
INCOMING CONCENTRATION WIRE TRANSFERS	930,000.00	(290,000.00)	—	(100,000.00)	(540,000.00)	—
MISC. INCOMING WIRE TRANSFERS	2,500,000.00	—	—	—	—	2,500,000.00
INVESTMENT MATURITIES	1,000,027.40	—	—	—	—	1,000,027.40
OTHER CASH INFLOWS	507,500.00	—	—	—	—	507,500.00
PROJECTED AVAILABLE BALANCE	**7,056,527.40**	**6,000.00**	**50,000.00**	**6,000.00**	**6,000.00**	**7,124,527.40**
LESS: CASH OUTFLOWS						
ACCOUNTS PAYABLE (CONTROLLED DISBURSEMENT)	—	2,003,000.00	1,742,000.00	—	—	3,745,000.00
PAYROLL	—	—	—	699,000.00	—	699,000.00
OUTGOING CONCENTRATION WIRES	4,444,000.00	(2,003,000.00)	(1,742,000.00)	(699,000.00)	—	—
MISC. WIRE/ACH PAYMENTS	—	—	—	—	—	—
SHORT- OR LONG-TERM INVESTMENT PURCHASES	—	—	—	—	—	—
DEBT AND INTEREST PAYMENTS	500,000.00	—	—	—	—	500,000.00
OTHER	800,000.00	—	—	—	—	800,000.00
TOTAL PROJECTED CASH OUTFLOWS	**5,744,000.00**	**—**	**—**	**—**	**—**	**5,744,000.00**
NET DAILY CASH POSITION	**1,312,527.40**	**6,000.00**	**50,000.00**	**6,000.00**	**6,000.00**	**1,380,527.40**

CREATED BY: ______________________________

REVIEWED BY: ______________________________

V. THE FORECASTING PROCESS

A. Cash Flow Components

Overall cash flow must be separated into its key components to produce an accurate forecast. One approach is to identify cash flows with operating, investing, and financing activities. These categories can be segregated further into inflows and outflows. For example, operating cash inflows might be segregated by product line, type of customer, and sales region. Operating cash outflows can be segregated into large-dollar vendor payments, small-dollar vendor payments, payroll, taxes, and other expense categories.

B. Degree of Certainty

Proper cash flow forecasting requires assigning degrees of certainty to the components:

- **Certain Cash Flows:** The timing and amounts of several types of cash flows are known in advance. Common examples are interest, principal repayments, dividends, royalties, and tax payments.
- **Predictable Cash Flows:** Cash collections from credit sales are an example of a cash flow component that can be predicted with reasonable accuracy. The cash flow on a given day depends on factors such as the level and pattern of past sales, age of accounts, number of customers, and payment histories. These factors enable reasonably accurate cash flow prediction. Disbursement for payroll and benefits tends to be very predictable because it is based on the number of employees, compensation method, and historical experience. Similarly, vendor check-clearing patterns can be predicted based on experience with clearing times.
- **Less Predictable Cash Flows:** Some cash flows, such as those related to sales of a new product, unexpected repairs, pending settlement of insurance claims, or the cost of settling a strike, are difficult to forecast. The experience and judgment of the forecaster are important in such situations.

C. Data Identification and Organization

The identification of suitable data is an important part of the forecasting process. The following factors should be considered:

- **Available Information:** Information may be gathered externally or internally. Sources include the company's banks, field managers, sales managers, and the A/P, A/R, payroll, FP&A, and tax departments. In many cases much of this data is available from internal systems, such as general ledger (G/L) systems, enterprise resource planning (ERP) systems, or treasury management systems (TMSs).
- **Assumptions:** It is important to understand what assumptions are being made about various projected input data to determine how accurate and useful the data may be. If sales managers are assuming that all accounts will be paid on time while the overall economy is slowing down, the treasury professional may need to adjust the underlying assumption to get an accurate forecast. Cash flows should be discussed with key participants to gain insight into any issues or quirks that need to be included in the forecast. For example, it may be important to know whether specific payments are made monthly, quarterly, or annually. For retailers, another example might be that 80% of their projected annual sales occur in the last two months of the year.
- **Desired Type of Forecast:** The data collected should be dictated by the desired cash flow forecast, not simply by what is available. For example, if preparing a short-term cash needs forecast, immediate A/P data may be important, but long-term capital acquisitions and planned securities offerings are probably not needed.

- **Source of Information:** Source identification is affected by the degree of centralization in the company's cash management structure. In a decentralized company, field managers usually have the most current financial data related to their operations. A centralized company is often less dependent on numerous field sources.
- **Account Structure:** Bank account structure is also important in that it may help group cash flows in a meaningful fashion and help identify potential changes. For example, using a concentration account to collect all cash inflows and disburse all cash outflows via ZBAs helps to facilitate cash flow forecasting compared to a system of multiple, stand-alone accounts.
- **Reporting Requirements:** To ensure the usefulness of the data selected, it is essential that the data are defined precisely and reported accurately in a timely manner. This should include an analysis of variances between the forecast and actual results to help track accuracy and improve future forecasts. A growing number of companies use company intranets and treasury websites to distribute management reports, including forecasts.
- **Historical Data:** A variety of data from prior periods are useful in predicting the amount and timing of cash inflows and outflows. Credit sales, payment histories, purchases, and scheduled payments are examples.

D. Selection and Validation of the Forecasting Method

The process of selecting a method of forecasting involves several key steps.

1. ESTABLISHING DATA RELATIONSHIPS

Before selecting the appropriate forecasting method, treasury professionals should ascertain the statistical relationship between the available data and the cash flow components to be forecasted. Data relationships can be found and evaluated by statistical procedures, or they can be estimated by graphing data or by employing the judgment of a treasury professional who has extensive experience with historical relationships. For example, cash disbursements can be related quantitatively to invoices received for payment, and cash collections can be related to prior-period credit sales.

2. SELECTING A METHOD

A method is selected after the data relationships are specified. Forecasting methods should be cost-effective. A forecasting system must be maintained along with the data required to produce the forecast. Forecasting software requires systems support. Time is required to collect and reconcile data, to interpret it (in some instances), and to input data to produce the periodic forecasts. The cost of increased sophistication of a forecasting system must be assessed in relation to the expected improvement in forecast accuracy.

3. TESTING AND VALIDATING RELATIONSHIPS

Ongoing testing and validation of any forecast is critical. Initial validation of a forecast and its internal assumptions is needed to ensure that the forecast actually works and provides worthwhile results. Ongoing feedback and testing is equally important to make sure that the forecast continues to match the real world and that the assumptions built into the cash flow forecast change to meet actual circumstances.

The following methods are often used for testing, validation, and refinement of the actual forecast:

- **In-Sample Validation:** The forecast is tested for accuracy using the historical data used to develop it. If the forecast accurately predicts one data series from one or more other series, the relationships among the data series are deemed to be validated. When a forecast is initially developed, however, there typically is no other data available to test it.
- **Out-of-Sample Validation:** The forecast is tested using data that were not used to develop it. For example, if three years of monthly data are available, the first thirty months of data could be used to develop the forecast. The forecast could then be used to "predict" the subsequent six months, which can then be compared to actual values for those months.
- **Ongoing Validation:** Continuing feedback from projected versus actual comparisons allows continuous evaluation and improvement of the forecast. This ongoing validation may be done on a daily basis for critical forecasts. Any reporting should include an analysis of forecast errors to help foster this process.
- **Documentation of the Process:** It is important to document how the forecast process works, as well as documenting the sources of data, contacts, etc. This enables others to understand and work with the forecast and allows future changes when needed.

4. USING TECHNOLOGY

Modern forecasting almost always takes advantage of computer technology to improve the process and help create needed models. Ranging from simple spreadsheets to sophisticated forecasting programs, computer technology provides tools to make forecasting faster and often more accurate. As discussed in Chapter 14, Information Technology in Treasury, most TMSs have a forecasting capability of some sort, and many ERP systems include tools to help create cash forecasts.

VI. FORECASTING METHODS

The method a company uses for a given forecast often depends on the forecasting horizon. The method most appropriate for making a daily cash forecast is probably not the best method for making a monthly forecast. Similarly, the best method for monthly forecasting will not be the best method for annual forecasting. It is also important to understand that while these forecasts provide a baseline for operational cash forecasting, any capital purchases, dividend payouts, debt repayment or collection, etc., must be layered onto these forecasts to obtain a more accurate projection of cash. For the purposes of discussion, this section will look at three basic categories of forecasting methods: (1) short-term methods, (2) medium- to long-term methods, and (3) statistical approaches.

A. Short-Term Forecasting Methods

For short-term forecasts, many companies use information relating to expected receipts and disbursements in the near future. There are several methods to develop short-term cash projections that incorporate factors affecting cash flow. Three of the more important methods include an A/R balance pattern forecast (which is covered in Chapter 9, Working

Capital Metrics), a receipts and disbursements forecast, and a distribution forecast. Statistical analysis of data relationships may be applied to methods applicable to all time horizons.

1. RECEIPTS AND DISBURSEMENTS FORECAST

Projecting receipts and disbursements is the core of short-term cash forecasting. It begins by creating separate schedules of cash receipts and disbursements. The schedules are prepared on a cash basis, rather than on an accrual basis, due to the need to forecast cash rather than earnings, especially when A/R and A/P data are incorporated. A good place to start is with the historic information provided in bank account statements, which by their nature are cash statements.

- **Receipts Schedule:** This schedule consists of a projection of collections from customers (e.g., cash sales or payments on A/R) and other cash inflows (e.g., interest or dividends received from investments). It also should include expected, nonrecurring cash inflows, such as the proceeds from asset sales and external financing activities.
- **Disbursements Schedule:** This schedule involves forecasting the cash disbursements for purchases and other cash outflows, such as payroll, taxes, interest, dividends, rent, and debt repayments. A/P systems are typically a good source for this type of information but A/P data must be adjusted to recognize that payments typically do not clear for some days after the actual disbursement.
- **Completed Forecast:** A completed forecast combines the receipts and disbursements schedules, and compares the result to a desired, minimum cash balance.

In Exhibit 13.2, a company has decided to maintain a $50,000 minimum cash balance to cushion it against unexpected expenses or enable it to take advantage of unanticipated opportunities. The beginning cash balance is the ending cash balance from the prior week. The final two lines of the forecast represent the forecasted deficit or surplus cash position in each week. With this information, a company can manage its borrowing and investing activity more accurately. In the example, the forecast shows a surplus of funds in Week 1 that could be invested to earn interest. In Weeks 2 and 3, the forecast projects a cash shortage that would require borrowing funds on a short-term basis or liquidating short-term investments.

EXHIBIT 13.2 **RECEIPTS AND DISBURSEMENTS FORECAST**

$ AMOUNTS IN THOUSANDS	WEEK 1	WEEK 2	WEEK 3
CASH RECEIPTS	$1,000	$ 1,000	$ 950
CASH DISBURSEMENTS	(870)	(1,350)	(1,000)
NET CASH FLOW	$ 130	$ (350)	$ (50)
BEGINNING CASH BALANCE	100	230	(120)
ENDING CASH BALANCE	$ 230	$ (120)	$ (170)
MINIMUM CASH REQ. (TARGET BALANCE)	50	50	50
FINANCING NEEDED (DEFICIT)		$ 170	$ 220
INVESTABLE FUNDS (SURPLUS)	$ 180		

2. DISTRIBUTION FORECAST

A distribution forecast estimates the daily impact that a single event has on cash flows over a specified period, based on historical patterns. The method is used widely for short-term forecasts. The distribution percentages can be calculated two different ways: (1) simple average, or (2) regression analysis.

With a simple average, the distribution percentages can be estimated by averaging past daily cash flows related to a particular category of disbursements. For example, the treasury professional may sample past clearings of A/P payments and discover that, on average, 40% of a certain category of payments cleared the day the payment was issued, 50% cleared the day after that, and 10% cleared after two or more days. The problem with taking a simple average is that actual payment posting dates may be influenced by more factors than the number of days after issuance.

While most distribution forecasts can be done using a simple average approach, when there are multiple factors involved (e.g., day-of-the-week or -month effects, or holidays), a more sophisticated approach such as regression analysis may be needed. An overview of regression analysis is provided in the statistical methods section that follows.

Exhibit 13.3 is an example of forecasting using the simple average distribution method.

EXHIBIT 13.3 FORECASTING USING THE DISTRIBUTION METHOD

A company has used regression analysis based on historical data to estimate the proportion of dollars that will clear on a given business day. It has determined that this proportion depends on the number of business days since the checks were distributed. The estimated proportions are given below.

BUSINESS DAYS SINCE DISTRIBUTION	% OF DOLLARS EXPECTED TO CLEAR
1	13%
2	38%
3	28%
4	13%
5	8%
TOTAL	**100%**

Therefore, if $100,000 in checks are distributed on Wednesday, May 1, the checks are estimated to clear according to the schedule below.

DATE	BUSINESS DAYS AFTER DISTRIBUTION	DAY OF THE WEEK	PERCENTAGE OF DOLLARS CLEARING	FORECAST OF DOLLARS CLEARING
MAY 2	1	THURSDAY	13%	$ 13,000
MAY 3	2	FRIDAY	38%	$ 38,000
MAY 6	3	MONDAY	28%	$ 28,000
MAY 7	4	TUESDAY	13%	$ 13,000
MAY 8	5	WEDNESDAY	8%	$ 8,000
		TOTAL	**100%**	**$100,000**

B. Medium- and Long-Term Forecasting Methods

Medium- and long-term forecasting methods primarily involve generating pro forma financial statements and are typically used in strategic planning or FP&A functions. As previously discussed, whether they are prepared in treasury or some other department, coordination of data and assumptions is important. The availability of internal accounting data provided by a typical ERP or integrated accounting and reporting system makes this task significantly easier. Many of the advanced reporting systems have sophisticated forecasting models as one of their options.

Projected income statements and balance sheets can be used to forecast cash flows over a longer time horizon. One of the easiest procedures for constructing pro forma financial statements is based on the percentage-of-sales method, as illustrated in Exhibits 13.4A, 13.4B, and 13.4C.

The percentage-of-sales method involves projecting financial statements based on the historical relationship between sales and liquid balance sheet accounts that tend to change in value along with sales. Cash, A/R, inventory, and A/P are the more important accounts. Account size (e.g., cash or inventory) is expressed as a percentage of sales, based on an examination of the historical relationship between account size and sales. This percentage is then used in conjunction with forecasted sales to produce a forecast of account size. The procedure is demonstrated in Exhibits 13.4A and 13.4B. Other balance sheet and income statement accounts are forecasted based on other factors (e.g., a known debt repayment schedule).

The percentage-of-sales method requires three steps:

- Forecast the income statement and balance sheet based on the relationships mentioned previously. (See Exhibits 13.4A and 13.4B.)
- Calculate the projected ending cash balance by determining how the forecasted income statement and balance sheet values impact cash (i.e., utilize a cash flow statement given the impact of changes to investments, capital/depreciation, and potential slowing of cash collections or payments). (See Exhibit 13.4C.)
- Compare the projected ending cash balance with the company's target cash balance, and adjust the pro forma statement to show the source of funding for a cash shortfall or the investment of a cash surplus. (See the note at the foot of Exhibit 13.4C.)

EXHIBIT 13.4A **FORECASTING WITH PRO FORMA FINANCIAL STATEMENTS**
(percentage-of-sales method)

Assume the following income statement and balance sheet (in thousands) represent a company's actual position as of December 31, 2xx1.

ACTUAL INCOME STATEMENT (IN THOUSANDS)—YEAR ENDING DECEMBER 31, 2xx1		
SALES	$ 2,000	
COST OF GOODS SOLD	(1,500)	[75% of sales]
SELLING & ADMIN. EXPENSE	(200)	[10% of sales]
DEPRECIATION	(100)	
INTEREST EXPENSE	(38)	[(0.12 x $150) + (0.10 x $200)]
INCOME BEFORE TAXES	$ 162	
TAXES	(55)	[34% tax rate]
NET INCOME	$ 107	

ACTUAL BALANCE SHEET (IN THOUSANDS)—YEAR ENDING DECEMBER 31, 2xx1			
CASH	$ 100	PAYABLES	$ 50
RECEIVABLES	300	NOTES (AT 12%)	150
INVENTORY	200	BONDS (AT 10%)	200
FIXED ASSETS	400	EQUITY	600
TOTAL ASSETS	$1,000	TOTAL LIABILITIES & EQUITY	$1,000

To generate the percentage-of-sales forecast, the following assumptions are made (all dollar amounts are in thousands) for the year 2xx1:

- **Sales will increase by 10% to $2,200.**
- Cost of goods sold, selling and administrative expenses, and current assets and liabilities (receivables, inventory, and payables) are a constant percentage of sales.
- **Cash balance is derived from the cash flow statement.**
- **Additional fixed assets in the amount of $100 will be purchased.**
- **Depreciation will be $50.**
- **Notes will be reduced to $100 at the beginning of the year.**
- **Dividends will be $24.**

EXHIBIT 13.4B FORECASTING WITH PRO FORMA FINANCIAL STATEMENTS *(continued)*

PROJECTED INCOME STATEMENT (IN THOUSANDS)—YEAR ENDING DECEMBER 31, 2xx1		
SALES	$2,200	
COST OF GOODS SOLD	(1,650)	[75% of sales]
SELLING & ADMIN. EXPENSE	(220)	[10% of sales]
DEPRECIATION	(50)	
INTEREST EXPENSE	(32)	[(0.12 x $100) + (0.10 x $200)]
INCOME BEFORE TAXES	$ 248	
TAXES	(84)	[34% tax rate]
NET INCOME	$ 164	
DIVIDENDS	(24)	
RETAINED EARNINGS	$ 140	

PROJECTED BALANCE SHEET (IN THOUSANDS)—YEAR ENDING DECEMBER 31, 2xx1			
CASH (FROM CASH FLOW STATEMENT)	$ 95	PAYABLES (2.5% OF SALES)	$ 55
RECEIVABLES (15% OF SALES)	330	NOTES (AT 12%)	100
INVENTORY (10% OF SALES)	220	BONDS (AT 10%)	200
NET FIXED ASSETS (NFA) (PRIOR NFA + NEW FIXED ASSETS – DEPRECIATION) ($400 + $100 – $50)	450	EQUITY (PRIOR EQUITY + RETAINED EARNINGS) ($600 + $140)	740
TOTAL ASSETS	$1,095	TOTAL LIABILITIES & EQUITY	$1,095

All of the projected account balances except cash are calculated based upon the given assumptions. The ending cash balance is determined by evaluating the impact on cash of the income statement activity and balance sheet changes and adjusting the beginning cash balance accordingly.

EXHIBIT 13.4C FORECASTING WITH PRO FORMA FINANCIAL STATEMENTS
(continued)

PROJECTED STATEMENT OF CASH FLOWS (IN THOUSANDS)—YEAR ENDING DECEMBER 31, 2xx1		
BEGINNING CASH BALANCE		$100
CASH FLOWS FROM OPERATING ACTIVITIES		
NET INCOME	$164	
ADJUSTMENTS TO RECONCILE NET INCOME TO CASH		
DEPRECIATION	$ 50	
INCREASE IN ACCOUNTS RECEIVABLE	(30)	
INCREASE IN INVENTORY	(20)	
INCREASE IN ACCOUNTS PAYABLE	5	
NET CASH PROVIDED (USED) IN OPERATING ACTIVITIES		169
CASH FLOWS FROM INVESTING ACTIVITIES		
PURCHASE OF FIXED ASSETS		(100)
CASH FLOWS FROM FINANCING ACTIVITIES		
NET REPAYMENT OF DEBT	$ (50)	
DIVIDENDS PAID	(24)	
NET CASH PROVIDED (USED) BY FINANCING ACTIVITIES		(74)
ENDING CASH BALANCE		$ 95

If the projected ending cash balance is less than the company's established target balance, the shortfall must be funded through taking on additional debt, issuing equity, or selling assets. Conversely, if the projected cash balance exceeds the target, the surplus may be invested in additional assets, used to reduce debt, and/or distributed to shareholders. In the above example, if the target cash balance were $110, then $15 in additional cash would need to be raised. If this were accomplished through an increase in notes payable, then the December 31, 2xx1 , balance sheet would appear as before, except that cash would be $110 and notes payable would be $115.

C. Statistical Methods in Forecasting

There are many statistical approaches that are available for forecasting purposes. In forecasting cash flows, there are several useful methods that can be applied. One of the most general statistical methods is that of extrapolation, where past trends are identified and used to predict the pattern of future cash flows. In forecasting, one of the more common applications of extrapolation is that of time series forecasting, with simple moving average and exponential smoothing as two of its primary models. Another popular statistical technique is that of correlation, along with regression analysis. These approaches are covered below.

1. TIME SERIES FORECASTING

A time series is a serial chain of values for some variable, such as sales. Every time series contains a trend, seasonal pattern, cyclical pattern, and random movement. A trend is the general direction that the values are moving (e.g., sales are increasing 5% year over year). A seasonal pattern repeats with regard to time of year. A cyclical pattern repeats without regard to time of year. It is possible that the series is stationary (i.e., the trend value is zero). The seasonal and cyclical patterns may be strong, moderate, or weak. Random movement is a change in the series not identifiable as a trend or a seasonal or cyclical influence. The source of random movement is usually unknown, but it may be a one-time event, such as a World's Fair, Olympic Games, or natural disaster.

The purpose of a time series model is to identify repetitive patterns in a historical series so that this pattern can be used to predict future values of the series. There are many kinds of time series models, and two of the primary models are described below.

a. Simple Moving Average

A simple moving average bases a forecast on a rolling average of past values for a series. The method has the advantage of being easy to use, but since a forecast is developed using an average of past values, it will lag a trend if one exists and tend to "dampen" or "smooth" turning points where seasonality or another irregular event is present. The larger the number of data points used to form the average, the greater the chance that random movement will be eliminated through averaging. However, the margin by which the trend will be missed will be greater, and the dampening of seasonal turning points will be stronger. An example of a five-day, moving average forecast is shown in Exhibit 13.5.

EXHIBIT 13.5 **FORECASTING WITH SIMPLE MOVING AVERAGES AND EXPONENTIAL SMOOTHING**

	FIVE-DAY MOVING AVERAGE FORECAST			FORECAST WITH EXPONENTIAL SMOOTHING	
DAY	**ACTUAL CASH FLOW (X_t)**	**FORECAST (N = 5)**	**ERROR**	**FORECAST (α = 0.40)**	**ERROR**
1	$110,000				
2	120,000				
3	115,000				
4	122,000				
5	126,000				
6	124,000	$118,600	$5,400	$118,600	$5,400
7	129,000	121,400	7,600	120,760	8,240
8	133,000	123,200	9,800	124,056	8,944
9	132,000	126,800	5,200	127,634	4,366

MOVING AVERAGE FORECAST

MOVING AVERAGE FORECAST FOR DAY 6 IS:

($110,000 + 120,000 + 115,000 + 122,000 + 126,000) / 5 = $118,600

WHICH RESULTS IN A FORECAST ERROR OF $124,000 – $118,600 = $5,400

EXPONENTIAL SMOOTHING FORECAST

THE EXPONENTIAL SMOOTHING FORECAST BEGINS WITH THE DAY 6 FORECAST OF $118,600 BASED ON THE MOVING AVERAGE FORECAST.

THEN, THE DAY 7 FORECAST USING EXPONENTIAL SMOOTHING IS:

0.40 ($124,000) + (1 – 0.40)($118,600) = $120,760

WHICH RESULTS IN A FORECAST ERROR OF $129,000 – $120,760 = $8,240

b. Exponential Smoothing

The exponential smoothing technique produces a forecasted value based on the most recent actual value, the most recent forecasted value, and a number between zero and one that is used to weight these two values. The weight, designated by the Greek letter alpha (α), is referred to as the *smoothing constant* and is calculated using a computer program such as a statistics package. This type of function is often built into many cash forecasting and TMS systems, which are discussed in more detail in Chapter 14, Information Technology in Treasury. The program selects the alpha value that weights past actual values and past forecasted values so as to produce the most accurate forecast of the variable's value in the next period. The model is developed using in-sample validation, discussed earlier. An example of exponential smoothing is shown in Exhibit 13.5.

The forecasted values are found in the following way:

Next Period Forecast = (Alpha)(Current-Period Actual) + (1 – Alpha)(Current-Period Forecast)

This formula can be expressed more formally as:

$$F_{t+1} = \alpha X_t + (1 - \alpha)(F_t)$$

Where:

t (subscript) = Time period (t = current period, t + 1 = next period, etc.)

F_{t+1} = Cash flow forecast for the next period (t + 1)

F_t = Cash flow forecast for the current period (t)

α = Smoothing constant ($0 < \alpha < 1$)

X_t = Actual cash flow for the current period (t)

As with a simple moving average forecast, exponential smoothing will yield a forecast that lags a trend in the series. If a trend in the series is mild, the lag effect will be minimal because, unlike a moving average, the forecast is made using values from the most recent period.

2. CORRELATION AND REGRESSION ANALYSIS

Correlation calculations involve a statistical identification of the degree of association between a cash flow and another variable. This is important to understand in determining what information can or should be used in building a forecast. For example, for many retail companies there is typically a high degree of correlation between prior-year cash receipts and current-year cash receipts. On the other hand, there may be a much lower correlation between sales forecasts and actual receipts. As a result, a forecast model would be more likely to use a prior year's sales than current sales forecasts to create an accurate forecast.

Once a relationship is established, the cash flow can be forecasted based on the actual or expected behavior of the other variable. Regression analysis is one of the primary methods that can be used to project cash flow after the quantified correlation between cash flow and another variable has been established.

Regression analysis is a statistical method that can be used to assess the impact that multiple variables (or causes) have on a value or an outcome. Regression is a sophisticated method that requires rather large amounts of data, and knowledge of the method's advantages and pitfalls. The explanatory model developed using regression must be reestimated when the underlying influences on cash flow change.

One of the most commonly used methods of regression analysis is known as the *linear least squares methodology.* Linear least squares is a method for finding the line *(linear)* that best fits a specific set of data points by minimizing *(least)* the sum of the squares *(squares)* of the differences *(the residuals)* of the data points from a particular line. The sum of the squares of the differences is used instead of the absolute values because this typically results in a straight line rather than one that "jigs and jags."

VII. BEST PRACTICES FOR CASH FORECASTING

There is a wide variation in cash forecasting methods as actually used by treasury professionals. As previously mentioned, forecasting is as much art as it is science. That being said, there are a number of best practices that high-performing treasury operations tend to follow. Some of these include:[2]

- **Use appropriate detail.** Perhaps the most important requirement is to make sure positions are forecasted in sufficient detail for the company's requirements. If the forecast is to be used to determine whether there is sufficient cash to meet obligations in different currencies, positions need to be forecasted in each of those currencies. On the other hand, if a company uses the forecast to manage its surplus balances, aggregated forecasts may be sufficient, even if this means some funds sit idle in bank accounts overnight.
- **Disclose assumptions.** Any significant assumptions (i.e., sales will increase by 5% per year) need to be disclosed, and the source of any information should also be documented. This is particularly useful in reviewing forecasts with someone who has not been involved in developing them.
- **Use the appropriate platform.** The organization should use the most appropriate platform to develop the forecast. In organizations where the cash flows are relatively stable and known in advance, there is very little need for sophisticated specialty tools to analyze the input data. On the other hand, where there are big fluctuations in data and significant variables involved, it may be necessary to use a system or software with greater processing power to generate the forecasted positions. Treasurers should always review the systems and solutions available to ensure they are being used to the maximum efficiency for the department as a whole. It might be appropriate when developing a global cash position forecast to use solutions that are already global in scope, such as an intranet, internal databases, or other proprietary tools. Alternatively, the organization could have access to additional functionality in a TMS or its ERP system. Even if a treasury department has a sophisticated forecasting system, it will not necessarily be worth deploying in all situations.
- **Invest the appropriate amount of resources.** A forecast that takes a few minutes first thing every day and provides a result that is 90% accurate most of the time may well be sufficient in many organizations. Only when there is more pressure for accuracy, to comply with covenants or manage limited liquidity, for example, will it be worthwhile to invest additional resources for a more accurate forecast. The costs of breaching a covenant or routinely overdrawing disbursement accounts may outweigh the investment necessary to develop a forecasting system to prevent this happening.
- **Validate the forecast.** Once the forecast period is over, treasury professionals should compare the forecast to actual results and determine the reason for any significant differences. Where possible, those reasons should be incorporated into future forecasts to improve long-term accuracy.
- **Cooperate and communicate.** Treasury is absolutely dependent on business units for accurate and timely information, and in turn the business units are often dependent on the reliability of cash forecasts provided by treasury. Clear expectations and common terminology should be established from the start of any forecasting effort.
- **Ensure the forecast is usable.** The investment in developing the forecast has to be justified by the outcome. It is no use investing lots of time and effort producing a forecast that is unusable because it is too late to act upon it. In addition, the forecast must be sufficiently robust to provide meaningful data.

2. Much of this material is taken from the *AFP Guide to Strategic Global Cash Position Forecasting*, published in 2012 and provided by AFP for its members through its Global Liquidity Guide series (http://www.afponline.org/GlobalLiquidityGuides/?terms=global_liquidity_guide).

VIII. SUMMARY

Cash forecasting is an important part of treasury management. Everybody does it, but it is difficult to do well. This is primarily due to the large number of assumptions and estimates that are required in producing any forecast. TMSs and other technology have simplified the process by making it easier to use relatively sophisticated analytical tools to produce forecasts, but the forecasts themselves are still only as accurate as the historical data and assumptions used in developing the forecast.

This chapter discussed the various types of forecasts typically used by treasury professionals and presented an overview of the typical forecasting process and available methodology. The chapter closed with a discussion of best practices in treasury forecasting, which can largely be summarized by saying that forecasts should be as simple as possible, given the intended purpose of the forecast, and must be timely enough and accurate enough to be usable.

TEST YOUR UNDERSTANDING: CHAPTER 13

Answers are on pages 697–701.

1. What are the primary tasks that require accurate forecasting?
2. What are three fundamental issues that need to be addressed in cash forecasting?
3. What is a forecast horizon, and what are the typical types of forecast horizons?
4. What is the difference between a static and a rolling forecast?
5. What are the key factors that need to be considered in identifying suitable data to be used in a forecast?
6. What are three of the more important methods of developing short-term cash projections?
7. What are the two methods of calculating distribution percentages for a forecast?
8. What is the percentage-of-sales method of forecasting, and what are the three basic steps in the method?
9. What is time series forecasting?
10. What is regression analysis?
11. Describe the three levels of cash flows based on their degree of certainty, and provide examples of each.
12. How can a treasury professional test and validate relationships in forecasting models?
13. What purpose does a closing cash position serve in cash management?

CHAPTER 14
Information Technology in Treasury

I. INTRODUCTION

II. INFORMATION TECHNOLOGY FOR TREASURY

A. The Role of Information Management in Treasury

B. Information Security

C. Types of Information Management Technology Solutions

D. Information Management Technology Platforms

E. Workflow Management

F. Technology Policies and Guidelines

III. TREASURY MANAGEMENT SYSTEMS (TMSs)

A. Background

B. Functionality

C. Technology Platforms

D. Costs

IV. E-COMMERCE

A. Basics of E-Commerce

B. Electronic Data Interchange (EDI)

C. E-Commerce Communication Standards

D. Electronic Bank Account Management (eBAM)

E. Mobile Banking

V. SUMMARY

I. INTRODUCTION

The modern treasury function is highly dependent upon various forms of technology to manage its diverse responsibilities. The advent of the electronic spreadsheet has transformed treasury from a manual function dependent upon pen and paper to a more automated environment that uses computers and technology for everything from daily cash positioning to account reconcilement and risk management. While many treasury professionals still rely heavily on electronic spreadsheets and personal computers, the available technology has grown to include such things as treasury management systems (TMSs), bank-specific workstations, the Internet, and company-wide ERP (enterprise resource planning) systems.

Whatever the platform, the use of technology allows treasury professionals to retrieve, review, analyze, and transmit large amounts of financial data in a timely manner while minimizing the potential for errors. It provides a standardized way to interact with various internal and external entities, including accounting, corporate finance, and financial institutions. It helps facilitate visibility in treasury operations and allows organizations to leverage external capabilities, such as SWIFT and online portals. It does, however, require an increased level of attention to control and security to safeguard against intrusion and fraud.

This chapter introduces some of the basics of information management and technology as they apply to treasury, including a discussion of security, treasury applications, technology platforms, and IT policies. The chapter then takes a detailed look at TMS functionality and cost. Finally, the chapter presents an overview of some of the issues involved in electronic commerce (e-commerce) and mobile or electronic banking, including a discussion of some of the various information standards that are important to treasury.

II. INFORMATION TECHNOLOGY FOR TREASURY

Information technology and information management have become an integral part of treasury management and the driving force in the development of TMSs. Since many companies view the finance area as the clearinghouse for a wide variety of intracompany information flows, one of treasury's major responsibilities is to integrate treasury operations with other operational areas, including accounting and finance.

A. The Role of Information Management in Treasury

To add value to a company, treasury professionals continue to expand information management beyond the narrow focus of the daily cash position. The added value comes from using information management and modern technology for tasks such as transaction initiation, as well as effecting FX transactions and managing commercial paper programs and financial risk management programs. The benefits of an IT-enhanced treasury department are magnified through collaboration with other departments and with various stakeholders and business partners. (Internal and external collaboration are discussed in Chapter 1, The Role of Treasury Management.)

With regards to information management, the treasury professional is commonly responsible for:

- Compiling data from a wide range of internal and external sources
- Sorting, analyzing, and storing information
- Initiating and validating transactions
- Obtaining account balances and transaction details from external sources
- Obtaining internal information that affects the cash flow timeline (e.g., receipts and disbursements)
- Consolidating information into the cash position worksheet
- Generating journal entries for accounting
- Reporting information to management
- Assisting other areas with any treasury-related research

B. Information Security

1. BASICS

Information security is the assurance that all information and messages are safe from intrusion, detection, and modification. Security must provide a number of basic elements:

- **Privacy:** The assurance that information is only accessible by authorized individuals and will not be used for unintended purposes
- **Authentication:** The ability to know, with a reasonable amount of certainty, who is accessing information or initiating a transaction
- **Authorization:** The ability to know and control what functions and data an authenticated individual can access and use
- **Integrity:** The ability to ensure that a message was not modified in transit and that stored information has not been improperly modified or deleted (data integrity is especially important for financial transactions)
- **Non-repudiation:** The inability of the sender or receiver of a message to deny having sent or received the message

2. MULTIFACTOR AUTHENTICATION

Authentication methods for information technology and network purposes are based on three basic factors:

- Something the individual **knows**, such as a password or personal fact
- Something the individual **has**, such as a token or a cell phone
- Something the individual **is**, such as a fingerprint or facial scan

Single-factor authentication uses only one of these factors, typically a password, to validate an individual attempting to access a system or network. Single-factor authentication is often acceptable for activities such as inquiries, which have no financial impact. Dual-factor authentication requires two of the three, such as a token and a password. A token is an electronic security device, discussed in more detail below. Since users demonstrate both possession of the token and the password, they are meeting the first two factors. Dual-factor authentication is currently the accepted standard for most financial systems, especially when actual transactions are being processed. Three-factor authentication requires the use of all three factors and is the strongest authentication available. It is typically reserved for access to high-security systems and locations.

A multifactor authentication methodology may also include "out-of-band" controls. *Out-of-band* refers to the use of additional steps or actions taken beyond the technology boundaries of a specific transaction and includes such things as callback verification using a previously registered phone number or a cell-phone-based challenge, in which a one-time access code is transmitted to a previously registered cell phone and must be entered to authenticate the user.

The success of any given authentication method depends on more than just technology. An effective authentication method should have customer acceptance, reliable performance, scalability to accommodate growth, and interoperability with existing systems and future plans. Otherwise, users will look for ways to defeat the system. For example, requiring a very long, complex, and random password as one factor is certainly more secure than short, simple passwords that can be easily discovered by hackers. This added security must be balanced against the tendency of many users to write long, random passwords down somewhere as they are difficult to remember, defeating the purpose of the password length.

3. ENCRYPTION

Encryption refers to the process of transforming information using some type of computer-based model to make it unreadable to anyone except those possessing special knowledge, similar to a password, usually referred to as a *key*. It addresses several of the security needs discussed above. First, encryption helps protect privacy. Second, properly designed encryption programs can also help with non-repudiation because the fact that a message has been encrypted and subsequently decrypted indicates that the originator possessed the specific key needed to originally encrypt the message, which implies at least single-factor authentication.

Many popular encryption programs are designed using what is called *public-key infrastructure (PKI)*. PKI involves the use of dual keys. One of the keys is private and is kept by an individual user or organization. The other key is public and is distributed to trading partners. Information encrypted with one key can only be decrypted and read using the other key. As a result, individuals encrypting data with the public key know that no one but the holder of the private key can access the data. Conversely, individuals who are able to decrypt messages using the public key have some assurance that the information came from the holder of the private key. These "keys" are typically computer files or certificates that are protected by some form of local password. PKI is designed to provide security over traditionally unsecure networks, such as the Internet.

4. DIGITAL SIGNATURES

A digital signature is a message encoded with the sender's secret, private key that the receiver can use to identify the source. As long as the private key is never shared with anyone, forgery of a digital signature is virtually impossible. A digital signature is tied to a document and to the signer, meaning the signer's digital signature will be different for each document signed.

Note that a digital signature is different from a digitized signature such as that used as a facsimile signature on laser-printed checks. In the United States, the Electronic Signatures in Global and National Commerce (E-Sign) Act gave digital signatures the same legal status as paper/ink signatures, sometimes referred to as *wet signatures*.

5. DIGITAL CERTIFICATES

Digital certificates tie the identity of the user (private key) to the user's public key and may also authenticate the devices used to create documents or transactions. The identification information is secured by a trusted third party's digital signature on the certificate. The trusted third party is known as the *certificate authority*.

Banks and other third parties are partnering with security companies, certificate authorities, software providers, and other technology firms to administer their public-key infrastructure and issue digital certificates. These initiatives serve as virtual passports to subscribers.

The main objective of this type of partnership is for corporations to trust the identity of digital partners through real-time authentication and validation of the transmission under legally binding contracts. These associations also let users verify unknown buyers through a trusted financial institution and establish multilateral trust through one bilateral customer agreement. Oftentimes, certificates are stored in a smart card with dual authentication. A combination of the smart card and an assigned PIN "unlock" the card. The next section (on tokens) describes authentication devices in more detail.

6. TOKENS

Tokens are electronic devices that contain circuitry that encodes assigned user-specific information or personal information to help ensure password protection. For example, one type of token contains a clock in a smart card that is synchronized to a clock on the host system where the data or application resides. When the user wants to log on to the system (whether locally or from a remote point), the token provides a unique code that, when entered with the user's PIN or password, ensures that the user is authorized to access the system. Alternatively, the token may be a device that is plugged in to a port on the user's computer and responds directly to the host system without the need for the user to enter, or even know, the challenge information. The use of a token meets the "something they have" criteria of multifactor authentication.

7. SINGLE SIGN-ON (SSO)

A single sign-on permits an individual to enter one user name and password in order to access multiple applications on the same network or at the same host. SSO has broad applicability to all technology, but can simplify access for treasury professionals that access multiple systems. For example, SSO is helpful when accessing a bank website or a hosted TMS provider with multiple applications, such as report generation and transaction initiation, because it allows an individual to sign on and authenticate one time and not have to authenticate with each individual application.

C. Types of Information Management Technology Solutions

Treasury professionals use a wide variety of technology solutions, ranging from simple spreadsheets to complex TMS packages. Each provides a range of functionality and capabilities at varying cost levels.

1. SPREADSHEETS

Computer-based spreadsheets, such as those created with Microsoft Excel, have almost universally replaced paper spreadsheets, but spreadsheets are still the mainstay of many treasury operations. They provide an inexpensive and convenient platform to consolidate and analyze the data that are essential to treasury, and many treasury professionals still use them to perform daily cash positioning and cash forecasting functions.

The major advantages of spreadsheets are their low initial cost, ubiquity, and ease of access, combined with an ability to modify and change spreadsheets as needed by the end user. The major drawbacks to spreadsheets are typically:

- Lack of security
- Lack of auditability
- Poor version control
- Minimal integration with other applications
- Lack of organized IT support and software maintenance
- Potential for corruption of data and internal formulas
- Lack of a common database, leading to duplication of data
- Lack of transaction initiation capabilities

While the spreadsheet software itself can be very inexpensive when compared to treasury-specific software, the total cost of ownership can be quite high based on the various drawbacks and the high potential for problems or mistakes.

2. BANK WORKSTATIONS AND ONLINE BANKING SOLUTIONS

Historically, many banks supplied their commercial customers with treasury applications that offered access to bank information and allowed for the initiation of various transactions. Most of these solutions started out as information reporting services. Over time, their capabilities were expanded in response to customer requests to provide broader access to information with inquiry capabilities, self-service capabilities for stop payments and other customer needs, and finally transaction initiation. In many cases, these bank-provided technology solutions offer functionality that can rival dedicated TMSs. Today, most of the bank-specific solutions have become online banking solutions typically offered over the Internet.

While bank-provided solutions overcome many of the drawbacks of spreadsheets, they are typically more expensive than spreadsheets over time due to ongoing fees for the use of the system. These fees are often based upon transaction volumes and usage, and can become significant if multiple users are frequently accessing bank information. The major drawback to bank-provided solutions is that they are typically limited to dealing with only one bank. Although some of the bank products can consolidate and report data from multiple banks, transaction initiation and inquiry capabilities are normally limited to the bank that provides the application. As a result, treasury operations that have multiple bank relationships may need to use multiple bank solutions, all with different security requirements and different user interfaces.

3. TREASURY MANAGEMENT SYSTEMS (TMSs)

TMSs, which are discussed in more detail below, were initially developed in response to the need to use one system to access multiple banks. Today, most TMSs not only provide access to multiple banks, but they also typically provide expanded functionality in terms of debt and investment management, FX management, and risk management, and often include the capability to directly connect with internal accounting and other financial systems. The expanded functionality usually comes at a higher cost point, however, and often requires some form of internal IT support to operate or configure the solution.

4. SPECIALTY SOFTWARE

In addition to full-featured TMSs, there are also a wide variety of specialty applications that are used by many treasury professionals. These include packages such as investment management software, escheatment tracking and reporting software, bank fee analysis tools, FX exposure tools, and risk management packages.

5. ENTERPRISE RESOURCE PLANNING (ERP) SYSTEMS

ERP systems are sophisticated information management, production, and accounting software packages that link different functional areas or operational divisions of a company on an enterprise-wide basis. They integrate large amounts of data into a common database, which helps eliminate multiple, duplicate copies of information. The greatest advantage of ERP systems is that they can provide a single processing platform for all of an organization's accounting and finance software, reducing the number of integration points required with stand-alone packages. Many ERP systems include some form of TMS application, which may include the ability to directly connect to an organization's banks to initiate payments and other transactions from A/P and to download and reconcile bank account information. One of the major advantages of ERP-based TMS solutions is the built-in integration with a company's accounting and financial applications. The disadvantages can include a higher cost point and a need for significant IT support.

6. DASHBOARDS

A dashboard is a user interface or display that, like a car's dashboard, organizes and presents information in a way that is easy to read and understand. Like a car's dashboard, it is often color coded to indicate the importance of specific information (e.g., green is normal and red requires immediate attention). Dashboards are intended to provide summary data that can be used to manage a function or process and often include the ability to "drill down" on specific pieces of information to get more detailed information about the specific item. For example, if one item on a dashboard were the number of payments over a specific dollar amount, clicking on the number would provide a detailed list of the individual payments.

A treasury management (TM) dashboard is intended to provide management immediate feedback on the overall status of treasury operations, while also publishing key financial information useful in running the business. The dashboard should be short and easy to read, and while the actual metrics and information published will vary from company to company, general categories of information can include:

- Interest, investment, and FX rates
- Cash flow and/or borrowing statistics
- Projected and/or large-dollar disbursements
- Key performance indicators (KPIs) or metrics, such as reconcilements completed, cash forecasting accuracy, wire transfer timing and accuracy, or transaction volumes
- Key deadlines and operational alerts (e.g., bank holidays; disbursement calendars; employee stock option [ESOP] exercise dates; and investment blackout periods, scheduled earnings announcements, and investor releases)

The principal challenges in implementing a TM dashboard include:

- Selecting the information and KPIs that are important to the specific organization
- Identifying the source(s) of information for each metric
- Automating the creation of the report so that it is produced and available in a timely manner

A sample TM dashboard is shown in Exhibit 14.1.

EXHIBIT 14.1 SAMPLE TREASURY MANAGEMENT DASHBOARD

XYZ Company Treasury Operations Dashboard

August 15, 2xx2

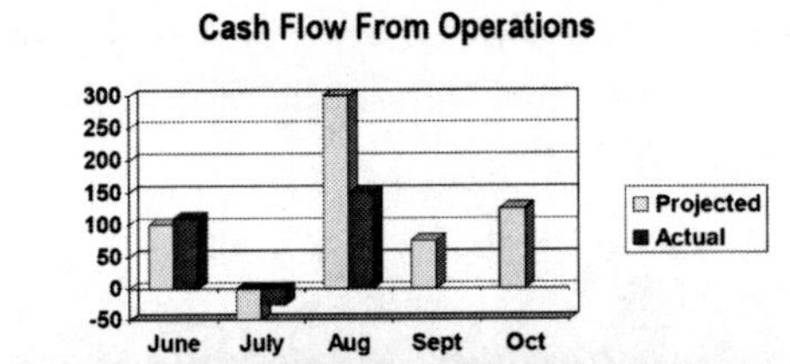

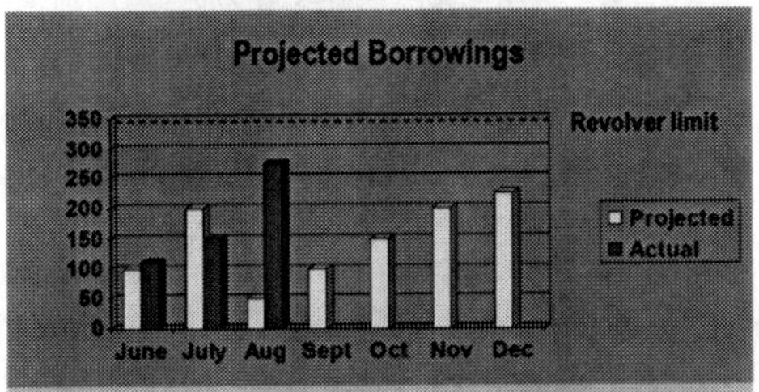

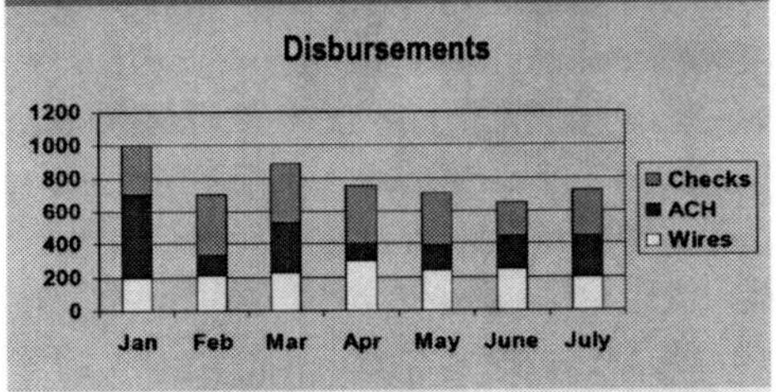

Operations Status

- Lockbox
- Wire Transfer
- Account Recon
- Cash Application
- Vendor Inquiries

XYZ Co. (NYSE:XYZ)

29.18 -0.19 / -0.38%

Open:	29.31	Volume:	7,300
High:	29.49	Volume Avg:	411,700
Low:	29.12	P/E Ratio:	12.00
Prev. Close:	29.37	Div. Yield	3.99%

52-Week Range (Low - High): 23.83 - 30.72

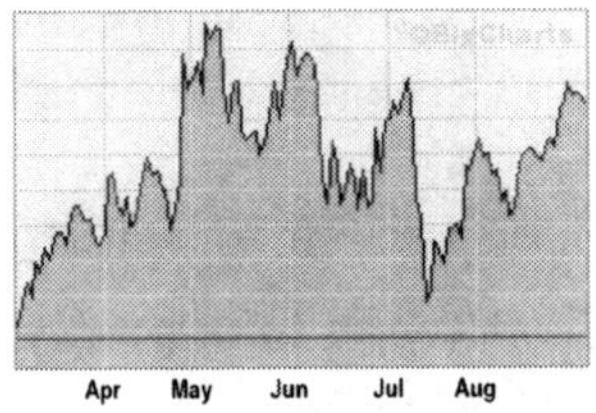

Key Metrics

	June	July	Aug.
DSO	38	40	41
DI	20	15	14
DPO	45	40	41

Key Rates

	Tues.	Wed.
Treasury Bills (90-day)	4.97	4.97
Commercial Paper (Finl. 90-day)	5.27	5.27
Commercial Paper (Non-Finl. 90-day)	5.22	5.23
Federal Funds (Overnight)	5.24	5.23
Eurodollars (90-day)	5.40	5.40
One-Month LIBOR	3.17	3.18

Pending Disbursements (over $100K)

Payee	Amount	Date
James Doe	$155,000.00	Aug. 16, 2xx2
Huntington Reserve	$215,986.55	Aug. 16, 2xx2
IBM	$200,000.00	Aug. 18, 2xx2
IRS	$750,000.00	Aug. 20, 2xx2
Monroe Printers	$125,000.00	Aug. 31, 2xx2
PPG	$425,000.00	Sep. 15, 2xx2

D. Information Management Technology Platforms

Most of the technology solutions available to treasury professionals can be provided on a variety of technology platforms or architectures. The options range from stand-alone personal computers to enterprise technology platforms and the Internet. Each platform has different pros and cons ranging from ease of access to cost.

1. STAND-ALONE TECHNOLOGY

Stand-alone technology refers to software or applications that are installed on an individual computer or workstation. This is typically the type of platform used for word processing and spreadsheet software. Some of the special application packages available for treasury professionals are also often available as stand-alone applications. The drawbacks to this type of application include the fact that the application can only be used by one person at a time and, unless special provisions are made, the information and data are stored locally in the computer itself, creating a potential risk of loss if something happens to the computer and complicating any potential integration with other applications. If multiple copies of the software are installed on multiple computers to allow for use by more than one person at a time, there can be significant cost and effort involved in making sure that all copies of the application, as well as all versions of the data being used, are kept in sync and are identical.

2. CLIENT/SERVER SOLUTION

In a client/server solution, individual workstations/computers are connected to a common server (a type of computer designed to handle the computing requirements of multiple users) over a local or wide area network with a shared database. This allows multiple users to access the application at the same time. The use of a common database ensures that everyone is using the same information and simplifies integration with other systems, such as G/L, A/R, and A/P systems.

This type of environment is normally referred to as an *installed system*, because the software being used is actually installed and resident on the company's server. One of the advantages of this is that the software being used can be customized or configured to meet the specific needs of the company that has purchased and installed it. The disadvantage is that as newer versions of the software with new or expanded capabilities are developed, they must be installed on the server and any modifications made to the older software must be made to the newer version as well. The cost is typically higher than for a stand-alone solution, due to the need for database services and networks, but security and backup can be handled at the server and are typically easier to control. A client/server solution can be installed on a departmental basis and provide service to just one area, such as treasury, or it can be much larger and provide computing capabilities to an entire organization or enterprise, as discussed next.

3. ENTERPRISE TECHNOLOGY

Enterprise technology is functionally the same as a departmental client/server environment but is expanded and typically has more computing capability to handle the overall information technology needs of an entire organization. The result may look the same to an end user, but normally involves centralized control of systems, applications, and security. This is the type of technology platform usually used for ERP systems.

Organizations with enterprise technology solutions often have a dedicated IT function that handles overall security, backup, and information control. They also typically have rules and requirements about the types of computers and software that can be installed on the enterprise network, as well as the types of data and information that can be stored on the network. In some cases, this IT function is outsourced to an external vendor who manages the organization's IT resources for a fee. Even if outsourced, enterprise technology is still considered installed software because the software is owned (or licensed) by a specific company and run on "its" equipment. The advantage to enterprise technology is that everything is centrally controlled and uniform across an organization. The disadvantage can be increased cost and the inability to get specific IT resources when needed due to competing demands from other areas of the organization.

4. HOSTED SOLUTION

Many software vendors, including most TMS vendors, also provide their solutions in a hosted environment. In fact, many vendors are now providing their solutions only in this fashion. In a hosted environment (also referred to as an *application service provider [ASP]* or *software-as-a-service [SaaS]* model), the vendor runs the application on its own technology platform, and companies access the software over the Internet using personal computers and Internet browser software. The vendor is responsible for updating and maintaining the software, as well as providing for appropriate backup and disaster recovery. Hosted solutions are also often referred to as *cloud computing*, since the applications are in the "cloud"[1] and accessed through the Internet.

Hosted software is typically charged for on a per-use fee, a per-user fee, or some combination of both. Some vendors also charge based on volume statistics, such as number of accounts or transactions, or services/modules actually used. This can result in higher ongoing processing fees but typically reduces or eliminates any upfront costs for software and hardware, since those belong to the vendor, as well as the cost and effort involved in installing new versions of the software as they become available. The largest drawback to a hosted solution is that it is typically not customizable. In other words, the user has exactly the same software and applications that all other users have. This is normally compensated for by making the software highly configurable, so that individual users can customize their own input screens and reports. In addition, unlike an installed solution where a company may pay for capabilities that are provided in the purchased software but not actually used, with hosted software, companies typically only pay for what is actually used.

E. Workflow Management

Workflow management is a function incorporated into many software packages that allows multistep processes to be automated, tracked, and managed. Although workflow software is available as independent software, it is more commonly seen as an integrated function of most TMS or ERP solutions.

Workflow management allows a company to use software to implement, monitor, and enforce the specific processes and procedures (i.e., the workflow) that it wants used throughout the company. For example, a company following best practices will normally require that all wire transfers be inputted by one individual and then approved and "released" by a second individual. Workflow management software will accept the initial transaction and then notify the appropriate approver(s) that a transaction is awaiting approval. Once the transaction is approved, the software will automatically release the transaction and may be set up to notify the original initiator that the

1. *The cloud* is a term often used to describe distributed computing provided over the Internet that allows multiple users to access and use the same software from a variety of locations. The software is actually running on a number of servers or computers that can be scaled up or down depending upon the number of users and their usage at any particular time.

transaction has been released. Management can view reports at any time to see how many transactions have been entered into the system and what their current status is (i.e., entered, approved, or released). Workflow management systems are typically capable of managing processes with many steps and multiple decisions points throughout the process. They not only help enforce proper procedures, but they also provide ongoing status reports that can be used to manage the overall process.

F. Technology Policies and Guidelines

Treasury policies and procedures are discussed in detail in Chapter 17. There are, however, several policies that apply specifically to treasury technology.

1. END-USER COMPUTING

Strictly speaking, an organization's end-user computing policy is usually owned by the IT department and not by treasury, and covers policies needed to control risk related to personal computers, laptops, mobile phones, and other portable devices. That being said, it is important for treasury to work with IT as a partner in dealing with the various issues covered in the policy and not blindly assume that IT is handling all of the details. An informed and cooperative treasury operation can help ensure that any problems related to technology are dealt with before becoming major issues. These policies typically cover:

- Password protection and update requirements
- Permitted use of company computer assets
- Permitted use of personal equipment
- Software version control and documentation requirements, including updates and patches
- Backup and recovery procedures
- Data integrity and security
- Use of antivirus software and update requirements
- Use of off-premise data controls for mobile devices and storage such as flash drives
- Permitted use of e-mail and Internet resources
- Documentation of end-user-developed software and spreadsheets

2. TREASURY SYSTEMS

In addition to end-user computing requirements, specific policies are needed regarding any TMS or other treasury-specific software an organization may have installed. While many of the issues involved are similar to those covered by a firm's IT policies, these policies typically are owned and managed by treasury due to the ability to access the firm's financial assets and bank accounts. Concerns typically include:

- Access to treasury systems
- Password requirements
- Segregation of duties
- Reconcilement with accounting and other books of record
- Backup and recovery procedures
- Off-premise access and use
- Reporting requirements

III. TREASURY MANAGEMENT SYSTEMS (TMSs)

A. Background

The simple treasury workstation of the 1980s that handled bank balance collection, daily cash positioning, and in some cases transaction initiation has expanded to an enterprise-wide TMS that now manages global liquidity, FX and financial risk management, derivatives, and bank accounts. Significant advances in technology have led to closer integration with other corporate applications, such as G/L and payroll, as well as single-function systems used for such things as escheatment and hedge accounting. While TMSs are available as independent solutions, many ERP systems now include TMSs as a part of their service offering.

Bank information is the core of a TMS regardless of how the data are received, and the real power of a TMS is the ability to collect, compile, synthesize, and relate the data to financial transactions and other treasury elements relevant to a particular organization. This section of the chapter takes a look at the functionality that can be expected from a TMS, however provided, and discusses some of the issues involved in selecting and implementing a TMS.

B. Functionality

TMSs can provide a wide variety of capabilities and functionality that are of value to the corporate practitioner. This functionality can be broken down into five major categories:

- Cash management
- Payments
- Financial transactions
- Accounting
- Bank account management (BAM)

1. CASH MANAGEMENT

Daily cash management includes cash positioning, funding, and investment. It starts with bank reporting, using SWIFT, BTRS (the replacement of *BAI2*), or other formats (discussed below in more detail) to gather previous- and current-day data from an organization's various banks. The TMS collects this information through direct bank connections (typically over the Internet), SWIFT, or some other third-party network. The value added by the TMS is that it eliminates the need for the organization to use multiple bank communication tools or manage the connectivity process. TMSs typically manage and report on the process so that users know if banks have failed to report, if files are incomplete, or if there are other problems collecting information (e.g., log-on or network issues).

Once data have been collected, TMSs typically have the ability to prepare and reconcile an organization's daily cash position based on bank and cash flow forecasting information. Most TMSs have the ability to provide a real-time or near real-time view of positions across banks, accounts, entities, and geographies.

Cash forecasting is an area of critical importance for most companies and a good example of where technology can provide significant benefits for treasury. A TMS should be able to accept direct input of forecast data by financial teams in a variety of locations, import data from the ERP or a data warehouse, and perhaps extrapolate based on past results. Validating and consolidating the various inputs improves both the quality and ease of forecast assembly.

In-house banking rounds out the suite of cash management capabilities provided by many TMSs. *In-house banking* refers to the company, or more typically the treasury department, acting as a "bank" for a group of the company's operating businesses. Functions performed by an in-house banking function, or IHB, can include cash pooling, inter/intracompany activity (including loans and license agreements), and foreign exchange. Having a technology-enabled IHB enables companies to benefit from functionality possible with an IHB without developing a large and expensive infrastructure to administer the operation. The IHB is the treasury structure that enables more strategic and flexible cash management for global-oriented businesses. IT is the mechanism that provides the ability to centralize cash management and function as an IHB without the use of an external service provider.

2. PAYMENTS

Meeting operational, compliance, and documentation demands for making basic payments can be time consuming, especially when multiple banks are involved, with a variety of access devices and user credentials. TMSs can help by providing the basic payment origination functionality and directly connecting to a company's various banks. Alternatively, many companies are using their ERP systems for A/P and payroll and using the TMS for purely treasury transactions, such as interbank transfers, funding, investing, and hedging. Some organizations take this functionality a step further and use their TMS as a payment factory (discussed in more detail in Chapter 10, Collections, Concentration, and Disbursements) to collect payment transactions from across the organization and sort/transmit them to appropriate banks and payment channels. This requires special workflows that are included in the functionality of some TMSs.

Multilateral netting, which is discussed in Chapter 8, Introduction to Working Capital Management, is a tool some companies use for managing inter/intracompany payment activity on a cost-effective basis. Most TMSs offer some form of netting system capable of working with payables, receivables, or a combination of the two (i.e., a hybrid system). In the event that the netting function is handled by an external provider such as a bank, the TMS can provide access to the transactions and information for posting and reporting purposes.

3. FINANCIAL TRANSACTIONS

TMSs typically provide the ability to manage debt and related derivative transactions. This includes portfolios of short- and long-term borrowings at fixed and floating rates, and lease contracts, as well as specialized functions such as calls, puts, and custom amortization schedules. Most TMS providers include a limited range of debt transactions within their base module. Additional capabilities not included in the base package are often available at an additional cost.

A TMS investment module supports the tracking and management of investment activity. Typically users can manage portfolios of short- and long-term investments, including money market funds, as well as interest-bearing, fixed-rate, floating-rate, and amortizing contracts. As with debt, a limited amount of investment functionality is incorporated in the base package, with additional functionality available as needed.

For those companies dealing in more than one currency, TMSs normally provide basic spot and forward FX transactions, and will generally support the tracking and management of non-deliverable forwards, "plain vanilla" options, and other related products. Transactions can be imported from single-bank or multibank portals to help in reconciliation and eliminate rekeying. Depending on the TMS, hedging and hedge effectiveness testing can be performed and mark-to-market valuations calculated.

4. ACCOUNTING

Transactions created by or imported to the TMS can normally be automatically transferred into the G/L through the generation of dual and multisided entries from the combination of bank and internal transactions within the TMS, increasing the potential for straight-through processing. Some systems support the independent reconcilement of bank transactions to accounting entries. Bank transactions imported each day are matched against accounting entries imported from the G/L based on user-defined rules, for a true bank-to-book reconciliation.

5. BANK ACCOUNT MANAGEMENT (BAM)

Good treasury practices require a firm handle on details of bank accounts, including signatories. Many TMSs offer a complete review and approval workflow to manage signature authorities for all accounts and produce the appropriate management, bank, and compliance reporting. The addition of electronic bank account management (eBAM) capabilities (also discussed below) provides an automated interface between the TMS and an organization's bank(s).

Additionally, some TMS vendors offer analysis and monitoring of bank fees. This capability is also available from certain specialized vendors but primarily for US banks, which typically use relatively standardized AFP fee categories (discussed in Chapter 7, Relationship Management and Vendor Selection). This US approach is becoming more common for global treasuries that take advantage of TWIST standards (discussed below). The functionality allows users to analyze and reconcile bank fees to compare monthly fees against internal benchmarks.

C. Technology Platforms

TMSs are typically available in all the same types of technology platforms discussed earlier in this chapter. The same advantages and drawbacks mentioned in the earlier discussion apply to TMS installations. In the case of TMSs, the available platforms typically include:

- **Stand-Alone:** TMS applications are installed on each user's workstation just as with other common business software such as word processors or spreadsheets.
- **Client/Server:** Individual workstations/computers are connected to a common server over a local or wide area network. The TMS is installed on the server with a single common database and is available to everyone on the network. This allows multiple users to access the same information simultaneously and ensures that everyone is using the same information.
- **Hosted (SaaS or ASP):** The application is hosted by an external vendor on its own site outside the company's infrastructure, sometimes referred to as *in the cloud* or *cloud computing*. The vendor is responsible for maintaining the hardware and the software, as well as providing needed security. Access is typically provided by an Internet browser.
- **ERP:** TMS applications are available as a module or modules of many ERP systems. One of the major benefits of an ERP solution is the integration with a company's other financial applications. A drawback can be the lack of specific features or functionality provided by a dedicated TMS solution.

D. Costs

The initial costs of implementing a TMS are directly influenced by the type of TMS and the specific platform used, and can include one-time costs such as system selection, software, hardware, installation, start-up, implementation, and personnel training expenses. Implementation costs for a TMS may be significant, and care should be taken to ensure these costs are not underestimated.

Ongoing TMS costs can include licensing, maintenance, and software usage. Fixed costs typically include administration, overhead, software maintenance, licensing, and upgrades. Variable costs include telecommunications charges, transaction service charges, and system security expenses.

When considering a TMS, it is important to consider the total cost of ownership for a particular solution. Installed systems often have higher up-front costs, but the ongoing costs can be significantly less since there are usually no usage fees. Hosted solutions, whether bank applications or TMSs, may have low initial costs, but ongoing costs can become significant for heavy users. Spreadsheets may appear to be a low-cost alternative until the lack of maintenance, security requirements, and auditability, and other risk factors are considered. ERP solutions can work well if the company already has an ERP system, but ERP solutions may not have all of the required functionality, leading to the need to purchase specialty software to fill any gaps.

Some of the issues involved in selecting a TMS package or vendor are discussed in Chapter 7, Relationship Management and Vendor Selection. However it is accomplished, the selection of a TMS should not be made using a strictly quantitative cost/benefit analysis, as many of the important benefits of a TMS are qualitative, including ease of use, the availability of ongoing support, and security.

Exhibit 14.2 provides a high-level comparison of the various TMS alternatives.

EXHIBIT 14.2 COMPARISON OF TMS ALTERNATIVES

Alternative	Features/ Functions	Complexity	Ongoing Support	Security/ Controls	Cost Visibility	Initial Cost	Ongoing Cost
Spreadsheets	Low	Low	None	Low/None	Low	Low	Potentially High
Bank Website	Medium	High	Medium	High	Low	Low	Medium to High
Installed TMS	High	High	Medium to High	High	High	Medium to High	Medium
Hosted/SaaS TMS	High	High	High	High	Medium	Low	Medium to High
ERP	Medium to High	High	High	High	High	High	Medium

SOURCE: Treasury Alliance Group LLC, "Trends in Technology," published in 2013 (http://www.treasuryalliance.com/publications).

IV. E-COMMERCE

A. Basics of E-Commerce

E-commerce is defined as the application of information and secure network technology for the purpose of facilitating business relationships, including buying and selling, among trading partners. E-commerce encompasses many types of channels and communications protocols, including traditional electronic data interchange (EDI) and Internet-based commerce. In addition to treasury, other functional areas impacted by e-commerce include supply chain management, online marketing, online transaction processing, automated inventory management, and automated data collection, mining, and warehousing systems.

1. BENEFITS OF E-COMMERCE

E-commerce can offer several benefits. It:

- Improves productivity, thereby enhancing working capital management
- Makes data reentry unnecessary, thereby reducing error rates and enabling faster data processing
- Eliminates mail time, thereby enhancing cash flow processes
- Improves communication capabilities
- Allows straight-through processing (STP)

Once data are entered at the beginning steps of any transaction, the same data can move from one business application system to another without manual intervention, so that information provided in a purchase order, for example, is automatically replicated in subsequent invoices, A/R systems, and A/P systems. E-commerce eliminates manual processes such as filing, matching, sorting, and retrieving material, as well as envelope stuffing, stamping, and mailing. It also significantly reduces cycle times because e-commerce transactions have no mail time delays, involve minimal processing time, and facilitate just-in-time (JIT) inventory management in many companies, all of which serve to meet key objectives of working capital management.

Since e-commerce makes data reentry unnecessary, it allows for straight-through processing, which reduces error rates and enables more efficient processing. For example, using e-commerce for the receipt of remittance information allows for greater accuracy in the posting of payments to the A/R ledger. E-commerce eliminates mail time in both receipts and disbursements, thereby reducing any uncertainty in cash flow timing, enabling more accurate cash flow forecasting, and improving working capital management.

It also offers improved communication capabilities. For example, acknowledgment that a customer has received an invoice helps to resolve issues of payment collection between buyers and sellers.[2]

2. USING THE INTERNET FOR E-COMMERCE

Increasingly, companies are using the Internet as a payment and financial information channel. Because the Internet is accessible by virtually anyone in the world who possesses the necessary hardware, software, and communications systems, it is attractive to many businesses as a means to reach more customers, and facilitate sales and service. However, the openness and accessibility of the Internet makes security a major concern. In addition, some countries may have restrictions on data shared via the Internet or across international boundaries. Many proprietary, Internet-based systems have sophisticated security schemes to ensure the confidentiality of information, protect company networks and databases from unauthorized access, and prevent fraud. Properly secured systems can handle business-to-business (B2B) or business-to-consumer (B2C) transmissions, or a combination of both. Whenever new communications services are established, the file transmission formats and languages must be agreed upon by all parties prior to implementation. In addition, rigorous testing routines should be in place in order to verify that all transmissions are secure.

A company must trust its e-commerce partners more than its paper-based trading partners for several reasons:

- Business dealings with an e-commerce trading partner often involve access to the company's internal systems and information.
- Errors can be made and propagated quickly through the electronic trading channel.
- There are many financial, reputational, and operational consequences of security breaches to a company's system.

B. Electronic Data Interchange (EDI)

EDI is a traditional building block of e-commerce that is based on an infrastructure using standardized communication formats to exchange business data between two trading partners. The following section includes a discussion of some of the common standards used in EDI and banking.

To send information electronically, companies must agree on a specific format and structure for electronic messages and data. In the early years of EDI, companies designed proprietary formats and communication interfaces, and either encouraged or mandated trading partners to participate. Proprietary data formats and technical requirements are used when a company deals with a small number of partners. However, when a company has many EDI partners, a common standard becomes necessary. EDI standards have evolved from proprietary standards to the current cross-industry and international standards, which are discussed in more detail in the next section.

2. Delivery acknowledgment is typically standard in e-commerce communications; however, in mail-based systems, such acknowledgment is only available as a special, extra-cost option (e.g., certified mail).

An important part of EDI transactions is the concept of acknowledgment. The most basic form of acknowledgment simply indicates that a message was received and complied with the basic EDI format being used. This is generally referred to as a *functional acknowledgment*. A second level of acknowledgment relates to the contents of the message. For example, a buyer may send an electronic payment and remittance advice to a supplier. The supplier would send back a functional acknowledgment that simply says it received the remittance information and was able to read it. A second-level acknowledgment would provide details including whether or not payment was properly applied and identify any open discrepancies in applying the remittance information. All EDI communication standards generally provide functional acknowledgments for all messages and then offer specific second-level or application acknowledgments for selected transactions or messages.

C. E-Commerce Communication Standards

Communication protocols, or standard languages, must be used in order for the many different types of systems to communicate with one another. Since treasury must often communicate with many internal and external entities in the conduct of its daily activities, it is important that treasury professionals have a basic understanding of the different communication standards they may encounter. Some examples of these languages are described in this section.

1. UNITED NATIONS/ELECTRONIC DATA INTERCHANGE FOR ADMINISTRATION, COMMERCE AND TRANSPORT (UN/EDIFACT) STANDARDS

Many countries have become involved in developing EDI standards, which has led to the development of the UN/EDIFACT rules. UN/EDIFACT is a set of internationally agreed-upon standards, directories, and guidelines for e-commerce. UN/EDIFACT has been adopted by the International Organization for Standardization (ISO) as ISO Standard 9735. UN/EDIFACT standards are used widely in Europe and in some Asian countries. (Most Asian countries use developing XML standards.) The UN/EDIFACT standards are not compatible with ASC X12 EDI standards (discussed below), but there is translation software available that allows for integration of EDI data with either standard.

2. INTERNATIONAL ORGANIZATION FOR STANDARDIZATION (ISO) 20022

ISO 20022 is an XML-based messaging standard for the financial services industry, whose intended use is transmitting information related to securities, payments, financial reporting, account management, international trade, and foreign exchange (FX). It is part of the ongoing development of Single Euro Payments Area (SEPA) payments standards and the next generation of the SWIFT messaging format. (SWIFT is discussed below, and both SWIFT and SEPA are covered in more detail in Chapter 4, Payment Systems.) ISO 20022 will initially be used for communications between organizations and their banks, as well as between the banks themselves.

3. SOCIETY FOR WORLDWIDE INTERBANK FINANCIAL TELECOMMUNICATION (SWIFT)

SWIFT is discussed in a number of other places in this book. The concern here has to do with telecommunication standards. While SWIFT is primarily a messaging system, it is also responsible for helping to develop standards regarding the types of messages that are carried on its, and other, telecommunications networks. In addition to being heavily involved in the development and management of the ISO 20022 standard discussed above, SWIFT also is responsible for the SWIFT MT (which simply stands for *message type*) messaging standard that is still widely used around the world.

The SWIFT network supports two broad types of transactions. The first—file-level transfers or FileAct—can be used to send and receive any type of bulk file that companies wish to transmit. The files transmitted using FileAct include both transaction data using the ISO 20022 standard, as well as bulk payment files and proprietary messages using nonstandard formats and data specifications agreed to by the various parties to the transmission. The second type of transaction is a traditional SWIFT MT message between two parties. Rather than bulk data, MT messages are predefined messages that provide specific information regarding individual transactions or specific information reporting. MTs are identified by number and cover such things as funds transfers, FX, securities, and bank balance and transaction reporting. Three of the most important messages from a treasury point of view are the MT 940, *Customer Statement Message*, the MT 941, *Balance Report*, and the MT 942, *Interim Transaction Report*. Traditionally, the MT 940 and MT 941 are used to provide previous-day and historical account information while the MT 942 is used to provide specific information regarding current-day transactions.

4. ASC X12 STANDARDS

The Accredited Standards Committee (ASC) X12 of the American National Standards Institute (ANSI) is the coordinating body that develops cross-industry EDI message standards in the United States. Development of the current US EDI standards began in 1968, with an initiative by the transportation industry to establish communications standards between and among railroads, ocean carriers, air carriers, and motor carriers. Following this lead, the grocery and retail industries also developed EDI standards. In 1979, ASC X12 was formed to develop general EDI standards that could be used cross-industry. Recently, the X12 groups have included XML standard usage in the financial services industry as part of their implementation and support efforts.

ASC X12's finance committee, ASC X12F, manages the following tasks:

- Develops and maintains X12 EDI and XML standards, including technical guidelines, focusing on financial e-commerce models
- Develops and maintains financial business models related to areas such as credit card processes, financial remittance delivery, and invoice and payment transactions (e.g., real estate and mortgage lending messages are developed and maintained using EDI and XML standards)
- Develops the payment systems architecture, which includes data security and data content management for financial standards
- Promotes the use of X12 EDI and XML standards across the financial services industry

5. ASC X12 FINANCIAL TRANSACTION SETS

By convention, numbers and letters are used to identify ASC X12 transaction sets. *Transaction sets* generally are defined as the electronic equivalent of a paper business document or form, with specific rules governing their formats. More information regarding the implementation and usage of X12 transaction sets is available on ASC X12's website (http://www.x12.org/).

6. BALANCE AND TRANSACTION REPORTING STANDARD (BTRS)[3]

BTRS is a communication protocol that has been developed by the ANSI ASC X9 committee to facilitate the transmission of balance and reporting information from banks and other financial institutions to their account holders. The predecessor to BTRS is the Bank Administration Institute (BAI) reporting format (often referred to as *BAI2* because it was the second such standard). BAI2 is not currently a standard; it is a commonly used format. BAI2 is widely used for information reporting of account balances, transactions, lockbox detail, and controlled disbursement detail. It has many optional fields and variations from bank to bank. Often banks require their clients to implement variations of the format, causing a large investment in scripting and resources to integrate these versions of the format into their back-office applications.

BTRS, the equivalent of BAI3, is a formal standard that was approved on June 7, 2012, and is administered by the ASC X9 committee. BTRS is intended to increase standardization of and improve upon BAI2. Major changes include:

- Modernization of text to include developments in banking and technology over the past 25 years
- Additional structure to support extended wire remittance (in corporate trade payments)
- Rationalization and reduction of the number of supported transaction codes
- Additional SEPA transaction codes to support new European payment types
- Additional balance codes to facilitate SWIFT and ISO 20022 XML interoperability
- Modified currency rules to make them mandatory and allow for multicurrency applications
- New 900 series code categories to define debits and credits

The standard builds upon the older BAI2 information-reporting format while retaining forward compatibility. Although a BTRS file with the above changes could not be interpreted with a BAI2 reader, a BAI2 file could be interpreted with a BTRS reader.

While the BAI2 code list is a domestic US format, many corporations have implemented the codes for their global reporting requirements. It is not uncommon to see information from other countries in a BAI format. The need for standardization of the BAI formats used for cross-border information is an industry objective and was one of the driving forces behind the transfer of the BAI format to the X9 committee and the globalization of BTRS. ASC X9 has international access and can promote national standards internationally to become ISO standards.

7. TRANSACTION WORKFLOW INNOVATION STANDARDS TEAM (TWIST)

TWIST is an industry group made up of corporations, public administrations, financial services providers (i.e., banks and nonbank financial institutions), and solutions providers (e.g., software vendors and consultancies) that is working to improve the flow of financial information between organizations and their financial institutions. The primary purpose of TWIST is to create XML-based communication standards for the exchange of data

3. Much of the information on BTRS is taken from the ASC X9 website (https://x9.org/standards/btrs/, accessed October 17, 2013).

throughout the financial supply chain. TWIST standards focus on payment and collection, cash management, working capital finance, and financial market access, and help reconcile and integrate treasury management operations with banking partners. The use of the standards are intended to allow treasurers to better position the cash flows of accounts and manage their timing, make short-term investments of unused cash, and manage commercial paper programs and other interactions with financial markets.

D. Electronic Bank Account Management (eBAM)

Bank account management refers to the management of all of the various facets of an organization's relationship with its bank(s), including opening and closing accounts, managing authorized signatories, and maintaining proper copies of documentation. As previously discussed, most TMSs provide functionality to facilitate bank account management. Even with this type of automated support, however, bank account management can be a challenge for any treasury operation due to the large amount of documents and paper that are typically part of the process. eBAM is an effort to replace the large amount of paper in the bank account management process with electronic messages and files exchanged between banks and their customers.

Conceptually, eBAM provides significant benefits to treasury operations, including:

- Eliminating the cost of creating, moving, reviewing, and storing paper
- Streamlining the process of managing complex, dispersed bank account and signatory information
- Improving the ability to quickly change bank accounts and their signatories across banks and geographies
- Strengthening internal control and improving related auditing and management reporting

A key roadblock to eBAM is that it does not eliminate the work required to establish an initial relationship between an organization and a specific bank. Due to the various regulatory and documentation requirements of different countries, discussed in more depth in Chapter 7, Relationship Management and Vendor Selection, companies must first establish a relationship with a given bank before eBAM can be used to manage accounts and related information.

Exhibit 14.3 illustrates the key elements of a conceptual eBAM workflow.

EXHIBIT 14.3 **KEY ELEMENTS OF eBAM**

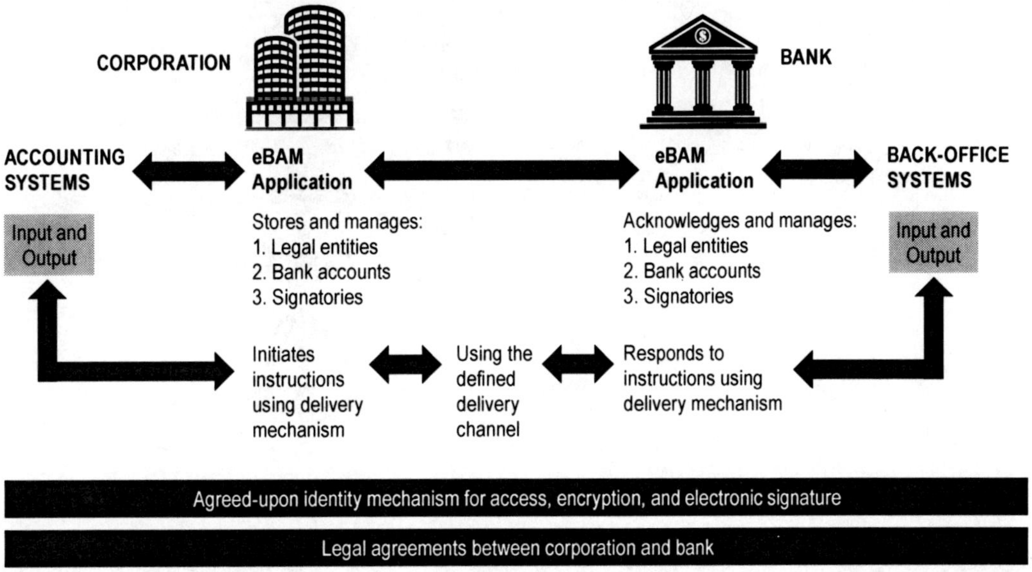

There are currently three major models of eBAM:

- **Corporate-Centric:** The corporation controls the technology and communicates with multiple banks electronically.
- **Bank-Centric:** A specific bank controls the process and communicates with multiple corporate account holders electronically.
- **Utility:** A third party such as SWIFT manages the process and communicates between multiple banks and multiple account holders electronically. In this model, some third parties also provide the ability to create and mail hard-copy documents to banks that are not able or not willing to accept electronic transmissions.

These three models are illustrated in Exhibits 14.4, 14.5, and 14.6, respectively. The entities on the left of each exhibit are corporations, and the entities on the right are banks.

EXHIBIT 14.4 **CORPORATE-CENTRIC eBAM MODEL**

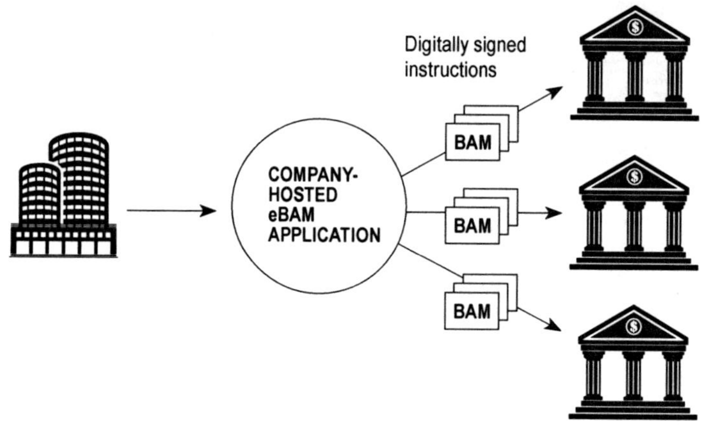

EXHIBIT 14.5 **BANK-CENTRIC eBAM MODEL**

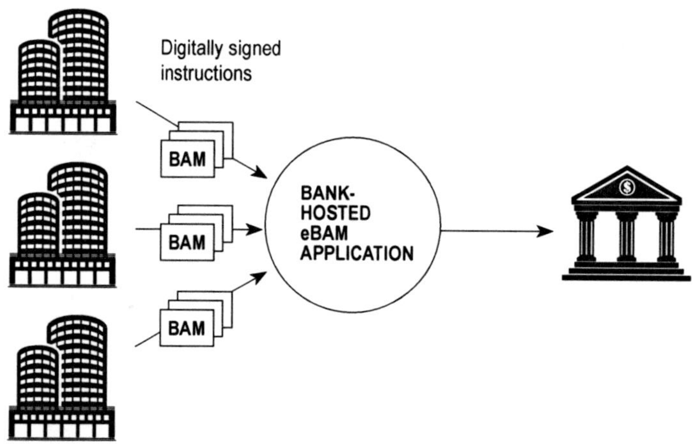

EXHIBIT 14.6 **UTILITY eBAM MODEL**

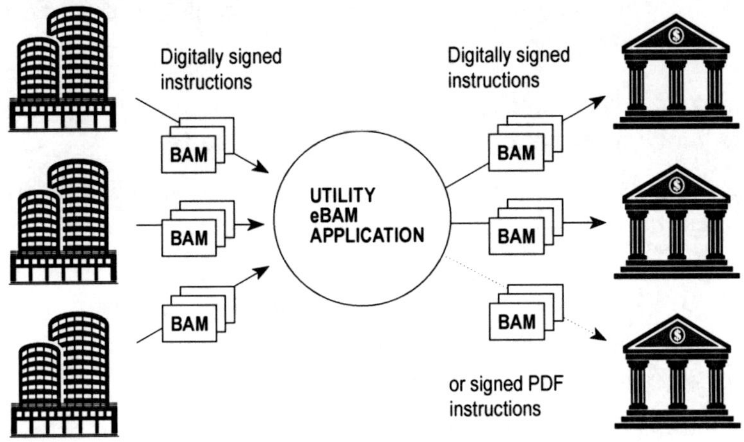

eBAM efforts are being led by SWIFT and a number of major multinational banks, providing a strong standards platform and a core base of bank users. A number of eBAM transaction sets have been added to the ISO 20022 format previously discussed. Although it holds significant promise, eBAM is still in its introductory stages as of the publication of this book. Several pilots have been in operation to test the concept, but more work is needed before eBAM becomes a broad reality.

E. Mobile Banking

Mobile banking refers to the provision of banking and financial services with the help of mobile telecommunication devices, such as mobile phones and tablets (including iPads), while *mobile payments* refers to the ability to use a mobile device to make a payment or transact business. Mobile banking has become a reality for consumer banking, and as a result many corporate bank customers are beginning to ask for mobile banking to address their needs. Some of the functions provided by mobile banking, such as transaction initiation and verification, remote deposit capture, and card acceptance, are discussed in Chapter 10, Collections, Concentration, and Disbursements. Mobile payments are critical to business because although companies typically do not make mobile payments, they are being asked to accept mobile payments from consumers.

Currently, the primary applications in the treasury area relate to information transmittal and transaction authorization. Treasury professionals are often on the go or are simply away from their desks at critical moments in the day when they need to control the disbursement of funds. Being able to do so from a mobile device is a significant benefit in terms of convenience. The informational feature of mobile computing provides instantaneous access to balance information, alerts on significant fund or market movements, and confirmation of important transaction events or credit line availability.

The major barriers to widespread acceptance of corporate mobile banking include security requirements for both the networks and, more importantly, the mobile devices (especially for the initiation of large-dollar transactions); technology issues related to the increased complexity and amount of data of corporate transactions; and the need to accommodate multiple users for a given bank account or relationship.

In addition to the basic Internet and mobile technology, there are a number of other technology innovations that have helped with the growth of mobile banking and mobile payments. These include:

- **Interactive Voice Response (IVR):** IVR is a technology that allows computers to interact with human beings through the use of voice recognition and touch-tone signals from a telephone (mobile or land line).
- **Short Message Service (SMS):** SMS is the text messaging service provided by most mobile telephones. It allows the exchange of short messages between mobile phones and other devices. While there are other messaging services available, such as multimedia messaging service (MMS) or enhanced messaging service (EMS), SMS is more widely used as it is typically available on all modern mobile phones.
- **Wireless Application Protocol (WAP):** WAP is a technical standard for the use and exchange of information over a mobile wireless network. Most mobile devices access the Internet using a WAP-based browser.
- **Near Field Communication (NFC):** NFC is a short-range wireless proximity technology that uses radio frequency signals to communicate between two devices, such as a mobile phone and a payment terminal, or two mobile phones.
- **Radio Frequency Identification (RFID):** RFID involves the use of noncontact wireless technology to transfer information, usually for the purposes of identifying and tracking ID tags attached to merchandise or other objects. RFID tags can be used to identify a specific mobile device for purposes of making and/or authenticating payments.
- **Quick Response (QR) Codes:** A QR code is a two-dimensional bar code that can be attached to an item or displayed on a mobile phone screen, and contains information that can be read by a QR reader or other optical scanner. When placed on an object, it can be scanned by a mobile phone and used to create an automated Internet link, which allows the user to obtain more information about the object or to purchase or pay for the object in a commercial transaction. When displayed on a mobile phone screen, it can be scanned at a point-of-sale terminal and used in place of a traditional payment card.

V. SUMMARY

The use of technology has become an essential part of any treasury professional's job due to the large amount of information that must be managed, compiled, and synthesized as part of routine treasury operations. This chapter provided an overview of some of the key technology issues that treasury professionals face, including security and information management. It then discussed TMSs and provided an overview of the functionality and capabilities that modern TMSs provide. The chapter closed with a discussion of a number of issues related to e-commerce and mobile banking, including an overview of a variety of communications standards that are commonly used in treasury operations.

TEST YOUR UNDERSTANDING: CHAPTER 14

Answers are on pages 702–707.

1. What roles are treasury professionals often responsible for with regards to information management?
2. What are the basic elements of information security?
3. What are the basic factors of multifactor authentication?
4. What is a digital signature?
5. What are tokens?
6. What are the major drawbacks to using spreadsheets as treasury technology?
7. What is a dashboard?
8. What are ERP systems?
9. What is a TMS?
10. List the basic platforms or architectures that are used to provide technology solutions for treasury.
11. What is workflow management?
12. What are the major categories of functionality that are typically provided by TMSs?
13. What are the principal benefits of e-commerce?
14. What is ISO 20022?
15. What is BTRS?
16. What is eBAM?
17. What is mobile banking?
18. What is NFC?

PART IV
Risk Management

CHAPTER 15
Operational and Enterprise Risk Management

CHAPTER 16
Financial Risk Management

CHAPTER 17
Treasury Policies and Procedures

CHAPTER 15
Operational and Enterprise Risk Management

I. INTRODUCTION

II. GENERAL RISK MANAGEMENT

A. The Risk Management Process
B. Techniques Used to Measure Risk
C. Risk Profile
D. Risk Management Policy and Governance

III. ENTERPRISE RISK MANAGEMENT (ERM)

A. Market Risk
B. Credit Risk
C. Operational Risk
D. Liquidity Risk
E. Legal and Regulatory Compliance Risk
F. Event Risk
G. Business Risk
H. Strategic Risk
I. Reputation Risk

IV. OPERATIONAL RISK MANAGEMENT

A. Internal Operational Risks
B. External Operational Risks
C. Fundamental Factors for Operational Risk Management Strategy

V. DISASTER RECOVERY AND BUSINESS CONTINUITY

A. Developing an Effective Disaster Recovery (DR) Plan

B. Creating a Communication Plan

C. Implementing the Plan

D. Performing Periodic Testing

VI. INSURANCE MANAGEMENT

A. Using Insurance Contracts to Manage Risk

B. Dealing with Insurance Providers

C. Insurance Risk Management Services

D. Risk-Financing Techniques

VII. SUMMARY

APPENDIX 15.1: DISASTER RECOVERY (DR) CHECKLIST

APPENDIX 15.2: TYPES OF INSURANCE COVERAGE

I. INTRODUCTION

Organizations are faced with a wide variety of risks. These risks can be physical, financial, or both. This chapter examines the basic concepts of risk management and discusses general operational risks. Financial risk management is discussed in Chapter 16.

In most organizations, treasury is responsible for financial risk management as well as general risk management for treasury operations. This typically includes payments risk, which is discussed in Chapter 10, Collections, Concentration, and Disbursements. In a growing number of organizations, treasury is also directly or indirectly involved in identifying and managing overall risk for the enterprise. This involvement may range from being asked to help identify and quantify various risk elements to being directly responsible for overall risk management for the entire company.

Effective risk management helps minimize the adverse effects of actual and potential losses by either preventing such losses from occurring (i.e., risk control) or financing the recovery from any losses that do occur (i.e., risk financing). The purpose of the risk management process in an organization is to:

- Help managers identify future events that create uncertainty
- Respond to negative possibilities by balancing the negative economic and/or regulatory effects of these possibilities with the costs that can be incurred to mitigate or eliminate them
- Provide direction to guide recovery actions when serious negative events occur

The term *enterprise risk management (ERM)* refers to a comprehensive, organization-wide approach to identifying, measuring, and managing the various risks that threaten the achievement of the organization's strategic objectives and therefore its overall operations. It is characterized by having a viewpoint that encompasses all areas of the organization.

In many organizations, the board of directors has a risk management committee that provides oversight to management regarding the identification and evaluation of ERM-related issues. Some organizations have also added the position of chief risk officer (CRO)—sometimes known as a *chief risk management officer (CRMO)*—whose primary responsibility is ERM. In these organizations, the CRO is the executive accountable to the board of directors for the efficient and effective governance of significant risks—and related opportunities—for the organization and its various segments.

The discussion in this chapter begins with general risk management principles, including techniques used to measure and monitor risk. That is followed by a discussion of the various types of enterprise and operational risk. The chapter closes with a brief discussion of disaster recovery and business continuity plans and a discussion of insurance as part of the risk management process.

II. GENERAL RISK MANAGEMENT

A. The Risk Management Process

The risk management process involves six steps:

- Determine an organization's risk tolerance.
- Identify potential exposures.
- Quantify the impact and level of exposures.
- Develop and implement an appropriate risk management strategy to manage those exposures.
- Monitor the exposures and evaluate the effectiveness of the strategy.
- Review and modify the strategy as needed.

1. DETERMINE RISK TOLERANCE

The first step in developing a risk management strategy is to determine the organization's risk tolerance. Organizations have different tolerances toward risk exposures that will directly impact their risk strategy:

- A new company in a rapidly evolving industry may be more aggressive in taking significant risks, in order to gain a competitive advantage.
- An established company in a mature industry may be more cautious about taking risks, in order to protect an existing competitive advantage.
- Government entities and not-for-profit organizations may be completely averse to taking or assuming even a small level of risk.
- A company's ability to accept risk may be limited by various covenants or indentures in agreements or charters.

2. IDENTIFY POTENTIAL EXPOSURES

Risk exposures in all areas of the organization need to be identified clearly both in terms of their likelihood (probability of occurrence) and their potential impact on the organization. For example, financial risks such as interest rate variations, FX rate changes, or fluctuations in commodity prices will vary depending on the industry and form of the business organization or government agency. Operational risk is also an important consideration, especially for organizations with significant treasury operations. Timely and accurate exposure information is critical for effective risk management.

3. QUANTIFY THE EXPOSURE

Once an exposure is identified, it must be measured and assessed both quantitatively and qualitatively. (Techniques for measuring risk are discussed later in this chapter.) The CRO and/or other senior management need to evaluate whether the organization can tolerate the risk, and whether it should reduce, transfer, or eliminate the exposure via an appropriate risk management strategy.

Quantitative assessment is important in order to:

- Assess the materiality, or level, of the exposure (i.e., high/medium/low)
- Identify the risk drivers (i.e., the factors that could or would cause the risk to materialize)
- Determine the probability/likelihood for losses due to the exposure
- Provide a benchmark for assessing risk mitigation strategies, generally in a cost-versus-benefit framework

\When quantifying materiality, a typical approach is to measure the cost or financial impact of a given risk. Material risks are those that exceed a predetermined level of financial impact (i.e., potential cost) or a predetermined level of risk (i.e., high risk with high-dollar exposure) to the organization. Materiality of risk exposure may vary significantly by company, industry, product, existing controls, etc., and should be assessed and reevaluated on a regular basis. The materiality of exposure will normally drive the frequency and amount of monitoring and testing needed.

Qualitative assessment is important to the overall design of appropriate risk mitigation strategies from both an economic and an accounting perspective. A qualitative assessment should:

- Examine basic operating procedures to determine where mitigation strategies, such as hedges, may be useful (e.g., a balance sheet hedge matches exposed liabilities against exposed assets and is referred to as *asset and liability management*)
- Determine how fundamental business processes contribute to risks and permit the identification of possible solutions
- Ensure that derivatives are structured and sized appropriately and proper accounting procedures are followed when derivatives are used as part of financial risk mitigation strategies

4. DEVELOP AND IMPLEMENT AN APPROPRIATE RISK MANAGEMENT STRATEGY

After identifying and measuring its risk exposures, an organization must develop, approve, and put into practice the right strategy to mitigate the exposures (refer also to the section on risk policy below). There are four basic approaches to managing risk:

- **Avoid the Risk:** This approach may involve a company deciding not to enter into a certain line of business or utilize a particular business or manufacturing process due to the risks involved.
- **Mitigate the Risk:** Mitigating risk generally involves putting appropriate controls in place to limit the potential risk exposure. In financial risk management, discussed in Chapter 16, approaches such as using derivatives or balance sheet hedges create a financial position (either a derivative instrument or a balance sheet item) that offsets the risk from an ongoing business process. For example, if a company expects to receive some amount of foreign currency as an accounts receivable, it could enter into a forward or futures contract that allows the company to convert the foreign currency into the home currency at a fixed rate that is known today. Other risk mitigation approaches include process and facility design, project management, education, and compliance management. An example of another risk mitigation approach would be the installation of sprinklers in a building to reduce the impact of a fire.
- **Transfer the Risk:** With this approach, the organization finds someone else who is willing to assume the risk. As discussed later in this chapter, the primary means of transferring risk is by using insurance of some type. A company may also contractually transfer risk by requiring that the risk be borne by another party in the supply/delivery chain.

- **Retain the Risk:** By their very nature, some lines of business carry inherent risks, and it may not be possible to completely avoid, transfer, or mitigate all the risks in certain types of operations. In these cases, businesses may opt to selectively bear some risks. For example, a power utility operating in an area prone to hurricanes has to deal with fact that its operations will likely be impacted by this risk at some point. In this case, disaster recovery and contingency planning become a key part of the utility's risk management strategy.

5. MONITOR THE EXPOSURES AND EVALUATE THE STRATEGY

An organization should monitor each material risk exposure. The frequency with which it does this depends on the likelihood of the risk, the materiality of the risk, and the organization's appetite for risk. For example, the frequency may be shortened or lengthened if the underlying asset's volatility decreases or increases, or if management's risk tolerance changes. An organization must evaluate the effectiveness of each strategy it has employed to reduce exposures. This evaluation should be performed with the organization's overall risk tolerance level in mind. The results of this assessment should be used to evaluate the overall effectiveness of the risk management strategy.

6. REVIEW AND MODIFY THE STRATEGY AS NEEDED

The risks that an organization faces change over time and its risk tolerance may also change. An effective risk management strategy must adapt to deal with these changes. Any risk strategy should be reviewed periodically in light of the quantitative results of the risk management program to determine what, if any, changes are needed. For example, if a company has decided to transfer risk through the use of insurance, it needs to review its insurance coverage to make sure that the coverage matches the current level of risk.

B. Techniques Used to Measure Risk

The following techniques are designed to evaluate the potential financial impact of risk-inducing events on a firm.

1. SENSITIVITY ANALYSIS

Sensitivity analysis examines the impact of a change in the value of a variable on a selected outcome measure (such as net cash flow), assuming all other variables are held constant. Sensitivity analysis is used to alter the value of a single variable in a spreadsheet or computer model to see how a change in that variable affects the outcome (net cash flow, in this example). For example, a company with variable-rate debt could perform a sensitivity analysis to determine the impact on cash flow if interest rates went up or down by 1%, 2%, and 4%.

These what-if exercises help to ascertain how sensitive net cash flow is to the amount of change that could reasonably be expected to occur in each variable. Sensitivity analysis helps to identify the variables that have the greatest influence on net cash flow. Once known, these variables can be categorized as *uncontrollable* or *somewhat controllable*. Steps can be taken to favorably control the variables that can be influenced. A monitoring protocol needs to be established to alert the firm to unfavorable movements in those variables that cannot be controlled so it can adjust operations as needed.

2. SCENARIO ANALYSIS

Scenario analysis is similar to sensitivity analysis, but more than one variable is altered at a time. Scenario analysis usually starts with a base case—an expected value for each input variable affecting the final value. People within the firm who are most familiar with each variable are asked to provide estimates of the highest and lowest possible values for those variables. Overall best- and worst-case scenarios can then be constructed to assess the range of possible outcomes for net cash flow or another value of interest. Sometimes, scenario analysis is formalized by asking those who supply best- and worst-case values for the variables to provide a subjective probability distribution to accompany their estimates. This makes the examination of the sensitivity of net cash flow to the variables more precise and, hopefully, more accurate.

3. VALUE AT RISK (VaR)

Another approach in determining how changing financial variables affect a company's value is called *value at risk (VaR)*. VaR is a statistical technique that was developed in the trading rooms of financial institutions to estimate the maximum potential losses of a trading operation or portfolio for a given period of time—in other words, the worst-case scenario. It was designed to incorporate a wide range of risk factors and summarize their impact in a single measure that answers the question, what is the most that I can expect to lose over a given period of time (e.g., a day or a year) with a reasonable amount of certainty? That amount is the value at risk.

For example, if a portfolio of securities has a one-day 5% VaR of $10 million, there is only a 5% probability that the securities will fall in value by more than $10 million in one day, absent any action by the owner of the securities (e.g., hedging or trading). Or to put it another way, there is a 95% probability that the most the investor will lose is $10 million on any given day. This does not imply that the owner will actually lose $10 million in a single day—just that $10 million is the most that the owner is likely to lose in a day. A VaR is always stated in terms of a probability, an amount, and a time period.

The VaR approach uses the probability and monetary impacts of specified events over a period of time to assess risk. A number of treasury and risk systems offer VaR modules, and basic market risk packages will sometimes provide VaR analysis for each hedge decision.

The most common approach to using VaR is called the variance-covariance method, which assumes that the future outcomes of some event are distributed normally. This approach only requires the estimation of two factors: an expected (i.e., average) value and a standard deviation for the distribution of these future outcomes.[1]

For example, Company A, whose functional currency is dollars, wants to determine the VaR of its foreign exchange exposure in its euro position, valued at $50 million, in order to determine whether it needs to hedge the exposure. (Hedges as a financial risk management tool are discussed in detail in Chapter 16.) Assume the company has determined, based on historical data, that the mean, or average, loss on any given day is zero. This is actually a reasonable result since the average change in currency value over a very short period of time is typically close to zero. Assume that the company has also determined that the standard deviation for a euro/dollar investment is $0.008. For this example, assume that the company wants to determine the VaR at the 5% level—in other words, what is the maximum dollar amount of risk that the company faces for this

1. Standard deviation is discussed in Chapter 12, Long-Term and Capital Investments.

investment 95% of the time? VaR is typically calculated at the 1%, 2.5%, or 5% level. At the 5% level, the value at risk is equal to 1.65 times the standard deviation of change in the currency. Using this information, the calculation becomes:

$$\begin{aligned} \text{VaR (5\%)} &= \text{Total Currency Value} \times [\text{Mean} - (1.65 \times \text{Standard Deviation})] \\ &= \$50{,}000{,}000 \times [0 - (1.65 \times \$0.008)] \\ &= \$50{,}000{,}000 \times -0.0132 \\ &= -\$660{,}000 \end{aligned}$$

Based on the information provided, the VaR at a 5% level for one day is $660,000. Another way to phrase this is to say that the company would expect— with a 95% confidence level—that its foreign exchange loss for any given day would not be more than $660,000. It could be less. It could, in fact, be a gain. But the worst loss that could be expected in a single day, 95% of the time, is $660,000.

Depending upon the circumstances, calculation of VaR can quickly become quite complex. As a result, most VaR calculations are typically performed through the use of computer software. Some treasury management systems include modules to calculate VaR and other risk models.

4. MONTE CARLO METHOD

A Monte Carlo method is a simulation method that uses probability and random numbers to solve a variety of problems. It uses computer models and random numbers to run repeated simulations of an event to determine the likelihood of specific outcomes. For example, given the probability distributions of revenue and cost variables based on past experience, what is the expected outcome of some measure, such as firm value, net cash flow, or economic value added?

If net cash flow is being simulated, historical experience is used to develop a range of outcomes and associated probability distributions for each variable in the set of variables that have a material impact on net cash flow. Then, values for each variable are randomly chosen by a computer software program in accordance with that variable's probability distribution. These values are combined per a specified formulation (e.g., revenues less all forms of cash outflow) to produce a measure of net cash flow. Simulation is useful because this process can be performed thousands of times. In each simulation run, the computer software selects a value for each variable derived from its probability distribution, assembles the values obtained, and produces a net cash flow number. A probability distribution for net cash flow emerges over the course of the many runs.

C. RISK PROFILE

A company's risk profile refers to how the company's overall value changes as the price of financial variables changes. The basic risk profile for a public company shows how the firm's earnings per share, common stock price, or overall value responds to changes in interest rates, FX rates, or commodity prices.

Risk profile analysis identifies the risks, classifies each risk into clearly defined categories, and quantifies the risks with respect to the probability of occurrence and the impact on value and/or cash flows. The analysis can be used to evaluate the effectiveness of the risk reduction measures that are employed. In some organizations, this process is known as a *risk self-assessment*. To demonstrate compliance with Sarbanes-Oxley (SOX) and similar requirements in various countries, many companies perform risk self-assessments and test against them regularly. These assessments are sometimes referred to as *risk and control self-assessments (RCSAs)*. For organizations that are not publicly traded (i.e., privately held, not-for-profit, or governmental), a risk profile is used to assess the impact on cash flow.

D. Risk Management Policy and Governance

Regardless of an organization's approach to risk, it is important for the firm's risk management committee and CRO (or equivalent) to have a clearly defined risk management policy endorsed and approved by the highest management level possible, preferably the board of directors. The policy should:

- Contain a concise statement of the organization's risk management goals and the overall scope of the risk management policy (e.g., eliminate, mitigate, and transfer risk)
- Define authorities and responsibilities (and the role of the CRO, if the organization has one)
- Identify the types of exposures to be managed
- Delineate the mitigation techniques and products that may be used
- Outline the process for determining specific strategies to be employed and exposures to be mitigated
- Summarize the process for monitoring performance of the strategies
- Outline contingency plans
- Require periodic review of the policy and testing of plans

In many companies, the CRO (or equivalent) reports directly to the CEO, the board of directors, or both. This is important for two reasons. First, the high level within the company adds authority to requests and recommendations related to risk management. Second, reporting to the CEO as opposed to someone directly responsible for risk management activities (such as the CFO or treasurer) helps creates an appropriate segregation of duties and responsibilities.

III. ENTERPRISE RISK MANAGEMENT (ERM)

As previously mentioned, ERM refers to a comprehensive, organization-wide approach to identifying, measuring, and managing the various risks that threaten the achievement of the organization's strategic objectives and therefore its overall operations. One purpose of ERM is to ascertain if and how each department contributes to, or is impacted by, a particular risk category (e.g., financial, operational, or market). Traditionally, risks have been addressed at the business department or other organizational subdivision level. ERM's comprehensive approach lets a business assess the full scope and implications of risks across division lines. Methods and models of ERM have become important tools for firms, and since they encompass the entire business, many aspects extend beyond the boundaries of treasury activities.[2]

ERM helps to ensure effective reporting and compliance with laws and regulations, and helps avoid damage to the entity's reputation and associated consequences. It also helps an entity achieve its goals while prudently managing the unexpected.

2. An important standards organization in the area of ERM and related internal controls is the Committee of Sponsoring Organizations of the Treadway Commission (COSO). This group operates under the auspices of the American Institute of Certified Public Accountants (AICPA) and is responsible for establishing COSO's standards for ERM.

When examining an organization's overall enterprise risk, there are many types of risk that must be considered. The important risks to consider are:

- Market risk (including financial risk)
- Credit risk
- Operational risk
- Liquidity risk
- Legal and regulatory compliance risk
- Event risk
- Business risk
- Strategic risk
- Reputation risk

A. Market Risk

Market risk is the possibility that fluctuations in financial market prices and rates will reduce the value of a security or a portfolio. It is usually divided into general risk (i.e., risk related to overall market rates and conditions) and firm-specific risk (i.e., risk related solely to an individual firm). The four basic types of market risk are:

- Equity price risk
- Interest rate risk
- Foreign exchange (FX) risk
- Commodity price risk

The last three of these risks (interest rate, FX, and commodity price) are generally referred to as *financial risk*. From the perspective of a treasury professional, *financial risk* is the general term for the impact on an organization from unexpected changes in interest rates, FX rates, or commodity prices. In most cases, treasury looks at financial risk as the probability that the value of a given asset/liability or some future transaction will be different from expectations (e.g., the value of a future payment on accounts receivable in euros for a US-based company will be dependent on the exchange rate between the euro and the US dollar). In many cases, these risks can be managed by some type of hedging, usually involving the use of a derivative contract or balance sheet hedge. This approach to financial risk, as well as some techniques to manage financial risk exposures, is covered in more detail in Chapter 16, Financial Risk Management.

Another view of financial risk is from the perspective of its impact on the overall market value of the firm or on a portfolio of investment assets. This view is somewhat broader in its approach and extends beyond just the transaction level. The important question to ask is, what impact would changes in interest rates, FX rates, or commodity prices have on the overall value of the portfolio in question? For a portfolio manager of primarily domestic equities, equity price risk (discussed below) is of primary concern. On the other hand, for a manager of a portfolio that contains international equities/bonds and commodities (e.g., gold and silver), all four of the components of market risk become important.

1. EQUITY PRICE RISK

Equity price risk is usually associated with volatility in stock prices. The general form of this risk refers to the sensitivity of an instrument or portfolio value to a change in broad stock market indices, while the firm-specific portion of this risk relates just to the company in question. As discussed in Chapter 12, Long-Term and Capital Investments, firm-specific risk can be mitigated by holding a portfolio of stocks, while general risk cannot be eliminated.

2. INTEREST RATE RISK

Interest rate risk relates to changes in investment values and borrowing costs, and potentially to overall firm value, as interest rates change.

3. FOREIGN EXCHANGE (FX) RISK

FX risk arises from the exposure an organization has as a result of transactions, assets, and liabilities that are denominated in a foreign currency. As exchange rates fluctuate, so too can the value of these items, ultimately impacting the overall value of a firm.

4. COMMODITY PRICE RISK

Commodity price risk differs considerably from interest rate and FX risk since most commodities are traded in markets where the concentration of supply in the hands of a few suppliers can magnify price volatility.

Exhibit 15.1 provides examples of general and firm-specific market risk for each of the four risks described above.

EXHIBIT 15.1 **EXAMPLES OF MARKET RISK BY CATEGORY**

	General Risk	Firm-Specific Risk
Equity Price Risk	The market as a whole declines due to general economic conditions.	The value of a company's stock declines because the company's chairman is indicted for stock fraud.
Interest Rate Risk	Interest rates increase broadly, impacting borrowing rates for all companies.	Interest rates for airplane leases rise, affecting the operating cost and related value of an airline whose entire fleet of planes is leased.
FX Risk	The value of the dollar falls in relation to other major currencies, affecting the market value of US companies.	The value of the South African rand falls in relation to the US dollar, affecting the value of a US-based company with major South African operations.
Commodity Price Risk	Petroleum prices are rising significantly, impacting the value of any company that uses large amounts of petroleum, such as airlines and petrochemical companies.	Orange crops are wiped out by frost damage, impacting a company whose sole product is orange juice.

B. Credit Risk

Credit risk is related to how a change in the credit quality of a company would affect the value of a security or portfolio of investments. Default on an investment or security is the extreme case of credit risk, but downgrading of a security can also be an issue. In some cases, the creditor may recover some value after default and the amount recovered is called the *recovery value or rate*. When given as a percentage, it is called the *loss given default*.

Credit risk arises both from transactions and from any risk in the portfolio due to concentration of similar assets. When the assets in a portfolio are all concentrated in a single area, industry, or type of security, the overall riskiness of the portfolio may increase significantly due to correlations between the investments (i.e., they all move together, thus increasing the overall volatility of the portfolio). Other risks in the credit area include risks related to specific security issues, the risks from specific issuers, and the probability of large (or multiple) failures on the part of counterparties to the transactions. Trade credit risks are covered in Chapter 8, Introduction to Working Capital Management. Default risks related to short-term investments and borrowing are covered in Chapter 11, Short-Term Investing and Borrowing. And risks related to long-term investments and borrowing are covered in Chapter 12, Long-Term and Capital Investments.

C. Operational Risk

Operational risk refers to potential losses resulting from inadequate systems, management failure, faulty controls, fraud and human error, and other related issues. Management of this type of risk exposure is covered in detail in the section on operational risk management later in this chapter.

D. Liquidity Risk

Liquidity risk is typically divided into two areas: funding liquidity risk and asset liquidity risk. Funding liquidity risk relates primarily to an organization's ability to raise necessary cash to meet its obligations as they come due. It is often linked to the ability to raise capital (both short- and long-term) in a timely manner, and it typically is managed by holding marketable securities or open (i.e., available) lines of credit. An example of liquidity risk would be a corporation with an active commercial paper program, which generally requires that the corporation must continually roll over this commercial paper. This program exposes the company to considerable funding liquidity risk, as many factors can affect the ability to refinance the commercial paper, such as a reduction in the credit rating of the company, narrowing spreads in short-term credit markets, or a deterioration in the credit markets themselves.

Asset liquidity risk relates to the ability to sell an asset quickly and at close to its true value. Asset liquidity risk is especially a problem for organizations holding portfolios of investment assets, particularly if those assets are less than liquid due to the type of asset (e.g., mortgage-backed securities during the Recession of 2009) or general market conditions (e.g., having to sell securities in a downward-trending market). This topic is covered in more detail in Chapter 11, Short-Term Investing and Borrowing.

E. Legal and Regulatory Compliance Risk

Legal and regulatory compliance risk is a type of operational risk and is typically managed by the compliance area of an organization. This topic is discussed later in this chapter's operational risk management section.

F. Event Risk

Event risk is the risk associated with unexpected events related to a given organization. Event risk includes such incidents as an unplanned corporate reorganization or a large natural disaster.

G. Business Risk

Business risk covers the classic risks to success in operating a business venture, such as uncertainty about the demand for products or services, the price that can be charged for those products or services, and the costs of producing and delivering the products or services. Business risk is primarily associated with the general day-to-day management of a company. Sometimes, strategic and reputation risks are viewed as components of business risk.

H. Strategic Risk

Strategic risk refers to the risk of major investments for which there is a significant uncertainty about success or profitability. Examples in this area would include entering into new markets, trying to spot and take advantage of trends, and investing in new technology.

I. Reputation Risk

Reputation risk is the risk that customers, suppliers, investors, and/or regulators may decide that a company has a bad reputation and decide not to do business with that company. For financial institutions, this type of risk is especially important and is specifically covered under Basel guidelines.[3] In some countries, companies are also under increasing pressure to demonstrate their ethical, social, and environmental responsibilities. Reputation risk also relates to how companies react to unexpected events that can impact their reputations and ultimately their futures.

IV. OPERATIONAL RISK MANAGEMENT

Generally, *operational risk* is defined as the risk of direct and indirect losses resulting either from external events that impact an organization's operations or from inadequate and failed internal processes, people, and systems. Operational risks do not ordinarily include market or credit risks. Usually, the internal sources of operational risk are related to the lack or failure of controls surrounding people, processes, or technology. External events can range from localized events (such as momentary communications failures) to negative global economic or political events.

Operational risk can be a significant cause of financial loss. Most financial disasters are attributed to a combination of exposure to market or credit risk, along with some failure of controls or the internal audit function. However, in many operational risk disasters, a single employee has been responsible for staggering losses that could have been prevented by appropriate oversight and controls. The problem is often the lack of management

3. Basel guidelines, promulgated by the Bank for International Settlements (BIS), are discussed in Chapter 2, Regulatory and Legal Environment, and Chapter 7, Relationship Management and Vendor Selection.

involvement in establishing financial controls and overseeing people who use financial tools such as derivatives or who have responsibilities relating to the trading of financial instruments and securities.

A. Internal Operational Risks

Internal risks involve an organization's employees, processes, or technology. The following are selected examples.

1. EMPLOYEE RISK

Employees can be a significant source of internal operational risk. The general risk of intentional employee fraud is typically referred to as *defalcation risk*, while the specific case of theft of money, securities, or property by an employee is known as *fidelity risk*. Employee fraud risk is not limited to the theft of company assets, but can also include the purposeful violation of company policies or procedures to improve performance ratings or compensation or to cover up errors and mistakes. An example of this type of fraud would be a "rogue" trader who violates company policy to indulge in risky and/or high-volume trades in an attempt to garner a larger year-end performance bonus. A more significant source of internal risk stems from unintentional actions by employees. Examples include employee errors in data entry or reentry, as well as transposition or deletion of numbers. Other potential sources of internal risk are the lack of knowledge or skills, and the loss of key personnel. Internal operational risk may arise from the employer's liability relative to employment law, as well as health and safety regulations. Once identified and assessed for materiality, most internal operational risks can be addressed by developing and implementing strong internal controls such as the segregation of duties, maker-checker controls,[4] periodic self-audits, and management oversight. In addition, some of the impact from this type of risk can be mitigated by insurance.

2. PROCESS RISK

Many organizations experience substantial exposure to losses related to the processes employed in day-to-day business operations. Process risk can arise from any functional area of a business, including procurement, manufacturing, sales, or fulfillment. The risk usually comes from a lack of proper controls or the failure of employees to follow procedures.

One source of process risk for the treasury area can result from accounting or financial reporting errors. Another source of process risk is a lack of timely reconciliation of bank accounts. These risks can be a potentially serious problem given the penalties introduced under SOX in the US and similar regulations put forth by other national stock exchanges. Organizations with high levels of manual processes have a significant risk of potential errors in data entry.

Process risk is not limited to manual processes. It can also occur when processes are so technical and complex that the people using them do not understand the processes, how to use them, or more importantly, what their limitations are and when they should not be used. An example of this latter type of risk would be complex computer models used to make investment decisions. In many cases the models are very helpful, but when the decisions being made go beyond the capabilities of the various models, the resulting risk can be significant. This type of process risk was demonstrated through the various credit risk models that were used by many companies to manage the risk of auction rate securities in the early part of the century. The models, which indicated little or no risk of default for most of the securities, turned out to be based on incorrect assumptions that most investors did not understand, resulting in large losses for many companies.

4. The practice of maker-checker controls involves one person performing a task while another person checks for accuracy. For example, in most companies one person is responsible for creating or entering wire transfer information into a TMS or bank terminal, and a second person is responsible for verifying and "releasing" the wire transfer.

Another type of process risk is incurred when an organization may not be able to meet the terms of contracts with customers and suppliers. This is often a problem in industries that deal in sparse commodities, where a supplier might not be able to meet demand. Also related to the production and delivery process is the risk of capacity error. Excess capacity increases overhead and fixed costs, which increases an organization's general business and operational risks. Conversely, insufficient capacity can lead to large backlogs, lost orders, increased errors, or unintended interruptions in the manufacturing and delivery process due to overtime or extra shifts.

Aside from the normal risk of nonpayment for goods or services, there can be errors in the actual clearing and settlement processes for financial transactions. On an internal basis, inbound payments may be posted to the wrong account or recorded improperly, which is sometimes a problem as organizations move from paper payment processes and implement new electronic processes. Outbound payments also may be misdirected, either unintentionally or as a result of employee fraud.

3. TECHNOLOGY RISK

As the treasury area of an organization relies increasingly on technology, the operational risk associated with the use of technology increases. Security breaches related to technology can be either internal or external types of risks. From an internal perspective, breaches are generally referred to as *security violations* and result when an employee bypasses or disobeys internal policies or guidelines related to technology use.

Another type of technology risk is the risk associated with the choice of a particular technology platform or vendor, including issues such as the need for after-sale installation and support or even the risk that a vendor may go out of business. A related issue is the risk associated with the potential failure or obsolescence of vendor-acquired hardware, software, and/or communications devices. This risk may also arise when a treasury system is selected without the support of, and consultation with, the organization's technology and legal staffs.

For example, a treasury information system vendor may offer a product that is suitable for the organization, but the vendor's stability and long-term viability may be questionable. It is sometimes preferable to purchase a good, but perhaps second-choice, software product from a known and stable provider rather than a superior product from a new and untested provider. There could also be risks related to capabilities, capacity, and compatibility of treasury technology with other systems in the organization.

Technology risk may also involve extensive use of computer-based spreadsheets in many parts of an organization's day-to-day operations. Spreadsheets can be extremely useful for many business functions and for data management, but there are some issues when they are used for mission-critical applications that require transactional and information processing. Complex spreadsheet models mixed with formula protection are often difficult to monitor and audit with respect to reliability and may provide an avenue for potential mistakes, file corruption, or employee fraud.

While spreadsheets may be appropriate for some treasury functions if proper controls are in place, critical treasury functions, especially those related to the payment/settlement process, should be performed on treasury systems or bank-provided payment systems rather than on spreadsheets.[5]

B. External Operational Risks

There are numerous external sources of operational risk, resulting primarily from an organization's need to interact with many types of external parties. Generally, these sources are categorized as financial institution, counterparty, legal and regulatory compliance, supplier, external theft/fraud, physical and electronic security, natural disaster, and terrorism.

1. FINANCIAL INSTITUTION RISK

Several key risks are associated with the use of financial institutions. The first is the potential failure of the financial institution and the resulting impact on the company (e.g., a loss of balances, diminished borrowing capabilities, or disrupted services). Other risks include potential operational failure on the part of the financial institution that performs daily transactions processing, communication failures between the company and the financial institution, risks related to the use of online banking portals, and the risk of loss or tampering with payment files.

2. COUNTERPARTY RISK

One of the key issues for treasury professionals in companies of all sizes is counterparty risk. Counterparty risk is the risk that the other party in a contract or financial transaction will not perform as promised. As covered earlier in this chapter, one component of counterparty risk is related to credit and default risk. In a generic context, however, the concept of counterparty risk extends to the risk related to any type of performance failure on the part of any of the counterparties with which an organization must interact. One resource available for guidance in this area is the *CTC Guide to Counterparty Risk Management* published by the Corporate Treasurers Council.

3. LEGAL AND REGULATORY COMPLIANCE RISK

Given the increasingly litigious business environment, a significant source of external operational risk is potential lawsuits or other legal actions instigated by customers, trade partners, or governmental agencies and regulators. This is exacerbated by the continuing growth in governmental regulation in many countries around the world. Multinational companies need to understand and comply with regulatory authorities in every jurisdiction in which they operate. The growth of laws dealing with terrorism and anti-money laundering has added significant regulatory and compliance overhead for organizations with large numbers of financial transactions, especially those transactions that cross international borders.

As discussed in Chapter 7, Relationship Management and Vendor Selection, *sovereign risk* is the risk of interference by a foreign government in the settlement or payment of a foreign transaction, and *political risk* refers to the economic impact that businesses may face due to political changes or decisions within a country. (The two terms are often used interchangeably.) This includes the risk of expropriation or other loss of foreign asset value. Also, tax risk (related to uncertainty about future tax liabilities) must be assessed, especially for multinational organizations that deal with a wide variety of sometimes conflicting tax codes and regulations. This risk can be substantial, given the penalties often assessed with missed filings or the underpayment of taxes.

5. The ISO 27001 standard provides an excellent framework for evaluating and managing IT security and risk.

4. SUPPLIER RISK

Risk related to an organization's suppliers and outsourcing arrangements is a specific type of counterparty risk that also entails significant operational risks. The more critical the supplier or commodity is in the production process, the more risk an organization faces if the supplier either fails to deliver according to plan or provides substandard products and services that result in customer dissatisfaction. These risks are even more important in an environment of shortened supply chains and just-in-time inventory management. Supplier failures or shortages quickly impact a company's customers, especially if the process being outsourced is critical to an organization's day-to-day operations. Also, the risk of a merger, acquisition, or divestiture of a particular supplier may result in disruptions in critical supplies or services. The trend toward outsourcing treasury functions has increased this aspect of operational risk significantly, as critical tasks are performed by outside parties rather than by company personnel.

5. EXTERNAL THEFT/FRAUD RISK

Traditionally, the primary source of risk in the area of external theft or fraud has been related to the payment process, often involving false invoices or check fraud. An organization should maintain an accounts payable environment with appropriate controls, such as proper authorization processes, segregation of duties, positive pay (preferably with payee verification), debit blocks, and daily reconciliation, to minimize losses due to invoice and check fraud.

Additionally, replacing paper-based payments with electronic payments can help to reduce potential check fraud. There are, however, potential fraud issues related to using electronic payments. To prevent potential automated clearinghouse (ACH) network fraud, organizations should use ACH debit blocks or filters, daily ACH reconciliation, and timely ACH returns. There are also fraud issues that can occur with business-to-business card payments and for organizations that accept electronic payments from consumers. The various aspects of payment risk are discussed in more detail in Chapter 10, Collections, Concentration, and Disbursements.

Organizations also run the risk of a breach or compromise of electronic databases due to computer hackers or other sources. A data breach or compromise occurs when there is a loss of data or other digital media from an organization's computer systems. The data breach could involve either sensitive internal information from the organization, or information about the organization's suppliers or customers (e.g., if a hacker steals customer credit card information). A related risk is that of corporate identity theft or account takeover, in which hackers use stolen information to access corporate bank accounts and financial assets.

There also may be the potential risk of loss from malfeasance, the collusion between external criminals and internal employees. Some of the typical crimes related to financial malfeasance include embezzlement, falsifying accounting data, corruption, money laundering, and counterfeiting. Among the preventative measures recommended by auditors are reinforcement of the corporate culture, ethical directives, and a strict code of conduct.

Retail environments routinely process large amounts of cash, and organizations dealing with large amounts of cash collections or disbursements run the risk of robbery or theft of those cash balances. The use of armored car services and automated store safes helps to reduce the risk of theft to the organization and robbery of its employees by controlling both the amount of available cash and the access to it.

6. PHYSICAL AND ELECTRONIC SECURITY RISK

Many organizations require physical security for their premises and employees to help prevent physical or electronic access to critical information (e.g., identity theft), as well as to ensure employees' safety. Security measures also may include biometric systems, using such technologies as fingerprint, face, or iris (eye) recognition to control physical access to facilities or key equipment. Physical security is especially important for financial institutions, utilities, and defense contractors.

In addition, many organizations have data-handling policies and procedures to address how staff should manage, store, and/or destroy restricted and sensitive information. Some organizations have records management officers and programs that address the review and classification of records and the controlled scheduled destruction of noncore records.

7. NATURAL DISASTER RISK

Natural disaster events leave organizations open to possible operational risk. These events could range from a temporary power outage to a major earthquake or hurricane. Every organization should have a contingency business resumption plan in place to manage and recover from impacts of such events. This plan should also be tested on a regular basis.

8. TERRORISM RISK

Terrorism has become a significant threat to the operations of many organizations. Many disaster recovery plans specifically include recovery from terrorist events, in addition to natural disasters. Most organizations try to manage exposure to terrorist activities by increasing the level of security for both their premises and employees.

C. Fundamental Factors for Operational Risk Management Strategy

Three critical factors determine an operational risk management strategy for an organization: culture, technology, and guidelines for the board of directors. The importance of each of these factors differs, depending upon the characteristics of an organization's business.

1. IMPORTANCE OF ORGANIZATIONAL CULTURE

Organizational culture plays an important role in managing overall operational risk. Employees who observe improper management behavior or board members who believe that senior management is not acting in shareholders' best interests must be free to report these activities without incurring significant personal or career risk. Both federal and state whistle-blower laws exist to protect employees who report unethical and illegal activities. As discussed in detail in Chapter 1, The Role of Treasury Management, a knowledgeable and independent board of directors is one of the best protections against managerial malfeasance.

Most risk management experts agree that the best approach is to develop a culture that promotes individual responsibility and is supportive of educated risk taking. One of the key characteristics of such a culture is a questioning approach to decision making that encourages anyone to ask legitimate questions or express genuine concerns related to the management of the organization. Another important characteristic is the willingness on the part of senior management to admit to a lack of sufficient information where applicable. Often, key decisions need to be made without complete information, but the decision maker must be aware of the information gaps and take some steps to mitigate this risk. Finally, the culture must provide all employees with written policies that set forth ethical behavior standards for every level of the organization.

2. IMPORTANCE OF TECHNOLOGY

While there are issues related to the use of technology (discussed earlier in this chapter), technology is also a critical factor in the formation of strategies related to operational risk management. Technology is necessary to help gather and analyze the information needed and then to monitor operational controls and procedures. Technology can help to reduce manual errors and, if properly implemented, can also serve to limit access by nonauthorized personnel.

3. IMPORTANCE OF GUIDELINES FOR THE BOARD OF DIRECTORS

Guidelines for the actions of the board of directors are especially important in reducing overall operating risk. For example, firms often place restrictions on how many board members and key executives may travel together in order to limit damage to corporate governance and control in the event of an accident. It is also important to address conflicts of interest, limit the number of internal board members, clarify personal responsibility, and facilitate the discussion and resolution of difficult or contentious issues. Many stock exchanges have explicit requirements regarding independence that must be adhered to if the company expects to continue to be listed on a given exchange. Lines of reporting should be clear, explicit, and known to all levels of the organization.

The importance of procedures is especially critical to any organization involved in trading activities because of the essential need to monitor and control these activities in relation to limits placed on authority and risk taking. Procedures for board behavior must be outlined clearly in trading policies and guidelines, as well as remaining subject to regular review and monitoring by auditors.

V. DISASTER RECOVERY AND BUSINESS CONTINUITY

Disaster recovery refers to the restoration of systems and communications after an event causes an outage. *Business continuity* refers to the actions taken with regard to crisis management, alternative operating procedures, and communications to staff and customers. The intent of disaster avoidance, recovery, and remediation measures is to preserve the firm's revenue stream. It is important that disaster recovery plans be tested and reevaluated on a regular basis to ensure that they are effective and current.

When organizations implement contingency plans, the focus is often on the business supply chain, ensuring that supplier linkages and production resources are restored and that customer service is maintained. While these are important factors, the business supply chain functions only as long as the related cash and information flows of the organization also continue.

The financial supply chain (purchase-to-pay cycle) is crucial to financial viability following a disaster. The treasury area plays a pivotal role in managing the organization's financial supply chain, through working capital management practices and by ensuring adequate liquidity sources. The key parties or resources involved in the financial chain generally are classified as either internal resources or external counterparties:

- **Internal resources** include treasury staff, computer systems, policies, procedures, processes (both automated and nonautomated), and office facilities.
- **External financial counterparties** include financial institutions, market information providers, vendors, and financial markets.

The infrastructure linking the two must be well designed and should include both internal and external networks, such as computers, servers, telecommunications, utilities, and vendor support services. An effective disaster recovery program encompasses each of these areas. Specific programs depend upon an organization's business, its treasury structure, and the specific risks the organization faces.

A. Developing an Effective Disaster Recovery (DR) Plan

1. IDENTIFY MISSION-CRITICAL FUNCTIONS

The first step in developing a DR plan is to identify mission-critical functions. An activity or function is mission critical when an interruption will create significant disruptions in an organization's business. Such disruptions have serious repercussions on an organization's ability to continue normal operations and ultimately to survive. Examples of mission-critical functions in treasury include the ability to initiate wire transfers for interest or bond payments, disbursement funding, and potentially payroll.

2. ASSESS RISKS

Once the critical functions have been identified, the potential risks that could disrupt these functions (e.g., inability to access a treasury workstation due to fire or flood) should be identified. The next step is to determine what would happen if the risk actually occurred. For example, what would be the impact if a denial-of-service attack by a hacker made it impossible to use the bank portal normally used to initiate wires?

In gauging risk levels, it is important to assess both the likelihood that something could go wrong and the consequences that would then occur.

3. EVALUATE CONTINGENCY MEASURES

After the risks have been assessed, the organization can then evaluate alternative measures to deal with the problem. In the previously cited example of inability to access the organization's lead bank via the bank's portal, alternatives could include initiating transactions by telephone or originating transactions through a backup bank that has not been affected. The goal is to understand and catalog the measures currently in place and evaluate their effectiveness, considering mission-critical functions and current risk levels. Bear in mind that during a disaster, cash is often king since banks, ATMs, and credit card systems may not be available. As a result, treasury has an important role in any DR plan in making sure that sufficient funds are available to meet the needs of any specific contingency measures.

4. PRIORITIZE CORRECTIVE ACTION

Once the potential contingency measures have been identified, assessed, and cataloged, the organization can determine the appropriate actions to take in the case of specific problems. These actions need to be prioritized in light of the impact on the organization and the previously determined risk level. For example, implementing corrective action for wires for interest and bond payments may have higher priority than implementing corrective action for trade payments, which may be delayed for some period of time before becoming a critical problem. And implementing high-cost alternatives for low-impact problems is probably not a good idea.

B. Creating a Communication Plan

A key element in developing and implementing any DR plan is to develop a parallel communication plan. In many disasters, normal phone systems and e-mail are not immediately available, and alternatives need to be planned for. The communication plan should include critical telephone numbers and contingency instructions for all staff. The organization should consider providing local service partners, regulatory agencies, and local law enforcement agencies copies of the communication plan. Contingency websites and/or call-in lines for staff, customers, and other key stakeholders can be extremely valuable in providing updates, calming tempers, and avoiding constant requests for situation updates.

C. Implementing the Plan

Once the DR plan and the related communication plan are developed, they need to be documented, distributed, and implemented. Implementation should include notifying all staff, not just key players, and providing appropriate training. No one knows who will be available at the time of a disaster, so it is important that all staff understand the contingency plans, how the plans are implemented, and who they should contact for instructions and guidance. There are many excellent online systems for documenting plans, but there should also be hard copies of the DR plan and communication numbers available in the event that the electronic systems have been compromised in the disaster. Implementation of the DR plan should also consider employee welfare and provide appropriate support for both emergency staff and their families. Key staff are much more likely to follow company policy in an emergency if they know that their families are also being taken care.

D. Performing Periodic Testing

A plan without testing is no plan, as there is no proof that the plan will actually work. DR plans need to be tested on a periodic basis, at least annually and preferably semiannually. These tests fulfill two functions: first, they identify problems with the plan that need to be corrected, and second, they help train staff and ingrain appropriate emergency responses. Appendix 15.1 includes a DR checklist that may be helpful in developing and testing DR plans.

VI. INSURANCE MANAGEMENT

Use of insurance is a very specific form of risk management in which financial protection (or reimbursement) for possible loss is purchased from another party. It is essentially a method of transferring risk from one party to another, though the term *risk transfer* has a very specific meaning in the insurance area and is discussed later in this chapter.

Insurance management is a decision or problem-solving process that identifies the possible losses and determines if insurance should be purchased against the risk of that loss and how much insurance is needed. Every organization needs some insurance risk management due to the possibility of accidental loss (i.e., loss exposures) that can disrupt operations and lower overall efficiency and profitability. As their level of involvement in overall risk management increases, treasury managers are being asked to become managers of comprehensive risk. The issue no longer is about what the year-over-year increase is in premium cost; rather, as with overall risk management, it is about the company's risk tolerance threshold and involves looking at concepts like total cost of risk (TCOR)[6] rather than just purchasing insurance coverage. It is therefore becoming increasingly common for the risk manager to be part of the treasury staff at companies with a significant exposure to risk.

The four objectives of insurance management (as it applies to risk mitigation) are to:

- Insure against catastrophic loss
- Decide when and what to insure
- Manage the purchase and use of insurance
- Obtain efficient pricing for insurance needs

A. Using Insurance Contracts to Manage Risk

Insurance contracts offer a traditional approach to managing and controlling operational risk. Although risk management typically seeks to reduce the possibility of losses, insurance usually is designed to compensate for losses, especially accidental losses, after they occur. Accidental losses, even if all are covered by insurance, have broad implications for the treasury area. Management often finds that accidents tend to reduce the firm's profitability, increase liquidity requirements, and impair financial security.

1. TYPES OF LOSSES AND POLICIES

Effective risk management helps to control or prevent losses, and adequate insurance helps to finance an organization's recovery when a loss occurs. Events resulting in a major loss generally disrupt an organization's operating and financial plans. Losses occur for a variety of reasons, and as a result there are different types of policies designed to cover specific losses. Appendix 15.2 provides a partial list of the various types of insurance. Examples of some of the types of loss that may be insured include:

- Property loss (e.g., from internal or external theft)
- Business interruption or net income loss
- Surety or breach-of-contract loss (e.g., from a contractor's failure to perform)
- Liability loss (e.g., from lawsuits by injured customers)
- Personnel loss (e.g., loss of the president or other key employees)
- Workers' compensation loss

6. TCOR is a metric that captures all the elements of risk management, including insurance premiums, self-retained losses, and any risk management administration expense.

2. WHY ORGANIZATIONS USE INSURANCE

Even if insurance eventually pays to repair or replace property, damage lowers the projected rate of return on the impaired assets. Any substantial business interruption is likely to lower profits because although an organization has business interruption insurance, cash inflows are slowed, putting pressure on the company's ability to meet its debt service obligations.

Liability losses can drain an organization's cash through the payment of uninsured claims, legal defense costs, or expenditures in negotiating with the involved insurers. Similarly, contractors' failure to complete projects deprives organizations of anticipated revenues and may impede growth, as can the death, disability, or resignation of a valuable, difficult-to-replace employee.

In addition to loss prevention and risk financing costs, the possibility of accidental losses imposes administrative costs on an organization. Management must decide where and how to apply loss prevention, select the proper types and amounts of insurance, and collect the insurance reimbursement when a covered loss occurs.

The total of all costs from both actual and potential losses constitutes an organization's cost of risk from losses. The total cost is often difficult to estimate. However, experts can assist organizations with this process by helping to identify the break-even point between the costs of insurance and the costs of uninsured losses for an organization.

B. Dealing with Insurance Providers

Most organizations purchase insurance through agents or brokers rather than directly from an insurance company. Although agents and brokers both receive commissions rather than salaries from insurers, an independent agent is legally an agent of the insurer while a broker is the legal agent of the applicant.

1. SELECTING INSURANCE—THE FINANCIAL PERSPECTIVE

When selecting among competing insurers, important factors to consider include:

- Long-term solvency of the insurer
- Rating for the insurer
- Service provided
- Cost versus exposure
- Industry knowledge and experience

a. Long-Term Solvency of the Insurer

Treasury professionals should investigate the financial solvency of all companies that insure the firm. Generally, state-guaranteed funds provide only limited protection when an insurer fails, and the delays involved in settling claims may be significant. Insurance coverage is only as good as the ability of the insurance company to pay claims, especially claims for large losses. Therefore, a firm's lenders may require credit agreements or loan covenants that stipulate minimum ratings for insurance carriers.

b. Rating for the Insurer

A.M. Best Company is the leading provider of ratings and financial information for the global insurance industry. It assigns two types of ratings: one for financial strength and one for indebtedness. Both are independent opinions based on the comprehensive quantitative and qualitative evaluation of an insurance company's balance sheet strength, operating performance, and business profile. Best's Financial Strength Ratings provide an opinion of an insurer's financial strength and ability to meet ongoing obligations to policyholders. Best's Debt Ratings provide the credit market with an opinion about the insurer's ability to meet its financial obligations to security holders when due. However, these are only opinions and do not guarantee a company's financial strength or its ability to meet obligations to policyholders and other financial claimants.

c. Service Provided

The ability of an insurer to provide loss control and/or claims service may help to reduce the overall cost of an insurance program. Service levels and specialization or expertise in a particular area of insurance should always be taken into consideration when selecting insurers, and many insurers will actually review operations and provide specific recommendations on risk mitigation. In some cases, failure to follow such recommendations can result in higher premiums and even termination of coverage.

d. Cost versus Exposure

The cost of an insurance policy or program should always be measured in relation to the financial stability, overall coverage, and quality of services offered by the prospective insurer.

e. Industry Knowledge and Experience

Insurance companies often specialize in specific industries and as a result have specific experience with the risks and issues faced by companies in that market segment. A prime example is Lloyd's of London, which got its start insuring against the loss of sailing ships and is historically known as an expert in the risks of the shipping industry.

2. SELECTING A DEDUCTIBLE

By selecting insurance coverage that has a deductible (also referred to as a *retention*, depending upon the type of insurance), an insured party can obtain a significantly lower premium when compared to the cost of first-dollar coverage,[7] especially in the case of property insurance. In essence, the deductible forces the insured to share some of the front-end risk from potential losses. The higher the deductible is, the lower the cost of the premium for insurance. It is important to weigh the frequency and types of losses that could fall within the deductible, as well as the uncertainty that accepting a policy with a deductible introduces relative to the premium savings obtained. Deductibles may also be set on a combination of:

- **Per-Occurrence Basis:** The deductible applies for each occurrence during the policy period.
- **Aggregate Basis:** The deductible is set on a per-period basis, regardless of the number of occurrences.

3. SELECTING A LIABILITY LIMIT

Liability limits determine the maximum amount that an insurance policy will pay for a specific loss. Selecting an appropriate limit is important because higher limits increase cost while lower limits can reduce potential recovery if the loss is greater than the policy limit. The challenge of selecting a liability limit may be made more complex if the amount of liability insurance the organization wishes to purchase is not available to it. In selecting a policy limit,

7. A policy that offers first-dollar coverage provides reimbursement for losses without any deductible.

management should consider the total potential risk, cost versus limits, and cost versus exposure. It should be noted that in some cases the insured company may not have a lot of choice in either limits or deductibles; rather, certain limits or deductibles may be forced on them by the insurer.

4. CLAIMS PAYMENT

Most policies provide coverage on a basic occurrence basis, where the eligibility of a claim is primarily based on the date of occurrence of the insured event. This type of policy has a term period, with a specified start and end date for the coverage, to cover losses that occur during the designated policy period. A policy that provides coverage on a claims-made basis, on the other hand, is driven by when the claims are made, regardless of when the actual loss event occurs. Thus, a valid claims-made policy can process a claim made today for an incident from five years ago, as long as there is not a retroactive date[8] that precludes it.

C. Insurance Risk Management Services

Most organizations maintain an in-house risk management information system and a complete set of internal records on insurance and losses. In lieu of in-house risk management, or as a means to supplement in-house expertise, insurance risk management consultants offer additional services, on a fee basis and as needed, to make and carry out insurance risk financing, management, and control decisions.

D. Risk-Financing Techniques

Risk-financing techniques involve resources that an organization may draw upon to finance recovery from losses and liabilities for which it is held responsible. Risk financing competes with other uses of corporate funds. Sound financial management requires integrating the organization's risk-financing needs with other more traditionally productive uses. This is necessary because without proper risk financing, profit-generating activities and assets are almost certain to be impaired, or even ruined, by accidents. As outlined below, the basic approaches to risk financing are risk retention and risk transfer.

1. RISK RETENTION

Risk retention involves the use of an organization's internal financial resources (including credit, if appropriate) to provide funds to finance a recovery from losses. In other words, the organization retains some or all of the loss, rather than transferring it by paying someone else (e.g., an insurance organization) to take it.

a. Noninsurance

One approach to risk retention is known as *noninsurance*. This technique involves relying on normal revenues to pay for small, normal losses as current expenses. Noninsurance is appropriate for losses that an organization can absorb readily as costs of doing business, but not for highly disruptive, potentially ruinous accidents.

8. A retroactive date is a date in some claims-made insurance policies that limits coverage to events that occur after that date. Claims for issues that happened before the date will not be covered.

b. Self-Insurance

Self-insurance is not technically a form of insurance because it does not involve a transfer of risk to an insurer or another separate entity. Also, the term *self-insurance* can describe any risk retention program, even quite informal, unfunded arrangements. Self-insured retention (SIR) is the component of loss covered by the insured in a policy. SIR differs from a deductible in that the insured is responsible for all aspects of a claim up to the defined limit. Self-insurance requires careful forecasting to ensure that adequate funds are available to meet future losses and that these funds are systematically maintained by the organization. Self-insurance differs from noninsurance in that the organization had made a conscious decision to self-insure and typically allocates specific assets to fund or pay for the costs of self-insuring, as opposed to noninsurance where the risks are ignored or assumed to be negligible.

Many large organizations use self-insurance to manage their employee health care expenses. This usually works well for organizations with a sizeable pool of diverse employees. Typically, the organization will contract with a third party to manage the provider network and claims processing. In addition, the organization may purchase some type of excess coverage to protect against unexpectedly high claims in a given period.

c. Single-Parent Captive

Another approach to risk retention is the use of a captive insurance company. A single-parent captive is a subsidiary owned for the purpose of insuring the risk of a parent company or its affiliates. The captive provides guaranteed access to insurance, may be used to provide unique types of insurance coverage or favorable rates, and often generates tax advantages for the parent company.

d. Group Captive

A group captive, also known as an *association captive*, resembles a single-parent captive except that it provides risk financing for multiple owners instead of just one. The captive may be owned jointly by the individual parents or by an association that the parent companies have formed. This shared ownership makes the group captive arrangement a form of insurance by virtue of the transfer of risk. In most cases, group captives are industry-based, which allows risk transfer across similar risks.

e. Risk Retention Group

A risk retention group is a special type of group captive formed under the terms of a US federal law that is designed to enable business firms to work together to jointly finance product liability claims. To the extent that risks are shared, this is considered insurance. These plans often are used in industries with a high potential for catastrophic losses, such as the airline industry and certain professional occupations (e.g., physicians in high-risk practice areas, accountants, or lawyers).

f. Claims Management

Many companies that self-insure (especially in the area of health insurance) contract out the claims approval and payment process to an insurance company or another third party. The primary benefits of this relationship are cost reduction, availability of specialty skills and technology, and access to a system of providers (especially in the health care area).

2. RISK TRANSFER

The essence of any risk transfer is a contract between a transferring organization (the transferor) and another entity (the transferee), under which the transferee agrees to pay designated types of the transferor's losses within contractual limits. The transferor may have to pay the transferee a fee (e.g., an insurance premium) for this promise of indemnity, or the transferor may have the bargaining power to secure this promise as a condition for agreeing to do business with the transferee. Such risk transfer arrangements are made frequently for tax or regulatory reasons, and may be accomplished through the purchase of reinsurance, either from a broker or directly from the market. It is important to note that the transfer of risk is only as good as the transferee's, or the insurance company's, ability to pay claims. As part of the transfer, the insured gives up all of the rights it may have to recover the loss from other parties. This is typically referred to as *subrogation*.

a. Contractual Transfer

Under contractual transfers, typified by hold-harmless agreements, the transferee is not an insurer and the transfer contract may take any form permitted by applicable law. Such contractual transfers may not provide transferors the degree of financial security they could obtain from a true insurer because most hold-harmless transferees are not in business to bear others' risk of loss. Additionally, these contracts and business activities are not as strictly regulated as insurers. This is a form of risk transfer, where the burden of the risks in question is transferred to another party. The other party can choose to purchase insurance of some type to mitigate those risks if it wishes.

b. Guaranteed Cost Insurance Program

In a guaranteed cost insurance program, the insured pays a fixed premium at the beginning of the policy period, and the insurer assumes the risk for paying all losses occurring during the policy period that fall within the scope and amount of the policy. The premium paid by the insured cannot be changed until the next policy period, although either the insurer or the insured may cancel coverage in the middle of the policy period under certain conditions. An insured that cancels this type of policy mid-period may not be entitled to a refund of premiums paid.

c. Retrospectively (Retro) Rated Insurance Program

In a retrospectively (retro) rated insurance program, the insured's cost of coverage for a policy period varies with the insured's losses during that period. Such programs are often used for workers' compensation and product liability insurance plans. The insured pays a standard, or deposit, premium at the beginning of the coverage period. At the end of the period, the insurer computes a final premium based on an agreed-upon formula that varies with the insured's actual costs or losses (subject to limits) for the policy period.

VII. SUMMARY

Operational risk management is a complex topic that is becoming increasingly important to the treasury professional as a growing number of organizations are turning to treasury for both direct and indirect management of operational risk. This chapter discussed the concept of enterprise risk management and presented the basic concepts behind risk management. It also reviewed the major categories of operational risk management and looked at how they might impact an organization. As part of this discussion, the chapter covered the need for a well-thought-out disaster recovery plan and presented the steps involved in creating such a plan. It also provided an overview of some of the key concepts of insurance management.

APPENDIX 15.1: DISASTER RECOVERY (DR) CHECKLIST[9]

The 2011 earthquake and subsequent tsunami in Japan have underscored once again the need for corporate treasurers no matter where they are located to always be ready to face unplanned service disruptions whether they be short-term outages or full-fledged disasters. Ensuring the business resiliency of your treasury operations is critical, and the processes for upgrading contingency plans should be ongoing, flexible, and dynamic. The questions below can help you assess your organization's readiness for business continuity in the event of a disaster—either man-made or natural.

Treasury Operations

- Have you reviewed your account information and your account structures—including authorized signers, security administrators, user IDs, and entitlements—with each of your banking partners to ensure that everything is accurate and up-to-date? Do you maintain this information off-site, as well as on-site?
- Are your locations geographically dispersed so you can rapidly shift treasury operations in the event of a crisis? Do your banking partners also have dispersed payments centers?
- If you lease your contingency site, how will space be allocated in the event of a major crisis (e.g., will it be on a first come, first served basis)?
- Will you have access to all necessary documentation and emergency procedures at off-site locations?

Contingency Plans

- Do you have contingency procedures in place so you can continue to process payments in the event of a crisis? Do you periodically test these procedures by logging on to your backup system and generating at least one real-time transaction? Are you reliant on a specific desktop PC, or do you maintain an alternate desktop PC as backup?
- Do you have an operational response plan? How often do you conduct a full end-to-end test to validate the recovery capabilities of staff and critical systems? Has the test been audited?
- In the event of a pandemic, which locations would be severely impacted if absentee rates were to reach between 30 to 50% of your organization? Having data on the number or percentage of your employees who rely on public transportation in high concentration areas will be helpful to you as you develop your contingency plans. In addition, as you review critical third-party organizations, be sure to check that they, too, have sufficient pandemic response plans.
- Have you tested your primary site against your contingency sites? Often, a single primary site requires recovery to multiple alternate sites. Recovery processes need to test coordination and communication procedures to ensure a full recovery of all components.
- In addition to contingency procedures for facilities, do you also have contingency procedures to ensure the security and protection of data?
- Do you have alternate power sources for your main server locations? Do you have a backup plan in the event your Internet provider goes down?
- Have you prepared other disaster contingencies, including a potable water supply, emergency food, flashlights, etc., on site?

9. Used with permission © 2013 JPMorgan Chase & Co. All rights reserved.

Crisis Communications

- Do you have an emergency management team in place? Do you have a clear, predetermined chain of command in the event of an emergency? Is this information documented and widely distributed within your organization? How often is it reviewed and updated?
- Does your crisis communication plan cover both internal and external procedures? Has it been documented and widely distributed throughout your organization?
- Have you provided your clients, colleagues, suppliers, financial and banking partners, and other key business contacts with emergency contact information?
- Have you established a dialogue with local fire, police, emergency medical services personnel, community leaders, government agencies, community organizations, and utilities regarding your disaster-preparedness procedures?
- Have you considered the emotional response your employees may have to a major crisis? A crisis could impact the ability of some of your employees to function. Consider cross-training personnel so that staff are ready to assume multiple roles if needed, and your organization is fully prepared to function in the event of an emergency.
- Have you reassessed all recovery plans to validate that assumptions and recovery solutions are still appropriate? An important step here is to include all constituents—both internal and external. In addition, business recovery time capabilities should be aligned with current recovery time objectives and should also ensure that the impact on clients is understood by all appropriate parties.

Other Factors for Consideration

- Have you considered how you would maintain liquidity if your primary provider were impacted by a disaster? How easily would you have access to cash in the event of a crisis?
- Have you conducted a comprehensive review of your insurance coverage? Does it include provisions for recovery and restoration?
- Do you use positive pay and stop payment capabilities to limit your exposure and help manage risk?
- Have you considered outsourcing your receivables collection to a provider with geographically dispersed network capabilities?

APPENDIX 15.2: TYPES OF INSURANCE COVERAGE

The list below describes some of the basic types of business insurance:

- **Business Interruption:** This coverage provides payments to an organization in the event it is unable to pursue a normal line of business for some period of time due to an unforeseen event. Business interruption insurance generally covers the loss of profits and continuing fixed expenses (e.g., debt or lease arrangements) while the organization is temporarily out of business. For example, if an organization suffered a fire at a main production facility, property insurance would pay for rebuilding the facility, and business interruption insurance would make payments to compensate the organization for lost profits and increased costs during the rebuilding process.
- **Casualty:** Concerned primarily with the legal liability of losses caused by personal injury or property damage, casualty insurance provides specific coverage for a variety of losses. Examples of typical casualty insurance include plate glass, crime, robbery, boiler or machinery, and aviation insurance. Many casualty insurers also write surety bonds and other forms of insurance not classified as property insurance.
- **Commercial Crime:** A principal of common law is that there can be no coverage for intentional or criminal acts. As a result, someone who commits a criminal act, such as stealing inventory, assaulting a customer, or poisoning products, will not be covered by insurance. There can, however, be coverage for the organization that employs the person committing the act, as long as that action is taken without the knowledge or approval of the organization. A crime insurance policy can cover the organization for such acts (refer also to fidelity and professional liability insurances).
- **Difference in Conditions (DIC):** DIC insurance covers property for perils not covered by basic property insurance policies. It is often purchased to fill voids in policies purchased overseas and to insure property in transit. Typically used in conjunction with multiple basic policies to make them uniform, DIC insurance does not provide additional limits of coverage for basic property perils (as an umbrella policy does for liability insurance).
- **Directors and Officers (D&O):** D&O policies cover situations in which a director or officer of an organization commits a negligent act or omission, or makes a misstatement or misleading statement, and a legal action is brought against the organization as a result. The policy provides coverage (usually with a large deductible) for directors' and officers' liability exposure if these individuals are sued. Coverage also is provided for defense costs, such as legal fees and other court costs, and may include coverage for an organization's subsidiaries.
- **Excess or Umbrella:** This coverage supplements basic or primary liability coverage. Policies generally pay after the primary policy's limits have been exhausted. For example, if the primary insurance policy has a $250,000 limit and claims exceed this amount, then an umbrella or excess policy would pay the excess claims up to the limit of the policy. Excess or umbrella policies can also be used to fill gaps in coverage provided by basic liability policies (i.e., the difference in coverage between two policies).
- **Fidelity:** Fidelity bonds provide coverage that guarantees payment for money or other property lost through dishonest acts of bonded employees, either by name or position. Whether employees act alone or in concert, the bond generally covers all dishonest acts, such as larceny, theft, embezzlement, forgery, misappropriation, wrongful abstraction, or willful misapplication. Because a fidelity bond makes up only part of the protection against theft, other crime insurance is often mandatory. A blanket bond could be used to cover all employees of an organization, while crime insurance provides specific coverage for the perils of burglary, theft, and robbery by external parties.

- **Key Person:** This type of life insurance (also known as *key man insurance*) names the organization as the beneficiary to insure against the loss of key personnel, such as a CEO or owner. This type of policy can also be used by partnerships to cover potential estate tax issues for private companies, or by ownerships to avoid forced dissolution of the company upon the death of an owner or partner.
- **Liability:** This coverage insures against damage to other parties that can arise from product defects; business practices; accidents; actions of the organization's employees, officers, or board of directors; and general negligence in the operation of the organization. Liability insurance typically includes defense costs in the event of litigation.
- **Professional Liability:** Commonly referred to as *errors and omissions (E&O) policies*, these policies protect service- and advice-providing individuals and companies, such as consultants, accounting firms, and investment advisors, from the cost of defending against a negligence claim made by a client, as well as from the cost of any damages that may be awarded in a civil lawsuit. While E&O coverage typically includes defense costs, coverage normally excludes criminal prosecution.
- **Property:** This insurance provides for reimbursement in the event of a loss of or damage to some type of asset (e.g., buildings, equipment, or inventory). Policies often cover the replacement value of the items in question, paying the costs of completely replacing those assets at their current market prices rather than at their historical or book value.
- **Transit/Ocean Marine:** Property insurance typically restricts coverage to specified locations listed within the policy. Transit, or transportation, insurance covers products or property while in transit. Marine insurance specifically covers property while on a boat.
- **Workers' Compensation:** Required by most states, this type of insurance covers employees' job-related injuries or diseases as a matter of right (without regard to fault). It generally provides benefits in the areas of medical care, death, disability, and rehabilitation.
- **Other Types of Insurance:** There are a variety of additional specialized types of insurance policies designed to meet an organization's specific needs. These include such things as fiduciary insurance for pension plans, crop insurance, etc.

TEST YOUR UNDERSTANDING: CHAPTER 15

Answers are on pages 708–713.

1. What are the purposes of the risk management process for an organization?
2. What are the roles of the risk management committee and the chief risk officer (CRO)?
3. What are the six steps in the risk management process?
4. What are the objectives of qualitative assessment with respect to measuring exposure as part of general risk management?
5. Describe the four basic approaches to developing and implementing a risk management strategy.
6. What is enterprise risk management?
7. What are the key elements that should be contained in an organization's risk management policy?
8. What is operational risk?
9. What are the four basic types of market risk?
10. Discuss the concepts of disaster recovery and business continuity.
11. Name three types of internal operational risk.
12. Name eight types of external operational risk.
13. What are three critical factors to consider in determining an operational risk management strategy?
14. What are the four goals of using insurance to mitigate risk?
15. What are the key factors to consider when selecting an insurer?
16. What is self-insurance?
17. Explain the concept of risk transfer.
18. What is value at risk (VaR)?
19. Explain the difference between sensitivity analysis and scenario analysis.

CHAPTER 16
Financial Risk Management

V. CURRENCY DERIVATIVES USED TO HEDGE FOREIGN EXCHANGE (FX) EXPOSURE

A. Currency or Foreign Exchange (FX) Forwards

B. Currency Futures

C. Currency Swaps

D. Currency Options

E. Hedging Tools Available for Exotic Currencies

VI. INTEREST RATE EXPOSURE AND RISK MANAGEMENT

A. Interest Rate Forwards

B. Interest Rate Futures

C. Interest Rate Swaps

D. Interest Rate Options

VII. COMMODITY RISK EXPOSURE

VIII. OTHER ISSUES RELATED TO FINANCIAL RISK MANAGEMENT

A. Accounting Issues

B. Tax Issues Related to Hedging

C. Hedging Policy Statement

IX. SUMMARY

I. INTRODUCTION

Chapter 15, Operational and Enterprise Risk Management, introduced the basic concepts of enterprise risk management, including a standard process for overall risk management: identify, measure, manage, and monitor. This chapter builds on that framework and discusses some of the tools and techniques available to the treasury professional to manage the specific area of financial risk.

In most companies, the management of financial risk is the responsibility of treasury. Since the treasury department is a clearinghouse for daily financial information, treasury professionals are in a good position to understand and help control an organization's exposure to various forms of financial risk. For domestic companies, financial risk has traditionally been in the area of interest rate risk, but the increased rate of globalization and international trade has created a corresponding need for managing foreign exchange (FX) risk. Fortunately this is an area that multinational companies have had to deal with for many years, and the processes and tools available to manage FX risk are well developed.

II. OVERVIEW OF FINANCIAL RISK MANAGEMENT IN TREASURY

Financial risk, also known as *economic or strategic exposure*, is the risk that the overall value of an organization may change in response to a change in interest or foreign exchange rates. In most organizations, financial risk is generally the responsibility of the treasury organization. Financial risk is typically broken down into three distinct categories (although many of the tools and techniques used to manage the different categories of financial risk are similar):

- Interest rate risk
- Foreign exchange (FX) risk
- Commodity price risk

A. Interest Rate Risk

As defined in Chapter 15, Operational and Enterprise Risk Management, interest rate risk is the risk related to changes in investment values or borrowing costs due to changes in interest rates. For example, as interest rates change, a firm may find that the overall value of its short-term and/or long-term investment portfolio changes. A positive change is good, but without adequate planning or protection, a change may be negative and reduce the company's overall value. Alternatively, a company that finances operating expenses using bank credit will be exposed to changes in overall expense as interest rates charged by the bank change. An increase in rates will lead to an increase in expense, and consequently to decreased earnings.

B. Foreign Exchange (FX) Risk

FX risk arises from the exposure an organization has as a result of transactions, assets, and liabilities that are denominated in a foreign currency. As exchange rates fluctuate, so too can the value of these items, ultimately impacting the overall value of a firm. FX risk is further broken down into three types of risk: economic, transaction, and translation risk.

1. ECONOMIC RISK

Economic risk exposure is the long-term effect of changes in exchange rates on the present value of future cash flows. Multinational corporations that conduct business in several different currencies are, in the long run, always subject to fluctuations in cash flows because of exchange rate changes. Even companies that only operate domestically are exposed to economic risk whenever there is foreign competition within the local market.

A company that purchases supplies locally and sells products locally is not affected by transaction or translation exposure. However, if the local currency appreciates against a foreign competitor's currency, then the company's earnings in the long run may be impacted when domestic demand shifts toward the less costly product or service of the foreign competitor.

2. TRANSACTION RISK

Transaction risk exposure arises when a company creates future receivables and/or payables that are denominated in a currency other than its home, or functional, currency. Thus, the ultimate value of these receivables or payables when they are collected or paid may be different from when they were created, due to possible changes in the exchange rate between the currency of denomination and the company's home currency.

This is the most common type of FX risk exposure to be hedged through the use of currency derivatives. Explicit transaction risk exposure begins when a receivable or payable is entered on the balance sheet and remains until cash is received or paid. For example, when a Japanese exporter sells merchandise to a French buyer and agrees to accept payment in euros (EUR) in three months, the transaction is recorded in revenue and in accounts receivable using the Japanese yen (JPY) equivalent value of the euro at that time. However, the value of the receivable changes as the value of the euro changes against the yen over the following three months. These gains and losses are typically recorded on the income statement at the end of each accounting period, creating earnings volatility.

3. TRANSLATION RISK

Translation risk exposure is created when a foreign subsidiary's financial statements are converted (translated) into the parent company's home currency as part of the process of consolidating a company's financial statements. In most countries, any company with an investment in operations in other countries must report its global income, assets, and liabilities on a consolidated basis in its home currency. This exposure is sometimes referred to as *accounting exposure*. The exposure occurs because the value of the foreign assets and liabilities may change from one accounting period to the next as the underlying FX rates change. For example, if a German company has a subsidiary in the United Kingdom, then the value of that subsidiary's assets and liabilities will change as the exchange rate between the euro (EUR) and the British pound (GBP) changes over a given accounting period. If the pound were to increase in value relative to the euro over the course of a year, then there would be a translation gain as a result of that change.

For most global companies, International Accounting Standard (IAS) 21: *The Effects of Changes in Foreign Exchange Rates* provides guidance for determining the impact of changing FX rates on translating financial statements from one currency to another. In the United States, the prevailing guideline is Accounting Standards Codification (ASC) Topic 830: *Foreign Currency Matters*. In both cases, the general approach is to try to insulate earnings for the period from the effects of translation gains and losses by placing those specific gains and losses into special equity accounts.

Using financial instruments to hedge this type of risk is difficult due to the large amounts of funds normally involved. However, a company can offset foreign asset exposures effectively by borrowing funds to finance the assets in the same currency. This approach is called a *balance sheet hedge*, or a *natural hedge*, and reduces the net exposure of the parent company.

4. IMPLICIT VERSUS EXPLICIT FX RISK

FX transaction risk can also be divided into implicit and explicit risk:

- **Implicit risk** is the risk that the value of future transactions will change due to changes in exchange rates. For example, a company may publish price lists in a foreign currency or make a firm quote in a foreign currency. These result in an implicit FX risk until such time as a sale is actually made and the sale recorded. For this reason, companies with extensive foreign currency transactions often manage their FX risk based on projected sales to account for implicit risk.
- **Explicit risk** is the risk that occurs due to changes in FX rates between the time a transaction occurs and the time it is finally settled. For example, a Canadian-based company sells a product denominated in Japanese yen (JPY) for payment in 30 days. The company is subject to explicit risk from the time of the sale until the receivable is actually collected.

C. Commodity Price Risk

Commodity price risk is the risk that a change in the price of a raw material used by a company will impact the income (and hence value) of a company that uses that raw material. For example, a plastics manufacturer may find its expenses going up more than anticipated if the price of oil (a raw material for most plastic) goes up unexpectedly. Factors that can affect commodity prices include political and regulatory changes, weather, technology, and overall market conditions.

D. Managing Financial Risk

Managing the exposure to financial risk typically involves some form of hedging and may involve speculation, both of which can alter a company's risk profile. In addition to these topics, this section also discusses the concept of arbitrage, which is used primarily to maintain efficiency in key financial markets.

1. PASSIVE OR NATURAL HEDGING

The first step in managing financial risk in many companies is to use passive, or natural, hedging. A natural hedge (typically used to address FX risk) occurs when a company holds both assets and liabilities in the same currency, allowing them to offset each other in the event of market fluctuation. For example, a non-European company that expects to earn future revenue in euros might arrange to finance part of its facilities with a euro-based loan. To the extent that the future earnings in euros match the loan payments in euros, the company is unaffected by changes in the value of the euro. Passive hedging strategies include borrowing and investing using currencies other than the organization's home currency (i.e., creating natural hedges), and can also include decisions around fixed versus floating borrowing, balance sheet matching, and fixed-price supplier agreements.

2. ACTIVE HEDGING

Active hedging is the process of using various financial instruments (discussed in more detail in the section below on derivatives as financial risk management tools) to reduce or eliminate risks associated with uncertain future cash flows. This is a core principle of treasury financial risk management. Hedging is similar to the concept of buying insurance to protect an asset, and the purpose of the hedge is to insure the asset's value (or minimize the risk on a liability) when its market value fluctuates.

In hedging a transaction, an organization essentially locks in a future FX rate, interest rate, or commodity price to minimize the risk in a transaction. For example, if a Japanese company sold EUR 6 million of product to a foreign trading partner with payment due in six months, the Japanese company might purchase a futures contract to deliver EUR 6 million in six months. By buying a futures contract[1] now (discussed in more detail later in this chapter), the company is locking in an FX rate so that if the value of the euro (EUR) declines in the next six months, the company will not lose any value on the deal. On the other hand, the company is also giving up any potential gain it might have made if the euro had gained in value over those same six months. In return, however, it has "insured" its payment and reduced its potential risk.

3. SPECULATION

While there is often some degree of speculation in hedging activities (given the difficulty in creating a "perfect" hedge), active speculation goes beyond hedging and involves taking a position on the direction of the market in the attempt to make a profit, which is not usually a treasury objective. Most companies use hedging to minimize risk, not to make a profit. But some companies go a step further and attempt to use the products to make a profit. This is referred to as *speculation*. In many companies, corporate hedging policies forbid this type of speculation. For some organizations, however, speculation in certain markets may be a treasury objective, as determined by the board of directors. For example, financial institutions often have a trading floor for stocks, FX contracts, or interest contracts where speculation is encouraged as a means of revenue generation. Another example might be an energy company that speculates in certain energy markets (e.g., oil and gas) as part of its corporate objectives.

A speculator should be an experienced market participant who is willing to assume significant risk. When expecting the price of an asset to increase, a speculator takes a long position in the asset, meaning the asset is purchased and held for a period of time in the hope that its price will rise. When expecting the price of an asset to decrease, however, a speculator takes a short position. That is, the asset is borrowed from a broker or dealer and then sold in the hope that its price will fall, after which it can be purchased at the lower price and returned to the broker or dealer from whom it was borrowed.

Speculators who are short the asset are referred to as being "naked" because they do not own the asset that they are required to return to the party that loaned it to them. If the price of the asset increases, then the speculator will have to purchase it for more than was obtained when it was sold, in order to return it to its lender. The same term is used to describe someone who purchases derivatives without owning the related asset. While derivatives can be an important tool in managing risk, "naked" derivatives involve speculation that can result in significant losses in the wrong circumstances.

1. Alternatively, this transaction can be hedged by buying a forward contract or option, both of which are also discussed later in this chapter.

4. ARBITRAGE

Arbitrage is the process by which an asset is purchased in one market and simultaneously sold in another market to produce a riskless profit. While making a profit is not usually a treasury objective, it is important for a treasury professional to understand the arbitrage process because arbitrage is the primary mechanism that ensures efficiency in financial markets.

In most cases, professional arbitrageurs do not assume risk; rather, they attempt to profit from market inefficiencies. For example, if Indian rupees (INR) can simultaneously be sold in London and purchased in Singapore to make a profit after transaction costs, then an arbitrage opportunity exists based on the inefficient market for rupees.

Another example of arbitrage is referred to as *covered interest arbitrage*. In this case an investor takes advantage of differences in the interest rates in two different currencies by using a forward contract (discussed later in this chapter) to eliminate any exposure to changes in the currencies (i.e., to "cover" the investor). In theory, the exchange rates (both long and short) in the two currencies should be such that an investor would earn exactly the same amount no matter which currency was used for the investment. This is referred to as *interest rate parity*. In the real world, there can, however, be situations where interest rate parity does not exist and investors can improve their returns by selecting the right currency.

For example, suppose the current spot[2] exchange rate is 1.3092 US dollars (USD) per euro (EUR), the six-month forward exchange rate is 1.3050 USD per EUR, and an investor has EUR 1,000,000 to invest. Assume also that the current euro deposit rate is 1.2% and the dollar deposit rate is 1.3% for six months. An investor can deposit the euros and earn EUR 6,000 in interest. However, the investor could also convert the euros to US dollars at the current spot rate and invest the resulting $1,309,200 at 1.3% for six months, returning $1,317,710, or EUR 1,009,739, for a profit of EUR 9,739. By investing in a covered forward, the investor increases his/her revenue by EUR 3,739 (less any fees charged for the forward), or 62%.

A true arbitrage transaction does not affect a company's overall risk profile. However, it is difficult for the majority of companies to take advantage of arbitrage opportunities because the market inefficiencies that lead to them are short-lived and lead only to small profits that are measured in basis points. Typically, only market participants with large amounts of capital and those who focus on watching for this type of opportunity can take advantage of such inefficiencies. For example, the major participants in the FX arbitrage market are large, global banks and third-party currency dealers.

E. The Benefits of Financial Risk Management

Managing a company's risk helps to reduce the variability of both a company's future cash flows and its profitability due to external changes in FX rates, interest rates, and commodity prices, which consequently increases the company's value. Hedging enables

2. A *spot exchange rate*, or just *spot rate*, is the rate quoted for an immediate exchange of currencies, or "on the spot" delivery. In reality, spot deals are normally consummated with a one- or two-day lag.

treasury to smooth uneven cash flows due to unexpected external changes and forecast financial results with greater confidence. Less variability in expected future cash flows increases a firm's value in three ways:

- Greater predictability in future cash flows makes the company more attractive to shareholders.
- The company gains an enhanced borrowing advantage in credit markets because lenders view the firm as being less risky.
- The company's probability of financial distress decreases because the firm can assess costs and revenues more accurately.

III. DERIVATIVE INSTRUMENTS USED AS FINANCIAL RISK MANAGEMENT TOOLS

A derivative instrument is a financial product that acquires its value by inference through a formulaic connection to another asset. The other asset is termed the *underlying asset*, and can be a financial instrument (e.g., a stock or bond), currency, or commodity. In the treasury area, the primary uses of these instruments are for managing FX (i.e., foreign currency), interest rate, and commodity price risks.

The use of derivatives may have an immediate impact on cash flow that is either favorable or unfavorable. Derivatives are complex and not always easy to understand, analyze, apply, account for, and report on. In considering the use of derivatives, a treasury professional must also consider the added cost of tax, regulatory, and reporting requirements related to the use of these instruments, which may dilute their value. Accordingly, many treasury professionals seek the advice of outside experts.

An organization that enters into a derivative contract typically must execute an agreement with the counterparty to that contract. The International Swaps and Derivatives Association (ISDA) is a trade organization made up of companies, dealers, and service providers that participate in the market for over-the-counter (OTC) derivative instruments. The organization created a standardized contract, the ISDA master agreement, and most derivatives in the global derivatives market are documented using ISDA agreements and related documentation. The master agreement consists of standardized items, which include general terms and conditions, and a schedule. The schedule is an integral part of the master agreement. It is used to customize the master agreement by amending the standard terms and specifying certain details for the standard terms. When the agreement is signed, it governs all past and future transactions entered into between the parties. Consequently, it must be negotiated with great prudence. It should be noted that the standard terms normally include an agreement to comply with Dodd-Frank requirements regarding derivatives (which are discussed in Chapter 2, Regulatory and Legal Environment), making them binding on both US and non-US organizations that sign an ISDA agreement. The master agreement has no fixed term—it is open ended. If the parties want to end their relationship, they may terminate the master agreement formally or simply not enter into further contracts with one another. In dealing with derivatives, any organization must also consider the potential for counterparty risk, which is discussed in Chapter 15, Operational and Enterprise Risk Management.

The four basic types of derivative instruments are forwards, futures, swaps, and options.

A. Forwards

A forward contract is an agreement between two parties to buy or sell a fixed amount of an asset to be delivered at a future date and at a price agreed upon today. This contrasts with a spot contract, which is an agreement between two parties to buy or sell a fixed amount of an asset immediately. The major difference between a forward and an option (discussed below) is that a forward transaction *must* occur while an option transaction *may* occur. In other words, settlement of a forward is mandatory, while the settlement of an option is optional at the discretion of the option holder. The underlying asset can be a financial instrument (e.g., a stock index fund or debt instrument), a currency (e.g., the euro or pound), or a commodity (e.g., gold or coffee). The future date is referred to as the contract's *maturity date*, and the price is called the *delivery price*. A company purchasing a forward contract is one party to the contract; the party selling the contract is referred to as the *counterparty*. In forward currency contracts, the counterparty is typically a bank or dealer in the FX markets. The party that intends to purchase the underlying asset is said to be in a *long forward contract position*; the counterparty is in a *short forward contract position*. The long position in a forward contract gains value when the price of the underlying asset rises, and loses value when the price of the underlying asset falls. Conversely, the short position gains value when the underlying asset price falls, and loses value when it rises. Exhibits 16.1A and 16.1B depict the payoff profiles in a forward contract from a long and a short position, respectively. Note how a gain in the value of one contract is offset by the loss of value in the other.

EXHIBIT 16.1A **FORWARD CONTRACT—LONG POSITION**

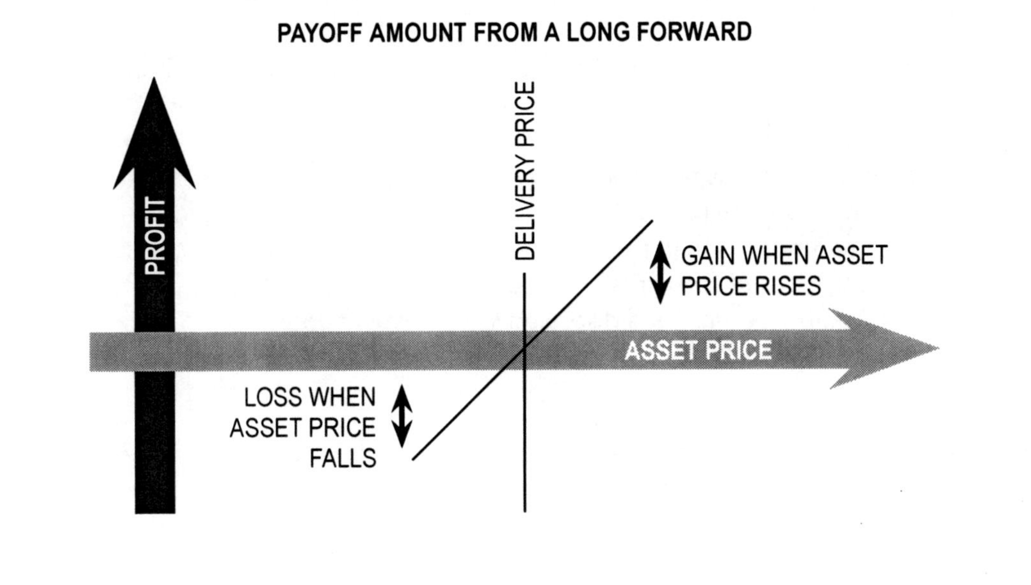

EXHIBIT 16.1B **FORWARD CONTRACT—SHORT POSITION**

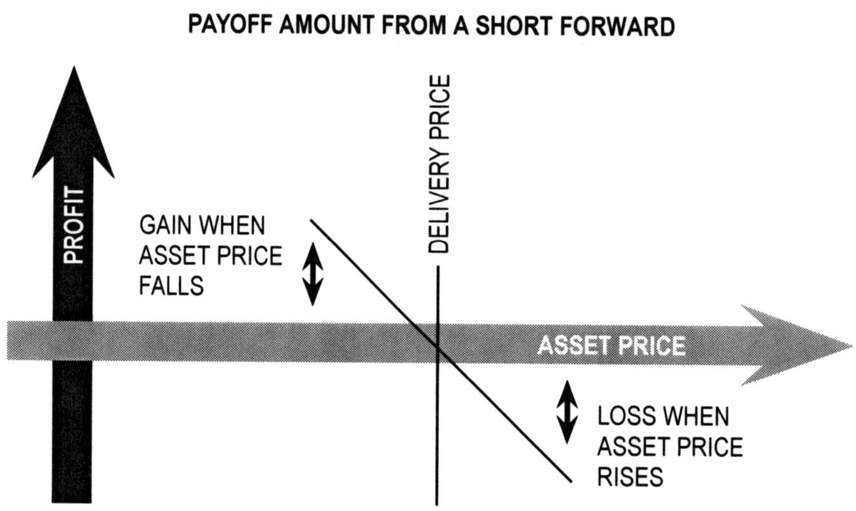

Forward markets are managed and supported by a group of banks, dealers, and traders that act as market makers (i.e., they quote both a bid and an ask price whenever requested to do so). Forward contracts are private contracts between two parties and are customized to each party's needs. The amount of the underlying asset and the maturity date of the contract are established when the contract is negotiated. In some cases, delivery of the underlying asset takes place at the maturity of the forward contract. In the case of forwards purchased purely for hedging purposes, the parties often agree to buy out, or "unwind," the transaction at the end of the contract rather than actually transferring the underlying asset. There are many different types of forwards, with currency forwards and interest rate forwards being the most common. These and other types of forwards are discussed later in this chapter.

B. Futures

Futures are similar to forwards in that the payoff profile from a long or short position in a futures contract looks exactly the same as the payoff in the respective forward contract (see Exhibits 16.1A and 16.1B). The main differences between futures and forwards are that futures are standardized contracts traded on organized exchanges and that the counterparty to all futures contracts is the exchange itself. The fact that the exchange is the counterparty increases the liquidity of the contract and virtually eliminates counterparty risk.

Futures contracts are standardized by the exchanges with respect to contract size and delivery dates. As a result, a limited range of delivery dates is available, which may not always match the exact needs of an organization. Relative to forward contracts, futures contracts are easier and less expensive to acquire. On the other hand, since contract sizes and maturities are standardized, it is probably not possible to create a "perfect" hedge,[3] as may be accomplished with a forward contract. For example, the size of a typical British pound (GBP) futures contract on the Chicago Mercantile Exchange is GBP 62,500, and delivery dates are listed for March, June, September, and December. If an organization has an exposure that is not a multiple of this number and/or the delivery date on the contract is not the date when pounds are required, using a futures contract to hedge will not precisely mitigate the exposure.

3. A *perfect hedge* is defined as a hedge that eliminates all market risk from a given transaction. In other words, the hedge is exactly the inverse of the base transaction. Perfect hedges are hard to create since many derivatives are traded in standard amounts or have standard settlement dates.

Futures trading requires a margin account that is marked to market on a daily basis using the closing price of the previous business day. *Marked to market* means that the hedger's gains or losses on the position are reflected on a daily basis. If the margin account drops below a specified amount, termed the *maintenance margin*, then a margin call is issued. A margin call requires the account holder to deposit cash sufficient to replenish the account to the initial level, or to close out the position with the exchange. Rarely are futures contracts settled by delivery; instead, they typically are closed out (i.e., settled financially between the two parties) prior to maturity. Currency futures are discussed in detail later in this chapter.

C. Swaps

A swap is an agreement between two parties to exchange (or swap) a set of cash flows at a future point in time. The most common type of swap is an interest rate swap. In this type of swap, Party X agrees to pay Party Y a stream of cash flows equal to a floating rate of interest on some mutually agreed-upon amount. This amount is referred to as *notional principal* because the principal amount does not exchange hands; instead, only interest payments are exchanged. At the same time, Party Y agrees to pay Party X a stream of cash flows equal to a fixed rate of interest on the same notional principal at the same future dates. In other words, Party X is swapping a fixed-rate loan for a floating-rate loan while Party Y is doing exactly the opposite.

Other types of swap arrangements include currency, commodity, and basis rate swaps. Currency swaps are agreements to convert an obligation in one currency to an obligation in another currency. Commodity swaps involve the exchange of a floating price on a commodity for a fixed price on the same commodity over a specified period of time. The actual commodity is not exchanged—the swap is a purely financial transaction based on any change in the price of the commodity. A basis rate swap is a type of interest rate swap that is used to manage interest rate risk and typically involves swapping one rate base for another (e.g., swapping the US prime rate for the London Interbank Offered Rate [LIBOR]). Examples of currency and interest rate swaps are discussed later in this chapter.

One of the risks in using swaps, as with any derivative, is counterparty risk (discussed in Chapter 15, Operational and Enterprise Risk Management). The value of the swap depends upon the other party fulfilling its obligation to make the agreed-upon payment stream. If the other party (the counterparty) does not make the payments, then the first party may still be liable for the original payment stream or cash flow. Using a trusted third party, such as a bank or FX dealer, helps mitigate the counterparty risk as the third party is responsible for evaluating the credit quality of each party involved in the swap.

D. Options

An option is a contract giving the buyer of the contract the right, but not the obligation, to buy or sell a fixed amount of an underlying asset at a fixed price on or before a specified date (see the discussion in the next paragraph regarding European versus American styles of options). The counterparty is called the *writer* of the option and receives the premium (price) paid for the contract. Options may be exchange-traded contracts or contracts negotiated with a specific counterparty. Exchange-traded options share many of the characteristics of futures contracts. They are standardized with respect to the quantity and delivery dates covered by the contract. In financial risk management, options can be used to manage FX, interest rate, and commodity risk for an organization. This section covers the basics of options and their valuation. The specific types of options used for FX and interest rate management are covered later in this chapter.

Unlike an American option that allows the contract to be exercised at any time on or before the delivery date, a European option may be exercised only on the delivery date. Under similar conditions, an American option will sell for a larger premium than a European option because the American option may be exercised at any time on or before its expiration date. Alternatively, a Bermuda option's exercise feature places it between American and European option contracts. It is exercisable only on specified dates that are spaced evenly over the option's life. Since its exercise feature is less liberal than an American option's but more liberal than a European option's, its premium is lower than the premium on an American option, but higher than the premium on a European option, for like circumstances.

1. CALL VERSUS PUT OPTIONS

A call option gives the contract owner the right, but not the obligation, to buy (call) the underlying asset from the contract writer at a fixed price through the delivery date. A put option gives the contract owner the right, but not the obligation, to sell (put) the underlying asset to the contract writer at a fixed price through the delivery date. This fixed price is called the *strike price* or *exercise price* of the contract. A call option is said to be "in the money" when the current market price is higher than the contract's strike price.

Assume for example that the current market price for oil is $95 per barrel. If an organization expects the price of oil to go up (or merely wants to protect against a rise in the price of oil since oil is used in production), it can purchase a call option to buy a specific quantity of oil, say 1,000 barrels at $100 per barrel. The strike price of the contract is $100, and the company will pay a premium of approximately $5 per barrel, or $5,000, for the contract. If the price of oil does not go up or actually falls, the option is not exercised, and the company loses the $5,000 option premium.

Assume instead that oil goes up to $111 per barrel. The company will exercise its option to buy oil at $100 per barrel and then sell it at $111, for a gross profit of $11 per barrel, less the premium, for a net profit of $6 per barrel, or $6,000. (If this had been a commodity hedge for raw materials, the company would have saved $6,000 in expense rather than making a profit.)

The break-even price for the company in this case is $105 per barrel, since that is the point at which the profit on the contract will offset the premium paid for the contract.[4]

2. OPTION PREMIUMS

The option buyer pays a premium to the option writer in exchange for the ability to call or put the option (i.e., buy or sell the underlying asset). The premium for an American option contract will assume a larger speculative premium[5] than will a European option contract because the American contract may be exercised any time through the delivery date. The owner of a European contract cannot gain from a rise in the price of the underlying asset until the delivery date because the contract may be exercised only on the delivery date. Thus, the speculative premium on a European option will be smaller. As discussed above, a Bermuda option will fall somewhere between these two extremes.

4. For purposes of illustration, this example ignores any broker's fees or other transaction costs that would typically increase the cost of the option to the buyer.

5. A speculative premium is that part of the premium that is based on speculation that the value of the underlying asset will increase or decrease over the life of the contract. The amount of the premium is based on the amount the writer of the option expects (or speculates) the price of the commodity to change over the life of the option.

There are five possible relationships between an option's premium and its strike (exercise) price:

- A call or put option is "at the money" if the underlying asset price is equal to the strike price of the option.
- A call option is "out of the money" if the asset price is less than the strike price of the option.
- A put option is "out of the money" if the asset price is greater than the strike price of the option.
- A call option is "in the money" if the asset price is greater than the strike price of the option.
- A put option is "in the money" if the asset price is less than the strike price of the option.

It is important to realize that the option premium is paid at the time the option contract is written, even if the underlying transaction is never completed because it is not in the money. This is in contrast with a forward contract where the underlying transaction is always completed, either through delivery of the asset or through unwinding, or buying out, the transaction.

3. OPTION PRICING

The premium (or price) of an option contract represents a combination of the strike price (plus a possible amount by which the option is in the money) and a speculative premium (depending upon the length of the contract, there may also be a component for the time value of money since the premium is being paid today for a contract that will settle sometime in the future). Suppose a call contract on a commodity has been written with a strike price of $50 per ton. If the commodity is now selling for $54 per ton, the option contract is said to be in the money by $4. If the owner sells the contract at this point, a buyer will pay at most $4 per ton for the contract because at that price the contract can be used to purchase the commodity at $50, resulting in a $54 per-ton cost to the buyer of the contract if it is exercised (the total of the $4 price for the option and the $50 cost to exercise the option)—the same as the price of the commodity in the open market. The seller of the contract will not accept less than $4 because the contract can be used to purchase the commodity for $50. If it is sold, the seller of the contract will have to pay $54 for the commodity in the open market.

Option pricing examples that illustrate the possible relationships between an option's premium and its strike price are shown in Exhibits 16.2A and 16.2B. The pure speculative premium is not included; only the relationship between the price of the underlying asset, the option premium, and the profit or loss position on the option is shown. Exhibit 16.2A follows the call option example given in the prior paragraph, and Exhibit 16.2B examines the corresponding put option.

EXHIBIT 16.2A **CALL OPTION PRICING**

A CALL OPTION WITH A $50 STRIKE PRICE IS PURCHASED WHEN THE UNDERLYING ASSET IS SELLING FOR $46 PER UNIT. THE PREMIUM PAID IS $1.

PRICE OF UNDERLYING ASSET ($)	PREMIUM PAID ($)	$50 CALL OPTION VALUE ($)	PROFIT (+) OR LOSS (-) ($)	CALL OPTION IS IN, AT, OR OUT OF THE MONEY
46	1	0	-1	OUT
47	1	0	-1	OUT
48	1	0	-1	OUT
49	1	0	-1	OUT
50	1	0	-1	AT
51	1	1	0	IN
52	1	2	+1	IN
53	1	3	+2	IN
54	1	4	+3	IN
55	1	5	+4	IN

EXHIBIT 16.2B **PUT OPTION PRICING**

A PUT OPTION WITH A $50 STRIKE PRICE IS PURCHASED WHEN THE UNDERLYING ASSET IS SELLING FOR $54 PER UNIT. THE PREMIUM PAID IS $1.

PRICE OF UNDERLYING ASSET ($)	PREMIUM PAID ($)	$50 PUT OPTION VALUE ($)	PROFIT (+) OR LOSS (-) ($)	CALL OPTION IS IN, AT, OR OUT OF THE MONEY
54	1	0	-1	OUT
53	1	0	-1	OUT
52	1	0	-1	OUT
51	1	0	-1	OUT
50	1	0	-1	AT
49	1	1	0	IN
48	1	2	+1	IN
47	1	3	+2	IN
46	1	4	+3	IN
45	1	5	+4	IN

A call option is purchased by a party that wishes to control its effective cost paid for a commodity (note that the actual cost will still vary but the company has limited its exposure to this change through buying an option). A put option is purchased by a party that wishes to control the effective price for which the commodity can be sold. This party may be in possession of the asset or may be speculating that the market price of the asset will decline.

In practice, the purchaser of a call contract normally does not exercise the option to buy, and the purchaser of a put contract normally does not exercise the option to sell. The actual commodity transaction occurs in the spot market. The option contract is sold and its value is used to offset losses if the commodity price is higher (call option) or lower (put option) than the strike price. If a party writes (sells) a call option contract, it is setting a ceiling on the commodity price it will receive in exchange for the premium obtained. The writer of a put contract is ensuring a floor on the price at which it is willing to sell the commodity in exchange for the premium.

Options are also useful for a company that is bidding on a business contract that would result in exchange rate exposures if the bid is accepted. For example, a US company bids on providing products or services priced in euros (EUR) to a French company. The US company is uncertain whether it will win the bid, but if its bid is accepted, then the company will have an exposure that results from euro-denominated receivables.

A currency call option lets the company lock in a minimum value of euros for a known premium amount. If the company does not win the bid, then the option can be closed out or allowed to expire if it is out of the money. The company is not obligated to exchange the currencies as it would be had it entered into a forward contract, nor has it exposed itself to possible losses as would be true had it purchased a futures contract. The price of these advantages is the premium paid for the currency call option contract.

E. Comparison of Forwards, Futures, and Options

	Forward Contract	Futures Contract	Option Contract
Definition	An agreement between two parties to buy or sell an asset at a fixed point in time for a specified price	A standardized contract to buy or sell an asset at a certain point in the future for a specified price	A contract that gives the buyer the option to buy (call) or sell (put) an asset at some point in the future for a specified price
Contract Size	Customized to the needs of the customer	Standardized size and time periods	Standardized if exchange-traded but customized if individually contracted
Expiration Date	Negotiable	Standardized	Standardized and negotiable are both available.
Market	Negotiated directly between the parties with no initial payment	Traded on an exchange with an initial margin deposit required	Exchange-traded or negotiated directly between two parties; if exchange-traded, typically requires a margin deposit
Regulation	Not regulated	Government-regulated (CFTC in the US)	Exchange-traded options are regulated by the exchange rules.
Settlement	Mandatory	Mandatory	Optional

IV. FOREIGN EXCHANGE (FX) RISK MANAGEMENT IN TREASURY

Managing the risks related to changing FX rates is a critical part of managing global treasury operations. This section discusses the risks and issues related to managing FX rate fluctuations.

A. Challenges in International/Global Treasury Management

The objectives of global treasury management are similar to those of domestic treasury management, with the main objective being the efficient use of an organization's global cash resources in a manner consistent with its strategic goals. A global treasury operation must also manage cross-border funds movement and use FX and liquidity management techniques that are different from those used within just one country. The selection of financial services providers that are capable of assisting a company with international operations is a critical aspect of the global treasury management process.

1. FOREIGN EXCHANGE (FX) RISK

International companies with cash flows in various foreign currencies are exposed to FX risk. A company must assess the volatility of the different types and levels of FX rate fluctuations for each specific currency involved and how changes in FX rates can impact its balance sheet and income statement. This analysis and methods for managing FX risk are covered elsewhere in this chapter. Companies that conduct business globally but only in their base, or home, currency sometimes falsely assume that they have eliminated their FX risk. In reality, they have only transferred the risk to their global trading partners, who will typically include the cost of any FX risk in making their trading decisions. As a result, companies that demand payment in their home currency may limit their explicit FX risk, but assume an implicit FX risk that can reduce the market competitiveness of their products.

2. CASH FLOW COMPLEXITY

A global company must manage the cash flows from subsidiaries, suppliers, and customers in each country in which it operates. Due to widely differing regulations, banking practices, payment systems, and levels of information availability, global companies must often manage treasury transactions in different currencies, as well as those transactions that cross national boundaries.

3. TAX ISSUES

Global companies face a myriad of tax laws and regulations. Global treasury operations often are required to seek expert tax and legal advice to interpret the rules and regulations of different, and sometimes conflicting, tax authorities. It is important to involve tax and legal experts in the development of any FX or global trading strategy.

B. Foreign Exchange (FX) Rates

1. FOREIGN CURRENCY QUOTATION FORMATS

FX rates, or spot rates, are quoted in several ways, depending on the currencies and the markets involved. An FX rate is typically expressed as the equivalent unit of one currency per unit of another currency at a given moment in time.

Foreign currency quotation formats tend to be structured as:

[Currency X] / [Currency Y] Rate

This can be read as "one unit of Currency X is equal to rate multiplied by Currency Y." To determine the cost in Currency Y of a given number of units of Currency X, just multiply that number by the rate. Conversely, to determine the amount of Currency X that could be purchased with a given amount of Currency Y, divide the amount of Currency Y by the rate.

From a US perspective, there are two ways to quote FX rates: the US dollar (USD) equivalent of one unit of foreign currency, or the foreign currency equivalent of one US dollar. If Currency Y is the US dollar, this is called a *USD equivalent quote*. If Currency X is the US dollar, this is called a *foreign currency equivalent quote*. To convert a foreign currency equivalent quote to a USD equivalent quote, use the following formula:

$$\text{USD Equivalent} = 1 \,/\, \text{Foreign Currency Equivalent}$$

In the spot market, the convention is that most currency rates are provided as USD equivalent rates (the number of foreign currency units that one US dollar will purchase), which is known as the *European quotation convention*. The British pound (GBP) and euro (EUR) are an exception to this rule and are quoted as foreign currency equivalent rates (the number of USD that the GPB or EUR will purchase), which is known as the *American quotation convention*. The following table displays examples of both types of quotation formats for selected foreign currencies, with the most common format used for each currency indicated in ***italic/bold type***.

Sample Foreign Currency Quotation Formats:

Currency	American Convention (Non-USD Equivalent)	European Convention (USD Equivalent)
British pound (GBP)	***GBP/USD 1.5322***	USD/GBP 0.6527
Canadian dollar (CAD)	CAD/USD 0.9841	***USD/CAD 1.0162***
Euro (EUR)	***EUR/USD 1.3086***	USD/EUR 0.7642
Japanese yen (JPY)	JPY/USD 0.0101	***USD/JPY 98.95***

Calculation Example: Foreign Exchange (FX) Conversion

In the table above, the quote for British pounds is:

GBP/USD 1.5322

This expression means that every British pound costs $1.5322. Since the USD cost of a single British pound is known, the USD cost of 250,000 pounds can be calculated by multiplying 250,000 by the rate, as in the following calculation:

GBP 250,000 = 250,000 × 1.5322 = USD 383,050

Similarly, to determine how many pounds can be purchased with $100,000, the following calculation would be used:

USD 100,000 = 100,000 / 1.5322 = GBP 65,266

2. BID-OFFER QUOTES

Banks and other dealers quote both bid and offer rates for foreign currency. The bid rate is the rate at which a dealer is willing to buy currency. The offer rate is the rate at which a dealer is willing to sell currency. The difference between the bid rate and the offer rate is referred to as the *bid-offer spread* or *bid-ask spread*. The spread covers the dealer's exposures, expenses, and profits.

The bid-offer quote is usually structured in the following format:

[Currency X] / [Currency Y] Bid Rate–Offer Rate

The bid rate is the rate at which the dealer is willing to buy Currency X and sell Currency Y. Conversely, the offer rate is the rate at which the dealer is willing to sell Currency X and buy Currency Y.

Calculation Example: Bid-Offer Quote

For this example, assume a dealer provides a bid-offer quote of USD/JPY 90.57–90.63 (often just abbreviated as USD/JPY 90.57–63). This means the dealer is willing to buy (bid) one US dollar (USD) at JPY 90.57 and sell (offer) one USD at JPY 90.63.

If a US organization wants to sell $50,000 to the dealer in exchange for Japanese yen (JPY), then the dealer buys (bids) the $50,000 from the organization for JPY 4,528,500. This is calculated as:

$$\text{JPY Amount} = \text{USD } 50{,}000 \times 90.57 = \text{JPY } 4{,}528{,}500$$

However, if the same US organization sells the JPY 4,528,500 back to the dealer in exchange for dollars, the dealer sells (offers) the organization only $49,967, calculated as:

$$\text{USD Amount} = \frac{\text{JPY } 4{,}528{,}500}{90.63} = \text{USD } 49{,}967$$

The difference of $33 (i.e., $50,000 – $49,967) represents the dealer's spread, or earnings, on the round-trip transaction.

3. HOW RATES ARE OBTAINED

Most companies that are active in the FX markets subscribe to one of the real-time rate reporting and/or electronic trading services, such as Bloomberg, Electronic Broking Services (EBS), or Reuters. Companies trading in the FX market on a less frequent basis may access FX rates through a bank or FX dealer or through online trading platforms such as FXall and 360 Treasury Systems AG (360T). Rates also are available on the Internet from a variety of sources. However, free services generally have a slight time delay.

4. FOREIGN EXCHANGE (FX) MARKETS

There are two basic FX markets: the spot market and the forward market. A rate quoted in the spot market is called the *spot FX rate* (also referred to as a *spot rate* or *spot contract*). Spot rates are quoted for the delivery (or settlement) of currency one or two business days following the date of the trade. For FX trades initiated from the United States, regular spot settlement of Canadian dollars and Mexican pesos is one business day, while regular spot settlement of European and Asian currencies is two business days. Faster settlement may be possible, but it is often at a less favorable rate than the spot rate.

A forward FX rate (forward rate) is a rate quoted for the delivery (or settlement) of currency beyond the terms of a spot contract. Deliveries under most forward FX contracts occur within a year of the trade date. Delivery dates beyond one year are available for actively traded currencies.

The forward rate is based on the spot rate, plus or minus forward points. Forward points reflect the difference between two countries' short-term money market interest rates (e.g., rates on short-term government borrowing or interbank rates) at the time the trade is executed. The interest rate differential between two countries determines if respective currencies will trade at par, at a discount, or at a premium in the forward market:

- **Par:** If the spot rate and forward rate are the same, then the forward rate is at par with the spot rate. In theory, this implies that the interest rate structure between the two countries is the same. Because this occurs only rarely, currencies generally trade at a discount or premium.
- **Discount:** A currency is at a discount when it is worth less in the forward market than in the spot market. The currency with the higher interest rate will trade at a discount in the forward market against a currency with a lower interest rate.
- **Premium:** A currency is at a premium when it is worth more in the forward market than in the spot market. The currency with the lower interest rate will trade at a premium in the forward market against a currency with a higher interest rate.
- **Points:** Premiums and discounts are commonly quoted in points (basis points, or 1 /100th of a percent). In the jargon of the industry, forward points are added to the spot rate when there is a premium and are subtracted from the spot rate in the case of a discount.

The relationship among the spot, forward, and money markets is known as *interest rate parity* (discussed earlier in this chapter). As long as FX and interest rate markets are efficient,[6] it should not be possible to take money from one country, invest it in another country's money market, return it to the original country, and generate a higher rate of return than could have been earned in the original country's money market. If an advantage to investing in another country's money market exists, it will be eliminated quickly because exchange rates adjust to the cross-border money flows created by investors as they attempt to capture the advantage. Thus, the difference observed between spot and forward market rates is not a prediction of the future movement of the spot rate; rather, it represents an adjustment of the exchange rate that gives economic recognition to the difference between short-term interest rates in the two countries.

C. Emerging Markets

For global companies operating in emerging markets, there may be some special challenges to managing the risk related to dealing with local currencies and governments in these markets. Some emerging economies have very tightly managed currencies, in terms of both exchange rates and availability. Management of FX exposures and risk in these situations may be very different from the more traditional FX risk management in more commonly traded currencies. It is important to be aware that organizations actually introduce greater elements of financial uncertainty when they fail to take adequate measures to address FX-related risk. Considering that emerging market FX risk is becoming more common within international enterprises, this is now more relevant to more businesses than ever before.

1. EMERGING MARKET CURRENCIES

On a broad level, emerging market currencies (often referred to as *exotic currencies* because they are not commonly traded) fall into one of several different categories contributing to the underlying risk profile:

- Free-floating currencies that are traded with some degree of transparency
- Currencies that trade subject to strict regulations imposed by monetary authorities in the country
- Currencies that are pegged to another currency in some form
- Currencies that trade within a band against other currencies
- Currencies that are not freely convertible

6. In this context, efficient markets would mean zero (or at least very low) transaction costs, perfect and costless information, no barriers to entry, and the ability of market participants to borrow or invest at some risk-free rate. While these conditions are not likely for the average investor, they may be possible for large institutional players, such as global banks and central banks.

Examples of exotic currencies currently include the Belarusian ruble (BYR), the Lebanese pound (LBP), the Samoan tala (WST), and the Iraqi dinar (IQD).

2. ISSUES WITH EXOTIC CURRENCIES

Emerging market FX risk may be a consideration for some multinationals, especially in view of the growth in business in emerging markets. Although FX exposures in major economies can be addressed using mainstream risk management instruments and techniques, the same is not necessarily the case with emerging markets. In particular, exotic currencies have unique characteristics that often impede more commonplace approaches to controlling FX risk.

The characteristics of exotic currencies typically include the following:

- Illiquidity
- Volatility
- Reduced transparency
- Limited derivative availability
- Capital controls
- Heightened carrying risk
- Pricing distortions
- Limited risk-sharing options
- Minimal internal hedging alternatives
- Transfer risks

Emerging market economies and their currencies are commonly afflicted with low levels of transaction activity, dramatic fluctuations (typically a depreciating trend), central bank restrictions, and less developed financial markets in general. All of these factors ultimately create conditions of elevated risk. The risk level is often magnified by potential event risk such as that created by political instability within the country.

V. CURRENCY DERIVATIVES USED TO HEDGE FOREIGN EXCHANGE (FX) EXPOSURE

Once a company has identified and quantified material exposures to exchange rate changes, it must decide whether to hedge each exposure. There are several instruments that a company can use to manage FX rate risk. While these tools are discussed briefly above, they are discussed in more detail in this section.

A. Currency or Foreign Exchange (FX) Forwards

A currency or FX forward is a commitment to buy or sell a specified amount of foreign currency on a future date at an agreed-upon exchange rate today. FX forwards are available through banks and other FX traders in most major currencies and in commonly available maturities of one, two, three, six, nine, and twelve months. Since these contracts are sold in the OTC market, they may be negotiated for most currencies and maturities, given a willing counterparty. Because forwards are credit instruments that relate to a company's ability to deliver at the end of the contract, the dealers or counterparties in FX forwards are often banks. As a result, the legal documentation concerning FX forwards usually involves credit-related risk issues and, in many cases, the dealer or counterparty may require the company to execute an ISDA master agreement before FX forward contracts can be initiated. The forward rate, or the rate at which the two currencies will be exchanged, depends upon three factors:

- The current spot rate
- The term of the forward contract
- The relative interest rates in the two countries during the term

Forward contracts are useful tools for managing currency exposure because uncertainty is exchanged for a certain outcome. The company is protected against losses if the currency moves against the underlying exposure, although it foregoes any benefit if the currency moves in favor of the underlying exposure. Forward contracts are best suited for known (or contracted) exposures and when there is a need to lock in the rate to eliminate uncertainty.

Calculation Example: Currency Forward

The following example assumes that a US importer has agreed to pay in British pounds (GBP). The US importer must pay an invoice for GBP 125,000 in 90 days.

- The importer could purchase a forward contract today for GBP quoted at $1.5332 in US dollars (USD) per GBP (i.e., GBP/USD 1.5322), deliverable in 90 days.
- At the end of 90 days, the importer would pay $191,650, calculated as follows:

$$\text{USD Amount} = 1.5332 \times \text{GBP } 125{,}000 = \text{USD } 191{,}650$$

- Upon payment of this amount on the contract, the US importer would receive GBP 125,000 to pay the invoice.
- Therefore, no matter what fluctuation occurred in the exchange rate during the next 90-day period, the purchase of the forward contract locks in the exchange rate for British pounds.

A window forward is a variation on the standard forward contract. In a window forward, rather than settling on a specific date, the forward allows settlement during a given period (or "window") of time. This type of forward allows some flexibility in dealing with potential production or legal delays but will typically cost more than a standard forward since the counterparty does not know exactly when the contract will settle and will typically price on the worst-case scenario.

An average-rate forward is a tool that is used when the hedger will be trading funds at some point in the future, but does not know the exact dates and volumes of the individual trades. An average-rate forward allows the buyer the ability to create a hedge rate for this unknown future exposure by locking in forward points and a spot rate today. At some specified point in the future, there is an averaging period of daily spot observations to determine an average rate that, when compared to the hedge rate, will set the payout.

B. Currency Futures

Currency futures contracts are similar to currency forwards except that futures are traded on organized exchanges and are standardized in terms of their amount and maturity date. Currency futures were initially offered at the Chicago Mercantile Exchange (CME), which is still the largest regulated currency futures marketplace in the world, but are now offered by a number of exchanges around the world. Typically the market price for a currency futures contract will be relatively the same no matter which broker is used.

Currency futures, like any other futures contracts, are marked to market and require the investor to maintain a margin account to protect against potential adverse changes in the value of the contract. With a margin account, currency traders are able to purchase contracts for some multiple of the amount in their margin account. Therefore, rather than paying the full purchase price at the time they purchase a contract, traders can purchase contracts for multiples of their margin account. In effect they "borrow" money from their broker to buy futures contracts and repay the loan on settlement. If the value of the contract ever falls below the amount in the margin account, the trader will be asked to deposit additional funds due to the margin call. If the trader is unable to do this, the broker or exchange will normally liquidate the trader's position immediately and charge any loss to the margin account. The size of the margin is dependent upon the rules of the specific exchange and broker, and in some cases the type of contract. For example, the Montreal Exchange requires a larger margin for speculative accounts than it does for hedging transactions.

An illustrative listing of some of the more common contracts available on the CME and their required margins is provided in Exhibit 16.3. Contracts are generally offered for six-month maturities on a quarterly cycle (i.e., March, June, September, and December).

EXHIBIT 16.3 **SELECTED CURRENCY CONTRACTS ON CME**

CURRENCY PAIR	CONTRACT SIZE	MARGIN REQUIRED
EUR/USD	EUR 125,000	$2,475
USD/JPY	JPY 12,500,000	$3,410
GBP/USD	GBP 62,500	$1,320
USD/CHF	CHF 125,000	$2,200
USD/CAD	CAD 100,000	$1,100

NOTE: CHF is the designation for the Swiss franc.

Calculation Example: Currency Future

Consider the example of a US import company that must pay an invoice for GBP 125,000 in 90 days. The company is uncertain regarding the future exchange rate and wishes to prevent exposure due to fluctuations in the value of the British pound (GBP). The company decides to purchase a futures contract for pounds today and hold the contract until the currency must be purchased in the spot market.

- If the value of the pound rises, causing an increase in the company's cost to pay the invoice, then the company could sell the futures contract (the price of which would also rise) for a profit. The profit gained on the futures contract is then used to offset the higher purchase price of the pounds in the spot market.
- Assume that a futures contract allows the company to purchase pounds at a rate of GBP/USD 1.5322, and assume that the information in Exhibit 16.3 is currently valid. The company would need to purchase two GBP futures contracts (at GBP 62,500 each) to fully hedge its exposure of GBP 125,000. In this case, the margin requirement for the position would be $1,320 per contract, for a total margin requirement of $2,640.
- If the GBP futures contracts decrease in value on a given day, money will be taken from the margin account. If the contracts increase in value on a given day, money will be added to the margin account when the position is marked to market.
- For example, suppose that at the end of the first day, the contract price settles at GBP/USD 1.5474. The value of the two contracts has increased by a total of $1,900, and the new value on the margin account after marking to market is $4,540, calculated as follows:

$$\text{Change in Contract Value} = (1.5474 - 1.5322) \times \text{GBP } 125{,}000 = \text{USD } 1{,}900$$

$$\text{New Margin Account Value} = \$2{,}640 + \$1{,}900 = \$4{,}540$$

- If the futures contract price decreases to GBP/USD 1.5425 the next day, then the resulting change in fair (or mark-to-market) value will be a negative $612.50, which must be subtracted from the margin account when it is marked to market. The value of the margin account after the second day will be $3,927.50, which still exceeds the minimum margin requirement. These calculations are illustrated below. Note that the process of marking the position to market at the end of each day will continue as long as the position is open.

$$\text{Change in Contract Value} = (1.5425 - 1.5474) \times \text{GBP } 125{,}000 = -\text{ USD } 612.50$$

$$\text{New Margin Account Value} = \$4{,}540.00 - \$612.50 = \$3{,}927.50$$

- Assume that when the company needs to buy pounds in 90 days, the exchange rate has risen to GBP/USD 1.6005. In this scenario, the company could buy the pounds in the spot market, paying GBP/USD 1.6005. The futures contract that the company holds to buy at GBP/USD 1.5322 has a profit of $0.0683 per pound, calculated as follows:

$$\text{Profit on Contract} = \$1.6005 - \$1.5322 = \$0.0683 \text{ per GBP}$$

- The company sells the contract back to the exchange and uses the profit of $0.0683 per GBP to offset the purchase price on the spot market, effectively achieving a net price of $1.5322 per pound.
- If, instead, the exchange rate has dropped to GBP/USD 1.5022, then the company would still buy the needed GBP in the spot market and would close the futures contract (i.e., sell the contract back to the exchange) at a loss of $0.0300 per pound, calculated as follows:

$$\text{Loss on Contract} = \$1.5022 - \$1.5322 = -\ \$0.0300 \text{ per GBP}$$

- In either case, the net cost of GBP to the company would still be GBP/USD 1.5322, and the total cost to pay the invoice would be $191,525 (1.5322 x GBP 125,000).

C. Currency Swaps

A currency swap typically involves the exchange of a cash flow denominated in one currency with a cash flow denominated in another currency, as well as an exchange of principal. The two cash flows can be at either fixed or floating rates. In the example below, both are fixed. A swap can also be used to change the value date of a forward when a company cannot meet the original delivery date due to unexpected circumstances, such as a late payment from a foreign customer.

Calculation Example: Currency Swap

Consider the following example of a currency swap, as illustrated in Exhibit 16.4. A US-based firm (Company A) wishes to borrow JPY 100 million for 10 years to fund an investment in Japan, and the current exchange rate is USD/JPY 99.0099. Since Company A is based in the United States, it has better access to the US capital markets and can borrow at a relatively lower interest rate in the United States. In this case, Company A may be able to lock in a lower interest rate by borrowing in US dollars (USD) and converting to Japanese yen (JPY) at the spot rate.

However, the company will face exchange rate risk throughout the life of the loan if yen-denominated cash flows from the Japanese investment are the anticipated source for interest and principal payments. Company A may use a currency swap to manage the FX exposure.

EXHIBIT 16.4 **CURRENCY SWAP**

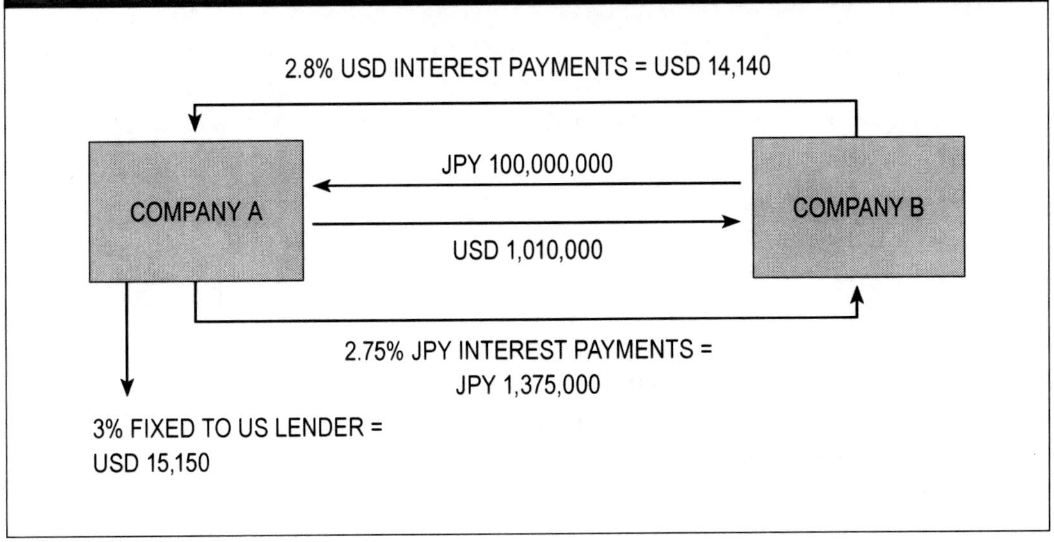

Suppose that Company A borrows $1,010,000 (the USD equivalent of JPY 100 million) for 10 years at a fixed interest rate of 3%. The company can then enter into a currency swap with a counterparty (Company B, typically a bank) to obtain the yen-denominated funding while limiting the exchange rate risk. Under the terms of the swap, Company A will make semiannual payments in yen to Company B (the counterparty) at a fixed rate of 2.75%, and Company B will make semiannual payments in US dollars to Company A at a fixed rate of 2.8%. A currency swap will typically specify that the company and counterparty exchange the notional principal at the beginning and end of the swap.

Therefore, the currency swap will consist of the following transactions:

- Company A will pay $1,010,000 to Company B, and Company B will pay Company A JPY 100 million. Company A can then use the JPY 100 million to make its investment in Japan.
- Every 6 months for 10 years, Company A and Company B will make the following payments:
  - Company A will pay Company B JPY 1,375,000 from local yen currency that it has obtained from its Japanese investment, calculated as:

$$0.0275 \times \text{JPY } 100{,}000{,}000 \times (180/360) = \text{JPY } 1{,}375{,}000$$

  - Company B will pay Company A $14,140, calculated as:

$$0.028 \times \$1{,}010{,}000 \times (180/360) = \$14{,}140$$

- At the end of 10 years, the Japanese investment will mature, returning to Company A the JPY 100 million principal, which Company A will then pay to Company B. Company B will pay Company A $1,010,000.

This structure will allow Company A to borrow in the market in which it has a comparative advantage (i.e., the United States), obtain the yen needed to finance operations in Japan, and minimize the risk associated with changes in the FX rate. Since Company A issued USD debt at 3%, the semiannual interest payment to the US creditors will be $15,150, calculated as:

$$0.03 \times \$1{,}010{,}000 \times (180/360) = \$15{,}150$$

Assuming the exchange rate continues to be USD/JPY 99.0099, Company A will also make semiannual interest payments of $13,887.50 (JPY 1,375,000/99.0099) to Company B, and will receive $14,140.00 every six months from Company B, under the terms of the swap. As a result, the net semiannual interest expense for Company A will be $14,897.50, calculated as:

$$\$15{,}150.00 + \$13{,}887.50 - \$14{,}140.00 = \$14{,}897.50$$

D. Currency Options

A currency option gives the buyer the right to buy (call) or sell (put) a fixed amount of a foreign currency at a fixed exchange rate (the strike price) on or before a specific future date. For example, a foreign currency call option sets a ceiling price to buy a foreign currency in terms of the domestic currency. The ceiling price is the strike price plus the premium paid for the call. Assume a call option on euros (EUR) has a strike price of $1.30 with a premium of $0.10. The maximum price, or ceiling, for this arrangement will be $1.40 ($1.30 + $0.10) per euro. Stated another way, the buyer will pay no more than $1.40 (net) to purchase EUR 1.00.

On the other hand, a foreign currency put option establishes a floor value to sell a foreign currency in terms of the domestic currency. The floor value is the exercise price less the premium paid for the put. Assume a put option on euros has a strike price of $1.35 with a premium of $0.05. The minimum value, or floor, for this arrangement will be $1.30 ($1.35 – $0.05) per euro. Stated another way, the seller will receive no less than $1.30 (net) for each euro sold.

As another example, assume a UK importer has an account payable due in three months in euros. The importer can ensure a maximum cost to obtain those euros by buying a call option on euros. If, at the time of payment, the spot market price of the euro is less than the strike price of the call option, the importer does not exercise the option and loses only the premium paid. The net cost of the euros to the importer is the spot price of the euro plus the option premium. The option acts as insurance against the spot price of the euro rising above a specific level. For this form of insurance, the importer pays the option premium (price). Note that as previously discussed, the buyer of the option will pay the option premium even if the contract is never exercised.

Option premiums have two components: intrinsic value and time value. The intrinsic value is the built-in value of an option and is calculated as the difference between the option strike price and the expected market price at the time the option can be exercised. The time value is equal to the option premium less the intrinsic value, and it reflects the risk that the option seller bears in selling the option to the buyer. Generally, the longer the time to maturity, the greater the time value because there is a greater chance that the value of the underlying asset may increase. An option that is close to maturity will have virtually no time value component in the premium pricing. This pricing relationship with respect to the time value also explains why a buyer would be willing to pay some premium for an option that at current market prices is out of the money (i.e., for a call option, the strike price is greater than the current market price). The longer the time to maturity, the greater the chance that the option will be in the money and thus provide additional value.

Calculation Example: Currency Option

Suppose a call option contract on GBP has been written with a strike price of $1.50 per pound (i.e., exchange rate is GBP/USD 1.50).

- Assuming this is an American option, if the spot exchange rate is GBP/USD 1.5372, then the option contract is said to be in the money by $0.0372 (spot rate minus the strike price, or $1.5372 – $1.50).
- A buyer of the contract will pay at least $0.0372 per GBP because at that price, the contract can be used to purchase GBP at $1.50, resulting in a GBP/USD 1.5372 cost to the buyer of the contract if it is exercised. This is the same price that would be paid for British pounds in the spot market. The seller of the contract will not accept less than $0.0372 per GBP because the contract can be used to purchase British pounds at GBP/USD 1.50. If the contract is exercised, the seller of the contract will have to pay GBP/USD 1.5372 in the spot market to purchase the British pounds for delivery.

- If there is some time until the contract expires, the premium for the contract will exceed $0.0372 per GBP because the party buying the contract has locked in a maximum price of GBP/USD 1.50 through the delivery date. No matter how much the value of the pound rises prior to the delivery date, the option holder can exercise the contract at GBP/USD 1.50. Accordingly, a buyer of the contract will be willing to pay some amount more than $0.0372 per GBP (the time value) for the option. If the market value of the British pound rises above GBP/USD 1.5372, then the option holder may gain by buying the currency at GBP/USD 1.50 or by selling the contract for more than was paid for it.
- For example, if the exchange rate rose to GBP/USD 1.6245 prior to the delivery date, then the option contract would sell for at least $0.1245 plus a speculative premium because the option is in the money by $0.1245 (e.g., $1.6245 – $1.50). The time value portion of the premium on an option will generally decline as the premium (option price) rises. As rising exchange rates cause the premium on the call option to increase, an option buyer who pays the higher price to acquire the contract has more money at risk should the value of the British pound subsequently decline. Accordingly, a call option buyer will be willing to pay a smaller time value premium as the price of the option increases.
- In the case of the call option in this example, the market value of the British pound may drop below GBP/USD 1.50, in which case the option is out of the money. If the price never recovers to rise above GBP/USD 1.50 by the delivery date, then the option will expire (i.e., it will not be exercised) because British pounds can be purchased in the spot market for less than $1.50 per pound. In this case, the party that purchased the option contract will experience a loss equal to the premium (price) paid for the contract. Again, as the price paid for the call contract increases as the exchange rate rises above GBP/USD 1.50, a buyer who pays the higher price to acquire the call contract has more money at risk should the exchange rate drop below GBP/USD 1.50 after the contract is purchased. Accordingly, a buyer will be willing to pay a smaller time value premium the higher the price of the option.
- The opposite is true of a put option. If a put option contract is purchased that permits the contract owner to sell GBP at $1.50 per pound, then the value of the contract will not increase as the exchange rate rises above GBP/USD 1.50. This is because an owner of the underlying asset (British pounds) will sell it in the market for the higher price rather than exercise the right to sell (put) the pounds at GBP/USD 1.50. If the spot exchange rate falls below GBP/USD 1.50, then the put contract will gain value because it lets the option's owner sell the currency at $1.50 per pound. The more the exchange rate declines below GBP/USD 1.50, the more value the put option gains.

E. Hedging Tools Available for Exotic Currencies

The principal derivative of choice for exotic currencies is the non-deliverable forward (NDF). The NDF is considered a synthetic instrument in that it is cash-settled in a major base currency (i.e., USD, EUR, etc.).[7] It is used as a proxy hedge in a situation in which an exotic currency is not actively traded in the forward market. In this case, a *proxy hedge* is defined as a hedge in an alternate currency that is actively traded and that typically moves in the same direction as the desired currency. The challenge is finding an appropriate proxy currency.

As NDF contracts are cash-settled, there is no actual exchange of the underlying currencies on settlement. Settlement simply reflects the difference between the previously agreed-upon NDF rate and the existing spot rate at time of fixing. This difference should approximately offset what occurred over the same time with respect to the underlying exotic currency relative to the base currency.

7. A synthetic security is created by combining one set of securities (usually including some type of derivative) to mimic the properties of another security.

For example, a Canadian company is importing products from China. The Canadian company is billed in Chinese renminbi (CNY) but pays its invoices in US dollars (USD). The company can purchase a USD/CNY NDF based on the amount and terms of its current invoice from its Chinese supplier to hedge against possible changes in the USD/CNY FX rate. At settlement time, the company will pay its supplier in USD and settle with its counterparty on the NDF in USD for any change in the FX rate. No renminbi will ever change hands.

In addition to NDFs (and similar to basic, "plain vanilla" option contracts), non-deliverable option (NDO) contracts can be used to address exotic FX risk. The NDO extends to the buyer the right, but not the obligation, to buy (via a call option) or sell (via a put option) a set amount of foreign currency at a specified rate, or strike price, on a predetermined future date. Fundamentally, the NDO serves as an insurance policy against undesirable market trends. The significant difference between an NDF and an NDO is that the NDO gives the user the right, but not the obligation, to buy or sell a prearranged amount of foreign currency at a specified rate and on a predetermined future date, while the NDF requires that the contract be consummated.

VI. INTEREST RATE EXPOSURE AND RISK MANAGEMENT

Many organizations face financial risks attributable to interest rate changes. The risk exposure arises from the nature of the firm's operating and/or financing activities. Organizations with variable interest rate investments face the possibility of lower earnings when interest rates fall, while organizations with debt tied to variable interest rates face higher borrowing costs when interest rates rise. Interest rate forwards (including forward rate agreements), futures, swaps, and options are typical instruments used to manage interest rate risk.

A. Interest Rate Forwards

1. BASICS OF INTEREST RATE FORWARDS

A forward contract allows its buyer to lock in today the future price of an asset, such as an interest-linked security. The buyer has to pay the agreed-upon price on the settlement date, whether or not the interest rate has moved in the buyer's favor. The seller is also required to deliver the asset on the settlement date, whatever that asset's price is in the spot market. There is generally no up-front fee or margin required on these types of contracts and no cash changes hands before the settlement date.

Interest rate forwards are typically cash-settled rather than settled through delivery. That is, one party is obligated to pay the other the difference between the contract value of the forward and its spot value at maturity date. The most popular of these is the forward rate agreement (FRA) outlined below.

2. FORWARD RATE AGREEMENTS (FRAs)

An FRA is a forward contract on interest rates in which two parties agree that a certain interest rate will apply to a certain principal during a specified, future period of time. The notional principal amounts are agreed upon, but they are never exchanged. If the actual rate is different from the agreed-upon rate in the contract at settlement, then one party pays the other a cash amount equal to the difference. The majority of FRAs are based on Eurodollar rates (typically LIBOR), although other rates are available. FRAs are very popular with short-term borrowers who are trying to fix today the effective interest rate they will have to pay at a future date. A corporation may use such an arrangement to lock in an interest rate today for future working capital financing scheduled in six months.

For example, a company may project that it will need to borrow $1,000,000 for six months starting three months from now. Because the company is concerned that current interest rates will rise over the next three months before it borrows the needed funds, it can purchase a 3+6 FRA to lock in current rates. In a 3+6 FRA, the 3 indicates that the effective or starting date of the FRA is three months from now, and the termination of the FRA will be nine (or 3+6) months from now.

B. Interest Rate Futures

Interest rate futures are contracts on an underlying asset whose price is dependent solely on the level of interest rates. The most popular short-term interest rate contracts are US Treasury bill (T-bill) contracts, and Eurodollar contracts traded on the Chicago Mercantile Exchange as bank certificates of deposit (CDs). The underlying asset in a T-bill futures contract is the 90-day T-bill rate. The underlying asset in a Eurodollar contract is the interest earned on a Eurodollar deposit (CD) at three-month LIBOR. The most actively traded long-term interest rate contracts are the 5- and 10-year US Treasury notes and the 30-year US Treasury bonds.

Like other futures contracts, interest rate futures contracts are typically traded on an exchange and require a margin account. Each day, the gains or losses on the contract are posted to the account (marked to market), and if the losses are large enough, the holder of the contract may receive a margin call, requiring the holder to either post additional funds to the account or have the position liquidated.

Investors will use these types of contracts because they allow the investors to protect open positions from adverse price movements. Any gains or losses on the open positions held by the investors are offset by the payoffs from the derivative contracts. If the actual interest rate at maturity is different from the predetermined rate, then money is paid or received, depending on whether the difference is positive or negative.

This type of contract allows a company to hedge a one-period rate change and is similar to the FRA discussed above. While short-term contracts are cash-settled, some long-term futures contracts involve settlement by delivering specific long-term bonds. The market for all these contracts is typically very competitive, with fairly narrow spreads.

An example of a typical interest rate futures contract is provided below.

Calculation Example: Interest Rate Futures

Futures contract pricing on a one-year T-bill is generally defined as 100 minus the promised interest rate.

- Assuming that the predetermined futures rate is 0.50%, the contract is for a predetermined price of 99.50 (100 – 0.50). This scenario assumes that the rate on a one-year T-bill will be 0.50% exactly one year from today and will thus sell for $99.50.

- However, if the actual rate on a one-year T-bill is 0.75% at end of the year, then the realized value is only 99.25 (100 – 0.75). The holder of the long position (i.e., the one who bought the futures contract) will be paid by the seller of the contract the difference between the contracted rate of 0.50% and the actual rate of 0.75%, or the difference of 99.50 – 99.25, which equals 0.25 per unit of the contract.
- If the rate had moved in the other direction, and instead of 0.50% the one-year T-bill was at 0.35%, then the realized value would be 99.65 (100 – 0.35). In this case the holder of the long position (i.e., the purchaser of the contract) would pay the seller of the contract the change between the contracted rate of 0.50% and the actual rate of 0.35%, which equals 0.15 per unit of the contract.

C. Interest Rate Swaps

An interest rate swap is an OTC agreement between two parties to exchange the cash flows of two different securities throughout the life of the contract. Interest rate swaps can be viewed as a series of forwards and, as with forwards, the contract is binding on both sides of the contract. Interest rate swaps are very flexible hedging instruments used by treasury professionals for asset/liability management, as well as by bond portfolio managers to reduce or extend the average maturity or exposure of an open position.

The most common type of interest rate swap is the fixed-floating swap, which is the exchange of a fixed interest rate cash flow for a floating interest rate cash flow (or vice versa), with both interest rates in the same currency. The fixed side pays a fixed interest rate on a notional amount, usually quarterly or semiannually, while the floating side pays a floating rate on the same notional amount. The reference rate is generally LIBOR, but could be any mutually agreed-upon rate. This is often referred to as a *vanilla swap*. If both interest rates are floating, then the exchange of cash flows is called a *basis rate swap*, which is less commonly used. An example of a basis rate swap is the exchange of interest payments based on LIBOR for interest payments based on the US prime rate. Note that there is no exchange of principal as it cancels out both at inception and at maturity.

Interest rate swaps are often used by treasury professionals to convert a fixed-rate investment or obligation into a floating-rate investment or obligation (or vice versa) in order to better match the particular needs of a company and the current offerings of the market.

Calculation Example: Interest Rate Swap

Assume two parties (A and B) enter into a five-year swap with a notional value of $100 million. Party A will take the fixed side of the transaction because it wants to have certainty about its future interest rate expense, and Party B will take the floating side of the transaction because it believes interest rates are likely to fall over the five-year period.

- In this example, Party A is exchanging its floating-rate exposure for a fixed rate, and Party B is exchanging its fixed-rate exposure for a floating rate. As a result, Party A will pay a fixed rate to Party B, and Party B will pay a floating rate to Party A. The reference rates are 3.75% on the fixed side and LIBOR + 3.50% on the floating side. This means that at the end of each year, Party A will owe Party B $100 million x 3.75%, while Party B will owe Party A $100 million x (LIBOR + 3.50%).
- In practice, there is a netting procedure and only the difference is settled. That is, if LIBOR is less than 0.25% (or 3.75% – 3.50%), then Party A pays Party B, and if LIBOR is greater than 0.25%, then Party B pays Party A. For example:
    - If LIBOR is 0.15%, then Party A pays Party B as follows:

$$[0.0375 - (0.0015 + 0.0350)] \times \$100{,}000{,}000 = \$100{,}000$$

    - If LIBOR is 0.45%, then Party B pays Party A as follows:

$$[(0.0045 + 0.0350) - 0.0375] \times \$100{,}000{,}000 = \$200{,}000$$

Alternatively, assume that the same two parties enter into an interest rate swap agreement because Party A has a comparative advantage in the fixed-rate market and Party B has a comparative advantage in the floating-rate market. The two parties agree to split the rate advantage 50/50. The following chart shows the fixed and floating rates available to each party:

	Fixed Rate	**Floating Rate**
Party A	2.25%	6-month LIBOR + 0.75%
Party B	3.25%	6-month LIBOR + 1.25%

Party A will enter into a fixed-rate loan for 2.25%, and Party B will enter into a floating-rate loan for LIBOR + 1.25%. Since the difference in their effective rates at the time of the swap is 0.50%,[8] they will split the advantage 50/50, or 0.25% each. Each party pays its lender directly. Party A will also pay Party B LIBOR + 0.25%, while Party B will pay Party A 2.00% fixed, based on their swap agreement.

Party A's net interest rate can be determined using the following calculation:

$$\begin{aligned}\text{Net Interest Rate} &= \text{Rate Paid to Lender} + \text{Rate Paid for Swap} - \text{Rate Received from Swap}\\ &= 2.25\% + (\text{LIBOR} + 0.25\%) - 2.00\%\\ &= \text{LIBOR} + 0.50\% \text{ (saving 0.25\% over the offered floating rate of LIBOR + 0.75\%)}\end{aligned}$$

Similarly, Party B's net interest rate can be calculated as:

$$\begin{aligned}\text{Net Interest Rate} &= \text{Rate Paid to Lender} + \text{Rate Paid for Swap} - \text{Rate Received from Swap}\\ &= (\text{LIBOR} + 1.25\%) + 2.00\% - (\text{LIBOR} + 0.25\%)\\ &= 3.00\% \text{ (saving 0.25\% over the offered fixed rate of 3.25\%)}\end{aligned}$$

8. The net advantage of the swap is calculated by taking the difference between the differences in the fixed and floating rates, as follows: (3.25% – 2.25%) – [(LIBOR + 1.25%) – (LIBOR + 0.75%)] = 0.50%.

D. Interest Rate Options

Interest rate options are option-type derivatives where the payoff depends on the level of interest rates. There are three basic types of interest rate options: caps, floors, and collars. They are similar to currency options (discussed earlier in this chapter), which can also be purchased as caps, floors, and collars, but their purpose is to help protect the user from unwanted interest rate fluctuations rather than currency fluctuations.

1. INTEREST RATE CAPS

Caps ensure that the borrower of a floating-rate loan pays no more than a predetermined maximum rate if interest rates rise above a ceiling level. This level is known as the *cap rate*. If rates fall, then the borrower is not obligated to exercise the option and can still enjoy the benefits of lower borrowing costs. The price of this insurance is the premium paid for the cap.

For example, assume a German firm is negotiating a borrowing agreement for a 10-year term loan that will have a floating rate set at the European Central Bank (ECB) benchmark lending rate plus 250 basis points. At the time the agreement is being signed, the ECB rate is only 0.25%, resulting in an all-in rate on the loan of 2.75%. The firm is worried that interest rates will rise in the future and asks for a cap of 6.00% on the all-in rate for the agreement. This cap will be in the form of an up-front premium based on the loan amount, typically for the period of the loan agreement. Assume a loan amount of EUR 50 million and a premium for the cap of 50 basis points. In this case, the firm will pay EUR 50,000,000 x 0.0050 = EUR 250,000 to obtain the cap.

2. INTEREST RATE FLOORS

Floors ensure that the owner of a floating-rate asset receives a minimum rate if interest rates fall below a floor level. If rates fall below this level, then the floating-rate asset is protected by a put option on interest rates. If interest rates rise, then the company can still benefit because it is not obligated to exercise the put option. The cost of this insurance is the premium paid for the interest rate floor.

For example, a Japanese investor is looking to purchase a JPY 100 million, five-year investment with a variable rate that is based on the Bank of Japan prime lending rate plus 200 basis points. At the time of the purchase, the Bank of Japan rate was 1.00%, resulting in a return to the investor of 3.00%. If the investor is worried that rates will fall in the future, the investor may wish to purchase a floor on the rate paid. If a floor of 2.75% (return to the investor) is offered for a premium of 5 basis points, then the investor would pay JPY 100,000,000 x 0.0005 = JPY 50,000 to obtain the floor.

3. INTEREST RATE COLLARS

A combination of an interest rate cap and an interest rate floor is called an *interest rate collar*. A company that buys an interest rate cap and sells an interest rate floor is effectively locking in a range for borrowing costs. The cap establishes a maximum borrowing rate, thereby protecting the company against higher interest rates, while the floor sets a minimum borrowing rate. A collar has no costs when the income received from selling the floor matches the premium paid for the cap. Costless collars are popular hedging vehicles providing some interest rate protection at zero cost. Besides caps, floors, and collars, there are other complex derivatives constantly being developed and marketed that are beyond the scope of this book.

VII. COMMODITY RISK EXPOSURE

Commodities used in production or operations processes are sold in commodities markets. The most common commodities markets are for agricultural and meat products, oil and gas, minerals, and metals. There are two major types of commodities risk: price exposure and delivery exposure.

The primary commodity exposure that organizations face is the potential for changes in the price of a commodity. If an organization uses commodities in the production process, then rising prices create an exposure for the organization. Conversely, if an organization sells the product, then falling prices create an exposure.

For certain organizations that are large users of energy products (e.g., oil, gas, and coal), a regular supply of the commodity is crucial. As examples, airlines depend upon the availability of jet fuel, and electricity-generating plants require natural gas or coal. In addition to price exposure, these organizations also may face delivery exposure, if the supplier is unable or unwilling to deliver when needed. Entering into a long-term agreement with a reliable and trusted energy producer can help to mitigate these exposures.

Like interest rate and FX risks, commodity price risk can be managed using forwards, futures, swaps, options, or combinations of these derivative instruments. Consider the following example. In an oil swap, two parties would agree on a notional principal expressed in barrels of oil (not dollars). Similar to currency or interest rate swaps, the parties make regular settlements on the basis of fixed and floating oil prices. The floating price used in an oil swap is usually the average price of oil over a specified period. To reduce the uncertainty associated with the change in the price of oil, a treasury professional may attempt to construct a costless collar (i.e., a combination of a cap and a floor).

VIII. OTHER ISSUES RELATED TO FINANCIAL RISK MANAGEMENT

A. Accounting Issues

Due to the strict rules around many of the instruments used in FX and other types of financial risk management, there are exacting accounting issues to consider. These are addressed by the International Accounting Standards Board (IASB) globally and by the Financial Accounting Standards Board (FASB) in the United States. Global and US accounting standards that relate to derivative and hedge accounting are discussed in more detail in Chapter 18, Financial Accounting and Reporting.

One of the primary problems in the valuation of, and subsequent accounting for, derivatives is determining their accurate value. For many years, especially as both financial markets and asset prices rose rapidly, the valuation approach of mark-to-market was used. This approach allowed buyers of derivatives to report large profits related to their trading activities and subsequently increase their compensation significantly.

The problems came as the markets fell and these same assets had to be written down, sometimes very quickly, resulting in large losses for these institutions. Through several iterations and amendments to accounting standards, both IASB and FASB are working to address these issues. The question sometimes comes down to something as simple as, what is the real market price of an asset?

As a general guideline, ASC Topic 820-10: *Fair Value Measurement—Overall* offers some updated guidance on this issue, especially in volatile or illiquid markets. A rapid deterioration in an asset class (e.g., specific commodities) can make market participants risk averse and cause illiquidity in otherwise liquid markets. These conditions set the stage for a very challenging environment for establishing reliable assumptions and inputs. Additional detail on ASC Topic 820 is provided in Chapter 18, Financial Accounting and Reporting.

With respect to improving the transparency of information disclosure relating to the use of derivatives and hedging, ASC Topic 815: *Derivatives and Hedging* is the prevailing guideline for US companies (with updates to International Financial Reporting Standards [IFRS] essentially matching these guidelines). It is designed to give a more accurate picture of a company's financial position by requiring additional information about how and why any derivative contracts are being used.

Specifically, Topic 815 requires the following disclosures:

- A discussion of the company's objectives and strategies for using derivatives
- The current fair market value of the company's derivative positions
- Any contingent, credit-related features of the company's derivative positions
- Locations and amounts of derivatives in a company's financial statement

B. Tax Issues Related to Hedging

Tax issues surrounding the use of hedges are complex, and errors in the accounting treatment of hedge transactions can be very costly. If an improper accounting treatment is used or documentation does not meet tax authority requirements, then the organization may not be able to treat the gains/losses from derivative holdings as an offset to operational gains/losses. This could result in a significantly higher tax liability from hedging activities. A treasury professional must be aware of these issues and should approach entering into hedge transactions with caution. In general, advice should be obtained from legal, tax, and accounting experts who specialize in this area.

Other tax-related problems are the tax liabilities that are incurred as a result of a restatement of financial information due to errors in applying very complex accounting guidelines for derivative instruments and hedging. This problem makes it even more imperative that global companies involved in active hedging strategies keep abreast of current developments in these areas and ensure that their external accountants and auditors are experts in tax issues related to their business.

C. Hedging Policy Statement

An effective hedging strategy requires both approval of the general hedging policy (typically at the board of director's level) and implementation of that policy (usually in the treasury area of the organization). This policy should provide general directives, targets to be achieved, or a mixture of both; and is essential for management oversight as well as regulatory compliance. As previously noted, most hedging policy statements will bar the use of derivatives for speculative purposes. The hedging policy statement is discussed in Chapter 17, Treasury Policies and Procedures, but should address the following items in the three key financial risk management areas:

- **For foreign currency hedging:**
    - o Known foreign currency exposures on the balance sheet (translation-related)
    - o Known foreign currency exposures related to existing transactions
    - o Currency exposures for forecasted transactions
    - o Currency exposures for projected, future acquisitions or divestitures
    - o Any currency exposure related to investment asset portfolios
- **For interest rate hedging:**
    - o Known interest rate exposures on existing short-term investments and borrowing
    - o Known interest rate exposures on existing long-term investments and borrowing
    - o Interest rate exposures on forecasted investments and borrowing
- **For commodity hedging:**
    - o Known and forecasted exposures related to commodity pricing
    - o Known and forecasted exposures related to commodity availability

Accounting issues related to hedging and the use of cash flow versus fair value approaches are covered in Chapter 18, Financial Accounting and Reporting.

IX. SUMMARY

Financial risk management is a complex and important part of many treasury professionals' daily jobs, and one that is growing increasingly important as business expands globally. Because treasury is often a central clearinghouse for financial information in many companies, it is well positioned to help manage financial risk.

This chapter discussed the basics of financial risk management (including foreign exchange and interest rate risk), covered the three types of FX exposure, and presented some of the tools that are available to the treasury professional to manage financial risk, including commonly available derivatives such as forwards, futures, swaps, and options. Although they are discussed in more detail in later chapters, some of the issues around accounting for derivatives and the need for appropriate corporate policies were also reviewed in this chapter.

TEST YOUR UNDERSTANDING: CHAPTER 16

Answers are on pages 714–717.

1. What are the three major categories of financial risk?
2. What are the three types of foreign exchange (FX) risk?
3. Discuss the concepts of active hedging, speculation, and arbitrage.
4. What are the benefits of financial risk management?
5. What is a forward contract?
6. What is a swap agreement?
7. What is the difference between a call option and a put option?
8. When are option contracts normally exercised?
9. Discuss the objectives of global treasury management.
10. What are the two basic FX markets?
11. What are forward points?
12. What is a currency swap?
13. Explain a forward rate agreement (FRA).
14. What are interest rate futures?
15. What is an interest rate collar?
16. What are the disclosures required by ASC Topic 815?
17. Compare implicit and explicit FX risk.
18. Discuss the challenges for global companies operating in emerging markets.
19. What are exotic currencies?

CHAPTER 17
Treasury Policies and Procedures

V. OVERVIEW OF KEY TREASURY POLICIES

A. Bank Account and Financial Services Authority Policies

B. Payments Policy

C. Collection and Concentration Policy

D. Investment Valuation and Impairment Policies

E. Payment Card Policies

F. Outsourcing Policy

G. Financial Risk Management Policies

H. Regulatory Compliance Policies

I. Funding/Financing Policies

J. Treasury Systems Policy

VI. SUMMARY

APPENDIX 17.1: SAMPLE SHORT-TERM INVESTMENT POLICY

I. INTRODUCTION

Organizations use policies to identify and describe their risks, and to establish the limits, guidelines, accountabilities, and risk management practices that the organization deems essential. A policy is intended to serve as a statement to guide activities in a particular area or function of an organization and to establish performance evaluation guidelines and process measurements. A procedure, sometimes referred to as a *standard operating procedure,* or *SOP,* is a specified series of actions or operations that should be executed in a consistent manner to achieve desired results identified in the policy. In other words, the procedures must follow the guidelines of the policy. Policies and procedures should be clearly stated and enforced—they are the basic principles, often approved by the board of directors, by which an organization operates.

This chapter provides an overview of treasury policies and procedures and discusses the key elements needed in developing an effective policy statement. It then presents a more detailed discussion of one specific policy statement to provide an overall example of policy development. Finally, this chapter provides a list of key treasury policies and the various elements that should be considered when developing them. An actual sample policy is included in Appendix 17.1.

II. OVERVIEW OF TREASURY POLICIES AND PROCEDURES

A. The Role of Treasury Policies and Procedures

Treasury policies and procedures provide a framework for the design of treasury workflows and controls that support an organization's operational, financial, and treasury management objectives. The behavior of treasury staff cannot be regulated merely by declaration. However, assigning specific duties and documenting the assignment of those duties to designated parties provides a baseline for acceptable behavior. The addition of specific penalties in the event of violations of that behavior also helps set appropriate expectations.

The formalization of policies and procedures is one way for an organization to inform employees, agents, contractors, and vendors of the expected behavior related to certain specific treasury activities. The standards outlined in an organization's treasury policies and procedures should be reviewed regularly for continued appropriateness and to make sure they incorporate relevant legislative, regulatory, or process changes/revisions. In addition, policies and procedures are often used as training tools to help document the organization's best practices and expectations.

B. Why Treasury Policies and Procedures Are Needed

There are four primary reasons why treasury policies and procedures are necessary:

- **Organizational Needs:** To provide a documented guide to best practices to ensure fundamental operational processes are performed in a consistent manner that meets the organization's needs. Additionally, policy statements are needed to grant and delegate the authority required to conduct essential treasury procedures.

- **Risk Management:** To provide a control process to mitigate identified risks in the operation.
- **Roles and Responsibilities:** To provide a clear definition of the roles and responsibilities within the treasury function. When problems occur, documented policies and procedures can provide some degree of protection for staff that are following the approved procedures.
- **Compliance:** To provide an effective internal audit and control tool that helps keep a company in compliance with regulatory and legal requirements, through well-defined and documented processes and guidelines.

III. GUIDELINES FOR CREATING POLICIES AND PROCEDURES

This section discusses guidelines for the development of formal policies and procedures governing treasury operational activities. At the start of the development process, it is important to determine the primary objective relating to each treasury function (e.g., investment management or foreign exchange [FX] risk management). It also helps to communicate the objectives for each treasury area throughout the organization and provide guidelines to ensure that the practices employed will support those objectives consistently. Finally, it is important to understand that the processes in each treasury area are generally influenced by factors outside that area, and perhaps even outside the treasury function as well. For example, processes related to the use of lockbox services and the management of remittance information passing through the lockbox are often influenced by requirements of the accounts receivable and credit departments.

A. Key Control Considerations

Regardless of the firm's organization or the structure of its treasury operations, there is a need for some fundamental level of controls, which should be in place and operating at all times. Well-written policy statements help document that these controls have been given appropriate consideration. Ultimately, a board of directors (or the owner/governing body of the organization) is responsible for ensuring that adequate internal controls are established and maintained to protect the company's assets. For financial institutions, board of directors and/or senior management responsibility for internal controls is a key element of the Basel Accords.[1] An example of a specific treasury department policy statement with supporting controls is provided in Appendix 17.1.

1. STRUCTURE OF CONTROLS

There is no standard structure for a company to follow in determining the levels of control that should be in place, but there are certain best-practice standards that should be followed—especially from an audit perspective. The analysis and understanding of the organization's operations gives rise to controls that can be implemented in a targeted and effective manner. Proper documentation of those controls in board-approved policy statements is a key step in that implementation. Correctly designed, operated, updated, and monitored controls can not only assist in preventing financial losses, but can also help to manage the organization more effectively. In establishing and documenting controls, some of the items to consider are:

- Internal and external controls
- Reporting and audit trails
- Controls on third-party service providers
- Compliance with regulatory requirements of major stock exchanges (e.g., Sarbanes-Oxley [SOX] Section 404[2] for organizations listed on a US exchange)

1. More detail on the Basel Accords is provided in Chapter 2, Regulatory and Legal Environment.
2. SOX Section 404 requires managers to state their responsibility for establishing and maintaining adequate internal controls for financial reporting.

2. DELEGATION OF AUTHORITY AND GOVERNANCE

One control factor that policies and procedures must address is the delegation of authority. Generally, this is accomplished by a board of directors' resolution outlining which responsibilities are delegated to a particular management position within the treasury operations area and identifying any designated limits, such as signing limits, on that authority. As an example, all decisions regarding the selection of financial institutions and related services might be delegated to the CFO or treasurer. The CFO or treasurer (with board approval) might then further delegate the authority for managing the request for proposal (RFP) and vendor selection process. The assistant treasurer or treasury manager might have the authority to select or manage certain services (e.g., lockboxes or controlled disbursement accounts) with a requirement that the CFO or treasurer provide final approval in the selection process. Signature authority on bank accounts is another common example of delegation of authority.

3. SEGREGATION OF DUTIES

Segregation of duties is another key control that should be addressed in policies and procedures. Segregation of duties is the concept of having more than one individual involved in a process to complete a task, which significantly reduces the risks of fraud and human error. This is a key concept of internal control in any financial operation. A typical example of a process requiring the segregation of duties would be the execution of a wire transfer, where one individual initiates the wire while another individual reviews and approves the wire.[3] Generally, at least two individuals should be involved in such a transaction. However, for large wire transfers, there are typically several levels of approval required to ensure the accuracy of the transaction. Another example is the approval of expense reports. An individual submitting an expense report should never be allowed to approve his/her own expense reimbursement request.

4. ROLES AND RESPONSIBILITIES

Another key control to be addressed by policies and procedures is the role of key personnel in the treasury organization, specifically identifying responsibilities and authority for each position and function. Individual policies should very specifically identify responsibilities of organizational positions (or functions). For example, the treasurer of an organization would be required to approve the hiring of an investment manager for the organization's short-term portfolio, but the assistant treasurer would be responsible for the day-to-day oversight of the investment manager.

5. RECORDS RETENTION POLICIES

There are many regulations relating to the retention of records, especially for compliance with regulatory and tax authorities. There are also severe penalties for failure to maintain proper workpapers, especially those related to audit activity, bankruptcies, and many government investigations. Retention policies also frequently include when and how specific key records should be destroyed (e.g., "disbursement requests and supporting documentation will be destroyed five years after payment has been made"). In addition

3. As discussed in Chapter 15, Operational and Enterprise Risk Management, these types of controls are typically called *maker-checker controls*.

to a general records retention policy, other treasury policies and procedures documents should contain requirements for the appropriate retention, safekeeping, and destruction of records, where appropriate.[4]

6. MOVING FROM CONTROLS TO POLICIES AND PROCEDURES

Given the importance of controls to the treasury area, the treasury policies development process should build in the desired controls for each function. As control requirements change over time in response to new developments and technology, so should the related policies and procedures.

B. Writing the Policy

1. PREDEVELOPMENT STAGE

It is essential to get authorization and support for the entire policy development process at the highest level possible in the organization before development begins. A vital step is to appoint an individual or group to take the lead and to whom primary responsibility for the development process can be assigned. Targeted individuals to fill this role typically include the general managers of the functional areas directly impacted by the policy. In addition, the active involvement and support of senior management will contribute greatly to the success of the development process and to producing a policy that is acceptable to all of the areas involved. Staff from the various functional areas directly affected by the policy should also be included in the policy development process.

2. IDENTIFYING ISSUES AND CONDUCTING ANALYSIS

Prior to drafting the policy, the issues relating to the proposed policy should be identified and analyzed. If membership on the development team includes all of the affected areas, then the chances of creating a policy that will be accepted by those affected are very good. The owners of all related processes should be included, and an agreed-upon flowchart (including workflows and organization charts) should be created for the proper execution of those processes.

3. DRAFTING THE POLICY

In the drafting stage, the development team creates the new basic policy or modifies an existing policy, using a common format and set of definitions. As a whole, the policies should represent a consistent, logical framework for organizational action. Some general guidelines for the creation of the policy include:

- Use clear, concise, simple language.
- Address what the rule will be, rather than how to implement it.
- Make the policy readily available to the organizational area.
- Describe clear lines of authority.
- Designate expert resources to interpret the policy if questions arise.
- Identify the parties who will review and approve the policy, and define any ongoing review process (e.g., "this policy will be reviewed and updated annually by the treasurer").

4. Treasury professionals should consult with their organizations' attorneys and tax professionals regarding appropriate record retention requirements since these may vary by country.

4. BASIC ELEMENTS OF A POLICY

Each organizational or functional area will have different needs for its policies, and the format will most likely vary considerably. There are, however, some general guidelines that should be followed regarding basic policy elements:

- **Objectives:** The objectives for the policy should be clearly stated at the beginning of the policy document.
- **Scope:** The scope of the policy should define, as precisely as possible, what areas and processes the policy will cover.
- **Basic Guidelines:** This section should provide a listing of all the areas covered by the policy, along with procedures for how each of the related processes should be performed and managed. These guidelines should also include how to manage exceptions (i.e., what constitutes an exception and how to handle it).
- **Roles and Responsibilities:** This section should provide a clear listing of the roles and responsibilities of the key participants in each policy. Included in this section should be an outline of the lines of authority, delegation, and segregation of duties.
- **Performance Measurement and Reporting:** This is an important part of the policy, especially where investments, derivatives, or trading activities are involved. The metrics or benchmarks used for performance measurement should be defined clearly, as well as the expectations for meeting the performance objectives. Any required reports should be discussed, including formats, timeframes, and deadlines.
- **Required Controls and Compliance Considerations:** One of the key aspects of developing policies and procedures is to ensure proper controls for processes used in the area in question. As previously mentioned, mandating a policy will not ensure compliance without appropriate oversight and controls. This section should also specify which, if any, external regulatory requirements are being addressed by the policy.
- **Exception Management:** No matter how comprehensive a policy statement is, there will always be exceptions to the rule. It is important that a policy statement identify who can approve exceptions and how they will be tracked and managed once they have been approved.
- **Review Cycle:** As discussed below in the section on policy review and updates, procedures change and evolve over time and the related policies must also change. An essential item in any policy is a statement of how frequently the policy will be reviewed and what approvals will be required (e.g., "this policy will be reviewed by the CFO annually and all changes approved by the board of directors"). The date of the last review should be included in the policy itself.
- **Policy Attachments:** A policy is most effective when it provides comprehensive information in the form of exhibits and appendices. These normally consist of glossaries, distribution lists, procedures manuals, organization charts, standard reports, and any other information needed to support or clarify the information provided in the body of the policy. It is important to keep the attachments as current as the policies.

C. Approval of the Policy

Once a policy has been developed, it should be reviewed as part of a four-level formal approval process:

- **Treasury Department Review:** Senior treasury staff should review and approve the policy, ensuring that it meets the intended purpose and objective, and that its content includes the required controls and consequences associated with the policy and related procedures. This review should include an assessment of reasonableness and functionality, as unreasonable policies are typically ignored.
- **Review by Other Functional Area Managers:** The policy should be reviewed and approved by accounting and legal, as well as by any areas other than treasury that are impacted by the policy. In addition, the policy should be reviewed by key financial managers in decentralized operating units. The focus of this review should be on the operational implications of the policy.
- **Review by Internal Audit and/or Compliance Group:** The internal audit group typically reviews policies for compliance with financial controls and regulatory requirements, including SOX in the United States. Many organizations have a compliance group separate from internal audit that is responsible for reviewing the firm's adherence with existing laws and regulations. In the investment area, the compliance group (and/or audit) is often a required level of control, monitoring trading restrictions and licensing.[5] General operational policies may not require this review, especially if they have no direct impact on the financial statements.
- **Final Approval:** Most treasury policies will need to be formally approved by the board of directors (or appropriate board committee) or equivalent, since they typically involve delegation of board authority and prerogatives (e.g., the authority to open or close a bank account). Policies with less of an impact may only require approval at a designated executive level. Final approval authority can vary depending upon existing delegations of board authority.

D. Policy Reviews, Updates, and Revisions

As organizations change and grow with the addition of staff and/or new products or services, the practices related to a given area may also undergo change. All policies should be reviewed, updated, and reapproved on a specified periodic basis, driven by the size and type of the organization. The review schedule and the required levels of review and approval should be included in the policy. A good practice, which is illustrated in the example in Appendix 17.1, is to include a revision-tracking section as part of the document. This should list all changes and updates in order to provide historical context and document any necessary regulatory compliance.

Policies should also be reevaluated and updated immediately following any major reorganization of the company's structure, material change in banking services, or relevant regulatory change. Implementation of the operational requirements dictated by a policy is most effectively accomplished through a detailed procedures manual, discussed in the next section, which can serve as a reference for daily activities and duties.

Policy compliance reviews are also important to the success of the policy. These reviews may be included within the scope of internal and/or external audits, but practice may vary by the type and size of the organization. The policy should clearly specify who is responsible for compliance testing, the scope of the testing, and to whom the results should be reported.

To ensure adequate compliance evaluation, many organizations assign compliance measurement to a specific person or unit outside the policy-related functional area. This is generally considered a best practice, as it ensures objectivity in the review process.

5. The compliance and/or audit group makes certain that items such as business licenses, securities licenses, and professional certifications are current and that any continuing education requirements are being met.

E. Procedure Development and Implementation

It is important to understand that policies drive the development of day-to-day procedures (often referred to as *standard operating procedures, or SOPs*) while procedures reinforce compliance with policy. An organization should make this relationship explicit by tying procedures to their underlying policies. Also, management should communicate how those procedures help the organization achieve its goals or strategic plan, and should ensure understanding and compliance on the part of managers and employees. The managers and employees affected should be involved in developing the procedures, as this will create a sense of ownership and, hopefully, better compliance.

Some of the more specific considerations in the development of procedures include the following:

- Procedures should be written so that they are clear and understandable to both existing and new managers and employees. They should be written in a concise manner with a minimum of verbiage, and all acronyms and technical terms should be spelled out clearly.
- Procedures that are unnecessarily restrictive may limit their usefulness, so when feasible, they should offer options.
- Documentation should be factual and double-checked for accuracy. Where possible, information that may become quickly outdated should not be included in the procedures.
- Where applicable, the procedures manual should include step-by-step instructions for completing any required forms (both paper and electronic).
- The procedures document itself should be structured so that users can focus quickly on the aspect of the procedure relevant to their decision/task at hand. Many organizations use a flexible, modular outline to make the document easy to modify and keep up to date.

IV. POLICY DEVELOPMENT EXAMPLE: SHORT-TERM INVESTMENT POLICY

A discussion of the elements of a short-term investment policy is provided to illustrate the various issues involved in developing a policy. The key issues driving an investment policy are discussed in Chapter 11, Short-Term Investing and Borrowing. This section will look at how those issues are converted into an actual policy statement. A sample short-term investment policy is provided in Appendix 17.1 to support this discussion.

For the treasury area, investment policy guidelines generally address management policies for the different types of securities that can be held by a company. The guidelines discussed in this section relate to the creation of a general investment policy and are appropriate for most types of organization.

A. The Importance of Having an Investment Policy

A formal investment policy establishes a clear understanding of the firm's investment philosophy and objectives. By establishing investment objectives, a firm can set clear parameters for its investments, allowing it to better manage liquidity, monitor compliance, and minimize risk, regardless of its structure (i.e., centralized or decentralized; domestic or global). This also serves to protect staff against blame for unforeseen problems as long as they are properly following documented policy.

In general, the more decentralized and geographically widespread the investment decision making, the more crucial an investment policy becomes to ensure a consistent, enterprise-wide approach. Formal written policies also help to delineate the relationship between the parent/holding company/corporate office and the subsidiary in decentralized operations.

B. Setting Investment Objectives

A common objective of most investment policies is to minimize the exposure to financial loss (i.e., safety or preservation of principal) while ensuring cash availability (i.e., liquidity) and maximizing returns. The objectives of an investment policy reflect the organization's philosophy about risk and return. Therefore, they must be tailored to accommodate its specific organizational structure, competitive environment, and overall objectives. For example, the objectives should reflect the business and environmental factors affecting the organization, such as company size, capital structure, and industry competition and regulation.[6]

1. SAFETY

Investment safety is usually viewed from the perspective of preservation of principal, but related factors such as credit quality and price volatility must also be considered. Credit quality can be measured in various ways and often indicates the probability of default, which means it can also be used to help measure the safety of the principal. Additionally, credit ratings are the primary mechanism used in measuring the quality of an investment portfolio. Oftentimes, minimum acceptable ratings levels for a portfolio or investment type are defined in the policy. Investment research is also used to evaluate credit risk. There is a wide variety of resources available to help in portfolio risk evaluation. Volatility, or the variability in the pricing of an investment, is also an important measure of both liquidity and safety. For fixed-income investments (bonds), volatility is usually related to maturity (i.e., longer maturity equates to higher price volatility). For stock investments, a commonly used measure of volatility is the beta (ß) for the stock. These topics are discussed in more detail in Chapter 12, Long-Term and Capital Investments.

2. LIQUIDITY

For a short-term investment portfolio, maintaining adequate liquidity is usually defined as the ability of an organization to convert assets into cash quickly and without a significant risk of loss. For long-term portfolios, especially where the maturity of the investments can be matched closely to the need for funds, liquidity may not be a primary objective. Liquidity needs may vary significantly from one company to another. Some organizations (e.g., broker-dealers) require daily liquidity, while others (e.g., pension funds or insurance companies) may have long-term liquidity requirements. Even companies within a specific industry (e.g., retail) may have differing liquidity requirements depending on their cash flow cycles, current profitability, and investment opportunities. Some companies may not have sufficient investment balances to consider alternatives such as external management or long-term investment horizons. Seasonality may also define an organization's liquidity needs (e.g., heavy cash flow only in the summer months). It is critical that both static and dynamic liquidity concerns be considered in the development of the investment policy.[7]

6. Regulations are constantly changing and can vary significantly from country to country. A discussion of major financial regulations is provided in Chapter 2, Regulatory and Legal Environment.

7. Static liquidity is measured at a particular point in time while dynamic liquidity is a measure of liquidity over a period of time into the future.

3. RISK/RETURN TRADE-OFF

An important objective of any investment policy is to achieve an acceptable return on invested capital. Companies must give careful consideration to how they rank investment return in relation to the other objectives of safety and liquidity. A key determinant in the return/safety/liquidity balance is the organization's philosophy regarding risk tolerance. Risk tolerance is an organization's willingness to take on additional risk in order to increase the expected rate of return on a portfolio. Risks to be considered include credit, counterparty, interest rate, reinvestment, prepayment, FX, and sovereign risk. The investment policy should address specific procedures that must be followed to minimize the various types of investment risk. Like many elements of the investment policy, guidelines pertaining to risk tolerance must be tailored to each organization.

Some organizations are more sensitive and susceptible to certain risks than others. Companies that engage in international commerce may face significant FX risks while other firms face none. Furthermore, every company has its own perspective and benchmarks on risk taking, principal preservation, and investment return, and ranks them in order of importance. Investment benchmarks are covered later in this chapter.

C. Developing a List of Permitted Investments

Once a company has established its investment objectives, it must decide which securities/instruments are suitable for investment and develop an approved list of permitted investments. Many organizations include the approved list in their investment policies. The list may name specific securities approved for investment (e.g., ABC Company commercial paper) or it may simply specify categories of qualified investment instruments (e.g., commercial paper). Lists are sometimes based on minimum credit ratings (e.g., commercial paper with a minimum rating of A-1/P-1). For global companies, the approved list may further specify acceptable issuer countries and in some cases specific industries within countries. As an example, investment in African manufacturing companies may be approved, but not mining companies in Africa, due to concerns about conflict minerals. Regardless of the approach taken to establish the list, it is important to review each approved instrument periodically to ensure that it remains compatible with the organization's stated investment objectives.

D. Investment Requirements

1. DIVERSIFICATION

Diversification is clearly one of the most important tools an investment manager possesses to protect the organization from the risks to which it is exposed. Diversification approaches include:

- Allocating investments by asset class (e.g., fixed income, equity, and cash), or among a variety of investment management firms (e.g., 25% with Company A and 75% with Company B)

- Holding a certain percentage of foreign securities so the company can minimize the impact that movements in a specific currency may have on the portfolio (e.g., the US dollar weakens by 5% against the euro)
- Limiting investments in issues from the same organization to a certain percentage of the total portfolio (e.g., 10% of the portfolio)
- Limiting investments from specific issuers and/or instruments in order to limit concentration risk (e.g., can invest up to $10 million in ABC Company commercial paper, or can invest up to 10% of the portfolio in a single currency or country)

Whatever approach is used, the diversification strategy should be defined clearly in the investment policy.

Many instruments in an investment portfolio may make periodic coupon or dividend payments. The organization must decide how the payments should be reinvested in order to achieve optimal asset allocation. The investment policy should stipulate guidelines and procedures governing the receipt of payments and their use. These rules may have important tax implications and should therefore be drafted in consultation with a corporate tax advisor.

2. INVESTMENT OR EXPOSURE HORIZON

A firm's investment horizon is the total length of time that it expects to or is willing to hold an investment. As discussed in Chapter 11, Short-Term Investing and Borrowing, and Chapter 12, Long-Term and Capital Investments, the longer the average time to maturity (i.e., duration) of investments in the portfolio, the greater the exposure to interest rate risk. An investment policy should specify any limitations that a firm may have regarding the maximum and average duration of the investments in its portfolio. This exposure horizon is a function of both the organization's risk philosophy and the total interest rate exposure already present in other areas of the organization. Short- and medium-term investment portfolios often consist of fixed-income securities and money market funds (MMFs). Since the price and/or return on those securities and MMFs are largely a function of the market interest rate, the portfolios are subject to significant interest rate exposure.

3. OTHER LIMITATIONS ON INVESTMENTS

In addition to decisions around diversification and investment/exposure horizons, organizations must make decisions regarding several other investment factors. These decisions should be outlined in the investment policy, as follows:

- Clearly state the organization's attitude toward maintaining simultaneous outstanding debt and investment positions. Some companies prohibit any investment activity while the organization has outstanding debt that can be paid off.
- Clearly specify any limits on the holding of less-than-liquid assets. These are assets for which there is a limited secondary or resale market.
- List financial and/or credit rating requirements for financial institutions and other companies in which investments are made.
- Define any special credit requirements and guidelines if foreign investments are allowed in the policy (i.e., direct investment in foreign companies or indirect investment through brokers/funds).
- Ensure that collateralization and guarantee guidelines are specified clearly. Collateralization partially protects the purchaser of the securities from loss of invested principal. When accepting securities or other assets as collateral, the purchaser must consider not only the value of the collateral, but also its liquidity.

- Specify how mutual funds are to be selected and whether their composition must adhere to the guidelines established in the investment policy (e.g., approved investments, diversification, and exposure horizon) when mutual funds are utilized for an investment portfolio.[8]

E. Other Issues in Developing an Investment Policy

1. VALUATION OF INVESTMENTS

The investment policy should state the process to be used for the valuation of investment portfolios and how to manage investments that may become impaired. This must comply with appropriate accounting guidelines, but it also helps document and support management choices where there are alternatives. Methods for valuing investments and the concept of other-than-temporary impairment are discussed in Chapter 11, Short-Term Investing and Borrowing, and Chapter 12, Long-Term and Capital Investments.

2. EXCEPTION MANAGEMENT

The investment policy must include provisions to accommodate exceptions. For example, when an investment opportunity arises that falls outside the approved list, the policy should dictate the appropriate procedure for obtaining exception approval. This can be as simple as obtaining a senior financial officer's (e.g., CFO's or treasurer's) written consent, or it may require a more formal approval. In addition, there should be guidelines on how to handle an investment that is downgraded, especially if the rating falls below investment policy guidelines.

There may be other cases where exceptions to the guidelines may be required. The investment policy should identify the individual or group whose approval is required for these exceptions. In addition, the policy should detail actions and procedures for dealing with exceptions found during compliance testing. For example, the policy might require that any exceptions found and determined to be high risk should be reported to the audit committee of the board of directors.

3. USE OF EXTERNAL MONEY MANAGERS

As an alternative to managing investments in-house, some firms may elect to use outside money managers. External money managers should be subject to the provisions of the corporate investment policy and are discussed in Chapter 11, Short-Term Investing and Borrowing.

It is critical that the policy clearly describe the roles and responsibilities of those involved in the investment process.[9] These include the roles of the person(s) involved in:

- Investment selection (e.g., investment manager, treasurer)
- Investment execution and reporting (e.g., treasury staff)
- Investment policy approvals or modifications, and exception management (e.g., CFO, board of directors)

8. Mutual funds and some of the issues related to using them for investment purposes are covered in Chapter 5, Money Markets.
9. A functional organizational chart or investment flowchart can also be very helpful in this process.

- Accounting and reconciliation of investment activity (e.g., controller)
- Overall management of the investment process (e.g., senior management)

Furthermore, the roles and responsibilities of internal or external parties that have peripheral or infrequent involvement with the process should be identified. A description of their related duties and when they are performed should also be listed (e.g., annual external audit of the investment balances).

4. PERFORMANCE MEASUREMENT AND REPORTING

The policy should specify benchmarks that will be used to evaluate performance. It should describe the types of reporting that are required, the frequency of each report, and the report recipients.

a. Performance Measurement

Portfolio performance should be evaluated against established benchmarks to measure and validate the success of an organization's investment practices in meeting the objectives stated in the policy. The benchmarks selected should be consistent with the company's agreed-upon goals and should be based on investment vehicles permitted by the investment policy. Common benchmarks include yields on US Treasury securities, which include Treasury bills (as a very short-term reference), Treasury notes, Treasury bonds, and 30-day commercial paper. Indices of a particular segment of the market may also be used as benchmarks. Some common indices are the Lipper Money Market Funds Index, the Standard & Poor's (S&P) 500, Barclays Capital Aggregate Bond Index, J.P. Morgan Government Bond Index, and the investment benchmarks provided by the Association for Financial Professionals (AFP). Depending upon portfolio mix, some companies develop a customized "blended" benchmark for use in evaluating performance.

Companies that authorize the use of foreign investment instruments should also select benchmarks that reflect their global market exposure. These might include reference rates such as the London Interbank Offered Rate (LIBOR) and Sterling Overnight Index Average (SONIA), as well as specific international bond rates (e.g., Eurobonds). Those companies should also report on the impact of currency movements on their portfolio holdings. Just as investment values shift with changes in interest rates, so too may their values fluctuate as a result of currency volatility.

b. Reporting

Reporting should be designed to accomplish specific goals. Accordingly, there should be different levels of reporting depending on the goals. For example, in a large organization with a significant investment portfolio, daily investment summaries may be prepared by the treasury or investment unit. These are intended to provide financial managers (e.g., controller, vice president of finance, director of treasury, and treasurer) with basic information about the daily portfolio composition, related interest rates, and maturities. Any breaches of investment limits and how those breaches were remedied should also be reported as quickly as possible. Weekly or monthly performance reports are another common form of investment reporting that provide a snapshot of portfolio holdings at a specific time. They also contain weekly or monthly average return information on the portfolio, comparisons to benchmarks, and narrative explanations of why the portfolio over- or underperformed relative to the benchmarks.

Furthermore, these reports often contain explanations of any fluctuation in average rates or invested balances and may include projections for the next period. This type of report would be distributed to financial managers, but might also be directed to senior management (e.g., CFO or CEO). Other reports may be designed to address issues for discussion at quarterly or annual meetings of the board of directors, or to meet regulatory and rating agency financial statement reporting requirements (including narrative in the notes to consolidated financial statements, as well as in the management's discussion and analysis section required in reports such as US SEC Form 10-K reports).

c. Calculating Returns

As a concluding point in the discussion of performance measurement and reporting, it is important to note that a variety of methods exist for calculating the return associated with a security or portfolio. Total return, current yield, and yield to maturity are the most popular methods. Various methods for calculating the return on investments are discussed in Chapter 11, Short-Term Investing and Borrowing, and Chapter 12, Long-Term and Capital Investments.

When comparing performance across time periods or across portfolios, it is essential that returns on the portfolios always be calculated the same way. Therefore, the investment policy should clearly state the method(s) that must be used to measure performance. Any differences related to taxable versus tax-exempt investments should also be considered, and any external investment managers should be required to report the same way.

5. POLICY COMPLIANCE

As with all policies, an investment policy should incorporate the need for regular policy compliance review and evaluation. Furthermore, it should identify the parties responsible for fulfilling this role. In some companies, this may be a responsibility of internal or external auditors. In others, it is the responsibility of a specific person or area outside the policy-related functional area, or perhaps a role of the compliance department. In certain firms, the internal or external auditors include investment policy compliance testing in their audits. When this is the case, the internal or external examiners should evaluate and review procedures, test individual transactions for compliance with the policy, confirm effectiveness and validity of selected investment reports, and make any appropriate recommendations to amend the policy or procedures. At the very least, examiners should test compliance and policy effectiveness annually, as well as immediately following periods of significant change in the company or following periods of major economic upheaval.

If internal or external auditors do not review investments for compliance with the policy, companies should assign the responsibility for investment policy compliance measurement to a specific person or unit outside the policy-related functional area. This approach clearly represents a best practice, as it ensures objectivity in the review process and does not rely on internal or external audit resources that may have other responsibilities that take precedence over compliance testing.

6. INTERNAL AND EXTERNAL CONTROLS

Controls should be established to ensure that assets and market-sensitive inside information are protected from loss, theft, or misuse. These controls should be described clearly in the investment policy. Segregation of duties is critical to ensuring sound internal controls. The separation of transaction authority from accounting and record keeping is essential to enforcing the checks and balances of the treasury department. Investment-related accounting activities should be segregated from the person and/or area responsible for managing investments. In addition, sound internal controls over the wire transfer process must be established and maintained. Again, these activities should be performed by someone outside the investment management process.

The monthly reconciliation of investment statements and records to an organization's internal general ledger accounts is considered a best practice and another significant safeguard in maintaining strong internal control. In addition to establishing internal safeguards against fraud and/or negligence, it is also important to understand the controls that third-party service providers have in place. Another recommended best practice is to conduct periodic audits of service providers to evaluate not only their service capabilities but also their internal controls. One approach for monitoring internal controls for providers is to require SSAE 16[10] audits of the providers' relevant operational controls. This topic is discussed in detail in Chapter 7, Relationship Management and Vendor Selection.

a. Custodial Service Providers

The investment policy should describe under what conditions a third-party custodian or safekeeping bank would be required to perform settlement of all investment transactions for external control purposes. A custodian will typically take possession of securities, receive delivery or book entry of principal and interest payments, perform record keeping, and provide maintenance services for the investment portfolio. These providers also play an important role in furnishing current electronic reporting on portfolio composition and performance. The custodian selection process usually includes reference checks and an analysis of financial stability, operating capabilities, quality of service, and services the custodian offers other than safekeeping (e.g., securities lending, reporting, FX, and short-term investment management services). Custodian performance is typically measured by the timeliness, completeness, and accuracy with which the custodian carries out its prescribed duties, and by compliance with established guidelines. As previously discussed, an organization may consider requesting an SSAE 16 report to help in the evaluation and review of any custodians.

b. Limitation of Liability

Limitation of liability is an area that should be addressed in the investment policy. For the purposes of an investment policy, limitation of liability relates to the measures designed to protect an organization involved in investment activity from financial loss due to negligence or crime. As such, it is important for organizations to specify in the investment policy what risk management steps should be taken (both internally and by outside parties) to limit exposure from negligence and crime (e.g., liability insurance).

7. EXTERNAL RESTRICTIONS

Regulatory or legal restrictions that may impact investment practices should be described clearly in the investment policy. Certain regulated entities (e.g., insurance companies, government agencies, and public utilities) may have specific investment constraints. For example, an insurance company may be required by NAIC (National Association of Insurance Commissioners) guidelines to limit investment activities to specific types of investments or impose concentration limits on permitted investments. Similarly, depending upon their legal structure and prevailing regulations, insurance companies, regulated entities, or state-sponsored institutions (e.g., universities and hospitals) may need to segregate their investments in separate accounts to comply with statutory commingling guidelines. The investment policy should clearly define all restrictions that affect the investment practices of the organization. Debt covenants may also place specific limitations on how a company manages investments. Restrictions may require the debt issuer to pay down the debt with any available cash, effectively prohibiting the company from making any short-term investments until the debt is retired.

10. Formerly Statement on Auditing Standards No. 70, or SAS 70.

V. OVERVIEW OF KEY TREASURY POLICIES

This section presents a list of key treasury policies that should be considered for any organization. An overview of the major factors that should be addressed in drafting the specific policies is also provided.

A. Bank Account and Financial Services Authority Policies

Bank account and financial services authority policies are essential for providing the appropriate delegation of authority regarding opening, closing, and managing accounts. Key items to be addressed in these policies include:

- Delegation of authority allowing treasury to manage financial services provider relationships
- Delegation of authority to open and close bank accounts
- Oversight and governance of banking relationships
- Duties and tasks involved in managing relationships
- Qualifying types of financial institutions
- Signing authority and reporting requirements
- Financial institution evaluation and reporting requirements
- Documentation requirements
- Records retention requirements

B. Payments Policy

A payments policy is important in order to provide consistent management of payments and payments risk across all payment processes. In addition to an overall payments policy, many companies provide a separate electronic funds transfer (wire transfer) policy and/or an international payments policy, due to the increased potential risks. Key elements include:

- Delegation of authority
- Permitted payment methods
- Payment and approval limits
- Joint approval requirements
- Payment authorization requirements
- Payment risk management
- Required documentation

C. Collection and Concentration Policy

A collection and concentration policy covers the issues involved in collecting customer payments and converting the receipts into accessible, available funds. Concerns to be addressed in this policy include:

- Control objectives
- Segregation of duties
- Customer satisfaction
- Acceptable payment types (e.g., cash or credit cards)
- Performance measurement
- Reporting requirements
- Exception management

D. Investment Valuation and Impairment Policies

Many companies find it important to have other investment policies, in addition to the short-term investment policy itself, that deal specifically with investment valuation and impairment. These policies should address:

- Identification of impaired investments, including OTTI (other-than-temporary impairment)
- Mark-to-market requirements
- Valuation of impaired securities
- Reporting requirements
- Exception management

E. Payment Card Policies

Card policies can cover both corporate cards issued and the receipt of card payments from customers. Policies for corporate cards should include:

- Types of cards issued
- Eligibility and approved uses
- Definition of responsibilities
- Card and transaction limits
- Review and reconcilement requirements
- Purchase restrictions, if any
- Prohibited uses
- PCI DSS compliance requirements[11]
- Payment and fraud risk management

11. The Payment Card Industry Data Security Standard (PCI DSS) is discussed in Chapter 4, Payment Systems.

Policies for receipt of card payments should include:

- Types of cards accepted, if any
- Definition of responsibilities
- Transaction limits, if any
- Review and reconcilement requirements
- PCI DSS compliance requirements
- Payment and fraud risk management
- Any requirements regarding merchant services providers

F. Outsourcing Policy

As more and more companies outsource various operating units, outsourcing policies help manage risk and maintain appropriate control. Key issues to be addressed in an outsourcing policy include:

- Delegation of authority
- Reporting requirements
- Vendor and operational risk management
- Information security and confidentiality requirements
- Performance measurement

G. Financial Risk Management Policies

Financial risk management policies apply to any financial instruments but are especially necessary if any financial derivatives or hedging activities occur, as policies may be a requirement for proper accounting and tax purposes. Firms involved in hedging or otherwise using derivatives may want to consider specific policies covering just their use. Key items to be incorporated in financial risk management policies include:

- Scope of permitted hedging and derivative activities
- Delegation of authority
- Segregation of duties
- Authorized derivatives
- Performance measurement and evaluation
- Management reporting
- Accounting and disclosure
- Trade/deal limits and monitoring
- Exception management
- Approved counterparties and related limits

H. Regulatory Compliance Policies

Regulatory compliance policies cover activities needed to comply with regulatory requirements that exist in a growing number of countries, including regulations related to money laundering, trade, and corruption. Key policy elements include:

- Statement of policy and required compliance
- Subcontractor and vendor compliance requirements
- Compliance monitoring activities
- Audit requirements
- Exception management
- Disciplinary processes

I. Funding/Financing Policies

Funding/financing policies pertain to the execution of strategies for long-term funding of the organization and should include:

- Funding objectives
- Limits and targets for committed funding
- Limits and targets for different sources of funding (e.g., banks and capital markets)
- Structural considerations of fixed- versus variable-rate debt
- Covenants
- Tax and other compliance mandates
- Authorization/approval processes and any related delegation of authority
- Refinancing or prepayment processes
- Uses of derivatives
- References to standard documentation

J. Treasury Systems Policy

In addition to end-user computing requirements, which are discussed in Chapter 14, Information Technology in Treasury, companies may want a specific policy regarding any treasury management systems (TMSs) they have installed. Concerns to be addressed in this policy include:

- Access to treasury systems
- Password requirements
- Segregation of duties
- Reconcilement with accounting and other books of record
- Backup and recovery
- Off-premise access and use
- Reporting requirements

VI. SUMMARY

Written treasury policies and procedures are an important part of the internal controls and risk management activities of any organization. This chapter covered the key elements of a well-written policy statement and how to go about developing and documenting treasury policies and procedures. A short-term investment policy was provided as a sample policy and used to illustrate how to develop a policy statement. The chapter closed with a high-level description of essential treasury policies, which included the key items that need to be addressed in those policy statements. A sample investment policy is provided in Appendix 17.1 for further illustration and reference.

APPENDIX 17.1: SAMPLE SHORT-TERM INVESTMENT POLICY

Policy Title: Short-Term Investment Policy for ABC Inc.

Created: January 3, 2xx0

Revision History

Version	Board Approval	Comments
1.0	January 3, 2xx0	Initial policy
1.1	January 4, 2xx1	Revised list of approved investments
2.0	July 5, 2xx2	Compliance update
3.0	March 17, 2xx3	Revised roles and responsibilities

Table of Contents

1.0 Purpose

The purpose of this policy is to set guidelines for the parameters, responsibilities, and controls for the short-term (12 months or less) investment of corporate funds.

2.0 Objectives

A. To ensure the safety and preservation of principal
B. To maintain adequate liquidity to meet cash flow requirements
C. To obtain the best available return consistent with safety and liquidity
D. To maintain standardized guidelines throughout the company

3.0 Scope

This policy applies to ABC Inc. and all of its wholly owned subsidiaries, including foreign subsidiaries. Investments are restricted to short-term investments as defined in the policy and as governed by ABC Inc.'s treasury department for all of its subsidiaries. For the purposes of this policy, the chief financial officer (CFO), treasurer, assistant treasurer, manager of treasury operations, and any of their appointees have the roles and responsibilities as defined in the policy for the investment activities of the company as a whole. This policy does not cover 401(k), profit-sharing, deferred compensation, stock purchase, or deferred director fee plans of ABC Inc., which are covered by separate policies.

4.0 Approved List of Short-Term Investments

The following instruments are approved for short-term investment:

- Bank deposits
- Domestic certificates of deposit
- Domestic commercial paper (rated A-1/P-1)
- Banker's acceptances
- US Treasury bills and notes
- Collateralized repurchase agreements
- Eurodollar time deposits
- Mutual funds that invest exclusively in securities approved under this policy

5.0 Investment Requirements

- Active investments with outside money managers are prohibited, with the exception of mutual funds (as stated in Section 4.0).
- To minimize foreign exchange exposure, all investments must be denominated in the functional currency of the entity making the investment.
- All issuers of commercial paper must be US corporations.
- Repurchase agreements must be fully collateralized by any of the securities approved under this investment policy. The current market value of the collateral must cover the principal amount of the investment at all times during the term of the investment.
- The composition of any mutual fund must meet the criteria for approved securities.
- The average duration of any short-term investment portfolio must not exceed nine months.
- ABC Inc. may take simultaneous debt and investment positions. The CFO has full discretion in determining the size of those positions.
- No more than 25% of the portfolio may be invested in securities lacking an active secondary market. Securities that have no active secondary market must mature in periods during which the company has high working capital requirements. Selection of the appropriate maturity schedule is left to the discretion of the CFO.
- All new types of investments must pass a formal review process that evaluates all related risks.
- Cash receipts from coupon and interest payments shall be handled by accounting. An accrued tax liability shall be recorded and the proceeds returned to the portfolio for reinvestment.

Investments in banks and domestic corporations under this policy are subject to the following additional limitations:

- US banks must have total assets of at least $40 billion or have a credit relationship with the company.
- Foreign banks must have total assets of at least $50 billion or have a credit relationship with the company. Foreign banks must have an agency, branch, or representative office with a domestic US license.
- Issuing corporations must have a commercial paper rating of P-1 or better by Moody's Investors Service and A-1 or better by Standard & Poor's, or an equivalent rating by another nationally recognized rating agency. (At least two ratings are required.) If the rating is supported by a bank letter of credit (L/C), then the L/C must be issued by a bank having a minimum long-term debt rating of Aa by Moody's and AA by Standard & Poor's.

Any exceptions to the above must be approved by the CFO.

Diversification
The approved types of investment instruments must be allocated among the following three categories, but not exceed the percentages indicated:

Category	Not More Than % of Total	Portfolio Instrument Types
US Government	95%	Treasury bills, Treasury notes, collateralized repurchase agreements backed by Treasuries
Corporate	55%	Domestic commercial paper, collateralized repurchase agreements backed by commercial paper
Bank	95%	Bank accounts, Eurodollar time deposits, money market accounts, banker's acceptances, certificates of deposit, collateralized repurchase agreements backed by any of the above bank-related securities
Concentration per Organization: To provide for diversification, investments are limited to $5 million per issuing entity for corporate-related instruments.		
Concentration per Mutual Fund: Up to $60 million may be invested in any single well-diversified mutual fund that invests exclusively in securities authorized under this investment policy.		

6.0 Custody of Securities

All of the financial institutions in which the company is eligible to invest, subject to the investment requirements listed in Section 5.0 of this document, are also authorized to hold investments in custody on behalf of the company. The company shall not take physical possession of investment securities.

7.0 Exception Management

Any exceptions to this policy must be approved in writing. For minor exceptions, such as exceeding investment limits on approved investments, the written approval of the CFO or treasurer is required. For major exceptions, such as purchasing a new investment instrument or exceeding portfolio diversification requirements, the written approval of the board of directors is required.

8.0 Performance Measurement and Reporting

The performance of the short-term investment portfolio shall be benchmarked against the total return and yield to maturity of the Lipper Money Market Funds Index, the Merrill Lynch 1-3 Year Corporate/Government Index, and the Barclays Capital Aggregate Bond Index. Money market mutual funds shall be benchmarked against the iMoneyNet Money Fund Report All-Taxable Average.

The treasury staff shall prepare weekly performance reports under the guidance of the assistant treasurer. The manager of treasury operations shall deliver a monthly report to the CFO and board of directors detailing the short-term investment portfolio's composition and performance. In addition, the manager of treasury operations is charged with disclosure of portfolio holdings in the 10-K and 10-Q reports that must be filed with the US Securities and Exchange Commission.

9.0 Roles and Responsibilities

Roles and responsibilities of the parties involved are specified below:

ROLE: **Board of Directors**

- Approving the policy
- Approving major policy exceptions (e.g., new investment types)
- Approving policy revisions
- Setting performance metrics

ROLE: **Chief Financial Officer**

- Developing the investment strategy
- Approving minor policy exceptions (e.g., amounts and terms)

ROLE: **Treasurer**

- Serving as policy custodian
- Developing the investment strategy
- Distributing the policy and revisions

ROLE: **Assistant Treasurer**

- Overseeing investment activities
- Recommending variations in set amounts and/or terms
- Collecting performance information

ROLE: **Manager of Treasury Operations**

- Keeping abreast of developments in the money market
- Keeping the assistant treasurer and treasurer informed of developments in the money market
- Providing investment reports to management as requested
- Investing excess funds as provided herein
- Determining the amount and maturity of an investment
- Distributing performance information

10.0 Internal Controls

The following internal controls must be enforced:

- The separation of transaction authority from accounting and record keeping shall be enforced.
- The separation of wire transfer and investment transaction duties shall be maintained. Wire transfers must be performed by a party outside the investment management process.
- All physical deliveries or book entries of principal and/or interest shall be performed by a third-party custodian.
- A monthly reconciliation of investment statements to the general ledger accounts shall be performed, and the results shall be delivered to the CFO and the treasurer.
- All investment portfolios must be covered by the company's liability and crime coverage insurance policies.
- All banks, brokers, and custodians must carry adequate liability and crime coverage, and provide a detailed review and assessment of their internal controls.

The manager of treasury operations shall have responsibility and authority over internal controls; however, controls may be removed only with the written consent of the CFO.

11.0 Compliance

Internal auditors shall include policy compliance in their audits. Auditors shall review procedures and performance and make recommendations for changes, as appropriate. Compliance testing shall be performed annually.

A copy of the policy and related procedures manual shall be placed on file in the treasurer's office, and an electronic version shall be posted on the company's intranet.

TEST YOUR UNDERSTANDING: CHAPTER 17

Answers are on pages 718–722.

1. What are the four primary reasons that treasury policies and procedures are required?
2. What are some key control issues to consider when developing treasury policy guidelines and objectives?
3. What are the basic elements of a policy?
4. Once a treasury policy has been developed, what are the typical steps in a formal approval process for that policy?
5. When should an existing policy be reviewed and updated?
6. What issues should be considered when writing treasury procedures?
7. Why should a company have a formal investment policy?
8. What is an investment horizon, and why should it be included in a firm's short-term investment policy?
9. What are the three typical objectives that must be considered in an investment policy?
10. What are some typical approaches to diversification that must be considered in an investment policy?
11. What are some common benchmarks used in the measurement of performance in an investment policy?
12. What are the key elements that should be included in a payments policy?
13. What elements should be included in an outsourcing policy?
14. What elements should be included in a regulatory compliance policy?
15. Why are records retention policy guidelines important?

PART V
Financial Management

CHAPTER 18

Financial Accounting and Reporting

I. INTRODUCTION

Financial statements, whether internal or external, summarize a company's operating results and financial position at a point in time. Analyzing these statements provides insight into:

- How well the company has managed its liquidity position
- How effectively it used and financed its assets
- Whether it had a proper balance between debt and equity financing compared to peers
- How well it controlled operating and financing costs
- Whether the profit it earned was satisfactory in relation to the levels of revenue it experienced and the investment in assets that support its operations

Financial statements are records of historical performance that provide insight into how markets form performance expectations and place a value on the company. In addition, many companies must file financial statements quarterly and annually with various regulatory agencies. For both reasons, it is important that financial statements be prepared carefully and accurately.

External financial statements are the primary basis from which an organization's external constituencies form opinions about its financial condition and management effectiveness. Lenders analyze statements to see if the company has been managed prudently so that debts can be repaid. Equity investors examine statements for operating effectiveness and profit earned on their investments. Suppliers look to financial statements to see if the company has adequate liquidity and cash flow to pay for purchases.

Internal financial statements are used by owners and staff to manage the day-to-day operation of an organization. They are used for analyzing the organization's performance and position, in order to take appropriate measures to improve overall results.

Vendors also use statement analysis to help determine a potential customer's creditworthiness, to assess competitors' operating and financing policies, to compare the company's financial performance with the stock market's assessment of its performance, and to identify and evaluate candidates for acquisition or merger.

This chapter introduces the accounting principles that global companies use to govern the creation of financial statements. Because of the size of the US market and the number of global companies that operate within US jurisdiction, an overview of US accounting principles and how they differ from international accounting standards is also provided. The next section of the chapter discusses financial reporting statements, as well as the opinions independent auditors render about the statements and how auditors reach those opinions. A brief discussion of accounting for derivatives, hedges, and FX is provided, due to its impact on what treasury professionals do. The chapter concludes with a brief discussion of accounting for governmental units and not-for-profit organizations.

II. ACCOUNTING CONCEPTS AND STANDARDS

This section covers the basics of accounting concepts and standards, both on a global basis and for organizations located in the United States specifically. The primary objective of the section is to provide treasury professionals with a better understanding of those accounting issues that have a major impact on the treasury function of an organization.

A. Global Accounting Standards

Accounting procedures provide the information used to measure a company's performance and analyze its financial position. Accounting applies methods for recording a company's assets, liabilities, shareholder equity, revenues, expenses, and cash flows. It is important to understand that standards provide consistency in accounting for activities that are common to all, or most, commercial enterprises. Being able to compare "apples to apples" by using commonly accepted accounting principles is the point of accounting, and of the global and US accounting standards boards.

On a global level, the International Accounting Standards Board (IASB) determines general accounting standards and is made up of board members from nine countries. Based in London, England, the IASB's mission is to develop a single set of global accounting standards published as pronouncements called *International Financial Reporting Standards* (*IFRS*).

Unlike US Generally Accepted Accounting Principles (GAAP) discussed below, which is rules-based, IFRS is principles-based. That is, rather than laying out specific rules that must be followed by rote (and can therefore lead to loopholes), IFRS lays out a series of general principles which all accounting statements must attempt to meet. While this could, in theory, result in different interpretations of specific situations, in practice it provides reasonable guidance to finding the "correct" solution to specific accounting transactions that are not spelled out in the rules.

B. International Financial Reporting Standards (IFRS) Basic Principles

The basic principles of IFRS are laid out in the Conceptual Framework published by the IASB. Under IFRS, there are a number of qualitative characteristics that accountants (and other financial professionals) are expected to follow in selecting and applying appropriate accounting policies for their organization. These characteristics include:

- **Relevance:** Information provided must be of value to decision makers and have predictive value, confirmatory value, or both.
- **Materiality:** Information presented must be material, or in other words, must have a significant impact on the financial position of the entity being reported. Materiality of specific information should be judged in regards to the circumstances of the entity and the transaction.
- **Faithful Representation:** Financial information should faithfully represent the transactions it represents. To the extent possible, it should be complete, neutral, and free from error.
- **Comparability:** Information must be presented in a form that allows it to be compared with prior periods and with other companies in a similar business. Financial statements should be appropriately restated to reflect changes in accounting policy that may impact comparability.
- **Verifiability:** Information presented must be neutral and unbiased, and must fairly represent the business transactions being reported.

- **Timeliness:** Information should be presented to decision makers in time to be capable of influencing their decisions within the limits of reliability and completeness.
- **Understandability:** Information must be presented in the manner that will make it as understandable as possible for non-accountants with a reasonable knowledge of business. Relevant information, however, should not be omitted just because it is complex and hard to understand.
- **Completeness (The Cost Constraint):** Within the limits of reasonable cost, information must be complete enough to make it usable and reliable.

In addition to these qualitative characteristics, IFRS lays out key elements that must be reported in financial statements. The basic elements of the balance sheet are defined as:

- **Assets:** Resources controlled by an entity that can be reasonably expected to produce future economic benefits
- **Liabilities:** Obligations of the entity resulting from past events that can reasonably be expected to result in the outflow of economic benefits
- **Equity:** The residual interest an entity has in its assets after deducting liabilities

Elements must be reported if they are likely to create future economic impacts (probable) and can be reliably measured.

C. US Accounting Standards

US accounting standards are relevant for any entity that conducts business in or is publicly traded in the United States. US accounting standards are governed by a detailed set of rules referred to as *GAAP*. These principles are developed, agreed upon, and published in the form of Accounting Standards Codification (ASC) Topics (formerly known as *Financial Accounting Standards [FASs])* by the Financial Accounting Standards Board (FASB), an independent, self-regulating organization formed in 1973. A list of key ASC Topics is provided in Appendix 18.1.

Authority for enforcing US accounting principles is the responsibility of the SEC, which relies on the FASB to develop accounting standards. All companies whose securities are traded publicly must file audited financial statements with the SEC using Form 10-K annually and Form 10-Q quarterly. SEC filings for specific companies may be obtained through the SEC's Electronic Data Gathering, Analysis, and Retrieval (EDGAR) database.[1] Many companies also provide copies of their filings on their company website.

The SEC enjoys broad powers with respect to prescribing accounting practices for required financial statement filings. It issues specific reporting guidance within its Financial Reporting Releases (FRRs). SEC Regulation S-X outlines reporting requirements, and additional guidance can be gleaned from decisions the SEC renders on various cases.

However, the SEC's philosophy is that the private sector retains the initiative for establishing and improving accounting standards. Therefore, the SEC relies on the FASB for this purpose. Financial Reporting Release No. 1 (FRR 1) recognizes accounting standards issued by the

1. The EDGAR database is located on the SEC's website at http://www.sec.gov/edgar.shtml.

FASB as the authoritative standards for financial reporting. Accordingly, financial statements conforming to GAAP presumably satisfy the SEC's requirements. Adherence to GAAP is crucial since investors, lenders, and trade creditors must have confidence that accounting information is created across companies consistently.

The four basic principles underlying GAAP are the:

- **Historical-Cost Principle:** Most assets and liabilities are reported at historical cost (i.e., there must be an evidentiary basis such as an invoice, receipt, or record of payment made or funds received). An important exception to this principle is the reporting for certain marketable securities, which must be reported at current market value (as discussed in Section IV of this chapter).
- **Full-Disclosure Principle:** Any information that may influence the judgment and decisions of a user of financial information should be disclosed.
- **Revenue Recognition Principle:** Revenue is reported when (1) cash or a claim for cash is received in exchange for goods or services, and (2) the earnings process is substantially complete. A *claim for cash* typically refers to accounts receivable—the assets that represent revenues from sales that have been recognized, but not yet collected. When funds are collected from the customer, the accounts receivable balance decreases and the cash balance increases, without any impact on income. This is because the revenue was recognized when the receivable was generated.
- **Matching Principle:** Expenses must be reported when the revenues with which they are associated are recognized. Long-lived or fixed assets are capitalized (i.e., recorded as assets on the balance sheet) and depreciated over time because they produce revenues over many accounting periods. This practice matches an asset's cost to the revenues it produces. Under the revenue recognition and matching principles, sales are reported even though cash has not been received. Similarly, expenses are reported even though cash has not been paid out. This forms the basis for accrual accounting.

Accrual accounting conforms to GAAP and is used by most businesses. Alternatively, non-GAAP accounting methods may be used by certain nonpublic businesses, and include both strict cash basis accounting and modified cash basis accounting. Using strict cash basis accounting, revenues and expenses are reported only when cash is received or disbursed. Modified cash basis accounting adopts some elements of accrual accounting, such as reporting accounts receivable as revenues, and capitalizing and depreciating fixed assets. Professional service firms use modified cash basis accounting extensively.[2]

If revenues and expenses were reported only when cash is transferred, the timing and amounts could be determined objectively. Accrual accounting requires the extensive use of supportable estimates and judgments, providing flexibility in the timing and the amounts reported in the financial statements. Accrual-based income is more useful to external decision makers because it provides a better basis for assessing historical activity and possibly for making predictions about a company's future earnings and cash flows.

FASB's guidelines also provide a permissible range of latitude for making estimates and judgments required in accrual accounting. Managers can take advantage of the latitudes allowed in timing revenues and expenses in order to report the highest level of accounting income (i.e., net income or net profit after tax). This practice is referred to as *earnings management*. However, if an accountant intentionally distorts the timing of revenues or expenses, or creates distortions in other ways to alter reported accounting income (e.g., possibly to earn a bonus, enhance a career, make the company's earnings appear to be less volatile, or please a superior or stockholders), this is called *earnings manipulation*. This practice may result in serious legal consequences for the accountant and the company, as well as professional consequences for the accountant.

2. Restrictions on the use of non-GAAP or cash accounting methods are effectively set by the Internal Revenue Service (IRS) in terms of which accounting methods are allowed for certain types and sizes of businesses. While cash accounting is typically used by small businesses, the IRS allows its use in businesses (including corporations) with up to $5 million in annual revenues and in farm businesses of any size. It should also be noted that any corporation that has inventory is required to use accrual accounting for at least the inventory accounting.

D. US Generally Accepted Accounting Principles (GAAP) versus International Financial Reporting Standards (IFRS)

While both the IASB and FASB continue to discuss and work toward the convergence of GAAP and IFRS, there do not appear to be any current plans to require US-based companies to change from GAAP to IFRS. As a result, companies that operate in the United States will be required to continue to comply with GAAP but may still need to produce IFRS statements if they also operate outside of the United States.

On July 13, 2012, the Staff of the SEC's Office of the Chief Accountant published its final report (called the *Final Staff Report*) on its "IFRS Work Plan." In its conclusions, that report stated that adopting IFRS as authoritative guidance in the United States is not supported by the vast majority of participants in the US capital markets, and would not be consistent with the methods of incorporation followed by other major capital markets (e.g., the endorsement process followed by the European Commission). The report also stated that while IFRS is generally perceived to be of high quality, there are areas where differences remain and inconsistencies exist in the application of IFRS globally.

While there is substantial overlap between IFRS and GAAP, there are also some key differences. Key differences include:[3]

- IFRS does not permit last-in, first-out (LIFO) accounting.
- IFRS uses a single-step method for impairment write-downs rather than the two-step method used in US GAAP, making write-downs more likely.
- IFRS requires capitalization of development costs once certain qualifying criteria are met. US GAAP generally requires development costs to be expensed as incurred, except for costs related to the development of computer software, for which capitalization is required once certain criteria are met.

III. Financial Reporting Statements

The form and content of a company's financial statements are determined by the end user's requirements (e.g., investors, regulators, and the general public). For example, a US business with public securities must conform to the SEC reporting requirements outlined in Regulation S-X. Nonpublic businesses also generate financial statements periodically to meet the needs of private lenders, bondholders, regulators, trade creditors, venture capitalists, and outside shareholders. Most outside end users with a significant stake in a business require an independent auditor to audit the financial statements. A firm may produce its own financial reporting statements, or it may employ an accountant or an accounting firm to produce them. Firms large enough to employ professional accountants typically produce the statements themselves. The statements are unaudited, even if produced by a certified accountant.

3. From "IFRS FAQs" on AICPA's IFRS Resources website (http://www.ifrs.com/ifrs_faqs.html, accessed July 16, 2013).

A. Auditing and Financial Statement Reliability

Confidence in the integrity of financial reports is critical in an open, market-driven economy. Investors, lenders, regulators, and the general public look to published financial statements to obtain information about a company's financial condition and performance.

Historically, certification of financial statements' accuracy by independent auditors was the main source of this confidence. However, the accounting manipulations that resulted in the downfall of several major public companies eroded this confidence.[4] In response, the US Congress passed the Sarbanes-Oxley Act (SOX), with the purpose of restoring confidence in published financial statements by establishing a set of controls over audit procedures and disclosure requirements, and an administrative vehicle to implement and oversee them.

Although most countries have their own national accounting and auditing certifications, there are a number of internationally recognized certifications. These certifications are especially valuable in transitional and developing economies where the quality of the national certification is low. The most popular international accounting certification is offered by the Association of Chartered Certified Accountants (ACCA). Until a few years ago, this certification was the only truly international accounting certification. However, in recent years, a few other certifications have started to become internationally recognized. In the United States, the primary accounting certification is the Certified Public Accountant (CPA), while in the United Kingdom, Canada, India, and many other former British colonies, it is the Chartered Accountant (CA). Regulatory requirements in many jurisdictions, including the United States, often require that in addition to being certified, public accountants and external auditors must also be licensed by the appropriate regulatory body.

1. AUDIT PROCESS

An audit is an examination of the firm's financial statements by an independent accountant in accordance with generally accepted auditing standards.[5] The purpose of conducting an audit is to produce an audit report in which an independent audit firm indicates the scope of the audit and renders an opinion regarding the relevance, completeness, and accuracy of the income statement, statement of financial position, statement of cash flows, any other statements, and all supporting material. In addition, the auditor will examine the strengths of the organization's internal controls and processes. The auditor's opinion does not comment on the company's financial fitness, but rather on whether the financial statements fairly reflect the company's financial position and are comparable to prior periods. Readers of financial statements should know who the auditors are and what accounting standards were applied in conducting the audit.

An independent auditor, often a public accounting firm, begins an audit by studying the business. This approach helps to ensure that the audit achieves the objectives listed previously. First, the auditor examines internal control procedures for reliability. Based on that information, the auditor establishes procedures for reconciling accounting entries against the evidence in support of them (e.g., invoices, bank statements, or customer orders). This is done on a sample basis, with the sample size based on the strengths of the internal controls. Weak internal controls require a larger sample; strong internal controls require a smaller sample.

4. Some of the more notable examples were Enron, Tyco International, WorldCom (now MCI), Parmalat, HealthSouth Corporation, Anglo Irish Bank, and Satyam Computer Services.

5. The global organization that coordinates auditing standards is the International Auditing and Assurance Standards Board (IAASB). In the United States, audits are generally done in accordance with the generally accepted auditing standards (GAAS) promulgated by the Auditing Standards Board (ASB) of the American Institute of Certified Public Accountants (AICPA).

It is also important to understand the concept of materiality as it relates to the auditing process. In most accounting applications, there is usually a significant degree of judgment involved in the preparation of the accounts. Where decisions are required about the appropriateness of a particular accounting judgment, the materiality convention suggests that this should only be an issue if the judgment is *significant* or *material* to the presentation of the accounts. The concept of materiality is therefore an important issue for auditors of financial accounts.

Next, the independent auditor determines that the method of accounting for items recorded in financial statements complies with the appropriate accounting rules (e.g., IFRS or GAAP). The auditor confirms that all information contained in the financial statements is proper and that all matters material to an assessment of the company's financial position are included, as well as any accompanying explanatory notes and tables. Finally, the auditor issues a report to the board of directors that discusses items of interest arising from the audit, and the auditor may also issue an opinion about the relevance, completeness, and accuracy of the financial statements and supporting notes. In addition to the report to the board, the auditor will also provide a letter to the management of the organization that discusses significant policies and estimates used, as well as any specific difficulties encountered during the review.

2. AUDIT OPINIONS

Auditors provide five types of opinions:

- **Standard Unqualified Opinion:** The auditor concludes that the financial statements fairly represent the business's activities and that the following conditions were met:
    - All required financial statements were provided.
    - Generally accepted auditing standards (GAAS) were followed in conducting the audit.
    - The statements were presented in accordance with the appropriate accounting standards (e.g., GAAP or IFRS).
    - The statements are consistent and comparable to the prior year's statements.
    - If a standard unqualified opinion cannot be rendered, then the appropriate opinion depends on the nature and materiality (i.e., degree) of the exceptions identified by the auditor.
- **Unqualified Opinion with Explanatory Paragraph, or Modified Unqualified Opinion:** When immaterial deviations from appropriate standards occur, an unqualified opinion with explanatory paragraph, or modified unqualified opinion, is appropriate. This happens when:
    - Some information requires special emphasis.
    - There is a change in who performs the audit.
    - The auditor questions the business's ability to continue.

- **Qualified Opinion:** If exceptions are material but do not overshadow the usefulness of the information, then a qualified opinion is given. Exceptions are noted in the written opinion.
- **Adverse Opinion:** An adverse opinion is required when exceptions are so material that the auditor determines the financial statements may be misleading.
- **Disclaimer of Opinion:** A disclaimer is a statement that the auditor cannot render an opinion. A disclaimer is required if the auditor is not independent of the company being audited or if the scope of the audit is so limited that no basis for forming an opinion exists.

First-year audits for public companies represent a unique situation in that the external auditors can only express the limited opinion that the financials are fair and accurate but cannot comment on their comparability to prior financial statements since those do not exist.

Generally, investors and creditors give more credence to audited financial statements than unaudited financial statements, and in turn give more credence to audited financials with an unqualified opinion versus those that are qualified. Even so, since the opinion is not a comment on financial fitness, an investor or creditor must still analyze the information contained in financial statements carefully when making decisions. As noted earlier, leeway in GAAP principles may paint a rosier picture of a company's condition than is warranted.

It should be noted that only publicly traded companies are required to have their financial statements audited. While some nonpublic companies may have their statements audited, they are not typically required to do so, unless there are regulatory or debt requirements that mandate an audit. Non-audited financial statements prepared by an external accountant are referred to as *compilations* and do not include any form of auditor's opinion. While companies that do not require an audit may have external accounting firms assist in the preparation of financial statements, these statements are not considered audited financial statements because they do not involve the level of review or verification required for an audit.

B. Types of Financial Statements

In most countries, the regulatory authorities require any issuer of securities to include the following in its annual and quarterly filings: a statement of financial position (e.g., a balance sheet), an income statement, the reconciliation of changes in shareholders' equity (statement of changes to shareholders' equity), and a statement of cash flows, along with the accompanying notes. In addition, a section known as the *management's discussion and analysis (MD&A)* must be included within the notes or presented as a separate statement.[6]

1. BALANCE SHEET

A balance sheet, or statement of financial position, reports a company's financial condition—including assets, liabilities, and shareholders' equity—at a point in time. Every account on the balance sheet is understood to be the value of that account as of that point in time. This is why a balance sheet is headed by the date the valuations occurred (e.g., December 31, 2xx1). Assets represent the resources the company can use to produce benefits, while liabilities and shareholders' equity are the means by which assets are financed. The following formula, known as the *accounting equation*, always holds:

$$\text{Total Assets} = \text{Liabilities} + \text{Shareholders' Equity}$$

6. The statement formats used here represent the requirements by the SEC (Regulation S-X) for companies publicly traded in the United States.

EXHIBIT 18.1 **SAMPLE BALANCE SHEET**

AS OF DECEMBER 31, 2XX1

ASSETS	CURRENT YEAR	PRIOR YEAR	CHANGE
CASH	$ 1,500,000	$ 1,000,000	$ 500,000
SHORT-TERM INVESTMENTS	1,300,000	1,500,000	(200,000)
ACCOUNTS RECEIVABLE	1,700,000	1,300,000	400,000
INVENTORY	2,600,000	2,100,000	500,000
PREPAID EXPENSES	900,000	900,000	0
TOTAL CURRENT ASSETS	**$ 8,000,000**	**$ 6,800,000**	**$1,200,000**
GROSS PROPERTY, PLANT & EQUIPMENT	9,000,000	8,100,000	900,000
LESS: ACCUMULATED DEPRECIATION	1,500,000	1,300,000	200,000
NET PROPERTY, PLANT & EQUIPMENT	7,500,000	6,800,000	700,000
INTANGIBLE ASSETS	0	0	0
TOTAL ASSETS	**$15,500,000**	**$13,600,000**	**$1,900,000**

LIABILITIES AND OWNERS' EQUITY	CURRENT YEAR	PRIOR YEAR	CHANGE
ACCOUNTS PAYABLE	$ 1,600,000	$ 1,200,000	$ 400,000
SHORT-TERM NOTES PAYABLE	1,800,000	1,300,000	500,000
TOTAL CURRENT LIABILITIES	**$ 3,400,000**	**$ 2,500,000**	**$ 900,000**
LONG-TERM DEBT	3,900,000	3,500,000	400,000
TOTAL LIABILITIES	**$ 7,300,000**	**$ 6,000,000**	**$1,300,000**
COMMON STOCK AT PAR VALUE	200,000	200,000	0
PAID-IN CAPITAL	3,600,000	3,600,000	0
RETAINED EARNINGS	4,400,000	3,800,000	600,000
TOTAL EQUITY	**$ 8,200,000**	**$ 7,600,000**	**$ 600,000**
TOTAL LIABILITIES AND EQUITY	**$15,500,000**	**$13,600,000**	**$1,900,000**

Exhibit 18.1 presents an example of a balance sheet.

a. Assets

Assets are company-owned economic resources that are expected to provide future economic benefits. To be reported as an asset on the balance sheet, the resource must be objectively quantifiable with a reasonable degree of accuracy. The valuation of most nonfinancial assets is based on historical cost. Assets are listed on the balance sheet in order of decreasing liquidity or convertibility into cash. There are several types of assets:

- **Current assets** are defined as cash or assets that are reasonably expected to be converted into cash within one year (i.e., an operating and accounting cycle). Current assets include cash, marketable securities, and any operating assets (e.g., accounts receivable, inventories, and prepaid expenses such as insurance premiums).
- **Fixed assets** are a company's investment in property, buildings, machinery, and equipment, and are often titled "Property, Plant, and Equipment" on the balance sheet. Also known as *capital assets*, fixed assets cannot be turned into cash as readily as current assets and are recorded at cost when they are acquired. Depreciable fixed assets (i.e., those that are used up or decline in value over time) are depreciated or expensed over their useful lives. Land is one example of an asset that is not depreciated. The book or carrying value of a depreciable asset is its cost minus the accumulated depreciation.[7] Other noncurrent assets include investments in long-term debt (bonds) and equity (stocks) of other companies, and intangible assets.
- **Intangible assets** lack physical substance, and there is often a high degree of uncertainty concerning their future value. Examples are goodwill, trademarks, and patents. An intangible asset with a finite and useful life is amortized over its legal or useful life, but if the intangible asset has an indefinite useful life, it is not amortized. However, it must be evaluated annually for any decline in value, which must be charged against income when identified.

b. Liabilities

Liabilities, which represent the business's obligations, generally consist of operating liability accounts and financing supplied by creditors, primarily lenders and suppliers. Liabilities are obligations or debts that will be paid with assets or services in the future. In the case of current liabilities, the obligation is expected to be repaid out of current assets or fulfilled within one year.

A note on terminology is warranted: the term *liability* refers to an amount that is owed, regardless of the form. Debt refers only to obligations that require interest payments, and should therefore be considered a subset of liabilities. Accounts payable is a liability, but not a debt, and notes payable are both a liability and a debt.

Current liabilities include obligations such as accounts payable, short-term loans, wages payable, taxes payable, deferred revenue, and the current portion of long-term debt. Accounts payable (also referred to as *trade payables*) are amounts due to vendors for purchased items. Accounts payable, together with operating accruals such as wages payable and taxes payable, are operating liability accounts. Short-term notes payable are typically short-term bank loans or commercial paper. Deferred revenue is an accounting for revenue the organization has received but for which it has not yet delivered the related product or service. An example may be a software company that is paid for a program before it is delivered and installed. Until the program is accepted by the customer, the revenue related to it is considered to be *deferred*.

Long-term liabilities are obligations, such as term loans, capital lease obligations, mortgages, and bonds, that are due beyond one year.

c. Shareholders' Equity

Shareholders' equity is the difference between total assets and total liabilities, and represents what would remain if all assets were sold and all creditors paid off in liquidation. It is, in effect, the financing provided by the company's owners and from ongoing company operations. The shareholders' equity section of the balance sheet contains a number of items, with two of the primary categories being the following:

7. Note that accumulated depreciation on the balance sheet is considered a *contra account* (more specifically, a *contra asset*), because it is subtracted from gross fixed assets to arrive at net fixed assets. This concept is covered later in this chapter in the section on the statement of cash flows.

- **Contributed capital** is the cash or other assets invested by shareholders. This section is further subdivided as needed to show various classes of stock, if any, such as common and preferred stock (discussed in Chapter 6, Capital Markets), with any preferred stock listed first.
- **Retained earnings** represent the changes in shareholders' equity arising from the retention of profits or losses of the company, less any dividends paid out to shareholders.

The statement of changes in shareholders' equity summarizes transactions affecting shareholders' equity and reconciles the ending balance to the beginning balance for each shareholders' equity account.

2. INCOME STATEMENT

The income statement, also called the *statement of earnings*, the *statement of operations*, or the *profit and loss statement*, summarizes:

- Revenues earned
- Expenses incurred
- Gains and losses arising from conversions of assets and liabilities over an accounting period

All accounts on the income statement must be measured over a span of time to have meaning. If, for example, a revenue number is quoted, it would not have meaning if one did not know whether it represented monthly, quarterly, or annual revenue. That is why the span of time over which income and expense items are measured is noted at the top of the income statement (e.g., "January 1–December 31, 2xx1," or "For the Year Ending December 31, 2xx1").

The order of items on the income statement progresses from those activities most closely associated with the primary revenue-generating activities to those with a less direct relationship.

Exhibit 18.2 presents an example of an income statement. While expenses appearing on the income statement vary from business to business, brief descriptions of the major line items portrayed in Exhibit 18.2 follow the exhibit.

EXHIBIT 18.2 **SAMPLE INCOME STATEMENT**

FOR THE YEAR ENDING DECEMBER 31, 2XX1

INCOME STATEMENT

	CURRENT YEAR	PRIOR YEAR	CHANGE
REVENUES	$15,000,000	$12,500,000	$2,500,000
LESS: COST OF GOODS SOLD	9,200,000	7,400,000	1,800,000
GROSS PROFIT	5,800,000	5,100,000	700,000
LESS: OPERATING EXPENSES	4,000,000	3,500,000	500,000
EBITDA (EBIT BEFORE DEP AND AMORT)	1,800,000	1,600,000	200,000
LESS: DEPRECIATION AND AMORTIZATION	200,000	150,000	50,000
OPERATING INCOME/EBIT	1,600,000	1,450,000	150,000
LESS: INTEREST EXPENSE	300,000	245,000	55,000
NET PROFIT BEFORE TAXES	1,300,000	1,205,000	95,000
LESS: PROVISION FOR INCOME TAXES	450,000	370,000	80,000
NET INCOME	$ 850,000	$ 835,000	$ 15,000

STATEMENT OF RETAINED EARNINGS

	CURRENT YEAR	PRIOR YEAR	CHANGE
BEGINNING RETAINED EARNINGS	$ 3,800,000	$ 3,215,000	$ 585,000
EARNINGS AVAILABLE FOR COMMON SHAREHOLDERS	850,000	835,000	15,000
LESS: COMMON STOCK DIVIDENDS PAID	250,000	250,000	0
PLUS/MINUS CURRENCY TRANSLATION ADJUSTMENT	0	0	0
ADDITION TO RETAINED EARNINGS	600,000	585,000	15,000
ENDING RETAINED EARNINGS	$ 4,400,000	$ 3,800,000	$ 600,000
EARNINGS PER SHARE (100,000 SHARES OUTSTANDING)	$8.50	$8.35	$0.15

Revenues represent amounts earned from the sale of merchandise or services to customers. The cost of goods sold (COGS) is the expense associated with providing the goods or services whose sale is recognized as revenues. COGS includes labor and material directly used in manufacturing the product sold, as well as any indirect or allocated manufacturing expenses. These costs are called *product costs*. The term *gross profit* is usually used for revenues less the COGS. Service companies typically do not have COGS.

Operating expenses (e.g., selling or administrative expenses) represent general expenses incurred in the course of running a business, but are not directly associated with the production of goods and services. Most operating expenses are considered period expenses because they occur over a period of time and cannot be attributed to specific units of goods or services sold.

One of the common measures for operating profitability is *earnings before interest, taxes, depreciation, and amortization (EBITDA)*. Once depreciation and amortization are subtracted, the remaining amount is referred to as *earnings before interest and taxes (EBIT)*. The term *operating income* refers to EBIT.

EBIT has traditionally been the measure used to evaluate a firm's ability to generate operating profits and to meet its financial and tax obligations. EBITDA first came into common use with leveraged buyouts in the 1980s, when it was used to indicate the ability of a company to service debt. As time passed, it became popular in industries with expensive assets that had to be written down over long periods. Many companies, especially in the technology sector, now commonly quote EBITDA.

The income statement also may include other income and expenses (e.g., interest income and expense, or realized currency gains and losses). These amounts typically arise from nonoperating activities such as those related to financing. Income before taxes is operating income, adjusted for other income and expenses. Net income is income before taxes minus income tax expenses.

In addition to net income, GAAP requires companies to report comprehensive income, which is net income adjusted for various gains and losses not reported on the income statement. These adjustments include:

- Unrealized gains and losses from other-than-temporarily impaired investments (ASC Topics 320 and 325)
- Minimum pension liability adjustments (ASC Topic 715)
- Foreign currency translation adjustments (ASC Topic 830)
- Changes in the market values of certain futures contracts qualifying as hedges (ASC Topic 815)

Comprehensive income must be reported as part of the income statement in the statement of changes in shareholders' equity (also referred to as the *statement of retained earnings*) or in a separate statement of comprehensive income.

As noted earlier, the balance sheet presents the accounting value of asset, liability, and equity accounts at a point in time. In contrast, all elements of income, including comprehensive income, capture economic activities that occur over a period of time. These economic flows explain the differences between the beginning-of-period and the end-of-period balance sheet account levels. The statement of cash flows details transactions that explain changes in the cash balance from the beginning of the accounting period to the end of the accounting period.

3. STATEMENT OF CASH FLOWS

Under accrual accounting, the reporting period when a revenue or expense item is recognized often differs from the reporting period when the corresponding cash transaction occurs. An income statement based on accrual accounting is a useful indication of a company's performance. However, lenders, creditors, and investors are concerned with a company's cash flow because cash, not earnings, repays debt, pays bills, and may be distributed as dividends.

The statement of cash flows provides a detailed picture of the sources of a company's cash flows and how these sources are used, and breaks them down into three categories:

- Operating activities
- Investing activities
- Financing activities

Sources and uses of funds, calculated from changes in balance sheet accounts from one period to the next, are used to create the statement of cash flows. A decrease in an asset account or an increase in a liability account is a funds source, while an increase in an asset account or a decrease in a liability account is a use of funds, as follows:

Sources of Funds:

- **Decrease in an Asset:** Funds are invested in assets or are freed up if the investment in the asset is reduced. For example, inventory sales reduce the amount of funds tied up in inventory (assuming no corresponding change in accounts receivable).
- **Increase in a Liability:** Liabilities represent financing for the firm, so an increase in a liability increases available funds. Examples include the purchase of inventory using trade credit, a bank loan, or stock sale.

Uses of Funds:

- **Increase in an Asset:** Investment in an asset can increase only by committing more funds to it, so an increase in an asset is a use of funds. For example, an increase in property reduces the amount of available funds.
- **Decrease in a Liability:** Funds are used to reduce a liability, whether to pay off debt or pay on accounts payable. Examples include the redemption of long-term bonds or a decrease in accounts payable.

Accumulated depreciation appears on the asset side of the balance sheet, but it is a source of funds when it increases. While depreciation is technically a noncash expense (i.e., there is no actual payment for depreciation), it does have a cash flow impact because it reduces the company's income taxes by lowering pretax income. Depreciation is also known as a *contra account*. When it increases, total assets decrease because it is subtracted, rather than added, when determining total assets.

The statement of cash flows includes flows from the income statement (net income and dividends) and changes in the balance sheet accounts measured from the end of one accounting period to the next. It is divided into three sections (operating, investing, and financing activities) and may be prepared using either the direct or the indirect method:

- The **direct method** reports the gross cash receipts and disbursements without examining any adjustments needed to calculate accrued net income. Operating activities are examined, and the total cash flow attributable to each activity is computed. To begin the direct method, accrual accounts must be converted to a cash amount. The direct method generally provides users more information about actual uses of cash. As a result, FASB and IASB have discussed requiring the direct method of cash flows. As of the publication of this book, this proposal has not been approved, due to the widespread use of the indirect method and the very large expense required for modifying financial reporting systems to present cash flows directly.
- The **indirect method** starts with net income taken from a firm's income statement and adjusts it to reflect the impact of noncash transactions during the reporting period. Net income is adjusted by any changes in balance sheet accounts from the prior period. Adjustments are made for changes in depreciation, amortization, accounts receivable, inventory, accounts payable, accrued wages payable, prepaid insurance, and income taxes payable. One difference between GAAP rules and IFRS principles is that under GAAP, dividends received from a company's investing activities are reported as an operating activity, not an investing activity.

Most companies prefer to use the indirect method because it is much easier to prepare, and because under GAAP rules, public companies must still provide a supplementary report very similar to the indirect cash flow report even if they use the direct method.

Exhibit 18.3 is based on information from the balance sheet in Exhibit 18.1 and the income statement in Exhibit 18.2, and is prepared using the indirect method. Similar to the income statement, the statement of cash flows is for a specific period, as shown in the exhibit.

EXHIBIT 18.3 **SAMPLE STATEMENT OF CASH FLOWS**

FOR THE YEAR ENDING DECEMBER 31, 2XX1

CASH FLOWS FROM OPERATING ACTIVITIES		
NET INCOME	$ 850,000	
ADJUSTMENTS TO RECONCILE NET INCOME TO NET CASH		
DEPRECIATION	200,000	
INCREASE IN ACCOUNTS RECEIVABLE	(400,000)	
INCREASE IN INVENTORY	(500,000)	
INCREASE IN ACCOUNTS PAYABLE	400,000	
NET CASH PROVIDED (USED) IN OPERATING ACTIVITIES		$ 550,000
CASH FLOWS FROM INVESTING ACTIVITIES		
CAPITAL EXPENDITURES	$(900,000)	
DECREASE IN SHORT-TERM INVESTMENTS	200,000	
NET CASH PROVIDED (USED) IN INVESTING ACTIVITIES		$(700,000)
CASH FLOWS FROM FINANCING ACTIVITIES		
NET SHORT-TERM BORROWING (NOTES PAYABLE)	$ 500,000	
PROCEEDS FROM ISSUANCE OF LONG-TERM DEBT	400,000	
DIVIDENDS PAID	(250,000)	
NET CASH PROVIDED BY FINANCING ACTIVITIES		$ 650,000
NET CASH INCREASE (DECREASE)		$ 500,000
CASH AT BEGINNING OF YEAR		$1,000,000
CASH AT END OF YEAR		$1,500,000

A viable organization must generate positive cash flow from operating activities in most years. Investing and financing activities support present and future operations, but the purpose of the business is to operate, and a negative cash flow from operations cannot be sustained for long by investing and financing cash flows.

To understand the structure of the statement of cash flows, look at some of the entries in Exhibit 18.3. For example, the balance sheet shows that the investment in inventory increased by $500,000 during the last year. Accordingly, the entry in the statement of cash flows shows that $500,000 of funds was used in the last year to pay for this added investment. As another example, accounts payable increased by $400,000 in the last year. Thus, cash was increased by this amount of supplier-based financing. Changes in inventory and accounts payable are attributable to operations, so they are recorded in the statement's operating activities section.

To calculate cash flow from operating activities, the current period's depreciation expense (from the income statement) and any other noncash charges reported on the income statement are added to net income. In a similar manner, noncash gains, if any, such as an increase in goodwill, are deducted from net income. Next, any changes in accounts receivable, inventories, and accounts payable are added or subtracted, along with changes in other operating accruals. These items represent the cash inflows and outflows related to daily operations.

Cash flows from investing activities relate to changes in nonoperating assets. Exhibit 18.3 shows that $900,000 was used to purchase capital or long-term assets, but that $200,000 of cash was gained by reducing the amount of short-term investments held. Alternatively stated, $200,000 was released from short-term investments—no doubt from selling or allowing them to mature. The changes in cash resulting from investing activities are netted. Exhibit 18.3 includes a net use of cash, due to the large capital expenditure amount.

Financing activities are related to interest-bearing debt and equity. When a debt or equity account increases, the firm has received cash. If debt or equity accounts decrease, the firm must have used cash to reduce them. Cash dividends are a discharge of cash from the company to its owners, so it is a use or reduction in the cash account. Entries in the statement's financing activities section are netted to arrive at an increase or decrease in the cash balance.

Exhibit 18.3 shows that the sample company generated a cash flow from operations of $550,000, had a net cash outflow of $700,000 based on changes in nonoperating assets (i.e., investing activities), and gained a net $650,000 of cash from financing activities, including the payment of dividends. Summing the inflows and outflows of cash shows a $500,000 net increase in cash. A look at the balance sheet in Exhibit 18.1 similarly shows a $500,000 increase in the cash account during the last year, but the statement of cash flows explains the causes of this change.

4. INTERNAL VERSUS EXTERNAL FINANCIAL STATEMENTS

External (or published) financial statements are used to provide the investors and other outsiders with information about the financial status of an entity. By their nature, these statements must comply with the appropriate financial standards, either IFRS or GAAP. Internal (or management) financial statements are those used by owners or other executives to manage the operation of an entity. Internal statements are not audited and can be in any format that management finds helpful in dealing with ongoing operations. While these two classes of statements come from the same basic financial information, their uses are quite different. At the end of the day, the two types of statements must reconcile to each other, but they can, and often do, provide very different types of information.

Internal financial statements typically consist of management reports, budgets, and forecasts, as well as the traditional financial statements already outlined. These reports are used for analyzing the organization's performance and position, and for taking appropriate measures to improve overall results.

IV. ACCOUNTING FOR DERIVATIVES, HEDGES, AND FOREIGN EXCHANGE (FX) TRANSLATION

As markets for derivatives and hedging products have expanded, so have the accounting guidelines for reporting their use. These accounting issues and guidelines will typically affect many organizations of all sizes and structures.

A. Derivatives and Hedge Accounting

A derivative is a financial instrument whose value is derived from some underlying financial asset. Derivatives can be forward, futures, option, and swap contracts. For companies that follow IASB regulations, the applicable guideline is International Accounting Standard (IAS) 39: *Financial Instruments: Recognition and Measurement*.[8] This statement covers accounting for both derivatives and hedging. Under US GAAP, the applicable guidelines are found in ASC Topic 815: *Derivatives and Hedging*. Initially, these guidelines required that all derivative instruments be carried on the balance sheet as an asset or a liability at fair market value (referred to as *mark-to-market accounting*), but were modified to some extent in reaction to the Recession of 2009 in ASC Topic 820: *Fair Value Measurement* and ASC Topic 825: *Financial Instruments*.

Under either IAS or ASC Topic guidelines, the accounting for the gains and losses arising from changes in a derivative's fair value generally depends on the instrument's intended use. Gains and losses arising from any revaluation of derivatives are reported in current-period income, provided the derivatives do not qualify as hedge instruments. If a derivative is used to hedge fluctuations in the value of a specific asset or liability on the balance sheet, then gains and losses of the revaluation are recognized as income or expense together with the offsetting gains and losses of the hedged item. This type of hedge is a *fair value hedge*.

Hedges designed to minimize fluctuations in the cash flow values of forecasted transactions include cash flow hedges and foreign currency transaction hedges. Gains and losses on such hedges are reported in comprehensive income and are not reported in current income until the related transactions impact current income. Rules for classifying derivative transactions are complex and detailed. ASC Topic 815 in its current form was developed from several FAS statements and amendments as the area of derivative instruments evolved over the last 25 years.

ASC Topic 820 clarifies the definition and application of fair value measurement. Prior to this guideline, multiple definitions and applications of fair value measurement could be applied to assets and liabilities. Under Topic 820, fair value of an asset or liability is defined by determining the price that would be received in an asset sale or the price paid to transfer a liability. The valuation price must be market-based and take into consideration all observable valuation inputs, such as competition and risk. ASC Topic 825 later expanded this application by stating that fair value should be applied to all financial assets and liabilities except for certain specified types of assets.[9]

IFRS handles hedge accounting similarly to GAAP. Assets and liabilities must be carried on the balance sheet at fair market value. Effective hedges[10] are booked within comprehensive income on the income statement, while the gain or loss on the noneffective portion of a hedge is booked within net income.

8. IFRS 9: *Financial Instruments* will replace IAS 39 for reporting periods beginning on or after January 1, 2015.
9. Topic 825 was codified from FAS 159. More information on the specifics of these guidelines can be found on the FASB website (http://www.fasb.org/st/summary/stsum159.shtml).
10. Hedge effectiveness is the degree to which changes in fair value or cash flows of the hedged item that are attributable to a hedged risk are offset by changes in the fair value or cash flows of the hedging instrument.

B. Foreign Exchange (FX) Translation Accounting

Companies that consolidate the results of foreign operations or subsidiaries denominated in the currency of the foreign country must generally translate the foreign financial statements into their functional or base currency (sometimes referred to as their *home currency*). IAS 21: *The Effects of Changes in Foreign Exchange Rates* provides the basis for doing this. IAS 21 is substantially similar to accounting treatment under US GAAP (ASC Topic 830: *Foreign Currency Matters*).

The task of foreign currency translation is essentially determining the correct exchange rate to be used in converting each financial statement line item from the foreign currency to the parent company's functional currency. The translation adjustment is an inherent result of this process, in which balance sheet and income statement items are translated at different rates. The basic steps in this process are:

- Determine the functional currency of the subsidiary: The *functional currency* is defined as the currency of the primary economic environment in which the entity operates. Normally, the majority of the subsidiary's business activities are transacted in that currency. This task can be more difficult than it seems and may require significant judgment. The subsidiary's functional currency is not necessarily its home currency (i.e., the currency of the country in which the subsidiary's headquarters are located) or the currency in which the subsidiary keeps its books.
- Determine whether the functional currency of the subsidiary is also its home currency:
    - If the subsidiary's functional currency is its home currency, then the current method is used to translate financial statement line items to the parent company's currency. The current method translates all assets and liabilities at the current spot rate at the date of translation. Equity items other than retained earnings are translated at the spot rates in effect on each related transaction date (known as *specific identification*). Retained earnings are translated at the weighted average rate for the relevant year, with the exception of any components that are identifiable with specific dates, in which case the spot rates for those dates are used. Income statement items are translated at the average rate for the period, except where specific identification is practicable. The resulting adjustment is not recognized in current earnings, but rather as a component of other comprehensive income.
    - If the functional currency of the subsidiary is not its home currency, then the temporal (historical) method is used. Under this method, nonmonetary balance sheet accounts and related income statement accounts are remeasured using historical exchange rates. The resulting translation adjustment is recognized in current earnings.

Foreign currency translation is more than a simple mechanical exercise. A thorough understanding of IAS 21 is required, and many aspects of this process require significant management judgment (and footnoting in the financial statements), especially as it relates to determining the functional currency of the subsidiary.

Accounting for foreign currency translation hedges is also covered under ASC Topic 830. Specifically, Topic 830 requires firms to account for all effective hedges of FX risk as hedges, as prescribed in ASC Topic 815, regardless of the form the hedge takes. A gain or loss on an effective hedge of FX risk is not recognized in net income. Rather, the gain or loss is reconciled within comprehensive income in the firm's shareholder equity.

V. ACCOUNTING FOR US GOVERNMENTAL AND NOT-FOR-PROFIT (G/NFP) ORGANIZATIONS

Governmental and not-for-profit (G/NFP) organizations do not have shareholders or other owners, but are organized to serve a collective group. Governmental agencies provide goods, services, or information to benefit the public as a whole or its particular segments. They raise cash primarily through taxes and fees paid by members of the community, regardless of whether those paying such taxes and fees derive any benefit from the resulting goods or services. In most cases, the accounting concepts covered earlier in this chapter are generally applicable to G/NFP organizations. Some of the key areas of difference are noted in this section. In general, G/NFP organizations must be audited on a regular basis just like for-profit entities.

Nongovernmental, not-for-profit organizations serve specific constituencies who pay for some or all the benefits provided. For example, professional associations (e.g., AFP) charge their members dues and raise revenues from various fees for services and from sponsorships for conferences. Other nongovernmental not-for-profits, such as many United Way agencies, rely entirely on altruism and grants to fund their operations.

The key feature distinguishing G/NFPs from profit-oriented businesses is that they provide as many goods or services as their resources allow. Another key difference is that these types of organizations typically use the term *fund balance* or *net worth* rather than *equity* in their accounting statements. Consequently, G/NFPs' financial accounting processes differ from those of for-profit enterprises. G/NFP reporting focuses on compliance and accountability rather than profitability. Because it is principles-based rather than rules-based, IFRS applies to G/NFPs as well as to for-profit entities in most of the world. In the United States, not-for-profits typically must comply with GAAP, while governments follow the rules and procedures developed by the Governmental Accounting Standards Board (GASB). The GASB is the authoritative standard-setting body for state and local governments, as well as for public schools, state universities, and other government-affiliated agencies.

The Financial Accounting Foundation (FAF) selects members, provides funds, and exercises general oversight for both the GASB and the FASB. The FASB has issued guidance for nongovernmental not-for-profits, such as private colleges, universities, and health care organizations, since the early 1990s. GAAP accounting standards also apply to nongovernmental entities. Many standards have specific provisions directed at these entities; therefore, their financial reports closely resemble those of for-profit organizations.

VI. SUMMARY

Sound financial reporting is essential to the ongoing operation of any organization, whether for internal or external use. This chapter introduced the basic concepts behind both international and US accounting principles and examined some of the key differences between them. The structure of key external financial statements was presented, along with a discussion of how those statements are audited for external validation. Finally, some treasury-specific topics regarding hedge accounting and FX reporting were presented.

APPENDIX 18.1: LISTING OF SELECTED FINANCIAL ACCOUNTING PRONOUNCEMENTS

The table below provides a list of selected financial accounting topics of interest to treasury professionals.[11] Although there is not always a direct one-to-one correspondence between ASC and IFRS, this table also provides the IFRS pronouncements that align with the various ASC Topics.

ASC Topics	IFRS Standards[12]
105 Generally Accepted Accounting Principles	IAS 1 Presentation of Financial Statements
220 Comprehensive Income	IAS 1 Presentation of Financial Statements
230 Statement of Cash Flows	IAS 7 Statement of Cash Flows
260 Earnings Per Share	IAS 33 Earnings per Share
280 Segment Reporting	IFRS 8 Operating Segments
320 Investments—Debt and Equity Securities	IAS 32 Financial Instruments: Presentation
330 Inventory	IAS 2 Inventories
350 Intangibles—Goodwill and Other	IAS 38 Intangible Assets
360 Property, Plant, and Equipment	IAS 16 Property, Plant and Equipment
410 Asset Retirement and Environmental Obligations	IAS 37 Provisions, Contingent Liabilities and Contingent Assets
420 Exit or Disposal Cost Obligations	IAS 37 Provisions, Contingent Liabilities and Contingent Assets
450 Contingencies	IAS 37 Provisions, Contingent Liabilities and Contingent Assets
470 Debt	IAS 39 Financial Instruments: Recognition and Measurement
480 Distinguishing Liabilities from Equity	IAS 1 Presentation of Financial Statements

11. Information in this appendix was obtained from the SEC Staff Paper, "Work Plan for the Consideration of Incorporating International Financial Reporting Standards in the Financial Reporting System for US Issuers: A Comparison of US GAAP and IFRS," November 16, 2011 (http://www.sec.gov/spotlight/globalaccountingstandards/ifrs-work-plan-paper-111611-gaap.pdf).
12. At the time of its formation in 2001, the IASB adopted the 41 existing International Accounting Standards (IAS 1–41). Subsequent pronouncements are numbered as IFRS standards.

ASC Topics	IFRS Standards
710 Compensation—General	IAS 19 Employee Benefits
715 Compensation—Retirement Benefits	IAS 26 Accounting and Reporting by Retirement Benefit Plans
718 Compensation—Stock Compensation	IFRS 2 Share-based Payment
730 Research and Development	IAS 38 Intangible Assets
740 Income Taxes	IAS 12 Income Taxes
805 Business Combinations	IAS 31 Interests in Joint Ventures
815 Derivatives and Hedging	IAS 39 Financial Instruments: Recognition and Measurement
820 Fair Value Measurement	IAS 36 Impairment of Assets, and IFRS 13 Fair Value Measurement
825 Financial Instruments	IAS 39 Financial Instruments: Recognition and Measurement
830 Foreign Currency Matters	IAS 21 The Effects of Changes in Foreign Exchange Rates
840 Leases	IAS 17 Leases, and 2013 Exposure Draft on Leases

TEST YOUR UNDERSTANDING: CHAPTER 18

Answers are on pages 723–727.

1. What kinds of insights can be provided by analyzing financial statements?
2. What is the IASB?
3. What are the basic principles of IFRS?
4. What are the four principles of GAAP?
5. What are the key differences between IFRS and GAAP?
6. What is shareholders' equity?
7. Compare and contrast internal and external financial statements.
8. Why are financial audits important?
9. What are the five types of audit opinions?
10. What are the basic types of financial statements?
11. Compare and contrast EBIT and EBITDA.
12. What are the two methods of preparing the statement of cash flows?
13. What is a derivative?
14. What is ASC Topic 820?
15. Describe the basic steps in preparing a foreign currency translation adjustment for financial statement purposes.
16. What is the key feature that distinguishes governmental and not-for-profit (G/NFP) organizations from profit-oriented businesses?

CHAPTER 19
Financial Planning and Analysis

I. INTRODUCTION

II. COST BEHAVIOR
A. Cost Types and Behaviors
B. Operating Leverage
C. Economies of Scale
D. Financial Leverage

III. DECISION EVALUATION
A. Identifying Relevant Costs and Revenues
B. Cost/Benefit Analysis

IV. DEVELOPING OPERATING AND FINANCIAL BUDGETS
A. Treasury's Role in Budgeting
B. Budgets and Financial Plans
C. The Budgeting Process
D. Uses of Budgets and Financial Plans

V. FINANCIAL STATEMENT ANALYSIS
A. Common-Size Statements and Ratios
B. Liquidity or Working Capital Ratios
C. Efficiency or Asset Management Ratios
D. Debt Management Ratios
E. Performance Ratios
F. Integrated Ratio Analysis
G. Service Industry Ratios
H. Strengths and Limitations of Ratio Analysis

I. INTRODUCTION

Financial planning and analysis (FP&A) is an important part of corporate finance. While many organizations have formal FP&A functions and staff, in many other companies much of the duties of FP&A are part of the treasury function. And even in companies that do have a formal FP&A function, there is frequently significant overlap between FP&A and treasury. Treasury plays an important role in an organization's planning and decision-making processes. For example, treasury professionals not only develop and implement financial and operating plans for the treasury area, but they also incorporate the financial and operating plans of all other departments in order to forecast the requirements for enterprise-wide liquidity. As part of this role, treasury professionals must identify and arrange financing sources, and analyze potential investment opportunities, while balancing liquidity requirements.

The budget process typically provides the foundation for FP&A, but it is only a part of the job. FP&A also plays a key role in the management of an organization's risk. Properly developed financial plans and forecasts are required to determine expected future cash flows, the timing of those cash flows, and any volatility related to those cash flows. These forecasts often impact hedging decisions about items such as foreign exchange (FX), interest rate, and commodity price/availability exposures, which are the backbone of financial risk management.

This chapter discusses how financial information is used for internal planning, decision making, and performance measurement. The chapter begins with an examination of cost behavior in a typical organization. The next sections examine operating and financial budgets, as well as financial statement analysis, including a discussion of key ratios used in that process. The chapter concludes by introducing some commonly used internal performance measures, such as return on investment (ROI) and economic value added (EVA), and by briefly discussing how financial analysis is used by external parties, such as rating agencies.

II. COST BEHAVIOR

Product planning, capital budgeting, cost/benefit analysis, and financial plan development all require an understanding of cost behavior. Cost behavior describes the relationship between costs and business activities (i.e., cost drivers), and varies with changes in a particular operating or financing activity.

A. Cost Types and Behaviors

Costs are classified into three categories:

- Fixed
- Variable
- Semi-variable (or mixed)

Fixed costs do not vary in total over a wide range of activity and are not immediately impacted by changes in business activities. One example of a fixed cost is the monthly account maintenance fee banks charge on deposit accounts. The fee remains the same regardless of the number of transactions on the account.

A fixed cost is treated as a lump sum when used in decision analysis. However, the fixed cost per unit of activity decreases as the activity level increases. The account maintenance fee will be the same regardless of the number of deposits made to an account. Consequently, the cost per deposit of a $100 maintenance fee is $10 if 10 deposits are made during the statement cycle and only $1 if 100 deposits are made.

Another consideration in fixed costs is that they may come from the addition of fixed assets in very specific sizes. For example, a utility company must determine the proper size of a generating plant that it needs for a particular location. The company can scale the plant size by the number of generating units it places in the plant. Each unit has a generating capacity of 50 megawatts (MW) of power, which will service approximately 10,000 households and has an acquisition cost of $25 million. Within a 50 MW range, therefore, the acquisition costs are essentially fixed, but there is a large jump in cost if the size is increased to the next range. This is referred to as the *step-up concept* of fixed costs.

Variable costs are costs whose total amount changes in direct proportion to the level of business activity. The cost of goods sold (COGS) is generally a variable cost. COGS generally increases as sales and production levels increase, and decreases if sales and production levels decrease. Many companies express COGS as a cost per unit produced. Total variable costs change with the volume of activity, while per-unit variable costs do not.

Some costs are semi-variable (or mixed) with both a fixed and variable component, and increase in stair-step fashion (similar to the step-up fixed costs discussed above). An example of semi-variable costs would be a machine company that has milling machines that produce widgets. Each milling machine costs $50,000 and can produce 10,000 widgets a month, and each widget consumes $1 of raw materials. The first widget will cost $50,001 to produce ($50,000 for the milling machine and $1 for the raw materials). Each additional widget will only cost $1 to manufacture until the production volume exceeds 10,000 widgets per month. Since the 10,001 widget will require the purchase of another milling machine, its marginal cost will again be $50,001 ($50,000 for the second milling machine and $1 for raw materials). Once the second machine is purchased, the next 10,000 widgets will only have a marginal cost of $1 each to manufacture. Every 10,000-widget increase in production volume will require an additional $50,000 plus the cost of the individual raw materials. Consequently, the semi-variable cost has both fixed and variable cost elements.

Exhibit 19.1 displays the behavior of the three cost types in relation to business volume. The horizontal axis measures output units, which may be any measurable activity. Examples include physical units in factory production or the number of transactions processed by tellers, ATMs, or remote deposit capture. The vertical axis measures the total cost of the activity itself.

EXHIBIT 19.1 **COST BEHAVIOR**

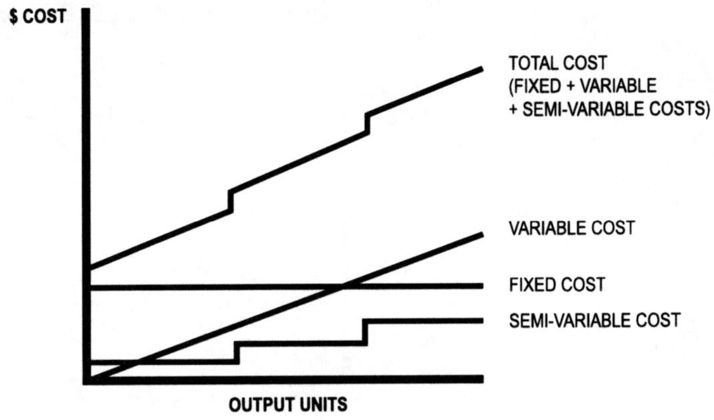

B. Operating Leverage

The relative levels of fixed and variable costs define a company's operating cost structure. Operating leverage is determined by the extent to which fixed costs are used in a company's operating cost structure. The higher the proportion of fixed costs, the higher the company's operating leverage. If a production process is characterized by high fixed costs and low variable costs, then profits will expand rapidly after the company earns enough to cover its fixed costs. However, if the process is characterized by low fixed costs and high variable costs, then the volume of business does not need to be as great to cover fixed costs, but additional business volume will not cause profits to rise as rapidly, because variable costs are high.

High fixed costs generally are associated with equipment-intensive operations (e.g., auto manufacturing), while high variable costs are associated with labor-intensive operations (e.g., restaurants or brokerage firms). A company with high operating leverage can achieve a large percentage increase in profits from a small increase in revenues, but it will experience a rapid decline in profits if sales decrease. For companies with low levels of operating leverage, the changes in operating profits will not be as volatile as sales levels change.

Exhibit 19.2 shows the impact of operating leverage on operating profit. To simplify each graph, semi-variable costs are omitted and variable cost lines are not shown. The total cost lines represent the sum of fixed and variable costs. Further, each graph assumes an economic process that is basically profitable, so revenues rise faster than costs.

EXHIBIT 19.2 **OPERATING LEVERAGE**

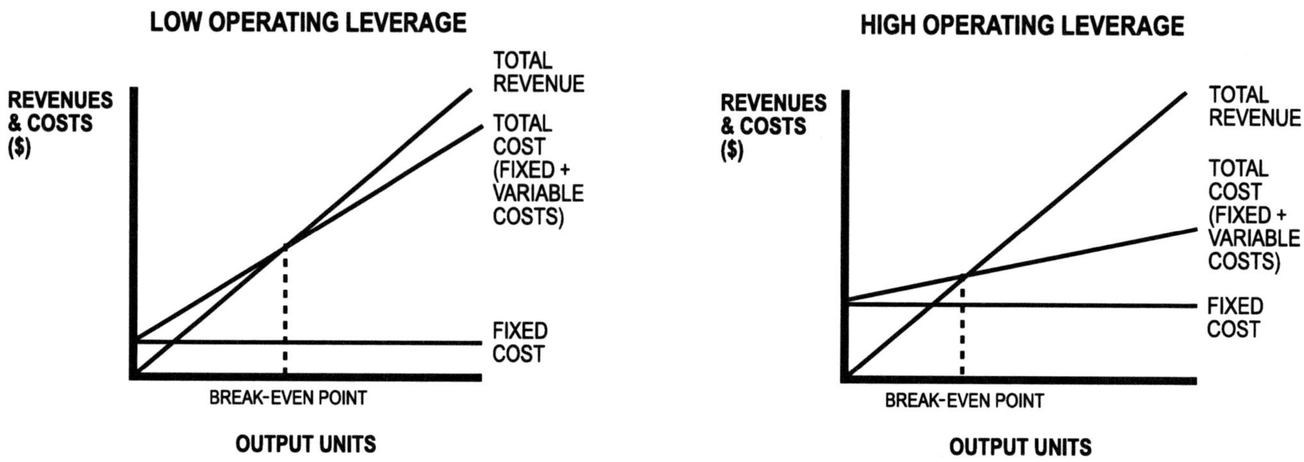

The two graphs in Exhibit 19.2 represent alternative methods for producing revenue from an activity. Therefore, the total revenue lines have the same slope in each graph. To understand the two graphs in the context of a situation, imagine that a manufacturing process is characterized by extensive use of labor and little use of equipment. Labor costs tend to be variable and equipment costs tend to be fixed. This situation represents low leverage, as shown in the graph on the left.

Now suppose an investment in equipment is made that reduces the number of workers. Variable costs per transaction will decrease, but the fixed costs associated with equipment will increase. The graph on the right shows this situation. Operating profit is defined as the difference between revenues and costs, or the vertical distance between the revenue and cost lines at any particular level of output units.

The point of intersection between the total revenue and total cost lines represents a break-even level of activity (i.e., operating profit is zero). As the number of units changes, operating profit changes more rapidly in the high operating leverage situation than in the low operating leverage situation. This implies more risk because operating profit is more sensitive to the level of business activity and because losses expand rapidly as activity drops below the break-even level.

On the other hand, operating profit will be larger in the high operating leverage case if the break-even level of output is exceeded. This explains why firms make heavy investments in equipment that reduce labor costs. However, choosing a cost structure that increases operating leverage will produce higher operating profit only if the firm exceeds the break-even level of activity. A measure known as the *degree of operating leverage* is discussed in Chapter 20, Financial Decisions and Management.

C. Economies of Scale

Economies of scale occur when an increase in sales lowers the average cost per unit sold. If a business has mostly variable costs, then the average cost remains fairly stable when sales increase. On the other hand, companies with high operating leverage and high levels of fixed costs experience declining average costs as sales increase. This is because the fixed costs are distributed over more units sold. Fixed costs tend to be associated with capital equipment, buildings, lease payments, interest payments, and property insurance. Therefore, economies of scale result when additional sales can be generated from the existing asset base.

D. Financial Leverage

Just as operating leverage looks at the use of fixed costs of production, financial leverage examines the fixed costs of financing. Generally, the higher the level of debt capital used in a company, the higher the interest costs and the greater the amount of financial leverage. As is discussed in more detail in Chapter 20, Financial Decisions and Management, the trade-off between the use of debt financing and equity financing, and thus the use of financial leverage, is one of the key financial decisions made by companies. A measure of the impact of debt use, known as the *degree of financial leverage*, is also discussed in Chapter 20.

III. DECISION EVALUATION

The decision-making process of most organizations is based on a financial comparison of the costs and benefits of alternatives. Qualitative factors enter into business decisions, but this discussion is restricted to quantitative elements (i.e., those that can be expressed in numerical terms). Because of the potential cash flow and working capital impacts, treasury professionals often play a central role in the financial analysis of corporate decisions, such as product line changes, the selection of banking relationships/third-party providers, and the decision to acquire or divest business units.

A. Identifying Relevant Costs and Revenues

Relevant data in evaluating decisions are the expected future cash costs and revenues among investment alternatives. There are two criteria that a cost or revenue must meet to be relevant:

- The cost or revenue must affect future cash flows. For example, if a company is considering a project using a previously purchased piece of equipment that has no alternative use, then the equipment cost is not relevant to the current decision because it does not affect future cash flows. Instead, this is referred to as a *sunk cost* (i.e., a historical cost that has already been incurred).
- The cost or revenue must differ among the alternatives. For example, if a package delivery company is looking at acquiring new trucks, only the factors that are different between the choices are relevant to the analysis. If there are two choices available and both have the same carrying capacity, then that factor should not be part of the consideration. Instead, the analysis should focus on the items that are different (e.g., acquisition costs, or fuel and maintenance costs).

Opportunity costs must also be considered when making choices. If a treasury professional decides to pay down debt that is not due, then the opportunity to invest that amount is gone. If this opportunity cost is not considered, then debt may be repaid that costs less than the return the company could earn from an available investment.

B. Cost/Benefit Analysis

Nearly all business decisions are based on a cost/benefit analysis, which assesses whether the relevant economic benefits of a given course of action exceed the relevant economic costs. A break-even analysis is a type of cost/benefit analysis that establishes the level of activity at which benefits and costs are equal.

A cost/benefit analysis typically attempts to measure the net benefit (i.e., benefits minus costs) of a proposed asset acquisition at a forecasted level of activity. An example of a cost/benefit analysis is a capital budgeting decision that relates the present value of cash benefits to the present value of cash costs. Other treasury decisions requiring a cost/ benefit analysis include ascertaining the minimum size for a commercial paper issue, purchasing a new treasury information system, and determining whether to outsource a given business process or perform it in-house.

1. BREAK-EVEN ANALYSIS

The break-even point is the level of activity for an operation at which the costs equal the benefits. A break-even analysis is used by businesses in product decisions to determine what level of sales, at a given price, is required to cover costs. The general formula for a break-even analysis is:

$$\text{Unit Break-Even Point} = \frac{\text{Fixed Costs}}{\text{Selling Price Per Unit} - \text{Variable Cost Per Unit}}$$

If a company makes a product or delivers a service for \$10 per unit, but the variable cost is only \$6 per unit, then it can determine how many units it must sell to cover \$10,000 of fixed costs by calculating the unit break-even point as follows:

$$\text{Unit Break-Even Point} = \frac{\$10{,}000}{\$10 - \$6} = 2{,}500 \text{ Units}$$

If the company sells more than 2,500 units, then its operating profit will expand by \$4 per unit because that is the amount by which the selling price exceeds the variable cost.

There are numerous applications for break-even analysis in treasury. One example is the calculation of the break-even amount of funds required to justify a wire transfer. Consider a company that usually uses an automated clearinghouse (ACH) network transfer to move funds from local field depository banks to its principal concentration bank. (Assume the local field and concentration banks are different institutions.) Because a wire transfer is more expensive than an ACH but results in quicker funds availability, a treasury professional should determine the quantity of funds that must be transferred to justify using the wire. (An example of this calculation is provided in Chapter 9, Working Capital Metrics.)

2. CAPITAL BUDGETING

Capital budgeting is the process by which proposed large-dollar investments in long-term assets are evaluated. These investments are often strategic because they commit the firm to a course of business that is not changed easily. Examples include the purchase of new equipment, replacement of existing equipment, introduction of a new product line, or acquisition of another firm (or a division of another firm). Capital budgeting decisions are a type of cost/benefit analysis, and treasury professionals employ several methods to evaluate them, including:

- Payback period
- Net present value
- Profitability index
- Internal rate of return

Each of these methods is discussed below and is illustrated using the project information in Exhibit 19.3.

EXHIBIT 19.3 **PROJECTED CASH FLOWS OF CAPITAL INVESTMENT PROJECTS**

	PROJECTED CASH FLOWS	
	PROJECT A	PROJECT B
Year 0	$(1,000)	$(1,000)
Year 1	$300	$300
Year 2	$300	$300
Year 3	$400	$400
Year 4	$100	$1,000
Year 5	$100	$1,000

3. PAYBACK PERIOD

The payback period equals the number of years required to recover the initial investment. There is no specific criterion for a right or wrong payback period. An acceptable payback period is a management judgment based on a variety of factors. The measure is significant because (1) the faster the investment is repaid, the faster the funds can be invested in another opportunity, and (2) investments with short payback periods are considered to be less risky than those with longer payback periods.

Project A in Exhibit 19.3 has a payback period of three years because it is expected that three years will elapse before the $1,000 investment is recovered. A glance at Exhibit 19.3 indicates that Projects A and B have the same payback period, but Project B is more desirable given the projected cash flows in Years 4 and 5 (after payback).

For illustration purposes, suppose the total project cost of each project increased to $1,500. In this case, Project A's payback period is unknown, since the projected revenue never exceeds the projected cost (although if it could be assumed that the $100 per year revenue projected in Years 4 and 5 continued at the same rate, then the payback period would be 8 years). In the case of Project B, $1,000 of the $1,500 is still recovered in the first three years, and the remaining $500 is recovered in the first half of Year 4 (assuming the cash flow takes place equally throughout the year), meaning the payback period is 3.5 years. Now Project B has a much shorter payback period than Project A.

The payback period method suffers from two shortcomings: (1) it does not consider the time value of money, and (2) it fails to consider cash flows beyond the payback period.

While the decision to accept or reject a proposed investment in an asset should not be made on the basis of payback alone, the method's shortcomings do not void its usefulness. The method also estimates the time required to recover the amount of cash invested and provides helpful information when used in conjunction with measures that calculate a project's economic value.

4. NET PRESENT VALUE (NPV)

NPV is calculated by netting the present value (or PV, discussed in Chapter 9, Working Capital Metrics) of anticipated cash inflows with the PV of cash outflows. For many investments, the only cash outflow is the initial cost that occurs at the time the investment is made (i.e., present time). In this case, the cost is already the PV because it occurs now. Costs may be incurred over two or more years for large projects (e.g., a pipeline or a refinery), in which case it is necessary to compute the PV of the cost outlays in periods beyond the present time.

The weighted average cost of capital (or WACC, discussed in Chapter 20, Financial Decisions and Management) is used as the discount rate because it is the company's cost of funds as derived from investor expectations. Accordingly, the PV of cash inflows discounted at the WACC represents the value of the cash flow stream to the firm's investors. When cost is subtracted, the net amount represents the value that will be created or destroyed by accepting and funding the proposed investment. If NPV is positive, then the firm's value will increase by this amount. Alternatively, if NPV is negative, then the amount equals that by which the firm's value will decrease. In the latter case, the investment would not be funded. The general formula for NPV is:

$$\text{NPV} = \text{PV of Cash Inflows} - \text{PV of Cash Outflows}$$

If the only cash outflow takes place in the present (e.g., a cost or investment as in Exhibit 19.3), then the equation is:

$$\text{NPV} = \frac{C_1}{(1+i)^1} + \frac{C_2}{(1+i)^2} + \frac{C_3}{(1+i)^3} \cdots + \frac{C_n}{(1+i)^n} - \text{Cost}$$

Where:

C = Net cash flow

i = Discount rate

n = Number of periods

If the desired discount rate (e.g., WACC) is 10%, then the NPVs for Projects A and B, respectively, are:

$$NPV_A = \frac{\$300}{(1+0.10)^1} + \frac{\$300}{(1+0.10)^2} + \frac{\$400}{(1+0.10)^3} + \frac{\$100}{(1+0.10)^4} + \frac{\$100}{(1+0.10)^5} - \$1{,}000$$

$$= \frac{\$300}{1.100} + \frac{\$300}{1.210} + \frac{\$400}{1.331} + \frac{\$100}{1.464} + \frac{\$100}{1.611} - \$1{,}000$$

$$= \$272.73 + \$247.93 + \$300.53 + \$68.31 + \$62.07 - \$1{,}000$$

$$= \$951.57 - \$1{,}000 = -\$48.43$$

$$NPV_B = \frac{\$300}{(1+0.10)^1} + \frac{\$300}{(1+0.10)^2} + \frac{\$400}{(1+0.10)^3} + \frac{\$1{,}000}{(1+0.10)^4} + \frac{\$1{,}000}{(1+0.10)^5} - \$1{,}000$$

$$= \frac{\$300}{1.100} + \frac{\$300}{1.210} + \frac{\$400}{1.331} + \frac{\$1{,}000}{1.464} + \frac{\$1{,}000}{1.611} - \$1{,}000$$

$$= \$272.73 + \$247.93 + \$300.53 + \$683.06 + \$620.73 - \$1{,}000$$

$$= \$2{,}124.98 - \$1{,}000 = \$1{,}124.98$$

Generally a project should only be considered for funding if it increases the firm's value and if NPV is positive (i.e., greater than zero). So while Project A's total cash inflows are $1,200 and its costs are $1,000, it ultimately reduces the value of the firm by $48.43. Based on the timing and amount of cash flows, the project is not justified given the firm's cost of capital. Project B, alternatively, is economically justifiable and should be funded because it is expected to contribute $1,124.98 to the firm's value in the present.

Based on NPV alone, Project A should be rejected and Project B should be implemented. However, funding decisions are usually made on a variety of factors, not just NPV. These might include competitive pressure, expected customer demand, or regulatory requirements.

5. PROFITABILITY INDEX (PI)

The PI is a cost/benefit measurement that is similar to NPV. It uses information generated by NPV analysis, but it views that information from a different perspective. NPV measures the total change in value in the present expected to result from an investment. PI is a ratio of the PV gained to the cost required to obtain that value. It shows value gained per dollar of investment and is calculated as follows:

$$PI = \frac{\text{Present Value of Cash Inflows}}{\text{Present Value of Cash Outflows}}$$

In cases where the only cash outflow is in the present (Period 0), the calculation is:

$$PI = \frac{\text{Present Value of Cash Inflows}}{\text{Cost}}$$

Therefore, for the projects in Exhibit 19.3, the PIs can be calculated as:

$$PI_A = \frac{\$951.57}{\$1{,}000.00} = 0.952$$

$$PI_B = \frac{\$2{,}124.98}{\$1{,}000.00} = 2.125$$

Project A contributes $0.952 of value for every $1.00 invested, so it should not be funded. Project B, on the other hand, contributes $2.125 of value for every $1.00 invested and should, therefore, be considered for funding. The decision criterion for using PI, therefore, is to accept a proposed project only if it contributes more value than it costs (i.e., if the PI ratio exceeds one).

Note that PI is not a rate of return measure; it is only a ratio of benefit to cost that is similar to the common-size ratios discussed later in this chapter.

6. INTERNAL RATE OF RETURN (IRR)

IRR is the discount rate that makes the NPV equal to zero or, equivalently, makes the PV of cash inflows equal to the PV of cash outflows. Consider the following situation. A proposed investment costs $100 in Period 0 and is expected to generate a cash flow of $110 in Period 1. The rate of return is an unambiguous 10%. To determine the PV of the $110 cash inflow at a discount rate of 10%, follow this calculation:

$$PV = \frac{\$110}{(1 + 0.10)^1} = \frac{\$110}{1.10} = \$100$$

Given this situation, NPV would be zero:

$$NPV = \text{PV of Cash Inflow} - \text{Cost} = \$100 - \$100 = \$0$$

In this simple situation, the internal rate of return is 10%. If the firm also requires a 10% discount rate, NPV will equal zero because the discount rate is the same as the rate of return.

To determine the rate of return on an investment, find the discount rate that makes the PV of its inflows equal to its cost or, equivalently, where the NPV equals zero.

For a problem with cash flows in multiple periods, such as the projects in Exhibit 19.3, finding the rate of return is typically done using a financial calculator, spreadsheet, or computer program. The important point here is to understand what a rate of return represents. The calculations used to find the rate of return and the solutions are shown below. The calculation programs that find the solutions to these types of problems usually use a trial-and-error process to find the specific interest rate (i) that results in an NPV of $0:

$$NPV_A = \frac{\$300}{(1+i)^1} + \frac{\$300}{(1+i)^2} + \frac{\$400}{(1+i)^3} + \frac{\$100}{(1+i)^4} + \frac{\$100}{(1+i)^5} - \$1,000 = \$0$$

Therefore:

$i = 7.7\%$

$$NPV_B = \frac{\$300}{(1+i)^1} + \frac{\$300}{(1+i)^2} + \frac{\$400}{(1+i)^3} + \frac{\$1,000}{(1+i)^4} + \frac{\$1,000}{(1+i)^5} - \$1,000 = \$0$$

Therefore:

$i = 38.1\%$

Recollect that the WACC in this example is 10%. This is the hurdle rate presented to the firm by its investors. An investment is justifiable only if it promises a rate of return greater than the desired hurdle rate.[1] Project A is not an acceptable investment, but Project B is quite acceptable. When using IRR to evaluate investments, the accept/reject decision criterion compares the rate of return to the cost of capital. A company should therefore accept and fund an investment if IRR is greater than the WACC.

Note that IRR does not reveal anything directly about the expected value change associated with an investment proposal. Instead, it is a comparison of the rate of return (IRR) to the rate of cost (WACC). There will be a value increase if IRR is greater than the WACC, but that amount will be unknown. NPV, on the other hand, measures a change in value. In the end, value is what matters because securities markets will determine the value change in the share price. As previously discussed, a positive NPV is one of the factors that determines value, but it should be recognized that projects with higher IRRs normally result in higher return ratios overall. Value is a combination of all factors discussed in this section.

1. Note that the hurdle rate used for IRR purposes does not have to be WACC, but can be any rate that firm management thinks is appropriate, such as average borrowing rate or even an arbitrary hurdle rate that represents the return management wants from new projects.

7. THE NEED FOR MULTIFACTOR COMPARISON

Most treasury professionals will compute some or all of these measures. If the initial cash flow estimates are reliable, then a proposed investment that has a short payback period, a sizeable NPV, a large PI, and an IRR that is significantly in excess of the WACC is almost sure to be an economic choice that will increase the firm's value and stock price. Of course, some investments are made out of necessity (e.g., crisis investments) or are made to comply with regulatory requirements. In these cases, the decision is not made on the basis of economic benefit measures.

From Exhibit 19.4, it is clear that Project B is superior to Project A. Project B should be considered for funding because it is acceptable under all criteria, including adding value to the company. Project A must be rejected because it fails under all criteria and would reduce the value of the company. If Project A contributed value, then it should be accepted even if its contribution to value is less than that of Project B. If both projects are acceptable per the decision criteria, then the only circumstances in which both should not be selected is if the firm is rationing capital among projects competing for funding or if the projects represent alternative ways of accomplishing the same objective (e.g., if they are mutually exclusive).

EXHIBIT 19.4 **SUMMARY OF CAPITAL EXPENDITURE ANALYSIS**

METHOD	PROJECT ACCEPTANCE CRITERION	PROJECT A	PROJECT B
NET PRESENT VALUE (NPV)	NPV > 0	$(48.43)	$1,124.98
PROFITABILITY INDEX (PI)	PI > 1	0.952	2.125
INTERNAL RATE OF RETURN (IRR)	IRR > WACC*	7.7%	38.1%

*Weighted Average Cost of Capital (WACC) = 10% in the example

Typically there will be more than two projects competing for capital resources as illustrated here. Additionally, most companies do not have an unlimited amount of capital available to invest in new projects. As a result, projects that meet or exceed the basic decision criteria may not be funded in any given year. One way to evaluate this is using a capital budget constraints analysis, as shown in Exhibit 19.5. In this example, the company had eight potential projects to evaluate (each represented by a diamond in the chart). The projects were first sorted by expected rate of return (i.e., IRR) and then graphed based on cumulative budget requirements to fund the projects, starting with the highest IRR. Assuming a hurdle rate of 5% (horizontal dashed line in the chart), the company would fund the top five projects as they all have an IRR over 5%. In the example shown, the company also has a budget limit of $10 million (vertical dotted line in the chart), and so will only fund the first two projects as they both exceed the hurdle rate and fall within the budget constraints. Other projects may be funded in the future when more funds are available.

EXHIBIT 19.5 **CAPITAL BUDGET CONSTRAINTS ANALYSIS**

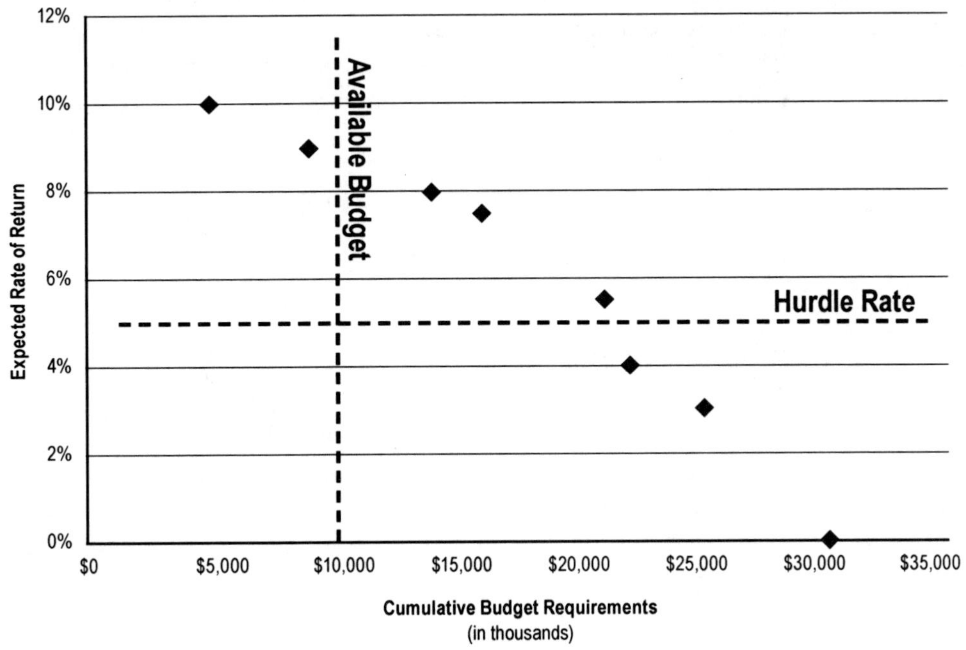

8. INVESTMENT RISK ANALYSIS

Real asset investments are risky because future cash flows are uncertain. Risk is associated with the degree of confidence one has in cash flow predictions. The less confidence one has in predicted cash flows and the wider the possible variation of those flows, the greater the investment risk. Risk tends to increase with the length of the investment period because the level of confidence in predicted cash flows decreases with how distant they are in the future. The three main methods for assessing investment risk are:

- Sensitivity analysis
- Scenario analysis
- Simulation

a. Sensitivity Analysis

Sensitivity analysis determines how a final outcome, such as NPV, is influenced by changes in the value of a particular variable (e.g., sales, or an operating or financing cost) and how vulnerable the expected outcome is to changes in a specific assumption. Sensitivity analysis can identify and evaluate the areas of greatest vulnerability, and permits the decision maker to determine the likelihood that an unacceptable outcome will occur.

In the previous Project A/B example using Exhibit 19.3, assume that the decision maker evaluating the capital expenditure for Project B has little confidence in the estimated cost of capital because of high financial leverage (i.e., the use of a large proportion of long-term debt in the capital structure) in a rising interest rate environment. A sensitivity analysis can reveal the impact of varying the discount rate while holding all other values constant at their expected levels. (Note that with sensitivity analysis only one variable at a time is changed, rather than a set of variables as in scenario analysis.) Given the cost of capital of 10%, a sensitivity analysis using a possible range of ±5% for the cost of capital would project the NPV to be between $1,509.59 and $819.65. The calculations are:

$$NPV_{B,-5\%} = -\$1,000 + \frac{\$300}{(1.05)^1} + \frac{\$300}{(1.05)^2} + \frac{\$400}{(1.05)^3} + \frac{\$1,000}{(1.05)^4} + \frac{\$1,000}{(1.05)^5} = \$1,509.59$$

$$NPV_{B,+5\%} = -\$1,000 + \frac{\$300}{(1.15)^1} + \frac{\$300}{(1.15)^2} + \frac{\$400}{(1.15)^3} + \frac{\$1,000}{(1.15)^4} + \frac{\$1,000}{(1.15)^5} = \$819.65$$

Sensitivity analysis may also be combined with a break-even analysis to estimate the maximum that could be paid for an investment before a negative NPV results. A break-even discount rate is determined by computing an IRR. One could find the discount rate that makes NPV equal zero given a set of expected future cash flows and an investment amount.

As determined previously, Project B has a PV of $2,124.98 at a discount rate of 10%. Therefore, the maximum amount that could be paid for the cash flows is $2,124.98. Paying more would generate a negative NPV. If the cost of capital increased, the firm would discount at the higher rate. A higher discount rate reduces the PV of the cash flows. If the discount rate rose to 12% because the cost of funds to the company increased, then the PV of the project's expected cash inflows would fall to $1,994.67. This figure would then be the maximum amount to invest without incurring a loss of value (a negative NPV).

b. Scenario Analysis

Scenario analysis is a type of what-if analysis that assesses possible outcomes under a range of circumstances. It is used frequently to establish the lower bound (i.e., worst case) and upper bound (i.e., best case) of outcomes.

To illustrate, consider Project B in the previous example. Assume the decision maker determines that the cost of capital may vary over the life of the project by as much as ±5% and that the forecasted cash inflows may be 25% lower or 10% higher than predicted, depending on market conditions. The best- and worst-case NPVs are calculated as follows:

$$NPV_{Best} = -\$1,000 + \frac{\$330}{(1.05)^1} + \frac{\$330}{(1.05)^2} + \frac{\$440}{(1.05)^3} + \frac{\$1,100}{(1.05)^4} + \frac{\$1,100}{(1.05)^5} = \$1,760.55$$

$$NPV_{Worst} = -\$1,000 + \frac{\$225}{(1.15)^1} + \frac{\$225}{(1.15)^2} + \frac{\$300}{(1.15)^3} + \frac{\$750}{(1.15)^4} + \frac{\$750}{(1.15)^5} = \$364.74$$

While the analysis projects $1,124.98 as the most likely NPV for the project, the range of probable outcomes is between $1,760.55 (the best case) and $364.74 (the worst case).

c. Simulation

The simulation method of assessment combines scenario and sensitivity analyses, allowing certain assumptions in a decision model to fluctuate simultaneously. Simulation models are complex, but numerous firms have written software that is available at reasonable prices to perform such analyses.

The most commonly used model is Monte Carlo simulation (discussed in Chapter 15, Operational and Enterprise Risk Management). It is an analytical technique in which a large number of simulations are run using random quantities selected from a probability distribution of values for specified variables. Next, a probability distribution of results is analyzed to infer which values are most likely to occur. A Monte Carlo simulation requires the estimation of probability distributions for all the input variables (e.g., revenues, operating costs, financing costs, and tax rates). Specific information about the distributions—in particular, the shape of the distribution and the expected parameter values, such as minimum, maximum, mean, and variance—is input into the simulation program. The program randomly combines variable values and generates an output distribution for the decision variable, such as NPV or IRR. This output distribution can be used to provide a quantitative assessment of the risk for the decision variable (i.e., the probability of a negative NPV or an IRR below some minimum value).

9. RISK-ADJUSTED DISCOUNT RATE (RADR)

The RADR approach essentially requires high-risk endeavors to earn a higher rate of return in order to justify the investment. When properly applied, RADR allows a firm to more closely match its capital needs to available sources and to better manage its overall levels of risk and return.

For example, in the analysis methods described above, such as NPV and IRR, the discount rate (or rate of return) used for calculations and/or comparisons was the WACC. While this rate is appropriate for large projects that are generally in line with a firm's overall risk level, it may not be the best to use for projects that are significantly higher or lower in risk. RADR can be a more effective method. RADR is also valuable when the analysis is being done in a large, multidivisional firm, where each division has a distinctly different risk profile.

In these cases, the analyst may want to adjust the discount rate (or cost of capital) used in calculations and comparisons. As a simple example, assume a large corporation has determined that each of its divisions will be categorized as low, average, or high risk for capital budgeting purposes. Further, it has decided to use a risk adjustment factor of ±2% to the overall firm's WACC to determine the RADR for each division. If the overall firm's WACC is 10%, then the divisional WACCs will be as follows:

- Low-Risk Divisions: WACC = 8%
- Average-Risk Divisions: WACC = 10%
- High-Risk Divisions: WACC = 12%

This same type of adjustment could also be done at a project level within each division, with high-risk projects being allocated a higher required return level and low-risk projects being allocated a lower required return.

10. RISK-ADJUSTED RETURN ON CAPITAL (RAROC)

Risk-adjusted return on capital, or RAROC, is an economic metric developed in the 1980s by the consulting firm Oliver Wyman to help measure the expected profitability of a project from a risk-adjusted standpoint. Although initially developed for financial institutions to use in identifying investment projects, it is increasingly being used by other types of organizations in making capital allocations. RAROC is a method of measuring the return on a project based upon the overall risk of the project.

As noted in the discussion of RADR, riskier projects should have higher returns than less risky projects. RADR accounts for this by setting a higher hurdle rate for riskier projects, but does nothing to adjust project returns to account for the expected risk. RAROC estimates the risk of the project and uses that to adjust the return on capital calculations. In other words, RADR sets the evaluation bar, in terms of hurdle rate, higher for riskier projects, while RAROC actually adjusts the expected return from each project based on its project risk to permit projects to be compared to each other.

Although the actual calculation is beyond the scope of this book, RAROC adjusts the projected revenues of a project based upon some measure of how likely the project is to succeed and calculates a return on investment based on those adjusted revenues. In the actual calculation, an expected loss (EL) is developed for each project based upon a number of factors, including the inherent risk of the project. This EL is then used to reduce projected cash flows, and an internal rate of return is calculated.

11. NONFINANCIAL ISSUES

While all of the calculations outlined above provide a numerical measure of the value of investment projects, it is also important to consider nonfinancial factors that may be relevant for a given project. For example, what if the market is not ready for the product or service that is to be launched by the investment decision? Or, what if the underlying technology is not yet ready for introduction to the public? More importantly, if there are regulatory requirements that must be met, projects may be funded even if they have negative financial impacts.

IV. DEVELOPING OPERATING AND FINANCIAL BUDGETS

Long-term planning is essential for both for-profit and not-for-profit organizations. A strategic plan establishes an organization's overall goals and objectives, and charts a course of action for achieving those objectives over a period of time, generally for two to ten years. Strategic plans are important because they establish the business framework necessary for developing detailed financial plans. The business strategy over the expected time horizon drives the financial forecast and budget.

A. Treasury's Role in Budgeting

Treasury is both directly and indirectly responsible for many portions of the planning and budgeting process, as well as for managing the budget's impact on cash flows. As plans and budgets are developed, there may also be changing impacts to the projected cash flow streams for the organization. A treasury professional must manage short-term assets and liabilities to ensure a company has adequate funds and liquidity in order to meet these changes. In addition, a treasury professional may be required to assess the impact of plans on debt covenants and credit ratings. Finally, a treasury professional must manage the financing of the company's long-term assets through debt and equity issues.

B. Budgets and Financial Plans

A budget is an in-depth plan that details how economic resources will be procured and deployed over a specific time period. Budgets typically cover periods ranging from one month to two years; long-range financial plans extend the process out many years. Most organizations use a detailed annual budget for planning and control purposes. The annual budget provides specific details underlying the first year of the long-range plan. It usually is organized further into shorter time divisions, such as months or quarters. An annual budget for an entire organization is called the *master budget.* As the process expands to the long term, financial plans get less detailed and focus more on the big picture.

Long-range financial plans quantify the elements of the strategic plan in the form of forecasted financial statements over a five- to ten-year period. These projected financial statements incorporate major debt and equity financing actions, as well as high-level business activities, such as acquisitions and/or divestitures of assets, products, services, divisions, or business lines. Since long-range financial plans quantify the business or strategic plan, projected balance sheets reflect the target capital structure, and projected income statements reflect the expected revenues and expenses. These pro forma financial statements serve as the basis for operating and financial budgets.

It should also be noted that most budgets are static plans that are frozen or fixed as a frame of reference to help manage the organization. To be truly effective, however, forecasts should be updated continually to reflect changes in the underlying economy, market conditions, and firm-specific issues, especially during times of financial uncertainty. Under these circumstances, static budgets can become meaningless and a more relevant forecast needs to be used as the new benchmark to measure progress, as well as to direct any necessary course correction.

C. The Budgeting Process

The master budget has two chief components: (1) the operating budget, and (2) the financial budget. The operating budget, or profit plan, focuses on day-to-day operations, while the financial budget addresses an organization's financing and investing activities. The planning process begins by constructing the elements of the operating budget. These include sales/revenue, production/purchases, and operating expense budgets.

Because the costs that must be budgeted depend upon the expected sales level, the first step in developing an operating budget is to generate a sales budget. If a business sells goods or services on credit, then a critical step in developing the sales budget is the cash collections schedule. This schedule details cash sales, accounts receivable balances, and cash collections of accounts receivable. The expenses necessary to support expected operations can be forecasted after the sales budget is established.

The financial budget can be constructed after the operating budget is complete.[2] The first step in constructing the financial budget is to develop the capital budget, which details the forecasted costs of expected investments. Capital investments may be necessary to acquire new facilities, replace aging or obsolete equipment, or initiate longer-term projects required under the long-range plan. The second step in constructing a financial budget is to develop the cash budget, which translates information from the operating and capital budgets into sources and uses of cash. The final step is to identify financing sources for any forecasted cash needs. If the cash budget projects a surplus, then management must decide whether to use the cash for future investments, pay down debt, distribute cash to shareholders through dividends, or increase the share price through stock repurchases. If the cash budget projects a deficit, then management must decide how to finance the deficit and/or reduce costs.

When combined, the operating and financial budgets form the master budget, which constitutes a set of pro forma financial statements for the budget period. Exhibit 19.6 illustrates how the information from the operating and financial budgets is used to construct financial statements. A full example of a pro forma financial plan is provided in Chapter 13, Cash Forecasting.

EXHIBIT 19.6 **CONSTRUCTING PRO FORMA FINANCIAL STATEMENTS FROM BUDGETS**

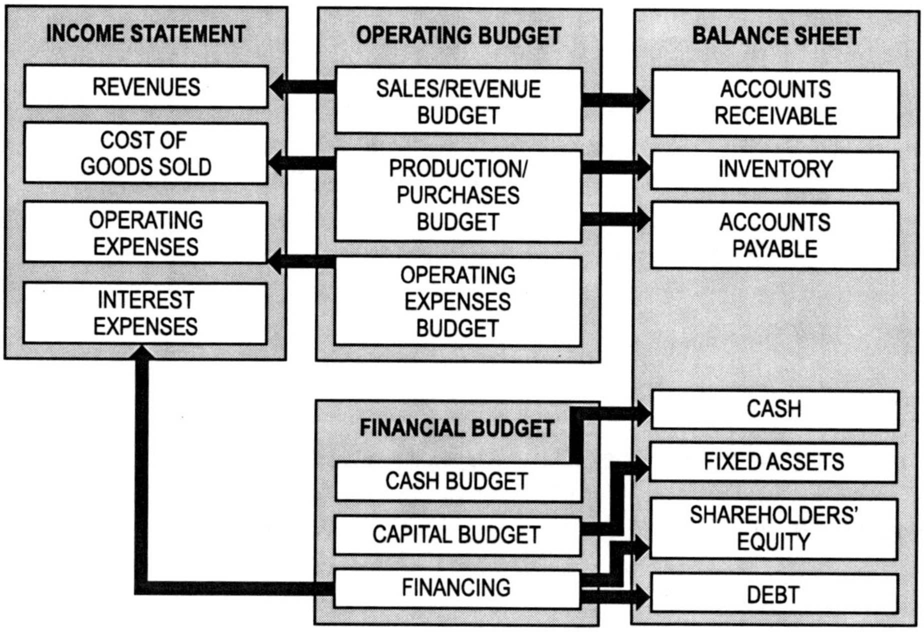

D. Uses of Budgets and Financial Plans

While budgets are used for various purposes, most are either planning- or control-related. Budgets discipline managers to plan and assess what resources are needed and how they will be funded. Because managers often are evaluated based on their ability to manage their budgets within plan, the budgeting process also requires managers to anticipate changing conditions and contingencies.

2. The steps outlined here are primarily oriented toward large organizations. Smaller organizations may not necessarily go through all of the steps outlined, or may follow a more streamlined or informal process.

Another use of budgets is resource allocation. All organizations encounter constraints on their resources, so budgets are enlisted to assist in allocation decisions. For example, local, state, and federal government agencies use budgets to allocate funds raised from taxes and other sources, as well as provide the requisite authority for the use of funds. Finally, a budget serves as a communication and coordination tool, informing all areas of an organization of each department's plans during a given budget period.

While the planning aspects of budgeting are forward looking, the control aspects of budgeting are retrospective. A budget serves as the primary benchmark against which actual results are compared. Any difference between actual results and the budgeted figure is called a *variance*. The process of identifying and analyzing budget variances is referred to as *variance analysis*.

Small variances are inevitable in the course of running a business. Large variances, however, may be an early indication of more serious problems, such as changes in economic conditions, the competitive environment, or customer buying patterns. Variances also may indicate a flaw in the forecasting method used. A company's optimal performance can be maintained only if the causes of the variances are identified and addressed quickly and effectively.

Budgets are a type of forecast and, as discussed in Chapter 13, Cash Forecasting, need to be updated and refreshed periodically as more current information becomes available. It is a common practice in many companies to update budgets on a quarterly basis as part of their variance analysis. Other companies only update their budgets if a major factor or assumption changes, such as the purchase or acquisition of a major subsidiary. While it is a best practice to update budgets periodically, some companies never update their budget outside of the annual budget cycle, and instead count on explanations of variances to cover major changes.

Modern ERP systems can simplify budget analysis by allowing for easy manipulation of budget numbers and assumptions. Managers can change assumptions and look at budget numbers in a variety of different formats that can be useful for analysis purposes. For example, once a base budget is developed, pro forma budgets can easily be produced by product, department, or geographic unit to identify issues and trends and to isolate potential problems.

V. FINANCIAL STATEMENT ANALYSIS

Financial statements provide information to existing and potential stakeholders who must make informed decisions about allocating economic resources:

- Suppliers must determine whether to make sales on credit.
- Trading partners must assess a counterparty's financial ability to meet contractual obligations.
- Lenders must determine whether to enter into or maintain credit relationships.
- Rating agencies must assess the credit risks of issued securities.
- Investors must make decisions about purchasing and selling corporate debt and equity securities.

Financial statements provide a great deal of the information required for making these decisions. Ratio and cash flow analyses are two of the most commonly used tools for analyzing financial statements. Cash flow analysis entails developing pro forma financial statements and using the statement of cash flows to assess future liquidity needs and resources. Financial ratio analysis helps to evaluate historical performance. Ratios fall into four general categories:

- **Liquidity or working capital ratios** measure the firm's ability to meet its payment obligations on short-term debt and help ascertain whether cash is being used effectively.
- **Efficiency or asset management ratios** measure how effectively assets are utilized.
- **Debt management ratios** measure the firm's degree of indebtedness and its ability to service its debt.
- **Performance ratios** measure profitability in relation to revenue and investment.

Since ratios are relative measures, they must be evaluated by comparing them to industry averages or the ratios of direct competitors. This process is generally referred to as *comparative analysis*. Industry averages are widely available and are commonly used as benchmarks. While averages are important reference points, they should not be thought of as targets, because a successful firm is often intentionally different in some way. Industry average ratios are available from traditional sources, such as Dun & Bradstreet, Moody's Investors Service, and Standard & Poor's, as well as through many types of online sources.

Some ratios assume special importance because covenants in debt contracts may require that a ratio be met as a minimum while another ratio may not be exceeded. It is also important to track a ratio's trend over time, usually three to five years. This process is generally referred to as a *trend analysis*. A ratio is based on a set of financial statements associated with the end of an accounting period. As such, it is a point estimate in time and provides no information about direction.

All of the sample calculations that follow use data (dollars expressed in thousands) from the financial statements provided in Exhibits 18.1, 18.2, and 18.3 from Chapter 18, Financial Accounting and Reporting. Data from the most recently completed year are used exclusively. For demonstration purposes, this chapter will forego computing a ratio more than once to examine its trend.

The calculations below use period-end figures for all balance sheet items. An alternative approach is to use the average figure (beginning balance plus ending balance, divided by two) for many of the balance sheet items. Using the average figures will help to smooth any balance sheet fluctuations, but the averages may not be relevant if the company's financial position has changed dramatically.

A. Common-Size Statements and Ratios

Common-size ratios can be useful to express account entries in a statement as a percentage, thus producing what is termed *common-size financial statements*. A common-size income statement expresses every line item on the statement as a percentage of revenue, and a common-size balance sheet expresses each account as a percentage of total assets. Exhibit 19.7 shows an example of a common-size balance sheet based on the information provided in Exhibit 18.1.

EXHIBIT 19.7 SAMPLE COMMON-SIZE BALANCE SHEET

AS OF DECEMBER 31, 2XX1

ASSETS	CURRENT YEAR	PRIOR YEAR	CHANGE
CASH	9.68%	7.35%	2.33%
SHORT-TERM INVESTMENTS	8.39%	11.03%	-2.64%
ACCOUNTS RECEIVABLE	10.97%	9.56%	1.41%
INVENTORY	16.77%	15.44%	1.33%
PREPAID EXPENSES	5.81%	6.62%	-0.81%
TOTAL CURRENT ASSETS	**51.61%**	**50.00%**	**1.61%**
GROSS PROPERTY, PLANT & EQUIPMENT	58.06%	59.56%	-1.50%
LESS: ACCUMULATED DEPRECIATION	9.68%	9.56%	0.12%
NET PROPERTY, PLANT & EQUIPMENT	48.39%	50.00%	-1.61%
INTANGIBLE ASSETS	0.00%	0.00%	0.00%
TOTAL ASSETS	**100.00%**	**100.00%**	**0.00%**
LIABILITIES & OWNERS' EQUITY	**CURRENT YEAR**	**PRIOR YEAR**	**CHANGE**
ACCOUNTS PAYABLE	10.32%	8.82%	1.50%
SHORT-TERM NOTES PAYABLE	11.61%	9.56%	2.05%
TOTAL CURRENT LIABILITIES	**21.94%**	**18.38%**	**3.56%**
LONG-TERM DEBT	25.16%	25.74%	-0.58%
TOTAL LIABILITIES	**47.10%**	**44.12%**	**2.98%**
COMMON STOCK AT PAR VALUE	1.29%	1.47%	-0.18%
PAID-IN CAPITAL	23.23%	26.47%	-3.24%
RETAINED EARNINGS	28.39%	27.94%	0.45%
TOTAL EQUITY	**52.90%**	**55.88%**	**-2.98%**
TOTAL LIABILITIES & EQUITY	**100.00%**	**100.00%**	**0.00%**

Common-size statements enable direct comparisons of financial data for firms of different sizes. Expenses as a percentage of revenues reveal which firm has the best expense controls in various areas. Asset categories expressed as a percentage of total assets can similarly be compared across companies, as can liability categories expressed as a percentage of total assets. Companies know from planning and experience what value expenditures should be in relation to revenues and how much should be invested in various asset categories as a percentage of the total investment in assets. Common-size statements can help a firm monitor itself and its competitors in this regard.

Some of the percentages in common-size income statements constitute profit margins, which are measures of profitability or performance. These include the gross profit, operating profit, net profit, and earnings before interest, taxes, depreciation, and amortization (EBITDA) margins. The formulas and examples of these ratios are provided later in this chapter in the section on performance ratios.

Financial ratios can be formed from virtually any combination of values from financial statements. Knowing which specific values are associated with a ratio can be helpful when interpreting that ratio's meaning.

B. Liquidity or Working Capital Ratios

A company's liquidity (i.e., its ability to meet present obligations when due) is measured using liquidity or working capital ratios and related calculations. These ratios and their calculations are discussed in Chapter 9, Working Capital Metrics. *Working capital* is defined as the sum of a company's current asset accounts (primarily cash, accounts receivable, and inventory) less the sum of its current liability accounts (primarily payables and accrual accounts). These are the accounts through which cash flows during a company's cash conversion cycle.

Liquidity or working capital ratios are standardized and widely used formulas that allow a company's management to:

- Determine adequate liquidity levels
- Establish liquidity policies and guidelines
- Continually monitor liquidity

Banks, other creditors, investors, analysts, and rating agencies use working capital and liquidity measures to assess a company's creditworthiness and short-term financial soundness.

C. Efficiency or Asset Management Ratios

The cash turnover ratio encourages firms to minimize their investments in cash consistent with maintaining adequate cash and overall liquidity. The same principle applies to all other assets and leads to the use of efficiency, or asset management, ratios. Understanding the balance sheet reveals that every dollar invested in assets must be supported by one dollar of financing. Such financing is not free, however. Investors who supply debt and equity to the firm expect a rate of return on their investment, and that represents a cost to the firm. The more the firm invests in assets, the greater the cost. Of course, assets support sales, but it is neither necessary nor desirable to have an asset base that exceeds the level appropriate to support those sales.

Efficiency is measured by turnover ratios. What is important here is how intensively firms use assets. The most common measures of asset utilization involve dividing the flow of revenue by the stock of investment in the asset.

1. TOTAL ASSET TURNOVER

Total asset turnover measures how many times the firm's asset base was used (i.e., turned over) in generating the flow of revenue during the period. This is a measure of how effectively the firm's assets are used to generate revenue. Total asset turnover is calculated as follows:

$$\text{Total Asset Turnover} = \frac{\text{Revenues}}{\text{Total Assets}} = \frac{\$15{,}000}{\$15{,}500} = 0.968 \text{ Times}$$

The higher the ratio, the more intensively the firm uses its assets. An alternative way to view the ratio is to observe that the firm generated $0.968 of revenue for every dollar of investment in assets.

2. FIXED ASSET TURNOVER

Fixed asset turnover focuses on how efficiently fixed assets (or property, plant, and equipment) are used. This ratio can be calculated as follows:

$$\text{Fixed Asset Turnover} = \frac{\text{Revenues}}{\text{Net Property, Plant, and Equipment}} = \frac{\$15{,}000}{\$7{,}500} = 2.0 \text{ Times}$$

The firm in the example turned over net property, plant, and equipment two times. Viewed alternatively, it generated $2.00 of revenue for each dollar invested in fixed assets. Sufficient productive assets are required to meet customers' demands for products or services, but not more. Idle capacity does not generate revenue; rather, it generates operating and financing expenses. This is why a company builds a manufacturing plant and operates it in shifts rather than builds multiple plants at which only single shifts operate.

3. CURRENT ASSET TURNOVER

Current asset turnover measures how many times the firm has turned over the stock of its most liquid assets with the flow of revenue. The following example shows how to calculate this ratio:

$$\text{Current Asset Turnover} = \frac{\text{Revenues}}{\text{Current Assets}} = \frac{\$15{,}000}{\$8{,}000} = 1.88 \text{ Times}$$

The firm turned over current assets 1.88 times or generated $1.88 of revenue per dollar invested in current asset accounts.

4. CASH CONVERSION EFFICIENCY

Cash conversion efficiency measures how effectively a company has converted sales (or revenues) into cash. The cash flow generated by operations (i.e., operating cash flow from the statement of cash flows) is viewed as a percentage of revenue. The higher the cash conversion efficiency ratio, the greater the net cash generated per dollar of revenue. This ratio, also called the *cash profit margin*, can be calculated as follows:

$$\text{Cash Conversion Efficiency} = \frac{\text{Cash Flow from Operations}}{\text{Revenues}}$$

$$= \frac{\$550}{\$15{,}000} = 0.037\text{, or } 3.7\%$$

The calculation reveals that $0.037 of cash was carved out of each revenue dollar.

D. Debt Management Ratios

When used prudently, there are several advantages to financing with debt: (1) debt sources cost less than equity sources, (2) the interest paid on debt normally is tax deductible, and (3) financing with debt does not dilute earnings because the number of common stock shares does not increase as it would if issuing stock.

Two types of ratios can help assess how much debt is prudent. The first type examines the degree of indebtedness (i.e., how much debt the firm has relative to assets or equity). The second type measures the firm's ability to service the debt it has (sometimes referred to as *coverage ratios*). A treasury professional can compare the ratios of his/her firm to those of competitors or industry average ratios to judge whether the company is using debt prudently, is capable of carrying more debt, or should reduce its indebtedness.

1. DEBT RATIOS MEASURING INDEBTEDNESS

As mentioned earlier in this chapter, a company's use of debt is generally referred to as *financial leverage*. There are several ratios that can be used to measure the level of indebtedness (i.e., debt usage) by a company. More details on the impact of financial leverage on the value of a company are provided in Chapter 20, Financial Decisions and Management.

a. Total Liabilities to Total Assets

The total liabilities to total assets ratio measures the percentage of all liabilities to total investments or total assets. The higher the percentage, the more the firm relies on debt to finance its assets. The following example shows how to calculate the ratio:

$$\text{Total Liabilities to Total Assets} = \frac{\text{Total Liabilities}}{\text{Total Assets}} = \frac{\$7,300}{\$15,500} = 0.471, \text{ or } 47.1\%$$

Short- and long-term liabilities are 47.1% of assets. In other words, some form of debt supplies $0.471 of each dollar of assets.

b. Long-Term Debt to Capital

Long-term debt to capital is used by financial analysts and credit rating agencies. Where *capital* is defined as the sum of long-term debt and equity, the ratio measures the percentage of a company's capital that is provided by long-term debt. Long-term debt includes such liabilities as long-term notes and bonds, term loans, capitalized lease obligations, and pension and retirement obligations. Equity capital consists of all preferred and common equity accounts, including retained earnings. The higher the long-term debt to capital ratio, the greater the percentage of debt a company uses in its capital structure, or mix of long-term debt and equity.

$$\text{Long-Term Debt to Capital} = \frac{\text{Long-Term Debt}}{\text{Long-Term Debt + Equity}}$$

$$= \frac{\$3,900}{\$3,900 + \$8,200} = \frac{\$3,900}{\$12,100} = 0.322, \text{ or } 32.2\%$$

The calculation reveals that long-term debt supplied 32.2% of total capital. Chapter 20, Financial Decisions and Management, discusses capital structure further.

c. Debt to Tangible Net Worth

Some assets are difficult to value or are not easily converted into cash. Goodwill, patents, trademarks, and copyrights represent such intangible assets because they are neither physical nor financial in form. Since their value as recorded on the balance sheet may be suspect and/or not realizable, it is reasonable to deduct their value from the equity value on the balance sheet.

When making this deduction, the remaining equity balance is called *tangible net worth*. For companies with significant levels of intangible assets, debt to tangible net worth typically shows debt to be a higher percentage of capital because of the adjustment to equity. The balance sheet in Exhibit 18.1 does not contain any intangible assets, so this calculation of the measure subtracts intangible assets of $0, as follows:

$$\text{Debt to Tangible Net Worth} = \frac{\text{Total Debt}}{\text{Total Equity} - \text{Intangible Assets}}$$

$$= \frac{\$1{,}800 + \$3{,}900}{\$8{,}200 - \$0} = \frac{\$5{,}700}{\$8{,}200} = 0.695\text{, or } 69.5\%$$

The sum of short- and long-term interest-bearing debt (i.e., total debt) is 69.5% of tangible net worth, or total equity in this case. Commercial banks and other lenders rely on this measure because it cleanses the indebtedness measure of the effects of intangible assets and a possible inflation of the actual value of equity.

2. MEASURES OF ABILITY TO SERVICE DEBT (COVERAGE RATIOS)

While the measures above examine the level of debt relative to assets or capital, coverage ratios are primarily concerned with measuring a company's ability to make payments on (i.e., service) its debt.

a. Times Interest Earned (TIE) Ratio

The TIE ratio measures a firm's ability to service its debt through interest payments. The numerator in the equation is operating income (i.e., earnings before interest and taxes [EBIT]). The purpose here is to isolate the amount available to pay interest charges on debt. Refer to the income statement in Exhibit 18.2. Just to conduct business, a company must pay suppliers (i.e., cost of goods sold) and operating expenses (e.g., salaries and wages, selling and administrative, travel and entertainment, vehicle, and utility). What remains after paying these expenses are the funds available to pay interest. The following calculation determines what multiple EBIT is of the interest the company is obligated to pay:

$$\text{Times Interest Earned} = \frac{\text{Operating Income}}{\text{Interest Expense}} = \frac{\text{EBIT}}{\text{Interest Expense}}$$

$$= \frac{\$1{,}600}{\$300} = 5.33 \text{ Times}$$

The firm has 5.33 times the funds available to pay interest as the amount of interest that was paid. The larger the TIE ratio, the more capable the firm is of paying interest in the event EBIT were to decline due to a business downturn or competitive shock. For example, if TIE was 5.00 times, EBIT could decline to one-fifth of its current amount and the firm could still pay the interest on its debt.

The TIE can also be calculated using EBITDA rather than EBIT. This configuration is often used by bondholders in bond covenant agreements, with one of the typical measures being the EBITDA to interest coverage ratio. Its application is similar to that of the TIE ratio, but it may be more appropriate for firms with high levels of depreciation and amortization. It was initially used by investment bankers financing leveraged buyouts (LBOs) to determine the ability of a new firm to service its debt in the short term.

b. Fixed-Charge Coverage Ratio

The fixed-charge coverage ratio is similar to the TIE, except it also takes into account fixed charges other than interest, such as payments on leases. The rationale is that lease payments represent a fixed obligation similar to debt service, so they should be included in examining a firm's indebtedness. The following calculation would result, assuming that the firm being used for these examples has annual lease payments of $500,000 (as with other numbers used in the calculations, the 000 will be omitted):

$$\text{Fixed-Charge Coverage} = \frac{\text{EBIT + Fixed Charges}}{\text{Interest + Fixed Charges}}$$

$$= \frac{\$1{,}600 + \$500}{\$300 + \$500} = \frac{\$2{,}100}{\$800} = 2.625 \text{ Times}$$

The interpretation of the fixed-charge coverage ratio is similar to that of the TIE. The bigger the ratio, the better able the firm is to meet its fixed-charge obligations. Note that the amount of the lease payments must be added back into EBIT in the numerator because these payments were deducted in the determination of EBIT on the income statement.

E. Performance Ratios

Profit is important and crucial to a firm's endurance, but it is just an amount rather than a comment on financial performance. Like most things, performance is relative. A race car driver's speedometer reading is interesting, but what counts is how fast the driver's car travels relative to other cars in the race. Posting a speed of 200 miles per hour (mph) is no good if the other cars travel at 202 mph.

Similarly, performance ratios measure profit relative to the amount of revenue or the level of financing. They show how much profit a firm earned per dollar of revenue or investment. What follows are six of the most commonly computed and quoted performance ratios.

1. GROSS PROFIT MARGIN

The gross profit margin shows the percentage of revenues remaining after the cost of goods sold is deducted from revenue. It is computed as follows:

$$\text{Gross Profit Margin} = \frac{\text{Gross Profit}}{\text{Revenues}} = \frac{\$5{,}800}{\$15{,}000} = 0.387\text{, or } 38.7\%$$

2. OPERATING PROFIT MARGIN

The operating profit margin shows the percentage of revenue remaining after both the cost of goods sold and all operating expenses are deducted from revenue. The calculation for operating profit margin is:

$$\text{Operating Profit Margin} = \frac{\text{EBIT}}{\text{Revenues}} = \frac{\$1{,}600}{\$15{,}000} = 0.107\text{, or } 10.7\%$$

3. EBITDA MARGIN

As discussed in Chapter 18, Financial Accounting and Reporting, EBITDA is sometimes used as a measure of operating profits for a company, especially in some industries like high technology. An alternative measure of operating profitability is known as the *EBITDA margin*, which is calculated as follows:

$$\text{EBITDA Margin} = \frac{\text{EBITDA}}{\text{Revenues}} = \frac{\$1{,}800}{\$15{,}000} = 0.120\text{, or } 12.0\%$$

4. NET PROFIT MARGIN

The net profit margin, also known as *return on sales* or *return on revenues*, shows the percentage of profits earned after all expenses and taxes are deducted from revenues. It is computed as:

$$\text{Net Profit Margin} = \frac{\text{Net Income}}{\text{Revenues}} = \frac{\$850}{\$15{,}000} = 0.057\text{, or } 5.7\%$$

To summarize, gross profit is $0.387 per dollar of revenue, operating profit is $0.107 per dollar of revenue, EBITDA is $0.120 per dollar of revenue, and net profit is $0.057 per dollar of revenue. Whether these results are satisfactory depends upon how they compare to a company's profit plan at the beginning of the accounting year and how its competitors are faring, as determined by direct comparison with them or by comparing the firm to industry averages.

5. RETURN ON TOTAL ASSETS (ROTA)

The ROTA ratio measures the company's amount of net income in relation to the level of total assets. The greater the ratio, the larger the net income is per dollar invested in assets. In the following example, every dollar in total assets generates $0.055 in net income:

$$\text{Return on Total Assets} = \frac{\text{Net Income}}{\text{Total Assets}} = \frac{\$850}{\$15{,}500} = 0.055\text{, or } 5.5\%$$

6. RETURN ON COMMON EQUITY

The return on common equity ratio measures the amount of earnings available to common shareholders relative to the level of their investment in the company. If a company issues preferred stock, then the dividends due to its preferred shareholders must be paid before any dividends are paid to common shareholders. Accordingly, the preferred share dividends must be deducted from net income to arrive at the *earnings available to common shareholders* value in the numerator of the following calculation. The measure *common equity* in the denominator represents total equity less the balance sheet book value of preferred equity. No preferred stock appears in the Exhibit 18.1 balance sheet. Therefore, the earnings available to common shareholders equal the net income, and common equity equals total equity.

$$\text{Return on Common Equity} = \frac{\text{Earnings Available to Common Shareholders}}{\text{Common Equity}}$$

$$= \frac{\text{Net Income} - \text{Preferred Dividends}}{\text{Total Equity} - \text{Preferred Stock}}$$

$$= \frac{\$850 - \$0}{\$8{,}200 - \$0} = 0.104\text{, or } 10.4\%$$

This calculation reveals that the firm earned $0.104 of net profit for each dollar of common equity investment.

F. Integrated Ratio Analysis

Companies can gain valued insight by looking at ratios in pairs or groups. The most commonly used example is the DuPont equation, which looks at ROTA as a product of the return on sales (i.e., net profit margin) and total asset turnover.

ROTA is computed as net income divided by total assets. If a company's ROTA is unsatisfactory, then the ratio provides little guidance as to the cause of poor performance. Alternatively, the relationship can be expressed in the DuPont form using the ratio data computed earlier:

$$\text{Return on Total Assets} = \text{Return on Sales} \times \text{Total Asset Turnover}$$

$$= \frac{\text{Net Income}}{\text{Revenues}} \times \frac{\text{Revenues}}{\text{Total Assets}}$$

$$= 0.057 \times 0.968 = 0.055\text{, or } 5.5\%$$

ROTA, a fundamental measure of performance, is really based on cost control in the income statement (return on sales) and the effective or efficient use of assets (total asset turnover). Of course, the firm must realize its budgeted sales levels. Assuming it has realized the sales levels, the key to performance then becomes effective cost control and good asset utilization. Each factor is a prerequisite to achieving a good overall financial result.

Suppose that the ROTA ratio was below standard because the return on sales was also too low. Analysts would then know to look deeper into the income statement, into gross and operating profit margins, and at accounts in the common-size income statement to compare them against those of the firm's competitors or those from an overall industry common-size statement. This process would identify expense categories that the company failed to control.

If total asset turnover was too low, then the firm had more investment in assets than a well-managed firm needed to support the experienced revenues. Treasury analysts should look at measures like cash turnover, working capital turnover, and fixed asset turnover to see if any of them are too low (i.e., if there is excessive investment). Similarly, analysts could compare the firm's common-size balance sheet to that of other firms to identify asset categories that appear to be too large.

G. Service Industry Ratios

Ratio analysis is often taught using manufacturing firms as examples, but the service sector is now very large. As a result, some contrasts in ratios merit mention. Pure service organizations, such as executive search firms, software firms, or education and training companies, rely on human talent much more than physical assets. These kinds of companies typically have small investments in buildings and land, and many prefer to lease facilities rather than own them.

Balance sheets of service companies have proportionately higher levels of current assets and lower levels of fixed assets, and they often have a large proportion of current assets, particularly accounts receivable. These firms frequently display little debt because they do not have much investment in fixed assets to support and they ordinarily have no investment in operating inventory to finance.

Income statements of service companies show large amounts for salaries and wages because employees are their biggest cost. Depending upon the type of business, supply costs can be proportionately large, but the types of operating and financing expenses that are typical for a manufacturing firm are much smaller for service companies.

Ratio analysis for service firms is quite valid, but the numerical values for the ratios will be different and the relative importance of certain ratios will also be different. In the context of the DuPont equation, profit margin and asset turnover are still important, but profit margin is more important and asset turnover is less important compared to a manufacturing firm. This is because the service firm has relatively few assets, but the firm must take great care to control salary expenses because this is its dominant expense category.

Relative to a manufacturing firm, working capital turnover will have more importance and fixed asset turnover will have less importance for a service firm, and the current and quick ratios will be a bit more important. This is because liquidity concerns tend to be most important in businesses primarily characterized by short-term assets and liabilities.

H. Strengths and Limitations of Ratio Analysis

Financial ratios and performance measurement calculations reveal a great deal about a company's financial and operating condition. Their primary advantages include the following:

- They are easily computed and widely used.
- The information necessary for calculations is obtained easily.
- They facilitate comparisons between companies.

On the other hand, ratio analysis has limitations. The significant disadvantages include the following:

- Ratios assess historical performance at fixed points in time. Therefore, they do not capture intra-period variations, nor are they necessarily indicative of future performance.
- Ratios should not be used in isolation; instead, they must be analyzed on either a comparative basis (i.e., compared with other companies or industry averages) or on a trend basis (i.e., compared to values in prior periods).
- Ratios summarize accounting information, but may not reflect economic value.
- Ratios do not reflect qualitative values, such as business strategies or managerial talent.
- The use of different accounting methods may reduce the validity of comparisons between firms.

VI. PERFORMANCE MEASUREMENT

Once planning is complete and decisions are made, the ongoing performance of a company's operations must be monitored and evaluated. Budgets provide one benchmark against which performance is assessed. Several other measures, which are described below, are used frequently for evaluating projects, divisions, subsidiaries, or business units.

To illustrate these measures, consider information from the balance sheet in Exhibit 18.1 and the income statement in Exhibit 18.2.

A. Return on Investment (ROI)

ROI is calculated as the profit per dollar of invested capital:

$$\text{ROI} = \frac{\text{Net Income}}{\text{Invested Capital}} = \frac{\text{Net Income}}{\text{Long-Term Debt + Equity}}$$

$$= \frac{\$850}{\$3{,}900 + \$8{,}200} = \frac{\$850}{\$12{,}100} = 0.0702\text{, or } 7.02\%$$

ROI has intuitive appeal, but suffers as a performance measure for several reasons.

First, if the ROI calculation does not include the full period being measured, then it may provide a misleading indication of performance in cases where cash flows are not distributed evenly over time. For example, if the ROI in the example was calculated over a six-month period, and $520 of the $850 expected over the year occurred during that period, then the computed six-month ROI would be $520/$12,100 (or 4.3%), which would represent an 8.6% annual rate. An estimated ROI of 8.6% annually exaggerates the actual annual ROI.

Second, ROI does not include a charge for the cost of the capital invested in the project. By not considering this cost, funds supporting the assets are implicitly free.

The third and greatest limitation of ROI as a performance measure is that it may lead a company's management to reject a positive NPV project if the project results in the decline of a given business unit's ROI. Suppose a business unit experiences a 20% ROI, but a proposed addition to this unit promises a 16% ROI. If the investment is funded, then it will increase the business unit's assets and reduce its ROI. If the cost of capital is 10%, then the asset investment will increase the firm's value because it will have a positive NPV and should therefore be made.

B. Residual Income (RI)

RI overcomes two limitations of ROI. First, it assigns a charge to the invested capital. Second, RI is an amount of profit (or loss), whereas ROI is a rate of return. If profit exceeds the charge for capital, then RI is an amount of profit—a residual above the capital cost. If it is less, then RI is an amount of loss. The formula for RI is:

$$\text{RI} = \text{Net Income} - (\text{Invested Capital} \times \text{Cost of Capital})$$

The previous example was based on a $12,100 investment and an $850 profit. Determine RI by adding a capital cost of 10%, as follows:

$$\text{RI} = \$850 - (\$12{,}100 \times 0.10) = \$850 - \$1{,}210 = -\$360$$

The RI after the capital charge is a negative $360. In other words, the firm has lost $360 of accounting value after the capital cost is deducted. RI shows why a comparison of value cannot be performed meaningfully without considering the cost of capital. The biggest drawback to RI is that it only reflects the absolute profit with no mention of the amount of capital needed to earn that profit. An RI of $100 on an investment of $100 is more valuable than an RI of $100 on an investment of $1,000,000.

C. Free Cash Flow (FCF)

FCF is also a type of RI analysis, but in addition to accounting for capital costs, it also includes adjustments for noncash items and for working capital investments. Its primary objective is to determine the amount of effective cash flow available to a company after all necessary investments have been accounted for. To this end, it is used extensively in the analysis of new or high-growth companies, especially by the providers of venture capital. The most commonly used version of the FCF calculation is as follows:

$$\text{FCF} = \text{Net Income} + (\text{Depreciation and Amortization}) - \text{Change in Working Capital} - \text{Capital Expenditures}$$

Using the information from the sample financial statements, the FCF for the company is calculated as follows:[3]

$$\text{FCF} = \$850 + \$200 - \$500 - \$900 = -\$350$$

3. The change in working capital is the net of the changes in the working capital accounts (A/R, inventory, and A/P), as shown on the statement of cash flows.

FCF can also be calculated using the operating cash flow figure from the statement of cash flows and then subtracting capital expenditures, yielding the same result:

$$\text{FCF} = \text{Cash from Operating Activities} - \text{Capital Expenditures}$$

$$= \$550 - \$900 = -\ \$350$$

Because FCF represents the cash that a company is able to generate after laying out the money required to maintain or expand its asset base, it is considered a better representation of the value of the firm to shareholders.

The FCF calculated above is negative, but it is important to note that negative FCF is not bad in and of itself. If free cash flow is negative, then it could be a sign that a company is growing quickly and/or making large investments. If this growth can be supported and the investments earn a high return, then the strategy has the potential to pay off in the long run. In this example, the company's revenues have grown by 20% from the prior to the current year, and the company has made large investments in both working capital and fixed assets. As has been indicated, a negative FCF is not unusual in this situation.

D. Economic Value Added (EVA)

EVA isolates the funds available to all suppliers of capital and then relates that total to the amount of capital supplied. The reason it is termed *economic value* is because value is created only if the firm earns a rate of return that exceeds its cost of capital (WACC). RI approaches this idea, but it does not provide the best measure of "profit."

The return measure typically used in EVA is operating income, or EBIT. One assumption in EVA analysis is that reinvestment in assets must occur in the amount of the depreciation and amortization if the business is to continue in its present form and size. The reinvestment in assets does not appear on the income statement because it is not an expense. Nonetheless, it is a cash outflow, which makes EBIT the appropriate measure for the purpose of computing EVA.[4] The amount of cash available to all suppliers of long-term debt and equity is found by multiplying EBIT by the difference of one minus the tax rate.

EVA (in thousands) can be computed using the information from the balance sheet in Exhibit 18.1 and the income statement in Exhibit 18.2, and assuming a 10% WACC. The tax rate needed in the formula that follows is found by dividing taxes by net profit before taxes in the income statement (i.e., \$450/\$1,300, or 34.615%).

$$\text{EVA} = \text{EBIT}(1 - \text{Tax Rate}) - (\text{WACC})(\text{Long-Term Debt} + \text{Equity})$$

$$= \$1,600\ (1 - 0.34615) - (0.10)(\$3,900 + \$8,200)$$

$$= \$1,600\ (0.65385) - (0.10)(\$12,100)$$

$$= \$1,046 - \$1,210 = -\ \$164$$

In this example, the company has a negative EVA. As with the case of the negative FCF, this is not necessarily a problem, as the negative EVA could be due to increases in the capital base that have not yet generated earnings. While growth can cause a negative EVA, a negative EVA is usually due to the expansion in capital base required to fund the growth. If revenue is growing, but the capital base is not expanding significantly and the company still has a negative EVA, then it could indicate that the additional sales are not generating sufficient profit to add value.

4. There are many variations for EVA calculations and some instances where EBITDA is used rather than EBIT in the calculation, especially for companies with high levels of depreciation/amortization or for LBOs. The formula presented in this section is the one that is most commonly used for EVA.

In the absence of this growth, however, a different interpretation could be made. Based on the WACC and the amount of long-term funds invested in the firm, investors expect the firm to generate $1,210 as a return on their investment. When this amount, termed a *capital charge*, is levied against the amount available, as measured by *EBIT(1 – Tax Rate)*, EVA is determined to be a negative $164. While this may not be a problem in the short run, if the firm were to continue to generate a negative EVA after the growth has slowed down to a more normal rate, then investors will bid down the firm's stock price because the firm's management failed to produce the amount of value expected. This would be the case even if the firm had positive returns on sales and assets.

EVA is a true measure of economic profit or loss, and is accepted in the professional financial community. Many firms use it to gauge their performance, to test the economic advantage of proposed investments, or in some cases, to determine management compensation. There are three generic ways in which EVA can be increased through intelligent asset management:

- Improve operating efficiency so that more EBIT is generated on the existing asset base.
- Invest additional capital in assets that earn a rate of return that exceeds the cost of capital.
- Eliminate assets that earn a rate of return that is less than the cost of capital.

Many companies implement EVA as a management tool to provide a practical, periodic performance measure for the overall company and for individual divisions and/or operating units. When used at the divisional and/or operating unit level, the parent company allocates capital to the individual units. EVA is used by the parent to determine the difference between the unit's net operating profit (EBIT) and a charge for capital (WACC). Managers are encouraged to devise and implement plans that increase EVA.

EVA is also useful for assessing management's longer-term performance because it can be linked to a company's stock price through a measure called *market value added (MVA)*. EVA is a year-by-year computation, but MVA represents the accumulated impact of successive EVA results since the firm's inception.

MVA is observable and measured as the market value of a company's debt and equity less its book value of debt and equity. If the market value of the firm's long-term debt and equity exceeds the book value, then the company's management has created value for shareholders; if it is less, then management has reduced shareholder value. Many large, well-known companies report positive accounting profits and produce positive cash flows while reducing shareholder value because they fail to earn their cost of capital.

VII. FINANCIAL ANALYSIS AND RATING AGENCIES

Most publicly issued debt by corporations and municipalities is rated by one or more of the credit rating agencies, which are companies that assign credit ratings for issuers of certain types of debt obligations, as well as for the debt instruments themselves. (These agencies are discussed in more detail in Chapter 11, Short-Term Investing and Borrowing).

In some cases, the ratings will apply to a specific issue and in other cases to the issuer in general. The common format is for the issuer to contract with a rating agency, which evaluates the creditworthiness of an issue or the issuer and provides a rating that can be made available to potential investors in that organization's debt issues.

While the ratings and their meanings are covered in more detail in Chapter 11, the purpose of this section is to understand what part the analysis of the organization's accounting statements and ratios play in the ratings process. The purpose of most debt ratings is to attempt to provide the investor with a measure of the credit risk involved in a debt issue (or with the issuer in general). The first part of this risk is the probability of default, or the chance that the issuer will not be able to make payments on the debt as promised. The second part of the risk is known as *loss given default*, or in the event of a default, how much of the money owed to the lender can be recovered either through the seizure and sale of any collateral assets, or through the settlement or bankruptcy process. In most cases, credit rating agencies include both considerations as part of their analyses and in the ratings they assign to publicly issued debt.

Credit ratings are also assigned internally by banks and other lenders, as well as by trade creditors to a business. Regardless of the entity that assigns these ratings, they generally have both quantitative and qualitative factors as part of their analyses. While the quantitative factors are often based on either financial variables or on ratios related to these variables, this is only part of the overall analysis. Depending on the type of credit involved, the qualitative factors may be even more important in the overall analysis. The two largest rating agencies, Moody's and Standard & Poor's, both state that their ratings are produced using a balanced mix of both quantitative and qualitative factors, and that these factors vary significantly by issue, issuer, industry, and country of location. For many other lenders to corporations and government entities, the approach is similar in that an analysis of financial information is only a part of the credit ratings (or credit-granting) decision.

VIII. SUMMARY

The basic function of FP&A is to perform budgeting and forecasting to inform management, manage external expectations, and keep the company on track toward its financial goals. This chapter discussed cost behavior in typical organizations and looked at how financial information is used for internal planning, decision making, and performance measurement. As part of that discussion, financial statement analysis and the ratios typically used for financial statement analysis were introduced. This was followed by an overview of some commonly used internal performance measures, such as return on investment (ROI) and economic value added (EVA). The chapter closed with a review of financial analysis as it applies to external parties such as credit rating agencies and lenders.

TEST YOUR UNDERSTANDING: CHAPTER 19

Answers are on pages 728–731.

1. What are the three categories of costs (and examples of each) that must be considered in product planning, capital budgeting, cost/benefit analysis, and financial plan development?
2. What are the differences between operating leverage and financial leverage?
3. What is a break-even analysis, and how is it used in a cost/benefit analysis?
4. What are the differences between net present value (NPV) and internal rate of return (IRR)?
5. How is sensitivity analysis used in investment risk analysis?
6. What are the three main methods of assessing investment risk?
7. What is RAROC?
8. What is the difference between total asset turnover and current asset turnover?
9. What is the cash conversion efficiency ratio, and how is it used?
10. Compare and contrast the times interest earned (TIE) ratio and the fixed-charge coverage ratio.
11. How are performance ratios (e.g., gross profit margin and operating profit margin) utilized in evaluating a firm's performance?
12. What is integrated ratio analysis?
13. What makes service industry ratios different from typical manufacturing firm ratios?
14. What are the primary advantages and disadvantages of ratio analysis?
15. Compare and contrast return on investment (ROI) and residual income (RI) as measures of performance.
16. What is the economic value added (EVA) concept?
17. What are the two chief components of the master budget?

CHAPTER 20
Financial Decisions and Management

I. INTRODUCTION

II. CAPITAL STRUCTURE OF A COMPANY
A. Optimal and Target Capital Structures
B. Trade-Offs Between Financing with Long-Term Debt and Common Stock
C. Capital Structure Theory
D. Business and Financial Risk
E. Target Capital Structure
F. Other Considerations in the Capital Structure Decision
G. Capital Structure in Not-For-Profit Organizations

III. RAISING AND MANAGING LONG-TERM CAPITAL
A. Raising Capital
B. Managing Outstanding Capital

IV. COST OF CAPITAL AND FIRM VALUE
A. Capital Components and Costs
B. Cost of Debt
C. Cost of Common Equity
D. Weighted Average Cost of Capital (WACC)
E. Firm Value

V. LEASE FINANCING AND MANAGEMENT

A. Why Companies Lease
B. Types of Leases
C. Estimated Residual Value
D. Tax Considerations for Leases
E. Lease versus Borrow-and-Buy Decision

VI. EQUITY FINANCING AND MANAGEMENT

A. Initial Public Offerings (IPOs) and the Decision to List Stock in the United States
B. Shareholder Rights
C. Mergers and Acquisitions
D. At the Market (ATM) Programs

VII. OTHER TOPICS IN FINANCIAL DECISIONS

A. Tax Strategies
B. Dividend Policy
C. Repatriation of Capital for Multinational Companies (MNCs)
D. Market Analysis and Research Tools

VIII. SUMMARY

I. INTRODUCTION

Among the most critical financial decisions an organization must make are those involving financing capital structure and asset investments. For all for-profit corporations, decisions related to the mix of debt versus equity and dividends must also be considered. While the management of these issues is not always part of treasury's responsibility, treasury is frequently involved with them, and in some companies directly responsible. Whether directly responsible or not, it is important that treasury professionals have a grasp of the basic issues involved because of their potential impact on treasury operations and the overall success of an organization.

While some of this material is introduced in Chapter 19, Financial Planning and Analysis, this chapter takes a deeper look into the issues related to capital management. Discussions in this chapter include capital structure, as well as the overall cost of capital and its impact on firm value, lease financing, and equity management. The chapter concludes with an overview of tax strategy, dividend policy, and repatriation of capital.

II. CAPITAL STRUCTURE OF A COMPANY

Any company requires new capital to finance growth. Capital can be acquired externally through debt issuance or stock sales, or internally through profit retention. The term *capital structure* of a company refers to the mix of long-term debt (in the form of term loans and various types of bonds) and equity (in the form of preferred stock, common stock, and retained earnings). The mix of long-term debt and equity influences the cost of each form and the overall cost of capital. The decision on what this mix should be is sometimes referred to as *the financing decision*. This section of the chapter discusses:

- Optimal capital structure
- Target capital structure
- How the cost of funds and the overall capital structure change as the degree of indebtedness changes
- How a company should raise funds in a particular circumstance to increase firm value

A. Optimal and Target Capital Structures

An optimal capital structure is the mix of long-term debt and equity that produces the lowest overall weighted average cost of capital (WACC). As discussed in Chapter 9, Working Capital Metrics, firm value depends partly upon the spread between the return on total assets (ROTA) and WACC. Therefore, the firm should attempt to identify the debt-equity mix that minimizes WACC and finance itself using that mix. Although much research has been conducted on the theory of optimal capital structure, what has emerged is, at best, a general understanding of how debt and equity interplay to influence WACC in the debt-equity mix. The most widely accepted explanation is discussed later in the chapter.

Chief financial officers and treasurers should attempt to identify the optimal capital structure. Then, they must factor in all of the following:

- The company's operating risks
- Its immediate and expected long-term financing needs
- The relative costs of debt and equity at the time funds must be raised
- The risk-taking attitude of the board of directors and senior management

After completing the analysis, financial managers can estimate the best practical mix of long-term debt and equity. This estimated "best" mix is known as the *target capital structure*. If the firm does not use the target capital structure presently, it should consider it when choosing between debt and equity financing in the future. Issuing debt will increase relative indebtedness, whereas issuing equity or financing via retained earnings will reduce it.

B. Trade-Offs Between Financing with Long-Term Debt and Common Stock

Considerations surrounding the use of long-term debt versus equity deserve mention before discussing capital structure theory. The advantages of using long-term debt (especially from the perspective of equity shareholders) are:

- Debt costs less than equity because it has historically been less risky to investors and the interest payments on debt are tax deductible to the firm (whereas dividends paid are not deductible).
- Long-term debt instruments provide either a fixed or floating rate of return to investors. If funds obtained through debt are invested to earn a rate of return in excess of the interest rate on the debt, earnings above those needed to service the debt go to the shareholders.
- Capital markets for long-term debt are generally efficient, especially for debt issues that are well rated. In normal markets, there is typically an adequate supply of investor funds to purchase large debt issues across a broad range of risk and repayment characteristics.[1]
- If funds are raised by selling debt rather than equity, the number of outstanding shares of common stock will not be increased, and earnings will therefore not be diluted. Stock dilution is discussed in more detail later in this chapter.
- Owners of the company's debt do not vote in elections for members of the board of directors or for any other matter put before shareholders for a vote. This is viewed as an advantage by the equity shareholders of the company.

The disadvantages of financing with long-term debt (from the equity shareholders' perspective) are:

- Debt has priority of claim over equity. In the event of liquidation, debt claims are paid before any equity claims. Payments for debt service are paid from pretax earnings, while equity payments (usually in the form of dividends) are paid from after-tax earnings.
- Required interest and principal payments on debt must be paid in full and in a timely fashion or the suppliers of debt have cause for action against the company. In the extreme, an inability to make required debt payments may lead to bankruptcy.
- Debt increases the financial risk of the company and if used beyond a certain amount relative to equity will increase the cost of capital (WACC).

1. The Recession of 2009 demonstrated that efficient operation of capital markets can be impacted severely by unusual economic conditions. Markets in developing countries may also be inefficient due to the local conditions and market participants. Over the long run, however, most capital markets (especially those in developed countries) have proven to be broad-based and efficient.

- Debt can be accompanied by liens on assets. Consequently, it limits management's flexibility in managing the assets.
- Debt suppliers place monitoring requirements on the company to ensure it adheres to the covenant and reporting requirements specified in the indenture or loan agreement. These monitoring requirements entail a cost borne by the company.

The advantages of financing with common stock are:

- Stock does not obligate a company to make fixed payments to investors.
- Stock does not mature.
- For creditors, stock offers a cushion against losses (i.e., the larger the amount of equity, the greater the losses that can be absorbed without the company becoming insolvent). Additionally, if a company expects to be profitable in the future, equity may be raised on attractive terms.

The disadvantages of common stock financing are:

- The sale of common stock may extend voting rights and control to more shareholders.
- The dilution of shareholder value may be an issue. (Dilution is discussed in more detail later in this chapter.)
- The cost of underwriting, or issuing, common stock is significant when compared with other sources of capital (i.e., stocks are expensive to issue relative to bonds).
- Common equity financing does not enjoy the tax shield (i.e., deductibility of interest expense) that debt financing provides, and the after-tax cost of equity capital is usually higher than that for debt capital.
- Increasing the number of common shares will automatically reduce earnings per share in the short run, assuming that income remains constant. This can lead to a reduction in stock price if the market reacts negatively to that reduction and assumes that the company will not be able to use the new capital to increase earnings enough to maintain or increase the expected earnings per share.

C. Capital Structure Theory

There are several theories that attempt to explain how companies arrive at the capital structures they exhibit. In terms of research and discussion in traditional financial management texts, the trade-off theory is the approach most often used to illustrate capital structure for a company.

The theory's essential idea is that companies "trade off" the use of debt and equity in their capital structures until they obtain the lowest WACC. Suppose a firm was financed entirely by equity. The capital cost is simply the cost of equity. If a small amount of debt was then substituted for equity in the capital structure, the WACC would decrease because (1) debt costs less than equity, and (2) the cost of each source would still be low since the capital structure would represent little risk. The debt ratio would be very low, and coverage ratios, such as times interest earned, would be very high. (Capital and debt ratios are discussed in Chapter 19, Financial Planning and Analysis.) As more debt is substituted for equity, the WACC would continue to decline because less expensive debt is substituted for more expensive equity, even though the cost of debt and equity rises slightly as the company's debt ratio increases and as coverage ratios decrease. The WACC decreases as indebtedness increases.

At some degree of indebtedness, however, adding more debt will cause the WACC to increase. The rising cost of debt and equity in response to the increasing risk to investors will cause their weighted average to increase. After this point, adding debt will lead to higher debt, equity, and overall capital costs. So as debt is substituted for equity in the firm's capital structure, as illustrated in Exhibit 20.1, the overall cost of capital (WACC) at first decreases as debt is increased and then rises as more debt is added. The mix of debt and equity associated with the lowest WACC is technically the optimal capital structure.

EXHIBIT 20.1 **COST OF CAPITAL**

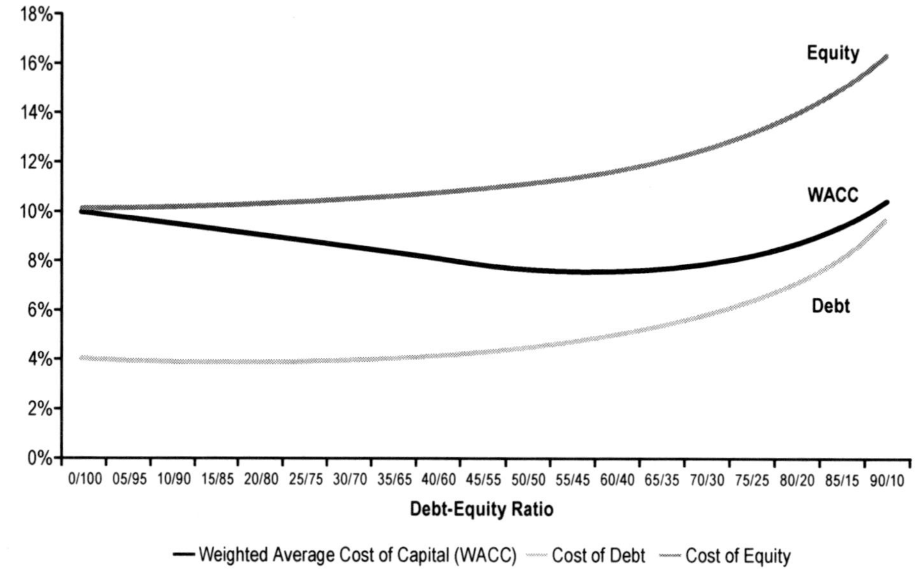

While the idea of an optimal capital structure based on this trade-off between the benefits and costs of debt is appealing as a theory, in the real world there are other factors that must be considered. For example, some industries (e.g., regulated power utilities) often have generally high debt ratios due to a large asset base that can be used as collateral and as a stable stream of cash flow. For most companies, the trade-off approach is used along with other factors relevant to both the firm individually and its industry, which are then used to arrive at a target capital structure. This target is used to raise new capital as the firm requires it. This concept of a target capital structure is covered in detail later in this chapter.

D. Business and Financial Risk

In determining a company's capital structure policy, the total risk of the company's operations and financing must be considered. Total risk comprises business and financial risks. Business risk is related to the stability and predictability of a company's revenue stream. The greater the revenue volatility, the greater the business risk. This is the primary reason that a seller of staple foods (e.g., a bread baker) has a lower stock beta[2] than a seller of microprocessors operating in a volatile and competitive computer market. Financial risk is related to the variability in net profit after tax, usually due to fixed costs of financing. These types of risk, or leverage, are discussed in this chapter; other forms of risk are discussed in Chapter 15, Operational and Enterprise Risk Management, and Chapter 16, Financial Risk Management.

1. OPERATING RISK AND OPERATING LEVERAGE

Operating risk is a function of the mix of variable and fixed costs in a company's operations. It is assessed by looking at how operating income (i.e., earnings before interest and taxes, or EBIT) responds to revenue changes. A firm with high fixed operating costs and low variable operating costs will have an EBIT that varies more in response to sales changes than one with high variable costs and low fixed costs. This is because fixed costs are imbedded costs that must be covered by revenue before operating profit is positive, but when they are combined with low variable costs, operating profit is able to expand rapidly after fixed costs are covered by revenue. Operating profit can be leveraged off of fixed costs. The measure of this leverage, called the *degree of operating leverage*, shows the responsiveness of operating profit to changes in sales. The measure is computed as:

$$\text{Degree of Operating Leverage} = \frac{\text{\% Change in EBIT}}{\text{\% Change in Sales}}$$

Exhibit 20.2 shows a firm whose sales have increased 20%, but whose operating profit has increased 33% because fixed costs are stable at $2,000. For these particular levels of revenue, the degree of operating leverage is:

$$\text{Degree of Operating Leverage} = \frac{33\%}{20\%} = 1.65$$

The percentage change in EBIT is 1.65 times as much as the percentage change in sales. Alternatively expressed, EBIT is 1.65 times as volatile as sales, in a proportionate sense. Note that operating leverage works when sales decrease, too. If sales decline, EBIT will decline proportionately faster.

2. Beta is a measure of stock price volatility and is covered in Chapter 12, Long-Term and Capital Investments.

EXHIBIT 20.2 **OPERATING AND FINANCIAL LEVERAGE**

OPERATING LEVERAGE (OL) IS THE RESULT OF FIXED COSTS IN OPERATIONS.
FINANCIAL LEVERAGE (FL) RESULTS FROM FIXED FINANCING COSTS (INTEREST).

ASSUMPTIONS:
VARIABLE OPERATING COSTS ARE 50% OF SALES.
FIXED OPERATING COSTS ARE $2,000.
INTEREST EXPENSE IS $1,000.
THE TAX RATE IS 40%.

ACCOUNT	YEAR 2XX0 $ AMOUNT		YEAR 2XX1 $ AMOUNT			CHANGE
SALES		10,000		12,000	OL	+20%
LESS: VARIABLE COSTS (50%)	(5,000)		(6,000)			
FIXED COSTS	(2,000)	(7,000)	(2,000)	(8,000)		
OPERATING PROFIT (EBIT)		3,000		4,000	FL	+33%
LESS: INTEREST		(1,000)		(1,000)		
TAXABLE INCOME		2,000		3,000		
LESS: TAXES (40%)		(800)		(1,200)		
NET INCOME		1,200		1,800		+50%

2. FINANCIAL RISK AND FINANCIAL LEVERAGE

Financial risk is a function of the mix of capital sources used to finance a company and is assessed by looking at how net income responds to changes in operating income, or EBIT. Just as operating leverage results from fixed operating expenses, financial leverage results from fixed financing expenses (e.g., interest). The more debt in the capital structure, the higher the interest payment(s). Larger fixed interest expense will cause net income to be more volatile in response to changes in operating income. Interest is a fixed financing cost of $1,000 in Exhibit 20.2. As a result, a 33% increase in EBIT results in a 50% increase in net income.

The relationship between the change in operating profit and the change in net income is termed the *degree of financial leverage*. It is defined as:

$$\text{Degree of Financial Leverage} = \frac{\text{\% Change in Net Income}}{\text{\% Change in EBIT}}$$

Using the information in Exhibit 20.2, the degree of financial leverage can be calculated as follows:

$$\text{Degree of Financial Leverage} = \frac{50\%}{33\%} = 1.515$$

Net income will increase proportionately 1.515 times as fast as EBIT. Again, the dynamic works in reverse. If EBIT declines, net income will decline proportionately faster.

Exhibit 20.2 shows that operating and financial leverage work together. The percentage increase in net income is 2.50 times that of revenue when revenue increases from $10,000 to $12,000 (+50% versus +20%). Since the two types of leverage work together, a firm must take careful note of its degree of operating leverage when deciding on a capital structure.

The best operating processes for most companies are dictated by the nature of their business. For example, manufacturing companies tend to have high fixed costs. This is because a heavy investment in equipment generally is necessary to obtain the lowest overall unit cost at the expected level of sales. And a large investment in equipment tends to be accompanied by high fixed costs. Alternatively, agricultural operations can have high variable and lower fixed costs because the costs of sowing, tending, and harvesting crops can be variable. A firm with high operating leverage, therefore, can tolerate less financial leverage than a firm with low operating leverage. As a result, firms with high operating leverage tend to have proportionately less debt in their capital structures than firms with low operating leverage.

E. Target Capital Structure

In addition to leverage, there are a number of other factors that companies need to consider in determining the best mix of debt and equity for raising new capital. These include:

1. Asset structure
2. Overall business risk
3. Shareholder control
4. Profitability (both historic and projected)
5. Market conditions

1. ASSET STRUCTURE

The asset structure of the company is also important to the capital structure decision. Companies, and industries in general, will have a composition of assets that is required for their line of business. By their nature, large manufacturers must have a large base of fixed assets (e.g., plant and equipment) to produce their products. Retailers need buildings and inventory; large oil companies need wells, refineries, and perhaps a network of retail outlets to sell their fuel; and service industries may need little in the way of physical assets for their operations. In some cases, the assets held by a company may be suitable for using as collateral for long-term debt. In this case, the company may use those assets to support a higher level of debt than would a company of similar size in a less capital-intensive industry.

2. OVERALL BUSINESS RISK

The overall business risk of a company usually relates to its variability in operating profitability. The less general the business risk, and thus the more stable the cash flow stream, the easier it is for a firm to consistently have funds available to service the fixed nature of long-term debt. Therefore, a company with a very stable operating profit stream would be able to have a higher debt level than a similar firm with a more variable stream. A regulated power utility is normally an example of a company with very stable operating profitability. Its revenues (rates) may be regulated, but as a monopoly, there is little uncertainty about the continuation of those revenues. The primary operating expense is often fuel costs, and while these may be unpredictable, the utility can typically pass these fluctuations on to their customers. Combine this stability of profits with a large asset base that can be used as collateral, and it is easy to see why these types of companies can usually support high levels of debt.

3. SHAREHOLDER CONTROL

The next general issue relating to capital structure is that of a desire on the part of management and the existing shareholders to maintain control of the company. Issuing new debt or equity has differing impacts relating to control of the company. In general, when new equity is issued, the existing shareholders may find their ownership stake in the company diluted. This dilution occurs because as new shareholders are brought into the company, the percentage ownership and earnings per share (EPS) of the existing shareholders decline.[3] Current shareholders may therefore prefer that new capital be raised in the form of debt rather than equity, to avoid this dilution problem.

4. PROFITABILITY

The next factor to be considered in relation to capital structure is that of profitability. Profitability is important because it represents a possible source of funding for the company, and it is an internal, rather than an external, source (i.e., the firm does not have go to the capital markets to raise these funds). The primary example of this type of funding is retained earnings, which are accumulated profits that have not been distributed to shareholders as dividends, but rather have been kept by the firm.

The retained earnings that appear in the equity section of a balance sheet are not immediately accessible funds. These funds have been distributed throughout the firm's assets through reinvestment. When profits are high, managers tend to finance a company's growth by retaining earnings rather than by borrowing funds. Then, as profits return to a normal level and/or as interest rates decline, managers may prefer to borrow funds. Over the long run, therefore, a company's use of debt may be impacted significantly by that company's ability to generate profits and keep retained earnings (e.g., equity) as part of its capital structure.

A related issue is the impact that new shares can have on earnings per share (EPS). While increasing capital by selling additional shares can be the right decision from a cost and profitability point of view, it also has the potential to reduce EPS unless the firm is able to use the new capital to produce sufficient additional earnings to offset the dilutive effect of the new shares. And even if overall profitability increases, reduced EPS can lower the market value of the firm's stock.

5. MARKET CONDITIONS

Overall market conditions also play a part in the question of debt versus equity in a company's capital structure. There are times when the stock market has been "booming" (e.g., the US stock market in the late 1990s), resulting in high stock prices and relatively "cheap" equity as a source of capital. During these periods, companies may choose to issue new stock because of its relatively low cost compared to market interest rates. There are also times when the stock

3. Some corporate charters provide preemptive rights to existing shareholders that require them to have the first rights to buy any new equity issues in proportion to their current ownership. While this right is included in many corporations, it is not a standard right in many US-based companies. Even where there are preemptive rights, the existing shareholders must still provide additional capital to the company if they want to maintain their current percentage ownership. Shareholders that either cannot or will not come up with the additional investment will find their ownership in the company diluted.

market is low and interest rates are very low (e.g., 2009 to 2010), giving debt a relative advantage. Company management should always look at current and expected market conditions in determining which source of capital can be raised most easily and inexpensively. Investment bankers can be a good source of expertise in assessing current and projected market conditions.

6. DETERMINING THE TARGET CAPITAL STRUCTURE

Based on an analysis of all of these factors, the board and management of a company will determine a target capital structure that will be used for raising new capital as it is needed. In most cases, the target is generally a range of values (e.g., a debt percentage between 40% and 60%) that the company may move between over time. Though this range may vary considerably between industries and from company to company within an industry, the range is set so that the value of the company and its WACC will not vary significantly within this range. When companies are toward the lower end of their debt range, they are usually said to have significant debt capacity. This means that they can add debt easily without negatively impacting the company's value. Companies that are toward the high end of this range are said to have little debt capacity, meaning that issuing more debt will likely cause a decrease in the company's value.

Needless to say, financial managers would generally choose to be at the lower end of the range, as this offers the most flexibility in terms of being able to raise capital. The other consideration, however, is that there are many forces over which the company may have little or no control that move it along this range. A period of high profitability might move the company toward the lower end, as it has more retained earnings and thus higher levels of equity financing. The availability of capital (long-term) investments will also have an impact. A company that is growing quickly, and is making large investments in fixed assets and working capital, may not be able to generate sufficient internal funding (e.g., retained earnings). It therefore may have to raise external debt and/or equity to maintain its growth. As mentioned previously, the general costs and market availability of debt and equity capital will also have an impact on how capital is raised. And while the obvious goal is to minimize the cost of capital (WACC), this must often be balanced against the need to preserve overall financial flexibility to meet future needs. In the end, the capital structure observed for a given firm at any point in time may be more a function of historical profits, investments, and markets than a conscious decision on management's part to maintain a specific mix of debt and equity.

F. Other Considerations in the Capital Structure Decision

In addition to the major factors just discussed, there are some additional items that can impact the financing decision (i.e., the determination of the target capital structure). These include rating agency and lender requirements, control of the firm, and regulatory restrictions, including minimum capital requirements.

1. RATING AGENCY AND LENDER CONSIDERATIONS

Because rating agencies, by implication, and lenders, per loan requirements, often impose constraints on management's actions, they impact a company's capital structure. Regardless of what management or equity holders believe is the optimal capital structure, lenders may require a more conservative level of debt to protect their interests. For example, debt covenants may specify a required maximum debt ratio, minimum coverage ratios, conditions to be met before dividends can be paid or increased, and limitations on increased indebtedness or the types of debt that can be issued. Rating agencies will also provide guidelines on capital ratios needed to qualify for particular ratings. As a result, management has to bear in mind its desired rating when it evaluates changing the company's capital structure.

For some companies, the various debt covenants of different lenders, or the requirements to maintain an investment-grade bond rating, leave management with limited flexibility in establishing a target capital structure. Management may decide to limit certain actions so as to keep in line with expected covenants. Therefore, if the company does have to borrow, it will be able to qualify for the best possible rate.

Lenders routinely include a ratings trigger in loan agreements. These triggers are clauses in financing agreements that require a company to maintain a certain credit rating. Failure to maintain a specified rating may trigger a higher loan rate or force the company to post additional collateral, take another specified action, or pay back the debt in full.

Such obligations have come under increased scrutiny by the financial community because they can force a company to artificially contort its liquidity position and can contribute to the inability to meet financial obligations. (Ratings triggers contributed significantly in many high-profile financial collapses.) Rating agencies routinely require companies to disclose triggers that they have in financing arrangements to evaluate whether the company can survive a ratings downgrade. A ratings downgrade is serious because it may initiate a spiral of events that result in a series of cross defaults[4] on debt.

2. THE ISSUE OF CONTROL

Control of a company is an important issue in determining capital structure. If a company issues too much equity, it dilutes the stock value, creating the potential for new shareholders to purchase shares at a lower price and potentially take control. A lower stock price also makes a company more vulnerable to unwelcome takeover attempts and activist shareholder activities. On the other hand, if management uses too much debt, it risks bankruptcy, resulting in creditors taking control. Too much debt will also eventually limit an organization's access to further debt financing for future projects. This can lead to having to choose between financing new projects with stock offerings that may result in loss of control or forgoing profitable growth opportunities that could benefit the firm.

3. REGULATORY RESTRICTIONS AND MINIMUM CAPITAL REQUIREMENTS

Countries often have regulatory restrictions that must be met to do business within that country. A major concern in this area is so-called thinly capitalized, or thin cap, subsidiaries of multinational companies. A thin cap company has more debt and therefore makes higher interest payments than would normally be possible if it were a stand-alone company. Thin capitalization is typically seen in multinational companies that have a choice of how much debt and how much equity to use in financing foreign subsidiaries since much of the debt and equity is coming from the parent company. The subsidiary is only able to carry the debt load because it is either borrowing from related parties or borrowing from third parties on the strength of group support in the form of guarantees from the parent company. The high level of debt leads to high interest expense paid to the parent, which in turn leads to "excessive" interest deductions in determining local taxes. Because of this, many countries have restrictions on thin capitalization and

4. *Cross default* refers to provisions in a bond indenture or loan agreement that put the borrower in default if the borrower defaults on another obligation.

either require higher rates of capital or limit the interest deductions that may be taken by the subsidiary. In some cases, the interest payments of thin cap subsidiaries are treated as a deemed dividend to the parent company. (Deemed dividends are discussed in more detail later in the chapter.)

In addition, various countries—or even regional governments such as states or provinces—may have specific capital requirements for specific industries. As is discussed in Chapter 2, Regulatory and Legal Environment, commercial banks and other depository institutions typically have restrictions imposed on the type of capital and the minimum levels of capital that must be maintained. Many government entities also impose minimum capital requirements on various types of insurance companies operating within their boundaries. Such requirements ensure that the insurance companies have adequate capital and reserves to meet any claims made against the policies they write. Other industries that typically have regulatory restrictions on capital include utilities, education, and transportation services.

G. Capital Structure in Not-For-Profit Organizations

In not-for-profit organizations (NFPs, which include most charities), capital structure is just as important an issue as it is in for-profit corporations. Though NFPs cannot issue common stock for equity financing, they often can and do have retained earnings (technically referred to as *accumulated excess of income over expenses*). They can also raise the equivalent of equity capital (technically referred to as *net assets*) through government grants and charitable contributions. For example, many governments are concerned about the provision of health care services to their general population. As a result, they often make grants to NFP providers to help offset the costs of services rendered to patients who cannot pay for those services. Further, international organizations often make grants to NFP health providers to help them operate. While some of these grants are nonspecific, they often provide specific services, such as neonatal intensive care to needy infants.

As for charitable contributions, individuals as well as companies are motivated to contribute to NFPs for a variety of reasons. Some of these include concern for the well-being of others, the recognition that often accompanies large contributions, and tax deductibility. As a result, charitable contributions are a significant source of capital for some NFPs.

In addition, the availability of tax-exempt financing provides some NFPs[5] with their own tax-based incentives to issue debt. Depending on the projects the NFP is pursuing and its other sources of capital, the directors of the organization will most likely arrive at a target level of debt for the organization. There may also be targets for the levels of short-term versus long-term debt in the overall financing of the NFP.

5. While many NFPs are tax-exempt (i.e., most charities), many are not (e.g., unions or homeowners associations).

III. RAISING AND MANAGING LONG-TERM CAPITAL

A. Raising Capital

For any company, the ability to raise capital at a reasonable price is one of the primary determinants of long-term success. While small companies primarily use personal capital and borrowed funds from banks, most midsize to large companies also issue some type of debt or equity securities. Many government entities and some not-for-profits use bond issues to raise needed capital in the private or public markets.

Some companies sell debt and equity instruments in the private market rather than (or in addition to) to the general public. The purchaser in a private sale is usually an institutional investor, such as a pension fund, insurance company, bank, or trust company.

The reasons why private placement may be preferred over public issuance include:

- Less restrictive covenants
- Relatively small issue size
- Reduced time to issuance
- Minimal reporting, agency rating, or public disclosure requirements
- Lower costs
- Control over who holds the debt
- Greater flexibility of terms and maturities

There are advantages and disadvantages to raising capital through public offerings. One of the principal advantages is that access to capital markets offers the potential to raise large amounts of debt and equity at prevailing rates. One of the primary disadvantages is the significant cost involved in managing the reporting, disclosure, and rating agency requirements for public security issues.

Initial public offerings (IPOs) require significant disclosure of a company's ownership, business activities, and financial statements. Publicly held companies are required by various regulators, such as the Securities and Exchange Commission (SEC) in the United States, to file a wide variety of forms and reports (e.g., SEC Forms 10-K, 8-K, and 10-Q) on a regular basis. A more detailed discussion of the role of regulators is provided in Chapter 2, Regulatory and Legal Environment. A more detailed discussion of the required regulatory reporting is provided in Chapter 18, Financial Accounting and Reporting.

In addition, the price of capital for a company may fluctuate widely due to factors over which a company has no control. Among these factors are the general economic environment, new technologies, industry issues, government regulations, and public perceptions of a company's future prospects.

When raising and managing capital, an organization must deal with a wide variety of different external parties, including investment bankers, corporate bankers, regulatory agencies, market analysts, rating agencies, auditors, shareholders, and bondholders. Each of these parties requires different types and degrees of information, and each views a corporation from a different perspective. In order for an organization to raise needed capital successfully, the company's treasury professionals must be able to respond to all parties' needs and expectations.

B. Managing Outstanding Capital

Once a company has issued stocks, bonds, or other securities, it must manage the legal and payment requirements for each type of security. To meet this need, treasury professionals often have to manage trustee relationships and responsibilities relative to a company's securities, as well as act as a disbursing agent for shareholder or bondholder payments. Shareholders must receive dividends as declared for preferred and common stock. Bondholders must receive interest and principal payments. Also, any sinking fund obligations (i.e., funds accumulated in a custodial account to retire debt instruments according to a predetermined schedule) or covenants on bond issues must be met. Financial reports must be completed and sent to interested parties in a timely manner, and various reports must be prepared and sent to regulatory agencies. Management also must plan for the future retirement of maturing issues and manage bank credit relationships.

In addition to its trustee and disbursing responsibilities, the treasury department may be responsible for investor relations, including participating in presentations to potential investors to raise capital, sometimes referred to as "road shows." These responsibilities include:

- Maintaining shareholder lists
- Sending out financial statements, annual reports, and other required filings
- Communicating with shareholders and bondholders
- Addressing investors' questions

IV. COST OF CAPITAL AND FIRM VALUE

The overall cost of capital has many applications in the valuation of assets and companies. It is the basic target number that asset returns must exceed if the company is to create shareholder value. In basic terms, financial markets "tell" a company what returns are expected on various types of debt and equity instruments because market return expectations are interpreted as a demand on the company. Such expectations must be met or the market will reduce firm value by bidding down the stock price.[6] The return expectation for a security becomes that source's cost of funds from the company's perspective. The overall cost of capital (or WACC) is obtained by weighting the costs of various funds sources by their proportionate dollar contribution to the company's total long-term financing sources.

A. Capital Components and Costs

The primary sources of a company's "permanent" capital are long-term debt, primarily in the form of bonds, and equity capital in the form of common stock and retained earnings. The relevant cost of these sources is their marginal cost (i.e., the rate of return the market would demand if funds were raised today). It is also important to compute the cost of capital using after-tax costs because they are the relevant costs to a firm.

6. It is important to note that firm value can be affected (often negatively) by industry perceptions or anticipated future trends, even though the company's own financials may be strong.

B. Cost of Debt

The relevant cost of debt is its after-tax cost. For a bond, the pretax rate of cost is its yield to maturity (YTM), or the rate of return earned over a bond's remaining life based on its market price at the date the measure is taken.

YTM is converted to an after-tax rate using the firm's marginal tax rate, as follows:

$$\text{After-Tax } r_D = r_D(1 - T)$$

Where:

After-Tax r_D = After-tax cost of debt

r_D = Yield to maturity on newly issued debt (before tax)

T = Company's marginal income tax rate

Calculation Example: After-Tax Cost of Debt

For example, assuming the before-tax cost of debt (i.e., YTM on bonds) is 5% and the marginal tax rate is 30%, the calculation of the after-tax cost of debt is as follows:

$$\text{After-Tax } r_D = r_D(1 - T)$$

$$= 0.05(1 - 0.30) = 0.035, \text{ or } 3.5\%$$

For this firm, the after-tax cost of debt is 3.5%, which means that the ability to treat interest as a tax-deductible expense has effectively lowered this company's debt costs by 1.5% on an overall basis.

In many companies with complicated tax liabilities, the marginal tax rate may be difficult to estimate from standard financial statements. If the analysis is performed internally, then a company's tax or accounting department may be able to provide an appropriate figure.

The effective cost of debt is its after-tax cost because the interest payments on debt are an expense for tax purposes. The issuance, or flotation, costs associated with debt may be significant for some companies. If so, these costs should be included in the determination of the cost of debt. For most large firms, however, the debt issues are large enough that the flotation cost per dollar raised is not material. In such cases, flotation costs normally are not considered when computing the effective cost of debt. This was assumed in the preceding computations.

C. Cost of Common Equity

Funds from common equity can be raised using two techniques:

- Retain earnings during the period (instead of paying earnings out in dividends).
- Issue new common stock.

The market's required rate of return on equity applies to retained earnings and common stock. The board of directors has the option to pay earnings to stockholders as dividends. If the board chooses to reinvest all or some of the earnings in the business, stockholders expect a rate of return on this investment just as they do when they purchase shares in the stock market. More detailed discussions of equity financing and dividend policy are provided in later sections of this chapter.

The capital asset pricing model (CAPM, introduced in Chapter 12, Long-Term and Capital Investments) may be used to estimate the market's required rate of return on equity. This is the cost that applies to equity funds that are obtained through retained earnings. The cost of issuing new, additional common stock will be a bit higher because the company will receive less per share when shares are sold, due to flotation expenses. Flotation costs are not considered in the CAPM formula that follows:

$$r_E = r_{RF} + (r_M - r_{RF})\beta$$

Where:

r_E = Required rate of return on stockholders' equity

r_{RF} = Expected rate of return on the risk-free asset (e.g., US T-bill rate)

r_M = Expected rate of return on the market portfolio (e.g., S&P 500 index)

ß= Beta value for the company's stock

Calculation Example: Equity Cost of Capital

Assume that the risk-free (e.g., T-bill) rate is 4.0%, the return on the overall stock market is 10.0%, and the beta for the company in question is 1.20. In this case, the cost of equity capital would be determined as follows:

$$r_E = r_{RF} + (r_M - r_{RF})\beta$$

$$= 0.04 + (0.10 - 0.04)(1.20) = 0.112, \text{ or } 11.2\%$$

For this firm, the cost of equity capital is 11.2%, which means any equity funds it raises through retained earnings effectively cost the company 11.2%. In addition, this company's stockholders require an 11.2% equity rate of return from the company.

D. Weighted Average Cost of Capital (WACC)

To determine a company's cost of capital, the company calculates a weighted average of the costs of long-term debt and equity where the weights represent the proportion that each contributes to total long-term financing:

$$WACC = W_D r_D(1 - T) + W_E r_E$$

Where:

W = Percent, or weight, of each financing source (D = debt, and E = equity) in relation to the sum of debt and equity financing

$(r_D)(1 - T)$ = After-tax cost of debt

r_E = Cost of equity (common stock and retained earnings)

Calculation Example: WACC

The following example uses information for the cost of debt and equity as determined in the earlier examples. It also assumes that one-third (33.3%) of total long-term financing is provided by debt and two-thirds (66.7%) is provided by equity:

$$WACC = W_D r_D (1 - T) + W_E r_E$$

$$= [0.333 \times 0.05 \times (1 - 0.3)] + (0.667 \times 0.112) = 0.0864, \text{ or } 8.64\%$$

For this firm, the WACC, or overall cost of capital, is 8.64%. It is an estimate of the market's overall return expectation for this company.

E. Firm Value

In the economic value added (EVA) discussion presented in Chapter 19, Financial Planning and Analysis, it is emphasized that the firm must earn a rate of return on assets that exceeds the cost of capital in order to create shareholder value. The firm in the preceding WACC computation must earn a rate of return on assets above 8.64%. If it earns less, then firm value will fall because market return expectations were not met.

The formula for EVA is:

$$EVA = EBIT(1 - \text{Tax Rate}) - (WACC)(\text{Long-Term Debt} + \text{Equity})$$

Calculation Example: EVA

EVA is determined by after-tax profitability relative to the cost of capital and how much capital is employed. As an example, in addition to the previously calculated WACC and an assumed tax rate of 30%, assume that $50,000,000 of capital (long-term debt and equity) is employed and that the company generated an operating profit of $6,800,000. EVA in this case would be:

$$EVA = EBIT(1 - \text{Tax Rate}) - (WACC)(\text{Long-Term Debt} + \text{Equity})$$

$$= \$6{,}800{,}000(1 - 0.30) - (0.0864)(\$50{,}000{,}000)$$

$$= \$4{,}760{,}000 - \$4{,}320{,}000 = \$440{,}000$$

The positive EVA of $440,000 will cause the company's share price to increase because it is the amount by which the after-tax profit exceeds the required amount of $4,320,000 needed just to satisfy market expectations. The after-tax return on total capital (i.e., net revenue after taxes, divided by long-term debt and equity) can be computed as $4,760,000/$50,000,000, or 9.52%. This result is directly comparable to the 8.64% WACC, which also is computed on an after-tax basis. Value was created (the positive EVA) because the return on capital exceeded the cost of capital.

If the after-tax operating profit was positive but less than $4,320,000, then accounting statements would have reported the profit, and a positive return on assets would have resulted. There may have been positive cash flow as well, but the share price would have been bid down and firm value would have fallen because the return on assets did not meet market expectations.

V. LEASE FINANCING AND MANAGEMENT

For many types of equipment acquisitions, leasing may be considered a substitute for debt. The lease versus borrow-and-buy decision is one of the most important types of analysis for companies acquiring capital assets. The capital asset acquisition process has two general stages:

- **Acquisition:** This is the process by which a company decides to acquire a particular building or other asset, basing the decision on regular capital budgeting procedures. In leasing, the issue of whether to acquire the asset is not a question to be analyzed because the decision to proceed with the project has been made already.
- **Finance:** Once the asset acquisition has been justified, the asset must be financed through borrowing or leasing. (Assets can also be purchased for cash, but then borrowing or leasing is not an issue.) For capital structure purposes, leasing normally has the same effect on capital structure as borrowing, so the cash flows from leasing usually are compared with the cash flows from borrowing funds to purchase the asset.

A. Why Companies Lease

In leasing, the owner of the asset is called the *lessor* and receives lease payments from the *lessee* who has use of the asset. A key reason for leasing is the tax benefit for both the lessor and the lessee. There may be an advantage to using leasing as a source of off-balance-sheet financing or for certain tax incentives.[7] In most cases, long-term lease arrangements may be considered a direct substitute for debt in a company's capital structure. This is especially true for companies with poor credit, which might limit their access to more traditional borrowing. Also, loan and debt covenants may dictate the form and structure of leases for many corporations, although in return, leases may offer fewer restrictions than direct lending covenants.

Leasing is generally an appealing choice for assets with a high potential for technological obsolescence, such as computers, medical equipment, and communications equipment. In this case, when the equipment becomes obsolete, the lease can be terminated and the equipment returned to the lessor. Leasing also may be attractive to start-up companies or companies beginning sales in a new area that have a high level of uncertainty about future demand and where the cancellation provisions of a lease may offer substantial protection.

A company also may choose to lease assets that are needed to conduct business but that fall outside the company's area of expertise. For example, a food wholesaler may choose to lease a fleet of delivery trucks rather than purchase the assets. The lessor takes care of financing and maintaining the fleet while the wholesaler focuses on operating its business. In many cases, lease financing may be offered simultaneously to the acquisition of the asset, making it an easy, one-stop shopping arrangement. While this type of arrangement may not be available for all types of leases, it can be a desirable option if available.

7. Tax advantages from leasing are dependent on the tax codes in effect for the organization. Lease financing and tax advantages under US Generally Accepted Accounting Principles (GAAP) and International Financial Reporting Standards (IFRS) are explained later in this chapter.

Finally, companies may consider leasing purely from a desire for more flexible financing options. The actual terms available on a lease, combined with the ability to "walk away" from the asset at the end of the lease term, may be more valuable than any residual value of the asset itself.

B. Types of Leases

The primary differences among lease types are:

- Length of lease period
- Which party is responsible for maintenance and upkeep of the asset
- Residual value of the asset (i.e., the estimated value of the asset at the end of the lease)
- Relevant tax treatment (though this may differ significantly for not-for-profits and municipalities)
- Who retains the assets at the end of the lease and under what terms

1. SALE-AND-LEASEBACK ARRANGEMENTS

Under a sale-and-leaseback arrangement, equipment owned by a company is sold to another party (lessor) and then immediately leased back by the original owner (lessee). This type of lease arrangement aids companies that need a cash infusion or that cannot take full advantage of the tax benefits from depreciation due to excessive operating losses. The sale-and-leaseback arrangement can move the cash flow stream (income or costs) to different periods, as well.

2. OPERATING OR SERVICE LEASES

Operating leases, also known as *service leases*, are established in such a way that the lessor may maintain the equipment and retain ownership thereof at the end of the lease. These arrangements are often done on an off-balance-sheet basis, meaning that lease payments are reflected only on the income statement. Neither the assets nor the lease appears on the lessee's balance sheet, but the lease payments appear as an expense on the income statement.

Operating leases usually run for periods substantially shorter than the life of the equipment, but tend to run three to five years on average for equipment and may be up to fifteen years for real estate leases. Consequently, lease payments usually are not sufficient to fully pay for the original cost of the equipment, meaning there is some residual value of the asset at the end of the lease term. Significant operating lease arrangements and the financial value of future lease commitments must be reported in a footnote to the financial statements, further ensuring that no investor or lender is unaware of leasing arrangements. In analyzing operating leases, it is important to consider the flexibility of cancellation policies carefully.

3. CAPITAL OR FINANCIAL LEASES

Capital leases, also known as *financial leases*, have terms that are different from those of operating leases. Capital leases are essentially an alternative to borrowing the funds and purchasing the asset in question.

For US organizations, Accounting Standards Codification (ASC) Topic 840-10-15: *Leases: Scope and Scope Exceptions*[8] specifies that any lease meeting any one of the following four conditions must be classified as a capital lease:

- The length of the lease is at least 75% of the estimated useful life of the asset.
- There is a transfer of ownership to the lessee at the end of the lease.

8. For discussion purposes, this book will focus on ASC Topic 840-10-15, issued by the Financial Accounting Standards Board (FASB). The International Accounting Standards Board (IASB) has comparable requirements in International Accounting Standard (IAS) 17: *Leases*. At the time of publication of this book, both FASB and IASB have issued exposure drafts for lease accounting that may cause significant changes in this area.

- The lease agreement contains a provision that allows the lessee to purchase the asset per a bargain purchase option during or at the end of the lease's life. A bargain price is one that is sufficiently less than fair market value, such that an expectation is created at the outset that the option will be exercised.
- The present value of the discounted lease payments at the beginning of the lease term exceeds 90% of the asset's fair market value.

A lease that does not meet any of these conditions may be classified as an operating lease.

The residual value is generally the estimated value of the asset at the end of a capital lease. The amortization of the asset's value considers the residual value in the computation of lease payments. The lessee generally is responsible for maintaining the asset and must pay any applicable taxes and insurance.

A capital lease is sometimes referred to as a *double-net lease* because the lessor receives payment after expenses are paid (e.g., maintenance, operating, and insurance expenses). When this type of lease is used in real estate, it may be referred to as a *triple-net lease* because it includes taxes, insurance, and utilities. This type of lease is an alternative to borrowing funds to finance the acquisition of a capital asset.[9]

Under certain conditions, leases may be considered a source of off-balance-sheet financing, thus avoiding the appearance of additional debt on a company's balance sheet, as well as increasing its return on assets. To correct this problem, the FASB issued Topic 840-10-15, which requires US companies entering into financial leases to capitalize the lease. This process restates a company's balance sheet to show the leased asset as a fixed asset and the present value of the lease payments as a liability.

The logic behind the FASB requirement is that when a company signs a financial lease agreement, the obligation to make lease payments is just as binding as in a long-term loan agreement. Thus, for most purposes, capitalized leases are a direct substitute for a company's long-term debt financing.

Exhibit 20.3 summarizes lease characteristics by type of lease.

9. Double- and triple-net leases may also be operating leases if properly structured, but are more likely to be capital leases due to the lessee's acceptance of maintenance and risk.

EXHIBIT 20.3 CHARACTERISTICS OF LEASES BY TYPE

CHARACTERISTIC	SALE AND LEASEBACK	CAPITAL LEASE	OPERATING LEASE
LEASE CRITERIA:* OWNERSHIP	N/A. Can be either capital or operating lease based on lease agreement.	Ownership of the asset is transferred to the lessee at the end of the lease term.	Ownership is retained by the lessor during and after the lease term.
LEASE CRITERIA: BARGAIN PURCHASE OPTION	N/A. Can be either capital or operating lease based on lease agreement.	The lease contains a bargain purchase option to buy the asset at less than fair market value.	The lease cannot contain a bargain purchase option.
LEASE CRITERIA: LENGTH OF LEASE PERIOD	N/A. Can be either capital or operating lease based on lease agreement.	The lease term equals or exceeds 75% of the asset's estimated useful life.	The lease term is less than 75% of the estimated useful life of the asset.
LEASE CRITERIA: PRESENT VALUE	N/A. Can be either capital or operating lease based on lease agreement.	The present value of the lease payments exceeds 90% of the total original cost of the asset.	The present value of lease payments is less than 90% of the asset's fair market value.
MAINTENANCE	Depends upon the lease agreement.	Transferred to lessee. Lessee pays maintenance, insurance, and taxes.	Right to use only. Lessor takes risks and benefits and often pays maintenance costs.
ACCOUNTING	May be sale and financial leaseback, or sale and operating leaseback. If the lessee classifies the lease-back as an operating lease, any gain or loss on sale is recognized immediately. If the leaseback is classified as a financial lease, the lessee defers and amortizes any gain on sale over the lease term.	Lease is considered an asset (leased asset) and liability (lease payments). Payments are shown in balance sheet.	No risk of ownership. Payments are considered operating expenses and shown in income statement.
TAX TREATMENT	Depends upon the type of lease.	Lessee is considered to be the owner of the equipment and therefore claims depreciation expense and interest expense.	Lessee is considered to be renting the equipment and therefore the lease payment is considered a rental expense.

* A lease that meets any one of the four lease criteria must be characterized as a capital lease.

C. Estimated Residual Value

The lessor owns the property upon expiration of the lease and has a primary claim on the asset's residual value (i.e., the amount remaining after all allowable depreciation charges have been subtracted from a depreciable asset). In most cases, the estimated residual value is built into the leasing arrangement. Assets with potentially high residual values generally have lower lease payments than similar assets with lower values.

Setting the residual value may impact the lease's tax status, as well as requirements for listing the lease as an on- or off-balance-sheet item. In lease analysis, it is critical to know the asset's assumed residual value at the end of the lease. There might be a requirement that the lessee reimburse the lessor for any difference between the estimated residual value and the actual residual value of the asset (e.g., if it is lower than the estimate). In vehicle leases, this requirement may be tied to the mileage (requiring the lessee to pay for any mileage above the agreed maximum) or to the general condition of the vehicle (especially if the lessee failed to properly maintain the vehicle according to the lease agreement).

D. Tax Considerations for Leases

Tax considerations for leases can vary by country. In the United States, the full amount of an annual operating lease payment is a tax-deductible expense for the lessee, provided the Internal Revenue Service (IRS) agrees that a particular contract is a genuine operating lease (based upon GAAP requirements outlined above) and not simply an installment loan in the guise of a lease. The primary reason for IRS restrictions on lease terms is to prevent a company (the lessee) from setting up a lease arrangement that allows for the more rapid write-off of an asset than that allowed by the IRS's depreciation rules.

Other countries have similar requirements that distinguish between capital or finance leases (also referred to as *funding leases* or *hire-purchase agreements*) and operating leases, typically now based upon IFRS[10] guidelines. IFRS lease guidelines focus on the overall substance of a particular transaction. Lease classification as an operating lease or a finance lease (i.e., the equivalent of a capital lease under US GAAP) depends on whether the lease transfers substantially all of the risks and rewards of ownership to the lessee. Although lease classification criteria are similar to those identified in US GAAP, there are no quantitative breakpoints in IFRS (e.g., 90% of the total cost). A lease of special-purpose assets that only the lessee can use without major modification generally would be classified as a finance lease, as would any lease that does not subject the lessor to significant risk with respect to the residual value of the leased property.

In general, most tax legislation is intended to deny deductions for interest (i.e., require treatment as a capital lease) when the avoidance of tax is deemed one of the main purposes for the lease transaction. Local tax treatment should always be confirmed before making any lease versus borrow-and-buy decision.

10. IFRS is discussed in Chapter 18, Financial Accounting and Reporting.

E. Lease versus Borrow-and-Buy Decision

When a company needs the use of an asset, it may purchase or lease it. Since a lease is a form of debt obligation, the appropriate way to evaluate the decision is to compare the costs of leasing with the costs of borrowing to buy the asset. The most common approach to comparing a lease to a borrow-and-buy scenario involves examining the net present value of cash flows associated with each alternative. Assuming the value of using the asset to the organization is the same whether it is leased or bought, the present value of each scenario would be computed and the one with the lowest net present value of costs would be chosen.

Calculation Example: Lease versus Borrow-and-Buy

For example, assume that a company needs to buy a new piece of machinery with a total cost of $50,000. The company will only need the machine for three years and can then resell it for its residual value of $20,000. The company can borrow the needed funds at 6%, with annual interest payments and a final principal repayment at the end of three years. For tax purposes, assume that the firm has a marginal tax rate of 30% and that depreciation for the machine will be $10,000 the first year, $16,000 the second year, and $6,000 the third year. Maintenance expenses on the machine will be $5,000 per year.

Alternatively, the company can lease the machine for $16,000 per year for three years with the payment due at the beginning of each year. If it does that, there will be no maintenance expense, and the company will return the machine to the leasing company at the end of the three years.

To compare the two options, the company first calculates the annual cash flow from each option and then compares the NPV of the two sets of cash flows, as illustrated below. (NPV is discussed in Chapter 19, Financial Planning and Analysis.)

Cost to Own:

		Year 1	Year 2	Year 3
1	Interest Payments ($50,000 x 6%)	(3,000)	(3,000)	(3,000)
2	Less: Tax Savings @ 30%	900	900	900
3	Equals: After-Tax Interest Cost	(2,100)	(2,100)	(2,100)
4	Principal Repayment			(50,000)
5	Maintenance Expense	(5,000)	(5,000)	(5,000)
6	Less: Tax Savings @ 30%	1,500	1,500	1,500
7	Equals: After-Tax Maintenance Expense	(3,500)	(3,500)	(3,500)
8	Depreciation Expense	(10,000)	(16,000)	(6,000)
9	Tax Savings on Depreciation (30% x Depreciation)	3,000	4,800	1,800
10	Residual Value of Machine			20,000
11	Book Value of Machine (Purchase Price Less Depreciation)			18,000
12	Taxable Gain on Sale			2,000
13	Tax on Gain @ 30%			(600)
	Net Cash Flow (Line 3+4+7+9+10+13)	(2,600)	(800)	(34,400)

The net present value of owning can be calculated as:

$$\text{NPV of Owning @ 6\%} = \frac{-\$2,600}{(1+0.06)^1} + \frac{-\$800}{(1+0.06)^2} + \frac{-\$34,400}{(1+0.06)^3}$$

$$= -\$2,453 + -\$712 + -\$28,883 = -\$32,048$$

Cost to Lease:

Note that the lease payments are made at the beginning of each year instead of the end, so the first payment is made immediately, which is considered Year 0.

		Year 0	Year 1	Year 2
1	Lease Payments	(16,000)	(16,000)	(16,000)
2	Less: Tax Savings @ 30%	4,800	4,800	4,800
3	Equals: Net Cash Flow	(11,200)	(11,200)	(11,200)

The net present value of leasing can be calculated as:

$$\text{NPV of Leasing @ 6\%} = \frac{-\$11{,}200}{(1+0.06)^0} + \frac{-\$11{,}200}{(1+0.06)^1} + \frac{-\$11{,}200}{(1+0.06)^2}$$

$$= -\$11{,}200 + -\$10{,}566 + -\$9{,}968 = -\$31{,}734$$

Comparison of Cost to Own versus Lease:

$$\text{Difference} = \$32{,}048 - \$31{,}734 = \$314$$

Based on the information in this example, the company will save $314 by leasing the machine instead of buying it and then reselling it at the end of three years. Although not quantified in this example, the company will also save the time and effort involved in reselling the machine at the end of the period.

VI. EQUITY FINANCING AND MANAGEMENT

As is covered in Chapter 6, Capital Markets, equity represents ownership in the organization. Equity has a very different payment stream to the investor and cost structure to the organization from debt financing (i.e., after-tax dividends rather than before-tax interest).

The purpose of this section is to cover some of the topics related to equity financing and management for organizations that use this type of financing. The first topic is related to the decision to issue stock, including going public (i.e., selling stock on the open market), issuing IPOs, listing stock, and choosing exchanges or off-exchange/over-the-counter (OTC) trading. The other topics covered in this section are shareholder rights and the financing of mergers and acquisitions.

A. Initial Public Offerings (IPOs) and the Decision to List Stock in the United States[11]

1. THE INITIAL PUBLIC OFFERING (IPO)

Although the common usage of the term tends to be limited to common stock, the term *IPO* describes an issuer's first, or initial, public offering of a security of any class. For companies with equity securities that are not currently available to the public or are not listed on one of the various exchanges, the decision to go public and/or to list the company's securities can be critical to a company's future growth.

11. Additional discussion regarding global equity markets is provided in Chapter 6, Capital Markets.

2. ADVANTAGES OF GOING PUBLIC

For a private or closely held company, the decision to go public offers several advantages. Owners of closely held companies usually have most of their wealth tied up in one company and thus are not adequately diversified. By selling a portion of stock to the general public, owners may invest the proceeds in other areas, increase their personal diversification, and raise capital for the business.

For investors in closely held companies, the stock of a company is very illiquid. It can be sold only to certain types of investors; hence, there is no intermediary to help in the sale. As a result, such companies' ability to raise capital when needed is difficult because the stock generally is not as attractive to outside investors. Going public can help to resolve this liquidity problem.

The problems of diversification and liquidity are less of an issue for publicly traded companies. A company must meet certain levels of disclosure of information and regulatory requirements by the SEC in order for its stock to become listed publicly. Transparency and outside regulation make investors more willing to purchase the stock of a publicly traded company and greatly facilitate a company's ability to raise new capital.

Making the stock of a company publicly available allows its value to be determined by the market and establishes a company's stock price.

IPOs can also be used to spin off a division or wholly owned subsidiary of a company that is already public. This process is often used by large, diversified companies when it is determined that a particular part of the company might be more valuable as a stand-alone entity. For example, the information technology section of a large manufacturing company may have developed highly regarded software for computer-aided design. In order to realize the full value of this software, the company may find it advantageous to spin off that part of the company so that it can sell the software throughout the industry more easily.

3. DISADVANTAGES OF GOING PUBLIC

The decision to trade the stock of a company publicly does have some disadvantages, primarily related to the disclosure required for the public issue. Going public also reduces managerial flexibility and forces the existing owners/managers to surrender some control.

a. Regulatory Disclosure

Owners/managers of closely/privately held companies may not be comfortable with the level of disclosure required for publicly held corporations for four reasons. First, competitors gain access to greater amounts of information about a company due to public disclosure requirements. Second, the compensation and net worth of the owners is determined more easily by outside parties. Third, in most countries, public companies must adhere to strict financial reporting attestation and internal control requirements. Fourth, the registration and disclosure process can be very expensive for an IPO, especially for smaller companies when compared to their pre-IPO reporting levels.

b. Managerial Flexibility

When a company's stock is held closely, the owners/managers have great flexibility with respect to how the company is managed. In a privately held company, large management salaries or generous perks do not produce the kind of conflicts between management and shareholders that may occur in a publicly held company.

c. Control

Owners/managers of closely held companies surrender some control by going public, even if majority ownership is retained. In publicly held companies and/or companies in industries with strong labor union representation, minority shareholders may have significant rights with respect to the operation of a company and representation on the board of directors. Also, there are many examples of publicly held companies being taken private by management to increase the level of control. This is especially true when a company is incorporated in a state where cumulative voting is allowed. This type of voting provides minority interests with a better opportunity to gain board representation. This topic is covered in more detail in the section below on shareholder rights.

d. Other Factors

Although increased liquidity of a company's stock may be one reason for going public, stocks of smaller companies may not be especially liquid. If there is a small market for the stock and/or it is not traded often, then the market price may not reflect its true value. For markets to price efficiently, trading should be regular and frequent with many buyers and sellers. In addition, a company going public with debt securities may be required to have the debt rated to sell it publicly. These costs may be significant, especially for smaller companies when they first go public. The company's investment banker should be raising/resolving these issues.

4. THE DECISION TO LIST STOCK

For most companies, the decision to go public with a company's stock coincides with the decision to have the stock (or other securities) listed on one of the organized exchanges, such as the New York Stock Exchange (NYSE) or the London Stock Exchange. Although the various national and regional exchanges have much in common, rules and requirements can vary by exchange and by country. In addition, tax consequences can vary by country. Therefore, it is important to consider the cost of complying with the regulatory requirements and tax regimes when choosing an exchange. Increasingly, companies are foregoing organized exchanges and listing securities on automated quotation systems, such as NASDAQ or JASDAQ, which started out as computer-based OTC trading systems and are now officially recognized exchanges.

Whichever market is chosen, it is important to work with sell-side analysts (discussed in Chapter 3, Banks and Financial Institutions) to help ensure that the stock is followed and rated in a manner consistent with the company's objectives. Failure to interest any analysts in an issue will typically have a negative impact on the potential value of the stock once it is being actively traded, as the stock becomes what is referred to as an "orphan" stock.

a. Advantages of Listing Stock

The primary advantage of having a company's stock listed on one of the organized exchanges is that the stock's marketability increases. In general, listing is advantageous to both a company and the public because a company's stock can be traded more widely and more investors can access it. Listing also can result in higher sales for a company because of increased public exposure. Additionally, the increased level of disclosure required for public listing has a tendency to reduce the perceived market risk of a company, which in turn may lower the weighted average cost of capital (WACC) on the company's common stock and bonds, thereby increasing the company's overall market value.

b. Disadvantages of Listing Stock

Most organized exchanges have their own rules and regulations, typically reporting and governance requirements, that can go well beyond any government regulation of public companies. Given these additional requirements and the higher costs charged by the exchanges, some companies decide to remain in the OTC market rather than to list stock on an organized exchange. Additionally, trading and liquidity in the OTC market has increased significantly since the early 1990s; hence, many companies have decided to be traded as OTC entities.

5. DELISTING OF STOCK

Stocks can be delisted from an exchange. In some cases, a stock is forced to be delisted (an involuntary delisting) because it has fallen out of compliance with the exchange's requirements (e.g., the company's share price falls below $1 per share for some specified period of time). Most exchanges have procedures for companies that want to maintain their listing to try to get back into compliance. However, if the requirements are not met within a set time period, then the company will be dropped from the exchange. Delisted stock may still be traded on the OTC market.

Some companies choose to have their stock delisted (a voluntary delisting). For example, the added disclosure requirements and expense of audit and reporting compliance on the NYSE have caused some smaller companies to go through the delisting process. Some foreign companies also have decided to delist their American depositary receipts (ADRs) to avoid exchange compliance requirements.

6. CHOICE OF EXCHANGES

Once a company has decided to list its stock rather than use the OTC market, it must decide on which exchanges the stock will be listed. There are requirements for joining the various exchanges, and companies must abide by the rules of each exchange on which they want their stocks traded.

For companies wishing to raise capital globally, there are stock exchanges in most of the world's money centers, including New York, Toronto, London, Tokyo, Frankfurt, Paris, Zurich, Singapore, Taiwan, and Hong Kong. Stocks of major US companies may be listed and traded on stock exchanges outside the United States. Similarly, stocks of large, foreign multinational companies may be listed and traded in the US markets.[12]

7. TYPE OF STOCK

In addition to deciding where and when to list, a firm that is going public has to determine what types of stock to issue. As discussed in Chapter 6, Capital Markets, stock can be issued in various classes, referred to as a *dual- or multi-class stock*, which can provide different rights to different shareholders. This is typically done to try to retain voting control of a company while raising capital in the market. In a dual-class system, two types of stock are issued: typically Class A and Class B stock. One class is sold to the general market and has limited voting rights, but may have preferential dividends in compensation. The second class is typically reserved for the original owners and executives, and has greater voting power to maintain majority control of the company.

12. A listing of the major exchanges in the world is provided in Chapter 6, Capital Markets.

B. Shareholder Rights

Treasury professionals should be familiar with shareholder rights and privileges because investor relations sometimes becomes part of their responsibilities and because equity is a key capital component. Generally, common stockholders have all or some of the following legal rights and privileges:

- **Control of the Company:** As owners of a company, stockholders have the right to elect a company's directors, who in turn select the officers to manage the business. There are numerous regulations, which can vary by legal jurisdiction, concerning the election of directors and procedures to be followed in doing so.
- **Cumulative Voting:** Corporate bylaws typically permit one vote per share of stock and, sometimes, cumulative voting. Cumulative voting allows a shareholder as many votes per share owned as there are open positions on the board in the same election. It also allows shareholders to cast these votes in any way they see fit. For example, if six places on the board are to be filled, then the holder of one share receives six votes. The shareholder could cast all six votes for one candidate or split them among candidates in any way desired. The purpose of cumulative voting is to increase the possibility that a minority of shareholders can elect someone to the board. Since they are concentrating their votes on one or two candidates, they virtually ensure that they will elect at least one board member and thereby have a minority position on the board of directors, allowing their viewpoints to be expressed during board deliberations.
- **Proxy:** The right to vote at the annual meeting can be assigned to another individual through a proxy. When stockholders are satisfied with the board's conduct and management's performance, they assign their proxies to the chief executive officer or another designated company executive. If a shareholder group is dissatisfied, then it will retain its votes and solicit the proxy votes of other shareholders in an attempt to elect candidates it favors to the board. When stockholder groups aggressively solicit the proxies of other shareholders, it is referred to as a *proxy fight*.
- **Staggered Election of Directors:** A system of staggered elections is when board members hold office for multiple years, but a minority of board seats is open in a single election. For example, on a twelve-person board, members may be elected to serve for three years, with four members elected to three-year terms each year. Staggered elections are used either to make it difficult to take over the board or because it is felt that continuity on the board is conducive to its making well-considered decisions.
- **Preemptive Right:** A preemptive right provides that existing shareholders shall have the first right to purchase shares of any new stock issue on a pro rata basis and based on the proportion of shares owned. Existing shareholders do not have to exercise the right, but they do possess a right of first refusal. The stock issue usually is conducted through a rights offering, in which existing shareholders declare their intention to subscribe to a certain number of shares when they are issued. The right conveys the opportunity to purchase shares at the subscription price. Rights are negotiable, so a shareholder who does not wish to purchase stock can sell the rights to third parties. A rights offering provides existing shareholders with the opportunity to maintain their proportionate share of ownership if they choose to do so. It is not a requirement in all jurisdictions, but it is incorporated into many corporate charters in places where it is not required.

C. Mergers and Acquisitions

Mergers and acquisitions typically involve major financial decisions on the part of the organizations that must deal with them. The merger or acquisition itself is a major decision that will impact an organization's future significantly. In addition, there are generally financing implications to these decisions, as the acquiring organization must often raise capital to pay for the merger or acquisition.

1. TYPES OF TRANSACTIONS

Whether a purchase is considered a merger or an acquisition really depends on whether the purchase is friendly or hostile, and how it is announced. In other words, the real difference lies in how the purchase is communicated to and received by the target company's board of directors, employees, and shareholders.

a. Merging Two Companies

In the pure sense of the term, a *merger* happens when two firms, often of about the same size, agree to go forward as a single new company rather than remain separately owned and operated. This kind of action is more precisely referred to as a *merger of equals*. Both companies' stocks are surrendered, and new company stock is issued in its place. In practice, however, actual mergers of equals do not happen very often. Usually, one company, the acquirer, will buy another and, as part of the deal's terms, simply allow the acquired firm to proclaim that the action is a merger of equals, even if it is technically an acquisition. Being bought out often carries negative connotations; therefore, by describing the deal as a merger, deal makers and top managers try to make the takeover more palatable.

b. Acquisition of a Company

An acquisition results when one company buys a majority of the voting shares of another company. An acquisition may be friendly or hostile.

In a friendly acquisition, the bidding company will typically inform the other company's board of directors of its intention to acquire. A good takeover candidate includes a cash-rich business, a company with a low debt to equity ratio, and a company with significant growth potential. In a friendly acquisition, with the board of the target company cooperating, the acquiring company may conduct extensive due diligence into the financial and other affairs of the target company. The acquirer may negotiate with the management of the prospective acquired company, which is the preferred approach.

c. Hostile Takeover

In cases where the target is expected to strongly fight a takeover attempt, the acquiring company will normally make a tender offer directly to the shareholders of the target, bypassing the target's management. In a hostile takeover, the acquiring firm may know only the publicly available information about the target and therefore may assume greater risk due to limited due diligence. A tender offer represents a cash offer for the common shares held by stockholders.

Generally, tender offers are more expensive than negotiated mergers and acquisitions, due to the resistance of target management and the fact that the target is now "in play" and may attract other bidders.

A second approach is to engage in a proxy fight prior to the target's annual shareholders meeting. A proxy gives the holder the right to vote those shares at the meeting where the board of directors will be selected. If the acquiring firm can obtain enough of the proxies (usually a simple majority), then it can elect a new board of directors that, presumably, will approve the acquisition. Another approach is known as a *creeping tender offer*, which involves quietly purchasing sufficient stock on the open market to enable a change in the management. Regardless of the approach, the key similarity is that the existing board and management are resistant to the acquisition.

d. Leveraged Buyout (LBO)

A leveraged buyout occurs when an entity finances the acquisition of a company primarily through borrowings typically collateralized by the assets of the company being acquired. The debt is normally carried on the balance sheet of the acquired company rather than that of the purchaser, and repayments of the debt are made from the operating funds flow of the acquired company. In limited cases, a leveraged buyout may also be made when the acquiring company uses its own assets as security for the loan. An LBO can also be used if a firm wishes to go private, in which case the firm uses the borrowed funds to buy back all of the acquired firm's outstanding stock. In most cases, the stockholders of the acquired company will receive an amount greater than the current price of the stock. An LBO often involves more risk than an acquisition paid for through the issuance of equity securities, due to the high level of debt and the need to generate ongoing operating profits to make the debt payments.

Leveraged buyouts differ from ordinary acquisitions in two major ways:

- First, a large fraction of the purchase price is debt-financed. Some, often all, of this debt is junk (i.e., below investment grade).
- Second, the LBO goes private, and its shares no longer trade on the open market. The LBO's stock is typically held by a partnership of investors. When this group is led by the company's management, the acquisition is called a *management buyout (MBO).*

Many LBO investor groups hope to capture value for themselves by selling off the company's assets in pieces to firms that believe they can incorporate these assets and experience synergies. Some groups try to raise cash by selling poorer performing assets, and building sales and profits of the remaining assets, hoping to sell them for a substantial profit at a later date. Though some LBOs may remain private for an extended period, most tend to be more of a short-term duration of less than five years.

2. FINANCING THE TRANSACTION

The transaction can be financed using existing cash, equity, debt, or a combination of all three. Common structures include:

- All-cash transaction
- Stock transaction (i.e., merger through exchange of stock)
- Mixed stock/cash transaction
- Leveraged cash transaction, financed through debt issue
- Leveraged buyout, with the majority of equity replaced by debt
- Debt transaction (i.e., debt offered to selling company shareholders)
- Mixed cash/debt transaction
- Preferred stock transaction

When cash is involved in paying for the acquired firm, it may come from a variety of sources:

- Cash from the acquiring firm
- Excess cash from the acquired firm
- Cash from the sale of some of the acquired firm's assets
- Issuance of investment-grade bonds
- Issuance of below-investment-grade bonds (i.e., junk bonds) that have an amortization schedule supported by a forecast of operating cash flows[13]

There are also a variety of funding resources that may consider making equity investments (e.g., common or preferred stocks). Unlike with debt, there are no scheduled payments for equity funding; however, equity investors have residual interests in the company and may exercise their controlling rights.

D. At the Market (ATM) Programs

As an alternative to a traditional underwritten offering of a fixed number of shares at a fixed price all at once, some organizations have turned to "at the market," or ATM, programs, which allow for the issuance of a specific amount of equity over time that is sold into the existing secondary market at the current market price on an as-needed basis.

In an ATM program, the issuer still needs to file appropriate disclosure documents, but in this case files a "shelf registration" to cover the potential issuance of stock. Once the registration and prospectus are approved, the company authorizes a specific broker-dealer to issue new stock for sale at current market prices as the company needs the additional capital. Because the stock is issued in small increments to avoid impacting the market price of the stock, these plans are also sometimes referred to as *dribble plans*.

VII. OTHER TOPICS IN FINANCIAL DECISIONS

A. Tax Strategies

For any corporation, tax and accounting issues will have a major impact on financial decision making. Many of the accounting issues are covered in Chapter 18, Financial Accounting and Reporting, and the basics of taxes and related regulations are covered in Chapter 2, Regulatory and Legal Environment. This section focuses primarily on general tax strategies that global corporations typically employ.

Companies involved in international business need an effective global tax strategy or they risk incurring highly unfavorable tax consequences. The choice of the proper tax strategy is important for both large global companies and smaller firms that are significantly involved in export-import activities. Effective international tax planning can reduce a company's global tax costs by minimizing the potential for paying double taxes (i.e., to a foreign jurisdiction and the company's home country). An effective global tax strategy will balance home country and foreign tax considerations in the context of a company's broader business and financial objectives.

13. The low rating usually results from higher debt ratios, a lower interest coverage ratio (e.g., times interest earned), and less than full confidence on the part of the rating agency that the forecasted operating cash flows will be sufficient to meet amortization requirements.

All of the world's taxing jurisdictions are seeking their share of the increasingly important cross-border revenue stream. A good example of this is the development during the last decade of widespread and complex international transfer pricing rules, which require companies to document their annual compliance with strict "arm's length" standards for the pricing of intercompany transfers of goods and services. Another problem area is that of deemed dividends, where payments on loans, sales of stock, or other transactions may be interpreted by tax authorities as an attempt on the part of a company to avoid paying taxes on dividends. The payments may then be determined to be deemed dividends, and appropriate taxes charged. These and other international tax rules are constantly changing, which becomes a challenge for uninformed companies that are engaged in cross-border business.

Proper international tax planning requires a company to develop a global tax strategy that facilitates its global business objectives. The starting point is to develop a solid understanding of the company's business and financial position, its international operating strategy, and where and how it intends to operate outside its home country. With this knowledge, a company (and its tax accountants) can develop an overall global tax strategy that makes good business sense and is practical. International tax planning for specific situations can then be approached in a coherent manner, taking into account the company's broader global tax and operating strategies.

Companies that are not familiar with international tax rules, cross-border transfer pricing requirements, and double-tax treaties are much more likely to suffer unnecessarily high global tax costs, including increased tax compliance burdens and tax penalties. Transfer pricing is the price that one subsidiary of a company charges another subsidiary of the same company for intracompany transactions. By managing transfer pricing, it is possible for the parent company to concentrate profits in a lower-tax country and thereby reduce its overall tax burden. Most tax authorities closely monitor transfer pricing to make sure they get their fair share of taxes. For example, many less developed countries do not have a good international tax treaty network, so it takes careful cross-border tax planning to minimize tax burdens, including high foreign corporate tax rates and high withholding taxes applied to a wide spectrum of outbound payments from such countries. The same holds true with transfer pricing.

The United States and most developed countries have had clearly defined transfer pricing rules for many years, including potential transfer pricing adjustment penalties and interest charges. In recent years, many developing nations have initiated their own sets of transfer price rules. So, it is no longer just a matter of being focused on the home country side of the transfer pricing equation, but also making sure that foreign transfer pricing problems are not created. An experienced international tax adviser can help a company establish a tax-effective cross-border transfer pricing strategy.

B. Dividend Policy

Dividend policies are typically set at the CEO/board of directors level, often with input from the treasurer, but can have a significant impact on treasury operations due to their impact on cash flows. Additionally, a company's decisions regarding dividend policy can have a significant impact on capital structure. Steadily increasing dividends may make a company's common stock more attractive to certain institutional investors and may increase the stock price. However, increasing dividends reduces the amount of cash flow (in the form of retained earnings) that a company has available for expansion. This may slow a company's growth and, hence, its ability to provide capital appreciation for investors. A company may then become less attractive to investors who prefer high levels of capital gains to regular income in the form of dividends. In effect, dividend policy determines the type of investor who is likely to be interested in being a shareholder.

The optimal dividend policy is one that:

- Maximizes shareholder value
- Retains sufficient profits to fund future asset expansion
- Distributes an appropriate amount of corporate income to investors
- Provides information to investors about the future earnings of the firm (i.e., "signaling")[14]

1. DIVIDEND PAYMENT PROCEDURES

When a company plans to pay a dividend, the board of directors declares a dividend amount, a payment date, and a shareholder-of-record date. This action results in four dates:

- **Declaration Date:** This is the date when the board of directors announces (declares) the dividend.
- **Record Date:** Also known as a *shareholder-of-record date*, or just *holder-of-record date*, this is the date when shareholders of record are entitled to receive the declared dividend.
- **Ex-Dividend Date:** This is the date on which the stock is sold without entitlement to the upcoming dividend. The ex-dividend date is usually two business days prior to the shareholder-of-record date, thereby enabling brokerage firms to send an updated list of shareholders to a company on time. Theoretically, there is a drop in the stock price equivalent to the dividend on the ex-dividend date. However, this is difficult to measure because other factors may influence the market price.
- **Payment Date:** This is the date when the dividend is paid, which is usually a week or more after the record date, to allow the company time to process and disburse the dividend.

For example, on June 3, 2xx1, a company announces that it will pay a $0.25 quarterly cash dividend on July 1, 2xx1 to shareholders of record on June 14, 2xx1. In this example:

- The declaration date is June 3, 2xx1.
- The record date is June 14, 2xx1.
- The ex-dividend date is June 12, 2xx1.[15]
- The payment date is July 1, 2xx1.

2. DIVIDEND REINVESTMENT PLANS (DRIPs)

Many firms provide a DRIP as a way for investors to increase their ownership of shares in the company. A DRIP enables existing shareholders to purchase additional shares directly from the company on a when-desired basis, normally with no commission or with only a small processing charge. These plans also allow investors to elect to reinvest dividends automatically in additional shares of company stock. Shares that the company distributes

14. Signaling can be either positive or negative, and often depends upon the context of the dividend (e.g., is the company returning capital that will not be needed in the future, or is the company expecting growth in overall earnings).
15. This assumes that June 12, 13, and 14 are business days.

under these plans may be held in the treasury (i.e., treasury stock), be repurchased by the company in the market and intended for this purpose, or be new, authorized shares of stock that have not been issued yet (i.e., "shelf-registered" stock).

These plans benefit smaller shareholders because transaction costs are low or nonexistent. Also, a few companies sell shares to DRIP investors at a discount to market price. From the company's point of view, this method of raising capital is significantly less expensive than issuing new stock to the general public (due to no underwriting costs), thus saving cash for the issuing company. One negative aspect of this type of plan, however, is that it may increase the number of small shareholders, resulting in more expensive shareholder relations and increasing the cost of maintaining shareholder records.

3. TYPES OF DIVIDENDS

Companies may employ many different methods to pay dividends to shareholders. Regular cash dividends are the most common, but there are other types, including stock, special, and liquidating dividends. Although not technically dividends, stock splits often are considered part of a dividend policy.

a. Cash Dividends

As mentioned previously, the most common form of dividend payment is a regular cash dividend. Corporate dividends usually are paid on a quarterly basis. Historically, they were paid by check, but are increasingly paid electronically.

b. Stock Dividends

When a company pays shareholders additional shares of stock rather than cash dividends, it is termed a *stock dividend.* Analytically, a stock dividend is the same as a stock split (discussed further in this section). The stock's per-share price in the market is reduced because additional shares are in circulation, but there is no real impact on shareholder wealth since the added shares do not alter the company's overall value. However, there may be additional costs to a company for managing the record keeping for the new shares. The dilution in earnings caused by the stock dividend will cause a fall in share price that is exactly proportionate to the increase in the number of shares outstanding. If a company is in a period of rapid growth and needs to retain all earnings for reinvestment, stock dividends may be a means of compensating shareholders for their loyalty. For example, if a company that follows a stable dividend policy has many attractive but expensive investment alternatives, it creates a dilemma for itself because it has conditioned shareholders to expect a cash dividend. One way out of the dilemma is to pay the dividend in stock rather than cash. This does not impart added value for shareholders, but may make them feel as though they have benefited. In addition, the investor will not have any taxes owed on the stock dividend.

c. Special Dividends

As previously discussed, dividend policy provides information to shareholders, especially if dividends change unexpectedly. For this reason, most companies that pay regular dividends attempt to avoid sudden dividend changes. If a company has a one-time earnings spike, paying a higher dividend for just one period will send mixed signals to shareholders. It may also cause a false expectation that dividends were increased permanently, which eventually will impact the company's stock price negatively. Therefore, a company usually declares a "special" dividend, which, by definition, is meant to be a one-time payment rather than an ongoing dividend increase.

d. Liquidating Dividends

A liquidating dividend[16] is one that is paid out of capital rather than earnings. This sometimes occurs when a company or one of its divisions is going out of business and management decides to pay off shareholders through a liquidating dividend. As the name implies, the company liquidates the remaining assets (capital) of the failed company or division to pay the dividend. This approach may also be used by the acquiring company in an LBO to liquidate the acquired company in order to meet debt service requirements.

e. Stock Splits

The basic idea behind a stock split is that an optimal trading range exists for a stock's price. When management deems that the share price has become too high for smaller shareholders to purchase the company's stock in round lots (i.e., multiples of 100 shares), it will recommend to the board of directors that the stock be split to reduce the share price. By reducing the price, it is possible that latent demand may become active and cause some increase in share price, although there is little evidence to support this effect.

Like a stock dividend, a stock split has no impact on company value in and of itself. Each causes earnings dilution, but the aggregate market value of shares will be the same after the split as before. Sometimes, a company whose share price has declined will initiate a reverse split to increase the price. A primary motivation for a reverse split is to avoid having the firm's shares be delisted by an exchange (i.e., removed from trading) under the exchange's minimum price policy.

4. STOCK REPURCHASES

As an alternative to paying cash dividends, the board of directors can authorize a stock repurchase, whereby the company uses some of its profits to enter the market and buy its own shares. For non-dividend-paying companies, this is an important means of returning capital to shareholders. There are typically regulatory and potentially covenant restrictions with which a company repurchasing its own shares must comply.

5. INTRACOMPANY DIVIDENDS

Large companies with wholly owned subsidiaries often use intracompany dividends to transfer profits from subsidiaries to the parent company. Subsidiaries may be required to pay a stated percentage of earnings to the parent, although these may be subject to thin capitalization rules, as previously discussed, which restrict payments to the parent if the subsidiary would become undercapitalized as a result. Intracompany dividends are a movement of funds between related companies that may be subject to taxes or regulatory restrictions. Intracompany dividend payments also may impact covenants with lenders. It should be noted that cross-border repatriation of dividends may not always be permitted by local regulators, and where permitted, may be heavily scrutinized (see discussion below on capital repatriation). Tax consequences must be balanced with the profit potential, and companies should seek advice from qualified tax professionals. Global financial institutions often offer services in this area for their customers.

16. Securities laws in some jurisdictions (sovereign and/or sub-sovereign) have specific regulations around the use of the term *liquidating dividend* versus *return of capital*.

6. TAXES ON DIVIDENDS

There are numerous tax considerations for dividend payments, mainly impacting recipients. For the average investor, dividends are usually taxable income and may be taxed at a different rate than capital gains. In some countries, tax rates on dividends received by corporations may be adjusted to reduce the potential double-taxation effect on those dividends. Tax regulations on dividends change constantly, and tax experts should be consulted for the latest information.

C. Repatriation of Capital for Multinational Companies (MNCs)

For MNCs, a major treasury issue is whether or when to repatriate cash from foreign subsidiaries to the domestic parent's country. Repatriation involves the actual transfer of funds between countries. The principal method of repatriation is the use of dividends. However, there may be expensive tax restrictions on this approach. Some countries, such as the United States, have tax policies that effectively discourage the repatriation of foreign income, and most countries prefer to see local earnings retained and reinvested locally. Therefore, other methods, such as management fees, royalties, licensing, transfer pricing, and intracompany loans, can be used for repatriation purposes. Most repatriation policies are related to the transfer of funds back to the parent company from wholly or partially owned global subsidiaries of the parent MNC. The objectives are to ensure that the MNC is compensated fairly for the foreign investment and that the host country benefits from the local reinvestment of funds.

1. MNC DIVIDENDS

The use of dividends to transfer profits from global subsidiaries is often restricted by host governments. Usually, there are either significant taxes (e.g., a 35% tax in the United States) charged on cross-border dividend payments, or outright restrictions on the repatriation of funds via dividend payments. Dividend payments to the parent company take subsidiary profits out of a country, but host governments prefer to see earnings reinvested locally.

To counter this problem, MNCs unbundle the cash flows from subsidiaries into separate items that are justified more easily to foreign governments than outright dividends. The techniques for separating items are management fees, transfer pricing, and intracompany loans.

2. MANAGEMENT FEES

Many MNCs charge global subsidiaries licensing and/or management fees in order to justify to host governments the flow of funds from a subsidiary to the parent company. Oftentimes, these fees are negotiated with the host government prior to when the MNC invests in the country.

3. TRANSFER PRICING

Transfer pricing is the price that subsidiaries of a large corporation charge one another for components sold among them. The benefit for MNCs is that transfer pricing can be used as a mechanism to locate profits in subsidiaries in low-tax countries and to move them out of subsidiaries in high-tax countries. Host governments resent these actions; hence, they frequently place restrictions on transfer pricing or changes in transfer prices made by MNCs within their jurisdictions. The implication for MNC management is that most transfer pricing for global subsidiaries must be done at "arm's length." This means setting transfer prices at the same level at which a company would buy or sell similar products from an unaffiliated company. This assures host governments that the profits from the MNC will be distributed fairly among all global subsidiaries. The complexity of transfer pricing is such that MNCs often seek the advice of highly specialized tax consultants to establish policies and procedures.

4. INTRACOMPANY LOANS

Another way to transfer funds between foreign subsidiaries is to use intracompany loans. When funds are required by a foreign subsidiary in a country whose government restricts dividends or other transfers from the subsidiary but permits the transfer of funds for the servicing of a loan, the parent (or another subsidiary) may loan funds rather than contribute equity. Subsequent loan and interest payments effectively replace the dividends that the subsidiary cannot pay the parent company. Should repayment of intracompany loans also be restricted, an MNC can sometimes bring a third-party intermediary into the process. Intracompany loans often produce tax advantages because foreign governments do not impose taxes on loan repayments, as would be the case with cross-border dividend payments. A company must be cautious that repeated intracompany loans are not viewed as deemed dividends (see discussion below) by the relevant tax authorities and taxed as such. This is particularly likely to happen if the loans are not paid back in a timely or routine fashion. Intracompany loans may be supported by tax treaties between the countries involved.

5. DEEMED DIVIDENDS

Deemed dividends occur when payments on loans, sales of stock, or other transactions may be interpreted by tax authorities as an attempt by a company to avoid paying taxes on dividends. The payments may be considered (i.e., "deemed") dividends and appropriate taxes charged. Deemed dividends are a potential issue for any global company and can vary significantly from country to country.

For example, a US MNC with offshore-controlled foreign corporations (OFCs) has some of the following issues with deemed dividends:

- Borrowings from OFCs by the parent may be considered dividends (i.e., deemed dividends) rather than borrowings, and thus taxable distributions as far as the tax authorities are concerned.
- Under Section 956 of the US tax code, a US shareholder of an OFC is currently required to include in income (as a deemed dividend) its pro rata share of any increase in the earnings of the OFC that are invested in US property.

6. RESTRICTIONS ON DIVIDENDS

There may be restrictions on the dividends that can be paid from different types of companies. Many borrowing arrangements include restrictive covenants on the payment of dividends unless certain financial ratios are maintained.

There may also be dividend restrictions oriented toward certain industries or classes of companies imposed by financial and regulatory authorities. Financial institutions and insurance companies often have restrictions on their dividends to protect their capital base in the event of loan or policy losses.

D. Market Analysis and Research Tools

Financial professionals can use various market analysis and research tools to help them make financial decisions. These are typically resources that are available to help with (1) portfolio investment decisions (i.e., when purchasing/selling investments or managing the portfolio), (2) acquisition and divestment decisions, (3) evaluation of trading partners for credit and counterparty risk, and (4) comparisons with other companies or industry averages.

Some of the analysis and research tools, such as Bloomberg, Thomson Reuters, and Dow Jones Financial Information Services, provide a wide range of services, including real-time news and information on financial markets (e.g., interest rates, foreign exchange rates, and market indices), as well as historical data. Some of the services also include platforms that allow for the execution of trades for stocks, bonds, currencies, and derivatives.

Other analysis and research tools, provided by companies such as Standard & Poor's (S&P) and Mergent, focus more on the provision of historical data for research purposes. Fee-based companies like Dun & Bradstreet (D&B) and CreditRiskMonitor provide information for those wanting to perform a credit analysis on potential customers or borrowers. Financial information on publicly traded companies is available from a wide range of sources as well. While many financial reporting services charge fees, there are also a large number of free sources, such as AOL Finance, Yahoo!Finance, and MSN Money. Financial statements (Form 10-K and 10-Q reports) for companies that are publicly traded in the United States are available at no charge through the SEC's Electronic Data Gathering, Analysis, and Retrieval (EDGAR) system.

VIII. SUMMARY

This chapter covered a number of topics related to corporate financial management, with an emphasis on capital structure and related issues, such as dividends. Although treasury professionals may not have direct responsibility for some of these issues, it is important that they are aware of their potential impact on treasury, especially on cash flows and payments. The topics covered in this chapter include theoretical capital structure and issues surrounding raising and managing capital, such as cost of capital, capital leases, regulatory restrictions (e.g., thin capitalization rules), and equity financing. The chapter closed with a discussion of a number of related issues that impact MNCs, including international tax strategies, deemed dividends, and repatriation of international earnings. A common element in all of this discussion is that while there are similarities in the treatment of these issues in many countries, local treatment, especially of tax issues, can vary. It is important that any treasury professional be aware of how local authorities and regulators will react before making specific decisions.

TEST YOUR UNDERSTANDING: CHAPTER 20

Answers are on pages 732–738.

1. Discuss the concepts of optimal and target capital structure.
2. What are the advantages of financing with common stock?
3. What is the trade-off approach to the use of debt and equity financing in a company's capital structure?
4. What is operating risk, and how can it be measured?
5. In addition to the trade-off between the costs and benefits of using financial leverage, what other factors should be considered as part of determining a company's target capital structure?
6. What is a ratings trigger?
7. Discuss the issue of capital structure as it relates to not-for-profit organizations (NFPs).
8. What are the reasons that private placement may be preferred over public issuance?
9. What are the four key characteristics of an optimal dividend policy?
10. What is a capital lease?
11. Discuss the lease versus borrow-and-buy decision for capital assets.
12. Why might a stock be delisted?
13. What are the four important dates relating to the payment of dividends?
14. What is a DRIP?
15. What is a stock repurchase?
16. What are the primary issues related to the repatriation of capital for multinational companies?
17. What is a deemed dividend?
18. What is an LBO?
19. Discuss the importance of a global tax strategy for a multinational company.

TEST YOUR UNDERSTANDING

Answers

CHAPTER 1 The Role of Treasury Management

1. What are the major objectives of treasury management?

The major objectives of treasury management include:

- Maintain liquidity.
- Optimize cash resources.
- Maintain access to short-term financing.
- Manage investments.
- Maintain access to medium- and long-term financing.
- Manage financial risk.
- Coordinate financial functions and share financial information.
- Manage external vendors.

2. Which of these objectives make up working capital management?

Collectively, the first four objectives listed above are often referred to as *working capital management*:

- Maintain liquidity.
- Optimize cash resources.
- Maintain access to short-term financing.
- Manage investments.

3. Why is effective management of working capital critical to an organization?

Working capital management is the foundation of effective treasury management. Without access to cash to pay vendors and employees, companies cannot operate. Many profitable companies have been forced to close their doors because of insufficient liquidity due to poor cash management.

4. What are the typical primary responsibilities of a treasurer?

A treasurer is primarily responsible for:

- Managing overall financial risk, including FX risk
- Arranging external financing, both short- and long-term
- Managing relationships with banks and other service providers
- Overseeing day-to-day liquidity and cash management
- Investing for the short and long term
- Developing and implementing treasury policies and procedures
- Managing domestic and international payments

5. What are the typical responsibilities of a credit manager?

The credit manager preserves and collects accounts receivable, sets corporate credit policies, approves the extension of credit terms and exposure limits to customers, and establishes information systems to monitor accounts receivable.

6. What are some typical activities for which a board of directors might grant authority to individuals within treasury operations?

The board of directors may grant the authority to:

- Open, close, and modify bank accounts
- Establish credit facilities
- Oversee investments
- Issue debt and equity securities
- Devise, implement, and execute risk management strategies

7. What are the six tasks involved in daily cash management?

Daily cash management typically involves the following tasks:

- Preparing a cash position worksheet
- Monitoring cash balances on deposit at financial institutions
- Collecting, concentrating, and disbursing cash
- Investing and borrowing funds on a short-term basis when needed
- Researching and reconciling exception items, such as unexpected charges on bank accounts, missing deposits, and uncleared checks
- Coordinating efforts with other finance areas, such as accounts receivable, accounts payable, tax, and accounting

8. What is the downside of making treasury a cost center?

The downside to making treasury a cost center is that management may focus on the cost of treasury operations and not the value provided by the function, leading to difficulties in obtaining appropriate budget and staff.

9. Why are shared services centers (SSCs) typically deployed?

Shared service centers are typically deployed for a variety of reasons:

- To reduce the costs of multiple or duplicate operations
- To standardize processes
- To increase the quality and timeliness of services
- To create a higher degree of strategic flexibility

10. Define corporate governance.

Corporate governance refers to the principles and processes by which any organization (for-profit or not-for profit) is governed. It provides the guidelines for managing a company so that it can fulfill its stated goals and objectives in a manner that adds to the value of the company and is also beneficial for all stakeholders in the long term.

11. What is required for a director to be considered independent under NYSE standards?

For a director to be considered independent under the NYSE standards, the board must determine that the director has no material relationship with the listed company, either directly or as a partner, shareholder, or officer of the organization.

12. What are the major checks and balances that limit and monitor management performance?

To protect stockholders, corporate governance procedures establish a set of checks and balances to place limits on executive prerogatives and monitor management performance. Important components include the board of directors (especially independent directors), shareholder meetings, independent external auditors, and regulatory agencies.

CHAPTER 2 Regulatory and Legal Environment

1. What is the primary role that financial institutions (FIs) play in the economy, and why are they regulated?

Their primary role is to provide a mechanism for savers of capital to transfer that capital to those who might best use it. In one instance, it may be some consumer's savings being used to help other consumers purchase a house or car. In another instance, it may be the pension savings of a worker being used to provide the equity capital for a company to expand its production facilities. Because this vital role of capital transfer is fundamental to the efficient functioning of the economy, FIs generally are regulated closely by monetary and other government authorities.

2. What is a central bank?

A central bank (sometimes referred to as a *monetary authority*) is an entity that is responsible for implementing and managing a country's monetary policy—in other words, the country's money supply and interest rates. In many countries, the central bank is also responsible for overseeing its country's commercial banking and payment systems.

3. What is the Financial Stability Board?

The FSB (based in Basel, Switzerland) was established to provide international coordination of national financial authorities and international standard-setting bodies. It works to develop and promote the implementation of effective regulatory, supervisory, and other financial sector policies.

4. What are the principal committees of the Bank for International Settlements?

- Group of Governors and Heads of Supervision (GHOS)
- Committee on the Global Financial System (CGFS)
- Committee on Payment and Settlement Systems (CPSS)

5. Describe the main features of the third Basel Accords (Basel III).

Basel III is a comprehensive set of reform measures, developed in 2011 in response to the global financial crisis of the late 2000s (referred to in this book as the *Recession of 2009*) and scheduled to be implemented through 2018, to strengthen the regulation, supervision, and risk management of the banking sector. As part of Basel III, core capital requirements were increased by approximately 2%, and minimum leverage and liquidity requirements were introduced.

Basel III's stated goals are to:

- Improve the banking sector's ability to absorb shocks arising from financial and economic stress, whatever the source
- Improve risk management and governance
- Strengthen banks' transparency and disclosures

The reforms target:

- Bank-level regulation, which will help raise the resilience of individual banking institutions to periods of stress
- System-wide risks that can build up across the banking sector, as well as the procyclical amplification of these risks over time

6. What is SEPA?

The Single Euro Payments Area (SEPA) is the name of the European Union (EU) payments integration initiative. The SEPA vision was set out by EU governments in the Lisbon agenda in March 2000, which aimed to make Europe more dynamic and competitive. The legislative framework of SEPA is contained in the European Payment Services Directive (PSD).

Following the introduction of euro notes and coins in 2002, the political drivers of the SEPA initiative—EU governments, the European Commission (EC), and the European Central Bank (ECB)—have focused on the integration of the euro payments market. Since then, the political drivers have called upon the payments industry to bolster the common currency by developing a set of harmonized payment schemes and frameworks for electronic euro payments, in line with the following overall vision for SEPA:

- Integrating the multitude of existing national euro credit transfer and euro direct debit schemes into a single set of European payment schemes is a natural step toward making the euro a single and fully operational currency. The PSD currently sets February 2014 as the final date for migration of both credit transfers and direct debits to the SEPA debit and credit schemes.
- Creating a single standard for payment cards across national borders aims at ensuring a consistent customer experience when making or accepting payments with cards throughout the euro area.
- The SEPA program seeks to incentivize increased use of electronic payment instruments by standardizing practices while reducing the cost of wholesale cash distribution.

7. What is the FATF, and what does it do?

The Financial Action Task Force (FATF) is an international organization composed of members from more than 30 countries. The primary purpose of this intergovernmental group is the development and promotion of policies, at both national and international levels, to combat money laundering and terrorist financing.

Since its creation, the FATF has spearheaded the effort to adopt and implement measures designed to counter the use of the financial system by criminals, primarily through anti-money laundering efforts. It monitors members' progress in implementing necessary measures, reviews money laundering and terrorist-financing techniques and countermeasures, and promotes the adoption and implementation of appropriate measures globally. In performing these activities, the FATF collaborates with other international bodies involved in combating both money laundering and the financing of terrorism.

8. Describe the three stages of money laundering.

- **Placement**: The physical deposit of cash proceeds from illegal activities into an FI
- **Layering**: A series of financial transactions designed to separate cash proceeds from their criminal or terrorist origins
- **Integration**: Creating what appears to be a legitimate explanation for the source of funds (e.g., showing that funds were donated for a charitable purpose)

9. What are the five general areas in which financial institution regulation is typically concentrated?

- Monitoring and managing the overall safety and soundness of the banking system
- Setting and implementing monetary policy
- Determining guidelines for the chartering of banks and other depository FIs
- Allocating credit toward certain sectors of the economy and protecting consumers
- Protecting investors purchasing securities through FIs

10. What are the major provisions of the Gramm-Leach-Bliley Act?

The Gramm-Leach-Bliley Act eliminates many of the provisions of the Glass-Steagall Act, especially those that created barriers among the functions of commercial banking, investment banking, and insurance. Specifically, it:

- Permits the creation of financial holding companies (FHCs) that can engage in any activity that the Fed considers financial in nature or incidental to it
- Establishes the Fed as the primary regulator of FHCs, which are subject to consolidated capital requirements at the parent company level and bank-style risk management at all levels
- Allows easier entry by foreign banks into the US financial services market
- Includes key provisions relating to consumer protection, including specific regulations regarding the protection of nonpublic personal information

11. What is the Durbin Amendment?

The Durbin Amendment is an amendment to the Dodd-Frank Act. It is a provision intended to limit debit card interchange fees and increase competition in payment processing.

12. What are the main provisions of the USA PATRIOT Act?

Provisions of the USA PATRIOT Act are that it:

- Imposes significant obligations upon nonbank FIs, including broker-dealers, credit card companies, and check-cashing services (nonbank FIs were not covered previously by BSA). It also includes nonfinancial entities potentially handling large-value transactions, such as car, boat, plane, and jewelry dealers.
- Makes all foreign banks with accounts in the United States subject to US jurisdiction, including the power to obtain records and information regarding customers.
- Prohibits US banks from maintaining, either directly or indirectly, correspondent accounts for any foreign shell banks, which are defined as foreign banks without a physical presence in any country.
- Prevents US credit card system operators from authorizing foreign banks to issue or accept US credit cards without taking steps to prevent usage by terrorists.
- Requires banks to know their customers, resulting in increased due diligence before taking on new business.

13. What is the Red Flags Rule?

The Federal Trade Commission (FTC), the federal bank regulatory agencies, and the National Credit Union Administration (NCUA) have issued US regulations (the Red Flags Rule) requiring FIs and creditors to develop and implement written identity theft prevention programs, as part of the Fair and Accurate Credit Transactions Act of 2003 (FACT). The programs must provide for the identification of, detection of, and response to patterns, practices, or specific activities—known as *red flags*—that could indicate identity theft.

14. Discuss the impact of Sarbanes-Oxley (SOX) legislation on publicly traded firms.

The primary purpose of SOX is to improve disclosure and financial reporting in the wake of a series of dramatic financial scandals between the years 2000 and 2002. SOX brought about numerous changes to Securities and Exchange Commission (SEC) rules and regulations and created the Public Company Accounting Oversight Board (PCAOB). Specifically, publicly traded firms must:

- Disclose in annual reports the code of ethics applicable to senior financial officers. Companies that change or waive the code must disclose the event by filing a Form 8-K with the SEC or posting a notice on the company's website.
- Disclose in annual reports whether the audit committee has a financial expert.
- Establish and maintain adequate internal controls for financial reporting.
- Require audit committees to preapprove all audit and non-audit services provided by the auditor, and be briefed by auditors on the company's accounting, including alternative approaches that might be preferable to the company's current methods.

15. List and discuss the key Fed regulations that impact treasury professionals.

The Fed defines and enforces several key US banking regulations that impact treasury professionals. Some of the major regulations include the following:

Regulation D implements the reserve requirement provision of the Federal Reserve Act of 1913, and imposes uniform reserve requirements on all depository institutions, with different levels of reserves for different types of deposits. The Fed uses this regulation to control the supply of money.

Regulation E implements provisions of the Electronic Fund Transfer Act of 1978, which establishes the rights, responsibilities, and liabilities of parties engaging in consumer-related EFTs, and also protects consumers using systems such as ATMs, automated clearinghouse (ACH), and credit cards. Regulation E also establishes the guidelines for the documentation of electronic transfers.

Regulation J implements the check collection and settlement provision of the Federal Reserve Act of 1913, and establishes procedures, duties, and responsibilities for check collection and settlement through the Federal Reserve System.

Regulation Q implemented the interest-bearing account restriction of the Glass-Steagall Act of 1933 and barred the paying of interest on any corporate demand deposit accounts. Interest rate ceilings initially set by this regulation on all commercial bank deposit accounts were partially phased out in 1986 by the Depository Institution Deregulation and Monetary Control Act (DIDMCA), and the final restrictions on corporate demand deposits were removed by the Dodd-Frank Act in 2010.

Regulation Y implements various provisions of the Bank Holding Company Act of 1956, the Change in Bank Control Act of 1978, and subsequent revisions covering the acquisition of control of banks and bank holding companies. It defines and regulates the nonbanking activities in which bank holding companies and foreign banking organizations in the United States may engage, including anti-tying restrictions.

Regulation Z applies to the Truth in Lending Act of 1968 (TILA), which is concerned with promoting informed use of credit by consumers. This regulation covers the use of all types of consumer lending, including credit cards, home mortgages, student loans, and installment loans. For treasury professionals, the primary impact of this regulation relates to credit cards offered to their customers; for educational institutions, the impact relates to the use of student loans.

Regulation Z was updated in February of 2010 in order to implement the Credit Card Accountability Responsibility and Disclosure Act of 2009 (Credit CARD Act). As a result, Regulation Z also:

- Protects consumers from unexpected increases in credit card interest rates by generally prohibiting increases in a rate during the first year after an account is opened, as well as any increases in a rate that applies to an existing credit card balance
- Prohibits creditors from issuing a credit card to a consumer who is under the age of 21 unless the consumer can make the required payments or obtains the signature of a parent or other cosigner who is able to do so
- Requires creditors to obtain a consumer's consent before charging fees for transactions that exceed the credit limit
- Limits the high fees associated with subprime credit cards
- Bans creditors from using the two-cycle billing method to impose interest charges
- Prohibits creditors from allocating payments in ways that maximize interest charges

Regulation BB implements the provisions of the Community Reinvestment Act of 1977, as revised in 1995, and requires banks to help meet the credit needs of the entire community in which they do business.

Regulation CC implements the provisions of the Expedited Funds Availability Act of 1987, which establishes rules designed to speed the collection and return of checks, and mandates banks to return unpaid checks expeditiously. This regulation also imposes the same return procedures to payable through drafts (PTDs) that apply to checks, and establishes endorsement standards for banks and companies to follow when depositing and clearing checks.

16. What is the Uniform Commercial Code?

The Uniform Commercial Code (UCC) is a uniform set of laws governing commercial transactions in the United States. It defines the rights and duties of all parties in a commercial transaction and provides a statutory definition of commonly accepted business practices. Because of the size of the US economy, the UCC has significant impact globally, and various portions of it have been used as a model in developing global trade agreements, such as the United Nations (UN) Convention on Contracts for the International Sale of Goods and international standards regarding letters of credit.

17. What are escheatment statutes, and how do they impact banks and companies?

In the business world, escheat statutes primarily impact banks or companies that hold unclaimed assets of customers or employees. The most general occurrence of escheat is when an entity (e.g., a bank) holds money or property (e.g., an account in that bank) and the property goes unclaimed for some specified period of time (generally referred to as a *dormant account*). In many jurisdictions, if the owner cannot be located, such property can be escheated to the government. Many states maintain websites and databases that allow individuals and companies to search for funds that have been escheated.

For nonbank organizations, escheat is the process of turning over to a state authority (in the United States) unclaimed or abandoned payroll checks, stocks and shares whose owners cannot be traced, or unclaimed/unused rebates, customer purchase deposits or down payments, and gift cards/certificates. It is important to realize that the state involved is the residence state of the customer or owner of the item being escheated, not the state of residence of the organization holding the property. Every company is required to file unclaimed property reports with each appropriate state annually and to make a good faith effort to find the owners of dormant accounts. The escheating criteria are driven by individual state regulations and, in many cases, the penalties and interest assessed by the state for failure to comply are often more than the actual amount of unclaimed property.

18. List the most common types of bankruptcies allowed by US federal legislation.

In the United States, there are several types of bankruptcy available for corporations, municipalities, and individuals. The following are the most common:

- **Chapter 7:** Liquidation of a firm
- **Chapter 9:** Financially distressed municipalities (city, county, and state government bankruptcies)
- **Chapter 11:** Business reorganization
- **Chapter 13:** Adjustment of debts for individuals with regular income (personal bankruptcy)
- **Chapter 15:** Establishment of bankruptcy trustees (for bankruptcies that involve companies, assets, or individuals in more than one country)

19. Describe the three types of formal bankruptcy.

- **Freefall:** In this case, a firm goes (or is forced) into bankruptcy and has no structured plan for coming out of bankruptcy.
- **Prearranged:** In this case, management has arranged a tentative deal with some of the creditors or parties, but not with all of them. Generally, these deals are done on an informal basis and are not legally binding.
- **Prepackaged (Prepac):** In this case, management files with the SEC a formal plan that all classes of creditors have voted on and accepted. Essentially, the firm goes to court with all of the details worked out and with everyone agreeing to the plan.

20. What is a capital tax?

In some foreign countries, particularly those experiencing an upsurge in economic growth, companies are assessed a capital tax on the initial capital used to establish a new venture, and on subsequent incoming capital or repatriated capital. A capital tax is used as a fiscal tool by some countries to augment tax collections. The tax can also be used by a government to slow foreign direct investment in a country.

CHAPTER 3 Banks and Financial Institutions

1. What is a global financial institution, and what are the primary services that it offers?

For the purpose of this book, a *global FI* is defined as one that operates in multiple countries in more than one part of the world, providing services to both domestic and multinational corporations. An FI with substantial operations outside its home country would be considered a global bank or FI according to this definition.

The primary services offered by global FIs are depository accounts, transaction services, lending, foreign exchange (FX), information reporting, and investment banking.

2. What are the two types of depository accounts?

There are two basic types of depository accounts:

- Current accounts, referred to as *checking or demand deposit accounts (DDAs)* in the United States
- Noncurrent or time deposit accounts (TDAs)

a. Current or Demand Deposit Accounts (DDAs)

A DDA, or checking account, is both a store of value (deposits) and, perhaps more importantly for treasury management purposes, a vehicle through which an account holder uses a bank to transfer funds to, and receive deposits from, a third party. The method of payment can be by cash, check, debit card, internal book transfer, or electronic transfer.

Depending upon the local regulations, DDAs may be interest-bearing or non-interesting-bearing. Prior to 2010 and the passage of the Dodd-Frank Act, the US Federal Reserve prohibited the payment of interest on demand deposits held by for-profit companies in the United States, in what was known as *Reg Q*. While Reg Q has since been repealed, most US-based corporate DDAs still do not earn interest on deposited funds. In addition, most large government or not-for-profit entities do not earn interest on their deposits because they use the same types of deposit accounts that are used by large corporations. In lieu of actual interest payments, many US-based banks provide earnings credits or analysis credits, which can be used to offset charges for bank services.

It is also important to note that another major difference between DDAs in the United States and those in other countries is the process of handling overdrafts. An overdraft occurs when items are presented against a DDA in excess of the balance in that account. In most countries, the general practice is to incorporate both an investment rate and a credit agreement with the DDA so that any positive balances are paid interest, while negative DDA balances result in an automatic loan and are charged some rate of interest. This type of arrangement is not generally available in the United States for corporate holders of DDA accounts unless specific lending arrangements have been previously agreed upon.

b. Noncurrent or Time Deposit Accounts (TDAs)

Time deposit accounts are accounts that must be maintained at an FI for a contractually specified period of time. These accounts usually allow withdrawal only with prior notification and may charge a penalty if the withdrawal requirements are not met. A certificate of deposit (CD) is a type of TDA and is used widely by savers. It represents the bank's obligation to pay a fixed or variable interest rate over some period of time.

For CDs under $100,000, the rate is typically nonnegotiable by the depositor and is generally fixed through the tenor of the certificate. The maturity date is a specified date in the future, not a length of time. Interest rates and maturities on CDs valued at more than $100,000 are typically negotiable, and the interest rate may be fixed or variable. For larger institutional investors, fully negotiable CDs are offered generally in $1 million blocks with maturities ranging from 14 days to 5 years. Most are offered with maturities of 12 or fewer months and are traded in an active secondary market.

FIs also offer other types of TDAs, such as savings accounts and money market deposit accounts (MMDAs), primarily for their retail and small business customers.

3. What are the different types of credit services offered by commercial banks?

Commercial banks, by definition, are broad-based lenders. They offer a wide range of business loans that vary by type of borrower, use of proceeds, and loan maturities. Banks provide medium- to long-term secured and unsecured loans to businesses for the purchase of property, plant, and equipment. The source of repayment is generally from cash flows of the company, but in some cases may be restricted to cash flows generated by the asset being financed. The loans are typically collateralized by the company's property, plant, or equipment, but again in some cases the collateral may be limited to the specific asset that is being financed (e.g., equipment loans or property loans). Leasing divisions of banks provide an alternative to medium- and long-term loans for financing capital equipment. FIs also provide mortgage financing for commercial real estate.

In addition, banks offer short-term working capital loans to fund cash shortfalls that occur when cash outflows precede cash inflows. In seasonal businesses, an expansion of the investment in inventory and accounts receivable precedes the cash inflow that occurs when accounts receivable convert to cash.

Short-term business borrowing (typically with a term of less than a year) can take several forms. For example, a business may borrow a specific amount to be repaid by a specific date (commonly referred to as a *term loan or note*). Alternatively, a business may secure a revolving line of credit (commonly referred to as a *revolver*), meaning it can borrow up to a specified amount, repay all or part of the outstanding balance, and borrow again at any time. In this case, the business typically must pay off the revolver in full by a specified date.

4. What are the typical trade services offered by large financial institutions?

Large FIs often provide a wide range of services to facilitate the payment and collection of trade obligations. These are more typically used for international business, but sometimes they are also used domestically.

- **Trade or commercial letters of credit (L/Cs)** are documents issued by a bank, guaranteeing the payment of a customer's draft up to a stated amount for a specified period, provided that certain conditions are met. In effect, the issuing bank is substituting its good name and credit on behalf of its customer's.
- **Standby L/Cs or guarantees** (also known as *clean L/Cs*) are performance contracts issued by banks ensuring that certain terms and conditions will be met by the bank's customer. Though these guarantees are generally used by companies involved in large capital construction projects, they are suitable any time certain contract conditions must be met and when there is no tangible collateral to seize for nonpayment or nonperformance.
- A **documentary collection** is a trade-services payment method that processes the collection of a draft and accompanying shipping documents through international correspondent banks. Instructions regarding the specifics of the transaction are contained in a collection letter that accompanies the documentation. It is the responsibility of the seller (exporter) to determine the specific instructions used in the collection letter.

- A **bankers' acceptance (BA)** is a negotiable, short-term instrument used primarily to finance the import of foreign goods, the export of domestic goods, or the storage of readily marketable staples. A BA is created when a bank "accepts" payment responsibility for a draft issued in connection with an L/C or documentary collection.

5. What are the three components of the investment banking process?

The investment banking process relating to the issuance of stocks and bonds generally has three distinct components: origination, underwriting, and distribution.

a. Origination

Origination involves consultation with a company raising funds about the characteristics of the issue and any underlying documents. The investment bank also monitors market conditions and advises the company about the best time to bring the issue to market in order to maximize the price per issued share and the amount of funds the firm wishes to raise.

b. Underwriting

Underwriting is the act of purchasing all or part of a block of securities issued by a company. Under a full-underwriting arrangement, the investment bank or syndicate (group) of investment banks owns the entire issue. The company has all the money it will receive and may set about the business of using the money as it intends. At that point, the investment bank (or syndicate) assumes the price and marketability risks of the issue. Price risk means it may not be possible for the investment bank to sell the entire issue of bonds or stock at the anticipated market price, which can jeopardize its profitability. Marketing risk means that it may not be possible to sell all the shares, which also places profitability at risk.

If the investment bank or syndicate is not confident it can sell the entire issue, it may try to assist the company on a best-efforts basis. In this case, the company pays a fee directly to the investment bank as compensation for advising the firm and marketing the issue. The investment bank does not underwrite the issue. Rather, it simply sells as many shares as possible through a selling group of brokerage firms up to a specified limit.

c. Distribution

Distribution is the term applied to a securities sale to investors by an investment bank or a syndicate of investment banks. When a syndicate is formed, one of the investment banks serves as the lead bank (also called the *lead underwriter*). The lead bank assumes most management functions and receives most of the fees. Once the underwriting syndicate owns the new securities, each member investment bank uses its distribution system to sell the issue.

6. Describe the services offered by commercial bank trust departments to their commercial customers.

- Establishing and managing employee pension plans or qualified employee benefit plans
- Acting as a corporate trustee for corporate bond or preferred stock issues
- Monitoring compliance with bond indenture agreements, which are the contractual arrangements between bond issuers and bondholders
- Acting as a transfer agent by keeping records of each purchase and sale of stocks and bonds, including maintaining records of a corporation's shareholders by name, address, and number of shares
- Acting as a registrar by compiling and maintaining lists of current stockholders and bondholders for the purpose of remitting dividend and interest payments

- Acting as a paying agent, whereby an FI receives funds from an issuer of stocks or bonds to pay dividends to stockholders and to pay principal and interest to bondholders
- Offering custody services (such as providing safekeeping for securities), and buying, selling, receiving, and delivering securities based on terms outlined in a custody agreement

7. What is a bank identification code? Describe the most commonly used bank identification code.

The Bank Identification Code, or BIC, is a unique identifier that specifies precisely the financial institutions involved—in some cases down to the branch level—in a financial transaction. The most commonly used BIC is known as the *SWIFT code* because the system is administered by the Society for Worldwide Interbank Financial Telecommunication (SWIFT).

A SWIFT code consists of eight or eleven characters, as follows:

- First four characters—bank code (alphabetic only)
- Next two characters—ISO 3166-1 alpha-2 country code (alphabetic only)
- Next two characters—location code (alphanumeric)
- Last three characters—branch code, optional ("XXX" for primary office) (alphanumeric)

When an eight-character code is used, it refers to the primary or head office of a given bank.

8. What is an IBAN?

The International Bank Account Number (IBAN) is a way to identify bank accounts across national borders. It was originally adopted by the European Committee for Banking Standards (ECBS), and later adopted as an international standard by the International Organization for Standardization (ISO). As with the BIC, the current standard is managed by SWIFT. The IBAN was initially developed to simplify payments within the European Union under the Single Euro Payments Area (SEPA). It has since also been implemented by most European countries and many other countries, especially in the Middle East and in the Caribbean.

The IBAN consists of up to 34 alphanumeric characters: first the two-letter ISO 3166-1 alpha-2 country code, then two check digits, and finally a country-specific Basic Bank Account Number (BBAN). The BBAN format is decided by each national banking community under the restriction that it must be of a fixed length of case-insensitive alphanumeric characters. It includes the domestic bank account number, branch identifier, and potential routing information.

9. What is a captive finance company?

A captive finance company is a type of industrial bank that is a subsidiary of a large industrial corporation and that finances purchases solely of the corporation's products. These FIs typically raise funds in the CP market and lend to other companies and individuals that purchase products from the parent corporation. Having a captive finance company allows a company to extend credit to customers without putting itself directly at risk. Companies such as Ford Motor Credit, General Electric (GE) Capital, and Hyundai Motor Finance are examples of captive finance companies.

CHAPTER 4 Payment Systems

1. What is a payment system?

A payment system is a series of processes and technologies that transfer monetary value from one party to another. Payments are typically made in exchange for the provision of goods or services, or to satisfy a legal obligation. They can be made in any number of currencies, using a variety of methods, such as cash, checks, electronic transfers, and cards. What makes a payment system a system is that it uses cash substitutes, such as checks or electronic messages, to instruct the debits and credits that transfer value from one party to another.

2. Is cash a payment system? Why or why not?

Cash payments are not, per se, a payment system, since the value transfer happens as part of the transfer of the coin or currency, but they constitute a critical payment method nonetheless. In fact, because of the inherent value of cash and the associated need for accounting and safekeeping, most companies have implemented significant processes around the handling of cash payments.

3. Name the four basic participants in a payment.

- The **payor** makes the payment and has his/her account debited for the value of the transaction.
- The **payor's financial institution** (often referred to as the *paying bank*) processes the value transfer on the payor's behalf.
- The **payee or beneficiary** is the receiver of the payment whose account is credited for the value of the transaction.
- The **payee's financial institution** (often referred to as the *receiving bank* or *receiving FI*) processes the transaction on behalf of the payee and generally holds the value in an account.

4. What are the four key elements of the payment process?

- **Payment instructions** are the information contained in an electronic transfer (e.g., a wire or ACH [automated clearinghouse] transaction) or a check. These instructions are from the payor and tell the paying bank to transfer value to the beneficiary through the receiving bank.
- **Payment generation** is where the instructions are entered into the payment system itself.
- **Clearing** is the process where the FIs use the payment information to transfer money between themselves on behalf of the payor and the beneficiary, either directly or through some external network.
- **Settlement** is the final step in the process and occurs when the beneficiary's bank account is credited and the payor's bank account is charged.

5. Discuss the difference between settlement and finality.

Settlement or *availability* refers to the actual movement of funds from the payor's account to the payee's account—in other words, the time at which the payee can actually use the money involved. *Finality* refers to the point in time when the payor knows that the money involved cannot be taken back or retracted by the payor or the payor's bank. Settlement becomes final when a payment is unconditional and irrevocable.

Finality varies depending on the payment system and the parties involved in the transaction. Payment systems that offer immediate and irrevocable value are called *real-time gross settlement (RTGS) systems* and are typically wire transfer systems. Others, such as check- or card-based systems, typically provide immediate information, with value following at a later time. But the value is contingent on the payor or the payor's bank not attempting to retract the payment, a right which can exist for several months or more, depending upon the specific payment system.

6. List the four major categories of payments, other than cash.

- **Checks or drafts** are payments that are initiated when one party writes a check to pay another, and they are one of the oldest forms of noncash payment systems. They are still used throughout the world and are most widely used in the United States, where they still represent the largest number of commercial or business payments.
- **RTGS (real-time gross settlement) or large-value electronic payments** are what most people mean when they refer to *wire transfers*. Wires have existed since the late 1800s with the invention of the telegraph, but did not become widely used until the early 1900s.
- **Low-value electronic payments,** often referred to as **automated clearinghouse, or ACH, payments,** were introduced in the early 1970s and were designed to replace checks with electronic payments. Unlike wires, which are processed individually and immediately (in real time), ACH payments are value-dated and processed in batches, and typically take one to two days to settle. Originally ACH payments were intended for "small" payments, such as payroll and consumer transactions. Today, many companies use ACH transactions to replace wires and other payment systems when the payment amount is known at least one day prior to the transaction date, due to the lower cost of ACH transactions.
- **Card-based payments** are payments that settle through one of the large card-processing networks such as Visa, MasterCard, China UnionPay, or American Express, or through one of the ATM (automated teller machine) or POS (point-of-sale) systems such as STAR, NYCE, or PULSE in the United States, Interac in Canada, or Telstra in Australia. Originally, card transactions were all credit card payments and were initiated through the presentment of a plastic credit card. Today, card payments come in a wide variety of alternatives, such as debit cards, prepaid cards, and payroll cards—some of which, despite the name, no longer use a physical card.

7. What are on-us and on-we check clearing?

"On-us" check clearing involves a single bank and occurs when a payee deposits a check in an account at the same bank on which it is drawn. The bank simultaneously debits the payor's account and credits the payee's account. The depositor typically receives same-day or immediate availability, if funds are available, and processing fees are often lower than for other checks that require additional processing.

"On-we" check clearing is similar to on-us but involves a group of banks that use a common third-party vendor to process their checks for them. Since all of the banks' checks are processed at the same time and same place, they can be treated as if they were on-us items, typically resulting in same-day or immediate availability for the depositing company.

8. What are the four major clearing channels for transit checks in the United States?

- **Clearinghouse:** Clearinghouses are either formal or informal associations formed by banks in a geographic area to permit the exchange of items drawn on the member participants. Member banks make daily, or sometimes more frequent, presentments to the clearinghouse. The net value (i.e., face amount of items submitted less items received, calculated on a bank-by-bank basis) is transferred between the banks by debiting and crediting correspondent accounts or through reserve accounts that each bank maintains with the local Federal Reserve Bank.

- **Correspondent Bank:** In correspondent bank clearing, the collecting bank maintains a depository account with another bank. The collecting bank sends cash letters to the correspondent bank, which presents the items to the paying bank through a local clearinghouse or the Fed. The collecting bank's depository account at the correspondent bank is then credited with the proceeds of the checks.
- **Direct Send or Direct Exchange:** As an alternative to using the clearing channels just discussed, collecting banks may arrange to send cash letters directly to a paying bank or to a nonlocal Federal Reserve Bank. This process, also referred to as *direct presentment*, enables banks to meet various deposit deadlines and achieve faster clearing times. The collecting bank maintains a depository account with the paying bank or nonlocal Federal Reserve Bank, which is credited with the proceeds of the checks. If the cash letter arrives early enough in the day, the paying bank must settle the same day.
- **Federal Reserve System (Fed):** The Fed also acts as a check-clearing agent. Depository banks can send cash letters to the Fed, which will then clear the checks and transfer values from paying banks to depository banks.

9. Describe continuous linked settlement (CLS) and why it was developed.

Beginning in the mid-1990s, central banks became increasingly concerned that the high level of settlement risk in existing practices, coupled with an unexpected event or failure, could trigger a serious disruption of the global FX markets and financial system liquidity. In an FX transaction, settlement risk is the risk that one party to the transaction pays out the currency it sold but does not receive the currency it bought. The exposure to a single counterparty, even if for a limited time, can be very large relative to the capital of the parties to the transaction. The solution to address this concern was the development of a risk-reducing, multicurrency FX settlement service. This solution is called *continuous linked settlement (CLS)*. CLS allows a simultaneous exchange of the payments for both sides of the underlying financial transactions (e.g., FX contracts, non-deliverable forward [NDF] contracts, and over-the-counter [OTC] derivative contracts), thereby eliminating settlement risk.

10. What is SWIFT?

The Society for Worldwide Interbank Financial Telecommunication (SWIFT) is not, strictly speaking, a payment system. It is a communication system used by most of the banks in the world to transmit payment instructions, among other things, and is therefore often thought of, incorrectly, as an international wire transfer or funds transfer system. SWIFT is an industry-owned, cooperative, interbank telecommunication network that enables banks to send authenticated electronic messages in standard formats. The information that moves through SWIFT ultimately results in value being transferred from one party to another, generally through correspondent banks, hence the perception that it is a payment system.

11. What are small-value transfer or ACH systems?

Small-value transfer systems are electronic networks for the exchange of smaller payment instructions among FIs, typically on behalf of consumers. Many countries have small-value transfer systems—Bacs in the United Kingdom, ECG (Electronic Clearing) in Hong Kong, and ACH in the United States. Small-value transfer payments, usually referred to as *ACH payments* or *non-time-critical payments*, are payment instructions to either debit or credit a deposit account. They are typically batch-processed, value-dated electronic funds transfers between originating and receiving FIs. An additional feature of most ACH systems is that an ACH transaction is capable of transferring more information about a payment than can normally be transmitted via most paper-based instruments or most wire transfers.

12. What are the three major currency options available for FedGlobal ACH payments?

- **Fixed-to-Variable:** US dollars are converted to a variable amount of a destination currency based on a competitive exchange rate. Settlement is between participating US financial institutions and the Federal Reserve Banks, in US dollars.
- **Fixed-to-Fixed—US Dollar to US Dollar:** Payments are both transferred and received in US dollars. Settlement is between participating US financial institutions and the Federal Reserve Banks, in US dollars.
- **Fixed-to-Fixed—Foreign Currency to Foreign Currency:** Payments are both transferred and received in foreign currency. The FX rate and settlement are managed and processed by participating US financial institutions and the respective foreign gateway operators via their foreign correspondent banks.

13. What are the primary differences between credit, debit, and charge cards?

A credit card is issued against a line of credit that the institution or merchant has extended, whereas a debit card is issued against a deposit account belonging to the cardholder. Charge cards are a special type of credit card in which the outstanding balance must be paid off each month.

14. What are purchasing cards, and what are their principal benefits?

Purchasing cards (also known as *procurement cards* or *p-cards*) are credit cards used by businesses for the purchase of supplies, inventory, equipment, and service contracts. Typically, p-cards are used for varying purchases, either low- or high-value, with spending limits established on an individual card basis. Purchases can be limited to approved vendors and suppliers, as determined by the merchant category code of the vendor or supplier. The principal benefit of a p-card for a company is the replacement of the traditional time-consuming, labor-intensive, paper-based requisition process. Additionally, companies may negotiate a rebate based on charge volume and average transaction size, and they may be able to effectively delay payment since purchased items will not be paid for until the end of the billing cycle. The principal benefit for an employee is that essential goods and services can be obtained quickly and conveniently without a complicated purchase order process.

15. What is PCI DSS?

As a result of several system breaches and compromises of data in card networks, the card industry created a governing body to establish and administer a series of strict requirements for the security of card data. Merchants are required to go through an audit of their systems and applications to confirm they are compliant with the Payment Card Industry Data Security Standard (PCI DSS).

The PCI DSS is a worldwide information security standard defined by the Payment Card Industry Security Standards Council. The standard was created to help organizations that process card payments prevent payment card fraud through increased controls around the data they hold and exchange. The standard applies to all organizations that store, process, or transmit cardholder information from any card branded with the logo of one of the major card brands.

Failure to comply with standards or a breach of security can result in substantial fines and possible termination of the acceptance of payment cards.

16. List the major components of merchant card fees.

The major components of merchant card fees are:

- Interchange fees (referred to simply as *interchange*)
- Assessments
- Processor fees or markups

CHAPTER 5 Money Markets

1. Who are the primary participants in the money market?

Issuers of money market instruments include government entities, securities dealers, commercial banks, and other corporations (including not-for-profits) that raise funds by borrowing in the money market. These organizations also invest in this market directly through purchases of money market instruments and indirectly by investing in money market funds (MMFs).

In the money markets, investors are lenders, while issuers are borrowers. Thus, investors purchasing money market instruments are making short-term loans to issuers. In many cases, large organizations participating in the money markets are both issuers and investors, depending on their needs at a specific point in time.

A broker-dealer is an entity that trades securities for its own account or on behalf of its customers. When executing trade orders on behalf of a customer, the institution is said to be acting as a *broker*. When executing trades for its own account, the institution is said to be acting as a *dealer*. Securities bought from clients or other firms in the capacity of a dealer may be sold to clients or to other firms, acting again in the capacity of a dealer, or they may become a part of the broker-dealer's own holdings.

2. What is a central securities depository?

Central securities depositories (CSDs) are companies that hold securities, in either certificated or noncertificated (dematerialized) form, to enable book-entry transfer of securities. CSDs may also provide a variety of other services—such as trade matching, and clearing and settlement—to facilitate money market transactions. Examples of CSDs include the Depository Trust Company (DTC) in the United States, Euroclear in Belgium, and the Singapore Exchange (SGX) in Singapore. Nearly all short-term securities are issued in noncertificated or book-entry form.

3. What are the major categories of investment risk?

- Credit or default risk
- Liquidity risk
- Price/interest rate risk
- Foreign exchange (FX) risk

4. What is a repurchase agreement (repo), and how does it work?

In a typical repo, a bank or securities dealer sells government securities it owns to an investor and agrees to repurchase them at a later date and at a slightly higher price. In most cases, this type of agreement is referred to as a *repo agreement* from the perspective of the entity selling the securities and agreeing to repurchase them at a later date. From the perspective of the entity that buys the securities with a promise to sell them back at a later date, it is generally known as a *reverse repo*. Thus, the repo side of the transaction is actually a short-term borrowing arrangement while the reverse repo side is a short-term investment arrangement.

5. What is CP?

Commercial paper (or *CP*) refers to tradable promissory notes issued by companies, as opposed to banks, and is normally an unsecured obligation or debt of the issuing company (i.e., the CP is not backed or "secured" by any collateral of the issuing company). Maturity can range from overnight to 270 days for publicly traded CP (issued in the United States under the SEC Securities Act of 1933 Section 3(a)(3)) and up to 397 days for private-placement CP (issued under Section 4(a)(2) of the same act), but most paper issued matures in less than 45 days. CP does not usually pay interest during its term. Instead, it is issued at a discounted price and the face value is paid at maturity. Therefore, the yield is a factor of the difference between the price paid and the face value over the term. Most CP is purchased for a specific maturity and is held for the full term. However, CP can be traded on the secondary market if an investor needs to access its capital value before maturity.

6. What is bank paper?

Banks raise funds in the money markets through time deposits, repurchase agreements (repos), and banker's acceptances (BAs). These are sometimes collectively referred to as *bank paper* or *bank obligations*. Examples of time deposits include savings accounts, certificates of deposit (CDs), and negotiable CDs. Negotiable CDs are large-value time deposits issued by banks and other financial institutions that are bought and sold on the open market. Negotiable CDs are usually traded in multiples of 100,000 or more (USD or foreign currency equivalent). While all CDs have a fixed maturity, there is an active secondary market for negotiable CDs. Nonnegotiable CDs, or retail CDs, which are issued in many different denominations to consumers and businesses, generally cannot be redeemed prior to maturity without a penalty and lack a secondary market.

7. Describe government paper.

State and local government agencies and authorities, as well as other government entities, raise funds in the short-term money market by issuing a range of short-term paper, generally referred to as *treasury bills* or *government-issued promissory notes*.

The market for government paper in most countries tends to be liquid and highly active, with investors having the ultimate reassurance of a sovereign issuer, although sovereign risk (i.e., the risk that a government itself may default) is a growing issue. In most cases, short-term government paper is issued on a discount basis. A variety of maturities is generally available, depending on a government's borrowing requirements, allowing investors to match their liquidity requirements very closely. However, government issuers generally do not need to offer much relative yield to attract investors, and returns will tend to be lower than other instruments of the same maturity because of the generally low default risk.

UK gilts, US Treasuries, German bunds, Japanese government bonds (JGBs), and Brazilian government bonds are all examples of sovereign government bonds. The United States, Japan, and Europe have historically been the biggest issuers in the government bond market. While US Treasury issues include T-bills, notes, and bonds, only those maturing within one year are classified as money market instruments. Because their liquidity and default risk are so low as to be considered near zero by the rating agencies, US Treasury securities are generally considered risk-free and serve as the benchmark against which interest rates on other debt securities are compared.

T-bills are money market instruments that are sold at a discount to their maturity value (i.e., par) and issued with original maturities of less than one year. At the time of this writing, T-bills are issued with maturities of 4, 13, 26, and 52 weeks. Newly issued Treasury offerings are sold through a multiple-price, sealed-bid auction. T-bills can be purchased on either a competitive or a noncompetitive basis. For investors submitting competitive bids, the bids are accepted starting with the highest price (i.e., lowest yield) offered, down to the lowest price necessary to sell the entire issue. Noncompetitive bids may also be submitted. In this case, the bidder is guaranteed to receive the desired amount of bills at the average price from the competitive-bid process.

8. What is an FRN?

Both companies and banks issue floating-rate notes (FRNs) to raise funds in the short-term market. FRNs sit at the longer end of the money market maturity spectrum, with maturities typically of one year or longer. FRNs pay a regular coupon, as well as the promise of a return of their face value at maturity. The actual return, or margin, on an FRN is a combination of the coupon interest rate and the capital gain or loss that results from an FRN transaction, since FRNs are traded on the secondary market at a discount. If an FRN is trading at par (i.e., at full face value), then the return is identical to the coupon rate.

The name *floating-rate note* derives from the fact that the rate of interest resets periodically, based on a reference rate such as the London Interbank Offered Rate (LIBOR) or the Euro Interbank Offered Rate (Euribor). As a result, FRNs are sold at a quoted spread over the stated reference rate. The spread is a rate that remains constant while the reference rate can vary. FRNs can have a variety of special features, such as minimum or maximum coupon rates. Perpetual FRNs are a type of FRN that is issued with no maturity date, and investors can only recapture their capital by selling them on the secondary market.

9. What is meant by the phrase "breaking the buck"?

Money market funds (MMFs) generally have a net asset value (NAV) set at one unit of the currency of the offering, such as dollars, pounds (sterling), or euros (hence the term *unit trust*). MMFs typically strive for stability and security. As long as the NAV of a particular MMF does not fall below one unit (e.g., $1), referred to as "breaking the buck," the investor's initial investment is secure. Historically, MMFs have been secure investments, and many treasury professionals (as well as individual investors) tend to regard them as the equivalent of cash in the bank. However, MMFs are not insured, and various regulators, such as the Securities and Exchange Commission (SEC) in the United States and the Committee of European Securities Regulators (CESR), are looking at changing the regulations regarding NAV and other MMF features.

10. Describe the Commercial Book-Entry System (CBES).

Operated by the US Treasury, CBES is a multi-tiered, automated system for purchasing, holding, and transferring marketable Treasury securities. CBES exists as a delivery system that provides for the simultaneous transfer of securities against the settlement of funds. Securities owners (or their brokers on their behalf) receive interest and redemption payments wired directly to their linked accounts.

At the top tier of CBES is the National Book-Entry System (NBES), which is operated by the Fed. For Treasury securities, the Fed operates the NBES in its capacity as the fiscal agent of the US Treasury. The Federal Reserve Banks maintain book-entry accounts for depository institutions, the US Treasury, foreign central banks, and most government-sponsored enterprises (GSEs).

At the middle tier of CBES, depository institutions hold book-entry accounts for their customers, which include brokers, dealers, institutional investors, and trusts. At the lower tier, each broker, dealer, and financial institution maintains book-entry accounts for individual customers, corporations, and other entities.

When an investor purchases securities through a broker, dealer, or financial institution, the securities are held on the book-entry system of that firm. Holding Treasury securities in this manner is known as *indirect holding* since there are one or more entities between the investor and the issuer (US Treasury). The CBES has succeeded in replacing paper securities with electronic records, eliminating the potential for theft, loss, or counterfeiting.

CHAPTER 6 Capital Markets

1. What are the two basic segments of the capital markets?

The capital markets can be divided into two basic segments:

- **Debt market**, which includes fixed-income capital, such as bond securities and term loans
- **Equity market**, which includes securities such as shares of common and preferred stock

2. Who are the key participants in the capital markets?

The key participants in the capital markets are the issuers of the securities, the investors who buy those securities, the broker-dealers who help to make the market function, and the regulators who help to ensure a level playing field and adherence to the rules.

3. List the different issuers of securities in the capital markets.

The primary issuers of capital market securities are governments and central banks, corporations, state-owned enterprises, sub-sovereign entities, and mutual fund companies.

4. What is the difference between retail and institutional investors?

Retail investors are typically individuals buying small amounts of stocks or bonds for their own investment portfolios. They are a large source of demand for investment vehicles and, in large measure, are relied upon by issuers as a very important source of capital. On the other hand, institutional investors come in various forms, but they can generally be described as large-scale investors (e.g., mutual fund companies, insurance companies, money managers, pension funds, corporations, and banks) that purchase large blocks of securities on behalf of others, as well as for their own portfolios.

5. Discuss the concept of primary markets versus secondary markets.

Primary markets offer newly issued debt and equity securities to investors when firms or government units sell securities to raise funds. An investment bank or a syndicate of investment banks underwrites (purchases) a securities issue and then sells shares of that issue to the investing public.

After the initial offering is sold to investors, the securities can be bought and sold on the secondary market. Existing debt and equity issues are traded by retail and institutional investors in secondary markets through established exchanges or through OTC markets. Since the securities are bought and sold among investors, the issuing firm neither experiences a cash flow nor a change in the number of securities outstanding.

6. What is a QIB?

According to guidelines set forth by the US Securities and Exchange Commission (SEC) in Rule 144A, a qualified institutional buyer (QIB) is an institution that manages at least $100 million in securities, and can be a bank, thrift institution, pension fund, corporation, insurance company, investment company, or employee benefit plan, or an entity owned entirely by qualified investors. A QIB can also be a registered broker-dealer that owns and invests, on a discretionary basis, at least $10 million in the securities of issuers that are not affiliated with the broker-dealer. Private placements often require that an investor attest to its status as a QIB because such private placements may not be marketed to non-QIBs. Outside the United States, QIBs are often referred to as *qualified institutional investors (QIIs)*.

7. What are the principal benefits of organized securities exchanges?

Organized exchanges function in various ways and provide four principal benefits:

- They provide a market system where the competitive forces of supply and demand determine securities prices.
- They sustain a market where frequent trading minimizes price volatility between individual trades.
- They maintain a market large enough to enable issuers to raise large amounts of capital through securities offerings.
- They furnish a regulated environment to help ensure fairness for exchange participants.

8. What are the purposes of a bond indenture?

Bonds represent a contract between the issuing entity and the bondholders. This contract is known as a *bond indenture*, which serves several purposes. It:

- Describes the bond issue
- Lists collateral (when applicable)
- Makes representations and warranties
- Specifies covenants
- States the terms by which the company will provide funds for redemption
- Sets forth the schedule of interest payment dates and amounts, the scheduled maturity date, and any early redemption or call provisions

9. What are sovereign bonds?

Bonds issued by a national government are referred to as *sovereign bonds* or *sovereign debt*, and are typically denominated in the currency of the issuing government. This category would include all types of government debt ranging from US government bonds to bonds issued by developing countries around the world. In addition to the traditional credit risk associated with bonds of any sort, sovereign debt also carries sovereign or political risk, and potentially foreign exchange or currency risk if issued in a currency other than the home currency of the investor. Sovereign risk is the risk that while the country may still exist at the maturity of the bond, there may be a change in monetary policy that may affect the value of the bond.

10. What are Eurobonds?

A Eurobond (sometimes called an *external bond*) is an international bond that is denominated in a currency other than that of the country in which it is issued. Eurobonds are named based on their face currency (e.g., Euroyen or Eurodollar). An example of this would be a Eurodollar bond that is dominated in US dollars and issued in India by a UK-based company. In this example, the UK company could issue the bond in any country other than the United States because it is denominated in US dollars.

11. What are floating-rate securities?

Floating-rate securities (or floaters) carry interest payments that reset periodically, based on movement in a representative interest rate index, such as the London Interbank Offered Rate (LIBOR) or the US T-bill. The rate on these securities is usually stated as a spread of difference from the base index rate (e.g., LIBOR + 3%). The interest rate on floating-rate debt may be reset daily, weekly, monthly, quarterly, semiannually, or annually, typically based on the index that is used for the security.

12. What are representations and warranties?

Representations and warranties are the existing conditions at the time when the loan agreement is executed, as attested to by the borrower. Such conditions generally include:

- Affirmation of the valid, legal existence of the borrowing company
- A resolution by the borrower's board of directors authorizing the borrowing
- The authority of the corporate officers signing the documents
- The borrower's confirmation of compliance with all applicable regulations
- An indemnity protecting the lender from environmental liabilities
- Representation that the execution of the loan agreement does not violate or conflict with the charter or bylaws of the borrower, or any other loan agreements to which the borrower is a party

13. What is a MAC clause?

A material adverse change (MAC) clause lets a lender refuse funding or declare a borrower to be in default, even if all agreements are in full compliance, if the lender believes a material adverse change has occurred in the borrower's condition. Examples of material adverse changes that might trigger a MAC clause could include changes in laws or regulations that have a significant negative impact on the borrower or the loss of a borrower's primary customer. MAC clauses are often used as a way to renegotiate the terms of an agreement when something negative happens, rather than being used to entirely cancel the agreement.

14. What is a loan guarantee?

When a subsidiary of a larger company borrows funds or issues bonds, lenders may require that the parent corporation (or sister subsidiary, supplier, customer, or other entity) provide a guarantee of principal for the arrangement. (In some cases, a subsidiary may provide a guarantee for the parent.) This requirement allows lenders recourse to the parent company (or guaranteeing party) to obtain payment in the event the subsidiary is in default. There are several levels of guarantees that the parent corporation or others (i.e., the guarantee party) can make regarding the degree of protection offered to a lender:

- **Full Guarantee:** The guarantee party fully guarantees any borrowing arrangement by the subsidiary and agrees to take over the loan if the subsidiary fails to make timely payments.
- **Specific-Project Guarantee:** The guarantee party guarantees only loans relating to specific projects of the subsidiary, rather than all loans.
- **Guarantee of Payment or Collection:** The guarantee party guarantees to make payment on the loan or collect payment from the subsidiary, but only if the subsidiary formally defaults on the loan. This agreement usually requires the lender to initiate default proceedings on the subsidiary and initiate collection efforts before the parent becomes involved.
- **Comfort Letter:** A comfort letter is a letter from another party stating actions that it will or will not take on behalf of the borrower. This type of agreement is not legally enforceable.
- **Performance Guarantee:** In some cases, the lender may ask for specific performance guarantees relative to the assets being financed. Under a full guarantee, the parent fully guarantees performance by the subsidiary. Under a best-efforts guarantee, the parent agrees to use its best efforts to persuade the subsidiary to perform, but it does not guarantee subsidiary performance.

- **Personal Guarantee:** In some cases, especially for smaller, privately held companies, the lender may require a personal guarantee on the part of the owner or other principals in the business before granting a loan.

15. Define par value, retained earnings, and additional paid-in capital.

Treasury professionals must be aware of three key accounting terms relating to common stock: par value, retained earnings, and additional paid-in capital (APIC). The total amount of stockholders' equity is the sum of these accounts. It is important to realize that these accounts represent only the historical accounting value of the equity and not the current market value.

The three accounting terms are defined as follows:

- **Par Value:** Par value is an arbitrary amount (usually stated in the corporate charter) that indicates the minimum amount stockholders have put up (or must put up) in the event of bankruptcy. For many publicly traded companies, this is $1 per share or $0 (no par value).
- **Retained Earnings:** This balance sheet account represents the accumulated net earnings of a corporation since its inception, less dividends paid to stockholders. This is part of the stockholders' equity and is an accounting of the money reinvested in a company in lieu of dividends paid out. It is important to understand that retained earnings are recorded as an accounting entry in the equity section of the balance sheet to reflect profits that have been invested in assets. However, they are not an available pool of funds.
- **Additional Paid-in Capital (APIC):** This account reflects the difference at the time of issue between the par value and the issuance price (less underwriting costs) of any new stock sold by a company. For example, if a company were to sell a new issue of stock with a par value of $1 and the company nets $25 per share, then a $1 per-share increase would be shown in the par value account and a $24 per-share increase would be shown in the APIC account.

16. What is preferred stock?

Preferred stock is equity, but it is different from common stock in terms of stockholder rights and its dividend payment streams. Preferred stock normally does not have voting rights. The general purpose is to raise capital through the issue of new equity while still maintaining control of a company. In terms of cash flows, it is more like debt than equity because of the fixed dividend payments. Unlike with debt, where missing interest payments can trigger loan covenants and even bankruptcy, a company does not risk bankruptcy by missing a preferred stock dividend. Another difference is that dividend payments on preferred stock do not have the tax deductibility feature that interest payments on debt do; therefore, the cost is generally much higher than that of a similar debt issue.

17. What are convertible securities?

Convertible securities are usually bonds or preferred stock that may be exchangeable at the holder's or issuer's option for a company's common stock under certain terms and conditions, and at a pre-stated price. The conversion does not provide any new capital for a company. Rather, it simply converts existing debt or preferred stock into common equity. The conversion ratio states the number of stock shares that one bond may be converted to if the owner chooses. The maturity value of the bond and the conversion ratio determine the issue's conversion price. For example, a $1,000 par value bond with a conversion ratio of 20 (i.e., 20 shares of common stock per bond) implies a stock conversion price of $50 (i.e., $1,000 divided by 20 shares).

18. What are depositary receipts?

Typically equity securities, depositary receipts (DRs) are negotiable financial instruments that trade on a local exchange but actually represent stock ownership in a foreign, publicly listed company. In order to expand the holdings of stock on a global basis, many stock exchanges offer different types of DRs. One of the most common DRs is the American depositary receipt (ADR), which allows US investors to effectively own stocks traded on foreign exchanges. These securities are known as *global depositary receipts (GDRs)* outside the United States.

CHAPTER 7 Relationship Management and Vendor Selection

1. What are the major factors that contribute to a successful long-term mutual relationship between companies and vendors?

Success in every long-term relationship involves mutual accommodation. Factors that increase the mutual benefit and profitability of the relationship are:

- Open and frequent two-way communications
- Regular and timely feedback
- Documentation of expectations of both parties in agreements and legal contracts
- Fairly priced, efficient, and effective financial services/products
- Complete, candid, and timely disclosure of information by both parties

2. What factors affect the pricing of bank loans?

The pricing of bank loans is often based on interdependent factors such as:

- Cost of funds
- Credit rating
- Total loans committed and outstanding
- Service fees
- Deposit balances maintained
- Range of other services used (e.g., foreign currency or derivatives trading)
- Loan maturity
- Revenue size and importance of the overall relationship to the lending institution
- Competition

3. What factors impact the number of bank relationships that an organization needs?

Decision factors include the existence of multi-country operations, the costs of maintaining multiple relationships, the risk of having a "single point of failure" (concentration risk), the relative strengths and capabilities of each bank, and the organization's credit needs. Companies with a complex, over-the-counter/field bank collection and concentration system involving multiple geographies may have to deal with a large number of small FIs to obtain appropriate geographic coverage. Multinational companies may need to have multiple bank relationships to provide product and service coverage in all the countries where the company has a presence.

4. List some of the important documents required as part of a relationship with an FI.

Among the important documents integral to an FI relationship are service agreements, account resolutions, signature cards, articles of incorporation from the customer, and contracts for depository accounts. The complexity and number of documents required typically increases as the number of countries involved increases. For example, FIs in many European countries will require a statement of beneficial interest.

5. What is an SLA?

A service level agreement, or SLA, may be a separate document or part of the service agreement. The SLA is primarily concerned with the definition of the specific services being provided and the operating metrics that can be used to measure the level of service being provided. SLAs also typically include a description of any penalties for failure to comply with the requirements of the agreement. The elements of an SLA often include:

- Operational policies and procedures (including the detailed processing requirements for each service; a list of required information and related reports; a list of individuals authorized to make changes; and a description of the issue escalation and resolution process)
- Performance standards and calculations that define agreed-upon levels of service performance and quality

6. What is meant by KYC?

Largely in response to money laundering and other related financial crimes, most countries have significantly strengthened their requirements around new bank relationships and the opening of bank accounts. These activities go under the general title of "*know your customer*" (or *KYC*) and require financial institutions to perform varying amounts of due diligence to determine the legitimacy of any new customers, as well as the identities of the individuals who have access or control over the funds in those accounts. Collectively, these due diligence efforts are usually referred to as *customer identification programs*, or *CIPs*. The nature and extent of the CIP may vary by country but will typically require a firm to provide copies of its articles of incorporation and identification of all signers on any bank accounts—through provision of copies (often certified) of driver's licenses or passports, as well as formal statements of beneficial ownership. A statement of beneficial ownership identifies the individuals that actually own or control a given bank account, which may be different from the name or names on the account.

7. What is a vendor scorecard?

A vendor scorecard is a management tool used to measure a vendor's performance in both a qualitative and quantitative method. The primary purpose of a scorecard is to provide a quantitative measure of the service provided and the benefit received, but it also provides feedback for the service provider to better understand how the customer perceives the value/quality/cost of the service(s) provided. In addition, the scorecard provides a tool to measure the relative value of current service relationships and evaluate service providers on those issues that the organization deems to be important. Finally, the scorecard can be used in support of continuous improvement and communication between both parties, and as a way to clarify how well the service provider delivers services and deals with issues. Although treasury is typically the focal point of the scorecard process, it is important to get input and feedback from any other area of the organization that may be affected by the vendor, such as accounting, accounts payable, or accounts receivable.

8. What are the four major vendor selection methods, and what is the main purpose of each?

- **Informal review** is intended to solicit vendors for potential solutions to existing problems.
- A **request for information (RFI)** is intended to identify vendors that are willing and able to provide products and services. It is typically used as a prelude to an RFP or RFQ.
- A **request for quote (RFQ)** is intended to solicit binding price quotes from vendors on comparable products and services.
- A **request for proposal (RFP)** is intended to solicit proposed solutions and proposed pricing from selected vendors.

9. In addition to treasury, who are the major stakeholders in a treasury RFP?

- **Business Operations:** Local or regional business managers from sales, operations, or finance who will be using the services being solicited have the first-line contact with customers and vendors. It is up to them to assist in defining the types of receivable and payable services and account locations needed. They can also provide valuable feedback on how banks and other vendors perform and are perceived in various localities around the world.
- **Tax and Legal:** Legal review of all documents and contracts is always critical. When the RFP is international and involves the movement of funds across borders and between entities, the legal and tax personnel become especially important. They will play an essential role in the initial development of the structure and should be involved in the review of bank proposals. Documentation is a mandatory part of setting up new accounts and services, and the legal department needs to participate in this process.
- **Accounting:** Bank accounts and business processes must be integrated with the company's ERP system, and all banking transactions will ultimately be reflected in the company's books, so it is important that accounting be involved with the project. Reconcilement, cash application, and payment processing are some of the key areas where bank or third-party service selection impacts accounting.
- **Systems:** IT professionals control the ERP system and govern the types of technology within the company, such as SaaS (software as a service) and client/server. They will be critical players in setting up file connectivity with the treasury's partners, such as SWIFT or host-to-host. IT is also an excellent resource in helping with an assessment of a potential vendor's systems and technology. Since IT resources can be quite scarce, it is a good idea to get them involved with the project early so they commit the necessary resources to support treasury.
- **Regulatory Compliance and Internal Audit:** The growing number and complexity of regulatory requirements, especially for multinational companies, requires input from whatever group in the firm has overall compliance responsibilities, such as for OFAC and anti-money laundering compliance requirements.
- **Supply Chain/Procurement:** This area within the organization plays a growing role in treasury projects, performing due diligence on vendor stability and negotiating contracts.

10. Describe value dating.

Outside the United States, banks often use value dating as compensation for services provided to customers. Under a value-dating system, a bank sets a forward value date on which the value of funds credited to an account is determined and establishes a back value date on which the value of funds debited from an account is determined. For example, when a deposit is forward valued, the date of the credit to the customer's account is later than the actual date the item is added to the customer's ledger balance at the bank. Similarly, when a withdrawal is back valued, the date of the debit to the customer's account is earlier than the actual date the item is deducted from the customer's ledger balance at the bank. This reduces available balances, which in turn reduces interest earned on the account. In effect, the bank is compensated during the value-dating period either by not having to pay interest on positive balances or by earning interest charged on negative balances. In some countries, value dating is standardized among the major clearing banks, while in other countries, it is negotiated on a customer-by-customer or item-by-item basis.

11. What is an account analysis statement?

An account analysis statement is, in effect, a bank's "bill" for services rendered, but is typically referred to as an *analysis statement. Analysis* is the name of the process that most US banks use to determine both earnings credits and charges for services rendered. An account analysis is, therefore, a record of the services provided to the customer by the bank, along with detailed information on balances and related earnings credits for those balances. This practice is typically not seen outside of the United States where invoices for services are more common. The account analysis statement typically provides the following information to a bank's commercial customers:

- Services provided
- Balances maintained
- Transaction/item volumes processed
- Charges assessed
- Earnings credit allowances

12. Compare and contrast average ledger balance and average collected balance.

- **Average Ledger Balance:** This is the sum of the daily ending ledger balances (both positive and negative) divided by the number of days in the analysis period. Balances used in the calculation are net of any current-period adjustments.
- **Average Collected Balance:** This is the sum of the daily ending collected balances (both positive and negative) divided by the number of days in the analysis period. In many account analysis statements, this item is calculated as the average ledger balance minus the average deposit float.

13. Compare and contrast fee compensation and balance compensation in the United States.

Given the account analysis system and earnings credit allowance as described, there has long been a debate over whether it is better to pay for banking services with excess balances or to aggressively manage bank balances and directly invest the funds. The advantages and disadvantages of providing compensation for services using the earnings credit or direct fee payments differ depending upon whether the perspective of a company or an FI is taken.

A company may favor fee compensation when it is able to earn more interest on its investments than it can obtain in an earnings credit on collected balances. The use of fees for compensation is even more compelling when a company can use excess balances to pay down short-term debt, which typically has a significantly higher opportunity cost than the ECR. In addition, fees can be budgeted and compared with other costs, while balances are not as directly comparable.

From a company's point of view, balance compensation lets the company take advantage of excess collected balances that arise from unanticipated deposits or precautionary transaction balances. Additional reasons why a company may prefer balance compensation are:

- Some FIs price loans and other services more favorably if collected balances are maintained.
- Balance compensation is not as visible as fee expenditures for budgeting purposes, thereby "masking" or hiding the actual compensation and eliminating the need for budget dollars to cover the services.
- Earnings credits used to determine the value of collected balances to the company are not taxable, while interest earned on short-term investments or sweep accounts generally is taxable.
- ECRs may exceed available short-term investment rates.

Some of the disadvantages of balance compensation for a company include:

- ECRs are not always known until after the applicable billing period.
- Earnings in excess of analysis fees are unusable and lost to the company.
- Balances in excess of the FDIC insurance limit may be at risk of loss in the event the bank is closed.

Some FIs prefer fee compensation because deposit balances increase the liabilities on their balance sheet. This may lead to a need for additional capital to meet regulatory or other requirements. A second reason why FIs often prefer fee compensation is that fees from deposit services are viewed as a low-risk source of earnings.

The principal reason why a bank may prefer balance compensation is that deposits may be used to fund loans and investments at rates exceeding the ECR provided to an account holder.

14. What is political risk?

Political risk is the term applied to the variety of actions that a government may take that negatively impact a company's operations and/or value. It includes the risk that a company's operations in a foreign country may be nationalized or expropriated by the government of that country. *Nationalization* refers to a government takeover of all companies in a specific industry, often involving ore extraction, petroleum, transportation, or power generation and distribution businesses. *Expropriation* refers to a government takeover of a single company, with or without compensation. Experience suggests that when compensation is made, it is significantly less than the market value of the expropriated company. Other types of political risk include:

- **Blocked Currencies:** Profits cannot be converted from the local currency into a major trading currency.
- **Forced Reinvestment:** Funds cannot be transferred out of the country in any form, or the amount that can be transferred is limited.
- **Required Majority Ownership:** Companies must be owned by resident nationals.

Multinational companies are exposed to varying degrees of political risk depending upon attitudes and policies of the host country and the nature of the business. A company with operations in foreign countries must be knowledgeable about the laws, regulations, taxes, and customs that govern business activities, as well as the overall political and social dynamics of the countries where capital is invested.

15. What is an SSAE 16 report?

An SSAE 16 report (also known as an *SOC [Service Organization Control] 1 Report*) is a third-party audit report that reports on a service provider's internal controls. The Statement on Standards for Attestation Engagements (SSAE) No. 16, *Reporting on Controls at a Service Organization*, was finalized by the Auditing Standards Board of the American Institute of Certified Public Accountants (AICPA) in January 2010 and effectively replaced the previous SAS 70 as the authoritative guidance for reporting on service organizations.

SSAE 16 complies with the International Standard on Assurance Engagements (ISAE) No. 3402, *Assurance Reports on Controls at a Service Organization*, which was issued in December 2009 by the International Auditing and Assurance Standards Board (IAASB), part of the International Federation of Accountants (IFAC). ISAE 3402 was developed to provide an international assurance standard for allowing public accountants to issue a report for use by user organizations and their auditors (user auditors) on the controls at a service organization that are likely to be a part of the user organization's system of internal controls over financial reporting.

16. What concerns should a treasurer have about service provider access to confidential information?

Service providers often have access to confidential information about an organization's customer base. A treasurer must know if, and under what conditions, this information may be shared with affiliates of the service provider or other parties to prevent any loss of confidentiality.

CHAPTER 8 Introduction to Working Capital Management

1. What is meant by the term *working capital*? How can working capital be increased or decreased?

The term *working capital* is defined as current assets less current liabilities. It is the cash and other liquid assets required by any organization to continue its operations by satisfying both upcoming operational expenses and maturing short-term debt. Working capital can be obtained (increased) by:

- Collecting cash flow from operations
- Increasing debt
- Selling assets and investments
- Selling equity

And it is used (reduced) by:

- Using cash flow in operations
- Repaying debt
- Purchasing assets and investments
- Paying dividends and buying back stock/equity

2. What is meant by the term *permanent current assets*?

While it may seem strange to talk about "permanent" current assets, the concept is important when considering financing. For any given organization, there will be a certain minimum amount of current assets that it must have to do business. This number will vary by company and industry, but one way of identifying it is to examine the balance sheet and determine the lowest amount of current assets that a given company has had in the past several years. This base is considered *permanent current assets* and anything over that amount is considered *fluctuating current assets*. Because the company can reasonably assume that, barring major problems, the value of its current assets will not fall below the permanent base, it can consider financing current assets with longer-term debt.

3. Compare and contrast the three current asset financing strategies.

- **Maturity-Matching Financing Strategy:** Under a maturity-matching financing strategy, the total of permanent current assets and fixed assets are financed with long-term financing (e.g., debt and equity). Short-term financing is used to finance fluctuating current assets. This means that the amount of short-term financing at a given time mirrors the amount of fluctuating current assets at that time.
- **Conservative Financing Strategy:** Under a conservative financing strategy, long-term financing supports fixed assets, permanent current assets, and some portion of fluctuating current assets. A company usually tries to finance the average level of fluctuating current assets with long-term sources. Short-term financing is used for the remainder of the fluctuating current assets.
- **Aggressive Financing Strategy:** Under an aggressive financing strategy, a company finances all fixed assets with long-term debt and equity, but finances only a portion of permanent current assets with long-term financing. Short-term financing supports the remainder of the permanent current assets and all temporary current assets. This strategy utilizes more ongoing short-term financing than other financing strategies.

4. What are two key considerations when determining credit extension policies?

The key considerations are as follows:

- If a company implements credit standards that are too strict, it may decline trade credit to customers that represent an acceptable credit risk, thereby limiting sales opportunities.
- If a company implements credit standards that are too lenient, it may grant trade credit to customers that represent an unacceptable credit risk, thereby increasing the risk of late payments and bad debt expenses.

5. What are the five Cs of credit?

- Character
- Capacity
- Capital
- Collateral
- Conditions

6. What are the four steps in the credit scoring process?

Credit scoring involves a four-step process:

- Differentiating standard and high-risk accounts based on the applicant's monthly income, outstanding obligations, and employment history
- Weighting the characteristics of applicants who fit into each category to establish creditworthiness
- Setting cutoff scores for clear approval or denial of credit
- Applying further analysis to applicants whose scores fall between the cutoff points

7. Compare and contrast the four basic forms of credit extension.

There are four basic forms of credit extension:

- **Open Account:** Open account, sometimes called *open book credit*, is the most common type of commercial trade credit. A seller issues an invoice as formal evidence of the obligation and records the sale as an A/R. The buyer is billed for each transaction by an invoice and/or monthly statement. Full payment of invoiced amounts is expected within the specified credit terms unless certain discounts or deductions are available to the buyer. A buyer's creditworthiness is reviewed periodically, but the buyer does not need to apply for credit each time it places an order.
- **Installment Credit:** Installment credit requires a customer to make equal periodic payments, each of which contains principal and interest components. Installment credit is used frequently for the purchase of high-value consumer durables, such as automobiles. Installment credit is liquidating, in that normal payments will eventually pay off the balance of the account over time. The seller requires the buyer to sign a contract, which specifies the credit terms of the obligation, discloses the interest rate, and lists all other costs.

- **Revolving Credit:** Under revolving credit terms, a company grants credit without requiring specific transaction approval, as long as the account remains current. An account usually is considered current if the credit outstanding is below an established credit limit and minimum payments are made on time. If the account is not paid in full by the due date, an interest charge is calculated based on the average amount outstanding over the entire period. Unlike installment credit, revolving credit is not automatically liquidating, as new purchases are added to the balance even as payments for older purchases are received and processed.
- **Letter of Credit (L/C):** The most complex form of credit extension is a commercial L/C. L/Cs are most commonly used in import/export transactions.

8. What is an open item system of cash application?

An open item system is most commonly used in business-to-business (B2B) sales. Each invoice sent to a customer is recorded in the A/R file. When a payment is received, it is matched with the specific invoices being paid. Any payment discrepancies are noted (e.g., discounts, allowances, adjustments, or returns). Remittance information, which typically accompanies payments, indicates which invoices are being paid, as well as any adjustments to the payment. This application process may be manual, automated, or a combination of both.

9. What are the most common terms of sale?

The most common sales terms are:

- Cash before delivery (CBD)
- Cash on delivery (COD)
- Cash terms
- Net terms
- Discount terms
- Monthly billing
- Draft/bill of lading
- Seasonal dating
- Consignment

10. What are some of the advantages and disadvantages of accepting credit cards in a business-to-business (B2B) setting?

The advantages of accepting credit cards rather than maintaining A/R in a B2B setting are:

- The seller bears no direct costs of running a credit department.
- The seller does not have to finance A/R.
- As long as proper authorization procedures are followed, the credit card issuer absorbs bad debt losses.
- Sales typically increase by making it easier for customers to charge purchases.
- The seller is paid more quickly—typically in one to two business days following the transaction.

The disadvantages of accepting credit cards for customer financing include:

- The seller relinquishes control over the credit decision (e.g., the sale could be lost if credit is not granted).
- The seller loses promotional opportunities by not having access to a list of credit customers.
- The seller incurs discount costs and transaction fees.
- There is an expense associated with maintaining compliance with credit card data security standards.

11. What is factoring?

Factoring involves the outright sale of receivables to a factor, a company that specializes in the financing and management of receivables. In most factoring arrangements, the buyer of the receivables has no recourse to the seller. *No recourse* or *without recourse* means that the factor must absorb the loss if a customer fails to pay. In some cases, however, the factoring arrangement stipulates that the factor has recourse, in which case the seller is liable for any bad debts the factor cannot collect.

12. What are the four principal types of cash flows with which treasury professionals must work?

There are four principal types of cash flows that treasury professionals must consider:

- **Cash outflows** include funds disbursed to employees, vendors, and suppliers; lenders; local, state, and federal tax agencies; bondholders; and shareholders. This process is typically referred to as the *purchase-to-pay timeline*. Inventory can be a by-product of the purchase-to-pay timeline.
- **Cash inflows** include funds collected from customers, obtained from financial sources (e.g., loans or investment income), and/or received from other sources. This is typically referred to as the *order-to-cash timeline*.
- **Concentration/funding flows** involve internal transfers among operating units of a company and between a firm's various bank accounts, with the objectives of pooling funds for other purposes or funding various disbursement accounts.
- **Liquidity management flows** involve using the organization's liquidity reserves in the most effective manner. If there is a surplus of funds, treasury may either (1) invest in suitable investments, or (2) pay down existing debt. If there is a shortage of funds, then treasury may either (1) sell off investments, or (2) draw on available debt sources (e.g., credit lines or commercial paper issuance).

13. What is float?

Float refers to the time interval, or delay, between the start and the completion of a specific phase or process occurring along the cash flow timeline. Float is often the result of wait time (e.g., the time lost while waiting for someone else to take action or the time needed to transmit information between two parties) and inefficiencies within a specific process, but is also often increased by the use of paper processes and delivery systems, such as the mailing of invoices to a business's customers.

14. What is the working capital cash conversion cycle? Identify its major components.

The continuous flow of cash through working capital accounts results in the cash conversion cycle (CCC), which explains and calculates how much time elapses from when funds are disbursed in direct support of a revenue-generating activity until the time when funds are recovered from revenues.

The major elements of the CCC are:

- Days' inventory, or inventory conversion period
- Days' receivables, or receivables conversion period
- Days' payables, or payables conversion period

15. What are the elements of a basic inventory policy?

The inventory policy of most companies includes elements such as:

- Reasons for holding inventory
- Types of inventory
- Levels of inventory
- Obsolescence and spoilage
- Benefits and costs of inventory

16. Describe the basic types of inventory.

The types of inventory generally are categorized as follows:

- **Raw Materials:** Raw materials inventory represents the basic input to the manufacturing process and allows arrivals to be separated from production scheduling. Partially completed components, such as subassemblies, may fall into this category instead of work in progress to give the company more flexibility in the production process.
- **Work in Progress (WIP):** WIP inventory represents items or materials that are in the process of being manufactured. This type of inventory allows different phases of the production process to be separated. The use and amount of WIP inventory are generally functions of the production process. A short, continuous process such as chemical production may have very little WIP, whereas a long batch-production process such as furniture manufacturing has a large level of WIP. WIP inventory also serves as a buffer between production stages with different processing speeds.
- **Finished Goods:** This type of inventory consists of completed items or materials available for sale, and lets a company fill orders when received rather than depend upon product completion to satisfy customer demands. Companies can manage highly variable or unpredictable demand levels more easily, which is extremely valuable in a retail environment because it allows the retailer to maintain a wide variety of goods for customers. It is important to note a significant difference in the management of finished goods inventory for generic products versus customized products. Due to limited resale value, customized product inventories must be managed much more tightly than more generic, easily sold goods.

- **Scrap or Obsolete Items:** In industries such as steel and aluminum manufacturing, scrap from production can be reused in later batches or sold to recyclers. Also, a portion of a company's inventories may become obsolete or damaged, especially in environments where there are rapid changes in existing products or introductions of new products. Obsolete or scrap inventories must be identified and dealt with independently. These inventories may be turned into cash through sales to scrap dealers or by taking tax deductions through write-offs.
- **Stores and Supplies:** Stores and supplies inventories are sometimes referred to as *indirect purchases*. These items are not used directly; rather, they support the production process. Examples include lubricating oils or maintenance materials for production machinery in a manufacturing business, or paper and other office supplies in a service business.

17. What are multicurrency accounts?

Multicurrency accounts are a special arrangement between a bank and a company, in which the bank lets the customer receive or make payments in a range of currencies from a single account or multiple subsidiary accounts. A multicurrency agreement generally specifies four stipulations:

- The base currency in which the account is denominated
- The portfolio of currencies accepted
- The spread or margin over the spot rate to use in exchanging each currency back to the base currency
- The value date to apply to debits and credits for each transaction type and currency

These accounts simplify the management of multinational working capital by allowing a company to make and receive payments in a variety of currencies without having to worry about the foreign exchange (FX) implications of every transaction.

18. What are the principal benefits of using a netting system in managing multinational working capital?

There are three principal benefits of using a netting system:

- A reduction in the number of FX transactions and cross-border wire transfers, and the resulting benefits from natural hedging
- More favorable FX rates due to the potential for larger FX trades resulting from consolidation
- Improved cash and currency exposure forecasting for both the subsidiary and the parent company as a result of the ability to preplan cross-border payments

19. In designing a disbursement system, what four goals must an organization keep in mind?

The four goals to keep in mind include:

- **Information Access:** Obtaining access to timely and accurate information regarding the status of disbursement accounts and disbursement clearings lets a company manage its cash position more effectively.
- **Fraud Prevention:** Preventing fraud means protecting company funds from unauthorized use, through written policies and internal controls, prompt bank reconciliation, and appropriate banking services (e.g., positive pay and debit blocks).

- **Relationship Maintenance with Payees:** Maintaining good relationships with payees means ensuring timely payments to employees, vendors, suppliers, lenders, tax agencies, bondholders, and shareholders, as well as filing any necessary tax or other legal forms.
- **Timing of Payments:** While it is important to pay vendors in a timely fashion, it can be equally important that payments not be made before they are due. Scheduling of payments is an important function of any disbursement system. Making payments early reduces available working capital, while deferring payments increases working capital by maximizing trade credit.

20. What is an export credit agency?

Export credit agencies (ECAs) are entities established by governments to provide services such as export loans or credit guarantees (or a combination of both) to support the country's export activities. ECAs are typically established to assist in the financing of goods and services from their country to international markets, often with a focus on smaller companies that are developing international capabilities. The basic services that the ECAs typically provide are working capital guarantees (pre-export financing), export credit insurance, and loan guarantees and direct loans (buyer financing).

21. What are the benefits of establishing an in-house bank?

Many large global companies have found it beneficial to establish in-house banks. In this arrangement, treasury becomes the main provider of banking services for all the company's operating entities. Because treasury manages all banking services, individual transactions of various subsidiaries can be aggregated, netted, and processed in bulk, resulting in fewer transactions and lower fees. The primary benefit is a reduction in overall banking costs. Secondary benefits include improved visibility and control over subsidiary cash assets, minimized borrowing, and an improved ability to manage internal and external FX risk. There may also be potential tax benefits to using this type of structure, as it provides for better information and tax planning related to international transactions, and some countries provide tax advantages for in-house banking facilities.

CHAPTER 9 Working Capital Metrics

1. What is meant by the term *time value of money*?

The time value of money is a basic financial concept that recognizes the fact that a given amount of money received today is more valuable than the same amount of money received a year from now. This is due to the fact that the money earned today can be used to earn more money, resulting in a larger amount of money in the future.

2. Explain the meaning of the term *opportunity cost*.

Opportunity cost is defined as the value of the best alternative not taken when two or more mutually exclusive alternatives are available. For example, if an investor has $100 to invest for one year and has to choose between investing in a stock that is expected to return 10% and a CD that will return 8%, the investor's opportunity cost of investing in the stock is the return that the investor would have made on the CD but did not (in other words, $8.00).

3. Compare and contrast the current ratio and the quick ratio.

The *current ratio* is defined as total current assets divided by total current liabilities. It is therefore the ratio of cash and assets expected to become cash in one year or less, to short-term liabilities that must be paid in one year or less. This ratio measures a company's ability to meet its current obligations or the degree to which current obligations are covered by current assets.

The *quick ratio* is defined as cash plus short-term investments and accounts receivable, divided by total current liabilities. It is also known as the *acid test ratio* because it is a more stringent measure of liquidity than the current ratio. The quick ratio measures the degree to which a company's current liabilities are covered by its most liquid current assets (i.e., cash and assets that will convert to cash most quickly).

4. How is days' receivables calculated?

Days' receivables is calculated by determining how many days of sales reside in A/R. Accordingly, the period ending value for A/R is divided by the amount of sales (or revenues) per day. In this calculation, note that revenues are used rather than cost of goods sold (COGS) because A/R is carried on the balance sheet based on the selling price. Year-end A/R is used here, but some users average the A/R balance from the most recent two balance sheets.

5. What is the formula for the cash conversion cycle?

Cash Conversion Cycle = Days' Inventory + Days' Receivables – Days' Payables

6. What is cash conversion efficiency?

Cash conversion efficiency measures how effectively a company has converted sales (or revenues) into cash. The cash flow generated by operations (i.e., operating cash flow from the statement of cash flows) is viewed as a percentage of revenue. The higher the cash conversion efficiency ratio, the greater the net cash generated per dollar of revenue.

7. What are the three situations where it makes economic sense to forego taking a cash discount?

To generalize, there are only three situations where it makes economic sense to forgo the offered discount:

- If the organization can earn a rate of return exceeding the discount rate by investing the funds in the short term instead of paying early and earning the discount.
- If the organization does not have cash available to take the discount, but has to borrow the necessary funds at an interest rate higher than the approximate cost of not taking the discount.
- If the organization has the ability to effectively change the terms by stretching out its accounts payable (A/P) terms. By paying the net amount at a later date, the paying organization is effectively reducing the implied interest rate on the transaction. However, this alternative is not one that should be exercised in the normal course of events due to the potential negative impact on vendor relations and ultimately on credit ratings.

8. Why is it important to monitor individual accounts receivable?

It is important to monitor individual accounts in order to identify:

- Errors or delays in the invoicing or payment process that are slowing collections
- Customers who may delay payment intentionally until follow-up is initiated
- A change in financial condition that may alter a customer's ability to make timely payments and require the curtailment of future credit sales

9. What is an A/R aging schedule?

An aging schedule separates accounts receivable (A/R) into current and past-due receivables using set periods (typically 30-day increments) and is a method for measuring A/R. Companies can analyze the aging of receivables in aggregate or on a customer-by-customer basis. An aging analysis identifies past-due accounts, which become less collectible as the age of each increases.

10. When conducting a lockbox cost/benefit calculation, what are the three elements that determine the opportunity cost of float?

Three factors determine the opportunity cost of float:

- The dollar amount of the collected items
- The total collection time for items
- A company's current opportunity cost of funds (usually its short-term investment or borrowing rate)

CHAPTER 10 Collections, Concentration, and Disbursements

1. What is a ZBA?

Zero balance accounts, or ZBAs, are bank accounts in which the end-of-day balance is maintained at zero. Credits and debits that post to the ZBA are netted at the close of each business day. From the account holder's perspective, if there is a credit balance in the ZBA, then the ZBA will be debited and the master account will be credited. This brings the balance in the ZBA back to zero. If there is a debit balance in the ZBA, then the ZBA will be credited and the master account will be debited. Again, this end-of-day transaction returns the balance in the ZBA to zero. Funding of the ZBA is generally done automatically by the bank and typically involves only an accounting entry by the bank and the company.

2. What is positive pay?

Positive pay is a disbursement service used to combat payment (primarily check, but increasingly ACH) fraud. With this service, the company transmits a file of payment information to the disbursement bank either at or before the time of the physical distribution of checks or anticipated ACH debits. The bank matches check serial numbers and dollar amounts of checks presented for payment against the issue database and pays only those checks or ACH transactions that match all relevant criteria. Many positive pay services also offer the ability to match against the payee field (known as *payee positive pay*), as well as the serial number and the amount, in an effort to detect an altered payee. In the case of ACH positive pay, transactions are matched based on dollar amount and originator.

3. What is controlled disbursement?

Controlled disbursement is a bank service that provides same-day notification to a company of the amount of checks that will clear against its disbursement account on a given day. This product is unique to the United States and was developed due to the specific characteristics of US corporate checking accounts (i.e., the historic regulatory ban on paying interest on positive balances and the limitations on overdrawing current accounts).

4. What are the different categories of wire transfers? Describe each.

- **Repetitive Wires:** Repetitive wire transfers are used when a company makes frequent transfers to the same credit parties. In a repetitive wire, only the date and dollar amount of the wire change—all other information remains constant. The bank (or payment system, such as a treasury management system [TMS], used by the customer to originate wires) maintains a record of the debit and credit bank accounts and accepts instructions either electronically (most banks offer a web-based wire transfer system) or via telephone to initiate the transfer. A unique identifier is assigned to each instruction template that contains all of the standing information. Since only the date and the dollar amount can be changed on a repetitive wire, this type of transfer provides significant assurance that funds will not be sent to an unknown or fraudulent party.
- **Semi-Repetitive Wires:** The debit and credit parties remain the same in a semi-repetitive wire transfer, but the description (e.g., a customer or an invoice number) may be changed, along with the date and the dollar amount. Semi-repetitive transfers combine the controls of repetitive transfers with the flexibility of non-repetitive transfers.

- **Non-Repetitive (Free-Form) Wires:** The debit and credit parties are different each time in a non-repetitive wire. Because all of the information is variable, this type of transfer has the highest degree of payment risk due to fraud or simple data entry errors. As a result, additional security measures are typically required to guard against both fraud and input errors. Examples of such measures are callbacks, secondary levels of approval, and segregation of duties.
- **Drawdown Wires:** A drawdown wire transfer is a request sent by a company's bank to a second bank requesting that the second bank initiate a wire transfer from either the company's account or another party's account at the second bank, sending the funds back to the first bank. The party being debited must pre-authorize the transfer; therefore, drawdown wires are most frequently used as part of a company's concentration system, since the company can authorize both sides of the transaction.
- **Standing Wires:** With a standing wire, a company establishes repetitive transfer instructions to move funds between two specified accounts automatically when previously determined criteria are met. Standing wires typically are used for concentrating funds, and the criteria could address either timing (e.g., all funds in the account at the end of the day) or a designated balance level (e.g., all funds in excess of $50,000).

5. What are freight payments?

Some banks and third parties offer a payment service called *freight payment* in which specialists pay all of a shipper's freight bills, audit bills for possible overcharges and duplicate payments, and provide reports that help a company compare costs for different routes and carriers. Manufacturers and wholesale distributors typically use this service.

6. What is a payment factory?

A payment factory is essentially a centralized accounts payable (A/P) processing center. It is often part of a centralized treasury operation known as an *in-house bank*, or it may be set up as part of an organization's enterprise resource planning (ERP) system. Payment factories are often used in multinational organizations with a large number of cross-border payments. They can also be linked to multilateral netting systems or re-invoicing programs in order to reduce the number of transactions between subsidiaries of a company, as well as better control overall exposures from foreign currencies. To send payments outside the organization, a single payment file from all the operating units can be sent to a global or regional bank, which can then arrange for payments to be made in local currencies to the vendors.

7. Describe the major issues that must be addressed in any collection system.

There are a number of major issues that must be addressed in any collection system:

- **Speed of Collection:** Minimizing the time it takes to collect the actual payment and have the funds available for use is a key goal for a collection system.
- **Security of the Payment:** The collection system should ensure that the payment is not diverted or stolen during the collection process. This is especially important when cash payments are involved.
- **Availability of Remittance Information:** Collecting a payment is important, but it is equally important to know who made the payment and why, especially if the payment is for less than anticipated.
- **Cost of Collection:** Minimizing the cost of any collection system is important, but the cost must be balanced against the prior items.

8. What is a virtual vault?

Companies with multiple retail locations use armored cars to collect deposits from their retail outlets to ensure the safety of both the collections and their staff. Because of the high cost of armored carriers, companies typically use them only for outlets with large amounts of cash receipts or where there are specific security concerns regarding the safety of employees taking deposits to local depository banks. The desire to speed up the collection cycle by having daily armored carrier pickups must be balanced against the cost of each individual pickup.

One solution to this problem that is becoming increasingly common is a product referred to as a *virtual vault*. The armored carrier, working in conjunction with the company's depository bank, provides a special safe to the retail outlet that records deposits into the safe and reports them to the armored carrier and the bank. The bank provides provisional credit at the time of the deposit into the safe, and the armored carrier picks up the contents of the safe on a reduced schedule, perhaps weekly instead of daily.

Virtual vaults also provide the ability for a bank to service retail outlets that are not near any of its branches. Working through the armored carrier, the bank can effectively accept deposits in any location that the armored carrier can service and is not limited to the geography of the bank's branches. As a result, this can also help geographically dispersed retailers handle their cash consolidation needs.

9. What is meant by the term *merchant services*?

Merchant services is the term typically used to describe the products offered by a bank, Internet service provider, or other firm (referred to as a *merchant processor*) that processes credit and debit card transactions. While the term principally refers to the acceptance and processing of card transactions, it also often includes ancillary services such as returns and adjustments, POS terminals, supplies, and customer support.

10. What is RDC?

Remote deposit capture (RDC) involves using a check scanner to capture an image of check payments and then depositing them by sending the images to the company's depository bank(s). This service eliminates the need to gather the checks and take them to the bank or send them via mail or overnight delivery service. This speeds up collection time, reduces the risk that the checks will be lost or stolen in transit, and typically reduces the overall cost of check processing. As with a virtual vault, RDC allows a depository bank to service locations that are physically distant from a bank facility, alleviating the need for subsequent cash consolidation from a local field bank. In some cases, RDC scanners are being incorporated into the electronic safes used for virtual vault services, providing a consolidated service for retail organizations. The product is limited to checks denominated in US dollars.

11. List the major steps in processing mail payments involving checks.

Mail payments can be processed internally or outsourced to a lockbox processor. In an internal company processing center, check and payment card processing, along with deposit preparation, are performed in-house. For checks, the processing generally involves the following steps:

- Receiving and opening the mail
- Separating the payment (i.e., check) from the remittance advice, which provides information on who is paying and what they are paying
- Forwarding the remittance advice, amount, and date of payment to the A/R department
- Preparing the check for deposit (i.e., endorsement and deposit preparation), or in the case of consumer payments, preparing the check for possible conversion into an ACH debit
- Transporting the check to the organization's deposit bank, employing remote deposit capture, or converting an eligible check into an ACH debit

12. What is check conversion?

Check conversion involves scanning the payor's check and converting it to an ACH debit. The benefit of this is that ACH transactions are typically less expensive than check processing. Checks can be converted at the point of presentment (e.g., the retail sales counter), in the back office or deposit-processing operation, or in a lockbox operation that is receiving bill payments. Each type of conversion has a different standard entry class (SEC) code. As with RDC, check conversion is limited to checks drawn on US-domiciled accounts. Unlike RDC, which is available for both consumer and commercial checks, check conversion is limited to consumer checks under $25,000.

13. What are EBPP and EIPP?

EBPP is electronic bill presentment and payment, and EIPP is electronic invoice presentment and payment. Although often thought of as disbursement products since they allow consumers or businesses to make payments electronically, EBPP and EIPP are actually a bridge between collections and disbursements that enable companies to send electronic statements and receive electronic remittances from their customers. With both products (EBPP for retail customers and EIPP for corporate customers), a company sends billing data to its customer, typically through an e-mail with a link to the company's billing portal (website). The customer can review the billing information, ask questions, and modify payment amounts as needed. Once satisfied, the customer authorizes payment electronically, typically triggering an EFT debit. EBPP and EIPP may be provided through a company's own website or a third-party vendor, often referred to as a *payment portal*. Because the collecting company, or the third-party vendor, controls both the transmission of the billing data and the subsequent collection, the remittance information is already linked to the payment, simplifying subsequent posting to A/R and reducing any exception processing.

14. Describe consolidated remittance processing.

Because payments come in many forms and types, organizations are often forced to deal with multiple sources of remittance information and payment data, often in widely different formats. This can result in processing delays and expensive exception item processing. One solution to this is a product often referred to as *consolidated remittance processing*, or *CRP*. The predecessor of CRP was a service often referred to as an *electronic lockbox*. An electronic lockbox provides a single collection point for all ACH and wire payments, and it can also process remittance advices from a variety of incoming formats into a single format for transmission to the organization's A/R department for posting and reconciliation. CRP takes this a step further by consolidating all remittance information into one stream of data in a common format. This can include not only EFT but check and card payments as well.

In some versions of CRP, the vendor (often a bank) providing the service also provides a service called *receivables matching*, in which the vendor matches a processed payment against the company's open invoices, applies the payment, and updates the A/R record.

15. What are the advantages of using a lockbox?

The major advantages of a lockbox system over an internal company payment-processing center include:

- Reduced mail and processing float
- Improved access to remittance information
- Reduced risk and improved security since payments are no longer received internally
- Improved control and record-keeping capabilities
- Uninterrupted service
- Scalability
- Proper segregation of duties

16. What information is normally included in a documentary collection letter?

The typical information disclosed in a documentary collection letter includes:

- Name of the seller (exporter)
- Name and address of the buyer (importer)
- Information regarding the collecting bank
- Details of the documentation accompanying the collection
- Date, tenor, and value of the collection
- Details of bank and other charges to be paid by the exporter, importer, or both
- Recourse procedures in the event of nonacceptance or nonpayment
- Any nonstandard terms or conditions

17. What is a letter of credit?

A letter of credit (L/C) is a document issued by a bank, guaranteeing the payment of a customer's draft up to a stated amount for a specified period, provided certain conditions are met. The L/C substitutes a bank's credit for that of the buyer, virtually eliminating the credit risk to the seller. L/Cs are a widely used method of payment for import and export shipments and are used frequently as a financing vehicle for cross-border trade transactions.

18. What is the difference between a revocable and irrevocable letter of credit?

L/Cs may be revocable or irrevocable. A revocable L/C can be canceled by the bank or the buyer at any time. This limits the credit protection available to the beneficiary of the L/C (i.e., the seller), who might ship goods only to find that the related L/C has been canceled. An irrevocable L/C can only be canceled if all parties to the transaction (i.e., the buyer, the seller, the issuing bank, and if the L/C is confirmed, the confirming bank) agree, thus providing maximum protection to the seller. Most L/Cs are irrevocable.

19. What is countertrade?

Countertrade is a method of payment used by companies that do not have access to sufficient hard currencies (i.e., internationally traded currencies) to pay for imports from other countries. For example, an exporter ships merchandise to the countertrading country. In exchange, it takes merchandise that may be sold elsewhere in the world. Pricing and foreign exchange rates are established between the trading parties.

20. Describe the three basic forms of pooling.

Pooling has three basic forms:

- **Physical Pooling:** In physical pooling, funds in separate subaccounts are automatically transferred to/from a header or concentration account in order to eliminate idle cash and fund cash outflows. The participating entities are either in surplus or deficit from a transactional perspective, but the bank accounts themselves are zero balanced. Physical pooling can be used across multiple legal entities located in the same or different countries, but the funds must be in the same currency. The funds movement between the participating entities is accounted for via intercompany loans, which must be at an "arm's length" or market rate. This is somewhat analogous to a ZBA account structure, but differs in that there is no requirement that all the accounts belong to one entity, hence the need for intercompany loans.
- **Notional Pooling:** Notional pooling achieves the same result, but it is accomplished by making balancing entries on a set of virtual accounts with no changes to the bank accounts held by company entities. The bank managing the notional pool provides an interest statement that reflects the net offset, which is similar to what would have been achieved with physical pooling. As there is no physical movement of money, intercompany loans are not required to account for the notional transactions. Banks usually require credit facilities to support any deficit balances in the pool, and notional pooling often requires extensive cross-guarantees among subsidiaries, which many companies find very difficult to implement. Some countries, including the United States, Germany, Mexico, Japan, and Brazil, disallow notional pooling. In these cases, the physical pooling method must be used.
- **Bank Overlay Structure:** A bank overlay structure is an approach that combines both sweeping and pooling. It is typically used when a company's primary bank has branches in several countries, but the branches do not provide a full range of domestic banking services. A local bank is used to provide collection and disbursement transactions and accounts, and to sweep surplus funds to the primary bank. The primary bank (overlay bank) then notionally pools or physically transfers cash balances in overlay accounts, providing a multi-country solution. The exact structure of this arrangement will depend on the bank agreement and possible tax considerations.

21. Describe some of the best practices that can be used to control payments fraud.

Positive pay (preferably with payee verification), ACH filters and blocks, and daily reconciliations are among the methods most used to help detect and control payments fraud. Other best practices for fraud control include:

- Use of check stock with built-in security features, such as microprinting, holograms, and other non-photo-reproducible features
- Appropriate segregation of duties so that the person reconciling accounts is not the person who can initiate transactions from the account
- The use of dual authentication for all EFT transactions, where one person originates a transaction and a second person reviews and releases the transaction
- The reduction or elimination of non-repetitive wires
- The use of separate accounts for deposits and disbursements
- The use of a dedicated computer (i.e., not used for other purposes) for the initiation of online EFT transactions

CHAPTER 11 Short-Term Investing and Borrowing

1. Compare and contrast in-house and outsourced investment management.

When using in-house management of short-term investments, an organization assumes responsibility for directly managing its own portfolio, including strategy choice, security and maturity selection, quality standards, and compliance monitoring to ensure the investment policy is followed and regulatory requirements are met. Although these decisions are guided by the organization's investment policy, the organization must be prepared to make specific decisions at all times based on current market conditions.

In-house management is generally appropriate only to the extent that the individuals charged with this responsibility have sufficient resources, training, and experience to effectively involve themselves in the relevant markets and accounting considerations or consequences for each investment choice.

The alternative to in-house management is to assign short-term investment portfolio duties to a third party, such as a money market fund manager or an outside money manager (e.g., an investment bank or registered investment advisor). While management costs or fees will be incurred, these need to be balanced against the cost needed to hire and maintain appropriate internal expertise. The use of external managers may also be dictated by the size and complexity of the organization's portfolio. External fund and money managers will typically have greater resources and experience than those usually found within an organization's treasury department.

2. What is the difference between a broker-dealer and a registered investment advisor?

A broker-dealer is an organization that trades securities for its own account and on behalf of its customers. A broker-dealer may provide investment recommendations to its customers, but does not have the fiduciary duty that a registered advisor does. As a result, broker-dealer recommendations are potentially going to be based upon securities that the broker-dealer has available for sale and may not address the actual wants or needs of the customer.

A registered investment advisor is someone who is paid a fee to make investment recommendations for a client or group of clients. When an organization hires an investment advisor to manage its short-term portfolio, the normal practice of the industry is to have a written agreement with that advisor making the relationship between the parties clear and specifying fees, investment guidelines, and any restrictions or operating policies that the advisor must follow. Such an investment advisor has a fiduciary duty to the customer that a broker-dealer does not.

3. What are the key elements in a short-term investment policy?

Formulating a short-term investment policy requires an organization to determine its tolerance for the types of risk borne, but no prudent short-term investment policy should be without the primary objective of principal preservation. Additionally, a board-approved investment policy should include the following:

- Investment objectives with respect to risk and return
- Permissible and prohibited investment vehicles or classes of investments
- Minimum and acceptable security ratings
- Maximum maturity for individual securities
- Maximum weighted average maturity or duration for the portfolio

- Maximum amounts (either by percentage, total dollar amount, or both) of the portfolio that may be invested in individual securities, companies, instrument classes, geographic areas, or industries
- Policies/guidelines for investing in foreign securities
- Specific responsibilities for implementing the policy, by organizational title
- Methods of monitoring compliance with policies, procedures, and internal controls
- Provisions for performance measurement, evaluation, and reporting
- Guidance for classification of investments in accordance with appropriate local regulatory and accounting guidance, such as the International Accounting Standards Board (IASB) guidelines globally, or the Financial Accounting Standards Board (FASB) and Governmental Accounting Standards Board (GASB) rules in the United States
- Responsibilities and reporting requirements for custodians, external investment managers, broker-dealers, and other investment counterparties
- Exception management and related approval processes

4. Describe the basic short-term investment strategies that are available to an organization.

A variety of short-term investment strategies is available to an organization, depending on its strategic objectives:

- A conservative investor may prefer a passive strategy, such as employing a buy-and-hold-to-maturity approach or investing in money market funds (MMFs). As previously discussed, a company without the resources to actively manage a portfolio of short-term investments may choose to simply hold one or more MMFs.
- A more aggressive investor may prefer active portfolio management to meet specific needs or potentially earn a higher rate of return by investing in securities that might be considered too risky by other investors.
- A corporate investor that is in a high tax bracket may favor tax-based strategies in addition to those described above.

These strategies may be used individually or in combination, depending on the organization's investment needs and objectives.

5. What is a yield curve?

A yield curve is a plot of the yields to maturity on the same investment instrument or class of instruments, but with varying maturities, as of a specific date. For example, a yield curve for US Treasury instruments is a plot of yields to maturity for US Treasury bond issues with varying periods to maturity as of the close of business on a particular date. Similarly, a plot of yields to maturity for AA rated industrial bonds with various maturities is a yield curve for that class of instruments.

6. Yield on a short-term investment is a function of what three factors?

The yield on any short-term investment instrument is a function of the:

- Cash flows received from the investment
- Amount paid for that investment
- Maturity or holding period

7. Name the principal types of short-term funding available to most companies.

- Trade credit
- Internal borrowing
- Selling of receivables
- Commercial bank credit
- Single payment notes
- Repurchase agreements (repos)
- Commercial paper (CP) issuance
- Asset-based borrowing

8. What are the costs typically involved with a line of credit?

A line-of-credit lender will typically charge interest and a commitment fee on the line on an annual basis. While there may be other fees, they tend to be one-time charges rather than annual fees. Interest is charged on the used portion of the line. The commitment fee may be charged on the line or its unused portion. The overall interest rate on the line is determined by the total interest paid on the line's used portion and the amount paid for the commitment fee relative to the average used portion of the credit line over the borrowing period.

9. What are the basic components of interest rates for borrowing?

Interest rates depend on many factors. Some of these factors come from general economic conditions, and some are dependent upon individual organization variables, such as financial position, industry, overall debt use, and environmental liabilities. To help form a basic understanding of these factors, the model below incorporates some of the most common factors into a calculation of an underlying borrowing rate on a specific issue.

For most companies, organizations, or government entities, the underlying cost of borrowing is a function of the following factors, which can be expressed as the variable r, where r is defined as:

$$r = r^*_{RF} + IP + DP + LP + MP$$

Where:

r^*_{RF} = Real risk-free rate of interest

IP = Inflation premium

DP = Default premium

LP = Liquidity premium

MP = Maturity premium

10. Compare and contrast short-term and long-term borrowing.

Historically, short-term interest rates are usually lower than long-term rates, so yield curves are usually normal, meaning they slope upward with maturity. This implies that there is a cost advantage to using short-term credit. When short-term rates are higher than long-term rates, the yield curve is inverted and slopes downward with maturity.

A significant responsibility for treasury professionals is to monitor interest rate cycles and the yield curve in order to make effective decisions about short- versus long-term financing. Depending on interest rate cycles and the prevailing yield curve for interest rates, a company may secure long-term, low-rate bank or institutional financing and/or obtain fixed- versus floating-rate financing. There are also several short-term financing sources (e.g., accounts payable and accruals) that have little or no interest costs.

Borrowing on a short-term basis carries two types of risks to the borrower that are avoided in longer-term borrowing:

- The first risk relates to fluctuations in market interest rates. If the company borrows on a short-term, floating-rate basis, then it will borrow at the prevailing interest rate and risk dramatic rate swings in either direction. Many companies negotiate short-term borrowing risk reduction techniques such as interest rate caps, collars, swaps, and floors to protect themselves against interest rate fluctuations.
- The second risk of short-term financing concerns the availability of funds. If a company relies heavily on short-term borrowing, then the short-term funds may not be available at some future point due to tightening credit standards on the part of lenders. Also, a company's credit quality may decline, thus endangering the future rollover or renewal of the credit arrangement. Some companies counter this risk by negotiating multiyear credit line commitments known as *revolving credit agreements*, which guarantee the availability of funds over a longer term.

In contrast to short-term borrowing, long-term borrowing on a fixed-rate basis stabilizes interest costs, or it provides a narrow range for fluctuation in interest costs on a variable-rate, long-term loan with an interest rate collar.

11. What are loan covenants?

Loan covenants impose either restrictions (known as *restrictive or negative covenants*) and/or obligations (known as *affirmative or positive covenants*) on the part of an organization's management. Loan covenants generally serve as a protection for the lenders (or investors) by preventing management (acting on behalf of the equity holders) from increasing the organization's credit risk, thereby reducing the value of any existing debt securities. Because the lenders do not typically have a voice in the organization's management, they must protect themselves through covenants at the time the loan is made. For bonds, the covenants typically are determined from negotiations with the rating agency as part of the ratings process. Depending on the covenants, there may be significant restrictions on the financial decision making for an organization. These restrictions could include limits or restrictions on the:

- Ability to sell certain assets
- Right of an organization to issue additional bonds
- Use of second or junior mortgages
- Key ratios that limit flexibility in financial decision making
- Payment of dividends

12. What are the two major classes of credit ratings?

- **Issuer Credit Ratings**: The rating is an opinion on the obligor's (issuer's) overall capacity to meet its financial obligations. These include counterparty, corporate credit, and sovereign credit ratings. Counterparty ratings are made on key counterparties in financial transactions, such as financial institutions and insurance companies. Corporate credit ratings are on corporate debt issuers, and sovereign ratings are on government debt issuers.
- **Issue-Specific Credit Ratings**: These ratings of specific long- and short-term securities consider the attributes of the issuer, as well as the specific terms of the issue, the quality of the collateral, and the creditworthiness of the guarantors.

CHAPTER 12 Long-Term and Capital Investments

1. What are the typical ways of stating a return objective for a long-term portfolio?

The return objective may be stated in terms of:

- An absolute return (e.g., an annualized return of 2.5%)
- A relative return (e.g., exceeds the return on 10-year US Treasuries by 50 basis points)
- A general goal (e.g., current income, capital appreciation, capital preservation, or total return)

2. What are the issues that should be considered in setting capital market investment objectives?

As a general guideline, treasury professionals should consider the following issues when setting their capital market investment objectives:

- Risk preferences for portfolio
- Return objectives
- Liquidity needs
- Time horizons or future needs for funds
- Tax issues
- Legal or regulatory factors (especially for pension fund investments)

3. Discuss asset allocation.

One of the key decisions in managing a portfolio of long-term, capital market investments is that of asset allocation, or the mix between fixed-income (debt) and equity (stock) securities. Although there are some variations, fixed-income securities generally tend to provide their returns in the form of income while equity investments are usually a mix of both income and capital appreciation (and potentially depreciation or loss). As a result, fixed-income securities, as the name implies, provide a relatively predictable stream of income over time.

Equities, on the other hand, have a higher potential for long-term gain, since the investor is benefiting from any increase in value of the underlying company, but equities also run the risk of a loss if the investment must be liquidated at a time when the value of the stock has declined.

The basic structure of the long-term asset allocation for any portfolio will be highly dependent on the objectives outlined for that portfolio. Generally, the longer the desired maturity of the portfolio and the greater the tolerance for risk, the higher the level of equity used in the portfolio, since equity has no maturity date and may have greater risk of short-term loss. Taxes must also be considered, especially when there are significant differences between tax rates on interest income versus capital gains.

4. What is duration?

Duration is one of the key measures of risk for a bond or fixed-income portfolio. It is important because it gives an estimate of the volatility of an investment, since bonds with higher durations typically have greater price volatility than bonds with lower durations (given equal credit, inflation, and reinvestment risk). Generally, the longer the duration, the more sensitive the bond or portfolio is to changes in interest rates.

Duration measures the number of years required to recover the true cost of a bond, considering the present value of all coupon and principal payments received in the future. Duration, in its simplest form, is the weighted average time to receipt of all future cash flows associated with a bond investment, including interest payments, discount accretion, premium amortization, and payment of principal. Because a bond generally pays interest periodically and may accrue additional principal if purchased at a discount to its maturity value (or depreciate if bought at a premium), it can be viewed as having an average maturity of all these cash flows that is different from its final maturity. Duration is simply the weighted average amount of time needed before all of the various cash flows from the bond pay back the initial cost of the bond.

5. What is the importance of the fixed-debt to floating-debt ratio?

Many fixed-income portfolio managers use the ratio of fixed-rate obligations to floating-rate obligations to monitor their portfolios. This relation is usually expressed in terms of a target fixed/floating ratio. In general, the ratio of fixed-rate to floating-rate investments tends to correspond to an organization's views on long-term interest rates. A firm that thinks interest rates are going to rise is likely to have more floating-rate than fixed-rate investments in its portfolio, while a firm that expects rates to drop is more likely to invest in a higher percentage of fixed-rate obligations. In addition, companies tend to use more floating-rate debt when they have sufficient financial strength to support the additional interest rate exposure. However, the proportion of fixed- to floating-rate debt varies widely among companies, suggesting that there is as much art as science in determining the appropriate mix.

The drawback to managing a portfolio solely on the ratio of fixed-rate debt to floating-rate debt is that it only considers one operational target and fails to take into account the terms of the actual securities in the portfolio. Since bonds can vary in maturity from 1 to 30 years (or longer), the ratio of fixed-rate debt to total debt reveals very little about the debt's maturity profile and the risks associated with it. As a result, it is also important to take into account the average term to maturity of the portfolio, as well as the overall duration of the portfolio.

6. Describe securities lending.

A technique that is available to help manage long-term assets, securities lending is a practice where the owner of specific securities lends them to another party. The terms of the securities lending agreement normally require the borrower to provide the lender of the securities with collateral, in the form of other securities or a letter of credit, equal to or greater in value than the securities that are being lent. The primary purpose of the loan is to allow the borrower to hedge or short-sell securities that it does not own, in anticipation of the value of the security declining. In return, the borrower pays the lender a negotiated fee. Loaned securities are also used to cover or eliminate "failed transactions." The practice allows owners of long-term securities to earn additional income on holdings that they cannot or do not want to actually sell out of their portfolio.

7. What is CAPM?

The capital asset pricing model (CAPM) describes one possible relationship between risk and the required rate of return on an asset. In the case of common stock, the CAPM is based on the concept that a sensible investor holds a diversified portfolio of stocks to mitigate risk. As more stocks are added to a portfolio, the overall riskiness and variability of the portfolio is reduced. Many studies show that company-specific return variation is almost completely eliminated in portfolios when 25 to 40 stocks in a variety of industries are owned.

8. How is the value of a long-term security established?

Publicly traded corporate securities are valued by financial markets. A security, or any economic asset, derives its value from the cash flow stream expected by investors over the asset's life and the risk associated with the possibility that the cash stream may not be realized as expected. The valuation of the anticipated cash benefit stream involves discounting the stream at the market's required rate of return, which is a function of the stream's risk. This rate of return represents an investor's opportunity cost (i.e., the rate of return that can be earned on investments of the same risk). That said, the asset's market value is the present value of the anticipated cash stream that is discounted using a rate appropriate to the stream's risk. Expressed algebraically, this idea may be represented as the summation of all the asset's cash flows over the investor's holding period, discounted at the appropriate opportunity cost. This concept can be written using the following formula:

$$PV_0 = \sum_{t=1}^{n} \frac{CF_t}{(1+k_i)^t} = \frac{CF_1}{(1+k_i)^1} + \frac{CF_2}{(1+k_i)^2} + \dots + \frac{CF_n}{(1+k_i)^n}$$

Where:

PV_0 = Current value of the asset

CF_t = Cash flow for the asset for Periods 1 through n

k_i = Opportunity cost or required rate of return for asset type i

NOTE: In this equation, the Σ sign indicates a summation of the factor following the symbol. In this case, the variable t runs from 1 to n in the summation.

9. How is the value of a bond established?

The valuation of bonds, or any other fixed-income security, is straightforward because the amount and timing of future cash flows are specified. In the case of a fixed-rate bond, the amount and timing of interest (coupon) payments and principal repayments are stated in the indenture. Bond interest payments usually are made semiannually. A bond's market price is the present value of the stream of interest payments plus the present value of the principal repayment, where discounting occurs at the market's required rate of return.

10. How is the value of common stock established?

Common stock valuation differs from bond and preferred stock valuation because both the timing and amount of cash flows associated with stock ownership are neither fixed nor known with certainty. A corporation's dividend policy is set by its board of directors, and the actual dividend paid may change over time. A stock investor would expect to sell the shares at some point in the future, but the selling price at that time is unknown today.

To value common stock, it is necessary to estimate the dividend stream and liquidation price, and then assign a required rate of return in order to determine the present value of the estimates. CAPM can be used to determine the required rates of return on common equity.

In the most general case of valuing stock, the price an investor would be willing to pay is the present value of the future dividend stream (i.e., the summation of all future dividends), discounted by the firm's cost of equity.

CHAPTER 13 Cash Forecasting

1. What are the primary tasks that require accurate forecasting?

- **Managing Liquidity:** Forecasting a company's net cash position at different intervals to identify potential cash excesses or shortages is essential for scheduling investment decisions and anticipating borrowing requirements to meet daily obligations. It is the most important reason for cash forecasting.
- **Controlling Financial Activities:** Variance analysis that compares actual cash flows with projected cash flows can help identify problems such as unanticipated inventory changes, delays in A/R collection, the mistiming of payments, and fraud or embezzlement. Early identification lets a company initiate corrective measures.
- **Meeting Strategic Objectives:** Cash flow forecasts are used to project future funding requirements and make operating decisions to support a company's strategic plan.
- **Budgeting Capital:** Forecasts of revenue, expenditures, and funding are needed to help evaluate proposed capital expenditures.
- **Managing Costs:** Cash forecasts are used to help minimize excess bank balances, reduce short-term borrowing costs, and increase short-term investment income.
- **Managing Currency Exposure:** Cash flow forecasts attributable to foreign operations are used to assess the degree of foreign currency exposure and provide information for policies designed to control currency risk.
- **Complying with Regulatory Requirements:** Cash flow forecasts are frequently part of internal control procedures needed to meet various regulatory requirements, such as minimum capital requirements or requirements for imprest tax accounts. This is especially important for publicly traded companies.

2. What are three fundamental issues that need to be addressed in cash forecasting?

- Simplicity
- Collaboration and communication
- Duplication

3. What is a forecast horizon, and what are the typical types of forecast horizons?

The forecast horizon is the time interval over which information is to be forecasted. It is an important forecasting consideration because a method appropriate for a short-term forecast will not be appropriate for longer-term forecasts, and vice versa. In most companies, short-term forecasting is the responsibility of treasury while longer-term forecasts are often done by FP&A or capital budgeting.

- **Short-Term Forecasting:** Short-term forecasts typically range from one to thirty days in length and predict cash receipts and disbursements, as well as the resulting balances, on a daily, weekly, or monthly basis. They aid in scheduling cash transfers, funding disbursement accounts, and making short-term investing and borrowing decisions. Short-term forecasting is also important for establishing and managing target balances for purposes of bank compensation. There is a growing trend on the part of some companies to create intraday cash forecasts in an attempt to reduce potential overdrafts and other related bank fees. This trend is supported by the availability of intraday balance reporting data from many banks.

- **Medium-Term Forecasting:** Cash flow forecasts from one to twelve months in length are an integral part of cash budgeting and are considered medium-term forecasts. They project the inflows (e.g., collections from sales and other sources of funds) and outflows (e.g., expenses and other uses of funds) on a monthly basis. They are used to determine the company's need for short-term credit or the availability of funds for short-term investing. They also serve as a benchmark for performance by comparing actual cash flows to projected cash flows based on the cash budget.
- **Long-Term Forecasting:** Long-term forecasts cover any period beyond one year. They take into consideration projections of long-term sales and expenditures, as well as market factors. These forecasts are of strategic importance because they help inform decisions about which type and amount of long-term financing to obtain, and the timing of obtaining funds. Financial institutions and rating agencies also use long-term forecasts for credit analysis and evaluation purposes.

4. What is the difference between a static and a rolling forecast?

As the name implies, a static forecast is one in which the time period of the forecast does not change but remains static even though the actual numbers or data in the forecast change over time. The period of time used in the forecast remains constant, and the forecast is updated at the end of the forecast period to show the subsequent period. A monthly (horizon) cash forecast that is done each month (frequency) is an example of a static forecast. An annual budget is another typical example of a static forecast in that the budget, which is a type of forecast, is normally always for the same 12-month period (e.g., January through December), even if the numbers are updated during the year.

In contrast, a rolling forecast is one with a constant number of periods (weeks, months, etc.) that is updated on a regular basis and "rolls" forward. An example of a rolling forecast would be a 13-month cash forecast that is updated monthly. Assume that the initial forecast covers the 13 months from January 2xx1 through January 2xx2. Sometime during January 2xx1, the forecast will be updated and will now cover the 13 months from February 2xx1 through February 2xx2. If nothing has changed, all that happens is that January 2xx1 is dropped from the forecast and the projection for February 2xx2 is added. In reality, the forecast data for the other months in the report are typically also updated because newer information is now available.

5. What are the key factors that need to be considered in identifying suitable data to be used in a forecast?

- **Available Information:** Information may be gathered externally or internally. Sources include the company's banks, field managers, sales managers, and the A/P, A/R, payroll, FP&A, and tax departments. In many cases much of this data is available from internal systems, such as general ledger (G/L) systems, enterprise resource planning (ERP) systems, or treasury management systems (TMSs).
- **Assumptions:** It is important to understand what assumptions are being made about various projected input data to determine how accurate and useful the data may be. If sales managers are assuming that all accounts will be paid on time while the overall economy is slowing down, the treasury professional may need to adjust the underlying assumption to get an accurate forecast. Cash flows should be discussed with key participants to gain insight into any issues or quirks that need to be included in the forecast. For example, it may be important to know whether specific payments are made monthly, quarterly, or annually. For retailers, another example might be that 80% of their projected annual sales occur in the last two months of the year.

- **Desired Type of Forecast:** The data collected should be dictated by the desired cash flow forecast, not simply by what is available. For example, if preparing a short-term cash needs forecast, immediate A/P data may be important, but long-term capital acquisitions and planned securities offerings are probably not needed.
- **Source of Information:** Source identification is affected by the degree of centralization in the company's cash management structure. In a decentralized company, field managers usually have the most current financial data related to their operations. A centralized company is often less dependent on numerous field sources.
- **Account Structure:** Bank account structure is also important in that it may help group cash flows in a meaningful fashion and help identify potential changes. For example, using a concentration account to collect all cash inflows and disburse all cash outflows via ZBAs helps to facilitate cash flow forecasting compared to a system of multiple, stand-alone accounts.
- **Reporting Requirements:** To ensure the usefulness of the data selected, it is essential that the data are defined precisely and reported accurately in a timely manner. This should include an analysis of variances between the forecast and actual results to help track accuracy and improve future forecasts. A growing number of companies use company intranets and treasury websites to distribute management reports, including forecasts.
- **Historical Data:** A variety of data from prior periods are useful in predicting the amount and timing of cash inflows and outflows. Credit sales, payment histories, purchases, and scheduled payments are examples.

6. What are three of the more important methods of developing short-term cash projections?

There are several methods to develop short-term cash projections that incorporate factors affecting cash flow. Three of the more important methods include an accounts receivable (A/R) balance pattern forecast, a receipts and disbursements forecast, and a distribution forecast.

7. What are the two methods of calculating distribution percentages for a forecast?

The distribution percentages can be calculated two different ways: (1) simple average, or (2) regression analysis.

8. What is the percentage-of-sales method of forecasting, and what are the three basic steps in the method?

The percentage-of-sales method involves projecting financial statements based on the historical relationship between sales and liquid balance sheet accounts that tend to change in value along with sales. Cash, A/R, inventory, and A/P are the more important accounts. Account size (e.g., cash or inventory) is expressed as a percentage of sales, based on an examination of the historical relationship between account size and sales. This percentage is then used in conjunction with forecasted sales to produce a forecast of account size. Other balance sheet and income statement accounts are forecasted based on other factors (e.g., a known debt repayment schedule).

The percentage-of-sales method requires three steps:

- Forecast the income statement and balance sheet based on the relationships mentioned previously.
- Calculate the projected ending cash balance by determining how the forecasted income statement and balance sheet values impact cash (i.e., utilize a cash flow statement given the impact of changes to investments, capital/depreciation, and potential slowing of cash collections or payments).
- Compare the projected ending cash balance with the company's target cash balance, and adjust the pro forma statement to show the source of funding for a cash shortfall or the investment of a cash surplus.

9. What is time series forecasting?

Time series forecasting is a forecasting model used to identify repetitive patterns in a historical series, so that this pattern can be used to predict future values of the series.

A time series is a serial chain of values for some variable, such as sales. Every time series contains a trend, seasonal pattern, cyclical pattern, and random movement. A trend is the general direction that the values are moving (e.g., sales are increasing 5% year over year). A seasonal pattern repeats with regard to time of year. A cyclical pattern repeats without regard to time of year. It is possible that the series is stationary (i.e., the trend value is zero). The seasonal and cyclical patterns may be strong, moderate, or weak. Random movement is a change in the series not identifiable as a trend or a seasonal or cyclical influence. The source of random movement is usually unknown, but it may be a one-time event, such as a World's Fair, Olympic Games, or natural disaster.

10. What is regression analysis?

Regression analysis is a statistical method that can be used to assess the impact that multiple variables (or causes) have on a value or an outcome. Regression is a sophisticated method that requires rather large amounts of data, and knowledge of the method's advantages and pitfalls. The explanatory model developed using regression must be reestimated when the underlying influences on cash flow change.

11. Describe the three levels of cash flows based on their degree of certainty, and provide examples of each.

- **Certain Cash Flows:** The timing and amounts of several types of cash flows are known in advance. Common examples are interest, principal repayments, dividends, royalties, and tax payments.
- **Predictable Cash Flows:** Cash collections from credit sales are an example of a cash flow component that can be predicted with reasonable accuracy. The cash flow on a given day depends on factors such as the level and pattern of past sales, age of accounts, number of customers, and payment histories. These factors enable reasonably accurate cash flow prediction. Disbursement for payroll and benefits tends to be very predictable because it is based on the number of employees, compensation method, and historical experience. Similarly, vendor check-clearing patterns can be predicted based on experience with clearing times.
- **Less Predictable Cash Flows:** Some cash flows, such as those related to sales of a new product, unexpected repairs, pending settlement of insurance claims, or the cost of settling a strike, are difficult to forecast. The experience and judgment of the forecaster are important in such situations.

12. How can a treasury professional test and validate relationships in forecasting models?

- **In-Sample Validation:** The forecast is tested for accuracy using the historical data used to develop it. If the forecast accurately predicts one data series from one or more other series, the relationships among the data series are deemed to be validated. When a forecast is initially developed, however, there typically is no other data available to test it.
- **Out-of-Sample Validation:** The forecast is tested using data that were not used to develop it. For example, if three years of monthly data are available, the first thirty months of data could be used to develop the forecast. The forecast could then be used to "predict" the subsequent six months, which can then be compared to actual values for those months.
- **Ongoing Validation:** Continuing feedback from projected versus actual comparisons allows continuous evaluation and improvement of the forecast. This ongoing validation may be done on a daily basis for critical forecasts. Any reporting should include an analysis of forecast errors to help foster this process.

- **Documentation of the Process:** It is important to document how the forecast process works, as well as documenting the sources of data, contacts, etc. This enables others to understand and work with the forecast and allows future changes when needed.

13. What purpose does a closing cash position serve in cash management?

A projected closing cash position statement, also known as the *daily cash forecast* or merely the *cash report*, is used to determine whether there will be a cash surplus or a cash deficit in a particular bank at the end of the day. The projected closing cash position is calculated by taking the day's opening available bank balance(s), adding any expected settlements in the collection and concentration accounts (depository banks), and deducting any projected disbursement totals. Information about receipts in the process of collection, whether checks, cards, or electronic, is typically available from the prior day's balance reports. Same-day receipts, such as wire transfers and controlled disbursement totals, are typically reported on a same-day basis.

Clearings of disbursements made from accounts other than controlled disbursement accounts must be estimated. Since wire transfers are real-time transactions, notice of incoming and outgoing wires is often available through a bank reporting system or TMS.

CHAPTER 14 Information Technology in Treasury

1. What roles are treasury professionals often responsible for with regards to information management?

With regards to information management, the treasury professional is commonly responsible for:

- Compiling data from a wide range of internal and external sources
- Sorting, analyzing, and storing information
- Initiating and validating transactions
- Obtaining account balances and transaction details from external sources
- Obtaining internal information that affects the cash flow timeline (e.g., receipts and disbursements)
- Consolidating information into the cash position worksheet
- Generating journal entries for accounting
- Reporting information to management
- Assisting other areas with any treasury-related research

2. What are the basic elements of information security?

Security must provide a number of basic elements:

- **Privacy:** The assurance that information is only accessible by authorized individuals and will not be used for unintended purposes
- **Authentication:** The ability to know, with a reasonable amount of certainty, who is accessing information or initiating a transaction
- **Authorization:** The ability to know and control what functions and data an authenticated individual can access and use
- **Integrity:** The ability to ensure that a message was not modified in transit and that stored information has not been improperly modified or deleted (data integrity is especially important for financial transactions)
- **Non-repudiation:** The inability of the sender or receiver of a message to deny having sent or received the message

3. What are the basic factors of multifactor authentication?

Authentication methods for information technology and network purposes are based on three basic factors:

- Something the individual **knows**, such as a password or personal fact
- Something the individual **has**, such as a token or a cell phone
- Something the individual **is**, such as a fingerprint or facial scan

4. What is a digital signature?

A digital signature is a message encoded with the sender's secret, private key that the receiver can use to identify the source. As long as the private key is never shared with anyone, forgery of a digital signature is virtually impossible. A digital signature is tied to a document and to the signer, meaning the signer's digital signature will be different for each document signed.

Note that a digital signature is different from a digitized signature such as that used as a facsimile signature on laser-printed checks. In the United States, the Electronic Signatures in Global and National Commerce (E-Sign) Act gave digital signatures the same legal status as paper/ink signatures, sometimes referred to as *wet signatures*.

5. What are tokens?

Tokens are electronic devices that contain circuitry that encodes assigned user-specific information or personal information to help ensure password protection. For example, one type of token contains a clock in a smart card that is synchronized to a clock on the host system where the data or application resides. When the user wants to log on to the system (whether locally or from a remote point), the token provides a unique code that, when entered with the user's PIN or password, ensures that the user is authorized to access the system. Alternatively, the token may be a device that is plugged in to a port on the user's computer and responds directly to the host system without the need for the user to enter, or even know, the challenge information. The use of a token meets the "something they have" criteria of multifactor authentication.

6. What are the major drawbacks to using spreadsheets as treasury technology?

The major drawbacks to spreadsheets are typically:

- Lack of security
- Lack of auditability
- Poor version control
- Minimal integration with other applications
- Lack of organized IT support and software maintenance
- Potential for corruption of data and internal formulas
- Lack of a common database, leading to duplication of data
- Lack of transaction initiation capabilities

7. What is a dashboard?

A dashboard is a user interface or display that, like a car's dashboard, organizes and presents information in a way that is easy to read and understand. Like a car's dashboard, it is often color coded to indicate the importance of specific information (e.g., green is normal and red requires immediate attention). Dashboards are intended to provide summary data that can be used to manage a function or process and often include the ability to "drill down" on specific pieces of information to get more detailed information about the specific item. For example, if one item on a dashboard were the number of payments over a specific dollar amount, clicking on the number would provide a detailed list of the individual payments.

A treasury management (TM) dashboard is intended to provide management immediate feedback on the overall status of treasury operations, while also publishing key financial information useful in running the business. The dashboard should be short and easy to read, and while the actual metrics and information published will vary from company to company, general categories of information can include:

- Interest, investment, and FX rates
- Cash flow and/or borrowing statistics
- Projected and/or large-dollar disbursements
- Key performance indicators (KPIs) or metrics, such as reconcilements completed, cash forecasting accuracy, wire transfer timing and accuracy, or transaction volumes
- Key deadlines and operational alerts (e.g., bank holidays; disbursement calendars; employee stock option [ESOP] exercise dates; and investment blackout periods, scheduled earnings announcements, and investor releases)

8. What are ERP systems?

Enterprise resource planning (ERP) systems are sophisticated information management, production, and accounting software packages that link different functional areas or operational divisions of a company on an enterprise-wide basis. They integrate large amounts of data into a common database, which helps eliminate multiple, duplicate copies of information. The greatest advantage of ERP systems is that they can provide a single processing platform for all of an organization's accounting and finance software, reducing the number of integration points required with stand-alone packages. Many ERP systems include some form of treasury management system (TMS) application, which may include the ability to directly connect to an organization's banks to initiate payments and other transactions from A/P and to download and reconcile bank account information. One of the major advantages of ERP-based TMS solutions is the built-in integration with a company's accounting and financial applications. The disadvantages can include a higher cost point and a need for significant IT support.

9. What is a TMS?

A treasury management system (TMS) is a computer system that provides treasury professionals with the ability to collect, compile, synthesize, and relate data provided by an organization's bank and other external partners to financial transactions and other treasury elements relevant to a particular organization. TMSs were initially developed in response to the need to use one system to access multiple banks. Today, most TMSs not only provide access to multiple banks, but they also typically provide expanded functionality in terms of debt and investment management, FX management, and risk management, and often include the capability to directly connect with internal accounting and other financial systems. The expanded functionality usually comes at a higher cost point, however, and often requires some form of internal IT support to operate or configure the solution.

10. List the basic platforms or architectures that are used to provide technology solutions for treasury.

Most of the technology solutions available to treasury professionals can be provided on a variety of technology platforms or architectures:

- Stand-alone technology
- Client/server solution
- Enterprise technology
- Hosted solution

11. What is workflow management?

Workflow management is a function incorporated into many software packages that allows multistep processes to be automated, tracked, and managed. Although workflow software is available as independent software, it is more commonly seen as an integrated function of most TMS or ERP solutions.

Workflow management allows a company to use software to implement, monitor, and enforce the specific processes and procedures (i.e., the workflow) that it wants used throughout the company. For example, a company following best practices will normally require that all wire transfers be inputted by one individual and then approved and "released" by a second individual. Workflow management software will accept the initial transaction and then notify the appropriate approver(s) that a transaction is awaiting approval. Once the transaction is approved, the software will automatically release the transaction and may be set up to notify the original initiator that the transaction has been released. Management can view reports at any time to see how many transactions have been entered into the system and what their current status is (i.e., entered, approved, or released). Workflow management systems are typically capable of managing processes with many steps and multiple decisions points throughout the process. They not only help enforce proper procedures, but they also provide ongoing status reports that can be used to manage the overall process.

12. What are the major categories of functionality that are typically provided by TMSs?

TMSs can provide a wide variety of capabilities and functionality that are of value to the corporate practitioner. This functionality can be broken down into five major categories:

- Cash management
- Payments
- Financial transactions
- Accounting
- Bank account management (BAM)

13. What are the principal benefits of e-commerce?

E-commerce can offer several benefits. It:

- Improves productivity, thereby enhancing working capital management
- Makes data reentry unnecessary, thereby reducing error rates and enabling faster data processing
- Eliminates mail time, thereby enhancing cash flow processes
- Improves communication capabilities
- Allows straight-through processing (STP)

14. What is ISO 20022?

ISO 20022 is an XML-based messaging standard for the financial services industry, whose intended use is transmitting information related to securities, payments, financial reporting, account management, international trade, and foreign exchange (FX). It is part of the ongoing development of Single Euro Payments Area (SEPA) payments standards and the next generation of the SWIFT messaging format. ISO 20022 will initially be used for communications between organizations and their banks, as well as between the banks themselves. (*ISO* stands for International Organization for Standardization, and *SWIFT* stands for Society for Worldwide Interbank Financial Telecommunication.)

15. What is BTRS?

The Balance and Transaction Reporting Standard (BTRS) is a communication protocol that has been developed by the American National Standards Institute (ANSI) Accredited Standards Committee (ASC) X9 committee to facilitate the transmission of balance and reporting information from banks and other financial institutions to their account holders. The predecessor to BTRS is the Bank Administration Institute (BAI) reporting format (often referred to as *BAI2* because it was the second such standard). BAI2 is not currently a standard; it is a commonly used format. BAI2 is widely used for information reporting of account balances, transactions, lockbox detail, and controlled disbursement detail. It has many optional fields and variations from bank to bank. Often banks require their clients to implement variations of the format, causing a large investment in scripting and resources to integrate these versions of the format into their back-office applications.

BTRS, the equivalent of BAI3, is a formal standard that was approved on June 7, 2012, and is administered by the ASC X9 committee. BTRS is intended to increase standardization of and improve upon BAI2. Major changes include:

- Modernization of text to include developments in banking and technology over the past 25 years
- Additional structure to support extended wire remittance (in corporate trade payments)
- Rationalization and reduction of the number of supported transaction codes
- Additional SEPA transaction codes to support new European payment types
- Additional balance codes to facilitate SWIFT and ISO 20022 XML interoperability
- Modified currency rules to make them mandatory and allow for multicurrency applications
- New 900 series code categories to define debits and credits

The standard builds upon the older BAI2 information-reporting format while retaining forward compatibility. Although a BTRS file with the above changes could not be interpreted with a BAI2 reader, a BAI2 file could be interpreted with a BTRS reader.

While the BAI2 code list is a domestic US format, many corporations have implemented the codes for their global reporting requirements. It is not uncommon to see information from other countries in a BAI format. The need for standardization of the BAI formats used for cross-border information is an industry objective and was one of the driving forces behind the transfer of the BAI format to the X9 committee and the globalization of BTRS. ASC X9 has international access and can promote national standards internationally to become ISO standards.

16. What is eBAM?

Electronic bank account management, or eBAM, is an effort to replace the large amount of paper in the bank account management process with electronic messages and files exchanged between banks and their customers.

Conceptually, eBAM provides significant benefits to treasury operations, including:

- Eliminating the cost of creating, moving, reviewing, and storing paper
- Streamlining the process of managing complex, dispersed bank account and signatory information
- Improving the ability to quickly change bank accounts and their signatories across banks and geographies
- Strengthening internal control and improving related auditing and management reporting

17. What is mobile banking?

Mobile banking refers to the provision of banking and financial services with the help of mobile telecommunication devices, such as mobile phones and tablets (including iPads), while *mobile payments* refers to the ability to use a mobile device to make a payment or transact business. Mobile banking has become a reality for consumer banking, and as a result many corporate bank customers are beginning to ask for mobile banking to address their needs.

18. What is NFC?

Near field communication (NFC) is a short-range wireless proximity technology that uses radio frequency signals to communicate between two devices, such as a mobile phone and a payment terminal, or two mobile phones.

CHAPTER 15 Operational and Enterprise Risk Management

1. What are the purposes of the risk management process for an organization?

The purpose of the risk management process in an organization is to:

- Help managers identify future events that create uncertainty
- Respond to negative possibilities by balancing the negative economic and/or regulatory effects of these possibilities with the costs that can be incurred to mitigate or eliminate them
- Provide direction to guide recovery actions when serious negative events occur

2. What are the roles of the risk management committee and the chief risk officer (CRO)?

In many organizations, the board of directors has a risk management committee that provides oversight to management regarding the identification and evaluation of issues related to enterprise risk management (ERM). Some organizations have also added the position of chief risk officer (CRO)—sometimes known as a *chief risk management officer (CRMO)*—whose primary responsibility is ERM. In these organizations, the CRO is the executive accountable to the board of directors for the efficient and effective governance of significant risks—and related opportunities—for the organization and its various segments.

3. What are the six steps in the risk management process?

The risk management process involves six steps:

- Determine an organization's risk tolerance.
- Identify potential exposures.
- Quantify the impact and level of exposures.
- Develop and implement an appropriate risk management strategy to manage those exposures.
- Monitor the exposures and evaluate the effectiveness of the strategy.
- Review and modify the strategy as needed.

4. What are the objectives of qualitative assessment with respect to measuring exposure as part of general risk management?

A qualitative assessment should:

- Examine basic operating procedures to determine where mitigation strategies, such as hedges, may be useful (e.g., a balance sheet hedge matches exposed liabilities against exposed assets and is referred to as *asset and liability management*)
- Determine how fundamental business processes contribute to risks and permit the identification of possible solutions
- Ensure that derivatives are structured and sized appropriately and proper accounting procedures are followed when derivatives are used as part of financial risk mitigation strategies

5. Describe the four basic approaches to developing and implementing a risk management strategy.

- **Avoid the Risk:** This approach may involve a company deciding not to enter into a certain line of business or utilize a particular business or manufacturing process due to the risks involved.
- **Mitigate the Risk:** Mitigating risk generally involves putting appropriate controls in place to limit the potential risk exposure. In financial risk management, approaches such as using derivatives or balance sheet hedges create a financial position (either a derivative instrument or a balance sheet item) that offsets the risk from an ongoing business process. For example, if a company expects to receive some amount of foreign currency as an accounts receivable, it could enter into a forward or futures contract that allows the company to convert the foreign currency into the home currency at a fixed rate that is known today. Other risk mitigation approaches include process and facility design, project management, education, and compliance management. An example of another risk mitigation approach would be the installation of sprinklers in a building to reduce the impact of a fire.
- **Transfer the Risk:** With this approach, the organization finds someone else who is willing to assume the risk. The primary means of transferring risk is by using insurance of some type. A company may also contractually transfer risk by requiring that the risk be borne by another party in the supply/delivery chain.
- **Retain the Risk:** By their very nature, some lines of business carry inherent risks, and it may not be possible to completely avoid, transfer, or mitigate all the risks in certain types of operations. In these cases, businesses may opt to selectively bear some risks. For example, a power utility operating in an area prone to hurricanes has to deal with fact that its operations will likely be impacted by this risk at some point. In this case, disaster recovery and contingency planning become a key part of the utility's risk management strategy.

6. What is enterprise risk management?

The term *enterprise risk management (ERM)* refers to a comprehensive, organization-wide approach to identifying, measuring, and managing the various risks that threaten the achievement of the organization's strategic objectives and therefore its overall operations. One purpose of ERM is to ascertain if and how each department contributes to, or is impacted by, a particular risk category (e.g., financial, operational, or market). Traditionally, risks have been addressed at the business department or other organizational subdivision level. ERM's comprehensive approach lets a business assess the full scope and implications of risks across division lines. Methods and models of ERM have become important tools for firms, and since they encompass the entire business, many aspects extend beyond the boundaries of treasury activities.

ERM helps to ensure effective reporting and compliance with laws and regulations, and helps avoid damage to the entity's reputation and associated consequences. It also helps an entity achieve its goals while prudently managing the unexpected.

7. What are the key elements that should be contained in an organization's risk management policy?

Regardless of an organization's approach to risk, it is important for the firm's risk management committee and CRO (or equivalent) to have a clearly defined risk management policy endorsed and approved by the highest management level possible, preferably the board of directors. The policy should:

- Contain a concise statement of the organization's risk management goals and the overall scope of the risk management policy (e.g., eliminate, mitigate, and transfer risk)
- Define authorities and responsibilities (and the role of the CRO, if the organization has one)

- Identify the types of exposures to be managed
- Delineate the mitigation techniques and products that may be used
- Outline the process for determining specific strategies to be employed and exposures to be mitigated
- Summarize the process for monitoring performance of the strategies
- Outline contingency plans
- Require periodic review of the policy and testing of plans

8. What is operational risk?

Operational risk refers to potential losses resulting from inadequate systems, management failure, faulty controls, fraud and human error, and other related issues.

9. What are the four basic types of market risk?

The four basic types of market risk are:

- Equity price risk
- Interest rate risk
- Foreign exchange (FX) risk
- Commodity price risk

10. Discuss the concepts of disaster recovery and business continuity.

Disaster recovery refers to the restoration of systems and communications after an event causes an outage. *Business continuity* refers to the actions taken with regard to crisis management, alternative operating procedures, and communications to staff and customers. The intent of disaster avoidance, recovery, and remediation measures is to preserve the firm's revenue stream. It is important that disaster recovery plans be tested and reevaluated on a regular basis to ensure that they are effective and current.

11. Name three types of internal operational risk.

- Employee risk
- Process risk
- Technology risk

12. Name eight types of external operational risk.

- Financial institution risk
- Counterparty risk
- Legal and regulatory compliance risk
- Supplier risk
- External theft/fraud risk
- Physical and electronic security risk
- Natural disaster risk
- Terrorism risk

13. What are three critical factors to consider in determining an operational risk management strategy?

Three critical factors determine an operational risk management strategy for an organization:

- Organizational culture
- Technology
- Guidelines for the board of directors

14. What are the four goals of using insurance to mitigate risk?

The four objectives of insurance management (as it applies to risk mitigation) are to:

- Insure against catastrophic loss
- Decide when and what to insure
- Manage the purchase and use of insurance
- Obtain efficient pricing for insurance needs

15. What are the key factors to consider when selecting an insurer?

When selecting among competing insurers, important factors to consider include:

- Long-term solvency of the insurer
- Rating for the insurer
- Service provided
- Cost versus exposure
- Industry knowledge and experience

16. What is self-insurance?

Self-insurance is not technically a form of insurance because it does not involve a transfer of risk to an insurer or another separate entity. Also, the term *self-insurance* can describe any risk retention program, even quite informal, unfunded arrangements. Self-insured retention (SIR) is the component of loss covered by the insured in a policy. SIR differs from a deductible in that the insured is responsible for all aspects of a claim up to the defined limit. Self-insurance requires careful forecasting to ensure that adequate funds are available to meet future losses and that these funds are systematically maintained by the organization. Self-insurance differs from noninsurance in that the organization had made a conscious decision to self-insure and typically allocates specific assets to fund or pay for the costs of self-insuring, as opposed to noninsurance where the risks are ignored or assumed to be negligible.

Many large organizations use self-insurance to manage their employee health care expenses. This usually works well for organizations with a sizeable pool of diverse employees. Typically, the organization will contract with a third party to manage the provider network and claims processing. In addition, the organization may purchase some type of excess coverage to protect against unexpectedly high claims in a given period.

17. Explain the concept of risk transfer.

The essence of any risk transfer is a contract between a transferring organization (the transferor) and another entity (the transferee), under which the transferee agrees to pay designated types of the transferor's losses within contractual limits. The transferor may have to pay the transferee a fee (e.g., an insurance premium) for this promise of indemnity, or the transferor may have the bargaining power to secure this promise as a condition for agreeing to do business with the transferee. Such risk transfer arrangements are made frequently for tax or regulatory reasons, and may be accomplished through the purchase of reinsurance, either from a broker or directly from the market. It is important to note that the transfer of risk is only as good as the transferee's, or the insurance company's, ability to pay claims. As part of the transfer, the insured gives up all of the rights it may have to recover the loss from other parties. This is typically referred to as *subrogation*.

18. What is value at risk (VaR)?

An approach used in determining how changing financial variables affect a company's value, value at risk (VaR) is a statistical technique that was developed in the trading rooms of financial institutions to estimate the maximum potential losses of a trading operation or portfolio for a given period of time—in other words, the worst-case scenario. It was designed to incorporate a wide range of risk factors and summarize their impact in a single measure that answers the question, what is the most that I can expect to lose over a given period of time (e.g., a day or a year) with a reasonable amount of certainty? That amount is the value at risk. The VaR approach uses the probability and monetary impacts of specified events over a period of time to assess risk.

19. Explain the difference between sensitivity analysis and scenario analysis.

Sensitivity analysis examines the impact of a change in the value of a variable on a selected outcome measure (such as net cash flow), assuming all other variables are held constant. Sensitivity analysis is used to alter the value of a single variable in a spreadsheet or computer model to see how a change in that variable affects the outcome (net cash flow, in this example).

Scenario analysis is similar to sensitivity analysis, but more than one variable is altered at a time. Scenario analysis usually starts with a base case—an expected value for each input variable affecting the final value. People within the firm who are most familiar with each variable are asked to provide estimates of the highest and lowest possible values for those variables. Overall best- and worst-case scenarios can then be constructed to assess the range of possible outcomes for net cash flow or another value of interest. Sometimes, scenario analysis is formalized by asking those who supply best- and worst-case values for the variables to provide a subjective probability distribution to accompany their estimates. This makes the examination of the sensitivity of net cash flow to the variables more precise and, hopefully, more accurate.

CHAPTER 16 Financial Risk Management

1. What are the three major categories of financial risk?

- Interest rate risk
- Foreign exchange (FX) risk
- Commodity price risk

2. What are the three types of foreign exchange (FX) risk?

- Economic risk
- Transaction risk
- Translation risk

3. Discuss the concepts of active hedging, speculation, and arbitrage.

Active hedging is the process of using various financial instruments to reduce or eliminate risks associated with uncertain future cash flows. This is a core principle of treasury financial risk management. Hedging is similar to the concept of buying insurance to protect an asset, and the purpose of the hedge is to insure the asset's value (or minimize the risk on a liability) when its market value fluctuates.

While there is often some degree of speculation in hedging activities (given the difficulty in creating a "perfect" hedge), active speculation goes beyond hedging and involves taking a position on the direction of the market in the attempt to make a profit, which is not usually a treasury objective. Most companies use hedging to minimize risk, not to make a profit. But some companies go a step further and attempt to use the products to make a profit. This is referred to as *speculation*. In many companies, corporate hedging policies forbid this type of speculation. For some organizations, however, speculation in certain markets may be a treasury objective, as determined by the board of directors. For example, financial institutions often have a trading floor for stocks, FX contracts, or interest contracts where speculation is encouraged as a means of revenue generation. Another example might be an energy company that speculates in certain energy markets (e.g., oil and gas) as part of its corporate objectives.

Arbitrage is the process by which an asset is purchased in one market and simultaneously sold in another market to produce a riskless profit. While making a profit is not usually a treasury objective, it is important for a treasury professional to understand the arbitrage process because arbitrage is the primary mechanism that ensures efficiency in financial markets.

4. What are the benefits of financial risk management?

Managing a company's risk helps to reduce the variability of both a company's future cash flows and its profitability due to external changes in FX rates, interest rates, and commodity prices, which consequently increases the company's value. Hedging enables treasury to smooth uneven cash flows due to unexpected external changes and forecast financial results with greater confidence. Less variability in expected future cash flows increases a firm's value in three ways:

- Greater predictability in future cash flows makes the company more attractive to shareholders.
- The company gains an enhanced borrowing advantage in credit markets because lenders view the firm as being less risky.
- The company's probability of financial distress decreases because the firm can assess costs and revenues more accurately.

5. What is a forward contract?

A forward contract is an agreement between two parties to buy or sell a fixed amount of an asset to be delivered at a future date and at a price agreed upon today. This contrasts with a spot contract, which is an agreement between two parties to buy or sell a fixed amount of an asset immediately. The underlying asset can be a financial instrument (e.g., a stock index fund or debt instrument), a currency (e.g., the euro or pound), or a commodity (e.g., gold or coffee). The future date is referred to as the contract's *maturity date*, and the price is called the *delivery price*.

6. What is a swap agreement?

A swap is an agreement between two parties to exchange (or swap) a set of cash flows at a future point in time. The most common type of swap is an interest rate swap. In this type of swap, Party X agrees to pay Party Y a stream of cash flows equal to a floating rate of interest on some mutually agreed-upon amount. This amount is referred to as *notional principal* because the principal amount does not exchange hands; instead, only interest payments are exchanged. At the same time, Party Y agrees to pay Party X a stream of cash flows equal to a fixed rate of interest on the same notional principal at the same future dates. In other words, Party X is swapping a fixed-rate loan for a floating-rate loan while Party Y is doing exactly the opposite. Other types of swap arrangements include currency, commodity, and basis rate swaps.

7. What is the difference between a call option and a put option?

A call option gives the contract owner the right, but not the obligation, to buy (call) the underlying asset from the contract writer at a fixed price through the delivery date. A put option gives the contract owner the right, but not the obligation, to sell (put) the underlying asset to the contract writer at a fixed price through the delivery date. This fixed price is called the *strike price* or *exercise price* of the contract.

8. When are option contracts normally exercised?

In practice, the purchaser of a call contract normally does not exercise the option to buy, and the purchaser of a put contract normally does not exercise the option to sell. The actual commodity transaction occurs in the spot market. The option contract is sold and its value is used to offset losses if the commodity price is higher (call option) or lower (put option) than the strike price. If a party writes (sells) a call option contract, it is setting a ceiling on the commodity price it will receive in exchange for the premium obtained. The writer of a put contract is ensuring a floor on the price at which it is willing to sell the commodity in exchange for the premium.

9. Discuss the objectives of global treasury management.

The objectives of global treasury management are similar to those of domestic treasury management, with the main objective being the efficient use of an organization's global cash resources in a manner consistent with its strategic goals. A global treasury operation must also manage cross-border funds movement and use FX and liquidity management techniques that are different from those used within just one country. The selection of financial services providers that are capable of assisting a company with international operations is a critical aspect of the global treasury management process.

10. What are the two basic FX markets?

There are two basic FX markets: the spot market and the forward market. A rate quoted in the spot market is called the *spot FX rate* (also referred to as a *spot rate* or *spot contract*). Spot rates are quoted for the delivery (or settlement) of currency one or two business days following the date of the trade. For FX trades initiated from the United States, regular spot settlement of Canadian dollars and Mexican pesos is one business day, while regular spot settlement of European and Asian currencies is two business days. Faster settlement may be possible, but it is often at a less favorable rate than the spot rate.

A forward FX rate (forward rate) is a rate quoted for the delivery (or settlement) of currency beyond the terms of a spot contract. Deliveries under most forward FX contracts occur within a year of the trade date. Delivery dates beyond one year are available for actively traded currencies.

11. What are forward points?

Forward points reflect the difference between two countries' short-term money market interest rates (e.g., rates on short-term government borrowing or interbank rates) at the time the trade is executed. The interest rate differential between two countries determines if respective currencies will trade at par, at a discount, or at a premium in the forward market. Premiums and discounts are commonly quoted in points (basis points, or 1 /100th of a percent). In the jargon of the industry, forward points are added to the spot rate when there is a premium and are subtracted from the spot rate in the case of a discount.

12. What is a currency swap?

A currency swap typically involves the exchange of a cash flow denominated in one currency with a cash flow denominated in another currency, as well as an exchange of principal. The two cash flows can be at either fixed or floating rates. A swap can also be used to change the value date of a forward when a company cannot meet the original delivery date due to unexpected circumstances, such as a late payment from a foreign customer.

13. Explain a forward rate agreement (FRA).

A forward rate agreement (FRA) is a forward contract on interest rates in which two parties agree that a certain interest rate will apply to a certain principal during a specified, future period of time. The notional principal amounts are agreed upon, but they are never exchanged. If the actual rate is different from the agreed-upon rate in the contract at settlement, then one party pays the other a cash amount equal to the difference.

14. What are interest rate futures?

Interest rate futures are contracts on an underlying asset whose price is dependent solely on the level of interest rates. The most popular short-term interest rate contracts are US Treasury bill (T-bill) contracts, and Eurodollar contracts traded on the Chicago Mercantile Exchange as bank certificates of deposit (CDs). The underlying asset in a T-bill futures contract is the 90-day T-bill rate. The underlying asset in a Eurodollar contract is the interest earned on a Eurodollar deposit (CD) at three-month LIBOR. The most actively traded long-term interest rate contracts are the 5- and 10-year US Treasury notes and the 30-year US Treasury bonds.

15. What is an interest rate collar?

An interest rate collar is a combination of an interest rate cap and an interest rate floor. A company that buys an interest rate cap and sells an interest rate floor is effectively locking in a range for borrowing costs. The cap establishes a maximum borrowing rate, thereby protecting the company against higher interest rates, while the floor sets a minimum borrowing rate. A collar has no costs when the income received from selling the floor matches the premium paid for the cap. Costless collars are popular hedging vehicles providing some interest rate protection at zero cost.

16. What are the disclosures required by ASC Topic 815?

Accounting Standards Codification (ASC) Topic 815 requires the following disclosures:

- A discussion of the company's objectives and strategies for using derivatives
- The current fair market value of the company's derivative positions
- Any contingent, credit-related features of the company's derivative positions
- Locations and amounts of derivatives in a company's financial statement

17. Compare implicit and explicit FX risk.

- **Implicit risk** is the risk that the value of future transactions will change due to changes in exchange rates. For example, a company may publish price lists in a foreign currency or make a firm quote in a foreign currency. These result in an implicit FX risk until such time as a sale is actually made and the sale recorded. For this reason, companies with extensive foreign currency transactions often manage their FX risk based on projected sales to account for implicit risk.
- **Explicit risk** is the risk that occurs due to changes in FX rates between the time a transaction occurs and the time it is finally settled. For example, a Canadian-based company sells a product denominated in Japanese yen (JPY) for payment in 30 days. The company is subject to explicit risk from the time of the sale until the receivable is actually collected.

18. Discuss the challenges for global companies operating in emerging markets.

For global companies operating in emerging markets, there may be some special challenges to managing the risk related to dealing with local currencies and governments in these markets. Some emerging economies have very tightly managed currencies, in terms of both exchange rates and availability. Management of FX exposures and risk in these situations may be very different from the more traditional FX risk management in more commonly traded currencies.

19. What are exotic currencies?

Emerging market currencies are often referred to as *exotic currencies* because they are not commonly traded. On a broad level, emerging market currencies fall into one of several different categories contributing to the underlying risk profile:

- Free-floating currencies that are traded with some degree of transparency
- Currencies that trade subject to strict regulations imposed by monetary authorities in the country
- Currencies that are pegged to another currency in some form
- Currencies that trade within a band against other currencies
- Currencies that are not freely convertible

CHAPTER 17 Treasury Policies and Procedures

1. What are the four primary reasons that treasury policies and procedures are required?

There are four primary reasons why treasury policies and procedures are necessary:

- **Organizational Needs:** To provide a documented guide to best practices to ensure fundamental operational processes are performed in a consistent manner that meets the organization's needs. Additionally, policy statements are needed to grant and delegate the authority required to conduct essential treasury procedures.
- **Risk Management:** To provide a control process to mitigate identified risks in the operation.
- **Roles and Responsibilities:** To provide a clear definition of the roles and responsibilities within the treasury function. When problems occur, documented policies and procedures can provide some degree of protection for staff that are following the approved procedures.
- **Compliance:** To provide an effective internal audit and control tool that helps keep a company in compliance with regulatory and legal requirements, through well-defined and documented processes and guidelines.

2. What are some key control issues to consider when developing treasury policy guidelines and objectives?

Key control considerations include:

- Structure of controls
- Delegation of authority and governance
- Segregation of duties
- Roles and responsibilities
- Records retention policies
- Moving from controls to policies and procedures

3. What are the basic elements of a policy?

Basic policy elements include:

- **Objectives:** The objectives for the policy should be clearly stated at the beginning of the policy document.
- **Scope:** The scope of the policy should define, as precisely as possible, what areas and processes the policy will cover.
- **Basic Guidelines:** This section should provide a listing of all the areas covered by the policy, along with procedures for how each of the related processes should be performed and managed. These guidelines should also include how to manage exceptions (i.e., what constitutes an exception and how to handle it).
- **Roles and Responsibilities:** This section should provide a clear listing of the roles and responsibilities of the key participants in each policy. Included in this section should be an outline of the lines of authority, delegation, and segregation of duties.
- **Performance Measurement and Reporting:** This is an important part of the policy, especially where investments, derivatives, or trading activities are involved. The metrics or benchmarks used for performance measurement should be defined clearly, as well as the expectations for meeting the performance objectives. Any required reports should be discussed, including formats, timeframes, and deadlines.

- **Required Controls and Compliance Considerations:** One of the key aspects of developing policies and procedures is to ensure proper controls for processes used in the area in question. Mandating a policy will not ensure compliance without appropriate oversight and controls. This section should also specify which, if any, external regulatory requirements are being addressed by the policy.
- **Exception Management:** No matter how comprehensive a policy statement is, there will always be exceptions to the rule. It is important that a policy statement identify who can approve exceptions and how they will be tracked and managed once they have been approved.
- **Review Cycle:** Procedures change and evolve over time and the related policies must also change. An essential item in any policy is a statement of how frequently the policy will be reviewed and what approvals will be required (e.g., "this policy will be reviewed by the CFO annually and all changes approved by the board of directors"). The date of the last review should be included in the policy itself.
- **Policy Attachments:** A policy is most effective when it provides comprehensive information in the form of exhibits and appendices. These normally consist of glossaries, distribution lists, procedures manuals, organization charts, standard reports, and any other information needed to support or clarify the information provided in the body of the policy. It is important to keep the attachments as current as the policies.

4. Once a treasury policy has been developed, what are the typical steps in a formal approval process for that policy?

The approval process steps include:

- Treasury department review
- Review by other functional area managers
- Review by the internal audit and/or compliance group
- Final approval

5. When should an existing policy be reviewed and updated?

All policies should be reviewed, updated, and reapproved on a specified periodic basis, driven by the size and type of the organization. The review schedule and the required levels of review and approval should be included in the policy. A good practice is to include a revision-tracking section as part of the document. This should list all changes and updates in order to provide historical context and document any necessary regulatory compliance.

Policies should also be reevaluated and updated immediately following any major reorganization of the company's structure, material change in banking services, or relevant regulatory change. Implementation of the operational requirements dictated by a policy is most effectively accomplished through a detailed procedures manual, which can serve as a reference for daily activities and duties.

6. What issues should be considered when writing treasury procedures?

Some of the more specific considerations in the development of procedures include the following:

- Procedures should be written so that they are clear and understandable to both existing and new managers and employees. They should be written in a concise manner with a minimum of verbiage, and all acronyms and technical terms should be spelled out clearly.
- Procedures that are unnecessarily restrictive may limit their usefulness, so when feasible, they should offer options.
- Documentation should be factual and double-checked for accuracy. Where possible, information that may become quickly outdated should not be included in the procedures.
- Where applicable, the procedures manual should include step-by-step instructions for completing any required forms (both paper and electronic).
- The procedures document itself should be structured so that users can focus quickly on the aspect of the procedure relevant to their decision/task at hand. Many organizations use a flexible, modular outline to make the document easy to modify and keep up to date.

7. Why should a company have a formal investment policy?

A formal investment policy establishes a clear understanding of the firm's investment philosophy and objectives. By establishing investment objectives, a firm can set clear parameters for its investments, allowing it to better manage liquidity, monitor compliance, and minimize risk, regardless of its structure (i.e., centralized or decentralized; domestic or global). This also serves to protect staff against blame for unforeseen problems as long as they are properly following documented policy.

In general, the more decentralized and geographically widespread the investment decision making, the more crucial an investment policy becomes to ensure a consistent, enterprise-wide approach. Formal written policies also help to delineate the relationship between the parent/holding company/corporate office and the subsidiary in decentralized operations.

8. What is an investment horizon, and why should it be included in a firm's short-term investment policy?

A firm's investment horizon is the total length of time that it expects to or is willing to hold an investment. The longer the average time to maturity (i.e., duration) of investments in the portfolio, the greater the exposure to interest rate risk. An investment policy should specify any limitations that a firm may have regarding the maximum and average duration of the investments in its portfolio. This exposure horizon is a function of both the organization's risk philosophy and the total interest rate exposure already present in other areas of the organization. Short- and medium-term investment portfolios often consist of fixed-income securities and money market funds (MMFs). Since the price and/or return on those securities and MMFs are largely a function of the market interest rate, the portfolios are subject to significant interest rate exposure.

9. What are the three typical objectives that must be considered in an investment policy?

The three objectives include:

- Safety
- Liquidity
- Risk/return trade-off

10. What are some typical approaches to diversification that must be considered in an investment policy?

Diversification approaches include:

- Allocating investments by asset class (e.g., fixed income, equity, and cash), or among a variety of investment management firms (e.g., 25% with Company A and 75% with Company B)
- Holding a certain percentage of foreign securities so the company can minimize the impact that movements in a specific currency may have on the portfolio (e.g., the US dollar weakens by 5% against the euro)
- Limiting investments in issues from the same organization to a certain percentage of the total portfolio (e.g., 10% of the portfolio)
- Limiting investments from specific issuers and/or instruments in order to limit concentration risk (e.g., can invest up to $10 million in ABC Company commercial paper, or can invest up to 10% of the portfolio in a single currency or country)

11. What are some common benchmarks used in the measurement of performance in an investment policy?

Common benchmarks include yields on US Treasury securities, which include Treasury bills (as a very short-term reference), Treasury notes, Treasury bonds, and 30-day commercial paper. Indices of a particular segment of the market may also be used as benchmarks. Some common indices are the Lipper Money Market Funds Index, the Standard & Poor's (S&P) 500, Barclays Capital Aggregate Bond Index, J.P. Morgan Government Bond Index, and the investment benchmarks provided by the Association for Financial Professionals (AFP). Depending upon portfolio mix, some companies develop a customized "blended" benchmark for use in evaluating performance.

12. What are the key elements that should be included in a payments policy?

Key elements to be addressed in a payments policy include:

- Delegation of authority
- Permitted payment methods
- Payment and approval limits
- Joint approval requirements
- Payment authorization requirements
- Payment risk management
- Required documentation

13. What elements should be included in an outsourcing policy?

Key issues to be addressed in an outsourcing policy include:

- Delegation of authority
- Reporting requirements
- Vendor and operational risk management
- Information security and confidentiality requirements
- Performance measurement

14. What elements should be included in a regulatory compliance policy?

Key elements to be included in a regulatory compliance policy include:

- Statement of policy and required compliance
- Subcontractor and vendor compliance requirements
- Compliance monitoring activities
- Audit requirements
- Exception management
- Disciplinary processes

15. Why are records retention policy guidelines important?

There are many regulations relating to the retention of records, especially for compliance with regulatory and tax authorities. There are also severe penalties for failure to maintain proper workpapers, especially those related to audit activity, bankruptcies, and many government investigations. Retention policies also frequently include when and how specific key records should be destroyed (e.g., "disbursement requests and supporting documentation will be destroyed five years after payment has been made"). In addition to a general records retention policy, other treasury policies and procedures documents should contain requirements for the appropriate retention, safekeeping, and destruction of records, where appropriate.

CHAPTER 18 Financial Accounting and Reporting

1. What kinds of insights can be provided by analyzing financial statements?

Analyzing financial statements provides insight into:

- How well the company has managed its liquidity position
- How effectively it used and financed its assets
- Whether it had a proper balance between debt and equity financing compared to peers
- How well it controlled operating and financing costs
- Whether the profit it earned was satisfactory in relation to the levels of revenue it experienced and the investment in assets that support its operations

2. What is the IASB?

On a global level, the International Accounting Standards Board (IASB) determines general accounting standards and is made up of board members from nine countries. Based in London, England, the IASB's mission is to develop a single set of global accounting standards published as pronouncements called International Financial Reporting Standards (IFRS).

3. What are the basic principles of IFRS?

The basic principles of International Financial Reporting Standards (IFRS) are laid out in the Conceptual Framework published by the IASB. Under IFRS, there are a number of qualitative characteristics that accountants (and other financial professionals) are expected to follow in selecting and applying appropriate accounting policies for their organization. These characteristics include:

- **Relevance:** Information provided must be of value to decision makers and have predictive value, confirmatory value, or both.
- **Materiality:** Information presented must be material, or in other words, must have a significant impact on the financial position of the entity being reported. Materiality of specific information should be judged in regards to the circumstances of the entity and the transaction.
- **Faithful Representation:** Financial information should faithfully represent the transactions it represents. To the extent possible, it should be complete, neutral, and free from error.
- **Comparability:** Information must be presented in a form that allows it to be compared with prior periods and with other companies in a similar business. Financial statements should be appropriately restated to reflect changes in accounting policy that may impact comparability.
- **Verifiability:** Information presented must be neutral and unbiased, and must fairly represent the business transactions being reported.
- **Timeliness:** Information should be presented to decision makers in time to be capable of influencing their decisions within the limits of reliability and completeness.
- **Understandability:** Information must be presented in the manner that will make it as understandable as possible for non-accountants with a reasonable knowledge of business. Relevant information, however, should not be omitted just because it is complex and hard to understand.
- **Completeness (The Cost Constraint):** Within the limits of reasonable cost, information must be complete enough to make it usable and reliable.

4. What are the four principles of GAAP?

The four basic principles underlying the US's Generally Accepted Accounting Principles (GAAP) are the:

- Historical-cost principle
- Full-disclosure principle
- Revenue recognition principle
- Matching principle

5. What are the key differences between IFRS and GAAP?

Key differences include:

- IFRS does not permit last-in, first-out (LIFO) accounting.
- IFRS uses a single-step method for impairment write-downs rather than the two-step method used in US GAAP, making write-downs more likely.
- IFRS requires capitalization of development costs once certain qualifying criteria are met. US GAAP generally requires development costs to be expensed as incurred, except for costs related to the development of computer software, for which capitalization is required once certain criteria are met.

6. What is shareholders' equity?

Shareholders' equity is the difference between total assets and total liabilities, and represents what would remain if all assets were sold and all creditors paid off in liquidation. It is, in effect, the financing provided by the company's owners and from ongoing company operations. The shareholders' equity section of the balance sheet contains a number of items, with two of the primary categories being the following:

- **Contributed capital** is the cash or other assets invested by shareholders. This section is further subdivided as needed to show various classes of stock, if any, such as common and preferred stock, with any preferred stock listed first.
- **Retained earnings** represent the changes in shareholders' equity arising from the retention of profits or losses of the company, less any dividends paid out to shareholders.

7. Compare and contrast internal and external financial statements.

External (or published) financial statements are used to provide the investors and other outsiders with information about the financial status of an entity. By their nature, these statements must comply with the appropriate financial standards, either IFRS or GAAP. Internal (or management) financial statements are those used by owners or other executives to manage the operation of an entity. Internal statements are not audited and can be in any format that management finds helpful in dealing with ongoing operations. While these two classes of statements come from the same basic financial information, their uses are quite different. At the end of the day, the two types of statements must reconcile to each other, but they can, and often do, provide very different types of information.

Internal financial statements typically consist of management reports, budgets, and forecasts, as well as the traditional financial statements already outlined. These reports are used for analyzing the organization's performance and position, and for taking appropriate measures to improve overall results.

8. Why are financial audits important?

Confidence in the integrity of financial reports is critical in an open, market-driven economy. Investors, lenders, regulators, and the general public look to published financial statements to obtain information about a company's financial condition and performance.

Historically, certification of financial statements' accuracy by independent auditors was the main source of this confidence. However, the accounting manipulations that resulted in the downfall of several major public companies eroded this confidence. In response, the US Congress passed the Sarbanes-Oxley Act (SOX), with the purpose of restoring confidence in published financial statements by establishing a set of controls over audit procedures and disclosure requirements, and an administrative vehicle to implement and oversee them.

Although most countries have their own national accounting and auditing certifications, there are a number of internationally recognized certifications. These certifications are especially valuable in transitional and developing economies where the quality of the national certification is low. The most popular international accounting certification is offered by the Association of Chartered Certified Accountants (ACCA). Until a few years ago, this certification was the only truly international accounting certification. However, in recent years, a few other certifications have started to become internationally recognized. In the United States, the primary accounting certification is the Certified Public Accountant (CPA), while in the United Kingdom, Canada, India, and many other former British colonies, it is the Chartered Accountant (CA). Regulatory requirements in many jurisdictions, including the United States, often require that in addition to being certified, public accountants and external auditors must also be licensed by the appropriate regulatory body.

9. What are the five types of audit opinions?

Auditors provide five types of opinions:

- Standard unqualified opinion
- Unqualified opinion with explanatory paragraph, or modified unqualified opinion
- Qualified opinion
- Adverse opinion
- Disclaimer of opinion

10. What are the basic types of financial statements?

The basic financial statements are:

- Balance sheet
- Income statement
- A reconciliation of changes in shareholders' equity (statement of changes to shareholders' equity)
- Statement of cash flows

In addition, while not a statement per se, the financial filings of public companies normally include a management's discussion and analysis section (MD&A), which is either included in the notes to the financial statements or presented as a separate statement.

11. Compare and contrast EBIT and EBITDA.

One of the common measures for operating profitability is *earnings before interest, taxes, depreciation, and amortization (EBITDA)*. Once depreciation and amortization are subtracted, the remaining amount is referred to as *earnings before interest and taxes (EBIT)*. The term *operating income* refers to EBIT.

EBIT has traditionally been the measure used to evaluate a firm's ability to generate operating profits and to meet its financial and tax obligations. EBITDA first came into common use with leveraged buyouts in the 1980s, when it was used to indicate the ability of a company to service debt. As time passed, it became popular in industries with expensive assets that had to be written down over long periods. Many companies, especially in the technology sector, now commonly quote EBITDA.

12. What are the two methods of preparing the statement of cash flows?

The statement of cash flows is generally prepared using either the direct or indirect approach:

- The **direct method** reports the gross cash receipts and disbursements without examining any adjustments needed to calculate accrued net income. Operating activities are examined, and the total cash flow attributable to each activity is computed. To begin the direct method, accrual accounts must be converted to a cash amount. The direct method generally provides users more information about actual uses of cash. As a result, FASB and IASB have discussed requiring the direct method of cash flows. As of the publication of this book, this proposal has not been approved, due to the widespread use of the indirect method and the very large expense required for modifying financial reporting systems to present cash flows directly.
- The **indirect method** starts with net income taken from a firm's income statement and adjusts it to reflect the impact of noncash transactions during the reporting period. Net income is adjusted by any changes in balance sheet accounts from the prior period. Adjustments are made for changes in depreciation, amortization, accounts receivable, inventory, accounts payable, accrued wages payable, prepaid insurance, and income taxes payable. One difference between GAAP rules and IFRS principles is that under GAAP, dividends received from a company's investing activities are reported as an operating activity, not an investing activity.

13. What is a derivative?

A derivative is a financial instrument whose value is derived from some underlying financial asset. Derivatives can be forward, futures, option, and swap contracts. For companies that follow IASB regulations, the applicable guideline is International Accounting Standard (IAS) 39: *Financial Instruments: Recognition and Measurement*. This statement covers accounting for both derivatives and hedging. Under US GAAP, the applicable guidelines are found in Accounting Standards Codification (ASC) Topic 815: *Derivatives and Hedging*. Initially, these guidelines required that all derivative instruments be carried on the balance sheet as an asset or a liability at fair market value (referred to as *mark-to-market accounting*), but were modified to some extent in reaction to the Recession of 2009 in ASC Topic 820: *Fair Value Measurement* and ASC Topic 825: *Financial Instruments*.

Under either IAS or ASC Topic guidelines, the accounting for the gains and losses arising from changes in a derivative's fair value generally depends on the instrument's intended use. Gains and losses arising from any revaluation of derivatives are reported in current-period income, provided the derivatives do not qualify as hedge instruments. If a derivative is used to hedge fluctuations in the value of a specific asset or liability on the balance sheet, then gains and losses of the revaluation are recognized as income or expense together with the offsetting gains and losses of the hedged item. This type of hedge is a *fair value hedge*.

14. What is ASC Topic 820?

Accounting Standards Codification (ASC) Topic 820 clarifies the definition and application of fair value measurement. Prior to this guideline, multiple definitions and applications of fair value measurement could be applied to assets and liabilities. Under Topic 820, fair value of an asset or liability is defined by determining the price that would be received in an asset sale or the price paid to transfer a liability. The valuation price must be market-based and take into consideration all observable valuation inputs, such as competition and risk. ASC Topic 825 later expanded this application by stating that fair value should be applied to all financial assets and liabilities except for certain specified types of assets.

15. Describe the basic steps in preparing a foreign currency translation adjustment for financial statement purposes.

The task of foreign currency translation is essentially determining the correct exchange rate to be used in converting each financial statement line item from the foreign currency to the parent company's functional currency. The translation adjustment is an inherent result of this process, in which balance sheet and income statement items are translated at different rates. The basic steps in this process are:

- Determine the functional currency of the subsidiary: The *functional currency* is defined as the currency of the primary economic environment in which the entity operates. Normally, the majority of the subsidiary's business activities are transacted in that currency. This task can be more difficult than it seems and may require significant judgment. The subsidiary's functional currency is not necessarily its home currency (i.e., the currency of the country in which the subsidiary's headquarters are located) or the currency in which the subsidiary keeps its books.
- Determine whether the functional currency of the subsidiary is also its home currency:
    - If the subsidiary's functional currency is its home currency, then the current method is used to translate financial statement line items to the parent company's currency. The current method translates all assets and liabilities at the current spot rate at the date of translation. Equity items other than retained earnings are translated at the spot rates in effect on each related transaction date (known as *specific identification*). Retained earnings are translated at the weighted average rate for the relevant year, with the exception of any components that are identifiable with specific dates, in which case the spot rates for those dates are used. Income statement items are translated at the average rate for the period, except where specific identification is practicable. The resulting adjustment is not recognized in current earnings, but rather as a component of other comprehensive income.
    - If the functional currency of the subsidiary is not its home currency, then the temporal (historical) method is used. Under this method, nonmonetary balance sheet accounts and related income statement accounts are remeasured using historical exchange rates. The resulting translation adjustment is recognized in current earnings.

16. What is the key feature that distinguishes governmental and not-for-profit (G/NFP) organizations from profit-oriented businesses?

The key feature distinguishing G/NFPs from profit-oriented businesses is that they provide as many goods or services as their resources allow. Another key difference is that these types of organizations typically use the term *fund balance* or *net worth* rather than *equity* in their accounting statements. Consequently, G/NFPs' financial accounting processes differ from those of for-profit enterprises. G/NFP reporting focuses on compliance and accountability rather than profitability.

CHAPTER 19 Financial Planning and Analysis

1. What are the three categories of costs (and examples of each) that must be considered in product planning, capital budgeting, cost/benefit analysis, and financial plan development?

Costs are classified into three categories:

- **Fixed costs** do not vary in total over a wide range of activity and are not immediately impacted by changes in business activities. One example of a fixed cost is the monthly account maintenance fee banks charge on deposit accounts. The fee remains the same regardless of the number of transactions on the account.
- **Variable costs** are costs whose total amount changes in direct proportion to the level of business activity. The cost of goods sold (COGS) is generally a variable cost. COGS generally increases as sales and production levels increase, and decreases if sales and production levels decrease.
- **Semi-variable (or mixed) costs** have both a fixed and variable component and increase in stair-step fashion. An example of semi-variable costs would be a machine company that has milling machines that produce widgets. Each milling machine costs $50,000 and can produce 10,000 widgets a month, and each widget consumes $1 of raw materials. The first widget will cost $50,001 to produce ($50,000 for the milling machine and $1 for the raw materials). Each additional widget will only cost $1 to manufacture until the production volume exceeds 10,000 widgets per month. Since the 10,001 widget will require the purchase of another milling machine, its marginal cost will again be $50,001 ($50,000 for the second milling machine and $1 for raw materials). Once the second machine is purchased, the next 10,000 widgets will only have a marginal cost of $1 each to manufacture. Every 10,000-widget increase in production volume will require an additional $50,000 plus the cost of the individual raw materials. Consequently, the semi-variable cost has both fixed and variable cost elements.

2. What are the differences between operating leverage and financial leverage?

Operating leverage is determined by the extent to which fixed costs are used in a company's operating cost structure. The higher the proportion of fixed costs, the higher the company's operating leverage.

Just as operating leverage looks at the use of fixed costs of production, financial leverage examines the fixed costs of financing. Generally, the higher the level of debt capital used in a company, the higher the interest costs and the greater the amount of financial leverage.

3. What is a break-even analysis, and how is it used in a cost/benefit analysis?

A break-even analysis is a type of cost/benefit analysis that establishes the level of activity at which benefits and costs are equal. The break-even point is the level of activity for an operation at which the costs equal the benefits. A break-even analysis is used by businesses in product decisions to determine what level of sales, at a given price, is required to cover costs.

4. What are the differences between net present value (NPV) and internal rate of return (IRR)?

NPV is calculated by netting the present value (PV) of anticipated cash inflows with the PV of cash outflows. IRR is the discount rate that makes the NPV equal to zero or, equivalently, makes the PV of cash inflows equal to the PV of cash outflows.

5. How is sensitivity analysis used in investment risk analysis?

Sensitivity analysis determines how a final outcome, such as NPV, is influenced by changes in the value of a particular variable (e.g., sales, or an operating or financing cost) and how vulnerable the expected outcome is to changes in a specific assumption. Sensitivity analysis can identify and evaluate the areas of greatest vulnerability, and permits the decision maker to determine the likelihood that an unacceptable outcome will occur.

6. What are the three main methods of assessing investment risk?

The three main methods for assessing investment risk are:

- Sensitivity analysis
- Scenario analysis
- Simulation

7. What is RAROC?

Risk-adjusted return on capital, or RAROC, is an economic metric developed in the 1980s by the consulting firm Oliver Wyman to help measure the expected profitability of a project from a risk-adjusted standpoint. Although initially developed for financial institutions to use in identifying investment projects, it is increasingly being used by other types of organizations in making capital allocations. RAROC is a method of measuring the return on a project based upon the overall risk of the project.

8. What is the difference between total asset turnover and current asset turnover?

Total asset turnover measures how many times the firm's asset base was used (i.e., turned over) in generating the flow of revenue during the period. This is a measure of how effectively the firm's assets are used to generate revenue. It is calculated as revenues divided by total assets.

Current asset turnover measures how many times the firm has turned over the stock of its most liquid assets with the flow of revenue. It is calculated as revenues divided by current assets.

9. What is the cash conversion efficiency ratio, and how is it used?

Cash conversion efficiency measures how effectively a company has converted sales (or revenues) into cash. The cash flow generated by operations (i.e., operating cash flow from the statement of cash flows) is viewed as a percentage of revenue. The higher the cash conversion efficiency ratio, the greater the net cash generated per dollar of revenue. This ratio is also called the *cash profit margin*.

10. Compare and contrast the times interest earned (TIE) ratio and the fixed-charge coverage ratio.

The TIE ratio measures a firm's ability to service its debt through interest payments. The numerator in the equation is operating income (i.e., earnings before interest and taxes [EBIT]). The purpose here is to isolate the amount available to pay interest charges on debt.

The fixed-charge coverage ratio is similar to the TIE, except it also takes into account fixed charges other than interest, such as payments on leases. The rationale is that lease payments represent a fixed obligation similar to debt service, so they should be included in examining a firm's indebtedness.

11. How are performance ratios (e.g., gross profit margin and operating profit margin) utilized in evaluating a firm's performance?

Profit is important and crucial to a firm's endurance, but it is just an amount rather than a comment on financial performance. Like most things, performance is relative. A race car driver's speedometer reading is interesting, but what counts is how fast the driver's car travels relative to other cars in the race. Posting a speed of 200 miles per hour (mph) is no good if the other cars travel at 202 mph.

Similarly, performance ratios measure profit relative to the amount of revenue or the level of financing. They show how much profit a firm earned per dollar of revenue or investment.

12. What is integrated ratio analysis?

Companies can gain valued insight by looking at ratios in pairs or groups. The most commonly used example is the DuPont equation, which looks at return on total assets (ROTA) as a product of the return on sales (i.e., net profit margin) and total asset turnover.

ROTA is computed as net income divided by total assets. If a company's ROTA is unsatisfactory, then the ratio provides little guidance as to the cause of poor performance.

13. What makes service industry ratios different from typical manufacturing firm ratios?

Ratio analysis is often taught using manufacturing firms as examples, but the service sector is now very large. As a result, some contrasts in ratios merit mention. Pure service organizations, such as executive search firms, software firms, or education and training companies, rely on human talent much more than physical assets. These kinds of companies typically have small investments in buildings and land, and many prefer to lease facilities rather than own them.

Balance sheets of service companies have proportionately higher levels of current assets and lower levels of fixed assets, and they often have a large proportion of current assets, particularly accounts receivable. These firms frequently display little debt because they do not have much investment in fixed assets to support and they ordinarily have no investment in operating inventory to finance.

Income statements of service companies show large amounts for salaries and wages because employees are their biggest cost. Depending upon the type of business, supply costs can be proportionately large, but the types of operating and financing expenses that are typical for a manufacturing firm are much smaller for service companies.

Ratio analysis for service firms is quite valid, but the numerical values for the ratios will be different and the relative importance of certain ratios will also be different. In the context of the DuPont equation, profit margin and asset turnover are still important, but profit margin is more important and asset turnover is less important compared to a manufacturing firm. This is because the service firm has relatively few assets, but the firm must take great care to control salary expenses because this is its dominant expense category.

Relative to a manufacturing firm, working capital turnover will have more importance and fixed asset turnover will have less importance for a service firm, and the current and quick ratios will be a bit more important. This is because liquidity concerns tend to be most important in businesses primarily characterized by short-term assets and liabilities.

14. What are the primary advantages and disadvantages of ratio analysis?

The primary advantages of ratio analysis include the following:

- The ratios are easily computed and widely used.
- The information necessary for calculations is obtained easily.
- It facilitates comparisons between companies.

The significant disadvantages of ratio analysis include the following:

- Ratios assess historical performance at fixed points in time. Therefore, they do not capture intra-period variations, nor are they necessarily indicative of future performance.
- Ratios should not be used in isolation; instead, they must be analyzed on either a comparative basis (i.e., compared with other companies or industry averages) or on a trend basis (i.e., compared to values in prior periods).
- Ratios summarize accounting information, but may not reflect economic value.
- Ratios do not reflect qualitative values, such as business strategies or managerial talent.
- The use of different accounting methods may reduce the validity of comparisons between firms.

15. Compare and contrast return on investment (ROI) and residual income (RI) as measures of performance.

ROI is calculated as the profit per dollar of invested capital. ROI has intuitive appeal, but suffers as a performance measure for several reasons. First, if the ROI calculation does not include the full period being measured, then it may provide a misleading indication of performance in cases where cash flows are not distributed evenly over time. Second, ROI does not include a charge for the cost of the capital invested in the project. By not considering this cost, funds supporting the assets are implicitly free. The third and greatest limitation of ROI as a performance measure is that it may lead a company's management to reject a positive NPV project if the project results in the decline of a given business unit's ROI.

RI overcomes two limitations of ROI. First, it assigns a charge to the invested capital. Second, RI is an amount of profit (or loss), whereas ROI is a rate of return. If profit exceeds the charge for capital, then RI is an amount of profit—a residual above the capital cost. If it is less, then RI is an amount of loss.

16. What is the economic value added (EVA) concept?

EVA isolates the funds available to all suppliers of capital and then relates that total to the amount of capital supplied. The reason it is termed *economic value* is because value is created only if the firm earns a rate of return that exceeds its cost of capital (WACC). RI approaches this idea, but it does not provide the best measure of "profit."

17. What are the two chief components of the master budget?

The master budget has two chief components: (1) the operating budget, and (2) the financial budget. The operating budget, or profit plan, focuses on day-to-day operations, while the financial budget addresses an organization's financing and investing activities.

CHAPTER 20 Financial Decisions and Management

1. Discuss the concepts of optimal and target capital structure.

An optimal capital structure is the mix of long-term debt and equity that produces the lowest overall weighted average cost of capital (WACC). Firm value depends partly upon the spread between the return on total assets (ROTA) and WACC. Therefore, the firm should attempt to identify the debt-equity mix that minimizes WACC and finance itself using that mix.

Chief financial officers and treasurers should attempt to identify the optimal capital structure. Then, they must factor in all of the following:

- The company's operating risks
- Its immediate and expected long-term financing needs
- The relative costs of debt and equity at the time funds must be raised
- The risk-taking attitude of the board of directors and senior management

After completing the analysis, financial managers can estimate the best practical mix of long-term debt and equity. This estimated "best" mix is known as the *target capital structure*. If the firm does not use the target capital structure presently, it should consider it when choosing between debt and equity financing in the future. Issuing debt will increase relative indebtedness, whereas issuing equity or financing via retained earnings will reduce it.

2. What are the advantages of financing with common stock?

The advantages of financing with common stock are:

- Stock does not obligate a company to make fixed payments to investors.
- Stock does not mature.
- For creditors, stock offers a cushion against losses (i.e., the larger the amount of equity, the greater the losses that can be absorbed without the company becoming insolvent). Additionally, if a company expects to be profitable in the future, equity may be raised on attractive terms.

3. What is the trade-off approach to the use of debt and equity financing in a company's capital structure?

In terms of research and discussion in traditional financial management texts, the trade-off theory is the approach most often used to illustrate capital structure for a company.

The theory's essential idea is that companies "trade off" the use of debt and equity in their capital structures until they obtain the lowest WACC. Suppose a firm was financed entirely by equity. The capital cost is simply the cost of equity. If a small amount of debt was then substituted for equity in the capital structure, the WACC would decrease because (1) debt costs less than equity, and (2) the cost of each source would still be low since the capital structure would represent little risk. The debt ratio would be very low, and coverage ratios, such as times interest earned, would be very high. As more debt is substituted for equity, the WACC would continue to decline because less expensive debt is substituted for more expensive equity, even though the cost of debt and equity rises slightly as the company's debt ratio increases and as coverage ratios decrease. The WACC decreases as indebtedness increases.

At some degree of indebtedness, however, adding more debt will cause the WACC to increase. The rising cost of debt and equity in response to the increasing risk to investors will cause their weighted average to increase. After this point, adding debt will lead to higher debt, equity, and overall capital costs. So as debt is substituted for equity in the firm's capital structure, the overall cost of capital (WACC) at first decreases as debt is increased and then rises as more debt is added. The mix of debt and equity associated with the lowest WACC is technically the optimal capital structure.

4. What is operating risk, and how can it be measured?

Operating risk is a function of the mix of variable and fixed costs in a company's operations. It is assessed by looking at how operating income (i.e., earnings before interest and taxes, or EBIT) responds to revenue changes. A firm with high fixed operating costs and low variable operating costs will have an EBIT that varies more in response to sales changes than one with high variable costs and low fixed costs. This is because fixed costs are imbedded costs that must be covered by revenue before operating profit is positive, but when they are combined with low variable costs, operating profit is able to expand rapidly after fixed costs are covered by revenue. Operating profit can be leveraged off of fixed costs. The measure of this leverage, called the *degree of operating leverage*, shows the responsiveness of operating profit to changes in sales.

5. In addition to the trade-off between the costs and benefits of using financial leverage, what other factors should be considered as part of determining a company's target capital structure?

In addition to leverage, there are a number of other factors that companies need to consider in determining the best mix of debt and equity for raising new capital. These include:

- Asset structure
- Overall business risk
- Shareholder control
- Profitability (both historic and projected)
- Market conditions

6. What is a ratings trigger?

Lenders routinely include a ratings trigger in loan agreements. These triggers are clauses in financing agreements that require a company to maintain a certain credit rating. Failure to maintain a specified rating may trigger a higher loan rate or force the company to post additional collateral, take another specified action, or pay back the debt in full.

Such obligations have come under increased scrutiny by the financial community because they can force a company to artificially contort its liquidity position and can contribute to the inability to meet financial obligations. (Ratings triggers contributed significantly in many high-profile financial collapses.) Rating agencies routinely require companies to disclose triggers that they have in financing arrangements to evaluate whether the company can survive a ratings downgrade.

7. Discuss the issue of capital structure as it relates to not-for-profit organizations (NFPs).

In not-for-profit organizations (NFPs, which include most charities), capital structure is just as important an issue as it is in for-profit corporations. Though NFPs cannot issue common stock for equity financing, they often can and do have retained earnings (technically referred to as *accumulated excess of income over expenses*). They can also raise the equivalent of equity capital (technically referred to as *net assets*) through government grants and charitable contributions. For example, many governments are concerned about the provision of health care services to their general population. As a result, they often make grants to NFP providers to help offset the costs of services rendered to patients who cannot pay for those services. Further, international organizations often make grants to NFP health providers to help them operate. While some of these grants are nonspecific, they often provide specific services, such as neonatal intensive care to needy infants.

As for charitable contributions, individuals as well as companies are motivated to contribute to NFPs for a variety of reasons. Some of these include concern for the well-being of others, the recognition that often accompanies large contributions, and tax deductibility. As a result, charitable contributions are a significant source of capital for some NFPs.

In addition, the availability of tax-exempt financing provides some NFPs with their own tax-based incentives to issue debt. Depending on the projects the NFP is pursuing and its other sources of capital, the directors of the organization will most likely arrive at a target level of debt for the organization. There may also be targets for the levels of short-term versus long-term debt in the overall financing of the NFP.

8. What are the reasons that private placement may be preferred over public issuance?

The reasons why private placement may be preferred over public issuance include:

- Less restrictive covenants
- Relatively small issue size
- Reduced time to issuance
- Minimal reporting, agency rating, or public disclosure requirements
- Lower costs
- Control over who holds the debt
- Greater flexibility of terms and maturities

9. What are the four key characteristics of an optimal dividend policy?

The optimal dividend policy is one that:

- Maximizes shareholder value
- Retains sufficient profits to fund future asset expansion
- Distributes an appropriate amount of corporate income to investors
- Provides information to investors about the future earnings of the firm (i.e., "signaling")

10. What is a capital lease?

Capital leases, also known as *financial leases*, have terms that are different from those of operating leases. Capital leases are essentially an alternative to borrowing the funds and purchasing the asset in question.

For US organizations, Accounting Standards Codification (ASC) Topic 840-10-15: *Leases: Scope and Scope Exceptions* specifies that any lease meeting any one of the following four conditions must be classified as a capital lease:

- The length of the lease is at least 75% of the estimated useful life of the asset.
- There is a transfer of ownership to the lessee at the end of the lease.
- The lease agreement contains a provision that allows the lessee to purchase the asset per a bargain purchase option during or at the end of the lease's life. A bargain price is one that is sufficiently less than fair market value, such that an expectation is created at the outset that the option will be exercised.
- The present value of the discounted lease payments at the beginning of the lease term exceeds 90% of the asset's fair market value.

A lease that does not meet any of these conditions may be classified as an operating lease.

11. Discuss the lease versus borrow-and-buy decision for capital assets.

When a company needs the use of an asset, it may purchase or lease it. Since a lease is a form of debt obligation, the appropriate way to evaluate the decision is to compare the costs of leasing with the costs of borrowing to buy the asset. The most common approach to comparing a lease to a borrow-and-buy scenario involves examining the net present value of cash flows associated with each alternative. Assuming the value of using the asset to the organization is the same whether it is leased or bought, the present value of each scenario would be computed and the one with the lowest net present value of costs would be chosen.

12. Why might a stock be delisted?

Stocks can be delisted from an exchange. In some cases, a stock is forced to be delisted (an involuntary delisting) because it has fallen out of compliance with the exchange's requirements (e.g., the company's share price falls below $1 per share for some specified period of time). Most exchanges have procedures for companies that want to maintain their listing to try to get back into compliance. However, if the requirements are not met within a set time period, then the company will be dropped from the exchange. Delisted stock may still be traded on the over-the-counter (OTC) market.

Some companies choose to have their stock delisted (a voluntary delisting). For example, the added disclosure requirements and expense of audit and reporting compliance on the New York Stock Exchange (NYSE) have caused some smaller companies to go through the delisting process. Some foreign companies also have decided to delist their American depositary receipts (ADRs) to avoid exchange compliance requirements.

13. What are the four important dates relating to the payment of dividends?

When a company plans to pay a dividend, the board of directors declares a dividend amount, a payment date, and a shareholder-of-record date. This action results in four dates:

- **Declaration Date:** This is the date when the board of directors announces (declares) the dividend.
- **Record Date:** Also known as a *shareholder-of-record date*, or just *holder-of-record date*, this is the date when shareholders of record are entitled to receive the declared dividend.
- **Ex-Dividend Date:** This is the date on which the stock is sold without entitlement to the upcoming dividend. The ex-dividend date is usually two business days prior to the shareholder-of-record date, thereby enabling brokerage firms to send an updated list of shareholders to a company on time. Theoretically, there is a drop in the stock price equivalent to the dividend on the ex-dividend date. However, this is difficult to measure because other factors may influence the market price.
- **Payment Date:** This is the date when the dividend is paid, which is usually a week or more after the record date, to allow the company time to process and disburse the dividend.

14. What is a DRIP?

Many firms provide a dividend reinvestment plan, or DRIP, as a way for investors to increase their ownership of shares in the company. A DRIP enables existing shareholders to purchase additional shares directly from the company on a when-desired basis, normally with no commission or with only a small processing charge. These plans also allow investors to elect to reinvest dividends automatically in additional shares of company stock. Shares that the company distributes under these plans may be held in the treasury (i.e., treasury stock), be repurchased by the company in the market and intended for this purpose, or be new, authorized shares of stock that have not been issued yet (i.e., "shelf-registered" stock).

These plans benefit smaller shareholders because transaction costs are low or nonexistent. Also, a few companies sell shares to DRIP investors at a discount to market price. From the company's point of view, this method of raising capital is significantly less expensive than issuing new stock to the general public (due to no underwriting costs), thus saving cash for the issuing company. One negative aspect of this type of plan, however, is that it may increase the number of small shareholders, resulting in more expensive shareholder relations and increasing the cost of maintaining shareholder records.

15. What is a stock repurchase?

As an alternative to paying cash dividends, the board of directors can authorize a stock repurchase, whereby the company uses some of its profits to enter the market and buy its own shares. For non-dividend-paying companies, this is an important means of returning capital to shareholders.

16. What are the primary issues related to the repatriation of capital for multinational companies?

For MNCs, a major treasury issue is whether or when to repatriate cash from foreign subsidiaries to the domestic parent's country. Repatriation involves the actual transfer of funds between countries. The principal method of repatriation is the use of dividends. However, there may be expensive tax restrictions on this approach. Some countries, such as the United States, have tax policies that effectively discourage the repatriation of foreign income, and most countries prefer to see local earnings retained and reinvested locally. Therefore, other methods, such as management fees, royalties, licensing, transfer pricing, and intracompany loans, can be used for repatriation purposes. Most repatriation policies are related to the transfer of funds back to the parent company from wholly or partially owned global subsidiaries of the parent MNC. The objectives are to ensure that the MNC is compensated fairly for the foreign investment and that the host country benefits from the local reinvestment of funds.

17. What is a deemed dividend?

Deemed dividends occur when payments on loans, sales of stock, or other transactions may be interpreted by tax authorities as an attempt by a company to avoid paying taxes on dividends. The payments may be considered (i.e., "deemed") dividends and appropriate taxes charged. Deemed dividends are a potential issue for any global company and can vary significantly from country to country.

18. What is an LBO?

A leveraged buyout, or LBO, occurs when an entity finances the acquisition of a company primarily through borrowings typically collateralized by the assets of the company being acquired. The debt is normally carried on the balance sheet of the acquired company rather than that of the purchaser, and repayments of the debt are made from the operating funds flow of the acquired company. In limited cases, a leveraged buyout may also be made when the acquiring company uses its own assets as security for the loan. An LBO can also be used if a firm wishes to go private, in which case the firm uses the borrowed funds to buy back all of the acquired firm's outstanding stock. In most cases, the stockholders of the acquired company will receive an amount greater than the current price of the stock. An LBO often involves more risk than an acquisition paid for through the issuance of equity securities, due to the high level of debt and the need to generate ongoing operating profits to make the debt payments.

Leveraged buyouts differ from ordinary acquisitions in two major ways:

- First, a large fraction of the purchase price is debt-financed. Some, often all, of this debt is junk (i.e., below investment grade).
- Second, the LBO goes private, and its shares no longer trade on the open market. The LBO's stock is typically held by a partnership of investors. When this group is led by the company's management, the acquisition is called a *management buyout (MBO)*.

Many LBO investor groups hope to capture value for themselves by selling off the company's assets in pieces to firms that believe they can incorporate these assets and experience synergies. Some groups try to raise cash by selling poorer performing assets, and building sales and profits of the remaining assets, hoping to sell them for a substantial profit at a later date. Though some LBOs may remain private for an extended period, most tend to be more of a short-term duration of less than five years.

19. Discuss the importance of a global tax strategy for a multinational company.

Companies involved in international business need an effective global tax strategy or they risk incurring highly unfavorable tax consequences. The choice of the proper tax strategy is important for both large global companies and smaller firms that are significantly involved in export-import activities. Effective international tax planning can reduce a company's global tax costs by minimizing the potential for paying double taxes (i.e., to a foreign jurisdiction and the company's home country). An effective global tax strategy will balance home country and foreign tax considerations in the context of a company's broader business and financial objectives.

LIST OF ACRONYMS AND ABBREVIATIONS

ABA	American Bankers Association
ABCP	Asset-Backed Commercial Paper
ABS	Asset-Backed Securities
ACCA	Association of Chartered Certified Accountants
ACH	Automated Clearinghouse
ADR	American Depositary Receipt
AICPA	American Institute of Certified Public Accountants
Amex	American Express
ANSI	American National Standards Institute
A/P	Accounts Payable
APIC	Additional Paid-In Capital
A/R	Accounts Receivable
ARP	Account Reconciliation Program
ASC	Accounting Standards Codification
ASC X9	Accredited Standards Committee X9
ASC X12	Accredited Standards Committee X12
ASC X12F	ASC X12's Finance Committee
ASP	Application Service Provider
AT	Assistant Treasurer
ATM	Automated Teller Machine
ATM Program	At the Market Program
AVS	Address Verification Service
B2B	Business-to-Business
B2C	Business-to-Consumer
B2G	Business-to-Government
BA	Banker's Acceptance
BAI	Bank Administration Institute
BAM	Bank Account Management
BAN	Bond Anticipation Note
BBAN	Basic Bank Account Number
BCBS	Basel Committee on Banking Supervision
BEY	Bond Equivalent Yield
BIC	Bank Identification Code
BIS	Bank for International Settlements
BSA	Bank Secrecy Act
BSB	Bank Services Billing
BTRS	Balance and Transaction Reporting Standard
C2B	Consumer-to-Business
C2C	Consumer-to-Consumer
C2G	Consumer-to-Government
CA	Chartered Accountant
CAPM	Capital Asset Pricing Model
CBD	Cash before Delivery
CBES	Commercial Book-Entry System
CCC	Cash Conversion Cycle
CD	Certificate of Deposit
CDARS	Certificate of Deposit Account Registry Service
CDS	Credit Default Swap
CEO	Chief Executive Officer
CFO	Chief Financial Officer
CFPB	Consumer Financial Protection Bureau
CFTC	Commodity Futures Trading Commission

CGFS	Committee on the Global Financial System
CHIPS	Clearing House Interbank Payments System
CIP	Customer Identification Program
CLS	Continuous Linked Settlement
COD	Cash on Delivery
COGS	Cost of Goods Sold
CP	Commercial Paper
CPSS	Committee on Payment and Settlement Systems
CRA	Credit Rating Agency
CRMO	Chief Risk Management Officer
CRO	Chief Risk Officer
CRP	Consolidated Remittance Processing
CSD	Central Securities Depository
CTR	Currency Transaction Report
CVV/CVC	Card Verification Value/Code
D/A	Documents against Acceptance
DDA	Demand Deposit Account
DI	Days' Inventory
DIC	Difference in Conditions
DIDMCA	Depository Institution Deregulation and Monetary Control Act
DIF	Deposit Insurance Fund
D&O	Directors and Officers
DOJ	Department of Justice
DP	Days' Payables
D/P	Documents against Payment
DPO	Day's Payable Outstanding
DR	Days' Receivables
DR	Depositary Receipt
DR	Disaster Recovery
DRIP	Dividend Reinvestment Plan
DSI	Days' Sales In Inventory
DSO	Days' Sales Outstanding
DTC	Depository Trust Company
DTCC	Depository Trust & Clearing Corporation
DWC	Days of Working Capital
EBA	European Banking Authority
eBAM	Electronic Bank Account Management
EBIT	Earnings Before Interest and Taxes
EBITDA	Earnings Before Interest, Taxes, Depreciation, and Amortization
EBPP	Electronic Bill Presentment and Payment
EBS	Electronic Broking Services
EBT	Electronic Benefit Transfer
EC	European Commission
ECA	Earnings Credit Analysis
ECA	Export Credit Agency
ECB	European Central Bank
ECBS	European Committee for Banking Standards
ECR	Earnings Credit Rate
EDGAR	Electronic Data Gathering, Analysis, and Retrieval [Database]
EDI	Electronic Data Interchange
EFT	Electronic Funds Transfer
EFTA	Electronic Fund Transfer Act
EFTPOS	Electronic Funds Transfer at the Point of Sale
EFTPS	Electronic Federal Tax Payment System
EIOPA	European Insurance and Occupational Pensions Authority
EIPP	Electronic Invoice Presentment and Payment
EL	Expected Loss
EMIR	European Market Infrastructure Regulation
EMS	European Monetary System
EMU	Economic and Monetary Union
EMV	Europay, MasterCard, Visa
EOQ	Economic Order Quantity

EPC	European Payments Council
EPC	External Processing Code
EPN	Electronic Payment Network
EPS	Earnings Per Share
EPU	European Payments Union
ERM	Enterprise Risk Management
ERP	Enterprise Resource Planning
ERS	Evaluated Receipts Settlement
E-SIGN Act	Electronic Signatures in Global and National Commerce Act
ESMA	European Securities and Markets Authority
ESOP	Employee Stock Option
ESRB	European Systemic Risk Board
ETF	Exchange-Traded Fund
EU	European Union
Euribor	Euro Interbank Offered Rate
EVA	Economic Value Added
FACT	Fair and Accurate Credit Transactions Act
FAF	Financial Accounting Foundation
FASB	Financial Accounting Standards Board
FATCA	Foreign Account Tax Compliance Act
FATF	Financial Action Task Force
FBAR	Report of Foreign Bank and Financial Accounts
FBI	Federal Bureau of Investigation
FCA	Financial Conduct Authority
FCF	Free Cash Flow
FCPA	Foreign Corrupt Practices Act
FDIC	Federal Deposit Insurance Corporation
FFIEC	Federal Financial Institutions Examination Council
FHC	Financial Holding Company
FHLMC (Freddie Mac)	Federal Home Loan Mortgage Corporation
FI	Financial Institution
FinCEN	Financial Crimes Enforcement Network
FINRA	Financial Industry Regulatory Authority
FIU	Financial Intelligence Unit
FNMA (Fannie Mae)	Federal National Mortgage Association
FOMC	Federal Open Market Committee
FP&A	Financial Planning & Analysis
FRA	Forward Rate Agreement
FRN	Floating-Rate Note
FRR	Financial Reporting Release
FSA	Financial Services Authority
FSB	Financial Stability Board
FSOC	Financial Stability Oversight Council
FSP	Financial Services Provider
FTC	Federal Trade Commission
FV	Future Value
FX	Foreign Exchange
G2B	Government-to-Business
G2C	Government-to-Consumer
GAAP	Generally Accepted Accounting Principles
GAAS	Generally Accepted Auditing Standards
GASB	Governmental Accounting Standards Board
GDR	Global Depositary Receipt
GHOS	Group of Governors and Heads of Supervision
G/L	General Ledger
GLB	Gramm-Leach-Bliley Act
G/NFP	Governmental/Not-For-Profit
GNMA (Ginnie Mae)	Government National Mortgage Association
GSE	Government-Sponsored Enterprise
HR	Human Resources
HTML	Hypertext Markup Language

IAASB	International Auditing and Assurance Standards Board
IADI	International Association of Deposit Insurers
IAIS	International Association of Insurance Supervisors
IAS	International Accounting Standard
IASB	International Accounting Standards Board
IBAN	International Bank Account Number
IBRD	International Bank for Reconstruction and Development
ICC	International Chamber of Commerce
ICSD	International Central Securities Depository
IFAC	International Federation of Accountants
IFRS	International Financial Reporting Standards
IMF	International Monetary Fund
IOSCO	International Organization of Securities Commissions
IPO	Initial Public Offering
IRD	Image Replacement Document
IRR	Internal Rate of Return
ISAE	International Standard on Assurance Engagements
ISDA	International Swaps and Derivatives Association
ISO	International Organization for Standardization
ISP	International Standby Practices
IT	Information Technology
IVR	Interactive Voice Response
JCB	Japan Credit Bureau
JIT	Just-in-Time
KPI	Key Performance Indicator
KYC	Know Your Customer
LBO	Leveraged Buyout
L/C	Letter of Credit
LIBOR	London Interbank Offered Rate
LVTS	Large Value Transfer System
MAC	Material Adverse Change
MBO	Management Buyout
MBS	Mortgage-Backed Security
MD&A	Management's Discussion & Analysis
MFN	Most Favored Nation
MICR	Magnetic Ink Character Recognition
MIGA	Multilateral Investment Guarantee Agency
MLCA	Money Laundering Control Act
MMDA	Money Market Deposit Account
MMF	Money Market Fund
MMY	Money Market Yield
MNC	Multinational Company
MNPI	Material Nonpublic Information
MOF	Ministry of Finance
MOTO	Mail Order or Telephone Order
MPS	Material Planning System
MT	Message Type
Muni	Municipal Bond/Security
MVA	Market Value Added
NAIC	National Association of Insurance Commissioners
NASD	National Association of Securities Dealers
NAV	Net Asset Value
NBES	National Book-Entry System
NCI	Noncash Item/Not Cash Item
NCUA	National Credit Union Administration
NCUSIF	National Credit Union Share Insurance Fund
NDF	Non-Deliverable Forward
NDO	Non-Deliverable Option
NFC	Near Field Communication

NFP	Not-for-Profit
NPV	Net Present Value
NRSRO	Nationally Recognized Statistical Rating Organization
NSCC	National Securities Clearing Corporation
NSF	Not Sufficient Funds/ Non-Sufficient Funds
NYSE	New York Stock Exchange
OBSA	Off-Balance-Sheet Arrangement
OCC	Office of the Comptroller of the Currency
OCR	Optical Character Recognition
ODFI	Originating Depository Financial Institution
OECD	Organisation for Economic Co-operation and Development
OFAC	Office of Foreign Assets Control
OFC	Offshore-Controlled Foreign Corporation
OTC	Over-the-Counter
OTTI	Other-Than-Temporary Impairment
P2P	Person-to-Person
PCAOB	Public Company Accounting Oversight Board
PCI DSS	Payment Card Industry Data Security Standard
PI	Profitability Index
PID	Payable-if-Desired
PIN	Personal Identification Number
PKI	Public-Key Infrastructure
POD	Proof of Deposit
POS	Point of Sale
P&Ps	Policies and Procedures
PRA	Prudential Regulation Authority
PSD	Payment Services Directive
PTD	Payable through Draft
PV	Present Value
QIB	Qualified Institutional Buyer
QII	Qualified Institutional Investor
QR Code	Quick Response Code
RADR	Risk-Adjusted Discount Rate
RAROC	Risk-Adjusted Return on Capital
RCC	Remotely Created Check
RCSA	Risk and Control Self-Assessment
RDC	Remote Deposit Capture
RDFI	Receiving Depository Financial Institution
REMIC	Real Estate Mortgage Investment Conduit
Repo	Repurchase Agreement
RFI	Request for Information
RFID	Radio Frequency Identification
RFP	Request for Proposal
RFQ	Request for Quote
RI	Residual Income
ROI	Return on Investment
ROTA	Return on Total Assets
RTGS	Real-Time Gross Settlement
RTM	Refer to Maker
RTN	Routing Transit Number
SaaS	Software as a Service
SDR	Special Drawing Right
SEC	Securities and Exchange Commission
SEC Code	Standard Entry Class Code
SEPA	Single Euro Payments Area
SIR	Self-Insured Retention
SLA	Service Level Agreement
SMS	Short Message Service
SOC	Service Organization Control
SOE	State-Owned Enterprise
SONIA	Sterling Overnight Index Average
SOP	Standard Operating Procedure
SOX	Sarbanes-Oxley Act

SPDR	Standard and Poor's Depositary Receipt
SSAE	Statement on Standards for Attestation Engagements
SSC	Shared Services Center
SSO	Single Sign-On
STP	Straight-Through Processing
SVC	Stored-Value Card
SWF	Sovereign Wealth Fund
SWIFT	Society for Worldwide Interbank Financial Telecommunication
TAN	Tax Anticipation Note
TARGET2	Trans-European Automated Real-time Gross settlement Express Transfer (TARGET) System (2nd generation)
TCOR	Total Cost of Risk
TDA	Time Deposit Account
T&E Card	Travel and Entertainment Card
TIE	Times Interest Earned
TIF	Tax Increment Financing
TILA	Truth in Lending Act
TMS	Treasury Management System
TRADES	Treasury/Reserve Automated Debt Entry System
TWIST	Transaction Workflow Innovation Standards Team
TXP	Tax Payment [Banking Convention]
UBPR	Uniform Bank Performance Report
UCC	Uniform Commercial Code
UCF	Uncollected Funds
UCP	Uniform Customs and Practice for Documentary Credits
UF	Uncollected Funds
UFH	Uncollected Funds Hold
UN/EDIFACT	United Nations/Electronic Data Interchange for Administration, Commerce and Transport
USA PATRIOT Act	Uniting and Strengthening America by Providing Appropriate Tools Required to Intercept and Obstruct Terrorism Act
UTL	Unable to Locate
VaR	Value at Risk
VAT	Value-Added Tax
VRDO	Variable-Rate Demand Obligation
WACC	Weighted Average Cost of Capital
WAP	Wireless Application Protocol
WIP	Work in Progress
XML	eXtensible Markup Language
YTC	Yield to Call
YTM	Yield to Maturity
YTW	Yield to Worst
ZBA	Zero Balance Account

LIST OF GLOSSARY TERMS

acceptance: A drawee's signed agreement to pay a negotiable instrument (typically a letter of credit or related draft) as presented. Acceptance acknowledges that all of the terms of the instrument, other than time, have been met and the instrument will be paid at the proper time. - CH10

account analysis: Largely unique to the US banking system, this is a record of the services provided to the customers of a bank, along with detailed information on balances and credits earned for those balances. The terms *account analysis* and *account analysis statement* are often used synonymously. *Account analysis* can also refer to the process used by the bank to determine earnings credits and service charges in creating this statement. - CH7

account analysis statement: A periodic statement that lists the fees for banking services provided to the account holder and any offsetting credits for deposited funds. - CH7

Account Analysis Transaction Set 822: A standardized format for financial institutions to use when sending account analysis statements to account holders electronically. It is developed by the Accredited Standards Committee (ASC) X12, and is often referred to as *ASC X12 822*. - CH7

account reconciliation program (ARP): A service offered by a financial institution that matches issue information to paid check information and reports outstanding/unpaid items. - CH10

account resolution: Usually made at the board of director's level, this is the basic account or service authorization empowering a representative of the business to enter into agreements for financial services. It usually specifies the functions that can be performed by specific individuals or job titles, the persons authorized to open and close accounts, and the entire scope and limitations of the relationship. An account resolution is a specific type of board resolution. - CH7

account takeover: A type of fraud in which a hacker gains access to a company's bank account information and uses that information to remove funds from the account. - CH15

Accounting Standards Codification (ASC): The detailed set of rules in the United States, referred to as *Generally Accepted Accounting Principles*, that are developed, agreed upon, and published in the form of ASC Topics by the Financial Accounting Standards Board, an independent, self-regulating organization formed in 1973. - CH18

accounts receivable (A/R) balance pattern: A forecasting tool that specifies the percentage of credit sales during a time period (e.g., one month) that remain outstanding at the end of the current time period and each subsequent time period. - CH9

Accounts Receivable Conversion (ARC): The US automated clearinghouse (ACH) format used to convert eligible checks received at a lockbox into electronic debits and process them as automated clearinghouse (ACH) transactions. The company receiving the checks must notify the check writer that checks will be converted. *ARC* is the standard entry class (SEC) code for this format. - CH10

account-to-account transfer: Under the FedGlobal ACH Payments system, this is the standard option for distributing payments between deposit accounts. - CH4

account-to-receiver transfer: Under the FedGlobal ACH Payments system, this type of transfer allows funds from accounts at a US depository financial institution to be retrieved by any receiver either at a participating bank location or at a trusted, third-party provider in certain receiving countries. - CH4

Accredited Standards Committee (ASC) X9: A not-for-profit organization chartered by the American National Standards Institute (ANSI), responsible for developing and maintaining financial industry standards, such as the size of a paper check and protocols for messaging, electronic security systems, and paperless contracts. ASC X9 is responsible for the Balance and Transaction Reporting Standard (BTRS), which has replaced the prior Bank Administration Institute reporting standard (BAI2). - CH14

Accredited Standards Committee (ASC) X12: A not-for-profit organization chartered by the American National Standards Institute (ANSI), responsible for developing and maintaining cross-industry electronic data interchange (EDI) message standards in the United States. - CH14

Accredited Standards Committee (ASC) X12 822: A major standardized format currently in use for the transmission of commercial account analysis information and used primarily by US financial institutions. The ASC X12 title is *Account Analysis Transaction Set 822*. - CH7

accrual accounting: The accounting approach under which expenses must be reported when the revenues with which they are associated are recognized. Long-lived or fixed assets are capitalized (i.e., recorded as assets on the balance sheet) and depreciated over time because they produce revenues over many accounting periods. This practice matches an asset's cost to the revenues it produces. Under the revenue recognition and matching principles, sales are reported even though cash has not been received. Similarly, expenses are reported even though cash has not been paid out. - CH18

accumulated depreciation: An asset account that records the amount of depreciation previously expensed on a company's assets. It appears on the asset side of the balance sheet, but it is a source of funds when it increases. While depreciation is technically a noncash expense (i.e., there is no actual payment for depreciation), it does have a cash flow impact because it reduces the company's income taxes by lowering pretax income. - CH18

additional paid-in capital (APIC): An equity account that reflects the difference at the time of issue between the par value and the issuance price (less underwriting costs) of any new stock sold by a company. - CH6

address verification service (AVS): A system used to verify the identity of the person claiming to own the credit card being used in a transaction. The system will check the billing address of the credit card provided by the user with the address on file at the credit card company. - CH10

advising bank: In a letter of credit (L/C) transaction, this is the bank that advises the seller of an L/C in its favor. - CH10

aggregate basis: A method of establishing insurance policy deductibles in which the deductible is set on a per-period basis, regardless of the number of occurrences (claims). - CH15

aggressive financing strategy: A current asset financing strategy that involves a company financing all fixed assets with long-term debt and equity, but financing only a portion of permanent current assets with long-term financing. Short-term financing supports the remainder of the permanent current assets and all temporary current assets. - CH8

aging schedule: A schedule that separates accounts receivable (A/R) into current and past-due receivables using set periods (typically 30-day increments), and is used for measuring A/R. - CH9

all-in rate: An interest rate that consists of a base rate, such as the London Interbank Offer Rate (LIBOR), the US prime rate, or the Fed funds rate, plus a spread that is added to, or occasionally subtracted from, the base rate. Rates on lines of credit are normally variable and adjust immediately to changes in the base rate. - CH11

alpha (smoothing constant): In an exponential smoothing forecasting methodology, this is the weight assigned to the most recent actual value and the most recent forecasted value. It is calculated using a computer program. The program selects the alpha value that weights past actual values and past forecasted values so as to produce the most accurate forecast of the variable's value in the next period. - CH13

American Bankers Association (ABA) number: In the United States, the ABA number (also known as the *routing transit number*) is a nine-digit number that identifies the paying bank for a check and provides the depository bank with the information it requires to route the check back to the paying bank through the clearing system. - CH4

American option: A type of option contract that can be executed or settled on or any time prior to the stated expiration date of the contract. Contrast with *European option* and *Bermuda option*. - CH16

application service provider (ASP): A business that provides computer-based services to customers over a network. - CH14

arbitrage: The process by which an asset is purchased in one financial market and sold in another market to produce a riskless profit. Arbitrage is the primary mechanism that ensures efficiency in financial markets. - CH16

as-of adjustment: The practice of a bank adding additional time as part of the collected-balance calculation when a check takes longer to clear than the initial availability that was granted. - CH4

asset liquidity risk: The risk that a security investment cannot be sold quickly without experiencing an unacceptable loss. This risk can also affect the yield and pricing on a security. By definition, a *liquid security* is one that can be converted quickly and easily into cash with very little exposure to market price risk and for a small transaction cost. Also referred to as *liquidity risk*. - CH5

asset tax: A tax owed on the value of accumulated real property or business equipment, or on the value of a financial portfolio. This tax may be charged in some countries in order to impose tax liabilities on a business even through that business may not show a profit or owe income tax on an international project. - CH2

asset-backed commercial paper (ABCP): An investment that has most of the features of standard commercial paper (CP), but is secured against specific assets—usually short-term trade receivables from a single company or a range of companies. ABCP may be classified as either *single seller*, if it is backed by assets from a single institution, or *multi-seller*, if it is backed by assets purchased from a number of issuers. - CH5

asset-based lending: A type of lending that involves commercial loans or lines of credit that are backed by liens on specific assets of the borrowing company. Asset-based lines of credit in the working capital area are typically secured by accounts receivable or inventory, and can support temporary financing needs. - CH8

asset/liability management: The process of managing and coordinating the assets and liabilities held in an investment portfolio to maximize earnings and minimize risk. Whenever an investment portfolio utilizes borrowed funds as part of its overall strategy, the issue of asset/liability management arises. This is primarily an issue for banks and large financial institutions that fund their investments with either deposits or borrowed funds. In many cases, the issue is expressed in terms of a maturity mismatch; that is, the institution may be borrowing funds in the short-term markets (e.g., by using commercial paper) while using the proceeds from the financing to purchase long-term assets. - CH12

at the market (ATM) program: A type of stock sales program that allows listed companies to sell additional shares of company stock over time through a designated broker-dealer at the current or prevailing market price to raise additional capital. - CH20

auditor's opinion: An opinion on a company's financial statements that is provided by an independent auditor (or audit firm) based on a financial audit. The purpose of conducting an audit is to produce an audit report in which an independent audit firm indicates the scope of the audit and renders an opinion regarding the relevance, completeness, and accuracy of the income statement, statement of financial position, statement of cash flows, any other statements, and all supporting material. In addition, the auditor will examine the strengths of the organization's internal controls and processes. The auditor's opinion does not comment on the company's financial fitness, but rather on whether the financial statements fairly reflect the company's financial position and are comparable to prior periods. - CH18

authentication: In electronic payment security, this is the ability to know, with a reasonable amount of certainty, who is accessing information or initiating a transaction. - CH14

automated clearinghouse (ACH): A batch-processing clearinghouse that traditionally has been used for high-volume, low-value transactions. - CH4

automated clearinghouse (ACH) credit transaction: An electronic message that instructs the originating depository financial institution to move funds from the originator's account to the receiver's account at the receiving depository financial institution. - CH4

automated clearinghouse (ACH) debit transaction: An electronic message that instructs the originating depository financial institution to move funds from the receiver's account to the originator's account. - CH4

availability: In a payment system, this is the point in time when the payee can use the funds provided by the payment, even though the payment may not be final. - CH4

availability float: The time interval or delay between the day when a payment is deposited into a bank account and the day when the payee's account is credited with collected funds. - CH8

availability schedule: A schedule that specifies, for each drawee endpoint, when a bank grants available credit or collected balances for deposited items. - CH4

available balance: The available balance (sometimes referred to as the *investable balance*) represents the balances in the customer's account that the bank was able to invest in income-producing assets during the account analysis period. *Available balance* is also defined as the amount of funds available for withdrawal from an account, based on the bank's availability schedule and/or local regulations that require specific availability for certain funds (e.g., Federal Reserve Regulation CC in the United States; other countries typically have similar regulations). - CH4

average collected balance: The sum of the daily ending collected balances (both positive and negative) divided by the number of days in the analysis period. In many account analysis statements, this item is calculated as the average ledger balance minus the average deposit float. - CH7

average collection period: The average number of days required to convert a credit sale into a cash inflow. Also referred to as *days' sales outstanding*. - CH9

average daily float: The sum of the dollar-days of float for all items received in a certain period divided by the number of days in the period. - CH9

average deposit float: The sum of the daily dollar amount of items in the process of collection (primarily checks) divided by the number of calendar or business days in the account analysis period. - CH7

average ledger balance: The sum of the daily ending ledger balances (both positive and negative) divided by the number of days in the account analysis period. Balances used in the calculation are net of any current-period adjustments. - CH7

Back Office Conversion (BOC): The US automated clearinghouse (ACH) format used to convert eligible checks received by retailers at the point of sale or presentment into electronic debits and process them as automated clearinghouse (ACH) transactions when the conversion is not done at the point of sale. Retailers and other entities that accept checks at the point of purchase or other manned bill payment locations can convert eligible checks to automated clearinghouse (ACH) debits in the back office. Explanatory signage must be present at the point of presentment, and the merchant/originator must put specific verbiage on the customer receipt indicating that the check may be converted and may clear as soon as the same day. *BOC* is the standard entry class (SEC) code for this format. - CH10

Balance and Transaction Reporting Standard (BTRS): A standard format used by financial institutions for reporting bank balance and transaction information to corporate customers. BTRS is administered by the American National Standards Institute (ANSI) via its Accredited Standards Committee (ASC) X9, and replaces the previous Bank Administration Institute reporting standard (BAI2). - CH14

balance sheet: A financial statement that reports a company's financial condition—including assets, liabilities, and stockholders' equity—at a point in time. Also called a *statement of financial position*. - CH6

balance-forward system: A cash application process (most commonly used in consumer transactions) in which payments are applied to the total outstanding balance on an accounts receivable account rather than to specific items. The remaining balance, if any, is then carried forward to the next billing cycle. The balance-forward system is most common in revolving credit situations, such as retail credit cards. - CH8

Bank Administration Institute (BAI) BAI2 format: An electronic reporting format used widely for reporting information about account balances, transactions, and lockbox and controlled disbursement details. BAI2 is superceded by the Balance and Transaction Reporting Standard (BTRS). - CH14

bank capital requirements: Rules or regulations that specify the amount of capital (usually defined as equity funds) the owners of a bank must contribute to the business. This is typically in the form of a ratio of capital to at-risk assets (loans and other investments). The higher the ratio of capital to assets, the lower the risk on the part of the bank. - CH2

Bank for International Settlements (BIS): An organization that fosters international monetary and financial cooperation and serves as a bank for central banks. The BIS is also the sponsoring organization for the Basel Committee on Banking Supervision. - CH2

Bank Identification Code (BIC): An international standard for uniquely identifying banks, including country and branch locations. - CH3

bank obligation: A debt instrument issued by a bank to raise funds. Banks raise funds in the money markets through time deposits, repurchase agreements (repos), and banker's acceptances, collectively referred to as *bank obligations* or *bank paper*. Examples of time deposits include savings accounts, certificates of deposit (CDs), and negotiable CDs. Negotiable CDs are large-value time deposits issued by banks and other financial institutions that are bought and sold on the open market. - CH5

bank of first deposit: In processing checks, this is the bank in which a check is initially deposited as part of the clearing process. Also known as the *depository bank* or *collecting bank*. - CH4

bank overlay structure: A type of pooling structure that combines both sweeping and pooling. It is typically used when a company's primary bank has branches in several countries, but the branches do not provide a full range of domestic banking services. A local bank is used to provide collection and disbursement transactions and accounts, and to sweep surplus funds to the primary bank. The primary bank (overlay bank) then notionally pools or physically transfers cash balances in overlay accounts, providing a multi-country solution. - CH10

bank scorecard: A vendor scorecard used by a company to measure the performance of its bank. See *vendor scorecard.*

Bank Secrecy Act of 1970 (BSA): A US legislative act under which US banks (and, in many cases, companies and individuals) are required to perform due diligence by determining a customer's identity and monitoring transactions for suspicious activity. The primary intent of the BSA is to deter money laundering and the use of secret foreign bank accounts. - CH2

banker's acceptance (BA): A cross-border financing instrument that can be used to finance the import, export, or domestic shipment of goods, as well as the storage of properly titled goods. BAs are used frequently in conjunction with letters of credit (L/Cs) requiring a time draft drawn on a bank. A BA is created when one person signs an unconditional written order directing a bank to pay a certain sum of money on demand or at a definite time to another person, usually to finance the shipment or temporary storage of goods. The unconditional written order, also known as a *time draft*, is stamped "accepted" by the bank. - CH10

banker's acceptance (BA) rate: The rate at which BAs trade in the secondary market. BAs are sold at a nominal spread over US Treasury bills. - CH10

bankruptcy: A condition of financial failure involving the inability to pay one's debts in a timely manner. This form of financial distress affects many organizations each year. In addition to the typical financial problems that may force a firm into bankruptcy, many management teams use the bankruptcy laws in innovative ways to protect either the firm's stakeholders or its management. The bankruptcy process is typically under the control of national bankruptcy laws and generally begins when the firm has not been able to meet scheduled payments on its debt. Bankruptcy may also occur when a firm's projections of cash flows indicate that it will not be able to meet debt payments at some time in the near future. - CH2

barter: A trade payment method that involves the direct exchange of goods or services between two parties without the exchange of money. It is most frequently used when funds cannot be repatriated due to currency controls or other legal limitations. - CH10

Basel Accords: A series of recommendations, issued by the Basel Committee on Banking Supervision, regarding the creation of international standards and regulations for how much capital financial institutions must put aside to reduce risks associated with investing and lending, as well as operational risk. There are currently three sets of Basel Accords, referred to as *Basel I, Basel II, and Basel III*. - CH2

Basel Committee on Banking Supervision (BCBS): A standards-setting body that operates under the Bank for International Settlements and provides a forum for regular cooperation on banking supervisory matters. - CH2

beneficial ownership (beneficial interest): Control over funds or accounts, which may be separate from signature authority or legal title. It recognizes that the entity in whose name an account is opened with a bank is not necessarily the person who ultimately controls the funds or who is ultimately entitled to the funds. - CH7

Bermuda option: A type of option contract that is exercisable only on specified dates that are spaced evenly over the option's life, in contrast with both American and European options. - CH16

beta: A measure of the volatility, or systematic risk, of a security or a portfolio in comparison to the market as a whole. - CH12

bid-offer quote: A price quote in which a dealer or other entity provides both the price at which it is willing to purchase (bid) and sell (offer) a specific commodity or security. The difference between the two is referred to as the *bid-offer spread* or *bid-ask spread*. - CH16

bilateral netting system: A type of netting system in which purchases between two subsidiaries of the same company are netted against each other so that periodically, typically once or twice per month on preset dates, only the net difference is transferred. - CH8

blocked currencies: A type of political risk, this is the practice of a government not allowing the conversion from the local currency into a major trading currency. - CH7

board of directors: A group of individuals that are elected as, or elected to act as, representatives of the stockholders to establish corporate management-related policies and to make decisions on major company issues. Such issues include the hiring/firing of executives, dividend policies, options policies, and executive compensation. Every public company must have a board of directors. - CH1

Board of Governors: The controlling entity for the US Federal Reserve System; the Board of Governors is responsible for the discount rate and reserve requirements. - CH2

board/corporate resolution: A resolution usually approved by an enterprise's board of directors that gives a specific individual (or individuals) the authority to facilitate the business of the enterprise. See also *account resolution*. - CH7

bond: A debt investment in which an investor loans money to an entity (corporate or governmental) that borrows the funds for a defined period of time at a fixed interest rate. - CH6

bond anticipation note (BAN): A short-term, interest-bearing security issued in the anticipation of larger future bond issues. - CH5

bond equivalent yield (BEY): A calculation for restating semiannual, quarterly, or monthly discount bond or note yields into an annual yield. This type of yield is calculated on a 365-day year basis, while the money market yield is based on a 360-day year. - CH11

bond indenture: A legal document that outlines the rights and obligations of the borrower (bond issuer) and lender (bondholder). It is a contract between the company and the bondholders, which includes various restrictive covenants that impose constraints on the actions of a company's management. - CH6

bond rating: A quality rating that is assigned to a bond issue to reflect both the probability of default and the loss given default on the issue. - CH6

book value per share: Total common stockholders' equity divided by the number of shares outstanding. - CH6

break-even analysis: A type of cost/benefit analysis that establishes the level of activity at which benefits and costs are equal. - CH19

brokerage firms: Institutions/firms that specialize in the sale of securities to institutional and retail customers by executing the distribution, or selling, side of an investment bank's intermediation function. - CH3

broker-dealer: A company or other organization that trades securities for its own account or on behalf of its customers. - CH5

budget: An in-depth plan that details how economic resources will be procured and deployed over a specific time period. Budgets typically cover periods ranging from one month to two years. - CH13

business continuity: Actions taken with regard to crisis management, alternative operating procedures, and communications to staff and customers. The intent of disaster avoidance, recovery, and remediation measures is to preserve the firm's revenue stream. - CH15

business interruption insurance: A type of insurance coverage that provides payments to an organization in the event it is unable to pursue a normal line of business for some period of time due to an unforeseen event. Business interruption insurance generally covers the loss of profits and continuing fixed expenses (e.g., debt or lease arrangements) while the organization is temporarily out of business. - CH15

business risk: A type of risk that represents the classic risks to success in operating a business venture, such as uncertainty about the demand for products or services, the price that can be charged for those products or services, and the costs of producing and delivering the products or services. Business risk is primarily associated with the general day-to-day management of a company. - CH15

call option: A type of option contract that gives the contract owner the right, but not the obligation, to buy (call) the underlying asset from the contract writer at a fixed price through the delivery date. - CH16

call provision: A bond provision that gives the issuing entity the right to call in a bond or other issue for redemption prior to the original maturity. As compensation to investors for early redemption, a call premium is generally paid when a bond is called. The call premium usually is set on a sliding scale, with larger premiums above par required the earlier an issue is called. - CH6

capital: The more permanent sources of funds used by a company, such as long-term debt, preferred stock, and common equity. - CH9

capital adequacy: A factor that measures whether the amount of capital maintained relative to the nature and extent of an institution's risks is sufficient given management's ability to identify, measure, monitor, and control these risks. - CH2

capital asset pricing model (CAPM): A model that describes one possible relationship between risk and the required rate of return on an asset. In the case of common stock, the CAPM is based on the concept that a sensible investor holds a diversified portfolio of stocks to mitigate risk. As more stocks are added to a portfolio, the overall riskiness and variability of the portfolio is reduced. - CH12

capital budgeting: The process by which proposed large-dollar investments in long-term assets are evaluated. - CH19

capital investment: Money used by a business to purchase long-term, typically fixed assets, such as land, machinery, or buildings. Capital investment may also refer to investments in long-term securities that are typically used to finance the purchase of such assets. Also known as *long-term investment*. - CH12

capital lease: A type of lease that has terms that are different from those of operating leases. Capital leases are essentially an alternative to borrowing the funds and purchasing the asset in question. Also known as a *financial lease* or *finance lease*. - CH20

capital market: A market in which individuals and institutions trade financial securities. Organizations/institutions in the public and private sectors also often sell long-term (debt and/or equity) securities on the capital markets in order to raise funds. Thus, this type of market is composed of both the primary and secondary markets. - CH6

capital preservation: An investment goal in which investors want to maintain the purchasing power of their investments while minimizing the risk of loss. While this is a suitable short-term investment management strategy, it may not always fit into the guidelines for capital investments. - CH12

capital structure: The mix of long-term debt (in the form of term loans and various types of bonds) and equity (in the form of preferred stock, common stock, and retained earnings). - CH20

capital tax: In some foreign countries, particularly those experiencing an upsurge in economic growth, companies are assessed a capital tax on the initial capital used to establish a new venture, and on subsequent incoming capital or repatriated capital. - CH2

captive finance company: A type of industrial bank that is a subsidiary of a large industrial corporation and whose sole purpose is to finance purchases of the corporation's products. - CH3

card verification value/code (CVV/CVC): A number usually printed on the reverse side of a payment card and used as an anti-fraud security feature to help verify possession of the actual payment card by the individual using the card. - CH10

cash application: The process of applying a customer's payment against outstanding invoices or receivables. - CH8

cash basis accounting: A major accounting method that recognizes revenues and expenses at the time physical cash is actually received or disbursed. - CH18

cash before delivery (CBD): A term of sale that requires the buyer to make full and final payment before the shipment or receipt of goods. Also known as *prepayment terms*. - CH8

cash concentration system: A system typically used to transfer funds from outlying depository locations (often at different banks) to a central bank account at a company's primary bank, commonly referred to as a *concentration account*. These systems are used in situations where companies may have to deal with a number of separate banks in disbursed geographic locations. - CH10

cash conversion cycle (CCC): In working capital management, this formula explains and calculates how much time elapses from when funds are disbursed in direct support of a revenue-generating activity until the time when funds are recovered from revenues. It is calculated as days' receivables plus days' inventory minus days' payables. The result is the average number of days between the cash outflow for the acquisition of materials and supplies, and the cash inflow from the sale of products or services. - CH8

cash conversion efficiency: An efficiency/asset management ratio that measures how effectively a company has converted sales (or revenues) into cash. It is computed as cash flow from operations divided by revenues. - CH19

cash dividend: The most common form of dividend payment, typically paid on a quarterly basis either by check or electronically. - CH20

cash flow statement: See *statement of cash flows*. - CH18

cash flow timeline: The interval that begins with the purchase of raw materials or parts from vendors and suppliers at the start of the operating cycle and ends when payment is received from customers at the completion of the operating cycle. - CH8

cash flow to total debt ratio: A ratio that measures the liquidity of a company as a function of cash flow and the level of total debt. It is calculated as net income plus depreciation (and other noncash expenses, such as amortization and depletion), divided by total long- and short-term debt. - CH9

cash inflows: Funds collected from customers, obtained from financial sources (e.g., loans or investment income), and/or received from other sources. - CH8

cash letter: In a check-clearing process, a file of check images or a bundle of checks accompanied by a list of individual items and other control documents. - CH4

cash management: The subset of treasury management that specifically deals with managing the daily liquidity (available cash) of a company or organization. - CH1

cash on delivery (COD): A term of sale whereby the seller ships the goods and the buyer pays upon receipt. If the buyer refuses to pay, the goods are returned and the seller must pay the shipping and handling costs. - CH8

cash outflows: Funds disbursed to employees, vendors, and suppliers; lenders; local, state, and federal tax agencies; bondholders; and shareholders. - CH8

cash terms: A term of sale whereby the buyer generally has 7 to 10 days to make payment. - CH8

cash turnover ratio: A ratio that indicates the number of cash cycles a firm experiences in one year, generally defined as the days in the year (365) divided by the cash conversion cycle. - CH9

cashier's check: A payment instrument in the form of a check drawn on a bank's own funds. Also known as an *official bank check*. - CH4

casualty insurance: Concerned primarily with the legal liability of losses caused by personal injury or property damage, this type of insurance provides specific coverage for a variety of losses. Examples of typical casualty insurance include plate glass, crime, robbery, boiler or machinery, and aviation insurance. Many casualty insurers also write surety bonds and other forms of insurance not classified as property insurance. - CH15

central bank (monetary authority): An entity that is responsible for implementing and managing a country's monetary policy—in other words, the country's money supply and interest rates. - CH2

central securities depository (CSD): A financial services company that holds securities, in either certificated or noncertificated (dematerialized) form, on behalf of their actual owners in order to enable book-entry transfer of securities. - CH5

century bonds: Bonds with a term of 100 years or greater. - CH6

certificate authority: A trusted third party that secures the identification information used in a digital certificate. - CH14

certificate of deposit (CD): A bank obligation that pays the bearer some stated rate (either fixed or variable) of interest over its maturity. It may be issued in any denomination, with maturities generally ranging from one month to five years. CDs under $100,000 are usually not negotiable, but large-denomination CDs, also referred to as *jumbos*, issued to corporations, banks, and institutional investors may be negotiable. In the United States, CDs are covered by the Federal Deposit Insurance Corporation up to the current deposit limits. - CH3

Certificate of Deposit Account Registry Service (CDARS): A private service that makes it possible to receive full Federal Deposit Insurance Corporation insurance coverage on amounts up to $50 million by distributing the funds among certificates of deposit issued by a participating network of US banks. - CH5

certificate of incumbency: A document (authorized by the board of directors) confirming the authority of a corporate officer to perform certain actions on behalf of the enterprise. - CH7

certified check: A payment instrument drawn on a depositor's checking account; funds are withdrawn from the depositor's account at the time of certification, to assure payment with a certification or guarantee by the bank. - CH4

Chapter 7 bankruptcy: A US bankruptcy petition for liquidation filed by a company, which protects the debtor from legal actions by creditors. In a Chapter 7 bankruptcy, all remaining assets are liquidated, and the company ceases to exist. - CH2

Chapter 11 bankruptcy: A US bankruptcy petition filed by a company that allows it to reorganize under court protection to restructure debts and emerge from bankruptcy after meeting certain conditions imposed by the court. - CH2

Chapter 13 bankruptcy: A US bankruptcy petition filed by a consumer that allows the consumer to file for bankruptcy and reorganization. - CH2

character: As part of the five Cs of credit, this is the perceived honesty or integrity of an individual applicant or a corporate applicant's officers. Character indicates an intent or willingness to pay, as evidenced by personal or corporate payment history. - CH8

Check Clearing for the 21st Century Act (Check 21): A US law that provided the basis for electronic clearing of checks by allowing the substitution of a copy or image of a check for the original document in the clearing process. It created a new negotiable instrument called an *image replacement document*. - CH2

check conversion: The process of converting a paper check to an electronic form, typically an ACH debit. It does not include an image used for check image processing. - CH10

chief executive officer (CEO): The highest ranking executive in a company whose main responsibilities include developing and implementing high-level strategies, making major corporate decisions, managing the overall operations and resources of a company, and acting as the main point of communication between the board of directors and the corporate operations. - CH1

chief financial officer (CFO): The senior manager who is responsible for overseeing the financial activities of an entire company. This includes signing checks, monitoring cash flow, and financial planning. - CH1

chief risk officer (CRO): The executive accountable to the board of directors for the efficient and effective governance of significant risks—and related opportunities—for an organization and its various segments. Sometimes known as the *chief risk management officer* (*CRMO*). - CH15

cleanup period: In relation to a commercial line of credit, this is a period of time, usually annually, during which the borrower must pay down all outstanding borrowings and reduce the balance of the loan to zero. - CH11

clearing: The process in which FIs use the information contained in a payment instruction, such as a check or wire transfer, to transfer money between themselves on behalf of the payor and the beneficiary, either directly or through some external network. - CH4

clearing channel: In a payment system, this is the method used to move either the payment instrument or information related to the instrument between parties involved in the transaction, as well as their banks. - CH4

clearing float: The time interval or delay between the day when a check is deposited by the payee and the day when the payor's account is debited. - CH8

Clearing House Interbank Payments System (CHIPS): A bank-owned, large-dollar funds transfer network operated by The Clearing House Payments Company. - CH4

clearinghouse: In a payment clearing process, this is a group of banks or other financial institutions that agree to exchange payment instruments (paper or electronic). - CH4

closed-loop card: A card issued by a gas company, department store, and other retailer that is accepted only by the issuing company. - CH4

cloud computing: The storing and accessing of computer software and data through an Internet browser rather than running installed software on a local computer. The software and data are typically housed on a distributed network managed by a third-party vendor. The vendor is responsible for updating and maintaining the software, as well as providing for appropriate backup and disaster recovery. - CH14

collateral: Assets used as security for a loan or bond issue. They may include physical assets (e.g., plant, equipment, and inventory) or financial assets (e.g., receivables and marketable securities). - CH6

collateral trust bond: A type of bond backed by securities of other companies that are owned by the firm issuing the bond. - CH6

collateralized loan: In inventory financing, this is a type of loan that is arranged using inventory as collateral for the loan, with the lender providing financing for some predetermined percentage of the inventory's value. - CH8

collected balance: An aggregate of bank account balances that is calculated as the average ledger balance minus the deposit float. - CH4

collecting bank (presenting bank): (1) In the check clearing process, this is the bank that accepts a check for deposit and collects the funds from the payee's bank. The collecting bank is also referred to as the *bank of first deposit* or *depository bank*. (2) In a documentary collection process, this is the bank (the buyer's bank) that presents the documents to the buyer. The collecting bank is also referred to as the *presenting bank*. - CH4,CH10

collection float: The time interval or delay between the time the buyer/payor initiates payment and the time the seller/payee receives good funds; it consists of mail float, processing float, and availability float. - CH8

collection letter: A document in a documentary collection process that specifies the exact procedures to be followed before shipping documents are released to the importer. - CH10

comfort letter: A letter from another party stating actions that it will or will not take on behalf of the borrower. This type of agreement is not legally enforceable. - CH6

commercial bank: A financial institution that accepts deposits from both businesses and consumers, and then lends some portion of those deposits to other businesses and consumers. - CH2

Commercial Book-Entry System (CBES): A multi-tiered, automated system for purchasing, holding, and transferring marketable securities. CBES exists as a delivery system that provides for the simultaneous transfer of securities against the settlement of funds. Securities owners (or their brokers on their behalf) receive interest and redemption payments wired directly to their linked accounts. CBES is operated by the US Treasury and is also known as the *Treasury/Reserve Automated Debt Entry System,* or *TRADES*. - CH5

commercial letter of credit (L/C): A commercial (or documentary) L/C is issued by a bank as the intended mechanism of payment in relation to a trade transaction involving the domestic or international shipment of merchandise. L/Cs are most commonly used in import/export transactions and are sometimes referred to as *trade L/Cs*. - CH10

commercial paper (CP): Tradable promissory notes issued by companies, as opposed to banks. Companies raise funds in the short-term money market through the issuance of CP. Maturity can range from overnight to 270 days for publicly traded CP and up to 397 days for private-placement CP, but most paper issued matures in less than 45 days. CP does not usually pay interest during its term. Instead, it is issued at a discounted price and the face value is paid at maturity. - CH5

commitment fee: A fee assessed based on the total amount or unused portion of a committed line of credit. A committed line usually involves a formal loan agreement that specifies the terms and conditions of the credit facility. - CH11

Committee on Payment and Settlement Systems (CPSS): A standards-setting body for payment and securities settlement systems. The CPSS is hosted by the Bank for International Settlements. - CH2

Committee on the Global Financial System (CGFS): A central bank forum for the monitoring and examination of broad issues relating to financial markets and systems. It helps to elaborate appropriate policy recommendations to support the central banks in the fulfillment of their responsibilities for monetary and financial stability. In carrying out this task, the committee places particular emphasis on assisting central bank governors in recognizing, analyzing, and responding to threats to the stability of financial markets and the global financial system. - CH2

Commodity Futures Trading Commission (CFTC): An independent US government agency with the mandate to regulate commodity futures and option markets in the United States. - CH2

commodity price risk: A type of risk related to the impact of changing commodity prices on the value of an organization. It differs considerably from interest rate and foreign exchange risk since most commodities are traded in markets where the concentration of supply in the hands of a few suppliers can magnify price volatility. - CH15

common equity: The capital contributed by stockholders and earnings retained in the business. Also refers to an account on corporate financial statements that reflects this amount. - CH9

common stock: A security that represents ownership in a company. The management of a company acts as an agent for shareholders to protect their interests. Equity in the form of common stock usually represents a significant portion of a publicly traded company's capital base. - CH6

common-size financial statement: A financial statement analysis technique that involves stating line items as percentages rather than amounts. A common-size income statement expresses every line item on the statement as a percentage of revenue, and a common-size balance sheet expresses each account as a percentage of total assets. Common-size statements enable direct comparisons of financial data for firms of different sizes. - CH19

common-size ratios: Ratios that express financial statement relationships in a percentage format that allows for easy comparison between companies of different sizes. - CH19

company processing center: A business function where check and payment card processing, along with deposit preparation, are performed in-house. - CH10

compensating balance: A balance maintained in a company's deposit accounts at a bank for the purpose of increasing the bank's overall revenue on the account. Compensating balances generally do not earn interest or offset depository service charges. - CH11

concentration (funding flows): A practice involving internal transfers among operating units of a company and between a firm's various bank accounts, with the objectives of pooling funds for other purposes or to fund various disbursement accounts. - CH8

concentration account: An account used by an organization to receive funds from collection accounts or to provide funding for disbursement accounts. These accounts are sometimes referred to as *master accounts*, especially when used in conjunction with a zero balance account. - CH10

confirming bank: In a letter of credit (L/C) transaction, this is the bank that commits to the seller that payment will be made if documents meet the terms and conditions of the L/C, regardless of the issuing bank's ability to pay. - CH10

conservative financing strategy: A current asset financing strategy that involves using long-term financing (e.g., debt and equity) to finance fixed assets, permanent current assets, and some portion of fluctuating current assets. Short-term financing is used for the remainder of the fluctuating current assets. - CH8

consignment: A term of sale whereby the supplier (sometimes referred to as the *consignor*) ships goods to another party (sometimes referred to as the *consignee*) who has no obligation to pay until the goods have been sold. - CH8

consolidated remittance processing (CRP): A service that provides a single collection point for all types of remittance payments (both electronic and paper) and consolidates all remittance information into one stream of data in a common format. - CH10

Consumer Financial Protection Bureau (CFPB): An independent consumer protection entity within the Federal Reserve that was created as part of the Dodd-Frank Act. The primary reason behind the CFPB's creation was to consolidate and strengthen consumer protection responsibilities and oversee the enforcement of federal laws intended to ensure the fair, equitable, and nondiscriminatory access to credit for individuals and communities. - CH2

continuous linked settlement (CLS): A process that allows a simultaneous exchange of the payments for both sides of underlying financial transactions (e.g., foreign exchange contracts, non-deliverable forward contracts, and over-the-counter derivative contracts), thereby eliminating settlement risk. - CH4

controlled disbursement: A bank service (unique to the United States) that provides same-day notification to a company of the amount of checks that will clear against its disbursement account on a given day. The disbursement account is typically not funded each day until after the daily notification is received. - CH10

convertible bond: A type of corporate debt security that can be converted by the holder, or sometimes the issuer, into shares of common or preferred stock at a fixed ratio of shares per bond. - CH6

Corporate Credit or Debit (CCD) or CCD Plus Addendum (CCD+): A US automated clearinghouse (ACH) format used for the concentration and disbursement of funds within or between companies (business-to-business). Only a limited amount of remittance information can be sent with the CCD format. The CCD+ is essentially a CCD with an addendum record that can hold up to 80 characters of remittance data. *CCD* and *CCD+* are the standard entry class (SEC) codes for these formats, respectively. - CH10

Corporate Trade Exchange (CTX): A US automated clearinghouse (ACH) format designed for business-to-business trade payments. It consists of a standard ACH payment transaction and a variable-length message addendum designed to convey remittance information in the Accredited Standards Committee (ASC) X12 data standard. The addendum can accommodate 9,999 records of 80 characters each. *CTX* is the standard entry class (SEC) code for this format. - CH10

correlation: As part of regression analysis (a statistical cash forecasting methodology), correlation calculations involve a statistical identification of the degree of association between a cash flow and another variable. Once this relationship is established, the cash flow can be forecasted based on the actual or expected behavior of the other variable. - CH13

correspondent bank: In a payment clearing process, this is one of two banks that have accounts with each other for the purpose of clearing and settlement of payment items between the banks. - CH4

cost of capital: A measure of the cost a company would incur to raise funds to make investments in assets. The overall cost of capital for a company is a function of the mix of capital components used and the individual costs of each component. - CH9

cost of goods sold (COGS): The expense associated with providing the goods or services whose sale is recognized as revenues. COGS includes labor and material directly used in manufacturing the product sold, as well as any indirect or allocated manufacturing expenses. - CH18

cost-benefit analysis: A business decision process that assesses whether the relevant economic benefits of a given course of action exceed the relevant economic costs. - CH19

counterparty risk: The risk that the other party in a contract or financial transaction will not perform as promised. One component of counterparty risk is related to credit and default risk. In a generic context, however, the concept of counterparty risk extends to the risk related to any type of performance failure on the part of any of the counterparties with which an organization must interact. - CH15

countertrade: A trade payment method used by companies that do not have access to sufficient hard currencies (i.e., internationally traded currencies) to pay for imports from other countries. As an example, an exporter ships merchandise to the countertrading country. In exchange, it takes merchandise that may be sold elsewhere in the world. - CH10

covenant: An additional requirement that is placed on debt or bond issues and that imposes constraints on the actions of the company's management. Covenants may be negative (i.e., actions the company cannot take, such as the double pledging of collateral) or affirmative (i.e., actions the company must take, such as providing regular financial statements or maintaining certain financial ratios). - CH6

coverage ratios: Financial ratios concerned primarily with measuring a company's ability to make payments on (i.e., service) its debt. - CH19

cram-down procedure: A type of procedure for formulating a reorganization plan in a US Chapter 11 bankruptcy filing. This procedure is generally executed by secured creditors and comes into play when a reorganization plan fails to meet the standard for approval by all classes of creditors under the unanimous consent procedure, or when the firm is insolvent and the old equity must be eliminated. In a cram-down case, if at least one class of creditors has voted in favor of a plan, then the court may confirm the plan (or a modified version of it) as long as each dissenting class is treated fairly and equitably. - CH2

credit card: A payment card issued by a company that provides the holder of the card the ability to borrow funds, typically at the point of sale, to pay for a transaction. - CH4

Credit Card Accountability Responsibility and Disclosure Act of 2009 (Credit CARD Act): A US law designed to protect consumers from arbitrary pricing and notification practices by credit card companies. - CH2

credit enhancement: An addition to a borrowing arrangement or debt securities issue meant to improve the overall credit rating on the loan or issue. It generally provides either a guarantee of payment in the event of default or an agreement to provide financing to roll over the debt issue. - CH6

credit manager: A credit management function/position that administers policies that establish credit standards, defines the terms of trade credit extension, approves customers for credit sales, and sets individual and aggregate credit limits within policy guidelines. - CH8

credit risk (default risk): A form of risk that is related to how a change in the credit quality of a company, including its ability to make payments in a timely manner, would affect the value of a security or portfolio of investments. Credit risk arises both from transactions and from any risk in the portfolio due to concentration of similar assets. Higher yields are typically associated with higher risk, as investors will require a higher return to compensate for a higher chance of loss. - CH5,CH15

credit scheme: The term used in the Single Euro Payments Area (SEPA) initiative to describe a pre-authorized credit program in which one person or company authorizes another to automatically credit its bank account for payments that are due. - CH4

credit transfer: In an electronic payment system, this is the process of a payor pushing funds from its account to the account of the payee. - CH4

credit unions: Not-for-profit financial corporations in the United States, chartered by either federal or state agencies, that originally were intended to restrict membership to individuals with a common affiliation (e.g., an employer, association, community organization, or geographic location) but may now include businesses as members. - CH3

cross-default (provision): A type of provision in a loan agreement or bond indenture that states that if a default occurs under any borrowing agreement, then all credit facilities with cross-default provisions are in default and subject to the remedies applicable to payment default. - CH20

cross-industry electronic data interchange (EDI): A set of format standards that addresses the needs of many different users in many industries. - CH14

cumulative voting: A form of voting that allows a shareholder as many votes per share owned as there are open positions on the board in the same election. - CH20

cure period: A period of time, often specified in a loan agreement, in which an event of default may be corrected before the lender may pursue default remedies. - CH6

currency derivative: A derivative instrument that allows trading partners to establish predetermined exchange rates for set periods, which effectively hedges against foreign exchange risk. Currency derivatives include option, futures, swap, and forward contracts. - CH16

current account: A bank depository account that is both a store of value (deposits) and, perhaps more importantly for treasury management purposes, a vehicle through which an account holder uses a bank to transfer funds to, and receive deposits from, a third party. Referred to as a *checking or demand deposit account (DDA)* in the United States. - CH3

current asset turnover ratio: An efficiency/asset management ratio that measures how many times the firm has turned over the stock of its most liquid assets with the flow of revenue. It is computed as revenues divided by current assets. - CH19

current assets: A term that generally refers to assets that are expected to be converted into cash within one year. - CH8

current liabilities: A term that generally refers to liabilities that are required to be paid for within one year. - CH8

current ratio: A ratio defined as total current assets divided by total current liabilities. It is therefore the ratio of cash and assets expected to become cash in one year or less, to short-term liabilities that must be paid in one year or less. - CH9

custodian: A third party that typically takes possession of securities, receives delivery or book entry of principal and interest payments, performs record keeping, and provides maintenance services for an investment portfolio. - CH17

customer identification program (CIP): The processes used by a financial institution to verify and validate the stated identity of a customer. CIP is normally part of the anti-money laundering processes of a financial institution. - CH7

Customer Transfer Plus (CTP): A Fedwire format implemented in late 2010 that provides the ability to send large amounts of remittance data in either a structured or unstructured format along with the payment. - CH4

Customer-Initiated Entry (CIE): The US automated clearinghouse (ACH) format used for pre-authorized payments that are initiated by consumers using telephone bill-paying services. *CIE* is the standard entry class (SEC) code for this format. - CH10

cutoff time: A time by which a specific process, such as depositing payments, must be completed for processing in the current cycle. For example, checks deposited after the current day's cutoff time will typically be processed the next day. - CH4

dashboard: An easy-to-read, typically graphical, report or online display that shows the current status of key performance indicators. - CH14

days' inventory (inventory conversion period): In the cash conversion cycle, this is the average number of days that elapse from the purchase of raw materials until the sale of finished goods. Also referred to as *days' sales in inventory*, or *DSI*. - CH8

days' payables (payables conversion period): In the cash conversion cycle, this is the average number of days between the purchase/receipt of materials or supplies and issuance of payment for them. - CH8

days' receivables (receivables conversion period): In the cash conversion cycle, this is the average number of days required to convert a credit sale into a collection. - CH8

days' sales outstanding (DSO): The average number of days required to convert a credit sale into a cash inflow. Also referred to as *average collection period*. - CH9

debentures: Unsecured bonds that represent general claims against the issuer organization's assets and/or cash flows and may carry a higher interest cost (to the issuer) than secured bonds. - CH6

debit card: A card that allows access to funds directly from a cardholder's checking or savings deposit account and can be either signature-based or personal identification number (PIN)-based. Often referred to as *EFTPOS* in many parts of the world. *EFTPOS* refers to electronic funds transfer (EFT) at the point of sale (POS). - CH4

debit scheme: The term used in the Single Euro Payments Area (SEPA) initiative to describe a pre-authorized debit program in which one person or company authorizes another to automatically debit its bank account for payments that are due. - CH4

debit transfer: In an electronic payments system, this is the process of a payor authorizing payees to initiate value transfers from the payor's account to the account of the payee. - CH4

debt management ratio: A type of ratio that measures the firm's degree of indebtedness and its ability to service its debt. - CH19

debt to tangible net worth ratio: A type of debt management ratio that reflects the impact of intangible assets (e.g., goodwill, patents, trademarks, and copyrights) on the balance sheet. It is computed as total debt, divided by total equity minus intangible assets. - CH19

deemed dividend: A situation that occurs when payments on loans, sales of stock, or other transactions are interpreted by tax authorities as an attempt by a company to avoid paying taxes on dividends. The payments may be considered (i.e., "deemed") dividends and appropriate taxes charged. Deemed dividends are a potential issue for any global company and can vary significantly from country to country. - CH20

default premium: An adjustment to the base interest rate to account for possible default on an investment. - CH11

defeasance of debt: A financial management method that removes debt from an organization's balance sheet without actually retiring the debt issue. In this arrangement, the borrower places sufficient funds in escrow, usually in government securities, to pay for interest and principal on the debt issue. Because control of both the debt and escrow funds is relinquished, and payment and retirement of the debt issue is now guaranteed, this debt and the related securities can be removed from the balance sheet and do not need to be considered in relation to any restrictive covenants the organization may have regarding debt. - CH6

degree of certainty: In the cash flow forecasting process, this is the practice of designating cash flows as certain flows, predictable flows, or less predictable flows. - CH13

demand deposit account (DDA): An account through which an account holder uses a bank to transfer funds to, and receive deposits from, a third party. Also known as a *checking account* or a *current account*. - CH3

departmental (unnamed) card: A variation on the purchasing card in which each department is given its own purchasing card for general use by that department. - CH4

deposit deadline: The time within the banking day when an item must be ready for transit at the depository bank's processing center to qualify for the availability stated in the availability schedule. - CH4

deposit insurance (deposit guarantee): A regulatory safeguard that protects the assets of smaller deposit customers (typically consumers, although corporate accounts are also typically covered up to a certain amount) who would be most harmed by a bank failure. - CH2

depositary receipt (DR): A type of negotiable financial instrument (typically equity securities) that trades on a local exchange but actually represents stock ownership in a foreign, publicly listed company. There are American and global DRs (ADRs and GDRs, respectively). - CH6

depository bank: The bank or financial institution in which a check is deposited for processing and clearing. Also known as the *bank of first deposit* or *collecting bank*. - CH4

Depository Institution Deregulation and Monetary Control Act of 1980 (DIDMCA): A US legislative act that provided for a phase-out of interest rate ceilings for financial institutions, mandated that all depository institutions hold reserves at the Federal Reserve (Fed), and mandated that the Fed price or eliminate its float in the check-clearing system. The act is also referred to as the *Monetary Control Act*. - CH2

Depository Trust & Clearing Corporation (DTCC): An investment-industry-owned corporation that works through its subsidiaries to provide clearing, settlement, and information services for equities, corporate and municipal bonds, government and mortgage-backed securities, money market instruments, and over-the-counter derivatives. It was formed in 1999 by the combination of the Depository Trust Company (DTC) and the National Securities Clearing Corporation (NSCC). - CH5

derivative: A financial product that acquires its value by inference through a formulaic connection to another asset. The other asset is termed the *underlying asset*, and can be a financial instrument (e.g., a stock or bond), currency, or commodity. - CH16

Destroyed Check Entry (XCK): A US automated clearinghouse (ACH) format used to clear and settle items that originated as checks, but the original paper item was lost or destroyed due to a catastrophic event (e.g., fire, flood, or hurricane). *XCK* is the standard entry class (SEC) code for this format. - CH10

difference in conditions (DIC): A type of insurance that covers property for perils not covered by basic property insurance policies. It is often purchased to fill voids in policies purchased overseas and to insure property in transit. Typically used in conjunction with multiple basic policies to make them uniform, DIC insurance does not provide additional limits of coverage for basic property perils (as an umbrella policy does for liability insurance). - CH15

digital certificate: An electronic commerce security product that ties the identity of the user (private key) to the user's public key and may also authenticate the devices used to create documents or transactions. - CH14

digital signature: A message encoded with the sender's secret, private key that the receiver can use to identify the source. A digital signature is essentially an electronic signature used in place of a written signature and is tied to a document and to the signer, meaning the signer's digital signature will be different for each document signed. - CH14

digitized signature: A scanned version of a written signature. A digitized signature should not be confused with a digital signature, which is an electronic signature used in place of a written signature. - CH14

direct deposit: A transfer made from a company's account to the account of an employee, shareholder, vendor, or trading partner using an automated clearinghouse credit transaction. - CH10

direct exchange: A process in which collecting banks arrange to send cash letters directly to a paying bank or to a nonlocal Federal Reserve Bank (in the United States) rather than using typical clearing channels. This process, also referred to as *direct presentment*, enables banks to meet various deposit deadlines and achieve faster clearing times. Also referred to as *direct send*. - CH4

directors and officers (D&O) insurance: A type of insurance that covers situations in which a director or officer or an organization commits a negligent act or omission, or makes a misstatement or misleading statement, and a legal action is brought against the organization as a result. The policy provides coverage (usually with a large deductible) for directors' and officers' liability exposure if these individuals are sued. Coverage also is provided for defense costs, such as legal fees and other court costs, and may include coverage for an organization's subsidiaries. - CH15

disaster recovery: The restoration of systems and communications after an event causes an outage. - CH15

disbursement float: The time interval or delay between the day when a payment is initiated and the day when funds are debited from the payor's account. - CH8

disbursements schedule: A schedule that involves forecasting the cash disbursements for purchases and other cash outflows, such as payroll, taxes, interest, dividends, rent, and debt repayments. It is a component of the receipts and disbursements forecast process. - CH13

discount brokerage: A brokerage firm that lets investors make trades at reduced prices, but provides little or no investment advice. - CH3

discount rate: Used in the valuation of discount investments such as US Treasury bills, commercial paper, and banker's acceptances, this is the rate used to determine the present value or purchase price of the instrument. In calculations, the discount rate is defined as the dollar discount divided by par, or maturity, value and then annualized using a 360-day year. - CH9

discount terms: A term of sale whereby the seller offers a discount on payments made prior to the net due date. Terms of 2/10 net 30 mean that the total amount is due within 30 days of the invoice date, but the buyer can take a 2% discount if it pays within 10 days. - CH8

distribution: An investment bank function that involves a securities sale to investors by an investment bank or syndicate of investment banks. - CH3

distribution forecast: A short-term forecasting methodology that estimates the daily impact that a single event has on cash flows over a specified period, based on historical patterns. - CH13

diversification: A method of managing risk by including a wide variety of investments with differing characteristics in a portfolio so that the risk of loss due to the failure of any one individual security is minimized. - CH12

dividend capture: A tax-motivated, short-term investment strategy that is available to corporations that pay taxes in the United States. A corporation may exclude from its taxable income 70–80% of the dividends received from stock owned in another corporation, as long as it owns the stock for at least 46 days of the 91-day period starting 45 days prior to the ex-dividend date. Even though dividend capture requires an equity investment, the strategy is considered a short-term investment because the stock is held only long enough to capture the dividend and qualify for the dividend exclusion. - CH11

dividend declaration date: The date when the board of directors announces (declares) a dividend. - CH20

dividend payment date: The date when a dividend is paid. - CH20

dividend policy: A company's policy regarding whether to pay dividends and, if so, how much and when to pay. - CH20

dividend record date: The date when shareholders of record are entitled to receive a declared dividend. Also known as a *shareholder-of-record date*, or *just holder-of-record date*. - CH20

dividend reinvestment plan (DRIP): A plan that enables existing shareholders to purchase additional shares directly from the company on a when-desired basis, normally with no commission or with only a small processing charge. These plans also allow investors to elect to reinvest dividends automatically in additional shares of company stock. - CH20

dividend signaling: A theory that dividends have information content or a signaling effect. Dividends are observed to contain information that signals management's intentions to investors and may provide information regarding expected future earnings. - CH20

documentary collection: A trade-services payment method that processes the collection of a draft and accompanying shipping documents through international correspondent banks. - CH3

documents against acceptance: A type of collection letter (in a documentary collection process) that uses a time draft, which is a draft payable on a specified future date, that must be accepted by the importer before the collecting bank may release documents. Upon maturity of the time draft, it is presented to the importer for payment. - CH10

documents against payment: A type of collection letter (in a documentary collection process) that uses a sight draft, which is a draft payable on demand, that requires the collecting bank to receive full and final payment of the amount owed prior to releasing the documents. - CH10

Dodd-Frank Wall Street Reform and Consumer Protection Act of 2010: Legislation enacted in the United States in response to concerns related to the financial services industry in the wake of the Recession of 2009. The act had a major impact on the regulation of banks and other FIs, and brought financial consumer protection under a single authority. - CH2

dollar discount: The difference between the purchase price and the par, or maturity, value on discounted investment instruments, such as US Treasury bills, commercial paper, and banker's acceptances. This difference represents interest earned on the investment. - CH11

dollar-days: A unit of measurement that reflects both a transaction's dollar amount and the number of days of float delay. The dollar-days of float on an individual check are calculated by multiplying the dollar amount of the check by the number of days from the time the payor mails the check to the time when the payee is granted credit, or availability, of collected funds. - CH9

draft/bill of lading: A term of sale whereby sellers collect payments through banking channels in what is known as a *documentary collection*. - CH8

drawdown wire: A type of wire transfer that is a request sent by a company's bank to a second bank requesting that the second bank initiate a wire transfer from either the company's account or another party's account at the second bank, sending the funds back to the first bank. The party being debited must pre-authorize the transfer. - CH10

DuPont equation: An integrated ratio analysis technique that looks at the return on total assets (ROTA) ratio as a product of the return on sales (i.e., net profit margin) and total asset turnover. - CH19

duration: A measure of the number of years required to recover the true cost of a bond, considering the present value of all coupon and principal payments received in the future. Duration, in its simplest form, is the weighted average time to receipt of all future cash flows associated with a bond investment, but it can also provide a measure of the sensitivity of the investment to changes in underlying interest rates. This is one of the primary measures of risk for a bond or fixed-income portfolio. - CH12

Durbin Amendment: An amendment to the Dodd-Frank Act in the United States that restricts interchange fees, or fees that financial institutions may charge for processing debit card payments. - CH2

earnings before interest and taxes (EBIT): A measure of operating income or profit that is calculated as gross profit less operating expenses, depreciation, and amortization. EBIT has traditionally been the measure used to evaluate a firm's ability to generate operating profits and to meet its financial and tax obligations. - CH18

earnings before interest, taxes, depreciation, and amortization (EBITDA): A measure of operating profitability that is calculated as gross profit less operating expenses (but not subtracting depreciation and amortization). EBITDA first came into common use with leveraged buyouts in the 1980s, when it was used to indicate the ability of a company to service debt. As time passed, it became popular in industries with expensive assets that had to be written down over long periods. Many companies, especially in the technology sector, now commonly quote EBITDA. - CH18

earnings credit allowance: The total dollar value of earnings credit (imputed interest) that can be used by a company to offset the bank service charges incurred during the account analysis period. - CH7

earnings credit rate: A short-term rate (most commonly the 90-day US Treasury bill rate) that is multiplied by the investable balance to determine the earnings credit allowance for the period, as part of the account analysis process. - CH7

EBIT: See *earnings before interest and taxes*. - CH18

EBITDA: See *earnings before interest, taxes, depreciation, and amortization*. - CH18

EBITDA margin: A measure of operating profitability calculated by dividing EBITDA (earnings before interest, taxes, depreciation, and amortization) by total revenues. - CH 19

e-commerce (electronic commerce): The application of information and secure network technology for the purpose of facilitating business relationships, including buying and selling, among trading partners. E-commerce encompasses many types of channels and communications protocols, including traditional electronic data interchange (EDI) and Internet-based commerce. - CH14

economic development bond: A type of bond typically issued by a developing country or sponsoring organization, such as the World Bank or the International Monetary Fund, for the express purpose of fostering development of infrastructure and related projects. - CH6

economic order quantity (EOQ) model: A model used to calculate optimal inventory levels, given specified ordering and holding costs. - CH8

economic risk: The risk that an asset will be affected by external conditions such as government regulation, exchange rates, or political stability, especially in international trade. - CH16

economic risk exposure (economic exposure): A form of risk that represents the long-term effect of changes in exchange rates on the present value of future cash flows. Multinational corporations that conduct business in several different currencies are, in the long run, always subject to fluctuations in cash flows because of exchange-rate changes. Even companies that only operate domestically are exposed to economic risk whenever there is foreign competition within the local market. - CH16

economic value added (EVA): A performance measurement ratio that isolates the funds available to all suppliers of capital and then relates that total to the amount of capital supplied. It can be computed as earnings before interest and taxes (EBIT), times one minus the company's tax rate, and then subtracting the product of the weighted average cost of capital and long-term debt and equity. - CH19

economies of scale: A relationship that occurs when an increase in sales lowers the average cost per unit sold. - CH19

efficiency/asset management ratio: A type of ratio that measures how effectively assets are utilized. - CH19

electronic bank account management (eBAM): A type of bank account management process that attempts to replace the large amount of paper in the process with electronic messages and files exchanged between banks and their customers. *Bank account management* refers to the management of all of the various facets of an organization's relationship with its bank(s), including opening and closing accounts, managing authorized signatories, and maintaining proper copies of documentation. - CH14

electronic bill presentment and payment (EBPP): A system for integrating the billing and payment processes, thereby enabling companies to send electronic statements and receive electronic remittances from customers. It is the retail consumer version of electronic invoice presentment and payment. - CH10

electronic commerce: See *e-commerce*. - CH14

Electronic Data Gathering, Analysis, and Retrieval (EDGAR) database: A database that contains a searchable listing of US Securities and Exchange Commission filings for public companies. - CH18

electronic data interchange (EDI): A traditional building block of e-commerce that is based on an infrastructure using standardized communication formats to exchange business data between two trading partners. - CH14

Electronic Federal Tax Payment System (EFTPS): A system that serves as the primary method for collecting and accounting for US federal taxes withheld by employers from individuals' salaries and wages, as well as corporate business, sales, and excise taxes. - CH10

electronic invoice presentment and payment (EIPP): A system for integrating the billing and payment processes, thereby enabling companies to send electronic statements and receive electronic remittances from customers. - CH10

electronic lockbox:, A variation of the lockbox approach that provides a single collection point for all automated clearinghouse (ACH) and wire payments for organizations with a large number of electronic funds transfer (EFT) collections. It can also process remittance advices from a variety of incoming formats into a single format for transmission to the organization's accounts receivable department for posting and reconciliation. - CH10

Electronic Signatures in Global and National Commerce Act of 2000 (E-SIGN Act): US legislation that was enacted to support electronic commerce (e-commerce) initiatives and grant digital signatures the same legal status as handwritten ink signatures. It establishes the legal certainty of e-commerce transactions and provides a measure of confidence around the enforceability of electronic transactions. - CH2

employee risk: A type of risk that is related to employees and represents a significant source of internal operational risk. The general risk of intentional employee fraud is typically referred to as *defalcation risk*, while the specific case of theft of money, securities, or property by an employee is known as *fidelity risk*. A more significant source of internal risk stems from unintentional actions by employees. Examples include employee errors in data entry or reentry, as well as transposition or deletion of numbers. - CH15

EMV: An acronym for *Europay, MasterCard, and Visa* that refers to a global standard for the use of smart cards (or chip cards) as either debit or credit cards. - CH4

encryption: The process of transforming information using some type of computer-based model to make it unreadable to anyone except those possessing special knowledge, similar to a password, usually referred to as a *key*. - CH14

enterprise resource planning (ERP) system: A sophisticated information management, production, and accounting software package that links different functional areas or operational divisions of a company on an enterprise-wide basis. - CH14

enterprise risk management (ERM): A comprehensive, organization-wide approach to identifying, measuring, and managing the various risks that threaten the achievement of an organization's strategic objectives and therefore its overall operations. It is characterized as having a viewpoint that encompasses all areas of the organization. - CH15

equipment trust certificate: A type of bond that is secured by movable equipment (e.g., a fleet of trucks or railroad equipment). Each certificate is backed by a specific asset or group of assets (i.e., there is no blanket lien securing the issue). - CH6

equity capital: The invested capital of an organization (as contrasted with borrowed or debt capital). From an accounting point of view, equity capital consists of all preferred and common equity accounts, including retained earnings, and is typically represented by securities such as shares of common and preferred stock. - CH19

equity price risk: A type of risk usually associated with volatility in stock prices. The general form of this risk refers to the sensitivity of an instrument or portfolio value to a change in broad stock market indices, while the firm-specific portion of this risk relates just to the company in question. - CH15

escheatment: The process of turning over unclaimed assets to the government, in specific instances. In the business world, escheat statutes primarily impact banks or companies that hold unclaimed assets of customers or employees. The most general occurrence of escheat is when an entity (e.g., a bank) holds money or property (e.g., an account in that bank) and the property goes unclaimed for some specified period of time (generally referred to as a *dormant account*). In many jurisdictions, if the owner cannot be located, such property must be escheated to the government. - CH2

Eurobond: A type of bond sold simultaneously in many countries outside the country of the borrower. Usually, a Eurobond is issued by an international syndicate and categorized according to the currency in which it is denominated. - CH6

eurodeposit: Originally defined as the deposit of non-euro currency in a European bank, this term has come to mean the deposit of any type of currency in a financial institution outside of the currency's home market (e.g., the deposit of US dollars or Japanese yen in a London bank account). - CH5

Eurodollar: A deposit denominated in US dollars held in a financial institution outside of the United States, typically in Europe. It may be issued as a negotiable Eurodollar certificate of deposit or as a nonnegotiable Eurodollar time deposit, both of which are interest-bearing. - CH5

European Central Bank (ECB): The central bank for the Economic and Monetary Union (EMU). The ECB conducts a unified monetary policy for the euro zone, which includes all EMU members that have adopted the euro as their common currency. - CH2

European option: A type of option contract that may only be executed (settled) on the actual option date specified in the contract. European options can be contrasted with American options, which may be settled any time before or on the specified option date. Contrast also with *Bermuda option*. - CH16

European Payments Council (EPC): The coordination and decision-making body of the European banking industry in relation to payments. The purpose of the EPC is to support and promote the Single Euro Payments Area (SEPA). The EPC develops payment schemes and frameworks that help to realize the integrated euro payments market. In particular, the EPC defines common positions for the cooperative space of payment services. - CH2

European Union (EU): A union of 28 member countries in Europe that have organized to work toward common political, social, and economic interests. - CH2

evaluated receipts settlement (ERS): A payment method designed to eliminate the need for a supplier to provide an invoice to its customer. The transfer of value amount for an ERS payment is not based on an invoice, but rather on a calculation of the quantity actually received by a customer multiplied by the agreed-upon price on the purchase order. - CH8

excess balance: A situation that occurs in an account when its average collected balance is greater than either the amount that the financial institution requires as a compensating balance or the target level that a company has chosen to maintain. - CH7

excess (umbrella) insurance: A type of insurance coverage that supplements basic or primary liability coverage. Policies generally pay after the primary policy's limits have been exhausted. For example, if the primary insurance policy has a $250,000 limit and claims exceed this amount, then an umbrella or excess policy would pay the excess claims up to the limit of the policy. Excess or umbrella policies can also be used to fill gaps in coverage provided by basic liability policies (i.e., the difference in coverage between two policies). - CH15

ex-dividend date: The date on which a stock is sold without entitlement to the upcoming dividend. The ex-dividend date is usually two business days prior to the shareholder-of-record date, thereby enabling brokerage firms to send an updated list of shareholders to a company on time. - CH20

exotic currency: A foreign exchange term used for a currency that is not widely traded (sometimes referred to as a *thinly traded currency*). These currencies can be difficult and expensive to trade due to a lack of liquidity or available counterparties. - CH16

exponential smoothing: A statistical cash forecasting technique that produces a forecasted value based on the most recent actual value, the most recent forecasted value, and a number between zero and one that is used to weight these two values. The weight, designated by the Greek letter alpha (α), is referred to as the *smoothing constant* and is calculated using a computer program such as a statistics package. - CH13

export credit agencies (ECAs): The general term for entities that are established by governments to support export activities through export loans, credit guarantees, or a combination of both. - CH8

Export-Import (Ex-Im) Bank of the United States: The official export credit agency of the United States. - CH8

expropriation: A government takeover of a single company, with or without compensation. - CH7

eXtensible markup language (XML): A computer-based language that is an extension of hypertext markup language (HTML) that allows the content and structure to be defined. - CH14

external theft/fraud risk: The risk of theft or fraud involving individuals external to the targeted company. Traditionally, the primary source of external theft or fraud has been related to the payment process, often involving false invoices or check fraud. - CH15

extrapolation: One of the most general statistical methods, this process identifies past trends and predicts the pattern of future cash flows using these trends. - CH13

factor: A type of nonbank financial intermediary that provides short-term financing to companies by purchasing accounts receivable at a discount. - CH3

factoring: An accounts receivable (A/R) financing process that involves the outright sale of receivables to a factor, a company that specializes in the financing and management of receivables. The factoring may be performed on a *with or without recourse* basis. In a *with recourse* arrangement, the factor may return any uncollectible A/R to the seller for full credit. In a *without recourse* factoring arrangement, the factor takes all the risk of default on the A/R. - CH8

fair value: Under Accounting Standards Codification (ASC) Topic 820, the fair value of an asset or liability is defined by determining the price that would be received in an asset sale or the price paid to transfer a liability. The valuation price must be market-based and take into consideration all observable valuation inputs, such as competition and risk. ASC Topic 825 expands this application by stating that fair value should be applied to all financial assets and liabilities except for certain specified types of assets. - CH18

Federal Deposit Insurance Corporation (FDIC): An independent agency of the US federal government whose primary role is to protect depositors from losses caused by bank insolvency. The FDIC preserves and promotes public confidence in the US financial system by insuring deposits in banks and thrift institutions up to a maximum of $250,000 per depositor; by identifying, monitoring, and addressing risks to the Deposit Insurance Fund; and by limiting the effect on the economy and the financial system when a bank or thrift institution fails. - CH2

Federal Home Loan Mortgage Corporation (FHLMC, or Freddie Mac): A stockholder-owned, government-sponsored enterprise chartered by the US Congress in 1970 to keep money flowing to mortgage lenders in support of homeownership and rental housing for middle-income Americans. The FHLMC purchases, guarantees, and securitizes mortgages to form mortgage-backed securities (MBSs). - CH5

Federal National Mortgage Association (FNMA, or Fannie Mae): A US government-sponsored enterprise that was created in 1938 to expand the flow of mortgage money by creating a secondary mortgage market. Fannie Mae is a publicly traded company that operates under a congressional charter that directs Fannie Mae to channel its efforts into increasing the availability and affordability of homeownership for low-, moderate-, and middle-income Americans. - CH5

Federal Open Market Committee (FOMC): The committee of the US Federal Reserve that runs the open market operations which help to implement US monetary policy and control the money supply. - CH2

Federal Reserve (Fed): The central bank for the United States, from the perspective of monetary policy. - CH2

FedGlobal Automated Clearinghouse Payments (FedGlobal ACH Payments): A service offered by the US Federal Reserve Bank to provide a framework for sending cross-border ACH transactions to countries around the world (over 35 countries as of 2013). - CH4

Fedwire: A large-value, real-time gross settlement (RTGS) transfer system operated by the US Federal Reserve. - CH4

fidelity bond: A type of insurance coverage that guarantees payment for money or other property lost through dishonest acts of bonded employees, either by name or position. Whether employees act alone or in concert, the bond generally covers all dishonest acts, such as larceny, theft, embezzlement, forgery, misappropriation, wrongful abstraction, or willful misapplication. Because a fidelity bond makes up only part of the protection against theft, other crime insurance is often mandatory. A blanket bond could be used to cover all employees of an organization, while crime insurance provides specific coverage for the perils of burglary, theft, and robbery by external parties. - CH15

fiduciary: An individual or institution to which certain property is given to hold in trust according to a trust agreement. - CH3

finality: In a payment system, this is the point in time when a payment can no longer be taken back or retracted by a payor, and the payee has full use of the funds. - CH4

Financial Accounting Foundation (FAF): A US foundation that selects members, provides funds, and exercises general oversight for both the Governmental Accounting Standards Board (GASB) and the Financial Accounting Standards Board (FASB). - CH18

Financial Accounting Standards (FASs): The former name of Accounting Standards Codification (ASC) Topics. - CH18

Financial Accounting Standards Board (FASB): An independent, self-regulating US organization made up of accounting professionals that establishes financial accounting and reporting standards in the United States, collectively referred to as *Generally Accepted Accounting Principles (GAAP)*. - CH18

Financial Action Task Force (FATF): An international, intergovernmental organization composed of members from more than 30 countries, whose primary purpose is the development and promotion of policies, at both national and international levels, to combat money laundering and terrorist financing. - CH2

financial budget: A component of a master budget, this budget addresses an organization's financing and investing activities. - CH19

Financial Crimes Enforcement Network (FinCEN): The primary US government agency (operating as a bureau of the US Treasury) that oversees and implements policies to prevent and detect money laundering by criminal or terrorist organizations. FinCEN serves as the US financial intelligence unit (FIU). - CH2

Financial Industry Regulatory Authority (FINRA): The largest independent regulator for all securities firms and registered securities representatives doing business in the United States. - CH2

financial institution (FI): An organization that provides some type of financial services to the public. A commercial bank is the most common type of FI. - CH3

financial institution risk: The risk of loss to an organization associated with the failure, either operational or financial, of a financial institution used by an organization. - CH15

financial intelligence unit (FIU): A specialized government agency established in many countries to monitor and deal with the problems of money laundering and similar financial crimes. FinCEN in the United States is an FIU. - CH2

financial lease: See *capital lease*. - CH20

financial leverage: A concept that examines the fixed costs of financing. Generally, the higher the level of debt capital used in a company, the higher the interest costs and the greater the amount of financial leverage. Financial leverage is also the measure of a company's use of debt in its capital structure. - CH19

financial planning: An organizational function that involves determining the need for present and future funding to support operations. An important part of this function is the forecasting of revenues, income, and external financing required to support the company's planned growth. - CH1

financial risk: The risk that the overall value of an organization may change in response to a change in interest or foreign exchange rates. Financial risk is typically broken down into three distinct categories: interest rate risk, foreign exchange (FX) risk, and commodity price risk. Financial risk is also referred to as *economic or strategic exposure*. - CH16

financial services provider (FSP): A vendor that provides treasury-related services. - CH7

Financial Stability Board (FSB): A board established to provide international coordination of national financial authorities and international standard-setting bodies. It works to develop and promote the implementation of effective regulatory, supervisory, and other financial sector policies. - CH2

Financial Stability Oversight Council (FSOC): A US agency created under the Dodd-Frank Act, whose primary responsibility is to prevent systemic risk from threatening the financial system by identifying threats to financial stability and gaps in regulations, and facilitating coordination across federal and state agencies. - CH2

financial statements: Accounting reports that summarize a company's operating results and financial position at a point in time. Analyzing these statements provides insights into (1) how well the company has managed its liquidity position, (2) how effectively it used and financed its assets, (3) whether it had a proper balance between debt and equity financing compared to peers, (4) how well it controlled operating and financing costs, and (5) whether the profit it earned was satisfactory in relation to the levels of revenue it experienced and the investment in assets that support its operations. - CH18

financial supply chain: The connection of trading partners from order placement to receipt of payment. It refers to the flow of financial information and money in counterpoint to the flow of goods and services. The financial supply chain is crucial to financial viability following a disaster. The treasury area plays a pivotal role in managing the organization's financial supply chain, through working capital management practices and by ensuring adequate liquidity sources. - CH14

finished goods: A type of inventory that consists of completed items or materials available for sale. It lets a company fill orders when received rather than depend upon product completion to satisfy customer demands. - CH8

five Cs of credit: A credit analysis process that considers the character, capacity, capital, collateral, and conditions of the potential borrower. - CH8

fixed asset turnover ratio: An efficiency/asset management ratio that measures how efficiently fixed assets (or property, plant, and equipment) are used. It is computed as revenues divided by net property, plant, and equipment. - CH19

fixed costs: Costs that do not vary in total over a wide range of activity and are not immediately impacted by changes in business activities. In cost accounting, fixed costs are contrasted with variable costs, which do change based on volume or activity levels. - CH19

fixed-charge coverage ratio: A coverage ratio that is similar to the times interest earned ratio but also takes into account fixed charges other than interest, such as payments on leases. It is computed as earnings before interest and taxes (EBIT) plus fixed charges, divided by interest expense plus fixed charges. - CH19

fixed/floating ratio: A ratio that provides a measure of interest rate risk utilizing a debt portfolio's mix of fixed-rate obligations relative to floating-rate obligations. Though duration is a more common measure of interest rate risk, many debt portfolio managers also use this ratio. This relationship is usually expressed in terms of a target fixed/floating ratio. - CH12

fixed-income capital: A type of capital that has fixed payments and includes capital such as bond securities and term loans. - CH6

fixed-to-fixed—foreign currency to foreign currency: A transaction currency option available as part of the FedGlobal ACH Payments service, in which payments are both transferred and received in foreign currency. The foreign exchange rate and settlement are managed and processed by participating US financial institutions and the respective foreign gateway operators via their foreign correspondent banks. - CH4

fixed-to-fixed—US dollar to US dollar: A transaction currency option available as part of the FedGlobal ACH Payments service, in which payments are both transferred and received in US dollars. Settlement is between participating US financial institutions and the Federal Reserve Banks, in US dollars. - CH4

fixed-to-variable currency: A transaction currency option available as part of the FedGlobal ACH Payments service, in which US dollars are converted to a variable amount of a destination currency based on a competitive exchange rate. Settlement is between participating US financial institutions and the Federal Reserve Banks, in US dollars. - CH4

float: The time interval, or delay, between the start and the completion of a specific phase or process occurring along the cash flow timeline. - CH8

floating-rate debt: A type of debt issue in which the interest rate is tied to a common rate basis, such as the London Interbank Offered Rate or the US Treasury bill. - CH6

floating-rate note (FRN): A note with a variable interest rate. The adjustments to the interest rate are made periodically (usually every six months) and are tied to a certain money market index. - CH5

float-neutral terms: Sales terms offered for electronic payment in which either the timing (i.e., value date) of a payment is adjusted or a discount is offered so as to maintain whatever float the buyer was receiving with the paper payment. - CH8

floor planning: In inventory financing, this is a type of asset-based lending used for high-value durable goods, such as automobiles, trucks, or heavy equipment. Loans are made against each individual item, recorded by serial number, and are not fully repaid until the item is sold. - CH8

flotation costs: The costs of issuing a security (usually the underwriting costs), not related to direct interest or equity costs. - CH20

forced reinvestment: A type of political risk in which funds cannot be transferred out of a country in any form, or the amount that can be transferred is limited. - CH7

forecasting horizon: In the cash forecasting process, this is the time interval over which information is to be forecasted. - CH13

foreign bond: A type of bond sold in a particular country by a foreign borrower, but usually denominated in the domestic currency of the country where issued. These bonds are primarily regulated by the authorities in the country of issue. - CH6

Foreign Corrupt Practices Act (FCPA): US legislation that specifically prohibits payments to foreign officials or their family members for the purpose of gaining any improper business advantage. - CH7

foreign exchange (FX): The conversion of one country's currency into that of another. - CH3

foreign exchange (FX) forward rate: A rate quoted for the delivery (or settlement) of currency beyond two business days following the date of the trade. - CH16

foreign exchange (FX) risk: A type of risk that arises from the exposure an organization has as a result of transactions, assets, and liabilities that are denominated in a foreign currency. As exchange rates fluctuate, so too can the value of these items, ultimately impacting the overall value of a firm. - CH15

foreign exchange (FX) spot rate: A rate quoted for the delivery (or settlement) of currency one or two business days following the date of the trade. - CH16

foreign tax credit: A type of tax credit available to a company with foreign income that has already been taxed by the foreign jurisdiction. For example, a US company's income derived from its non-US operations typically is included in its tax return to determine the amount of US income tax due. If income from foreign sources has already been subjected to foreign income taxes, the same income is taxed twice. To relieve the effect of double taxation, US tax law grants a US company a tax credit against its total US income tax liability for foreign income taxes paid by the parent and its subsidiaries. This credit is called the *foreign tax credit*. - CH2

forward: An agreement between two parties to buy or sell a fixed amount of an asset to be delivered at a future date and at a price agreed upon today. The underlying asset in a forward contract can be a financial instrument (e.g., a stock index fund or debt instrument), a currency (e.g., the euro or pound), or a commodity (e.g., gold or coffee). - CH16

forward market: A financial market in which contracts for future delivery (futures) of currency or commodities are bought and sold. - CH3

forward rate agreement (FRA): A forward contract on interest rates in which two parties agree that a certain interest rate will apply to a certain principal during a specified, future period of time. The notional principal amounts are agreed upon, but they are never exchanged. If the actual rate is different from the agreed-upon rate in the contract at settlement, then one party pays the other a cash amount equal to the difference. - CH16

free cash flow (FCF): A performance measurement ratio that is similar to residual income analysis but which—in addition to accounting for capital costs—also includes adjustments for noncash items and for working capital investments. Its primary objective is to determine the amount of effective cash flow available to a company after all necessary investments have been accounted for. To this end, it is used extensively in the analysis of new or high-growth companies, especially by the providers of venture capital. It is most commonly computed by adding net income to depreciation and amortization, less the change in working capital and capital expenditures. - CH19

free-fall bankruptcy: A type of bankruptcy in which a firm goes (or is forced) into bankruptcy and has no structured plan for coming out of bankruptcy. - CH2

freight payment services: An outsourced form of accounts payable wherein specialists pay all of a shipper's freight bills, audit bills for possible overcharges and duplicate payments, and provide reports that help a company compare costs for different routes and carriers. - CH10

full guarantee: A level of guarantee for a subsidiary in which the guarantee party (the parent organization or another party) fully guarantees any borrowing arrangement by the subsidiary and agrees to take over the loan if the subsidiary fails to make timely payments. - CH6

full-service brokerage: A brokerage that has research analysts who are industry specialists and provides investment advice to institutions and individual investors. - CH3

functional currency: For determining foreign exchange translation exposure, this is the currency of the primary economic environment in which the entity operates. Normally, the majority of the entity's business activities are transacted in that currency. - CH18

future value (FV): For an investment made today, this is the expected value of the investment at a specified, future date. - CH9

futures: Similar to forwards, futures are agreements between two parties to buy or sell a fixed amount of an asset to be delivered at a future date and at a price agreed upon today. Futures differ, however, in the following ways. First, they are standardized contracts (i.e., standard contract sizes and delivery dates). Second, they are typically traded on organized exchanges rather than over the counter. Third, they are generally not settled with delivery of the underlying asset; instead, they typically are closed out (i.e., settled financially between the two parties) prior to maturity. - CH16

Generally Accepted Accounting Principles (GAAP): A detailed set of rules that govern US accounting standards. These principles are developed, agreed upon, and published in the form of Accounting Standards Codification (ASC) Topics by the Financial Accounting Standards Board (FASB). - CH18

ghost card: A variation on the purchasing card that does not involve the use of an actual card. With a ghost card system, a card number is given to a specific vendor and is then used for electronic purchasing and billing purposes. Also known as a *virtual card*. - CH4

giro: A method of transferring money by instructing a bank to directly transfer funds from one bank account to another without the use of checks. Giro payments are initiated by the payor and can be one-time payments or can be recurring standing instructions for a series of payments. A giro payment is the functional equivalent of an ACH credit. Also known as *postal giro*, since many giro systems are run by the postal system within a country. - CH4

global financial institution: A financial institution that operates in multiple countries in more than one part of the world, providing services to both domestic and multinational corporations. - CH3

good funds: Collected funds in an account that are immediately usable by the owner of the account. - CH8

goodwill: An account that can be found in the assets portion of a company's balance sheet. Goodwill can often arise when one company is purchased by another company. In an acquisition, the amount paid for the company over book value usually accounts for the target firm's intangible assets. - CH18

Government National Mortgage Association (GNMA, or Ginnie Mae): A wholly owned agency of the United States that provides liquidity for government-sponsored mortgage programs through its mortgage-backed securities plan. - CH5

government paper: A range of short-term paper, generally referred to as *treasury bills* or *government-issued promissory notes*, issued by state and local government agencies and authorities, as well as other government entities, in order to raise funds in the short-term money market. - CH5

government warrant: In government finance, this is an order to pay that instructs a treasurer to pay the warrant holder on demand or after a maturity date. Warrants deposited in a bank are routed (based on the magnetic ink character recognition line information) to a collecting bank that processes them as collection items. The collecting bank presents the warrants to the government entity's treasury department for payment each business day. - CH4

Governmental Accounting Standards Board (GASB): The authoritative standard-setting body for US state and local governments, as well as for public schools, state universities, and other government-affiliated agencies. - CH18

governmental or not-for-profit (G/NFP) organization: A type of organization that does not have shareholders or other owners, but is organized to serve a collective group. Governmental agencies provide goods, services, or information to benefit the public as a whole or its particular segments. They raise cash primarily through taxes and fees paid by members of the community, regardless of whether those paying such taxes and fees derive any benefit from the resulting goods or services. Nongovernmental, not-for-profit organizations serve specific constituencies who pay for some or all the benefits provided. - CH18

government-sponsored enterprise (GSE): A company that is created by a national government in order to participate in or help support various commercial activities on the government's behalf. These organizations are generally formed for a specific purpose and are designed to support a certain economic sector. In the United States, examples would include Freddie Mac and Fannie Mae. *GSE* is a US term; the more generic global term is *state-owned enterprise*. - CH6

gross profit margin: A performance ratio that shows the percentage of revenues remaining after the cost of goods sold is deducted from revenue. It is computed as gross profit divided by revenues. - CH19

gross settlement: A type of settlement in a payment system in which each transaction results in a separate value transfer between the payor and payee. In most gross settlement systems, the settlement is on a real-time basis, resulting in a real-time gross settlement (RTGS) system. - CH4

Group of Governors and Heads of Supervision (GHOS): The governing body of the Basel Committee on Banking Supervision. The GHOS is comprised of central bank governors and (non-central bank) heads of supervision from member countries. - CH2

guarantee of payment or collection: A guarantee by one party (usually a parent company) that another party (usually a subsidiary) will make payment on a loan or collection. The guarantor is only responsible in the event that the subsidiary formally defaults on the loan. - CH6

hedging: A risk management strategy used to limit the probability of loss from changes in the prices of commodities, currencies, or securities. In active hedging, an organization uses various financial instruments to reduce or eliminate risks associated with uncertain future cash flows. In passive (or natural) hedging, an organization holds both assets and liabilities in the same currency so that fluctuations offset each other. - CH16

Herstatt risk: Foreign or cross-currency settlement risk, especially between bank counterparties; the risk that one party to a transaction defaults and is not able to fulfill its obligation to settle the transaction, potentially triggering a string of other defaults. Herstatt risk is named after a German bank that failed in 1974, causing a cascading string of payment defaults. - CH2

high-yield bond: A high-paying bond with a lower credit rating than investment-grade corporate bonds, Treasury bonds, and municipal bonds. Because of the higher risk of default, these bonds pay a higher yield than investment-grade bonds. Also referred to as *junk bonds* or *below-investment-grade bonds* (i.e., an investment quality rating of BB+ or less from S&P, or Ba1 or less from Moody's). - CH6

"holder in due course" issue: A situation that arises when a third party, someone other than the payee or the depository bank, accepts or cashes a negotiable instrument (i.e., a check) in good faith that subsequently turns out to be fraudulent. This is a uniquely US problem that results from US law regarding negotiable instruments such as checks. - CH10

holding period: The expected period of time that a particular investor will hold a given investment or asset, generally the time between when the asset is purchased and when it is sold. - CH11

holding period yield: The yield computed for the time a security is held. However, yields are quoted on an annualized basis, so the holding period yield is adjusted by determining how many holding periods occur in one year and using that number to annualize the yield. - CH11

home currency: The currency of the country in which an entity's headquarters are located. In foreign exchange translation, if the functional currency of the subsidiary is the home currency, then the current method is used to translate financial statement line items to the parent company's currency. The current method translates all assets and liabilities at the current spot rate at the date of translation. - CH18

hybrid lockbox: A lockbox system (sometimes referred to as *wholetail*) that combines features of wholesale and retail lockboxes, and is configured, usually on a customized basis, to process both business-to-business and consumer-to-business payments. - CH10

hybrid security: A type of security that is generally created by combining the elements of two or more different types of securities into one. Typically, a hybrid will behave like a fixed-income security (bond) under certain circumstances and an equity security (stock) under other circumstances. - CH6

image processing: Processing of a document, such as a check, using an electronic image of the document in place of the original physical instrument. - CH4

image replacement document (IRD): In the United States, this is a paper reproduction of the original check that contains an image of the front and back of the original check and is the legal equivalent of the original check. - CH4

imaging technology: A technology that allows paper documents, such as checks and remittance advices, to be scanned, converted to digital images, and stored for subsequent distribution, handling, and processing. Also known as *image technology*. - CH10

impairment of capital rule: A regulatory restriction on the amount that an FI can lend or invest in a particular company or industry, based on the quality of the FI's existing loan portfolio. - CH2

imprest account: An account maintained at a fixed amount for a particular purpose or activity. Sometimes used as a petty cash account. - CH10

income bond: A type of bond that pays interest only if a company has profits, thus reducing some of the risk of issuing debt from a company's viewpoint. - CH6

income statement: A financial statement that summarizes revenues earned, expenses incurred, and gains and losses arising from conversions of assets and liabilities over an accounting period. Also called a *statement of earnings*, a *statement of operations*, or a *profit and loss statement*. - CH18

incumbency certificate: See *certificate of incumbency*. - CH7

indebtedness/debt ratio: A ratio used to measure the level of indebtedness (i.e., debt usage) by a company. - CH19

independent auditor: An external auditor with a certified public accounting designation that qualifies him or her to provide an auditor's report. May also be used to refer to a public accounting firm that employs qualified external auditors. - CH18

independent director: Under New York Stock Exchange standards, this is a director who has no material relationship with the listed company, either directly or as a partner, shareholder, or officer of the organization. - CH1

index bond: A type of bond that has interest rates tied to an economic index. Index bonds are used most often when a high level of price inflation is present or possible. - CH6

indirect purchases: Purchases of stores and supplies inventories, which are not used directly in a manufacturing/production process. Rather, they support the production process. - CH8

industrial bank: Also known as an *industrial loan company*, this is an FI with a limited scope of services. Industrial banks sell certificates that are labeled as *investment shares* and can also accept customer deposits. They then invest the proceeds in installment loans for consumers and small businesses. Industrial banks differ from commercial lenders because they accept deposits. They also differ from commercial banks because they do not offer checking accounts. Because of their limited scope of services, they do not fall under general banking regulatory authority, are locally chartered, and may be owned by nonbank holding companies. - CH3

industrial credit/capital company: A subsidiary of a large industrial corporation that raises funds in the commercial paper market and lends to companies or individuals. Also referred to as a *captive finance company*. - CH2

inflation premium: An adjustment to the base interest rate to account for projected inflation over the investment period. - CH11

informal bankruptcy: A form of bankruptcy handled outside the bankruptcy courts. In bankruptcy proceedings, it is possible to perform a reorganization or a liquidation informally. An informal reorganization typically involves a firm that is fundamentally sound, but is undergoing temporary financial difficulties. This is often done outside of bankruptcy in an agreed-upon write-off of some portion of the firm's debts by its creditors. - CH2

information float: The time between receiving good funds and the time the organization knows that it has the funds available and can actually make use of those funds. For a company receiving payments on accounts receivable, there may also be delays between the receipt of the payment and the posting of that payment to a customer's account. If the customer is close to its credit limit, this could, in turn, delay the ability of the company to sell more goods or services to that customer. - CH 8

in-house bank: The practice of having treasury become the main provider of banking services for all the company's operating entities. - CH8

initial public offering (IPO): The first sale of stock by a private company to the public. IPOs are often issued by smaller, younger companies seeking the capital to expand, but can also be done by large privately owned companies looking to become publicly traded. - CH6

in-sample validation: In the selection and validation of a forecasting model, this process tests a forecast for accuracy using the historical data used to develop it. If the forecast accurately predicts one data series from one or more other series, the relationships among the data series are deemed to be validated. When a forecast is initially developed, however, there typically is no other data available to test it. - CH13

insolvency: The inability to pay one's debts in a timely manner. The terms *bankruptcy* and *insolvency* are often used interchangeably, but in some jurisdictions, such as the United Kingdom, *bankruptcy* refers only to personal insolvency while the general term *insolvency* applies to both corporate and personal insolvency. - CH2

installment credit: A form of credit extension that requires a customer to make equal periodic payments, each of which contains principal and interest components. - CH8

insurance company: A type of nonbank financial institution that sells insurance products. From a corporate perspective, insurance companies are primarily long-term lenders to companies. They are significant investors in real estate, particularly commercial real estate (e.g., shopping centers), as well as long-term bonds. Insurance companies have started to compete with banks for short- and medium-term loans. They provide mortgage funding, leasing services, guaranteed investment contracts (similar to bank certificates of deposit, generally paying interest for one to five years), and universal life insurance policies with long-term savings features. - CH3

insurance management: A decision or problem-solving process that identifies possible risks and losses, and determines if insurance should be purchased against the risk of each loss and how much insurance is needed. - CH15

insurance risk management: A risk management technique in which financial protection (or reimbursement) for possible loss is purchased from another party in the form of insurance. It is essentially a method of transferring risk from one party to another. - CH15

intangible assets: Assets that lack physical substance and for which there is often a high degree of uncertainty concerning their future value. Examples are goodwill, trademarks, and patents. An intangible asset with a finite and useful life is amortized over its legal or useful life, but if the intangible asset has an indefinite useful life, it is not amortized. However, it must be evaluated annually for any decline in value, which must be charged against income when identified. - CH18

integrated ratio analysis: The practice of looking at various financial ratios in pairs or groups to gain better insight into a company's financial performance. - CH19

integrated/comprehensive accounts payable (A/P) service: A function in which a financial services provider (FSP) provides outsourced disbursement services to a company based on a transmission of payment information. The service allows a company to make multiple types of payments (e.g., check, electronic funds transfer, or card) through one channel. - CH10

interest rate forward: A type of forward contract, similar to a forward rate agreement, that allows its buyer to lock in today the future price of an asset, such as an interest-linked security. The buyer has to pay the agreed-upon price on the settlement date, whether or not the interest rate has moved in the buyer's favor. The seller is also required to deliver the asset on the settlement date, whatever that asset's price is in the spot market. - CH16

interest rate option: An option-type derivative where the payoff depends on the level of interest rates. There are three basic types of interest rate options: caps, floors, and collars. - CH16

interest rate risk: A type of risk that relates to changes in investment values and borrowing costs, and potentially to overall firm value, as interest rates change. - CH15

internal factoring: The practice of a company's internal factoring unit buying accounts receivable from the exporting unit and collecting funds from the importing unit. - CH8

internal rate of return (IRR): The discount rate that makes the net present value equal to zero or, equivalently, makes the present value (PV) of cash inflows equal to the PV of cash outflows. - CH19

International Accounting Standards Board (IASB): An international standards-setting body that determines general accounting standards and is made up of board members from nine countries. Based in London, England, the IASB's mission is to develop a single set of global accounting standards published as pronouncements called *International Financial Reporting Standards*. - CH11

International ACH Transaction (IAT): A US automated clearinghouse (ACH) format that is part of a payment transaction originating from, or transmitted to, an office of a financial agency located outside the territorial jurisdiction of the United States. *IAT* is the standard entry class (SEC) code for this format. - CH10

International Association of Deposit Insurers (IADI): An international not-for-profit organization formed to enhance the effectiveness of deposit insurance systems by promoting guidance and international cooperation. Members of IADI conduct research and produce guidance for the benefit of those jurisdictions seeking to establish or improve a deposit insurance system. Members also share their knowledge and expertise through participation in international conferences and other forums. - CH2

International Association of Insurance Supervisors (IAIS): The standards-setting group that represents insurance regulators and supervisory entities of some 190 jurisdictions in nearly 140 countries, constituting the great majority of the world's insurance premiums. - CH2

International Bank Account Number (IBAN): An international standard for identifying bank accounts across national borders. - CH3

International Chamber of Commerce (ICC) Publication 590: An ICC publication that deals with international standby practices and governs the administration of standby letters of credit. The current version is International Standby Practices (1998), or ISP98, which is contained in ICC Publication 590. - CH10

International Financial Reporting Standards (IFRS): A set of international accounting standards stating how particular types of transactions and other events should be reported in financial statements. IFRS are issued by the International Accounting Standards Board. - CH18

International Organization for Standardization (ISO): The world's largest developer of voluntary international standards for a variety of products and services, including financial reporting and payments. - CH3

International Organization for Standardization (ISO) 20022: An XML-based global messaging standard for the financial services industry whose intended use is transmitting information related to securities, payments, financial reporting, account management, international trade, and foreign exchange. - CH14

International Organization of Securities Commissions (IOSCO): An organization that is recognized as the international standard setter for securities markets. Its membership regulates more than 95% of the world's securities markets, and it is the primary international cooperative forum for securities market regulatory agencies. - CH2

International Standby Practices: ISP98: A set of rules that govern the administration of standby letters of credit (L/Cs). ISP98 is issued by the International Chamber of Commerce (ICC). See also *International Chamber of Commerce (ICC) Publication 590.* - CH10

International Swaps and Derivatives Association (ISDA): A trade organization made up of companies, dealers, and service providers that participate in the market for over-the-counter derivative instruments. - CH16

Internet-Initiated Entry (WEB): The US automated clearinghouse (ACH) format used for payments that are not pre-authorized, but are initiated by consumers using the Internet. *WEB* is the standard entry class (SEC) code for this format. - CH10

intracompany dividend: A type of dividend used in large companies with wholly owned subsidiaries to transfer profits from subsidiaries back to the parent company. - CH20

inventory conversion period: See *days' inventory.* - CH8

investment bank: A financial intermediary that performs a variety of services, such as (1) underwriting, by acting as an intermediary between an issuer of securities and the investing public; (2) facilitating mergers, acquisitions, divestitures, and other corporate reorganizations; and (3) acting as a broker/financial advisor for institutional clients. - CH3

investment banker: A professional who is responsible for assisting issuers in the design and placement of securities issuances. - CH6

invoicing float: The delay between the day that a customer places an order and the day that the customer actually receives an invoice for that order that can be processed for payment. - CH8

issuer credit rating: A credit rating that is an opinion on the obligor's (issuer's) overall capacity to meet its financial obligations. - CH11

issue-specific rating: A credit rating of a specific long- or short-term security that considers the attributes of the issuer, as well as the specific terms of the issue, the quality of the collateral, and the creditworthiness of the guarantors. - CH10

issuing bank: In a letter of credit (L/C) transaction, this is the buyer's (importer's) bank that issues the L/C in favor of the seller (exporter). - CH10

just-in-time (JIT) methodology: An inventory management approach that attempts to minimize inventory levels by reducing the costs or uncertainties that underlie the motives for holding inventory. - CH8

know your customer (KYC): The due diligence procedures that a financial institution must follow to determine or verify the identity of its customers. KYC is considered a key part of anti-money laundering compliance activities. - CH7

lagging: The executing of cross-border payments between subsidiaries after the scheduled payment date. Lagging is used when a subsidiary country's currency is expected to appreciate relative to the parent company's currency. - CH8

layering: The attempt to conceal the source of ownership of money by creating a complex series of transactions (layers) in order to provide anonymity. Used in relation to money laundering. - CH2

lead bank/institution: The financial institution that is responsible for managing a syndicated loan or securities sale that is funded by multiple financial institutions. - CH3

leading: The executing of cross-border payments between subsidiaries before the scheduled payment date. Leading is employed when a subsidiary country's currency is expected to depreciate relative to the parent company's currency. - CH8

ledger balance: A bank balance that reflects all entries to a bank account, regardless of whether the deposited items have been collected and are available for withdrawal. - CH4

ledger cutoff: The time of day when a bank deposit must be received in order to be posted to the ledger balance of the depositor's account. - CH4

legal risk: A type of operational risk that relates to legal actions against a company. Given the increasingly litigious business environment, a significant source of external operational risk is potential lawsuits or other legal actions instigated by customers, trade partners, or governmental agencies and regulators. Insurance may be used to mitigate this risk in some cases. - CH15

less predictable cash flow: In the cash flow forecasting process, this is a cash flow component that is difficult to forecast. Examples of these types of cash flows would be those related to sales of a new product, unexpected repairs, pending settlement of insurance claims, or the cost of settling a strike. - CH13

letter of credit (L/C): A promise by the issuing bank to pay a certain amount under specific circumstances. A commercial L/C (see definition earlier in glossary) is related to a business transaction, while a standby letter of credit (see definition later in the glossary) is typically used as a guarantee. - CH10

leveraged buyout (LBO): A type of transaction in which an entity buys or acquires a firm using a significant amount of borrowed funds in the process. In many cases, the assets of the acquired company may be used as collateral for the borrowed funds. - CH20

liability insurance: Any type of insurance policy that protects against damage to other parties that can arise from product defects; business practices; accidents; actions of the organization's employees, officers, or board of directors; and general negligence in the operation of the organization. Liability insurance typically includes defense costs in the event of litigation. Intentional damage and contractual liabilities are typically not covered in these types of policies. - CH15

lien: A legal claim on an asset or assets. In most types of secured lending, the lender has a lien or legal claim on the assets used as collateral in the event it cannot take physical possession of the assets. - CH6

line of credit: An agreement in which the lender gives the borrower access to funds up to a maximum amount over a specific period of time. Lines of credit are usually revolving, meaning the borrower may borrow, repay, and borrow funds again up to the established limit during the commitment period. - CH11

liquidating dividend: A dividend that is paid out of capital rather than earnings. This sometimes occurs when a company or one of its divisions is going out of business and management decides to pay off shareholders through a liquidating dividend. As the name implies, the company liquidates the remaining assets (capital) of the failed company or division to pay the dividend. This approach may also be used by the acquiring company in a leveraged buyout to liquidate the acquired company in order to meet debt service requirements. - CH20

liquidity: The ability of an organization to convert assets into cash quickly and without a significant risk of loss. - CH17

liquidity management flows: Cash flows that are employed to use an organization's liquidity reserves in the most effective manner. If there is a surplus of funds, treasury may either (1) invest them in suitable investments, or (2) pay down existing debt. Alternatively, if there is a shortage of funds, then treasury may either (1) sell off investments, or (2) draw on available debt sources (e.g., credit lines or commercial paper issuance). - CH8

liquidity premium: An adjustment to the base interest rate to account for the lack of liquidity on an investment. - CH11

liquidity risk: A type of risk that is typically divided into two areas: *funding liquidity risk* and *asset liquidity risk*. *Funding liquidity risk* relates primarily to an organization's ability to raise necessary cash to meet its obligations as they come due. It is often linked to the ability to raise capital (both short- and long-term) in a timely manner, and it typically is managed by holding marketable securities or open (i.e., available) lines of credit. *Asset liquidity* risk is defined earlier in the glossary. - CH15

liquidity/working capital ratio: A type of ratio that measures the firm's ability to meet its payment obligations on short-term debt and helps ascertain whether cash is being used effectively. - CH19

loan covenant: A requirement included in a loan agreement that serves to protect the lender. Loan covenants impose either restrictions (known as *restrictive or negative covenants*) and/or obligations (known as *affirmative or positive covenants*) on the part of an organization's management. They typically have a significant impact on an organization's financial decision making. - CH11

loan participation: A type of lending arrangement in which a financial institution purchases an interest in another lender's credit facility. The purchaser is called a *participant*, and the seller is the *lead institution*. The participant does not have a separate note and has only an indirect relationship with the borrower. - CH11

loan sales: An offering of commercial banks that involves the structuring of lending facilities so that short-term loans can be sold to other banks and investors. - CH3

loan syndication: A type of lending arrangement in which multiple financial institutions share the funding of a single credit facility. The syndicate, or group of lenders, is led by an agent who acts as the intermediary between the company and the syndicate to negotiate credit terms and documentation, make advances and collect payments on the loan, and disseminate information. - CH11

lockbox system: A collection tool in which a financial institution or third-party vendor receives payments at specified post office box (lockbox) addresses, processes the remittances, and credits the payments into a payee's account. - CH10

London Interbank Offered Rate (LIBOR): An interest rate at which banks can borrow funds, in marketable size, from other banks in the London interbank market. LIBOR is fixed on a daily basis by the British Bankers' Association. LIBOR is derived from a filtered average of the world's most creditworthy banks' interbank deposit rates for larger loans with maturities between overnight and one full year. - CH11

long-term debt to capital ratio: A type of debt management ratio that measures the percentage of a company's capital (where *capital* is defined as the sum of long-term debt and equity) that is provided by long-term debt. It is computed as long-term debt divided by long-term debt plus equity. - CH19

long-term forecasting: A type of cash forecasting in which the forecast covers any period beyond one year. It takes into consideration projections of long-term sales and expenditures, as well as market factors. - CH13

long-term investment: Any investment with a term greater than one year. See *capital investment*. - CH12

magnetic ink character recognition (MICR): A data capture process that translates the machine-readable information on a check into a digital data entry. See also *MICR line*. - CH4

mail float: The time interval or delay between the day a payment (and any related remittance information) is mailed and the day it is received by a payee or at a payee's processing site. - CH8

maker: The entity that creates a check or other negotiable instrument. - CH4

market risk: A type of risk that involves the possibility that fluctuations in financial market prices and rates will reduce the value of a security or a portfolio. It is usually divided into general risk (i.e., risk related to overall market rates and conditions) and firm-specific risk (i.e., risk related solely to an individual firm). - CH15

market value per share: The current price at which a share of stock is traded. Though this is not technically part of the accounting statements, it is often included in reports issued by a company and various financial reporting services. - CH6

master account: An account used by an organization to receive funds from collection accounts or to provide funding for disbursement accounts as part of a zero balance account (ZBA) arrangement. These accounts are sometimes referred to as *concentration accounts*. - CH10

master budget: An annual budget for an entire organization. The master budget has two chief components: (1) the operating budget, and (2) the financial budget. - CH19

matching process: An internal control method that involves the matching of an invoice to the original purchase order to help confirm the order was placed and that the invoice complies with the agreed terms. A further match against receiving records ensures the order was fulfilled. - CH8

material adverse change (MAC) clause: A clause in a loan agreement that allows a lender to refuse funding or declare a borrower to be in default, even if all agreements are in full compliance, if the lender believes a material adverse change has occurred in the borrower's condition. - CH6

materiality: An accounting concept that involves determining the significance of the impact of information on the financial position of the entity being reported. In most accounting applications, there is usually a significant degree of judgment involved in the preparation of the accounts. Where decisions are required about the appropriateness of a particular accounting judgment, the materiality convention suggests that this should only be an issue if the judgment is *significant* or *material* to the presentation of the accounts. The concept of materiality is therefore an important issue for auditors of financial accounts. - CH18

maturity premium: An adjustment to the base interest rate of a longer-term security to account for the increased price risk created by the longer maturity. - CH11

maturity-matching financing strategy: A current asset financing strategy that involves using long-term financing (e.g., debt and equity) to finance permanent current assets and fixed assets. Short-term financing is used to finance fluctuating current assets. - CH8

maturity-matching investment strategy: An investment strategy that involves matching the maturity of an investment to the future need for funds. - CH6

medium-term forecasting: A type of cash flow forecasting in which the forecasts are for periods of one to 12 months. These forecasts are an integral part of cash budgeting. They project the inflows (e.g., collections from sales and other sources of funds) and outflows (e.g., expenses and other uses of funds) on a monthly basis. They are used to determine the company's need for short-term credit or the availability of funds for short-term investing. They also serve as a benchmark for performance by comparing actual cash flows to projected cash flows based on the cash budget. - CH13

memo posting: The practice of noting a credit or debit entry early in the day when the actual credit or debit will not be applied to the account until after the close of business. - CH10

merchant acquirer: The financial institution that processes and settles payment card transactions on behalf of a merchant. - CH4

merchant services: The term typically used to describe the products offered by a bank, Internet service provider, or other firm (referred to as a *merchant processor*) that processes credit and debit card transactions. While the term principally refers to the acceptance and processing of card transactions, it also often includes ancillary services such as returns and adjustments, point-of-sale (POS) terminals, supplies, and customer support. - CH10

message authentication: An electronic commerce security element that provides the ability to know, with a reasonable amount of certainty, who sent or received a message. - CH14

MICR line: The machine-readable information on the bottom of a check. A MICR line is printed using a special font and magnetic ink. *MICR* is an acronym for *magnetic ink character recognition*. While initially read using special magnetic scanning equipment, many MICR lines are now processed using optical character recognition. - CH4

middleware: Computer-based software that links two different applications. - CH8

mobile banking: The provision of banking and financial services with the help of mobile telecommunication devices, such as mobile phones and tablets. - CH14

mobile payments: Electronic payments made using mobile devices, such as mobile phones or tablets. - CH14

Monetary Control Act: See *Depository Institution Deregulation and Monetary Control Act of 1980 (DIDMCA)*. - CH2

monetary policy: Government policy related to monitoring and controlling a country's money supply and interest rates. - CH2

money laundering: Any financial transaction that generates an asset or a value as the result of an illegal act, which may involve actions such as tax evasion or false accounting. - CH2

money market: That part of the global financial market that deals with financial instruments that are easily converted to cash (highly liquid) and have very short maturities, typically one year or less. In addition, most money market instruments are debt-type securities, which are also known as *fixed-income securities*. - CH5

money market deposit account (MMDA): A type of demand deposit account that pays an unregulated rate of interest determined by individual institutions. Generally, there can be no more than six withdrawals per calendar month or statement cycle, no more than three of which can be by check, draft, or debit card. - CH3

money market fund (MMF): A commingled pool of money market instruments, typically held by banks or investment firms, in which fund investors have an ownership interest. The funds may be offered in the local currency or, where allowed by local regulators, in a foreign currency. They generally have a net asset value set at one unit of the currency of the offering. Known as *unit trusts* in the United Kingdom and Europe. - CH5

money market yield (MMY): A calculation for restating semiannual, quarterly, or monthly discount bond or note yields into an annual yield. This type of yield is calculated on a 360-day year basis, while the bond equivalent yield is based on a 365-day year. - CH11

money order: A prepaid instrument issued by various third parties such as banks, postal services, or consumer outlets (e.g., convenience stores and check-cashing agencies), where the purchaser is the instrument's payor and the money order is the obligation of the issuer. - CH4

Monte Carlo simulation: A type of simulation/analytical technique in which a large number of simulations are run using random quantities selected from a probability distribution of values for specified variables. The resulting probability distribution is analyzed to infer which values are most likely to occur. - CH15

monthly billing: A term of sale whereby the seller issues a monthly statement covering all invoices prior to a cutoff date, typically toward the end of each month. - CH8

mortgage bond: A type of bond used to finance specific assets pledged as security against the issue. Mortgage bonds usually include substantial financial covenants or indenture agreements. - CH6

mortgage-backed security (MBS): A type of asset-backed security that uses pools of mortgages (mainly residential) as the source of cash flows to the investors. - CH5

multicurrency account: A special arrangement between a bank and a company, in which the bank lets the customer receive or make payments in a range of currencies from a single account or multiple subsidiary accounts. - CH8

multicurrency bond: A type of bond that is usually issued as (1) a currency option bond that allows investors to choose among several predetermined currencies, or (2) a currency cocktail bond that is denominated in a standard basket of several currencies (e.g., special drawing rights). - CH6

multifactor authentication: An authentication method for information technology and network purposes requiring the presence of different factors of authentication: (1) something the individual knows, such as a password or personal fact; (2) something the individual has, such as a token or a cell phone; and (3) something the individual is, such as a fingerprint or facial scan. - CH14

multilateral netting system: A type of netting system that is similar to a bilateral system but it involves more than two subsidiaries. Each subsidiary informs a central treasury management center of all planned cross-border payments through an electronic system. Multilateral netting is used primarily for intracompany transactions. - CH8

multiple-drawee check: A check that can be presented for payment at more than one bank. Normally, both bank names appear on the check as drawees. Also known as a *payable-if-desired check*. - CH10

municipal bond (muni): A sub-sovereign bond issued by a municipality, typically in the United States and usually in the form of a general obligation or revenue bond. General obligation bonds are paid from the proceeds of general tax revenues. Alternatively, revenue bonds are linked directly to, and repaid from, the revenues generated from specific public projects or services (e.g., stadiums, toll roads and bridges, or public utilities). Most municipal bonds are exempt from federal and, in some cases, state and local income taxes. - CH6

municipal securities: Types of debt (bonds or notes) issued by city, county, or state government entities that generally have some type of income tax exemption for any interest paid on them. Commonly called *munis*. - CH3

mutual fund: A company that brings together money from many people and invests it in stocks, bonds, or other assets. The combined holdings of stocks, bonds, or other assets the fund owns are known as its *portfolio*. - CH5

NACHA, the Electronic Payments Association: A US membership organization of financial institutions and other stakeholders that establishes and administers the rules, standards, and procedures that enable members to exchange automated clearinghouse (ACH) payments on a national basis. The organization also levies fines for violations of the rules. NACHA membership includes a number of regional ACH associations that provide various educational, rules guidance, and other support services to their local members. Formerly known as the National Automated Clearing House Association. - CH4

National Book-Entry System (NBES): A real-time gross settlement system used for the transfer of US Treasury, government agency, and other securities. - CH5

National Credit Union Administration (NCUA): An independent US federal agency that charters and supervises federal credit unions. The NCUA is backed by the full faith and credit of the US government. It also operates the National Credit Union Share Insurance Fund, insuring the savings of account holders in all federal credit unions and many state-chartered credit unions. - CH2

nationalization: A government takeover of all companies in a particular industry, often involving ore extraction, petroleum, transportation, or power generation and distribution businesses. - CH7

nationally recognized statistical rating organizations (NRSROs): Companies that assign credit ratings for issuers of certain types of short- and long-term debt obligations, as well as for the debt instruments themselves. Ratings can be on either a solicited or unsolicited basis. Also known as *credit rating agencies*. - CH11

natural disaster risk: A type of risk related to losses resulting from naturally occurring events, such as storms, floods, or earthquakes. Natural disaster events leave organizations open to possible operational risk. These events could range from a temporary power outage to a major earthquake or hurricane. Every organization should have a contingency business resumption plan in place to manage and recover from impacts of such events. This plan should also be tested on a regular basis. - CH15

natural hedge: The practice of offsetting foreign asset exposures effectively by borrowing funds to finance the assets in the same currency. This approach reduces the net exposure of the parent company. Also called a *balance sheet hedge*. - CH16

negotiating bank: In a letter of credit transaction, this is the bank that examines the documents presented by the beneficiary, receives payment from the issuing bank, and pays the beneficiary. - CH10

net asset value (NAV): A value that represents the price per share of a mutual fund or an exchange-traded fund. It is generally calculated as the total value of all the securities or assets in the fund (less any liabilities) divided by the number of shares outstanding. For most funds, the NAV will fluctuate as the market values of the securities in the fund portfolio change. The primary exception is a money market fund, which generally has a fixed NAV equivalent to one unit of the currency of denomination. - CH5

net present value (NPV): A type of financial analysis, this value is calculated by netting the present value (PV) of anticipated cash inflows with the PV of cash outflows. - CH19

net profit margin: A performance ratio that shows the percentage of profits earned after all expenses and taxes are deducted from revenues. It is defined as net income divided by revenues. Also known as *return on sales* or *return on revenues*. - CH19

net terms: A term of sale whereby the seller specifies a net due date by which the buyer must pay in full. - CH8

netting: An internal company (intracompany) payables system that is designed to reduce the number of cross-border payments among company units through the elimination or consolidation of funds denominated in different currencies. - CH8

noninsurance: An approach to risk retention, this technique involves relying on normal revenues to pay for small, normal losses as current expenses. Noninsurance is appropriate for losses that an organization can absorb readily as costs of doing business, but not for highly disruptive, potentially ruinous accidents. - CH15

non-repetitive (free-form) wire: A type of wire transfer where both the debit and credit parties can be changed for each transaction. As a result, additional security measures are typically required. Examples of such measures are callbacks, secondary levels of approval, and segregation of duties. - CH10

non-repudiation: The inability of the purported maker or originator of a statement, document, or payment to challenge the validity of the original item. The term may also be used to refer to the inability of a receiver to deny having received the item. - CH14

nonresident account: An account with a financial institution that is owned by a nonresident of the country in which the account is held. - CH3

not-for-profit (NFP) organization: An organization that does not earn profits for its owners and that serves specific constituencies who pay for some or all the benefits provided. All money earned or donated is used to further the organization's stated objectives. For example, professional associations (e.g., the Association for Financial Professionals) charge their members dues and raise revenues from various fees for services and from sponsorships for conferences. Other nongovernmental NFPs (e.g., many United Way agencies) rely entirely on altruism and grants to fund their operations. - CH18

notional pooling: A type of pooling that requires a company's subsidiaries to use branches of the same bank. All excess and deficit balances in the company's subsidiary accounts are summed each day to calculate the net interest earned or due. Funds are not actually transferred; rather, they are simply totaled for the purpose of calculating interest. - CH10

notional principal: The base amount of a financial transaction, used to calculate interest payments. The notional prinicipal is never actually exchanged, but is only used for calculation purposes, hence the term *notional*. In an interest rate swap, the notional principal is the dollar amount used to calculate the interest rate payments that are exchanged as part of the transaction. - CH16

off-balance-sheet arrangement (OBSA): A US Securities and Exchange Commission (SEC) term used to refer to any transaction, agreement, or other contractual arrangement that obligates the reporting company but does not appear on the balance sheet. It is intended to include off-balance-sheet arrangements for which a company may have contingent liabilities or obligations that are not readily apparent to an investor. These arrangements must be disclosed in the discussion portion of financial statements. - CH2

off-balance-sheet financing: A type of arrangement designed to provide financing that does not appear on the balance sheet. This is one type of off-balance-sheet arrangement. Examples of off-balance-sheet financing include joint ventures, research and development partnerships, sales of receivables (factoring), and operating leases (rather than purchases of capital equipment). - CH6

Office of Foreign Assets and Control (OFAC): An office of the US Department of the Treasury that administers and enforces economic and trade sanctions based on US foreign policy and national security goals. Its objective is to identify and target threats to the national security, foreign policy, or economy of the United States. - CH2

Office of the Comptroller of the Currency (OCC): A bureau of the US Treasury Department that was established by Congress in 1863 to regulate the national banking system. It is the primary chartering authority and regulator for national banks. - CH2

official bank check: A type of check that is issued by the bank that draws on the bank's own funds. Also known as a *cashier's check*. - CH4

ongoing validation: In the selection and validation of a forecasting model, this process involves using continuing feedback from projected versus actual comparisons and allows continuous evaluation and improvement of the forecast. - CH13

on-us check clearing: A type of check-clearing process that involves a single bank and occurs when a payee deposits a check in an account at the same bank on which it is drawn. - CH4

on-we check clearing: A type of check-clearing process that occurs when checks are deposited at a financial institution that are drawn on related financial institutions or on financial institutions that share a common check-processing system, thus eliminating the need to clear the checks through another bank. - CH4

open account (open book credit): A form of credit extension that is the most common type of commercial trade credit. A seller issues an invoice as formal evidence of the obligation and records the sale as an account receivable. The buyer is billed for each transaction by an invoice and/or monthly statement. Full payment of invoiced amounts is expected within the specified credit terms unless certain discounts or deductions are available to the buyer. A buyer's creditworthiness is reviewed periodically, but the buyer does not need to apply for credit each time it places an order. - CH8

open item system: A cash application process most commonly used in business-to-business sales. Each invoice sent to a customer is recorded in the accounts receivable file. When a payment is received, it is matched with the specific invoices being paid. Any payment discrepancies are noted (e.g., discounts, allowances, adjustments, or returns). - CH8

opening cash position: The sum of the available balances in a company's bank accounts. It is adjusted for the day's anticipated cash inflows and outflows to arrive at the projected closing cash position. - CH13

open-loop card: A credit card—either bank-issued credit card, American Express, or Discover—that is accepted anywhere the card logo is displayed. - CH4

operating budget: A component of a master budget, this budget focuses on day-to-day operations. Also known as a *profit plan*. - CH19

operating cycle: A representation of the flow of funds through a company from the acquisition of raw materials, through the production cycle and the sale of products or services, and finally to the collection of payments from customers. - CH8

operating lease (service lease): A type of lease that is established in such a way that the lessor may maintain the equipment and retain ownership thereof at the end of the lease. These arrangements are often done on an off-balance-sheet basis, meaning that lease payments are reflected only on the income statement. - CH20

operating leverage: A concept that examines the responsiveness of operating profits to changes in sales. Operating leverage is determined by the extent to which fixed costs are used in a company's operating cost structure. The higher the proportion of fixed costs, the higher the company's operating leverage. - CH19

operating profit margin: A performance ratio that shows the percentage of revenue remaining after both the cost of goods sold and all operating expenses are deducted from revenue. It is computed as earnings before interest and taxes (EBIT) divided by revenues. - CH19

operational risk: The risk of direct and indirect losses resulting either from external events that impact an organization's operations or from inadequate and failed internal processes, people, and systems. Operational risk can be a significant cause of financial loss. - CH15

opportunity cost: The value of the best alternative not taken when two or more mutually exclusive alternatives are available. - CH8

optical character recognition (OCR): A processing method for data entry that reads preprinted information on remittance documents and creates a digital data file. - CH4

optimal capital structure: The mix of long-term debt and equity that produces the lowest overall weighted average cost of capital for a firm. - CH20

option: A contract giving the buyer of the contract the right, but not the obligation, to buy or sell a fixed amount of an underlying asset at a fixed price on or before a specified date. - CH16

option premium: The price paid for an option contract. - CH16

order-to-cash timeline: The process or steps involved in converting orders or sales of goods into cash or good funds in the merchant's bank account. - CH8

originating depository financial institution (ODFI): In an automated clearinghouse transaction, this is the financial institution that initiates the transaction on the originator's behalf. - CH4

origination: An investment bank function that involves consultation with a company raising funds about the characteristics of a securities issue and any underlying documents. The investment bank also monitors market conditions and advises the company about the best time to bring the issue to market in order to maximize the price per issued share and the amount of funds the firm wishes to raise. - CH3

origination desk: A subset of trading professionals who are charged with evaluating, pricing, and managing the placement of new security issues. Also known as *originators*. - CH6

originator: (1) The party that creates an automated clearinghouse (ACH) transaction. (2) In investment banking, a subset of trading professionals who are charged with evaluating, pricing, and managing the placement of new security issues. Also known as an *origination desk*. - CH4,CH6

other-than-temporary impairment (OTTI): A classification for securities that are impaired (i.e., market value is less than adjusted cost) and whose impairment is not or cannot be expected to be cured in the foreseeable future. If a security is considered to be temporarily impaired due to market or credit conditions, then there is considerable flexibility in accounting for that security. If, on the other hand, the impairment is deemed to be other-than-temporary, then the Financial Accounting Standards Board has provided amended guidelines (ASC Codification Topic 325: *Investments—Other*) for the valuation of these securities. This forms the basis for OTTI. - CH11

out-of-sample validation: In the selection and validation of a forecasting model, this process tests the forecast using data that were not used to develop it. - CH13

outsourcing: Utilizing a third party to perform all or part of a core function. - CH1

overdraft: A situation that occurs when items are presented against a demand deposit account in excess of the balance in that account. - CH3

over-leveraged: A term used to describe a company that has taken on too much debt. - CH8

over-the-counter (OTC) market: A type of market that is more decentralized than a formal securities exchange. OTC markets also rely upon electronic communication to conduct trading activity in an auction-style market between participating brokers and dealers. Government, municipal, and corporate debt, and some equity issuances that are not traded on exchanges, are sometimes traded in the OTC markets. - CH6

par value: An arbitrary amount (usually stated in the corporate charter) that indicates the minimum amount stockholders have put up (or must put up) in the event of bankruptcy. - CH6

patterning: The practice of using a number of smaller cash transactions to avoid suspicion by regulatory authorities, typically as part of a money laundering scheme. - CH2

payable through draft (PTD): A payment instrument resembling a check that is drawn against the payor rather than the bank. It is handled like a check through the clearing process, but the responsibility for paying the draft lies with the payor, referred to as the *drawee* in the case of drafts. - CH4

payable-if-desired (PID) check: A check that can be presented for payment at more than one bank. Normally, both bank names appear on the check as drawees. Also known as a *multiple-drawee check*. - CH10

payables conversion period: See *days' payables*. - CH8

payback period: The number of years required to recover the initial investment in an asset or project. - CH19

payee: In a payment system, the one receiving the payment. - CH4

payee positive pay: A positive pay service that matches against the payee field, in addition to the serial number and amount of a check, in an effort to detect an altered payee. - CH10

paying bank: In a payment clearing process, the bank or financial institution where the payor's account resides. The paying bank processes the value transfer on the payor's behalf. - CH4

Payment Card Industry Data Security Standard (PCI DSS): A worldwide information security standard defined by the Payment Card Industry Security Standards Council. The standard was created to help organizations that process card payments prevent payment card fraud through increased controls around the data they hold and exchange. The standard applies to all organizations that store, process, or transmit cardholder information from any card branded with the logo of one of the major card brands. - CH4

payment card risk: A type of risk that arises due to the theft of card details and misuse of these details. Merchants that accept mail, phone, or Internet orders made with card payments may mitigate their risk of fraud by using an address verification service that matches the address provided by the cardholder with the account billing address on record with the issuer. - CH10

payment float: The period of time between the day that a bill or invoice is sent/received (depending on the perspective of the seller or buyer) and the day that payment is actually credited to the biller's bank account. - CH8

payment system: A series of processes and technologies (a payment instrument, a clearing channel, and a settlement mechanism) that transfer monetary value from one party to another. - CH4

payment systems risk (PSR): A term that encompasses all the different risks that can occur in a payment system. There are many components to PSR, including (1) systemic risk, which is the risk of the entire payment system collapsing due to the failure of one or more large financial institutions; (2) settlement risk, which is the risk that the counterparty to a transaction may fail to fund its side of the transaction; and (3) fraud risk, which is the risk of fraud from internal or external parties. - CH10

payor: In a payment system, the one making the payment. - CH4

payroll card (pay card): A prefunded stored-value card used to replace payroll checks or direct deposit of payroll. - CH4

pension fund: A fund that invests contributions from employers and/or employees for the future retirement needs of the employees. - CH2

pension plan: A type of retirement plan, usually tax-exempt, wherein an employer makes contributions toward a pool of funds set aside for an employee's future benefit. The pool of funds is then invested on the employee's behalf, allowing the employee to receive benefits upon retirement. - CH2

percentage-of-sales method: A medium-term cash forecasting technique that involves projecting financial statements based on the historical relationship between sales and liquid balance sheet accounts that tend to change in value along with sales. Cash, accounts receivable, inventory, and accounts payable are the more important accounts. Account size (e.g., cash or inventory) is expressed as a percentage of sales. This percentage is then used in conjunction with forecasted sales to produce a forecast of account size. - CH13

performance guarantee: A type of guarantee requested by a lender for a loan to a subsidiary of another organization. In some cases, the lender may ask for specific performance guarantees relative to the assets being financed. Under a full guarantee, the parent fully guarantees performance by the subsidiary. Under a best-efforts guarantee, the parent agrees to use its best efforts to persuade the subsidiary to perform, but it does not guarantee subsidiary performance. - CH6

performance measurement: The ongoing monitoring and evaluating of the performance of an investment, portfolio, individual, department, or organization. - CH7

performance ratio: A type of ratio that measures profit relative to the amount of revenue or the level of financing. - CH19

per-occurrence basis: A method for determining the deductible on an insurance policy claim, where the deductible applies for each occurrence during the policy period. - CH15

personal guarantee: A type of guarantee in which a lender may require a personal pledge on the part of the owner or other principals in a business before granting a loan to the business. This is more common for smaller, privately held companies. - CH6

Phoenix-Hecht's *The Blue Book of Bank Prices*: An annually published comparison of key bank service charges. - CH7

physical and electronic security risk: Risk related to unauthorized physical or electronic access to premises or information. Many organizations require physical security for their premises and employees to help prevent physical or electronic access to critical information (e.g., identity theft), as well as to ensure employees' safety. Security measures also may include biometric systems, using such technologies as fingerprint, face, or iris (eye) recognition to control physical access to facilities or key equipment. Physical security is especially important for financial institutions, utilities, and defense contractors. - CH15

physical pooling: A type of pooling that requires the use of a single currency because balances are physically transferred out of subaccounts and into a main account on a daily basis. This type of pooling can be used in cross-border structures. - CH10

Point-of-Purchase (POP) Check Conversion: A type of check conversion that occurs when customers' checks are scanned at the cash register (point of purchase, or POP), capturing the account information from the magnetic ink character recognition (MICR) line on the check. The MICR line data are converted into an automated clearinghouse (ACH) debit, and the check is voided and returned to the customer, who then signs a debit authorization in the form of a register receipt. Also, a US ACH format for the same process. *POP* is the standard entry class (SEC) code for this format. - CH10

political risk: A term applied to a variety of actions that a government may take that negatively impact a company's operations and/or value. It includes the risk that a company's operations in a foreign country may be nationalized or expropriated by the government of that country. - CH6

pooling: A typical method of cash concentration in countries where banks can pay interest on excess demand deposit balances and charge interest on deficit balances. - CH10

positive pay: A disbursement service used to combat payment (primarily check, but increasingly ACH) fraud, wherein a company transmits a file of payment information to the disbursement bank either at or before the time of the physical distribution of checks or anticipated ACH debits. The bank matches check serial numbers and dollar amounts of checks presented for payment against the issue database and pays only those checks or ACH transactions that match all relevant criteria. Any exceptions are conveyed to the company for its decision whether to pay or return the item. - CH10

positive pay with payee: See *payee positive pay*. - CH10

prearranged bankruptcy: A type of bankruptcy in which management arranges a tentative deal with some of the creditors or parties, but not with all of them. Generally, these deals are done on an informal basis and are not legally binding. - CH2

Prearranged Payment and Deposit (PPD): A US automated clearinghouse (ACH) format that acts as the payment application by which consumers authorize a company or a financial institution to credit or debit an account for normally recurring payments in fixed amounts. *PPD* is the standard entry class (SEC) code for this format. - CH10

pre-authorized draft: A payment instrument that authorizes the payee to draw/draft against the payor's account. Also known as a *remotely created check (RCC)*. - CH4

predictable cash flow: In the cash flow forecasting process, this is a cash flow component that can be predicted with reasonable accuracy. - CH13

preemptive right: A shareholder right that provides existing shareholders the first right to purchase shares of any new stock issue on a pro rata basis and based on the proportion of shares owned. - CH20

preferred stock: An investment security that is a type of equity, but is different from common stock in terms of stockholder rights and dividend payment streams. In terms of cash flows, it is more like debt than equity because of the fixed dividend payments. Unlike with debt, however, a company does not risk bankruptcy by missing a preferred stock dividend. Another difference is that dividend payments on preferred stock do not have the tax deductibility feature that interest payments on debt do; therefore, the cost is generally much higher than that of a similar debt issue. - CH6

prepackaged (prepac) bankruptcy: A type of bankruptcy in which management files with the US Securities and Exchange Commission a formal plan that all classes of creditors have voted on and accepted. Essentially, the firm goes to court with all of the details worked out and with everyone agreeing to the plan. - CH2

present value (PV): The value at the present time of anticipated future cash flows or payments. - CH9

price/interest rate risk: A type of risk that arises when interest rates change for securities that are identical or nearly identical to portfolio securities. Securities with longer maturities generally are subject to greater price risk than similar securities with shorter maturities because their market values are more responsive to changes in market interest rates. - CH5

primary market: A financial market that offers newly issued debt and equity securities to investors when firms or government units sell securities to raise funds. - CH6

private equity: An investment of either common or preferred stock in an operating company that is not publicly traded on an exchange. This investment sometimes involves the acquisition of an entire company. - CH2

private market: A financial market for private, or direct, placement, in which securities are offered and sold to a limited number of investors and not offered to the general public. The investment banking firm, acting as a broker to bring the issuer and investors together, meets with prospective buyers and confirms the details of the offering. - CH6

private placement: The practice of the direct sale of long-term loans to institutional investors, such as insurance companies and hedge funds. - CH3

process risk: A type of internal operational risk related to an organization's processes. Many organizations experience substantial exposure to losses related to the processes employed in day-to-day business operations. Process risk can arise from any functional area of a business, including procurement, manufacturing, sales, or fulfillment. The risk usually comes from a lack of proper controls or the failure of employees to follow procedures. - CH15

processing float: The time interval or delay between the time the payee or the payee's processing site receives the payment and the time the payment (typically a check) is deposited into the payee's account. - CH8

profitability index (PI): A cost/benefit measurement that is similar to net present value, PI is a ratio of the present value gained to the cost required to obtain that value. It shows value gained per dollar of investment. PI is calculated as present value of cash inflows divided by present value of cash outflows. - CH19

project financing: A type of financing that applies to large projects, often in the energy area (e.g., energy exploration, refineries, and utility power plants). Project financing is also used for private infrastructure (e.g., stadiums, shopping centers, toll roads, and commercial or residential developments). - CH6

projected closing cash position: A forecast of the day's ending cash position that is determined by taking the day's opening available bank balance(s), adding any expected settlements in the collection (lockbox, wire, and automated clearinghouse) and concentration accounts (depository banks), and deducting any projected disbursement totals. A projected closing cash position statement is also known as a *daily cash forecast* or merely a *cash report*. - CH13

promissory note: The legal portion of a debt contract; an unconditional promise to pay a specified amount plus interest at a defined rate either on demand or on a certain date. - CH6

proof of deposit (POD): An availability assignment method used in banking in which availability is assigned to each check as it is processed. - CH4

property insurance: A type of insurance that provides for reimbursement in the event of a loss of or damage to some type of asset (e.g., buildings, equipment, or inventory). Policies often cover the replacement value of the items in question, paying the costs of completely replacing those assets at their current market prices rather than at their historical or book value. - CH15

proxy: An instrument by which a shareholder can assign his/her right to vote at the annual meeting to another individual. - CH20

public-key infrastructure (PKI): A data encryption methodology designed to provide security over traditionally unsecure networks, such as the Internet. PKI involves the use of dual keys: a public key and a private key. - CH14

purchase price: The price that an investor pays for a security. This price is important as it is the main component in calculating the returns achieved by the investor. - CH11

purchase-to-pay timeline: The time from the purchase of raw materials, retail goods, or services until payment is received and collected. - CH8

purchasing card: A payment card, typically a credit card, used by a business for the purchase of supplies, inventory, equipment, and service contracts. Also known as a *procurement card* or *p-card*. - CH4

put option: A type of option contract that gives the contract owner the right, but not the obligation, to sell (put) the underlying asset to the contract writer at a fixed price through the delivery date. - CH16

qualified institutional buyer (QIB): In US law, this is an investor that is specifically recognized as being financially sophisticated and needing less protection than typical consumers. QIBs are primarily institutional investors that manage at least $100 million in securities, and can be financial institutions, pension funds, corporations, insurance companies, investment companies, or employee benefit plans, or an entity owned entirely by qualified investors. Known outside the United States as a *qualified institutional investor (QII)*. - CH6

quick ratio (acid test ratio): A liquidity ratio that is calculated as cash plus short-term investments and accounts receivable, divided by total current liabilities. It is also known as the *acid test ratio* because it is a more stringent measure of liquidity than the current ratio. - CH9

RAROC: See *risk-adjusted return on capital*. - CH19

ratings trigger: A clause in a financing agreement that requires a company to maintain a certain credit rating. Failure to maintain a specified rating may trigger a higher loan rate or force the company to post additional collateral, take another specified action, or pay back the debt in full. - CH20

real estate mortgage investment conduit (REMIC): An entity formed to pool mortgage loans based on risk and issue mortgage-backed bonds or other securities to investors. - CH5

real risk-free rate of interest: The rate demanded by savers (or investors) to compensate for delaying their use of the money today, in the absence of any risk or inflation, for a one-year maturity. - CH11

real-time gross settlement system (RTGS): A type of payment system in which each transaction results in a separate value transfer between the payor and payee, and the payment to the payee is final and irrevocable at the time the receiving bank's account is credited or at the time the receiving bank is notified of the payment, whichever is earlier. - CH4

receipts and disbursements forecast: A short-term cash forecasting model, this forecast begins by creating separate schedules of cash receipts and disbursements, and then combining them. The schedules are prepared on a cash basis, rather than on an accrual basis, due to the need to forecast cash rather than earnings. The model tends to forecast cash accurately in the short-term and near medium-term, especially when accounts receivable and accounts payable data are incorporated. - CH13

receipts schedule: A component of the receipts and disbursements forecast process, this is a projection of collections from customers (e.g., cash sales or payments on accounts receivable) and other cash inflows (e.g., interest or dividends received from investments). It also should include expected, nonrecurring cash inflows, such as the proceeds from asset sales and external financing activities. - CH13

receivables conversion period: See *days' receivables*. - CH8

receiver: The party whose account is affected by the automated clearinghouse transaction. - CH4

receiving bank: In a payment clearing process, this is the bank or financial institution where the payee's account resides. It processes the transaction on behalf of the payee. - CH4

receiving depository financial institution (RDFI): In an automated clearinghouse transaction, this is the financial institution that acts as an intermediary between the originator and the receiver, on the receiver's side of the transaction. - CH4

recourse: A term related to using a factoring arrangement. In this case, the seller is liable for any bad debts the factor cannot collect. - CH8

Red Flags Rule: US regulation requiring FIs and creditors to develop and implement written identity theft prevention programs that provide for the identification of, detection of, and response to patterns, practices, or specific activities (i.e., red flags) that could indicate identity theft. - CH2

refinancing: The replacement of an existing debt with a new obligation before the maturity of the original debt, typically with different terms. Refinancing of bonds is often done following periods of high interest rates. During high interest rate periods, many entities that must issue bonds attach call provisions that allow the bonds to be redeemed prior to maturity. - CH6

regression analysis: A statistical cash forecasting method that can be used to assess the impact that multiple variables (or causes) have on a value or an outcome. It is a sophisticated method that requires large amounts of data. - CH13

regulatory compliance risk: A type of operational risk that relates to compliance with regulatory requirements. Part of overall operational risk stems from the requirement to comply with many regulations of federal, state, local, and industry-specific regulatory agencies, as well as compliance with accounting rules and guidelines for financial transactions and money laundering. This also can include tax risk (related to uncertainty about future tax liabilities), especially for multinational organizations that deal with a wide variety of sometimes conflicting tax codes and regulations. There is also an operational risk component to tax risk, given the penalties often assessed with missed filings or the underpayment of taxes. - CH15

re-invoicing: An intracompany method of centralizing the responsibility for monitoring and collecting international accounts receivable to more effectively manage related foreign exchange exposures. - CH8

reject item: A check that is rejected by a bank's automated check-processing equipment. - CH4

relationship review: A periodic assessment of service levels and responsiveness, both quantitatively and qualitatively, of a financial services provider. Scorecards are a tool that is useful in conducting this type of review. - CH7

relaxed current asset investment strategy: A current asset management strategy in which a company maintains high levels of current assets relative to sales. A large investment in current assets is likely to lower investment returns, but the firm operates with less risk because of its larger liquid asset balances. - CH8

remitting bank: In a documentary collection process, this is the bank of the seller/exporter. It receives the collection documents from the seller. - CH10

remote deposit capture (RDC): In an over-the-counter field deposit system, this is a process that allows an organization to scan and image checks, then transmit those images to its depository bank for posting and clearing, instead of having to deposit physical checks. In the United States, the bank then transmits the images to the Federal Reserve or another image exchange network for clearing. - CH4

remotely created check (RCC): See *pre-authorized draft*. - CH4

repatriation of capital: The transfer of funds from foreign subsidiaries back to the parent company in the home country. - CH20

repetitive wire: A type of wire transfer used when a company makes frequent transfers to the same credit parties. Only the date and the dollar amount may be changed on a repetitive wire. - CH10

Re-Presented Check Entry (RCK): The US automated clearinghouse (ACH) format used to transmit ACH debit entries in place of a paper check that has been returned for insufficient or uncollected funds. The general requirements are that the item be less than $2,500 and be drawn on a consumer account. RCK originators must provide advance notice to the check writer (e.g., in a customer statement or at the point of sale) that any check returned for insufficient or uncollected funds may be collected electronically. *RCK* is the standard entry class (SEC) code for this format. - CH10

repurchase agreement (repo): An agreement in which a bank or securities dealer sells government securities it owns to an investor and agrees to repurchase them at a later date and at a slightly higher price. In most cases, this type of agreement is referred to as a *repo agreement* from the perspective of the entity selling the security and agreeing to repurchase it at a later date. From the perspective of the entity that buys the security with a promise to sell it back at a later date, it is generally known as a *reverse repo*. - CH5

reputation risk: The risk that customers, suppliers, investors, and/or regulators may decide that a company has a bad reputation and decide not to do business with that company. For financial institutions, this type of risk is especially important and is covered under Basel guidelines. Reputation risk also relates to how companies react to unexpected events that can impact their reputations and ultimately their futures. - CH15

request for information (RFI): A document requesting information about a vendor's interest in, and ability to, provide services. The requesting company provides a formal description of its needs and asks selected vendors to provide general information as to how they could meet the company's needs. - CH7

request for proposal (RFP): A formal document prepared by a sourcing company that outlines objectives, needs, and service requirements and may be used to obtain bids for anything ranging from one specific service to a company's entire relationship. - CH7

request for quote (RFQ): A document whose purpose is to invite suppliers into a bidding process on specific products or services. It is best suited to products and services that are essentially standardized and/or commoditized, which makes each supplier's quote easily comparable to others. - CH7

required majority ownership: A type of political risk in which a government requires that companies must be owned by resident nationals. - CH7

reserve requirement: A central bank requirement that establishes the minimum percentage of customer deposits that financial institutions must hold as reserves and not lend out to other customers. The reserve requirement is an important part of managing monetary policy. In the United States, the reserve requirement is also a factor in the computation of earnings credit computation, since it represents a US financial institution's compensation for the level of balances it is required to maintain with the Federal Reserve. As of the date of publication, the reserve requirement was 10% of collected balances. - CH2,CH7

residual income (RI): A performance measurement ratio that assigns a charge to the invested capital of a company and shows an amount of profit (or loss). It is computed by subtracting invested capital (i.e., long-term debt and equity) times the cost of capital from net income. - CH19

residual value: (1) The amount of value remaining after all allowable depreciation charges have been subtracted from a depreciable asset. (2) The estimated value of an asset at the end of a lease. - CH20

restrictive current asset investment strategy: A current asset management strategy in which a company maintains low levels of current assets relative to sales. This strategy is typically the most profitable as long as unexpected events do not drive down liquidity to the point that it causes severe problems. - CH6

retail lockbox: A lockbox system used primarily to process high-volume, small-dollar consumer remittances (consumer-to-business) that frequently involve recurring, monthly installment payments. - CH10

retained earnings: A balance sheet account that represents the accumulated net earnings of a corporation since its inception, less dividends paid to shareholders. It also represents the changes in shareholders' equity arising from the retention of profits and losses of the company, less any dividends paid out to shareholders. - CH6,CH18

retrospectively (retro) rated insurance program: A type of insurance program in which the insured's cost of coverage for a policy period varies with the insured's losses during that period. Such programs are used often for workers' compensation and product liability insurance plans. The insured pays a standard, or deposit, premium at the beginning of the coverage period. At the end of the period, the insurer computes a final premium based on an agreed-upon formula that varies with the insured's actual costs or losses (subject to limits) for the policy period. - CH15

return on common equity: A performance ratio that measures the amount of earnings available to common shareholders relative to the level of their investment in the company. It is computed as earnings available to common shareholders divided by common equity. - CH19

return on investment (ROI): A performance measurement ratio that calculates profit per dollar of invested capital. It is computed by dividing net income by invested capital (or long-term debt and equity). - CH19

return on total assets (ROTA): A performance ratio that measures a company's amount of net income in relation to the level of total assets. It is computed as net income divided by total assets. - CH19

reverse positive pay: A process whereby a company's bank transmits a file of the checks presented for payment to the company on a daily or intraday basis. Within a specified time deadline, the company matches this file to a list of checks issued and notifies the bank of any items to be returned. - CH10

revolver: See *revolving credit agreement*. - CH11

revolving credit: A form of credit extension whereby a company grants credit without requiring specific transaction approval, as long as the account remains current. - CH11

revolving credit agreement: A committed line of credit established for a specified period of time, often on a multiyear basis. Revolving credits are formal, contractual commitments with loan agreements, including covenants. Also known as a *revolver*. - CH11

risk and control self-assessment (RCSA): A risk profile analysis process that identifies the risks, classifies each risk into clearly defined categories, and quantifies the risks with respect to the probability of occurrence and the impact on value and/or cash flows. The analysis can be used to evaluate the effectiveness of the risk reduction measures that are employed. In some organizations, this process is known as a *risk self-assessment*. - CH15

risk financing: The process of identifying and/or raising the funds needed to recover from a loss. Risk-financing techniques involve resources that an organization may draw upon to finance recovery from losses and liabilities for which it is held responsible. Risk financing competes with other uses of corporate funds. Sound financial management requires integrating the organization's risk-financing needs with other more traditionally productive uses. - CH15

risk profile: An assessment of how a company's overall value changes as the price of financial variables changes. The basic risk profile for a public company shows how the firm's earnings per share, common stock price, or overall value respond to changes in interest rates, foreign exchange rates, or commodity prices. - CH15

risk retention: A risk-financing approach that involves the use of an organization's internal financial resources (including credit, if appropriate) to provide funds to finance a recovery from losses. In other words, the organization retains some or all of the loss, rather than transferring it by paying someone else (e.g., an insurance organization) to take it. - CH15

risk transfer: The shifting of responsibility for a risk from one party to another, often through insurance. The essence of any risk transfer is a contract between a transferring organization (the transferor) and another entity (the transferee), under which the transferee agrees to pay designated types of the transferor's losses within contractual limits. The transferor may have to pay the transferee a fee (e.g., an insurance premium) for this promise of indemnity, or the transferor may have the bargaining power to secure this promise as a condition for agreeing to do business with the transferee. - CH15

risk-adjusted discount rate (RADR): A type of cost/benefit analysis that essentially requires high-risk endeavors to earn a higher rate of return in order to justify the investment. When properly applied, RADR allows a firm to more closely match its capital needs to available sources and to better manage its overall levels of risk and return. - CH19

risk-adjusted return on capital (RAROC): A method of determining the economic value of a transaction or activity based upon the anticipated risk-adjusted performance of the activity. - CH19

risk-free asset: A type of asset that has a certain future return. US Treasuries (especially Treasury bills) are considered to be risk-free because they are backed by the US government. - CH12

rolling forecast: A type of forecast in which the period of the forecast assumptions are reviewed and the forecast is updated or "rolled" forward at the end of each period. Typically, the number of periods in the forecast (days, weeks, months, etc.) remains constant, but old periods are dropped and new periods are added as the forecast progresses. - CH13

sales tax: A type of tax that is charged at the point of purchase for certain goods and services. The tax amount is typically calculated by applying a percentage rate to the taxable price of a sale. - CH2

Sarbanes-Oxley Act of 2002 (SOX): US legislation that requires companies to evaluate and disclose their internal financial controls as they relate to financial reporting, and requires auditors to attest to, or confirm, the effectiveness of these controls. It further requires that chief executive officers and chief financial officers certify financial statements, and specifies fines and jail sentences for knowingly and willfully misstating information therein. The act also requires companies with publicly traded securities to maintain independent audit committees (of the board of directors) that can interact with the external auditor in an unfettered way. - CH2

Sarbanes-Oxley (SOX) Section 404: A section of SOX that requires managers to state their responsibility for establishing and maintaining adequate internal controls for financial reporting. - CH17

savings account: A type of interest-bearing depository account owned mainly by individuals and not-for-profit institutions. Historically, many of these accounts were known as *passbook savings accounts*. - CH3

scenario analysis: A method for assessing investment risk, this type of what-if analysis assesses possible outcomes under a range of circumstances. It is used frequently to establish the lower bound (i.e., worst case) and upper bound (i.e., best case) of outcomes. Scenario analysis is similar to sensitivity analysis, but more than one variable is altered at a time. Scenario analysis usually starts with a base case—an expected value for each input variable affecting the final value. - CH15,CH19

scrap/obsolete items: A category of inventory that includes items from the production process that are left over (i.e., scrap) or no longer useful (i.e., obsolete items). Scrap from production can be reused in later batches or sold to recyclers. A portion of a company's inventories may become obsolete or damaged, especially in environments where there are rapid changes in existing products or introductions of new products. - CH8

seasonal dating: A term of sale whereby the seller agrees to accept payment at the end of the buyer's selling season. - CH8

seasoned offering: A type of stock offering that occurs when a firm that already has outstanding stock issues new, additional equity in the market. - CH6

secondary market: A financial market that trades previously issued securities. Existing debt and equity issues are traded by retail and institutional investors in secondary markets through established exchanges or through over-the-counter markets. Since the securities are bought and sold among investors, the issuing firm neither experiences a cash flow nor a change in the number of securities outstanding. - CH6

Securities and Exchange Commission (SEC): A US federal agency designed to maintain a fair and orderly market for investors by regulating and supervising securities sales. - CH2

securities exchange: An organized stock exchange that facilitates the buying and selling of debt and equity securities. - CH6

securities trader: Within an investment bank or brokerage firms, this is a market participant who helps to maintain active, orderly, secondary markets for all equity and debt instruments. - CH6

securitization: The practice of pooling various debt contracts, such as consumer loans, credit card debt, and mortgages, and using them as a basis for issuing securities. Many types of debt instruments are securitized to increase liquidity, thus lowering the cost of capital to borrowers. The primary corporate applications of securitization are accounts receivable and inventory. These are bundled together to collateralize securities, making them more liquid and attractive to investors. - CH6

security device: In electronic payment security, this is a key or token used to guard against misuse or fraud. - CH14

segregation of duties: The concept of having more than one person required to complete a specific activity, such as making a vendor payment or collecting and posting revenue from customers. Segregation, or separation, of duties is a key internal control issue that is important in managing risk and reducing fraud. At an operational level, responsibilities such as approval, authorization, and verification functions, including expense approval, check-signing authority, and account reconciliation, should be separated. - CH10

seigniorage: Government revenue from the issuance of coin and currency, which is based on the difference between the value of the money and the cost to produce it. Historically, it arose from the manufacture of coins, which were worth more than the metal used to mint the coins. - CH2

self-insurance: An approach used by some organizations as an alternative to purchasing insurance, this practice is not technically a form of insurance because it does not involve a transfer of risk to an insurer or another separate entity; instead, the organization will cover its own losses. It is often used by large organizations to manage their employee health care expenses. The term *self-insurance* can describe any risk retention program, even quite informal, unfunded arrangements. Self-insured retention (SIR) is the component of loss covered by the insured in a policy. - CH15

semi-repetitive wire: A type of wire transfer where the debit and credit parties remain the same (as in a repetitive wire transfer), but the description (e.g., a customer or an invoice number) may be changed, along with the date and the dollar amount. - CH10

semi-variable costs: Costs that contain both a fixed and variable cost component so that total costs are fixed for a set level of production and vary after that. - CH19

sensitivity analysis: A method of assessing investment risk, this type of analysis determines how a final outcome, such as net present value, is influenced by changes in the value of a particular variable (e.g., sales, or an operating or financing cost) and how vulnerable the expected outcome is to changes in a specific assumption. Note that with sensitivity analysis only one variable at a time is changed, rather than a set of variables as in scenario analysis. - CH19

service agreement: A legal document (contract) that describes the requirements and expectations of both the purchaser and provider of a specific service or services. - CH7

service charge: An explicit fee or price charged for service(s) provided by a financial institution. Service charges are either expressed as a flat monthly fee or as a per-item or per-unit price. In the case of the latter, the unit price is multiplied by the volume to arrive at the analysis period total (in the account analysis process). - CH3

service industry ratios: Ratios used in ratio analysis of firms in the service sector. Service companies typically have small investments in buildings and land, and rely more on human talent than physical assets. - CH19

service lease: See *operating lease*. - CH20

service level agreement (SLA): An agreement (which may be a separate document or part of a service agreement) that specifies the level of service expected from a financial services provider, along with a description of any penalties for failure to comply with the requirements of the agreement. - CH7

settlement: In a payment system, this is the actual movement of funds from the payor's account to the payee's account. - CH4

settlement mechanism: In a payment system, this is the mechanism or operation used to complete the transfer of value from the payor to the payee. - CH4

settlement risk: A form of counterparty credit risk that is related to the probability that a party funding a particular transaction will default on the actual payment or settlement obligation. - CH4

shared services center (SSC): A department or operation within a multiunit organization tasked with supplying multiple business units and their respective divisions and departments with specialized services, such as information technology (IT), human resources (HR), or accounts payable (A/P) services. In some companies this includes day-to-day treasury operations (cash management) and other treasury functions, which may be operated as SSCs. - CH1

short-term financing: A financing strategy used to meet temporary cash needs for periods of one year or less. - CH11

short-term forecasting: A type of cash forecasting in which the forecasts typically range from one to thirty days in length and predict cash receipts and disbursements, as well as the resulting balances, on a daily, weekly, or monthly basis. - CH13

short-term investment: An investment using short-term instruments with a maturity of less than one-year. - CH5

sight draft: A draft that is payable upon presentment, provided all of the terms of the draft have been met. Sight drafts are often presented in combination with other documents, such as titles or bills of lading. If all the documentation is in order, then the draft is payable upon presentment (i.e., at sight). - CH4

signature card: A document businesses furnish to banks to show the signatures of authorized signers (or specimens of both facsimile and computerized signatures) for all accounts. - CH7

simple moving average: A statistical cash forecasting methodology (and type of time series forecasting) that bases the forecast on a rolling average of past values for a series. - CH13

simulation: A method of assessing investment risk, this method combines scenario and sensitivity analyses, allowing certain assumptions in a decision model to fluctuate simultaneously. - CH19

Single Euro Payments Area (SEPA): The name of the European Union (EU) payments integration initiative. SEPA focuses on the technical, legal, and commercial barriers to paying and/or receiving euros cross-border within SEPA boundaries. SEPA establishes minimum standards and common pricing for payments processing within the EU. - CH2

single payment note: A type of note that is usually granted for a short period of time and specific purpose, with both the principal and interest amounts paid at maturity. Because of the limited duration and precise maturity of a single payment note, a specific cash flow event is frequently identified as the repayment source at the time the funds are advanced. - CH11

single sign-on (SSO): A software technique that allows an individual to enter one user name and password in order to access multiple applications on the same network or at the same host. - CH14

single-use card: A disposable credit card number that looks like a regular credit card number, but includes an embedded expiration date and security code, and will only work for a single use. - CH4

sinking fund: A fund that is the result of a provision that may be attached to a bond issue. It generally requires the issuer to set aside this pool of funds, which can be used to repay the bond's principal at maturity. - CH6

smart card: A typical payment card with the addition of a computer chip with related circuitry that can be used to store information for security or transaction processing. Transactions made with a smart card can update the card's memory and be stored for future processing. Smart cards are used with special card readers that can read and write to the card. Also known as a *chip card*. - CH4

smart card authentication: See *token*. - CH14

Society for Worldwide Interbank Financial Telecommunication (SWIFT): A financial industry-owned, cooperative, interbank telecommunication network that enables banks and corporations to send authenticated electronic messages in standard formats. - CH4

software as a service (SaaS): A distribution model in which software is run on a hosted computer and provided to the end user on an as-needed basis. SaaS applications are typically accessed over the Internet using a web browser. - CH14

sovereign bond: A bond issued by a national government and typically denominated in the currency of the issuing government. Also referred to as *sovereign debt*. - CH6

sovereign fund: A government-owned investment fund composed of a wide variety of financial assets, sometimes known as a *sovereign wealth fund (SWF)*. - CH2

special dividend: A dividend that is paid on a one-time basis, rather than as a regular quarterly dividend. - CH20

special drawing right (SDR): An artificial currency created by the International Monetary Fund whose asset value is based on a basket of currencies consisting of the euro, Japanese yen, British pound sterling and US dollar. - CH6

specific-project guarantee: A type of loan guarantee in which the guarantee party guarantees only loans relating to specific projects of the subsidiary rather than all loans. - CH6

speculation: A practice that involves taking a position on the direction of the market in order to make a profit, which is not usually a treasury objective. In some organizations, however, speculation in certain markets may be a treasury objective, as determined by the board of directors. - CH16

spot market: The market for immediate trading of currency or commodities. - CH16

spread: The difference between the bid and ask price of a particular security or asset. - CH5

standard loan provision: See *loan covenant*. - CH11

standard operating procedure (SOP): The normal or usual way of completing a specific task or duty. SOPs are often documented so that they can be performed on a routine basis and executed in a consistent manner. - CH17

standby letter of credit (L/C): A variation of a commercial L/C that is issued primarily by US banks. Once issued, a standby L/C serves as a vehicle to ensure the financial performance of a bank's customer to a third-party beneficiary. Standby L/Cs are the equivalent of guarantees issued by non-US banks. - CH2

standing wire: A type of wire transfer where a company establishes repetitive transfer instructions to move funds between two specified accounts automatically when previously determined criteria are met. - CH10

statement of beneficial interest: A document that specifies who has control over funds or accounts. This may be separate from who has signature authority or legal title. - CH7

statement of cash flows: A financial statement that provides a detailed picture of the sources of a company's cash flows and how these sources are used. Also known as a *cash flow statement*. - CH18

state-owned enterprise (SOE): A company that is created by a national government in order to participate in or help support various commercial activities on the government's behalf. These organizations are generally formed for a specific purpose and are designed to support a certain economic sector. SOEs are also known as *crown corporations* (in Canada and the United Kingdom, for example) or *government-sponsored enterprises*, or *GSEs* (in the United States). - CH6

static forecast: A type of forecast in which the period being forecasted, such as a calendar year, does not change as the forecast is updated. - CH13

stock dividend: A dividend that pays shareholders additional shares of stock rather than cash dividends. - CH20

stock purchase warrant: An option to buy stock from a company at a stated price until a stated date. - CH6

stock repurchase: A practice where a company uses some of its profits to purchase existing shares of its stock, either on the open market or directly from shareholders. This usually tends to increase the price of the stock. - CH20

stock split: A process in which a company replaces one existing share of stock with multiple shares of new stock. It is often done when a company's stock price is determined to be too high. The basic idea is to get the price of the stock down to a better trading range. - CH20

stored-value card (SVC): A type of debit card that may be offered by financial institutions, retailers, and other service providers, and can be a branded, open-loop card (e.g., Visa or MasterCard), or a private-label, closed-loop card (e.g., Starbucks or other merchant gift card). Generally, an open-loop card can be used almost anywhere while a closed-loop card can only be used at one selected merchant or group of merchants. Gift cards are one of the most commonly used types of SVC. - CH4

stores and supplies: A category of inventories that are not used directly in a production process; rather, they support the production process. They are also known as *indirect purchases*. - CH8

straight-through processing (STP): An initiative used by companies in the financial industry to optimize the speed at which transactions are processed. STP refers to eliminating all manual intervention so that a particular process is totally electronic from beginning to end. - CH7

strategic risk: The risk of major investments for which there is a significant uncertainty about success or profitability. Examples in this area would include entering into new markets, trying to spot and take advantage of trends, and investing in new technology. - CH15

stress test: An analytical exercise that assumes an adverse change in one or more of the firm's funding sources, or a major shock to the company's core business due to a competitor's action, litigation crisis, product recall, production plant disaster, financial crisis, or other source of business trauma. The proposed change in funds availability may involve the loss of one or more of the firm's borrowing facilities, a sudden and large increase in borrowing costs, or both. Such changes may reduce the firm's credit rating, violate loan covenants, or cause a technical default on a credit facility. - CH2

sub-sovereign bond: A type of bond issued by a level of government below the national or central government, which includes regions, provinces, states, municipalities, etc. Sub-sovereign bonds are subject to a wide variety of national and regional provisions in their country of origin and may have tax implications. - CH6

sub-sovereign entity: A government entity that is smaller than and subordinate to a national government. Examples of sub-sovereign entities include states, provinces, counties, and territories. - CH6

supplier risk: Risk related to an organization's suppliers and outsourcing arrangements. Supplier risk is a specific type of counterparty risk that also entails significant operational risks. The more critical the supplier or commodity is in the production process, the more risk an organization faces if the supplier either fails to deliver according to plan or provides substandard products and services that result in customer dissatisfaction. - CH15

supplier-managed replenishment program: An inventory management process whereby the supplier maintains and tracks the inventory of materials it provides to a customer. Title to the product is transferred at the shipping dock. - CH8

swap: An agreement between two parties to exchange (or swap) a set of cash flows at a future point in time. The most common type of swap is an interest rate swap. - CH16

sweep account: An account used by an organization that has its depository institution sweep any excess, end-of-day funds into an investment account. Though sweep accounts are not actually a separate category of short-term investment, they are used widely and are diverse, offering investment in repos or other money market instruments, managed accounts, and mutual funds. Some sweeps offer tax-exempt, offshore investments. - CH5

systemic risk: The risk of collapse of an entire financial system or entire market, as opposed to risk associated with any one individual organization, group, or component of a system. It is a risk imposed by linkages and interdependencies in a market or an economy that lead to a potential cascading failure that could bring down an entire banking system or market. - CH2

target capital structure: The specific capital structure that a company has set as its desired structure. This is typically the mix of debt and equity the company will use in raising new capital. - CH20

tax anticipation note (TAN): A short-term debt security issued in anticipation of future tax collections. TANs are generally issued by state and municipal governments to provide immediate funding for a capital expenditure, such as highway construction. - CH5

tax increment financing (TIF) bond: A type of bond used primarily for local financing in which a municipality may use all or a portion of new property taxes within a designated district to assist in the project's financing. - CH6

tax payment (TXP) convention: The standard NACHA payment format for state tax payments in the United States via automated clearinghouse. Usage and specific formats vary from state to state. - CH10

technology risk: The risk an organization faces as a result of its use of technology. As the treasury area of an organization relies increasingly on technology, the operational risk associated with the use of technology increases. Technology risk includes risks associated with (1) security breaches, (2) use of computer-based spreadsheets, and (3) the choice of a particular technology platform or vendor. - CH15

Telephone-Initiated Entry (TEL): The US automated clearinghouse (ACH) format used for payments that are not pre-authorized, but are approved by consumers over the phone. *TEL* is the standard entry class (SEC) code for this format. - CH10

tender option bond: A type of bond (also known as a *put bond*) that allows the holder to redeem the bond (i.e., sell it back to the issuer) either once during its life or on specified dates. Redemption is usually at par value. - CH6

term loan: A type of loan with a fixed maturity, usually greater than one year, which can be repaid either in installments or in a single payment. - CH6

term note: A medium-term debt instrument, typically with terms from two to ten years, issued by an organization. In most cases, these notes pay interest at periodic intervals. - CH6

terrorism risk: Risk related to terrorist attacks or other terrorist activities. Terrorism has become a significant threat to the operations of many organizations. Many disaster recovery plans specifically include recovery from terrorist events, in addition to natural disasters. Most organizations try to manage exposure to terrorist activities by increasing the level of security for both their premises and employees. - CH15

thinly capitalized: A description of a company that has a very small amount of capital or initial investment in relation to the amount of business the company conducts. The term is often used by taxing authorities in referring to subsidiary companies run by foreign corporations with minimal initial investment. - CH20

thrift (savings) institutions: Historically, depository institutions that accept consumer deposits and loan money, traditionally in the form of mortgage loans, under the charge of promoting housing and home ownership. - CH3

time deposit account (TDA): A depository account that must be maintained at an FI for a contractually specified period of time. - CH3

time draft: A draft that is payable at some future date, provided all of the terms of the draft have been met. As with sight drafts, time drafts are often presented in combination with other documents, such as titles or bills of lading. If all the documentation is in order, then the draft is payable at the specified future date. - CH4

time series forecasting: A medium- or long-term statistical cash forecasting process where a serial chain of values (known as a *time series*) for some variable (e.g., sales) is identified. Every time series contains a trend, seasonal pattern, cyclical pattern, and random movement. A trend is the general direction that the values are moving. A seasonal pattern repeats with regard to time of year. A cyclical pattern repeats without regard to time of year. Random movement is a change in the series not identifiable as a trend, or a seasonal or cyclical influence. - CH13

time value of money: A fundamental finance principle that establishes the relationship between cash flows received at different times. For example, a dollar received today is worth more than a dollar received tomorrow because today's dollar can be invested to earn a return. Conversely, a dollar received tomorrow is worth less than a dollar received today because the opportunity to earn interest is lost. - CH9

times interest earned (TIE) ratio: A coverage ratio that measures a firm's ability to service its debt through interest payments. It is computed as operating income divided by interest expense. - CH19

token: A security device that the owner uses to authorize access to a network or online service. Tokens are electronic devices that contain circuitry that encodes assigned user-specific information or personal information to help ensure password protection. - CH14

total asset turnover ratio: An efficiency/asset management ratio that measures how many times a firm's asset base was used (i.e., turned over) in generating the flow of revenue during the period. It is computed as revenues divided by total assets. - CH19

total liabilities to total assets ratio: A type of debt management ratio that measures the percentage of all liabilities to total investments or total assets. It is computed as total liabilities divided by total assets. - CH19

tracking stock: A special type of stock that is a separate stock created by a parent company to track the financial progress of a particular piece of business. Despite being part of a publicly traded entity, tracking stocks trade under unique ticker symbols. These stocks are meant to create opportunities for investors to buy into a fast-growing unit without investing in the whole company. - CH6

trade acceptance: A financial instrument that is similar to a banker's acceptance (BA) except it is drawn on, and accepted by, a buyer (importer). - CH10

trade credit: A form of credit that arises when a buyer receives goods but payment is not made to the supplier until some later date. Trade credit is the primary source of short-term financing used by many businesses. - CH11

trade letter of credit (L/C): See *commercial letter of credit (L/C)*. - CH3

trading companies: A trade payment method whereby an exporter (seller) sells products at a discount to an export trading company, which then resells the products internationally. - CH10

transaction risk exposure: A type of exposure that arises when a company creates future receivables and/or payables that are denominated in a currency other than its home, or functional, currency. - CH16

Transaction Workflow Innovation Standards Team (TWIST) bank services billing (BSB) format: A format that was developed as a standard intended for use by banks and their wholesale transaction service users to facilitate a monthly electronic communication of banking fees to the banks' corporate customers and others incurring those fees. - CH7

Trans-European Automated Real-time Gross settlement Express Transfer 2 (TARGET2) system: A system that provides real-time settlement for cross-border electronic payments in euros. - CH4

transfer pricing: The setting of the price that subsidiaries of a large corporation charge one another for components sold among them. - CH20

transit check: A check deposited with a financial institution that is drawn on another financial institution. - CH4

translation risk exposure: A type of exposure that is created when a foreign subsidiary's financial statements are converted (translated) into a parent company's home currency as part of the process of consolidating a company's financial statements. The exposure occurs because the value of the foreign assets and liabilities may change from one accounting period to the next as the underlying foreign exchange rates change. - CH16

travel card: A credit card used by a business for employee travel purposes. Also known as a *travel and entertainment (T&E) card*. - CH4

traveler's check: A prepaid instrument, similar to a money order, where two signatures usually are required by the purchaser: one at issuance and one at the time the check is used to pay for goods or services. - CH4

Treasury bill (T-bill): A short-term debt obligation backed by the US government with a maturity of less than one year. T-bills are sold in denominations of $1,000 up to a maximum purchase of $5 million and commonly have maturities of 1 month (4 weeks), 3 months (13 weeks), or 6 months (26 weeks). - CH5

Treasury bond (T-bond): A marketable, fixed-interest US government debt security with a maturity of more than 10 years. T-bonds make interest payments semiannually and the income that holders receive is only taxed at the federal level. - CH16

treasury management (TM) dashboard: A type of financial dashboard intended to provide management immediate feedback on the overall status of treasury operations, while also publishing key financial information useful in running the business. - CH14

treasury management system (TMS): A computer system, typically a stand-alone personal computer- (PC-), client/server-, or cloud-based system, which has software that gathers information from both internal and external sources for use by the treasury area of an organization. - CH14

Treasury note (T-note): A marketable US government debt security with a fixed interest rate and a maturity between one and ten years. T-notes can be bought either directly from the US government or through a bank. - CH16

treasury policies and procedures (P&Ps): Policies (i.e., statements to guide activities in a particular area or function of an organization) and procedures (i.e., specified series of actions or operations) that provide a framework for the design of treasury workflow processes, systems, and controls that support a company's objectives. - CH17

treasury stock: Stock issued by a company and later reacquired. It may be held in the company's treasury indefinitely, reissued to the public, or retired. Treasury stock receives no dividends and does not carry voting power while held by the company. It is considered issued, but not outstanding; therefore, it is deducted from any capital calculations. - CH6

triple-net lease: A lease agreement in which the lessee pays all expenses of the underlying property, in addition to any rent payments to the property owner (lessor). These expenses usually include taxes, insurance, and maintenance costs, hence the term *triple*. - CH20

Truth in Lending Act of 1968 (TILA): A US legislative act that requires lenders to disclose the effective annual interest rate, termed the *annual percentage rate*, and the total dollar cost on loans. - CH2

turnover tax: A type of tax that is essentially a sales tax on goods and services. - CH2

tying: The act of requiring a purchaser to buy one product or service in order to be allowed to buy a second, typically unrelated, product or service. - CH2

unanimous consent procedure: A type of procedure for formulating a reorganization plan in a US Chapter 11 bankruptcy filing. Under this procedure, all classes of creditors and equity holders must consent to the reorganization plan, with a two-thirds vote of all members in each class required for consent. - CH2

underwriting: An investment bank function, this is the act of purchasing all or a part of a block of securities issued by a company and thereby becoming responsible for their ultimate distribution. The underwriter normally assumes all the risk or liability for the sale of the securities. - CH3

Uniform Bank Performance Report (UBPR): An analytical tool, published by the Federal Financial Institutions Examination Council (FFIEC), created for bank supervisory, examination, and management purposes. In a concise format, it shows the impact of management decisions and economic conditions on a bank's performance and balance sheet composition. The performance and composition data contained in the report can be used to help evaluate the adequacy of earnings, liquidity, capital, asset and liability management, and growth management. - CH7

Uniform Commercial Code (UCC): A uniform set of laws governing commercial transactions in the United States. It defines the rights and duties of all parties in a commercial transaction and provides a statutory definition of commonly accepted business practices. This code provides guidelines for paper-based contracts, business transactions, and payment instruments. - CH2

Uniform Customs and Practice for Documentary Credits (UCP) 600: A set of rules established by the International Chamber of Commerce (ICC) which govern the operation of commercial letters of credit, and are known as *UCP*. The current rules are outlined under UCP 600, and these rules affect almost every credit issued under the ICC's UCP. - CH10

United Nations/Electronic Data Interchange for Administration, Commerce and Transport (UN/EDIFACT) standards: A set of internationally agreed-upon standards, directories, and guidelines for electronic commerce. - CH14

use tax: A type of tax that is imposed directly on the consumer of goods that were purchased without paying sales tax (generally items purchased from a vendor in another state or over the Internet and delivered to the purchaser by mail or common carrier). - CH2

value dating: A process whereby a bank sets a forward value date on which the value of funds credited to an account is determined and establishes a back value date on which the value of funds debited from (or credited to) an account is determined. - CH7

value-added tax (VAT): A type of sales tax that involves charging a separate tax at each discrete stage of production and/or distribution based on the increased value (i.e., value added) occurring at that stage. - CH2

value-at-risk (VaR): A risk management measurement that is used to determine how changing financial variables will affect a company's value. It is designed specifically to incorporate a wide range of risk factors and summarize their impact in a single measure. The VaR approach uses the probability and monetary impacts of specified adverse events over a period of time to assess risk. - CH15

value-dated automated clearinghouse (ACH) transactions: ACH transactions where the payment instructions include settlement dates. - CH4

variable costs: Costs in a business whose total amount changes in direct proportion to the level of business activity. In cost accounting, variable costs are contrasted with fixed costs, which do not change based on volume or activity levels. - CH19

variable-rate demand obligation (VRDO): A type of security issued as a long-term bond that carries a short-term liquidity feature, or put. Generally, this put option, which is an investor's option to sell (or put) the instrument back to the issuer at par, allows for liquidation either weekly or monthly and is typically supported by a credit facility, such as a bank letter of credit. While interest from VRDOs is often tax-exempt, VRDOs exist as both taxable and nontaxable instruments. - CH5

vendor scorecard: A management tool used to measure a vendor's performance in both a qualitative and quantitative method. The primary purpose of a scorecard is to provide a quantitative measure of the service provided and the benefit received, but it also provides feedback for the service provider to better understand how the customer perceives the value, quality, and cost of the service(s) provided. - CH7

virtual vault services: In an over-the-counter field deposit system, this type of vault service may be offered by banks or through third-party, nonbank companies, such as armored car services. The basic approach is to utilize armored car and courier services to replace or enhance physical bank branch locations. In addition, many of these services offer immediate availability of any funds processed through their vaults. These services typically include a smart safe that verifies deposits to the safe. - CH10

weighted average cost of capital (WACC): Used in determining the overall cost of capital, this cost is computed as a weighted average of the effective cost of debt and the cost of equity. - CH9

wholesale lockbox: A lockbox system that is used primarily to process low-volume, large-dollar business-to-business payments that, unlike consumer payments, must often be matched to specific invoices (i.e., several invoices are paid with one check). - CH10

withholding tax: A type of tax that may be charged on funds being moved from one country to another. Companies may be required to pay such taxes when moving funds outside a foreign country. The amount can vary from 1% to almost 35% of the repatriated flow. - CH2

without recourse (no recourse): A term related to using a factoring arrangement. In this case, the factor must absorb the loss if a customer fails to pay. - CH8

work in progress (WIP): A type of inventory that represents items or materials that are in the process of being manufactured. - CH8

workflow management system: Technology that enables a company to use software to implement, monitor, and enforce the specific processes and procedures (i.e., the workflow) that it wants used throughout the company. - CH14

working capital: The sum of a company's current asset accounts (primarily cash, accounts receivable, and inventory) less the sum of its current liability accounts (primarily payables and accrual accounts). Also known as *net working capital*. - CH8

working capital gap: The time gap between a cash outflow and a cash inflow. - CH1

Yankee CD: A certificate of deposit that is denominated in US dollars and issued in the United States by a branch of a non-US bank. - CH5

year basis: The number of days in a year, when calculating the yield on an investment. Money market yield is traditionally based on a 360-day year, while bond equivalent yield is based on a 365-day year. - CH11

yield: The income return on an investment. This refers to the interest or dividends received from a security and is usually expressed annually as a percentage based on the investment's cost, its current market value, or its face value. - CH5

yield curve: A plot of the yields to maturity on the same investment instrument or class of instruments, but with varying maturities, as of a specific date. For example, a yield curve for US Treasury instruments is a plot of yields to maturity for US Treasury bond issues with varying periods to maturity as of the close of business on a particular date. - CH11

yield to call (YTC): The yield a bond would provide if the issuer calls it prior to maturity. Since callable bonds usually are called only if interest rates have fallen, the YTC is typically lower than the yield to maturity. - CH12

yield to maturity (YTM): The rate of return anticipated on a bond if it is held until the maturity date. YTM is considered a long-term bond yield expressed as an annual rate. The calculation of YTM takes into account the current market price, par value, coupon interest rate, and time to maturity. It is also assumed that all coupons are reinvested at the same rate. Sometimes, this is simply referred to as *yield*. - CH12

zero balance account (ZBA): A type of bank account (typically used for disbursements via check or electronic funds transfer) where the end-of-day balance in the account is maintained at zero. Transfers are made from a master account to fund this account, typically at the end of the day. A ZBA can also be set up as a depository account from which funds are debited and transferred to a master account at the end of each day. - CH10

zero-coupon bond: A debt security that does not pay interest (a coupon) but is traded at a deep discount, rendering a profit at maturity when the bond is redeemed for its full face value. - CH6

INDEX

Numbers

A

B

C

D

E

G

H

J

K

N

O

P

S

T

U

V

W

X

Y

Z

CPSIA information can be obtained at www.ICGtesting.com
Printed in the USA
BVOW01s0003070514

352234BV00001B/1/P

9 780615 800370